THE OXFORD PAPERBACK
SPANISH DICTIONARY

Also available

The Oxford Paperback French Dictionary

The Oxford Paperback German Dictionary

The Oxford Paperback Italian Dictionary

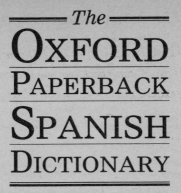

The Oxford Paperback Spanish Dictionary

Spanish–English
English–Spanish

Español–Inglés
Inglés–Español

CHRISTINE LEA

Oxford New York
OXFORD UNIVERSITY PRESS

Oxford University Press, Walton Street, Oxford OX2 6DP
Oxford New York
Athens Auckland Bangkok Bombay
Calcutta Cape Town Dar es Salaam Delhi
Florence Hong Kong Istanbul Karachi
Kuala Lumpur Madras Madrid Melbourne
Mexico City Nairobi Paris Singapore
Taipei Tokyo Toronto

and associated companies in
Berlin Ibadan

Oxford is a trade mark of Oxford University Press

First published 1993 as The Oxford Spanish Minidictionary
First issued as an Oxford University Press paperback 1994

British Library Cataloguing in Publication Data
Data available

Library of Congress Cataloging in Publication Data
Lea, Christine.
The Oxford paperback Spanish dictionary: Spanish-English, English-Spanish = Español-Inglés, Inglés-Español/Christine Lea.
p. cm.—(Oxford reference)
1. Spanish language—Dictionaries—English.
2. English language—Dictionaries—Spanish.
I. Title. II. Series.
463v.21—dc20 PC4640.L44 1994 93-30406
ISBN 0-19-280013-2

7 9 10 8

Printed in Great Britain by
Mackays of Chatham
Chatham, Kent

Contents · Índice

Preface

This dictionary has been written with speakers of both English and Spanish in mind and contains the most useful words and expressions of the English and Spanish languages of today. Wide coverage of culinary and motoring terms has been included to help the tourist.

Common abbreviations, names of countries, and other useful geographical names are included.

English pronunciation is given by means of the International Phonetic Alphabet. It is shown for all headwords and for those derived words whose pronunciation is not easily deduced from that of a headword. The rules for pronunciation of Spanish are given on page x.

I should like to thank particularly Mary-Carmen Beaven whose comments have been invaluable. I would also like to acknowledge the help given me unwittingly by Dr M. Janes and Mrs J. Andrews, whose French and Italian Minidictionaries have served as models for the present work.

C.A.L.

Prefacio

Este diccionario de Oxford se escribió tanto para los hispanohablantes como para los angloparlantes y contiene las palabras y frases más corrientes de ambas lenguas de hoy. Se incluyen muchos términos culinarios y de automovilismo que pueden servir al turista.

Las abreviaturas más corrientes, los nombres de países, y otros términos geográficos figuran en este diccionario.

La pronunciación inglesa sigue el Alfabeto Fonético Internacional. Se incluye para cada palabra clave y todas las derivadas cuya pronunciación no es fácil de deducir a partir de la palabra clave. Las reglas de la pronunciación española se encuentran en la página x.

Quisiera reconocer la ayuda de Mary-Carmen Beaven cuyas observaciones me han sido muy valiosas. También quiero agradecerles al Dr. M. Janes y a la Sra. J. Andrews cuyos minidiccionarios del francés y del italiano me han servido de modelo para el presente.

C.A.L.

Introduction

The swung dash (~) is used to replace a headword or that part of a headword preceding the vertical bar (|). In both English and Spanish only irregular plurals are given. Normally Spanish nouns and adjectives ending in an unstressed vowel form the plural by adding *s* (e.g. *libro*, *libros*). Nouns and adjectives ending in a stressed vowel or a consonant add *es* (e.g. *rubí*, *rubíes*; *pared*, *paredes*). An accent on the final syllable is not required when *es* is added (e.g. *nación*, *naciones*). Final *z* becomes *ces* (e.g. *vez*, *veces*). Spanish nouns and adjectives ending in *o* form the feminine by changing the final *o* to *a* (e.g. *hermano*, *hermana*). Most Spanish nouns and adjectives ending in anything other than final *o* do not have a separate feminine form with the exception of those denoting nationality etc; these add *a* to the masculine singular form (e.g. *español*, *española*). An accent on the final syllable is then not required (e.g. *inglés*, *inglesa*). Adjectives ending in *án*, *ón*, or *or* behave like those denoting nationality with the following exceptions: *inferior*, *mayor*, *mejor*, *menor*, *peor*, *superior* where the feminine has the same form as the masculine. Spanish verb tables will be found in the appendix.

The Spanish alphabet

In Spanish *ch*, *ll* and *ñ* are considered separate letters and in the Spanish-English section, therefore, they will be found after *cu*, *lu* and *ny* respectively.

Introducción

La tilde (~) se emplea para substituir a la palabra cabeza de artículo o aquella parte de tal palabra que precede a la barra vertical (|). Tanto en inglés como en español se dan los plurales solamente si son irregulares. Para formar el plural regular en inglés se añade la letra *s* al sustantivo singular, pero se añade *es* cuando se trata de una palabra que termina en *ch*, *sh*, *s*, *ss*, *us*, *x*, o *z* (p.ej. *sash*, *sashes*). En el caso de una palabra que termina en *y* precedida por una consonante, la *y* se cambia en *ies* (p.ej. *baby*, *babies*). Para formar el tiempo pasado y el participio pasado se añade *ed* al infinitivo de los verbos regulares ingleses (p.ej. *last*, *lasted*). En el caso de los verbos ingleses que terminan en *e* muda se añade sólo la *d* (p.ej. *move*, *moved*). En el caso de los verbos ingleses que terminan en *y* hay que cambiar la *y* en *ied* (p.ej. *carry*, *carried*). Los verbos irregulares se encuentran en el diccionario por orden alfabético remitidos al infinitivo, y también en la lista en el apéndice.

Pronunciation of Spanish

Vowels:

a is between pronunciation of *a* in English *cat* and *arm*
e is like *e* in English *bed*
i is like *ee* in English *see* but a little shorter
o is like *o* in English *hot* but a little longer
u is like *oo* in English *too*
y when a vowel is as Spanish **i**

Consonants:

b 1) in initial position or after nasal consonant is like English *b*
2) in other positions is between English *b* and English *v*
c 1) before **e** or **i** is like *th* in English *thin*
2) in other positions is like *c* in English *cat*
ch is like *ch* in English *chip*
d 1) in initial position, after nasal consonants and after **l** is like English *d*
2) in other positions is like *th* in English *this*
f is like English *f*
g 1) before **e** or **i** is like *ch* in Scottish *loch*
2) in initial position is like *g* in English *get*
3) in other positions is like 2) but a little softer
h is silent in Spanish but see also **ch**
j is like *ch* in Scottish *loch*
k is like English *k*
l is like English *l* but see also **ll**
ll is like *lli* in English *million*
m is like English *m*
n is like English *n*
ñ is like *ni* in English *opinion*
p is like English *p*
q is like English *k*
r is rolled or trilled
s is like *s* in English *sit*
t is like English *t*
v 1) in initial position or after nasal consonant is like English *b*
2) in other positions is between English *b* and English *v*

w is like Spanish **b** or **v**
x is like English *x*
y is like English *y*
z is like *th* in English *thin*

Pronunciación Inglesa

Símbolos fonéticos

Vocales y diptongos

iː	s*ee*	ə	*a*go
ɪ	s*i*t	eɪ	p*a*ge
e	t*e*n	əʊ	h*o*me
æ	h*a*t	aɪ	f*i*ve
ɑː	*ar*m	aɪə	f*ire*
ɒ	g*o*t	aʊ	n*ow*
ɔː	s*aw*	aʊə	fl*our*
ʊ	p*u*t	ɔɪ	j*oi*n
uː	t*oo*	ɪə	n*ear*
ʌ	c*u*p	eə	h*air*
ɜː	f*ur*	ʊə	p*oor*

Consonantes

p	*p*en	s	*s*o
b	*b*ad	z	*z*oo
t	*t*ea	ʃ	*sh*e
d	*d*ip	ʒ	mea*s*ure
k	*c*at	h	*h*ow
g	*g*ot	m	*m*an
tʃ	*ch*in	n	*n*o
dʒ	*J*une	ŋ	si*ng*
f	*f*all	l	*l*eg
v	*v*oice	r	*r*ed
θ	*th*in	j	*y*es
ð	*th*en	w	*w*et

Abbreviations · Abreviaturas

adjective	*a*	adjetivo
abbreviation	*abbr/abrev*	abreviatura
administration	*admin*	administración
adverb	*adv*	adverbio
American	*Amer*	americano
anatomy	*anat*	anatomía
architecture	*archit/arquit*	arquitectura
definite article	*art def*	artículo definido
indefinite article	*art indef*	artículo indefinido
astrology	*astr*	astrología
motoring	*auto*	automóvil
auxiliary	*aux*	auxiliar
aviation	*aviat/aviac*	aviación
biology	*biol*	biología
botany	*bot*	botánica
commerce	*com*	comercio
conjunction	*conj*	conjunción
cookery	*culin*	cocina
electricity	*elec*	electricidad
school	*escol*	enseñanza
Spain	*Esp*	España
feminine	*f*	femenino
familiar	*fam*	familiar
figurative	*fig*	figurado
philosophy	*fil*	filosofía
photography	*foto*	fotografía
geography	*geog*	geografía
geology	*geol*	geología
grammar	*gram*	gramática
humorous	*hum*	humorístico
interjection	*int*	interjección
interrogative	*inter*	interrogativo
invariable	*invar*	invariable
legal, law	*jurid*	jurídico
Latin American	*LAm*	latinoamericano
language	*lang*	lengua(je)
masculine	*m*	masculino
mathematics	*mat(h)*	matemáticas
mechanics	*mec*	mecánica
medicine	*med*	medicina
military	*mil*	militar
music	*mus*	música
mythology	*myth*	mitología
noun	*n*	nombre
nautical	*naut*	náutica
oneself	*o.s.*	uno mismo, se
proprietary term	*P*	marca registrada

pejorative	*pej*	peyorativo
philosophy	*phil*	filosofía
photography	*photo*	fotografía
plural	*pl*	plural
politics	*pol*	política
possessive	*poss*	posesivo
past participle	*pp*	participio de pretérito
prefix	*pref*	prefijo
preposition	*prep*	preposición
present participle	*pres p*	participio de presente
pronoun	*pron*	pronombre
psychology	*psych*	psicología
past tense	*pt*	tiempo pasado
railway	*rail*	ferrocarril
relative	*rel*	relativo
religion	*relig*	religión
school	*schol*	enseñanza
singular	*sing*	singular
slang	*sl*	argot
someone	*s.o.*	alguien
something	*sth*	algo
technical	*tec*	técnico
television	*TV*	televisión
university	*univ*	universidad
auxiliary verb	*v aux*	verbo auxiliar
verb	*vb*	verbo
intransitive verb	*vi*	verbo intransitivo
pronominal verb	*vpr*	verbo pronominal
transitive verb	*vt*	verbo transitivo
transitive & intransitive verb	*vti*	verbo transitivo e intransitivo

Proprietary terms

This dictionary includes some words which are, or are asserted to be, proprietary names or trade marks. Their inclusion does not imply that they have acquired for legal purposes a non-proprietary or general significance, nor is any other judgement implied concerning their legal status. In cases where the editor has some evidence that a word is used as a proprietary name or trade mark this is indicated by the letter (P), but no judgement concerning the legal status of such words is made or implied thereby.

Marcas registradas

Este diccionario incluye algunas palabras que son o pretenden ser marcas registradas. No debe atribuirse ningún valor jurídico ni a la presencia ni a la ausencia de tal designación.

ESPAÑOL-INGLÉS
SPANISH-ENGLISH

A

a *prep* in, at; (*dirección*) to; (*tiempo*) at; (*hasta*) to, until; (*fecha*) on; (*más tarde*) later; (*medio*) by; (*precio*) for, at. **~ 5 km** 5 km away. **¿~ cuántos estamos?** what's the date? **~l día siguiente** the next day. **~ la francesa** in the French fashion. **~ las 2** at 2 o'clock. **~ los 25 años** (*edad*) at the age of 25; (*después de*) after 25 years. **~ no ser por** but for. **~ que** I bet. **~ 28 de febrero** on the 28th of February
ábaco *m* abacus
abad *m* abbot
abadejo *m* (*pez*) cod
abad|esa *f* abbess. **~ía** *f* abbey
abajo *adv* (down) below; (*dirección*) down(wards); (*en casa*) downstairs. ● *int* down with. **calle ~** down the street. **el ~ firmante** the undersigned. **escaleras ~** downstairs. **la parte de ~** the bottom part. **los de ~** those at the bottom. **más ~** below.
abalanzarse [10] *vpr* rush towards
abalorio *m* glass bead
abanderado *m* standard-bearer
abandon|ado *adj* abandoned; (*descuidado*) neglected; ‹*personas*› untidy. **~ar** *vt* leave ‹*un lugar*›; abandon ‹*personas, cosas*›. ● *vi* give up. **~arse** *vpr* give in; (*descuidarse*) let o.s. go. **~o** *m* abandonment; (*estado*) abandon
abani|car [7] *vt* fan. **~co** *m* fan. **~queo** *m* fanning
abarata|miento *m* reduction in price. **~r** *vt* reduce. **~rse** *vpr* ‹*precios*› come down
abarca *f* sandal
abarcar [7] *vt* put one's arms around, embrace; (*comprender*) embrace; (*LAm, acaparar*) monopolize
abarquillar *vt* warp. **~se** *vpr* warp
abarrotar *vt* overfill, pack full
abarrotes *mpl* (*LAm*) groceries
abast|ecer [11] *vt* supply. **~ecimiento** *m* supply; (*acción*) supplying. **~o** *m* supply. **dar ~o a** supply
abati|do *a* depressed. **~miento** *m* depression. **~r** *vt* knock down, demolish; (*fig, humillar*) humiliate. **~rse** *vpr* swoop (**sobre** on); (*ponerse abatido*) get depressed
abdica|ción *f* abdication. **~r** [7] *vt* give up. ● *vi* abdicate
abdom|en *m* abdomen. **~inal** *a* abdominal
abec|é *m* (*fam*) alphabet, ABC. **~edario** *m* alphabet
abedul *m* birch (tree)
abej|a *f* bee. **~arrón** *m* bumble-bee. **~ón** *m* drone. **~orro** *m* bumble-bee; (*insecto coleóptero*) cockchafer
aberración *f* aberration
abertura *f* opening
abet|al *m* fir wood. **~o** *m* fir (tree)
abierto *pp véase* **abrir.** ● *a* open
abigarra|do *a* multi-coloured; (*fig, mezclado*) mixed. **~miento** *m* variegation
abigeato *m* (*Mex*) rustling
abism|al *a* abysmal; (*profundo*) deep. **~ar** *vt* throw into an abyss; (*fig, abatir*) humble. **~arse** *vpr* be absorbed (**en** in), be lost (**en** in). **~o** *m* abyss; (*fig, diferencia*) world of difference
abizcochado *a* spongy
abjura|ción *f* abjuration. **~r** *vt* forswear. ● *vi*. **~r de** forswear
ablanda|miento *m* softening. **~r** *vt* soften. **~rse** *vpr* soften
ablución *f* ablution
abnega|ción *f* self-sacrifice. **~do** *a* self-sacrificing
aboba|do *a* silly. **~miento** *m* silliness
aboca|do *a* ‹*vino*› medium. **~r** [7] *vt* pour out
abocetar *vt* sketch
abocinado *a* trumpet-shaped

abochornar *vt* suffocate; (*fig, avergonzar*) embarrass. **~se** *vpr* feel embarassed; ‹*plantas*› wilt

abofetear *vt* slap

aboga|cía *f* legal profession. **~do** *m* lawyer; (*notario*) solicitor; (*en el tribunal*) barrister, attorney (*Amer*). **~r** [12] *vi* plead

abolengo *m* ancestry

aboli|ción *f* abolition. **~cionismo** *m* abolitionism. **~cionista** *m & f* abolitionist. **~r** [24] *vt* abolish

abolsado *a* baggy

abolla|dura *f* dent. **~r** *vt* dent

abomba|do *a* convex; (*Arg, borracho*) drunk. **~r** *vt* make convex. **~rse** *vpr* (*LAm, corromperse*) start to rot, go bad

abomina|ble *a* abominable. **~ción** *f* abomination. **~r** *vt* detest. ● *vi*. **~r de** detest

abona|ble *a* payable. **~do** *a* paid. ● *m* subscriber

abonanzar *vi* ‹*tormenta*› abate; ‹*tiempo*› improve

abon|ar *vt* pay; (*en agricultura*) fertilize. **~aré** *m* promissory note. **~arse** *vpr* subscribe. **~o** *m* payment; (*estiércol*) fertilizer; (*a un periódico*) subscription

aborda|ble *a* reasonable; ‹*persona*› approachable. **~je** *m* boarding. **~r** *vt* tackle ‹*un asunto*›; approach ‹*una persona*›; (*naut*) come alongside

aborigen *a & m* native

aborrascarse [7] *vpr* get stormy

aborrec|er [11] *vt* hate; (*exasperar*) annoy. **~ible** *a* loathsome. **~ido** *a* hated. **~imiento** *m* hatred

aborregado *a* ‹*cielo*› mackerel

abort|ar *vi* have a miscarriage. **~ivo** *a* abortive. **~o** *m* miscarriage; (*voluntario*) abortion; (*fig, monstruo*) abortion. **hacerse ~ar** have an abortion

abotaga|miento *m* swelling. **~rse** [12] *vpr* swell up

abotonar *vt* button (up)

aboveda|do *a* vaulted. **~r** *vt* vault

abra *f* cove

abracadabra *m* abracadabra

abrasa|dor *a* burning. **~r** *vt* burn; (*fig, consumir*) consume. **~rse** *vpr* burn

abrasi|ón *f* abrasion; (*geología*) erosion. **~vo** *a* abrasive

abraz|adera *f* bracket. **~ar** *vt* [10] embrace; (*encerrar*) enclose. **~arse** *vpr* embrace. **~o** *m* hug. **un fuerte ~o de** (*en una carta*) with best wishes from

abrecartas *m* paper-knife

ábrego *m* south wind

abrelatas *m invar* tin opener (*Brit*), can opener

abreva|dero *m* watering place. **~r** *vt* water ‹*animales*›. **~rse** *vpr* ‹*animales*› drink

abrevia|ción *f* abbreviation; (*texto abreviado*) abridged text. **~do** *a* brief; ‹*texto*› abridged. **~r** *vt* abbreviate; abridge ‹*texto*›; cut short ‹*viaje etc*›. ● *vi* be brief. **~tura** *f* abbreviation

abrig|ada *f* shelter. **~adero** *m* shelter. **~ado** *a* ‹*lugar*› sheltered; ‹*personas*› well wrapped up. **~ar** [12] *vt* shelter; cherish ‹*esperanza*›; harbour ‹*duda, sospecha*›. **~arse** *vpr* (take) shelter; (*con ropa*) wrap up. **~o** *m* (over)coat; (*lugar*) shelter

abril *m* April. **~eño** *a* April

abrillantar *vt* polish

abrir [*pp* **abierto**] *vt/i* open. **~se** *vpr* open; (*extenderse*) open out; ‹*el tiempo*› clear

abrocha|dor *m* buttonhook. **~r** *vt* do up; (*con botones*) button up

abrojo *m* thistle

abroncar [7] *vt* (*fam*) tell off; (*abuchear*) boo; (*avergonzar*) shame. **~se** *vpr* be ashamed; (*enfadarse*) get annoyed

abroquelarse *vpr* shield o.s.

abruma|dor *a* overwhelming. **~r** *vt* overwhelm

abrupto *a* steep; (*áspero*) harsh

abrutado *a* brutish

absceso *m* abscess

absentismo *m* absenteeism

ábside *m* apse

absintio *m* absinthe

absolución *f* (*relig*) absolution; (*jurid*) acquittal

absolut|amente *adv* absolutely, completely. **~ismo** *m* absolutism. **~ista** *a & m & f* absolutist. **~o** *a* absolute. **~orio** *a* of acquittal. **en ~o** (*de manera absoluta*) absolutely; (*con sentido negativo*) (not) at all

absolver [2, *pp* **absuelto**] *vt* (*relig*) absolve; (*jurid*) acquit

absor|bente *a* absorbent; (*fig, interesante*) absorbing. **~ber** *vt* absorb. **~ción** *f* absorption. **~to** *a* absorbed

abstemio *a* teetotal. ● *m* teetotaller

absten|ción *f* abstention. **~erse** [40] *vpr* abstain, refrain (**de** from)
abstinen|cia *f* abstinence. **~te** *a* abstinent
abstra|cción *f* abstraction. **~cto** *a* abstract. **~er** [41] *vt* abstract. **~erse** *vpr* be lost in thought. **~ído** *a* absent-minded
abstruso *a* abstruse
absuelto *a* (*relig*) absolved; (*jurid*) acquitted
absurdo *a* absurd. ● *m* absurd thing
abuche|ar *vt* boo. **~o** *m* booing
abuel|a *f* grandmother. **~o** *m* grandfather. **~os** *mpl* grandparents
ab|ulia *f* lack of willpower. **~úlico** *a* weak-willed
abulta|do *a* bulky. **~miento** *m* bulkiness. **~r** *vt* enlarge; (*hinchar*) swell; (*fig, exagerar*) exaggerate. ● *vi* be bulky
abunda|ncia *f* abundance. **~nte** *a* abundant, plentiful. **~r** *vi* be plentiful. **nadar en la ~ncia** be rolling in money
aburguesa|miento *m* conversion to a middle-class way of life. **~rse** *vpr* become middle-class
aburri|do *a* (*con estar*) bored; (*con ser*) boring. **~miento** *m* boredom; (*cosa pesada*) bore. **~r** *vt* bore. **~rse** *vpr* be bored, get bored
abus|ar *vi* take advantage. **~ar de la bebida** drink too much. **~ivo** *a* excessive. **~o** *m* abuse. **~ón** *a* (*fam*) selfish
abyec|ción *f* wretchedness. **~to** *a* abject
acá *adv* here; (*hasta ahora*) until now. **~ y allá** here and there. **de ~ para allá** to and fro. **de ayer ~** since yesterday
acaba|do *a* finished; (*perfecto*) perfect; (*agotado*) worn out. ● *m* finish. **~miento** *m* finishing; (*fin*) end. **~r** *vt/i* finish. **~rse** *vpr* finish; (*agotarse*) run out; (*morirse*) die. **~r con** put an end to. **~r de** (+ *infinitivo*) have just (+ *pp*). **~ de llegar** he has just arrived. **~r por** (+ *infinitivo*) end up (+ *gerundio*). **¡se acabó!** that's it!
acabóse *m*. **ser el ~** be the end, be the limit
acacia *f* acacia
acad|emia *f* academy. **~émico** *a* academic
acaec|er [11] *vi* happen. **~imiento** *m* occurrence
acalora|damente *adv* heatedly. **~do** *a* heated. **~miento** *m* heat. **~r** *vt* warm up; (*fig, excitar*) excite. **~rse** *vpr* get hot; (*fig, excitarse*) get excited
acallar *vt* silence
acampanado *a* bell-shaped
acampar *vi* camp
acanala|do *a* grooved. **~dura** *f* groove. **~r** *vt* groove
acantilado *a* steep. ● *m* cliff
acanto *m* acanthus
acapara|r *vt* hoard; (*monopolizar*) monopolize. **~miento** *m* hoarding; (*monopolio*) monopolizing
acaracolado *a* spiral
acaricia|dor *a* caressing. **~r** *vt* caress; (*rozar*) brush; ‹*proyectos etc*› have in mind
ácaro *m* mite
acarre|ar *vt* transport; ‹*desgracias etc*› cause. **~o** *m* transport
acartona|do *a* ‹*persona*› wizened. **~rse** *vpr* (*ponerse rígido*) go stiff; ‹*persona*› become wizened
acaso *adv* maybe, perhaps. ● *m* chance. **~ llueva mañana** perhaps it will rain tomorrow. **al ~** at random. **por si ~** in case
acata|miento *m* respect (**a** for). **~r** *vt* respect
acatarrarse *vpr* catch a cold, get a cold
acaudalado *a* well off
acaudillar *vt* lead
acceder *vi* agree; (*tener acceso*) have access
acces|ibilidad *f* accessibility. **~ible** *a* accessible; ‹*persona*› approachable. **~o** *m* access, entry; (*med, ataque*) attack; (*llegada*) approach
accesorio *a & m* accessory
accidentado *a* ‹*terreno*› uneven; (*agitado*) troubled; ‹*persona*› injured
accident|al *a* accidental. **~arse** *vpr* have an accident. **~e** *m* accident
acci|ón *f* (*incl jurid*) action; (*hecho*) deed. **~onar** *vt* work. ● *vi* gesticulate. **~onista** *m & f* shareholder
acebo *m* holly (tree)
acebuche *m* wild olive tree
acecinar *vt* cure ‹*carne*›. **~se** *vpr* become wizened
acech|ar *vt* spy on; (*aguardar*) lie in wait for. **~o** *m* spying. **al ~o** on the look-out

acedera *f* sorrel
acedía *f* (*pez*) plaice; (*acidez*) heartburn
aceit|ar *vt* oil; (*culin*) add oil to. **~e** *m* oil; (*de oliva*) olive oil. **~era** *f* oil bottle; (*para engrasar*) oilcan. **~ero** *a* oil. **~oso** *a* oily
aceitun|a *f* olive. **~ado** *a* olive. **~o** *m* olive tree
acelera|ción *f* acceleration. **~damente** *adv* quickly. **~dor** *m* accelerator. **~r** *vt* accelerate; (*fig*) speed up, quicken
acelga *f* chard
ac|émila *f* mule; (*como insulto*) ass (*fam*). **~emilero** *m* muleteer
acendra|do *a* pure. **~r** *vt* purify; refine ‹*metales*›
acensuar *vt* tax
acent|o *m* accent; (*énfasis*) stress. **~uación** *f* accentuation. **~uar** [21] *vt* stress; (*fig*) emphasize. **~uarse** *vpr* become noticeable
aceña *f* water-mill
acepción *f* meaning, sense
acepta|ble *a* acceptable. **~ción** *f* acceptance; (*aprobación*) approval. **~r** *vt* accept
acequia *f* irrigation channel
acera *f* pavement (*Brit*), sidewalk (*Amer*)
acerado *a* steel; (*fig, mordaz*) sharp
acerca de *prep* about
acerca|miento *m* approach; (*fig*) reconciliation. **~r** [7] *vt* bring near. **~rse** *vpr* approach
acería *f* steelworks
acerico *m* pincushion
acero *m* steel. **~ inoxidable** stainless steel
acérrimo *a* (*fig*) staunch
acert|ado *a* right, correct; (*apropiado*) appropriate. **~ar** [1] *vt* hit ‹*el blanco*›; (*adivinar*) get right, guess. ● *vi* get right. **~ar a** happen to. **~ar con** hit on. **~ijo** *m* riddle
acervo *m* pile; (*bienes*) common property
acetato *m* acetate
acético *a* acetic
acetileno *m* acetylene
acetona *m* acetone
aciago *a* unlucky
aciano *m* cornflower
ac|íbar *m* aloes; (*planta*) aloe; (*fig, amargura*) bitterness. **~ibarar** *vt* add aloes to; (*fig, amargar*) embitter
acicala|do *a* dressed up, overdressed. **~r** *vt* dress up. **~rse** *vpr* get dressed up
acicate *m* spur
acid|ez *f* acidity. **~ificar** [7] *vt* acidify. **~ificarse** *vpr* acidify
ácido *a* sour. ● *m* acid
acierto *m* success; (*idea*) good idea; (*habilidad*) skill
aclama|ción *f* acclaim; (*aplausos*) applause. **~r** *vt* acclaim; (*aplaudir*) applaud
aclara|ción *f* explanation. **~r** *vt* lighten ‹*colores*›; (*explicar*) clarify; (*enjuagar*) rinse. ● *vi* ‹*el tiempo*› brighten up. **~rse** *vpr* become clear. **~torio** *a* explanatory
aclimata|ción *f* acclimatization, acclimation (*Amer*). **~r** *vt* acclimatize, acclimate (*Amer*). **~rse** *vpr* become acclimatized, become acclimated (*Amer*)
acné *m* acne
acobardar *vt* intimidate. **~se** *vpr* get frightened
acocil *m* (*Mex*) freshwater shrimp
acod|ado *a* bent. **~ar** *vt* (*doblar*) bend; (*agricultura*) layer. **~arse** *vpr* lean on (**en** on). **~o** *m* layer
acog|edor *a* welcoming; ‹*ambiente*› friendly. **~er** [14] *vt* welcome; (*proteger*) shelter; (*recibir*) receive. **~erse** *vpr* take refuge. **~ida** *f* welcome; (*refugio*) refuge
acogollar *vi* bud. **~se** *vpr* bud
acolcha|do *a* quilted. **~r** *vt* quilt, pad
acólito *m* acolyte; (*monaguillo*) altar boy
acomet|edor *a* aggressive; (*emprendedor*) enterprising. **~er** *vt* attack; (*emprender*) undertake; (*llenar*) fill. **~ida** *f* attack. **~ividad** *f* aggression; (*iniciativa*) enterprise
acomod|able *a* adaptable. **~adizo** *a* accommodating. **~ado** *a* well off. **~ador** *m* usher. **~adora** *f* usherette. **~amiento** *m* suitability. **~ar** *vt* arrange; (*adaptar*) adjust. ● *vi* be suitable. **~arse** *vpr* settle down; (*adaptarse*) conform. **~aticio** *a* accommodating. **~o** *m* position
acompaña|do *a* accompanied; (*concurrido*) busy. **~miento** *m* accompaniment. **~nta** *f* companion. **~nte** *m* companion; (*mus*) accompanist. **~r** *vt* accompany; (*adjuntar*) enclose. **~rse** *vpr* (*mus*) accompany o.s.

acompasa|do *a* rhythmic. **~r** *vt* keep in time; (*fig*, *ajustar*) adjust

acondiciona|do *a* equipped. **~miento** *m* conditioning. **~r** *vt* fit out; (*preparar*) prepare

acongojar *vt* distress. **~se** *vpr* get upset

acónito *m* aconite

aconseja|ble *a* advisable. **~do** *a* advised. **~r** *vt* advise. **~rse** *vpr* take advice. **~rse con** consult

aconsonantar *vt/i* rhyme

acontec|er [11] *vi* happen. **~imiento** *m* event

acopi|ar *vt* collect. **~o** *m* store

acopla|do *a* coordinated. **~miento** *m* coupling; (*elec*) connection. **~r** *vt* fit; (*elec*) connect; (*rail*) couple

acoquina|miento *m* intimidation. **~r** *vt* intimidate. **~rse** *vpr* be intimidated

acoraza|do *a* armour-plated. ● *m* battleship. **~r** [10] *vt* armour

acorazonado *a* heart-shaped

acorcha|do *a* spongy. **~rse** *vpr* go spongy; ‹*parte del cuerpo*› go to sleep

acord|ado *a* agreed. **~ar** [2] *vt* agree (upon); (*decidir*) decide; (*recordar*) remind. **~e** *a* in agreement; (*mus*) harmonious. ● *m* chord

acorde|ón *m* accordion. **~onista** *m & f* accordionist

acordona|do *a* ‹*lugar*› cordoned off. **~miento** *m* cordoning off. **~r** *vt* tie, lace; (*rodear*) surround, cordon off

acorrala|miento *m* (*de animales*) rounding up; (*de personas*) cornering. **~r** *vt* round up ‹*animales*›; corner ‹*personas*›

acorta|miento *m* shortening. **~r** *vt* shorten; (*fig*) cut down

acos|ar *vt* hound; (*fig*) pester. **~o** *m* pursuit; (*fig*) pestering

acostar [2] *vt* put to bed; (*naut*) bring alongside. ● *vi* (*naut*) reach land. **~se** *vpr* go to bed; (*echarse*) lie down; (*Mex*, *parir*) give birth

acostumbra|do *a* (*habitual*) usual. **~do a** used to, accustomed to. **~r** *vt* get used. **me ha acostumbrado a levantarme por la noche** he's got me used to getting up at night. ● *vi*. **~r (a)** be accustomed to. **acostumbro comer a la una** I usually have lunch at one o'clock. **~rse** *vpr* become accustomed, get used

acota|ción *f* (*nota*) marginal note; (*en el teatro*) stage direction; (*cota*) elevation mark. **~do** *a* enclosed. **~r** *vt* mark out ‹*terreno*›; (*anotar*) annotate

ácrata *a* anarchistic. ● *m & f* anarchist

acre *m* acre. ● *a* ‹*olor*› pungent; ‹*sabor*› sharp, bitter

acrecenta|miento *m* increase. **~r** [1] *vt* increase. **~rse** *vpr* increase

acrec|er [11] *vt* increase. **~imiento** *m* increase

acredita|do *a* reputable; (*pol*) accredited. **~r** *vt* prove; accredit ‹*representante diplomático*›; (*garantizar*) guarantee; (*autorizar*) authorize. **~rse** *vpr* make one's name

acreedor *a* worthy (**a** of). ● *m* creditor

acribillar *vt* (*a balazos*) riddle (**a** with); (*a picotazos*) cover (**a** with); (*fig*, *a preguntas etc*) pester (**a** with)

acrimonia *f* (*de sabor*) sharpness; (*de olor*) pungency; (*fig*) bitterness

acrisola|do *a* pure; (*fig*) proven. **~r** *vt* purify; (*confirmar*) prove

acritud *f* (*de sabor*) sharpness; (*de olor*) pungency; (*fig*) bitterness

acr|obacia *f* acrobatics. **~obacias aéreas** aerobatics. **~óbata** *m & f* acrobat. **~obático** *a* acrobatic. **~obatismo** *m* acrobatics

acrónimo *m* acronym

acróstico *a & m* acrostic

acta *f* minutes; (*certificado*) certificate

actinia *f* sea anemone

actitud *f* posture, position; (*fig*) attitude, position

activ|ación *f* speed-up. **~amente** *adv* actively. **~ar** *vt* activate; (*acelerar*) speed up. **~idad** *f* activity. **~o** *a* active. ● *m* assets

acto *m* act; (*ceremonia*) ceremony. **en el ~** immediately

act|or *m* actor. **~riz** *f* actress

actuación *f* action; (*conducta*) behaviour; (*theat*) performance

actual *a* present; ‹*asunto*› topical. **~idad** *f* present. **~idades** *fpl* current affairs. **~ización** *f* modernization. **~izar** [10] *vt* modernize. **~mente** *adv* now, at the present time. **en la ~idad** nowadays

actuar [21] *vt* work. ● *vi* act. **~ como, ~ de** act as

actuario *m* clerk of the court. ~ **(de seguros)** actuary
acuarel|a *f* watercolour. **~ista** *m & f* watercolourist
acuario *m* aquarium. **A~** Aquarius
acuartela|do *a* quartered. **~miento** *m* quartering. **~r** *vt* quarter, billet; (*mantener en cuartel*) confine to barracks
acuático *a* aquatic
acuci|ador pressing. **~ar** *vt* urge on; (*dar prisa a*) hasten. **~oso** *a* keen
acuclillarse *vpr* crouch down, squat down
acuchilla|do *a* slashed; ‹*persona*› stabbed. **~r** *vt* slash; stab ‹*persona*›; (*alisar*) smooth
acudir *vi*. ~ **a** go to, attend; keep ‹*una cita*›; (*en auxilio*) go to help
acueducto *m* aqueduct
acuerdo *m* agreement. • *vb véase* **acordar**. **¡de ~!** OK! **de ~ con** in accordance with. **estar de ~** agree. **ponerse de ~** agree
acuesto *vb véase* **acostar**
acuidad *f* acuity, sharpness
acumula|ción *f* accumulation. **~dor** *a* accumulative. • *m* accumulator. **~r** *vt* accumulate. **~rse** *vpr* accumulate
acunar *vt* rock
acuña|ción *f* minting, coining. **~r** *vt* mint, coin
acuos|idad *f* wateriness. **~o** *a* watery
acupuntura *f* acupuncture
acurrucarse [7] *vpr* curl up
acusa|ción *f* accusation. **~do** *a* accused; (*destacado*) marked. • *m* accused. **~dor** *a* accusing. • *m* accuser. **~r** *vt* accuse; (*mostrar*) show; (*denunciar*) denounce. **~rse** *vpr* confess; (*notarse*) become marked. **~torio** *a* accusatory
acuse *m*. **~ de recibo** acknowledgement of receipt
acus|ica *m & f* (*fam*) telltale. **~ón** *a & m* telltale
acústic|a *f* acoustics. **~o** *a* acoustic
achacar [7] *vt* attribute
achacoso *a* sickly
achaflanar *vt* bevel
achantar *vt* (*fam*) intimidate. **~se** *vpr* hide; (*fig*) back down
achaparrado *a* stocky
achaque *m* ailment
achares *mpl* (*fam*). **dar ~** make jealous
achata|miento *m* flattening. **~r** *vt* flatten
achica|do *a* childish. **~r** [7] *vt* make smaller; (*fig, empequeñecer, fam*) belittle; (*naut*) bale out. **~rse** *vpr* become smaller; (*humillarse*) be humiliated
achicopalado *a* (*Mex*) depressed
achicoria *f* chicory
achicharra|dero *m* inferno. **~nte** *a* sweltering. **~r** *vt* burn; (*fig*) pester. **~rse** *vpr* burn
achispa|do *a* tipsy. **~rse** *vpr* get tipsy
achocolatado *a* (chocolate-)brown
achuch|ado *a* (*fam*) hard. **~ar** *vt* jostle, push. **~ón** *m* shove, push
achulado *a* cocky
adagio *m* adage, proverb; (*mus*) adagio
adalid *m* leader
adamascado *a* damask
adapta|ble *a* adaptable. **~ción** *f* adaptation. **~dor** *m* adapter. **~r** *vt* adapt; (*ajustar*) fit. **~rse** *vpr* adapt o.s.
adecentar *vt* clean up. **~se** *vpr* tidy o.s. up
adecua|ción *f* suitability. **~damente** *adv* suitably. **~do** *a* suitable. **~r** *vt* adapt, make suitable
adelant|ado *a* advanced; ‹*niño*› precocious; ‹*reloj*› fast. **~amiento** *m* advance(ment); (*auto*) overtaking. **~ar** *vt* advance, move forward; (*acelerar*) speed up; put forward ‹*reloj*›; (*auto*) overtake. • *vi* advance, go forward; ‹*reloj*› gain, be fast. **~arse** *vpr* advance, move forward; ‹*reloj*› gain; (*auto*) overtake. **~e** *adv* forward. • *int* come in!; (*¡siga!*) carry on! **~o** *m* advance; (*progreso*) progress. **más ~e** (*lugar*) further on; (*tiempo*) later on. **pagar por ~ado** pay in advance.
adelfa *f* oleander
adelgaza|dor *a* slimming. **~miento** *m* slimming. **~r** [10] *vt* make thin. • *vi* lose weight; (*adrede*) slim. **~rse** *vpr* lose weight; (*adrede*) slim
ademán *m* gesture. **ademanes** *mpl* (*modales*) manners. **en ~ de** as if to
además *adv* besides; (*también*) also. **~ de** besides
adentr|arse *vpr*. **~ en** penetrate into; study thoroughly ‹*tema etc*›. **~o** *adv* in(side). **mar ~o** out at sea. **tierra ~o** inland
adepto *m* supporter

aderez|ar [10] *vt* flavour ‹*bebidas*›; (*condimentar*) season; dress ‹*ensalada*›. **~o** *m* flavouring; (*con condimentos*) seasoning; (*para ensalada*) dressing
adeud|ar *vt* owe. **~o** *m* debit
adhe|rencia *f* adhesion; (*fig*) adherence. **~rente** *a* adherent. **~rir** [4] *vt* stick on. ● *vi* stick. **~rirse** *vpr* stick; (*fig*) follow. **~sión** *f* adhesion; (*fig*) support. **~sivo** *a & m* adhesive
adici|ón *f* addition. **~onal** *a* additional. **~onar** *vt* add
adicto *a* devoted. ● *m* follower
adiestra|do *a* trained. **~miento** *m* training. **~r** *vt* train. **~rse** *vpr* practise
adinerado *a* wealthy
adiós *int* goodbye!; (*al cruzarse con alguien*) hello!
adit|amento *m* addition; (*accesorio*) accessory. **~ivo** *m* additive
adivin|ación *f* divination; (*por conjeturas*) guessing. **~ador** *m* fortune-teller. **~anza** *f* riddle. **~ar** *vt* foretell; (*acertar*) guess. **~o** *m* fortune-teller
adjetivo *a* adjectival. ● *m* adjective
adjudica|ción *f* award. **~r** [7] *vt* award. **~rse** *vpr* appropriate. **~tario** *m* winner of an award
adjunt|ar *vt* enclose. **~o** *a* enclosed; (*auxiliar*) assistant. ● *m* assistant
adminículo *m* thing, gadget
administra|ción *f* administration; (*gestión*) management. **~dor** *m* administrator; (*gerente*) manager. **~dora** *f* administrator; manageress. **~r** *vt* administer. **~tivo** *a* administrative
admira|ble *a* admirable. **~ción** *f* admiration. **~dor** *m* admirer. **~r** *vt* admire; (*asombrar*) astonish. **~rse** *vpr* be astonished. **~tivo** *a* admiring
admi|sibilidad *f* admissibility. **~sible** *a* acceptable. **~sión** *f* admission; (*aceptación*) acceptance. **~tir** *vt* admit; (*aceptar*) accept
adobar *vt* (*culin*) pickle; (*fig*) twist
adobe *m* sun-dried brick. **~ra** *f* mould for making (sun-dried) bricks
adobo *m* pickle
adocena|do *a* common. **~rse** *vpr* become common
adoctrinamiento *m* indoctrination
adolecer [11] *vi* be ill. **~ de** suffer with
adolescen|cia *f* adolescent. **~te** *a & m & f* adolescent
adonde *conj* where
adónde *adv* where?
adop|ción *f* adoption. **~tar** *vt* adopt. **~tivo** *a* adoptive; ‹*patria*› of adoption
adoqu|ín *m* paving stone; (*imbécil*) idiot. **~inado** *m* paving. **~inar** *vt* pave
adora|ble *a* adorable. **~ción** *f* adoration. **~dor** *a* adoring. ● *n* worshipper. **~r** *vt* adore
adormec|edor *a* soporific; ‹*droga*› sedative. **~er** [11] *vt* send to sleep; (*fig, calmar*) calm, soothe. **~erse** *vpr* fall asleep; (*un miembro*› go to sleep. **~ido** *a* sleepy; ‹*un miembro*› numb. **~imiento** *m* sleepiness; (*de un miembro*) numbness
adormidera *f* opium poppy
adormilarse *vpr* doze
adorn|ar *vt* adorn (**con, de** with). **~o** *m* decoration
adosar *vt* lean (**a** against)
adqui|rido *a* acquired. **~rir** [4] *vt* acquire; (*comprar*) buy. **~sición** *f* acquisition; (*compra*) purchase. **~sitivo** *a* acquisitive. **poder** *m* **~sitivo** purchasing power
adrede *adv* on purpose
adrenalina *f* adrenalin
adscribir [*pp* **adscrito**] *vt* appoint
aduan|a *f* customs. **~ero** *a* customs. ● *m* customs officer
aducir [47] *vt* allege
adueñarse *vpr* take possession
adul|ación *f* flattery. **~ador** *a* flattering. ● *m* flatterer. **~ar** *vt* flatter
ad|ulteración *f* adulteration. **~ulterar** *vt* adulterate. ● *vi* commit adultery. **~ulterino** *a* adulterous. **~ulterio** *m* adultery. **~últera** *f* adulteress. **~últero** *a* adulterous. ● *m* adulterer
adulto *a & m* adult, grown-up
adusto *a* severe, harsh
advenedizo *a & m* upstart
advenimiento *m* advent, arrival; (*subida al trono*) accession
adventicio *a* accidental
adverbi|al *a* adverbial. **~o** *m* adverb
advers|ario *m* adversary. **~idad** *f* adversity. **~o** *a* adverse, unfavourable
advert|encia *f* warning; (*prólogo*) foreword. **~ido** *a* informed. **~ir** [4] *vt* warn; (*notar*) notice

adviento *m* Advent
advocación *f* dedication
adyacente *a* adjacent
aéreo *a* air; (*photo*) aerial; ‹*ferrocarril*› overhead; (*fig*) flimsy
aeróbica *f* aerobics
aerodeslizador *m* hovercraft
aerodinámic|a *f* aerodynamics. **~o** *a* aerodynamic
aeródromo *m* aerodrome, airdrome (*Amer*)
aero|espacial *a* aerospace. **~faro** *m* beacon. **~lito** *m* meteorite. **~nauta** *m* & *f* aeronaut. **~náutica** *f* aeronautics. **~náutico** *a* aeronautical. **~nave** *f* airship. **~puerto** *m* airport. **~sol** *m* aerosol
afab|ilidad *f* affability. **~le** *a* affable
afamado *a* famous
af|án *m* hard work; (*deseo*) desire. **~anar** *vt* (*fam*) pinch. **~anarse** *vpr* strive (**en, por** to). **~anoso** *a* laborious
afea|miento *m* disfigurement. **~r** *vt* disfigure, make ugly; (*censurar*) censure
afección *f* disease
afecta|ción *f* affectation. **~do** *a* affected. **~r** *vt* affect
afect|ísimo *a* affectionate. **~ísimo amigo** (*en cartas*) my dear friend. **~ividad** *f* emotional nature. **~ivo** *a* sensitive. **~o** *m* (*cariño*) affection. • *a*. **~o a** attached to. **~uosidad** *f* affection. **~uoso** *a* affectionate. **con un ~uoso saludo** (*en cartas*) with kind regards. **suyo ~ísimo** (*en cartas*) yours sincerely
afeita|do *m* shave. **~dora** *f* electric razor. **~r** *vt* shave. **~rse** *vpr* (have a) shave
afelpado *a* velvety
afemina|do *a* effeminate. • *m* effeminate person. **~miento** *m* effeminacy. **~rse** *vpr* become effeminate
aferrar [1] *vt* grasp
afgano *a* & *m* Afghan
afianza|miento *m* (*reforzar*) strengthening; (*garantía*) guarantee. **~rse** [10] *vpr* become established
afici|ón *f* liking; (*conjunto de aficionados*) fans. **~onado** *a* keen (**a** on), fond (**a** of). • *m* fan. **~onar** *vt* make fond. **~onarse** *vpr* take a liking to. **por ~ón** as a hobby
afila|do *a* sharp. **~dor** *m* knife-grinder. **~dura** *f* sharpening. **~r** *vt* sharpen. **~rse** *vpr* get sharp; (*ponerse flaco*) grow thin
afilia|ción *f* affiliation. **~do** *a* affiliated. **~rse** *vpr* become a member (**a** of)
afiligranado *a* filigreed; (*fig*) delicate
afín *a* similar; (*próximo*) adjacent; ‹*personas*› related
afina|ción *f* refining; (*auto, mus*) tuning. **~do** *a* finished; (*mus*) in tune. **~r** *vt* refine; (*afilar*) sharpen; (*acabar*) finish; (*auto, mus*) tune. • *vi* be in tune. **~rse** *vpr* become more refined
afincarse [7] *vpr* settle
afinidad *f* affinity; (*parentesco*) relationship
afirma|ción *f* affirmation. **~r** *vt* make firm; (*asentir*) affirm. **~rse** *vpr* steady o.s.; (*confirmar*) confirm. **~tivo** *a* affirmative
aflic|ción *f* affliction. **~tivo** *a* distressing
afligi|do *a* distressed. • *m* afflicted. **~r** [14] *vt* distress. **~rse** *vpr* grieve
afloja|miento *m* loosening. **~r** *vt* loosen; (*relajar*) ease. • *vi* let up
aflora|miento *m* outcrop. **~r** *vi* appear on the surface
aflu|encia *f* flow. **~ente** *a* flowing. • *m* tributary. **~ir** [17] *vi* flow (**a** into)
af|onía *f* hoarseness. **~ónico** *a* hoarse
aforismo *m* aphorism
aforo *m* capacity
afortunado *a* fortunate, lucky
afrancesado *a* francophile
afrent|a *f* insult; (*vergüenza*) disgrace. **~ar** *vt* insult. **~oso** *a* insulting
África *f* Africa. **~ del Sur** South Africa
africano *a* & *m* African
afrodisíaco *a* & *m*, **afrodisiaco** *a* & *m* aphrodisiac
afrontar *vt* bring face to face; (*enfrentar*) face, confront
afuera *adv* out(side). **¡~!** out of the way! **~s** *fpl* outskirts.
agachar *vt* lower. **~se** *vpr* bend over
agalla *f* (*de los peces*) gill. **~s** *fpl* (*fig*) guts
agarrada *f* row
agarrader|a *f* (*LAm*) handle. **~o** *m* handle. **tener ~as** (*LAm*), **tener ~os** have influence

agarr|ado *a* (*fig, fam*) mean. **~ador** *a* (*Arg*) ‹*bebida*› strong. **~ar** *vt* grasp; (*esp LAm*) take, catch. ● *vi* ‹*plantas*› take root. **~arse** *vpr* hold on; (*reñirse, fam*) fight. **~ón** *m* tug; (*LAm, riña*) row

agarrota|miento *m* tightening; (*auto*) seizing up. **~r** *vt* tie tightly; ‹*el frío*› stiffen; garotte ‹*un reo*›. **~rse** *vpr* go stiff; (*auto*) seize up

agasaj|ado *m* guest of honour. **~ar** *vt* look after well. **~o** *m* good treatment

ágata *f* agate

agavilla|dora *f* (*máquina*) binder. **~r** *vt* bind

agazaparse *vpr* hide

agencia *f* agency. **~ de viajes** travel agency. **~ inmobiliaria** estate agency (*Brit*), real estate agency (*Amer*). **~r** *vt* find. **~rse** *vpr* find (out) for o.s.

agenda *f* notebook

agente *m* agent; (*de policía*) policeman. **~ de aduanas** customs officer. **~ de bolsa** stockbroker

ágil *a* agile

agilidad *f* agility

agita|ción *f* waving; (*de un líquido*) stirring; (*intranquilidad*) agitation. **~do** *a* ‹*el mar*› rough; (*fig*) agitated. **~dor** *m* (*pol*) agitator

agitanado *a* gypsy-like

agitar *vt* wave; shake ‹*botellas etc*›; stir ‹*líquidos*›; (*fig*) stir up. **~se** *vpr* wave; ‹*el mar*› get rough; (*fig*) get excited

aglomera|ción *f* agglomeration; (*de tráfico*) traffic jam. **~r** *vt* amass. **~rse** *vpr* form a crowd

agn|osticismo *m* agnosticism. **~óstico** *a & m* agnostic

agobi|ador *a* ‹*trabajo*› exhausting; ‹*calor*› oppressive. **~ante** *a* ‹*trabajo*› exhausting; ‹*calor*› oppressive. **~ar** *vt* weigh down; (*fig, abrumar*) overwhelm. **~o** *m* weight; (*cansancio*) exhaustion; (*opresión*) oppression

agolpa|miento *m* (*de gente*) crowd; (*de cosas*) pile. **~rse** *vpr* crowd together

agon|ía *f* death throes; (*fig*) agony. **~izante** *a* dying; ‹*luz*› failing. **~izar** [10] *vi* be dying

agor|ar [16] *vt* prophesy. **~ero** *a* of ill omen. ● *m* soothsayer

agostar *vt* wither

agosto *m* August. **hacer su ~** feather one's nest

agota|do *a* exhausted; ‹*libro*› out of print. **~dor** *a* exhausting. **~miento** *m* exhaustion. **~r** *vt* exhaust. **~rse** *vpr* be exhausted; ‹*libro*› go out of print

agracia|do *a* attractive; (*que tiene suerte*) lucky. **~r** make attractive

agrada|ble *a* pleasant, nice. **~r** *vi* please. **esto me ~** I like this

agradec|er [11] *vt* thank ‹*persona*›; be grateful for ‹*cosa*›. **~ido** *a* grateful. **~imiento** *m* gratitude. **¡muy ~ido!** thanks a lot!

agrado *m* pleasure; (*amabilidad*) friendliness

agrandar *vt* enlarge; (*fig*) exaggerate. **~se** *vpr* get bigger

agrario *a* agrarian, land; ‹*política*› agricultural

agrava|miento *m* worsening. **~nte** *a* aggravating. ● *f* additional problem. **~r** *vt* aggravate; (*aumentar el peso*) make heavier. **~rse** *vpr* get worse

agravi|ar *vt* offend; (*perjudicar*) wrong. **~arse** *vpr* be offended. **~o** *m* offence

agraz *m*. **en ~** prematurely

agredir [24] *vt* attack. **~ de palabra** insult

agrega|do *m* aggregate; (*funcionario diplomático*) attaché. **~r** [12] *vt* add; (*unir*) join; appoint ‹*persona*›

agremiar *vt* form into a union. **~se** *vpr* form a union

agres|ión *f* aggression; (*ataque*) attack. **~ividad** *f* aggressiveness. **~ivo** aggressive. **~or** *m* aggressor

agreste *a* country

agria|do *a* (*fig*) embittered. **~r** [*regular, o raramente* 20] *vt* sour. **~rse** *vpr* turn sour; (*fig*) become embittered

agr|ícola *a* agricultural. **~icultor** *a* agricutural. ● *m* farmer. **~icultura** *f* agriculture, farming

agridulce *a* bitter-sweet; (*culin*) sweet-and-sour

agriera *f* (*LAm*) heartburn

agrietar *vt* crack. **~se** *vpr* crack; ‹*piel*› chap

agrimens|or *m* surveyor. **~ura** *f* surveying

agrio *a* sour; (*fig*) sharp. **~s** *mpl* citrus fruits

agronomía *f* agronomy

agropecuario *a* farming
agrupa|ción *f* group; (*acción*) grouping. **~r** *vt* group. **~rse** *vpr* form a group
agua *f* water; (*lluvia*) rain; (*marea*) tide; (*vertiente del tejado*) slope. **~ abajo** downstream. **~ arriba** upstream. **~ bendita** holy water. **~ caliente** hot water. **estar entre dos ~s** sit on the fence. **hacer ~** (*naut*) leak. **nadar entre dos ~s** sit on the fence
aguacate *m* avocado pear; (*árbol*) avocado pear tree
aguacero *m* downpour, heavy shower
agua *f* **corriente** running water
aguachinarse *vpr* (*Mex*) ‹*cultivos*› be flooded
aguada *f* watering place; (*naut*) drinking water; (*acuarela*) water-colour
agua *f* **de colonia** eau-de-Cologne
aguad|o *a* watery. **~ucho** *m* refreshment kiosk
agua: ~ dulce fresh water. **~fiestas** *m & f invar* spoil-sport, wet blanket. **~ fría** cold water. **~fuerte** *m* etching
aguaje *m* spring tide
agua: ~mala *f*, **~mar** *m* jellyfish
aguamarina *f* aquamarine
agua: ~miel *f* mead. **~ mineral con gas** fizzy mineral water. **~ mineral sin gas** still mineral water. **~nieve** *f* sleet
aguanoso *a* watery; ‹*tierra*› waterlogged
aguant|able *a* bearable. **~aderas** *fpl* patience. **~ar** *vt* put up with, bear; (*sostener*) support. ● *vi* hold out. **~arse** *vpr* restrain o.s. **~e** *m* patience; (*resistencia*) endurance
agua: ~pié *m* watery wine. **~ potable** drinking water. **~r** [15] *vt* water down. **~ salada** salt water.
aguardar *vt* wait for. ● *vi* wait
agua: ~rdiente *m* (cheap) brandy. **~rrás** *m* turpentine, turps (*fam*). **~turma** *f* Jerusalem artichoke. **~zal** *m* puddle
agud|eza *f* sharpness; (*fig, perspicacia*) insight; (*fig, ingenio*) wit. **~izar** [10] *vt* sharpen. **~izarse** *vpr* ‹*enfermedad*› get worse. **~o** *a* sharp; ‹*ángulo, enfermedad*› acute; ‹*voz*› high-pitched
agüero *m* omen. **ser de buen ~** augur well
aguij|ada *f* goad. **~ar** *vt* (*incl fig*) goad. **~ón** *m* point of a goad. **~onazo** *m* prick. **~onear** *vt* goad
águila *f* eagle; (*persona perspicaz*) astute person
aguileña *f* columbine
aguil|eño *a* aquiline. **~ucho** *m* eaglet
aguinaldo *m* Christmas box
aguja *f* needle; (*del reloj*) hand; (*arquit*) steeple. **~s** *fpl* (*rail*) points
agujer|ear *vt* make holes in. **~o** *m* hole
agujetas *fpl* stiffness. **tener ~** be stiff
agujón *m* hairpin
agusanado *a* full of maggots
agutí *m* (*LAm*) guinea pig
aguza|do *a* sharp. **~miento** *m* sharpening. **~r** [10] *vt* sharpen
ah *int* ah!, oh!
aherrojar *vt* (*fig*) oppress
ahí *adv* there. **de ~ que** so that. **por ~** over there; (*aproximadamente*) thereabouts
ahija|da *f* god-daughter, godchild. **~do** *m* godson, godchild. **~r** *vt* adopt
ahínco *m* enthusiasm; (*empeño*) insistence
ahíto *a* full up
ahog|ado *a* (*en el agua*) drowned; (*asfixiado*) suffocated. **~ar** [12] *vt* (*en el agua*) drown; (*asfixiar*) suffocate; put out ‹*fuego*›. **~arse** *vpr* (*en el agua*) drown; (*asfixiarse*) suffocate. **~o** *m* breathlessness; (*fig, angustia*) distress; (*apuro*) financial trouble
ahondar *vt* deepen; ● *vi* go deep. **~ en** (*fig*) examine in depth. **~se** *vpr* get deeper
ahora *adv* now; (*hace muy poco*) just now; (*dentro de poco*) very soon. **~ bien** but. **~ mismo** right now. **de ~ en adelante** from now on, in future. **por ~** for the time being
ahorca|dura *f* hanging. **~r** [7] *vt* hang. **~rse** *vpr* hang o.s.
ahorita *adv* (*fam*) now. **~ mismo** right now
ahorquillar *vt* shape like a fork
ahorr|ador *a* thrifty. **~ar** *vt* save. **~arse** *vpr* save o.s. **~o** *m* saving; (*cantidad ahorrada*) savings. **~os** *mpl* savings
ahuecar [7] *vt* hollow; fluff up ‹*colchón*›; deepen ‹*la voz*›; (*marcharse, fam*) clear off (*fam*)

ahuizote *m* (*Mex*) bore
ahulado *m* (*LAm*) oilskin
ahuma|do *a* (*culin*) smoked; (*de colores*) smoky. **~r** *vt* (*culin*) smoke; (*llenar de humo*) fill with smoke. ● *vi* smoke. **~rse** *vpr* become smoky; ‹*comida*› acquire a smoky taste; (*emborracharse, fam*) get drunk
ahusa|do *a* tapering. **~rse** *vpr* taper
ahuyentar *vt* drive away; banish ‹*pensamientos etc*›
airado *a* annoyed
aire *m* air; (*viento*) breeze; (*corriente*) draught; (*aspecto*) appearance; (*mus*) tune, air. **~ación** *f* ventilation. **~ acondicionado** air-conditioned. **~ar** *vt* air; (*ventilar*) ventilate; (*fig, publicar*) make public. **~arse** *vpr*. **salir para ~arse** go out for some fresh air. **al ~ libre** in the open air. **darse ~s** give o.s. airs
airón *m* heron
airos|amente *adv* gracefully. **~o** *a* draughty; (*fig*) elegant
aisla|do *a* isolated; (*elec*) insulated. **~dor** *a* (*elec*) insulating. ● *m* (*elec*) insulator. **~miento** *m* isolation; (*elec*) insulation. **~nte** *a* insulating. **~r** [23] *vt* isolate; (*elec*) insulate
ajajá *int* good! splendid!
ajar *vt* crumple; (*estropear*) spoil
ajedre|cista *m & f* chess-player. **~z** *m* chess. **~zado** *a* chequered, checked
ajenjo *m* absinthe
ajeno *a* (*de otro*) someone else's; (*de otros*) other people's; (*extraño*) alien
ajetre|arse *vpr* be busy. **~o** *m* bustle
ají *m* (*LAm*) chilli; (*salsa*) chilli sauce
aj|iaceite *m* garlic sauce. **~ilimójili** *m* piquant garlic sauce. **~illo** *m* garlic. **al ~illo** cooked with garlic. **~o** *m* garlic. **~o-a-rriero** *m* cod in garlic sauce
ajorca *f* bracelet
ajuar *m* furnishings; (*de novia*) trousseau
ajuma|do *a* (*fam*) drunk. **~rse** *vpr* (*fam*) get drunk
ajust|ado *a* right; ‹*vestido*› tight. **~ador** *m* fitter. **~amiento** *m* fitting; (*adaptación*) adjustment; (*acuerdo*) agreement; (*de una cuenta*) settlement. **~ar** *vt* fit; (*adaptar*) adapt; (*acordar*) agree; settle ‹*una cuenta*›; (*apretar*) tighten. ● *vi* fit. **~arse** *vpr* fit; (*adaptarse*) adapt o.s.; (*acordarse*) come to an agreement. **~e** m fitting; (*adaptación*) *f* adjustment; (*acuerdo*) agreement; (*de una cuenta*) settlement
ajusticiar *vt* execute
al = **a**; **el**
ala *f* wing; (*de sombrero*) brim; (*deportes*) winger
alaba|ncioso *a* boastful. **~nza** *f* praise. **~r** *vt* praise. **~rse** *vpr* boast
alabastro *m* alabaster
álabe *m* (*paleta*) paddle; (*diente*) cog
alabe|ar *vt* warp. **~arse** *vpr* warp. **~o** *m* warping
alacena *f* cupboard (*Brit*), closet (*Amer*)
alacrán *m* scorpion
alacridad *f* alacrity
alado *a* winged
alambi|cado *a* distilled; (*fig*) subtle. **~camiento** *m* distillation; (*fig*) subtlety. **~car** [7] *vt* distil. **~que** *m* still
alambr|ada *f* wire fence; (*de alambre de espinas*) barbed wire fence. **~ar** *vt* fence. **~e** *m* wire. **~e de espinas** barbed wire. **~era** *f* fireguard
alameda *f* avenue; (*plantío de álamos*) poplar grove
álamo *m* poplar. **~ temblón** aspen
alano *m* mastiff
alarde *m* show. **~ar** *vi* boast
alarga|dera *f* extension. **~do** *a* long. **~dor** *m* extension. **~miento** *m* lengthening. **~r** [12] *vt* lengthen; stretch out ‹*mano etc*›; (*dar*) give, pass. **~rse** *vpr* lengthen, get longer
alarido *m* shriek
alarm|a *f* alarm. **~ante** *a* alarming. **~ar** *vt* alarm, frighten. **~arse** *vpr* be alarmed. **~ista** *m & f* alarmist
alba *f* dawn
albacea *m* executor. ● *f* executrix
albacora (*culin*) tuna(-fish)
albahaca *f* basil
albanés *a & m* Albanian
Albania *f* Albania
albañal *m* sewer, drain
albañil *m* bricklayer. **~ería** *f* (*arte*) bricklaying
albarán *m* delivery note
albarda *f* packsaddle; (*Mex*) saddle. **~r** *vt* saddle
albaricoque *m* apricot. **~ro** *m* apricot tree
albatros *m* albatross
albedrío *m* will. **libre ~** free will

albéitar *m* veterinary surgeon (*Brit*), veterinarian (*Amer*), vet (*fam*)
alberca *f* tank, reservoir
alberg|ar [12] *vt* (*alojar*) put up; ‹*viviendas*› house; (*dar asilo*) shelter. **~arse** *vpr* stay; (*refugiarse*) shelter. **~ue** *m* accommodation; (*refugio*) shelter. **~ue de juventud** youth hostel
albóndiga *f* meatball, rissole
albor *m* dawn. **~ada** *f* dawn; (*mus*) dawn song. **~ear** *vi* dawn
albornoz *m* (*de los moros*) burnous; (*para el baño*) bathrobe
alborot|adizo *a* excitable. **~ado** *a* excited; (*aturdido*) hasty. **~ador** *a* rowdy. ● *m* trouble-maker. **~ar** *vt* disturb, upset. ● *vi* make a racket. **~arse** *vpr* get excited; ‹*el mar*› get rough. **~o** *m* row, uproar
alboroz|ado *a* overjoyed. **~ar** [10] *vt* make laugh; (*regocijar*) make happy. **~arse** *vpr* be overjoyed. **~o** *m* joy
albufera *f* lagoon
álbum *m* (*pl* **~es** *o* **~s**) album
alcachofa *f* artichoke
alcald|e *m* mayor. **~esa** *f* mayoress. **~ía** *f* mayoralty; (*oficina*) mayor's office
álcali *m* alkali
alcalino *a* alkaline
alcance *m* reach; (*de arma, telescopio etc*) range; (*déficit*) deficit
alcancía *f* money-box
alcantarilla *f* sewer; (*boca*) drain
alcanzar [10] *vt* (*llegar a*) catch up; (*coger*) reach; catch ‹*un autobús*›; ‹*bala etc*› strike, hit. ● *vi* reach; (*ser suficiente*) be enough. **~ a** manage
alcaparra *f* caper
alcaucil *m* artichoke
alcayata *f* hook
alcazaba *f* fortress
alcázar *m* fortress
alcoba *f* bedroom
alcoh|ol *m* alcohol. **~ol desnaturalizado** methylated spirits, meths (*fam*). **~ólico** *a* & *m* alcoholic. **~olímetro** *m* breathalyser (*Brit*). **~olismo** *m* alcoholism. **~olizarse** [10] *vpr* become an alcoholic
Alcorán *m* Koran
alcornoque *m* cork-oak; (*persona torpe*) idiot
alcuza *f* (olive) oil bottle
aldaba *f* door-knocker. **~da** *f* knock at the door
alde|a *f* village. **~ano** *a* village; (*campesino*) rustic, country. **~huela** *f* hamlet
alea|ción *f* alloy. **~r** *vt* alloy
aleatorio *a* uncertain
alecciona|dor *a* instructive. **~miento** *m* instruction. **~r** *vt* instruct
aledaños *mpl* outskirts
alega|ción *f* allegation; (*Arg, Mex, disputa*) argument. **~r** [12] *vt* claim; (*jurid*) allege. ● *vi* (*LAm*) argue. **~to** *m* plea
aleg|oría *f* allegory. **~órico** *a* allegorical
alegr|ar *vt* make happy; (*avivar*) brighten up. **~arse** *vpr* be happy; (*emborracharse*) get merry. **~e** *a* happy; (*achispado*) merry, tight. **~emente** *adv* happily. **~ía** *f* happiness. **~ón** *m* sudden joy, great happiness
aleja|do *a* distant. **~miento** *m* removal; (*entre personas*) estrangement; (*distancia*) distance. **~r** *vt* remove; (*ahuyentar*) get rid of; (*fig, apartar*) separate. **~rse** *vpr* move away
alela|do *a* stupid. **~r** *vt* stupefy. **~rse** *vpr* be stupefied
aleluya *m* & *f* alleluia
alemán *a* & *m* German
Alemania *f* Germany. **~ Occidental** (*historia*) West Germany. **~ Oriental** (*historia*) East Germany
alenta|dor *a* encouraging. **~r** [1] *vt* encourage. ● *vi* breathe
alerce *m* larch
al|ergia *f* allergy. **~érgico** *a* allergic
alero *m* (*del tejado*) eaves
alerón *m* aileron
alerta *adv* alert, on the alert. ¡**~**! look out! **~r** *vt* alert
aleta *f* wing; (*de pez*) fin
aletarga|do *a* lethargic. **~miento** *m* lethargy. **~r** [12] *vt* make lethargic. **~rse** *vpr* become lethargic
alet|azo *m* (*de un ave*) flap of the wings; (*de un pez*) flick of the fin. **~ear** *vi* flap its wings, flutter. **~eo** *m* flapping (of the wings)
aleve *a* treacherous
alevín *m* young fish
alevos|ía *f* treachery. **~o** *a* treacherous
alfab|ético *a* alphabetical. **~etizar** [10] *vt* alphabetize; teach to read

and write ‹*a uno*›. **~eto** *m* alphabet. **~eto Morse** Morse code

alfalfa *f* lucerne (*Brit*), alfalfa (*Amer*)

alfar *m* pottery. **~ería** *f* pottery. **~ero** *m* potter

alféizar *m* window-sill

alferecía *f* epilepsy

alférez *m* second lieutenant

alfil *m* (*en ajedrez*) bishop

alfile|r *m* pin. **~razo** *m* pinprick. **~tero** *m* pin-case

alfombr|a *f* (*grande*) carpet; (*pequeña*) rug, mat. **~ar** *vt* carpet. **~illa** *f* rug, mat; (*med*) German measles

alforja *f* saddle-bag

algas *fpl* seaweed

algarabía *f* (*fig, fam*) gibberish, nonsense

algarada *f* uproar

algarrob|a *f* carob bean. **~o** *m* carob tree

algazara *f* uproar

álgebra *f* algebra

algebraico *a* algebraic

álgido *a* (*fig*) decisive

algo *pron* something; (*en frases interrogativas*) anything. • *adv* rather. **¿~ más?** is there anything else? **¿quieres tomar algo?** (*de beber*) would you like a drink?; (*de comer*) would you like something to eat?

algod|ón *m* cotton. **~ón de azúcar** candy floss (*Brit*), cotton candy (*Amer*). **~onero** *a* cotton. • *m* cotton plant. **~ón hidrófilo** cotton wool

alguacil *m* bailiff

alguien *pron* someone, somebody; (*en frases interrogativas*) anyone, anybody

alguno *a* (*delante de nombres masculinos en singular* **algún**) some; (*en frases interrogativas*) any; (*pospuesto al nombre en frases negativas*) at all. **no tiene idea alguna** he hasn't any idea at all. • *pron* one; (*en plural*) some; (*alguien*) someone. **alguna que otra vez** from time to time. **algunas veces, alguna vez** sometimes

alhaja *f* piece of jewellery; (*fig*) treasure. **~r** *vt* deck with jewels; (*amueblar*) furnish

alharaca *f* fuss

alhelí *m* wallflower

alheña *f* privet

alhucema *f* lavender

alia|do *a* allied. • *m* ally. **~nza** *f* alliance; (*anillo*) wedding ring. **~r** [20] *vt* combine. **~rse** *vpr* be combined; (*formar una alianza*) form an alliance

alias *adv & m* alias

alicaído *a* (*fig, débil*) weak; (*fig, abatido*) depressed

alicates *mpl* pliers

aliciente *m* incentive; (*de un lugar*) attraction

alien|ado *a* mentally ill. **~ista** *m & f* psychiatrist

aliento *m* breath; (*ánimo*) courage

aligera|miento *m* lightening; (*alivio*) alleviation. **~r** *vt* make lighter; (*aliviar*) alleviate, ease; (*apresurar*) quicken

alij|ar *vt* (*descargar*) unload; smuggle ‹*contrabando*›. **~o** *m* unloading; (*contrabando*) contraband

alimaña *f* vicious animal

aliment|ación *f* food; (*acción*) feeding. **~ar** *vt* feed; (*nutrir*) nourish. • *vi* be nourishing. **~arse** *vpr* feed (**con, de** on). **~icio** *a* nourishing. **~o** *m* food. **~os** *mpl* (*jurid*) alimony. **productos** *mpl* **~icios** foodstuffs

alimón. al ~ *adv* jointly

alinea|ción *f* alignment; (*en deportes*) line-up. **~r** *vt* align, line up

aliñ|ar *vt* (*culin*) season. **~o** *m* seasoning

alioli *m* garlic sauce

alisar *vt* smooth

alisios *apl.* **vientos** *mpl* **~** trade winds

aliso *m* alder (tree)

alista|miento *m* enrolment. **~r** *vt* put on a list; (*mil*) enlist. **~rse** *vpr* enrol; (*mil*) enlist

aliteración *f* alliteration

alivi|ador *a* comforting. **~ar** *vt* lighten; relieve ‹*dolor, etc*›; (*hurtar, fam*) steal, pinch (*fam*). **~arse** *vpr* ‹*dolor*› diminish; ‹*persona*› get better. **~o** *m* relief

aljibe *m* tank

alma *f* soul; (*habitante*) inhabitant

almac|én *m* warehouse; (*LAm, tienda*) grocer's shop; (*de un arma*) magazine. **~enes** *mpl* department store. **~enaje** *m* storage; (*derechos*) storage charges. **~enamiento** *m* storage; (*mercancías almacenadas*) stock. **~enar** *vt* store; stock up with

‹*provisiones*›. **~enero** *m* (*Arg*) shopkeeper. **~enista** *m & f* shopkeeper
almádena *f* sledge-hammer
almanaque *m* almanac
almeja *f* clam
almendr|a *f* almond. **~ado** *a* almond-shaped. **~o** *m* almond tree
almiar *m* haystack
alm|íbar *m* syrup. **~ibarado** *a* syrupy. **~ibarar** *vt* cover in syrup
almid|ón *m* starch. **~onado** *a* starched; (*fig, estirado*) starchy
alminar *m* minaret
almirant|azgo *m* admiralty. **~e** *m* admiral
almirez *m* mortar
almizcle *m* musk
almohad|a *f* cushion; (*de la cama*) pillow; (*funda*) pillowcase. **~illa** *f* small cushion; (*acerico*) pincushion. **~ón** *m* large pillow, bolster. **consultar con la ~a** sleep on it
almorranas *fpl* haemorrhoids, piles
alm|orzar [2 & 10] *vt* (*a mediodía*) have for lunch; (*desayunar*) have for breakfast. ● *vi* (*a mediodía*) have lunch; (*desayunar*) have breakfast. **~uerzo** *m* (*a mediodía*) lunch; (*desayuno*) breakfast
alocado *a* scatter-brained
alocución *f* address, speech
aloja|do *m* (Mex) lodger, guest. **~miento** *m* accommodation. **~r** *vt* put up. **~rse** *vpr* stay
alondra *f* lark
alpaca *f* alpaca
alpargat|a *f* canvas shoe, espadrille. **~ería** *f* shoe shop
Alpes *mpl* Alps
alpin|ismo *m* mountaineering, climbing. **~ista** *m & f* mountaineer, climber. **~o** *a* Alpine
alpiste *m* birdseed
alquil|ar *vt* (*tomar en alquiler*) hire ‹*vehículo*›, rent ‹*piso, casa*›; (*dar en alquiler*) hire (out) ‹*vehículo*›, rent (out) ‹*piso, casa*›. **~arse** *vpr* ‹*casa*› be let; ‹*vehículo*› be on hire. **se alquila** to let (*Brit*), for rent (*Amer*). **~er** *m* (*acción de alquilar un piso etc*) renting; (*acción de alquilar un vehículo*) hiring; (*precio por el que se alquila un piso etc*) rent; (*precio por el que se alquila un vehículo*) hire charge. **de ~er** for hire
alquimi|a *f* alchemy. **~sta** *m* alchemist
alquitara *f* still. **~r** *vt* distil
alquitr|án *m* tar. **~anar** *vt* tar
alrededor *adv* around. **~ de** around; (*con números*) about. **~es** *mpl* surroundings; (*de una ciudad*) outskirts
alta *f* discharge
altamente *adv* highly
altaner|ía *f* (*orgullo*) pride. **~o** *a* proud, haughty
altar *m* altar
altavoz *m* loudspeaker
altera|bilidad *f* changeability. **~ble** *a* changeable. **~ción** *f* change, alteration. **~do** *a* changed, altered; (*perturbado*) disturbed. **~r** *vt* change, alter; (*perturbar*) disturb; (*enfadar*) anger, irritate. **~rse** *vpr* change, alter; (*agitarse*) get upset; (*enfadarse*) get angry; ‹*comida*› go off
alterca|do *m* argument. **~r** [7] *vi* argue
altern|ado *a* alternate. **~ador** *m* alternator. **~ante** *a* alternating. **~ar** *vt/i* alternate. **~arse** *vpr* take turns. **~ativa** *f* alternative. **~ativo** *a* alternating. **~o** *a* alternate
alteza *f* height. **A~** (*título*) Highness
altibajos *mpl* (*de terreno*) unevenness; (*fig*) ups and downs
altiplanicie *f* high plateau
altísimo *a* very high. ● *m*. **el A~** the Almighty
altisonante *a*, **altísono** *a* pompous
altitud *f* height; (*aviat, geog*) altitude
altiv|ez *f* arrogance. **~o** *a* arrogant
alto *a* high; ‹*persona*› tall; ‹*voz*› loud; (*fig, elevado*) lofty; (*mus*) ‹*nota*› high(-pitched); (*mus*) ‹*voz, instrumento*› alto; ‹*horas*› early. **tiene 3 metros de ~** it is 3 metres high. ● *adv* high; (*de sonidos*) loud(ly). ● *m* height; (*de un edificio*) high floor; (*viola*) viola; (*voz*) alto; (*parada*) stop. ● *int* halt!, stop! **en lo ~ de** on the top of
altoparlante *m* (*esp LAm*) loudspeaker
altruis|mo *m* altruism. **~ta** *a* altruistic. ● *m & f* altruist
altura *f* height; (*altitud*) altitude; (*de agua*) depth; (*fig, cielo*) sky. **a estas ~s** at this stage. **tiene 3 metros de ~** it is 3 metres high
alubia *f* French bean
alucinación *f* hallucination
alud *m* avalanche

aludi|do *a* in question. **darse por ~do** take it personally. **no darse por ~do** turn a deaf ear. **~r** *vi* mention

alumbra|do *a* lit; (*achispado, fam*) tipsy. • *m* lighting. **~miento** *m* lighting; (*parto*) childbirth. **~r** *vt* light. • *vi* give birth. **~rse** *vpr* (*emborracharse*) get tipsy

aluminio *m* aluminium (*Brit*), aluminum (*Amer*)

alumno *m* pupil; (*univ*) student

aluniza|je *m* landing on the moon. **~r** [10] *vi* land on the moon

alusi|ón *f* allusion. **~vo** *a* allusive

alverja *f* vetch; (*LAm, guisante*) pea

alza *f* rise. **~cuello** *m* clerical collar, dog-collar (*fam*). **~da** *f* (*de caballo*) height; (*jurid*) appeal. **~do** *a* raised; ‹*persona*› fraudulently bankrupt; (*Mex, soberbio*) vain; ‹*precio*› fixed. **~miento** *m* raising; (*aumento*) rise, increase; (*pol*) revolt. **~r** [10] *vt* raise, lift (up); raise ‹*precios*›. **~rse** *vpr* rise; (*ponerse en pie*) stand up; (*pol*) revolt; (*quebrar*) go fraudulently bankrupt; (*apelar*) appeal

allá *adv* there. **¡~ él!** that's his business. **~ fuera** out there. **~ por el 1970** around about 1970. **el más ~** the beyond. **más ~** further on. **más ~ de** beyond. **por ~** over there

allana|miento *m* levelling; (*de obstáculos*) removal. **~miento de morada** burglary. **~r** *vt* level; remove ‹*obstáculos*›; (*fig*) iron out ‹*dificultades etc*›; burgle ‹*una casa*›. **~rse** *vpr* level off; (*hundirse*) fall down; (*ceder*) submit (**a** to)

allega|do *a* close. • *m* relation. **~r** [12] vt collect

allí *adv* there; (*tiempo*) then. **~ donde** wherever. **~ fuera** out there. **por ~** over there

ama *f* lady of the house. **~ de casa** housewife. **~ de cría** wet-nurse. **~ de llaves** housekeeper

amab|ilidad *f* kindness. **~le** *a* kind; (*simpático*) nice

amado *a* dear. **~r** *m* lover

amaestra|do *a* trained; (*en circo*) performing. **~miento** *m* training. **~r** *vt* train

amag|ar [12] *vt* (*amenazar*) threaten; (*mostrar intención de*) show signs of. • *vi* threaten; ‹*algo bueno*› be in the offing. **~o** *m* threat; (*señal*) sign; (*med*) sympton

amalgama *f* amalgam. **~r** *vt* amalgamate

amamantar *vt* breast-feed

amancebarse *vpr* live together

amanecer *m* dawn. • *vi* dawn; ‹*persona*› wake up. **al ~** at dawn, at daybreak

amanera|do *a* affected. **~miento** *m* affectation. **~rse** *vpr* become affected

amanezca *f* (*Mex*) dawn

amansa|dor *m* tamer. **~miento** *m* taming. **~r** *vt* tame; break in ‹*un caballo*›; soothe ‹*dolor etc*›. **~rse** *vpr* calm down

amante *a* fond. • *m & f* lover

amañ|ar *vt* arrange. **~o** *m* scheme

amapola *f* poppy

amar *vt* love

amara|je *m* landing on the sea; (*de astronave*) splash-down. **~r** *vt* land on the sea; ‹*astronave*› splash down

amarg|ado *a* embittered. **~ar** [12] *vt* make bitter; embitter ‹*persona*›. **~arse** *vpr* get bitter. **~o** *a* bitter. • *m* bitterness. **~ura** *f* bitterness

amariconado *a* effeminate

amarill|ear *vi* go yellow. **~ento** *a* yellowish; ‹*tez*› sallow. **~ez** *f* yellow; (*de una persona*) paleness. **~o** *a & m* yellow

amarra *f* mooring rope. **~s** *fpl* (*fig, fam*) influence. **~do** *a* (*LAm*) mean. **~r** *vt* moor; (*atar*) tie. • *vi* (*empollar, fam*) study hard, swot (*fam*)

amartillar *vt* cock (*arma de fuego*)

amas|ar *vt* knead; (*fig, tramar, fam*) concoct, cook up (*fam*). **~ijo** *m* dough; (*acción*) kneading; (*fig, mezcla, fam*) hotchpotch

amate *m* (*Mex*) fig tree

amateur *a & m & f* amateur

amatista *f* amethyst

amazona *f* Amazon; (*mujer varonil*) mannish woman; (*que monta a caballo*) horsewoman

Amazonas *m*. **el río ~** the Amazon

ambages *mpl* circumlocutions. **sin ~** in plain language

ámbar *m* amber

ambarino *a* amber

ambici|ón *f* ambition. **~onar** *vt* strive after. **~onar ser** have an ambition to be. **~oso** *a* ambitious. • *m* ambitious person

ambidextro *a* ambidextrous. • *m* ambidextrous person

ambient|ar *vt* give an atmosphere to. **~arse** *vpr* adapt o.s. **~e** *m* atmosphere; (*medio*) environment

ambig|uamente *adv* ambiguously. **~üedad** *f* ambiguity. **~uo** *a* ambiguous; (*fig, afeminado, fam*) effeminate

ámbito *m* ambit

ambos *a & pron* both. **~ a dos** both (of them)

ambulancia *f* ambulance; (*hospital móvil*) field hospital

ambulante *a* travelling

ambulatorio *m* out-patients' department

amedrentar *vt* frighten, scare. **~se** *vpr* be frightened

amén *m* amen. ● *int* amen! **en un decir ~** in an instant

amenaza *f* threat. **~dor** *a*, **~nte** *a* threatening. **~r** [10] *vt* threaten

amen|idad *f* pleasantness. **~izar** [10] *vt* brighten up. **~o** *a* pleasant

América *f* America. **~ Central** Central America. **~ del Norte** North America. **~ del Sur** South America. **~ Latina** Latin America

american|a *f* jacket. **~ismo** *m* Americanism. **~ista** *m & f* Americanist. **~o** *a* American

amerindio *a & m & f* Amerindian, American Indian

ameriza|je *m* landing on the sea; (*de astronave*) splash-down. **~r** [10] *vt* land on the sea; ‹*astronave*› splash down

ametralla|dora *f* machine-gun. **~r** *vt* machine-gun

amianto *m* asbestos

amig|a *f* friend; (*novia*) girl-friend; (*amante*) lover. **~able** *a* friendly. **~ablemente** *adv* amicably. **~rse** [12] *vpr* live together

am|ígdala *f* tonsil. **~igdalitis** *f* tonsillitis

amigo *a* friendly. ● *m* friend; (*novio*) boy-friend; (*amante*) lover. **ser ~ de** be fond of. **ser muy ~s** be good friends

amilanar *vt* frighten, scare. **~se** *vpr* be frightened

aminorar *vt* lessen; slow down ‹*velocidad*›

amist|ad *f* friendship. **~ades** *mpl* friends. **~osamente** *adv* amicably. **~oso** *a* friendly

amnesia *f* amnesia

amnist|ía *f* amnesty. **~iar** [20] *vt* grant an amnesty to

amo *m* master; (*dueño*) owner; (*jefe*) boss; (*cabeza de familia*) head of the family

amodorra|miento *m* sleepiness. **~rse** *vpr* get sleepy

amojonar *vt* mark out

amola|dor *m* knife-grinder. **~r** [2] *vt* sharpen; (*molestar, fam*) annoy

amoldar *vt* mould; (*acomodar*) fit

amonedar *vt* coin, mint

amonesta|ción *f* rebuke, reprimand; (*de una boda*) banns. **~r** *vt* rebuke, reprimand; (*anunciar la boda*) publish the banns

amoniaco *m*, **amoníaco** *m* ammonia

amontillado *m* Amontillado, pale dry sherry

amontona|damente *adv* in a heap. **~miento** *m* piling up. **~r** *vt* pile up; (*fig, acumular*) accumulate. **~rse** *vpr* pile up; ‹*gente*› crowd together; (*amancebarse, fam*) live together

amor *m* love. **~es** *mpl* (*relaciones amorosas*) love affairs. **con mil ~es, de mil ~es** with (the greatest of) pleasure. **hacer el ~** make love. **por (el) ~ de Dios** for God's sake

amorata|do *a* purple; (*de frío*) blue. **~rse** *vpr* go black and blue

amorcillo *m* Cupid

amordazar [10] *vt* gag; (*fig*) silence

amorfo *a* amorphous, shapeless

amor: ~ío *m* affair. **~oso** *a* loving; ‹*cartas*› love

amortajar *vt* shroud

amortigua|dor *a* deadening. ● *m* (*auto*) shock absorber. **~miento** *m* deadening; (*de la luz*) dimming. **~r** [15] *vt* deaden ‹*ruido*›; dim ‹*luz*›; cushion ‹*golpe*›; tone down ‹*color*›

amortiza|ble *a* redeemable. **~ción** *f* (*de una deuda*) repayment; (*recuperación*) redemption. **~r** [10] *vt* repay ‹*una deuda*›

amoscarse [7] *vpr* (*fam*) get cross, get irritated

amostazarse [10] *vpr* get cross

amotina|do *a & m* insurgent, rebellious. **~miento** *m* riot; (*mil*) mutiny. **~r** *vt* incite to riot. **~rse** *vpr* rebel; (*mil*) mutiny

ampar|ar *vt* help; (*proteger*) protect. **~arse** *vpr* seek protection; (*de la lluvia*) shelter. **~o** *m* protection; (*de la lluvia*) shelter. **al ~o de** under the protection of

amperio *m* ampere, amp (fam)

amplia|ción *f* extension; (*photo*) enlargement. **~r** [20] *vt* enlarge, extend; (*photo*) enlarge

amplifica|ción *f* amplification. **~dor** *m* amplifier. **~r** [7] amplify
ampli|o *a* wide; (*espacioso*) spacious; ‹*ropa*› loose-fitting. **~tud** *f* extent; (*espaciosidad*) spaciousness; (*espacio*) space
ampolla *f* (*med*) blister; (*frasco*) flask; (*de medicamento*) ampoule, phial
ampuloso *a* pompous
amputa|ción *f* amputation; (*fig*) deletion. **~r** *vt* amputate; (*fig*) delete
amueblar *vt* furnish
amuinar *vt* (*Mex*) annoy
amuralla|do *a* walled. **~r** *vt* build a wall around
anacardo *m* (*fruto*) cashew nut
anaconda *f* anaconda
anacr|ónico *a* anachronistic. **~onismo** *m* anachronism
ánade *m* & *f* duck
anagrama *m* anagram
anales *mpl* annals
analfabet|ismo *m* illiteracy. **~o** *a* & *m* illiterate
analgésico *a* & *m* analgesic, pain-killer
an|álisis *m invar* analysis. **~álisis de sangre** blood test. **~alista** *m* & *f* analyst. **~alítico** *a* analytical. **~alizar** [10] *vt* analyze
an|alogía *f* analogy. **~álogo** *a* analogous
ananás *m* pineapple
anaquel *m* shelf
anaranjado *a* orange
an|arquía *f* anarchy. **~árquico** *a* anarchic. **~arquismo** *m* anarchism. **~arquista** *a* anarchistic. ● *m* & *f* anarchist
anatema *m* anathema
anat|omía *f* anatomy. **~ómico** *a* anatomical
anca *f* haunch; (*parte superior*) rump; (*nalgas*, *fam*) bottom. **~s** *fpl* **de rana** frogs' legs
ancestral *a* ancestral
anciano *a* elderly, old. ● *m* elderly man, old man; (*relig*) elder. **los ~s** old people
ancla *f* anchor. **~dero** *m* anchorage. **~r** *vi* anchor, drop anchor. **echar ~s** anchor. **levar ~s** weigh anchor
áncora *f* anchor; (*fig*) refuge
ancho *a* wide; ‹*ropa*› loose-fitting; (*fig*) relieved; (*demasiado grande*) too big; (*ufano*) smug. ● *m* width; (*rail*) gauge. **a mis anchas, a sus anchas etc** comfortable, relaxed. **quedarse tan ancho** behave as if nothing has happened. **tiene 3 metros de ~** it is 3 metres wide
anchoa *f* anchovy
anchura *f* width; (*medida*) measurement
andaderas *fpl* baby-walker
andad|or *a* good at walking. ● *m* baby-walker. **~ura** *f* walking; (*manera de andar*) walk
Andalucía *f* Andalusia
andaluz *a* & *m* Andalusian
andamio *m* platform. **~s** *mpl* scaffolding
andar [25] *vt* (*recorrer*) cover, go. ● *vi* walk; ‹*máquina*› go, work; (*estar*) be; (*moverse*) move. ● *m* walk. **¡anda!** go on! come on! **~iego** *a* fond of walking; (*itinerante*) wandering. **~ por** be about. **~se** *vpr* (*marcharse*) go away
andén *m* platform; (*de un muelle*) quayside; (*LAm, acera*) pavement (*Brit*), sidewalk (*Amer*)
Andes *mpl* Andes
andino *a* Andean
Andorra *f* Andorra
andrajo *m* rag. **~so** *a* ragged
andurriales *mpl* (*fam*) out-of-the-way place
anduve *vb véase* **andar**
anécdota *f* anecdote
anega|dizo *a* subject to flooding. **~r** [12] *vt* flood. **~rse** *vpr* be flooded, flood
anejo *a* attached. ● *m* annexe; (*de libro etc*) appendix
an|emia *f* anaemia. **~émico** *a* anaemic
anest|esia *f* anaesthesia. **~ésico** *a* & *m* anaesthetic. **~esista** *m* & *f* anaesthetist
anex|ión *f* annexation. **~ionar** *vt* annex. **~o** *a* attached. ● *m* annexe
anfibio *a* amphibious. ● *m* amphibian
anfiteatro *m* amphitheatre; (*en un teatro*) upper circle
anfitri|ón *m* host. **~ona** *f* hostess
ángel *m* angel; (*encanto*) charm
angelical *a*, **angélico** *a* angelic
angina *f*. **~ de pecho** angina (pectoris). **tener ~s** have tonsillitis
anglicano *a* & *m* Anglican
anglicismo *m* Anglicism
anglófilo *a* & *m* Anglophile
anglo|hispánico *a* Anglo-Spanish. **~sajón** *a* & *m* Anglo-Saxon

angosto *a* narrow
anguila *f* eel
angula *f* elver, baby eel
angular *a* angular
ángulo *m* angle; (*rincón, esquina*) corner; (*curva*) bend
anguloso *a* angular
angusti|a *f* anguish. **~ar** *vt* distress; (*inquietar*) worry. **~arse** *vpr* get distressed; (*inquietarse*) get worried. **~oso** *a* anguished; (*que causa angustia*) distressing
anhel|ante *a* panting; (*deseoso*) longing. **~ar** *vt* (+ *nombre*) long for; (+ *verbo*) long to. ● *vi* pant. **~o** *m* (*fig*) yearning. **~oso** *a* panting; (*fig*) eager
anidar *vi* nest
anill|a *f* ring. **~o** *m* ring. **~o de boda** wedding ring
ánima *f* soul
anima|ción *f* (*de personas*) life; (*de cosas*) liveliness; (*bullicio*) bustle; (*en el cine*) animation. **~do** *a* lively; ‹*sitio etc*› busy. **~dor** *m* compère, host
animadversión *f* ill will
animal *a* animal; (*fig, torpe, fam*) stupid. ● *m* animal; (*fig, idiota, fam*) idiot; (*fig, bruto, fam*) brute
animar *vt* give life to; (*dar ánimo*) encourage; (*dar vivacidad*) liven up. **~se** *vpr* (*decidirse*) decide; (*ponerse alegre*) cheer up. **¿te animas a venir al cine?** do you fancy coming to the cinema?
ánimo *m* soul; (*mente*) mind; (*valor*) courage; (*intención*) intention. **¡~!** come on!, cheer up! **dar ~s** encourage
animosidad *f* animosity
animoso *a* brave; (*resuelto*) determined
aniquila|ción *f* annihilation. **~miento** *m* annihilation. **~r** *vt* annihilate; (*acabar con*) ruin. **~rse** *vpr* deteriorate
anís *m* aniseed; (*licor*) anisette
aniversario *m* anniversary
ano *m* anus
anoche *adv* last night, yesterday evening
anochecer [11] *vi* get dark; ‹*persona*› be at dusk. **anochecí en Madrid** I was in Madrid at dusk. ● *m* nightfall, dusk. **al ~** at nightfall
anodino *a* indifferent
an|omalía *f* anomaly. **~ómalo** *a* anomalous
an|onimato *m* anonymity. **~ónimo** *a* anonymous; ‹*sociedad*› limited. ● *m* anonymity; (*carta*) anonymous letter
anormal *a* abnormal; (*fam*) stupid, silly. **~idad** *f* abnormality
anota|ción *f* noting; (*acción de poner notas*) annotation; (*nota*) note. **~r** *vt* (*poner nota*) annotate; (*apuntar*) make a note of
anquilosa|miento *m* paralysis. **~r** *vt* paralyze. **~rse** *vpr* become paralyzed
ansi|a *f* anxiety, worry; (*anhelo*) yearning. **~ar** [20 *o regular*] *vt* long for. **~edad** *f* anxiety. **~oso** *a* anxious; (*deseoso*) eager
antag|ónico *a* antagonistic. **~onismo** *m* antagonism. **~onista** *m & f* antagonist
antaño *adv* in days gone by
antártico *a & m* Antarctic
ante *prep* in front of, before; (*en comparación con*) compared with; (*frente a peligro, enemigo*) in the face of; (*en vista de*) in view of. ● *m* (*piel*) suede. **~anoche** *adv* the night before last. **~ayer** *adv* the day before yesterday. **~brazo** *m* forearm
ante... *pref* ante...
antece|dente *a* previous. ● *m* antecedent. **~dentes** *mpl* history, background. **~dentes penales** criminal record. **~der** *vt* precede. **~sor** *m* predecessor; (*antepasado*) ancestor
antedicho *a* aforesaid
antelación *f* advance. **con ~** in advance
antemano *adv*. **de ~** beforehand
antena *f* antenna; (*radio, TV*) aerial
anteojeras *fpl* blinkers
anteojo *m* telescope. **~s** *mpl* (*gemelos*) opera glasses; (*prismáticos*) binoculars; (*LAm, gafas*) glasses, spectacles
ante: ~pasados *mpl* forebears, ancestors. **~pecho** *m* rail; (*de ventana*) sill. **~poner** [34] *vt* put in front (**a** of); (*fig*) put before, prefer. **~proyecto** *m* preliminary sketch; (*fig*) blueprint. **~puesto** *a* put before
anterior *a* previous; (*delantero*) front, fore. **~idad** *f*. **con ~idad** previously. **~mente** *adv* previously
antes *adv* before; (*antiguamente*) in days gone by; (*mejor*) rather; (*primero*) first. **~ de** before. **~ de ayer**

the day before yesterday. **~ de que** + *subj* before. **~ de que llegue** before he arrives. **cuanto ~, lo ~ posible** as soon as possible

antesala *f* anteroom; (*sala de espera*) waiting-room. **hacer ~** wait (to be received)

anti... *pref* anti...

anti: ~aéreo *a* anti-aircraft. **~biótico** *a & m* antibiotic. **~ciclón** *m* anticyclone

anticip|ación *f* anticipation. **con ~ación** in advance. **con media hora de ~ación** half an hour early. **~adamente** *adv* in advance. **~ado** *a*. **por ~ado** in advance. **~ar** *vt* bring forward; advance ‹*dinero*›. **~arse** *vpr* be early. **~o** *m* (*dinero*) advance; (*fig*) foretaste

anti: ~concepcional *a & m* contraceptive. **~conceptivo** *a & m* contraceptive. **~congelante** *m* antifreeze

anticua|do *a* old-fashioned. **~rio** *m* antique dealer. **~rse** *vpr* go out of date

anticuerpo *m* antibody

antídoto *m* antidote

anti: ~estético *a* ugly. **~faz** *m* mask. **~gás** *a invar*. **careta ~gás** gas mask

antig|ualla *f* old relic. **~uamente** *adv* formerly; (*hace mucho tiempo*) long ago. **~üedad** *f* antiquity; (*objeto*) antique; (*en un empleo*) length of service. **~uo** *a* old, ancient. **chapado a la ~ua** old-fashioned

antílope *m* antelope

Antillas *fpl* West Indies

antinatural *a* unnatural

antip|atía *f* dislike; (*cualidad de antipático*) unpleasantness. **~ático** *a* unpleasant, unfriendly

anti: ~semita *m & f* anti-Semite. **~semítico** *a* anti-Semitic. **~semitismo** *m* anti-Semitism. **~séptico** *a & m* antiseptic. **~social** *a* antisocial

antítesis *f invar* antithesis

antoj|adizo *a* capricious. **~arse** *vpr* fancy. **se le ~a un caramelo** he fancies a sweet. **~o** *m* whim; (*de embarazada*) craving

antología *f* anthology

antorcha *f* torch

antro *m* cavern; (*fig*) dump, hole. **~ de perversión** den of iniquity

antropófago *m* cannibal

antrop|ología *f* anthropology. **~ólogo** *m & f* anthropologist

anua|l *a* annual. **~lidad** *f* annuity. **~lmente** *adv* yearly. **~rio** *m* yearbook

anudar *vt* tie, knot; (*fig, iniciar*) begin; (*fig, continuar*) resume. **~se** *vpr* get into knots. **~se la voz** get a lump in one's throat

anula|ción *f* annulment, cancellation. **~r** *vt* annul, cancel. ● *a* ‹*dedo*› ring. ● *m* ring finger

Anunciación *f* Annunciation

anunci|ante *m & f* advertiser. **~ar** *vt* announce; advertise ‹*producto comercial*›; (*presagiar*) be a sign of. **~arse** *vpr* promise to be. **~o** *m* announcement; (*para vender algo*) advertisement, advert (*fam*); (*cartel*) poster

anzuelo *m* (fish)hook; (*fig*) bait. **tragar el ~** be taken in, fall for it

añadi|do *a* added. **~dura** *f* addition. **~r** *vt* add. **por ~dura** besides

añejo *a* ‹*vino*› mature; ‹*jamón etc*› cured

añicos *mpl* bits. **hacer ~** (*romper*) smash (to pieces); (*dejar cansado*) wear out

añil *m* indigo

año *m* year. **~ bisiesto** leap year. **~ nuevo** new year. **al ~** per year, a year. **¿cuántos ~s tiene? tiene 5 ~s** how old is he? he's 5 (years old). **el ~ pasado** last year. **el ~ que viene** next year. **entrado en ~s** elderly. **los ~s 60** the sixties

añora|nza *f* nostalgia. **~r** *vt* miss. ● *vi* pine

apabullar *vt* crush; (*fig*) intimidate

apacentar [1] *vt* graze. **~se** *vpr* graze

apacib|ilidad *f* gentleness; (*calma*) peacefulness. **~le** *a* gentle; ‹*tiempo*› mild

apacigua|dor *a* pacifying. **~miento** *m* appeasement. **~r** [15] *vt* pacify; (*calmar*) calm; relieve ‹*dolor etc*›. **~rse** *vpr* calm down

apadrina|miento *m* sponsorship. **~r** *vt* sponsor; be godfather to ‹*a un niño*›; (*en una boda*) be best man for

apaga|dizo *a* slow to burn. **~do** *a* extinguished; ‹*color*› dull; ‹*aparato eléctrico*› off; ‹*persona*› lifeless; ‹*sonido*› muffled. **~r** [12] *vt* put out ‹*fuego, incendio*›; turn off, switch off ‹*aparato eléctrico*›; quench ‹*sed*›; muffle ‹*sonido*›. **~rse** *vpr* ‹*fuego*› go

out; ‹*luz*› go out; ‹*sonido*› die away; (*fig*) pass away
apagón *m* blackout
apalabrar *vt* make a verbal agreement; (*contratar*) engage. **~se** *vpr* come to a verbal agreement
apalanca|miento *m* leverage. **~r** [7] *vt* (*levantar*) lever up; (*abrir*) lever open
apalea|miento *m* (*de grano*) winnowing; (*de alfombras, frutos, personas*) beating. **~r** *vt* winnow ‹*grano*›; beat ‹*alfombras, frutos, personas*›; (*fig*) be rolling in ‹*dinero*›
apantallado *a* (*Mex*) stupid
apañ|ado *a* handy. **~ar** *vt* (*arreglar*) fix; (*remendar*) mend; (*agarrar*) grasp, take hold of. **~arse** *vpr* get along, manage. **¡estoy ~ado!** that's all I need!
aparador *m* sideboard
aparato *m* apparatus; (*máquina*) machine; (*teléfono*) telephone; (*rad, TV*) set; (*ostentación*) show, pomp. **~samente** *adv* ostentatiously; (*impresionante*) spectacularly. **~sidad** *f* ostentation. **~so** *a* showy, ostentatious; ‹*caída*› spectacular
aparca|miento *m* car park (*Brit*), parking lot (*Amer*). **~r** [7] *vt/i* park
aparea|miento *m* pairing off. **~r** *vt* pair off; mate ‹*animales*›. **~rse** *vpr* match; ‹*animales*› mate
aparecer [11] *vi* appear. **~se** *vpr* appear
aparej|ado *a* ready; (*adecuado*) fitting. **llevar ~ado, traer ~ado** mean, entail. **~o** *m* preparation; (*avíos*) equipment
aparent|ar *vt* (*afectar*) feign; (*parecer*) look. • *vi* show off. **~a 20 años** she looks like she's 20. **~e** *a* apparent; (*adecuado, fam*) suitable
apari|ción *f* appearance; (*visión*) apparition. **~encia** *f* appearance; (*fig*) show. **cubrir las ~encias** keep up appearances
apartad|ero *m* lay-by; (*rail*) siding. **~o** *a* separated; (*aislado*) isolated. • *m* (*de un texto*) section. **~o (de correos)** post-office box, PO box
apartamento *m* flat (*Brit*), apartment
apart|amiento *m* separation; (*LAm, piso*) flat (*Brit*), apartment; (*aislamiento*) seclusion. **~ar** *vt* separate; (*quitar*) remove. **~arse** *vpr* leave; abandon ‹*creencia*›; (*quitarse de en medio*) get out of the way; (*aislarse*) cut o.s. off. **~e** *adv* apart; (*por separado*) separately; (*además*) besides. • *m* aside; (*párrafo*) new paragraph. **~e de** apart from. **dejar ~e** leave aside. **eso ~e** apart from that
apasiona|do *a* passionate; (*entusiasta*) enthusiastic; (*falto de objetividad*) biassed. • *m* lover (**de** of). **~miento** *m* passion. **~r** *vt* excite. **~rse** *vpr* get excited (**de, por** about), be mad (**de, por** about); (*ser parcial*) become biassed
ap|atía *f* apathy. **~ático** *a* apathetic
apea|dero *m* (*rail*) halt. **~r** *vt* fell ‹*árbol*›; (*disuadir*) dissuade; overcome ‹*dificultad*›; sort out ‹*problema*›. **~rse** *vpr* (*de un vehículo*) get off
apechugar [12] *vi* push (with one's chest). **~ con** put up with
apedrear *vt* stone
apeg|ado *a* attached. **~o** *m* (*fam*) affection. **tener ~o a** be fond of
apela|ción *f* appeal. **~r** appeal; (*recurrir*) resort (**a** to)
apelmazar [10] *vt* compress
apellid|ar *vt* call. **~arse** *vpr* be called. **¿cómo te apellidas?** what's your surname? **~o** *m* surname
apenar *vt* pain. **~se** *vpr* grieve
apenas *adv* hardly, scarcely; (*enseguida que*) as soon as. **~ si** (*fam*) hardly
ap|éndice *m* (*med*) appendix; (*fig*) appendage; (*de un libro*) appendix. **~endicitis** *f* appendicitis
apercibi|miento *m* warning. **~r** *vt* warn (**de** of, about); (*amenazar*) threaten. **~rse** *vpr* prepare; (*percatarse*) provide o.s. (**de** with)
apergaminado *a* ‹*piel*› wrinkled
aperitivo *m* (*bebida*) aperitif; (*comida*) appetizer
aperos *mpl* agricultural equipment
apertura *f* opening
apesadumbrar *vt* upset. **~se** *vpr* be upset
apestar *vt* stink out; (*fastidiar*) pester. • *vi* stink (**a** of)
apet|ecer [11] *vt* long for; (*interesar*) appeal to. **¿te ~ece una copa?** do you fancy a drink? do you feel like a drink?. • *vi* be welcome. **~ecible** *a* attractive. **~ito** *m* appetite; (*fig*) desire. **~itoso** *a* tempting
apiadarse *vpr* feel sorry (**de** for)

ápice *m* (*nada, en frases negativas*) anything. **no ceder un ~** not give an inch

apicult|or *m* bee-keeper. **~ura** *f* bee-keeping

apilar *vt* pile up

apiñar *vt* pack in. **~se** *vpr* ‹*personas*› crowd together; ‹*cosas*› be packed tight

apio *m* celery

apisonadora *f* steamroller

aplacar [7] *vt* placate; relieve ‹*dolor*›

aplanar *vt* smooth. **~se** *vpr* become smooth; ‹*persona*› lose heart

aplasta|nte *a* overwhelming. **~r** *vt* crush. **~rse** *vpr* flatten o.s.

aplatanarse *vpr* become lethargic

aplau|dir *vt* clap, applaud; (*fig*) applaud. **~so** *m* applause; (*fig*) praise

aplaza|miento *m* postponement. **~r** [10] *vt* postpone; defer ‹*pago*›

aplebeyarse *vpr* lower o.s.

aplica|ble *a* applicable. **~ción** *f* application. **~do** *a* ‹*persona*› diligent. **~r** [7] *vt* apply; (*fijar*) attach. **~rse** *vpr* apply o.s.

aplom|ado *a* self-confident; (*vertical*) vertical. **~o** *m* (self-) confidence, aplomb; (*verticalidad*) verticality

apocado *a* timid

Apocalipsis *f* Apocalypse

apocalíptico *a* apocalyptic

apoca|miento *m* diffidence. **~r** [7] *vt* belittle ‹*persona*›. **~rse** *vpr* feel small

apodar *vt* nickname

apodera|do *m* representative. **~r** *vt* authorize. **~rse** *vpr* seize

apodo *m* nickname

apogeo *m* (*fig*) height

apolilla|do *a* moth-eaten. **~rse** *vpr* get moth-eaten

apolítico *a* non-political

apología *f* defence

apoltronarse *vpr* get lazy

apoplejía *f* stroke

apoquinar *vt/i* (*fam*) fork out

aporrear *vt* hit, thump; beat up ‹*persona*›

aporta|ción *f* contribution. **~r** *vt* contribute

aposent|ar *vt* put up, lodge. **~o** *m* room, lodgings

apósito *m* dressing

aposta *adv* on purpose

apostar[1] [2] *vt/i* bet

apostar[2] *vt* station. **~se** *vpr* station o.s.

apostilla *f* note. **~r** *vt* add notes to

apóstol *m* apostle

apóstrofo *m* apostrophe

apoy|ar *vt* lean (**en** against); (*descansar*) rest; (*asentar*) base; (*reforzar*) support. **~arse** *vpr* lean, rest. **~o** *m* support

apreci|able *a* appreciable; (*digno de estima*) worthy. **~ación** *f* appreciation; (*valoración*) appraisal. **~ar** *vt* value; (*estimar*) appreciate. **~ativo** *a* appreciative. **~o** *m* appraisal; (*fig*) esteem

aprehensión *f* capture

apremi|ante *a* urgent, pressing. **~ar** *vt* urge; (*obligar*) compel; (*dar prisa a*) hurry up. ● *vi* be urgent. **~o** *m* urgency; (*obligación*) obligation

aprender *vt/i* learn. **~se** *vpr* learn (by heart)

aprendiz *m* apprentice. **~aje** *m* apprenticeship

aprensi|ón *f* apprehension; (*miedo*) fear. **~vo** *a* apprehensive, fearful

apresa|dor *m* captor. **~miento** *m* capture. **~r** *vt* seize; (*prender*) capture

aprestar *vt* prepare. **~se** *vpr* prepare

apresura|damente *adv* hurriedly, in a hurry. **~do** *a* in a hurry; (*hecho con prisa*) hurried. **~miento** *m* hurry. **~r** *vt* hurry. **~rse** *vpr* hurry

apret|ado *a* tight; (*difícil*) difficult; (*tacaño*) stingy, mean. **~ar** [1] *vt* tighten; press ‹*botón*›; squeeze ‹*persona*›; (*comprimir*) press down. ● *vi* be too tight. **~arse** *vpr* crowd together. **~ón** *m* squeeze. **~ón de manos** handshake

aprieto *m* difficulty. **verse en un ~** be in a tight spot

aprisa *adv* quickly

aprisionar *vt* imprison

aproba|ción *f* approval. **~r** [2] *vt* approve (of); pass ‹*examen*›. ● *vi* pass

apropia|do *a* appropriate. **~rse** *vpr*. **~rse de** appropriate, take

aprovecha|ble *a* usable. **~do** *a* (*aplicado*) diligent; (*ingenioso*) resourceful; (*egoísta*) selfish; (*económico*) thrifty. **~miento** *m* advantage; (*uso*) use. **~r** *vt* take advantage of; (*utilizar*) make use of. ● *vi* be useful. **~rse** *vpr* make the most of it. **~rse de** take advantage of. **¡que aproveche!** enjoy your meal!

aprovisionar *vt* supply (**con, de** with)

aproxima|ción *f* approximation; (*proximidad*) closeness; (*en la lotería*) consolation prize. **~damente** *adv* roughly, approximately. **~do** *a* approximate, rough. **~r** *vt* bring near; (*fig*) bring together ‹*personas*›. **~rse** *vpr* come closer, approach

apt|itud *f* suitability; (*capacidad*) ability. **~o** *a* (*capaz*) capable; (*adecuado*) suitable

apuesta *f* bet

apuesto *m* smart. ● *vb véase* **apostar**

apunta|ción *f* note. **~do** *a* sharp. **~dor** *m* prompter

apuntalar *vt* shore up

apunt|amiento *m* aiming; (*nota*) note. **~ar** *vt* aim ‹*arma*›; (*señalar*) point at; (*anotar*) make a note of, note down; (*sacar punta*) sharpen; (*en el teatro*) prompt. **~arse** *vpr* put one's name down; score ‹*triunfo, tanto etc*›. **~e** *m* note; (*bosquejo*) sketch. **tomar ~s** take notes

apuñalar *vt* stab

apur|adamente *adv* with difficulty. **~ado** *a* difficult; (*sin dinero*) hard up; (*agotado*) exhausted; (*exacto*) precise, carefully done. **~ar** *vt* exhaust; (*acabar*) finish; drain ‹*vaso etc*›; (*fastidiar*) annoy; (*causar vergüenza*) embarrass. **~arse** *vpr* worry; (*esp LAm, apresurarse*) hurry up. **~o** *m* tight spot, difficult situation; (*vergüenza*) embarrassment; (*estrechez*) hardship, want; (*esp LAm, prisa*) hurry

aquejar *vt* trouble

aquel *a* (*f* **aquella,** *mpl* **aquellos,** *fpl* **aquellas**) that; (*en plural*) those; (*primero de dos*) former

aquél *pron* (*f* **aquélla,** *mpl* **aquéllos,** *fpl* **aquéllas**) that one; (*en plural*) those; (*primero de dos*) the former

aquello *pron* that; (*asunto*) that business

aquí *adv* here. **de ~** from here. **de ~ a 15 días** in a fortnight's time. **de ~ para allí** to and fro. **de ~ que** so that. **hasta ~** until now. **por ~** around here

aquiescencia *f* acquiescence

aquietar *vt* calm (down)

aquí: ~ fuera out here. **~ mismo** right here

árabe *a & m & f* Arab; (*lengua*) Arabic

Arabia *f* Arabia. **~ saudita, ~ saudí** Saudi Arabia

arábigo *a* Arabic

arado *m* plough. **~r** *m* ploughman

Aragón *m* Aragon

aragonés *a & m* Aragonese

arancel *m* tariff. **~ario** *a* tariff

arandela *f* washer

araña *f* spider; (*lámpara*) chandelier

arañar *vt* scratch

arar *vt* plough

arbitra|je *m* arbitration; (*en deportes*) refereeing. **~r** *vt/i* arbitrate; (*en fútbol etc*) referee; (*en tenis etc*) umpire

arbitr|ariedad *f* arbitrariness. **~ario** *a* arbitrary. **~io** *m* (free) will; (*jurid*) decision, judgement

árbitro *m* arbitrator; (*en fútbol etc*) referee; (*en tenis etc*) umpire

árbol *m* tree; (*eje*) axle; (*palo*) mast

arbol|ado *m* trees. **~adura** *f* rigging. **~eda** *f* wood

árbol: ~ genealógico family tree. **~ de navidad** Christmas tree

arbusto *m* bush

arca *f* (*caja*) chest. **~ de Noé** Noah's ark

arcada *f* arcade; (*de un puente*) arches; (*náuseas*) retching

arca|ico *a* archaic. **~ísmo** *m* archaism

arcángel *m* archangel

arcano *m* mystery. ● *a* mysterious, secret

arce *m* maple (tree)

arcén *m* (*de autopista*) hard shoulder; (*de carretera*) verge

arcilla *f* clay

arco *m* arch; (*de curva*) arc; (*arma, mus*) bow. **~ iris** *m* rainbow

archipiélago *m* archipelago

archiv|ador *m* filing cabinet. **~ar** *vt* file (away). **~o** *m* file; (*de documentos históricos*) archives

arder *vt/i* burn; (*fig, de ira*) seethe. **~se** *vpr* burn (up). **estar que arde** be very tense. **y va que arde** and that's enough

ardid *m* trick, scheme

ardiente *a* burning. **~mente** *adv* passionately

ardilla *f* squirrel

ardor *m* heat; (*fig*) ardour. **~ del estómago** *m* heartburn. **~oso** *a* burning
arduo *a* arduous
área *f* area
arena *f* sand; (*en deportes*) arena; (*en los toros*) (bull)ring. **~l** *m* sandy area
arenga *f* harangue. **~r** [12] *vt* harangue
aren|isca *f* sandstone. **~isco** *a*, **~oso** *a* sandy
arenque *m* herring. **~ ahumado** kipper
argamasa *f* mortar
Argel *m* Algiers. **~ia** *f* Algeria
argelino *a* & *m* Algerian
argentado *a* silver-plated
Argentina *f*. **la ~** Argentina
argentin|ismo *m* Argentinism. **~o** *a* silvery; (*de la Argentina*) Argentinian, Argentine. ● *m* Argentinian
argolla *f* ring
argot *m* slang
argucia *f* sophism
argüir [19] *vt* (*deducir*) deduce; (*probar*) prove, show; (*argumentar*) argue; (*echar en cara*) reproach. ● *vi* argue
argument|ación *f* argument. **~ador** *a* argumentative. **~ar** *vt/i* argue. **~o** *m* argument; (*de libro, película etc*) story, plot; (*resumen*) synopsis
aria *f* aria
aridez *f* aridity, dryness
árido *a* arid, dry. ● *m*. **~s** *mpl* dry goods
Aries *m* Aries
arisco *a* ‹*persona*› unsociable; ‹*animal*› vicious
arist|ocracia *f* aristocracy. **~ócrata** *m* & *f* aristocrat. **~ocrático** *a* aristocratic
aritmética *f* arithmetic
arma *f* arm, weapon; (*sección*) section. **~da** *f* navy; (*flota*) fleet. **~ de fuego** firearm. **~do** *a* armed (**de** with). **~dura** *f* armour; (*de gafas etc*) frame; (*tec*) framework. **~mento** *m* arms, armaments; (*acción de armar*) armament. **~r** *vt* arm (**de** with); (*montar*) put together. **~r un lío** kick up a fuss. **La A~da Invencible** the Armada
armario *m* cupboard; (*para ropa*) wardrobe. **~ ropero** wardrobe
armatoste *m* monstrosity, hulk (*fam*)
armazón *m* & *f* frame(work)
armer|ía *f* gunsmith's shop; (*museo*) war museum. **~o** *m* gunsmith
armiño *m* ermine
armisticio *m* armistice
armonía *f* harmony
armónica *f* harmonica, mouth organ
armoni|oso harmonious. **~zación** *f* harmonizing. **~zar** [10] *vt* harmonize. ● *vi* harmonize; ‹*personas*› get on well (**con** with); ‹*colores*› go well (**con** with)
arnés *m* armour. **arneses** *mpl* harness
aro *m* ring, hoop; (*Arg, pendiente*) ear-ring
arom|a *m* aroma; (*de vino*) bouquet. **~ático** *a* aromatic. **~atizar** [10] *vt* perfume; (*culin*) flavour
arpa *f* harp
arpado *a* serrated
arpía *f* harpy; (*fig*) hag
arpillera *f* sackcloth, sacking
arpista *m* & *f* harpist
arp|ón *m* harpoon. **~onar** *vt*, **~onear** *vt* harpoon
arque|ar *vt* arch, bend. **~arse** *vpr* arch, bend. **~o** *m* arching, bending
arque|ología *f* archaeology. **~ológico** *a* archaeological. **~ólogo** *m* archaeologist
arquería *f* arcade
arquero *m* archer; (*com*) cashier
arqueta *f* chest
arquetipo *m* archetype; (*prototipo*) prototype
arquitect|o *m* architect. **~ónico** *a* architectural. **~ura** *f* architecture
arrabal *m* suburb; (*LAm, tugurio*) slum. **~es** *mpl* outskirts. **~ero** *a* suburban; (*de modales groseros*) common
arracima|do *a* in a bunch; (*apiñado*) bunched together. **~rse** *vpr* bunch together
arraiga|damente *adv* firmly. **~r** [12] *vi* take root. **~rse** *vpr* take root; (*fig*) settle
arran|cada *f* sudden start. **~car** [7] *vt* pull up ‹*planta*›; extract ‹*diente*›; (*arrebatar*) snatch; (*auto*) start. ● *vi* start. **~carse** *vpr* start. **~que** *m* sudden start; (*auto*) start; (*de emoción*) outburst
arras *fpl* security
arrasa|dor *a* overwhelming, devastating. **~r** *vt* level, smooth; raze to the ground ‹*edificio etc*›; (*llenar*) fill to the brim. ● *vi* ‹*el cielo*› clear.

~rse *vpr* ‹*el cielo*› clear; ‹*los ojos*› fill with tears; (*triunfar*) triumph

arrastr|ado *a* (*penoso*) wretched. **~ar** *vt* pull; (*rozar contra el suelo*) drag (along); give rise to ‹*consecuencias*›. ● *vi* trail on the ground. **~arse** *vpr* crawl; (*humillarse*) grovel. **~e** *m* dragging; (*transporte*) haulage. **estar para el ~e** (*fam*) have had it, be worn out. **ir ~ado** be hard up

arrayán *m* myrtle

arre *int* gee up! **~ar** *vt* urge on; give ‹*golpe*›

arrebañar *vt* scrape together; scrape clean ‹*plato etc*›

arrebat|ado *a* enraged; (*irreflexivo*) impetuous; ‹*cara*› flushed. **~ar** *vt* snatch (away); ‹*el viento*› blow away; (*fig*) win (over); captivate ‹*corazón etc*›. **~arse** *vpr* get carried away. **~o** *m* (*de cólera etc*) fit; (*éxtasis*) extasy

arrebol *m* red glow

arreciar *vi* get worse, increase

arrecife *m* reef

arregl|ado *a* neat; (*bien vestido*) well-dressed; (*moderado*) moderate. **~ar** *vt* arrange; (*poner en orden*) tidy up; sort out ‹*asunto, problema etc*›; (*reparar*) mend. **~arse** *vpr* (*ponerse bien*) improve; (*prepararse*) get ready; (*apañarse*) manage, make do; (*ponerse de acuerdo*) come to an agreement. **~árselas** manage, get by. **~o** *m* (*incl mus*) arrangement; (*acción de reparar*) repair; (*acuerdo*) agreement; (*orden*) order. **con ~o a** according to

arrellanarse *vpr* lounge, sit back

arremangar [12] *vt* roll up ‹*mangas*›; tuck up ‹*falda*›. **~se** *vpr* roll up one's sleeves

arremet|er *vt/i* attack. **~ida** *f* attack

arremolinarse *vpr* mill about

arrenda|dor *m* (*que da en alquiler*) landlord; (*que toma en alquiler*) tenant. **~miento** *m* renting; (*contrato*) lease; (*precio*) rent. **~r** [1] *vt* (*dar casa en alquiler*) let; (*dar cosa en alquiler*) hire out; (*tomar en alquiler*) rent. **~tario** *m* tenant

arreos *mpl* harness

arrepenti|miento *m* repentance, regret. **~rse** [4] *vpr*. **~rse de** be sorry, regret; repent ‹*pecados*›

arrest|ar *vt* arrest, detain; (*encarcelar*) imprison. **~o** *m* arrest; (*encarcelamiento*) imprisonment

arriar [20] *vt* lower ‹*bandera, vela*›; (*aflojar*) loosen; (*inundar*) flood. **~se** *vpr* be flooded

arriba *adv* (up) above; (*dirección*) up(wards); (*en casa*) upstairs. ● *int* up with; (*¡levántate!*) up you get!; (*¡ánimo!*) come on! **¡~ España!** long live Spain! **~ mencionado** aforementioned. **calle ~** up the street. **de ~ abajo** from top to bottom. **de 100 pesetas para ~** more than 100 pesetas. **escaleras ~** upstairs. **la parte de ~** the top part. **los de ~** those at the top. **más ~** above

arribar *vi* ‹*barco*› reach port; (*esp LAm, llegar*) arrive

arribista *m & f* self-seeking person, arriviste

arribo *m* (*esp LAm*) arrival

arriero *m* muleteer

arriesga|do *a* risky. **~r** [12] *vt* risk; (*aventurar*) venture. **~rse** *vpr* take a risk

arrim|ar *vt* bring close(r); (*apartar*) move out of the way ‹*cosa*›; (*apartar*) push aside ‹*persona*›. **~arse** *vpr* come closer, approach; (*apoyarse*) lean (**a** on). **~o** *m* support. **al ~o de** with the support of

arrincona|do *a* forgotten. **~rse** *vt* put in a corner; (*perseguir*) corner; (*arrumbar*) put aside; (*apartar a uno*) leave out, ignore. **~rse** *vpr* become a recluse

arriscado *a* ‹*terreno*› uneven

arrobar *vt* entrance. **~se** *vpr* be enraptured

arrocero *a* rice

arrodillarse *vpr* kneel (down)

arrogan|cia *f* arrogance; (*orgullo*) pride. **~te** *a* arrogant; (*orgulloso*) proud

arrogarse [12] *vpr* assume

arroj|ado *a* brave. **~ar** *vt* throw; (*dejar caer*) drop; (*emitir*) give off, throw out; (*producir*) produce. ● *vi* (*esp LAm, vomitar*) be sick. **~arse** *vpr* throw o.s. **~o** *m* courage

arrolla|dor *a* overwhelming. **~r** *vt* roll (up); (*atropellar*) run over; ‹*ejército*› crush; ‹*agua*› sweep away; (*tratar sin respeto*) have no respect for

arropar *vt* wrap up; (*en la cama*) tuck up; (*fig, amparar*) protect. **~se** *vpr* wrap (o.s.) up

arroy|o *m* stream; (*de una calle*) gutter; (*fig, de lágrimas*) flood; (*fig, de sangre*) pool. **poner en el ~o** throw into the street. **~uelo** *m* small stream

arroz *m* rice. **~al** *m* rice field. **~ con leche** rice pudding

arruga *f* (*en la piel*) wrinkle, line; (*en tela*) crease. **~r** [12] *vt* wrinkle; crumple ‹*papel*›; crease ‹*tela*›. **~rse** *vpr* ‹*la piel*› wrinkle, get wrinkled; ‹*tela*› crease, get creased

arruinar *vt* ruin; (*destruir*) destroy. **~se** *vpr* ‹*persona*› be ruined; ‹*edificio*› fall into ruins

arrullar *vt* lull to sleep. ● *vi* ‹*palomas*› coo. **~se** *vpr* bill and coo

arrumaco *m* caress; (*zalamería*) flattery

arrumbar *vt* put aside

arsenal *m* (*astillero*) shipyard; (*de armas*) arsenal; (*fig*) store

arsénico *m* arsenic

arte *m en singular, f en plural* art; (*habilidad*) skill; (*astucia*) cunning. **bellas ~s** fine arts. **con ~** skilfully. **malas ~s** trickery. **por amor al ~** for nothing, for love

artefacto *m* device

arter|amente *adv* artfully. **~ía** *f* cunning

arteria *f* artery; (*fig, calle*) main road

artero *a* cunning

artesan|al *a* craft. **~ía** *f* handicrafts. **~o** *m* artisan, craftsman. **objeto** *m* **de ~ía** hand-made article

ártico *a & m* Arctic

articula|ción *f* joint; (*pronunciación*) articulation. **~damente** *adv* articulately. **~do** *a* articulated; ‹*lenguaje*› articulate. **~r** *vt* articulate

articulista *m & f* columnist

artículo *m* article. **~s** *mpl* (*géneros*) goods. **~ de exportación** export commodity. **~ de fondo** editorial, leader

artificial *a* artificial

artificiero *m* bomb-disposal expert

artificio *m* (*habilidad*) skill; (*dispositivo*) device; (*engaño*) trick. **~so** *a* clever; (*astuto*) artful

artilugio *m* gadget

artiller|ía *f* artillery. **~o** *m* artilleryman, gunner

artimaña *f* trap

art|ista *m & f* artist; (*en espectáculos*) artiste. **~ísticamente** *adv* artistically. **~ístico** *a* artistic

artr|ítico *a* arthritic. **~itis** *f* arthritis

arveja *f* vetch; (*LAm, guisante*) pea

arzobispo *m* archbishop

as *m* ace

asa *f* handle

asad|o *a* roast(ed). ● *m* roast (meat), joint. **~o a la parrilla** grilled. **~o al horno** (*sin grasa*) baked; (*con grasa*) roast. **~or** *m* spit. **~ura** *f* offal

asalariado *a* salaried. ● *m* employee

asalt|ante *m* attacker; (*de un banco*) robber. **~ar** *vt* storm ‹*fortaleza*›; attack ‹*persona*›; raid ‹*banco etc*›; (*fig*) ‹*duda*› assail; (*fig*) ‹*idea etc*› cross one's mind. **~o** *m* attack; (*en boxeo*) round

asamble|a *f* assembly; (*reunión*) meeting; (*congreso*) conference. **~ísta** *m & f* member of an assembly

asapán *m* (*Mex*) flying squirrel

asar *vt* roast; (*fig, acosar*) pester (**a** with). **~se** *vpr* be very hot. **~ a la parrilla** grill. **~ al horno** (*sin grasa*) bake; (*con grasa*) roast

asbesto *m* asbestos

ascendencia *f* descent

ascend|ente *a* ascending. **~er** [1] *vt* promote. ● *vi* go up, ascend; ‹*cuenta etc*› come to, amount to; (*ser ascendido*) be promoted. **~iente** *m & f* ancestor; (*influencia*) influence

ascens|ión *f* ascent; (*de grado*) promotion. **~ional** *a* upward. **~o** *m* ascent; (*de grado*) promotion. **día** *m* **de la A~ión** Ascension Day

ascensor *m* lift (*Brit*), elevator (*Amer*). **~ista** *m & f* lift attendant (*Brit*), elevator operator (*Amer*)

asc|eta *m & f* ascetic. **~ético** *a* ascetic

asco *m* disgust. **dar ~** be disgusting; (*fig, causar enfado*) be infuriating. **estar hecho un ~** be disgusting. **hacer ~s de algo** turn up one's nose at sth. **me da ~ el ajo** I can't stand garlic. **¡qué ~!** how disgusting! **ser un ~** be a disgrace

ascua *f* ember. **estar en ~s** be on tenterhooks

asea|damente *adv* cleanly. **~do** *a* clean; (*arreglado*) neat. **~r** *vt* (*lavar*) wash; (*limpiar*) clean; (*arreglar*) tidy up

asedi|ar *vt* besiege; (*fig*) pester. **~o** *m* siege

asegura|do *a & m* insured. **~dor** *m* insurer. **~r** *vt* secure, make safe; (*decir*) assure; (*concertar un seguro*)

insure; (*preservar*) safeguard. **~rse** *vpr* make sure
asemejarse *vpr* be alike
asenta|da *f*. **de una ~da** at a sitting. **~do** *a* situated; (*arraigado*) established. **~r** [1] *vt* place; (*asegurar*) settle; (*anotar*) note down. ● *vi* be suitable. **~rse** *vpr* settle; (*estar situado*) be situated
asenti|miento *m* consent. **~r** [4] *vi* agree (**a** to). **~r con la cabeza** nod
aseo *m* cleanliness. **~s** *mpl* toilets
asequible *a* obtainable; ‹*precio*› reasonable; ‹*persona*› approachable
asesin|ar *vt* murder; (*pol*) assassinate. **~ato** *m* murder; (*pol*) assassination. **~o** *m* murderer; (*pol*) assassin
asesor *m* adviser, consultant. **~amiento** *m* advice. **~ar** *vt* advise. **~arse** *vpr*. **~arse con/de** consult. **~ía** *f* consultancy; (*oficina*) consultant's office
asestar *vt* aim ‹*arma*›; strike ‹*golpe etc*›; (*disparar*) fire
asevera|ción *f* assertion. **~r** *vt* assert
asfalt|ado *a* asphalt. **~ar** *vt* asphalt. **~o** *m* asphalt
asfixia *f* suffocation. **~nte** *a* suffocating. **~r** *vt* suffocate. **~rse** *vpr* suffocate
así *adv* so; (*de esta manera*) like this, like that. ● *a* such. **~ ~, ~ asá, ~ asado** so-so. **~ como** just as. **~... como** both... and. **~ pues** so. **~ que** so; (*enseguida*) as soon as. **~ sea** so be it. **~ y todo** even so. **aun ~** even so. **¿no es ~?** isn't that right? **y ~ (sucesivamente)** and so on
Asia *f* Asia
asiático *a* & *m* Asian
asidero *m* handle; (*fig, pretexto*) excuse
asidu|amente *adv* regularly. **~idad** *f* regularity. **~o** *a* & *m* regular
asiento *m* seat; (*situación*) site. **~ delantero** front seat. **~ trasero** back seat. **tome Vd ~** please take a seat
asigna|ción *f* assignment; (*sueldo*) salary. **~r** *vt* assign; allot ‹*porción, tiempo etc*›
asignatura *f* subject. **~ pendiente** (*escol*) failed subject; (*fig*) matter still to be resolved
asil|ado *m* inmate. **~ado político** refugee. **~o** *m* asylum; (*fig*) shelter; (*de ancianos etc*) home. **~o de huérfanos** orphanage. **pedir ~o político** ask for political asylum
asimétrico *a* asymmetrical
asimila|ción *f* assimilation. **~r** *vt* assimilate. **~rse** *vpr* be assimilated. **~rse a** resemble
asimismo *adv* in the same way, likewise
asir [45] *vt* grasp. **~se** *vpr* grab hold (**a, de** of)
asist|encia *f* attendance; (*gente*) people (present); (*en un teatro etc*) audience; (*ayuda*) assistance. **~encia médica** medical care. **~enta** *f* assistant; (*mujer de la limpieza*) charwoman. **~ente** *m* assistant. **~ente social** social worker. **~ido** *a* assisted. **~ir** *vt* assist, help; ‹*un médico*› treat. ● *vi*. **~ir a** attend, be present at
asm|a *f* asthma. **~ático** *a* & *m* asthmatic
asn|ada *f* (*fig*) silly thing. **~o** *m* donkey; (*fig*) ass
asocia|ción *f* association; (*com*) partnership. **~do** *a* associated; ‹*miembro etc*› associate. ● *m* associate. **~r** *vt* associate; (*com*) take into partnership. **~rse** *vpr* associate; (*com*) become a partner
asolador *a* destructive
asolar[1] [1] *vt* destroy. **~se** *vpr* be destroyed
asolar[2] *vt* dry up ‹*plantas*›
asoma|da *f* brief appearance. **~r** *vt* show. ● *vi* appear, show. **~rse** *vpr* ‹*persona*› lean out (**a, por** of); ‹*cosa*› appear
asombr|adizo *a* easily frightened. **~ar** *vt* (*pasmar*) amaze; (*sorprender*) surprise. **~arse** *vpr* be amazed; (*sorprenderse*) be surprised. **~o** *m* amazement, surprise. **~osamente** *adv* amazingly. **~oso** *a* amazing, astonishing
asomo *m* sign. **ni por ~** by no means
asonada *f* mob; (*motín*) riot
aspa *f* cross, X-shape; (*de molino*) (windmill) sail. **~do** *a* X-shaped
aspaviento *m* show, fuss. **~s** *mpl* gestures. **hacer ~s** make a big fuss
aspecto *m* look, appearance; (*fig*) aspect
aspereza *f* roughness; (*de sabor etc*) sourness
áspero *a* rough; ‹*sabor etc*› bitter
aspersión *f* sprinkling

aspiración *f* breath; (*deseo*) ambition

aspirador *a* suction. **~a** *f* vacuum cleaner

aspira|nte *m* candidate. **~r** *vt* breathe in; ‹*máquina*› suck up. ● *vi* breathe in; ‹*máquina*› suck. **~r a** aspire to

aspirina *f* aspirin

asquear *vt* sicken. ● *vi* be sickening. **~se** *vpr* be disgusted

asqueros|amente *adv* disgustingly. **~idad** *f* filthiness. **~o** *a* disgusting

asta *f* spear; (*de la bandera*) flagpole; (*mango*) handle; (*cuerno*) horn. **a media ~** at half-mast. **~do** *a* horned

asterisco *m* asterisk

astilla *f* splinter. **~s** *fpl* firewood. **~r** *vt* splinter. **hacer ~s** smash. **hacerse ~s** shatter

astillero *m* shipyard

astringente *a & m* astringent

astro *m* star

astr|ología *f* astrology. **~ólogo** *m* astrologer

astrona|uta *m & f* astronaut. **~ve** *f* spaceship

astr|onomía *f* astronomy. **~onómico** *a* astronomical. **~ónomo** *m* astronomer

astu|cia *f* cleverness; (*ardid*) cunning. **~to** *a* astute; (*taimado*) cunning

asturiano *a & m* Asturian

Asturias *fpl* Asturias

asueto *m* time off, holiday

asumir *vt* assume

asunción *f* assumption. **A~** Assumption

asunto *m* subject; (*cuestión*) matter; (*de una novela*) plot; (*negocio*) business. **~s** *mpl* **exteriores** foreign affairs. **el ~ es que** the fact is that

asusta|dizo *a* easily frightened. **~r** *vt* frighten. **~rse** *vpr* be frightened

ataca|nte *m & f* attacker. **~r** [7] *vt* attack

atad|ero *m* rope; (*cierre*) fastening; (*gancho*) hook. **~ijo** *m* bundle. **~o** *a* tied; (*fig*) timid. ● *m* bundle. **~ura** *f* tying; (*cuerda*) string

ataj|ar *vi* take a short cut. **~o** *m* short cut; (*grupo*) bunch. **echar por el ~o** take the easy way out

atalaya *f* watch-tower; (*fig*) vantage point

atañer [22] *vt* concern

ataque *m* attack; (*med*) fit, attack. **~ al corazón** heart attack. **~ de nervios** hysterics

atar *vt* tie (up). **~se** *vpr* get tied up

atardecer [11] *vi* get dark. ● *m* dusk. **al ~** at dusk

atarea|do *a* busy. **~rse** *vpr* work hard

atasc|adero *m* (*fig*) stumbling block. **~ar** [7] *vt* block; (*fig*) hinder. **~arse** *vpr* get stuck; ‹*tubo etc*› block. **~o** *m* obstruction; (*auto*) traffic jam

ataúd *m* coffin

atav|iar [20] *vt* dress up. **~iarse** *vpr* dress up, get dressed up. **~ío** *m* dress, attire

atemorizar [10] *vt* frighten. **~se** *vpr* be frightened

Atenas *fpl* Athens

atenazar [10] *vt* (*fig*) torture; ‹*duda, miedo*› grip

atención *f* attention; (*cortesía*) courtesy, kindness; (*interés*) interest. **¡~!** look out! **~ a** beware of. **llamar la ~** attract attention, catch the eye. **prestar ~** pay attention

atender [1] *vt* attend to; heed ‹*consejo etc*›; (*cuidar*) look after. ● *vi* pay attention

atenerse [40] *vpr* abide (**a** by)

atentado *m* offence; (*ataque*) attack. **~ contra la vida de uno** attempt on s.o.'s life

atentamente *adv* attentively; (*con cortesía*) politely; (*con amabilidad*) kindly. **le saluda ~** (*en cartas*) yours faithfully

atentar *vi* commit an offence. **~ contra la vida de uno** make an attempt on s.o.'s life

atento *a* attentive; (*cortés*) polite; (*amable*) kind

atenua|nte *a* extenuating. ● *f* extenuating circumstance. **~r** [21] *vt* attenuate; (*hacer menor*) diminish, lessen. **~rse** *vpr* weaken

ateo *a* atheistic. ● *m* atheist

aterciopelado *a* velvety

aterido *a* frozen (stiff), numb (with cold)

aterra|dor *a* terrifying. **~r** *vt* terrify. **~rse** *vpr* be terrified

aterriza|je *m* landing. **~je forzoso** emergency landing. **~r** [10] *vt* land

aterrorizar [10] *vt* terrify

atesorar *vt* hoard

atesta|do *a* packed, full up. ● *m* sworn statement. **~r** *vt* fill up, pack; (*jurid*) testify

atestiguar [15] *vt* testify to; (*fig*) prove
atiborrar *vt* fill, stuff. **~se** *vpr* stuff o.s.
ático *m* attic
atilda|do *a* elegant, neat. **~r** *vt* put a tilde over; (*arreglar*) tidy up. **~rse** *vpr* smarten o.s. up
atina|damente *adv* rightly. **~do** *a* right; (*juicioso*) wise, sensible. **~r** *vt/i* hit upon; (*acertar*) guess right
atípico *a* exceptional
atiplado *a* high-pitched
atirantar *vt* tighten
atisb|ar *vt* spy on; (*vislumbrar*) make out. **~o** *m* spying; (*indicio*) hint, sign
atizar [10] *vt* poke; give ‹*golpe*›; (*fig*) stir up; arouse, excite ‹*pasión etc*›
atlántico *a* Atlantic. **el (océano) A~** the Atlantic (Ocean)
atlas *m* atlas
atl|eta *m & f* athlete. **~ético** *a* athletic. **~etismo** *m* athletics
atm|ósfera *f* atmosphere. **~osférico** *a* atmospheric
atolondra|do *a* scatter-brained; (*aturdido*) bewildered. **~miento** *m* bewilderment; (*irreflexión*) thoughtlessness. **~r** *vt* bewilder; (*pasmar*) stun. **~rse** *vpr* be bewildered
atolladero *m* bog; (*fig*) tight corner
at|ómico *a* atomic. **~omizador** *m* atomizer. **~omizar** [10] *vt* atomize
átomo *m* atom
atónito *m* amazed
atonta|do *a* bewildered; (*tonto*) stupid. **~r** *vt* stun. **~rse** *vpr* get confused
atormenta|dor *a* tormenting. ● *m* tormentor. **~r** *vt* torture. **~rse** *vpr* worry, torment o.s.
atornillar *vt* screw on
atosigar [12] *vt* pester
atracadero *m* quay
atracador *m* bandit
atracar [7] *vt* (*amarrar*) tie up; (*arrimar*) bring alongside; rob ‹*banco, persona*›. ● *vi* ‹*barco*› tie up; ‹*astronave*› dock. **~se** *vpr* stuff o.s. **(de** with)
atracci|ón *f* attraction. **~ones** *fpl* entertainment, amusements
atrac|o *m* hold-up, robbery. **~ón** *m*. **darse un ~ón** stuff o.s.
atractivo *a* attractive. ● *m* attraction; (*encanto*) charm
atraer [41] *vt* attract
atragantarse *vpr* choke (**con** on). **la historia se me atraganta** I can't stand history
atranc|ar [7] *vt* bolt ‹*puerta*›; block up ‹*tubo etc*›. **~arse** *vpr* get stuck; ‹*tubo*› get blocked. **~o** *m* difficulty
atrapar *vt* trap; (*fig*) land ‹*empleo etc*›; catch ‹*resfriado*›
atrás *adv* behind; (*dirección*) backwards); (*tiempo*) previously, before. ● *int* back! **dar un paso ~** step backwards. **hacia ~, para ~** backwards
atras|ado *a* behind; ‹*reloj*› slow; (*con deudas*) in arrears; ‹*país*› backward. **llegar ~ado** arrive late. **~ar** *vt* slow down; (*retrasar*) put back; (*demorar*) delay, postpone. ● *vi* ‹*reloj*› be slow. **~arse** *vpr* be late; ‹*reloj*› be slow; (*quedarse atrás*) be behind. **~o** *m* delay; (*de un reloj*) slowness; (*de un país*) backwardness. **~os** *mpl* arrears
atravesa|do *a* lying across; (*bizco*) cross-eyed; (*fig, malo*) wicked. **~r** [1] *vt* cross; (*traspasar*) go through; (*poner transversalmente*) lay across. **~rse** *vpr* lie across; (*en la garganta*) get stuck, stick; (*entrometerse*) interfere
atrayente *a* attractive
atrev|erse *vpr* dare. **~erse con** tackle. **~ido** *a* daring, bold; (*insolente*) insolent. **~imiento** *m* daring, boldness; (*descaro*) insolence
atribución *f* attribution. **atribuciones** *fpl* authority
atribuir [17] *vt* attribute; confer ‹*función*›. **~se** *vpr* take the credit for
atribular *vt* afflict. **~se** *vpr* be distressed
atribut|ivo *a* attributive. **~o** *m* attribute; (*símbolo*) symbol
atril *m* lectern; (*mus*) music stand
atrincherar *vt* fortify with trenches. **~se** *vpr* entrench (o.s.)
atrocidad *f* atrocity. **decir ~es** make silly remarks. **¡qué ~!** how terrible!
atrochar *vi* take a short cut
atrojarse *vpr* (*Mex*) be cornered
atrona|dor *a* deafening. **~r** [2] *vt* deafen
atropell|adamente *adv* hurriedly. **~ado** *a* hasty. **~ar** *vt* knock down, run over; (*empujar*) push aside; (*maltratar*) bully; (*fig*) outrage, insult. **~arse** *vpr* rush. **~o** *m* (*auto*) accident; (*fig*) outrage

atroz *a* atrocious; (*fam*) huge. **~mente** *adv* atrociously, awfully
atuendo *m* dress, attire
atufar *vt* choke; (*fig*) irritate. **~se** *vpr* be overcome; (*enfadarse*) get cross
atún *m* tuna (fish)
aturdi|do *a* bewildered; (*irreflexivo*) thoughtless. **~r** *vt* bewilder, stun; ‹*ruido*› deafen. **~rse** *vpr* be stunned; (*intentar olvidar*) try to forget
atur(r)ullar *vt* bewilder
atusar *vt* smooth; trim ‹*pelo*›
auda|cia *f* boldness, audacity. **~z** *a* bold
audib|ilidad *f* audibility. **~le** *a* audible
audición *f* hearing; (*concierto*) concert
audiencia *f* audience; (*tribunal*) court
auditor *m* judge-advocate; (*de cuentas*) auditor
auditorio *m* audience; (*sala*) auditorium
auge *m* peak; (*com*) boom
augur|ar *vt* predict; ‹*cosas*› augur. **~io** *m* omen. **~ios** *mpl*. **con nuestros ~ios para** with our best wishes for
augusto *a* august
aula *f* class-room; (*univ*) lecture room
aulaga *f* gorse
aull|ar [23] *vi* howl. **~ido** *m* howl
aument|ar *vt* increase; put up ‹*precios*›; magnify ‹*imagen*›; step up ‹*producción, voltaje*›. ● *vi* increase. **~arse** *vpr* increase. **~ativo** *a & m* augmentative. **~o** *m* increase; (*de sueldo*) rise
aun *adv* even. **~ así** even so. **~ cuando** although. **más ~** even more. **ni ~** not even
aún *adv* still, yet. **~ no ha llegado** it still hasn't arrived, it hasn't arrived yet
aunar [23] *vt* join. **~se** *vpr* join together
aunque *conj* although, (even) though
aúpa *int* up! **de ~** wonderful
aureola *f* halo
auricular *m* (*de teléfono*) receiver. **~es** *mpl* headphones
aurora *f* dawn
ausen|cia *f* absence. **~tarse** *vpr* leave. **~te** *a* absent. ● *m & f* absentee; (*jurid*) missing person. **en ~ de** in the absence of
auspicio *m* omen. **bajo los ~s de** sponsored by
auster|idad *f* austerity. **~o** *a* austere
austral *a* southern. ● *m* (*unidad monetaria argentina*) austral
Australia *m* Australia
australiano *a & m* Australian
Austria *f* Austria
austriaco, austríaco *a & m* Austrian
aut|enticar [7] authenticate. **~enticidad** *f* authenticity. **~éntico** *a* authentic
auto *m* sentence; (*auto, fam*) car. **~s** *mpl* proceedings
auto... *pref* auto...
auto|ayuda *f* self-help. **~biografía** *f* autobiography. **~biográfico** *a* autobiographical. **~bombo** *m* self-glorification
autobús *m* bus. **en ~** by bus
autocar *m* coach (*Brit*), (long-distance) bus (*Amer*)
aut|ocracia *f* autocracy. **~ócrata** *m & f* autocrat. **~ocrático** *a* autocratic
autóctono *a* autochthonous
auto: ~determinación *f* self-determination. **~defensa** *f* self-defence. **~didacto** *a* self-taught. ● *m* autodidact. **~escuela** *f* driving school. **~giro** *m* autogiro
autógrafo *m* autograph
automación *f* automation
autómata *m* robot
autom|ático *a* automatic. ● *m* press-stud. **~atización** *f* automation. **~atizar** [10] *vt* automate
automotor *a* (*f* **automotriz**) self-propelled. ● *m* diesel train
autom|óvil *a* self-propelled. ● *m* car. **~ovilismo** *m* motoring. **~ovilista** *m & f* driver, motorist
aut|onomía *f* autonomy. **~onómico** *a*, **~ónomo** *a* autonomous
autopista *f* motorway (*Brit*), freeway (*Amer*)
autopsia *f* autopsy
autor *m* author. **~a** *f* author(ess)
autori|dad *f* authority. **~tario** *a* authoritarian. **~tarismo** *m* authoritarianism
autoriza|ción *f* authorization. **~damente** *adv* officially. **~do** *a* authorized, offical; ‹*opinión etc*› authoritative. **~r** [10] *vt* authorize

auto: ~rretrato *m* self-portrait. **~servicio** *m* self-service restaurant. **~stop** *m* hitch-hiking. **hacer ~stop** hitch-hike
autosuficien|cia *f* self-sufficiency. **~te** *a* self-sufficient
autovía *f* dual carriageway
auxili|ar *a* assistant; ‹*servicios*› auxiliary. ● *m* assistant. ● *vt* help. **~o** *m* help. **¡~o!** help! **~os espirituales** last rites. **en ~o de** in aid of. **pedir ~o** shout for help. **primeros ~os** first aid
Av. *abrev* (*Avenida*) Ave, Avenue
aval *m* guarantee
avalancha *f* avalanche
avalar *vt* guarantee
avalorar *vt* enhance; (*fig*) encourage
avance *m* advance; (*en el cine*) trailer; (*balance*) balance; (*de noticias*) early news bulletin. **~ informativo** publicity hand-out
avante *adv* (*esp LAm*) forward
avanza|do *a* advanced. **~r** [10] *vt* move forward. ● *vi* advance
avar|icia *f* avarice. **~icioso** *a*, **~iento** *a* greedy; (*tacaño*) miserly. **~o** *a* miserly. ● *m* miser
avasalla|dor *a* overwhelming. **~r** *vt* dominate
Avda. *abrev* (*Avenida*) Ave, Avenue
ave *f* bird. **~ de paso** (*incl fig*) bird of passage. **~ de presa**, **~ de rapiña** bird of prey
avecinarse *vpr* approach
avecindarse *vpr* settle
avejentarse *vpr* age
avellan|a *f* hazel-nut. **~o** *m* hazel (tree)
avemaría *f* Hail Mary. **al ~** at dusk
avena *f* oats
avenar *vt* drain
avenida *f* (*calle*) avenue; (*de río*) flood
avenir [53] *vt* reconcile. **~se** *vpr* come to an agreement
aventaja|do *a* outstanding. **~r** *vt* surpass
aventar [1] *vt* fan; winnow ‹*grano etc*›; ‹*viento*› blow away
aventur|a *f* adventure; (*riesgo*) risk. **~a amorosa** love affair. **~ado** *a* risky. **~ar** *vt* risk. **~arse** *vpr* dare. **~a sentimental** love affair. **~ero** *a* adventurous. ● *m* adventurer
avergonza|do *a* ashamed; (*embarazado*) embarrassed. **~r** [10 & 16] *vt* shame; (*embarazar*) embarrass. **~rse** *vpr* be ashamed; (*embarazarse*) be embarrassed
aver|ía *f* (*auto*) breakdown; (*daño*) damage. **~iado** *a* broken down; ‹*fruta*› damaged, spoilt. **~iar** [20] *vt* damage. **~iarse** *vpr* get damaged; ‹*coche*› break down
averigua|ble *a* verifiable. **~ción** *f* verification; (*investigación*) investigation; (*Mex, disputa*) argument. **~dor** *m* investigator. **~r** [15] *vt* verify; (*enterarse de*) find out; (*investigar*) investigate. ● *vi* (*Mex*) quarrel
aversión *f* aversion (**a, hacia, por** for)
avestruz *m* ostrich
aviación *f* aviation; (*mil*) air force
aviado *a* (*Arg*) well off. **estar ~** be in a mess
aviador *m* (*aviat*) member of the crew; (*piloto*) pilot; (*Arg, prestamista*) money-lender; (*Arg, de minas*) mining speculator
aviar [20] *vt* get ready, prepare; (*arreglar*) tidy; (*reparar*) repair; (*LAm, prestar dinero*) lend money; (*dar prisa*) hurry up. **~se** *vpr* get ready. **¡avíate!** hurry up!
av|ícula *a* poultry. **~icultor** *m* poultry farmer. **~icultura** *f* poultry farming
avidez *f* eagerness, greed
ávido *a* eager, greedy
avieso *a* (*maligno*) wicked
avinagra|do *a* sour. **~r** *vt* sour; (*fig*) embitter. **~rse** *vpr* go sour; (*fig*) become embittered
avío *m* preparation. **~s** *mpl* provisions; (*utensilios*) equipment
avi|ón *m* aeroplane (*Brit*), airplane (*Amer*). **~oneta** *f* light aircraft
avis|ado *a* wise. **~ar** *vt* warn; (*informar*) notify, inform; call ‹*medico etc*›. **~o** *m* warning; (*anuncio* notice. **estar sobre ~o** be on the alert. **mal ~ado** ill-advised. **sin previo ~o** without notice
avisp|a *f* wasp. **~ado** *a* sharp. **~ero** *m* wasps' nest; (*fig*) mess. **~ón** *m* hornet
avistar *vt* catch sight of
avitualla|miento *m* supplying. **~r** *vt* provision
avivar *vt* stoke up ‹*fuego*›; brighten up ‹*color*›; arouse ‹*interés, pasión*›; intensify ‹*dolor*›. **~se** *vpr* revive; (*animarse*) cheer up
axila *f* axilla, armpit

axiom|a *m* axiom. **~ático** *a* axiomatic
ay *int* (*de dolor*) ouch!; (*de susto*) oh!; (*de pena*) oh dear! **~ de** poor. **¡~ de tí!** poor you!
aya *f* governess, child's nurse
ayer *adv* yesterday. ● *m* past. **antes de ~** the day before yesterday. **~ por la mañana** yesterday morning. **~ (por la) noche** last night
ayo *m* tutor
ayote *m* (*Mex*) pumpkin
ayuda *f* help, aid. **~ de cámara** valet. **~nta** *f*, **~nte** *m* assistant; (*mil*) adjutant. **~nte técnico sanitario (ATS)** nurse. **~r** *vt* help
ayun|ar *vi* fast. **~as** *fpl*. **estar en ~as** have had no breakfast; (*fig, fam*) be in the dark. **~o** *m* fasting
ayuntamiento *m* town council, city council; (*edificio*) town hall
azabache *m* jet
azad|a *f* hoe. **~ón** *m* (large) hoe
azafata *f* air hostess
azafrán *m* saffron
azahar *m* orange blossom
azar *m* chance; (*desgracia*) misfortune. **al ~** at random. **por ~** by chance
azararse *vpr* go wrong; (*fig*) get flustered
azaros|amente *adv* hazardously. **~o** *a* hazardous, risky; ‹*persona*› unlucky
azoga|do *a* restless. **~rse** [12] *vpr* be restless
azolve *m* (*Mex*) obstruction
azora|do *a* flustered, excited, alarmed. **~miento** *m* confusion, embarrassment. **~r** *vt* embarrass; (*aturdir*) alarm. **~rse** *vpr* get flustered, be alarmed
Azores *fpl* Azores
azot|aina *f* beating. **~ar** *vt* whip, beat. **~e** *m* whip; (*golpe*) smack; (*fig, calamidad*) calamity
azotea *f* flat roof. **estar mal de la ~** be mad
azteca *a* & *m* & *f* Aztec
az|úcar *m* & *f* sugar. **~ucarado** *a* sweet. **~ucarar** *vt* sweeten. **~ucarero** *m* sugar bowl
azucena *f* (white) lily
azufre *m* sulphur
azul *a* & *m* blue. **~ado** *a* bluish. **~ de lavar** (washing) blue. **~ marino** navy blue
azulejo *m* tile
azuzar *vt* urge on, incite

B

bab|a *f* spittle. **~ear** *vi* drool, slobber; ‹*niño*› dribble. **caerse la ~a** be delighted
babel *f* bedlam
babe|o *m* drooling; (*de un niño*) dribbling. **~ro** *m* bib
Babia *f*. **estar en ~** have one's head in the clouds
babieca *a* stupid. ● *m* & *f* simpleton
babor *m* port. **a ~** to port, on the port side
babosa *f* slug
babosada *f* (*Mex*) silly remark
babos|ear *vt* slobber over; ‹*niño*› dribble over. **~eo** *m* drooling; (*de niño*) dribbling. **~o** *a* slimy; (*LAm, tonto*) silly
babucha *f* slipper
babuino *m* baboon
baca *f* luggage rack
bacaladilla *f* small cod
bacalao *m* cod
bacon *m* bacon
bacteria *f* bacterium
bache *m* hole; (*fig*) bad patch
bachillerato *m* school-leaving examination
badaj|azo *m* stroke (of a bell). **~o** *m* clapper; (*persona*) chatterbox
bagaje *m* baggage; (*animal*) beast of burden; (*fig*) knowledge
bagatela *f* trifle
Bahamas *fpl* Bahamas
bahía *f* bay
bail|able *a* dance. **~ador** *a* dancing. ● *m* dancer. **~aor** *m* Flamenco dancer. **~ar** *vt/i* dance. **~arín** dancer. **~arina** *f* dancer; (*de baile clásico*) ballerina. **~e** *m* dance. **~e de etiqueta** ball. **ir a ~ar** go dancing
baja *f* drop, fall; (*mil*) casualty. **~ por maternidad** maternity leave. **~da** *f* slope; (*acto de bajar*) descent. **~mar** *m* low tide. **~r** *vt* lower; (*llevar abajo*) get down; bow ‹*la cabeza*›. **~r la escalera** go downstairs. ● *vi* go down; ‹*temperatura, precio*› fall. **~rse** *vpr* bend down. **~r(se) de** get out of ‹*coche*›; get off ‹*autobús, caballo, tren, bicicleta*›. **dar(se) de ~** take sick leave
bajeza *f* vile deed
bajío *m* sandbank

bajo *a* low; (*de estatura*) short, small; ‹*cabeza, ojos*› lowered; (*humilde*) humble, low; (*vil*) vile, low; ‹*color*› pale; ‹*voz*› low; (*mus*) deep. ● *m* lowland; (*bajío*) sandbank; (*mus*) bass. ● *adv* quietly; ‹*volar*› low. ● *prep* under; (*temperatura*) below. **~ la lluvia** in the rain. **los ~s fondos** the low district. **por lo ~** under one's breath; (*fig*) in secret

bajón *m* drop; (*de salud*) decline; (*com*) slump

bala *f* bullet; (*de algodón etc*) bale. **~ perdida** stray bullet. **como una ~** like a shot

balada *f* ballad

baladí *a* trivial

baladrón *a* boastful

baladron|ada *f* boast. **~ear** *vi* boast

balan|ce *m* swinging; (*de una cuenta*) balance; (*documento*) balance sheet. **~cear** *vt* balance. ● *vi* hesitate. **~cearse** *vpr* swing; (*vacilar*) hesitate. **~ceo** *m* swinging. **~za** *f* scales; (*com*) balance

balar *vi* bleat

balaustrada *f* balustrade, railing(s); (*de escalera*) banisters

balay *m* (*LAm*) wicker basket

balazo *m* (*disparo*) shot; (*herida*) bullet wound

balboa *f* (*unidad monetaria panameña*) balboa

balbuc|ear *vt/i* stammer; ‹*niño*› babble. **~eo** *m* stammering; (*de niño*) babbling. **~iente** *a* stammering; ‹*niño*› babbling. **~ir** [24] *vt/i* stammer; ‹*niño*› babble

balc|ón *m* balcony. **~onada** *f* row of balconies. **~onaje** *m* row of balconies

balda *f* shelf

baldado *a* disabled, crippled; (*rendido*) shattered. ● *m* disabled person, cripple

baldaquín *m*, **baldaquino** *m* canopy

baldar *vt* cripple

balde *m* bucket. **de ~** free (of charge). **en ~** in vain. **~ar** *vt* wash down

baldío *a* ‹*terreno*› waste; (*fig*) useless

baldosa *f* (floor) tile; (*losa*) flagstone

balduque *m* (*incl fig*) red tape

balear *a* Balearic. ● *m* native of the Balearic Islands. **las Islas** *fpl* **B~es** the Balearics, the Balearic Islands

baleo *m* (*LAm, tiroteo*) shooting; (*Mex, abanico*) fan

balido *m* bleat; (*varios sonidos*) bleating

bal|ín *m* small bullet. **~ines** *mpl* shot

balística *f* ballistics

baliza *f* (*naut*) buoy; (*aviat*) beacon

balneario *m* spa; (*con playa*) seaside resort. ● *a*. **estación** *f* **balnearia** spa; (*con playa*) seaside resort

balompié *m* football (*Brit*), soccer

bal|ón *m* ball, football. **~oncesto** *m* basketball. **~onmano** *m* handball. **~volea** *m* volleyball

balotaje *m* (*LAm*) voting

balsa *f* (*de agua*) pool; (*plataforma flotante*) raft

bálsamo *m* balsam; (*fig*) balm

balsón *m* (*Mex*) stagnant water

baluarte *m* (*incl fig*) bastion

balumba *f* mass, mountain

ballena *f* whale

ballesta *f* crossbow

ballet /ba'le/ (*pl* **ballets** uba'le/) *m* ballet

bambole|ar *vi* sway; ‹*mesa etc*› wobble. **~arse** *vpr* sway; ‹*mesa etc*› wobble. **~o** *m* swaying; (*de mesa etc*) wobbling

bambú *m* (*pl* **bambúes**) bamboo

banal *a* banal. **~idad** *f* banality

banan|a *f* (*esp LAm*) banana. **~o** *m* (*LAm*) banana tree

banast|a *f* large basket. **~o** *m* large round basket

banc|a *f* banking; (*en juegos*) bank; (*LAm, asiento*) bench. **~ario** *a* bank, banking. **~arrota** *f* bankruptcy. **~o** *m* (*asiento*) bench; (*com*) bank; (*bajío*) sandbank. **hacer ~arrota, ir a la ~arrota** go bankrupt

banda *f* (*incl mus, radio*) band; (*grupo*) gang, group; (*lado*) side. **~da** *f* (*de aves*) flock; (*de peces*) shoal. **~ de sonido, ~ sonora** sound-track

bandeja *f* tray; (*LAm, plato*) serving dish. **servir algo en ~ a uno** hand sth to s.o. on a plate

bandera *f* flag; (*estandarte*) banner, standard

banderill|a *f* banderilla. **~ear** *vt* stick the banderillas in. **~ero** *m* banderillero

banderín *m* pennant, small flag, banner

bandido *m* bandit

bando *m* edict, proclamation; (*partido*) faction. **~s** *mpl* banns. **pasarse al otro ~** go over to the other side

bandolero *m* bandit

bandolina *f* mandolin

bandoneón *m* large accordion

banjo *m* banjo

banquero *m* banker

banqueta *f* stool; (*LAm, acera*) pavement (*Brit*), sidewalk (*Amer*)

banquete *m* banquet; (*de boda*) wedding reception. **~ar** *vt/i* banquet

banquillo *m* bench; (*jurid*) dock; (*taburete*) footstool

bañ|ado *m* (*LAm*) swamp. **~ador** *m* (*de mujer*) swimming costume; (*de hombre*) swimming trunks. **~ar** *vt* bathe, immerse; bath ‹*niño*›; (*culin, recubrir*) coat. **~arse** *vpr* go swimming, have a swim; (*en casa*) have a bath. **~era** *f* bath, bath-tub. **~ero** *m* life-guard. **~ista** *m & f* bather. **~o** *m* bath; (*en piscina, mar etc*) swim; (*bañera*) bath, bath-tub; (*capa*) coat(ing)

baptisterio *m* baptistery; (*pila*) font

baquet|a *f* (*de fusil*) ramrod; (*de tambor*) drumstick. **~ear** *vt* bother. **~eo** *m* nuisance, bore

bar *m* bar

barahúnda *f* uproar

baraja *f* pack of cards. **~r** *vt* shuffle; juggle, massage ‹*cifras etc*›. ● *vi* argue (**con** with); (*enemistarse*) fall out (**con** with). **~s** *fpl* argument. **jugar a la ~** play cards. **jugar a dos ~s, jugar con dos ~s** be deceitful, indulge in double-dealing

baranda *f*, **barandal** *m*, **barandilla** *f* handrail; (*de escalera*) banisters

barat|a *f* (*Mex*) sale. **~ija** *f* trinket. **~illo** *m* junk shop; (*géneros*) cheap goods. **~o** *a* cheap. ● *m* sale. ● *adv* cheap(ly). **~ura** *f* cheapness

baraúnda *f* uproar

barba *f* chin; (*pelo*) beard. **~do** *a* bearded

barbacoa *f* barbecue; (*Mex, carne*) barbecued meat

bárbaramente *adv* savagely; (*fig*) tremendously

barbari|dad *f* barbarity; (*fig*) outrage; (*mucho, fam*) awful lot (*fam*). **¡qué ~dad!** how awful! **~e** *f* barbarity; (*fig*) ignorance. **~smo** *m* barbarism

bárbaro *a* barbaric, cruel; (*bruto*) uncouth; (*estupendo, fam*) terrific (*fam*). ● *m* barbarian. **¡qué ~!** how marvellous!

barbear *vt* (*afeitar*) shave; (*Mex, lisonjear*) fawn on

barbecho *m* fallow

barber|ía *f* barber's (shop). **~o** *m* barber; (*Mex, adulador*) flatterer

barbi|lampiño *a* beardless; (*fig*) inexperienced, green. **~lindo** *m* dandy

barbilla *f* chin

barbitúrico *m* barbiturate

barbo *m* barbel. **~ de mar** red mullet

barbot|ar *vt/i* mumble. **~ear** *vt/i* mumble. **~eo** *m* mumbling

barbudo *a* bearded

barbullar *vi* jabber

barca *f* (small) boat. **~ de pasaje** ferry. **~je** *m* fare. **~za** *f* barge

Barcelona *f* Barcelona

barcelonés *a* of Barcelona, from Barcelona. ● *m* native of Barcelona

barco *m* boat; (*navío*) ship. **~ cisterna** tanker. **~ de vapor** steamer. **~ de vela** sailing boat. **ir en ~** go by boat

bario *m* barium

barítono *m* baritone

barman *m* (*pl* **barmans**) barman

barniz *m* varnish; (*para loza etc*) glaze; (*fig*) veneer. **~ar** [10] *vt* varnish; glaze ‹*loza etc*›

bar|ométrico *a* barometric. **~ómetro** *m* barometer

bar|ón *m* baron. **~onesa** *f* baroness

barquero *m* boatman

barra *f* bar; (*pan*) French bread; (*de oro o plata*) ingot; (*palanca*) lever. **~ de labios** lipstick. **no pararse en ~s** stop at nothing

barrabasada *f* mischief, prank

barraca *f* hut; (*vivienda pobre*) shack, shanty

barranco *m* ravine, gully; (*despeñadero*) cliff, precipice

barre|dera *f* road-sweeper. **~dura** *f* rubbish. **~minas** *m invar* mine-sweeper

barren|a *f* drill, bit. **~ar** *vt* drill. **~o** *m* large (mechanical) drill. **entrar en ~a** ‹*avión*› go into a spin

barrer *vt* sweep; (*quitar*) sweep aside

barrera *f* barrier. **~ del sonido** sound barrier

barriada *f* district

barrica *f* barrel
barricada *f* barricade
barrido *m* sweeping
barrig|a *f* (pot-)belly. **~ón** *a*, **~udo** *a* pot-bellied
barril *m* barrel. **~ete** *m* keg, small barrel
barrio *m* district, area. **~bajero** *a* vulgar, common. **~s bajos** poor quarter, poor area. **el otro ~** (*fig*, *fam*) the other world
barro *m* mud; (*arcilla*) clay; (*arcilla cocida*) earthenware
barroco *a* Baroque. ● *m* Baroque style
barrote *m* heavy bar
barrunt|ar *vt* sense, have a feeling. **~e** *m*, **~o** *m* sign; (*presentimiento*) feeling
bartola *f*. **tenderse a la ~, tumbarse a la ~** take it easy
bártulos *mpl* things. **liar los ~** pack one's bags
barullo *m* uproar; (*confusión*) confusion. **a ~** galore
basa *f*, **basamento** *m* base; (*fig*) basis
basar *vt* base. **~se** *vpr*. **~se en** be based on
basc|a *f* crowd. **~as** *fpl* nausea. **~osidad** *f* filth. **la ~a** the gang
báscula *f* scales
bascular *vi* tilt
base *f* base; (*fig*) basis, foundation. **a ~ de** thanks to; (*mediante*) by means of; (*en una receta*) as the basic ingredient(s). **a ~ de bien** very well. **partiendo de la ~ de, tomando como ~** on the basis of
básico *a* basic
basílica *f* basilica
basilisco *m* basilisk. **hecho un ~** furious
basta *f* tack, tacking stitch
bastante *a* enough; (*varios*) quite a few, quite a lot of. ● *adv* rather, fairly; (*mucho tiempo*) long enough; (*suficiente*) enough; (*Mex*, *muy*) very
bastar *vi* be enough. **¡basta!** that's enough! **basta decir que** suffice it to say that. **basta y sobra** that's more than enough
bastardilla *f* italics. **poner en ~** italicize
bastardo *m* bastard; (*fig*, *vil*) mean, base
bastidor *m* frame; (*auto*) chassis. **~es** *mpl* (*en el teatro*) wings. **entre ~es** behind the scenes
bastión *f* (*incl fig*) bastion
basto *a* coarse. **~s** *mpl* (*naipes*) clubs
bast|ón *m* walking stick. **empuñar el ~ón** take command. **~onazo** *m* blow with a stick
basur|a *f* rubbish, garbage (*Amer*); (*en la calle*) litter. **~ero** *m* dustman (*Brit*), garbage collector (*Amer*); (*sitio*) rubbish dump; (*recipiente*) dustbin (*Brit*), garbage can (*Amer*). **cubo** *m* **de la ~a** dustbin (*Brit*), garbage can (*Amer*)
bata *f* dressing-gown; (*de médico etc*) white coat. **~ de cola** Flamenco dress
batall|a *f* battle. **~a campal** pitched battle. **~ador** *a* fighting. ● *m* fighter. **~ar** *vi* battle, fight. **~ón** *m* battalion. ● *a*. **cuestión** *f* **batallona** vexed question. **de ~a** everyday
batata *f* sweet potato
bate *m* bat. **~ador** *m* batter; (*cricket*) batsman
batería *f* battery; (*mus*) percussion. **~ de cocina** kitchen utensils, pots and pans
batido *a* beaten; ‹*nata*› whipped. ● *m* batter; (*bebida*) milk shake. **~ra** *f* beater. **~ra eléctrica** mixer
batín *m* dressing-gown
batir *vt* beat; (*martillar*) hammer; mint ‹*monedas*›; whip ‹*nata*›; (*derribar*) knock down. **~ el récord** break the record. **~ palmas** clap. **~se** *vpr* fight
batuta *f* baton. **llevar la ~** be in command, be the boss
baúl *m* trunk; (*LAm*, *auto*) boot (*Brit*), trunk (*Amer*)
bauti|smal *a* baptismal. **~smo** *m* baptism, christening. **~sta** *a* & *m* & *f* Baptist. **~zar** [10] *vt* baptize, christen
baya *f* berry
bayeta *f* (floor-)cloth
bayoneta *f* bayonet. **~zo** *m* (*golpe*) bayonet thrust; (*herida*) bayonet wound
baza *f* (*naipes*) trick; (*fig*) advantage. **meter ~** interfere
bazar *m* bazaar
bazofia *f* leftovers; (*basura*) rubbish
beat|itud *f* (*fig*) bliss. **~o** *a* blessed; (*de religiosidad afectada*) sanctimonious
bebé *m* baby
beb|edero *m* drinking trough; (*sitio*) watering place. **~edizo** *a*

drinkable. ● *m* potion; (*veneno*) poison. **~edor** *a* drinking. ● *m* heavy drinker. **~er** *vt/i* drink. **dar de ~er a uno** give s.o. a drink. **~ida** *f* drink. **~ido** *a* tipsy, drunk

beca *f* grant, scholarship. **~rio** *m* scholarship holder, scholar

becerro *m* calf

befa *f* jeer, taunt. **~r** *vt* scoff at. **~rse** *vpr*. **~rse de** scoff at. **hacer ~ de** scoff at

beige /beis, bes/ *a* & *m* beige

béisbol *m* baseball

beldad *f* beauty

belén *m* crib, nativity scene; (*barullo*) confusion

belga *a* & *m* & *f* Belgian

Bélgica *f* Belgium

bélico *a*, **belicoso** *a* warlike

beligerante *a* belligerent

bella|co *a* wicked. ● *m* rogue. **~quear** *vi* cheat. **~quería** *f* dirty trick

bell|eza *f* beauty. **~o** *a* beautiful. **~as artes** *fpl* fine arts

bellota *f* acorn

bemol *m* flat. **tener (muchos) ~es** be difficult

bencina *f* (*Arg*, *gasolina*) petrol (*Brit*), gasoline (*Amer*)

bend|ecir [46 *pero imperativo* **bendice**, *futuro*, *condicional y pp regulares*] *vt* bless. **~ición** *f* blessing. **~ito** *a* blessed, holy; (*que tiene suerte*) lucky; (*feliz*) happy

benefactor *m* benefactor. **~a** *f* benefactress

benefic|encia *f* (*organización pública*) charity. **~iar** *vt* benefit. **~iarse** *vpr* benefit. **~iario** *m* beneficiary; (*de un cheque etc*) payee. **~io** *m* benefit; (*ventaja*) advantage; (*ganancia*) profit, gain. **~ioso** *a* beneficial, advantageous

benéfico *a* beneficial; (*de beneficencia*) charitable

benemérito *a* worthy

beneplácito *m* approval

ben|evolencia *f* benevolence. **~évolo** *a* benevolent

bengala *f* flare. **luz** *f* **de B~** flare

benign|idad *f* kindness; (*falta de gravedad*) mildness. **~o** *a* kind; (*moderado*) gentle, mild; ‹*tumor*› benign

beodo *a* drunk

berberecho *m* cockle

berenjena *f* aubergine (*Brit*), eggplant. **~l** *m* (*fig*) mess

bermejo *a* red

berr|ear *vi* ‹*animales*› low, bellow; ‹*niño*› howl; (*cantar mal*) screech. **~ido** *m* bellow; (*de niño*) howl; (*de cantante*) screech

berrinche *m* temper; (*de un niño*) tantrum

berro *m* watercress

berza *f* cabbage

besamel(a) *f* white sauce

bes|ar *vt* kiss; (*rozar*) brush against. **~arse** *vpr* kiss (each other); (*tocarse*) touch each other. **~o** *m* kiss

bestia *f* beast; (*bruto*) brute; (*idiota*) idiot. **~ de carga** beast of burden. **~l** *a* bestial, animal; (*fig*, *fam*) terrific. **~lidad** *f* bestiality; (*acción brutal*) horrid thing

besugo *m* sea-bream. **ser un ~** be stupid

besuquear *vt* cover with kisses

betún *m* bitumen; (*para el calzado*) shoe polish

biberón *m* feeding-bottle

Biblia *f* Bible

bíblico *a* biblical

bibliografía *f* bibliography

biblioteca *f* library; (*librería*) bookcase. **~ de consulta** reference library. **~ de préstamo** lending library. **~rio** *m* librarian

bicarbonato *m* bicarbonate. **~ sódico** bicarbonate of soda

bici *f* (*fam*) bicycle, bike (*fam*). **~cleta** *f* bicycle. **ir en ~cleta** go by bicycle, cycle. **montar en ~cleta** ride a bicycle

bicolor *a* two-colour

bicultural *a* bicultural

bicho *m* (*animal*) small animal, creature; (*insecto*) insect. **~ raro** odd sort. **cualquier ~ viviente, todo ~ viviente** everyone

bidé *m*, **bidet** *m* bidet

bidón *m* drum, can

bien *adv* (**mejor**) well; (*muy*) very, quite; (*correctamente*) right; (*de buena gana*) willingly. ● *m* good; (*efectos*) property; (*provecho*) advantage, benefit. **¡~!** fine!, OK!, good! **~... (o) ~** either... or. **~ que** although. **¡está ~!** fine! alright! **más ~** rather. **¡muy ~!** good! **no ~** as soon as. **¡qué ~!** marvellous!, great! (*fam*). **si ~** although

bienal *a* biennial

bien: ~aventurado *a* fortunate. **~estar** *m* well-being. **~hablado** *a* well-spoken. **~hechor** *m* benefactor.

~hechora *f* benefactress. **~intencionado** *a* well-meaning
bienio *m* two years, two year-period
bien: ~quistar *vt* reconcile. **~quistarse** *vpr* become reconciled. **~quisto** *a* well-liked
bienvenid|a *f* welcome. **~o** *a* welcome. **¡~o!** welcome! **dar la ~a a uno** welcome s.o.
bife *m* (*Arg*), **biftek** *m* steak
bifurca|ción *f* fork, junction. **~rse** [7] *vpr* fork
b|igamia *f* bigamy. **~ígamo** *a* bigamous. ● *m & f* bigamist
bigot|e *m* moustache. **~udo** *a* with a big moustache
bikini *m* bikini; (*culin*) toasted cheese and ham sandwich
bilingüe *a* bilingual
billar *m* billiards
billete *m* ticket; (*de banco*) note (*Brit*), bill (*Amer*). **~ de banco** banknote. **~ de ida y vuelta** return ticket (*Brit*), round-trip ticket (*Amer*). **~ sencillo** single ticket (Brit), one-way ticket (*Amer*). **~ro** *m*, **~ra** *f* wallet, billfold (*Amer*)
billón *m* billion (*Brit*), trillion (*Amer*)
bimbalete *m* (*Mex*) swing
bi|mensual *a* fortnightly, twice-monthly. **~mestral** *a* two-monthly. **~motor** *a* twin-engined. ● *m* twin-engined plane
binocular *a* binocular. **~es** *mpl* binoculars
biodegradable *a* biodegradable
bi|ografía *f* biography. **~ográfico** *a* biographical. **~ógrafo** *m* biographer
bi|ología *f* biology. **~ológico** *a* biological. **~ólogo** *m* biologist
biombo *m* folding screen
biopsia *f* biopsy
bioquímic|a *f* biochemistry; (*persona*) biochemist. **~o** *m* biochemist
bípedo *m* biped
biplano *m* biplane
biquini *m* bikini
birlar *vt* (*fam*) steal, pinch (*fam*)
birlibirloque *m*. **por arte de ~** (as if) by magic
Birmania *f* Burma
birmano *a & m* Burmese
biromen *m* (*Arg*) ball-point pen
bis *m* encore. ● *adv* twice. **¡~!** encore! **vivo en el 3 ~** I live at 3A
bisabuel|a *f* great-grandmother. **~o** *m* great-grandfather. **~os** *mpl* great-grandparents
bisagra *f* hinge
bisar *vt* encore
bisbise|ar *vt* whisper. **~o** *m* whisper(ing)
bisemanal *a* twice-weekly
bisiesto *a* leap. **año** *m* **~** leap year
bisniet|a *f* great-granddaughter. **~o** *m* great-grandson. **~os** *mpl* great-grandchildren
bisonte *m* bison
bisté *m*, **bistec** *m* steak
bisturí *m* scalpel
bisutería *f* imitation jewellery, costume jewellery
bizco *a* cross-eyed. **quedarse ~** be dumbfounded
bizcocho *m* sponge (cake); (*Mex, galleta*) biscuit
bizquear *vi* squint
blanc|a *f* white woman; (*mus*) minim. **~o** *a* white; ‹*tez*› fair. ● *m* white; (*persona*) white man; (*intervalo*) interval; (*espacio*) blank; (*objetivo*) target. **~o de huevo** white of egg, egg-white. **dar en el ~o** hit the mark. **dejar en ~o** leave blank. **pasar la noche en ~o** have a sleepless night. **~o y negro** black and white. **~ura** *f* whiteness. **~uzco** *a* whitish
blandir [24] *vt* brandish
bland|o *a* soft; ‹*carácter*› weak; (*cobarde*) cowardly; ‹*palabras*› gentle, tender. **~ura** *f* softness. **~uzco** *a* softish
blanque|ar *vt* whiten; white-wash ‹*paredes*›; bleach ‹*tela*›. ● *vi* turn white; (*presentarse blanco*) look white. **~cino** *a* whitish. **~o** *m* whitening
blasfem|ador *a* blasphemous. ● *m* blasphemer. **~ar** *vi* blaspheme. **~ia** *f* blasphemy. **~o** *a* blasphemous. ● *m* blasphemer
blas|ón *m* coat of arms; (*fig*,) honour, glory. **~onar** *vt* emblazon. ● *vi* boast (**de** of, about)
bledo *m* nothing. **me importa un ~, no se me da un ~** I couldn't care less
blinda|je *m* armour. **~r** *vt* armour
bloc *m* (*pl* **blocs**) pad
bloque *m* block; (*pol*) bloc. **~ar** *vt* block; (*mil*) blockade; (*com*) freeze. **~o** *m* blockade; (*com*) freezing. **en ~** en bloc
blusa *f* blouse
boato *m* show, ostentation

bob|ada *f* silly thing. **~alicón** *a* stupid. **~ería** *f* silly thing. **decir ~adas** talk nonsense

bobina *f* bobbin, reel; (*foto*) spool; (*elec*) coil

bobo *a* silly, stupid. • *m* idiot, fool

boca *f* mouth; (*fig, entrada*) entrance; (*de cañón*) muzzle; (*agujero*) hole. **~ abajo** face down. **~ arriba** face up. **a ~ de jarro** point-blank. **con la ~ abierta** dumbfounded

bocacalle *f* junction. **la primera ~ a la derecha** the first turning on the right

bocad|illo *m* sandwich; (*comida ligera, fam*) snack. **~o** *m* mouthful; (*mordisco*) bite; (*de caballo*) bit

boca: ~jarro. a ~jarro point-blank. **~manga** *f* cuff

bocanada *f* puff; (*de vino etc*) mouthful

bocaza *f invar*, **bocazas** *f invar* big-mouth

boceto *m* outline, sketch

bocina *f* horn. **~zo** *m* toot, blast. **tocar la ~** sound one's horn

bock *m* beer mug

bocha *f* bowl. **~s** *fpl* bowls

bochinche *m* uproar

bochorno *m* sultry weather; (*fig, vergüenza*) embarrassment. **~so** *a* oppressive; (*fig*) embarrassing. **¡qué ~!** how embarrassing!

boda *f* marriage; (*ceremonia*) wedding

bodeg|a *f* cellar; (*de vino*) wine cellar; (*almacén*) warehouse; (*de un barco*) hold. **~ón** *m* cheap restaurant; (*pintura*) still life

bodoque *m* pellet; (*tonto, fam*) thickhead

bofes *mpl* lights. **echar los ~** slog away

bofet|ada *f* slap; (*fig*) blow. **dar una ~ada a uno** slap s.o. in the face. **darse de ~adas** clash. **~ón** *m* punch

boga *m & f* rower; (*hombre*) oarsman; (*mujer*) oarswoman; (*moda*) fashion. **estar en ~** be in fashion, be in vogue. **~da** *f* stroke (of the oar). **~dor** rower, oarsman. **~r** [12] *vt* row. **~vante** *m* (*crustáceo*) lobster

Bogotá *f* Bogotá

bogotano *a* from Bogotá. • *m* native of Bogotá

bohemio *a & m* Bohemian

bohío *m* (*LAm*) hut

boicot *m* (*pl* **boicots**) boycott. **~ear** *vt* boycott. **~eo** *m* boycott. **hacer el ~** boycott

boina *f* beret

boîte /bwat/ *m* night-club

bola *f* ball; (*canica*) marble; (*naipes*) slam; (*betún*) shoe polish; (*mentira*) fib; (*Mex, reunión desordenada*) rowdy party. **~ del mundo** (*fam*) globe. **contar ~s** tell fibs. **dejar que ruede la ~** let things take their course. **meter ~s** tell fibs

bolas *fpl* (*LAm*) bolas

boleada *f* (*Mex*) polishing of shoes

boleadoras (*LAm*) *fpl* bolas

bolera *f* bowling alley

bolero *m* (*baile, chaquetilla*) bolero; (*fig, mentiroso, fam*) liar; (*Mex, limpiabotas*) bootblack

boletín *m* bulletin; (*publicación periódica*) journal; (*escolar*) report. **~ de noticias** news bulletin. **~ de precios** price list. **~ informativo** news bulletin. **~ meteorológico** weather forecast

boleto *m* (*esp LAm*) ticket

boli *m* (*fam*) Biro (P), ball-point pen

boliche *m* (*juego*) bowls; (*bolera*) bowling alley

bolígrafo *m* Biro (P), ball-point pen

bolillo *m* bobbin; (*Mex, panecillo*) (bread) roll

bolívar *m* (*unidad monetaria venezolana*) bolívar

Bolivia *f* Bolivia

boliviano *a* Bolivian. • *m* Bolivian; (*unidad monetaria de Bolivia*) boliviano

bolo *m* skittle

bolsa *f* bag; (*monedero*) purse; (*LAm, bolsillo*) pocket; (*com*) stock exchange; (*cavidad*) cavity. **~ de agua caliente** hot-water bottle

bolsillo *m* pocket; (*monedero*) purse. **de ~** pocket

bolsista *m & f* stockbroker

bolso *m* (*de mujer*) handbag

boll|ería *f* baker's shop. **~ero** *m* baker. **~o** *m* roll; (*con azúcar*) bun; (*abolladura*) dent; (*chichón*) lump; (*fig, jaleo, fam*) fuss

bomba *f* bomb; (*máquina*) pump; (*noticia*) bombshell. **~ de aceite** (*auto*) oil pump. **~ de agua** (*auto*) water pump. **~ de incendios** fire-engine. **pasarlo ~** have a marvellous time

bombach|as *fpl* (*LAm*) knickers, pants. **~o** *m* (*esp Mex*) baggy trousers, baggy pants (*Amer*)

bombarde|ar *vt* bombard; (*mil*) bomb. **~o** *m* bombardment; (*mil*) bombing. **~ro** *m* (*avión*) bomber
bombazo *m* explosion
bombear *vt* pump; (*mil*) bomb
bombero *m* fireman. **cuerpo** *m* **de ~s** fire brigade (*Brit*), fire department (*Amer*)
bombilla *f* (light) bulb; (*LAm, para maté*) pipe for drinking maté; (*Mex, cucharón*) ladle
bombín *m* pump; (*sombrero, fam*) bowler (hat) (*Brit*), derby (*Amer*)
bombo *m* (*tambor*) bass drum. **a ~ y platillos** with a lot of fuss
bomb|ón *m* chocolate. **ser un ~ón** be a peach. **~ona** *f* container. **~onera** *f* chocolate box
bonachón *a* easygoing; (*bueno*) good-natured
bonaerense *a* from Buenos Aires. • *m* native of Buenos Aires
bonanza *f* (*naut*) fair weather; (*prosperidad*) prosperity. **ir en ~** (*naut*) have fair weather; (*fig*) go well
bondad *f* goodness; (*amabilidad*) kindness. **tenga la ~ de** would you be kind enough to. **~osamente** *adv* kindly. **~oso** *a* kind
bongo *m* (*LAm*) canoe
boniato *m* sweet potato
bonito *a* nice; (*mono*) pretty. **¡muy ~!**, **¡qué ~!** that's nice!, very nice!. • *m* bonito
bono *m* voucher; (*título*) bond. **~ del Tesoro** government bond
boñiga *f* dung
boqueada *f* gasp. **dar las ~s** be dying
boquerón *m* anchovy
boquete *m* hole; (*brecha*) breach
boquiabierto *a* open-mouthed; (*fig*) amazed, dumbfounded. **quedarse ~** be amazed
boquilla *f* mouthpiece; (*para cigarillos*) cigarette-holder; (*filtro de cigarillo*) tip
borboll|ar *vi* bubble. **~ón** *m* bubble. **hablar a ~ones** gabble. **salir a ~ones** gush out
borbot|ar *vt* bubble. **~ón** *m* bubble. **hablar a ~ones** gabble. **salir a ~ones** gush out
bordado *a* embroidered. • *m* embroidery. **quedar ~, salir ~** come out very well
bordante *m* (*Mex*) lodger
bordar *vt* embroider; (*fig, fam*) do very well
bord|e *m* edge; (*de carretera*) side; (*de plato etc*) rim; (*de un vestido*) hem. **~ear** *vt* go round the edge of; (*fig*) border on. **~illo** *m* kerb. **al ~e de** on the edge of; (*fig*) on the brink of
bordo *m* board. **a ~** on board
borinqueño *a & m* Puerto Rican
borla *f* tassel
borra *f* flock; (*pelusa*) fluff; (*sedimento*) sediment
borrach|era *f* drunkenness. **~ín** *m* drunkard. **~o** *a* drunk. • *m* drunkard; (*temporalmente*) drunk. **estar ~o** be drunk. **ni ~o** never in a million years. **ser ~o** be a drunkard
borrador *m* rough copy; (*libro*) rough notebook
borradura *f* crossing-out
borrajear *vt/i* scribble
borrar *vt* rub out; (*tachar*) cross out
borrasc|a *f* storm. **~oso** *a* stormy
borreg|o *m* year-old lamb; (*fig*) simpleton; (*Mex, noticia falsa*) hoax. **~uil** *a* meek
borric|ada *f* silly thing. **~o** *m* donkey; (*fig, fam*) ass
borrón *m* smudge; (*fig, imperfección*) blemish; (*de una pintura*) sketch. **~ y cuenta nueva** let's forget about it!
borroso *a* blurred; (*fig*) vague
bos|caje *m* thicket. **~coso** *a* wooded. **~que** *m* wood, forest. **~quecillo** *m* copse
bosquej|ar *vt* sketch. **~o** *m* sketch
bosta *f* dung
bostez|ar [10] *vi* yawn. **~o** *m* yawn
bota *f* boot; (*recipiente*) leather wine bottle
botadero *m* (*Mex*) ford
botánic|a *f* botany. **~o** *a* botanical. • *m* botanist
botar *vt* launch. • *vi* bounce. **estar que bota** be hopping mad
botarat|ada *f* silly thing. **~e** *m* idiot
bote *m* bounce; (*golpe*) blow; (*salto*) jump; (*sacudida*) jolt; (*lata*) tin, can; (*vasija*) jar; (*en un bar*) jar for tips; (*barca*) boat. **~ salvavidas** lifeboat. **de ~ en ~** packed
botell|a *f* bottle. **~ita** *f* small bottle
botica *f* chemist's (shop) (*Brit*), drugstore (*Amer*). **~rio** *m* chemist (*Brit*), druggist (*Amer*)
botija *f*, **botijo** *m* earthenware jug
botín *m* half boot; (*despojos*) booty; (*LAm, calcetín*) sock

botiquín *m* medicine chest; (*de primeros auxilios*) first aid kit

bot|ón *m* button; (*yema*) bud. **~onadura** *f* buttons. **~ón de oro** buttercup. **~ones** *m invar* bellboy (*Brit*), bellhop (*Amer*)

botulismo *m* botulism

boutique /bu'tik/ *m* boutique

bóveda *f* vault

boxe|ador *m* boxer. **~ar** *vi* box. **~o** *m* boxing

boya *f* buoy; (*corcho*) float. **~nte** *a* buoyant

bozal *m* (*de perro etc*) muzzle; (*de caballo*) halter

bracear *vi* wave one's arms; (*nadar*) swim, crawl

bracero *m* labourer. **de ~** (*fam*) arm in arm

braga *f* underpants, knickers; (*cuerda*) rope. **~dura** *f* crotch. **~s** *fpl* knickers, pants. **~zas** *m invar* (*fam*) henpecked man

bragueta *f* flies

braille /breil/ *m* Braille

bram|ar *vi* roar; ‹*vaca*› moo; ‹*viento*› howl. **~ido** *m* roar

branquia *f* gill

bras|a *f* hot coal. **a la ~a** grilled. **~ero** *m* brazier; (*LAm, hogar*) hearth

Brasil *m*. **el ~** Brazil

brasile|ño *a & m* Brazilian. **~ro** *a & m* (*LAm*) Brazilian

bravata *f* boast

bravío *a* wild; ‹*persona*› coarse, uncouth

brav|o *a* brave; ‹*animales*› wild; ‹*mar*› rough. **¡~!** *int* well done! bravo! **~ura** *f* ferocity; (*valor*) courage

braz|a *f* fathom. **nadar a ~a** do the breast-stroke. **~ada** *f* waving of the arms; (*en natación*) stroke; (*cantidad*) armful. **~ado** *m* armful. **~al** *m* arm-band. **~alete** *m* bracelet; (*brazal*) arm-band. **~o** *m* arm; (*de animales*) foreleg; (*rama*) branch. **~o derecho** right-hand man. **a ~o** by hand. **del ~o** arm in arm

brea *f* tar, pitch

brear *vt* ill-treat

brécol *m* broccoli

brecha *f* gap; (*mil*) breach; (*med*) gash. **estar en la ~** be in the thick of it

brega *f* struggle. **~r** [12] *vi* struggle; (*trabajar mucho*) work hard, slog away. **andar a la ~** work hard

breña *f*, **breñal** *m* scrub

Bretaña *f* Brittany. **Gran ~** Great Britain

breve *a* short. **~dad** *f* shortness. **en ~** soon, shortly. **en ~s momentos** soon

brez|al *m* moor. **~o** *m* heather

brib|ón *m* rogue, rascal. **~onada** *f*, **~onería** *f* dirty trick

brida *f* bridle. **a toda ~** at full speed

bridge /britʃ/ *m* bridge

brigada *f* squad; (*mil*) brigade. **general de ~** brigadier (*Brit*), brigadier-general (*Amer*)

brill|ante *a* brilliant. • *m* diamond. **~antez** *f* brilliance. **~ar** *vi* shine; (*centellear*) sparkle. **~o** *m* shine; (*brillantez*) brilliance; (*centelleo*) sparkle. **dar ~o, sacar ~o** polish

brinc|ar [7] *vi* jump up and down. **~o** *m* jump. **dar un ~o** jump. **estar que brinca** be hopping mad. **pegar un ~o** jump

brind|ar *vt* offer. • *vi*. **~ar por** toast, drink a toast to. **~is** *m* toast

br|ío *m* energy; (*decisión*) determination. **~ioso** *a* spirited; (*garboso*) elegant

brisa *f* breeze

británico *a* British. • *m* Briton, British person

brocado *m* brocade

bróculi *m* broccoli

brocha *f* paintbrush; (*para afeitarse*) shaving-brush

broche *m* clasp, fastener; (*joya*) brooch; (*Arg, sujetapapeles*) paper-clip

brocheta *f* skewer

brom|a *f* joke. **~a pesada** practical joke. **~ear** *vi* joke. **~ista** *a* fun-loving. • *m & f* joker. **de ~a, en ~a** in fun. **ni de ~a** never in a million years

bronca *f* row; (*reprensión*) telling-off

bronce *m* bronze. **~ado** *a* bronze; (*por el sol*) tanned, sunburnt. **~ar** *vt* tan ‹*piel*›. **~arse** *vpr* get a suntan

bronco *a* rough

bronquitis *f* bronchitis

broqueta *f* skewer

brot|ar *vi* ‹*plantas*› bud, sprout; (*med*) break out; ‹*líquido*› gush forth; ‹*lágrimas*› well up. **~e** *m* bud, shoot; (*med*) outbreak; (*de líquido*) gushing; (*de lágrimas*) welling-up

bruces *mpl*. **de ~** face down(wards). **caer de ~** fall flat on one's face

bruj|a *f* witch. • *a* (*Mex*) penniless. **~ear** *vi* practise witchcraft. **~ería** *f* witchcraft. **~o** *m* wizard, magician; (*LAm*) medicine man
brújula *f* compass
brum|a *f* mist; (*fig*) confusion. **~oso** *a* misty, foggy
bruñi|do *m* polish. **~r** [22] *vt* polish
brusco *a* (*repentino*) sudden; ‹*persona*› brusque
Bruselas *fpl* Brussels
brusquedad *f* abruptness
brut|al *a* brutal. **~alidad** *f* brutality; (*estupidez*) stupidity. **~o** *a* (*estúpido*) stupid; (*tosco*) rough, uncouth; ‹*peso, sueldo*› gross
bucal *a* oral
buce|ar *vi* dive; (*fig*) explore. **~o** *m* diving
bucle *m* curl
budín *m* pudding
budis|mo *m* Buddhism. **~ta** *m & f* Buddhist
buen *véase* **bueno**
buenamente *adv* easily; (*voluntariamente*) willingly
buenaventura *f* good luck; (*adivinación*) fortune. **decir la ~ a uno, echar la ~ a uno** tell s.o.'s fortune
bueno *a* (*delante de nombre masculino en singular* **buen**) good; (*apropiado*) fit; (*amable*) kind; ‹*tiempo*› fine. • *int* well!; (*de acuerdo*) OK!, very well! **¡buena la has hecho!** you've gone and done it now! **¡buenas noches!** good night! **¡buenas tardes!** (*antes del atardecer*) good afternoon!; (*después del atardecer*) good evening! **¡~s días!** good morning! **estar de buenas** be in a good mood. **por las buenas** willingly
Buenos Aires *m* Buenos Aires
buey *m* ox
búfalo *m* buffalo
bufanda *f* scarf
bufar *vi* snort. **estar que bufa** be hopping mad
bufete *m* (*mesa*) writing-desk; (*despacho*) lawyer's office
bufido *m* snort; (*de ira*) outburst
buf|o *a* comic. **~ón** *a* comical. • *m* buffoon. **~onada** *f* joke
bugle *m* bugle
buharda *f*, **buhardilla** *f* attic; (*ventana*) dormer window
búho *m* owl
buhoner|ía *f* pedlar's wares. **~o** *m* pedlar
buitre *m* vulture
bujía *f* candle; (*auto*) spark(ing)-plug
bula *f* bull
bulbo *m* bulb
bulevar *m* avenue, boulevard
Bulgaria *f* Bulgaria
búlgaro *a & m* Bulgarian
bulo *m* hoax
bulto *m* (*volumen*) volume; (*tamaño*) size; (*forma*) shape; (*paquete*) package; (*protuberancia*) lump. **a ~** roughly
bulla *f* uproar; (*muchedumbre*) crowd
bullicio *m* hubbub; (*movimiento*) bustle. **~so** *a* bustling; (*ruidoso*) noisy
bullir [22] *vt* stir, move. • *vi* boil; (*burbujear*) bubble; (*fig*) bustle
buñuelo *m* doughnut; (*fig*) mess
BUP *abrev* (*Bachillerato Unificado Polivalente*) secondary school education
buque *m* ship, boat
burbuj|a *f* bubble. **~ear** *vi* bubble; ‹*vino*› sparkle. **~eo** *m* bubbling
burdel *m* brothel
burdo *a* rough, coarse; ‹*excusa*› clumsy
burgu|és *a* middle-class, bourgeois. • *m* middle-class person. **~esía** *f* middle class, bourgeoisie
burla *f* taunt; (*broma*) joke; (*engaño*) trick. **~dor** *a* mocking. • *m* seducer. **~r** *vt* trick, deceive; (*seducir*) seduce. **~rse** *vpr*. **~rse de** mock, make fun of
burlesco *a* funny
burlón *a* mocking
bur|ocracia *f* civil service. **~ócrata** *m & f* civil servant. **~ocrático** *a* bureaucratic
burro *m* donkey; (*fig*) ass
bursátil *a* stock-exchange
bus *m* (*fam*) bus
busca *f* search. **a la ~ de** in search of. **en ~ de** in search of
busca: ~pié *m* feeler. **~pleitos** *m invar* (*LAm*) trouble-maker
buscar [7] *vt* look for. • *vi* look. **buscársela** ask for it. **ir a ~ a uno** fetch s.o.
buscarruidos *m invar* trouble-maker
buscona *f* prostitute
busilis *m* snag
búsqueda *f* search
busto *m* bust

butaca *f* armchair; (*en el teatro etc*) seat
butano *m* butane
buzo *m* diver
buzón *m* postbox (*Brit*), mailbox (*Amer*)

C

C/ *abrev* (*Calle*) St, Street, Rd, Road
cabal *a* exact; (*completo*) complete. **no estar en sus ~es** not be in one's right mind
cabalga|dura *f* mount, horse. **~r** [12] *vt* ride. ● *vi* ride, go riding. **~ta** *f* ride; (*desfile*) procession
cabalmente *adv* completely; (*exactamente*) exactly
caballa *f* mackerel
caballada *f* (*LAm*) stupid thing
caballeresco *a* gentlemanly. **literatura** *f* **caballeresca** books of chivalry
caballer|ía *f* mount, horse. **~iza** *f* stable. **~izo** *m* groom
caballero *m* gentleman; (*de orden de caballería*) knight; (*tratamiento*) sir. **~samente** *adv* like a gentleman. **~so** *a* gentlemanly
caballete *m* (*del tejado*) ridge; (*de la nariz*) bridge; (*de pintor*) easel
caballito *m* pony. **~ del diablo** dragonfly. **~ de mar** sea-horse. **los ~s** (*tiovivo*) merry-go-round
caballo *m* horse; (*del ajedrez*) knight; (*de la baraja española*) queen. **~ de vapor** horsepower. **a ~** on horseback
cabaña *f* hut
cabaret /kaba're/ *m* (*pl* **cabarets** /kaba're/) night-club
cabece|ar *vi* nod; (*para negar*) shake one's head. **~o** *m* nodding, nod; (*acción de negar*) shake of the head
cabecera *f* (*de la cama, de la mesa*) head; (*en un impreso*) heading
cabecilla *m* leader
cabell|o *m* hair. **~os** *mpl* hair. **~udo** *a* hairy
caber [28] *vi* fit (**en** into). **los libros no caben en la caja** the books won't fit into the box. **no cabe duda** there's no doubt
cabestr|illo *m* sling. **~o** *m* halter
cabeza *f* head; (*fig, inteligencia*) intelligence. **~da** *f* butt; (*golpe recibido*) blow; (*saludo, al dormirse*) nod. **~zo** *m* butt; (*en fútbol*) header. **andar de ~** have a lot to do. **dar una ~da** nod off
cabida *f* capacity; (*extensión*) area. **dar ~ a** leave room for, leave space for
cabina *f* (*de avión*) cabin, cockpit; (*electoral*) booth; (*de camión*) cab. **~ telefónica** telephone box (*Brit*), telephone booth (*Amer*)
cabizbajo *a* crestfallen
cable *m* cable
cabo *m* end; (*trozo*) bit; (*mil*) corporal; (*mango*) handle; (*geog*) cape; (*naut*) rope. **al ~** eventually. **al ~ de una hora** after an hour. **de ~ a rabo** from beginning to end. **llevar(se) a ~** carry out
cabr|a *f* goat. **~a montesa** *f* mountain goat. **~iola** *f* jump, skip. **~itilla** *f* kid. **~ito** *m* kid
cabrón *m* cuckold
cabuya *f* (*LAm*) pita, agave
cacahuate *m* (*Mex*), **cacahuete** *m* peanut
cacao *m* (*planta y semillas*) cacao; (*polvo*) cocoa; (*fig*) confusion
cacare|ar *vt* boast about. ● *vi* ‹*gallo*› crow; ‹*gallina*› cluck. **~o** *m* (*incl fig*) crowing; (*de gallina*) clucking
cacería *f* hunt
cacerola *f* casserole, saucepan
caciqu|e *m* cacique, Indian chief; (*pol*) cacique, local political boss. **~il** *a* despotic. **~ismo** *m* caciquism, despotism
caco *m* pickpocket, thief
cacof|onía *f* cacophony. **~ónico** *a* cacophonous
cacto *m* cactus
cacumen *m* acumen
cacharro *m* earthenware pot; (*para flores*) vase; (*coche estropeado*) wreck; (*cosa inútil*) piece of junk; (*chisme*) thing. **~s** *mpl* pots and pans
cachear *vt* frisk
cachemir *m*, **cachemira** *f* cashmere
cacheo *m* frisking
cachetada *f* (*LAm*), **cachete** *m* slap
cachimba *f* pipe
cachiporra *f* club, truncheon. **~zo** *m* blow with a club
cachivache *m* thing, piece of junk
cacho *m* bit, piece; (*LAm, cuerno*) horn; (*miga*) crumb
cachondeo *m* (*fam*) joking, joke
cachorro *m* (*perrito*) puppy; (*de otros animales*) young

cada *a invar* each, every. **~ uno** each one, everyone. **uno de ~ cinco** one in five

cadalso *m* scaffold

cadáver *m* corpse. **ingresar ~** be dead on arrival

cadena *f* chain; (*TV*) channel. **~ de fabricación** production line. **~ de montañas** mountain range. **~ perpetua** life imprisonment

cadencia *f* cadence, rhythm

cadera *f* hip

cadete *m* cadet

caduc|ar [7] *vi* expire. **~idad** *f*. **fecha** *f* **de ~idad** sell-by date. **~o** *a* decrepit

cae|dizo *a* unsteady. **~r** [29] *vi* fall. **~rse** *vpr* fall (over). **dejar ~r** drop. **estar al ~r** be about to happen. **este vestido no me ~ bien** this dress doesn't suit me. **hacer ~r** knock over. **Juan me ~ bien** I get on well with Juan. **su cumpleaños cayó en Martes** his birthday fell on a Tuesday

café *m* coffee; (*cafetería*) café. ● *a*. **color ~** coffee-coloured. **~ con leche** white coffee. **~ cortado** coffee with a little milk. **~ (solo)** black coffee

cafe|ína *f* caffeine. **~tal** *m* coffee plantation. **~tera** *f* coffee-pot. **~tería** *f* café. **~tero** *a* coffee

caíd|a *f* fall; (*disminución*) drop; (*pendiente*) slope. **~o** *a* fallen; (*abatido*) dejected. ● *m* fallen

caigo *vb véase* **caer**

caimán *m* cayman, alligator

caj|a *f* box; (*grande*) case; (*de caudales*) safe; (*donde se efectúan los pagos*) cash desk; (*en supermercado*) check-out. **~a de ahorros** savings bank. **~a de caudales**, **~a fuerte** safe. **~a postal de ahorros** post office savings bank. **~a registradora** till. **~ero** *m* cashier. **~etilla** *f* packet. **~ita** *f* small box. **~ón** *m* large box; (*de mueble*) drawer; (*puesto de mercado*) stall. **ser de ~ón** be a matter of course

cal *m* lime

cala *f* cove

calaba|cín *m* marrow; (*fig, idiota, fam*) idiot. **~za** *f* pumpkin; (*fig, idiota, fam*) idiot

calabozo *m* prison; (*celda*) cell

calado *a* soaked. ● *m* (*naut*) draught. **estar ~ hasta los huesos** be soaked to the skin

calamar *m* squid

calambre *m* cramp

calami|dad *f* calamity, disaster. **~toso** *a* calamitous, disastrous

calar *vt* soak; (*penetrar*) pierce; (*fig, penetrar*) see through; sample ‹*fruta*›. **~se** *vpr* get soaked; ‹*zapatos*› leak; (*auto*) stall

calavera *f* skull

calcar [7] *vt* trace; (*fig*) copy

calceta *f*. **hacer ~** knit

calcetín *m* sock

calcinar *vt* burn

calcio *m* calcium

calco *m* tracing. **~manía** *f* transfer. **papel** *m* **de ~** tracing-paper

calcula|dor *a* calculating. **~dora** *f* calculator. **~dora de bolsillo** pocket calculator. **~r** *vt* calculate; (*suponer*) reckon, think

cálculo *m* calculation; (*fig*) reckoning

caldea|miento *m* heating. **~r** *vt* heat, warm. **~rse** *vpr* get hot

calder|a *f* boiler; (*Arg, para café*) coffee-pot; (*Arg, para té*) teapot. **~eta** *f* small boiler

calderilla *f* small change, coppers

calder|o *m* small boiler. **~ón** *m* large boiler

caldo *m* stock; (*sopa*) soup, broth. **poner a ~ a uno** give s.o. a dressing-down

calefacción *f* heating. **~ central** central heating

caleidoscopio *m* kaleidoscope

calendario *m* calendar

caléndula *f* marigold

calenta|dor *m* heater. **~miento** *m* heating; (*en deportes*) warm-up. **~r** [1] *vt* heat, warm. **~rse** *vpr* get hot, warm up

calentur|a *f* fever, (high) temperature. **~iento** *a* feverish

calibr|ar *vt* calibrate; (*fig*) measure. **~e** *m* calibre; (*diámetro*) diameter; (*fig*) importance

calidad *f* quality; (*función*) capacity. **en ~ de** as

cálido *a* warm

calidoscopio *m* kaleidoscope

caliente *a* hot, warm; (*fig, enfadado*) angry

califica|ción *f* qualification; (*evaluación*) assessment; (*nota*) mark. **~r** [7] *vt* qualify; (*evaluar*) assess; mark ‹*examen etc*›. **~r de** describe as, label. **~tivo** *a* qualifying. ● *m* epithet

caliz|a *f* limestone. **~o** *a* lime

calm|a *f* calm. **¡~a!** calm down! **~ante** *a & m* sedative. **~ar** *vt* calm, soothe. ● *vi* ‹*viento*› abate. **~arse** *vpr* calm down; ‹*viento*› abate. **~oso** *a* calm; (*flemático, fam*) phlegmatic. **en ~a** calm. **perder la ~a** lose one's composure

calor *m* heat, warmth. **hace ~** it's hot. **tener ~** be hot

caloría *f* calorie

calorífero *m* heater

calumni|a *f* calumny; (*oral*) slander; (*escrita*) libel. **~ar** *vt* slander; (*por escrito*) libel. **~oso** *a* slanderous; ‹*cosa escrita*› libellous

caluros|amente *adv* warmly. **~o** *a* warm

calv|a *f* bald patch. **~ero** *m* clearing. **~icie** *f* baldness. **~o** *a* bald; ‹*terreno*› barren

calza *f* (*fam*) stocking; (*cuña*) wedge

calzada *f* road

calza|do *a* wearing shoes. ● *m* footwear, shoe. **~dor** *m* shoehorn. **~r** [10] *vt* put shoes on; (*llevar*) wear. ● *vi* wear shoes. ● *vpr* put on. **¿qué número calza Vd?** what size shoe do you take?

calz|ón *m* shorts; (*ropa interior*) knickers, pants. **~ones** *mpl* shorts. **~oncillos** *mpl* underpants

calla|do *a* quiet. **~r** *vt* silence; keep ‹*secreto*›; hush up ‹*asunto*›. ● *vi* be quiet, keep quiet, shut up (*fam*). **~rse** *vpr* be quiet, keep quiet, shut up (*fam*). **¡cállate!** be quiet! shut up! (*fam*)

calle *f* street, road; (*en deportes, en autopista*) lane. **~ de dirección única** one-way street. **~ mayor** high street, main street. **abrir ~** make way

callej|a *f* narrow street. **~ear** *vi* wander about the streets. **~ero** *a* street. ● *m* street plan. **~ón** *m* alley. **~uela** *f* back street, side street. **~ón sin salida** cul-de-sac

call|ista *m & f* chiropodist. **~o** *m* corn, callus. **~os** *mpl* tripe. **~oso** *a* hard, rough

cama *f* bed. **~ de matrimonio** double bed. **~ individual** single bed. **caer en la ~** fall ill. **guardar ~** be confined to bed

camada *f* litter; (*fig, de ladrones*) gang

camafeo *m* cameo

camaleón *m* chameleon

cámara *f* room; (*de reyes*) royal chamber; (*fotográfica*) camera; (*de armas, pol*) chamber. **~ fotográfica** camera. **a ~ lenta** in slow motion

camarada *f* colleague; (*amigo*) companion

camarer|a *f* chambermaid; (*de restaurante etc*) waitress; (*en casa*) maid. **~o** *m* waiter

camarín *m* dressing-room; (*naut*) cabin

camarón *m* shrimp

camarote *m* cabin

cambi|able *a* changeable; (*com etc*) exchangeable. **~ante** *a* variable. **~ar** *vt* change; (*trocar*) exchange. ● *vi* change. **~ar de idea** change one's mind. **~arse** *vpr* change. **~o** *m* change; (*com*) exchange rate; (*moneda menuda*) (small) change. **~sta** *m & f* money-changer. **en ~o** on the other hand

camelia *f* camellia

camello *m* camel

camilla *f* stretcher; (*sofá*) couch

camina|nte *m* traveller. **~r** *vt* cover. ● *vi* travel; (*andar*) walk; ‹*río, astros etc*› move. **~ta** *f* long walk

camino *m* road; (*sendero*) path, track; (*dirección, medio*) way. **~ de** towards, on the way to. **abrir ~** make way. **a medio ~, a la mitad del ~** half-way. **de ~** on the way. **ponerse en ~** set out

cami|ón *m* lorry; (*Mex, autobús*) bus. **~onero** *m* lorry-driver. **~oneta** *f* van

camis|a *f* shirt; (*de un fruto*) skin. **~a de dormir** nightdress. **~a de fuerza** strait-jacket. **~ería** *f* shirt shop. **~eta** *f* T-shirt; (*ropa interior*) vest. **~ón** *m* nightdress

camorra *f* (*fam*) row. **buscar ~** look for trouble, pick a quarrel

camote *m* (*LAm*) sweet potato

campamento *m* camp

campan|a *f* bell. **~ada** *f* stroke of a bell; (*de reloj*) striking. **~ario** *m* bell tower, belfry. **~eo** *m* peal of bells. **~illa** *f* bell. **~udo** *a* bell-shaped; ‹*estilo*› bombastic

campaña *f* countryside; (*mil, pol*) campaign. **de ~** (*mil*) field

campe|ón *a & m* champion. **~onato** *m* championship

campes|ino *a* country. ● *m* peasant. **~tre** *a* country

camping /'kampin/ *m* (*pl* **campings** /'kampin/) camping; (*lugar*) campsite. **hacer ~** go camping

campiña *f* countryside
campo *m* country; (*agricultura, fig*) field; (*de tenis*) court; (*de fútbol*) pitch; (*de golf*) course. **~santo** *m* cemetery
camufla|do *a* camouflaged. **~je** *m* camouflage. **~r** *vt* camouflage
cana *f* grey hair, white hair. **echar una ~ al aire** have a fling. **peinar ~s** be getting old
Canadá *m*. **el ~** Canada
canadiense *a & m* Canadian
canal *m* (*incl TV*) channel; (*artificial*) canal; (*del tejado*) gutter. **~ de la Mancha** English Channel. **~ de Panamá** Panama Canal. **~ón** *m* (*horizontal*) gutter; (*vertical*) drain-pipe
canalla *f* rabble. ● *m* (*fig, fam*) swine. **~da** *f* dirty trick
canapé *m* sofa, couch; (*culin*) canapé
Canarias *fpl*. **(las islas) ~** the Canary Islands, the Canaries
canario *a* of the Canary Islands. ● *m* native of the Canary Islands; (*pájaro*) canary
canast|a *f* (large) basket. **~illa** *f* small basket; (*para un bebé*) layette. **~illo** *m* small basket. **~o** *m* (large) basket
cancela *f* gate
cancela|ción *f* cancellation . **~r** *vt* cancel; write off ‹*deuda*›; (*fig*) forget
cáncer *m* cancer. **C~** Cancer
canciller *m* chancellor; (*LAm, ministro de asuntos exteriores*) Minister of Foreign Affairs
canci|ón *f* song. **~ón de cuna** lullaby. **~onero** *m* song-book. **¡siempre la misma ~ón!** always the same old story!
cancha *f* (*de fútbol*) pitch, ground; (*de tenis*) court
candado *m* padlock
candel|a *f* candle. **~ero** *m* candlestick. **~illa** *f* candle
candente *a* (*rojo*) red-hot; (*blanco*) white-hot; (*fig*) burning
candidato *m* candidate
candidez *f* innocence; (*ingenuidad*) naïvety
cándido *a* naïve
candil *m* oil-lamp; (*Mex, araña*) chandelier. **~ejas** *fpl* footlights
candinga *m* (*Mex*) devil
candor *m* innocence; (*ingenuidad*) naïvety. **~oso** *a* innocent; (*ingenuo*) naïve
canela *f* cinnamon. **ser ~** be beautiful
cangrejo *m* crab. **~ de río** crayfish
canguro *m* kangaroo; (*persona*) baby-sitter
can|íbal *a & m* cannibal. **~ibalismo** *m* cannibalism
canica *f* marble
canijo *m* weak
canino *a* canine. ● *m* canine (tooth)
canje *m* exchange. **~ar** *vt* exchange
cano *a* grey-haired
canoa *f* canoe; (*con motor*) motor boat
canon *m* canon
can|ónigo *m* canon. **~onizar** [10] *vt* canonize
canoso *a* grey-haired
cansa|do *a* tired. **~ncio** *m* tiredness. **~r** *vt* tire; (*aburrir*) bore. ● *vi* be tiring; (*aburrir*) get boring. **~rse** *vpr* get tired
cantábrico *a* Cantabrian. **el mar ~** the Bay of Biscay
canta|nte *a* singing. ● *m* singer; (*en óperas*) opera singer. **~or** *m* Flamenco singer. **~r** *vt/i* sing. ● *m* singing; (*canción*) song; (*poema*) poem. **~rlas claras** speak frankly
cántar|a *f* pitcher. **~o** *m* pitcher. **llover a ~os** pour down
cante *m* folk song. **~ flamenco**, **~ jondo** Flamenco singing
cantera *f* quarry
cantidad *f* quantity; (*número*) number; (*de dinero*) sum. **una ~ de** lots of
cantilena *f*, **cantinela** *f* song
cantimplora *f* water-bottle
cantina *f* canteen; (*rail*) buffet
canto *m* singing; (*canción*) song; (*borde*) edge; (*de un cuchillo*) blunt edge; (*esquina*) corner; (*piedra*) pebble. **~ rodado** boulder. **de ~** on edge
cantonés *a* Cantonese
cantor *a* singing. ● *m* singer
canturre|ar *vt/i* hum. **~o** *m* humming
canuto *m* tube
caña *f* stalk, stem; (*planta*) reed; (*vaso*) glass; (*de la pierna*) shin. **~ de azúcar** sugar-cane. **~ de pescar** fishing-rod
cañada *f* ravine; (*camino*) track
cáñamo *m* hemp. **~ índio** cannabis
cañ|ería *f* pipe; (*tubería*) piping. **~o** *m* pipe, tube; (*de fuente*) jet. **~ón** *m* pipe, tube; (*de órgano*) pipe; (*de

chimenea) flue; (*arma de fuego*) cannon; (*desfiladero*) canyon. **~onazo** *m* gunshot. **~onera** *f* gunboat
caoba *f* mahogany
ca|os *m* chaos. **~ótico** *a* chaotic
capa *f* cloak; (*de pintura*) coat; (*culin*) coating; (*geol*) stratum, layer
capacidad *f* capacity; (*fig*) ability
capacitar *vt* qualify, enable; (*instruir*) train
caparazón *m* shell
capataz *m* foreman
capaz *a* capable, able; (*espacioso*) roomy. **~ para** which holds, with a capacity of
capazo *m* large basket
capcioso *a* sly, insidious
capellán *m* chaplain
caperuza *f* hood; (*de pluma*) cap
capilla *f* chapel; (*mus*) choir
capita *f* small cloak, cape
capital *a* capital, very important. ● *m* (*dinero*) capital. ● *f* (*ciudad*) capital; (*LAm*, *letra*) capital (letter). **~ de provincia** county town
capitali|smo *m* capitalism. **~sta** *a* & *m* & *f* capitalist. **~zar** [10] *vt* capitalize
capit|án *m* captain. **~anear** *vt* lead, command; (*un equipo*) captain
capitel *m* (*arquit*) capital
capitulaci|ón *f* surrender; (*acuerdo*) agreement. **~ones** *fpl* marriage contract
capítulo *m* chapter. **~s matrimoniales** marriage contract
capó *m* bonnet (*Brit*), hood (*Amer*)
capón *m* (*pollo*) capon
caporal *m* chief, leader
capota *f* (*de mujer*) bonnet; (*auto*) folding top, sliding roof
capote *m* cape
Capricornio *m* Capricorn
capricho *m* whim. **~so** *a* capricious, whimsical. **a ~** capriciously
cápsula *f* capsule
captar *vt* harness ‹*agua*›; grasp ‹*sentido*›; hold ‹*atención*›; win ‹*confianza*›; (*radio*) pick up
captura *f* capture. **~r** *vt* capture
capucha *f* hood
capullo *m* bud; (*de insecto*) cocoon
caqui *m* khaki
cara *f* face; (*de una moneda*) obverse; (*de un objeto*) side; (*aspecto*) look, appearance; (*descaro*) cheek. **~ a** towards; (*frente a*) facing. **~ a ~** face to face. **~ o cruz** heads or tails. **dar la ~** face up to. **hacer ~ a** face. **no volver la ~ atrás** not look back. **tener ~ de** look, seem to be. **tener ~ para** have the face to. **tener mala ~** look ill. **volver la ~** look the other way
carabela *f* caravel, small light ship
carabina *f* rifle; (*fig*, *señora*, *fam*) chaperone
Caracas *m* Caracas
caracol *m* snail; (*de pelo*) curl. **¡~es!** Good Heavens! **escalera** *f* **de ~** spiral staircase
carácter *m* (*pl* **caracteres**) character. **con ~ de**, **por su ~ de** as
característic|a *f* characteristic; (*LAm*, *teléfonos*) dialling code. **~o** *a* characteristic, typical
caracteriza|do *a* characterized; (*prestigioso*) distinguished. **~r** [10] *vt* characterize
cara: ~ dura cheek, nerve. **~dura** *m* & *f* cheeky person, rotter (*fam*)
caramba *int* good heavens!, goodness me!
carámbano *m* icicle
caramelo *m* sweet (*Brit*), candy (*Amer*); (*azúcar fundido*) caramel
carancho *m* (*Arg*) vulture
carapacho *m* shell
caraqueño *a* from Caracas. ● *m* native of Caracas
carátula *f* mask; (*fig*, *teatro*) theatre; (*Mex*, *esfera del reloj*) face
caravana *f* caravan; (*fig*, *grupo*) group; (*auto*) long line, traffic jam
caray *int* (*fam*) good heavens!, goodness me!
carb|ón *m* coal; (*papel*) carbon (paper); (*para dibujar*) charcoal. **~oncillo** *m* charcoal. **~onero** *a* coal. ● *m* coal-merchant. **~onizar** [10] *vt* (*fig*) burn (to a cinder). **~ono** *m* carbon
carburador *m* carburettor
carcajada *f* burst of laughter. **reírse a ~s** roar with laughter. **soltar una ~** burst out laughing
cárcel *m* prison, jail; (*en carpintería*) clamp
carcel|ario *a* prison. **~ero** *a* prison. ● *m* prison officer
carcom|a *f* woodworm. **~er** *vt* eat away; (*fig*) undermine. **~erse** *vpr* be eaten away; (*fig*) waste away
cardenal *m* cardinal; (*contusión*) bruise
cárdeno *a* purple

cardiaco, **cardíaco** *a* cardiac, heart. ● *m* heart patient
cardinal *a* cardinal
cardiólogo *m* cardiologist, heart specialist
cardo *m* thistle
carear *vt* bring face to face ‹*personas*›; compare ‹*cosas*›
carecer [11] *vi.* **~ de** lack. **~ de sentido** not to make sense
caren|cia *f* lack. **~te** *a* lacking
carero *a* expensive
carestía *f* (*precio elevado*) high price; (*escasez*) shortage
careta *f* mask
carey *m* tortoiseshell
carga *f* load; (*fig*) burden; (*acción*) loading; (*de barco*) cargo; (*obligación*) obligation. **~do** *a* loaded; (*fig*) burdened; ‹*tiempo*› heavy; ‹*hilo*› live; ‹*pila*› charged. **~mento** *m* load; (*acción*) loading; (*de un barco*) cargo. **~nte** *a* demanding. **~r** [12] *vt* load; (*fig*) burden; (*mil, elec*) charge; fill ‹*pluma etc*›; (*fig, molestar, fam*) annoy. ● *vi* load. **~r con** pick up. **~rse** *vpr* (*llenarse*) fill; ‹*cielo*› become overcast; (*enfadarse, fam*) get cross. **llevar la ~ de algo** be responsible for sth
cargo *m* load; (*fig*) burden; (*puesto*) post; (*acusación*) accusation, charge; (*responsabilidad*) charge. **a ~ de** in the charge of. **hacerse ~ de** take responsibility for. **tener a su ~** be in charge of
carguero *m* (*Arg*) beast of burden; (*naut*) cargo ship
cari *m* (*LAm*) grey
cariacontecido *a* crestfallen
caria|do *a* decayed. **~rse** *vpr* decay
caribe *a* Caribbean. **el mar** *m* **C~** the Caribbean (Sea)
caricatura *f* caricature
caricia *f* caress
caridad *f* charity. **¡por ~!** for goodness sake!
caries *f invar* (dental) decay
carilampiño *a* clean-shaven
cariño *m* affection; (*caricia*) caress. **~ mío** my darling. **~samente** *adv* tenderly, lovingly; (*en carta*) with love from. **~so** *a* affectionate. **con mucho ~** (*en carta*) with love from. **tener ~ a** be fond of. **tomar ~ a** take a liking to. **un ~** (*en carta*) with love from
carism|a *m* charisma. **~ático** *a* charismatic
caritativo *a* charitable
cariz *m* look
carlinga *f* cockpit
carmesí *a & m* crimson
carmín *m* (*de labios*) lipstick; (*color*) red
carnal *a* carnal; ‹*pariente*› blood, full. **primo ~** first cousin
carnaval *m* carnival. **~esco** *a* carnival. **martes** *m* **de ~** Shrove Tuesday
carne *f* (*incl de frutos*) flesh; (*para comer*) meat. **~ de cerdo** pork. **~ de cordero** lamb. **~ de gallina** gooseflesh. **~ picada** mince. **~ de ternera** veal. **~ de vaca** beef. **me pone la ~ de gallina** it gives me the creeps. **ser de ~ y hueso** be only human
carné *m* card; (*cuaderno*) notebook. **~ de conducir** driving licence (*Brit*), driver's license (*Amer*). **~ de identidad** identity card.
carnero *m* sheep; (*culin*) lamb
carnet /kar'ne/ *m* card; (*cuaderno*) notebook. **~ de conducir** driving licence (*Brit*), driver's license (*Amer*). **~ de identidad** identity card
carnicer|ía *f* butcher's (shop); (*fig*) massacre. **~o** *a* carnivorous; (*fig, cruel*) cruel, savage. ● *m* butcher; (*animal*) carnivore
carnívoro *a* carnivorous. ● *m* carnivore
carnoso *a* fleshy
caro *a* dear. ● *adv* dear, dearly. **costar ~ a uno** cost s.o. dear
carpa *f* carp; (*tienda*) tent
carpeta *f* file, folder. **~zo** *m*. **dar ~zo a** shelve, put on one side
carpinter|ía *f* carpentry. **~o** *m* carpinter, joiner
carraspe|ar *vi* clear one's throat. **~ra** *f*. **tener ~ra** have a frog in one's throat
carrera *f* run; (*prisa*) rush; (*concurso*) race; (*recorrido, estudios*) course; (*profesión*) profession, career
carreta *f* cart. **~da** *f* cart-load
carrete *m* reel; (*película*) 35mm film
carretera *f* road. **~ de circunvalación** bypass, ring road. **~ nacional** A road (*Brit*), highway (*Amer*). **~ secundaria** B road (*Brit*), secondary road (*Amer*)
carret|illa *f* trolley; (*de una rueda*) wheelbarrow; (*de bebé*) baby-walker. **~ón** *m* small cart

carril *m* rut; (*rail*) rail; (*de autopista etc*) lane
carrillo *m* cheek; (*polea*) pulley
carrizo *m* reed
carro *m* cart; (*LAm, coche*) car. **~ de asalto**, **~ de combate** tank
carrocería *f* (*auto*) bodywork; (*taller*) car repairer's
carroña *f* carrion
carroza *f* coach, carriage; (*en desfile de fiesta*) float
carruaje *m* carriage
carrusel *m* merry-go-round
carta *f* letter; (*documento*) document; (*lista de platos*) menu; (*lista de vinos*) list; (*geog*) map; (*naipe*) card. **~ blanca** free hand. **~ de crédito** credit card
cartearse *vpr* correspond
cartel *m* poster; (*de escuela etc*) wall-chart. **~era** *f* hoarding; (*en periódico*) entertainments. **~ito** *m* notice. **de ~** celebrated. **tener ~** be a hit, be successful
cartera *f* wallet; (*de colegial*) satchel; (*para documentos*) briefcase
cartería *f* sorting office
carterista *m & f* pickpocket
cartero *m* postman, mailman (*Amer*)
cartílago *m* cartilage
cartilla *f* first reading book. **~ de ahorros** savings book. **leerle la ~ a uno** tell s.o. off
cartón *m* cardboard
cartucho *m* cartridge
cartulina *f* thin cardboard
casa *f* house; (*hogar*) home; (*empresa*) firm; (*edificio*) building. **~ de correos** post office. **~ de huéspedes** boarding-house. **~ de socorro** first aid post. **amigo** *m* **de la ~** family friend. **ir a ~** go home. **salir de ~** go out
casad|a *f* married woman. **~o** *a* married. • *m* married man. **los recién ~os** the newly-weds
casamentero *m* matchmaker
casa|miento *m* marriage; (*ceremonia*) wedding. **~r** *vt* marry. • *vi* get married. **~rse** *vpr* get married
cascabel *m* small bell. **~eo** *m* jingling
cascada *f* waterfall
cascado *a* broken; ‹*voz*› harsh
cascanueces *m invar* nutcrackers
cascar [7] *vt* break; crack ‹*frutos secos*›; (*pegar*) beat. • *vi* (*fig, fam*) chatter, natter (*fam*). **~se** *vpr* crack
cáscara *f* (*de huevo, frutos secos*) shell; (*de naranja*) peel; (*de plátano*) skin
casco *m* helmet; (*de cerámica etc*) piece, fragment; (*cabeza*) head; (*de barco*) hull; (*envase*) empty bottle; (*de caballo*) hoof; (*de una ciudad*) part, area
cascote *m* rubble
caserío *m* country house; (*conjunto de casas*) hamlet
casero *a* home-made; (*doméstico*) domestic, household; (*amante del hogar*) home-loving; ‹*reunión*› family. • *m* owner; (*vigilante*) caretaker
caseta *f* small house, cottage. **~ de baño** bathing hut
caset(t)e *m & f* cassette
casi *adv* almost, nearly; (*en frases negativas*) hardly. **~ ~** very nearly. **~ nada** hardly any. **¡~ nada!** is that all! **~ nunca** hardly ever
casilla *f* small house; (*cabaña*) hut; (*de mercado*) stall; (*en ajedrez etc*) square; (*departamento de casillero*) pigeon-hole
casillero *m* pigeon-holes
casimir *m* cashmere
casino *m* casino; (*sociedad*) club
caso *m* case; (*atención*) notice. **~ perdido** hopeless case. **~ urgente** emergency. **darse el ~ (de) que** happen. **el ~ es que** the fact is that. **en ~ de** in the event of. **en cualquier ~** in any case, whatever happens. **en ese ~** in that case. **en todo ~** in any case. **en último ~** as a last resort. **hacer ~ de** take notice of. **poner por ~** suppose
caspa *f* dandruff
cáspita *int* good heavens!, goodness me!
casquivano *a* scatter-brained
cassette *m & f* cassette
casta *f* (*de animal*) breed; (*de persona*) descent
castaña *f* chestnut
castañet|a *f* click of the fingers. **~ear** *vi* ‹*dientes*› chatter
castaño *a* chestnut, brown. • *m* chestnut (tree)
castañuela *f* castanet
castellano *a* Castilian. • *m* (*persona*) Castilian; (*lengua*) Castilian, Spanish. **~parlante** *a* Castilian-speaking, Spanish-speaking. **¿habla Vd ~?** do you speak Spanish?

castidad *f* chastity
castig|ar [12] *vt* punish; (*en deportes*) penalize. **~o** *m* punishment; (*en deportes*) penalty
Castilla *f* Castille. **~ la Nueva** New Castille. **~ la Vieja** Old Castille
castillo *m* castle
cast|izo *a* true; ‹*lengua*› pure. **~o** *a* pure
castor *m* beaver
castra|ción *f* castration. **~r** *vt* castrate
castrense *m* military
casual *a* chance, accidental. **~idad** *f* chance, coincidence. **~mente** *adv* by chance. **dar la ~idad** happen. **de ~idad, por ~idad** by chance. **¡qué ~idad!** what a coincidence!
cataclismo *m* cataclysm
catador *m* taster; (*fig*) connoisseur
catalán *a & m* Catalan
catalejo *m* telescope
catalizador *m* catalyst
cat|alogar [12] *vt* catalogue; (*fig*) classify. **~álogo** *m* catalogue
Cataluña *f* Catalonia
catamarán *m* catamaran
cataplúm *int* crash! bang!
catapulta *f* catapult
catar *vt* taste, try
catarata *f* waterfall, falls; (*med*) cataract
catarro *m* cold
cat|ástrofe *m* catastrophe. **~astrófico** *a* catastrophic
catecismo *m* catechism
catedral *f* cathedral
catedrático *m* professor; (*de instituto*) teacher, head of department
categ|oría *f* category; (*clase*) class. **~órico** *a* categorical. **de ~oría** important. **de primera ~oría** first-class
catinga *f* (*LAm*) bad smell
catita *f* (*Arg*) parrot
catoche *m* (*Mex*) bad mood
cat|olicismo *m* catholicism. **~ólico** *a* (Roman) Catholic. ● *m* (Roman) Catholic
catorce *a & m* fourteen
cauce *m* river bed; (*fig, artificial*) channel
caución *f* caution; (*jurid*) guarantee
caucho *m* rubber
caudal *m* (*de río*) flow; (*riqueza*) wealth. **~oso** *a* ‹*río*› large
caudillo *m* leader, caudillo
causa *f* cause; (*motivo*) reason; (*jurid*) lawsuit. **~r** *vt* cause. **a ~ de, por ~ de** because of
cáustico *a* caustic
cautel|a *f* caution. **~arse** *vpr* guard against. **~osamente** *adv* warily, cautiously. **~oso** *a* cautious, wary
cauterizar [10] *vt* cauterize; (*fig*) apply drastic measures to
cautiv|ar *vt* capture; (*fig, fascinar*) captivate. **~erio** *m*, **~idad** *f* captivity. **~o** *a & m* captive
cauto *a* cautious
cavar *vt/i* dig
caverna *f* cave, cavern
caviar *m* caviare
cavidad *f* cavity
cavil|ar *vi* ponder, consider. **~oso** *a* worried
cayado *m* (*de pastor*) crook; (*de obispo*) crozier
caza *f* hunting; (*una expedición*) hunt; (*animales*) game. ● *m* fighter. **~dor** *m* hunter. **~dora** *f* jacket. **~ mayor** big game hunting. **~ menor** small game hunting. **~r** [10] *vt* hunt; (*fig*) track down; (*obtener*) catch, get. **andar a (la) ~ de** be in search of. **dar ~** chase, go after
cazo *m* saucepan; (*cucharón*) ladle. **~leta** *f* (small) saucepan
cazuela *f* casserole
cebada *f* barley
ceb|ar *vt* fatten (up); (*con trampa*) bait; prime ‹*arma de fuego*›. **~o** *m* bait; (*de arma de fuego*) charge
ceboll|a *f* onion. **~ana** *f* chive. **~eta** *f* spring onion. **~ino** *m* chive
cebra *f* zebra
cece|ar *vi* lisp. **~o** *m* lisp
cedazo *m* sieve
ceder *vt* give up. ● *vi* give in; (*disminuir*) ease off; (*fallar*) give way, collapse. **ceda el paso** give way
cedilla *f* cedilla
cedro *m* cedar
cédula *f* document; (*ficha*) index card
CE(E) *abrev* (*Comunidad* (*Económica*) *Europea*) E(E)C, European (Economic) Community
cefalea *f* severe headache
ceg|ador *a* blinding. **~ar** [1 & 12] *vt* blind; (*tapar*) block up. **~arse** *vpr* be blinded (**de** by). **~ato** *a* short-sighted. **~uera** *f* blindness
ceja *f* eyebrow
cejar *vi* move back; (*fig*) give way
celada *f* ambush; (*fig*) trap
cela|dor *m* (*de niños*) monitor; (*de cárcel*) prison warder; (*de museo etc*) attendant. **~r** *vt* watch

celda *f* cell
celebra|ción *f* celebration. **~r** *vt* celebrate; (*alabar*) praise. **~rse** *vpr* take place
célebre *a* famous; (*fig, gracioso*) funny
celebridad *f* fame; (*persona*) celebrity
celeridad *f* speed
celest|e *a* heavenly. **~ial** *a* heavenly. **azul ~e** sky-blue
celibato *m* celibacy
célibe *a* celibate
celo *m* zeal. **~s** *mpl* jealousy. **dar ~s** make jealous. **papel** *m* **~** adhesive tape, Sellotape (P). **tener ~s** be jealous
celofán *m* cellophane
celoso *a* enthusiastic; (*que tiene celos*) jealous
celta *a* Celtic. ● *m & f* Celt
céltico *a* Celtic
célula *f* cell
celular *a* cellular
celuloide *m* celluloid
celulosa *f* cellulose
cellisca *f* sleetstorm
cementerio *m* cemetery
cemento *m* cement; (*hormigón*) concrete; (*LAm, cola*) glue
cena *f* dinner; (*comida ligera*) supper. **~duría** *f* (*Mex*) restaurant
cenag|al *m* marsh, bog; (*fig*) tight spot. **~oso** *a* muddy
cenar *vt* have for dinner; (*en cena ligera*) have for supper. ● *vi* have dinner; (*tomar cena ligera*) have supper
cenicero *m* ashtray
cenit *m* zenith
ceniz|a *f* ash. **~o** *a* ashen. ● *m* jinx
censo *m* census. **~ electoral** electoral roll
censura *f* censure; (*de prensa etc*) censorship. **~r** *vt* censure; censor ‹*prensa etc*›
centavo *a & m* hundredth; (*moneda*) centavo
centell|a *f* flash; (*chispa*) spark. **~ar** *vi*, **~ear** *vi* sparkle. **~eo** *m* sparkle, sparkling
centena *f* hundred. **~r** *m* hundred. **a ~res** by the hundred
centenario *a* centenary; ‹*persona*› centenarian. ● *m* centenary; (*persona*) centenarian
centeno *m* rye
centésim|a *f* hundredth. **~o** *a* hundredth; (*moneda*) centésimo
cent|ígrado *a* centigrade, Celsius. **~igramo** *m* centigram. **~ilitro** *m* centilitre. **~ímetro** *m* centimetre
céntimo *a* hundredth. ● *m* cent
centinela *f* sentry
centolla *f*, **centollo** *m* spider crab
central *a* central. ● *f* head office. **~ de correos** general post office. **~ eléctrica** power station. **~ nuclear** nuclear power station. **~ telefónica** telephone exchange. **~ismo** *m* centralism. **~ita** *f* switchboard
centraliza|ción *f* centralization. **~r** [10] *vt* centralize
centrar *vt* centre
céntrico *a* central
centrífugo *a* centrifugal
centro *m* centre. **~ comercial** shopping centre
Centroamérica *f* Central America
centroamericano *a & m* Central American
centuplicar [7] *vt* increase a hundredfold
ceñi|do *a* tight. **~r** [5 & 22] *vt* surround, encircle; ‹*vestido*› be a tight fit. **~rse** *vpr* limit o.s. (**a** to)
ceñ|o *m* frown. **~udo** *a* frowning. **fruncir el ~o** frown
cepill|ar *vt* brush; (*en carpintería*) plane. **~o** *m* brush; (*en carpintería*) plane. **~o de dientes** toothbrush
cera *f* wax
cerámic|a *f* ceramics; (*materia*) pottery; (*objeto*) piece of pottery. **~o** *a* ceramic
cerca *f* fence. ● *adv* near, close. **~s** *mpl* foreground. **~ de** *prep* near; (*con números, con tiempo*) nearly. **de ~** from close up, closely
cercado *m* enclosure
cercan|ía *f* nearness, proximity. **~ías** *fpl* outskirts. **tren** *m* **de ~ías** local train. **~o** *a* near, close. **C~o Oriente** *m* Near East
cercar [7] *vt* fence in, enclose; ‹*gente*› surround, crowd round; (*asediar*) besiege
cerciorar *vt* convince. **~se** *vpr* make sure, find out
cerco *m* (*grupo*) circle; (*cercado*) enclosure; (*asedio*) siege
Cerdeña *f* Sardinia
cerdo *m* pig; (*carne*) pork
cereal *m* cereal
cerebr|al *a* cerebral. **~o** *m* brain; (*fig, inteligencia*) intelligence, brains

ceremoni|a *f* ceremony. **~al** *a* ceremonial. **~oso** *a* ceremonious, stiff
céreo *a* wax
cerez|a *f* cherry. **~o** cherry tree
cerill|a *f* match. **~o** *m* (*Mex*) match
cern|er [1] *vt* sieve. **~erse** *vpr* hover; (*fig*, *amenazar*) hang over. **~idor** *m* sieve
cero *m* nought, zero; (*fútbol*) nil (*Brit*), zero (*Amer*); (*tenis*) love; (*persona*) nonentity. **partir de ~** start from scratch
cerquillo *m* (*LAm*, *flequillo*) fringe
cerquita *adv* very near
cerra|do *a* shut, closed; (*espacio*) shut in, enclosed; ‹*cielo*› overcast; ‹*curva*› sharp. **~dura** *f* lock; (*acción de cerrar*) shutting, closing. **~jero** *m* locksmith. **~r** [1] *vt* shut, close; (*con llave*) lock; (*con cerrojo*) bolt; (*cercar*) enclose; turn off ‹*grifo*›; block up ‹*agujero etc*›. ● *vi* shut, close. **~rse** *vpr* shut, close; ‹*herida*› heal. **~r con llave** lock
cerro *m* hill. **irse por los ~s de Úbeda** ramble on
cerrojo *m* bolt. **echar el ~** bolt
certamen *m* competition, contest
certero *a* accurate
certeza *f*, **certidumbre** *f* certainty
certifica|do *a* ‹*carta etc*› registered. ● *m* certificate; (*carta*) registered letter. **~r** [7] *vt* certify; register ‹*carta etc*›
certitud *f* certainty
cervato *m* fawn
cerve|cería *f* beerhouse, bar; (*fábrica*) brewery. **~za** *f* beer. **~za de barril** draught beer. **~za de botella** bottled beer
cesa|ción *f* cessation, suspension. **~nte** *a* out of work. **~r** *vt* stop. ● *vi* stop, cease; (*dejar un empleo*) give up. **sin ~r** incessantly
cesáreo *a* Caesarian. **operación** *f* **cesárea** Caesarian section
cese *m* cessation; (*de un empleo*) dismissal
césped *m* grass, lawn
cest|a *f* basket. **~ada** *f* basketful. **~o** *m* basket. **~o de los papeles** wastepaper basket
cetro *m* sceptre; (*fig*) power
cianuro *m* cyanide
ciática *f* sciatica
cibernética *f* cibernetics
cicatriz *f* scar. **~ación** *f* healing. **~ar** [10] *vt/i* heal. **~arse** *vpr* heal
ciclamino *m* cyclamen
cíclico *a* cyclic(al)
ciclis|mo *m* cycling. **~ta** *m & f* cyclist
ciclo *m* cycle; (*LAm*, *curso*) course
ciclomotor *m* moped
ciclón *m* cyclone
ciclostilo *m* cyclostyle, duplicating machine
ciego *a* blind. ● *m* blind man, blind person. **a ciegas** in the dark
cielo *m* sky; (*relig*) heaven; (*persona*) darling. **¡~s!** good heavens!, goodness me!
ciempiés *m invar* centipede
cien *a* a hundred. **~ por ~** (*fam*) completely, one hundred per cent. **me pone a ~** it drives me mad
ciénaga *f* bog, swamp
ciencia *f* science; (*fig*) knowledge. **~s** *fpl* (*univ etc*) science. **~s empresariales** business studies. **saber a ~ cierta** know for a fact, know for certain
cieno *m* mud
científico *a* scientific. ● *m* scientist
ciento *a & m* (*delante de nombres, y numerales a los que multiplica* **cien**) a hundred, one hundred. **por ~** per cent
cierne *m* blossoming. **en ~** in blossom; (*fig*) in its infancy
cierre *m* fastener; (*acción de cerrar*) shutting, closing. **~ de cremallera** zip, zipper (*Amer*)
cierro *vb véase* **cerrar**
cierto *a* certain; (*verdad*) true. **estar en lo ~** be right. **lo ~ es que** the fact is that. **no es ~** that's not true. **¿no es ~?** right? **por ~** certainly, by the way. **si bien es ~ que** although
ciervo *m* deer
cifra *f* figure, number; (*cantidad*) sum. **~do** *a* coded. **~r** *vt* code; (*resumir*) summarize. **en ~** code, in code
cigala *f* (Norway) lobster
cigarra *f* cicada
cigarr|illo *m* cigarette. **~o** *m* (*cigarillo*) cigarette; (*puro*) cigar
cigüeña *f* stork
cil|índrico *a* cylindrical. **~indro** *m* cylinder; (*Mex*, *organillo*) barrel organ
cima *f* top; (*fig*) summit
címbalo *m* cymbal
cimbrear *vt* shake. **~se** *vpr* sway
cimentar [1] *vt* lay the foundations of; (*fig*, *reforzar*) strengthen
cimer|a *f* crest. **~o** *a* highest

cimiento *m* foundations; (*fig*) source. **desde los ~s** from the very beginning
cinc *m* zinc
cincel *m* chisel. **~ar** *vt* chisel
cinco *a* & *m* five
cincuent|a *a* & *m* fifty; (*quincuagésimo*) fiftieth. **~ón** *a* about fifty
cine *m* cinema. **~matografiar** [20] *vt* film
cinético *a* kinetic
cínico *a* cynical; (*desvergonzado*) shameless. • *m* cynic
cinismo *m* cynicism; (*desvergüenza*) shamelessness
cinta *f* band; (*adorno de pelo etc*) ribbon; (*película*) film; (*magnética*) tape; (*de máquina de escribir etc*) ribbon. **~ aisladora**, **~ aislante** insulating tape. **~ magnetofónica** magnetic tape. **~ métrica** tape measure
cintur|a *f* waist. **~ón** *m* belt. **~ón de seguridad** safety belt. **~ón salvavidas** lifebelt
ciprés *m* cypress (tree)
circo *m* circus
circuito *m* circuit; (*viaje*) tour. **~ cerrado** closed circuit. **corto ~** short circuit
circula|ción *f* circulation; (*vehículos*) traffic. **~r** *a* circular. • *vt* circulate. • *vi* circulate; ‹*líquidos*› flow; (*conducir*) drive; ‹*autobús etc*› run
círculo *m* circle. **~ vicioso** vicious circle. **en ~** in a circle
circunci|dar *vt* circumcise. **~sión** *f* circumcision
circunda|nte *a* surrounding. **~r** *vt* surround
circunferencia *f* circumference
circunflejo *m* circumflex
circunscri|bir [*pp* **circunscrito**] *vt* confine. **~pción** *f* (*distrito*) district. **~pción electoral** constituency
circunspecto *a* wary, circumspect
circunstan|cia *f* circumstance. **~te** *a* surrounding. • *m* bystander. **los ~tes** those present
circunvalación *f*. **carretera** *f* **de ~** bypass, ring road
cirio *m* candle
ciruela *f* plum. **~ claudia** greengage. **~ damascena** damson
ciru|gía *f* surgery. **~jano** *m* surgeon
cisne *m* swan
cisterna *f* tank, cistern
cita *f* appointment; (*entre chico y chica*) date; (*referencia*) quotation. **~ción** *f* quotation; (*jurid*) summons. **~do** *a* aforementioned. **~r** *vt* make an appointment with; (*mencionar*) quote; (*jurid*) summons. **~rse** *vpr* arrange to meet
cítara *f* zither
ciudad *f* town; (*grande*) city. **~anía** *f* citizenship; (*habitantes*) citizens. **~ano** *a* civic • *m* citizen, inhabitant; (*habitante de ciudad*) city dweller
cívico *a* civic
civil *a* civil. • *m* civil guard. **~idad** *f* politeness
civiliza|ción *f* civilization. **~r** [10] *vt* civilize. **~rse** *vpr* become civilized
civismo *m* community spirit
cizaña *f* (*fig*) discord
clam|ar *vi* cry out, clamour. **~or** *m* cry; (*griterío*) noise, clamour; (*protesta*) outcry. **~oroso** *a* noisy
clandestin|idad *f* secrecy. **~o** *a* clandestine, secret
clara *f* (*de huevo*) egg white
claraboya *f* skylight
clarear *vi* dawn; (*aclarar*) brighten up. **~se** *vpr* be transparent
clarete *m* rosé
claridad *f* clarity; (*luz*) light
clarifica|ción *f* clarification. **~r** [7] *vt* clarify
clarín *m* bugle
clarinet|e *m* clarinet; (*músico*) clarinettist. **~ista** *m* & *f* clarinettist
clarividen|cia *f* clairvoyance; (*fig*) far-sightedness. **~te** *a* clairvoyant; (*fig*) far-sighted
claro *a* (*con mucha luz*) bright; (*transparente, evidente*) clear; ‹*colores*› light; ‹*líquido*› thin. • *m* (*en bosque etc*) clearing; (*espacio*) gap. • *adv* clearly. • *int* of course! **~ de luna** moonlight. **¡~ que sí!** yes of course! **¡~ que no!** of course not!
clase *f* class; (*aula*) classroom. **~ media** middle class. **~ obrera** working class. **~ social** social class. **dar ~s** teach. **toda ~ de** all sorts of
clásico *a* classical; (*fig*) classic. • *m* classic
clasifica|ción *f* classification; (*deportes*) league. **~r** [7] *vt* classify; (*seleccionar*) sort
claudia *f* greengage
claudicar [7] (*ceder*) give in; (*cojear*) limp

claustro *m* cloister; (*univ*) staff
claustrof|obia *f* claustrophobia. **~óbico** *a* claustrophobic
cláusula *f* clause
clausura *f* closure; (*ceremonia*) closing ceremony. **~r** *vt* close
clava|do *a* fixed; (*con clavo*) nailed. **~r** *vt* knock in ‹*clavo*›; (*introducir a mano*) stick; (*fijar*) fix; (*juntar*) nail together. **es ~do a su padre** he's the spitting image of his father
clave *f* key; (*mus*) clef; (*clavicémbalo*) harpsichord
clavel *m* carnation
clavicémbalo *m* harpsichord
clavícula *f* collar bone, clavicle
clavija *f* peg; (*elec*) plug
clavo *m* nail; (*culin*) clove
claxon *m* (*pl* **claxons** /ˈklakson/) horn
clemen|cia *f* clemency, mercy. **~te** *a* clement, merciful
clementina *f* tangerine
cleptómano *m* kleptomaniac
cler|ecía *f* priesthood. **~ical** *a* clerical
clérigo *m* priest
clero *m* clergy
cliché *m* cliché; (*foto*) negative
cliente *m & f* client, customer; (*de médico*) patient. **~la** *f* clientele, customers; (*de médico*) patients, practice
clim|a *m* climate. **~ático** *a* climatic. **~atizado** *a* air-conditioned. **~atológico** *a* climatological
clínic|a *f* clinic. **~o** *a* clinical. ● *m* clinician
clip *m* (*pl* **clips**) clip
clo *m* cluck. **hacer ~ ~** cluck
cloaca *f* drain, sewer
cloque|ar *vi* cluck. **~o** *m* clucking
cloro *m* chlorine
club *m* (*pl* **clubs** *o* **clubes**) club
coacci|ón *f* coercion, compulsion. **~onar** *vt* coerce, compel
coagular *vt* coagulate; clot ‹*sangre*›; curdle ‹*leche*›. **~se** *vpr* coagulate; ‹*sangre*› clot; ‹*leche*› curdle
coalición *f* coalition
coartada *f* alibi
coartar *vt* hinder; restrict ‹*libertad etc*›
cobard|e *a* cowardly. ● *m* coward. **~ía** *f* cowardice
cobaya *f*, **cobayo** *m* guinea pig
cobert|era *f* (*tapadera*) lid. **~izo** *m* lean-to, shelter. **~or** *m* bedspread; (*manta*) blanket. **~ura** *f* covering
cobij|a *f* (*LAm, ropa de cama*) bedclothes; (*Mex, manta*) blanket. **~ar** *vt* shelter. **~arse** *vpr* shelter, take shelter. **~o** *m* shelter
cobra *f* cobra
cobra|dor *m* conductor. **~dora** *f* conductress. **~r** *vt* collect; (*ganar*) earn; charge ‹*precio*›; cash ‹*cheque*›; (*recuperar*) recover. ● *vi* be paid. **~rse** *vpr* recover
cobre *m* copper; (*mus*) brass (instruments)
cobro *m* collection; (*de cheque*) cashing; (*pago*) payment. **ponerse en ~** go into hiding. **presentar al ~** cash
cocada *f* (*LAm*) sweet coconut
cocaína *f* cocaine
cocción *f* cooking; (*tec*) baking, firing
cocear *vt/i* kick
coc|er [2 & 9] *vt/i* cook; (*hervir*) boil; (*en horno*) bake. **~ido** *a* cooked. ● *m* stew
cociente *m* quotient. **~ intelectual** intelligence quotient, IQ
cocin|a *f* kitchen; (*arte de cocinar*) cookery, cuisine; (*aparato*) cooker. **~a de gas** gas cooker. **~a eléctrica** electric cooker. **~ar** *vt/i* cook. **~ero** *m* cook
coco *m* coconut; (*árbol*) coconut palm; (*cabeza*) head; (*duende*) bogeyman. **comerse el ~** think hard
cocodrilo *m* crocodile
cocotero *m* coconut palm
cóctel *m* (*pl* **cóctels** *o* **cócteles**) cocktail; (*reunión*) cocktail party
coche *m* car (*Brit*), motor car (*Brit*), automobile (*Amer*); (*de tren*) coach, carriage. **~-cama** sleeper. **~ fúnebre** hearse. **~ra** *f* garage; (*de autobuses*) depot. **~ restaurante** dining-car. **~s de choque** dodgems
cochin|ada *f* dirty thing. **~o** *a* dirty, filthy. ● *m* pig
cod|azo *m* nudge (with one's elbow); (*Mex, aviso secreto*) tip-off. **~ear** *vt/i* elbow, nudge
codici|a *f* greed. **~ado** *a* coveted, sought after. **~ar** *vt* covet. **~oso** *a* greedy (**de** for)
código *m* code. **~ de la circulación** Highway Code
codo *m* elbow; (*dobladura*) bend. **hablar por los ~s** talk too much. **hasta los ~s** up to one's neck
codorniz *m* quail
coeducación *f* coeducation

coerción *f* coercion
coetáneo *a & m* contemporary
coexist|encia *f* coexistence. **~ir** *vi* coexist
cofradía *f* brotherhood
cofre *m* chest
coger [14] *vt* (*España*) take; catch ‹*tren, autobús, pelota, catarro*›; (*agarrar*) take hold of; (*del suelo*) pick up; pick ‹*frutos etc*›. ● *vi* (*caber*) fit. **~se** *vpr* trap, catch
cogollo *m* (*de lechuga etc*) heart; (*fig, lo mejor*) cream; (*fig, núcleo*) centre
cogote *m* back of the neck
cohech|ar *vt* bribe. **~o** *m* bribery
coherente *a* coherent
cohesión *f* cohesion
cohete *m* rocket; (*Mex, pistola*) pistol
cohibi|ción *f* inhibition. **~r** *vt* restrict; inhibit ‹*persona*›. **~rse** *vpr* feel inhibited; (*contenerse*) restrain o.s.
coincid|encia *f* coincidence. **~ente** *a* coincidental. **~ir** *vt* coincide. **dar la ~encia** happen
coje|ar *vt* limp; ‹*mueble*› wobble. **~ra** *f* lameness
coj|ín *m* cushion. **~inete** *m* small cushion. **~inete de bolas** ball bearing
cojo *a* lame; ‹*mueble*› wobbly. ● *m* lame person
col *f* cabbage. **~es de Bruselas** Brussel sprouts
cola *f* tail; (*fila*) queue; (*para pegar*) glue. **a la ~** at the end. **hacer ~** queue (up). **tener ~**, **traer ~** have serious consequences
colabora|ción *f* collaboration. **~dor** *m* collaborator. **~r** *vi* collaborate
colada *f* washing. **hacer la ~** do the washing
colador *m* strainer
colapso *m* collapse; (*fig*) stoppage
colar [2] *vt* strain ‹*líquidos*›; (*lavar*) wash; pass ‹*moneda falsa etc*›. ● *vi* ‹*líquido*› seep through; (*fig*) be believed, wash (*fam*). **~se** *vpr* slip; (*no hacer caso de la cola*) jump the queue; (*en fiesta*) gatecrash; (*meter la pata*) put one's foot in it
colch|a *f* bedspread. **~ón** *m* mattress. **~oneta** *f* mattress
colear *vi* wag its tail; ‹*asunto*› not be resolved. **vivito y coleando** alive and kicking
colecci|ón *f* collection; (*fig, gran número de*) a lot of. **~onar** *vt* collect. **~onista** *m & f* collector
colecta *f* collection
colectiv|idad *f* community. **~o** *a* collective. ● *m* (*Arg*) minibus
colector *m* (*en las alcantarillas*) main sewer
colega *m & f* colleague
colegi|al *m* schoolboy. **~ala** *f* schoolgirl. **~o** *m* private school; (*de ciertas profesiones*) college. **~o mayor** hall of residence
colegir [5 & 14] *vt* gather
cólera *f* cholera; (*ira*) anger, fury. **descargar su ~** vent one's anger. **montar en ~** fly into a rage
colérico *a* furious, irate
colesterol *m* cholesterol
coleta *f* pigtail
colga|nte *a* hanging. ● *m* pendant. **~r** [2 & 12] *vt* hang; hang out ‹*colada*›; hang up ‹*abrigo etc*›. ● *vi* hang; (*teléfono*) hang up, ring off. **~rse** *vpr* hang o.s. **dejar a uno ~do** let s.o. down
cólico *m* colic
coliflor *m* cauliflower
colilla *f* cigarette end
colina *f* hill
colinda|nte *a* adjacent. **~r** *vt* border (**con** on)
colisión *f* collision, crash; (*fig*) clash
colmar *vt* fill to overflowing; (*fig*) fulfill. **~ a uno de amabilidad** overwhelm s.o. with kindness
colmena *f* beehive, hive
colmillo *m* eye tooth, canine (tooth); (*de elefante*) tusk; (*de otros animales*) fang
colmo *m* height. **ser el ~** be the limit, be the last straw
coloca|ción *f* positioning; (*empleo*) job, position. **~r** [7] *vt* put, place; (*buscar empleo*) find work for. **~rse** *vpr* find a job
Colombia *f* Colombia
colombiano *a & m* Colombian
colon *m* colon
colón *m* (*unidad monetaria de Costa Rica y El Salvador*) colón
Colonia *f* Cologne
coloni|a *f* colony; (*agua de colonia*) eau-de-Cologne; (*LAm, barrio*) suburb. **~a de verano** holiday camp. **~al** *a* colonial. **~ales** *mpl* imported foodstuffs; (*comestibles en general*) groceries. **~alista** *m & f* colonialist. **~zación** *f* colonization. **~zar** [10] colonize
coloqui|al *a* colloquial. **~o** *m* conversation; (*congreso*) conference

color *m* colour. **~ado** *a* (*rojo*) red. **~ante** *m* colouring. **~ar** *vt* colour. **~ear** *vt/i* colour. **~ete** *m* rouge. **~ido** *m* colour. **de ~** colour. **en ~** (*fotos, película*) colour

colosal *a* colossal; (*fig, magnífico, fam*) terrific

columna *f* column; (*fig, apoyo*) support

columpi|ar *vt* swing. **~arse** *vpr* swing. **~o** *m* swing

collar *m* necklace; (*de perro etc*) collar

coma *f* comma. ● *m* (*med*) coma

comadre *f* midwife; (*madrina*) godmother; (*vecina*) neighbour. **~ar** *vi* gossip

comadreja *f* weasel

comadrona *f* midwife

comand|ancia *f* command. **~ante** *m* commander. **~o** *m* command; (*soldado*) commando

comarca *f* area, region

comba *f* bend; (*juguete*) skipping-rope. **~r** *vt* bend. **~rse** *vpr* bend. **saltar a la ~** skip

combat|e *m* fight; (*fig*) struggle. **~iente** *m* fighter. **~ir** *vt/i* fight

combina|ción *f* combination; (*bebida*) cocktail; (*arreglo*) plan, scheme; (*prenda*) slip. **~r** *vt* combine; (*arreglar*) arrange; (*armonizar*) match, go well with. **~rse** *vpr* combine; (*ponerse de acuerdo*) agree (**para** to)

combustible *m* fuel

comedia *f* comedy; (*cualquier obra de teatro*) play. **hacer la ~** pretend

comedi|do *a* reserved. **~rse** [5] *vpr* be restrained

comedor *m* dining-room; (*restaurante*) restaurant; (*persona*) glutton. **ser buen ~** have a good appetite

comensal *m* companion at table, fellow diner

comentar *vt* comment on; (*anotar*) annotate. **~io** *m* commentary; (*observación*) comment; (*fam*) gossip. **~ista** *m & f* commentator

comenzar [1 & 10] *vt/i* begin, start

comer *vt* eat; (*a mediodía*) have for lunch; (*corroer*) eat away; (*en ajedrez*) take. ● *vi* eat; (*a mediodía*) have lunch. **~se** *vpr* eat (up). **dar de ~ a** feed

comerci|al *a* commercial. **~ante** *m* trader; (*de tienda*) shopkeeper. **~ar** *vt* trade (**con, en** in); (*con otra persona*) do business. **~o** *m* commerce; (*actividad*) trade; (*tienda*) shop; (*negocio*) business

comestible *a* edible. **~s** *mpl* food. **tienda de ~s** grocer's (shop) (*Brit*), grocery (*Amer*)

cometa *m* comet. ● *f* kite

comet|er *vt* commit; make ‹*falta*›. **~ido** *m* task

comezón *m* itch

comicastro *m* poor actor, ham (*fam*)

comicios *mpl* elections

cómico *a* comic(al). ● *m* comic actor; (*cualquier actor*) actor

comida *f* food; (*a mediodía*) lunch. **hacer la ~** prepare the meals

comidilla *f* topic of conversation. **ser la ~ del pueblo** be the talk of the town

comienzo *m* beginning, start. **a ~s de** at the beginning of

comil|ón *a* greedy. **~ona** *f* feast

comillas *fpl* inverted commas

comino *m* cumin. **(no) me importa un ~** I couldn't care less

comisar|ía *f* police station. **~io** *m* commissioner; (*deportes*) steward. **~io de policía** police superintendent

comisión *f* assignment; (*comité*) commission, committee; (*com*) commission

comisura *f* corner. **~ de los labios** corner of the mouth

comité *m* committee

como *adv* like, as. ● *conj* as; (*en cuanto*) as soon as. **~ quieras** as you like. **~ sabes** as you know. **~ si** as if

cómo *a* how? **¿~?** I beg your pardon? **¿~ está Vd?** how are you? **¡~ no!** (*esp LAm*) of course! **¿~ son?** what are they like? **¿~ te llamas?** what's your name? **¡y ~!** and how!

cómoda *f* chest of drawers

comodidad *f* comfort. **a su ~** at your convenience

cómodo *a* comfortable; (*útil*) handy

comoquiera *conj*. **~ que** since. **~ que sea** however it may be

compacto *a* compact; (*denso*) dense; ‹*líneas etc*› close

compadecer [11] *vt* feel sorry for. **~se** *vpr*. **~se de** feel sorry for

compadre *m* godfather; (*amigo*) friend

compañ|ero *m* companion; (*de trabajo*) colleague; (*amigo*) friend. **~ía** *f* company. **en ~ía de** with

compara|ble *a* comparable. **~ción** *f* comparison. **~r** *vt* compare. **~tivo** *a & m* comparative. **en ~ción con** in comparison with, compared with
comparecer [11] *vi* appear
comparsa *f* group; (*en el teatro*) extra
compartimiento *m* compartment
compartir *vt* share
compás *m* (*instrumento*) (pair of) compasses; (*ritmo*) rhythm; (*división*) bar (*Brit*), measure (*Amer*); (*naut*) compass. **a ~** in time
compasi|ón *f* compassion, pity. **tener ~ón de** feel sorry for. **~vo** *a* compassionate
compatib|ilidad *f* compatibility. **~le** *a* compatible
compatriota *m & f* compatriot
compeler *vt* compel, force
compendi|ar *vt* summarize. **~o** *m* summary
compenetración *f* mutual understanding
compensa|ción *f* compensation. **~ción por despido** redundancy payment. **~r** *vt* compensate
competen|cia *f* competition; (*capacidad*) competence; (*terreno*) field, scope. **~te** *a* competent; (*apropiado*) appropriate, suitable
competi|ción *f* competition. **~dor** *m* competitor. **~r** [5] *vi* compete
compilar *vt* compile
compinche *m* accomplice; (*amigo, fam*) friend, mate (*fam*)
complac|encia *f* pleasure; (*indulgencia*) indulgence. **~er** [32] *vt* please; (*prestar servicio*) help. **~erse** *vpr* have pleasure, be pleased. **~iente** *a* helpful; ‹*marido*› complaisant
complej|idad *f* complexity. **~o** *a & m* complex
complement|ario *a* complementary. **~o** *m* complement; (*gram*) object, complement
complet|ar *vt* complete. **~o** *a* complete; (*lleno*) full; (*perfecto*) perfect
complexión *f* disposition; (*constitución*) constitution
complica|ción *f* complication. **~r** [7] *vt* complicate; involve ‹*persona*›. **~rse** *vpr* become complicated
cómplice *m* accomplice
complot *m* (*pl* **complots**) plot
compon|ente *a* component. ● *m* component; (*culin*) ingredient; (*miembro*) member. **~er** [34] *vt* make up; (*mus, literatura etc*) write, compose; (*reparar*) mend; (*culin*) prepare; (*arreglar*) restore; settle ‹*estómago*›; reconcile ‹*diferencias*›. **~erse** *vpr* be made up; (*arreglarse*) get ready. **~érselas** manage
comporta|miento *m* behaviour. **~r** *vt* involve. **~rse** *vpr* behave. **~rse como es debido** behave properly. **~rse mal** misbehave
composi|ción *f* composition. **~tor** *m* composer
compostelano *a* from Santiago de Compostela. ● *m* native of Santiago de Compostela
compostura *f* composition; (*arreglo*) repair; (*culin*) condiment; (*comedimiento*) composure
compota *f* stewed fruit
compra *f* purchase. **~ a plazos** hire purchase. **~dor** *m* buyer; (*en una tienda*) customer. **~r** *vt* buy. **~venta** *f* dealing. **hacer la ~, ir a la ~, ir de ~s** do the shopping, go shopping. **negocio** *m* **de ~venta** second-hand shop
compren|der *vt* understand; (*incluir*) include. **~sible** *a* understandable. **~sión** *f* understanding. **~sivo** *a* understanding; (*que incluye*) comprehensive
compresa *f* compress; (*de mujer*) sanitary towel
compr|esión *f* compression. **~imido** *a* compressed. ● *m* pill, tablet. **~imir** *vt* compress; keep back ‹*lágrimas*›; (*fig*) restrain
comproba|nte *m* (*recibo*) receipt. **~r** *vt* check; (*confirmar*) confirm
compromet|er *vt* compromise; (*arriesgar*) endager. **~erse** *vpr* compromise o.s.; (*obligarse*) agree to. **~ido** *a* ‹*situación*› awkward, embarrassing
compromiso *m* obligation; (*apuro*) predicament; (*cita*) appointment; (*acuerdo*) agreement. **sin ~** without obligation
compuesto *a* compound; ‹*persona*› smart. ● *m* compound
compungido *a* sad, sorry
computador *m*, **computadora** *f* computer
computar *vt* calculate
cómputo *m* calculation
comulgar [12] *vi* take Communion
común *a* common. ● *m* community. **en ~** in common. **por lo ~** generally

comunal *a* municipal, communal
comunica|ción *f* communication. **~do** *m* communiqué. **~do a la prensa** press release. **~r** [7] *vt/i* communicate; pass on ‹*enfermedad, información*›. **~rse** *vpr* communicate; ‹*enfermedad*› spread. **~tivo** *a* communicative. **está ~ndo** (*al teléfono*) it's engaged, the line's engaged
comunidad *f* community. **~ de vecinos** residents' association. **C~ (Económica) Europea** European (Economic) Community. **en ~** together
comunión *f* communion; (*relig*) (Holy) Communion
comunis|mo *m* communism. **~ta** *a & m & f* communist
comúnmente *adv* generally, usually
con *prep* with; (*a pesar de*) in spite of; (+ *infinitivo*) by. **~ decir la verdad** by telling the truth. **~ que** so. **~ tal que** as long as
conato *m* attempt
concatenación *f* chain, linking
cóncavo *a* concave
concebir [5] *vt/i* conceive
conceder *vt* concede, grant; award ‹*premio*›; (*admitir*) admit
concej|al *m* councillor. **~o** *m* town council
concentra|ción *f* concentration. **~do** *m* concentrated. **~r** *vt* concentrate. **~rse** *vpr* concentrate
concep|ción *f* conception. **~to** *m* concept; (*opinión*) opinion. **bajo ningún ~to** in no way. **en mi ~to** in my view. **por ningún ~to** in no way
concerniente *a* concerning. **en lo ~ a** with regard to
concertar [1] *vt* (*mus*) harmonize; (*coordinar*) coordinate; (*poner de acuerdo*) agree. ● *vi* be in tune; (*fig*) agree. **~se** *vpr* agree
concertina *f* concertina
concesión *f* concession
conciencia *f* conscience; (*conocimiento*) consciousness. **~ción** *f* awareness. **~ limpia** clear conscience. **~ sucia** guilty conscience. **a ~ de que** fully aware that. **en ~** honestly. **tener ~ de** be aware of. **tomar ~ de** become aware of
concienzudo *a* conscientious
concierto *m* concert; (*acuerdo*) agreement; (*mus, composición*) concerto
concilia|ble *a* reconcilable. **~ción** *f* reconciliation. **~r** *vt* reconcile. **~r el sueño** get to sleep. **~rse** *vpr* gain
concilio *m* council
conciso *m* concise
conciudadano *m* fellow citizen
conclu|ir [17] *vt* finish; (*deducir*) conclude. ● *vi* finish, end. **~irse** *vpr* finish, end. **~sión** *f* conclusion. **~yente** *a* conclusive
concord|ancia *f* agreement. **~ar** [2] *vt* reconcile. ● *vi* agree. **~e** *a* in agreement. **~ia** *f* harmony
concret|amente *adv* specifically, to be exact. **~ar** *vt* make specific. **~arse** *vpr* become definite; (*limitarse*) confine o.s. **~o** *a* concrete; (*determinado*) specific, particular. ● *m* (*LAm, hormigón*) concrete. **en ~o** definite; (*concretamente*) to be exact; (*en resumen*) in short
concurr|encia *f* coincidence; (*reunión*) crowd, audience. **~ido** *a* crowded, busy. **~ir** *vi* meet; (*asistir*) attend; (*coincidir*) coincide; (*contribuir*) contribute; (*en concurso*) compete
concurs|ante *m & f* competitor, contestant. **~ar** *vi* compete, take part. **~o** *m* competition; (*concurrencia*) crowd; (*ayuda*) help
concha *f* shell; (*carey*) tortoiseshell
condado *m* county
conde *m* earl, count
condena *f* sentence. **~ción** *f* condemnation. **~do** *m* convict. **~r** *vt* condemn; (*jurid*) convict
condensa|ción *f* condensation. **~r** *vt* condense. **~rse** *vpr* condense
condesa *f* countess
condescende|ncia *f* condescension; (*tolerancia*) indulgence. **~r** [1] *vi* agree; (*dignarse*) condescend
condici|ón *f* condition; (*naturaleza*) nature. **~onado** *a*, **~onal** *a* conditional. **~onar** *vt* condition. **a ~ón de (que)** on the condition that
condiment|ar *vt* season. **~o** *m* condiment
condolencia *f* condolence
condominio *m* joint ownership
condón *m* condom
condonar *vt* (*perdonar*) reprieve; cancel ‹*deuda*›
conducir [47] *vt* drive ‹*vehículo*›; carry ‹*electricidad, gas, agua etc*›. ● *vi* drive; (*fig, llevar*) lead. **~se** *vpr* behave. **¿a qué conduce?** what's the point?

conducta *f* behaviour
conducto *m* pipe, tube; (*anat*) duct. **por ~ de** through
conductor *m* driver; (*jefe*) leader; (*elec*) conductor
conduzco *vb véase* **conducir**
conectar *vt/i* connect; (*enchufar*) plug in
conejo *m* rabbit
conexión *f* connection
confabularse *vpr* plot
confecci|ón *f* making; (*prenda*) ready-made garment. **~ones** *fpl* clothing, clothes. **~onado** *a* ready-made. **~onar** *vt* make
confederación *f* confederation
conferencia *f* conference; (*al teléfono*) long-distance call; (*univ etc*) lecture. **~ cumbre**, **~ en la cima**, **~ en la cumbre** summit conference. **~nte** *m & f* lecturer
conferir [4] *vt* confer; award ‹*premio*›
confes|ar [1] *vt/i* confess. **~arse** *vpr* confess. **~ión** *f* confession. **~ional** *a* confessional. **~ionario** *m* confessional. **~or** *m* confessor
confeti *m* confetti
confia|do *a* trusting; (*seguro de sí mismo*) confident. **~nza** *f* trust; (*en sí mismo*) confidence; (*intimidad*) familiarity. **~r** [20] *vt* entrust. • *vi* trust. **~rse** *vpr* put one's trust in
confiden|cia *f* confidence, secret. **~cial** *a* confidential. **~te** *m & f* close friend; (*de policía*) informer
configuración *f* configuration, shape
conf|ín *m* border. **~inar** *vt* confine; (*desterrar*) banish. • *vi* border (**con** on). **~ines** *mpl* outermost parts
confirma|ción *f* confirmation. **~r** *vt* confirm
confiscar [7] *vt* confiscate
confit|ería *f* sweet-shop (*Brit*), candy store (*Amer*). **~ura** *f* jam
conflagración *f* conflagration
conflicto *m* conflict
confluencia *f* confluence
conforma|ción *f* conformation, shape. **~r** *vt* (*acomodar*) adjust. • *vi* agree. **~rse** *vpr* conform
conform|e *a* in agreement; (*contento*) happy, satisfied; (*según*) according (**con** to). • *conj* as. • *int* OK! **~e a** in accordance with, according to. **~idad** *f* agreement; (*tolerancia*) resignation. **~ista** *m & f* conformist
conforta|ble *a* comfortable. **~nte** *a* comforting. **~r** *vt* comfort
confronta|ción *f* confrontation; (*comparación*) comparison. **~r** *vt* confront; (*comparar*) compare
confu|ndir *vt* blur; (*equivocar*) mistake, confuse; (*perder*) lose; (*mezclar*) mix up, confuse. **~ndirse** *vpr* become confused; (*equivocarse*) make a mistake. **~sión** *f* confusion; (*vergüenza*) embarrassment. **~so** *a* confused; (*avergonzado*) embarrassed
congela|do *a* frozen. **~dor** *m* freezer. **~r** *vt* freeze
congeniar *vi* get on
congesti|ón *f* congestion. **~onado** *a* congested. **~onar** *vt* congest. **~onarse** *vpr* become congested
congoja *f* distress
congraciar *vt* win over. **~se** *vpr* ingratiate o.s.
congratular *vt* congratulate
congrega|ción *f* gathering; (*relig*) congregation. **~rse** [12] *vpr* gather, assemble
congres|ista *m & f* delegate, member of a congress. **~o** *m* congress, conference. **C~o de los Diputados** House of Commons
cónico *a* conical
conífer|a *f* conifer. **~o** *a* coniferous
conjetura *f* conjecture, guess. **~r** *vt* conjecture, guess
conjuga|ción *f* conjugation. **~r** [12] *vt* conjugate
conjunción *f* conjunction
conjunto *a* joint. • *m* collection; (*mus*) band; (*ropa*) suit, outfit. **en ~** altogether
conjura *f*, **conjuración** *f* conspiracy
conjurar *vt* plot, conspire
conmemora|ción *f* commemoration. **~r** *vt* commemorate. **~tivo** *a* commemorative
conmigo *pron* with me
conminar *vt* threaten; (*avisar*) warn
conmiseración *f* commiseration
conmo|ción *f* shock; (*tumulto*) upheaval; (*terremoto*) earthquake. **~cionar** *vt* shock. **~ cerebral** concussion. **~ver** [2] *vt* shake; (*emocionar*) move
conmuta|dor *m* switch. **~r** *vt* exchange
connivencia *f* connivance
connota|ción *f* connotation. **~r** *vt* connote
cono *m* cone

conoc|edor *a & m* expert. **~er** [11] *vt* know; (*por primera vez*) meet; (*reconocer*) recognize, know. **~erse** *vpr* know o.s.; ‹*dos personas*› know each other; (*notarse*) be obvious. **dar a ~er** make known. **darse a ~er** make o.s. known. **~ido** *a* well-known. ● *m* acquaintance. **~imiento** *m* knowledge; (*sentido*) consciousness; (*conocido*) acquaintance. **perder el ~imiento** faint. **se ~e que** apparently. **tener ~imiento de** know about

conozco *vb véase* **conocer**

conque *conj* so

conquense *a* from Cuenca. ● *m* native of Cuenca

conquista *f* conquest. **~dor** *a* conquering. ● *m* conqueror; (*de América*) conquistador; (*fig*) lady-killer. **~r** *vt* conquer, win

consabido *a* well-known

consagra|ción *f* consecration. **~r** *vt* consecrate; (*fig*) devote. **~rse** *vpr* devote o.s.

consanguíneo *m* blood relation

consciente *a* conscious

consecución *f* acquisition; (*de un deseo*) realization

consecuen|cia *f* consequence; (*firmeza*) consistency. **~te** *a* consistent. **a ~cia de** as a result of. **en ~cia, por ~cia** consequently

consecutivo *a* consecutive

conseguir [5 & 13] *vt* get, obtain; (*lograr*) manage; achieve ‹*objetivo*›

conseja *f* story, fable

consej|ero *m* adviser; (*miembro de consejo*) member. **~o** *m* advice; (*pol*) council. **~o de ministros** cabinet

consenso *m* assent, consent

consenti|do *a* ‹*niño*› spoilt. **~miento** *m* consent. **~r** [4] *vt* allow. ● *vi* consent. **~rse** *vpr* break

conserje *m* porter, caretaker. **~ría** *f* porter's office

conserva *f* preserves; (*mermelada*) jam, preserve; (*en lata*) tinned food. **~ción** *f* conservation; (*de alimentos*) preservation; (*de edificio*) maintenance. **en ~** preserved

conservador *a & m* (*pol*) conservative

conservar *vt* keep; preserve ‹*alimentos*›. **~se** *vpr* keep; ‹*costumbre etc*› survive

conservatorio *m* conservatory

considera|ble *a* considerable. **~ción** *f* consideration; (*respeto*) respect. **~do** *a* considered; (*amable*) considerate; (*respetado*) respected. **~r** *vt* consider; (*respetar*) respect. **de ~ción** considerable. **de su ~ción** (*en cartas*) yours faithfully. **tomar en ~ción** take into consideration

consigna *f* order; (*rail*) left luggage office (*Brit*), baggage room (*Amer*); (*eslogan*) slogan

consigo *pron* (*él*) with him; (*ella*) with her; (*Ud, Uds*) with you; (*uno mismo*) with o.s.

consiguiente *a* consequent. **por ~** consequently

consist|encia *f* consistency. **~ente** *a* consisting (**en** of); (*firme*) solid. **~ir** *vi* consist (**en** of); (*deberse*) be due (**en** to)

consola|ción *f* consolation. **~r** [2] *vt* console, comfort

consolidar *vt* consolidate. **~se** *vpr* consolidate

consomé *m* clear soup, consommé

consonan|cia *f* consonance. **~te** *a* consonant. ● *f* consonant

consorcio *m* consortium

consorte *m & f* consort

conspicuo *a* eminent; (*visible*) visible

conspira|ción *f* conspiracy. **~dor** *m* conspirator. **~r** *vi* conspire

constan|cia *f* constancy. **~te** *a* constant

constar *vi* be clear; (*figurar*) appear, figure; (*componerse*) consist. **hacer ~** point out. **me consta que** I'm sure that. **que conste que** believe me

constatar *vt* check; (*confirmar*) confirm

constelación *f* constellation

consternación *f* consternation

constipa|do *m* cold. ● *a*. **estar ~do** have a cold. **~rse** *vpr* catch a cold

constitu|ción *f* constitution; (*establecimiento*) setting up. **~cional** *a* constitutional. **~ir** [17] *vt* constitute; (*formar*) form; (*crear*) set up, establish. **~irse** *vpr* set o.s. up (**en** as); (*presentarse*) appear. **~tivo** *a*, **~yente** *a* constituent

constreñir [5 & 22] *vt* force, oblige; (*restringir*) restrain

constricción *f* constriction

constru|cción *f* construction. **~ctor** *m* builder. **~ir** [17] *vt* construct; build ‹*edificio*›

consuelo *m* consolation, comfort
consuetudinario *a* customary
cónsul *m* consul
consula|do *m* consulate. **~r** *a* consular
consult|a *f* consultation. **~ar** *vt* consult. **~orio** *m* surgery. **~orio sentimental** problem page. **horas** *fpl* **de ~a** surgery hours. **obra** *f* **de ~a** reference book
consumar *vt* complete; commit ‹*crimen*›; consummate ‹*matrimonio*›
consum|ición *f* consumption; (*bebida*) drink; (*comida*) food. **~ido** *a* ‹*persona*› skinny, wasted; ‹*frutas*› shrivelled. **~idor** *m* consumer. **~ir** *vt* consume. **~irse** *vpr* ‹*persona*› waste away; ‹*cosa*› wear out; (*quedarse seco*) dry up. **~ismo** *m* consumerism. **~o** *m* consumption
contab|ilidad *f* book-keeping; (*profesión*) accountancy. **~le** *m* & *f* accountant
contacto *m* contact. **ponerse en ~ con** get in touch with
contado *a* counted. **~s** *apl* few. **~r** *m* meter; (*LAm, contable*) accountant. **al ~** cash
contagi|ar *vt* infect ‹*persona*›; pass on ‹*enfermedd*›; (*fig*) contaminate. **~o** *m* infection. **~oso** *a* infectious
contamina|ción *f* contamination, pollution. **~r** *vt* contaminate, pollute
contante *a*. **dinero** *m* **~** cash
contar [2] *vt* count; tell ‹*relato*›. ● *vi* count. **~ con** rely on, count on. **~se** *vpr* be included (**entre** among); (*decirse*) be said
contempla|ción *f* contemplation. **~r** *vt* look at; (*fig*) contemplate. **sin ~ciones** unceremoniously
contemporáneo *a* & *m* contemporary
contend|er [1] *vi* compete. **~iente** *m* & *f* competitor
conten|er [40] *vt* contain; (*restringir*) restrain. **~erse** *vpr* restrain o.s. **~ido** *a* contained. ● *m* contents
content|ar *vt* please. **~arse** *vpr*. **~arse de** be satisfied with, be pleased with. **~o** *a* (*alegre*) happy; (*satisfecho*) pleased
contesta|ción *f* answer. **~dor** *m*. **~ automático** answering machine. **~r** *vt/i* answer; (*replicar*) answer back
contexto *m* context
contienda *f* struggle
contigo *pron* with you
contiguo *a* adjacent
continen|cia *f* continence. **~tal** *a* continental. **~te** *m* continent
contingen|cia *f* contingency. **~te** *a* contingent. ● *m* contingent; (*cuota*) quota
continu|ación *f* continuation. **~ar** [21] *vt* continue, resume. ● *vi* continue. **~ará** (*en revista, TV etc*) to be continued. **~idad** *f* continuity. **~o** *a* continuous; (*muy frecuente*) continual. **a ~ación** immediately after. **corriente** *f* **~a** direct current
contorno *m* outline; (*geog*) contour. **~s** *mpl* surrounding area
contorsión *f* contortion
contra *adv* & *prep* against. ● *m* cons. **en ~** against
contraalmirante *m* rear-admiral
contraata|car [7] *vt/i* counter-attack. **~que** *m* counter-attack
contrabajo *m* double-bass; (*persona*) double-bass player
contrabalancear *vt* counterbalance
contraband|ista *m* & *f* smuggler. **~o** *m* contraband
contracción *f* contraction
contrachapado *m* plywood
contrad|ecir [46] *vt* contradict. **~icción** *f* contradiction. **~ictorio** *a* contradictory
contraer [41] *vt* contract. **~ matrimonio** marry. **~se** *vpr* contract; (*limitarse*) limit o.s.
contrafuerte *m* buttress
contragolpe *m* backlash
contrahecho *a* fake; ‹*moneda*› counterfeit; ‹*persona*› hunch-backed
contraindicación *f* contraindication
contralto *m* alto. ● *f* contralto
contramano. **a ~** in the wrong direction
contrapartida *f* compensation
contrapelo. **a ~** the wrong way
contrapes|ar *vt* counterbalance. **~o** *m* counterbalance
contraponer [34] oppose; (*comparar*) compare
contraproducente *a* counter-productive
contrari|ar [20] *vt* oppose; (*molestar*) annoy. **~edad** *f* obstacle; (*disgusto*) annoyance. **~o** *a* contrary; ‹*dirección*› opposite; ‹*persona*› opposed. **al ~o** on the contrary. **al**

~o de contrary to. **de lo ~o** otherwise. **en ~o** against. **llevar la ~a** contradict. **por el ~o** on the contrary

contrarrestar *vt* counteract

contrasentido *m* contradiction

contraseña *f* secret mark; (*palabra*) password

contrast|ar *vt* check, verify. ● *vi* contrast. **~e** *m* contrast; (*en oro, plata etc*) hallmark

contratar *vt* sign a contract for; engage ‹*empleados*›

contratiempo *m* setback; (*accidente*) accident

contrat|ista *m & f* contractor. **~o** *m* contract

contraven|ción *f* contravention. **~ir** [53] *vi*. **~ir a** contravene

contraventana *f* shutter

contribu|ción *f* contribution; (*tributo*) tax. **~ir** [17] *vt/i* contribute. **~yente** *m & f* contributor; (*que paga impuestos*) taxpayer

contrincante *m* rival, opponent

contrito *a* contrite

control *m* control; (*inspección*) check. **~ar** *vt* control; (*examinar*) check

controversia *f* controversy

contundente *a* ‹*arma*› blunt; ‹*argumento etc*› convincing

conturbar *vt* perturb

contusión *f* bruise

convalec|encia *f* convalescence. **~er** [11] *vi* convalesce. **~iente** *a & m & f* convalescent

convalidar *vt* confirm; recognize ‹*título*›

convenc|er [9] *vt* convince. **~imiento** *m* conviction

convenci|ón *f* convention. **~onal** *a* conventional

conveni|encia *f* convenience; (*aptitud*) suitability. **~encias (sociales)** conventions. **~ente** *a* suitable; (*aconsejable*) advisable; (*provechoso*) useful, advantageous. **~o** *m* agreement. **~r** [53] *vt* agree. ● *vi* agree; (*ser conveniente*) be convenient for, suit; (*ser aconsejable*) be advisable

convento *m* (*de monjes*) monastery; (*de monjas*) convent

convergente *a* converging

converger [14] *vi*, **convergir** [14] *vi* converge

conversa|ción *f* conversation. **~r** *vi* converse, talk

conver|sión *f* conversion. **~so** *a* converted. ● *m* convert. **~tible** *a* convertible. **~tir** [4] *vt* convert. **~tirse** *vpr* be converted

convexo *a* convex

convic|ción *f* conviction. **~to** *a* convicted

convida|do *m* guest. **~r** *vt* invite. **te convido a un helado** I'll treat you to an ice-cream

convincente *a* convincing

convite *m* invitation; (*banquete*) banquet

conviv|encia *f* coexistence. **~ir** *vi* live together

convocar [7] *vt* convene ‹*reunión*›; summon ‹*personas*›

convoy *m* convoy; (*rail*) train; (*vinagrera*) cruet

convulsión *f* convulsion; (*fig*) upheaval

conyugal *a* conjugal; (*vida*› married

cónyuge *m* spouse. **~s** *mpl* (married) couple

coñac *m* (*pl* **coñacs**) brandy

coopera|ción *f* co-operation. **~r** *vi* co-operate. **~tiva** *f* co-operative. **~tivo** *a* co-operative

coord|enada *f* coordinate. **~inación** *f* co-ordination. **~inar** *vt* co-ordinate

copa *f* glass; (*deportes, fig*) cup. **~s** *fpl* (*naipes*) hearts. **tomar una ~** have a drink

copia *f* copy. **~ en limpio** fair copy. **~r** *vt* copy. **sacar una ~** make a copy

copioso *a* copious; ‹*lluvia, nevada etc*› heavy

copla *f* verse; (*canción*) song

copo *m* flake. **~ de nieve** snowflake. **~s de maíz** cornflakes

coquet|a *f* flirt; (*mueble*) dressing-table. **~ear** *vi* flirt. **~eo** *m* flirtation. **~o** *a* flirtatious

coraje *m* courage; (*rabia*) anger. **dar ~** make mad, make furious

coral *a* choral. ● *m* (*materia, animal*) coral

Corán *m* Koran

coraza *f* (*naut*) armour-plating; (*de tortuga*) shell

coraz|ón *m* heart; (*persona*) darling. **~onada** *f* hunch; (*impulso*) impulse. **sin ~ón** heartless. **tener buen ~ón** be good-hearted

corbata *f* tie, necktie (*esp Amer*). **~ de lazo** bow tie

corcova *f* hump. **~do** *a* hunch-backed
corchea *f* quaver
corchete *m* fastener, hook and eye; (*gancho*) hook; (*paréntesis*) square bracket
corcho *m* cork
cordel *m* cord, thin rope
cordero *m* lamb
cordial *a* cordial, friendly. ● *m* tonic. **~idad** *f* cordiality, warmth
cordillera *f* mountain range
córdoba *m* (*unidad monetaria de Nicaragua*) córdoba
Córdoba *f* Cordova
cordón *m* string; (*de zapatos*) lace; (*cable*) flex; (*fig*) cordon. **~ umbilical** umbilical cord
corear *vt* chant
coreografía *f* choreography
corista *m* & *f* member of the chorus. ● *f* (*bailarina*) chorus girl
cornet|a *f* bugle. **~ín** *m* cornet
Cornualles *m* Cornwall
cornucopia *f* cornucopia
cornudo *a* horned. ● *m* cuckold
coro *m* chorus; (*relig*) choir
corona *f* crown; (*de flores*) wreath, garland. **~ción** *f* coronation. **~r** *vt* crown
coronel *m* colonel
coronilla *f* crown. **estar hasta la ~** be fed up
corporación *f* corporation
corporal *a* corporal
corpulento *a* stout
corpúsculo *m* corpuscle
corral *m* pen. **aves** *fpl* **de ~** poultry
correa *f* strap; (*de perro*) lead; (*cinturón*) belt
correc|ción *f* correction; (*reprensión*) rebuke; (*cortesía*) good manners. **~to** *a* correct; (*cortés*) polite
corre|dizo *a* running. **nudo ~dizo** slip knot. **puerta** *f* **~diza** sliding door. **~dor** *m* runner; (*pasillo*) corridor; (*agente*) agent, broker. **~dor automovilista** racing driver
corregir [5 & 14] *vt* correct; (*reprender*) rebuke
correlaci|ón *f* correlation. **~onar** *vt* correlate
correo *m* courier; (*correos*) post, mail; (*tren*) mail train. **~s** *mpl* post office. **echar al ~** post
correr *vt* run; (*viajar*) travel; draw ‹*cortinas*›. ● *vi* run; ‹*agua, electricidad etc*› flow; ‹*tiempo*› pass. **~se** *vpr* (*apartarse*) move along; (*pasarse*) go too far; ‹*colores*› run. **~se una juerga** have a ball
correspond|encia *f* correspondence. **~er** *vi* correspond; (*ser adecuado*) be fitting; (*contestar*) reply; (*pertenecer*) belong; (*incumbir*) fall to. **~erse** *vpr* (*amarse*) love one another. **~iente** *a* corresponding
corresponsal *m* correspondent
corrid|a *f* run. **~a de toros** bullfight. **~o** *a* ‹*peso*› good; (*continuo*) continuous; (*avergonzado*) embarrassed. **de ~a** from memory
corriente *a* ‹*agua*› running; ‹*monedas, publicación, cuenta, año etc*› current; (*ordinario*) ordinary. ● *f* current; (*de aire*) draught; (*fig*) tendency. ● *m* current month. **al ~** (*al día*) up-to-date; (*enterado*) aware
corr|illo *m* small group, circle. **~o** *m* circle
corroborar *vt* corroborate
corroer [24 & 37] *vt* corrode; (*geol*) erode; (*fig*) eat away. **~se** *vpr* corrode
corromper *vt* rot ‹*madera*›; turn bad ‹*alimentos*›; (*fig*) corrupt. ● *vi* (*fam*) stink. **~se** *vpr* ‹*madera*› rot; ‹*alimentos*› go bad; (*fig*) be corrupted
corrosi|ón *f* corrosion. **~vo** *a* corrosive
corrupción *f* (*de madera etc*) rot; (*soborno*) bribery; (*fig*) corruption
corsé *m* corset
cortacésped *m invar* lawn-mower
cortad|o *a* cut; ‹*leche*› sour; (*avergonzado*) embarrassed; (*confuso*) confused. ● *m* coffee with a little milk. **~ura** *f* cut
corta|nte *a* sharp; ‹*viento*› biting; ‹*frío*› bitter. **~r** *vt* cut; (*recortar*) cut out; (*aislar, detener*) cut off; (*interrumpir*) cut in. ● *vi* cut. **~rse** *vpr* cut o.s.; ‹*leche etc*› curdle; (*al teléfono*) be cut off; (*fig*) be embar rassed, become tongue-tied. **~rse el pelo** have one's hair cut. **~rse las uñas** cut one's nails
cortaúñas *m invar* nail-clippers
corte *m* cutting; (*de instrumento cortante*) cutting edge; (*de corriente*) cut; (*de prendas de vestir*) cut; (*de tela*) length. ● *f* court. **~ de luz** power cut. **~ y confección** dress-making. **hacer la ~** court. **las C~s** the Spanish parliament

cortej|ar *vt* court. **~o** *m* (*de rey etc*) entourage. **~o fúnebre** cortège, funeral procession. **~o nupcial** wedding procession

cortés *a* polite

cortesan|a *f* courtesan. **~o** *m* courtier

cortesía *f* courtesy

corteza *f* bark; (*de naranja etc*) peel, rind; (*de pan*) crust

cortijo *m* farm; (*casa*) farmhouse

cortina *f* curtain

corto *a* short; (*escaso*) scanty; (*apocado*) shy. **~circuito** *m* short circuit. **~ de alcances** dim, thick. **~ de oído** hard of hearing. **~ de vista** short-sighted. **a la corta o a la larga** sooner or later. **quedarse ~** fall short; (*miscalcular*) under-estimate

Coruña *f*. **La ~** Corunna

corvo *a* bent

cosa *f* thing; (*asunto*) business; (*idea*) idea. **~ de** about. **como si tal ~** just like that; (*como si no hubiera pasado nada*) as if nothing had happened. **decirle a uno cuatro ~s** tell s.o. a thing or two. **lo que son las ~s** much to my surprise

cosaco *a* & *m* Cossack

cosech|a *f* harvest; (*de vino*) vintage. **~ar** *vt* harvest. **~ero** *m* harvester

coser *vt/i* sew. **~se** *vpr* stick to s.o. **eso es ~ y cantar** it's as easy as pie

cosmético *a* & *m* cosmetic

cósmico *a* cosmic

cosmonauta *m* & *f* cosmonaut

cosmopolita *a* & *m* & *f* cosmopolitan

cosmos *m* cosmos

cosquillas *fpl* ticklishness. **buscar a uno las ~** provoke s.o. **hacer ~** tickle. **tener ~** be ticklish

costa *f* coast. **a ~ de** at the expense of. **a toda ~** at any cost

costado *m* side

costal *m* sack

costar [2] *vt/i* cost. **~ caro** be expensive. **cueste lo que cueste** at any cost

Costa Rica *f* Costa Rica

costarricense *a* & *m*, **costarriqueño** *a* & *m* Costa Rican

coste *m* cost. **~ar** *vt* pay for; (*naut*) sail along the coast

costero *a* coastal

costilla *f* rib; (*chuleta*) chop

costo *m* cost. **~so** *a* expensive

costumbre *f* custom, habit. **de ~** *a* usual. ● *adv* usually

costur|a *f* sewing; (*línea*) seam; (*confección*) dressmaking. **~era** *f* dressmaker. **~ero** *m* sewing box

cotejar *vt* compare

cotidiano *a* daily

cotille|ar *vt* gossip. **~o** *m* gossip

cotiza|ción *f* quotation, price. **~r** [10] *vt* (*en la bolsa*) quote. ● *vi* pay one's subscription. **~rse** *vpr* fetch; (*en la bolsa*) stand at; (*fig*) be valued

coto *m* enclosure; (*de caza*) preserve. **~ de caza** game preserve

cotorr|a *f* parrot; (*urraca*) magpie; (*fig*) chatterbox. **~ear** *vi* chatter

coyuntura *f* joint; (*oportunidad*) opportunity; (*situación*) situation; (*circunstancia*) occasion, juncture

coz *f* kick

cráneo *m* skull

cráter *m* crater

crea|ción *f* creation. **~dor** *a* creative. ● *m* creator. **~r** *vt* create

crec|er [11] *vi* grow; (*aumentar*) increase. **~ida** *f* (*de río*) flood. **~ido** *a* ‹*persona*› grown-up; ‹*número*› large, considerable; ‹*plantas*› fully-grown. **~iente** *a* growing; ‹*luna*› crescent. **~imiento** *m* growth

credencial *a* credential. **~es** *fpl* credentials

credibilidad *f* credibility

crédito *m* credit. **digno de ~** reliable, trustworthy

credo *m* creed. **en un ~** in a flash

crédulo *a* credulous

cre|encia *f* belief. **~er** [18] believe; (*pensar*) think. **~o que no** I don't think so, I think not. **~o que sí** I think so. ● *vi* believe. **~erse** *vpr* consider o.s. **no me lo ~o** I don't believe it. **~íble** *a* credible. **¡ya lo ~o!** I should think so!

crema *f* cream; (*culin*) custard. **~ bronceadora** sun-tan cream

cremación *f* cremation; (*de basura*) incineration

cremallera *f* zip, zipper (*Amer*)

crematorio *m* crematorium; (*de basura*) incinerator

crepitar *vi* crackle

crepúsculo *m* twilight

crescendo *m* crescendo

cresp|o *a* frizzy. **~ón** *m* crêpe

cresta *f* crest; (*tupé*) toupee; (*geog*) ridge

Creta *f* Crete

cretino *m* cretin

creyente *m* believer

cría *f* breeding; (*animal*) baby animal
cria|da *f* maid, servant. **~dero** *m* nursery. **~do** *a* brought up. ● *m* servant. **~dor** *m* breeder. **~nza** *f* breeding. **~r** [20] *vt* suckle; grow ‹*plantas*›; breed ‹*animales*›; (*educar*) bring up. **~rse** *vpr* grow up
criatura *f* creature; (*niño*) baby
crim|en *m* crime. **~inal** *a & m & f* criminal
crin *m* mane; (*relleno*) horsehair
crinolina *f* crinoline
crío *m* child
criollo *a & m* Creole
cripta *f* crypt
crisantemo *m* chrysanthemum
crisis *f* crisis
crisol *m* melting-pot
crispar *vt* twitch; (*irritar, fam*) annoy. **~ los nervios a uno** get on s.o.'s nerves
cristal *m* crystal; (*vidrio*) glass; (*de una ventana*) pane of glass. **~ de aumento** magnifying glass. **~ino** *a* crystalline; (*fig*) crystal-clear. **~izar** [10] crystallize. **limpiar los ~es** clean the windows
cristian|amente *adv* in a Christian way. **~dad** *f* Christianity. **~ismo** *m* Christianity. **~o** *a & m* Christian
Cristo *m* Christ
cristo *m* crucifix
criterio *m* criterion; (*opinión*) opinion
cr|ítica *f* criticism; (*reseña*) review. **~iticar** [7] *vt* criticize. **~ítico** *a* critical. ● *m* critic
croar *vi* croak
crom|ado *a* chromium-plated. **~o** *m* chromium, chrome
cromosoma *m* chromosome
crónic|a *f* chronicle; (*de periódico*) news. **~o** *a* chronic
cronista *m & f* reporter
cronol|ogía *f* chronology. **~ógico** *a* chronological
cron|ometraje *m* timing. **~ometrar** *vt* time. **~ómetro** *m* chronometer; (*en deportes*) stop-watch
croquet /'kroket/ *m* croquet
croqueta *f* croquette
cruce *m* crossing; (*de calles, de carreteras*) crossroads; (*de peatones*) (pedestrian) crossing
crucial *a* cross-shaped; (*fig*) crucial
crucifi|car [7] *vt* crucify. **~jo** *m* crucifix. **~xión** *f* crucifiction
crucigrama *m* crossword (puzzle)
crudo *a* raw; (*fig*) crude. **petróleo** *m* **~** crude oil
cruel *a* cruel. **~dad** *f* cruelty
cruji|do *m* (*de seda, de hojas secas etc*) rustle; (*de muebles etc*) creak. **~r** *vi* ‹*seda, hojas secas etc*› rustle; ‹*muebles etc*› creak
cruz *f* cross; (*de moneda*) tails. **~ gamada** swastika. **la C~ Roja** the Red Cross
cruzada *f* crusade
cruzar [10] *vt* cross; (*poner de un lado a otro*) lay across. **~se** *vpr* cross; (*pasar en la calle*) pass
cuaderno *m* exercise book; (*para apuntes*) notebook
cuadra *f* (*caballeriza*) stable; (*LAm, manzana*) block
cuadrado *a & m* square
cuadragésimo *a* fortieth
cuadr|ar *vt* square. ● *vi* suit; (*estar de acuerdo*) agree. **~arse** *vpr* (*mil*) stand to attention; (*fig*) dig one's heels in. **~ilátero** *a* quadrilateral. ● *m* quadrilateral; (*boxeo*) ring
cuadrilla *f* group; (*pandilla*) gang
cuadro *m* square; (*pintura*) painting; (*de obra de teatro, escena*) scene; (*de jardín*) bed; (*de números*) table; (*de mando etc*) panel; (*conjunto del personal*) staff. **~ de distribución** switchboard. **a ~s, de ~s** check. **en ~** in a square. **¡qué ~!, ¡vaya un ~!** what a sight!
cuadrúpedo *m* quadruped
cuádruple *a & m* quadruple
cuajar *vt* thicken; clot ‹*sangre*›; curdle ‹*leche*›; (*llenar*) fill up. ● *vi* ‹*nieve*› settle; (*fig, fam*) work out. **cuajado de** full of. **~se** *vpr* coagulate; ‹*sangre*› clot; ‹*leche*› curdle. **~ón** *m* clot
cual *pron*. **el ~, la ~ etc** (*animales y cosas*) that, which; (*personas, sujeto*) who, that; (*personas, objeto*) whom. ● *adv* as, like. ● *a* such as. **~ si** as if. **~... tal** like... like. **cada ~** everyone. **por lo ~** because of which
cuál *pron* which
cualidad *f* quality; (*propiedad*) property
cualquiera *a* (*delante de nombres* **cualquier**, *pl* **cualesquiera**) any. ● *pron* (*pl* **cualesquiera**) anyone, anybody; (*cosas*) whatever, whichever. **un ~** a nobody
cuando *adv* when. ● *conj* when; (*aunque*) even if. **~ más** at the most.

~ menos at the least. **~ no** if not. **aun ~** even if. **de ~ en ~** from time to time

cuándo *adv & conj* when. **¿de ~ acá?**, **¿desde ~?** since when?

cuant|ía *f* quantity; (*extensión*) extent. **~ioso** *a* abundant

cuanto *a* as much... as, as many... as. ● *pron* as much as, as many as. ● *adv* as much as. **~ más, mejor** the more the merrier. **en ~** as soon as. **en ~ a** as for. **por ~** since. **unos ~s** a few, some

cuánto *a* (*interrogativo*) how much?; (*interrogativo en plural*) how many?; (*exclamativo*) what a lot of! ● *pron* how much?; (*en plural*) how many? ● *adv* how much. **¿~ tiempo?** how long? **¡~ tiempo sin verte!** it's been a long time! **¿a ~?** how much? **¿a ~s estamos?** what's the date today? **un Sr. no sé ~s** Mr So-and-So

cuáquero *m* Quaker

cuarent|a *a & m* forty; (*cuadragésimo*) fortieth. **~ena** *f* (about) forty; (*med*) quarantine. **~ón** *a* about forty

cuaresma *f* Lent

cuarta *f* (*palmo*) span

cuartear *vt* quarter, divide into four; (*zigzaguear*) zigzag. **~se** *vpr* crack

cuartel *m* (*mil*) barracks. **~ general** headquarters. **no dar ~** show no mercy

cuarteto *m* quartet

cuarto *a* fourth. ● *m* quarter; (*habitación*) room. **~ de baño** bathroom. **~ de estar** living room. **~ de hora** quarter of an hour. **estar sin un ~** be broke. **menos ~** (a) quarter to. **y ~** (a) quarter past

cuarzo *m* quartz

cuatro *a & m* four. **~cientos** *a & m* four hundred

Cuba *f* Cuba

cuba: ~libre *m* rum and Coke (P). **~no** *a & m* Cuban

cúbico *a* cubic

cubículo *m* cubicle

cubiert|a *f* cover, covering; (*de la cama*) bedspread; (*techo*) roof; (*neumático*) tyre; (*naut*) deck. **~o** *a* covered; ‹*cielo*› overcast. ● *m* place setting, cutlery; (*comida*) meal. **a ~o** under cover. **a ~o de** safe from

cubis|mo *m* cubism. **~ta** *a & m & f* cubist

cubil *m* den, lair. **~ete** *m* bowl; (*molde*) mould; (*para echar los dados*) cup

cubo *m* bucket; (*en geometría y matemáticas*) cube

cubrecama *m* bedspread

cubrir *vt* [*pp* **cubierto**] cover; ‹*sonido*› drown; fill ‹*vacante*›. **~se** *vpr* cover o.s.; (*ponerse el sombrero*) put on one's hat; ‹*el cielo*› cloud over, become overcast

cucaracha *f* cockcroach

cuclillas. en ~ *adv* squatting

cuclillo *m* cuckoo

cuco *a* shrewd; (*mono*) pretty, nice. ● *m* cuckoo; (*insecto*) grub

cucurucho *m* cornet

cuchar|a *f* spoon. **~ada** *f* spoonful. **~adita** *f* teaspoonful. **~illa** *f*, **~ita** *f* teaspoon. **~ón** *m* ladle

cuchiche|ar *vi* whisper. **~o** *m* whispering

cuchill|a *f* large knife; (*de carnicero*) cleaver; (*hoja de afeitar*) razor blade. **~ada** *f* slash; (*herida*) knife wound. **~o** *m* knife

cuchitril *m* pigsty; (*fig*) hovel

cuello *m* neck; (*de camisa*) collar. **cortar el ~ a uno** cut s.o.'s throat

cuenc|a *f* hollow; (*del ojo*) (eye) socket; (*geog*) basin. **~o** *m* hollow; (*vasija*) bowl

cuenta *f* count; (*acción de contar*) counting; (*factura*) bill; (*en banco, relato*) account; (*asunto*) affair; (*de collar etc*) bead. **~ corriente** current account, checking account (*Amer*). **ajustar las ~s** settle accounts. **caer en la ~ de que** realize that. **darse ~ de** realize. **en resumidas ~s** in short. **por mi ~** for myself. **tener en ~, tomar en ~** bear in mind

cuentakilómetros *m invar* milometer

cuent|ista *m & f* story-writer; (*de mentiras*) fibber. **~o** *m* story; (*mentira*) fib, tall story. ● *vb véase* **contar**

cuerda *f* rope; (*más fina*) string; (*mus*) string. **~ floja** tightrope. **dar ~ a** wind up ‹*un reloj*›

cuerdo *a* ‹*persona*› sane; ‹*acción*› sensible

cuern|a *f* horns. **~o** *m* horn

cuero *m* leather; (*piel*) skin; (*del grifo*) washer. **~ cabelludo** scalp. **en ~s (vivos)** stark naked

cuerpo *m* body

cuervo *m* crow

cuesta *f* slope, hill. **~ abajo** downhill. **~ arriba** uphill. **a ~s** on one's back

cuesti|ón *f* matter; (*altercado*) quarrel; (*dificultad*) trouble. **~onario** *m* questionnaire

cueva *f* cave; (*sótano*) cellar

cuida|do *m* care; (*preocupación*) worry; (*asunto*) affair. **¡~do!** (be) careful! **~doso** *a* careful. **~dosamente** *adv* carefully. **~r** *vt* look after. ● *vi*. **~r de** look after. **~rse** *vpr* look after o.s. **~rse de** be careful to. **tener ~do** be careful

culata *f* (*de arma de fuego*) butt; (*auto*) cylinder head. **~zo** *m* recoil

culebra *f* snake

culebrón *m* (*LAm*) soap opera

culinario *a* culinary

culmina|ción *f* culmination. **~r** *vi* culminate

culo *m* (*fam*) bottom. **ir de ~** go downhill

culpa *f* fault; (*jurid*) guilt. **~bilidad** *f* guilt. **~ble** *a* guilty. ● *m* culprit. **~r** *vt* blame (**de** for). **echar la ~** blame. **por ~ de** because of. **tener la ~ de** be to blame for

cultiv|ar *vt* farm; grow ‹*plantas*›; (*fig*) cultivate. **~o** *m* farming; (*de plantas*) growing

cult|o *a* ‹*tierra etc*› cultivated; ‹*persona*› educated. ● *m* cult; (*homenaje*) worship. **~ura** *f* culture. **~ural** *a* cultural

culturismo *m* body-building

cumbre *f* summit; (*fig*) height

cumpleaños *m invar* birthday

cumplido *a* perfect; (*grande*) large; (*cortés*) polite. ● *m* compliment. **~r** *a* reliable. **de ~** courtesy. **por ~** out of politeness

cumplim|entar *vt* carry out; (*saludar*) pay a courtesy call to; (*felicitar*) congratulate. **~iento** *m* carrying out, execution

cumplir *vt* carry out; observe ‹*ley*›; serve ‹*condena*›; reach ‹*años*›; keep ‹*promesa*›. ● *vi* do one's duty. **~se** *vpr* expire; (*realizarse*) be fulfilled. **hoy cumple 3 años** he's 3 (years old) today. **por ~** as a mere formality

cumulativo *a* cumulative

cúmulo *m* pile, heap

cuna *f* cradle; (*fig, nacimiento*) birthplace

cundir *vi* spread; (*rendir*) go a long way

cuneta *f* gutter

cuña *f* wedge

cuñad|a *f* sister-in-law. **~o** *m* brother-in-law

cuño *m* stamp. **de nuevo ~** new

cuota *f* quota; (*de sociedad etc*) subscription, fees

cupe *vb véase* **caber**

cupé *m* coupé

Cupido *m* Cupid

cupo *m* cuota

cupón *m* coupon

cúpula *f* dome

cura *f* cure; (*tratamiento*) treatment. ● *m* priest. **~ble** *a* curable. **~ción** *f* healing. **~ndero** *m* faith-healer. **~r** *vt* (*incl culin*) cure; dress ‹*herida*›; (*tratar*) treat; (*fig*) remedy; tan ‹*pieles*›. ● *vi* ‹*persona*› get better; ‹*herida*› heal; (*fig*) be cured. **~rse** *vpr* get better

curios|ear *vi* pry; (*mirar*) browse. **~idad** *f* curiosity; (*limpieza*) cleanliness. **~o** *a* curious; (*raro*) odd, unusual; (*limpio*) clean

curriculum vitae *m* curriculum vitae

cursar *vt* send; (*estudiar*) study

cursi *a* pretentious, showy. ● *m* affected person

cursillo *m* short course

cursiva *f* italics

curso *m* course; (*univ etc*) year. **en ~** under way; ‹*año etc*› current

curtir *vt* tan; (*fig*) harden. **~se** *vpr* become tanned; (*fig*) become hardened

curv|a *f* curve; (*de carretera*) bend. **~o** *a* curved

cúspide *f* peak

custodi|a *f* care, safe-keeping. **~ar** *vt* take care of. **~o** *a & m* guardian

cutáneo *a* skin. **enfermedad** *f* **cutánea** skin disease

cutícula *f* cuticle

cutis *m* skin, complexion

cuyo *pron* (*de persona*) whose, of whom; (*de cosa*) whose, of which. **en ~ caso** in which case

CH

chabacano *a* common; ‹*chiste etc*› vulgar. ● *m* (*Mex, albaricoque*) apricot

chabola *f* shack. **~s** *fpl* shanty town

chacal *m* jackal

chacota *f* fun. **echar a ~** make fun of

chacra *f* (*LAm*) farm
cháchara *f* chatter
chacharear *vt* (*Mex*) sell. ● *vi* chatter
chafar *vt* crush. **quedar chafado** be nonplussed
chal *m* shawl
chalado *a* (*fam*) crazy
chalé *m* house (with a garden), villa
chaleco *m* waistcoat, vest (*Amer*). ~ **salvavidas** life-jacket
chalequear *vt* (*Arg*, *Mex*) trick
chalet *m* (*pl* **chalets**) house (with a garden), villa
chalón *m* (*LAm*) shawl
chalote *m* shallot
chalupa *f* boat
chamac|a *f* (*esp Mex*) girl. **~o** *m* (*esp Mex*) boy
chamagoso *a* (*Mex*) filthy
chamarr|a *f* sheepskin jacket. **~o** *m* (*LAm*) coarse blanket
chamba *f* (*fam*) fluke; (*Mex*, *empleo*) job. **por ~** by fluke
champán *m*, **champaña** *m* champagne
champiñón *m* mushroom
champú *m* (*pl* **champúes** *o* **champús**) shampoo
chamuscar [7] *vt* scorch; (*Mex*, *vender*) sell cheaply
chance *m* (*esp LAm*) chance
chanclo *m* clog; (*de caucho*) rubber overshoe
chancho *m* (*LAm*) pig
chanchullo *m* swindle, fiddle (*fam*)
chandal *m* tracksuit
chanquete *m* whitebait
chantaj|e *m* blackmail. **~ista** *m & f* blackmailer
chanza *f* joke
chapa *f* plate, sheet; (*de madera*) plywood; (*de botella*) metal top. **~do** *a* plated. **~do a la antigua** old-fashioned. **~do de oro** gold-plated
chaparrón *m* downpour. **llover a chaparrones** pour (down), rain cats and dogs
chapotear *vi* splash
chapuce|ar *vt* botch; (*Mex*, *engañar*) deceive. **~ro** *a* ‹*persona*› careless; ‹*cosas*› shoddy. ● *m* careless worker
chapurrar *vt*, **chapurrear** *vt* speak badly, speak a little; mix ‹*licores*›
chapuza *f* botched job, mess; (*de poca importancia*) odd job
chaqueta *f* jacket. **cambiar la ~** change sides
chaquetero *m* turncoat
charada *f* charade
charc|a *f* pond, pool. **~o** *m* puddle, pool. **cruzar el ~o** cross the water; (*ir a América*) cross the Atlantic
charla *f* chat; (*conferencia*) talk. **~dor** *a* talkative. **~r** *vi* (*fam*) chat
charlatán *a* talkative. ● *m* chatterbox; (*curandero*) charlatan
charol *m* varnish; (*cuero*) patent leather
chárter *a* charter
chascar [7] *vt* crack ‹*látigo*›; click ‹*lengua*›; snap ‹*dedos*›. ● *vi* ‹*látigo*› crack; (*con la lengua*) click one's tongue; ‹*los dedos*› snap
chascarrillo *m* joke, funny story
chasco *m* disappointment; (*broma*) joke; (*engaño*) trick
chasis *m* (*auto*) chassis
chasqu|ear *vt* crack ‹*látigo*›; click ‹*lengua*›; snap ‹*dedos*›. ● *vi* ‹*látigo*› crack; (*con la lengua*) click one's tongue; ‹*los dedos*› snap. **~ido** *m* crack; (*de la lengua*) click; (*de los dedos*) snap
chatarra *f* scrap iron; (*fig*) scrap
chato *a* ‹*nariz*› snub; ‹*persona*› snub-nosed; ‹*objetos*› flat. ● *m* wine glass; (*niño*, *mujer*, *fam*) dear, darling; (*hombre*, *fam*) mate (*fam*)
chaval *m* (*fam*) boy, lad. **~a** *f* girl, lass
che *int* (*Arg*) listen!, hey!
checo *a & m* Czech. **la república** *f* **Checa** the Czech Republic
checoslovaco *a & m* (*history*) Czechoslovak
Checoslovaquia *f* (*history*) Czechoslovakia
chelín *m* shilling
chelo *a* (*Mex*, *rubio*) fair
cheque *m* cheque. **~ de viaje** traveller's cheque. **~ra** *f* cheque-book
chica *f* girl; (*criada*) maid, servant
chicano *a & m* Chicano, Mexican-American
chicle *m* chewing-gum
chico *a* (*fam*) small. ● *m* boy. **~s** *mpl* children
chicoleo *m* compliment
chicoria *f* chicory
chicharra *f* cicada; (*fig*) chatterbox
chicharrón *m* (*de cerdo*) crackling; (*fig*) sunburnt person
chichón *m* bump, lump
chifla|do *a* (*fam*) crazy, daft. **~r** *vt* (*fam*) drive crazy. **~rse** *vpr* be mad (**por** about). **le chifla el chocolate**

he's mad about chocolate. **le tiene chiflado esa chica** he's crazy about that girl
Chile *m* Chile
chile *m* chilli
chileno *a & m* Chilean
chill|ar *vi* scream, shriek; ‹*gato*› howl; ‹*ratón*› squeak; ‹*cerdo*› squeal. **~ido** *m* scream, screech; (*de gato etc*) howl. **~ón** *a* noisy; ‹*colores*› loud; ‹*sonido*› shrill
chimenea *f* chimney; (*hogar*) fireplace
chimpancé *m* chimpanzee
China *f* China
chinch|ar *vt* (*fam*) annoy, pester. **~e** *m* drawing-pin (*Brit*), thumbtack (*Amer*); (*insecto*) bedbug; (*fig*) nuisance. **~eta** *f* drawing-pin (*Brit*), thumbtack (*Amer*)
chinela *f* slipper
chino *a & m* Chinese
Chipre *m* Cyprus
chipriota *a & m & f* Cypriot
chiquillo *a* childish. ● *m* child, kid (*fam*)
chiquito *a* small, tiny. ● *m* child, kid (*fam*)
chiribita *f* spark. **estar que echa ~s** be furious
chirimoya *f* custard apple
chiripa *f* fluke. **por ~** by fluke
chirivía *f* parsnip
chirri|ar *vi* creak; ‹*pájaro*› chirp. **~do** *m* creaking; (*al freír*) sizzling; (*de pájaros*) chirping
chis *int* sh!, hush!; (*para llamar a uno, fam*) hey!, psst!
chism|e *m* gadget, thingumajig (*fam*); (*chismorreo*) piece of gossip. **~es** *mpl* things, bits and pieces. **~orreo** *m* gossip. **~oso** *a* gossipy. ● *m* gossip
chispa *f* spark; (*gota*) drop; (*gracia*) wit; (*fig*) sparkle. **estar que echa ~(s)** be furious
chispea|nte *a* sparkling. **~r** *vi* spark; (*lloviznar*) drizzle; (*fig*) sparkle
chisporrotear *vt* throw out sparks; ‹*fuego*› crackle; ‹*aceite*› sizzle
chistar *vi* speak. **sin ~** without saying a word
chiste *m* joke, funny story. **hacer ~ de** make fun of. **tener ~** be funny
chistera *f* (*fam*) top hat, topper (*fam*)
chistoso *a* funny
chiva|r *vi* inform ‹*policía*›; ‹*niño*› tell. **~tazo** *m* tip-off. **~to** *m* informer; (*niño*) telltale
chivo *m* kid, young goat
choca|nte *a* surprising; ‹*persona*› odd. **~r** [7] *vt* clink ‹*vasos*›; shake ‹*la mano*›. ● *vi* collide, hit. **~r con**, **~r contra** crash into. **lo ~nte es que** the surprising thing is that
chocolate *m* chocolate. **tableta** *f* **de ~** bar of chocolate
choch|ear *vi* be senile. **~o** *a* senile; (*fig*) soft
chófer *m* chauffeur; (*conductor*) driver
cholo *a & m* (*LAm*) half-breed
chopo *m* poplar
choque *m* collision; (*fig*) clash; (*eléctrico*) shock; (*auto, rail etc*) crash, accident; (*sacudida*) jolt
chorizo *m* salami
chorr|ear *vi* gush forth; (*fig*) be dripping. **~o** *m* jet, stream; (*caudal pequeño*) trickle; (*fig*) stream. **a ~os** (*fig*) in abundance. **hablar a ~os** jabber
chovinis|mo *m* chauvinism. **~ta** *a* chauvinistic. ● *m & f* chauvinist
choza *f* hut
chubas|co *m* squall, heavy shower; (*fig*) bad patch. **~quero** *m* raincoat, anorak
chuchería *f* trinket; (*culin*) sweet
chufa *f* tiger nut
chuleta *f* chop
chulo *a* insolent; (*vistoso*) showy. ● *m* ruffian; (*rufián*) pimp
chumbo *m* prickly pear; (*fam*) bump. **higo** *m* **~** prickly pear
chup|ada *f* suck; (*al cigarro etc*) puff. **~ado** *a* skinny; (*fácil, fam*) very easy. **~ar** *vt* suck, lick; puff at ‹*cigarro etc*›; (*absorber*) absorb. **~arse** *vpr* lose weight. **~ete** *m* dummy (*Brit*), pacifier (*Amer*)
churro *m* fritter; (*fam*) mess. **me salió un ~** I made a mess of it
chusco *a* funny
chusma *f* riff-raff
chutar *vi* shoot. **¡va que chuta!** it's going well!

D

dactilógrafo *m* typist
dado *m* dice. ● *a* given; ‹*hora*› gone. **~ que** since, given that
dalia *f* dahlia
daltoniano *a* colour-blind

dama *f* lady; (*en la corte*) lady-in-waiting. **~s** *fpl* draughts (*Brit*), checkers (*Amer*)
damasco *m* damask
danés *a* Danish. ● *m* Dane; (*idioma*) Danish
danza *f* dance; (*acción*) dancing; (*enredo*) affair. **~r** [10] *vt/i* dance
dañ|ado *a* damaged. **~ar** *vt* damage; harm ‹*persona*›. **~ino** *a* harmful. **~o** *m* damage; (*a una persona*) harm. **~oso** *a* harmful. **~os y perjuicios** damages. **hacer ~o a** harm; hurt ‹*persona*›. **hacerse ~o** hurt o.s.
dar [26] *vt* give; (*producir*) yield; strike ‹*la hora*›. ● *vi* give. **da igual** it doesn't matter. **¡dale!** go on! **da lo mismo** it doesn't matter. **~ a** ‹*ventana*› look on to; ‹*edificio*› face. **~ a luz** give birth. **~ con** meet ‹*persona*›; find ‹*cosa*›; **~ de cabeza** fall flat on one's face. **~ por** assume; (+ *infinitivo*) decide. **~se** *vpr* give o.s. up; (*suceder*) happen. **dárselas de** make o.s. out to be. **~se por** consider o.s. **¿qué más da?** it doesn't matter!
dardo *m* dart
dársena *f* dock
datar *vt* date. ● *vi*. **~ de** date from
dátil *m* date
dato *m* fact. **~s** *mpl* data, information
de *prep* of; (*procedencia*) from; (*suposición*) if. **~ día** by day. **~ dos en dos** two by two. **~ haberlo sabido** if I (you, he etc) had known. **~ niño** as a child. **el libro ~ mi amigo** my friend's book. **las 2 ~ la madrugada** 2 (o'clock) in the morning. **un puente ~ hierro** an iron bridge. **soy ~ Loughborough** I'm from Loughborough
deambular *vi* stroll
debajo *adv* underneath. **~ de** underneath, under. **el de ~** the one underneath. **por ~** underneath. **por ~ de** below
debat|e *m* debate. **~ir** *vt* debate
deber *vt* owe. ● *vi* have to, must. ● *m* duty. **~es** *mpl* homework. **~se** *vpr*. **~se a** be due to. **debo marcharme** I must go, I have to go
debido *a* due; (*correcto*) proper. **~ a** due to. **como es ~** as is proper. **con el respeto ~** with due respect
débil *a* weak; ‹*ruido*› faint; ‹*luz*› dim
debili|dad *f* weakness. **~tar** *vt* weaken. **~tarse** *vpr* weaken, get weak
débito *m* debit; (*deuda*) debt
debutar *vi* make one's debut
década *f* decade
deca|dencia *f* decline. **~dente** *a* decadent. **~er** [29] *vi* decline; (*debilitarse*) weaken. **~ído** *a* depressed. **~imiento** *m* decline, weakening
decano *m* dean; (*miembro más antiguo*) senior member
decantar *vt* decant ‹*vino etc*›
decapitar *vt* behead
decena *f* ten; (*aproximadamente*) about ten
decencia *f* decency, honesty
decenio *m* decade
decente *a* ‹*persona*› respectable, honest; ‹*cosas*› modest; (*limpio*) clean, tidy
decepci|ón *f* disappointment. **~onar** *vt* disappoint
decibelio *m* decibel
decidi|do *a* decided; ‹*persona*› determined, resolute. **~r** *vt* decide; settle ‹*cuestión etc*›. ● *vi* decide. **~rse** *vpr* make up one's mind
decimal *a* & *m* decimal
décimo *a* & *m* tenth. ● *m* (*de lotería*) tenth part of a lottery ticket
decimo: ~ctavo *a* & *m* eighteenth. **~cuarto** *a* & *m* fourteenth. **~nono** *a* & *m*, **~noveno** *a* & *m* nineteenth. **~quinto** *a* & *m* fifteenth. **~séptimo** *a* & *m* seventeenth. **~sexto** *a* & *m* sixteenth. **~tercero** *a* & *m*, **~tercio** *a* & *m* thirteenth
decir [46] *vt* say; (*contar*) tell. ● *m* saying. **~se** *vpr* be said. **~ que no** say no. **~ que sí** say yes. **dicho de otro modo** in other words. **dicho y hecho** no sooner said than done. **¿dígame?** can I help you? **¡dígame!** (*al teléfono*) hello! **digamos** let's say. **es ~** that is to say. **mejor dicho** rather. **¡no me digas!** you don't say!, really! **por así ~, por ~lo así** so to speak, as it were. **querer ~** mean. **se dice que** it is said that, they say that
decisi|ón *f* decision. **~vo** *a* decisive
declamar *vt* declaim
declara|ción *f* statement. **~ción de renta** income tax return. **~r** *vt/i* declare. **~rse** *vpr* declare o.s.; (*epidemia etc*) break out
declina|ción *f* (*gram*) declension. **~r** *vt/i* decline; ‹*salud*› deteriorate

declive *m* slope; (*fig*) decline. **en ~** sloping
decolorar *vt* discolour, fade. **~se** *vpr* become discoloured, fade
decora|ción *f* decoration. **~do** *m* (*en el teatro*) set. **~dor** *m* decorator. **~r** *vt* decorate. **~tivo** *a* decorative
decoro *m* decorum; (*respeto*) respect. **~so** *a* proper; (*modesto*) modest; ‹*profesión*› honourable
decrecer [11] *vi* decrease, diminish; ‹*aguas*› subside
decrépito *a* decrepit
decret|ar *vt* decree. **~o** *m* decree
dedal *m* thimble
dedica|ción *f* dedication. **~r** [7] *vt* dedicate; devote ‹*tiempo*›. **~toria** *f* dedication, inscription
ded|il *m* finger-stall. **~illo** *m*. **al ~illo** at one's fingertips. **~o** *m* finger; (*del pie*) toe. **~o anular** ring finger. **~ corazón** middle finger. **~o gordo** thumb. **~o índice** index finger. **~o meñique** little finger. **~o pulgar** thumb
deduc|ción *f* deduction. **~ir** [47] *vt* deduce; (*descontar*) deduct
defect|o *m* fault, defect. **~uoso** *a* defective
defen|der [1] *vt* defend. **~sa** *f* defence. **~sivo** *a* defensive. **~sor** *m* defender. **abogado** *m* **~sor** defence counsel
deferen|cia *f* deference. **~te** *a* deferential
deficien|cia *f* deficiency. **~cia mental** mental handicap. **~te** *a* deficient; (*imperfecto*) defective. **~te mental** mentally handicapped
déficit *m invar* deficit
defini|ción *f* definition. **~do** *a* defined. **~r** *vt* define; (*aclarar*) clarify. **~tivo** *a* definitive. **en ~tiva** (*en resumen*) in short
deflación *f* deflation
deform|ación *f* deformation; (*TV etc*) distortion. **~ar** *vt* deform; (*TV etc*) distort. **~arse** *vpr* go out of shape. **~e** *a* deformed; (*feo*) ugly
defraudar *vt* cheat; (*decepcionar*) disappoint; evade ‹*impuestos etc*›
defunción *f* death
degenera|ción *f* degeneration; (*moral*) degeneracy. **~do** *a* degenerate. **~r** *vi* degenerate
deglutir *vt/i* swallow
degollar [16] *vt* cut s.o.'s throat; (*fig, arruinar*) ruin
degradar *vt* degrade. **~se** *vpr* lower o.s.
degusta|ción *f* tasting. **~r** *vt* taste
dehesa *f* pasture
dei|dad *f* deity. **~ficar** [7] *vt* deify
deja|ción *f* surrender. **~dez** *f* abandon; (*pereza*) laziness. **~do** *a* negligent. **~r** *vt* leave; (*abandonar*) abandon; (*prestar*) lend; (*permitir*) let. **~r aparte**, **~r a un lado** leave aside. **~r de** stop. **no ~r de** not fail to
dejo *m* aftertaste; (*tonillo*) accent
del = **de**; **el**
delantal *m* apron
delante *adv* in front; (*enfrente*) opposite. **~ de** in front of. **de ~** front
delanter|a *f* front; (*de teatro etc*) front row; (*ventaja*) advantage. **coger la ~a** get ahead. **~o** *a* front. • *m* forward. **llevar la ~a** be ahead
delat|ar *vt* denounce. **~or** *m* informer
delega|ción *f* delegation; (*sucursal*) branch. **~do** *m* delegate; (*com*) agent, representative. **~r** [12] *vt* delegate
deleit|ar *vt* delight. **~e** *m* delight
deletéreo *a* deleterious
deletre|ar *vt* spell (out). **~o** *m* spelling
deleznable *a* brittle, crumbly; ‹*argumento etc*› weak
delfín *m* dolphin
delgad|ez *f* thinness. **~o** *a* thin; (*esbelto*) slim. **~ucho** *a* skinny
delibera|ción *f* deliberation. **~r** *vt* discuss, decide. • *vi* deliberate
delicad|eza *f* delicacy; (*fragilidad*) frailty; (*tacto*) tact. **~o** *a* delicate; (*sensible* sensitive; (*discreto*) tactful, discreet. **falta de ~eza** tactlessness
delici|a *f* delight. **~oso** *a* delightful; ‹*sabor etc*› delicious; (*gracioso, fam*) funny
delimitar *vt* delimit
delincuen|cia *f* delinquency. **~te** *a & m* delinquent
delinea|nte *m* draughtsman. **~r** *vt* outline; (*dibujar*) draw
delinquir [8] *vi* commit an offence
delir|ante *a* delirious. **~ar** *vi* be delirious; (*fig*) talk nonsense. **~io** *m* delirium; (*fig*) frenzy
delito *m* crime, offence
delta *f* delta
demacrado *a* emaciated

demagogo *m* demagogue

demanda *f*. **en ~ de** asking for; (*en busca de*) in search of. **~nte** *m & f* (*jurid*) plaintiff. **~r** *vt* (*jurid*) bring an action against

demarca|ción *f* demarcation. **~r** [7] *vt* demarcate

demás *a* rest of the, other. ● *pron* rest, others. **lo ~** the rest. **por ~** useless; (*muy*) very. **por lo ~** otherwise

demasía *f* excess; (*abuso*) outrage; (*atrevimiento*) insolence. **en ~** too much

demasiado *a* too much; (*en plural*) too many. ● *adv* too much; (*con adjetivo*) too

demen|cia *f* madness. **~te** *a* demented, mad

dem|ocracia *f* democracy. **~ócrata** *m & f* democrat. **~ocrático** *a* democratic

demol|er [2] *vt* demolish. **~ición** *f* demolition

demonio *m* devil, demon. **¡~s!** hell! **¿cómo ~s?** how the hell? **¡qué ~s!** what the hell!

demora *f* delay. **~r** *vt* delay. ● *vi* stay on. **~rse** *vpr* be a long time

demostra|ción *f* demonstration, show. **~r** [2] *vt* demonstrate; (*mostrar*) show; (*probar*) prove. **~tivo** *a* demonstrative

denegar [1 & 12] *vt* refuse

deng|oso *a* affected, finicky. **~ue** *m* affectation

denigrar *vt* denigrate

denomina|ción *f* denomination. **~do** *a* called. **~dor** *m* denominator. **~r** *vt* name

denotar *vt* denote

dens|idad *f* density. **~o** *a* dense, thick

denta|dura *f* teeth. **~dura postiza** denture, false teeth. **~l** *a* dental

dentera *f*. **dar ~ a uno** set s.o.'s teeth on edge; (*dar envidia*) make s.o. green with envy

dentífrico *m* toothpaste

dentista *m & f* dentist

dentro *adv* inside; (*de un edificio*) indoors. **~ de** in. **~ de poco** soon. **por ~** inside

denuncia *f* report; (*acusación*) accusation. **~r** *vt* report (a crime); ‹*periódico etc*› denounce; (*indicar*) indicate

departamento *m* department; (*Arg, piso*) flat (*Brit*), apartment (*Amer*)

dependencia *f* dependence; (*sección*) section; (*sucursal*) branch

depender *vi* depend (**de** on)

dependient|a *f* shop assistant. **~e** *a* dependent (**de** on). ● *m* employee; (*de oficina*) clerk; (*de tienda*) shop assistant

depila|ción *f* depilation. **~r** *vt* depilate. **~torio** *a* depilatory

deplora|ble *a* deplorable. **~r** *vt* deplore, regret

deponer [34] *vt* remove from office. ● *vi* give evidence

deporta|ción *f* deportation. **~r** *vt* deport

deport|e *m* sport. **~ista** *m* sportsman. ● *f* sportswoman. **~ivo** *a* sports. ● *m* sports car. **hacer ~e** take part in sports

deposición *f* deposition; (*de un empleo*) removal from office

dep|ositador *m* depositor. **~ositante** *m & f* depositor. **~ositar** *vt* deposit; (*poner*) put, place. **~ósito** *m* deposit; (*conjunto de cosas*) store; (*almacén*) warehouse; (*mil*) depot; (*de líquidos*) tank

deprava|ción *f* depravity. **~do** *a* depraved. **~r** *vt* deprave. **~rse** *vpr* become depraved

deprecia|ción *f* depreciation. **~r** *vt* depreciate. **~rse** *vpr* depreciate

depresión *f* depression

deprim|ente *a* depressing. **~ido** *a* depressed. **~ir** *vt* depress. **~irse** *vpr* get depressed

depura|ción *f* purification; (*pol*) purging. **~r** *vt* purify; (*pol*) purge

derech|a *f* (*mano*) right hand; (*lado*) right. **~ista** *a* right-wing. ● *m & f* right-winger. **~o** *a* right; (*vertical*) upright; (*recto*) straight. ● *adv* straight. ● *m* right; (*ley*) law; (*lado*) right side. **~os** *mpl* dues. **~os de autor** royalties. **a la ~a** on the right; (*hacia el lado derecho*) to the right. **todo ~o** straight on

deriva *f* drift. **a la ~** drifting, adrift

deriva|ción *f* derivation; (*cambio*) diversion. **~do** *a* derived. ● *m* derivative, by-product. **~r** *vt* derive; (*cambiar la dirección de*) divert. ● *vi*. **~r de** derive from, be derived from. **~rse** *vpr* be derived

derram|amiento *m* spilling. **~amiento de sangre** bloodshed. **~ar** *vt* spill; (*verter*) pour; shed ‹*lágrimas*›. **~arse** *vpr* spill. **~e** *m* spilling; (*pérdida*) leakage; (*cantidad perdida*) spillage; (*med*) discharge; (*med, de sangre*) haemorrhage

derretir [5] vt melt. **~se** *vpr* melt; (*enamorarse*) fall in love (**por** with)

derriba|do *a* fallen down. **~r** *vt* knock down; bring down, overthrow ‹*gobierno etc*›. **~rse** *vpr* fall down

derrocar [7] *vt* bring down, overthrow ‹*gobierno etc*›

derroch|ar *vt* squander. **~e** *m* waste

derrot|a *f* defeat; (*rumbo*) course. **~ar** *vt* defeat. **~ado** *a* defeated; ‹*vestido*› shabby. **~ero** *m* course

derrumba|miento *m* collapse. **~r** *vt* (*derribar*) knock down. **~rse** *vpr* collapse

desaborido *a* tasteless; ‹*persona*› dull

desabotonar *vt* unbutton, undo. ● *vi* bloom. **~se** *vpr* come undone

desabrido *a* tasteless; ‹*tiempo*› unpleasant; ‹*persona*› surly

desabrochar *vt* undo. **~se** *vpr* come undone

desacat|ar *vt* have no respect for. **~o** *m* disrespect

desac|ertado *a* ill-advised; (*erróneo*) wrong. **~ertar** [1] *vt* be wrong. **~ierto** *m* mistake

desaconseja|ble *a* inadvisable. **~do** *a* unwise, ill-advised. **~r** *vt* advise against, dissuade

desacorde *a* discordant

desacostumbra|do *a* unusual. **~r** *vt* give up

desacreditar *vt* discredit

desactivar *vt* defuse

desacuerdo *m* disagreement

desafiar [20] *vt* challenge; (*afrontar*) defy

desafilado *a* blunt

desafina|do *a* out of tune. **~r** *vi* be out of tune. **~rse** *vpr* go out of tune

desafío *m* challenge; (*combate*) duel

desaforado *a* ‹*comportamiento*› outrageous; (*desmedido*) excessive; ‹*sonido*› loud; (*enorme*) huge

desafortunad|amente *adv* unfortunately. **~o** *a* unfortunate

desagrada|ble *a* unpleasant. **~r** *vt* displease. ● *vi* be unpleasant. **me ~ el sabor** I don't like the taste

desagradecido *a* ungrateful

desagrado *m* displeasure. **con ~** unwillingly

desagravi|ar *vt* make amends to. **~o** *m* amends; (*expiación*) atonement

desagregar [12] *vt* break up. **~se** *vpr* disintegrate

desagüe *m* drain; (*acción*) drainage. **tubo** *m* **de ~** drain-pipe

desaguisado *a* illegal. ● *m* offence; (*fam*) disaster

desahog|ado *a* roomy; (*adinerado*) well-off; (*fig, descarado, fam*) impudent. **~ar** [12] *vt* relieve; vent ‹*ira*›. **~arse** *vpr* (*desfogarse*) let off steam. **~o** *m* comfort; (*alivio*) relief

desahuci|ar *vt* deprive of hope; give up hope for ‹*enfermo*›; evict ‹*inquilino*›. **~o** *m* eviction

desair|ado *a* humiliating; ‹*persona*› humiliated, spurned. **~ar** *vt* snub ‹*persona*›; disregard ‹*cosa*›. **~e** *m* rebuff

desajuste *m* maladjustment; (*avería*) breakdown

desal|entador *a* disheartening. **~entar** [1] *vt* (*fig*) discourage. **~iento** *m* discouragement

desaliño *m* untidiness, scruffiness

desalmado *a* wicked

desalojar *vt* eject ‹*persona*›; evacuate ‹*sitio*›. ● *vi* move (house)

desampar|ado *a* helpless; (*abandonado*) abandoned. **~ar** *vt* abandon. **~o** *m* helplessness; (*abandono*) abandonment

desangelado *a* insipid, dull

desangrar *vt* bleed. **~se** *vpr* bleed

desanima|do *a* down-hearted. **~r** *vt* discourage. **~rse** *vpr* lose heart

desánimo *m* discouragement

desanudar *vt* untie

desapacible *a* unpleasant; ‹*sonido*› harsh

desapar|ecer [11] *vi* disappear; ‹*efecto*› wear off. **~ecido** *a* disappeared. ● *m* missing person. **~ecidos** *mpl* missing. **~ición** *f* disappearance

desapasionado *a* dispassionate

desapego *m* indifference

desapercebido *a* unnoticed

desaplicado *a* lazy

desaprensi|ón *f* unscrupulousness. **~vo** *a* unscrupulous

desaproba|ción *f* disapproval. **~r** [2] *vt* disapprove of; (*rechazar*) reject.

desaprovecha|do *a* wasted; ‹*alumno*› lazy. **~r** *vt* waste

desarm|ar *vt* disarm; (*desmontar*) take to pieces. **~e** *m* disarmament

desarraig|ado *a* rootless. **~ar** [12] *vt* uproot; (*fig, erradicar*) wipe out. **~o** *m* uprooting; (*fig*) eradication

desarregl|ado *a* untidy; (*desordenado*) disorderly. **~ar** *vt* mess up; (*deshacer el orden*) make untidy. **~o** *m* disorder; (*de persona*) untidiness
desarroll|ado *a* (well-) developed. **~ar** *vt* develop; (*desenrollar*) unroll, unfold. **~arse** *vpr* (*incl foto*) develop; (*desenrollarse*) unroll; ‹*suceso*› take place. **~o** *m* development
desarrugar [12] *vt* smooth out
desarticular *vt* dislocate ‹*hueso*›; (*fig*) break up
desaseado *a* dirty; (*desordenado*) untidy
desasirse [45] *vpr* let go (**de** of)
desasos|egar [1 & 12] *vt* disturb. **~egarse** *vpr* get uneasy. **~iego** *m* anxiety; (*intranquilidad*) restlessness
desastr|ado *a* scruffy. **~e** *m* disaster. **~oso** *a* disastrous
desata|do *a* untied; (*fig*) wild. **~r** *vt* untie; (*fig, soltar*) unleash. **~rse** *vpr* come undone
desatascar [7] *vt* pull out of the mud; unblock ‹*tubo etc*›
desaten|ción *f* inattention; (*descortesía*) discourtesy. **~der** [1] *vt* not pay attention to; neglect ‹*deber etc*›. **~to** *a* inattentive; (*descortés*) discourteous
desatin|ado *a* silly. **~o** *m* silliness; (*error*) mistake
desatornillar *vt* unscrew
desatracar [7] *vt/i* cast off
desautorizar [10] *vt* declare unauthorized; (*desmentir*) deny
desavenencia *f* disagreement
desayun|ar *vt* have for breakfast. ● *vi* have breakfast. **~o** *m* breakfast
desazón *m* (*fig*) anxiety
desbandarse *vpr* (*mil*) disband; (*dispersarse*) disperse
desbarajust|ar *vt* throw into confusion. **~e** *m* confusion
desbaratar *vt* spoil
desbloquear *vt* unfreeze
desbocado *a* ‹*vasija etc*› chipped; ‹*caballo*› runaway; ‹*persona*› foul-mouthed
desborda|nte *a* overflowing. **~r** *vt* go beyond; (*exceder*) exceed. ● *vi* overflow. **~rse** *vpr* overflow
descabalgar [12] *vi* dismount
descabellado *a* crazy
descabezar [10] *vt* behead
descafeinado *a* decaffeinated. ● *m* decaffeinated coffee
descalabr|ar *vt* injure in the head; (*fig*) damage. **~o** *m* disaster
descalificar [7] *vt* disqualify; (*desacreditar*) discredit
descalz|ar [10] *vt* take off ‹*zapato*›. **~o** *a* barefoot
descaminar *vt* misdirect; (*fig*) lead astray
descamisado *a* shirtless; (*fig*) shabby
descampado *a* open. ● *m* open ground
descans|ado *a* rested; ‹*trabajo*› easy. **~apiés** *m* footrest. **~ar** *vt/i* rest. **~illo** *m* landing. **~o** *m* rest; (*descansillo*) landing; (*en deportes*) half-time; (*en el teatro etc*) interval
descapotable *a* convertible
descarado *a* insolent, cheeky; (*sin vergüenza*) shameless
descarg|a *f* unloading; (*mil, elec*) discharge. **~ar** [12] *vt* unload; (*mil, elec*) discharge, shock; deal ‹*golpe etc*›. ● *vi* flow into. **~o** *m* unloading; (*recibo*) receipt; (*jurid*) evidence
descarnado *a* scrawny, lean; (*fig*) bare
descaro *m* insolence, cheek; (*cinismo*) nerve, effrontery
descarriar [20] *vt* misdirect; (*fig*) lead astray. **~se** *vpr* go the wrong way; ‹*res*› stray; (*fig*) go astray
descarrila|miento *m* derailment. **~r** *vi* be derailed. **~se** *vpr* be derailed
descartar *vt* discard; (*rechazar*) reject. **~se** *vpr* discard
descascarar *vt* shell
descen|dencia *f* descent; (*personas*) descendants. **~dente** *a* descending. **~der** [1] *vt* lower, get down; go down ‹*escalera etc*›. ● *vi* go down; (*provenir*) be descended (**de** from). **~diente** *m & f* descendent. **~so** *m* descent; (*de temperatura, fiebre etc*) fall, drop
descentralizar [10] *vt* decentralize
descifrar *vt* decipher; decode ‹*clave*›
descolgar [2 & 12] *vt* take down; pick up ‹*el teléfono*›. **~se** *vpr* let o.s. down; (*fig, fam*) turn up
descolorar *vt* discolour, fade
descolori|do *a* discoloured, faded; ‹*persona*› pale. **~r** *vt* discolour, fade
descomedido *a* rude; (*excesivo*) excessive, extreme

descomp|ás *m* disproportion. **~asado** *a* disproportionate

descomp|oner [34] *vt* break down; decompose ‹*substancia*›; distort ‹*rasgos*›; (*estropear*) break; (*desarreglar*) disturb, spoil. **~onerse** *vpr* decompose; ‹*persona*› lose one's temper. **~osición** *f* decomposition; (*med*) diarrhoea. **~ostura** *f* breaking; (*de un motor*) breakdown; (*desorden*) disorder. **~uesto** *a* broken; (*podrido*) decomposed; (*encolerizado*) angry. **estar ~uesto** have diarrhoea

descomunal *a* (*fam*) enormous

desconc|ertante *a* disconcerting. **~ertar** [1] *vt* disconcert; (*dejar perplejo*) puzzle. **~ertarse** *vpr* be put out, be disconcerted; ‹*mecanismo*› break down. **~ierto** *m* confusion

desconectar *vt* disconnect

desconfia|do *a* distrustful. **~nza** *f* distrust, suspicion. **~r** [20] *vi*. **~r de** not trust; (*no creer*) doubt

descongelar *vt* defrost; (*com*) unfreeze

desconoc|er [11] *vt* not know, not recognize. **~ido** *a* unknown; (*cambiado*) unrecognizable. ● *m* stranger. **~imiento** *m* ignorance

desconsidera|ción *f* lack of consideration. **~do** *a* inconsiderate

descons|olado *a* distressed. **~olar** [2] *vt* distress. **~olarse** *vpr* despair. **~uelo** *m* distress; (*tristeza*) sadness

desconta|do *a*. **dar por ~do** take for granted. **por ~do** of course. **~r** [2] *vt* discount

descontent|adizo *a* hard to please. **~ar** *vt* displease. **~o** *a* unhappy (**de** about), discontented (**de** with). ● *m* discontent

descontrolado *a* uncontrolled

descorazonar *vt* discourage. **~se** *vpr* lose heart

descorchar *vt* uncork

descorrer *vt* draw ‹*cortina*›. **~ el cerrojo** unbolt the door

descort|és *a* rude, discourteous. **~esía** *f* rudeness

descos|er *vt* unpick. **~erse** *vpr* come undone. **~ido** *a* unstitched; (*fig*) disjointed. **como un ~ido** a lot

descoyuntar *vt* dislocate

descrédito *m* disrepute. **ir en ~ de** damage the reputation of

descreído *a* unbelieving

descremar *vt* skim

descri|bir [*pp* **descrito**] *vt* describe. **~pción** *f* description. **~ptivo** *a* descriptive

descuartizar [10] *vt* cut up

descubierto *a* discovered; (*no cubierto*) uncovered; (*expuesto*) exposed; ‹*cielo*› clear; (*sin sombrero*) bareheaded. ● *m* overdraft; (*déficit*) deficit. **poner al ~** expose

descubri|miento *m* discovery. **~r** [*pp* **descubierto**] *vt* discover; (*quitar lo que cubre*) uncover; (*revelar*) reveal; unveil ‹*estatua*›. **~rse** *vpr* be discovered; ‹*cielo*› clear; (*quitarse el sombrero*) take off one's hat

descuento *m* discount

descuid|ado *a* careless; ‹*aspecto etc*› untidy; (*desprevenido*) unprepared. **~ar** *vt* neglect. ● *vi* not worry. **~arse** *vpr* be careless; (*no preocuparse*) not worry. **¡~a!** don't worry! **~o** *m* carelessness; (*negligencia*) negligence. **al ~o** nonchalantly. **estar ~ado** not worry, rest assured

desde *prep* (*lugar etc*) from; (*tiempo*) since, from. **~ hace poco** for a short time. **~ hace un mes** for a month. **~ luego** of course. **~ Madrid hasta Barcelona** from Madrid to Barcelona. **~ niño** since childhood

desdecir [46, *pero imperativo* **desdice**, *futuro y condicional regulares*] *vi*. **~ de** be unworthy of; (*no armonizar*) not match. **~se** *vpr*. **~ de** take back ‹*palabras etc*›; go back on ‹*promesa*›

desd|én *m* scorn. **~eñable** *a* contemptible. **~eñar** *vt* scorn. **~eñoso** *a* scornful

desdicha *f* misfortune. **~do** *a* unfortunate. **por ~** unfortunately

desdoblar *vt* straighten; (*desplegar*) unfold

desea|ble *a* desirable. **~r** *vt* want; wish ‹*algo a uno*›. **de ~r** desirable. **le deseo un buen viaje** I hope you have a good journey. **¿qué desea Vd?** can I help you?

desecar [7] *vt* dry up

desech|ar *vt* throw out. **~o** *m* rubbish

desembalar *vt* unpack

desembarazar [10] *vt* clear. **~se** *vpr* free o.s.

desembarca|dero *m* landing stage. **~r** [7] *vt* unload. ● *vi* disembark

desemboca|dura *f* (*de río*) mouth; (*de calle*) opening. **~r** [7] *vi*. **~r en**

‹*río*› flow into; ‹*calle*› join; (*fig*) lead to, end in
desembols|ar *vt* pay. **~o** *m* payment
desembragar [12] *vi* declutch
desembrollar *vt* unravel
desembuchar *vi* tell, reveal a secret
desemejan|te *a* unlike, dissimilar. **~za** *f* dissimilarity
desempapelar *vt* unwrap
desempaquetar *vt* unpack, unwrap
desempat|ar *vi* break a tie. **~e** *m* tie-breaker
desempeñ|ar *vt* redeem; play ‹*papel*›; hold ‹*cargo*›; perform, carry out ‹*deber etc*›. **~arse** *vpr* get out of debt. **~o** *m* redemption; (*de un papel, de un cargo*) performance
desemple|ado *a* unemployed. ● *m* unemployed person. **~o** *m* unemployment. **los ~ados** *mpl* the unemployed
desempolvar *vt* dust; (*fig*) unearth
desencadenar *vt* unchain; (*fig*) unleash. **~se** *vpr* break loose; ‹*guerra etc*› break out
desencajar *vt* dislocate; (*desconectar*) disconnect. **~se** *vpr* become distorted
desencant|ar *vt* disillusion. **~o** *m* disillusionment
desenchufar *vt* unplug
desenfad|ado *a* uninhibited. **~ar** *vt* calm down. **~arse** *vpr* calm down. **~o** *m* openness; (*desenvoltura*) assurance
desenfocado *a* out of focus
desenfren|ado *a* unrestrained. **~arse** *vpr* rage. **~o** *m* licentiousness
desenganchar *vt* unhook
desengañ|ar *vt* disillusion. **~arse** *vpr* be disillusioned; (*darse cuenta*) realize. **~o** *m* disillusionment, disappointment
desengrasar *vt* remove the grease from. ● *vi* lose weight
desenla|ce *m* outcome. **~zar** [10] *vt* undo; solve ‹*problema*›
desenmarañar *vt* unravel
desenmascarar *vt* unmask
desenojar *vt* calm down. **~se** *vpr* calm down
desenred|ar *vt* unravel. **~arse** *vpr* extricate o.s. **~o** *m* denoument
desenrollar *vt* unroll, unwind
desenroscar [7] *vt* unscrew
desentenderse [1] *vpr* want nothing to do with; (*afectar ignorancia*) pretend not to know. **hacerse el desentendido** (*fingir no oir*) pretend not to hear
desenterrar [1] *vt* exhume; (*fig*) unearth
desenton|ar *vi* be out of tune; ‹*colores*› clash. **~o** *m* rudeness
desentrañar *vt* work out
desenvoltura *f* ease; (*falta de timidez*) confidence; (*descaro*) insolence
desenvolver [2, *pp* **desenvuelto**] *vt* unwrap; expound ‹*idea etc*›. **~se** *vpr* act with confidence
deseo *m* wish, desire. **~so** *a* desirous. **arder en ~s de** long for. **buen ~** good intentions. **estar ~so de** be eager to
desequilibr|ado *a* unbalanced. **~io** *m* imbalance
des|erción *f* desertion; (*pol*) defection. **~ertar** *vt* desert. **~értico** *a* desert-like. **~ertor** *m* deserter
desespera|ción *f* despair. **~do** *a* desperate. **~nte** *a* infuriating. **~r** *vt* drive to despair. ● *vi* despair (**de** of). **~rse** *vpr* despair
desestimar *vt* (*rechazar*) reject
desfachat|ado *a* brazen, impudent. **~ez** *f* impudence
desfalc|ar [7] *vt* embezzle. **~o** *m* embezzlement
desfallec|er [11] *vt* weaken. ● *vi* get weak; (*desmayarse*) faint. **~imiento** *m* weakness
desfas|ado *a* ‹*persona*› out of place, out of step; ‹*máquina etc*› out of phase. **~e** *m* jet-lag. **estar ~ado** have jet-lag
desfavor|able *a* unfavourable. **~ecer** [11] *vt* ‹*ropa*› not suit
desfigurar *vt* disfigure; (*desdibujar*) blur; (*fig*) distort
desfiladero *m* pass
desfil|ar *vi* march (past). **~e** *m* procession, parade. **~e de modelos** fashion show
desfogar [12] *vt* vent (**en**, **con** on). **~se** *vpr* let off steam
desgajar *vt* tear off; (*fig*) uproot ‹*persona*›. **~se** *vpr* come off
desgana *f* (*falta de apetito*) lack of appetite; (*med*) weakness, faintness; (*fig*) unwillingness
desgarr|ador *a* heart-rending. **~ar** *vt* tear; (*fig*) break ‹*corazón*›. **~o** *m* tear, rip; (*descaro*) insolence. **~ón** *m* tear

desgast|ar *vt* wear away; wear out ‹*ropa*›. **~arse** *vpr* wear away; ‹*ropa*› be worn out; ‹*persona*› wear o.s. out. **~e** *m* wear

desgracia *f* misfortune; (*accidente*) accident; (*mala suerte*) bad luck. **~damente** *adv* unfortunately. **~do** *a* unlucky; (*pobre*) poor; (*desagradable*) unpleasant. ● *m* unfortunate person, poor devil (*fam*). **~r** *vt* spoil. **caer en ~** fall from favour. **estar en ~** be unfortunate. **por ~** unfortunately. **¡qué ~!** what a shame!

desgranar *vt* shell ‹*guisantes etc*›

desgreñado *a* ruffled, dishevelled

desgua|ce *m* scrapyard. **~zar** [10] *vt* scrap

deshabitado *a* uninhabited

deshabituarse [21] *vpr* get out of the habit

deshacer [31] *vt* undo; strip ‹*cama*›; unpack ‹*maleta*›; (*desmontar*) take to pieces; break ‹*trato*›; (*derretir*) melt; (*en agua*) dissolve; (*destruir*) destroy; (*estropear*) spoil; (*derrotar*) defeat. **~se** *vpr* come undone; (*descomponerse*) fall to pieces; (*derretirse*) melt. **~se de algo** get rid of sth. **~se en lágrimas** burst into tears. **~se por hacer algo** go out of one's way to do sth

deshelar [1] *vt* thaw. **~se** *vpr* thaw

desheredar *vt* disinherit

deshidratar *vt* dehydrate. **~se** *vpr* become dehydrated

deshielo *m* thaw

deshilachado *a* frayed

deshincha|do *a* ‹*neumático*› flat. **~r** *vt* deflate. **~rse** *vpr* go down

deshollina|dor *m* (chimney-)sweep. **~r** *vt* sweep ‹*chimenea*›

deshon|esto *a* dishonest; (*obsceno*) indecent. **~or** *m*, **~ra** *f* disgrace. **~rar** *vt* dishonour

deshora *f*. **a ~** (*a hora desacostumbrada*) at an unusual time; (*a hora inoportuna*) at an inconvenient time; (*a hora avanzada*) very late

deshuesar *vt* bone ‹*carne*›; stone ‹*fruta*›

desidia *f* laziness

desierto *a* deserted. ● *m* desert

designa|ción *f* designation. **~r** *vt* designate; (*fijar*) fix

desigual *a* unequal; ‹*terreno*› uneven; (*distinto*) different. **~dad** *f* inequality

desilusi|ón *f* disappointment; (*pérdida de ilusiones*) disillusionment. **~onar** *vt* disappoint; (*quitar las ilusiones*) disillusion. **~onarse** *vpr* become disillusioned

desinfecta|nte *m* disinfectant. **~r** *vt* disinfect

desinfestar *vt* decontaminate

desinflar *vt* deflate. **~se** *vpr* go down

desinhibido *a* uninhibited

desintegra|ción *f* disintegration. **~r** *vt* disintegrate. **~rse** *vpr* disintegrate

desinter|és *m* impartiality; (*generosidad*) generosity. **~esado** *a* impartial; (*liberal*) generous

desistir *vi*. **~ de** give up

desleal *a* disloyal. **~tad** *f* disloyalty

desleír [51] *vt* thin down, dilute

deslenguado *a* foul-mouthed

desligar [12] *vt* untie; (*separar*) separate; (*fig, librar*) free. **~se** *vpr* break away; (*de un compromiso*) free o.s.

deslizar [10] *vt* slide, slip. **~se** *vpr* slide, slip; ‹*tiempo*› slide by, pass; (*fluir*) flow

deslucido *a* tarnished; (*gastado*) worn out; (*fig*) undistinguished

deslumbrar *vt* dazzle

deslustrar *vt* tarnish

desmadr|ado *a* unruly. **~arse** *vpr* get out of control. **~e** *m* excess

desmán *m* outrage

desmandarse *vpr* get out of control

desmantelar *vt* dismantle; (*despojar*) strip

desmañado *a* clumsy

desmaquillador *m* make-up remover

desmay|ado *a* unconscious. **~ar** *vi* lose heart. **~arse** *vpr* faint. **~o** *m* faint; (*estado*) unconsciousness; (*fig*) depression

desmedido *a* excessive

desmedrarse *vpr* waste away

desmejorarse *vpr* deteriorate

desmelenado *a* dishevelled

desmembrar *vt* (*fig*) divide up

desmemoriado *a* forgetful

desmentir [4] *vt* deny. **~se** *vpr* contradict o.s.; (*desdecirse*) go back on one's word

desmenuzar [10] *vt* crumble; chop ‹*carne etc*›

desmerecer [11] *vt* be unworthy of. ● *vi* deteriorate

desmesurado *a* excessive; (*enorme*) enormous

desmigajar *vt*, **desmigar** [12] *vt* crumble

desmonta|ble *a* collapsible. **~r** *vt* (*quitar*) remove; (*desarmar*) take to pieces; (*derribar*) knock down; (*allanar*) level. ● *vi* dismount

desmoralizar [10] *vt* demoralize

desmoronar *vt* wear away; (*fig*) make inroads into. **~se** *vpr* crumble

desmovilizar [10] *vt/i* demobilize

desnatar *vt* skim

desnivel *m* unevenness; (*fig*) difference, inequality

desnud|ar *vt* strip; undress, strip ‹*persona*›. **~arse** *vpr* get undressed. **~ez** *f* nudity. **~o** *a* naked; (*fig*) bare. ● *m* nude

desnutri|ción *f* malnutrition. **~do** *a* undernourished

desobed|ecer [11] *vt* disobey. **~iencia** *f* disobedience. **~iente** *a* disobedient

desocupa|do *a* ‹*asiento etc*› vacant, free; (*sin trabajo*) unemployed; (*ocioso*) idle. **~r** *vt* vacate

desodorante *m* deodorant

desoír [50] *vt* take no notice of

desola|ción *f* desolation; (*fig*) distress. **~do** *a* desolate; ‹*persona*› sorry, sad. **~r** *vt* ruin; (*desconsolar*) distress

desollar *vt* skin; (*fig*, *criticar*) criticize; (*fig*, *hacer pagar demasiado*, *fam*) fleece

desorbitante *a* excessive

desorden *m* disorder, untidiness; (*confusión*) confusion. **~ado** *a* untidy. **~ar** *vt* disarrange, make a mess of

desorganizar [10] *vt* disorganize; (*trastornar*) disturb

desorienta|do *a* confused. **~r** *vt* disorientate. **~rse** *vpr* lose one's bearings

desovar *vi* ‹*pez*› spawn; ‹*insecto*› lay eggs

despabila|do *a* wide awake; (*listo*) quick. **~r** *vt* (*despertar*) wake up; (*avivar*) brighten up. **~rse** *vpr* wake up; (*avivarse*) brighten up. **¡despabílate!** get a move on!

despaci|o *adv* slowly. ● *int* easy does it! **~to** *adv* slowly

despach|ar *vt* finish; (*tratar con*) deal with; (*vender*) sell; (*enviar*) send; (*despedir*) send away; issue ‹*billete*›. ● *vi* hurry up. **~arse** *vpr* get rid; (*terminar*) finish. **~o** *m* dispatch; (*oficina*) office; (*venta*) sale; (*del teatro*) box office

despampanante *a* stunning

desparejado *a* odd

desparpajo *m* confidence; (*descaro*) impudence

desparramar *vt* scatter; spill ‹*líquidos*›; squander ‹*fortuna*›

despavorido *a* terrified

despectivo *a* disparaging; ‹*sentido etc*› pejorative

despecho *m* spite. **a ~ de** in spite of. **por ~** out of spite

despedazar [10] *vt* tear to pieces

despedi|da *f* goodbye, farewell. **~da de soltero** stag-party. **~r** [5] *vt* say goodbye, see off; dismiss ‹*empleado*›; evict ‹*inquilino*›; (*arrojar*) throw; give off ‹*olor etc*›. **~rse** *vpr*. **~rse de** say goodbye to

despeg|ado *a* cold, indifferent. **~ar** [12] *vt* unstick. ● *vi* ‹*avión*› take off. **~o** *m* indifference. **~ue** *m* take-off

despeinar *vt* ruffle the hair of

despeja|do *a* clear; ‹*persona*› wide awake. **~r** *vt* clear; (*aclarar*) clarify. ● *vi* clear. **~rse** *vpr* (*aclararse*) become clear; ‹*cielo*› clear; ‹*tiempo*› clear up; ‹*persona*› liven up

despellejar *vt* skin

despensa *f* pantry, larder

despeñadero *m* cliff

desperdici|ar *vt* waste. **~o** *m* waste. **~os** *mpl* rubbish. **no tener ~o** be good all the way through

desperezarse [10] *vpr* stretch

desperfecto *m* flaw

desperta|dor *m* alarm clock. **~r** [1] *vt* wake up; (*fig*) awaken. **~rse** *vpr* wake up

despiadado *a* merciless

despido *m* dismissal

despierto *a* awake; (*listo*) bright

despilfarr|ar *vt* waste. **~o** *m* squandering; (*gasto innecesario*) extravagance

despista|do *a* (*con estar*) confused; (*con ser*) absent-minded. **~r** *vt* throw off the scent; (*fig*) mislead. **~rse** *vpr* go wrong; (*fig*) get confused

despiste *m* swerve; (*error*) mistake; (*confusión*) muddle

desplaza|do *a* out of place. **~miento** *m* displacement; (*de opinión etc*) swing, shift. **~r** [10] *vt* displace. **~rse** *vpr* travel

despl|egar [1 & 12] *vt* open out; spread ‹*alas*›; (*fig*) show. **~iegue** *m* opening; (*fig*) show
desplomarse *vpr* lean; (*caerse*) collapse
desplumar *vt* pluck; (*fig, fam*) fleece
despobla|do *m* deserted area. **~r** [2] *vt* depopulate
despoj|ar *vt* deprive ‹*persona*›; strip ‹*cosa*›. **~o** *m* plundering; (*botín*) booty. **~os** *mpl* left-overs; (*de res*) offal; (*de ave*) giblets
desposado *a & m* newly-wed
déspota *m & f* despot
despreci|able *a* despicable; ‹*cantidad*› negligible. **~ar** *vt* despise; (*rechazar*) scorn. **~o** *m* contempt
desprend|er *vt* remove; give off ‹*olor*›. **~erse** *vpr* fall off; (*fig*) part with; (*deducirse*) follow. **~imiento** *m* loosening; (*generosidad*) generosity
despreocupa|ción *f* carelessness. **~do** *a* unconcerned; (*descuidado*) careless. **~rse** *vpr* not worry
desprestigiar *vt* discredit
desprevenido *a* unprepared. **coger a uno ~** catch s.o. unawares
desproporci|ón *f* disproportion. **~onado** *a* disproportionate
despropósito *m* irrelevant remark
desprovisto *a*. **~ de** lacking, without
después *adv* after, afterwards; (*más tarde*) later; (*a continuación*) then. **~ de** after. **~ de comer** after eating. **~ de todo** after all. **~ que** after. **poco ~** soon after. **una semana ~** a week later
desquiciar *vt* (*fig*) disturb
desquit|ar *vt* compensate. **~arse** *vpr* make up for; (*vengarse*) take revenge. **~e** *m* compensation; (*venganza*) revenge
destaca|do *a* outstanding. **~r** [7] *vt* emphasize. ● *vi* stand out. **~rse** *vpr* stand out
destajo *m* piece-work. **hablar a ~** talk nineteen to the dozen
destap|ar *vt* uncover; open ‹*botella*›. **~arse** *vpr* reveal one's true self. **~e** *m* (*fig*) permissiveness
destartalado *a* ‹*habitación*› untidy; ‹*casa*› rambling
destell|ar *vi* sparkle. **~o** *m* sparkle; (*de estrella*) twinkle; (*fig*) glimmer
destemplado *a* out of tune; (*agrio*) harsh; ‹*tiempo*› unsettled; ‹*persona*› out of sorts
desteñir [5 & 22] *vt* fade; (*manchar*) discolour. ● *vi* fade. **~se** *vpr* fade; ‹*color*› run
desterra|do *m* exile. **~r** [1] *vt* banish
destetar *vt* wean
destiempo *m*. **a ~** at the wrong moment
destierro *m* exile
destil|ación *f* distillation. **~ar** *vt* distil. **~ería** *f* distillery
destin|ar *vt* destine; (*nombrar*) appoint. **~atario** *m* addressee. **~o** *m* (*uso*) use, function; (*lugar*) destination; (*empleo*) position; (*suerte*) destiny. **con ~o a** going to, bound for. **dar ~o a** find a use for
destitu|ción *f* dismissal. **~ir** [17] *vt* dismiss
destornilla|dor *m* screwdriver. **~r** *vt* unscrew
destreza *f* skill
destripar *vt* rip open
destroz|ar [10] *vt* ruin; (*fig*) shatter. **~o** *m* destruction. **causar ~os, hacer ~os** ruin
destru|cción *f* destruction. **~ctivo** *a* destructive. **~ir** [17] *vt* destroy; demolish ‹*edificio*›
desunir *vt* separate
desus|ado *a* old-fashioned; (*insólito*) unusual. **~o** *m* disuse. **caer en ~o** become obsolete
desvaído *a* pale; (*borroso*) blurred; ‹*persona*› dull
desvalido *a* needy, destitute
desvalijar *vt* rob; burgle ‹*casa*›
desvalorizar [10] *vt* devalue
desván *m* loft
desvanec|er [11] *vt* make disappear; tone down ‹*colores*›; (*borrar*) blur; (*fig*) dispel. **~erse** *vpr* disappear; (*desmayarse*) faint. **~imiento** *m* (*med*) fainting fit
desvariar [20] *vi* be delirious; (*fig*) talk nonsense
desvel|ar *vt* keep awake. **~arse** *vpr* stay awake, have a sleepless night. **~o** *m* insomnia, sleeplessness
desvencijar *vt* break; (*agotar*) exhaust
desventaja *f* disadvantage
desventura *f* misfortune. **~do** *a* unfortunate
desverg|onzado *a* impudent, cheeky. **~üenza** *f* impudence, cheek
desvestirse [5] *vpr* undress
desv|iación *f* deviation; (*auto*) diversion. **~iar** [20] *vt* deflect, turn aside.

~iarse *vpr* be deflected; (*del camino*) make a detour; (*del tema*) stray. **~ío** *m* diversion; (*frialdad*) *f* indifference
desvivirse *vpr* long (**por** for); (*afanarse*) strive, do one's utmost
detall|ar *vt* relate in detail. **~e** *m* detail; (*fig*) gesture. **~ista** *m & f* retailer. **al ~e** in detail; (*al por menor*) retail. **con todo ~e** in great detail. **en ~es** in detail. **¡qué ~e!** how thoughtful!
detect|ar *vt* detect. **~ive** *m* detective
deten|ción *f* stopping; (*jurid*) arrest; (*en la cárcel*) detention. **~er** [40] *vt* stop; (*jurid*) arrest; (*encarcelar*) detain; (*retrasar*) delay. **~erse** *vpr* stop; (*entretenerse*) spend a lot of time. **~idamente** *adv* carefully. **~ido** *a* (*jurid*) under arrest; (*minucioso*) detailed. ● *m* prisoner
detergente *a & m* detergent
deterior|ar *vt* damage, spoil. **~arse** *vpr* deteriorate. **~o** *m* damage
determina|ción *f* determination; (*decisión*) decison. **~nte** *a* decisive. **~r** *vt* determine; (*decidir*) decide; (*fijar*) fix. **tomar una ~ción** make a decision
detestar *vt* detest
detonar *vi* explode
detrás *adv* behind; (*en la parte posterior*) on the back. **~ de** behind. **por ~** on the back; (*detrás de*) behind
detrimento *m* detriment. **en ~ de** to the detriment of
detrito *m* debris
deud|a *f* debt. **~or** *m* debtor
devalua|ción *f* devaluation. **~r** [21] *vt* devalue
devanar *vt* wind
devasta|dor *a* devastating. **~r** *vt* devastate
devoción *f* devotion
devol|ución *f* return; (*com*) repayment, refund. **~ver** [5] (*pp* **devuelto**) *vt* return; (*com*) repay, refund; restore ‹*edificio etc*›. ● *vi* be sick
devorar *vt* devour
devoto *a* devout; ‹*amigo etc*› devoted. ● *m* enthusiast
di *vb véase* **dar**
día *m* day. **~ de fiesta** (public) holiday. **~ del santo** saint's day. **~ festivo** (public) holiday. **~ hábil, ~ laborable** working day. **al ~** up to date. **al ~ siguiente** (on) the following day. **¡buenos ~s!** good morning! **dar los buenos ~s** say good morning. **de ~** by day. **el ~ de hoy** today. **el ~ de mañana** tomorrow. **en pleno ~** in broad daylight. **en su ~** in due course. **todo el santo ~** all day long. **un ~ de estos** one of these days. **un ~ sí y otro no** every other day. **vivir al ~** live from hand to mouth
diab|etes *f* diabetes. **~ético** *a* diabetic
diab|lo *m* devil. **~lura** *f* mischief. **~ólico** *a* diabolical
diácono *m* deacon
diadema *f* diadem
diáfano *a* diaphanous
diafragma *m* diaphragm
diagn|osis *f* diagnosis. **~osticar** [7] *vt* diagnose. **~óstico** *a* diagnostic
diagonal *a & f* diagonal
diagrama *m* diagram
dialecto *m* dialect
diálisis *f* dialysis
di|alogar [12] *vi* talk. **~álogo** *m* dialogue
diamante *m* diamond
diámetro *m* diameter
diana *f* reveille; (*blanco*) bull's-eye
diapasón *m* (*para afinar*) tuning fork
diapositiva *f* slide, transparency
diari|amente *adv* every day. **~o** *a* daily. ● *m* newspaper; (*libro*) diary. **a ~o** daily. **~o hablado** (*en la radio*) news bulletin. **de ~o** everyday, ordinary
diarrea *f* diarrhoea
diatriba *f* diatribe
dibuj|ar *vt* draw. **~o** *m* drawing. **~os animados** cartoon (film)
diccionario *m* dictionary
diciembre *m* December
dictado *m* dictation
dictad|or *m* dictator. **~ura** *f* dictatorship
dictamen *m* opinion; (*informe*) report
dictar *vt* dictate; pronounce ‹*sentencia etc*›
dich|a *f* happiness. **~o** *a* said; (*susodicho*) aforementioned. ● *m* saying. **~oso** *a* happy; (*afortunado*) fortunate. **~o y hecho** no sooner said than done. **mejor ~o** rather. **por ~a** fortunately
didáctico *a* didactic

dieci|nueve *a & m* nineteen. **~ocho** *a & m* eighteen. **~séis** *a & m* sixteen. **~siete** *a & m* seventeen

diente *m* tooth; (*de tenedor*) prong; (*de ajo*) clove. **~ de león** dandelion. **hablar entre ~s** mumble

diesel /'disel/ *a* diesel

diestr|a *f* right hand. **~o** *a* (*derecho*) right; (*hábil*) skillful

dieta *f* diet

diez *a & m* ten

diezmar *vt* decimate

difama|ción *f* (*con palabras*) slander; (*por escrito*) libel. **~r** *vt* (*hablando*) slander; (*por escrito*) libel

diferen|cia *f* difference; (*desacuerdo*) disagreement. **~ciar** *vt* differentiate between. ● *vi* differ. **~ciarse** *vpr* differ. **~te** *a* different

difer|ido *a* (*TV etc*) recorded. **~ir** [4] *vt* postpone, defer. ● *vi* differ

dif|ícil *a* difficult. **~icultad** *f* difficulty; (*problema*) problem. **~icultar** *vt* make difficult

difteria *f* diphtheria

difundir *vt* spread; (*TV etc*) broadcast. **~se** *vpr* spread

difunto *a* late, deceased. ● *m* deceased

difusión *f* spreading

dige|rir [4] *vt* digest. **~stión** *f* digestion. **~stivo** *a* digestive

digital *a* digital; (*de los dedos*) finger

dignarse *vpr* deign. **dígnese Vd** be so kind as

dign|atario *m* dignitary. **~idad** *f* dignity; (*empleo*) office. **~o** *a* worthy; (*apropiado*) appropriate

digo *vb véase* **decir**

digresión *f* digression

dije *vb véase* **decir**

dila|ción *f* delay. **~tación** *f* dilation, expansion. **~tado** *a* extensive; ‹*tiempo*› long. **~tar** *vt* expand; (*med*) dilate; (*prolongar*) prolong. **~tarse** *vpr* expand; (*med*) dilate; (*extenderse*) extend. **sin ~ción** immediately

dilema *m* dilemma

diligen|cia *f* diligence; (*gestión*) job; (*historia*) stagecoach. **~te** *a* diligent

dilucidar *vt* explain; solve ‹*misterio*›

diluir [17] *vt* dilute

diluvio *m* flood

dimensión *f* dimension; (*tamaño*) size

diminut|ivo *a & m* diminutive. **~o** *a* minute

dimi|sión *f* resignation. **~tir** *vt/i* resign

Dinamarca *f* Denmark

dinamarqués *a* Danish. ● *m* Dane

din|ámica *f* dynamics. **~ámico** *a* dynamic. **~amismo** *m* dynamism

dinamita *f* dynamite

dínamo *m*, **dinamo** *m* dynamo

dinastía *f* dynasty

dineral *m* fortune

dinero *m* money. **~ efectivo** cash. **~ suelto** change

dinosaurio *m* dinosaur

diócesis *f* diocese

dios *m* god. **~a** *f* goddess. **¡D~ mío!** good heavens! **¡gracias a D~!** thank God! **¡válgame D~!** bless my soul!

diploma *m* diploma

diplomacia *f* diplomacy

diplomado *a* qualified

diplomático *a* diplomatic. ● *m* diplomat

diptongo *m* diphthong

diputa|ción *f* delegation. **~ción provincial** county council. **~do** *m* delegate; (*pol, en España*) member of the Cortes; (*pol, en Inglaterra*) Member of Parliament; (*pol, en Estados Unidos*) congressman

dique *m* dike

direc|ción *f* direction; (*señas*) address; (*los que dirigen*) management; (*pol*) leadership. **~ción prohibida** no entry. **~ción única** one-way. **~ta** *f* (*auto*) top gear. **~tiva** *f* directive, guideline. **~tivo** *m* executive. **~to** *a* direct; ‹*línea*› straight; ‹*tren*› through. **~tor** *m* director; (*mus*) conductor; (*de escuela etc*) headmaster; (*de periódico*) editor; (*gerente*) manager. **~tora** *f* (*de escuela etc*) headmistress. **en ~to** (*TV etc*) live. **llevar la ~ción de** direct

dirig|ente *a* ruling. ● *m & f* leader; (*de empresa*) manager. **~ible** *a & m* dirigible. **~ir** [14] *vt* direct; (*mus*) conduct; run ‹*empresa etc*›; address ‹*carta etc*›. **~irse** *vpr* make one's way; (*hablar*) address

discernir [1] *vt* distinguish

disciplina *f* discipline. **~r** *vt* discipline. **~rio** *a* disciplinary

discípulo *m* disciple; (*alumno*) pupil

disco *m* disc; (*mus*) record; (*deportes*) discus; (*de teléfono*) dial; (*auto*) lights; (*rail*) signal

disconforme *a* not in agreement

discontinuo *a* discontinuous

discord|ante *a* discordant. **~e** *a* discordant. **~ia** *f* discord
discoteca *f* discothèque, disco (*fam*); (*colección de discos*) record library
discreción *f* discretion
discrepa|ncia *f* discrepancy; (*desacuerdo*) disagreement. **~r** *vi* differ
discreto *a* discreet; (*moderado*) moderate; ‹*color*› subdued
discrimina|ción *f* discrimination. **~r** *vt* (*distinguir*) discriminate between; (*tratar injustamente*) discriminate against
disculpa *f* apology; (*excusa*) excuse. **~r** *vt* excuse, forgive. **~rse** *vpr* apologize. **dar ~s** make excuses. **pedir ~s** apologize
discurrir *vt* think up. ● *vi* think (**en** about); ‹*tiempo*› pass
discurs|ante *m* speaker. **~ar** *vi* speak (**sobre** about). **~o** *m* speech
discusión *f* discussion; (*riña*) argument. **eso no admite ~** there can be no argument about that
discuti|ble *a* debatable. **~r** *vt* discuss; (*argumentar*) argue about; (*contradecir*) contradict. ● *vi* discuss; (*argumentar*) argue
disec|ar [7] *vt* dissect; stuff ‹*animal muerto*›. **~ción** *f* dissection
disemina|ción *f* dissemination. **~r** *vt* disseminate, spread
disentería *f* dysentery
disenti|miento *m* dissent, disagreement. **~r** [4] *vi* disagree (**de** with) (**en** on)
diseñ|ador *m* designer. **~ar** *vt* design. **~o** *m* design; (*fig*) sketch
disertación *f* dissertation
disfraz *m* disguise; (*vestido*) fancy dress. **~ar** [10] *vt* disguise. **~arse** *vpr*. **~arse de** disguise o.s. as
disfrutar *vt* enjoy. ● *vi* enjoy o.s. **~ de** enjoy
disgregar [12] *vt* disintegrate
disgust|ar *vt* displease; (*molestar*) annoy. **~arse** *vpr* get annoyed, get upset; ‹*dos personas*› fall out. **~o** *m* annoyance; (*problema*) trouble; (*repugnancia*) disgust; (*riña*) quarrel; (*dolor*) sorrow, grief
disiden|cia *f* disagreement, dissent. **~te** *a & m & f* dissident
disímil *a* (*LAm*) dissimilar
disimular *vt* conceal. ● *vi* pretend
disipa|ción *f* dissipation; (*de dinero*) squandering. **~r** *vt* dissipate; (*derrochar*) squander
diskette *m* floppy disk
dislocarse [7] *vpr* dislocate
disminu|ción *f* decrease. **~ir** [17] *vi* diminish
disociar *vt* dissociate
disolver [2, *pp* **disuelto**] *vt* dissolve. **~se** *vpr* dissolve
disonante *a* dissonant
dispar *a* different
disparar *vt* fire. ● *vi* shoot (**contra** at)
disparat|ado *a* absurd. **~ar** *vi* talk nonsense. **~e** *m* silly thing; (*error*) mistake. **decir ~es** talk nonsense. **¡qué ~e!** how ridiculous! **un ~e** (*mucho, fam*) a lot, an awful lot (*fam*)
disparidad *f* disparity
disparo *m* (*acción*) firing; (*tiro*) shot
dispensar *vt* distribute; (*disculpar*) excuse. **¡Vd dispense!** forgive me
dispers|ar *vt* scatter, disperse. **~arse** *vpr* scatter, disperse. **~ión** *f* dispersion. **~o** *a* scattered
dispon|er [34] *vt* arrange; (*preparar*) prepare. ● *vi*. **~er de** have; (*vender etc*) dispose of. **~erse** *vpr* get ready. **~ibilidad** *f* availability. **~ible** *a* available
disposición *f* arrangement; (*aptitud*) talent; (*disponibilidad*) disposal; (*jurid*) order, decree. **~ de ánimo** frame of mind. **a la ~ de** at the disposal of. **a su ~** at your service
dispositivo *m* device
dispuesto *a* ready; (*hábil*) clever; (*inclinado*) disposed; (*servicial*) helpful
disputa *f* dispute. **~r** *vt* dispute. ● *vi*. **~r por** argue about; (*competir para*) compete for. **sin ~** undoubtedly
distan|cia *f* distance. **~ciar** *vt* space out; (*en deportes*) outdistance. **~ciarse** *vpr* ‹*dos personas*› fall out. **~te** *a* distant. **a ~cia** from a distance. **guardar las ~cias** keep one's distance
distar *vi* be away; (*fig*) be far. **dista 5 kilómetros** it's 5 kilometres away
distin|ción *f* distinction. **~guido** *a* distinguished; (*en cartas*) Honoured. **~guir** [13] *vt/i* distinguish. **~guirse** *vpr* distinguish o.s.; (*diferenciarse*) differ; (*verse*) be visible. **~tivo** *a* distinctive. ● *m* badge. **~to** *a* different; (*claro*) distinct
distorsión *f* distortion; (*med*) sprain
distra|cción *f* amusement; (*descuido*) absent-mindedness, inattention. **~er** [41] *vt* distract; (*divertir*)

amuse; embezzle ‹*fondos*›. ● *vi* be entertaining. **~erse** *vpr* amuse o.s.; (*descuidarse*) not pay attention. **~ído** *a* amusing; (*desatento*) absent-minded

distribu|ción *f* distribution. **~idor** *m* distributor, agent. **~idor automático** vending machine. **~ir** [17] *vt* distribute

distrito *m* district

disturbio *m* disturbance

disuadir *vt* dissuade

diurético *a & m* diuretic

diurno *a* daytime

divagar [12] *vi* (*al hablar*) digress

diván *m* settee, sofa

diverg|encia *f* divergence. **~ente** *a* divergent. **~ir** [14] *vi* diverge

diversidad *f* diversity

diversificar [7] *vt* diversify

diversión *f* amusement, entertainment; (*pasatiempo*) pastime

diverso *a* different

diverti|do *a* amusing; (*que tiene gracia*) funny; (*agradable*) enjoyable. **~r** [4] *vt* amuse, entertain. **~rse** *vpr* enjoy o.s.

dividir *vt* divide; (*repartir*) share out

divin|idad *f* divinity. **~o** *a* divine

divisa *f* emblem. **~s** *fpl* foreign exchange

divisar *vt* make out

divis|ión *f* division. **~or** *m* divisor. **~orio** *a* dividing

divorci|ado *a* divorced. ● *m* divorcee. **~ar** *vt* divorce. **~arse** *vpr* get divorced. **~o** *m* divorce

divulgar [12] *vt* divulge; (*propagar*) spread. **~se** *vpr* become known

do *m* C; (*solfa*) doh

dobl|adillo *m* hem; (*de pantalón*) turn-up (*Brit*), cuff (*Amer*). **~ado** *a* double; (*plegado*) folded; ‹*película*› dubbed. **~ar** *vt* double; (*plegar*) fold; (*torcer*) bend; turn ‹*esquina*›; dub ‹*película*›. ● *vi* turn; ‹*campana*› toll. **~arse** *vpr* double; (*encorvarse*) bend; (*ceder*) give in. **~e** *a* double. ● *m* double; (*pliegue*) fold. **~egar** [12] *vt* (*fig*) force to give in. **~egarse** *vpr* give in. **el ~e** twice as much

doce *a & m* twelve. **~na** *f* dozen. **~no** *a* twelfth

docente *a* teaching. ● *m & f* teacher

dócil *a* obedient

doct|o *a* learned. **~or** *m* doctor. **~orado** *m* doctorate. **~rina** *f* doctrine

document|ación *f* documentation, papers. **~al** *a & m* documentary. **~ar** *vt* document. **~arse** *vpr* gather information. **~o** *m* document. **D~o Nacional de Identidad** national identity card

dogm|a *m* dogma. **~ático** *a* dogmatic

dólar *m* dollar

dol|er [2] *vi* hurt, ache; (*fig*) grieve. **me duele la cabeza** my head hurts. **le duele el estómago** he has a pain in his stomach. **~erse** *vpr* regret; (*quejarse*) complain. **~or** *m* pain; (*sordo*) ache; (*fig*) sorrow. **~oroso** *a* painful. **~or de cabeza** headache. **~or de muelas** toothache

domar *vt* tame; break in ‹*caballo*›

dom|esticar [7] *vt* domesticate. **~éstico** *a* domestic. ● *m* servant

domicilio *m* home. **a ~** at home. **servicio a ~** home delivery service

domina|ción *f* domination. **~nte** *a* dominant; ‹*persona*› domineering. **~r** *vt* dominate; (*contener*) control; (*conocer*) have a good knowledge of. ● *vi* dominate; (*destacarse*) stand out. **~rse** *vpr* control o.s.

domin|go *m* Sunday. **~guero** *a* Sunday. **~ical** *a* Sunday

dominio *m* authority; (*territorio*) domain; (*fig*) good knowledge

dominó *m* (*juego*) dominoes

don *m* talent, gift; (*en un sobre*) Mr. **~ Pedro** Pedro. **tener ~ de lenguas** have a gift for languages. **tener ~ de gentes** have a way with people

donación *f* donation

donaire *m* grace, charm

dona|nte *m* (*de sangre*) donor. **~r** *vt* donate

doncella *f* (*criada*) maid

donde *adv* where

dónde *adv* where? **¿hasta ~?** how far? **¿por ~?** whereabouts?; (*¿por qué camino?*) which way? **¿a ~ vas?** where are you going? **¿de ~ eres?** where are you from?

dondequiera *adv* anywhere; (*en todas partes*) everywhere. **~ que** wherever. **por ~** everywhere

doña *f* (*en un sobre*) Mrs. **~ María** María

dora|do *a* golden; (*cubierto de oro*) gilt. **~dura** *f* gilding. **~r** *vt* gilt; (*culin*) brown

dormi|lón *m* sleepyhead. ● *a* lazy. **~r** [6] *vt* send to sleep. ● *vi* sleep. **~rse** *vpr* go to sleep. **~tar** *vi* doze. **~torio** *m* bedroom. **~r la siesta**

have an afternoon nap, have a siesta. **echarse a dormir** go to bed
dors|al *a* back. ● *m* (*en deportes*) number. **~o** *m* back
dos *a* & *m* two. **~cientos** *a* & *m* two hundred. **cada ~ por tres** every five minutes. **de ~ en ~** in twos, in pairs. **en un ~ por tres** in no time. **los dos, las dos** both (of them)
dosi|ficar [7] *vt* dose; (*fig*) measure out. **~s** *f* dose
dot|ado *a* gifted. **~ar** *vt* give a dowry; (*proveer*) endow (**de** with). **~e** *m* dowry
doy *vb véase* **dar**
dragar [12] *vt* dredge
drago *m* dragon tree
dragón *m* dragon
dram|a *m* drama; (*obra de teatro*) play. **~ático** *a* dramatic. **~atizar** [10] *vt* dramatize. **~aturgo** *m* playwright
drástico *a* drastic
droga *f* drug. **~dicto** *m* drug addict. **~do** *a* drugged. ● *m* drug addict. **~r** [12] *vt* drug. **~rse** *vpr* take drugs. **~ta** *m* & *f* (*fam*) drug addict
droguería *f* hardware shop (*Brit*), hardware store (*Amer*)
dromedario *m* dromedary
ducha *f* shower. **~rse** *vpr* have a shower
dud|a *f* doubt. **~ar** *vt/i* doubt. **~oso** *a* doubtful; (*sospechoso*) dubious. **poner en ~a** question. **sin ~a (alguna)** without a doubt
duelo *m* duel; (*luto*) mourning
duende *m* imp
dueñ|a *f* owner, proprietress; (*de una pensión*) landlady. **~o** *m* owner, proprietor; (*de una pensión*) landlord
duermo *vb véase* **dormir**
dul|ce *a* sweet; ‹*agua*› fresh; (*suave*) soft, gentle. ● *m* sweet. **~zura** *f* sweetness; (*fig*) gentleness
duna *f* dune
dúo *m* duet, duo
duodécimo *a* & *m* twelfth
duplica|do *a* in duplicate. ● *m* duplicate. **~r** [7] *vt* duplicate. **~rse** *vpr* double
duque *m* duke. **~sa** *f* duchess
dura|ción *f* duration, length. **~dero** *a* lasting
durante *prep* during, in; (*medida de tiempo*) for. **~ todo el año** all year round
durar *vi* last
durazno *m* (*LAm*, *fruta*) peach
dureza *f* hardness, toughness; (*med*) hard patch
durmiente *a* sleeping
duro *a* hard; (*culin*) tough; (*fig*) harsh. ● *adv* hard. ● *m* five-peseta coin. **ser ~ de oído** be hard of hearing

E

e *conj* and
ebanista *m* & *f* cabinet-maker
ébano *m* ebony
ebri|edad *f* drunkenness. **~o** *a* drunk
ebullición *f* boiling
eccema *m* eczema
eclesiástico *a* ecclesiastical. ● *m* clergyman
eclipse *m* eclipse
eco *m* echo. **hacer(se) ~** echo
ecolog|ía *f* ecology. **~ista** *m* & *f* ecologist
economato *m* cooperative store
econ|omía *f* economy; (*ciencia*) economics. **~ómicamente** *adv* economically. **~ómico** *a* economic(al); (*no caro*) inexpensive. **~omista** *m* & *f* economist. **~omizar** [10] *vt/i* economize
ecuación *f* equation
ecuador *m* equator. **el E~** Ecuador
ecuánime *a* level-headed; (*imparcial*) impartial
ecuanimidad *f* equanimity
ecuatoriano *a* & *m* Ecuadorian
ecuestre *a* equestrian
echar *vt* throw; post ‹*carta*›; give off ‹*olor*›; pour ‹*líquido*›; sprout ‹*hojas etc*›; (*despedir*) throw out; dismiss ‹*empleado*›; (*poner*) put on; put out ‹*raices*›; show ‹*película*›. **~se** *vpr* throw o.s.; (*tumbarse*) lie down. **~ a** start. **~ a perder** spoil. **~ de menos** miss. **~se atrás** (*fig*) back down. **echárselas de** feign
edad *f* age. **~ avanzada** old age. **E~ de Piedra** Stone Age. **E~ Media** Middle Ages. **¿qué ~ tiene?** how old is he?
edición *f* edition; (*publicación*) publication
edicto *m* edict
edific|ación *f* building. **~ante** *a* edifying. **~ar** [7] *vt* build; (*fig*) edify. **~io** *m* building; (*fig*) structure

Edimburgo *m* Edinburgh
edit|ar *vt* publish. **~or** *a* publishing. ● *m* publisher. **~orial** *a* editorial. ● *m* leading article. ● *f* publishing house
edredón *m* eiderdown
educa|ción *f* upbringing; (*modales*) (good) manners; (*enseñanza*) education. **~do** *a* polite. **~dor** *m* teacher. **~r** [7] *vt* bring up; (*enseñar*) educate. **~tivo** *a* educational. **bien ~do** polite. **falta de ~ción** rudeness, bad manners. **mal ~do** rude
edulcorante *m* sweetener
EE.UU. *abrev* (*Estados Unidos*) USA, United States (of America)
efect|ivamente *adv* really; (*por supuesto*) indeed. **~ivo** *a* effective; (*auténtico*) real; ‹*empleo*› permanent. ● *m* cash. **~o** *m* effect; (*impresión*) impression. **~os** *mpl* belongings; (*com*) goods. **~uar** [21] *vt* carry out, effect; make ‹*viaje, compras etc*›. **en ~o** in fact; (*por supuesto*) indeed
efervescente *a* effervescent; ‹*bebidas*› fizzy
efica|cia *f* effectiveness; (*de persona*) efficiency. **~z** *a* effective; ‹*persona*› efficient
eficien|cia *f* efficiency. **~te** *a* efficient
efigie *f* effigy
efímero *a* ephemeral
efluvio *m* outflow
efusi|ón *n* effusion. **~vo** *a* effusive; ‹*gracias*› warm
Egeo *m*. **mar ~** Aegean Sea
égida *f* aegis
egipcio *a* & *m* Egyptian
Egipto *m* Egypt
ego|céntrico *a* egocentric. ● *m* egocentric person. **~ísmo** *m* selfishness. **~ísta** *a* selfish. ● *m* selfish person
egregio *a* eminent
egresar *vi* (*LAm*) leave; (*univ*) graduate
eje *m* axis; (*tec*) axle
ejecu|ción *f* execution; (*mus etc*) performance. **~tante** *m* & *f* executor; (*mus etc*) performer. **~tar** *vt* carry out; (*mus etc*) perform; (*matar*) execute
ejecutivo *m* director, manager
ejempl|ar *a* exemplary. ● *m* (*ejemplo*) example, specimen; (*libro*) copy; (*revista*) issue, number. **~ificar** [7] *vt* exemplify. **~o** *m* example. **dar ~o** set an example. **por ~o** for example. **sin ~** unprecedented
ejerc|er [9] *vt* exercise; practise ‹*profesión*›; exert ‹*influencia*›. ● *vi* practise. **~icio** *m* exercise; (*de una profesión*) practice. **~itar** *vt* exercise. **~itarse** *vpr* exercise. **hacer ~icios** take exercise
ejército *m* army
el *art def m* (*pl* **los**) the. ● *pron* (*pl* **los**) the one. **~ de Antonio** Antonio's. **~ que** whoever, the one
él *pron* (*persona*) he; (*persona con prep*) him; (*cosa*) it. **el libro de ~** his book
elabora|ción *f* processing; (*fabricación*) manufacture. **~r** *vt* process; manufacture ‹*producto*›; (*producir*) produce
el|asticidad *f* elasticity. **~ástico** *a* & *m* elastic
elec|ción *f* choice; (*de político etc*) election. **~ciones** *fpl* (*pol*) election. **~tor** *m* voter. **~torado** *m* electorate. **~toral** *a* electoral
electrici|dad *f* electricity. **~sta** *m* & *f* electrician
eléctrico *a* electric; (*de la electricidad*) electrical
electrificar [7] *vt*, **electrizar** [10] *vt* electrify
electrocutar *vt* electrocute
electrodo *m* electrode
electrodoméstico *a* electrical household. **~s** *mpl* electrical household appliances
electrólisis *f* electrolysis
electrón *m* electron
electrónic|a *f* electronics. **~o** *a* electronic
elefante *m* elephant
elegan|cia *f* elegance. **~te** *a* elegant
elegía *f* elegy
elegi|ble *a* eligible. **~do** *a* chosen. **~r** [5 & 14] *vt* choose; (*por votación*) elect
element|al *a* elementary. **~o** *m* element; (*persona*) person, bloke (*fam*). **~os** *mpl* (*nociones*) basic principles
elenco *m* (*en el teatro*) cast
eleva|ción *f* elevation; (*de precios*) rise, increase; (*acción*) raising. **~dor** *m* (*LAm*) lift. **~r** *vt* raise; (*promover*) promote
elimina|ción *f* elimination. **~r** *vt* eliminate. **~toria** *f* preliminary heat
el|ipse *f* ellipse. **~íptico** *a* elliptical

élite /e'lit, e'lite/ *f* elite
elixir *m* elixir
elocución *f* elocution
elocuen|cia *f* eloquence. **~te** *a* eloquent
elogi|ar *vt* praise. **~o** *m* praise
elote *m* (*Mex*) corn on the cob
eludir *vt* avoid, elude
ella *pron* (*persona*) she; (*persona con prep*) her; (*cosa*) it. **~s** *pron pl* they; (*con prep*) them. **el libro de ~** her book. **el libro de ~s** their book
ello *pron* it
ellos *pron pl* they; (*con prep*) them. **el libro de ~** their book
emaciado *a* emaciated
emana|ción *f* emanation. **~r** *vi* emanate (**de** from); (*originarse*) originate (**de** from, in)
emancipa|ción *f* emancipation. **~do** *a* emancipated. **~r** *vt* emancipate. **~rse** *vpr* become emancipated
embadurnar *vt* smear
embajad|a *f* embassy. **~or** *m* ambassador
embalar *vt* pack
embaldosar *vt* tile
embalsamar *vt* embalm
embalse *m* dam; (*pantano*) reservoir
embaraz|ada *a* pregnant. ● *f* pregnant woman. **~ar** [10] *vt* hinder. **~o** *m* hindrance; (*de mujer*) pregnancy. **~oso** *a* awkward, embarrassing
embar|cación *f* boat. **~cadero** *m* jetty, pier. **~car** [7] *vt* embark ‹*personas*›; ship ‹*mercancías*›. **~carse** *vpr* embark. **~carse en** (*fig*) embark upon
embargo *m* embargo; (*jurid*) seizure. **sin ~** however
embarque *m* loading
embarullar *vt* muddle
embaucar [7] *vt* deceive
embeber *vt* absorb; (*empapar*) soak. ● *vi* shrink. **~se** *vpr* be absorbed
embelesar *vt* delight. **~se** *vpr* be delighted
embellecer [11] *vt* embellish
embesti|da *f* attack. **~r** [5] *vt/i* attack
emblema *m* emblem
embobar *vt* amaze
embobecer [11] *vt* make silly. **~se** *vpr* get silly
embocadura *f* (*de un río*) mouth
emboquillado *a* tipped
embolsar *vt* pocket
emborrachar *vt* get drunk. **~se** *vpr* get drunk
emborrascarse [7] *vpr* get stormy
emborronar *vt* blot
embosca|da *f* ambush. **~rse** [7] *vpr* lie in wait
embotar *vt* blunt; (*fig*) dull
embotella|miento *m* (*de vehículos*) traffic jam. **~r** *vt* bottle
embrague *m* clutch
embriag|ar [12] *vt* get drunk; (*fig*) intoxicate; (*fig, enajenar*) enrapture. **~arse** *vpr* get drunk. **~uez** *f* drunkenness; (*fig*) intoxication
embrión *m* embryo
embroll|ar *vt* mix up; involve ‹*personas*›. **~arse** *vpr* get into a muddle; *en un asunto*) get involved. **~o** *m* tangle; (*fig*) muddle. **~ón** *m* troublemaker
embromar *vt* make fun of; (*engañar*) fool
embruja|do *a* bewitched; ‹*casa etc*› haunted. **~r** *vt* bewitch
embrutecer [11] *vt* brutalize
embuchar *vt* wolf ‹*comida*›
embudo *m* funnel
embuste *m* lie. **~ro** *a* deceitful. ● *m* liar
embuti|do *m* (*culin*) sausage. **~r** *vt* stuff
emergencia *f* emergency; (*acción de emerger*) emergence. **en caso de ~** in case of emergency
emerger [14] *vi* appear, emerge; ‹*submarino*› surface
emigra|ción *f* emigration. **~nte** *m & f* emigrant. **~r** *vi* emigrate
eminen|cia *f* eminence. **~te** *a* eminent
emisario *m* emissary
emis|ión *f* emission; (*de dinero*) issue; (*TV etc*) broadcast. **~or** *a* issuing; (*TV etc*) broadcasting. **~ora** *f* radio station
emitir *vt* emit; let out ‹*grito*›; (*TV etc*) broadcast; (*expresar*) express; (*poner en circulación*) issue
emoci|ón *f* emotion; (*excitación*) excitement. **~onado** *a* moved. **~onante** *a* exciting; (*conmovedor*) moving. **~onar** *vt* excite; (*conmover*) move. **~onarse** *vpr* get excited; (*conmoverse*) be moved. **¡qué ~ón!** how exciting!
emotivo *a* emotional; (*conmovedor*) moving
empacar [7] *vt* (*LAm*) pack

empacho *m* indigestion; (*vergüenza*) embarrassment
empadronar *vt* register. **~se** *vpr* register
empalagoso *a* sickly; (*demasiado amable*) ingratiating; (*demasiado sentimental*) mawkish
empalizada *f* fence
empalm|ar *vt* connect, join. • *vi* meet. **~e** *m* junction; (*de trenes*) connection
empanad|a *f* (savoury) pie. **~illa** *f* (small) pie. **~o** *a* fried in breadcrumbs
empanizado *a* (*Mex*) fried in breadcrumbs
empantanar *vt* flood. **~se** *vpr* become flooded; (*fig*) get bogged down
empañar *vt* mist; dull ‹*metales etc*›; (*fig*) tarnish. **~se** *vpr* ‹*cristales*› steam up
empapar *vt* soak; (*absorber*) soak up. **~se** *vpr* be soaked
empapela|do *m* wallpaper. **~r** *vt* paper; (*envolver*) wrap (in paper)
empaquetar *vt* package; pack together ‹*personas*›
emparedado *m* sandwich
emparejar *vt* match; (*nivelar*) make level. **~se** *vpr* pair off
empast|ar *vt* fill ‹*muela*›. **~e** *m* filling
empat|ar *vi* draw. **~e** *m* draw
empedernido *a* inveterate; (*insensible*) hard
empedrar [1] *vt* pave
empeine *m* instep
empeñ|ado *a* in debt; (*decidido*) determined; (*acalorado*) heated. **~ar** *vt* pawn; pledge ‹*palabras*›; (*principiar*) start. **~arse** *vpr* (*endeudarse*) get into debt; (*meterse*) get involved; (*estar decidido a*) insist (**en** on). **~o** *m* pledge; (*resolución*) determination. **casa de ~s** pawnshop
empeorar *vt* make worse. • *vi* get worse. **~se** *vpr* get worse
empequeñecer [11] *vt* dwarf; (*fig*) belittle
empera|dor *m* emperor. **~triz** *f* empress
empezar [1 & 10] *vt/i* start, begin. **para ~** to begin with
empina|do *a* upright; ‹*cuesta*› steep. **~r** *vt* raise. **~rse** *vpr* ‹*persona*› stand on tiptoe; ‹*animal*› rear
empírico *a* empirical
emplasto *m* plaster
emplaza|miento *m* (*jurid*) summons; (*lugar*) site. **~r** [10] *vt* summon; (*situar*) site
emple|ado *m* employee. **~ar** *vt* use; employ ‹*persona*›; spend ‹*tiempo*›. **~arse** *vpr* be used; ‹*persona*› be employed. **~o** *m* use; (*trabajo*) employment; (*puesto*) job
empobrecer [11] *vt* impoverish. **~se** *vpr* become poor
empolvar *vt* powder
empoll|ar *vt* incubate ‹*huevos*›; (*estudiar, fam*) swot up (*Brit*), grind away at (*Amer*). • *vi* ‹*ave*› sit; ‹*estudiante*› swot (*Brit*), grind away (*Amer*). **~ón** *m* swot
emponzoñar *vt* poison
emporio *m* emporium; (*LAm, almacén*) department store
empotra|do *a* built-in, fitted. **~r** *vt* fit
emprendedor *a* enterprising
emprender *vt* undertake; set out on ‹*viaje etc*›. **~la con uno** pick a fight with s.o.
empresa *f* undertaking; (*com*) company, firm. **~rio** *m* impresario; (*com*) contractor
empréstito *m* loan
empuj|ar *vt* push; press ‹*botón*›. **~e** *m* push, shove; (*fig*) drive. **~ón** *m* push, shove
empuñar *vt* grasp; take up ‹*pluma, espada*›
emular *vt* emulate
emulsión *f* emulsion
en *prep* in; (*sobre*) on; (*dentro*) inside, in; (*con dirección*) into; (*medio de transporte*) by. **~ casa** at home. **~ coche** by car. **~ 10 días** in 10 days. **de pueblo ~ pueblo** from town to town
enagua *f* petticoat
enajena|ción *f* alienation; (*éxtasis*) rapture. **~r** *vt* alienate; (*volver loco*) drive mad; (*fig, extasiar*) enrapture. **~ción mental** insanity
enamora|do *a* in love. • *m* lover. **~r** *vt* win the love of. **~rse** *vpr* fall in love (**de** with)
enan|ito *m* dwarf. **~o** *a & m* dwarf
enardecer [11] *vt* inflame. **~se** *vpr* get excited (**por** about)
encabeza|miento *m* heading; (*de periódico*) headline. **~r** [10] *vt* introduce ‹*escrito*›; (*poner título a*) entitle; head ‹*una lista*›; lead ‹*revolución etc*›; (*empadronar*) register

encadenar *vt* chain; (*fig*) tie down
encaj|ar *vt* fit; fit together ‹*varias piezas*›. ● *vi* fit; (*estar de acuerdo*) tally. **~arse** *vpr* squeeze into. **~e** *m* lace; (*acción de encajar*) fitting
encajonar *vt* box; (*en sitio estrecho*) squeeze in
encalar *vt* whitewash
encallar *vt* run aground; (*fig*) get bogged down
encaminar *vt* direct. **~se** *vpr* make one's way
encandilar *vt* (*pasmar*) bewilder; (*estimular*) stimulate
encanecer [11] *vi* go grey
encant|ado *a* enchanted; (*hechizado*) bewitched; ‹*casa etc*› haunted. **~ador** *a* charming. ● *m* magician. **~amiento** *m* magic. **~ar** *vt* bewitch; (*fig*) charm, delight. **~o** *m* magic; (*fig*) delight. **¡~ado!** pleased to meet you! **me ~a la leche** I love milk
encapotado *a* ‹*cielo*› overcast
encapricharse *vpr*. **~ con** take a fancy to
encarar *vt* face. **~se** *vpr*. **~se con** face
encarcelar *vt* imprison
encarecer [11] *vt* put up the price of; (*alabar*) praise. ● *vi* go up
encarg|ado *a* in charge. ● *m* manager, attendant, person in charge. **~ar** [12] *vt* entrust; (*pedir*) order. **~arse** *vpr* take charge (**de** of). **~o** *m* job; (*com*) order; (*recado*) errand. **hecho de ~o** made to measure
encariñarse *vpr*. **~ con** take to, become fond of
encarna|ción *f* incarnation. **~do** *a* incarnate; (*rojo*) red. ● *m* red
encarnizado *a* bitter
encarpetar *vt* file; (*LAm, dar carpetazo*) shelve
encarrilar *vt* put back on the rails; (*fig*) direct, put on the right road
encasillar *vt* pigeonhole
encastillarse *vpr*. **~ en** (*fig*) stick to
encauzar [10] *vt* channel
encend|edor *m* lighter. **~er** [1] *vt* light; (*pegar fuego a*) set fire to; switch on, turn on ‹*aparato eléctrico*›; (*fig*) arouse. **~erse** *vpr* light; (*prender fuego*) catch fire; (*excitarse*) get excited; (*ruborizarse*) blush. **~ido** *a* lit; ‹*aparato eléctrico*› on; (*rojo*) bright red. ● *m* (*auto*) ignition
encera|do *a* waxed. ● *m* (*pizarra*) blackboard. **~r** *vt* wax
encerr|ar [1] *vt* shut in; (*con llave*) lock up; (*fig, contener*) contain. **~ona** *f* trap
encía *f* gum
encíclica *f* encyclical
enciclop|edia *f* encyclopaedia. **~édico** *a* enclyclopaedic
encierro *m* confinement; (*cárcel*) prison
encima *adv* on top; (*arriba*) above. **~ de** on, on top of; (*sobre*) over; (*además de*) besides, as well as. **por ~** on top; (*a la ligera*) superficially. **por ~ de todo** above all
encina *f* holm oak
encinta *a* pregnant
enclave *m* enclave
enclenque *a* weak; (*enfermizo*) sickly
encog|er [14] *vt* shrink; (*contraer*) contract. **~erse** *vpr* shrink. **~erse de hombros** shrug one's shoulders. **~ido** *a* shrunk; (*fig, tímido*) timid
encolar *vt* glue; (*pegar*) stick
encolerizar [10] *vt* make angry. **~se** *vpr* get angry, lose one's temper
encomendar [1] *vt* entrust
encomi|ar *vt* praise. **~o** *m* praise
encono *m* bitterness, ill will
encontra|do *a* contrary, conflicting. **~r** [2] *vt* find; (*tropezar con*) meet. **~rse** *vpr* meet; (*hallarse*) be. **no ~rse** feel uncomfortable
encorvar *vt* bend, curve. **~se** *vpr* stoop
encrespado *a* ‹*pelo*› curly; ‹*mar*› rough
encrucijada *f* crossroads
encuaderna|ción *f* binding. **~dor** *m* bookbinder. **~r** *vt* bind
encuadrar *vt* frame
encub|ierto *a* hidden. **~rir** [*pp* **encubierto**] *vt* hide, conceal; shelter ‹*delincuente*›
encuentro *m* meeting; (*colisión*) crash; (*en deportes*) match; (*mil*) skirmish
encuesta *f* survey; (*investigación*) inquiry
encumbra|do *a* eminent. **~r** *vt* (*fig, elevar*) exalt. **~rse** *vpr* rise
encurtidos *mpl* pickles
encharcar [7] *vt* flood. **~se** *vpr* be flooded
enchuf|ado *a* switched on. **~ar** *vt* plug in; fit together ‹*tubos etc*›. **~e** *m* socket; (*clavija*) plug; (*de tubos*

etc) joint; (*fig*, *empleo*, *fam*) cushy job; (*influencia*, *fam*) influence. **tener ~e** have friends in the right places

endeble *a* weak

endemoniado *a* possessed; (*malo*) wicked

enderezar [10] *vt* straighten out; (*poner vertical*) put upright (again); (*fig*, *arreglar*) put right, sort out; (*dirigir*) direct. **~se** *vpr* straighten out

endeudarse *vpr* get into debt

endiablado *a* possessed; (*malo*) wicked

endomingarse [12] *vpr* dress up

endosar *vt* endorse ‹*cheque etc*›; (*fig*, *fam*) lumber

endrogarse [12] *vpr* (*Mex*) get into debt

endulzar [10] *vt* sweeten; (*fig*) soften

endurecer [11] *vt* harden. **~se** *vpr* harden; (*fig*) become hardened

enema *m* enema

enemi|go *a* hostile. ● *m* enemy. **~stad** *f* enmity. **~star** *vt* make an enemy of. **~starse** *vpr* fall out (**con** with)

en|ergía *f* energy. **~érgico** *a* ‹*persona*› lively; ‹*decisión*› forceful

energúmeno *m* madman

enero *m* January

enervar *vt* enervate

enésimo *a* nth, umpteenth (*fam*)

enfad|adizo *a* irritable. **~ado** *a* cross, angry. **~ar** *vt* make cross, anger; (*molestar*) annoy. **~arse** *vpr* get cross. **~o** *m* anger; (*molestia*) annoyance

énfasis *m invar* emphasis, stress. **poner ~** stress, emphasize

enfático *a* emphatic

enferm|ar *vi* fall ill. **~edad** *f* illness. **~era** *f* nurse. **~ería** *f* sick bay. **~ero** *m* (male) nurse. **~izo** *a* sickly. **~o** *a* ill. ● *m* patient

enflaquecer [11] *vt* make thin. ● *vi* lose weight

enfo|car [7] *vt* shine on; focus ‹*lente etc*›; (*fig*) consider. **~que** *m* focus; (*fig*) point of view

enfrascarse [7] *vpr* (*fig*) be absorbed

enfrentar *vt* face, confront; (*poner frente a frente*) bring face to face. **~se** *vpr*. **~se con** confront; (*en deportes*) meet

enfrente *adv* opposite. **~ de** opposite. **de ~** opposite

enfria|miento *m* cooling; (*catarro*) cold. **~r** [20] *vt* cool (down); (*fig*) cool down. **~rse** *vpr* go cold; (*fig*) cool off

enfurecer [11] *vt* infuriate. **~se** *vpr* lose one's temper; ‹*mar*› get rough

enfurruñarse *vpr* sulk

engalanar *vt* adorn. **~se** *vpr* dress up

enganchar *vt* hook; hang up ‹*ropa*›. **~se** *vpr* get caught; (*mil*) enlist

engañ|ar *vt* deceive, trick; (*ser infiel*) be unfaithful. **~arse** *vpr* be wrong, be mistaken; (*no admitir la verdad*) deceive o.s. **~o** *m* deceit, trickery; (*error*) mistake. **~oso** *a* deceptive; ‹*persona*› deceitful

engarzar [10] *vt* string ‹*cuentas*›; set ‹*joyas*›; (*fig*) link

engatusar *vt* (*fam*) coax

engendr|ar *vt* breed; (*fig*) produce. **~o** *m* (*monstruo*) monster; (*fig*) brainchild

englobar *vt* include

engomar *vt* glue

engordar *vt* fatten. ● *vi* get fatter, put on weight

engorro *m* nuisance

engranaje *m* (*auto*) gear

engrandecer [11] *vt* (*enaltecer*) exalt, raise

engrasar *vt* grease; (*con aceite*) oil; (*ensuciar*) make greasy

engreído *a* arrogant

engrosar [2] *vt* swell. ● *vi* ‹*persona*› get fatter; ‹*río*› swell

engullir [22] *vt* gulp down

enharinar *vt* sprinkle with flour

enhebrar *vt* thread

enhorabuena *f* congratulations. **dar la ~** congratulate

enigm|a *m* enigma. **~ático** *a* enigmatic

enjabonar *vt* soap; (*fig*, *fam*) butter up

enjalbegar [12] *vt* whitewash

enjambre *m* swarm

enjaular *vt* put in a cage

enjuag|ar [12] *vt* rinse (out). **~atorio** *m* mouthwash. **~ue** *m* rinsing; (*para la boca*) mouthwash

enjugar [12] *vt* dry; (*limpiar*) wipe; cancel ‹*deuda*›

enjuiciar *vt* pass judgement on

enjuto *a* ‹*persona*› skinny

enlace *m* connection; (*matrimonial*) wedding

enlatar *vt* tin, can

enlazar [10] *vt* tie together; (*fig*) relate, connect
enlodar *vt*, **enlodazar** [10] *vt* cover in mud
enloquecer [11] *vt* drive mad. ● *vi* go mad. **~se** *vpr* go mad
enlosar *vt* (*con losas*) pave; (*con baldosas*) tile
enlucir [11] *vt* plaster
enluta|do *a* in mourning. **~r** *vt* dress in mourning; (*fig*) sadden
enmarañar *vt* tangle (up), entangle; (*confundir*) confuse. **~se** *vpr* get into a tangle; (*confundirse*) get confused
enmarcar [7] *vt* frame
enmascarar *vt* mask. **~se de** masquerade as
enm|endar *vt* correct. **~endarse** *vpr* mend one's way. **~ienda** *f* correction; (*de ley etc*) amendment
enmohecerse [11] *vpr* (*con óxido*) go rusty; (*con hongos*) go mouldy
enmudecer [11] *vi* be dumbstruck; (*callar*) say nothing
ennegrecer [11] *vt* blacken
ennoblecer [11] *vt* ennoble; (*fig*) add style to
enoj|adizo *a* irritable. **~ado** *a* angry, cross. **~ar** *vt* make cross, anger; (*molestar*) annoy. **~arse** *vpr* get cross. **~o** *m* anger; (*molestia*) annoyance. **~oso** *a* annoying
enorgullecerse [11] *vpr* be proud
enorm|e *a* enormous; (*malo*) wicked. **~emente** *adv* enormously. **~idad** *f* immensity; (*atrocidad*) enormity. **me gusta una ~idad** I like it enormously
enrabiar *vt* infuriate
enraizar [10 & 20] *vi* take root
enrarecido *a* rarefied
enrasar *vt* make level
enred|adera *f* creeper. **~adero** *a* climbing. **~ar** *vt* tangle (up), entangle; (*confundir*) confuse; (*comprometer a uno*) involve, implicate; (*sembrar la discordia*) cause trouble between. ● *vi* get up to mischief. **~ar con** fiddle with, play with. **~arse** *vpr* get into a tangle; (*confundirse*) get confused; ‹*persona*› get involved. **~o** *m* tangle; (*fig*) muddle, mess
enrejado *m* bars
enrevesado *a* complicated
enriquecer [11] *vt* make rich; (*fig*) enrich. **~se** *vpr* get rich
enrojecer [11] *vt* turn red, redden. **~se** *vpr* ‹*persona*› go red, blush
enrolar *vt* enlist
enrollar *vt* roll (up); wind ‹*hilo etc*›
enroscar [7] *vt* coil; (*atornillar*) screw in
ensalad|a *f* salad. **~era** *f* salad bowl. **~illa** *f* Russian salad. **armar una ~a** make a mess
ensalzar [10] *vt* praise; (*enaltecer*) exalt
ensambladura *f*, **ensamblaje** *m* (*acción*) assembling; (*efecto*) joint
ensamblar *vt* join
ensanch|ar *vt* widen; (*agrandar*) enlarge. **~arse** *vpr* get wider. **~e** *m* widening; (*de ciudad*) new district
ensangrentar [1] *vt* stain with blood
ensañarse *vpr*. **~ con** treat cruelly
ensartar *vt* string ‹*cuentas etc*›
ensay|ar *vt* test; rehearse ‹*obra de teatro etc*›. **~arse** *vpr* rehearse. **~o** *m* test, trial; (*composición literaria*) essay
ensenada *f* inlet, cove
enseña|nza *f* education; (*acción de enseñar*) teaching. **~nza media** secondary education. **~r** *vt* teach; (*mostrar*) show
enseñorearse *vpr* take over
enseres *mpl* equipment
ensillar *vt* saddle
ensimismarse *vpr* be lost in thought
ensoberbecerse [11] *vpr* become conceited
ensombrecer [11] *vt* darken
ensordecer [11] *vt* deafen. ● *vi* go deaf
ensortijar *vt* curl ‹*pelo etc*›
ensuciar *vt* dirty. **~se** *vpr* get dirty
ensueño *m* dream
entablar *vt* (*empezar*) start
entablillar *vt* put in a splint
entalegar [12] *vt* put into a bag; (*fig*) hoard
entallar *vt* fit ‹*un vestido*›. ● *vi* fit
entarimado *m* parquet
ente *m* entity, being; (*persona rara, fam*) odd person; (*com*) firm, company
entend|er [1] *vt* understand; (*opinar*) believe, think; (*querer decir*) mean. ● *vi* understand. **~erse** *vpr* make o.s. understood; (*comprenderse*) be understood. **~er de** know all about. **~erse con** get on with. **~ido** *a* understood; (*enterado*) well-informed. ● *interj* agreed!, OK! (*fam*). **~imiento** *m* understanding.

a mi ~er in my opinion. **dar a ~er** hint. **no darse por ~ido** pretend not to understand, turn a deaf ear
entenebrecer [11] *vt* darken. **~se** *vpr* get dark
enterado *a* well-informed; (*que sabe*) aware. **no darse por ~** pretend not to understand, turn a deaf ear
enteramente *adv* entirely, completely
enterar *vt* inform. **~se** *vpr*. **~se de** find out about, hear of. **¡entérate!** listen! **¿te enteras?** do you understand?
entereza *f* (*carácter*) strength of character
enternecer [11] *vt* (*fig*) move, touch. **~se** *vpr* be moved, be touched
entero *a* entire, whole; (*firme*) firm. **por ~** entirely, completely
enterra|dor *m* gravedigger. **~r** [1] *vt* bury
entibiar *vt* cool. **~se** *vpr* cool down; (*fig*) cool off
entidad *f* entity; (*organización*) organization; (*com*) company
entierro *m* burial; (*ceremonia*) funeral
entona|ción *f* intonation; (*fig*) arrogance. **~r** *vt* intone. ● *vi* (*mus*) be in tune; ‹*colores*› match. **~rse** *vpr* (*fortalecerse*) tone o.s. up; (*engreírse*) be arrogant
entonces *adv* then. **en aquel ~, por aquel ~** at that time, then
entontecer [11] *vt* make silly. **~se** *vpr* get silly
entornar *vt* half close; leave ajar ‹*puerta*›
entorpecer [11] *vt* ‹*frío etc*› numb; (*dificultar*) hinder
entra|da *f* entrance; (*acceso*) admission, entry; (*billete*) ticket; (*de datos, tec*) input. **~do** *a*. **~do en años** elderly. **ya ~da la noche** late at night. **~nte** *a* next, coming. **dar ~da a** (*admitir*) admit. **de ~da** right away.
entraña *f* (*fig*) heart. **~s** *fpl* entrails; (*fig*) heart. **~ble** *a* ‹*cariño etc*› deep; ‹*amigo*› close. **~r** *vt* involve
entrar *vt* put; (*traer*) bring. ● *vi* go in, enter; (*venir*) come in, enter; (*empezar*) start, begin. **no ~ ni salir en** have nothing to do with
entre *prep* (*de dos personas o cosas*) between; (*más de dos*) among(st)
entreab|ierto *a* half-open. **~rir** [*pp* **entreabierto**] *vt* half open
entreacto *m* interval
entrecano *a* ‹*pelo*› greying; ‹*persona*› who is going grey
entrecejo *m* forehead. **arrugar el ~, fruncir el ~** frown
entrecerrar [1] *vt* (*Amer*) half close
entrecortado *a* ‹*voz*› faltering; ‹*respiración*› laboured
entrecruzar [10] *vt* intertwine
entrega *f* handing over; (*de mercancías etc*) delivery; (*de novela etc*) instalment; (*dedicación*) commitment. **~r** [12] *vt* hand over, deliver, give. **~rse** *vpr* surrender, give o.s. up; (*dedicarse*) devote o.s. (**a** to)
entrelazar [10] *vt* intertwine
entremés *m* hors-d'oeuvre; (*en el teatro*) short comedy
entremet|er *vt* insert. **~erse** *vpr* interfere. **~ido** *a* interfering
entremezclar *vt* mix
entrena|dor *m* trainer. **~miento** *m* training. **~r** *vt* train. **~rse** *vpr* train
entrepierna *f* crotch
entresacar [7] *vt* pick out
entresuelo *m* mezzanine
entretanto *adv* meanwhile
entretejer *vt* interweave
entreten|er [40] *vt* entertain, amuse; (*detener*) delay, keep; (*mantener*) keep alive, keep going. **~erse** *vpr* amuse o.s.; (*tardar*) delay, linger. **~ido** *a* entertaining. **~imiento** *m* entertainment; (*mantenimiento*) upkeep
entrever [43] *vt* make out, glimpse
entrevista *f* interview; (*reunión*) meeting. **~rse** *vpr* have an interview
entristecer [11] *vt* sadden, make sad. **~se** *vpr* be sad
entromet|erse *vpr* interfere. **~ido** *a* interfering
entroncar [7] *vi* be related
entruchada *f*, **entruchado** *m* (*fam*) plot
entumec|erse [11] *vpr* go numb. **~ido** *a* numb
enturbiar *vt* cloud
entusi|asmar *vt* fill with enthusiasm; (*gustar mucho*) delight. **~asmarse** *vpr*. **~asmarse con** get enthusiastic about; (*ser aficionado a*) be mad about, love. **~asmo** *m* enthusiasm. **~asta** *a* enthusiastic.

● *m & f* enthusiast. **~ástico** *a* enthusiastic

enumera|ción *f* count, reckoning. **~r** *vt* enumerate

enuncia|ción *f* enunciation. **~r** *vt* enunciate

envainar *vt* sheathe

envalentonar *vt* encourage. **~se** *vpr* be brave, pluck up courage

envanecer [11] *vt* make conceited. **~se** *vpr* be conceited

envas|ado *a* tinned. ● *m* packaging. **~ar** *vt* package; (*en latas*) tin, can; (*en botellas*) bottle. **~e** *m* packing; (*lata*) tin, can; (*botella*) bottle

envejec|er [11] *vt* make old. ● *vi* get old, grow old. **~erse** *vpr* get old, grow old. **~ido** *a* aged, old

envenenar *vt* poison

envergadura *f* (*alcance*) scope

envés *m* wrong side

envia|do *a* sent. ● *m* representative; (*de la prensa*) correspondent. **~r** *vt* send

enviciar *vt* corrupt

envidi|a *f* envy; (*celos*) jealousy. **~able** *a* enviable. **~ar** *vt* envy, be envious of. **~oso** *a* envious. **tener ~a a** envy

envilecer [11] *vt* degrade

envío *m* sending, dispatch; (*de mercancías*) consignment; (*de dinero*) remittance. **~ contra reembolso** cash on delivery. **gastos** *mpl* **de envío** postage and packing (costs)

enviudar *vi* ‹*mujer*› become a widow, be widowed; ‹*hombre*› become a widower, be widowed

env|oltura *f* wrapping. **~olver** [2, *pp* **envuelto**] *vt* wrap; (*cubrir*) cover; (*fig, acorralar*) corner; (*fig, enredar*) involve; (*mil*) surround. **~olvimiento** *m* involvement. **~uelto** *a* wrapped (up)

enyesar *vt* plaster; (*med*) put in plaster

enzima *f* enzyme

épica *f* epic

epicentro *m* epicentre

épico *a* epic

epid|emia *f* epidemic. **~émico** *a* epidemic

epil|epsia *f* epilepsy. **~éptico** *a* epileptic

epílogo *m* epilogue

episodio *m* episode

epístola *f* epistle

epitafio *m* epitaph

epíteto *m* epithet

epítome *m* epitome

época *f* age; (*período*) period. **hacer ~** make history, be epoch-making

equidad *f* equity

equilátero *a* equilateral

equilibr|ar *vt* balance. **~io** *m* balance; (*de balanza*) equilibrium. **~ista** *m & f* tightrope walker

equino *a* horse, equine

equinoccio *m* equinox

equipaje *m* luggage (*esp Brit*), baggage (*esp Amer*); (*de barco*) crew

equipar *vt* equip; (*de ropa*) fit out

equiparar *vt* make equal; (*comparar*) compare

equipo *m* equipment; (*en deportes*) team

equitación *f* riding

equivale|ncia *f* equivalence. **~nte** *a* equivalent. **~r** [42] *vi* be equivalent; (*significar*) mean

equivoca|ción *f* mistake, error. **~do** *a* wrong. **~r** [7] *vt* mistake. **~rse** *vpr* be mistaken, be wrong, make a mistake. **~rse de** be wrong about. **~rse de número** dial the wrong number. **si no me equivoco** if I'm not mistaken

equívoco *a* equivocal; (*sospechoso*) suspicious. ● *m* ambiguity; (*juego de palabras*) pun; (*doble sentido*) double meaning

era *f* era. ● *vb véase* **ser**

erario *m* treasury

erección *f* erection; (*fig*) establishment

eremita *m* hermit

eres *vb véase* **ser**

erguir [48] *vt* raise. **~ la cabeza** hold one's head high. **~se** *vpr* straighten up

erigir [14] *vt* erect. **~se** *vpr* set o.s. up (**en** as)

eriza|do *a* prickly. **~rse** [10] *vpr* stand on end

erizo *m* hedgehog; (*de mar*) sea urchin. **~ de mar, ~ marino** sea urchin

ermita *f* hermitage. **~ño** *m* hermit

erosi|ón *f* erosion. **~onar** *vt* erode

er|ótico *a* erotic. **~otismo** *m* eroticism

errar [1, *la* **i** *inicial se escribe* **y**) *vt* miss. ● *vi* wander; (*equivocarse*) make a mistake, be wrong

errata *f* misprint

erróneo *a* erroneous, wrong

error *m* error, mistake. **estar en un ~** be wrong, be mistaken

eructar *vi* belch
erudi|ción *f* learning, erudition. **~to** *a* learned
erupción *f* eruption; (*med*) rash
es *vb véase* **ser**
esa *a véase* **ese**
ésa *pron véase* **ése**
esbelto *a* slender, slim
esboz|ar [10] *vt* sketch, outline. **~o** *m* sketch, outline
escabeche *m* pickle. **en ~** pickled
escabroso *a* ‹*terreno*› rough; ‹*asunto*› difficult; (*atrevido*) crude
escabullirse [22] *vpr* slip away
escafandra *f*, **escafandro** *m* diving-suit
escala *f* scale; (*escalera de mano*) ladder; (*de avión*) stopover. **~da** *f* climbing; (*pol*) escalation. **~r** *vt* scale; break into ‹*una casa*›. ● *vi* (*pol*) escalate. **hacer ~ en** stop at. **vuelo sin ~s** non-stop flight
escaldar *vt* scald
escalera *f* staircase, stairs; (*de mano*) ladder. **~ de caracol** spiral staircase. **~ de incendios** fire escape. **~ mecánica** escalator. **~ plegable** step-ladder
escalfa|do *a* poached. **~r** *vt* poach
escalinata *f* flight of steps
escalofrío *m* shiver
escal|ón *m* step; (*de escalera interior*) stair; (*de escala*) rung. **~onar** *vt* spread out
escalope *m* escalope
escam|a *f* scale; (*de jabón*) flake; (*fig*) suspicion. **~oso** *a* scaly
escamotear *vt* make disappear; (*robar*) steal, pinch (*fam*); disregard ‹*dificultad*›
escampar *vi* stop raining
esc|andalizar [10] *vt* scandalize, shock. **~andalizarse** *vpr* be shocked. **~ándalo** *m* scandal; (*alboroto*) uproar. **~andaloso** *a* scandalous; (*alborotador*) noisy
Escandinavia *f* Scandinavia
escandinavo *a* & *m* Scandinavian
escaño *m* bench; (*pol*) seat
escapa|da *f* escape; (*visita*) flying visit. **~do** *a* in a hurry. **~r** *vi* escape. **~rse** *vpr* escape; ‹*líquido, gas*› leak. **dejar ~r** let out
escaparate *m* (shop) window. **ir de ~s** go window-shopping
escapatoria *f* (*fig, fam*) way out
escape *m* (*de gas, de líquido*) leak; (*fuga*) escape; (*auto*) exhaust
escarabajo *m* beetle
escaramuza *f* skirmish
escarbar *vt* scratch; pick ‹*dientes, herida etc*›; (*fig, escudriñar*) delve (**en** into)
escarcha *f* frost. **~do** *a* ‹*fruta*› crystallized
escarlat|a *a invar* scarlet. **~ina** *f* scarlet fever
escarm|entar [1] *vt* punish severely. ● *vi* learn one's lesson. **~iento** *m* punishment; (*lección*) lesson
escarn|ecer [11] *vt* mock. **~io** *m* ridicule
escarola *f* endive
escarpa *f* slope. **~do** *a* steep
escas|ear *vi* be scarce. **~ez** *f* scarcity, shortage; (*pobreza*) poverty. **~o** *a* scarce; (*poco*) little; (*insuficiente*) short; (*muy justo*) barely
escatimar *vt* be sparing with
escayola *f* plaster. **~r** *vt* put in plaster
escena *f* scene; (*escenario*) stage. **~rio** *m* stage; (*en el cine*) scenario; (*fig*) scene
escénico *a* scenic
escenografía *f* scenery
esc|epticismo *m* scepticism. **~éptico** *a* sceptical. ● *m* sceptic
esclarecer [11] *vt* (*fig*) throw light on, clarify
esclavina *f* cape
esclav|itud *f* slavery. **~izar** [10] *vt* enslave. **~o** *m* slave
esclerosis *f* sclerosis
esclusa *f* lock
escoba *f* broom
escocer [2 & 9] *vt* hurt. ● *vi* sting
escocés *a* Scottish. ● *m* Scotsman
Escocia *f* Scotland
escog|er [14] *vt* choose, select. **~ido** *a* chosen; (*de buena calidad*) choice
escolar *a* school. ● *m* schoolboy. ● *f* schoolgirl. **~idad** *f* schooling
escolta *f* escort
escombros *mpl* rubble
escond|er *vt* hide. **~erse** *vpr* hide. **~idas. a ~idas** secretly. **~ite** *m* hiding place; (*juego*) hide-and-seek. **~rijo** *m* hiding place
escopeta *f* shotgun. **~zo** *m* shot
escoplo *m* chisel
escoria *f* slag; (*fig*) dregs
Escorpión *m* Scorpio
escorpión *m* scorpion
escot|ado *a* low-cut. **~adura** *f* low neckline. **~ar** *vt* cut out. ● *vi* pay

one's share. **~e** *m* low neckline. **ir a ~e, pagar a ~e** share the expenses

escozor *m* pain

escri|bano *m* clerk. **~biente** *m* clerk. **~bir** [*pp* **escrito**] *vt/i* write. **~bir a máquina** type. **~birse** *vpr* write to each other; (*deletrearse*) be spelt. **~to** *a* written. ● *m* writing; (*documento*) document. **~tor** *m* writer. **~torio** *m* desk; (*oficina*) office. **~tura** *f* (hand)writing; (*documento*) document; (*jurid*) deed. **¿cómo se escribe...?** how do you spell...? **poner por ~to** put into writing

escr|úpulo *m* scruple; (*escrupulosidad*) care, scrupulousness. **~uloso** *a* scrupulous

escrut|ar *vt* scrutinize; count ‹*votos*›. **~inio** *m* count. **hacer el ~inio** count the votes

escuadr|a *f* (*instrumento*) square; (*mil*) squad; (*naut*) fleet. **~ón** *m* squadron

escuálido *a* skinny; (*sucio*) squalid

escuchar *vt* listen to. ● *vi* listen

escudilla *f* bowl

escudo *m* shield. **~ de armas** coat of arms

escudriñar *vt* examine

escuela *f* school. **~ normal** teachers' training college

escueto *a* simple

escuincle *m* (*Mex*, *perro*) stray dog; (*Mex*, *muchacho*, *fam*) child, kid (*fam*)

escul|pir *vt* sculpture. **~tor** *m* sculptor. **~tora** *f* sculptress. **~tura** *f* sculpture; (*en madera*) carving

escupir *vt/i* spit

escurr|eplatos *m invar* plate-rack. **~idizo** *a* slippery. **~ir** *vt* drain; wring out ‹*ropa*›. ● *vi* drip; (*ser resbaladizo*) be slippery. **~irse** *vpr* slip

ese *a* (*f* **esa**, *mpl* **esos**, *fpl* **esas**) that; (*en plural*) those

ése *pron* (*f* **ésa**, *mpl* **ésos**, *fpl* **ésas**) that one; (*en plural*) those; (*primero de dos*) the former. **ni por ésas** on no account

esencia *f* essence. **~l** *a* essential. **lo ~l** the main thing

esf|era *f* sphere; (*de reloj*) face. **~érico** *a* spherical

esfinge *f* sphinx

esf|orzarse [2 & 10] *vpr* make an effort. **~uerzo** *m* effort

esfumarse *vpr* fade away; ‹*persona*› vanish

esgrim|a *f* fencing. **~ir** *vt* brandish; (*fig*) use

esguince *m* swerve; (*med*) sprain

eslab|ón *m* link. **~onar** *vt* link (together)

eslavo *a* Slav, Slavonic

eslogan *m* slogan

esmalt|ar *vt* enamel; varnish ‹*uñas*›; (*fig*) adorn. **~e** *m* enamel. **~ de uñas, ~e para las uñas** nail varnish (*Brit*), nail polish (*Amer*)

esmerado *a* careful

esmeralda *f* emerald

esmerarse *vpr* take care (**en** over)

esmeril *m* emery

esmero *m* care

esmoquin *m* dinner jacket, tuxedo (*Amer*)

esnob *a invar* snobbish. ● *m* & *f* (*pl* **esnobs**) snob. **~ismo** *m* snobbery

esnórkel *m* snorkel

eso *pron* that. **¡~ es!** that's it! **~ mismo** exactly. **¡~ no!** certainly not! **¡~ sí!** of course. **a ~ de** about. **en ~** at that moment. **¿no es ~?** isn't that right? **por ~** therefore. **y ~ que** although

esos *a pl véase* **ese**

ésos *pron pl véase* **ése**

espabila|do *a* bright. **~r** *vt* snuff ‹*vela*›; (*avivar*) brighten up; (*despertar*) wake up. **~rse** *vpr* wake up; (*apresurarse*) hurry up

espaci|al *a* space. **~ar** *vt* space out. **~o** *m* space. **~oso** *a* spacious

espada *f* sword. **~s** *fpl* (*en naipes*) spades

espagueti *m* spaghetti

espald|a *f* back. **~illa** *f* shoulder-blade. **a ~as de uno** behind s.o.'s back. **a las ~as** on one's back. **tener las ~as anchas** be broad-shouldered. **volver la ~a a uno, volver las ~as a uno** give s.o. the cold shoulder

espant|ada *f* stampede. **~adizo** *a* timid, timorous. **~ajo** *m*, **~apájaros** *m inv* scarecrow. **~ar** *vt* frighten; (*ahuyentar*) frighten away. **~arse** *vpr* be frightened; (*ahuyentarse*) be frightened away. **~o** *m* terror; (*horror*) horror. **~oso** *a* frightening; (*muy grande*) terrible. **¡qué ~ajo!** what a sight!

España *f* Spain

español *a* Spanish. ● *m* (*persona*) Spaniard; (*lengua*) Spanish. **los**

~es the Spanish. **~izado** *a* Hispanicized

esparadrapo *m* sticking-plaster, plaster (*Brit*)

esparci|do *a* scattered; (*fig*) widespread. **~r** [9] *vt* scatter; (*difundir*) spread. **~rse** *vpr* be scattered; (*difundirse*) spread; (*divertirse*) enjoy o.s.

espárrago *m* asparagus

esparto *m* esparto (grass)

espasm|o *m* spasm. **~ódico** *a* spasmodic

espátula *f* spatula; (*en pintura*) palette knife

especia *f* spice

especial *a* special. **~idad** *f* speciality (*Brit*), specialty (*Amer*). **~ista** *a* & *m* & *f* specialist. **~ización** *f* specialization. **~izar** [10] *vt* specialize. **~izarse** *vpr* specialize. **~mente** *adv* especially. **en ~** especially

especie *f* kind, sort; (*en biología*) species; (*noticia*) piece of news. **en ~** in kind

especifica|ción *f* specification. **~r** [7] *vt* specify

específico *a* specific

espect|áculo *m* sight; (*diversión*) entertainment, show. **~ador** *m* & *f* spectator. **~acular** *a* spectacular

espectro *m* spectre; (*en física*) spectrum

especula|ción *f* speculation. **~dor** *m* speculator. **~r** *vi* speculate. **~tivo** *a* speculative

espej|ismo *m* mirage. **~o** *m* mirror. **~o retrovisor** (*auto*) rear-view mirror

espeleólogo *m* potholer

espeluznante *a* horrifying

espera *f* wait. **sala** *f* **de ~** waiting room

espera|nza *f* hope. **~r** *vt* hope; (*aguardar*) wait for; (*creer*) expect. • *vi* hope; (*aguardar*) wait. **~r en uno** trust in s.o. **en ~ de** awaiting. **espero que no** I hope not. **espero que sí** I hope so

esperma *f* sperm

esperpento *m* fright; (*disparate*) nonsense

espes|ar *vt* thicken. **~arse** *vpr* thicken. **~o** *a* thick; ‹*pasta etc*› stiff. **~or** *m*, **~ura** *f* thickness; (*bot*) thicket

espetón *m* spit

esp|ía *f* spy. **~iar** [20] *vt* spy on. • *vi* spy

espiga *f* (*de trigo etc*) ear

espina *f* thorn; (*de pez*) bone; (*dorsal*) spine; (*astilla*) splinter; (*fig, dificultad*) difficulty. **~ dorsal** spine

espinaca *f* spinach

espinazo *m* spine

espinilla *f* shin; (*med*) blackhead

espino *m* hawthorn. **~ artificial** barbed wire. **~so** *a* thorny; ‹*pez*› bony; (*fig*) difficult

espionaje *m* espionage

espiral *a* & *f* spiral

espirar *vt/i* breathe out

esp|iritismo *m* spiritualism. **~iritoso** *a* spirited. **~iritista** *m* & *f* spiritualist. **~íritu** *m* spirit; (*mente*) mind; (*inteligencia*) intelligence. **~iritual** *a* spiritual. **~iritualismo** *m* spiritualism

espita *f* tap, faucet (*Amer*)

espl|éndido *a* splendid; ‹*persona*› generous. **~endor** *m* splendour

espliego *m* lavender

espolear *vt* (*fig*) spur on

espoleta *f* fuse

espolvorear *vt* sprinkle

esponj|a *f* sponge; (*tejido*) towelling. **~oso** *a* spongy. **pasar la ~a** forget about it

espont|aneidad *f* spontaneity. **~áneo** *a* spontaneous

esporádico *a* sporadic

espos|a *f* wife. **~as** *fpl* handcuffs. **~ar** *vt* handcuff. **~o** *m* husband. **los ~os** the couple

espuela *f* spur; (*fig*) incentive. **dar de ~s** spur on

espum|a *f* foam; (*en bebidas*) froth; (*de jabón*) lather. **~ar** *vt* skim. • *vi* foam; ‹*bebidas*› froth; ‹*jabón*› lather. **~oso** *a* ‹*vino*› sparkling. **echar ~a** foam, froth

esqueleto *m* skeleton

esquem|a *m* outline. **~ático** *a* sketchy

esqu|í *m* (*pl* **esquís**) ski; (*el deporte*) skiing. **~iador** *m* skier. **~iar** [20] *vi* ski

esquilar *vt* shear

esquimal *a* & *m* Eskimo

esquina *f* corner

esquirol *m* blackleg

esquiv|ar *vt* avoid. **~o** *a* aloof

esquizofrénico *a* & *m* schizophrenic

esta *a véase* **este**

ésta *pron véase* **éste**

estab|ilidad *f* stability. **~ilizador** *m* stabilizer. **~ilizar** [10] *vt* stabilize. **~le** *a* stable

establec|er [11] *vt* establish. **~erse** *vpr* settle; (*com*) start a business. **~imiento** *m* establishment
establo *m* cowshed
estaca *f* stake; (*para apalear*) stick. **~da** *f* (*cerca*) fence
estación *f* station; (*del año*) season; (*de vacaciones*) resort. **~ de servicio** service station
estaciona|miento *m* parking. **~r** *vt* station; (*auto*) park. **~rio** *a* stationary
estadio *m* stadium; (*fase*) stage
estadista *m* statesman. ● *f* stateswoman
estadístic|a *f* statistics. **~o** *a* statistical
estado *m* state. **~ civil** marital status. **~ de ánimo** frame of mind. **~ de cuenta** bank statement. **~ mayor** (*mil*) staff. **en buen ~** in good condition. **en ~ (interesante)** pregnant
Estados Unidos *mpl* United States
estadounidense *a* American, United States. ● *m & f* American
estafa *f* swindle. **~r** *vt* swindle
estafeta *f* (*oficina de correos*) (sub-) post office
estala|ctita *f* stalactite. **~gmita** *f* stalagmite
estall|ar *vi* explode; ‹*olas*› break; ‹*guerra, epidemia etc*› break out; (*fig*) burst. **~ar en llanto** burst into tears. **~ar de risa** burst out laughing. **~ido** *m* explosion; (*de guerra, epidemia etc*) outbreak; (*de risa etc*) outburst
estamp|a *f* print; (*aspecto*) appearance. **~ado** *a* printed. ● *m* printing; (*tela*) cotton print. **~ar** *vt* stamp; (*imprimir*) print. **dar a la ~a** (*imprimir*) print; (*publicar*) publish. **la viva ~a** the image
estampía. de ~ía suddenly
estampido *m* explosion
estampilla *f* stamp; (*Mex*) (postage) stamp
estanca|do *a* stagnant. **~miento** *m* stagnation. **~r** [7] *vt* stem; (*com*) turn into a monopoly
estanci|a *f* stay; (*Arg, finca*) ranch, farm; (*cuarto*) room. **~ero** *m* (*Arg*) farmer
estanco *a* watertight. ● *m* tobacconist's (shop)
estandarte *m* standard, banner
estanque *m* lake; (*depósito de agua*) reservoir
estanquero *m* tobacconist
estante *m* shelf. **~ría** *f* shelves; (*para libros*) bookcase
estañ|o *m* tin. **~adura** *f* tin-plating
estar [27] *vi* be; (*quedarse*) stay; (*estar en casa*) be in. **¿estamos?** alright? **estamos a 29 de noviembre** it's the 29th of November. **~ para** be about to. **~ por** remain to be; (*con ganas de*) be tempted to; (*ser partidario de*) be in favour of. **~se** *vpr* stay. **¿cómo está Vd?**, **¿cómo estás?** how are you?
estarcir [9] *vt* stencil
estatal *a* state
estático *a* static; (*pasmado*) dumbfounded
estatua *f* statue
estatura *f* height
estatut|ario *a* statutory. **~o** *m* statute
este *m* east; (*viento*) east wind. ● *a* (*f* **esta**, *mpl* **estos**, *fpl* **estas**) this; (*en plural*) these. ● *int* (*LAm*) well, er
éste *pron* (*f* **ésta**, *mpl* **éstos**, *fpl* **éstas**) this one, (*en plural*) these; (*segundo de dos*) the latter
estela *f* wake; (*arquit*) carved stone
estera *f* mat; (*tejido*) matting
est|éreo *a* stereo. **~ereofónico** *a* stereo, stereophonic
esterilla *f* mat
estereotip|ado *a* stereotyped. **~o** *m* stereotype
est|éril *a* sterile; ‹*mujer*› infertile; ‹*terreno*› barren. **~erilidad** *f* sterility; (*de mujer*) infertility; (*de terreno*) barrenness
esterlina *a* sterling. **libra** *f* **~** pound sterling
estético *a* aesthetic
estevado *a* bow-legged
estiércol *m* dung; (*abono*) manure
estigma *m* stigma. **~s** *mpl* (*relig*) stigmata
estilarse *vpr* be used
estil|ista *m & f* stylist. **~izar** [10] *vt* stylize. **~o** *m* style. **por el ~o** of that sort
estilográfica *f* fountain pen
estima *f* esteem. **~do** *a* esteemed. **~do señor** (*en cartas*) Dear Sir. **~r** *vt* esteem; have great respect for ‹*persona*›; (*valorar*) value; (*juzgar*) think
est|imulante *a* stimulating. ● *m* stimulant. **~imular** *vt* stimulate; (*incitar*) incite. **~ímulo** *m* stimulus
estipular *vt* stipulate

estir|ado *a* stretched; ‹*persona*› haughty. **~ar** *vt* stretch; (*fig*) stretch out. **~ón** *m* pull, tug; (*crecimiento*) sudden growth
estirpe *m* stock
estival *a* summer
esto *pron neutro* this; (*este asunto*) this business. **en ~** at this point. **en ~ de** in this business of. **por ~** therefore
estofa *f* class. **de baja ~** ‹*gente*› low-class
estofa|do *a* stewed. ● *m* stew. **~r** *vt* stew
estoic|ismo *m* stoicism. **~o** *a* stoical. ● *m* stoic
estómago *m* stomach. **dolor** *m* **de ~** stomach-ache
estorb|ar *vt* hinder, obstruct; (*molestar*) bother, annoy. ● *vi* be in the way. **~o** *m* hindrance; (*molestia*) nuisance
estornino *m* starling
estornud|ar *vi* sneeze. **~o** *m* sneeze
estos *a mpl véase* **este**
éstos *pron mpl véase* **éste**
estoy *vb véase* **estar**
estrabismo *m* squint
estrado *m* stage; (*mus*) bandstand
estrafalario *a* outlandish
estrag|ar [12] *vt* devastate. **~o** *m* devastation. **hacer ~os** devastate
estragón *m* tarragon
estrambótico *a* outlandish
estrangula|ción *f* strangulation. **~dor** *m* strangler; (*auto*) choke. **~miento** *m* blockage; (*auto*) bottleneck. **~r** *vt* strangle
estraperlo *m* black market. **comprar algo de ~** buy sth on the black market
estratagema *f* stratagem
estrateg|a *m & f* strategist. **~ia** *f* strategy
estratégic|amente *adv* strategically. **~o** *a* strategic
estrato *m* stratum
estratosfera *f* stratosphere
estrech|ar *vt* make narrower; take in ‹*vestido*›; (*apretar*) squeeze; hug ‹*persona*›. **~ar la mano a uno** shake hands with s.o. **~arse** *vpr* become narrower; (*apretarse*) squeeze up. **~ez** *f* narrowness; (*apuro*) tight spot; (*falta de dinero*) want. **~o** *a* narrow; ‹*vestido etc*› tight; (*fig, íntimo*) close. ● *m* straits. **~o de miras**, **de miras ~as** narrow-minded
estregar [1 & 12] *vt* rub
estrella *f* star. **~ de mar**, **~mar** *m* starfish
estrellar *vt* smash; fry ‹*huevos*›. **~se** *vpr* smash; (*fracasar*) fail. **~se contra** crash into
estremec|er [11] *vt* shake. **~erse** *vpr* tremble (**de** with). **~imiento** *m* shaking
estren|ar *vt* use for the first time; wear for the first time ‹*vestido etc*›; show for the first time ‹*película*›. **~arse** *vpr* make one's début; ‹*película*› have its première; ‹*obra de teatro*› open. **~o** *m* first use; (*de película*) première; (*de obra de teatro*) first night
estreñi|do *a* constipated. **~miento** *m* constipation
estr|épito *m* din. **~epitoso** *a* noisy; (*fig*) resounding
estreptomicina *f* streptomycin
estrés *m* stress
estría *f* groove
estribar *vt* rest (**en** on); (*consistir*) lie (**en** in)
estribillo *m* refrain; (*muletilla*) catchphrase
estribo *m* stirrup; (*de vehículo*) step; (*contrafuerte*) buttress. **perder los ~s** lose one's temper
estribor *m* starboard
estricto *a* strict
estridente *a* strident, raucous
estrofa *f* strophe
estropajo *m* scourer. **~so** *a* ‹*carne etc*› tough; ‹*persona*› slovenly
estropear *vt* spoil; (*romper*) break. **~se** *vpr* be damaged; ‹*fruta etc*› go bad; (*fracasar*) fail
estructura *f* structure. **~l** *a* structural
estruendo *m* din; (*de mucha gente*) uproar. **~so** *a* deafening
estrujar *vt* squeeze; (*fig*) drain
estuario *m* estuary
estuco *m* stucco
estuche *m* case
estudi|ante *m & f* student. **~antil** *a* student. **~ar** *vt* study. **~o** *m* study; (*de artista*) studio. **~oso** *a* studious
estufa *f* heater; (*LAm*) cooker
estupefac|ción *f* astonishment. **~iente** *a* astonishing. ● *m* narcotic. **~to** *a* astonished
estupendo *a* marvellous; (*hermoso*) beautiful
est|upidez *f* stupidity; (*acto*) stupid thing. **~úpido** *a* stupid

estupor *m* amazement
esturión *m* sturgeon
estuve *vb véase* **estar**
etapa *f* stage. **hacer ~ en** break the journey at. **por ~s** in stages
etc *abrev* (*etcétera*) etc
etcétera *adv* et cetera
éter *m* ether
etéreo *a* ethereal
etern|amente *adv* eternally. **~idad** *f* eternity. **~izar** [10] *vt* drag out. **~izarse** *vpr* be interminable. **~o** *a* eternal
étic|a *f* ethics. **~o** *a* ethical
etimología *f* etymology
etiqueta *f* ticket, tag; (*ceremonial*) etiquette. **de ~** formal
étnico *a* ethnic
eucalipto *m* eucalyptus
eufemismo *m* euphemism
euforia *f* euphoria
Europa *f* Europe
europe|o *a & m* European. **~izar** [10] *vt* Europeanize
eutanasia *f* euthanasia
evacua|ción *f* evacuation. **~r** [21 *o regular*] *vt* evacuate
evadir *vt* avoid. **~se** *vpr* escape
evaluar [21] *vt* evaluate
evang|élico *a* evangelical. **~elio** *m* gospel. **~elista** *m & f* evangelist
evapora|ción *f* evaporation. **~r** *vi* evaporate. **~rse** *vpr* evaporate; (*fig*) disappear
evasi|ón *f* evasion; (*fuga*) escape. **~vo** *a* evasive
evento *m* event. **a todo ~** at all events
eventual *a* possible. **~idad** *f* eventuality
eviden|cia *f* evidence. **~ciar** *vt* show. **~ciarse** *vpr* be obvious. **~te** *a* obvious. **~temente** *adv* obviously. **poner en ~cia** show; (*fig*) make a fool of
evitar *vt* avoid; (*ahorrar*) spare
evocar [7] *vt* evoke
evoluci|ón *f* evolution. **~onado** *a* fully-developed. **~onar** *vi* evolve; (*mil*) manoeuvre
ex *pref* ex-, former
exacerbar *vt* exacerbate
exact|amente *adv* exactly. **~itud** *f* exactness. **~o** *a* exact; (*preciso*) accurate; (*puntual*) punctual. **¡~!** exactly!. **con ~itud** exactly
exagera|ción *f* exaggeration. **~do** *a* exaggerated. **~r** *vt/i* exaggerate
exalta|do *a* exalted; (*fanático*) fanatical. **~r** *vt* exalt. **~rse** *vpr* get excited
exam|en *m* examination; (*escol, univ*) exam(ination). **~inador** *m* examiner. **~inar** *vt* examine. **~inarse** *vpr* take an exam
exánime *a* lifeless
exaspera|ción *f* exasperation. **~r** *vt* exasperate. **~rse** *vpr* get exasperated
excava|ción *f* excavation. **~dora** *f* digger. **~r** *vt* excavate
excede|ncia *f* leave of absence. **~nte** *a & m* surplus. **~r** *vi* exceed. **~rse** *vpr* go too far. **~rse a sí mismo** excel o.s.
excelen|cia *f* excellence; (*tratamiento*) Excellency. **~te** *a* excellent
exc|entricidad *f* eccentricity. **~éntrico** *a & m* eccentric
excepci|ón *f* exception. **~onal** *a* exceptional. **a ~ón de, con ~ón de** except (for)
except|o *prep* except (for). **~uar** [21] *vt* except
exces|ivo *a* excessive. **~o** *m* excess. **~o de equipaje** excess luggage (*esp Brit*), excess baggage (*esp Amer*)
excita|ble *a* excitable. **~ción** *f* excitement. **~nte** *a* exciting. • *m* stimulant. **~r** *vt* excite; (*incitar*) incite. **~rse** *vpr* get excited
exclama|ción *f* exclamation. **~r** *vi* exclaim
exclu|ir [17] *vt* exclude. **~sión** *f* exclusion. **~siva** *f* sole right; (*en la prensa* exclusive (story). **~sive** *adv* exclusive; (*exclusivamente*) exclusively. **~sivo** *a* exclusive
excomu|lgar [12] *vt* excommunicate. **~nión** *f* excommunication
excremento *m* excrement
exculpar *vt* exonerate; (*jurid*) acquit
excursi|ón *f* excursion, trip. **~onista** *m & f* day-tripper. **ir de ~ón** go on an excursion
excusa *f* excuse; (*disculpa*) apology. **~r** *vt* excuse. **presentar sus ~s** apologize
execra|ble *a* loathsome. **~r** *vt* loathe
exento *a* exempt; (*libre*) free
exequias *fpl* funeral rites
exhala|ción *f* shooting star. **~r** *vt* exhale, breath out; give off ‹*olor etc*›. **~rse** *vpr* hurry. **como una ~ción** at top speed

exhaust|ivo *a* exhaustive. **~o** *a* exhausted
exhibi|ción *f* exhibition. **~cionista** *m & f* exhibitionist. **~r** *vt* exhibit
exhortar *vt* exhort (**a** to)
exhumar *vt* exhume; (*fig*) dig up
exig|encia *f* demand. **~ente** *a* demanding. **~ir** [14] *vt* demand. **tener muchas ~encias** be very demanding
exiguo *a* meagre
exil|(i)ado *a* exiled. ● *m* exile. **~(i)arse** *vpr* go into exile. **~io** *m* exile
eximio *a* distinguished
eximir *vt* exempt; (*liberar*) free
existencia *f* existence. **~s** *fpl* stock
existencial *a* existential. **~ismo** *m* existentialism
exist|ente *a* existing. **~ir** *vi* exist
éxito *m* success. **no tener ~** fail. **tener ~** be successful
exitoso *a* successful
éxodo *m* exodus
exonerar *vt* (*de un empleo*) dismiss; (*de un honor etc*) strip
exorbitante *a* exorbitant
exorci|smo *m* exorcism. **~zar** [10] *vt* exorcise
exótico *a* exotic
expan|dir *vt* expand; (*fig*) spread. **~dirse** *vpr* expand. **~sión** *f* expansion. **~sivo** *a* expansive
expatria|do *a & m* expatriate. **~r** *vt* banish. **~rse** *vpr* emigrate; (*exiliarse*) go into exile
expectativa *f*. **estar a la ~** be on the lookout
expedición *f* dispatch; (*cosa expedida*) shipment; (*mil, científico etc*) expedition
expediente *m* expedient; (*jurid*) proceedings; (*documentos*) record, file
expedi|r [5] *vt* dispatch, send; issue ‹*documento*›. **~to** *a* clear
expeler *vt* expel
expende|dor *m* dealer. **~dor automático** vending machine. **~duría** *f* shop; (*de billetes*) ticket office. **~r** *vt* sell
expensas *fpl*. **a ~ de** at the expense of. **a mis ~** at my expense
experiencia *f* experience
experiment|al *a* experimental. **~ar** *vt* test, experiment with; (*sentir*) experience. **~o** *m* experiment
experto *a & m* expert
expiar [20] *vt* atone for
expirar *vi* expire; (*morir*) die
explana|da *f* levelled area; (*paseo*) esplanade. **~r** *vt* level
explayar *vt* extend. **~se** *vpr* spread out, extend; (*hablar*) be long-winded; (*confiarse*) confide (**a** in)
expletivo *m* expletive
explica|ción *f* explanation. **~r** [7] *vt* explain. **~rse** *vpr* understand; (*hacerse comprender*) explain o.s. **no me lo explico** I can't understand it
explícito *a* explicit
explora|ción *f* exploration. **~dor** *m* explorer; (*muchacho*) boy scout. **~r** *vt* explore. **~torio** *a* exploratory
explosi|ón *f* explosion; (*fig*) outburst. **~onar** *vt* blow up. **~vo** *a & m* explosive
explota|ción *f* working; (*abuso*) exploitation. **~r** *vt* work ‹*mina*›; farm ‹*tierra*›; (*abusar*) exploit. ● *vi* explode
expone|nte *m* exponent. **~r** [34] *vt* expose; display ‹*mercancías*›; (*explicar*) expound; exhibit ‹*cuadros etc*›; (*arriesgar*) risk. ● *vi* hold an exhibition. **~rse** *vpr* run the risk (**a** of)
exporta|ción *f* export. **~dor** *m* exporter. **~r** *vt* export
exposición *f* exposure; (*de cuadros etc*) exhibition; (*en escaparate etc*) display; (*explicación*) exposition, explanation
expresamente *adv* specifically
expres|ar *vt* express. **~arse** *vpr* express o.s. **~ión** *f* expression. **~ivo** *a* expressive; (*cariñoso*) affectionate
expreso *a* express. ● *m* express messenger; (*tren*) express
exprimi|dor *m* squeezer. **~r** *vt* squeeze; (*explotar*) exploit
expropiar *vt* expropriate
expuesto *a* on display; ‹*lugar etc*› exposed; (*peligroso*) dangerous. **estar ~ a** be liable to
expuls|ar *vt* expel; throw out ‹*persona*›; send off ‹*jugador*›. **~ión** *f* expulsion
expurgar [12] *vt* expurgate
exquisit|o *a* exquisite. **~amente** *adv* exquisitely
extasiar [20] *vt* enrapture
éxtasis *m invar* ecstasy
extático *a* ecstatic
extend|er [1] *vt* spread (out); draw up ‹*documento*›. **~erse** *vpr* spread;

‹*paisaje etc*› extend, stretch; (*tenderse*) stretch out. **~ido** *a* spread out; (*generalizado*) widespread; ‹*brazos*› outstretched

extens|amente *adv* widely; (*detalladamente*) in full. **~ión** *f* extension; (*amplitud*) expanse; (*mus*) range. **~o** *a* extensive

extenuar [21] *vt* exhaust

exterior *a* external, exterior; (*del extranjero*) foreign; ‹*aspecto etc*› outward. ● *m* exterior; (*países extranjeros*) abroad. **~izar** [10] *vt* show

extermin|ación *f* extermination. **~ar** *vt* exterminate. **~io** *m* extermination

externo *a* external; ‹*signo etc*› outward. ● *m* day pupil

extin|ción *f* extinction. **~guir** [13] *vt* extinguish. **~guirse** *vpr* die out; ‹*fuego*› go out. **~to** *a* extinguished; ‹*raza etc*› extinct. **~tor** *m* fire extinguisher

extirpa|r *vt* uproot; extract ‹*muela etc*›; remove ‹*tumor*›. **~ción** *f* (*fig*) eradication

extorsi|ón *f* (*fig*) inconvenience. **~onar** *vt* inconvenience

extra *a invar* extra; (*de buena calidad*) good-quality; ‹*huevos*› large. **paga** *f* **~** bonus

extrac|ción *f* extraction; (*de lotería*) draw. **~to** *m* extract

extradición *f* extradition

extraer [41] *vt* extract

extranjero *a* foreign. ● *m* foreigner; (*países*) foreign countries. **del ~** from abroad. **en el ~**, **por el ~** abroad

extrañ|ar *vt* surprise; (*encontrar extraño*) find strange; (*LAm, echar de menos*) miss; (*desterrar*) banish. **~arse** *vpr* be surprised (**de** at); ‹*2 personas*› grow apart. **~eza** *f* strangeness; (*asombro*) surprise. **~o** *a* strange. ● *m* stranger

extraoficial *a* unofficial

extraordinario *a* extraordinary. ● *m* (*correo*) special delivery; (*plato*) extra dish; (*de periódico etc*) special edition. **horas** *fpl* **extraordinarias** overtime

extrarradio *m* suburbs

extrasensible *a* extra-sensory

extraterrestre *a* extraterrestrial. ● *m* alien

extravagan|cia *f* oddness, eccentricity. **~te** *a* odd, eccentric

extravertido *a* & *m* extrovert

extrav|iado *a* lost; ‹*lugar*› isolated. **~iar** [20] *vt* lose. **~iarse** *vpr* get lost; ‹*objetos*› be missing. **~ío** *m* loss

extremar *vt* overdo. **~se** *vpr* make every effort

extremeño *a* from Extremadura. ● *m* person from Extremadura

extrem|idad *f* extremity. **~idades** *fpl* extremities. **~ista** *a* & *m* & *f* extremist. **~o** *a* extreme. ● *m* end; (*colmo*) extreme. **en ~o** extremely. **en último ~o** as a last resort

extrovertido *a* & *m* extrovert

exuberan|cia *f* exuberance. **~te** *a* exuberant

exulta|ción *f* exultation. **~r** *vi* exult

eyacular *vt/i* ejaculate

F

fa *m* F; (*solfa*) fah

fabada *f* Asturian stew

fábrica *f* factory. **marca** *f* **de ~** trade mark

fabrica|ción *f* manufacture. **~ción en serie** mass production. **~nte** *m* & *f* manufacturer. **~r** [7] *vt* manufacture; (*inventar*) fabricate

fábula *f* fable; (*mentira*) story, lie; (*chisme*) gossip

fabuloso *a* fabulous

facci|ón *f* faction. **~ones** *fpl* (*de la cara*) features

faceta *f* facet

fácil *a* easy; (*probable*) likely; ‹*persona*› easygoing

facili|dad *f* ease; (*disposición*) aptitude. **~dades** *fpl* facilities. **~tar** *vt* facilitate; (*proporcionar*) provide

fácilmente *adv* easily

facistol *m* lectern

facón *m* (*Arg*) gaucho knife

facsímil(e) *m* facsimile

factible *a* feasible

factor *m* factor

factoría *f* agency; (*esp LAm, fábrica*) factory

factura *f* bill, invoice; (*hechura*) manufacture. **~r** *vt* (*hacer la factura*) invoice; (*cobrar*) charge; (*en ferrocarril*) register (*Brit*), check (*Amer*)

faculta|d *f* faculty; (*capacidad*) ability; (*poder*) power. **~tivo** *a* optional

facha *f* (*aspecto, fam*) look

fachada *f* façade; (*fig*, *apariencia*) show
faena *f* job. **~s domésticas** housework
fagot *m* bassoon; (*músico*) bassoonist
faisán *m* pheasant
faja *f* (*de tierra*) strip; (*corsé*) corset; (*mil etc*) sash
fajo *m* bundle; (*de billetes*) wad
falang|e *f* (*política española*) Falange. **~ista** *m & f* Falangist
falda *f* skirt; (*de montaña*) side
fálico *a* phallic
fals|ear *vt* falsify, distort. **~edad** *f* falseness; (*mentira*) lie, falsehood. **~ificación** *f* forgery. **~ificador** *m* forger. **~ificar** [7] *vt* forge. **~o** *a* false; (*equivocado*) wrong; (*falsificado*) fake
falt|a *f* lack; (*ausencia*) absence; (*escasez*) shortage; (*defecto*) fault, defect; (*culpa*) fault; (*error*) mistake; (*en fútbol etc*) foul; (*en tenis*) fault. **~ar** *vi* be lacking; (*estar ausente*) be absent. **~o** *a* lacking (**de** in). **a ~a de** for lack of. **echar en ~a** miss. **hacer ~a** be necessary. **me hace ~a** I need. **¡no ~aba más!** don't mention it! (*naturalmente*) of course! **sacar ~as** find fault
falla *f* (*incl geol*) fault. **~r** *vi* fail; (*romperse*) break, give way; ‹*motor*, *tiro etc*› miss. **sin ~r** without fail
fallec|er [11] *vi* die. **~ido** *a* late. • *m* deceased
fallido *a* vain; (*fracasado*) unsuccessful
fallo *m* failure; (*defecto*) fault; (*jurid*) sentence
fama *f* fame; (*reputación*) reputation. **de mala ~** of ill repute. **tener ~ de** have the reputation of
famélico *a* starving
familia *f* family. **~ numerosa** large family. **~r** *a* familiar; (*de la familia*) family; (*sin ceremonia*) informal. **~ridad** *f* familiarity. **~rizarse** [10] *vpr* become familiar (**con** with)
famoso *a* famous
fanático *a* fanatical. • *m* fanatic
fanfarr|ón *a* boastful. • *m* braggart. **~onada** *f* boasting; (*dicho*) boast. **~onear** *vi* show off
fango *m* mud. **~so** *a* muddy
fantas|ear *vi* daydream; (*imaginar*) fantasize. **~ía** *f* fantasy. **de ~** fancy
fantasma *m* ghost
fantástico *a* fantastic
fantoche *m* puppet
faringe *f* pharynx
fardo *m* bundle
farfullar *vi* jabber, gabble
farmac|eútico *a* pharmaceutical. • *m* chemist (*Brit*), pharmacist, druggist (*Amer*). **~ia** *f* (*ciencia*) pharmacy; (*tienda*) chemist's (shop) (*Brit*), pharmacy, drugstore (*Amer*)
faro *m* lighthouse; (*aviac*) beacon; (*auto*) headlight
farol *m* lantern; (*de la calle*) street lamp. **~a** *f* street lamp. **~ita** *f* small street lamp
farsa *f* farce
fas *adv*. **por ~ o por nefas** rightly or wrongly
fascículo *m* instalment
fascina|ción *f* fascination. **~r** *vt* fascinate
fascis|mo *m* fascism. **~ta** *a & m & f* fascist
fase *f* phase
fastidi|ar *vt* annoy; (*estropear*) spoil. **~arse** *vpr* (*aguantarse*) put up with it; (*hacerse daño*) hurt o.s. **~o** *m* nuisance; (*aburrimiento*) boredom. **~oso** *a* annoying. **¡para que te ~es!** so there! **¡qué ~o!** what a nuisance!
fatal *a* fateful; (*mortal*) fatal; (*pésimo*, *fam*) terrible. **~idad** *f* fate; (*desgracia*) misfortune. **~ista** *m & f* fatalist
fatig|a *f* fatigue. **~as** *fpl* troubles. **~ar** [12] *vt* tire. **~arse** *vpr* get tired. **~oso** *a* tiring
fatuo *a* fatuous
fauna *f* fauna
fausto *a* lucky
favor *m* favour. **~able** *a* favourable. **a ~ de**, **en ~ de** in favour of. **haga el ~ de** would you be so kind as to, please. **por ~** please
favorec|edor *a* flattering. **~er** [11] *vt* favour; ‹*vestido*, *peinado etc*› suit. **~ido** *a* favoured
favorit|ismo *m* favouritism. **~o** *a & m* favourite
faz *f* face
fe *f* faith. **dar ~ de** certify. **de buena ~** in good faith
fealdad *f* ugliness
febrero *m* February
febril *a* feverish
fecund|ación *f* fertilization. **~ación artificial** artificial insemination. **~ar** *vt* fertilize. **~o** *a* fertile; (*fig*) prolific

fecha *f* date. **~r** *vt* date. **a estas ~s** now; (*todavía*) still. **hasta la ~** so far. **poner la ~** date
fechoría *f* misdeed
federa|ción *f* federation. **~l** *a* federal
feísimo *a* hideous
felici|dad *f* happiness. **~dades** *fpl* best wishes; (*congratulaciones*) congratulations. **~tación** *f* congratulation. **~tar** *vt* congratulate. **~tarse** *vpr* be glad
feligr|és *m* parishioner. **~esía** *f* parish
felino *a* & *m* feline
feliz *a* happy; (*afortunado*) lucky. **¡Felices Pascuas!** Happy Christmas! **¡F~ Año Nuevo!** Happy New Year!
felpudo *a* plush. ● *m* doormat
femeni|l *a* feminine. **~no** *a* feminine; (*biol, bot*) female. ● *m* feminine. **~nidad** *f* femeninity. **~sta** *a* & *m* & *f* feminist
fen|omenal *a* phenomenal. **~ómeno** *m* phenomenon; (*monstruo*) freak
feo *a* ugly; (*desagradable*) nasty; (*malo*) bad
féretro *m* coffin
feria *f* fair; (*verbena*) carnival; (*descanso*) holiday; (*Mex, cambio*) change. **~do** *a*. **día ~do** holiday
ferment|ación *f* fermentation. **~ar** *vt/i* ferment. **~o** *m* ferment
fero|cidad *f* ferocity. **~z** *a* fierce; ‹*persona*› savage
férreo *a* iron. **vía férrea** railway (*Brit*), railroad (*Amer*)
ferreter|ía *f* ironmonger's (shop) (*Brit*), hardware store (*Amer*). **~o** *m* ironmonger (*Brit*), hardware dealer (*Amer*)
ferro|bús *m* local train. **~carril** *m* railway (*Brit*), railroad (*Amer*). **~viario** *a* rail. ● *m* railwayman (*Brit*), railroad worker (*Amer*)
fértil *a* fertile
fertili|dad *f* fertility. **~zante** *m* fertilizer. **~zar** [10] *vt* fertilize
férvido *a* fervent
ferv|iente *a* fervent. **~or** *m* fervour
festej|ar *vt* celebrate; entertain ‹*persona*›; court ‹*novia etc*›; (*Mex, golpear*) beat. **~o** *m* entertainment; (*celebración*) celebration
festiv|al *m* festival. **~idad** *f* festivity. **~o** *a* festive; (*humorístico*) humorous. **día ~o** feast day, holiday
festonear *vt* festoon
fétido *a* stinking
feto *m* foetus
feudal *a* feudal
fiado *m*. **al ~** on credit. **~r** *m* fastener; (*jurid*) guarantor
fiambre *m* cold meat
fianza *f* (*dinero*) deposit; (*objeto*) surety. **bajo ~** on bail. **dar ~** pay a deposit
fiar [20] *vt* guarantee; (*vender*) sell on credit; (*confiar*) confide. ● *vi* trust. **~se** *vpr*. **~se de** trust
fiasco *m* fiasco
fibra *f* fibre; (*fig*) energy. **~ de vidrio** fibreglass
fic|ción *f* fiction. **~ticio** *a* fictitious; (*falso*) false
fich|a *f* token; (*tarjeta*) index card; (*en los juegos*) counter. **~ar** *vt* file. **~ero** *m* card index. **estar ~ado** have a (police) record
fidedigno *a* reliable
fidelidad *f* faithfulness. **alta ~** hi-fi (*fam*), high fidelity
fideos *mpl* noodles
fiebre *f* fever. **~ del heno** hay fever. **tener ~** have a temperature
fiel *a* faithful; ‹*memoria, relato etc*› reliable. ● *m* believer; (*de balanza*) needle. **los ~es** the faithful
fieltro *m* felt
fier|a *f* wild animal; (*persona*) brute. **~o** *a* fierce; (*cruel*) cruel. **estar hecho una ~a** be furious
fierro *m* (*LAm*) iron
fiesta *f* party; (*día festivo*) holiday. **~s** *fpl* celebrations. **~ nacional** bank holiday (*Brit*), national holiday
figura *f* figure; (*forma*) shape; (*en obra de teatro*) character; (*en naipes*) court-card. **~r** *vt* feign; (*representar*) represent. ● *vi* figure; (*ser importante*) be important. **~rse** *vpr* imagine. **¡figúrate!** just imagine! **~tivo** *a* figurative
fij|ación *f* fixing. **~ar** *vt* fix; stick ‹*sello*›; post ‹*cartel*›. **~arse** *vpr* settle; (*fig, poner atención*) notice. **¡fíjate!** just imagine! **~o** *a* fixed; (*firme*) stable; ‹*persona*› settled. **de ~o** certainly
fila *f* line; (*de soldados etc*) file; (*en el teatro, cine etc*) row; (*cola*) queue. **ponerse en ~** line up
filamento *m* filament
fil|antropía *f* philanthropy. **~antrópico** *a* philanthropic. **~ántropo** *m* philanthropist

filarmónico *a* philharmonic
filat|elia *f* stamp collecting, philately. **~élico** *a* philatelic. ● *m* stamp collector, philatelist
filete *m* fillet
filfa *f* (*fam*) hoax
filial *a* filial. ● *f* subsidiary
filigrana *f* filigree (work); (*en papel*) watermark
Filipinas *fpl*. **las (islas) ~** the Philippines
filipino *a* Philippine, Filipino
filmar *vt* film
filo *m* edge; (*de hoja*) cutting edge; (*Mex, hambre*) hunger. **al ~ de las doce** at exactly twelve o'clock. **dar ~ a, sacar ~ a** sharpen
filología *f* philology
filón *m* vein; (*fig*) gold-mine
fil|osofía *f* philosophy. **~osófico** *a* philosophical. **~ósofo** *m* philosopher
filtr|ar *vt* filter. **~arse** *vpr* filter; ‹*dinero*› disappear. **~o** *m* filter; (*bebida*) philtre
fin *m* end; (*objetivo*) aim. **~ de semana** weekend. **a ~ de** in order to. **a ~ de cuentas** all things considered. **a ~ de que** in order that. **a ~es de** at the end of. **al ~** finally. **al ~ y al cabo** after all. **dar ~ a** end. **en ~** in short. **poner ~ a** end. **por ~** finally. **sin ~** endless
final *a* final, last. ● *m* end. ● *f* final. **~idad** *f* aim. **~ista** *m & f* finalist. **~izar** [10] *vt/i* end. **~mente** *adv* finally
financi|ar *vt* finance. **~ero** *a* financial. ● *m* financier
finca *f* property; (*tierras*) estate; (*LAm, granja*) farm
finés *a* Finnish. ● *m* Finn; (*lengua*) Finnish
fingi|do *a* false. **~r** [14] *vt* feign; (*simular*) simulate. ● *vi* pretend. **~rse** *vpr* pretend to be
finito *a* finite
finlandés *a* Finnish. ● *m* (*persona*) Finn; (*lengua*) Finnish
Finlandia *f* Finland
fin|o *a* fine; (*delgado*) slender; (*astuto*) shrewd; ‹*sentido*› keen; (*cortés*) polite; ‹*jerez*› dry. **~ura** *f* fineness; (*astucia*) shrewdness; (*de sentido*) keenness; (*cortesía*) politeness
fiordo *m* fiord
firma *f* signature; (*empresa*) firm
firmamento *m* firmament
firmar *vt* sign
firme *a* firm; (*estable*) stable, steady; ‹*persona*› steadfast. ● *m* (*pavimento*) (road) surface. ● *adv* hard. **~za** *f* firmness. **de ~** hard. **en ~** firm, definite
fisc|al *a* fiscal. ● *m & f* public prosecutor. **~o** *m* treasury
fisg|ar [12] *vt* pry into ‹*asunto*›; spy on ‹*persona*›. ● *vi* pry. **~ón** *a* prying. ● *m* busybody
físic|a *f* physics. **~o** *a* physical. ● *m* physique; (*persona*) physicist
fisi|ología *f* physiology. **~ológico** *a* physiological. **~ólogo** *m* physiologist
fisioterap|euta *m & f* physiotherapist. **~ia** *f* physiotherapy. **~ista** *m & f* (*fam*) physiotherapist
fisonom|ía *f* physiognomy, face. **~ista** *m & f*. **ser buen ~ista** be good at remembering faces
fisura *f* (*Med*) fracture
fláccido *a* flabby
flaco *a* thin, skinny; (*débil*) weak
flagelo *m* scourge
flagrante *a* flagrant. **en ~** red-handed
flamante *a* splendid; (*nuevo*) brand-new
flamenco *a* flamenco; (*de Flandes*) Flemish. ● *m* (*música etc*) flamenco
flan *m* crème caramel
flaqueza *f* thinness; (*debilidad*) weakness
flash *m* flash
flato *m*, **flatulencia** *f* flatulence
flaut|a *f* flute. ● *m & f* (*músico*) flautist, flutist (*Amer*). **~ín** *m* piccolo. **~ista** *m & f* flautist, flutist (*Amer*)
fleco *m* fringe
flecha *f* arrow
flem|a *f* phlegm. **~ático** *a* phlegmatic
flequillo *m* fringe
fletar *vt* charter
flexib|ilidad *f* flexibility. **~le** *a* flexible. ● *m* flex, cable
flirte|ar *vi* flirt. **~o** *m* flirting
floj|ear *vi* ease up. **~o** *a* loose; (*poco fuerte*) weak; ‹*viento*› light; (*perezoso*) lazy
flor *f* flower; (*fig*) cream. **~a** *f* flora. **~al** *a* floral. **~ecer** [11] *vi* flower, bloom; (*fig*) flourish. **~eciente** *a* (*fig*) flourishing. **~ero** *m* flower vase. **~ido** *a* flowery; (*selecto*) select; ‹*lenguaje*› florid. **~ista** *m & f* florist

flota *f* fleet
flot|ador *m* float. **~ar** *vi* float. **~e** *m*. **a ~e** afloat
flotilla *f* flotilla
fluctua|ción *f* fluctuation. **~r** [21] *vi* fluctuate
flu|idez *f* fluidity; (*fig*) fluency. **~ido** *a* fluid; (*fig*) fluent. ● *m* fluid. **~ir** [17] *vi* flow. **~jo** *m* flow. **~o y reflujo** ebb and flow
fluorescente *a* fluorescent
fluoruro *m* fluoride
fluvial *a* river
fobia *f* phobia
foca *f* seal
foc|al *a* focal. **~o** *m* focus; (*lámpara*) floodlight; (*LAm, bombilla*) light bulb
fogón *m* (*cocina*) cooker
fogoso *a* spirited
folio *m* leaf
folkl|ore *m* folklore. **~órico** *a* folk
follaje *m* foliage
follet|ín *m* newspaper serial. **~o** *m* pamphlet
follón *m* (*lío*) mess; (*alboroto*) row
fomentar *vt* foment, stir up
fonda *f* (*pensión*) boarding-house
fondo *m* bottom; (*parte más lejana*) bottom, end; (*de escenario, pintura etc*) background; (*profundidad*) depth. **~s** *mpl* funds, money. **a ~** thoroughly. **en el ~** deep down
fonétic|a *f* phonetics. **~o** *a* phonetic
fono *m* (*LAm, del teléfono*) earpiece
fontaner|ía plumbing. **~o** *m* plumber
footing /'futin/ *m* jogging
forastero *a* alien. ● *m* stranger
forceje|ar *vi* struggle. **~o** *m* struggle
fórceps *m invar* forceps
forense *a* forensic
forjar *vt* forge
forma *f* form, shape; (*horma*) mould; (*modo*) way; (*de zapatero*) last. **~s** *fpl* conventions. **~ción** *f* formation; (*educación*) training. **dar ~ a** shape; (*expresar*) formulate. **de ~ que** so (that). **de todas ~s** anyway. **estar en ~** be in good form. **guardar ~s** keep up appearances
formal *a* formal; (*de fiar*) reliable; (*serio*) serious. **~idad** *f* formality; (*fiabilidad*) reliability; (*seriedad*) seriousness
formar *vt* form; (*hacer*) make; (*enseñar*) train. **~se** *vpr* form; (*desarrollarse*) develop
formato *m* format
formidable *a* formidable; (*muy grande*) enormous; (*muy bueno, fam*) marvellous
fórmula *f* formula; (*receta*) recipe
formular *vt* formulate; make ‹*queja etc*›; (*expresar*) express
fornido *a* well-built
forraje *m* fodder. **~ar** *vt/i* forage
forr|ar *vt* (*en el interior*) line; (*en el exterior*) cover. **~o** *m* lining; (*cubierta*) cover. **~o del freno** brake lining
fortale|cer [11] *vt* strengthen. **~za** *f* strength; (*mil*) fortress; (*fuerza moral*) fortitude
fortificar [7] *vt* fortify
fortuito *a* fortuitous. **encuentro** *m* **~** chance meeting
fortuna *f* fortune; (*suerte*) luck. **por ~** fortunately
forz|ado *a* hard. **~ar** [2 & 10] *vt* force. **~osamente** *adv* necessarily. **~oso** *a* inevitable; (*necesario*) necessary
fosa *f* grave
fosfato *m* phosphate
fósforo *m* phosphorus; (*cerilla*) match
fósil *a & m* fossil
fosilizarse [10] *vpr* fossilize
foso *m* ditch
foto *f* photo, photograph. **sacar ~s** take photographs
fotocopia *f* photocopy. **~dora** *f* photocopier. **~r** *vt* photocopy
fotogénico *a* photogenic
fot|ografía *f* photography; (*foto*) photograph. **~ografiar** [20] *vt* photograph. **~ográfico** *a* photographic. **~ógrafo** *m* photographer. **sacar ~ografías** take photographs
foyer *m* foyer
frac *m* (*pl* **fraques** *o* **fracs**) tails
fracas|ar *vi* fail. **~o** *m* failure
fracción *f* fraction; (*pol*) faction
fractura *f* fracture. **~r** *vt* fracture, break. **~rse** *vpr* fracture, break
fragan|cia *f* fragrance. **~te** *a* fragrant
fragata *f* frigate
fr|ágil *a* fragile; (*débil*) weak. **~agilidad** *f* fragility; (*debilidad*) weakness
fragment|ario *a* fragmentary. **~o** *m* fragment
fragor *m* din
fragoso *a* rough

fragua *f* forge. **~r** [15] *vt* forge; (*fig*) concoct. ● *vi* harden
fraile *m* friar; (*monje*) monk
frambuesa *f* raspberry
francés *a* French. ● *m* (*persona*) Frenchman; (*lengua*) French
Francia *f* France
franco *a* frank; (*com*) free. ● *m* (*moneda*) franc
francotirador *m* sniper
franela *f* flannel
franja *f* border; (*fleco*) fringe
franque|ar *vt* clear; stamp ‹*carta*›; overcome ‹*obstáculo*›. **~o** *m* stamping; (*cantidad*) postage
franqueza *f* frankness; (*familiaridad*) familiarity
franquis|mo *m* General Franco's regime; (*política*) Franco's policy. **~ta** *a* pro-Franco
frasco *m* small bottle
frase *f* phrase; (*oración*) sentence. **~ hecha** set phrase
fratern|al *a* fraternal. **~idad** *f* fraternity
fraud|e *m* fraud. **~ulento** *a* fraudulent
fray *m* brother, friar
frecuen|cia *f* frequency. **~tar** *vt* frequent. **~te** *a* frequent. **con ~cia** frequently
frega|dero *m* sink. **~r** [1 & 12] *vt* scrub; wash up ‹*los platos*›; mop ‹*el suelo*›; (*LAm, fig, molestar, fam*) annoy
freír [51, *pp* **frito**] *vt* fry; (*fig, molestar, fam*) annoy. **~se** *vpr* fry; ‹*persona*› be very hot, be boiling (*fam*)
frenar *vt* brake; (*fig*) check
fren|esí *m* frenzy. **~ético** *a* frenzied
freno *m* (*de caballería*) bit; (*auto*) brake; (*fig*) check
frente *m* front. ● *f* forehead. **~ a** opposite; (*en contra de*) opposed to. **~ por ~** opposite; (*en un choque*) head-on. **al ~** at the head; (*hacia delante*) forward. **arrugar la ~** frown. **de ~** forward. **hacer ~ a** face ‹*cosa*›; stand up to ‹*persona*›
fresa *f* strawberry
fresc|a *f* fresh air. **~o** *a* (*frío*) cool; (*nuevo*) fresh; (*descarado*) cheeky. ● *m* fresh air; (*frescor*) coolness; (*mural*) fresco; (*persona*) impudent person. **~or** *m* coolness. **~ura** *f* freshness; (*frío*) coolness; (*descaro*) cheek. **al ~o** in the open air. **hacer ~o** be cool. **tomar el ~o** get some fresh air
fresno *m* ash (tree)
friable *a* friable
frialdad *f* coldness; (*fig*) indifference
fricci|ón *f* rubbing; (*fig, tec*) friction; (*masaje*) massage. **~onar** *vt* rub
frigidez *f* coldness; (*fig*) frigidity
frígido *a* frigid
frigorífico *m* refrigerator, fridge (*fam*)
fríjol *m* bean. **~es refritos** (*Mex*) purée of black beans
frío *a & m* cold. **coger ~** catch cold. **hacer ~** be cold
frisar *vi*. **~ en** be getting on for, be about
frito *a* fried; (*exasperado*) exasperated. **me tiene ~** I'm sick of him
fr|ivolidad *f* frivolity. **~ívolo** *a* frivolous
fronda *f* foliage
fronter|a *f* frontier; (*fig*) limit. **~izo** *a* frontier. **~o** *a* opposite
frontón *m* pelota court
frotar *vt* rub; strike ‹*cerilla*›
fructífero *a* fruitful
frugal *a* frugal
fruncir [9] *vt* gather ‹*tela*›; wrinkle ‹*piel*›
fruslería *f* trifle
frustra|ción *f* frustration. **~r** *vt* frustrate. **~rse** *vpr* (*fracasar*) fail. **quedar ~do** be disappointed
frut|a *f* fruit. **~ería** *f* fruit shop. **~ero** *a* fruit. ● *m* fruiterer; (*recipiente*) fruit bowl. **~icultura** *f* fruit-growing. **~illa** *f* (*LAm*) strawberry. **~o** *m* fruit
fucsia *f* fuchsia
fuego *m* fire. **~s artificiales** fireworks. **a ~ lento** on a low heat. **tener ~** have a light
fuente *f* fountain; (*manantial*) spring; (*plato*) serving dish; (*fig*) source
fuera *adv* out; (*al exterior*) outside; (*en otra parte*) away; (*en el extranjero*) abroad. ● *vb véase* **ir** *y* **ser**. **~ de** outside; (*excepto*) except for, besides. **por ~** on the outside
fuerte *a* strong; ‹*color*› bright; ‹*sonido*› loud; ‹*dolor*› severe; (*duro*) hard; (*grande*) large; ‹*lluvia, nevada*› heavy. ● *m* fort; (*fig*) strong point. ● *adv* hard; (*con hablar etc*) loudly; (*mucho*) a lot
fuerza *f* strength; (*poder*) power; (*en física*) force; (*mil*) forces. **~ de**

voluntad will-power. **a ~ de** by dint of, by means of. **a la ~** by necessity. **por ~** by force; (*por necesidad*) by necessity. **tener ~s para** have the strength to

fuese *vb véase* **ir** *y* **ser**

fug|a *f* flight, escape; (*de gas etc*) leak; (*mus*) fugue. **~arse** [12] *vpr* flee, escape. **~az** *a* fleeting. **~itivo** *a & m* fugitive. **ponerse en ~a** take to flight

fui *vb véase* **ir** *y* **ser**

fulano *m* so-and-so. **~, mengano y zutano** Tom, Dick and Harry

fulgor *m* brilliance; (*fig*) splendour

fulminar *vt* strike by lightning; (*fig, mirar*) look daggers at

fuma|dor *a* smoking. ● *m* smoker. **~r** *vt/i* smoke. **~rse** *vpr* smoke; (*fig, gastar*) squander. **~rada** *f* puff of smoke. **~r en pipa** smoke a pipe. **prohibido ~r** no smoking

funámbulo *m* tightrope walker

funci|ón *f* function; (*de un cargo etc*) duties; (*de teatro*) show, performance. **~onal** *a* functional. **~onar** *vi* work, function. **~onario** *m* civil servant. **no ~ona** out of order

funda *f* cover. **~ de almohada** pillowcase

funda|ción *f* foundation. **~mental** *a* fundamental. **~mentar** *vt* lay the foundations of; (*fig*) base. **~mento** *m* foundation. **~r** *vt* found; (*fig*) base. **~rse** *vpr* be based

fundi|ción *f* melting; (*de metales*) smelting; (*taller*) foundry. **~r** *vt* melt; smelt ‹*metales*›; cast ‹*objeto*›; blend ‹*colores*›; (*fusionar*) merge. **~rse** *vpr* melt; (*unirse*) merge

fúnebre *a* funeral; (*sombrío*) gloomy

funeral *a* funeral. ● *m* funeral. **~es** *mpl* funeral

funicular *a & m* funicular

furg|ón *m* van. **~oneta** *f* van

fur|ia *f* fury; (*violencia*) violence. **~ibundo** *a* furious. **~ioso** *a* furious. **~or** *m* fury

furtivo *a* furtive

furúnculo *m* boil

fuselaje *m* fuselage

fusible *m* fuse

fusil *m* gun. **~ar** *vt* shoot

fusión *f* melting; (*unión*) fusion; (*com*) merger

fútbol *m* football

futbolista *m* footballer

fútil *a* futile

futur|ista *a* futuristic. ● *m & f* futurist. **~o** *a & m* future

G

gabán *m* overcoat

garbardina *f* raincoat; (*tela*) gabardine

gabinete *m* (*pol*) cabinet; (*en museo etc*) room; (*de dentista, médico etc*) consulting room

gacela *f* gazelle

gaceta *f* gazette

gachas *fpl* porridge

gacho *a* drooping

gaélico *a* Gaelic

gafa *f* hook. **~s** *fpl* glasses, spectacles. **~s de sol** sun-glasses

gaf|ar *vt* hook; (*fam*) bring bad luck to. **~e** *m* jinx

gaita *f* bagpipes

gajo *m* (*de naranja, nuez etc*) segment

gala|s *fpl* finery, best clothes. **estar de ~** be dressed up. **hacer ~ de** show off

galán *m* (*en el teatro*) male lead; (*enamorado*) lover

galante *a* gallant. **~ar** *vt* court. **~ría** *f* gallantry

galápago *m* turtle

galardón *m* reward

galaxia *f* galaxy

galeón *m* galleon

galera *f* galley

galería *f* gallery

Gales *m* Wales. **país de ~** Wales

gal|és *a* Welsh. ● *m* Welshman; (*lengua*) Welsh. **~esa** *f* Welshwoman

galgo *m* greyhound

Galicia *f* Galicia

galimatías *m invar* (*fam*) gibberish

galón *m* gallon; (*cinta*) braid; (*mil*) stripe

galop|ar *vi* gallop. **~e** *m* gallop

galvanizar [10] *vt* galvanize

gallard|ía *f* elegance. **~o** *a* elegant

gallego *a & m* Galician

galleta *f* biscuit (*Brit*), cookie (*Amer*)

gall|ina *f* hen, chicken; (*fig, fam*) coward. **~o** *m* cock

gama *f* scale; (*fig*) range

gamba *f* prawn (*Brit*), shrimp (*Amer*)

gamberro *m* hooligan

gamuza *f* (*piel*) chamois leather

gana *f* wish, desire; (*apetito*) appetite. **de buena ~** willingly. **de mala ~** reluctantly. **no me da la ~** I don't feel like it. **tener ~s de** (+ *infinitivo*) feel like (+ *gerundio*)

ganad|ería *f* cattle raising; (*ganado*) livestock. **~o** *m* livestock. **~o de cerda** pigs. **~o lanar** sheep. **~o vacuno** cattle

ganar *vt* earn; (*en concurso, juego etc*) win; (*alcanzar*) reach; (*aventajar*) beat. ● *vi* (*vencer*) win; (*mejorar*) improve. **~se la vida** earn a living. **salir ganando** come out better off

ganch|illo *m* crochet. **~o** *m* hook. **~oso** *a*, **~udo** *a* hooked. **echar el ~o a** hook. **hacer ~illo** crochet. **tener ~o** be very attractive

gandul *a & m & f* good-for-nothing

ganga *f* bargain; (*buena situación*) easy job, cushy job (*fam*)

gangrena *f* gangrene

gans|ada *f* silly thing. **~o** *m* goose

gañi|do *m* yelping. **~r** [22] *vi* yelp

garabat|ear *vt/i* (*garrapatear*) scribble. **~o** *m* (*garrapato*) scribble

garaj|e *m* garage. **~ista** *m & f* garage attendant

garant|e *m & f* guarantor. **~ía** *f* guarantee. **~ir** [24] *vt* (*esp LAm*), **~izar** [10] *vt* guarantee

garapiñado *a*. **almendras** *fpl* **garapiñadas** sugared almonds

garbanzo *m* chick-pea

garbo *m* poise; (*de escrito*) style. **~so** *a* elegant

garfio *m* hook

garganta *f* throat; (*desfiladero*) gorge; (*de botella*) neck

gárgaras *fpl*. **hacer ~** gargle

gargarismo *m* gargle

gárgola *f* gargoyle

garita *f* hut; (*de centinela*) sentry box

garito *m* gambling den

garra *f* (*de animal*) claw; (*de ave*) talon

garrafa *f* carafe

garrapata *f* tick

garrapat|ear *vi* scribble. **~o** *m* scribble

garrote *m* club, cudgel; (*tormento*) garrotte

gárrulo *a* garrulous

garúa *f* (*LAm*) drizzle

garza *f* heron

gas *m* gas. **con ~** fizzy. **sin ~** still

gasa *f* gauze

gaseosa *f* lemonade

gasfitero *m* (*Arg*) plumber

gas|óleo *m* diesel. **~olina** *f* petrol (*Brit*), gasoline (*Amer*), gas (*Amer*). **~olinera** *f* petrol station (*Brit*), gas station (*Amer*); (*lancha*) motor boat. **~ómetro** *m* gasometer

gast|ado *a* spent; ‹*vestido etc*› worn out. **~ador** *m* spendthrift. **~ar** *vt* spend; (*consumir*) use; (*malgastar*) waste; wear ‹*vestido etc*›; crack ‹*broma*›. ● *vi* spend. **~arse** *vpr* wear out. **~o** *m* expense; (*acción de gastar*) spending

gástrico *a* gastric

gastronomía *f* gastronomy

gat|a *f* cat. **a ~as** on all fours. **~ear** *vi* crawl

gatillo *m* trigger; (*de dentista*) (dental) forceps

gat|ito *m* kitten. **~o** *m* cat. **dar ~o por liebre** take s.o. in

gaucho *a & m* Gaucho

gaveta *f* drawer

gavilla *f* sheaf; (*de personas*) band, gang

gaviota *f* seagull

gazpacho *m* gazpacho, cold soup

géiser *m* geyser

gelatina *f* gelatine; (*jalea*) jelly

gelignita *f* gelignite

gema *f* gem

gemelo *m* twin. **~s** *mpl* (*anteojos*) binoculars; (*de camisa*) cuff-links. **G~s** Gemini

gemido *m* groan

Géminis *mpl* Gemini

gemir [5] *vi* groan; ‹*animal*› whine, howl

gen *m*, **gene** *m* gene

geneal|ogía *f* genealogy. **~ógico** *a* genealogical. **árbol** *m* **~ógico** family tree

generación *f* generation

general *a* general; (*corriente*) common. ● *m* general. **~ísimo** *m* generalissimo, supreme commander. **~ización** *f* generalization. **~izar** [10] *vt/i* generalize. **~mente** *adv* generally. **en ~** in general. **por lo ~** generally

generar *vt* generate

género *m* type, sort; (*biol*) genus; (*gram*) gender; (*producto*) product. **~s de punto** knitwear. **~ humano** mankind

generos|idad *f* generosity. **~o** *a* generous; ‹*vino*› full-bodied

génesis *m* genesis

genétic|a *f* genetics. **~o** *a* genetic

genial *a* brilliant; (*agradable*) pleasant
genio *m* temper; (*carácter*) nature; (*talento, persona*) genius
genital *a* genital. **~es** *mpl* genitals
gente *f* people; (*nación*) nation; (*familia, fam*) family; (*Mex, persona*) person
gentil *a* charming; (*pagano*) pagan. **~eza** *f* elegance; (*encanto*) charm; (*amabilidad*) kindness
gentío *m* crowd
genuflexión *f* genuflection
genuino *a* genuine
ge|ografía *f* geography. **~ográfico** *a* geographical. **~ógrafo** *m* geographer
ge|ología *f* geology. **~ólogo** *m* geologist
geom|etría *f* geometry. **~étrico** *a* geometrical
geranio *m* geranium
geren|cia *f* management. **~te** *m* manager
geriatría *f* geriatrics
germánico *a & m* Germanic
germen *m* germ
germicida *f* germicide
germinar *vi* germinate
gestación *f* gestation
gesticula|ción *f* gesticulation. **~r** *vi* gesticulate; (*hacer muecas*) grimace
gesti|ón *f* step; (*administración*) management. **~onar** *vt* take steps to arrange; (*dirigir*) manage
gesto *m* expression; (*ademán*) gesture; (*mueca*) grimace
Gibraltar *m* Gibraltar
gibraltareño *a & m* Gibraltarian
gigante *a* gigantic. ● *m* giant. **~sco** *a* gigantic
gimn|asia *f* gymnastics. **~asio** *m* gymnasium, gym (*fam*). **~asta** *m & f* gymnast. **~ástica** *f* gymnastics
gimotear *vi* whine
ginebra *f* gin
Ginebra *f* Geneva
ginec|ología *f* gynaecology. **~ólogo** *m* gynaecologist
gira *f* excursion; (*a varios sitios*) tour
girar *vt* spin; (*por giro postal*) transfer. ● *vi* rotate, go round; ‹*camino etc*› turn
girasol *m* sunflower
gir|atorio *a* revolving. **~o** *m* turn; (*com*) draft; (*locución*) expression. **~o postal** postal order
giroscopio *m* gyroscope
gis *m* chalk
gitano *a & m* gypsy
glacia|l *a* icy. **~r** *m* glacier
gladiador *m* gladiator
glándula *f* gland
glasear *vt* glaze; (*culin*) ice
glicerina *f* glycerine
glicina *f* wisteria
glob|al *a* global; (*fig*) overall. **~o** *m* globe; (*aeróstato, juguete*) balloon
glóbulo *m* globule; (*med*) corpuscle
gloria *f* glory. **~rse** *vpr* boast (**de** about)
glorieta *f* bower; (*auto*) roundabout (*Brit*), (traffic) circle (*Amer*)
glorificar [7] *vt* glorify
glorioso *a* glorious
glosario *m* glossary
glot|ón *a* gluttonous. ● *m* glutton. **~onería** *f* gluttony
glucosa *f* glucose
gnomo /'nomo/ *m* gnome
gob|ernación *f* government. **~ernador** *a* governing. ● *m* governor. **~ernante** *a* governing. **~ernar** [1] *vt* govern; (*dirigir*) manage, direct. **~ierno** *m* government; (*dirección*) management, direction. **~ierno de la casa** housekeeping. **Ministerio** *m* **de la G~ernación** Home Office (*Brit*), Department of the Interior (*Amer*)
goce *m* enjoyment
gol *m* goal
golf *m* golf
golfo *m* gulf; (*niño*) urchin; (*holgazán*) layabout
golondrina *f* swallow
golos|ina *f* titbit; (*dulce*) sweet. **~o** *a* fond of sweets
golpe *m* blow; (*puñetazo*) punch; (*choque*) bump; (*de emoción*) shock; (*acceso*) fit; (*en fútbol*) shot; (*en golf, en tenis, de remo*) stroke. **~ar** *vt* hit; (*dar varios golpes*) beat; (*con mucho ruido*) bang; (*con el puño*) punch. ● *vi* knock. **~ de estado** coup d'etat. **~ de fortuna** stroke of luck. **~ de mano** raid. **~ de vista** glance. **~ militar** military coup. **de ~** suddenly. **de un ~** at one go
gom|a *f* rubber; (*para pegar*) glue; (*anillo*) rubber band; (*elástico*) elastic. **~a de borrar** rubber. **~a de pegar** glue. **~a espuma** foam rubber. **~ita** *f* rubber band
gongo *m* gong
gord|a *f* (*Mex*) thick tortilla. **~iflón** *m* (*fam*), **~inflón** *m* (*fam*) fatty. **~o** *a* ‹*persona*› fat; ‹*carne*› fatty;

(*grande*) large, big. ● *m* first prize. **~ura** *f* fatness; (*grasa*) fat
gorila *f* gorilla
gorje|ar *vi* chirp. **~o** *m* chirping
gorra *f* cap
gorrión *m* sparrow
gorro *m* cap; (*de niño*) bonnet
got|a *f* drop; (*med*) gout. **~ear** *vi* drip. **~eo** *m* dripping. **~era** *f* leak. **ni ~a** nothing
gótico *a* Gothic
gozar [10] *vt* enjoy. ● *vi.* **~ de** enjoy. **~se** *vpr* enjoy
gozne *m* hinge
gozo *m* pleasure; (*alegría*) joy. **~so** *a* delighted
graba|ción *f* recording. **~do** *m* engraving, print; (*en libro*) illustration. **~r** *vt* engrave; record ‹*discos etc*›
gracejo *m* wit
graci|a *f* grace; (*favor*) favour; (*humor*) wit. **~as** *fpl* thanks. **¡~as!** thank you!, thanks! **~oso** *a* funny. ● *m* fool, comic character. **dar las ~as** thank. **hacer ~a** amuse; (*gustar*) please. **¡muchas ~as!** thank you very much! **tener ~a** be funny
grad|a *f* step; (*línea*) row; (*de anfiteatro*) tier. **~ación** *f* gradation. **~o** *m* degree; (*escol*) year (*Brit*), grade (*Amer*); (*voluntad*) willingness
gradua|ción *f* graduation; (*de alcohol*) proof. **~do** *m* graduate. **~l** *a* gradual. **~r** [21] *vt* graduate; (*medir*) measure; (*univ*) confer a degree on. **~rse** *vpr* graduate
gráfic|a *f* graph. **~o** *a* graphic. ● *m* graph
grajo *m* rook
gram|ática *f* grammar. **~atical** *a* grammatical
gramo *m* gram, gramme (*Brit*)
gramófono *m* record-player, gramophone (*Brit*), phonograph (*Amer*)
gran *a véase* **grande**
grana *f* (*color*) scarlet
granada *f* pomegranate; (*mil*) grenade
granate *m* garnet
Gran Bretaña *f* Great Britain
grande *a* (*delante de nombre en singular* **gran**) big, large; (*alto*) tall; (*fig*) great. ● *m* grandee. **~za** *f* greatness
grandioso *a* magnificent
granel *m.* **a ~** in bulk; (*suelto*) loose; (*fig*) in abundance
granero *m* barn
granito *m* granite; (*grano*) small grain
graniz|ado *m* iced drink. **~ar** [10] *vi* hail. **~o** *m* hail
granj|a *f* farm. **~ero** *m* farmer
grano *m* grain; (*semilla*) seed; (*de café*) bean; (*med*) spot. **~s** *mpl* cereals
granuja *m & f* rogue
gránulo *m* granule
grapa *f* staple
gras|a *f* grease; (*culin*) fat. **~iento** *a* greasy
gratifica|ción *f* (*propina*) tip; (*de sueldo*) bonus. **~r** [7] *vt* (*dar propina*) tip
gratis *adv* free
gratitud *f* gratitude
grato *a* pleasant; (*bienvenido*) welcome
gratuito *a* free; (*fig*) uncalled for
grava *f* gravel
grava|men *m* obligation. **~r** *vt* tax; (*cargar*) burden
grave *a* serious; (*pesado*) heavy; ‹*sonido*› low; ‹*acento*› grave. **~dad** *f* gravity
gravilla *f* gravel
gravita|ción *f* gravitation. **~r** *vi* gravitate; (*apoyarse*) rest **(sobre** on); (*fig, pesar*) weigh **(sobre** on)
gravoso *a* onerous; (*costoso*) expensive
graznar *vi* ‹*cuervo*› caw; ‹*pato*› quack
Grecia *f* Greece
gregario *a* gregarious
greguería *f* uproar
gremio *m* union
greñ|a *f* mop of hair. **~udo** *a* unkempt
gresca *f* uproar; (*riña*) quarrel
griego *a & m* Greek
grieta *f* crack
grifo *m* tap, faucet (*Amer*); (*animal fantástico*) griffin
grilletes *mpl* shackles
grillo *m* cricket; (*bot*) shoot. **~s** *mpl* shackles
grima *f.* **dar ~** annoy
gringo *m* (*LAm*) Yankee (*fam*), American
gripe *f* flu (*fam*), influenza
gris *a* grey. ● *m* grey; (*policía, fam*) policeman
grit|ar *vt* shout (for); (*como protesta*) boo. ● *vi* shout. **~ería** *f*, **~erío** *m*

uproar. **~o** *m* shout; (*de dolor, sorpresa*) cry; (*chillido*) scream. **dar ~s** shout

grosella *f* redcurrant. **~ negra** blackcurrant

groser|ía *f* coarseness; (*palabras etc*) coarse remark. **~o** *a* coarse; (*descortés*) rude

grosor *m* thickness

grotesco *a* grotesque

grúa *f* crane

grues|a *f* gross. **~o** *a* thick; ‹*persona*› fat, stout. ● *m* thickness; (*fig*) main body

grulla *f* crane

grumo *m* clot; (*de leche*) curd

gruñi|do *m* grunt; (*fig*) grumble. **~r** [22] *vi* grunt; ‹*perro*› growl; (*refunfuñar*) grumble

grupa *f* hindquarters

grupo *m* group

gruta *f* grotto

guacamole *m* (*Mex*) avocado purée

guadaña *f* scythe

guagua *f* trifle; (*esp LAm, autobús, fam*) bus

guante *m* glove

guapo *a* good-looking; ‹*chica*› pretty; (*elegante*) smart

guarapo *m* (*LAm*) sugar cane liquor

guarda *m & f* guard; (*de parque etc*) keeper. ● *f* protection. **~barros** *m invar* mudguard. **~bosque** *m* gamekeeper. **~costas** *m invar* coastguard vessel. **~dor** *a* careful. ● *m* keeper. **~espaldas** *m invar* bodyguard. **~meta** *m invar* goalkeeper. **~r** *vt* keep; (*vigilar*) guard; (*proteger*) protect; (*reservar*) save, keep. **~rse** *vpr* be on one's guard. **~rse de** (+ *infinitivo*) avoid (+ *gerundio*). **~rropa** *m* wardrobe; (*en local público*) cloakroom. **~vallas** *m invar* (*LAm*) goalkeeper

guardería *f* nursery

guardia *f* guard; (*custodia*) care. ● *f* guard. **G~ Civil** Civil Guard. **~ municipal** policeman. **~ de tráfico** traffic policeman. **estar de ~** be on duty. **estar en ~** be on one's guard. **montar la ~** mount guard

guardián *m* guardian; (*de parque etc*) keeper; (*de edificio*) caretaker

guardilla *f* attic

guar|ecer [11] (*albergar*) give shelter to. **~ecerse** *vpr* take shelter. **~ida** *f* den, lair; (*de personas*) hideout

guarn|ecer [11] *vt* provide; (*adornar*) decorate; (*culin*) garnish. **~ición** *m* decoration; (*de caballo*) harness; (*culin*) garnish; (*mil*) garrison; (*de piedra preciosa*) setting

guarro *m* pig

guasa *f* joke; (*ironía*) irony

guaso *a* (*Arg*) coarse

guasón *a* humorous. ● *m* joker

Guatemala *f* Guatemala

guatemalteco *a* from Guatemala. ● *m* person from Guatemala

guateque *m* party

guayaba *f* guava; (*dulce*) guava jelly

guayabera *f* (*Mex*) shirt

gubernamental *a*, **gubernativo** *a* governmental

güero *a* (*Mex*) fair

guerr|a *f* war; (*método*) warfare. **~a civil** civil war. **~ear** *vi* wage war. **~ero** *a* war; (*belicoso*) fighting. ● *m* warrior. **~illa** *f* band of guerillas. **~illero** *m* guerilla. **dar ~a** annoy

guía *m & f* guide. ● *f* guidebook; (*de teléfonos*) directory; (*de ferrocarriles*) timetable

guiar [20] *vt* guide; (*llevar*) lead; (*auto*) drive. **~se** *vpr* be guided (**por** by)

guij|arro *m* pebble. **~o** *m* gravel

guillotina *f* guillotine

guind|a *f* morello cherry. **~illa** *f* chilli

guiñapo *m* rag; (*fig, persona*) reprobate

guiñ|ar *vt/i* wink. **~o** *m* wink. **hacer ~os** wink

gui|ón *m* hyphen, dash; (*de película etc*) script. **~onista** *m & f* scriptwriter

guirnalda *f* garland

güiro *m* (*LAm*) gourd

guisa *f* manner, way. **a ~ de** as. **de tal ~** in such a way

guisado *m* stew

guisante *m* pea. **~ de olor** sweet pea

guis|ar *vt/i* cook. **~o** *m* dish

güisqui *m* whisky

guitarr|a *f* guitar. **~ista** *m & f* guitarist

gula *f* gluttony

gusano *m* worm; (*larva de mosca*) maggot

gustar *vt* taste. ● *vi* please. **¿te gusta?** do you like it? **me gusta el vino** I like wine

gusto *m* taste; (*placer*) pleasure. **~so** *a* tasty; (*agradable*) pleasant. **a ~** comfortable. **a mi ~** to my liking.

buen ~ (good) taste. **con mucho ~** with pleasure. **dar ~** please. **mucho ~** pleased to meet you

gutural *a* guttural

H

ha *vb véase* **haber**

haba *f* broad bean; (*de café etc*) bean

Habana *f*. **la ~** Havana

haban|era *f* habanera, Cuban dance. **~ero** *a* from Havana. ● *m* person from Havana. **~o** *m* (*puro*) Havana

haber *v aux* [30] have. ● *v impersonal* (*presente s & pl* **hay**, *imperfecto s & pl* **había**, *pretérito s & pl* **hubo**) be. **hay 5 bancos en la plaza** there are 5 banks in the square. **hay que hacerlo** it must be done, you have to do it. **he aquí** here is, here are. **no hay de qué** don't mention it, not at all. **¿qué hay?** (*¿qué pasa?*) what's the matter?; (*¿qué tal?*) how are you?

habichuela *f* bean

hábil *a* skilful; (*listo*) clever; (*adecuado*) suitable

habilidad *f* skill; (*astucia*) cleverness

habilita|ción *f* qualification. **~r** *vt* qualify

habita|ble *a* habitable. **~ción** *f* room; (*casa etc*) dwelling; (*cuarto de dormir*) bedroom; (*en biología*) habitat. **~ción de matrimonio**, **~ción doble** double room. **~ción individual** , **~ción sencilla** single room. **~do** *a* inhabited. **~nte** *m* inhabitant. **~r** *vt* live in. ● *vi* live

hábito *m* habit

habitual *a* usual, habitual; ‹*cliente*› regular. **~mente** *adv* usually

habituar [21] *vt* accustom. **~se** *vpr*. **~se a** get used to

habla *f* speech; (*idioma*) language; (*dialecto*) dialect. **al ~** (*al teléfono*) speaking. **ponerse al ~ con** get in touch with. **~dor** *a* talkative. ● *m* chatterbox. **~duría** *f* rumour. **~durías** *fpl* gossip. **~nte** *a* speaking. ● *m & f* speaker. **~r** *vt* speak. ● *vi* speak, talk (**con** to). **~rse** *vpr* speak. **¡ni ~r!** out of the question! **se ~ español** Spanish spoken

hacedor *m* creator, maker

hacendado *m* landowner; (*LAm*) farmer

hacendoso *a* hard-working

hacer [31] *vt* do; (*fabricar, producir etc*) make; (*en matemáticas*) make, be. ● *v impersonal* (*con expresiones meteorológicas*) be; (*con determinado periodo de tiempo*) ago. **~se** *vpr* become; (*acostumbrarse*) get used (**a** to); (*estar hecho*) be made. **~ de** act as. **~se a la mar** put to sea. **~se el sordo** pretend to be deaf. **hace buen tiempo** it's fine weather. **hace calor** it's hot. **hace frío** it's cold. **hace poco** recently. **hace 7 años** 7 years ago. **hace sol** it's sunny. **hace viento** it's windy. **¿qué le vamos a ~?** what are we going to do?

hacia *prep* towards; (*cerca de*) near; (*con tiempo*) at about. **~ abajo** down(wards). **~ arriba** up(wards). **~ las dos** at about two o'clock

hacienda *f* country estate; (*en LAm*) ranch; (*LAm, ganado*) livestock; (*pública*) treasury. **Ministerio** *m* **de H~** Ministry of Finance; (*en Gran Bretaña*) Exchequer; (*en Estados Unidos*) Treasury. **ministro** *m* **de H~** Minister of Finance; (*en Gran Bretaña*) Chancellor of the Exchequer; (*en Estados Unidos*) Secretary of the Treasury

hacinar *vt* stack

hacha *f* axe; (*antorcha*) torch

hachís *m* hashish

hada *f* fairy. **cuento** *m* **de ~s** fairy tale

hado *m* fate

hago *vb véase* **hacer**

Haití *m* Haiti

halag|ar [12] *vt* flatter. **~üeño** *a* flattering

halcón *m* falcon

hálito *m* breath

halo *m* halo

hall /xol/ *m* hall

halla|r *vt* find; (*descubrir*) discover. **~rse** *vpr* be. **~zgo** *m* discovery

hamaca *f* hammock; (*asiento*) deck-chair

hambr|e *f* hunger; (*de muchos*) famine. **~iento** *a* starving. **tener ~e** be hungry

Hamburgo *m* Hamburg

hamburguesa *f* hamburger

hamp|a *f* underworld. **~ón** *m* thug

handicap /'xandikap/ *m* handicap

hangar *m* hangar

haragán *a* lazy, idle. ● *m* layabout

harap|iento *a* in rags. **~o** *m* rag

harina *f* flour

harpa *f* harp

hart|ar *vt* satisfy; (*fastidiar*) annoy. **~arse** *vpr* (*comer*) eat one's fill; (*cansarse*) get fed up (**de** with). **~azgo** *m* surfeit. **~o** *a* full; (*cansado*) tired; (*fastidiado*) fed up (**de** with). ● *adv* enough; (*muy*) very. **~ura** *f* surfeit; (*abundancia*) plenty; (*de deseo*) satisfaction

hasta *prep* as far as; (*con tiempo*) until, till; (*Mex*) not until. ● *adv* even. **¡~ la vista!** goodbye!, see you! (*fam*). **¡~ luego!** see you later! **¡~ mañana!** see you tomorrow! **¡~ pronto!** see you soon!

hast|iar [20] *vt* annoy; (*cansar*) weary, tire; (*aburrir*) bore. **~iarse** *vpr* get fed up (**de** with). **~ío** *m* weariness; (*aburrimiento*) boredom; (*asco*) disgust

hat|illo *m* bundle (of belongings); (*ganado*) small flock. **~o** *m* belongings; (*ganado*) flock, herd

haya *f* beech (tree). ● *vb véase* **haber**

Haya *f*. **la ~** the Hague

haz *m* bundle; (*de trigo*) sheaf; (*de rayos*) beam

hazaña *f* exploit

hazmerreír *m* laughing-stock

he *vb véase* **haber**

hebdomadario *a* weekly

hebilla *f* buckle

hebra *f* thread; (*fibra*) fibre

hebreo *a* Hebrew; (*actualmente*) Jewish. ● *m* Hebrew; (*actualmente*) Jew; (*lengua*) Hebrew

hecatombe *m* (*fig*) disaster

hechi|cera *f* witch. **~cería** *f* witchcraft. **~cero** *a* magic. ● *m* wizard. **~zar** [10] *vt* cast a spell on; (*fig*) fascinate. **~zo** *m* witchcraft; (*un acto de brujería*) spell; (*fig*) fascination

hech|o *pp de* **hacer**. ● *a* mature; (*terminado*) finished; ‹*vestidos etc*› ready-made; (*culin*) done. ● *m* fact; (*acto*) deed; (*cuestión*) matter; (*suceso*) event. **~ura** *f* making; (*forma*) form; (*del cuerpo*) build; (*calidad de fabricación*) workmanship. **de ~o** in fact

hed|er [1] *vi* stink. **~iondez** *f* stench. **~iondo** *a* stinking, smelly. **~or** *m* stench

hela|da *f* freeze; (*escarcha*) frost. **~dera** *f* (*LAm*) refrigerator, fridge (*Brit, fam*). **~dería** *f* ice-cream shop. **~do** *a* frozen; (*muy frío*) very cold. ● *m* ice-cream. **~dora** *f* freezer. **~r** [1] *vt* freeze. **~rse** *vpr* freeze

helecho *m* fern

hélice *f* spiral; (*propulsor*) propeller

heli|cóptero *m* helicopter. **~puerto** *m* heliport

hembra *f* female; (*mujer*) woman

hemisferio *m* hemisphere

hemorragia *f* haemorrhage

hemorroides *fpl* haemorrhoids, piles

henchir [5] *vt* fill. **~se** *vpr* stuff o.s.

hend|er [1] *vt* split. **~idura** *f* crack, split; (*geol*) fissure

heno *m* hay

heráldica *f* heraldry

herb|áceo *a* herbaceous. **~olario** *m* herbalist. **~oso** *a* grassy

hered|ad *f* country estate. **~ar** *vt/i* inherit. **~era** *f* heiress. **~ero** *m* heir. **~itario** *a* hereditary

herej|e *m* heretic. **~ía** *f* heresy

herencia *f* inheritance; (*fig*) heritage

heri|da *f* injury. **~do** *a* injured, wounded. ● *m* injured person. **~r** [4] *vt* injure, wound; (*fig*) hurt. **~rse** *vpr* hurt o.s. **los ~dos** the injured; (*cantidad*) the number of injured

herman|a *f* sister. **~a política** sister-in-law. **~astra** *f* stepsister. **~astro** *m* stepbrother. **~dad** *f* brotherhood. **~o** *m* brother. **~o político** brother-in-law. **~os gemelos** twins

hermético *a* hermetic; (*fig*) watertight

hermos|o *a* beautiful; (*espléndido*) splendid; ‹*hombre*› handsome. **~ura** *f* beauty

hernia *f* hernia

héroe *m* hero

hero|ico *a* heroic. **~ína** *f* heroine; (*droga*) heroin. **~ismo** *m* heroism

herr|adura *f* horseshoe. **~amienta** *f* tool. **~ería** *f* smithy. **~ero** *m* blacksmith. **~umbre** *f* rust

herv|idero *m* (*manantial*) spring; (*fig*) hotbed; (*multitud*) throng. **~ir** [4] *vt/i* boil. **~or** *m* boiling; (*fig*) ardour

heterogéneo *a* heterogeneous

heterosexual *a & m & f* heterosexual

hex|agonal *a* hexagonal. **~ágono** *m* hexagon

hiato *m* hiatus

hiberna|ción *f* hibernation. **~r** *vi* hibernate
hibisco *m* hibiscus
híbrido *a & m* hybrid
hice *vb véase* **hacer**
hidalgo *m* nobleman
hidrata|nte *a* moisturizing. **~r** *vt* hydrate; ‹*crema etc*› moisturize. **crema** *f* **~nte** moisturizing cream
hidráulico *a* hydraulic
hidroavión *m* seaplane
hidroeléctrico *a* hydroelectric
hidrófilo *a* absorbent
hidr|ofobia *f* rabies. **~ófobo** *a* rabid
hidrógeno *m* hydrogen
hidroplano *m* seaplane
hiedra *f* ivy
hiel *f* (*fig*) bitterness
hielo *m* ice; (*escarcha*) frost; (*fig*) coldness
hiena *f* hyena; (*fig*) brute
hierba *f* grass; (*culin*, *med*) herb. **~buena** *f* mint. **mala ~** weed; (*gente*) bad people, evil people
hierro *m* iron
hígado *m* liver
higi|ene *f* hygiene. **~énico** *a* hygienic
hig|o *m* fig. **~uera** *f* fig tree
hij|a *f* daughter. **~a política** daughter-in-law. **~astra** *f* step-daughter. **~astro** *m* stepson. **~o** *m* son. **~o político** son-in-law. **~s** *mpl* sons; (*chicos y chicas*) children
hilar *vt* spin. **~ delgado** split hairs
hilaridad *f* laughter, hilarity
hilera *f* row; (*mil*) file
hilo *m* thread; (*elec*) wire; (*de líquido*) trickle; (*lino*) linen
hilv|án *m* tacking. **~anar** *vt* tack; (*fig*, *bosquejar*) outline
himno *m* hymn. **~ nacional** anthem
hincapié *m*. **hacer ~ en** stress, insist on
hincar [7] *vt* drive in. **~se** *vpr* sink into. **~se de rodillas** kneel down
hincha *f* (*fam*) grudge; (*aficionado*, *fam*) fan
hincha|do *a* inflated; (*med*) swollen; ‹*persona*› arrogant. **~r** *vt* inflate, blow up. **~rse** *vpr* swell up; (*fig*, *comer mucho*, *fam*) gorge o.s. **~zón** *f* swelling; (*fig*) arrogance
hindi *m* Hindi
hindú *a* Hindu
hiniesta *f* (*bot*) broom
hinojo *m* fennel
hiper... *pref* hyper...
hiper|mercado *m* hypermarket. **~sensible** *a* hypersensitive. **~tensión** *f* high blood pressure
hípico *a* horse
hipn|osis *f* hypnosis. **~ótico** *a* hypnotic. **~otismo** *m* hypnotism. **~otizador** *m* hypnotist. **~otizar** [10] *vt* hypnotize
hipo *m* hiccup. **tener ~** have hiccups
hipocondríaco *a & m* hypochondriac
hip|ocresía *f* hypocrisy. **~ócrita** *a* hypocritical. • *m & f* hypocrite
hipodérmico *a* hypodermic
hipódromo *m* racecourse
hipopótamo *m* hippopotamus
hipoteca *f* mortgage. **~r** [7] *vt* mortgage
hip|ótesis *f invar* hypothesis. **~otético** *a* hypothetical
hiriente *a* offensive, wounding
hirsuto *a* shaggy
hirviente *a* boiling
hispánico *a* Hispanic
hispano... *pref* Spanish
Hispanoamérica *f* Spanish America
hispano|americano *a* Spanish American. **~hablante** *a*, **~parlante** *a* Spanish-speaking
hist|eria *f* hysteria. **~érico** *a* hysterical. **~erismo** *m* hysteria
hist|oria *f* history; (*cuento*) story. **~oriador** *m* historian. **~órico** *a* historical. **~orieta** *f* tale; (*con dibujos*) strip cartoon. **pasar a la ~oria** go down in history
hito *m* milestone
hizo *vb véase* **hacer**
hocico *m* snout; (*fig*, *de enfado*) grimace
hockey *m* hockey. **~ sobre hielo** ice hockey
hogar *m* hearth; (*fig*) home. **~eño** *a* home; ‹*persona*› home-loving
hogaza *f* large loaf
hoguera *f* bonfire
hoja *f* leaf; (*de papel*, *metal etc*) sheet; (*de cuchillo*, *espada etc*) blade. **~ de afeitar** razor blade. **~lata** *f* tin. **~latería** *f* tinware. **~latero** *m* tinsmith
hojaldre *m* puff pastry, flaky pastry
hojear *vt* leaf through; (*leer superficialmente*) glance through
hola *int* hello!
Holanda *f* Holland
holand|és *a* Dutch. • *m* Dutchman; (*lengua*) Dutch. **~esa** *f* Dutchwoman

holg|ado *a* loose; (*fig*) comfortable. **~ar** [2 & 12] *vt* (*no trabajar*) not work, have a day off; (*sobrar*) be unnecessary. **~azán** *a* lazy. ● *m* idler. **~ura** *f* looseness; (*fig*) comfort; (*en mecánica*) play. **huelga decir que** needless to say

holocausto *m* holocaust

hollín *m* soot

hombre *m* man; (*especie humana*) man(kind). ● *int* Good Heavens!; (*de duda*) well. **~ de estado** statesman. **~ de negocios** businessman. **~ rana** frogman. **el ~ de la calle** the man in the street

hombr|era *f* epaulette; (*almohadilla*) shoulder pad. **~o** *m* shoulder

hombruno *a* masculine

homenaje *m* homage; (*fig*) tribute. **rendir ~ a** pay tribute to

home|ópata *m* homoeopath. **~opatía** *f* homoeopathy. **~opático** *a* homoeopathic

homicid|a *a* murderous. ● *m & f* murderer. **~io** *m* murder

homogéneo *a* homogeneous

homosexual *a & m & f* homosexual. **~idad** *f* homosexuality

hond|o *a* deep. **~onada** *f* hollow. **~ura** *f* depth

Honduras *fpl* Honduras

hondureño *a & m* Honduran

honest|idad *f* decency. **~o** *a* proper

hongo *m* fungus; (*culin*) mushroom; (*venenoso*) toadstool

hon|or *m* honour. **~orable** *a* honourable. **~orario** *a* honorary. **~orarios** *mpl* fees. **~ra** *f* honour; (*buena fama*) good name. **~radez** *f* honesty. **~rado** *a* honest. **~rar** *vt* honour. **~rarse** *vpr* be honoured

hora *f* hour; (*momento determinado, momento oportuno*) time. **~ avanzada** late hour. **~ punta** rush hour. **~s** *fpl* **de trabajo** working hours. **~s** *fpl* **extraordinarias** overtime. **a estas ~s** now. **¿a qué ~?** at what time? when? **de ~ en ~** hourly. **de última ~** last-minute. **en buena ~** at the right time. **media ~** half an hour. **¿qué ~ es?** what time is it? **¿tiene Vd ~?** can you tell me the time?

horario *a* time; (*cada hora*) hourly. ● *m* timetable. **a ~** (*LAm*) on time

horca *f* gallows

horcajadas. a ~ astride

horchata *f* tiger-nut milk

horda *f* horde

horizont|al *a & f* horizontal. **~e** *m* horizon

horma *f* mould; (*para fabricar calzado*) last; (*para conservar forma del calzado*) shoe-tree

hormiga *f* ant

hormigón *m* concrete

hormigue|ar *vt* tingle; (*bullir*) swarm. **me ~a la mano** I've got pins and needles in my hand. **~o** *m* tingling; (*fig*) anxiety

hormiguero *m* anthill; (*de gente*) swarm

hormona *f* hormone

horn|ada *f* batch. **~ero** *m* baker. **~illo** *m* cooker. **~o** *m* oven; (*para ladrillos, cerámica etc*) kiln; (*tec*) furnace

horóscopo *m* horoscope

horquilla *f* pitchfork; (*para el pelo*) hairpin

horr|endo *a* awful. **~ible** *a* horrible. **~ipilante** *a* terrifying. **~or** *m* horror; (*atrocidad*) atrocity. **~orizar** [10] *vt* horrify. **~orizarse** *vpr* be horrified. **~oroso** *a* horrifying. **¡qué ~or!** how awful!

hort|aliza *f* vegetable. **~elano** *m* market gardener. **~icultura** *f* horticulture

hosco *a* surly; ‹*lugar*› gloomy

hospeda|je *m* lodging. **~r** *vt* put up. **~rse** *vpr* lodge

hospital *m* hospital

hospital|ario *m* hospitable. **~idad** *f* hospitality

hostal *m* boarding-house

hostería *f* inn

hostia *f* (*relig*) host; (*golpe, fam*) punch

hostigar [12] *vt* whip; (*fig, excitar*) urge; (*fig, molestar*) pester

hostil *a* hostile. **~idad** *f* hostility

hotel *m* hotel. **~ero** *a* hotel. ● *m* hotelier

hoy *adv* today. **~ (en) día** nowadays. **~ mismo** this very day. **~ por ~** for the time being. **de ~ en adelante** from now on

hoy|a *f* hole; (*sepultura*) grave. **~o** *m* hole; (*sepultura*) grave. **~uelo** *m* dimple

hoz *f* sickle; (*desfiladero*) pass

hube *vb véase* **haber**

hucha *f* money box

hueco *a* hollow; (*vacío*) empty; (*esponjoso*) spongy; (*resonante*) resonant. ● *m* hollow

huelg|a *f* strike. **~a de brazos caídos** sit-down strike. **~a de celo** work-to-rule. **~a de hambre** hunger strike. **~uista** *m & f* striker. **declarar la ~a, declararse en ~a** come out on strike
huelo *vb véase* **oler**
huella *f* footprint; (*de animal, vehículo etc*) track. **~ dactilar, ~ digital** fingerprint
huérfano *a* orphaned. ● *m* orphan. **~ de** without
huero *a* empty
huert|a *f* market garden (*Brit*), truck farm (*Amer*); (*terreno de regadío*) irrigated plain. **~o** *m* vegetable garden; (*de árboles frutales*) orchard
huesa *f* grave
hueso *m* bone; (*de fruta*) stone. **~so** *a* bony
huésped *m* guest; (*que paga*) lodger; (*animal*) host
huesudo *a* bony
huev|a *f* roe. **~era** *f* eggcup. **~o** *m* egg. **~o duro** hard-boiled egg. **~o escalfado** poached egg. **~o estrellado, ~o frito** fried egg. **~o pasado por agua** boiled egg. **~os revueltos** scrambled eggs
hui|da *f* flight, escape. **~dizo** *a* (*tímido*) shy; (*fugaz*) fleeting. **~r** [17] *vt/i* flee, run away; (*evitar*) avoid
huipil *m* (*Mex*) embroidered smock
huitlacoche *m* (*Mex*) edible black fungus
hule *m* oilcloth, oilskin
human|idad *f* mankind; (*fig*) humanity. **~idades** *fpl* humanities. **~ismo** *m* humanism. **~ista** *m & f* humanist. **~itario** *a* humanitarian. **~o** *a* human; (*benévolo*) humane. ● *m* human (being)
hum|areda *f* cloud of smoke. **~ear** *vi* smoke; (*echar vapor*) steam
humed|ad *f* dampness (*en meteorología*) humidity. **~ecer** [11] *vt* moisten. **~ecerse** *vpr* become moist
húmedo *a* damp; ‹*clima*› humid; (*mojado*) wet
humi|ldad *f* humility. **~lde** *a* humble. **~llación** *f* humiliation. **~llar** *vt* humiliate. **~llarse** *vpr* humble o.s.
humo *m* smoke; (*vapor*) steam; (*gas nocivo*) fumes. **~s** *mpl* conceit
humor *m* mood, temper; (*gracia*) humour. **~ismo** *m* humour. **~ista** *m & f* humorist. **~ístico** *a* humorous. **estar de mal ~** be in a bad mood
hundi|do *a* sunken. **~miento** *m* sinking. **~r** *vt* sink; destroy ‹*edificio*›. **~rse** *vpr* sink; ‹*edificio*› collapse
húngaro *a & m* Hungarian
Hungría *f* Hungary
huracán *m* hurricane
huraño *a* unsociable
hurg|ar [12] *vt* poke; (*fig*) stir up. **~ón** *m* poker
hurón *m* ferret. ● *a* unsociable
hurra *int* hurray!
hurraca *f* magpie
hurtadillas. a ~ stealthily
hurt|ar *vt* steal. **~o** *m* theft; (*cosa robada*) stolen object
husmear *vt* sniff out; (*fig*) pry into
huyo *vb véase* **huir**

I

Iberia *f* Iberia
ibérico *a* Iberian
ibero *a & m* Iberian
íbice *m* ibex, mountain goat
Ibiza *f* Ibiza
iceberg /iθ'ber/ *m* iceberg
icono *m* icon
ictericia *f* jaundice
ida *f* outward journey; (*salida*) departure. **de ~ y vuelta** return (*Brit*), round-trip (*Amer*)
idea *f* idea; (*opinión*) opinion. **cambiar de ~** change one's mind. **no tener la más remota ~, no tener la menor ~** not have the slightest idea, not have a clue (*fam*)
ideal *a* ideal; (*imaginario*) imaginary. ● *m* ideal. **~ista** *m & f* idealist. **~izar** [10] *vt* idealize
idear *vt* think up, conceive; (*inventar*) invent
ídem *pron & adv* the same
idéntico *a* identical
identi|dad *f* identity. **~ficación** *f* identification. **~ficar** [7] *vt* identify. **~ficarse** *vpr*. **~ficarse con** identify with
ideol|ogía *f* ideology. **~ógico** *a* ideological
idílico *a* idyllic
idilio *m* idyll
idiom|a *m* language. **~ático** *a* idiomatic

idiosincrasia *f* idiosyncrasy
idiot|a *a* idiotic. ● *m & f* idiot. **~ez** *f* idiocy
idiotismo *m* idiom
idolatrar *vt* worship; (*fig*) idolize
ídolo *m* idol
idóneo *a* suitable (**para** for)
iglesia *f* church
iglú *m* igloo
ignición *f* ignition
ignomini|a *f* ignominy, disgrace. **~oso** *a* ignominious
ignora|ncia *f* ignorance. **~nte** *a* ignorant. ● *m* ignoramus. **~r** *vt* not know, be unaware of
igual *a* equal; (*mismo*) the same; (*similar*) like; (*llano*) even; (*liso*) smooth. ● *adv* easily. ● *m* equal. **~ que** (the same) as. **al ~ que** the same as. **da ~**, **es ~** it doesn't matter
igual|ar *vt* make equal; (*ser igual*) equal; (*allanar*) level. **~arse** *vpr* be equal. **~dad** *f* equality. **~mente** *adv* equally; (*también*) also, likewise; (*respuesta de cortesía*) the same to you
ijada *f* flank
ilegal *a* illegal
ilegible *a* illegible
ilegítimo *a* illegitimate
ileso *a* unhurt
ilícito *a* illicit
ilimitado *a* unlimited
ilógico *a* illogical
ilumina|ción *f* illumination; (*alumbrado*) lighting; (*fig*) enlightenment. **~r** *vt* light (up); (*fig*) enlighten. **~rse** *vpr* light up
ilusi|ón *f* illusion; (*sueño*) dream; (*alegría*) joy. **~onado** *a* excited. **~onar** *vt* give false hope. **~onarse** *vpr* have false hopes. **hacerse ~ones** build up one's hopes. **me hace ~ón** I'm thrilled; I'm looking forward to ‹*algo en el futuro*›
ilusionis|mo *m* conjuring. **~ta** *m & f* conjurer
iluso *a* easily deceived. ● *m* dreamer. **~rio** *a* illusory
ilustra|ción *f* learning; (*dibujo*) illustration. **~do** *a* learned; (*con dibujos*) illustrated. **~r** *vt* explain; (*instruir*) instruct; (*añadir dibujos etc*) illustrate. **~rse** *vpr* acquire knowledge. **~tivo** *a* illustrative
ilustre *a* illustrious
imagen *f* image; (*TV etc*) picture
imagina|ble *a* imaginable. **~ción** *f* imagination. **~r** *vt* imagine. **~rse** *vpr* imagine. **~rio** *m* imaginary. **~tivo** *a* imaginative
imán *m* magnet
imantar *vt* magnetize
imbécil *a* stupid. ● *m & f* imbecile, idiot
imborrable *a* indelible; ‹*recuerdo etc*› unforgettable
imbuir [17] *vt* imbue (**de** with)
imita|ción *f* imitation. **~r** *vt* imitate
impacien|cia *f* impatience. **~tarse** *vpr* lose one's patience. **~te** *a* impatient; (*intranquilo*) anxious
impacto *m* impact
impar *a* odd
imparcial *a* impartial. **~idad** *f* impartiality
impartir *vt* impart
impasible *a* impassive
impávido *a* fearless; (*impasible*) impassive
impecable *a* impeccable
impedi|do *a* disabled. **~menta** *f* (*esp mil*) baggage. **~mento** *m* hindrance. **~r** [5] *vt* prevent; (*obstruir*) hinder
impeler *vt* drive
impenetrable *a* impenetrable
impenitente *a* unrepentant
impensa|ble *a* unthinkable. **~do** *a* unexpected
imperar *vi* reign
imperativo *a* imperative; ‹*persona*› imperious
imperceptible *a* imperceptible
imperdible *m* safety pin
imperdonable *a* unforgivable
imperfec|ción *f* imperfection. **~to** *a* imperfect
imperial *a* imperial. ● *f* upper deck. **~ismo** *m* imperialism
imperio *m* empire; (*poder*) rule; (*fig*) pride. **~so** *a* imperious
impermeable *a* waterproof. ● *m* raincoat
impersonal *a* impersonal
impertérrito *a* undaunted
impertinen|cia *f* impertinence. **~te** *a* impertinent
imperturbable *a* imperturbable
ímpetu *m* impetus; (*impulso*) impulse; (*impetuosidad*) impetuosity
impetuos|idad *f* impetuosity; (*violencia*) violence. **~o** *a* impetuous; (*violento*) violent

impío *a* ungodly; ‹*acción*› irreverent
implacable *a* implacable
implantar *vt* introduce
implica|ción *f* implication. **~r** [7] *vt* implicate; (*significar*) imply
implícito *a* implicit
implora|ción *f* entreaty. **~r** *vt* implore
imponderable *a* imponderable; (*inapreciable*) invaluable
impon|ente *a* imposing; (*fam*) terrific. **~er** [34] *vt* impose; (*requerir*) demand; deposit ‹*dinero*›. **~erse** *vpr* be imposed; (*hacerse obedecer*) assert o.s.; (*hacerse respetar*) command respect. **~ible** *a* taxable
impopular *a* unpopular. **~idad** *f* unpopularity
importa|ción *f* import; (*artículo*) import. **~dor** *a* importing. ● *m* importer
importa|ncia *f* importance; (*tamaño*) size. **~nte** *a* important; (*en cantidad*) considerable. **~r** *vt* import; (*valer*) cost. ● *vi* be important, matter. **¡le importa...?** would you mind...? **no ~** it doesn't matter
importe *m* price; (*total*) amount
importun|ar *vt* bother. **~o** *a* troublesome; (*inoportuno*) inopportune
imposib|ilidad *f* impossibility. **~le** *a* impossible. **hacer lo ~le** do all one can
imposición *f* imposition; (*impuesto*) tax
impostor *m & f* impostor
impotable *a* undrinkable
impoten|cia *f* impotence. **~te** *a* powerless, impotent
impracticable *a* impracticable; (*intransitable*) unpassable
impreca|ción *f* curse. **~r** [7] *vt* curse
imprecis|ión *f* vagueness. **~o** *a* imprecise
impregnar *vt* impregnate; (*empapar*) soak; (*fig*) cover
imprenta *f* printing; (*taller*) printing house, printer's
imprescindible *a* indispensable, essential
impresi|ón *f* impression; (*acción de imprimir*) printing; (*tirada*) edition; (*huella*) imprint. **~onable** *a* impressionable. **~onante** *a* impressive; (*espantoso*) frightening. **~onar** *vt* impress; (*conmover*) move; (*foto*) expose. **~onarse** *vpr* be impressed; (*conmover*) be moved
impresionis|mo *m* impressionism. **~ta** *a & m & f* impressionist
impreso *a* printed. ● *m* printed paper, printed matter. **~ra** *f* printer
imprevis|ible *a* unforseeable. **~to** *a* unforeseen
imprimir [*pp* **impreso**] *vt* impress; print ‹*libro etc*›
improbab|ilidad *f* improbability. **~le** *a* unlikely, improbable
improcedente *a* unsuitable
improductivo *a* unproductive
improperio *m* insult. **~s** *mpl* abuse
impropio *a* improper
improvis|ación *f* improvisation. **~adamente** *adv* suddenly. **~ado** *a* improvised. **~ar** *vt* improvise. **~o** *a*. **de ~o** suddenly
impruden|cia *f* imprudence. **~te** *a* imprudent
impuden|cia *f* impudence. **~te** *a* impudent
imp|údico *a* immodest; (*desvergonzado*) shameless. **~udor** *m* immodesty; (*desvergüenza*) shamelessness
impuesto *a* imposed. ● *m* tax. **~ sobre el valor añadido** VAT, value added tax
impugnar *vt* contest; (*refutar*) refute
impulsar *vt* impel
impuls|ividad *f* impulsiveness. **~ivo** *a* impulsive. **~o** *m* impulse
impun|e *a* unpunished. **~idad** *f* impunity
impur|eza *f* impurity. **~o** *a* impure
imputa|ción *f* charge. **~r** *vt* attribute; (*acusar*) charge
inacabable *a* interminable
inaccesible *a* inaccessible
inaceptable *a* unacceptable
inacostumbrado *a* unaccustomed
inactiv|idad *f* inactivity. **~o** *a* inactive
inadaptado *a* maladjusted
inadecuado *a* inadequate; (*inapropiado*) unsuitable
inadmisible *a* inadmissible; (*intolerable*) intolerable
inadvert|ido *a* unnoticed. **~encia** *f* inadvertence
inagotable *a* inexhaustible
inaguantable *a* unbearable; ‹*persona*› insufferable
inaltera|ble unchangeable; ‹*color*› fast; ‹*carácter*› calm. **~do** *a* unchanged

inanimado *a* inanimate
inaplicable *a* inapplicable
inapreciable *a* imperceptible
inapropiado *a* inappropriate
inarticulado *a* inarticulate
inasequible *a* out of reach
inaudito *a* unheard-of
inaugura|ción *f* inauguration. **~l** *a* inaugural. **~r** *vt* inaugurate
inca *a* Incan. ● *m & f* Inca. **~ico** *a* Incan
incalculable *a* incalculable
incandescen|cia *f* incandescence. **~te** *a* incandescent
incansable *a* tireless
incapa|cidad *f* incapacity. **~citar** *vt* incapacitate. **~z** *a* incapable
incauto *a* unwary; (*fácil de engañar*) gullible
incendi|ar *vt* set fire to. **~arse** *vpr* catch fire. **~ario** *a* incendiary. ● *m* arsonist. **~o** *m* fire
incentivo *m* incentive
incertidumbre *f* uncertainty
incesante *a* incessant
incest|o *m* incest. **~uoso** *a* incestuous
inciden|cia *f* incidence; (*incidente*) incident. **~tal** *a* incidental. **~te** *m* incident
incidir *vi* fall; (*influir*) influence
incienso *m* incense
incierto *a* uncertain
incinera|ción *f* incineration; (*de cadáveres*) cremation. **~dor** *m* incinerator. **~r** *vt* incinerate; cremate ‹*cadáver*›
incipiente *a* incipient
incisión *f* incision
incisivo *a* incisive. ● *m* incisor
incitar *vt* incite
incivil *a* rude
inclemen|cia *f* harshness. **~te** *a* harsh
inclina|ción *f* slope; (*de la cabeza*) nod; (*fig*) inclination. **~r** *vt* incline. **~rse** *vpr* lean; (*encorvarse*) stoop; (*en saludo*) bow; (*fig*) be inclined. **~rse a** (*parecerse*) resemble
inclu|ido *a* included; ‹*precio*› inclusive; (*en cartas*) enclosed. **~ir** [17] *vt* include; (*en cartas*) enclose. **~sión** *f* inclusion. **~sive** *adv* inclusive. **hasta el lunes ~sive** up to and including Monday. **~so** *a* included; (*en cartas*) enclosed. ● *adv* including; (*hasta*) even
incógnito *a* unknown. **de ~** incognito
incoheren|cia *f* incoherence. **~te** *a* incoherent
incoloro *a* colourless
incólume *a* unharmed
incomestible *a*, **incomible** *a* uneatable, inedible
incomodar *vt* inconvenience; (*molestar*) bother. **~se** *vpr* trouble o.s.; (*enfadarse*) get angry
incómodo *a* uncomfortable; (*inoportuno*) inconvenient
incomparable *a* imcomparable
incompatib|ilidad *f* incompatibility. **~le** *a* incompatible
incompeten|cia *f* incompetence. **~te** *a* incompetent
incompleto *a* incomplete
incompren|dido *a* misunderstood. **~sible** *a* incomprehensible. **~sión** *f* incomprehension
incomunicado *a* isolated; ‹*preso*› in solitary confinement
inconcebible *a* inconceivable
inconciliable *a* irreconcilable
inconcluso *a* unfinished
incondicional *a* unconditional
inconfundible *a* unmistakable
incongruente *a* incongruous
inconmensurable *a* (*fam*) enormous
inconscien|cia *f* unconsciousness; (*irreflexión*) recklessness. **~te** *a* unconscious; (*irreflexivo*) reckless
inconsecuente *a* inconsistent
inconsiderado *a* inconsiderate
inconsistente *a* insubstantial
inconsolable *a* unconsolable
inconstan|cia *f* inconstancy. **~te** *a* changeable; ‹*persona*› fickle
incontable *a* countless
incontaminado *a* uncontaminated
incontenible *a* irrepressible
incontestable *a* indisputable
incontinen|cia *f* incontinence. **~te** *a* incontinent
inconvenien|cia *f* disadvantage. **~te** *a* inconvenient; (*inapropiado*) inappropriate; (*incorrecto*) improper. ● *m* difficulty; (*desventaja*) drawback
incorpora|ción *f* incorporation. **~r** *vt* incorporate; (*culin*) mix. **~rse** *vpr* sit up; join ‹*sociedad, regimiento etc*›
incorrecto *a* incorrect; ‹*acción*› improper; (*descortés*) discourteous
incorregible *a* incorrigible
incorruptible *a* incorruptible
incrédulo *a* incredulous

increíble *a* incredible
increment|ar *vt* increase. **~o** *m* increase
incriminar *vt* incriminate
incrustar *vt* encrust
incuba|ción *f* incubation. **~dora** *f* incubator. **~r** *vt* incubate; (*fig*) hatch
incuestionable *a* unquestionable
inculcar [7] *vt* inculcate
inculpar *vt* accuse; (*culpar*) blame
inculto *a* uncultivated; ‹*persona*› uneducated
incumplimiento *m* non-fulfilment; (*de un contrato*) breach
incurable *a* incurable
incurrir *vi*. **~ en** incur; fall into ‹*error*›; commit ‹*crimen*›
incursión *f* raid
indaga|ción *f* investigation. **~r** [12] *vt* investigate
indebido *a* undue
indecen|cia *f* indecency. **~te** *a* indecent
indecible *a* inexpressible
indecis|ión *f* indecision. **~o** *a* undecided
indefenso *a* defenceless
indefini|ble *a* indefinable. **~do** *a* indefinite
indeleble *a* indelible
indelicad|eza *f* indelicacy. **~o** *a* indelicate; (*falto de escrúpulo*) unscrupulous
indemn|e *a* undamaged; ‹*persona*› unhurt. **~idad** *f* indemnity. **~izar** [10] *vt* indemnify, compensate
independ|encia *f* independence. **~iente** *a* independent
independizarse [10] *vpr* become independent
indescifrable *a* indecipherable, incomprehensible
indescriptible *a* indescribable
indeseable *a* undesirable
indestructible *a* indestructible
indetermina|ble *a* indeterminable. **~do** *a* indeterminate
India *f*. **la ~** India. **las ~s** *fpl* the Indies
indica|ción *f* indication; (*sugerencia*) suggestion. **~ciones** *fpl* directions. **~dor** *m* indicator; (*tec*) gauge. **~r** [7] *vt* show, indicate; (*apuntar*) point at; (*hacer saber*) point out; (*aconsejar*) advise. **~tivo** *a* indicative. ● *m* indicative; (*al teléfono*) dialling code
índice *m* indication; (*dedo*) index finger; (*de libro*) index; (*catálogo*) catalogue; (*aguja*) pointer
indicio *m* indication, sign; (*vestigio*) trace
indiferen|cia *f* indifference. **~te** *a* indifferent. **me es ~te** it's all the same to me
indígena *a* indigenous. ● *m & f* native
indigen|cia *f* poverty. **~te** *a* needy
indigest|ión *f* indigestion. **~o** *a* undigested; (*difícil de digerir*) indigestible
indign|ación *f* indignation. **~ado** *a* indignant. **~ar** *vt* make indignant. **~arse** *vpr* be indignant. **~o** *a* unworthy; (*despreciable*) contemptible
indio *a & m* Indian
indirect|a *f* hint. **~o** *a* indirect
indisciplina *f* lack of discipline. **~do** *a* undisciplined
indiscre|ción *f* indiscretion. **~to** *a* indiscreet
indiscutible *a* unquestionable
indisoluble *a* indissoluble
indispensable *a* indispensable
indisp|oner [34] *vt* (*enemistar*) set against. **~onerse** *vpr* fall out; (*ponerse enfermo*) fall ill. **~osición** *f* indisposition. **~uesto** *a* indisposed
indistinto *a* indistinct
individu|al *a* individual; ‹*cama*› single. **~alidad** *f* individuality. **~alista** *m & f* individualist. **~alizar** [10] *vt* individualize. **~o** *a & m* individual
índole *f* nature; (*clase*) type
indolen|cia *f* indolence. **~te** *a* indolent
indoloro *a* painless
indomable *a* untameable
indómito *a* indomitable
Indonesia *f* Indonesia
inducir [47] *vt* induce; (*deducir*) infer
indudable *a* undoubted. **~mente** *adv* undoubtedly
indulgen|cia *f* indulgence. **~te** *a* indulgent
indult|ar *vt* pardon; exempt (*de un pago etc*). **~o** *m* pardon
industria *f* industry. **~l** *a* industrial. ● *m* industrialist. **~lización** *f* industrialization. **~lizar** [10] *vt* industrialize
industriarse *vpr* do one's best
industrioso *a* industrious

inédito *a* unpublished; (*fig*) unknown
ineducado *a* impolite
inefable *a* inexpressible
ineficaz *a* ineffective
ineficiente *a* inefficient
inelegible *a* ineligible
ineludible *a* inescapable, unavoidable
inept|itud *f* ineptitude. **~o** *a* inept
inequívoco *a* unequivocal
iner|cia *f* inertia
inerme *a* unarmed; (*fig*) defenceless
inerte *a* inert
inesperado *a* unexpected
inestable *a* unstable
inestimable *a* inestimable
inevitable *a* inevitable
inexacto *a* inaccurate; (*incorrecto*) incorrect; (*falso*) untrue
inexistente *a* non-existent
inexorable *a* inexorable
inexper|iencia *f* inexperience. **~to** *a* inexperienced
inexplicable *a* inexplicable
infalible *a* infallible
infam|ar *vt* defame. **~atorio** *a* defamatory. **~e** *a* infamous; (*fig, muy malo, fam*) awful. **~ia** *f* infamy
infancia *f* infancy
infant|a *f* infanta, princess. **~e** *m* infante, prince; (*mil*) infantryman. **~ería** *f* infantry. **~il** *a* (*de niño*) child's; (*como un niño*) infantile
infarto *m* coronary (thrombosis)
infatigable *a* untiring
infatua|ción *f* conceit. **~rse** *vpr* get conceited
infausto *a* unlucky
infec|ción *f* infection. **~cioso** *a* infectious. **~tar** *vt* infect. **~tarse** *vpr* become infected. **~to** *a* infected; (*fam*) disgusting
infecundo *a* infertile
infeli|cidad *f* unhappiness. **~z** *a* unhappy
inferior *a* inferior. • *m & f* inferior. **~idad** *f* lower; (*calidad*) inferiority
inferir [4] *vt* infer; (*causar*) cause
infernal *a* infernal, hellish
infestar *vt* infest; (*fig*) inundate
infi|delidad *f* unfaithfulness. **~el** *a* unfaithful
infierno *m* hell
infiltra|ción *f* infiltration. **~rse** *vpr* infiltrate
ínfimo *a* lowest
infini|dad *f* infinity. **~tivo** *m* infinitive. **~to** *a* infinite. • *m* infinite; (*en matemáticas*) infinity. **una ~dad de** countless
inflación *f* inflation; (*fig*) conceit
inflama|ble *a* (in)flammable. **~ción** *f* inflammation. **~r** *vt* set on fire; (*fig, med*) inflame. **~rse** *vpr* catch fire; (*med*) become inflamed
inflar *vt* inflate; (*fig, exagerar*) exaggerate
inflexi|ble *a* inflexible. **~ón** *f* inflexion
infligir [14] *vt* inflict
influ|encia *f* influence. **~enza** *f* flu (*fam*), influenza. **~ir** [17] *vt/i* influence. **~jo** *m* influence. **~yente** *a* influential
informa|ción *f* information. **~ciones** *fpl* (*noticias*) news; (*de teléfonos*) directory enquiries. **~dor** *m* informant
informal *a* informal; (*incorrecto*) incorrect
inform|ante *m & f* informant. **~ar** *vt/i* inform. **~arse** *vpr* find out. **~ática** *f* information technology. **~ativo** *a* informative
informe *a* shapeless. • *m* report; (*información*) information
infortun|ado *a* unfortunate. **~io** *m* misfortune
infracción *f* infringement
infraestructura *f* infrastructure
infranqueable *a* impassable; (*fig*) insuperable
infrarrojo *a* infrared
infrecuente *a* infrequent
infringir [14] *vt* infringe
infructuoso *a* fruitless
infundado *a* unfounded
infu|ndir *vt* instil. **~sión** *f* infusion
ingeniar *vt* invent
ingenier|ía *f* engineering. **~o** *m* engineer
ingenio *m* ingenuity; (*agudeza*) wit; (*LAm, de azúcar*) refinery. **~so** *a* ingenious
ingenu|idad *f* ingenuousness. **~o** *a* ingenuous
ingerir [4] *vt* swallow
Inglaterra *f* England
ingle *f* groin
ingl|és *a* English. • *m* Englishman; (*lengua*) English. **~esa** *f* Englishwoman
ingrat|itud *f* ingratitude. **~o** *a* ungrateful; (*desagradable*) thankless
ingrediente *m* ingredient

ingres|ar *vt* deposit. ● *vi.* **~ar en** come in, enter; join ‹*sociedad*›. **~o** *m* entry; (*en sociedad, hospital etc*) admission. **~os** *mpl* income

inh|ábil *a* unskillful; (*no apto*) unfit. **~abilidad** *f* unskillfulness

inhabitable *a* uninhabitable

inhala|ción *f* inhalation. **~dor** *m* inhaler. **~r** *vt* inhale

inherente *a* inherent

inhibi|ción *f* inhibition. **~r** *vt* inhibit

inhospitalario *a*, **inhóspito** *a* inhospitable

inhumano *a* inhuman

inicia|ción *f* beginning. **~l** *a & f* initial. **~r** *vt* initiate; (*comenzar*) begin, start. **~tiva** *f* initiative

inicio *m* beginning

inicuo *a* iniquitous

inigualado *a* unequalled

ininterrumpido *a* continuous

injer|encia *f* interference. **~ir** [4] *vt* insert. **~irse** *vpr* interfere

injert|ar *vt* graft. **~to** *m* graft

injuri|a *f* insult; (*ofensa*) offence. **~ar** *vt* insult. **~oso** *a* offensive

injust|icia *f* injustice. **~o** *a* unjust

inmaculado *a* immaculate

inmaduro *a* unripe; ‹*persona*› immature

inmediaciones *fpl* neighbourhood

inmediat|amente *adv* immediately. **~o** *a* immediate; (*contiguo*) next

inmejorable *a* excellent

inmemorable *a* immemorial

inmens|idad *f* immensity. **~o** *a* immense

inmerecido *a* undeserved

inmersión *f* immersion

inmigra|ción *f* immigration. **~nte** *a & m* immigrant. **~r** *vt* immigrate

inminen|cia *f* imminence. **~te** *a* imminent

inmiscuirse [17] *vpr* interfere

inmobiliario *a* property

inmoderado *a* immoderate

inmodesto *a* immodest

inmolar *vt* sacrifice

inmoral *a* immoral. **~idad** *f* immorality

inmortal *a* immortal. **~izar** [10] *vt* immortalize

inmóvil *a* immobile

inmueble *a*. **bienes ~s** property

inmund|icia *f* filth. **~icias** *fpl* rubbish. **~o** *a* filthy

inmun|e *a* immune. **~idad** *f* immunity. **~ización** *f* immunization. **~izar** [10] *vt* immunize

inmuta|ble *a* unchangeable. **~rse** *vpr* turn pale

innato *a* innate

innecesario *a* unnecessary

innegable *a* undeniable

innoble *a* ignoble

innova|ción *f* innovation. **~r** *vt/i* innovate

innumerable *a* innumerable

inocen|cia *f* innocence. **~tada** *f* practical joke. **~te** *a* innocent. **~tón** *a* naïve

inocuo *a* innocuous

inodoro *a* odourless. ● *m* toilet

inofensivo *a* inoffensive

inolvidable *a* unforgettable

inoperable *a* inoperable

inopinado *a* unexpected

inoportuno *a* untimely; (*incómodo*) inconvenient

inorgánico *a* inorganic

inoxidable *a* stainless

inquebrantable *a* unbreakable

inquiet|ar *vt* worry. **~arse** *vpr* get worried. **~o** *a* worried; (*agitado*) restless. **~ud** *f* anxiety

inquilino *m* tenant

inquirir [4] *vt* enquire into, investigate

insaciable *a* insatiable

insalubre *a* unhealthy

insanable *a* incurable

insatisfecho *a* unsatisfied; (*descontento*) dissatisfied

inscri|bir [*pp* **inscrito**] *vt* inscribe; (*en registro etc*) enrol, register. **~birse** *vpr* register. **~pción** *f* inscription; (*registro*) registration

insect|icida *m* insecticide. **~o** *m* insect

insegur|idad *f* insecurity. **~o** *a* insecure; (*dudoso*) uncertain

insemina|ción *f* insemination. **~r** *vt* inseminate

insensato *a* senseless

insensible *a* insensitive; (*med*) insensible; (*imperceptible*) imperceptible

inseparable *a* inseparable

insertar *vt* insert

insidi|a *f* trap. **~oso** *a* insidious

insigne *a* famous

insignia *f* badge; (*bandera*) flag

insignificante *a* insignificant

insincero *a* insincere

insinua|ción *f* insinuation. **~nte** *a* insinuating. **~r** [21] *vt* insinuate. **~rse** *vpr* ingratiate o.s. **~rse en** creep into

insípido *a* insipid
insist|encia *f* insistence. **~ente** *a* insistent. **~ir** *vi* insist; (*hacer hincapié*) stress
insolación *f* sunstroke
insolen|cia *f* rudeness, insolence. **~te** *a* rude, insolent
insólito *a* unusual
insoluble *a* insoluble
insolven|cia *f* insolvency. **~te** *a & m & f* insolvent
insomn|e *a* sleepless. **~io** *m* insomnia
insondable *a* unfathomable
insoportable *a* unbearable
insospechado *a* unexpected
insostenible *a* untenable
inspec|ción *f* inspection. **~cionar** *vt* inspect. **~tor** *m* inspector
inspira|ción *f* inspiration. **~r** *vt* inspire. **~rse** *vpr* be inspired
instala|ción *f* installation. **~r** *vt* install. **~rse** *vpr* settle
instancia *f* request
instant|ánea *f* snapshot. **~áneo** *a* instantaneous; ‹*café etc*› instant. **~e** *m* instant. **a cada ~e** constantly. **al ~e** immediately
instar *vt* urge
instaura|ción *f* establishment. **~r** *vt* establish
instiga|ción *f* instigation. **~dor** *m* instigator. **~r** [12] *vt* instigate; (*incitar*) incite
instint|ivo *a* instinctive. **~o** *m* instinct
institu|ción *f* institution. **~cional** *a* institutional. **~ir** [17] *vt* establish. **~to** *m* institute; (*escol*) (secondary) school. **~triz** *f* governess
instru|cción *f* instruction. **~ctivo** *a* instructive. **~ctor** *m* instructor. **~ir** [17] *vt* instruct; (*enseñar*) teach
instrument|ación *f* instrumentation. **~al** *a* instrumental. **~o** *m* instrument; (*herramienta*) tool
insubordina|ción *f* insubordination. **~r** *vt* stir up. **~rse** *vpr* rebel
insuficien|cia *f* insufficiency; (*inadecuación*) inadequacy. **~te** *a* insufficient
insufrible *a* insufferable
insular *a* insular
insulina *f* insulin
insulso *a* tasteless; (*fig*) insipid
insult|ar *vt* insult. **~o** *m* insult
insuperable *a* insuperable; (*excelente*) excellent
insurgente *a* insurgent
insurrec|ción *f* insurrection. **~to** *a* insurgent
intacto *a* intact
intachable *a* irreproachable
intangible *a* intangible
integra|ción *f* integration. **~l** *a* integral; (*completo*) complete; ‹*pan*› wholemeal (*Brit*), wholewheat (*Amer*). **~r** *vt* make up
integridad *f* integrity; (*entereza*) wholeness
íntegro *a* complete; (*fig*) upright
intelect|o *m* intellect. **~ual** *a & m & f* intellectual
inteligen|cia *f* intelligence. **~te** *a* intelligent
inteligible *a* intelligible
intemperancia *f* intemperance
intemperie *f* bad weather. **a la ~** in the open
intempestivo *a* untimely
intenci|ón *f* intention. **~onado** *a* deliberate. **~onal** *a* intentional. **bien ~onado** well-meaning. **mal ~onado** malicious. **segunda ~ón** duplicity
intens|idad *f* intensity. **~ificar** [7] *vt* intensify. **~ivo** *a* intensive. **~o** *a* intense
intent|ar *vt* try. **~o** *m* intent; (*tentativa*) attempt. **de ~o** intentionally
intercalar *vt* insert
intercambio *m* exchange
interceder *vt* intercede
interceptar *vt* intercept
intercesión *f* intercession
interdicto *m* ban
inter|és *m* interest; (*egoísmo*) self-interest. **~esado** *a* interested; (*parcial*) biassed; (*egoísta*) selfish. **~esante** *a* interesting. **~esar** *vt* interest; (*afectar*) concern. ● *vi* be of interest. **~esarse** *vpr* take an interest (**por** in)
interfer|encia *f* interference. **~ir** [4] *vi* interfere
interino *a* temporary; ‹*persona*› acting. ● *m* stand-in; (*médico*) locum
interior *a* interior. ● *m* inside. **Ministerio** *m* **del I~** Home Office (*Brit*), Department of the Interior (*Amer*)
interjección *f* interjection
interlocutor *m* speaker
interludio *m* interlude
intermediario *a & m* intermediary
intermedio *a* intermediate. ● *m* interval

interminable *a* interminable
intermitente *a* intermittent. ● *m* indicator
internacional *a* international
intern|ado *m* (*escol*) boarding-school. **~ar** *vt* intern; (*en manicomio*) commit. **~arse** *vpr* penetrate. **~o** *a* internal; (*escol*) boarding. ● *m* (*escol*) boarder
interpelar *vt* appeal
interponer [34] *vt* interpose. **~se** *vpr* intervene
int|erpretación *f* interpretation. **~erpretar** *vt* interpret. **~érprete** *m* interpreter; (*mus*) performer
interroga|ción *f* question; (*acción*) interrogation; (*signo*) question mark. **~r** [12] *vt* question. **~tivo** *a* interrogative
interru|mpir *vt* interrupt; (*suspender*) stop. **~pción** *f* interruption. **~ptor** *m* switch
intersección *f* intersection
interurbano *a* inter-city; ‹*conferencia*› long-distance
intervalo *m* interval; (*espacio*) space. **a ~s** at intervals
interven|ir [53] *vt* control; (*med*) operate on. ● *vi* intervene; (*participar*) take part. **~tor** *m* inspector; (*com*) auditor
intestino *m* intestine
intim|ar *vi* become friendly. **~idad** *f* intimacy
intimidar *vt* intimidate
íntimo *a* intimate. ● *m* close friend
intitular *vt* entitle
intolera|ble *a* intolerable. **~nte** *a* intolerant
intoxicar [7] *vt* poison
intranquil|izar [10] *vt* worry. **~o** *a* worried
intransigente *a* intransigent
intransitable *a* impassable
intransitivo *a* intransitive
intratable *a* intractable
intrépido *a* intrepid
intriga *f* intrigue. **~nte** *a* intriguing. **~r** [12] *vt/i* intrigue
intrincado *a* intricate
intrínseco *a* intrinsic
introduc|ción *f* introduction. **~ir** [47] *vt* introduce; (*meter*) insert. **~irse** *vpr* get into; (*entrometerse*) interfere
intromisión *f* interference
introvertido *a* & *m* introvert
intrus|ión *f* intrusion. **~o** *a* intrusive. ● *m* intruder
intui|ción *f* intuition. **~r** [17] *vt* sense. **~tivo** *a* intuitive
inunda|ción *f* flooding. **~r** *vt* flood
inusitado *a* unusual
in|útil *a* useless; (*vano*) futile. **~utilidad** *f* uselessness
invadir *vt* invade
inv|alidez *f* invalidity; (*med*) disability. **~álido** *a* & *m* invalid
invaria|ble *a* invariable. **~do** *a* unchanged
invas|ión *f* invasion. **~or** *a* invading. ● *m* invader
invectiva *f* invective
invencible *a* invincible
inven|ción *f* invention. **~tar** *vt* invent
inventario *m* inventory
invent|iva *f* inventiveness. **~ivo** *a* inventive. **~or** *m* inventor
invernadero *m* greenhouse
invernal *a* winter
inverosímil *a* improbable
inversión *f* inversion; (*com*) investment
inverso *a* inverse; (*contrario*) opposite. **a la inversa** the other way round
invertebrado *a* & *m* invertebrate
inverti|do *a* inverted; (*homosexual*) homosexual. ● *m* homosexual. **~r** [4] *vt* reverse; (*volcar*) turn upside down; (*com*) invest; spend ‹*tiempo*›
investidura *f* investiture
investiga|ción *f* investigation; (*univ*) research. **~dor** *m* investigator. **~r** [12] *vt* investigate
investir [5] *vt* invest
inveterado *a* inveterate
invicto *a* unbeaten
invierno *m* winter
inviolable *a* inviolate
invisib|ilidad *f* invisibility. **~le** *a* invisible
invita|ción *f* invitation. **~do** *m* guest. **~r** *vt* invite. **te invito a una copa** I'll buy you a drink
invoca|ción *f* invocation. **~r** [7] *vt* invoke
involuntario *a* involuntary
invulnerable *a* invulnerable
inyec|ción *f* injection. **~tar** *vt* inject
ion *m* ion
ir [49] *vi* go; ‹*ropa*› (*convenir*) suit. ● *m* going. **~se** *vpr* go away. **~ a hacer** be going to do. **~ a pie** walk. **~ de paseo** go for a walk. **~ en coche** go by car. **no me va ni me viene** it's all the same to me. **no**

vaya a ser que in case. **¡qué va!** nonsense! **va mejorando** it's gradually getting better. **¡vamos!**, **¡vámonos!** come on! let's go! **¡vaya!** fancy that! **¡vete a saber!** who knows? **¡ya voy!** I'm coming!
ira *f* anger. **~cundo** *a* irascible
Irak *m* Iraq
Irán *m* Iran
iraní *a & m & f* Iranian
iraquí *a & m & f* Iraqi
iris *m* (*anat*) iris; (*arco iris*) rainbow
Irlanda *f* Ireland
irland|és *a* Irish. ● *m* Irishman; (*lengua*) Irish. **~esa** *f* Irishwoman
ir|onía *f* irony. **~ónico** *a* ironic
irracional *a* irrational
irradiar *vt/i* radiate
irrazonable *a* unreasonable
irreal *a* unreal. **~idad** *f* unreality
irrealizable *a* unattainable
irreconciliable *a* irreconcilable
irreconocible *a* unrecognizable
irrecuperable *a* irretrievable
irreducible *a* irreducible
irreflexión *f* impetuosity
irrefutable *a* irrefutable
irregular *a* irregular. **~idad** *f* irregularity
irreparable *a* irreparable
irreprimible *a* irrepressible
irreprochable *a* irreproachable
irresistible *a* irresistible
irresoluto *a* irresolute
irrespetuoso *a* disrespectful
irresponsable *a* irresponsible
irrevocable *a* irrevocable
irriga|ción *f* irrigation. **~r** [12] *vt* irrigate
irrisorio *a* derisive; (*insignificante*) ridiculous
irrita|ble *a* irritable. **~ción** *f* irritation. **~r** *vt* irritate. **~rse** *vpr* get annoyed
irrumpir *vi* burst (**en** in)
irrupción *f* irruption
isla *f* island. **las I~s Británicas** the British Isles
Islam *m* Islam
islámico *a* Islamic
islandés *a* Icelandic. ● *m* Icelander; (*lengua*) Icelandic
Islandia *f* Iceland
isleño *a* island. ● *m* islander
Israel *m* Israel
israelí *a & m* Israeli
istmo /'ismo/ *m* isthmus
Italia *f* Italy
italiano *a & m* Italian
itinerario *a* itinerary
IVA *abrev* (*impuesto sobre el valor añadido*) VAT, value added tax
izar [10] *vt* hoist
izquierd|a *f* left(-hand); (*pol*) left (-wing). **~ista** *m & f* leftist. **~o** *a* left. **a la ~a** on the left; (*con movimiento*) to the left

J

ja *int* ha!
jabalí *m* wild boar
jabalina *f* javelin
jab|ón *m* soap. **~onar** *vt* soap. **~onoso** *a* soapy
jaca *f* pony
jacinto *m* hyacinth
jacta|ncia *f* boastfulness; (*acción*) boasting. **~rse** *vpr* boast
jadea|nte *a* panting. **~r** *vi* pant
jaez *m* harness
jaguar *m* jaguar
jalea *f* jelly
jaleo *m* row, uproar. **armar un ~** kick up a fuss
jalón *m* (*LAm, tirón*) pull; (*Mex, trago*) drink
Jamaica *f* Jamaica
jamás *adv* never; (*en frases afirmativas*) ever
jamelgo *m* nag
jamón *m* ham. **~ de York** boiled ham. **~ serrano** cured ham
Japón *m*. **el ~** Japan
japonés *a & m* Japanese
jaque *m* check. **~ mate** checkmate
jaqueca *f* migraine. **dar ~** bother
jarabe *m* syrup
jardín *m* garden. **~ de la infancia** kindergarten, nursery school
jardiner|ía *f* gardening. **~o** *m* gardener
jarocho *a* (*Mex*) from Veracruz
jarr|a *f* jug. **~o** *m* jug. **echar un ~o de agua fría a** throw cold water on. **en ~as** with hands on hips
jaula *f* cage
jauría *f* pack of hounds
jazmín *m* jasmine
jef|a *f* boss. **~atura** *f* leadership; (*sede*) headquarters. **~e** *m* boss; (*pol etc*) leader. **~e de camareros** head waiter. **~e de estación** stationmaster. **~e de ventas** sales manager
jengibre *m* ginger

jeque *m* sheikh
jer|arquía *f* hierarchy. **~árquico** *a* hierarchical
jerez *m* sherry. **al ~** with sherry
jerga *f* coarse cloth; (*argot*) jargon
jerigonza *f* jargon; (*galimatías*) gibberish
jeringa *f* syringe; (*LAm, molestia*) nuisance. **~r** [12] *vt* (*fig, molestar, fam*) annoy
jeroglífico *m* hieroglyph(ic)
jersey *m* (*pl* **jerseys**) jersey
Jerusalén *m* Jerusalem
Jesucristo *m* Jesus Christ. **antes de ~** BC, before Christ
jesuita *a & m & f* Jesuit
Jesús *m* Jesus. ● *int* good heavens!; (*al estornudar*) bless you!
jícara *f* small cup
jilguero *m* goldfinch
jinete *m* rider, horseman
jipijapa *f* straw hat
jirafa *f* giraffe
jirón *m* shred, tatter
jitomate *m* (*Mex*) tomato
jocoso *a* funny, humorous
jorna|da *f* working day; (*viaje*) journey; (*etapa*) stage. **~l** *m* day's wage; (*trabajo*) day's work. **~lero** *m* day labourer
joroba *f* hump. **~do** *a* hunchbacked. ● *m* hunchback. **~r** *vt* annoy
jota *f* letter J; (*danza*) jota, popular dance; (*fig*) iota. **ni ~** nothing
joven (*pl* **jóvenes**) *a* young. ● *m* young man, youth. ● *f* young woman, girl
jovial *a* jovial
joy|a *f* jewel. **~as** *fpl* jewellery. **~ería** *f* jeweller's (shop). **~ero** *m* jeweller; (*estuche*) jewellery box
juanete *m* bunion
jubil|ación *f* retirement. **~ado** *a* retired. **~ar** *vt* pension off. **~arse** *vpr* retire. **~eo** *m* jubilee
júbilo *m* joy
jubiloso *a* jubilant
judaísmo *m* Judaism
judía *f* Jewish woman; (*alubia*) bean. **~ blanca** haricot bean. **~ escarlata** runner bean. **~ verde** French bean
judicial *a* judicial
judío *a* Jewish. ● *m* Jewish man
judo *m* judo
juego *m* game; (*de niños, tec*) play; (*de azar*) gambling; (*conjunto*) set. ● *vb véase* **jugar**. **estar en ~** be at stake. **estar fuera de ~** be offside. **hacer ~** match
juerga *f* spree
jueves *m* Thursday
juez *m* judge. **~ de instrucción** examining magistrate. **~ de línea** linesman
juga|dor *m* player; (*en juegos de azar*) gambler. **~r** [3] *vt* play. ● *vi* play; (*a juegos de azar*) gamble; (*apostar*) bet. **~rse** *vpr* risk. **~r al fútbol** play football
juglar *m* minstrel
jugo *m* juice; (*de carne*) gravy; (*fig*) substance. **~so** *a* juicy; (*fig*) substantial
juguet|e *m* toy. **~ear** *vi* play. **~ón** *a* playful
juicio *m* judgement; (*opinión*) opinion; (*razón*) reason. **~so** *a* wise. **a mi ~** in my opinion
juliana *f* vegetable soup
julio *m* July
junco *m* rush, reed
jungla *f* jungle
junio *m* June
junt|a *f* meeting; (*consejo*) board, committee; (*pol*) junta; (*tec*) joint. **~ar** *vt* join; (*reunir*) collect. **~arse** *vpr* join; ‹*gente*› meet. **~o** *a* joined; (*en plural*) together. **~o a** next to. **~ura** *f* joint. **por ~o** all together
jura|do *a* sworn. ● *m* jury; (*miembro de jurado*) juror. **~mento** *m* oath. **~r** *vt/i* swear. **~r en falso** commit perjury. **jurárselas a uno** have it in for s.o. **prestar ~mento** take the oath
jurel *m* (type of) mackerel
jurídico *a* legal
juris|dicción *f* jurisdiction. **~prudencia** *f* jurisprudence
justamente *a* exactly; (*con justicia*) fairly
justicia *f* justice
justifica|ción *f* justification. **~r** [7] *vt* justify
justo *a* fair, just; (*exacto*) exact; ‹*ropa*› tight. ● *adv* just. **~ a tiempo** just in time
juven|il *a* youthful. **~tud** *f* youth; (*gente joven*) young people
juzga|do *m* (*tribunal*) court. **~r** [12] *vt* judge. **a ~r por** judging by

K

kilo *m*, **kilogramo** *m* kilo, kilogram
kil|ometraje *m* distance in kilometres, mileage. **~ométrico** *a* (*fam*) endless. **~ómetro** *m* kilometre. **~ómetro cuadrado** square kilometre
kilovatio *m* kilowatt
kiosco *m* kiosk

L

la *m* A; (*solfa*) lah. ● *art def f* the. ● *pron* (*ella*) her; (*Vd*) you; (*ello*) it. **~ de** the one. **~ de Vd** your one, yours. **~ que** whoever, the one
laberinto *m* labyrinth, maze
labia *f* glibness
labio *m* lip
labor *f* work; (*tarea*) job. **~able** *a* working. **~ar** *vi* work. **~es** *fpl* **de aguja** needlework. **~es** *fpl* **de ganchillo** crochet. **~es** *fpl* **de punto** knitting. **~es** *fpl* **domésticas** housework
laboratorio *m* laboratory
laborioso *a* laborious
laborista *a* Labour. ● *m & f* member of the Labour Party
labra|do *a* worked; ‹*madera*› carved; ‹*metal*› wrought; ‹*tierra*› ploughed. **~dor** *m* farmer; (*obrero*) labourer. **~nza** *f* farming. **~r** *vt* work; carve ‹*madera*›; cut ‹*piedra*›; till ‹*la tierra*›; (*fig, causar*) cause
labriego *m* peasant
laca *f* lacquer
lacayo *m* lackey
lacerar *vt* lacerate
lacero *m* lassoer; (*cazador*) poacher
lacio *a* straight; (*flojo*) limp
lacón *m* shoulder of pork
lacónico *a* laconic
lacra *f* scar
lacr|ar *vt* seal. **~e** *m* sealing wax
lactante *a* breast-fed
lácteo *a* milky. **productos** *mpl* **~s** dairy products
ladear *vt/i* tilt. **~se** *vpr* lean
ladera *f* slope
ladino *a* astute
lado *m* side. **al ~** near. **al ~ de** at the side of, beside. **los de al ~** the next door neighbours. **por otro ~** on the other hand. **por todos ~s** on all sides. **por un ~** on the one hand
ladr|ar *vi* bark. **~ido** *m* bark
ladrillo *m* brick; (*de chocolate*) block
ladrón *a* thieving. ● *m* thief
lagart|ija *f* (small) lizard. **~o** *m* lizard
lago *m* lake
lágrima *f* tear
lagrimoso *a* tearful
laguna *f* small lake; (*fig, omisión*) gap
laico *a* lay
lamé *m* lamé
lamedura *f* lick
lament|able *a* lamentable, pitiful. **~ar** *vt* be sorry about. **~arse** *vpr* lament; (*quejarse*) complain. **~o** *m* moan
lamer *vt* lick; ‹*olas etc*› lap
lámina *f* sheet; (*foto*) plate; (*dibujo*) picture
lamina|do *a* laminated. **~r** *vt* laminate
lámpara *f* lamp; (*bombilla*) bulb; (*lamparón*) grease stain. **~ de pie** standard lamp
lamparón *m* grease stain
lampiño *a* clean-shaven, beardless
lana *f* wool. **~r** *a*. **ganado** *m* **~r** sheep. **de ~** wool(len)
lanceta *f* lancet
lancha *f* boat. **~ motora** *f* motor boat. **~ salvavidas** lifeboat
lanero *a* wool(len)
langost|a *f* (*crustáceo marino*) lobster; (*insecto*) locust. **~ino** *m* prawn
languide|cer [11] *vi* languish. **~z** *f* languor
lánguido *a* languid; (*decaído*) listless
lanilla *f* nap; (*tela fina*) flannel
lanudo *a* woolly
lanza *f* lance, spear
lanza|llamas *m invar* flame-thrower. **~miento** *m* throw; (*acción de lanzar*) throwing; (*de proyectil, de producto*) launch. **~r** [10] *vt* throw; (*de un avión*) drop; launch ‹*proyectil, producto*›. **~rse** *vpr* fling o.s.
lapicero *m* (propelling) pencil
lápida *f* memorial tablet. **~ sepulcral** tombstone
lapidar *vt* stone
lápiz *m* pencil; (*grafito*) lead. **~ de labios** lipstick
Laponia *f* Lapland

lapso *m* lapse
larg|a *f*. **a la ~a** in the long run. **dar ~as** put off. **~ar** [12] *vt* slacken; (*dar, fam*) give; (*fam*) deal ‹*bofetada etc*›. **~arse** *vpr* (*fam*) go away, clear off (*fam*). **~o** *a* long; (*demasiado*) too long. ● *m* length. **¡~o!** go away! **~ueza** *f* generosity. **a lo ~o** lengthwise. **a lo ~o de** along. **tener 100 metros de ~o** be 100 metres long
laring|e *f* larynx. **~itis** *f* laryngitis
larva *f* larva
las *art def fpl* the. ● *pron* them. **~ de** those, the ones. **~ de Vd** your ones, yours. **~ que** whoever, the ones
lascivo *a* lascivious
láser *m* laser
lástima *f* pity; (*queja*) complaint. **dar ~** be pitiful. **ella me da ~** I feel sorry for her. **¡qué ~!** what a pity!
lastim|ado *a* hurt. **~ar** *vt* hurt. **~arse** *vpr* hurt o.s. **~ero** *a* doleful. **~oso** *a* pitiful
lastre *m* ballast
lata *f* tinplate; (*envase*) tin (*esp Brit*), can; (*molestia, fam*) nuisance. **dar la ~** be a nuisance. **¡qué ~!** what a nuisance!
latente *a* latent
lateral *a* side, lateral
latido *m* beating; (*cada golpe*) beat
latifundio *m* large estate
latigazo *m* (*golpe*) lash; (*chasquido*) crack
látigo *m* whip
latín *m* Latin. **saber ~** (*fam*) not be stupid
latino *a* Latin. **L~américa** *f* Latin America. **~americano** *a* & *m* Latin American
latir *vi* beat; ‹*herida*› throb
latitud *f* latitude
latón *m* brass
latoso *a* annoying; (*pesado*) boring
laucha *f* (*Arg*) mouse
laúd *m* lute
laudable *a* laudable
laureado *a* honoured; (*premiado*) prize-winning
laurel *m* laurel; (*culin*) bay
lava *f* lava
lava|ble *a* washable. **~bo** *m* wash-basin; (*retrete*) toilet. **~dero** *m* sink, wash-basin. **~do** *m* washing. **~do de cerebro** brainwashing. **~do en seco** dry-cleaning. **~dora** *f* washing machine. **~ndería** *f* laundry. **~ndería automática** launderette, laundromat (*esp Amer*). **~parabrisas** *m invar* windscreen washer (*Brit*), windshield washer (*Amer*). **~platos** *m & f invar* dishwasher; (*Mex, fregadero*) sink. **~r** *vt* wash. **~r en seco** dry-clean. **~rse** *vpr* have a wash. **~rse las manos** (*incl fig*) wash one's hands. **~tiva** *f* enema. **~vajillas** *m & f inv* dishwasher
lax|ante *a* & *m* laxative. **~o** *a* loose
laz|ada *f* bow. **~o** *m* knot; (*lazada*) bow; (*fig, vínculo*) tie; (*cuerda con nudo corredizo*) lasso; (*trampa*) trap
le *pron* (*acusativo, él*) him; (*acusativo, Vd*) you; (*dativo, él*) (to) him; (*dativo, ella*) (to) her; (*dativo, ello*) (to) it; (*dativo, Vd*) (to) you
leal *a* loyal; (*fiel*) faithful. **~tad** *f* loyalty; (*fidelidad*) faithfulness
lebrel *m* greyhound
lección *f* lesson; (*univ*) lecture
lect|or *m* reader; (*univ*) language assistant. **~ura** *f* reading
leche *f* milk; (*golpe*) bash. **~ condensada** condensed milk. **~ desnatada** skimmed milk. **~ en polvo** powdered milk. **~ra** *f* (*vasija*) milk jug. **~ría** *f* dairy. **~ro** *a* milk, dairy. ● *m* milkman. **~ sin desnatar** whole milk. **tener mala ~** be spiteful
lecho *m* bed
lechoso *a* milky
lechuga *f* lettuce
lechuza *f* owl
leer [18] *vt/i* read
legación *f* legation
legado *m* legacy; (*enviado*) legate
legajo *m* bundle, file
legal *a* legal. **~idad** *f* legality. **~izar** [10] *vt* legalize; (*certificar*) authenticate. **~mente** *adv* legally
legar [12] *vt* bequeath
legendario *a* legendary
legible *a* legible
legi|ón *f* legion. **~onario** *m* legionary
legisla|ción *f* legislation. **~dor** *m* legislator. **~r** *vi* legislate. **~tura** *f* legislature
leg|itimidad *f* legitimacy. **~ítimo** *a* legitimate; (*verdadero*) real
lego *a* lay; (*ignorante*) ignorant. ● *m* layman
legua *f* league
legumbre *f* vegetable
lejan|ía *f* distance. **~o** *a* distant
lejía *f* bleach
lejos *adv* far. **~ de** far from. **a lo ~** in the distance. **desde ~** from a distance, from afar

lelo *a* stupid
lema *m* motto
lencería *f* linen; (*de mujer*) lingerie
lengua *f* tongue; (*idioma*) language. **irse de la ~** talk too much. **morderse la ~** hold one's tongue. **tener mala ~** have a vicious tongue
lenguado *m* sole
lenguaje *m* language
lengüeta *f* (*de zapato*) tongue
lengüetada *f*, **lengüetazo** *m* lick
lente *f* lens. **~s** *mpl* glasses. **~s de contacto** contact lenses
lentej|a *f* lentil. **~uela** *f* sequin
lentilla *f* contact lens
lent|itud *f* slowness. **~o** *a* slow
leñ|a *f* firewood. **~ador** *m* woodcutter. **~o** *m* log
Leo *m* Leo
le|ón *m* lion. **León** Leo. **~ona** *f* lioness
leopardo *m* leopard
leotardo *m* thick tights
lepr|a *f* leprosy. **~oso** *m* leper
lerdo *a* dim; (*torpe*) clumsy
les *pron* (*acusativo*) them; (*acusativo, Vds*) you; (*dativo*) (to) them; (*dativo, Vds*) (to) you
lesbia(na) *f* lesbian
lesbiano *a*, **lesbio** *a* lesbian
lesi|ón *f* wound. **~onado** *a* injured. **~onar** *vt* injure; (*dañar*) damage
letal *a* lethal
letanía *f* litany
let|árgico *a* lethargic. **~argo** *m* lethargy
letr|a *f* letter; (*escritura*) handwriting; (*de una canción*) words, lyrics. **~a de cambio** bill of exchange. **~a de imprenta** print. **~ado** *a* learned. **~ero** *m* notice; (*cartel*) poster
letrina *f* latrine
leucemia *f* leukaemia
levadizo *a*. **puente** *m* **~** drawbridge
levadura *f* yeast. **~ en polvo** baking powder
levanta|miento *m* lifting; (*sublevación*) uprising. **~r** *vt* raise, lift; (*construir*) build; (*recoger*) pick up; (*separar*) take off. **~rse** *vpr* get up; (*ponerse de pie*) stand up; (*erguirse, sublevarse*) rise up
levante *m* east; (*viento*) east wind. **L~** Levant
levar *vt* weigh ‹*ancla*›. ● *vi* set sail
leve *a* light; ‹*enfermedad etc*› slight; (*de poca importancia*) trivial. **~dad** *f* lightness; (*fig*) slightness
léxico *m* vocabulary
lexicografía *f* lexicography
ley *f* law; (*parlamentaria*) act. **plata** *f* **de ~** sterling silver
leyenda *f* legend
liar [20] *vt* tie; (*envolver*) wrap up; roll ‹*cigarillo*›; (*fig, confundir*) confuse; (*fig, enredar*) involve. **~se** *vpr* get involved
libanés *a* & *m* Lebanese
Líbano *m*. **el ~** Lebanon
libel|ista *m* & *f* satirist. **~o** *m* satire
libélula *f* dragonfly
libera|ción *f* liberation. **~dor** *a* liberating. ● *m* liberator
liberal *a* & *m* & *f* liberal. **~idad** *f* liberality. **~mente** *adv* liberally
liber|ar *vt* free. **~tad** *f* freedom. **~tad de cultos** freedom of worship. **~tad de imprenta** freedom of the press. **~tad provisional** bail. **~tar** *vt* free. **en ~tad** free
libertino *m* libertine
Libia *f* Libya
libido *m* libido
libio *a* & *m* Libyan
libra *f* pound. **~ esterlina** pound sterling
Libra *f* Libra
libra|dor *m* (*com*) drawer. **~r** *vt* free; (*de un peligro*) rescue. **~rse** *vpr* free o.s. **~rse de** get rid of
libre *a* free; ‹*aire*› open; (*en natación*) freestyle. **~ de impuestos** tax-free. ● *m* (*Mex*) taxi
librea *f* livery
libr|ería *f* bookshop (*Brit*), bookstore (*Amer*); (*mueble*) bookcase. **~ero** *m* bookseller. **~eta** *f* notebook. **~o** *m* book. **~o de a bordo** logbook. **~o de bolsillo** paperback. **~o de ejercicios** exercise book. **~o de reclamaciones** complaints book
licencia *f* permission; (*documento*) licence. **~do** *m* graduate. **~ para manejar** (*LAm*) driving licence. **~r** *vt* (*mil*) discharge; (*echar*) dismiss. **~tura** *f* degree
licencioso *a* licentious
liceo *m* (*esp LAm*) (secondary) school
licita|dor *m* bidder. **~r** *vt* bid for
lícito *a* legal; (*permisible*) permissible
licor *m* liquid; (*alcohólico*) liqueur
licua|dora *f* liquidizer. **~r** [21] liquefy
lid *f* fight. **en buena ~** by fair means

líder *m* leader
liderato *m*, **liderazgo** *m* leadership
lidia *f* bullfighting; (*lucha*) fight; (*LAm, molestia*) nuisance. **~r** *vt/i* fight
liebre *f* hare
lienzo *m* linen; (*del pintor*) canvas; (*muro, pared*) wall
liga *f* garter; (*alianza*) league; (*mezcla*) mixture. **~dura** *f* bond; (*mus*) slur; (*med*) ligature. **~mento** *m* ligament. **~r** [12] *vt* tie; (*fig*) join; (*mus*) slur. ● *vi* mix. **~r con** (*fig*) pick up. **~rse** *vpr* (*fig*) commit o.s.
liger|eza *f* lightness; (*agilidad*) agility; (*rapidez*) swiftness; (*de carácter*) fickleness. **~o** *a* light; (*rápido*) quick; (*ágil*) agile; (*superficial*) superficial; (*de poca importancia*) slight. ● *adv* quickly. **a la ~a** lightly, superficially
liguero *m* suspender belt
lija *f* dogfish; (*papel de lija*) sandpaper. **~r** *vt* sand
lila *f* lilac
Lima *f* Lima
lima *f* file; (*fruta*) lime. **~duras** *fpl* filings. **~r** *vt* file (down)
limbo *m* limbo
limita|ción *f* limitation. **~do** *a* limited. **~r** *vt* limit. **~r con** border on. **~tivo** *a* limiting
límite *m* limit. **~ de velocidad** speed limit
limítrofe *a* bordering
limo *m* mud
lim|ón *m* lemon. **~onada** *f* lemonade
limosn|a *f* alms. **~ear** *vi* beg. **pedir ~a** beg
limpia *f* cleaning. **~botas** *m invar* bootblack. **~parabrisas** *m inv* windscreen wiper (*Brit*), windshield wiper (*Amer*). **~pipas** *m invar* pipe-cleaner. **~r** *vt* clean; (*enjugar*) wipe
limpi|eza *f* cleanliness; (*acción de limpiar*) cleaning. **~eza en seco** dry-cleaning. **~o** *a* clean; ‹*cielo*› clear; (*fig, honrado*) honest. ● *adv* fairly. **en ~o** (*com*) net. **jugar ~o** play fair
linaje *m* lineage; (*fig, clase*) kind
lince *m* lynx
linchar *vt* lynch
lind|ante *a* bordering (**con** on). **~ar** *vi* border (**con** on). **~e** *f* boundary. **~ero** *m* border
lindo *a* pretty, lovely. **de lo ~** (*fam*) a lot
línea *f* line. **en ~s generales** in broad outline. **guardar la ~** watch one's figure
lingote *m* ingot
lingü|ista *m & f* linguist. **~ística** *f* linguistics. **~ístico** *a* linguistic
lino *m* flax; (*tela*) linen
linóleo *m*, **linóeum** *m* lino, linoleum
linterna *f* lantern; (*de bolsillo*) torch, flashlight (*Amer*)
lío *m* bundle; (*jaleo*) fuss; (*embrollo*) muddle; (*amorío*) affair
liquen *m* lichen
liquida|ción *f* liquidation; (*venta especial*) (clearance) sale. **~r** *vt* liquify; (*com*) liquidate; settle ‹*cuenta*›
líquido *a* liquid; (*com*) net. ● *m* liquid
lira *f* lyre; (*moneda italiana*) lira
líric|a *f* lyric poetry. **~o** *a* lyric(al)
lirio *m* iris. **~ de los valles** lily of the valley
lirón *m* dormouse; (*fig*) sleepyhead. **dormir como un ~** sleep like a log
Lisboa *f* Lisbon
lisia|do *a* disabled. **~r** *vt* disable; (*herir*) injure
liso *a* smooth; ‹*pelo*› straight; ‹*tierra*› flat; (*sencillo*) plain
lisonj|a *f* flattery. **~eador** *a* flattering. ● *m* flatterer. **~ear** *vt* flatter. **~ero** *a* flattering
lista *f* stripe; (*enumeración*) list; (*de platos*) menu. **~ de correos** poste restante. **~do** *a* striped. **a ~s** striped
listo *a* clever; (*preparado*) ready
listón *m* ribbon; (*de madera*) strip
lisura *f* smoothness
litera *f* (*en barco*) berth; (*en tren*) sleeper; (*en habitación*) bunk bed
literal *a* literal
litera|rio *a* literary. **~tura** *f* literature
litig|ar [12] *vi* dispute; (*jurid*) litigate. **~io** *m* dispute; (*jurid*) litigation
litografía *f* (*arte*) lithography; (*cuadro*) lithograph
litoral *a* coastal. ● *m* coast
litro *m* litre
lituano *a & m* Lithuanian
liturgia *f* liturgy
liviano *a* fickle, inconstant
lívido *a* livid
lizo *m* warp thread

lo *art def neutro*. ~ **importante** what is important, the important thing. ● *pron* (*él*) him; (*ello*) it. ~ **que** what(ever), that which

loa *f* praise. **~ble** *a* praiseworthy. **~r** *vt* praise

lobo *m* wolf

lóbrego *a* gloomy

lóbulo *m* lobe

local *a* local. ● *m* premises; (*lugar*) place. **~idad** *f* locality; (*de un espectáculo*) seat; (*entrada*) ticket. **~izar** [10] *vt* localize; (*encontrar*) find, locate

loción *f* lotion

loco *a* mad; (*fig*) foolish. ● *m* lunatic. ~ **de alegría** mad with joy. **estar ~ por** be crazy about. **volverse ~** go mad

locomo|ción *f* locomotion. **~tora** *f* locomotive

locuaz *a* talkative

locución *f* expression

locura *f* madness; (*acto*) crazy thing. **con ~** madly

locutor *m* announcer

locutorio *m* (*de teléfono*) telephone booth

lod|azal *m* quagmire. **~o** *m* mud

logaritmo *m* logarithm, log

lógic|a *f* logic. **~o** *a* logical

logística *f* logistics

logr|ar *vt* get; win ‹*premio*›. **~ hacer** manage to do. **~o** *m* achievement; (*de premio*) winning; (*éxito*) success

loma *f* small hill

lombriz *f* worm

lomo *m* back; (*de libro*) spine; (*doblez*) fold. ~ **de cerdo** loin of pork

lona *f* canvas

loncha *f* slice; (*de tocino*) rasher

londinense *a* from London. ● *m* Londoner

Londres *m* London

loneta *f* thin canvas

longánimo *a* magnanimous

longaniza *f* sausage

longev|idad *f* longevity. **~o** *a* long-lived

longitud *f* length; (*geog*) longitude

lonja *f* slice; (*de tocino*) rasher; (*com*) market

lord *m* (*pl* **lores**) lord

loro *m* parrot

los *art def mpl* the. ● *pron* them. ~ **de Antonio** Antonio's. ~ **que** whoever, the ones

losa *f* slab; (*baldosa*) flagstone. ~ **sepulcral** tombstone

lote *m* share

lotería *f* lottery

loto *m* lotus

loza *f* crockery

lozano *a* fresh; ‹*vegetación*› lush; ‹*persona*› lively

lubri(fi)ca|nte *a* lubricating. ● *m* lubricant. **~r** [7] *vt* lubricate

lucero *m* (*estrella*) bright star; (*planeta*) Venus

lucid|ez *f* lucidity. **~o** *a* splendid

lúcido *a* lucid

luciérnaga *f* glow-worm

lucimiento *m* brilliance

lucir [11] *vt* (*fig*) show off. ● *vi* shine; ‹*lámpara*› give off light; ‹*joya*› sparkle. **~se** *vpr* (*fig*) shine, excel

lucr|ativo *a* lucrative. **~o** *m* gain

lucha *f* fight. **~dor** *m* fighter. **~r** *vi* fight

luego *adv* then; (*más tarde*) later. ● *conj* therefore. ~ **que** as soon as. **desde ~** of course

lugar *m* place. ~ **común** cliché. **~eño** *a* village. **dar ~ a** give rise to. **en ~ de** instead of. **en primer ~** in the first place. **hacer ~** make room. **tener ~** take place

lugarteniente *m* deputy

lúgubre *a* gloomy

lujo *m* luxury. **~so** *a* luxurious. **de ~** de luxe

lujuria *f* lust

lumbago *m* lumbago

lumbre *f* fire; (*luz*) light. **¿tienes ~?** have you got a light?

luminoso *a* luminous; (*fig*) brilliant

luna *f* moon; (*de escaparate*) window; (*espejo*) mirror. ~ **de miel** honeymoon. **~r** *a* lunar. ● *m* mole. **claro de ~** moonlight. **estar en la ~** be miles away

lunes *m* Monday. **cada ~ y cada martes** day in, day out

lupa *f* magnifying glass

lúpulo *m* hop

lustr|abotas *m inv* (*LAm*) bootblack. **~ar** *vt* shine, polish. **~e** *m* shine; (*fig, esplendor*) splendour. **~oso** *a* shining. **dar ~e a, sacar ~e a** polish

luto *m* mourning. **estar de ~** be in mourning

luxación *f* dislocation

Luxemburgo *m* Luxemburg

luz *f* light; (*electricidad*) electricity. **luces** *fpl* intelligence. ~ **antiniebla**

(*auto*) fog light. **a la ~ de** in the light of. **a todas luces** obviously. **dar a ~** give birth. **hacer la ~ sobre** shed light on. **sacar a la ~** bring to light

LL

llaga *f* wound; (*úlcera*) ulcer
llama *f* flame; (*animal*) llama
llamada *f* call; (*golpe*) knock; (*señal*) sign
llama|do *a* known as. **~miento** *m* call. **~r** *vt* call; (*por teléfono*) ring (up). ● *vi* call; (*golpear en la puerta*) knock; (*tocar el timbre*) ring. **~rse** *vpr* be called. **~r por teléfono** ring (up), telephone. **¿cómo te ~s?** what's your name?
llamarada *f* blaze; (*fig*) blush; (*fig, de pasión etc*) outburst
llamativo *a* loud, gaudy
llamear *vi* blaze
llan|eza *f* simplicity. **~o** *a* flat, level; ‹*persona*› natural; (*sencillo*) plain. ● *m* plain
llanta *f* (*auto*) (wheel) rim; (*LAm, neumático*) tyre
llanto *m* weeping
llanura *f* plain
llave *f* key; (*para tuercas*) spanner; (*grifo*) tap (*Brit*), faucet (*Amer*); (*elec*) switch. **~ inglesa** monkey wrench. **~ro** *m* key-ring. **cerrar con ~** lock. **echar la ~** lock up
llega|da *f* arrival. **~r** [12] *vi* arrive, come; (*alcanzar*) reach; (*bastar*) be enough. **~rse** *vpr* come near; (*ir*) go (round). **~r a** (*conseguir*) manage to. **~r a saber** find out. **~r a ser** become
llen|ar *vt* fill (up); (*rellenar*) fill in. **~o** *a* full. ● *m* (*en el teatro etc*) full house. **de ~** completely
lleva|dero *a* tolerable. **~r** *vt* carry; (*inducir, conducir*) lead; (*acompañar*) take; wear ‹*ropa*›; (*traer*) bring. **~rse** *vpr* run off with ‹*cosa*›. **~rse bien** get on well together. **¿cuánto tiempo ~s aquí?** how long have you been here? **llevo 3 años estudiando inglés** I've been studying English for 3 years
llor|ar *vi* cry; ‹*ojos*› water. **~iquear** *vi* whine. **~iqueo** *m* whining. **~o** *m* crying. **~ón** *a* whining. ● *m* cry-baby. **~oso** *a* tearful
llov|er [2] *vi* rain. **~izna** *f* drizzle. **~iznar** *vi* drizzle
llueve *vb véase* **llover**
lluvi|a *f* rain; (*fig*) shower. **~oso** *a* rainy; ‹*clima*› wet

M

maca *f* defect; (*en fruta*) bruise
macabro *a* macabre
macaco *a* (*LAm*) ugly. ● *m* macaque (monkey)
macadam *m*, **macadán** *m* Tarmac (*P*)
macanudo *a* (*fam*) great
macarrón *m* macaroon. **~es** *mpl* macaroni
macerar *vt* macerate
maceta *f* mallet; (*tiesto*) flowerpot
macilento *a* wan
macizo *a* solid. ● *m* mass; (*de plantas*) bed
macrobiótico *a* macrobiotic
mácula *f* stain
macuto *m* knapsack
mach /mak/ *m*. **(número de) ~** Mach (number)
machac|ar [7] *vt* crush. ● *vi* go on (**en** about). **~ón** *a* boring. ● *m* bore
machamartillo. a ~ *adv* firmly
machaqueo *m* crushing
machet|azo *m* blow with a machete; (*herida*) wound from a machete. **~e** *m* machete
mach|ista *m* male chauvinist. **~o** *a* male; (*varonil*) macho
machón *m* buttress
machucar [7] *vt* crush; (*estropear*) damage
madeja *f* skein
madera *m* (*vino*) Madeira. ● *f* wood; (*naturaleza*) nature. **~ble** *a* yielding timber. **~je** *m*, **~men** *m* woodwork
madero *m* log; (*de construcción*) timber
madona *f* Madonna
madr|astra *f* stepmother. **~e** *f* mother. **~eperla** *f* mother-of-pearl. **~eselva** *f* honeysuckle
madrigal *m* madrigal
madriguera *f* den; (*de liebre*) burrow
madrileño *a* of Madrid. ● *m* person from Madrid
madrina *f* godmother; (*en una boda*) chief bridesmaid
madroño *m* strawberry-tree

madrug|ada *f* dawn. **~ador** *a* who gets up early. ● *m* early riser. **~ar** [12] *vi* get up early. **~ón** *m*. **darse un ~ón** get up very early

madur|ación *f* maturing; (*de fruta*) ripening. **~ar** *vt/i* mature; ‹*fruta*› ripen. **~ez** *f* maturity; (*de fruta*) ripeness. **~o** *a* mature; ‹*fruta*› ripe

maestr|a *f* teacher. **~ía** *f* skill. **~o** *m* master. **~a, ~o (de escuela)** schoolteacher

mafia *f* Mafia

magdalena *f* madeleine, small sponge cake

magia *f* magic

mágico *a* magic; (*maravilloso*) magical

magín *m* (*fam*) imagination

magisterio *m* teaching (profession); (*conjunto de maestros*) teachers

magistrado *m* magistrate; (*juez*) judge

magistral *a* teaching; (*bien hecho*) masterly; ‹*lenguaje*› pedantic

magistratura *f* magistracy

magn|animidad *f* magnanimity. **~ánimo** *a* magnanimous

magnate *m* magnate

magnesia *f* magnesia. **~ efervescente** milk of magnesia

magnético *a* magnetic

magneti|smo *m* magnetism. **~zar** [10] *vt* magnetize

magnetofón *m*, **magnetófono** *m* tape recorder

magnificencia *f* magnificence

magnífico *a* magnificent

magnitud *f* magnitude

magnolia *f* magnolia

mago *m* magician. **los (tres) reyes ~s** the Magi

magr|a *f* slice of ham. **~o** *a* lean; ‹*tierra*› poor; ‹*persona*› thin

magulla|dura *f* bruise. **~r** *vt* bruise

mahometano *a* & *m* Muhammadan

maíz *m* maize, corn (*Amer*)

majada *f* sheepfold; (*estiércol*) manure; (*LAm*) flock of sheep

majader|ía *f* silly thing. **~o** *m* idiot; (*mano del mortero*) pestle. ● *a* stupid

majador *m* crusher

majagranzas *m* idiot

majar *vt* crush; (*molestar*) bother

majest|ad *f* majesty. **~uoso** *a* majestic

majo *a* nice

mal *adv* badly; (*poco*) poorly; (*difícilmente*) hardly; (*equivocadamente*) wrongly. ● *a* see **malo**. ● *m* evil; (*daño*) harm; (*enfermedad*) illness. **~ que bien** somehow (or other). **de ~ en peor** worse and worse. **hacer ~ en** be wrong to. **¡menos ~!** thank goodness!

malabar *a*. **juegos ~es** juggling. **~ismo** *m* juggling. **~ista** *m* & *f* juggler

malaconsejado *a* ill-advised

malacostumbrado *a* with bad habits

malagueño *a* of Málaga. ● *m* person from Málaga

malamente *adv* badly; (*fam*) hardly enough

malandanza *f* misfortune

malapata *m* & *f* nuisance

malaria *f* malaria

Malasia *f* Malaysia

malasombra *m* & *f* clumsy person

malavenido *a* incompatible

malaventura *f* misfortune. **~do** *a* unfortunate

malayo *a* Malay(an)

malbaratar *vt* sell off cheap; (*malgastar*) squander

malcarado *a* ugly

malcasado *a* unhappily married; (*infiel*) unfaithful

malcomer *vi* eat poorly

malcriad|eza *f* (*LAm*) bad manners. **~o** *a* ‹*niño*› spoilt

maldad *f* evil; (*acción*) wicked thing

maldecir [46 *pero imperativo* **maldice**, *futuro y condicional regulares, pp* **maldecido** *o* **maldito**] *vt* curse. ● *vi* speak ill (**de** of); (*quejarse*) complain (**de** about)

maldici|ente *a* backbiting; (*que blasfema*) foul-mouthed. **~ón** *f* curse

maldit|a *f* tongue. **¡~a sea!** damn it! **~o** *a* damned. ● *m* (*en el teatro*) extra

maleab|ilidad *f* malleability. **~le** *a* malleable

malea|nte *a* wicked. ● *m* vagrant. **~r** *vt* damage; (*pervertir*) corrupt. **~rse** *vpr* be spoilt; (*pervertirse*) be corrupted

malecón *m* breakwater; (*rail*) embankment; (*para atracar*) jetty

maledicencia *f* slander

maleficio *m* curse

maléfico *a* evil

malestar *m* indisposition; (*fig*) uneasiness

malet|a *f* (suit)case; (*auto*) boot, trunk (*Amer*); (*LAm, lío de ropa*)

bundle; (*LAm*, *de bicicleta*) saddle-bag. **hacer la ~a** pack one's bags. ● *m* & *f* (*fam*) bungler. **~ero** *m* porter; (*auto*) boot, trunk (*Amer*). **~ín** *m* small case
malevolencia *f* malevolence
malévolo *a* malevolent
maleza *f* weeds; (*matorral*) undergrowth
malgasta|dor *a* wasteful. ● *m* spendthrift. **~r** *vt* waste
malgeniado *a* (*LAm*) bad-tempered
malhablado *a* foul-mouthed
malhadado *a* unfortunate
malhechor *m* criminal
malhumorado *a* bad-tempered
malici|a *f* malice. **~arse** *vpr* suspect. **~as** *fpl* (*fam*) suspicions. **~oso** *a* malicious
malign|idad *f* malice; (*med*) malignancy. **~o** *a* malignant; ‹*persona*› malicious
malintencionado *a* malicious
malmandado *a* disobedient
malmirado *a* (*con estar*) disliked; (*con ser*) inconsiderate
malo *a* (*delante de nombre masculino en singular* **mal**) bad; (*enfermo*) ill. **~ de** difficult. **estar de malas** be out of luck; (*malhumorado*) be in a bad mood. **lo ~ es que** the trouble is that. **ponerse a malas con uno** fall out with s.o. **por las malas** by force
malogr|ar *vt* waste; (*estropear*) spoil. **~arse** *vpr* fall through. **~o** *m* failure
maloliente *a* smelly
malparto *m* miscarriage
malpensado *a* nasty, malicious
malquerencia *f* dislike
malquist|ar *vt* set against. **~arse** *vpr* fall out. **~o** *a* disliked
malsano *a* unhealthy; (*enfermizo*) sickly
malsonante *a* ill-sounding; (*grosero*) offensive
malta *f* malt; (*cerveza*) beer
maltés *a* & *m* Maltese
maltratar *vt* ill-treat
maltrecho *a* battered
malucho *a* (*fam*) poorly
malva *f* mallow. **(color de) ~** *a invar* mauve
malvado *a* wicked
malvavisco *m* marshmallow
malvender *vt* sell off cheap
malversa|ción *f* embezzlement. **~dor** *a* embezzling. ● *m* embezzler. **~r** *vt* embezzle
Malvinas *fpl*. **las islas ~** the Falkland Islands
malla *f* mesh. **cota de ~** coat of mail
mallo *m* mallet
Mallor|ca *f* Majorca. **~quín** *a* & *m* Majorcan
mama *f* teat; (*de mujer*) breast
mamá *f* mum(my)
mama|da *f* sucking. **~r** *vt* suck; (*fig*) grow up with; (*engullir*) gobble
mamario *a* mammary
mamarrach|adas *fpl* nonsense. **~o** *m* clown; (*cosa ridícula*) (ridiculous) sight
mameluco *a* Brazilian half-breed; (*necio*) idiot
mamífero *a* mammalian. ● *m* mammal
mamola *f*. **hacer la ~** chuck (under the chin); (*fig*) make fun of
mamotreto *m* notebook; (*libro voluminoso*) big book
mampara *f* screen
mamporro *m* blow
mampostería *f* masonry
mamut *m* mammoth
maná *f* manna
manada *f* herd; (*de lobos*) pack. **en ~** in crowds
manager /'manaʒer/ *m* manager
mana|ntial *m* spring; (*fig*) source. **~r** *vi* flow; (*fig*) abound. ● *vt* run with
manaza *f* big hand; (*sucia*) dirty hand. **ser un ~s** be clumsy
manceb|a *f* concubine. **~ía** *f* brothel. **~o** *m* youth; (*soltero*) bachelor
mancera *f* plough handle
mancilla *f* stain. **~r** *vt* stain
manco *a* (*de una mano*) one-handed; (*de las dos manos*) handless; (*de un brazo*) one-armed; (*de los dos brazos*) armless
mancomún *adv*. **de ~** jointly
mancomun|adamente *adv* jointly. **~ar** *vt* unite; (*jurid*) make jointly liable. **~arse** *vpr* unite. **~idad** *f* union
mancha *f* stain
Mancha *f*. **la ~** la Mancha (region of Spain). **el canal de la ~** the English Channel
mancha|do *a* dirty; ‹*animal*› spotted. **~r** *vt* stain. **~rse** *vpr* get dirty
manchego *a* of la Mancha. ● *m* person from la Mancha
manchón *m* large stain

manda *f* legacy
manda|dero *m* messenger. **~miento** *m* order; (*relig*) commandment. **~r** *vt* order; (*enviar*) send; (*gobernar*) rule. ● *vi* be in command. **¿mande?** (*esp LAm*) pardon?
mandarín *m* mandarin
mandarin|a *f* (*naranja*) mandarin; (*lengua*) Mandarin. **~o** *m* mandarin tree
mandat|ario *m* attorney. **~o** *m* order; (*jurid*) power of attorney
mandíbula *f* jaw
mandil *m* apron
mandioca *f* cassava
mando *m* command; (*pol*) term of office. **~ a distancia** remote control. **los ~s** the leaders
mandolina *f* mandolin
mandón *a* bossy
manducar [7] *vt* (*fam*) stuff oneself with
manecilla *f* needle; (*de reloj*) hand
manej|able *a* manageable. **~ar** *vt* handle; (*fig*) manage; (*LAm, conducir*) drive. **~arse** *vpr* behave. **~o** *m* handling; (*intriga*) intrigue
manera *f* way. **~s** *fpl* manners. **de ~ que** so (that). **de ninguna ~** not at all. **de otra ~** otherwise. **de todas ~s** anyway
manga *f* sleeve; (*tubo de goma*) hose(pipe); (*red*) net; (*para colar*) filter
mangante *m* beggar; (*fam*) scrounger
mangle *m* mangrove
mango *m* handle; (*fruta*) mango
mangonear *vt* boss about. ● *vi* (*entrometerse*) interfere
manguera *f* hose(pipe)
manguito *m* muff
manía *f* mania; (*antipatía*) dislike
maniaco *a*, **maníaco** *a* maniac(al). ● *m* maniac
maniatar *vt* tie s.o.'s hands
maniático *a* maniac(al); (*fig*) crazy
manicomio *m* lunatic asylum
manicura *f* manicure; (*mujer*) manicurist
manido *a* stale; ‹*carne*› high
manifesta|ción *f* manifestation; (*pol*) demonstration. **~nte** *m* demonstrator. **~r** [1] *vi* manifest; (*pol*) state. **~rse** *vpr* show; (*pol*) demonstrate
manifiesto *a* clear; ‹*error*› obvious; ‹*verdad*› manifest. ● *m* manifesto
manilargo *a* light-fingered
manilla *f* bracelet; (*de hierro*) handcuffs
manillar *m* handlebar(s)
maniobra *f* manoeuvring; (*rail*) shunting; (*fig*) manoeuvre. **~r** *vt* operate; (*rail*) shunt. ● *vi* manoeuvre. **~s** *fpl* (*mil*) manoeuvres
manipula|ción *f* manipulation. **~r** *vt* manipulate
maniquí *m* dummy. ● *f* model
manirroto *a* extravagant. ● *m* spendthrift
manita *f* little hand
manivela *f* crank
manjar *m* (*special*) dish
mano *f* hand; (*de animales*) front foot; (*de perros, gatos*) front paw. **~ de obra** work force. **¡~s arriba!** hands up! **a ~** by hand; (*próximo*) handy. **de segunda ~** second hand. **echar una ~** lend a hand. **tener buena ~ para** be good at
manojo *m* bunch
manose|ar *vt* handle; (*fig*) overwork. **~o** *m* handling
manotada *f*, **manotazo** *m* slap
manote|ar *vi* gesticulate. **~o** *m* gesticulation
mansalva. a ~ *adv* without risk
mansarda *f* attic
mansedumbre *f* gentleness; (*de animal*) tameness
mansión *f* stately home
manso *a* gentle; ‹*animal*› tame
manta *f* blanket. **~ eléctrica** electric blanket. **a ~ (de Dios)** a lot
mantec|a *f* fat; (*LAm*) butter. **~ado** *m* bun; (*helado*) ice-cream. **~oso** *a* greasy
mantel *m* tablecloth; (*del altar*) altar cloth. **~ería** *f* table linen
manten|er [40] *vt* support; (*conservar*) keep; (*sostener*) maintain. **~erse** *vpr* remain. **~ de/con** live off. **~imiento** *m* maintenance
mantequ|era *f* butter churn. **~ería** *f* dairy. **~illa** *f* butter
mantilla *f* mantilla
manto *m* cloak
mantón *m* shawl
manual *a* & *m* manual
manubrio *m* crank
manufactura *f* manufacture; (*fábrica*) factory
manuscrito *a* handwritten. ● *m* manuscript
manutención *f* maintenance

manzana *f* apple. **~r** *m* (*apple*) orchard
manzanilla *f* camomile tea; (*vino*) manzanilla, pale dry sherry
manzano *m* apple tree
maña *f* skill. **~s** *fpl* cunning
mañan|a *f* morning; (*el día siguiente*) tomorrow. ● *m* future. ● *adv* tomorrow. **~ero** *a* who gets up early. ● *m* early riser. **~a por la ~a** tomorrow morning. **pasado ~a** the day after tomorrow. **por la ~a** in the morning
mañoso *a* clever; (*astuto*) crafty
mapa *m* map. **~mundi** *m* map of the world
mapache *m* racoon
mapurite *m* skunk
maqueta *f* scale model
maquiavélico *a* machiavellian
maquilla|je *m* make-up. **~r** *vt* make up. **~rse** *vpr* make up
máquina *f* machine; (*rail*) engine. **~ de escribir** typewriter. **~ fotográfica** camera
maquin|ación *f* machination. **~al** *a* mechanical. **~aria** *f* machinery. **~ista** *m & f* operator; (*rail*) engine driver
mar *m & f* sea. **alta ~** high seas. **la ~ de** (*fam*) lots of
maraña *f* thicket; (*enredo*) tangle; (*embrollo*) muddle
maravedí *m* (*pl* **maravedís, maravedises**) maravedi, old Spanish coin
maravill|a *f* wonder. **~ar** *vt* astonish. **~arse** *vpr* be astonished (**con** at). **~oso** *a* marvellous, wonderful. **a ~a, a las mil ~as** marvellously. **contar/decir ~as de** speak wonderfully of. **hacer ~as** work wonders
marbete *m* label
marca *f* mark; (*de fábrica*) trademark; (*deportes*) record. **~do** *a* marked. **~dor** *m* marker; (*deportes*) scoreboard. **~r** [7] *vt* mark; (*señalar*) show; (*anotar*) note down; score ‹*un gol*›; dial ‹*número de teléfono*›. ● *vi* score. **de ~** brand name; (*fig*) excellent. **de ~ mayor** (*fam*) first-class
marcial *a* martial
marciano *a & m* Martian
marco *m* frame; (*moneda alemana*) mark; (*deportes*) goal-posts
marcha *f* (*incl mus*) march; (*auto*) gear; (*curso*) course. **a toda ~** at full speed. **dar/hacer ~ atrás** put into reverse. **poner en ~** start; (*fig*) set in motion
marchante *m* (*f* **marchanta**) dealer; (*LAm, parroquiano*) client
marchar *vi* go; (*funcionar*) work, go. **~se** *vpr* go away, leave
marchit|ar *vt* wither. **~arse** *vpr* wither. **~o** *a* withered
marea *f* tide. **~do** *a* sick; (*en el mar*) seasick; (*aturdido*) dizzy; (*borracho*) drunk. **~r** *vt* sail, navigate; (*baquetear*) annoy. **~rse** *vpr* feel sick; (*en un barco*) be seasick; (*estar aturdido*) feel dizzy; (*irse la cabeza*) feel faint; (*emborracharse*) get slightly drunk
marejada *f* swell; (*fig*) wave
maremagno *m* (*de cosas*) sea; (*de gente*) (noisy) crowd
mareo *m* sickness; (*en el mar*) seasickness; (*aturdimiento*) dizziness; (*fig, molestia*) nuisance
marfil *m* ivory. **~eño** *a* ivory. **torre** *f* **de ~** ivory tower
margarina *f* margarine
margarita *f* pearl; (*bot*) daisy
marg|en *m* margin; (*borde*) edge, border; (*de un río*) bank; (*de un camino*) side; (*nota marginal*) marginal note. **~inado** *a* on the edge. ● *m* outcast. **~inal** *a* marginal. **~inar** *vt* (*excluir*) exclude; (*dejar márgenes*) leave margins; (*poner notas*) write notes in the margin. **al ~en** (*fig*) outside
mariachi (*Mex*) *m* (*música popular de Jalisco*) Mariachi; (*conjunto popular*) Mariachi band
mariano *a* Marian
marica *f* (*hombre afeminado*) sissy; (*urraca*) magpie
maricón *m* homosexual, queer (*sl*)
marid|aje *m* married life; (*fig*) harmony. **~o** *m* husband
mariguana *f*, **marihuana** *f* marijuana
marimacho *m* mannish woman
marimandona *f* bossy woman
marimba *f* (type of) drum; (*LAm, especie de xilofón*) marimba
marimorena *f* (*fam*) row
marin|a *f* coast; (*cuadro*) seascape; (*conjunto de barcos*) navy; (*arte de navegar*) seamanship. **~era** *f* seamanship; (*conjunto de marineros*) crew. **~ero** *a* marine; ‹*barco*› seaworthy. ● *m* sailor. **~o** *a* marine. **~a de guerra** navy. **~a mercante** merchant navy. **a la ~era** in tomato

and garlic sauce. **azul ~o** navy blue
marioneta *f* puppet. **~s** *fpl* puppet show
maripos|a *f* butterfly. **~ear** *vi* be fickle; (*galantear*) flirt. **~n** *m* flirt. **~a nocturna** moth
mariquita *f* ladybird, ladybug (*Amer*)
marisabidilla *f* know-all
mariscador *m* shell-fisher
mariscal *m* marshal
maris|co *m* seafood, shellfish. **~quero** *m* (*persona que pesca mariscos*) seafood fisherman; (*persona que vende mariscos*) seafood seller
marital *a* marital
marítimo *a* maritime; ‹*ciudad etc*› coastal, seaside
maritornes *f* uncouth servant
marmit|a *f* pot. **~ón** *m* kitchen boy
mármol *m* marble
marmol|era *f* marblework, marbles. **~ista** *m & f* marble worker
marmóreo *a* marble
marmota *f* marmot
maroma *f* rope; (*LAm, función de volatines*) tightrope walking
marqu|és *m* marquess. **~esa** *f* marchioness. **~esina** *f* glass canopy
marquetería *f* marquetry
marrajo *a* ‹*toro*› vicious; ‹*persona*› cunning. ● *m* shark
marran|a *f* sow. **~ada** *f* filthy thing; (*cochinada*) dirty trick. **~o** *a* filthy. ● *m* hog
marrar *vt* (*errar*) miss; (*fallar*) fail
marrón *a & m* brown
marroquí *a & m & f* Moroccan. ● *m* (*tafilete*) morocco
marrubio *m* (*bot*) horehound
Marruecos *m* Morocco
marruller|ía *f* cajolery. **~o** *a* cajoling. ● *m* cajoler
marsopa *f* porpoise
marsupial *a & m* marsupial
marta *f* marten
martajar *vt* (*Mex*) grind ‹*maíz*›
Marte *m* Mars
martes *m* Tuesday
martill|ada *f* blow with a hammer. **~ar** *vt* hammer. **~azo** *m* blow with a hammer. **~ear** *vt* hammer. **~eo** *m* hammering. **~o** *m* hammer
martín *m* **pescador** kingfisher
martinete *m* (*macillo del piano*) hammer; (*mazo*) drop hammer
martingala *f* (*ardid*) trick
mártir *m & f* martyr
martir|io *m* martyrdom. **~izar** [10] *vt* martyr; (*fig*) torment, torture. **~ologio** *m* martyrology
marxis|mo *m* Marxism. **~ta** *a & m & f* Marxist
marzo *m* March
más *adv & a* (*comparativo*) more; (*superlativo*) most. **~ caro** dearer. **~ curioso** more curious. **el ~ caro** the dearest; (*de dos*) the dearer. **el ~ curioso** the most curious; (*de dos*) the more curious. ● *conj* and, plus. ● *m* plus (sign). **~ bien** rather. **~ de** (*cantidad indeterminada*) more than. **~ o menos** more or less. **~ que** more than. **~ y ~** more and more. **a lo ~** at (the) most. **de ~** too many. **es ~** moreover. **no ~** no more
masa *f* dough; (*cantidad*) mass; (*física*) mass. **en ~** en masse
masacre *f* massacre
masaj|e *m* massage. **~ista** *m* masseur. ● *f* masseuse
masca|da *f* (*LAm*) plug of tobacco. **~dura** *f* chewing. **~r** [7] *vt* chew
máscara *f* mask; (*persona*) masked figure/person
mascar|ada *f* masquerade. **~illa** *f* mask. **~ón** *m* (large) mask
mascota *f* mascot
masculin|idad *f* masculinity. **~o** *a* masculine; ‹*sexo*› male. ● *m* masculine
mascullar [3] *vt* mumble
masilla *f* putty
masivo *a* massive, large-scale
mas|ón *m* (free)mason. **~onería** *f* (free)masonry. **~ónico** *a* masonic
masoquis|mo *m* masochism. **~ta** *a* masochistic. ● *m & f* masochist
mastate *m* (*Mex*) loincloth
mastelero *m* topmast
mastica|ción *f* chewing. **~r** [7] *vt* chew; (*fig*) chew over
mástil *m* mast; (*palo*) pole; (*en instrumentos de cuerda*) neck
mastín *m* mastiff
mastitis *f* mastitis
mastodonte *m* mastodon
mastoides *a & f* mastoid
mastuerzo *m* cress
masturba|ción *f* masturbation. **~rse** *vpr* masturbate
mata *f* grove; (*arbusto*) bush
matad|ero *m* slaughterhouse. **~or** *a* killing. ● *m* killer; (*torero*) matador
matadura *f* sore

matamoscas *m invar* fly swatter
mata|nza *f* killing. **~r** *vt* kill ‹*personas*›; slaughter ‹*reses*›. **~rife** *m* butcher. **~rse** *vpr* commit suicide; (*en un acidente*) be killed. **estar a ~r con uno** be deadly enemies with s.o.
matarratas *m invar* cheap liquor
matasanos *m invar* quack
matasellos *m invar* postmark
match *m* match
mate *a* matt, dull; ‹*sonido*› dull. ● *m* (*ajedrez*) (check)mate; (*LAm, bebida*) maté
matemátic|as *fpl* mathematics, maths (*fam*), math (*Amer, fam*). **~o** *a* mathematical. ● *m* mathematician
materia *f* matter; (*material*) material. **~ prima** raw material. **en ~ de** on the question of
material *a & m* material. **~idad** *f* material nature. **~ismo** *m* materialism. **~ista** *a* materialistic. ● *m & f* materialist. **~izar** [10] *vt* materialize. **~izarse** *vpr* materialize. **~mente** *adv* materially; (*absolutamente*) absolutely
matern|al *a* maternal; (*como de madre*) motherly. **~idad** *f* motherhood; (*casa de maternidad*) maternity home. **~o** *a* motherly; ‹*lengua*› mother
matin|al *a* morning. **~ée** *m* matinée
matiz *m* shade. **~ación** *f* combination of colours. **~ar** [10] *vt* blend ‹*colores*›; (*introducir variedad*) vary; (*teñir*) tinge (**de** with)
matojo *m* bush
mat|ón *m* bully. **~onismo** *m* bullying
matorral *m* scrub; (*conjunto de matas*) thicket
matra|ca *f* rattle. **~quear** *vt* rattle; (*dar matraca*) pester. **dar ~ca** pester. **ser un(a) ~ca** be a nuisance
matraz *m* flask
matriarca|do *m* matriarchy. **~l** *a* matriarchal
matr|ícula *f* (*lista*) register, list; (*acto de matricularse*) registration; (*auto*) registration number. **~icular** *vt* register. **~icularse** *vpr* enrol, register
matrimoni|al *a* matrimonial. **~o** *m* marriage; (*pareja*) married couple
matritense *a* from Madrid
matriz *f* matrix; (*anat*) womb, uterus
matrona *f* matron; (*partera*) midwife
Matusalén *m* Methuselah. **más viejo que ~** as old as Methuselah
matute *m* smuggling. **~ro** *m* smuggler
matutino *a* morning
maula *f* piece of junk
maull|ar *vi* miaow. **~ido** *m* miaow
mauritano *a* & m Mauritanian
mausoleo *m* mausoleum
maxilar *a* maxillary. **hueso ~** jaw(bone)
máxima *f* maxim
máxime *adv* especially
máximo *a* maximum; (*más alto*) highest. ● *m* maximum
maya *f* daisy; (*persona*) Maya Indian
mayestático *a* majestic
mayo *m* May; (*palo*) maypole
mayólica *f* majolica
mayonesa *f* mayonnaise
mayor *a* (*más grande, comparativo*) bigger; (*más grande, superlativo*) biggest; (*de edad, comparativo*) older; (*de edad, superlativo*) oldest; (*adulto*) grown-up; (*principal*) main, major; (*mus*) major. ● *m & f* boss; (*adulto*) adult. **~al** *m* foreman; (*pastor*) head shepherd. **~azgo** *m* entailed estate. **al por ~** wholesale
mayordomo *m* butler
mayor|ía *f* majority. **~ista** *m & f* wholesaler. **~mente** *adv* especially
mayúscul|a *f* capital (letter). **~o** *a* capital; (*fig, grande*) big
maza *f* mace
mazacote *m* hard mass
mazapán *m* marzipan
mazmorra *f* dungeon
mazo *m* mallet; (*manojo*) bunch
mazorca *f*. **~ de maíz** corn on the cob
me *pron* (*acusativo*) me; (*dativo*) (to) me; (*reflexivo*) (to) myself
meandro *m* meander
mecánic|a *f* mechanics. **~o** *a* mechanical. ● *m* mechanic
mecani|smo *m* mechanism. **~zación** *f* mechanization. **~zar** [10] *vt* mechanize
mecanograf|ía *f* typing. **~iado** *a* typed, typewritten. **~iar** [20] *vt* type
mecanógrafo *m* typist
mecate *m* (*LAm*) (*pita*) rope
mecedora *f* rocking chair
mecenazgo *m* patronage

mecer [9] *vt* rock; swing ‹*columpio*›. **~se** *vpr* rock; (*en un columpio*) swing
mecha *f* (*de vela*) wick; (*de mina*) fuse
mechar *vt* stuff, lard
mechero *m* (cigarette) lighter
mechón *m* (*de pelo*) lock
medall|a *f* medal. **~ón** *m* medallion; (*relicario*) locket
media *f* stocking; (*promedio*) average
mediación *f* mediation
mediado *a* half full; ‹*trabajo etc*› halfway through. **a ~s de marzo** in the middle of March
mediador *m* mediator
medialuna *f* croissant
median|amente *adv* fairly. **~era** *f* party wall. **~ero** *a* ‹*muro*› party. **~a** *f* average circumstances. **~o** *a* average, medium; (*mediocre*) mediocre
medianoche *f* midnight; (*culin*) small sandwich
mediante *prep* through, by means of
mediar *vi* mediate; (*llegar a la mitad*) be halfway (**en** through)
mediatizar [10] *vt* annex
medic|ación *f* medication. **~amento** *m* medicine. **~ina** *f* medicine. **~inal** *a* medicinal. **~inar** *vt* administer medicine
medición *f* measurement
médico *a* medical. ● *m* doctor. **~ de cabecera** GP, general practitioner
medid|a *f* measurement; (*unidad*) measure; (*disposición*) measure, step; (*prudencia*) moderation. **~or** *m* (*LAm*) meter. **a la ~a** made to measure. **a ~a que** as. **en cierta ~a** to a certain point
mediero *m* share-cropper
medieval *a* medieval. **~ista** *m & f* medievalist
medio *a* half (a); (*mediano*) average. **~ litro** half a litre. ● *m* middle; (*manera*) means; (*en deportes*) half(-back). **en ~** in the middle (**de** of). **por ~ de** through
mediocr|e *a* (*mediano*) average; (*de escaso mérito*) mediocre. **~idad** *f* mediocrity
mediodía *m* midday, noon; (*sur*) south
medioevo *m* Middle Ages
Medio Oriente *m* Middle East
medir [5] *vt* medir; weigh up ‹*palabras etc*›. ● *vi* measure, be. **~se** *vpr* (*moderarse*) be moderate
medita|bundo *a* thoughtful. **~ción** *f* meditation. **~r** *vt* think about. ● *vi* meditate
Mediterráneo *m* Mediterranean
mediterráneo *a* Mediterranean
médium *m & f* medium
medrar *vi* thrive
medroso *a* (*con estar*) frightened; (*con ser*) fearful
médula *f* marrow
medusa *f* jellyfish
mefítico *a* noxious
mega... *pref* mega...
megáfono *m* megaphone
megal|ítico *a* megalithic. **~ito** *m* megalith
megal|omanía *f* megalomania. **~ómano** *m* megalomaniac
mejicano *a & m* Mexican
Méjico *m* Mexico
mejido *a* ‹*huevo*› beaten
mejilla *f* cheek
mejillón *m* mussel
mejor *a & adv* (*comparativo*) better; (*superlativo*) best. **~a** *f* improvement. **~able** *a* improvable. **~amiento** *m* improvement. **~ dicho** rather. **a lo ~** perhaps. **tanto ~** so much the better
mejorana *f* marjoram
mejorar *vt* improve, better. ● *vi* get better
mejunje *m* mixture
melanc|olía *f* melancholy. **~ólico** *a* melancholic
melaza *f* molasses, treacle (*Amer*)
melen|a *f* long hair; (*de león*) mane. **~udo** *a* long-haired
melifluo *a* mellifluous
melillense *a* of/from Melilla. ● *m* person from Melilla
melindr|e *m* (*mazapán*) sugared marzipan cake; (*masa frita con miel*) honey fritter. **~oso** *a* affected
melocot|ón *m* peach. **~onero** *m* peach tree
mel|odía *f* melody. **~ódico** *a* melodic. **~odioso** *a* melodious
melodram|a *m* melodrama. **~áticamente** *adv* melodramatically. **~ático** *a* melodramatic
melómano *m* music lover
mel|ón *m* melon; (*bobo*) fool. **~onada** *f* something stupid
meloncillo *m* (*animal*) mongoose
melos|idad *f* sweetness. **~o** *a* sweet

mella *f* notch. **~do** *a* jagged. **~r** *vt* notch
mellizo *a & m* twin
membran|a *f* membrane. **~oso** *a* membranous
membrete *m* letterhead
membrill|ero *m* quince tree. **~o** *m* quince
membrudo *a* burly
memez *f* something silly
memo *a* stupid. ● *m* idiot
memorable *a* memorable
memorando *m*, **memorándum** *m* notebook; (*nota*) memorandum
memoria *f* memory; (*informe*) report; (*tesis*) thesis. **~s** *fpl* (*recuerdos personales*) memoirs. **de ~** from memory
memorial *m* memorial. **~ista** *m* amanuensis
memor|ión *m* good memory. **~ista** *a* having a good memory. **~ístico** *a* memory
mena *f* ore
menaje *m* furnishings
menci|ón *f* mention. **~onado** *a* aforementioned. **~onar** *vt* mention
menda|cidad *f* mendacity. **~z** *a* lying
mendi|cante *a & m* mendicant. **~cidad** *f* begging. **~gar** [12] *vt* beg (for). ● *vi* beg. **~go** *m* beggar
mendrugo *m* (*pan*) hard crust; (*zoquete*) blockhead
mene|ar *vt* move, shake. **~arse** *vpr* move, shake. **~o** *m* movement, shake
menester *m* need. **~oso** *a* needy. **ser ~** be necessary
menestra *f* stew
menestral *m* artesan
mengano *m* so-and-so
mengua *f* decrease; (*falta*) lack; (*descrédito*) discredit. **~do** *a* miserable; (*falto de carácter*) spineless. **~nte** *a* decreasing; ‹*luna*› waning; ‹*marea*› ebb. ● *f* (*del mar*) ebb tide; (*de un río*) low water. **~r** [15] *vt/i* decrease, diminish
meningitis *f* meningitis
menisco *m* meniscus
menjurje *m* mixture
menopausia *f* menopause
menor *a* (*más pequeño, comparativo*) smaller; (*más pequeño, superlativo*) smallest; (*más joven, comparativo*) younger; (*más joven*) youngest; (*mus*) minor. ● *m & f* (*menor de edad*) minor. **al por ~** retail
Menorca *f* Minorca
menorquín *a & m* Minorcan
menos *a* (*comparativo*) less; (*comparativo, con plural*) fewer; (*superlativo*) least; (*superlativo, con plural*) fewest. ● *adv* (*comparativo*) less; (*superlativo*) least. ● *prep* except. **~cabar** *vt* lessen; (*fig, estropear*) damage. **~cabo** *m* lessening. **~preciable** *a* contemptible. **~preciar** *vt* despise. **~precio** *m* contempt. **a ~ que** unless. **al ~** at least. **ni mucho ~** far from it. **por lo ~** at least
mensaje *m* message. **~ro** *m* messenger
menso *a* (*Mex*) stupid
menstru|ación *f* menstruation. **~al** *a* menstrual. **~ar** [21] *vi* menstruate. **~o** *m* menstruation
mensual *a* monthly. **~idad** *f* monthly pay
ménsula *f* bracket
mensurable *a* measurable
menta *f* mint
mental *a* mental. **~idad** *f* mentality. **~mente** *adv* mentally
mentar [1] *vt* mention, name
mente *f* mind
mentecato *a* stupid. ● *m* idiot
mentir [4] *vi* lie. **~a** *f* lie. **~oso** *a* lying. ● *m* liar. **de ~ijillas** for a joke
mentís *m invar* denial
mentol *m* menthol
mentor *m* mentor
menú *m* menu
menudear *vi* happen frequently
menudencia *f* trifle
menudeo *m* retail trade
menudillos *mpl* giblets
menudo *a* tiny; ‹*lluvia*› fine; (*insignificante*) insignificant. **~s** *mpl* giblets. **a ~** often
meñique *a* ‹*dedo*› little. ● *m* little finger
meollo *m* brain; (*médula*) marrow; (*parte blanda*) soft part; (*fig, inteligencia*) brains
meramente *adv* merely
mercachifle *m* hawker; (*fig*) profiteer
mercader *m* (*LAm*) merchant
mercado *m* market. **M~ Común** Common Market. **~ negro** black market
mercan|cía *f* article. **~cías** *fpl* goods, merchandise. **~te** *a & m*

merchant. **~til** *a* mercantile, commercial. **~tilismo** *m* mercantilism
mercar [7] *vt* buy
merced *f* favour. **su/vuestra ~** your honour
mercenario *a & m* mercenary
mercer|ía *f* haberdashery, notions (*Amer*). **~o** *m* haberdasher
mercurial *a* mercurial
Mercurio *m* Mercury
mercurio *m* mercury
merec|edor *a* deserving. **~er** [11] *vt* deserve. ● *vi* be deserving. **~idamente** *adv* deservedly. **~ido** *a* well deserved. **~imiento** *m* (*mérito*) merit
merend|ar [1] vt have as an afternoon snack. ● *vi* have an afternoon snack. **~ero** *m* snack bar; (*lugar*) picnic area
merengue *m* meringue
meretriz *f* prostitute
mergo *m* cormorant
meridian|a *f* (*diván*) couch. **~o** *a* midday; (*fig*) dazzling. ● *m* meridian
meridional *a* southern. ● *m* southerner
merienda *f* afternoon snack
merino *a* merino
mérito *m* merit; (*valor*) worth
meritorio *a* meritorious. ● *m* unpaid trainee
merlo *m* black wrasse
merluza *f* hake
merma *f* decrease. **~r** *vt/i* decrease, reduce
mermelada *f* jam
mero *a* mere; (*Mex, verdadero*) real. ● *adv* (*Mex, precisamente*) exactly; (*Mex, verdaderamente*) really. ● *m* grouper
merode|ador *a* marauding. ● *m* marauder. **~ar** *vi* maraud. **~o** *m* marauding
merovingio *a & m* Merovingian
mes *m* month; (*mensualidad*) monthly pay
mesa *f* table; (*para escribir o estudiar*) desk. **poner la ~** lay the table
mesana *f* (*palo*) mizen-mast
mesarse *vpr* tear at one's hair
mesenterio *m* mesentery
meseta *f* plateau; (*descansillo*) landing
mesiánico *a* Messianic
Mesías *m* Messiah
mesilla *f* small table. **~ de noche** bedside table
mesón *m* inn
mesoner|a *f* landlady. **~o** *m* landlord
mestiz|aje *m* crossbreeding. **~o** *a* ‹*persona*› half-caste; ‹*animal*› cross-bred. ● *m* (*persona*) half-caste; (*animal*) cross-breed
mesura *f* moderation. **~do** *a* moderate
meta *f* goal; (*de una carrera*) finish
metabolismo *m* metabolism
metacarpiano *m* metacarpal
metafísic|a *f* metaphysics. **~o** *a* metaphysical
met|áfora *f* metaphor. **~afórico** *a* metaphorical
met|al *m* metal; (*instrumentos de latón*) brass; (*de la voz*) timbre. **~álico** *a* ‹*objeto*› metal; ‹*sonido*› metallic. **~alizarse** [10] *vpr* (*fig*) become mercenary
metal|urgia *f* metallurgy. **~úrgico** *a* metallurgical
metam|órfico *a* metamorphic. **~orfosear** *vt* transform. **~orfosis** *f* metamorphosis
metano *m* methane
metatarsiano *m* metatarsal
metátesis *f invar* metathesis
metedura *f*. **~ de pata** blunder
mete|órico *a* meteoric. **~orito** *m* meteorite. **~oro** *m* meteor. **~orología** *f* meteorology. **~orológico** meteorological. **~orólogo** *m* meteorologist
meter *vt* put, place; (*ingresar*) deposit; score ‹*un gol*›; (*enredar*) involve; (*causar*) make. **~se** *vpr* get; (*entrometerse*) meddle. **~se con uno** pick a quarrel with s.o.
meticulos|idad *f* meticulousness. **~o** *a* meticulous
metido *m* reprimand. ● *a*. **~ en años** getting on. **estar muy ~ con uno** be well in with s.o.
metilo *m* methyl
metódico *a* methodical
metodis|mo *m* Methodism. **~ta** *a & m & f* Methodist
método *m* method
metodología *f* methodology
metomentodo *m* busybody
metraje *m* length. **de largo ~** ‹*película*› feature
metrall|a *f* shrapnel. **~eta** *f* submachine gun
métric|a *f* metrics. **~o** *a* metric; ‹*verso*› metrical

metro *m* metre; (*tren*) underground, subway (*Amer*). ~ **cuadrado** cubic metre
metrónomo *m* metronome
metr|ópoli *f* metropolis. **~opolitano** *a* metropolitan. ● *m* metropolitan; (*tren*) underground, subway (*Amer*)
mexicano *a* & *m* (*LAm*) Mexican
México *m* (*LAm*) Mexico. ~ **D. F.** Mexico City
mezcal *m* (*Mex*) (type of) brandy
mezc|la *f* (*acción*) mixing; (*substancia*) mixture; (*argamasa*) mortar. **~lador** *m* mixer. **~lar** *vt* mix; shuffle ‹*los naipes*›. **~larse** *vpr* mix; (*intervenir*) interfere. **~olanza** *f* mixture
mezquin|dad *f* meanness. **~o** *a* mean; (*escaso*) meagre. ● *m* mean person
mezquita *f* mosque
mi *a* my. ● *m* (*mus*) E; (*solfa*) mi
mí *pron* me
miaja *f* crumb
miasma *m* miasma
miau *m* miaow
mica *f* (*silicato*) mica; (*Mex*, *embriaguez*) drunkenness
mico *m* (long-tailed) monkey
micro... *pref* micro...
microbio *m* microbe
micro: **~biología** *f* microbiology. **~cosmo** *m* microcosm. **~film(e)** *m* microfilm
micrófono *m* microphone
micrómetro *m* micrometer
microonda *f* microwave. **horno** *m* **de ~s** microwave oven
microordenador *m* microcomputer
microsc|ópico *a* microscopic. **~opio** *m* microscope
micro: **~surco** *m* long-playing record. **~taxi** *m* minicab
miedo *m* fear. **~so** *a* fearful. **dar ~** frighten. **morirse de ~** be scared to death. **tener ~** be frightened
miel *f* honey
mielga *f* lucerne, alfalfa (*Amer*)
miembro *m* limb; (*persona*) member
mientras *conj* while. ● *adv* meanwhile. **~ que** whereas. **~ tanto** in the meantime
miércoles *m* Wednesday. **~ de ceniza** Ash Wednesday
mierda *f* (*vulgar*) shit
mies *f* corn, grain (*Amer*)
miga *f* crumb; (*fig*, *meollo*) essence. **~jas** *fpl* crumbs. **~r** [12] *vt* crumble
migra|ción *f* migration. **~torio** *a* migratory
mijo *m* millet
mil *a* & *m* a/one thousand. **~es de** thousands of. **~ novecientos noventa y dos** nineteen ninety-two. **~ pesetas** a thousand pesetas
milagro *m* miracle. **~so** *a* miraculous
milano *m* kite
mildeu *m*, **mildiu** *m* mildew
milen|ario *a* millenial. **~io** *m* millennium
milenrama *f* milfoil
milésimo *a* & m thousandth
mili *f* (*fam*) military service
milicia *f* soldiering; (*gente armada*) militia
mili|gramo *m* milligram. **~litro** *m* millilitre
milímetro *m* millimetre
militante *a* militant
militar *a* military. ● *m* soldier. **~ismo** *m* militarism. **~ista** *a* militaristic. ● *m* & *f* militarist. **~izar** [10] *vt* militarize
milonga *f* (*Arg*, *canción*) popular song; (*Arg*, *baile*) popular dance
milord *m*. **vivir como un ~** live like a lord
milpies *m invar* woodlouse
milla *f* mile
millar *m* thousand. **a ~es** by the thousand
mill|ón *m* million. **~onada** *f* fortune. **~onario** *m* millionaire. **~onésimo** *a* & *m* millionth. **un ~n de libros** a million books
mimar *vt* spoil
mimbre *m* & *f* wicker. **~arse** *vpr* sway. **~ra** *f* osier. **~ral** *m* osier-bed
mimetismo *m* mimicry
mímic|a *f* mime. **~o** *a* mimic
mimo *m* mime; (*a un niño*) spoiling; (*caricia*) caress
mimosa *f* mimosa
mina *f* mine. **~r** *vt* mine; (*fig*) undermine
minarete *m* minaret
mineral *m* mineral; (*mena*) ore. **~ogía** *f* mineralogy. **~ogista** *m* & *f* mineralogist
miner|ía *f* mining. **~o** *a* mining. ● *m* miner
mini... *pref* mini...
miniar *vt* paint in miniature
miniatura *f* miniature
minifundio *m* smallholding
minimizar [10] *vt* minimize

mínim|o *a & m* minimum. **~um** *m* minimum
minino *m* (*fam*) cat, puss (*fam*)
minio *m* red lead
minist|erial *a* ministerial. **~erio** *m* ministry. **~ro** *m* minister
minor|ación *f* diminution. **~a** *f* minority. **~idad** *f* minority. **~ista** *m & f* retailer
minuci|a *f* trifle. **~osidad** *f* thoroughness. **~oso** *a* thorough; (*con muchos detalles*) detailed
minué *m* minuet
minúscul|a *f* small letter, lower case letter. **~o** *a* tiny
minuta *f* draft; (*menú*) menu
minut|ero *m* minute hand. **~o** *m* minute
mío *a & pron* mine. **un amigo ~** a friend of mine
miop|e *a* short-sighted. ● *m & f* short-sighted person. **~ía** *f* short-sightedness
mira *f* sight; (*fig, intención*) aim. **~da** *f* look. **~do** *a* thought of; (*comedido*) considerate; (*cirunspecto*) circumspect. **~dor** *m* windowed balcony; (*lugar*) viewpoint. **~miento** *m* consideration. **~r** *vt* look at; (*observar*) watch; (*considerar*) consider. **~r fijamente a** stare at. ● *vi* look; ‹*edificio etc*› face. **~rse** *vpr* ‹*personas*› look at each other. **a la ~** on the lookout. **con ~s a** with a view to. **echar una ~da a** glance at
mirilla *f* peephole
miriñaque *m* crinoline
mirlo *m* blackbird
mirón *a* nosey. ● *m* nosey-parker; (*espectador*) onlooker
mirra *f* myrrh
mirto *m* myrtle
misa *f* mass
misal *m* missal
mis|antropía *f* misanthropy. **~antrópico** *a* misanthropic. **~ántropo** *m* misanthropist
miscelánea *f* miscellany; (*Mex, tienda*) corner shop
miser|able *a* very poor; (*lastimoso*) miserable; (*tacaño*) mean. **~ia** *f* extreme poverty; (*suciedad*) squalor
misericordi|a *f* pity; (*piedad*) mercy. **~oso** *a* merciful
mísero *a* very poor; (*lastimoso*) miserable; (*tacaño*) mean
misil *m* missile
misi|ón *f* mission. **~onal** *a* missionary. **~onero** *m* missionary
misiva *f* missive
mism|amente *adv* just. **~ísimo** *a* very same. **~o** *a* same; (*después de pronombre personal*) myself, yourself, himself, herself, itself, ourselves, yourselves, themselves; (enfático) very. ● *adv* right. **ahora ~** right now. **aquí ~** right here
mis|oginia *f* misogyny. **~ógino** *m* misogynist
misterio *m* mystery. **~so** *a* mysterious
místic|a *f* mysticism. **~o** *a* mystical
mistifica|ción *f* falsification; (*engaño*) trick. **~r** [7] vt falsify; (*engañar*) deceive
mitad *f* half; (*centro*) middle
mítico *a* mythical
mitiga|ción *f* mitigation. **~r** [12] *vt* mitigate; quench ‹*sed*›; relieve ‹*dolor etc*›
mitin *m* meeting
mito *m* myth. **~logía** *f* mythology. **~lógico** *a* mythological
mitón *m* mitten
mitote *m* (*LAm*) Indian dance
mitra *f* mitre. **~do** *m* prelate
mixteca *f* (*Mex*) southern Mexico
mixt|o *a* mixed. ● *m* passenger and goods train; (*cerilla*) match. **~ura** *f* mixture
mnemotécnic|a *f* mnemonics. **~o** *a* mnemonic
moaré *m* moiré
mobiliario *m* furniture
moblaje *m* furniture
moca *m* mocha
moce|dad *f* youth. **~ro** *m* young people. **~tón** *m* strapping lad
moción *f* motion
moco *m* mucus
mochales *a invar*. **estar ~** be round the bend
mochila *f* rucksack
mocho *a* blunt. ● *m* butt end
mochuelo *m* little owl
moda *f* fashion. **~l** *a* modal. **~les** *mpl* manners. **~lidad** *f* kind. **de ~** in fashion
model|ado *m* modelling. **~ador** *m* modeller. **~ar** *vt* model; (*fig, configurar*) form. **~o** *m* model
modera|ción *f* moderation. **~do** *a* moderate. **~r** *vt* moderate; reduce ‹*velocidad*›. **~rse** *vpr* control oneself

modern|amente *adv* recently. **~idad** *f* modernity. **~ismo** *m* modernism. **~ista** *m & f* modernist. **~izar** [10] *vt* modernize. **~o** *a* modern
modest|ia *f* modesty. **~o** *a* modest
modicidad *f* reasonableness
módico *a* moderate
modifica|ción *f* modification. **~r** [7] *vt* modify
modismo *m* idiom
modist|a *f* dressmaker. **~o** *m & f* designer
modo *m* manner, way; (*gram*) mood; (*mus*) mode. **~ de ser** character. **de ~ que** so that. **de ningún ~** certainly not. **de todos ~s** anyhow
modorr|a *f* drowsiness. **~o** *a* drowsy
modoso *a* well-behaved
modula|ción *f* modulation. **~dor** *m* modulator. **~r** *vt* modulate
módulo *m* module
mofa *f* mockery. **~rse** *vpr*. **~rse de** make fun of
mofeta *f* skunk
moflet|e *m* chubby cheek. **~udo** *a* with chubby cheeks
mogol *m* Mongol. **el Gran M~** the Great Mogul
moh|ín *m* grimace. **~ino** *a* sulky. **hacer un ~ín** pull a face
moho *m* mould; (*óxido*) rust. **~so** *a* mouldy; ‹*metales*› rusty
moisés *m* Moses basket
mojado *a* damp, wet
mojama *f* salted tuna
mojar *vt* wet; (*empapar*) soak; (*humedecer*) moisten, dampen. ● *vi*. **~ en** get involved in
mojicón *m* blow in the face; (*bizcocho*) sponge cake
mojiganga *f* masked ball; (*en el teatro*) farce
mojigat|ería *f* hypocrisy. **~o** *m* hypocrite
mojón *m* boundary post; (*señal*) signpost
molar *m* molar
mold|e *m* mould; (*aguja*) knitting needle. **~ear** *vt* mould, shape; (*fig*) form. **~ura** *f* moulding
mole *f* mass, bulk. ● *m* (*Mex, guisado*) (Mexican) stew with chili sauce
mol|écula *f* molecule. **~ecular** *a* molecular
mole|dor *a* grinding. ● *m* grinder; (*persona*) bore. **~r** [2] grind; (*hacer polvo*) pulverize
molest|ar *vt* annoy; (*incomodar*) bother. **¿le ~a que fume?** do you mind if I smoke? **no ~ar** do not disturb. ● *vi* be a nuisance. **~arse** *vpr* bother; (*ofenderse*) take offence. **~ia** *f* bother, nuisance; (*inconveniente*) inconvenience; (*incomodidad*) discomfort. **~o** *a* annoying; (*inconveniente*) inconvenient; (*ofendido*) offended
molicie *f* softness; (*excesiva comodidad*) easy life
molido *a* ground; (*fig, muy cansado*) worn out
molienda *f* grinding
molin|ero *m* miller. **~ete** *m* toy windmill. **~illo** *m* mill; (*juguete*) toy windmill. **~o** *m* (water) mill. **~o de viento** windmill
molusco *m* mollusc
mollar *a* soft
molleja *f* gizzard
mollera *f* (*de la cabeza*) crown; (*fig, sesera*) brains
moment|áneamente *adv* momentarily; (*por el momento*) right now. **~áneo** *a* momentary. **~o** *m* moment; (*mecánica*) momentum
momi|a *f* mummy. **~ficación** *f* mummification. **~ficar** [7] *vt* mummify. **~ficarse** *vpr* become mummified
momio *a* lean. ● *m* bargain; (*trabajo*) cushy job
monaca|l *a* monastic. **~to** *m* monasticism
monada *f* beautiful thing; (*de un niño*) charming way; (*acción tonta*) silliness
monaguillo *m* altar boy
mon|arca *m & f* monarch. **~arquía** *f* monarchy. **~árquico** *a* monarchic(al). **~arquismo** *m* monarchism
mon|asterio *m* monastery. **~ástico** *a* monastic
monda *f* pruning; (*peladura*) peel
mond|adientes *m invar* toothpick. **~adura** *f* pruning; (*peladura*) peel. **~ar** *vt* peel ‹*fruta etc*›; dredge ‹*un río*›. **~o** *a* (*sin pelo*) bald; (*sin dinero*) broke; (*sencillo*) plain
mondongo *m* innards
moned|a *f* coin; (*de un país*) currency. **~ero** *m* minter; (*portamonedas*) purse

monetario *a* monetary
mongol *a & m* Mongolian
mongolismo *m* Down's syndrome
monigote *m* weak character; (*muñeca*) rag doll; (*dibujo*) doodle
monises *mpl* money, dough (*fam*)
monitor *m* monitor
monj|a *f* nun. **~e** *m* monk. **~il** *a* nun's; (*como de monja*) like a nun
mono *m* monkey; (*sobretodo*) overalls. ● *a* pretty
mono... *pref* mono...
monocromo *a & m* monochrome
monóculo *m* monocle
mon|ogamia *f* monogamy. **~ógamo** *a* monogamous
monografía *f* monograph
monograma *m* monogram
monol|ítico *a* monolithic. **~ito** *m* monolith
mon|ologar [12] *vi* soliloquize. **~ólogo** *m* monologue
monoman|ía *f* monomania. **~iaco** *m* monomaniac
monoplano *m* monoplane
monopoli|o *m* monopoly. **~zar** [10] *vt* monopolize
monos|ilábico *a* monosyllabic. **~ílabo** *m* monosyllable
monoteís|mo *m* monotheism. **~ta** *a* monotheistic. ● *m & f* monotheist
mon|otonía *f* monotony. **~ótono** *a* monotonous
monseñor *m* monsignor
monserga *f* boring talk
monstruo *m* monster. **~sidad** *f* monstrosity. **~so** *a* monstrous
monta *f* mounting; (*valor*) value
montacargas *m invar* service lift
monta|do *a* mounted. **~dor** *m* fitter. **~je** *m* assembly; (*cine*) montage; (*teatro*) staging, production
montañ|a *f* mountain. **~ero** *a* mountaineer. **~és** *a* mountain. ● *m* highlander. **~ismo** *m* mountaineering. **~oso** *a* mountainous. **~a rusa** big dipper
montaplatos *m invar* service lift
montar *vt* ride; (*subirse*) get on; (*ensamblar*) assemble; cock ‹*arma*›; set up ‹*una casa, un negocio*›. ● *vi* ride; (*subirse a*) mount. **~ a caballo** ride a horse
montaraz *a* ‹*animales*› wild; ‹*personas*› mountain
monte *m* (*montaña*) mountain; (*terreno inculto*) scrub; (*bosque*) forest. **~ de piedad** pawn-shop. **ingeniero** *m* **de ~s** forestry expert
montepío *m* charitable fund for dependents
monter|a *f* cloth cap. **~o** *m* hunter
montés *a* wild
Montevideo *m* Montevideo
montevideano *a &* m Montevidean
montículo *m* hillock
montón *m* heap, pile. **a montones** in abundance, lots of
montuoso *a* hilly
montura *f* mount; (*silla*) saddle
monument|al *a* monumental; (*fig, muy grande*) enormous. **~o** *m* monument
monzón *m & f* monsoon
moñ|a *f* hair ribbon. **~o** *m* bun
moque|o *m* runny nose. **~ro** *m* handkerchief
moqueta *f* fitted carpet
moquillo *m* distemper
mora *f* mulberry; (*zarzamora*) blackberry
morada *f* dwelling
morado *a* purple
morador *m* inhabitant
moral *m* mulberry tree. ● *f* morals. ● *a* moral. **~eja** *f* moral. **~idad** *f* morality. **~ista** *m & f* moralist. **~izador** *a* moralizing. ● *m* moralist. **~izar** [10] *vt* moralize
morapio *m* (*fam*) cheap red wine
morar *vi* live
moratoria *f* moratorium
morbidez *f* softness
mórbido *a* soft; (*malsano*) morbid
morbo *m* illness. **~sidad** *f* morbidity. **~so** *a* unhealthy
morcilla *f* black pudding
morda|cidad *f* bite. **~z** *a* biting
mordaza *f* gag
mordazmente *adv* bitingly
morde|dura *f* bite. **~r** [2] *vt* bite; (*fig, quitar porciones a*) eat into; (*denigrar*) gossip about. ● *vi* bite
mordis|car [7] *vt* nibble (at). ● *vi* nibble. **~co** *m* bite. **~quear** *vt* nibble (at)
morelense *a* (*Mex*) from Morelos. ● *m & f* person from Morelos
morena *f* (*geol*) moraine
moreno *a* dark; (*de pelo obscuro*) dark-haired; (*de raza negra*) negro
morera *f* mulberry tree
morería *f* Moorish lands; (*barrio*) Moorish quarter
moretón *m* bruise
morfema *m* morpheme
morfin|a *f* morphine. **~ómano** *a* morphine. ● *m* morphine addict

morfol|ogía *f* morphology. **~ógico** *a* morphological
moribundo *a* moribund
morillo *m* andiron
morir [6] (*pp* **muerto**) *vi* die; (*fig, extinguirse*) die away; (*fig, terminar*) end. **~se** *vpr* die. **~se de hambre** starve to death; (*fig*) be starving. **se muere por una flauta** she's dying to have a flute
moris|co *a* Moorish. ● *m* Moor. **~ma** *f* Moors
morm|ón *m* & *f* Mormon. **~ónico** *a* Mormon. **~onismo** *m* Mormonism
moro *a* Moorish. ● *m* Moor
moros|idad *f* dilatoriness. **~o** *a* dilatory
morrada *f* butt; (*puñetazo*) punch
morral *m* (*mochila*) rucksack; (*del cazador*) gamebag; (*para caballos*) nosebag
morralla *f* rubbish
morrillo *m* nape of the neck
morriña *f* homesickness
morro *m* snout
morrocotudo *a* (*esp Mex*) (*fam*) terrific (*fam*)
morsa *f* walrus
mortaja *f* shroud
mortal *a* & *m* & *f* mortal. **~idad** *f* mortality. **~mente** *adv* mortally
mortandad *f* death toll
mortecino *a* failing; ‹*color*› faded
mortero *m* mortar
mortífero *a* deadly
mortifica|ción *f* mortification. **~r** [7] *vt* (*med*) damage; (*atormentar*) plague; (*humillar*) humiliate. **~rse** *vpr* (*Mex*) feel embarassed
mortuorio *a* death
morueco *m* ram
moruno *a* Moorish
mosaico *a* of Moses, Mosaic. ● *m* mosaic
mosca *f* fly. **~rda** *f* blowfly. **~rdón** *m* botfly; (*mosca de cuerpo azul*) bluebottle
moscatel *a* muscatel
moscón *m* botfly; (*mosca de cuerpo azul*) bluebottle
moscovita *a* & *m* & *f* Muscovite
Moscú *m* Moscow
mosque|arse *vpr* get cross. **~o** *m* resentment
mosquete *m* musket. **~ro** *m* musketeer
mosquit|ero *m* mosquito net. **~o** *m* mosquito; (*mosca pequeña*) fly, gnat
mostacho *m* moustache
mostachón *m* macaroon
mostaza *f* mustard
mosto *m* must
mostrador *m* counter
mostrar [2] *vt* show. **~se** *vpr* (show oneself to) be. **se mostró muy amable** he was very kind
mostrenco *a* ownerless; ‹*animal*› stray; (*torpe*) thick; (*gordo*) fat
mota *f* spot, speck
mote *m* nickname; (*lema*) motto
motea|do *a* speckled. **~r** *vt* speckle
motejar *vt* call
motel *m* motel
motete *m* motet
motín *m* riot; (*rebelión*) uprising; (*de tropas*) mutiny
motiv|ación *f* motivation. **~ar** *vt* motivate; (*explicar*) explain. **~o** *m* reason. **con ~o de** because of
motocicl|eta *f* motor cycle, motor bike (*fam*). **~ista** *m* & *f* motorcyclist
motón *m* pulley
motonave *f* motor boat
motor *a* motor. ● *m* motor, engine. **~a** *f* motor boat. **~ de arranque** starter motor
motoris|mo *m* motorcycling. **~ta** *m* & *f* motorist; (*de una moto*) motorcyclist
motorizar [10] *vt* motorize
motriz *af* motive, driving
move|dizo *a* movable; (*poco firme*) unstable; ‹*persona*› fickle. **~r** [2] *vt* move; shake ‹*la cabeza*›; (*provocar*) cause. **~rse** *vpr* move; (*darse prisa*) hurry up. **arenas** *fpl* **~dizas** quicksand
movi|ble *a* movable. **~do** *a* moved; (*foto*) blurred; (*inquieto*) fidgety
móvil *a* movable. ● *m* motive
movili|dad *f* mobility. **~zación** *f* mobilization. **~zar** [10] *vt* mobilize
movimiento *m* movement, motion; (*agitación*) bustle
moza *f* girl; (*sirvienta*) servant, maid. **~lbete** *m* young lad
mozárabe *a* Mozarabic. ● *m* & *f* Mozarab
moz|o *m* boy, lad. **~uela** *f* young girl. **~uelo** *m* young boy/lad
muaré *m* moiré
mucam|a *f* (*Arg*) servant. **~o** *m* (*Arg*) servant
mucos|idad *f* mucus. **~o** *a* mucous
muchach|a *f* girl; (*sirvienta*) servant, maid. **~o** *m* boy, lad; (*criado*) servant

muchedumbre *f* crowd
muchísimo *a* very much. ● *adv* a lot
mucho *a* much (*pl* **many),** a lot of. ● *pron* a lot; (*personas*) many (people). ● *adv* a lot, very much; (*de tiempo*) long, a long time. **ni ~ menos** by no means. **por ~ que** however much
muda *f* change of clothing; (*de animales*) moult. **~ble** *a* changeable; ‹*personas*› fickle. **~nza** *f* change; (*de casa*) removal. **~r** *vt/i* change. **~rse** (*de ropa*) change one's clothes; (*de casa*) move (house)
mudéjar *a & m & f* Mudéjar
mud|ez *f* dumbness. **~o** *a* dumb; (*callado*) silent
mueble *a* movable. ● *m* piece of furniture
mueca *f* grimace, face. **hacer una ~** pull a face
muela *f* (*diente*) tooth; (*diente molar*) molar; (*piedra de afilar*) grindstone; (*piedra de molino*) millstone
muelle *a* soft. ● *m* spring; (*naut*) wharf; (*malecón*) jetty
muérdago *m* mistletoe
muero *vb véase* **morir**
muert|e *f* death; (*homicidio*) murder. **~o** *a* dead; (*matado, fam*) killed; ‹*colores*› pale. ● *m* dead person; (*cadáver*) body, corpse
muesca *f* nick; (*ranura*) slot
muestra *f* sample; (*prueba*) proof; (*modelo*) model; (*seal*) sign. **~rio** *m* collection of samples
muestro *vb véase* **mostrar**
muevo *vb véase* **mover**
mugi|do *m* moo. **~r** [14] *vi* moo; (*fig*) roar
mugr|e *m* dirt. **~iento** *a* dirty, filthy
mugrón *m* sucker
muguete *m* lily of the valley
mujer *f* woman; (*esposa*) wife. ● *int* my dear! **~iego** *a* ‹*hombre*› fond of the women. **~il** *a* womanly. **~ío** *m* (crowd of) women. **~zuela** *f* prostitute
mújol *m* mullet
mula *f* mule; (*Mex*) unsaleable goods. **~da** *f* drove of mules
mulato *a & m* mulatto
mulero *m* muleteer
mulet|a *f* crutch; (*fig*) support; (*toreo*) stick with a red flag
mulo *m* mule
multa *f* fine. **~r** *vt* fine
multi... *pref* multi...
multicolor *a* multicolour(ed)
multicopista *m* copying machine
multiforme *a* multiform
multilateral *a* multilateral
multilingüe *a* multilingual
multimillonario *m* multimillionaire
múltiple *a* multiple
multiplic|ación *f* multiplication. **~ar** [7] *vt* multiply. **~arse** *vpr* multiply; (*fig*) go out of one's way. **~idad** *f* multiplicity
múltiplo *a & m* multiple
multitud *f* multitude, crowd. **~inario** *a* multitudinous
mulli|do *a* soft. ● *m* stuffing. **~r** [22] *vt* soften
mund|ano *a* wordly; (*de la sociedad elegante*) society. ● *m* socialite. **~ial** *a* world-wide. **la segunda guerra ~ial** the Second World War. **~illo** *m* world, circles. **~o** *m* world. **~ología** *f* worldly wisdom. **todo el ~o** everybody
munición *f* ammunition; (*provisiones*) supplies
municip|al *a* municipal. **~alidad** *f* municipality. **~io** *m* municipality; (*ayuntamiento*) town council
mun|ificencia *f* munificence. **~ífico** *a* munificent
muñe|ca *f* (*anat*) wrist; (*juguete*) doll; (*maniquí*) dummy. **~co** *m* boy doll. **~quera** *f* wristband
muñón *m* stump
mura|l *a* mural, wall. ● *m* mural. **~lla** *f* (city) wall. **~r** *vt* wall
murciélago *m* bat
murga *f* street band; (*lata*) bore, nuisance. **dar la ~** bother, be a pain (*fam*)
murmullo *m* (*de personas*) whisper(ing), murmur(ing); (*del agua*) rippling; (*del viento*) sighing, rustle
murmura|ción *f* gossip. **~dor** *a* gossiping. ● *m* gossip. **~r** *vi* murmur; (*hablar en voz baja*) whisper; (*quejarse en voz baja*) mutter; (*criticar*) gossip
muro *m* wall
murri|a *f* depression. **~o** *a* depressed
mus *m* card game
musa *f* muse
musaraña *f* shrew
muscula|r *a* muscular. **~tura** *f* muscles
músculo *m* muscle
musculoso *a* muscular
muselina *f* muslin

museo *m* museum. **~ de arte** art gallery
musgaño *m* shrew
musgo *m* moss. **~so** *a* mossy
música *f* music
musical *a & m* musical
músico *a* musical. ● *m* musician
music|ología *f* musicology. **~ólogo** *m* musicologist
musitar *vt/i* mumble
muslímico *a* Muslim
muslo *m* thigh
mustela *a* weasel
musti|arse *vpr* wither, wilt. **~o** *a* ‹*plantas*› withered; ‹*cosas*› faded; ‹*personas*› gloomy; (*Mex, hipócrita*) hypocritical
musulmán *a & m* Muslim
muta|bilidad *f* mutability. **~ción** *f* change; (*en biología*) mutation
mutila|ción *f* mutilation. **~do** *a* crippled. ● *m* cripple. **~r** *vt* mutilate; cripple, maim ‹*persona*›
mutis *m* (*en el teatro*) exit. **~mo** *m* silence
mutu|alidad *f* mutuality; (*asociación*) friendly society. **~amente** *adv* mutually. **~o** *a* mutual
muy *adv* very; (*demasiado*) too

N

nab|a *f* swede. **~o** *m* turnip
nácar *m* mother-of-pearl
nac|er [11] *vi* be born; ‹*huevo*› hatch; ‹*planta*› sprout. **~ido** *a* born. **~iente** *a* ‹*sol*› rising. **~imiento** *m* birth; (*de río*) source; (*belén*) crib. **dar ~imiento a** give rise to. **lugar** *m* **de ~imiento** place of birth. **recien ~ido** newborn. **volver a ~er** have a narrow escape
naci|ón *f* nation. **~onal** *a* national. **~onalidad** *f* nationality. **~onalismo** *m* nationalism. **~onalista** *m & f* nationalist. **~onalizar** [10] *vt* nationalize. **~onalizarse** *vpr* become naturalized
nada *pron* nothing, not anything. ● *adv* not at all. **¡~ de eso!** nothing of the sort! **antes de ~** first of all. **¡de ~!** (*después de 'gracias'*) don't mention it! **para ~** (not) at all. **por ~ del mundo** not for anything in the world
nada|dor *m* swimmer. **~r** *vi* swim
nadería *f* trifle
nadie *pron* no one, nobody
nado *adv*. **a ~** swimming
nafta *f* (*LAm, gasolina*) petrol, (*Brit*), gas (*Amer*)
nailon *m* nylon
naipe *m* (playing) card. **juegos** *mpl* **de ~s** card games
nalga *f* buttock. **~s** *fpl* bottom
nana *f* lullaby
Nápoles *m* Naples
naranj|a *f* orange. **~ada** *f* orangeade. **~al** *m* orange grove. **~o** *m* orange tree
narcótico *a & m* narcotic
nariz *f* nose; (*orificio de la nariz*) nostril. **¡narices!** rubbish!
narra|ción *f* narration. **~dor** *m* narrator. **~r** *vt* tell. **~tivo** *a* narrative
nasal *a* nasal
nata *f* cream
natación *f* swimming
natal *a* birth; ‹*pueblo etc*› home. **~idad** *f* birth rate
natillas *fpl* custard
natividad *f* nativity
nativo *a & m* native
nato *a* born
natural *a* natural. ● *m* native. **~eza** *f* nature; (*nacionalidad*) nationality; (*ciudadanía*) naturalization. **~eza muerta** still life. **~idad** *f* naturalness. **~ista** *m & f* naturalist. **~izar** [10] *vt* naturalize. **~izarse** *vpr* become naturalized. **~mente** *adv* naturally. ● *int* of course!
naufrag|ar [12] *vi* ‹*barco*› sink; ‹*persona*› be shipwrecked; (*fig*) fail. **~io** *m* shipwreck
náufrago *a* shipwrecked. ● *m* shipwrecked person
náusea *f* nausea. **dar ~s a uno** make s.o. feel sick. **sentir ~s** feel sick
nauseabundo *a* sickening
náutico *a* nautical
navaja *f* penknife; (*de afeitar*) razor. **~zo** *m* slash
naval *a* naval
Navarra *f* Navarre
nave *f* ship; (*de iglesia*) nave. **~ espacial** spaceship. **quemar las ~s** burn one's boats
navega|ble *a* navigable; ‹*barco*› seaworthy. **~ción** *f* navigation. **~nte** *m & f* navigator. **~r** [12] *vi* sail; ‹*avión*› fly
Navid|ad *f* Christmas. **~eño** *a* Christmas. **en ~ades** at Christmas. **¡feliz ~ad!** Happy Christmas! **por ~ad** at Christmas

navío *m* ship
nazi *a & m & f* Nazi
neblina *f* mist
nebuloso *a* misty; (*fig*) vague
necedad *f* foolishness. **decir ~es** talk nonsense. **hacer una ~** do sth stupid
necesari|amente *adv* necessarily. **~o** *a* necessary
necesi|dad *f* necessity; (*pobreza*) poverty. **~dades** *fpl* hardships. **por ~dad** (out) of necessity. **~tado** *a* in need (**de** of); (*pobre*) needy. **~tar** *vt* need. ● *vi*. **~tar de** need
necio *a* silly. ● *m* idiot
necrología *f* obituary column
néctar *m* nectar
nectarina *f* nectarine
nefasto *a* unfortunate, ominous
nega|ción *f* negation; (*desmentimiento*) denial; (*gram*) negative. **~do** *a* incompetent. **~r** [1 & 12] *vt* deny; (*rehusar*) refuse. **~rse** *vpr*. **~rse a** refuse. **~tiva** *f* negative; (*acción*) denial; (*acción de rehusar*) refusal. **~tivo** *a & m* negative
negligen|cia *f* negligence. **~te** *a* negligent
negoci|able *a* negotiable. **~ación** *f* negotiation. **~ante** *m & f* dealer. **~ar** *vt/i* negotiate. **~ar en** trade in. **~o** *m* business; (*com, trato*) deal. **~os** *mpl* business. **hombre** *m* **de ~os** businessman
negr|a *f* Negress; (*mus*) crotchet. **~o** *a* black; ‹*persona*› Negro. ● *m* (*color*) black; (*persona*) Negro. **~ura** *f* blackness. **~uzco** *a* blackish
nene *m & f* baby, child
nenúfar *m* water lily
neo... *pref* neo...
neocelandés *a* from New Zealand. ● *m* New Zealander
neolítico *a* Neolithic
neón *m* neon
nepotismo *m* nepotism
nervio *m* nerve; (*tendón*) sinew; (*bot*) vein. **~sidad** *f*, **~sismo** *m* nervousness; (*impaciencia*) impatience. **~so** *a* nervous; (*de temperamento*) highly-strung. **crispar los ~s a uno** (*fam*) get on s.o.'s nerves. **ponerse ~so** get excited
neto *a* clear; ‹*verdad*› simple; (*com*) net
neumático *a* pneumatic. ● *m* tyre
neumonía *f* pneumonia
neuralgia *f* neuralgia
neur|ología *f* neurolgy. **~ólogo** *m* neurologist
neur|osis *f* neurosis. **~ótico** *a* neurotic
neutr|al *a* neutral. **~alidad** *f* neutrality. **~alizar** [10] *vt* neutralize. **~o** *a* neutral; (*gram*) neuter
neutrón *m* neutron
neva|da *f* snowfall. **~r** [1] *vi* snow. **~sca** *f* blizzard
nevera *f* fridge (*Brit, fam*), refrigerator
nevisca *f* light snowfall. **~r** [7] *vi* snow lightly
nexo *m* link
ni *conj* nor, neither; (*ni siquiera*) not even. **~... ~** neither... nor. **~ que** as if. **~ siquiera** not even
Nicaragua *f* Nicaragua
nicaragüense *a & m & f* Nicaraguan
nicotina *f* nicotine
nicho *m* niche
nido *m* nest; (*de ladrones*) den; (*escondrijo*) hiding-place
niebla *f* fog; (*neblina*) mist. **hay ~** it's foggy
niet|a *f* granddaughter. **~o** *m* grandson. **~os** *mpl* grandchildren
nieve *f* snow; (*LAm, helado*) ice-cream
Nigeria *f* Nigeria. **~no** *a* Nigerian
niki *m* T-shirt
nilón *m* nylon
nimbo *m* halo
nimi|edad *f* triviality. **~o** *a* insignificant
ninfa *f* nymph
ninfea *f* water lily
ningún *véase* **ninguno**
ninguno *a* (*delante de nombre masculino en singular* **ningún**) no, not any. ● *pron* none; (*persona*) no-one, nobody; (*de dos*) neither. **de ninguna manera, de ningún modo** by no means. **en ninguna parte** nowhere
niñ|a *f* (little) girl. **~ada** *f* childish thing. **~era** *f* nanny. **~ería** *f* childish thing. **~ez** *f* childhood. **~o** *a* childish. ● *m* (little) boy. **de ~o** as a child. **desde ~o** from childhood
níquel *m* nickel
níspero *m* medlar
nitidez *f* clearness
nítido *a* clear; (*foto*) sharp
nitrato *m* nitrate
nítrico *a* nitric
nitrógeno *m* nitrogen

nivel *m* level; (*fig*) standard. **~ar** *vt* level. **~arse** *vpr* become level. **~ de vida** standard of living

no *adv* not; (*como respuesta*) no. **¿~?** isn't it? **~ más** only. **¡a que ~!** I bet you don't! **¡cómo ~!** of course! **Felipe ~ tiene hijos** Felipe has no children. **¡que ~!** certainly not!

nob|iliario *a* noble. **~le** *a & m & f* noble. **~leza** *f* nobility

noción *f* notion. **nociones** *fpl* rudiments

nocivo *a* harmful

nocturno *a* nocturnal; ‹*clase*› evening; ‹*tren etc*› night. ● *m* nocturne

noche *f* night. **~ vieja** New Year's Eve. **de ~** at night. **hacer ~** spend the night. **media ~** midnight. **por la ~** at night

Nochebuena *f* Christmas Eve

nodo *m* (*Esp, película*) newsreel

nodriza *f* nanny

nódulo *m* nodule

nogal *m* walnut(-tree)

nómada *a* nomadic. ● *m & f* nomad

nombr|adía *f* fame. **~ado** *a* famous; (*susodicho*) aforementioned. **~amiento** *m* appointment. **~ar** *vt* appoint; (*citar*) mention. **~e** *m* name; (*gram*) noun; (*fama*) renown. **~e de pila** Christian name. **en ~e de** in the name of. **no tener ~e** be unspeakable. **poner de ~e** call

nomeolvides *m invar* forget-me-not

nómina *f* payroll

nomina|l *a* nominal. **~tivo** *a & m* nominative. **~tivo a** ‹*cheque etc*› made out to

non *a* odd. ● *m* odd number

nonada *f* trifle

nono *a* ninth

nordeste *a* ‹*región*› north-eastern; ‹*viento*› north-easterly. ● *m* north-east

nórdico *a* northern. ● *m* northerner

noria *f* water-wheel; (*en una feria*) ferris wheel

norma *f* rule

normal *a* normal. ● *f* teachers' training college. **~idad** normality (*Brit*), normalcy (*Amer*). **~izar** [10] *vt* normalize. **~mente** *adv* normally, usually

Normandía *f* Normandy

noroeste *a* ‹*región*› north-western; ‹*viento*› north-westerly. ● *m* north-west

norte *m* north; (*viento*) north wind; (*fig, meta*) aim

Norteamérica *f* (North) America

norteamericano *a & m* (North) American

norteño *a* northern. ● *m* northerner

Noruega *f* Norway

noruego *a & m* Norwegian

nos *pron* (*acusativo*) us; (*dativo*) (to) us; (*reflexivo*) (to) ourselves; (*recíproco*) (to) each other

nosotros *pron* we; (*con prep*) us

nost|algia *f* nostalgia; (*de casa, de patria*) homesickness. **~álgico** *a* nostalgic

nota *f* note; (*de examen etc*) mark. **~ble** *a* notable. **~ción** *f* notation. **~r** *vt* notice; (*apuntar*) note down. **de mala ~** notorious. **de ~** famous. **digno de ~** notable. **es de ~r** it should be noted. **hacerse ~r** stand out

notario *m* notary

notici|a *f* (piece of) news. **~as** *fpl* news. **~ario** *m* news. **~ero** *a* news. **atrasado de ~as** behind the times. **tener ~as de** hear from

notifica|ción *f* notification. **~r** [7] *vt* notify

notori|edad *f* notoriety. **~o** *a* well-known; (*evidente*) obvious

novato *m* novice

novecientos *a & m* nine hundred

noved|ad *f* newness; (*noticia*) news; (*cambio*) change; (*moda*) latest fashion. **~oso** *a* (*LAm*) novel. **sin ~ad** no news

novel|a *f* novel. **~ista** *m & f* novelist

noveno *a* ninth

novent|a *a & m* ninety; (*nonagésimo*) ninetieth. **~ón** *a & m* ninety-year-old

novia *f* girlfriend; (*prometida*) fiancée; (*en boda*) bride. **~zgo** *m* engagement

novicio *m* novice

noviembre *m* November

novilunio *m* new moon

novill|a *f* heifer. **~o** *m* bullock. **hacer ~os** play truant

novio *m* boyfriend; (*prometido*) fiancé; (*en boda*) bridegroom. **los ~s** the bride and groom

novísimo *a* very new

nub|arrón *m* large dark cloud. **~e** *f* cloud; (*de insectos etc*) swarm. **~lado** *a* cloudy, overcast. ● *m* cloud. **~lar** *vt* cloud. **~larse** *vpr* become cloudy. **~loso** *a* cloudy

nuca *f* back of the neck

nuclear *a* nuclear

núcleo *m* nucleus

nudillo *m* knuckle

nudis|mo *m* nudism. **~ta** *m & f* nudist

nudo *m* knot; (*de asunto etc*) crux. **~so** *a* knotty. **tener un ~ en la garganta** have a lump in one's throat

nuera *f* daughter-in-law

nuestro *a* our; (*pospuesto al sustantivo*) of ours. • *pron* ours. **~ coche** our car. **un coche ~** a car of ours

nueva *f* (piece of) news. **~s** *fpl* news. **~mente** *adv* newly; (*de nuevo*) again

Nueva York *f* New York

Nueva Zelanda *f*, **Nueva Zelandia** *f* (*LAm*) New Zealand

nueve *a & m* nine

nuevo *a* new. **de ~** again

nuez *f* nut; (*del nogal*) walnut; (*anat*) Adam's apple. **~ de Adán** Adam's apple. **~ moscada** nutmeg

nul|idad *f* incompetence; (*persona, fam*) nonentity. **~o** *a* useless; (*jurid*) null and void

num|eración *f* numbering. **~eral** *a & m* numeral. **~erar** *vt* number. **~érico** *a* numerical

número *m* number; (*arábigo, romano*) numeral; (*de zapatos etc*) size. **sin ~** countless

numeroso *a* numerous

nunca *adv* never, not ever. **~ (ja)más** never again. **casi ~** hardly ever. **más que ~** more than ever

nupcia|l *a* nuptial. **~s** *fpl* wedding. **banquete ~l** wedding breakfast

nutria *f* otter

nutri|ción *f* nutrition. **~do** *a* nourished, fed; (*fig*) large; ‹*aplausos*› loud; ‹*fuego*› heavy. **~r** *vt* nourish, feed; (*fig*) feed. **~tivo** *a* nutritious. **valor** *m* **~tivo** nutritional value

nylon *m* nylon

Ñ

ña *f* (*LAm, fam*) Mrs

ñacanina *f* (*Arg*) poisonous snake

ñame *m* yam

ñapindá *m* (*Arg*) mimosa

ñato (*LAm*) snub-nosed

ño *m* (*LAm, fam*) Mr

ñoñ|ería *f*, **~ez** *f* insipidity. **~o** *a* insipid; (*tímido*) bashful; (*quisquilloso*) prudish

ñu *m* gnu

O

o *conj* or. **~ bien** rather. **~... ~** either... or. **~ sea** in other words

oasis *m invar* oasis

obcecar [7] *vt* blind

obed|ecer [11] *vt/i* obey. **~iencia** *f* obedience. **~iente** *a* obedient

obelisco *m* obelisk

obertura *f* overture

obes|idad *f* obesity. **~o** *a* obese

obispo *m* bishop

obje|ción *f* objection. **~tar** *vt/i* object

objetiv|idad *f* objectivity. **~o** *a* objective. • *m* objective; (*foto etc*) lens

objeto *m* object

objetor *m* objector. **~ de conciencia** conscientious objector

oblicuo *a* oblique; ‹*mirada*› sidelong

obliga|ción *f* obligation; (*com*) bond. **~do** *a* obliged; (*forzoso*) obligatory; **~r** [12] *vt* force, oblige. **~rse** *vpr*. **~rse a** undertake to. **~torio** *a* obligatory

oboe *m* oboe; (*músico*) oboist

obra *f* work; (*de teatro*) play; (*construcción*) building. **~ maestra** masterpiece. **en ~s** under construction. **por ~ de** thanks to. **~r** *vt* do; (*construir*) build

obrero *a* labour; ‹*clase*› working. • *m* workman; (*en fábrica*) worker

obscen|idad *f* obscenity. **~o** *a* obscene

obscu... *véase* **oscu...**

obsequi|ar *vt* lavish attention on. **~ar con** give, present with. **~o** *m* gift, present; (*agasajo*) attention. **~oso** *a* obliging. **en ~o de** in honour of

observa|ción *f* observation; (*objeción*) objection. **~dor** *m* observer. **~ncia** *f* observance. **~nte** *a* observant. **~r** *vt* observe; (*notar*) notice. **~rse** *vpr* be noted. **~torio** *m* observatory. **hacer una ~ción** make a remark

obses|ión *f* obsession. **~ionar** *vt* obsess. **~ivo** *a* obsessive. **~o** *a* obsessed

obst|aculizar [10] *vt* hinder. **~áculo** *m* obstacle

obstante. no ~ *adv* however, nevertheless. ● *prep* in spite of

obstar *vi*. **~ para** prevent

obstétrico *a* obstetric

obstina|ción *f* obstinacy. **~do** *a* obstinate. **~rse** *vpr* be obstinate. **~rse en** (+ *infintivo*) persist in (+ *gerundio*)

obstru|cción *f* obstruction. **~ir** [17] *vt* obstruct

obtener [40] *vt* get, obtain

obtura|dor *m* (*foto*) shutter. **~r** *vt* plug; fill ‹*muela etc*›

obtuso *a* obtuse

obviar *vt* remove

obvio *a* obvious

oca *f* goose

ocasi|ón *f* occasion; (*oportunidad*) opportunity; (*motivo*) cause. **~onal** *a* chance. **~onar** *vt* cause. **aprovechar la ~ón** take the opportunity. **con ~ón de** on the occasion of. **de ~ón** bargain; (*usado*) second-hand. **en ~ones** sometimes. **perder una ~ón** miss a chance

ocaso *m* sunset; (*fig*) decline

occident|al *a* western. ● *m & f* westerner. **~e** *m* west

océano *m* ocean

ocio *m* idleness; (*tiempo libre*) leisure time. **~sidad** *f* idleness. **~so** *a* idle; (*inútil*) pointless

oclusión *f* occlusion

octano *m* octane. **índice** *m* **de ~** octane number, octane rating

octav|a *f* octave. **~o** *a & m* eighth

octogenario *a & m* octogenarian, eighty-year-old

oct|ogonal *a* octagonal. **~ógono** *m* octagon

octubre *m* October

oculista *m & f* oculist, optician

ocular *a* eye

ocult|ar *vt* hide. **~arse** *vpr* hide. **~o** *a* hidden; (*secreto*) secret

ocupa|ción *f* occupation. **~do** *a* occupied; ‹*persona*› busy. **~nte** *m* occupant. **~r** *vt* occupy. **~rse** *vpr* look after

ocurr|encia *f* occurrence, event; (*idea*) idea; (*que tiene gracia*) witty remark. **~ir** *vi* happen. **~irse** *vpr* occur. **¿qué ~e?** what's the matter? **se me ~e que** it occurs to me that

ochent|a *a & m* eighty. **~ón** *a & m* eighty-year-old

ocho *a & m* eight. **~cientos** *a & m* eight hundred

oda *f* ode

odi|ar *vt* hate. **~o** *m* hatred. **~oso** *a* hateful

odisea *f* odyssey

oeste *m* west; (*viento*) west wind

ofen|der *vt* offend; (*insultar*) insult. **~derse** *vpr* take offence. **~sa** *f* offence. **~siva** *f* offensive. **~sivo** *a* offensive

oferta *f* offer; (*en subasta*) bid; (*regalo*) gift. **~s de empleo** situations vacant. **en ~** on (special) offer

oficial *a* official. ● *m* skilled worker; (*funcionario*) civil servant; (*mil*) officer. **~a** *f* skilled (woman) worker

oficin|a *f* office. **~a de colocación** employment office. **~a de Estado** government office. **~a de turismo** tourist office. **~ista** *m & f* office worker. **horas** *fpl* **de ~a** business hours

oficio *m* job; (*profesión*) profession; (*puesto*) post. **~so** *a* (*no oficial*) unofficial

ofrec|er [11] *vt* offer; give ‹*fiesta, banquete etc*›; (*prometer*) promise. **~erse** *vpr* ‹*persona*› volunteer; ‹*cosa*› occur. **~imiento** *m* offer

ofrenda *f* offering. **~r** *vt* offer

ofusca|ción *f* blindness; (*confusión*) confusion. **~r** [7] *vt* blind; (*confundir*) confuse. **~rse** *vpr* be dazzled

ogro *m* ogre

oí|ble *a* audible. **~da** *f* hearing. **~do** *m* hearing; (*anat*) ear. **al ~do** in one's ear. **de ~das** by hearsay. **de ~do** by ear. **duro de ~do** hard of hearing

oigo *vb véase* **oír**

oír [50] *vt* hear. **~ misa** go to mass. **¡oiga!** listen!; (*al teléfono*) hello!

ojal *m* buttonhole

ojalá *int* I hope so! ● *conj* if only

ojea|da *f* glance. **~r** *vt* eye; (*para inspeccionar*) see; (*ahuyentar*) scare away. **dar una ~da a**, **echar una ~da a** glance at

ojeras *fpl* (*del ojo*) bags

ojeriza *f* ill will. **tener ~ a** have a grudge against

ojete *m* eyelet

ojo *m* eye; (*de cerradura*) keyhole; (*de un puente*) span. **¡~!** careful!
ola *f* wave
olé *int* bravo!
olea|da *f* wave. **~je** *m* swell
óleo *m* oil; (*cuadro*) oil painting
oleoducto *m* oil pipeline
oler [2, *las formas que empezarían por* **ue** *se escriben* **hue**] *vt* smell; (*curiosear*) pry into; (*descubrir*) discover. ● *vi* smell (**a** of)
olfat|ear *vt* smell, sniff; (*fig*) sniff out. **~o** *m* (sense of) smell; (*fig*) intuition
olimpiada *f*, **olimpíada** *f* Olympic games, Olympics
olímpico *a* ‹*juegos*› Olympic
oliv|a *f* olive; (*olivo*) olive tree. **~ar** *m* olive grove. **~o** *m* olive tree
olmo *m* elm (tree)
olor *m* smell. **~oso** *a* sweet-smelling
olvid|adizo *a* forgetful. **~ar** *vt* forget. **~arse** *vpr* forget; (*estar olvidado*) be forgotten. **~o** *m* oblivion; (*acción de olvidar*) forgetfulness. **se me ~ó** I forgot
olla *f* pot, casserole; (*guisado*) stew. **~ a/de presión**, **~ exprés** pressure cooker. **~ podrida** Spanish stew
ombligo *m* navel
ominoso *a* awful, abominable
omi|sión *f* omission; (*olvido*) forgetfulness. **~tir** *vt* omit
ómnibus *a* omnibus
omnipotente *a* omnipotent
omóplato *m*, **omoplato** *m* shoulder blade
once *a* & *m* eleven
ond|a *f* wave. **~a corta** short wave. **~a larga** long wave. **~ear** *vi* wave; ‹*agua*› ripple. **~ulación** *f* undulation; (*del pelo*) wave. **~ular** *vi* wave. **longitud** *f* **de ~a** wavelength
oneroso *a* onerous
ónice *m* onyx
onomástico *a*. **día ~**, **fiesta onomástica** name-day
ONU *abrev* (*Organización de las Naciones Unidas*) UN, United Nations
onza *f* ounce
opa *a* (*LAm*) stupid
opaco *a* opaque; (*fig*) dull
ópalo *m* opal
opción *f* option
ópera *f* opera
opera|ción *f* operation; (*com*) transaction. **~dor** *m* operator; (*cirujano*) surgeon; (*TV*) cameraman. **~r** *vt* operate on; work ‹*milagro etc*›. ● *vi* operate; (*com*) deal. **~rse** *vpr* occur; (*med*) have an operation. **~torio** *a* operative
opereta *f* operetta
opin|ar *vi* think. **~ión** *f* opinion. **la ~ión pública** public opinion
opio *m* opium
opone|nte *a* opposing. ● *m* & *f* opponent. **~r** *vt* oppose; offer ‹*resistencia*›; raise ‹*objeción*›. **~rse** *vpr* be opposed; ‹*dos personas*› oppose each other
oporto *m* port (wine)
oportun|idad *f* opportunity; (*cualidad de oportuno*) timeliness. **~ista** *m* & *f* opportunist. **~o** *a* opportune; (*apropiado*) suitable
oposi|ción *f* opposition. **~ciones** *fpl* competition, public examination. **~tor** *m* candidate
opres|ión *f* oppression; (*ahogo*) difficulty in breathing. **~ivo** *a* oppressive. **~o** *a* oppressed. **~or** *m* oppressor
oprimir *vt* squeeze; press ‹*botón etc*›; ‹*ropa*› be too tight for; (*fig*) oppress
oprobio *m* disgrace
optar *vi* choose. **~ por** opt for
óptic|a *f* optics; (*tienda*) optician's (shop). **~o** *a* optic(al). ● *m* optician
optimis|mo *m* optimism. **~ta** *a* optimisitic. ● *m* & *f* optimist
opuesto *a* opposite; (*enemigo*) opposed
opulen|cia *f* opulence. **~to** *a* opulent
oración *f* prayer; (*discurso*) speech; (*gram*) sentence
oráculo *m* oracle
orador *m* speaker
oral *a* oral
orar *vi* pray
oratori|a *f* oratory. **~o** *a* oratorical. ● *m* (*mus*) oratorio
orbe *m* orb
órbita *f* orbit
orden *m* & *f* order; (*Mex, porción*) portion. **~ado** *a* tidy. **~ del día** agenda. **órdenes** *fpl* **sagradas** Holy Orders. **a sus órdenes** (*esp Mex*) can I help you? **en ~** in order. **por ~** in turn
ordenador *m* computer
ordena|nza *f* order. ● *m* (*mil*) orderly. **~r** *vt* put in order; (*mandar*) order; (*relig*) ordain
ordeñar *vt* milk
ordinal *a* & *m* ordinal

ordinario *a* ordinary; (*grosero*) common
orear *vt* air
orégano *m* oregano
oreja *f* ear
orfanato *m* orphanage
orfebre *m* goldsmith, silversmith
orfeón *m* choral society
orgánico *a* organic
organigrama *m* flow chart
organillo *m* barrel-organ
organismo *m* organism
organista *m & f* organist
organiza|ción *f* organization. **~dor** *m* organizer. **~r** [10] *vt* organize. **~rse** *vpr* get organized
órgano *m* organ
orgasmo *m* orgasm
orgía *f* orgy
orgullo *m* pride. **~so** *a* proud
orientación *f* direction
oriental *a & m & f* oriental
orientar *vt* position. **~se** *vpr* point; ‹*persona*› find one's bearings
oriente *m* east. **O~ Medio** Middle East
orificio *m* hole
orig|en *m* origin. **~inal** *a* original; (*excéntrico*) odd. **~inalidad** *f* originality. **~inar** *vt* give rise to. **~inario** *a* original; (*nativo*) native. **dar ~en a** give rise to. **ser ~inario de** come from
orilla *f* (*del mar*) shore; (*de río*) bank; (*borde*) edge
orín *m* rust
orina *f* urine. **~l** *m* chamber-pot. **~r** *vi* urinate
oriundo *a*. **~ de** ‹*persona*› (originating) from; ‹*animal etc*› native to
orla *f* border
ornamental *a* ornamental
ornitología *f* ornithology
oro *m* gold. **~s** *mpl* Spanish card suit. **~ de ley** 9 carat gold. **hacerse de ~** make a fortune. **prometer el ~ y el moro** promise the moon
oropel *m* tinsel
orquesta *f* orchestra. **~l** *a* orchestral. **~r** *vt* orchestrate
orquídea *f* orchid
ortiga *f* nettle
ortodox|ia *f* orthodoxy. **~o** *a* orthodox
ortografía *f* spelling
ortop|edia *f* orthopaedics. **~édico** *a* orthopaedic
oruga *f* caterpillar
orzuelo *m* sty
os *pron* (*acusativo*) you; (*dativo*) (to) you; (*reflexivo*) (to) yourselves; (*recíproco*) (to) each other
osad|ía *f* boldness. **~o** *a* bold
oscila|ción *f* swinging; (*de precios*) fluctuation; (*tec*) oscillation. **~r** *vi* swing; ‹*precio*› fluctuate; (*tec*) oscillate; (*fig, vacilar*) hesitate
oscur|ecer [11] *vi* darken; (*fig*) obscure. **~ecerse** *vpr* grow dark; (*nublarse*) cloud over. **~idad** *f* darkness; (*fig*) obscurity. **~o** *a* dark; (*fig*) obscure. **a ~as** in the dark
óseo *a* bony
oso *m* bear. **~ de felpa**, **~ de peluche** teddy bear
ostensible *a* obvious
ostent|ación *f* ostentation. **~ar** *vt* show off; (*mostrar*) show. **~oso** *a* ostentatious
osteoartritis *f* osteoarthritis
oste|ópata *m & f* osteopath. **~opatía** *f* osteopathy
ostión *m* (*esp Mex*) oyster
ostra *f* oyster
ostracismo *m* ostracism
Otan *abrev* (*Organización del Tratado del Atlántico Norte*) NATO, North Atlantic Treaty Organization
otear *vt* observe; (*escudriñar*) scan, survey
otitis *f* inflammation of the ear
otoño *m* autumn (*Brit*), fall (*Amer*)
otorga|miento *m* granting; (*documento*) authorization. **~r** [12] *vt* give; (*jurid*) draw up
otorrinolaringólogo *m* ear, nose and throat specialist
otro *a* other; (*uno más*) another. • *pron* another (one); (*en plural*) others; (*otra persona*) someone else. **el ~** the other. **el uno al ~** one another, each other
ovación *f* ovation
oval *a* oval
óvalo *m* oval
ovario *m* ovary
oveja *f* sheep; (*hembra*) ewe
overol *m* (*LAm*) overalls
ovino *a* sheep
ovillo *m* ball. **hacerse un ~** curl up
OVNI *abrev* (*objeto volante no identificado*) UFO, unidentified flying object
ovulación *f* ovulation

oxida|ción *f* rusting. **~r** *vi* rust. **~rse** *vpr* go rusty
óxido *m* oxide
oxígeno *m* oxygen
oye *vb véase* **oír**
oyente *a* listening. ● *m & f* listener
ozono *m* ozone

P

pabellón *m* bell tent; (*edificio*) building; (*de instrumento*) bell; (*bandera*) flag
pabilo *m* wick
paceño *a* from La Paz. ● *m* person from La Paz
pacer [11] *vi* graze
pacien|cia *f* patience. **~te** *a & m & f* patient
pacificar [7] *vt* pacify; reconcile ‹*dos personas*›. **~se** *vpr* calm down
pacífico *a* peaceful. **el (Océano** *m* **) P~** the Pacific (Ocean)
pacifis|mo *m* pacifism. **~ta** *a & m & f* pacifist
pact|ar *vi* agree, make a pact. **~o** *m* pact, agreement
pachucho *a* ‹*fruta*› overripe; ‹*persona*› poorly
padec|er [11] *vt/i* suffer (**de** from); (*soportar*) bear. **~imiento** *m* suffering; (*enfermedad*) ailment
padrastro *m* stepfather
padre *a* (*fam*) great. ● *m* father. **~s** *mpl* parents
padrino *m* godfather; (*en boda*) best man
padrón *m* census
paella *f* paella
paga *f* pay, wages. **~ble** *a*, **~dero** *a* payable
pagano *a & m* pagan
pagar [12] *vt* pay; pay for ‹*compras*›. ● *vi* pay. **~é** *m* IOU
página *f* page
pago *m* payment
pagoda *f* pagoda
país *m* country; (*región*) region. **~ natal** native land. **el P~ Vasco** the Basque Country. **los P~es Bajos** the Low Countries
paisa|je *m* countryside. **~no** *a* of the same country. ● *m* compatriot
paja *f* straw; (*fig*) nonsense
pajarera *f* aviary
pájaro *m* bird. **~ carpintero** woodpecker
paje *m* page
Pakistán *m*. **el ~** Pakistan
pala *f* shovel; (*laya*) spade; (*en deportes*) bat; (*de tenis*) racquet
palabr|a *f* word; (*habla*) speech. **~ota** *f* swear-word. **decir ~otas** swear. **pedir la ~a** ask to speak. **soltar ~otas** swear. **tomar la ~a** (begin to) speak
palacio *m* palace; (*casa grande*) mansion
paladar *m* palate
paladino *a* clear; (*público*) public
palanca *f* lever; (*fig*) influence. **~ de cambio (de velocidades)** gear lever (*Brit*), gear shift (*Amer*)
palangana *f* wash-basin
palco *m* (*en el teatro*) box
Palestina *f* Palestine
palestino *a & m* Palestinian
palestra *f* (*fig*) arena
paleta *f* (*de pintor*) palette; (*de albañil*) trowel
paleto *m* yokel
paliativo *a & m* palliative
palide|cer [11] *vi* turn pale. **~z** *f* paleness
pálido *a* pale
palillo *m* small stick; (*de dientes*) toothpick
palique *m*. **estar de ~** be chatting
paliza *f* beating
palizada *f* fence; (*recinto*) enclosure
palma *f* (*de la mano*) palm; (*árbol*) palm (tree); (*de dátiles*) date palm. **~s** *fpl* applause. **~da** *f* slap. **~das** *fpl* applause. **dar ~(da)s** clap. **tocar las ~s** clap
palmera *f* date palm
palmo *m* span; (*fig, pequeña cantidad*) small amount. **~ a ~** inch by inch
palmote|ar *vi* clap, applaud. **~o** *m* clapping, applause
palo *m* stick; (*del teléfono etc*) pole; (*mango*) handle; (*de golf*) club; (*golpe*) blow; (*de naipes*) suit; (*mástil*) mast
paloma *f* pigeon, dove
palomitas *fpl* popcorn
palpa|ble *a* palpable. **~r** *vt* feel
palpita|ción *f* palpitation. **~nte** *a* throbbing. **~r** *vi* throb; (*latir*) beat
palta *f* (*LAm*) avocado pear
pal|údico *a* marshy; (*de paludismo*) malarial. **~udismo** *m* malaria
pamp|a *f* pampas. **~ear** *vi* (*LAm*) travel across the pampas. **~ero** *a* of the pampas

pan *m* bread; (*barra*) loaf. **~ integral** wholemeal bread (*Brit*), wholewheat bread (*Amer*). **~ tostado** toast. **~ rallado** breadcrumbs. **ganarse el ~** earn one's living
pana *f* corduroy
panacea *f* panacea
panader|ía *f* bakery; (*tienda*) baker's (shop). **~o** *m* baker
panal *m* honeycomb
Panamá *f* Panama
panameño *a & m* Panamanian
pancarta *f* placard
panda *m* panda; (*pandilla*) gang
pander|eta *f* (small) tambourine. **~o** *m* tambourine
pandilla *f* gang
panecillo *m* (bread) roll
panel *m* panel
panfleto *m* pamphlet
pánico *m* panic
panor|ama *m* panorama. **~ámico** *a* panoramic
panqué *m* (*LAm*) pancake
pantaletas *fpl* (*LAm*) underpants, knickers
pantal|ón *m* trousers. **~ones** *mpl* trousers. **~ón corto** shorts. **~ón tejano**, **~ón vaquero** jeans
pantalla *f* screen; (*de lámpara*) (lamp)shade
pantano *m* marsh; (*embalse*) reservoir. **~so** *a* boggy
pantera *f* panther
pantomima *f* pantomime
pantorrilla *f* calf
pantufla *f* slipper
panucho *m* (*Mex*) stuffed tortilla
panz|a *f* belly. **~ada** *f* (*hartazgo*, *fam*) bellyful; (*golpe*, *fam*) blow in the belly. **~udo** *a* fat, pot-bellied
pañal *m* nappy (*Brit*), diaper (*Amer*)
pañ|ería *f* draper's (shop). **~o** *m* material; (*de lana*) woollen cloth; (*trapo*) cloth. **~o de cocina** dishcloth; (*para secar*) tea towel. **~o higiénico** sanitary towel. **en ~os menores** in one's underclothes
pañuelo *m* handkerchief; (*de cabeza*) scarf
papa *m* pope. ● *f* (*esp LAm*) potato. **~s francesas** (*LAm*) chips
papá *m* dad(dy). **~s** *mpl* parents. **P~ Noel** Father Christmas
papada *f* (*de persona*) double chin
papado *m* papacy
papagayo *m* parrot
papal *a* papal
papanatas *m inv* simpleton
paparrucha *f* (*tontería*) silly thing
papaya *f* pawpaw
papel *m* paper; (*en el teatro etc*) role. **~ carbón** carbon paper. **~ celofán** celophane paper. **~ de calcar** carbon paper. **~ de embalar**, **~ de envolver** wrapping paper. **~ de plata** silver paper. **~ de seda** tissue paper. **~era** *f* waste-paper basket. **~ería** *f* stationer's (shop). **~eta** *f* ticket; (*para votar*) paper. **~ higiénico** toilet paper. **~ pintado** wallpaper. **~ secante** blotting paper. **blanco como el ~** as white as a sheet. **desempeñar un ~**, **hacer un ~** play a role
paperas *fpl* mumps
paquebote *m* packet (boat)
paquete *m* packet; (*paquebote*) packet (boat); (*Mex*, *asunto difícil*) difficult job. **~ postal** parcel
paquistaní *a & m* Pakistani
par *a* equal; ‹*número*› even. ● *m* couple; (*dos cosas iguales*) pair; (*igual*) equal; (*título*) peer. **a la ~** at the same time; ‹*monedas*› at par. **al ~ que** at the same time. **a ~es** two by two. **de ~ en ~** wide open. **sin ~** without equal
para *prep* for; (*hacia*) towards; (*antes del infinitivo*) (in order) to. **~ con** to(wards). **¿~ qué?** why? **~ que** so that
parabienes *mpl* congratulations
parábola *f* (*narración*) parable
parabrisas *m inv* windscreen (*Brit*), windshield (*Amer*)
paraca *f* (*LAm*) strong wind (from the Pacific)
paraca|ídas *m inv* parachute. **~idista** *m & f* parachutist; (*mil*) paratrooper
parachoques *m inv* bumper (*Brit*), fender (*Amer*); (*rail*) buffer
parad|a *f* (*acción*) stopping; (*sitio*) stop; (*de taxis*) rank; (*mil*) parade. **~ero** *m* whereabouts; (*alojamiento*) lodging. **~o** *a* stationary; ‹*obrero*› unemployed; (*lento*) slow. **dejar ~o** confuse. **tener mal ~ero** come to a sticky end
paradoja *f* paradox
parador *m* state-owned hotel
parafina *f* paraffin
par|afrasear *vt* paraphrase. **~áfrasis** *f inv* paraphrase
paraguas *m inv* umbrella
Paraguay *m* Paraguay
paraguayo *a & m* Paraguayan

paraíso *m* paradise; (*en el teatro*) gallery
paralel|a *f* parallel (line). **~as** *fpl* parallel bars. **~o** *a & m* parallel
par|álisis *f inv* paralysis. **~alítico** *a* paralytic. **~alizar** [10] *vt* paralyse
paramilitar *a* paramilitary
páramo *m* barren plain
parang|ón *m* comparison. **~onar** *vt* compare
paraninfo *m* hall
paranoi|a *f* paranoia. **~co** *a* paranoiac
parapeto *m* parapet; (*fig*) barricade
parapléjico *a & m* paraplegic
parar *vt/i* stop. **~se** *vpr* stop. **sin ~** continuously
pararrayos *m inv* lightning conductor
parásito *a* parasitic. • *m* parasite
parasol *m* parasol
parcela *f* plot. **~r** *vt* divide into plots
parcial *a* partial. **~idad** *f* prejudice; (*pol*) faction. **a tiempo ~** part-time
parco *a* sparing, frugal
parche *m* patch
pardo *a* brown
parear *vt* pair off
parec|er *m* opinion; (*aspecto*) appearance. • *vi* [11] seem; (*asemejarse*) look like; (*aparecer*) appear. **~erse** *vpr* resemble, look like. **~ido** *a* similar. • *m* similarity. **al ~er** apparently. **a mi ~er** in my opinion. **bien ~ido** good-looking. **me ~e** I think. **¿qué te parece?** what do you think? **según ~e** apparently
pared *f* wall. **~ón** *m* thick wall; (*de ruinas*) standing wall. **~ por medio** next door. **llevar al ~ón** shoot
parej|a *f* pair; (*hombre y mujer*) couple; (*la otra persona*) partner. **~o** *a* alike, the same; (*liso*) smooth
parente|la *f* relations. **~sco** *m* relationship
paréntesis *m inv* parenthesis; (*signo ortográfico*) bracket. **entre ~** (*fig*) by the way
paria *m & f* outcast
paridad *f* equality
pariente *m & f* relation, relative
parihuela *f*, **parihuelas** *fpl* stretcher
parir *vt* give birth to. • *vi* have a baby, give birth
París *m* Paris
parisiense *a & m & f*, **parisino** *a & m* Parisian
parking /'parkin/ *m* car park (*Brit*), parking lot (*Amer*)
parlament|ar *vi* discuss. **~ario** *a* parliamentary. • *m* member of parliament (*Brit*), congressman (*Amer*). **~o** *m* parliament
parlanchín *a* talkative. • *m* chatterbox
parmesano *a* Parmesan
paro *m* stoppage; (*desempleo*) unemployment; (*pájaro*) tit
parodia *f* parody. **~r** *vt* parody
parpadear *vi* blink; ‹*luz*› flicker; ‹*estrella*› twinkle
párpado *m* eyelid
parque *m* park. **~ de atracciones** funfair. **~ infantil** children's playground. **~ zoológico** zoo, zoological gardens
parqué *m* parquet
parquedad *f* frugality; (*moderación*) moderation
parra *f* grapevine
párrafo *m* paragraph
parrilla *f* grill; (*LAm, auto*) radiator grill. **~da** *f* grill. **a la ~** grilled
párroco *m* parish priest
parroquia *f* parish; (*iglesia*) parish church. **~no** *m* parishioner; (*cliente*) customer
parsimoni|a *f* thrift. **~oso** *a* thrifty
parte *m* message; (*informe*) report. • *f* part; (*porción*) share; (*lado*) side; (*jurid*) party. **dar ~** report. **de mi ~** for me. **de ~ de** from. **¿de ~ de quién?** (*al teléfono*) who's speaking? **en cualquier ~** anywhere. **en gran ~** largely. **en ~** partly. **en todas ~s** everywhere. **la mayor ~** the majority. **ninguna ~** nowhere. **por otra ~** on the other hand. **por todas ~s** everywhere
partera *f* midwife
partición *f* sharing out
participa|ción *f* participation; (*noticia*) notice; (*de lotería*) lottery ticket. **~nte** *a* participating. • *m & f* participant. **~r** *vt* notify. • *vi* take part
participio *m* participle
partícula *f* particle
particular *a* particular; ‹*clase*› private. • *m* matter. **~idad** *f* peculiarity. **~izar** [10] *vt* distinguish; (*detallar*) give details about. **en ~** in particular. **nada de ~** nothing special
partida *f* departure; (*en registro*) entry; (*documento*) certificate; (*juego*) game; (*de gente*) group. **mala ~** dirty trick

partidario *a & m* partisan. **~ de** keen on

parti|do *a* divided. ● *m* (*pol*) party; (*encuentro*) match, game; (*equipo*) team. **~r** *vt* divide; (*romper*) break; (*repartir*) share; crack ‹*nueces*›. ● *vi* leave; (*empezar*) start. **~rse** *vpr* (*romperse*) break; (*dividirse*) split. **a ~r de** (starting) from

partitura *f* (*mus*) score

parto *m* birth; (*fig*) creation. **estar de ~** be in labour

párvulo *m*. **colegio de ~s** nursery school

pasa *f* raisin. **~ de Corinto** currant. **~ de Esmirna** sultana

pasa|ble *a* passable. **~da** *f* passing; (*de puntos*) row. **~dero** *a* passable. **~dizo** *m* passage. **~do** *a* past; ‹*día, mes etc*› last; (*anticuado*) old-fashioned; ‹*comida*› bad, off. **~do mañana** the day after tomorrow. **~dor** *m* bolt; (*de pelo*) hair-slide; (*culin*) strainer. **de ~da** in passing. **el lunes ~do** last Monday

pasaje *m* passage; (*naut*) crossing; (*viajeros*) passengers. **~ro** *a* passing. ● *m* passenger

pasamano(s) *m* handrail; (*barandilla de escalera*) banister(s)

pasamontañas *m inv* Balaclava (helmet)

pasaporte *m* passport

pasar *vt* pass; (*poner*) put; (*filtrar*) strain; spend ‹*tiempo*›; (*tragar*) swallow; show ‹*película*›; (*tolerar*) tolerate, overlook; give ‹*mensaje, enfermedad*›. ● *vi* pass; (*suceder*) happen; (*ir*) go; (*venir*) come; ‹*tiempo*› go by. **~ de** have no interest in. **~se** *vpr* pass; (*terminarse*) be over; ‹*flores*› wither; ‹*comida*› go bad; spend ‹*tiempo*›; (*excederse*) go too far. **~lo bien** have a good time. **~ por alto** leave out. **como si no hubiese pasado nada** as if nothing had happened. **lo que pasa es que** the fact is that. **pase lo que pase** whatever happens. **¡pase Vd!** come in!, go in! **¡que lo pases bien!** have a good time! **¿qué pasa?** what's the matter?, what's happening?

pasarela *f* footbridge; (*naut*) gangway

pasatiempo *m* hobby, pastime

pascua *f* (*fiesta de los hebreos*) Passover; (*de Resurrección*) Easter; (*Navidad*) Christmas. **~s** *fpl* Christmas. **hacer la ~ a uno** mess things up for s.o. **¡y santas ~s!** and that's that!

pase *m* pass

pase|ante *m & f* passer-by. **~ar** *vt* take for a walk; (*exhibir*) show off. ● *vi* go for a walk; (*en coche etc*) go for a ride. **~arse** *vpr* go for a walk; (*en coche etc*) go for a ride. **~o** *m* walk; (*en coche etc*) ride; (*calle*) avenue. **~o marítimo** promenade. **dar un ~o** go for a walk. **¡vete a ~o!** (*fam*) go away!, get lost! (*fam*)

pasillo *m* passage

pasión *f* passion

pasiv|idad *f* passiveness. **~o** *a* passive

pasm|ar *vt* astonish. **~arse** *vpr* be astonished. **~o** *m* astonishment. **~oso** *a* astonishing

paso *a* ‹*fruta*› dried ● *m* step; (*acción de pasar*) passing; (*huella*) footprint; (*manera de andar*) walk; (*camino*) way through; (*entre montañas*) pass; (*estrecho*) strait(s). **~ a nivel** level crossing (*Brit*), grade crossing (*Amer*). **~ de cebra** Zebra crossing. **~ de peatones** pedestrian crossing. **~ elevado** flyover. **a cada ~** at every turn. **a dos ~s** very near. **al ~ que** at the same time as. **a ~ lento** slowly. **ceda el ~** give way. **de ~** in passing. **de ~ por** on the way through. **prohibido el ~** no entry

pasodoble *m* (*baile*) pasodoble

pasota *m & f* drop-out

pasta *f* paste; (*masa*) dough; (*dinero, fam*) money. **~s** *fpl* pasta; (*pasteles*) pastries. **~ de dientes**, **~ dentífrica** toothpaste

pastar *vt/i* graze

pastel *m* cake; (*empanada*) pie; (*lápiz*) pastel. **~ería** *f* cakes; (*tienda*) cake shop, confectioner's

paste(u)rizar [10] *vt* pasteurize

pastiche *m* pastiche

pastilla *f* pastille; (*de jabón*) bar; (*de chocolate*) piece

pastinaca *f* parsnip

pasto *m* pasture; (*hierba*) grass; (*Mex, césped*) lawn. **~r** *m* shepherd; (*relig*) minister. **~ral** *a* pastoral

pata *f* leg; (*pie*) paw, foot. **~s arriba** upside down. **a cuatro ~s** on all fours. **meter la ~** put one's foot in it. **tener mala ~** have bad luck

pataca *f* Jerusalem artichoke

pata|da *f* kick. **~lear** *vt* stamp; ‹*niño pequeño*› kick

pataplum *int* crash!
patata *f* potato. **~s fritas** chips (*Brit*), French fries (*Amer*). **~s fritas (a la inglesa)** (potato) crisps (*Brit*), potato chips (*Amer*)
patent|ar *vt* patent. **~e** *a* obvious. ● *f* licence. **~e de invención** patent
patern|al *a* paternal; ‹*cariño etc*› fatherly. **~idad** *f* paternity. **~o** *a* paternal; ‹*cariño etc*› fatherly
patético *a* moving
patillas *fpl* sideburns
patín *m* skate; (*juguete*) scooter
pátina *f* patina
patina|dero *m* skating rink. **~dor** *m* skater. **~je** *m* skating. **~r** *vi* skate; (*deslizarse*) slide. **~zo** *m* skid; (*fig, fam*) blunder
patio *m* patio. **~ de butacas** stalls (*Brit*), orchestra (*Amer*)
pato *m* duck
patol|ogía *f* pathology. **~ógico** *a* pathological
patoso *a* clumsy
patraña *f* hoax
patria *f* native land
patriarca *m* patriarch
patrimonio *m* inheritance; (*fig*) heritage
patri|ota *a* patriotic. ● *m & f* patriot. **~ótico** *a* patriotic. **~otismo** *m* patriotism
patrocin|ar *vt* sponsor. **~io** *m* sponsorship
patr|ón *m* patron; (*jefe*) boss; (*de pensión etc*) landlord; (*modelo*) pattern. **~onato** *m* patronage; (*fundación*) trust, foundation
patrulla *f* patrol; (*fig, cuadrilla*) group. **~r** *vt/i* patrol
paulatinamente *adv* slowly
pausa *f* pause. **~do** *a* slow
pauta *f* guideline
paviment|ar *vt* pave. **~o** *m* pavement
pavo *m* turkey. **~ real** peacock
pavor *m* terror. **~oso** *a* terrifying
payas|ada *f* buffoonery. **~o** *m* clown
paz *f* peace. **La P~** La Paz
peaje *m* toll
peatón *m* pedestrian
pebet|a *f* (*LAm*) little girl. **~e** *m* little boy
peca *f* freckle
peca|do *m* sin; (*defecto*) fault. **~dor** *m* sinner. **~minoso** *a* sinful. **~r** [7] *vi* sin
pecoso *a* freckled
pectoral *a* pectoral; (*para la tos*) cough
peculiar *a* peculiar, particular. **~idad** *f* peculiarity
pech|era *f* front. **~ero** *m* bib. **~o** *m* chest; (*de mujer*) breast; (*fig, corazón*) heart. **~uga** *f* breast. **dar el ~o** breast-feed ‹*a un niño*›; (*afrontar*) confront. **tomar a ~o** take to heart
pedagogo *m* teacher
pedal *m* pedal. **~ear** *vi* pedal
pedante *a* pedantic
pedazo *m* piece, bit. **a ~s** in pieces. **hacer ~s** break to pieces. **hacerse ~s** fall to pieces
pedernal *m* flint
pedestal *m* pedestal
pedestre *a* pedestrian
pediatra *m & f* paediatrician
pedicuro *m* chiropodist
pedi|do *m* order. **~r** [5] *vt* ask (for); (*com, en restaurante*) order. ● *vi* ask. **~r prestado** borrow
pegadizo *a* sticky; (*mus*) catchy
pegajoso *a* sticky
pega|r [12] *vt* stick (on); (*coser*) sew on; give ‹*enfermedad etc*›; (*juntar*) join; (*golpear*) hit; (*dar*) give. ● *vi* stick. **~rse** *vpr* stick; (*pelearse*) hit each other. **~r fuego a** set fire to. **~tina** *f* sticker
pein|ado *m* hairstyle. **~ar** *vt* comb. **~arse** *vpr* comb one's hair. **~e** *m* comb. **~eta** *f* ornamental comb
p.ej. *abrev* (*por ejemplo*) e.g., for example
pela|do *a* ‹*fruta*› peeled; ‹*cabeza*› bald; ‹*número*› exactly; ‹*terreno*› barren. ● *m* bare patch. **~dura** *f* (*acción*) peeling; (*mondadura*) peelings
pela|je *m* (*de animal*) fur; (*fig, aspecto*) appearance. **~mbre** *m* (*de animal*) fur; (*de persona*) thick hair
pelar *vt* cut the hair; (*mondar*) peel; (*quitar el pellejo*) skin
peldaño *m* step; (*de escalera de mano*) rung
pelea *f* fight; (*discusión*) quarrel. **~r** *vi* fight. **~rse** *vpr* fight
peletería *f* fur shop
peliagudo *a* difficult, tricky
pelícano *m*, **pelicano** *m* pelican
película *f* film (*esp Brit*), movie (*Amer*). **~ de dibujos (animados)** cartoon (film). **~ en colores** colour film
peligro *m* danger; (*riesgo*) risk. **~so** *a* dangerous. **poner en ~** endanger

pelirrojo *a* red-haired
pelma *m & f*, **pelmazo** *m* bore, nuisance
pel|o *m* hair; (*de barba o bigote*) whisker. **~ón** *a* bald; (*rapado*) with very short hair. **no tener ~os en la lengua** be outspoken. **tomar el ~o a uno** pull s.o.'s leg
pelota *f* ball; (*juego vasco*) pelota. **~ vasca** pelota. **en ~(s)** naked
pelotera *f* squabble
pelotilla *f*. **hacer la ~ a** ingratiate o.s. with
peluca *f* wig
peludo *a* hairy
peluquer|ía *f* (*de mujer*) hairdresser's; (*de hombre*) barber's. **~o** *m* (*de mujer*) hairdresser; (*de hombre*) barber
pelusa *f* down; (*celos, fam*) jealousy
pelvis *f* pelvis
pella *f* lump
pelleja *f*, **pellejo** *m* skin
pellizc|ar [7] *vt* pinch. **~o** *m* pinch
pena *f* sadness; (*dificultad*) difficulty. **~ de muerte** death penalty. **a duras ~s** with difficulty. **da ~ que** it's a pity that. **me da ~ que** I'm sorry that. **merecer la ~** be worthwhile. **¡qué ~!** what a pity! **valer la ~** be worthwhile
penacho *m* tuft; (*fig*) plume
penal *a* penal; (*criminal*) criminal. ● *m* prison. **~idad** *f* suffering; (*jurid*) penalty. **~izar** [10] *vt* penalize
penalty *m* penalty
penar *vt* punish. ● *vi* suffer. **~ por** long for
pend|er *vi* hang. **~iente** *a* hanging; ‹*terreno*› sloping; ‹*cuenta*› outstanding; (*fig*) ‹*asunto etc*› pending. ● *m* earring. ● *f* slope
pendón *m* banner
péndulo *a* hanging. ● *m* pendulum
pene *m* penis
penetra|nte *a* penetrating; ‹*sonido*› piercing; ‹*herida*› deep. **~r** *vt* penetrate; (*fig*) pierce; (*entender*) understand. ● *vi* penetrate; (*entrar*) go into
penicilina *f* penicillin
pen|ínsula *f* peninsula. **península Ibérica** Iberian Peninsula. **~insular** *a* peninsular
penique *m* penny
peniten|cia *f* penitence; (*castigo*) penance. **~te** *a & m & f* penitent
penoso *a* painful; (*difícil*) difficult

pensa|do *a* thought. **~dor** *m* thinker. **~miento** *m* thought. **~r** [1] *vt* think; (*considerar*) consider. ● *vi* think. **~r en** think about. **~tivo** *a* thoughtful. **bien ~do** all things considered. **cuando menos se piensa** when least expected. **menos ~do** least expected. **¡ni ~rlo!** certainly not! **pienso que sí** I think so
pensi|ón *f* pension; (*casa de huéspedes*) guest-house. **~ón completa** full board. **~onista** *m & f* pensioner; (*huésped*) lodger; (*escol*) boarder
pentágono *m* pentagon
pentagrama *m* stave
Pentecostés *m* Whitsun; (*fiesta judía*) Pentecost
penúltimo *a & m* penultimate, last but one
penumbra *f* half-light
penuria *f* shortage
peñ|a *f* rock; (*de amigos*) group; (*club*) club. **~ón** *m* rock. **el peñón de Gibraltar** The Rock (of Gibraltar)
peón *m* labourer; (*en ajedrez*) pawn; (*en damas*) piece; (*juguete*) (spinning) top
peonía *f* peony
peonza *f* (spinning) top
peor *a* (*comparativo*) worse; (*superlativo*) worst. ● *adv* worse. **~ que ~** worse and worse. **lo ~** the worst thing. **tanto ~** so much the worse
pepin|illo *m* gherkin. **~o** *m* cucumber. **(no) me importa un ~o** I couldn't care less
pepita *f* pip
pepitoria *f* fricassee
pequeñ|ez *f* smallness; (*minucia*) trifle. **~ito** *a* very small, tiny. **~o** *a* small, little. **de ~o** as a child. **en ~o** in miniature
pequinés *m* (*perro*) Pekingese
pera *f* (*fruta*) pear. **~l** *m* pear (tree)
percance *m* setback
percatarse *vpr*. **~ de** notice
perc|epción *f* perception. **~eptible** *a* perceptible. **~eptivo** *a* perceptive. **~ibir** *vt* perceive; earn ‹*dinero*›
percusión *f* percussion
percutir *vt* tap
percha *f* hanger; (*de aves*) perch. **de ~** off the peg
perde|dor *a* losing. ● *m* loser. **~r** [1] *vt* lose; (*malgastar*) waste; miss ‹*tren etc*›. ● *vi* lose; ‹*tela*› fade. **~rse** *vpr* get lost; (*desparecer*) disappear;

(*desperdiciarse*) be wasted; (*estropearse*) be spoilt. **echar(se) a ~r** spoil

pérdida *f* loss; (*de líquido*) leak; (*de tiempo*) waste

perdido *a* lost

perdiz *f* partridge

perd|ón *m* pardon, forgiveness. ● *int* sorry! **~onar** *vt* excuse, forgive; (*jurid*) pardon. **¡~one (Vd)!** sorry! **pedir ~ón** apologize

perdura|ble *a* lasting. **~r** *vi* last

perece|dero *a* perishable. **~r** [11] *vi* perish

peregrin|ación *f* pilgrimage. **~ar** *vi* go on a pilgrimage; (*fig*, fam) travel. **~o** *a* strange. ● *m* pilgrim

perejil *m* parsley

perengano *m* so-and-so

perenne *a* everlasting; (*bot*) perennial

perentorio *a* peremptory

perez|a *f* laziness. **~oso** *a* lazy

perfec|ción *f* perfection. **~cionamiento** *m* perfection; (*mejora*) improvement. **~cionar** *vt* perfect; (*mejorar*) improve. **~cionista** *m & f* perfectionist. **~tamente** *adv* perfectly. ● *int* of course! **~to** *a* perfect; (*completo*) complete. **a la ~ción** perfectly, to perfection

perfidia *f* treachery

pérfido *a* treacherous

perfil *m* profile; (*contorno*) outline; **~es** *mpl* (*fig*, *rasgos*) features. **~ado** *a* (*bien terminado*) well-finished. **~ar** *vt* draw in profile; (*fig*) put the finishing touches to

perfora|ción *f* perforation. **~do** *m* perforation. **~dora** *f* punch. **~r** *vt* pierce, perforate; punch ‹*papel, tarjeta etc*›

perfum|ar *vt* perfume. **~arse** *vpr* put perfume on. **~e** *m* perfume, scent. **~ería** *f* perfumery

pergamino *m* parchment

pericia *f* expertise

pericón *m* popular Argentinian dance

perif|eria *f* (*de población*) outskirts. **~érico** *a* peripheral

perilla *f* (*barba*) goatee

perímetro *m* perimeter

periódico *a* periodic(al). ● *m* newspaper

periodis|mo *m* journalism. **~ta** *m & f* journalist

período *m*, **periodo** *m* period

periquito *m* budgerigar

periscopio *m* periscope

perito *a & m* expert

perju|dicar [7] *vt* harm; (*desfavorecer*) not suit. **~dicial** *a* harmful. **~icio** *m* harm. **en ~icio de** to the detriment of

perjur|ar *vi* perjure o.s. **~io** *m* perjury

perla *f* pearl. **de ~s** *adv* very well. ● *a* excellent

permane|cer [11] *vi* remain. **~ncia** *f* permanence; (*estancia*) stay. **~nte** *a* permanent. ● *f* perm

permeable *a* permeable

permi|sible *a* permissible. **~sivo** *a* permissive. **~so** *m* permission; (*documento*) licence; (*mil etc*) leave. **~so de conducción**, **~so de conducir** driving licence (*Brit*), driver's license (*Amer*). **~tir** *vt* allow, permit. **~tirse** *vpr* be allowed. **con ~so** excuse me. **¿me ~te?** may I?

permutación *f* exchange; (*math*) permutation

pernicioso *a* pernicious; ‹*persona*› wicked

pernio *m* hinge

perno *m* bolt

pero *conj* but. ● *m* fault; (*objeción*) objection

perogrullada *f* platitude

perol *m* pan

peronista *m & f* follower of Juan Perón

perorar *vi* make a speech

perpendicular *a & f* perpendicular

perpetrar *vt* perpetrate

perpetu|ar [21] *vt* perpetuate. **~o** *a* perpetual

perplej|idad *f* perplexity. **~o** *a* perplexed

perr|a *f* (*animal*) bitch; (*moneda*) coin, penny (*Brit*), cent (*Amer*); (*rabieta*) tantrum. **~era** *f* kennel. **~ería** *f* (*mala jugada*) dirty trick; (*palabra*) harsh word. **~o** *a* awful ● *m* dog. **~o corredor** hound. **~o de aguas** spaniel. **~o del hortelano** dog in the manger. **~o galgo** greyhound. **de ~os** awful. **estar sin una ~a** be broke

persa *a & m & f* Persian

perse|cución *f* pursuit; (*tormento*) persecution. **~guir** [5 & 13] *vt* pursue; (*atormentar*) persecute

persevera|ncia *f* perseverance. **~nte** *a* persevering. **~r** *vi* persevere

persiana *f* (Venetian) blind

persist|encia *f* persistence. **~ente** *a* persistent. **~ir** *vi* persist

person|a *f* person. **~as** *fpl* people. **~aje** *m* (*persona importante*) important person; (*de obra literaria*) character. **~al** *a* personal; (*para una persona*) single. ● *m* staff. **~alidad** *f* personality. **~arse** *vpr* appear in person. **~ificar** [7] *vt* personify. **~ificación** *f* personification

perspectiva *f* perspective

perspica|cia *f* shrewdness; (*de vista*) keen eye-sight. **~z** *a* shrewd; ‹*vista*› keen

persua|dir *vt* persuade. **~sión** *f* persuasion. **~sivo** *a* persuasive

pertenecer [11] *vi* belong

pertinaz *a* persistent

pertinente *a* relevant

perturba|ción *f* disturbance. **~r** *vt* perturb

Perú *m*. **el ~** Peru

peruano *a* & *m* Peruvian

perver|sión *f* perversion. **~so** *a* perverse. ● *m* pervert. **~tir** [4] *vt* pervert

pervivir *vi* live on

pesa *f* weight. **~dez** *f* weight; (*de cabeza etc*) heaviness; (*lentitud*) sluggishness; (*cualidad de fastidioso*) tediousness; (*cosa fastidiosa*) bore, nuisance

pesadilla *f* nightmare

pesad|o *a* heavy; (*lento*) slow; (*duro*) hard; (*aburrido*) boring, tedious. **~umbre** *f* (*pena*) sorrow

pésame *m* sympathy, condolences

pesar *vt/i* weigh. ● *m* sorrow; (*remordimiento*) regret. **a ~ de (que)** in spite of. **me pesa que** I'm sorry that. **pese a (que)** in spite of

pesario *m* pessary

pesca *f* fishing; (*peces*) fish; (*pescado*) catch. **~da** *f* hake. **~dería** *f* fish shop. **~dilla** *f* whiting. **~do** *m* fish. **~dor** *a* fishing. ● *m* fisherman. **~r** [7] *vt* catch. ● *vi* fish. **ir de ~** go fishing

pescuezo *m* neck

pesebre *m* manger

pesero *m* (*Mex*) minibus taxi

peseta *f* peseta; (*Mex*) twenty-five centavos

pesimis|mo *m* pessimism. **~ta** *a* pessimistic. ● *m* & *f* pessimist

pésimo *a* very bad, awful

peso *m* weight; (*moneda*) peso. **~ bruto** gross weight. **~ neto** net weight. **a ~** by weight. **de ~** influential

pesquero *a* fishing

pesquisa *f* inquiry

pestañ|a *f* eyelash. **~ear** *vi* blink. **sin ~ear** without batting an eyelid

pest|e *f* plague; (*hedor*) stench. **~icida** *m* pesticide. **~ilencia** *f* pestilence; (*hedor*) stench

pestillo *m* bolt

pestiño *m* pancake with honey

petaca *f* tobacco case; (*LAm, maleta*) suitcase

pétalo *m* petal

petardo *m* firework

petición *f* request; (*escrito*) petition. **a ~ de** at the request of

petirrojo *m* robin

petrificar [7] *vt* petrify

petr|óleo *m* oil. **~olero** *a* oil. ● *m* oil tanker. **~olífero** *a* oil-bearing

petulante *a* arrogant

peyorativo *a* pejorative

pez *f* fish; (*substancia negruzca*) pitch. **~ espada** swordfish

pezón *m* nipple; (*bot*) stalk

pezuña *f* hoof

piada *f* chirp

piadoso *a* compassionate; (*devoto*) devout

pian|ista *m* & *f* pianist. **~o** *m* piano. **~o de cola** grand piano

piar [20] *vi* chirp

pib|a *f* (*LAm*) little girl. **~e** *m* (*LAm*) little boy

picad|illo *m* mince; (*guiso*) stew. **~o** *a* perforated; ‹*carne*› minced; (*ofendido*) offended; ‹*mar*› choppy; ‹*diente*› bad. **~ura** *f* bite, sting; (*de polilla*) moth hole

picante *a* hot; ‹*palabras etc*› cutting

picaporte *m* door-handle; (*aldaba*) knocker

picar [7] *vt* prick, pierce; ‹*ave*› peck; ‹*insecto, pez*› bite; ‹*avispa*› sting; (*comer poco*) pick at; mince ‹*carne*›. ● *vi* prick; ‹*ave*› peck; ‹*insecto, pez*› bite; ‹*sol*› scorch; ‹*sabor fuerte*› be hot. **~ alto** aim high

picard|ear *vt* corrupt. **~ía** *f* wickedness; (*travesura*) naughty thing

picaresco *a* roguish; ‹*literatura*› picaresque

pícaro *a* villainous; ‹*niño*› mischievous. ● *m* rogue

picatoste *m* toast; (*frito*) fried bread

picazón *f* itch

pico *m* beak; (*punta*) corner; (*herramienta*) pickaxe; (*cima*) peak.

~tear *vt* peck; (*comer, fam*) pick at. **y ~** (*con tiempo*) a little after; (*con cantidad*) a little more than

picudo *a* pointed

pich|ona *f* (*fig*) darling; **~ón** *m* pigeon

pido *vb véase* **pedir**

pie *m* foot; (*bot, de vaso*) stem. **~ cuadrado** square foot. **a cuatro ~s** on all fours. **al ~ de la letra** literally. **a ~** on foot. **a ~(s) juntillas** (*fig*) firmly. **buscarle tres ~s al gato** split hairs. **de ~** standing (up). **de ~s a cabeza** from head to foot. **en ~** standing (up). **ponerse de/en ~** stand up

piedad *f* pity; (*relig*) piety

piedra *f* stone; (*de mechero*) flint; (*granizo*) hailstone

piel *f* skin; (*cuero*) leather. **artículos de ~** leather goods

pienso *vb véase* **pensar**

pierdo *vb véase* **perder**

pierna *f* leg. **estirar las ~s** stretch one's legs

pieza *f* piece; (*parte*) part; (*obra teatral*) play; (*moneda*) coin; (*habitación*) room. **~ de recambio** spare part

pífano *m* fife

pigment|ación *f* pigmentation. **~o** *m* pigment

pigmeo *a & m* pygmy

pijama *m* pyjamas

pila *f* (*montón*) pile; (*recipiente*) basin; (*eléctrica*) battery. **~ bautismal** font

píldora *f* pill

pilot|ar *vt* pilot. **~o** *m* pilot

pilla|je *m* pillage. **~r** *vt* pillage; (*alcanzar, agarrar*) catch; (*atropellar*) run over

pillo *a* wicked. ● *m* rogue

pim|entero *m* (*vasija*) pepper-pot. **~entón** *m* paprika, cayenne pepper. **~ienta** *f* pepper. **~iento** *m* pepper. **grano** *m* **de ~ienta** peppercorn

pináculo *m* pinnacle

pinar *m* pine forest

pincel *m* paintbrush. **~ada** *f* brush-stroke. **la última ~ada** (*fig*) the finishing touch

pinch|ar *vt* pierce, prick; puncture ‹*neumático*›; (*fig, incitar*) push; (*med, fam*) give an injection to. **~azo** *m* prick; (*en neumático*) puncture. **~itos** *mpl* kebab(s); (*tapas*) savoury snacks. **~o** *m* point

ping|ajo *m* rag. **~o** *m* rag

ping-pong *m* table tennis, ping-pong

pingüino *m* penguin

pino *m* pine (tree)

pint|a *f* spot; (*fig, aspecto*) appearance. **~ada** *f* graffiti. **~ar** *vt* paint. **~arse** *vpr* put on make-up. **~or** *m* painter. **~or de brocha gorda** painter and decorator. **~oresco** *a* picturesque. **~ura** *f* painting. **no ~a nada** (*fig*) it doesn't count. **tener ~a de** look like

pinza *f* (clothes-)peg (*Brit*), (clothes-) pin (*Amer*); (*de cangrejo etc*) claw. **~s** *fpl* tweezers

pinzón *m* chaffinch

piñ|a *f* pine cone; (*ananás*) pineapple; (*fig, grupo*) group. **~ón** *m* (*semilla*) pine nut

pío *a* pious; ‹*caballo*› piebald. ● *m* chirp. **no decir (ni) ~** not say a word

piocha *f* pickaxe

piojo *m* louse

pionero *m* pioneer

pipa *f* pipe; (*semilla*) seed; (*de girasol*) sunflower seed

pipián *m* (*LAm*) stew

pique *m* resentment; (*rivalidad*) rivalry. **irse a ~** sink

piqueta *f* pickaxe

piquete *m* picket

piragua *f* canoe

pirámide *f* pyramid

pirata *m & f* pirate

Pirineos *mpl* Pyrenees

piropo *m* (*fam*) compliment

piruet|a *f* pirouette. **~ear** *vi* pirouette

pirulí *m* lollipop

pisa|da *f* footstep; (*huella*) footprint. **~papeles** *m invar* paperweight. **~r** *vt* tread on; (*apretar*) press; (*fig*) walk over. ● *vi* tread. **no ~r el césped** keep off the grass

piscina *f* swimming pool; (*para peces*) fish-pond

Piscis *m* Pisces

piso *m* floor; (*vivienda*) flat (*Brit*), apartment (*Amer*); (*de zapato*) sole

pisotear *vt* trample (on)

pista *f* track; (*fig, indicio*) clue. **~ de aterrizaje** runway. **~ de baile** dance floor. **~ de hielo** skating-rink. **~ de tenis** tennis court

pistacho *m* pistachio (nut)

pisto *m* fried vegetables

pistol|a *f* pistol. **~era** *f* holster. **~ero** *m* gunman

pistón *m* piston
pit|ar *vt* whistle at. ● *vi* blow a whistle; (*auto*) sound one's horn. **~ido** *m* whistle
pitill|era *f* cigarette case. **~o** *m* cigarette
pito *m* whistle; (*auto*) horn
pitón *m* python
pitorre|arse *vpr*. **~arse de** make fun of. **~o** *m* teasing
pitorro *m* spout
pivote *m* pivot
pizarr|a *f* slate; (*encerrado*) blackboard. **~ón** *m* (*LAm*) blackboard
pizca *f* (*fam*) tiny piece; (*de sal*) pinch. **ni ~** not at all
pizz|a *f* pizza. **~ería** *f* pizzeria
placa *f* plate; (*conmemorativa*) plaque; (*distintivo*) badge
pláceme *m* congratulations
place|ntero *a* pleasant. **~r** [32] *vt* please. **me ~** I like. ● *m* pleasure
plácido *a* placid
plaga *f* plague; (*fig, calamidad*) disaster; (*fig, abundancia*) glut. **~r** [12] *vt* fill
plagi|ar *vt* plagiarize. **~o** *m* plagiarism
plan *m* plan; (*med*) course of treatment. **a todo ~** on a grand scale. **en ~ de** as
plana *f* (*llanura*) plain; (*página*) page. **en primera ~** on the front page
plancha *f* iron; (*lámina*) sheet. **~do** *m* ironing. **~r** *vt/i* iron. **a la ~** grilled. **tirarse una ~** put one's foot in it
planeador *m* glider
planear *vt* plan. ● *vi* glide
planeta *m* planet. **~rio** *a* planetary. ● *m* planetarium
planicie *f* plain
planifica|ción *f* planning. **~r** [7] *vt* plan
planilla *f* (*LAm*) list
plano *a* flat. ● *m* plane; (*de ciudad*) plan. **primer ~** foreground; (*foto*) close-up
planta *f* (*anat*) sole; (*bot, fábrica*) plant; (*plano*) ground plan; (*piso*) floor. **~ baja** ground floor (*Brit*), first floor (*Amer*)
planta|ción *f* plantation. **~do** *a* planted. **~r** *vt* plant; deal ‹*golpe*›. **~r en la calle** throw out. **~rse** *vpr* stand; (*fig*) stand firm. **bien ~do** good-looking
plantear *vt* (*exponer*) expound; (*causar*) create; raise ‹*cuestión*›
plantilla *f* insole; (*modelo*) pattern; (*personal*) personnel
plaqué *m* plate
plasma *m* plasma
plástico *a* & *m* plastic
plata *f* silver; (*fig, dinero, fam*) money. **~ de ley** sterling silver. **~ alemana** nickel silver
plataforma *f* platform
plátano *m* plane (tree); (*fruta*) banana; (*platanero*) banana tree
platea *f* stalls (*Brit*), orchestra (*Amer*)
plateado *a* silver-plated; (*color de plata*) silver
pl|ática *f* chat, talk. **~aticar** [7] *vi* chat, talk
platija *f* plaice
platillo *m* saucer; (*mus*) cymbal. **~ volante** flying saucer
platino *m* platinum. **~s** *mpl* (*auto*) points
plato *m* plate; (*comida*) dish; (*parte de una comida*) course
platónico *a* platonic
plausible *a* plausible; (*loable*) praiseworthy
playa *f* beach; (*fig*) seaside
plaza *f* square; (*mercado*) market; (*sitio*) place; (*empleo*) job. **~ de toros** bullring
plazco *vb véase* **placer**
plazo *m* period; (*pago*) instalment; (*fecha*) date. **comprar a ~s** buy on hire purchase (*Brit*), buy on the installment plan (*Amer*)
plazuela *f* little square
pleamar *f* high tide
plebe *f* common people. **~yo** *a* & *m* plebeian
plebiscito *m* plebiscite
plectro *m* plectrum
plega|ble *a* pliable; ‹*silla etc*› folding. **~r** [1 & 12] *vt* fold. **~rse** *vpr* bend; (*fig*) give way
pleito *m* (court) case; (*fig*) dispute
plenilunio *m* full moon
plen|itud *f* fullness; (*fig*) height. **~o** *a* full. **en ~o día** in broad daylight. **en ~o verano** at the height of the summer
pleuresía *f* pleuresy
plieg|o *m* sheet. **~ue** *m* fold; (*en ropa*) pleat
plinto *m* plinth
plisar *vt* pleat

plom|ero *m* (*esp LAm*) plumber. **~o** *m* lead; (*elec*) fuse. **de ~o** lead
pluma *f* feather; (*para escribir*) pen. **~ estilográfica** fountain pen. **~je** *m* plumage
plúmbeo *a* leaden
plum|ero *m* feather duster; (*para plumas, lapices etc*) pencil-case. **~ón** *m* down
plural *a & m* plural. **~idad** *f* plurality; (*mayoría*) majority. **en ~** in the plural
pluriempleo *m* having more than one job
plus *m* bonus
pluscuamperfecto *m* pluperfect
plusvalía *f* appreciation
plut|ocracia *f* plutocracy. **~ócrata** *m & f* plutocrat. **~ocrático** *a* plutocratic
plutonio *m* plutonium
pluvial *a* rain
pobla|ción *f* population; (*ciudad*) city, town; (*pueblo*) village. **~do** *a* populated. • *m* village. **~r** [2] *vt* populate; (*habitar*) inhabit. **~rse** *vpr* get crowded
pobre *a* poor. • *m & f* poor person; (*fig*) poor thing. **¡~cito!** poor (little) thing! **¡~ de mí!** poor (old) me! **~za** *f* poverty
pocilga *f* pigsty
poción *f* potion
poco *a* not much, little; (*en plural*) few; (*unos*) a few. • *m* (a) little. • *adv* little, not much; (*con adjetivo*) not very; (*poco tiempo*) not long. **~ a ~** little by little, gradually. **a ~ de** soon after. **dentro de ~** soon. **hace ~** not long ago. **poca cosa** nothing much. **por ~** (*fam*) nearly
podar *vt* prune
poder [33] *vi* be able. **no pudo venir** he couldn't come. **¿puedo hacer algo?** can I do anything? **¿puedo pasar?** may I come in? • *m* power. **~es** *mpl* **públicos** authorities. **~oso** *a* powerful. **en el ~** in power. **no ~ con** not be able to cope with; (*no aguantar*) not be able to stand. **no ~ más** be exhausted; (*estar harto de algo*) not be able to manage any more. **no ~ menos que** not be able to help. **puede que** it is possible that. **puede ser** it is possible. **¿se puede ...?** may I ...?
podrido *a* rotten
po|ema *m* poem. **~esía** *f* poetry; (*poema*) poem. **~eta** *m* poet. **~ético** *a* poetic

polaco *a* Polish. • *m* Pole; (*lengua*) Polish
polar *a* polar. **estrella ~** polestar
polarizar [10] *vt* polarize
polca *f* polka
polea *f* pulley
pol|émica *f* controversy. **~émico** *a* polemic(al). **~emizar** [10] *vi* argue
polen *m* pollen
policía *f* police (force); (*persona*) policewoman. • *m* policeman. **~co** *a* police; ‹*novela etc*› detective
policlínica *f* clinic, hospital
policromo, polícromo *a* polychrome
polideportivo *m* sports centre
poliéster *m* polyester
poliestireno *m* polystyrene
polietileno *m* polythene
pol|igamia *f* polygamy. **~ígamo** *a* polygamous
polígloto *m & f* polyglot
polígono *m* polygon
polilla *f* moth
polio(mielitis) *f* polio(myelitis)
pólipo *m* polyp
politécnic|a *f* polytechnic. **~o** *a* polytechnic
polític|a *f* politics. **~o** *a* political; ‹*pariente*› -in-law. • *m* politician. **padre** *m* **~o** father-in-law
póliza *f* document; (*de seguros*) policy
polo *m* pole; (*helado*) ice lolly (*Brit*); (*juego*) polo. **~ helado** ice lolly (*Brit*). **~ norte** North Pole
Polonia *f* Poland
poltrona *f* armchair
polución *f* (*contaminación*) pollution
polv|areda *f* cloud of dust; (*fig, escándalo*) scandal. **~era** *f* compact. **~o** *m* powder; (*suciedad*) dust. **~os** *mpl* powder. **en ~o** powdered. **estar hecho ~o** be exhausted. **quitar el ~o** dust
pólvora *f* gunpowder; (*fuegos artificiales*) fireworks
polvor|iento *a* dusty. **~ón** *m* Spanish Christmas shortcake
poll|ada *f* brood. **~era** *f* (*para niños*) baby-walker; (*LAm, falda*) skirt. **~ería** *f* poultry shop. **~o** *m* chicken; (*gallo joven*) chick
pomada *f* ointment
pomelo *m* grapefruit
pómez *a*. **piedra** *f* **~** pumice stone
pomp|a *f* bubble; (*esplendor*) pomp. **~as fúnebres** funeral. **~oso** *a* pompous; (*espléndido*) splendid

pómulo *m* cheek; (*hueso*) cheekbone

poncha|do *a* (*Mex*) punctured, flat. **~r** *vt* (*Mex*) puncture

ponche *m* punch

poncho *m* poncho

ponderar *vt* (*alabar*) speak highly of

poner [34] *vt* put; put on ‹*ropa, obra de teatro, TV etc*›; (*suponer*) suppose; lay ‹*la mesa, un huevo*›; (*hacer*) make; (*contribuir*) contribute; give ‹*nombre*›; show ‹*película, interés*›; open ‹*una tienda*›; equip ‹*una casa*›. ● *vi* lay. **~se** *vpr* put o.s.; (*volverse*) get; put on ‹*ropa*›; ‹*sol*› set. **~ con** (*al teléfono*) put through to. **~ en claro** clarify. **~ por escrito** put into writing. **~ una multa** fine. **~se a** start to. **~se a mal con uno** fall out with s.o. **pongamos** let's suppose

pongo *vb véase* **poner**

poniente *m* west; (*viento*) west wind

pont|ificado *m* pontificate. **~ifical** *a* pontifical. **~ificar** [7] *vi* pontificate. **~ífice** *m* pontiff

pontón *m* pontoon

popa *f* stern

popelín *m* poplin

popul|acho *m* masses. **~ar** *a* popular; ‹*lenguaje*› colloquial. **~aridad** *f* popularity. **~arizar** [10] *vt* popularize. **~oso** *a* populous

póquer *m* poker

poquito *m* a little bit. ● *adv* a little

por *prep* for; (*para*) (in order) to; (*a través de*) through; (*a causa de*) because of; (*como agente*) by; (*en matemática*) times; (*como función*) as; (*en lugar de*) instead of. **~ la calle** along the street. **~ mí** as for me, for my part. **~ si** in case. **~ todo el país** throughout the country. **50 kilómetros ~ hora** 50 kilometres per hour

porcelana *f* china

porcentaje *m* percentage

porcino *a* pig. ● *m* small pig

porción *f* portion; (*de chocolate*) piece

pordiosero *m* beggar

porf|ía *f* persistence; (*disputa*) dispute. **~iado** *a* persistent. **~iar** [20] *vi* insist. **a ~ía** in competition

pormenor *m* detail

pornogr|afía *f* pornography. **~áfico** *a* pornographic

poro *m* pore. **~so** *a* porous

poroto *m* (*LAm, judía*) bean

porque *conj* because; (*para que*) so that

porqué *m* reason

porquería *f* filth; (*basura*) rubbish; (*grosería*) dirty trick

porra *f* club; (*culin*) fritter

porrón *m* wine jug (with a long spout)

portaaviones *m invar* aircraft-carrier

portada *f* façade; (*de libro*) title page

portador *m* bearer

porta|equipaje(s) *m invar* boot (*Brit*), trunk (*Amer*); (*encima del coche*) roof-rack. **~estandarte** *m* standard-bearer

portal *m* hall; (*puerta principal*) main entrance; (*soportal*) porch

porta|lámparas *m invar* socket. **~ligas** *m invar* suspender belt. **~monedas** *m invar* purse

portarse *vpr* behave

portátil *a* portable

portavoz *m* megaphone; (*fig, persona*) spokesman

portazgo *m* toll

portazo *m* bang. **dar un ~** slam the door

porte *m* transport; (*precio*) carriage. **~ador** *m* carrier

portento *m* marvel

porteño *a* (*de Buenos Aires*) from Buenos Aires. ● *m* person from Buenos Aires

porter|ía *f* caretaker's lodge, porter's lodge; (*en deportes*) goal. **~o** *m* caretaker, porter; (*en deportes*) goalkeeper. **~o automático** intercom (*fam*)

portezuela *f* small door; (*auto*) door

pórtico *m* portico

portill|a *f* gate; (*en barco*) porthole. **~o** *m* opening

portorriqueño *a* Puerto Rican

Portugal *m* Portugal

portugués *a & m* Portuguese

porvenir *m* future

posada *f* guest house; (*mesón*) inn

posaderas *fpl* (*fam*) bottom

posar *vt* put. ● *vi* ‹*pájaro*› perch; ‹*modelo*› sit. **~se** *vpr* settle

posdata *f* postscript

pose|edor *m* owner. **~er** [18] *vt* have, own; (*saber*) know well. **~ído** *a* possessed. **~sión** *f* possession. **~sionar** *vt*. **~sionar de** hand over. **~sionarse** *vpr*. **~sionarse de** take possession of. **~sivo** *a* possessive

posfechar *vt* postdate

posguerra *f* post-war years
posib|ilidad *f* possibility. **~le** *a* possible. **de ser ~le** if possible. **en lo ~le** as far as possible. **hacer todo lo ~le para** do everything possible to. **si es ~le** if possible
posición *f* position
positivo *a* positive
poso *m* sediment
posponer [34] *vt* put after; (*diferir*) postpone
posta *f*. **a ~** on purpose
postal *a* postal. ● *f* postcard
poste *m* pole
postergar [12] *vt* pass over; (*diferir*) postpone
posteri|dad *f* posterity. **~or** *a* back; (*ulterior*) later. **~ormente** *adv* later
postigo *m* door; (*contraventana*) shutter
postizo *a* false, artificial. ● *m* hairpiece
postra|do *a* prostrate. **~r** *vt* prostrate. **~rse** *vpr* prostrate o.s.
postre *m* dessert, sweet (*Brit*). **de ~** for dessert
postular *vt* postulate; collect ‹*dinero*›
póstumo *a* posthumous
postura *f* position, stance
potable *a* drinkable; ‹*agua*› drinking
potaje *m* vegetable stew
potasio *m* potassium
pote *m* jar
poten|cia *f* power. **~cial** *a* & *m* potential. **~te** *a* powerful. **en ~cia** potential
potingue *m* (*fam*) concoction
potr|a *f* filly. **~o** *m* colt; (*en gimnasia*) horse. **tener ~a** be lucky
pozo *m* well; (*hoyo seco*) pit; (*de mina*) shaft
pozole *m* (*Mex*) stew
práctica *f* practice; (*destreza*) skill. **en la ~** in practice. **poner en ~** put into practice
practica|ble *a* practicable. **~nte** *m* & *f* nurse. **~r** [7] *vt* practise; play ‹*deportes*›; (*ejecutar*) carry out
práctico *a* practical; (*diestro*) skilled. ● *m* practitioner
prad|era *f* meadow; (*terreno grande*) prairie. **~o** *m* meadow
pragmático *a* pragmatic
preámbulo *m* preamble
precario *a* precarious
precaución *f* precaution; (*cautela*) caution. **con ~** cautiously
precaver *vt* guard against
precede|ncia *f* precedence; (*prioridad*) priority. **~nte** *a* preceding. ● *m* precedent. **~r** *vt/i* precede
precepto *m* precept. **~r** *m* tutor
precia|do *a* valuable; (*estimado*) esteemed. **~rse** *vpr* boast
precinto *m* seal
precio *m* price. **~ de venta al público** retail price. **al ~ de** at the cost of. **no tener ~** be priceless. **¿qué ~ tiene?** how much is it?
precios|idad *f* value; (*cosa preciosa*) beautiful thing. **~o** *a* precious; (*bonito*) beautiful. **¡es una ~idad!** it's beautiful!
precipicio *m* precipice
precipita|ción *f* precipitation. **~damente** *adv* hastily. **~do** *a* hasty. **~r** *vt* hurl; (*acelerar*) accelerate; (*apresurar*) hasten. **~rse** *vpr* throw o.s.; (*correr*) rush; (*actuar sin reflexionar*) act rashly
precis|amente *a* exactly. **~ar** *vt* require; (*determinar*) determine. **~ión** *f* precision; (*necesidad*) need. **~o** *a* precise; (*necesario*) necessary
preconcebido *a* preconceived
precoz *a* early; ‹*niño*› precocious
precursor *m* forerunner
predecesor *m* predecessor
predecir [46]; *o* [46, *pero imperativo* **predice**, *futuro y condicional regulares*] *vt* foretell
predestina|ción *f* predestination. **~r** *vt* predestine
prédica *f* sermon
predicamento *m* influence
predicar [7] *vt/i* preach
predicción *f* prediction; (*del tiempo*) forecast
predilec|ción *f* predilection. **~to** *a* favourite
predisponer [34] *vt* predispose
predomin|ante *a* predominant. **~ar** *vt* dominate. ● *vi* predominate. **~io** *m* predominance
preeminente *a* pre-eminent
prefabricado *a* prefabricated
prefacio *m* preface
prefect|o *m* prefect. **~ura** *f* prefecture
prefer|encia *f* preference. **~ente** *a* preferential. **~ible** *a* preferable. **~ido** *a* favourite. **~ir** [4] *vt* prefer. **de ~encia** preferably
prefigurar *vt* foreshadow
prefij|ar *vt* fix beforehand; (*gram*) prefix. **~o** *m* prefix; (*telefónico*) dialling code

preg|ón *m* announcement. **~onar** *vt* announce
pregunta *f* question. **~r** *vt/i* ask. **~rse** *vpr* wonder. **hacer ~s** ask questions
prehistórico *a* prehistoric
preju|icio *m* prejudice. **~zgar** [12] *vt* prejudge
prelado *m* prelate
preliminar *a & m* preliminary
preludio *m* prelude
premarital *a*, **prematrimonial** *a* premarital
prematuro *a* premature
premedita|ción *f* premeditation. **~r** *vt* premeditate
premi|ar *vt* give a prize to; (*recompensar*) reward. **~o** *m* prize; (*recompensa*) reward; (*com*) premium. **~o gordo** first prize
premonición *f* premonition
premura *f* urgency; (*falta*) lack
prenatal *a* antenatal
prenda *f* pledge; (*de vestir*) article of clothing, garment; (*de cama etc*) linen. **~s** *fpl* (*cualidades*) talents; (*juego*) forfeits. **~r** *vt* captivate. **~rse** *vpr* be captivated (**de** by); (*enamorarse*) fall in love (**de** with)
prender *vt* capture; (*sujetar*) fasten. • *vi* catch; (*arraigar*) take root. **~se** *vpr* (*encenderse*) catch fire
prensa *f* press. **~r** *vt* press
preñado *a* pregnant; (*fig*) full
preocupa|ción *f* worry. **~do** *a* worried. **~r** *vt* worry. **~rse** *vpr* worry. **~rse de** look after. **¡no te preocupes!** don't worry!
prepara|ción *f* preparation. **~do** *a* prepared. • *m* preparation. **~r** *vt* prepare. **~rse** *vpr* get ready. **~tivo** *a* preparatory. • *m* preparation. **~torio** *a* preparatory
preponderancia *f* preponderance
preposición *f* preposition
prepotente *a* powerful; (*fig*) presumptuous
prerrogativa *f* prerogative
presa *f* (*acción*) capture; (*cosa*) catch; (*embalse*) dam
presagi|ar *vt* presage. **~o** *m* omen; (*premonición*) premonition
présbita *a* long-sighted
presb|iteriano *a & m* Presbyterian. **~iterio** *m* presbytery. **~ítero** *m* priest
prescindir *vi*. **~ de** do without; (*deshacerse de*) dispense with
prescri|bir (*pp* **prescrito**) *vt* prescribe. **~pción** *f* prescription
presencia *f* presence; (*aspecto*) appearance. **~r** *vt* be present at; (*ver*) witness. **en ~ de** in the presence of
presenta|ble *a* presentable. **~ción** *f* presentation; (*aspecto*) appearance; (*de una persona a otra*) introduction. **~dor** *m* presenter. **~r** *vt* present; (*ofrecer*) offer; (*hacer conocer*) introduce; show ‹*película*›. **~rse** *vpr* present o.s.; (*hacerse conocer*) introduce o.s.; (*aparecer*) turn up
presente *a* present; (*este*) this. • *m* present. **los ~s** those present. **tener ~** remember
presenti|miento *m* presentiment; (*de algo malo*) foreboding. **~r** [4] *vt* have a presentiment of
preserva|ción *f* preservation. **~r** *vt* preserve. **~tivo** *m* condom
presiden|cia *f* presidency; (*de asamblea*) chairmanship. **~cial** *a* presidential. **~ta** *f* (woman) president. **~te** *m* president; (*de asamblea*) chairman. **~te del gobierno** leader of the government, prime minister
presidi|ario *m* convict. **~o** *m* prison
presidir *vt* preside over
presilla *f* fastener
presi|ón *f* pressure. **~onar** *vt* press; (*fig*) put pressure on. **a ~ón** under pressure. **hacer ~ón** press
preso *a* under arrest; (*fig*) stricken. • *m* prisoner
presta|do *a* (*a uno*) lent; (*de uno*) borrowed. **~mista** *m & f* moneylender. **pedir ~do** borrow
préstamo *m* loan; (*acción de pedir prestado*) borrowing
prestar *vt* lend; give ‹*ayuda etc*›; pay ‹*atención*›. • *vi* lend
prestidigita|ción *f* conjuring. **~dor** *m* magician
prestigio *m* prestige. **~so** *a* prestigious
presu|mido *a* presumptuous. **~mir** *vt* presume. • *vi* be conceited. **~nción** *f* presumption. **~nto** *a* presumed. **~ntuoso** *a* presumptuous
presup|oner [34] *vt* presuppose. **~uesto** *m* budget
presuroso *a* quick
preten|cioso *a* pretentious. **~der** *vt* try to; (*afirmar*) claim; (*solicitar*) apply for; (*cortejar*) court. **~dido** *a* so-called. **~diente** *m* pretender; (*a*

una mujer) suitor. **~sión** *f* pretension; (*aspiración*) aspiration

pretérito *m* preterite, past

pretexto *m* pretext. **a ~ de** on the pretext of

prevalec|er [11] *vi* prevail. **~iente** *a* prevalent

prevalerse [42] *vpr* take advantage

preven|ción *f* prevention; (*prejuicio*) prejudice. **~ido** *a* ready; (*precavido*) cautious. **~ir** [53] *vt* prepare; (*proveer*) provide; (*precaver*) prevent; (*advertir*) warn. **~tivo** *a* preventive

prever [43] *vt* foresee; (*prepararse*) plan

previo *a* previous

previs|ible *a* predictable. **~ión** *f* forecast; (*prudencia*) prudence. **~ión de tiempo** weather forecast. **~to** *a* foreseen

prima *f* (*pariente*) cousin; (*cantidad*) bonus

primario *a* primary

primate *m* primate; (*fig, persona*) important person

primavera *f* spring. **~l** *a* spring

primer *a véase* **primero**

primer|a *f* (*auto*) first (gear); (*en tren etc*) first class. **~o** *a* (*delante de nombre masculino en singular* **primer**) first; (*principal*) main; (*anterior*) former; (*mejor*) best. ● *n* (the) first. ● *adv* first. **~a enseñanza** primary education. **a ~os de** at the beginning of. **de ~a** first-class

primitivo *a* primitive

primo *m* cousin; (*fam*) fool. **hacer el ~** be taken for a ride

primogénito *a & m* first-born, eldest

primor *m* delicacy; (*cosa*) beautiful thing

primordial *a* basic

princesa *f* princess

principado *m* principality

principal *a* principal. ● *m* (*jefe*) head, boss (*fam*)

príncipe *m* prince

principi|ante *m & f* beginner. **~ar** *vt/i* begin, start. **~o** *m* beginning; (*moral, idea*) principle; (*origen*) origin. **al ~o** at first. **a ~o(s) de** at the beginning of. **dar ~o a** start. **desde el ~o** from the outset. **en ~o** in principle. **~os** *mpl* (*nociones*) rudiments

pring|oso *a* greasy. **~ue** *m* dripping; (*mancha*) grease mark

prior *m* prior. **~ato** *m* priory

prioridad *f* priority

prisa *f* hurry, haste. **a ~** quickly. **a toda ~** (*fam*) as quickly as possible. **correr ~** be urgent. **darse ~** hurry (up). **de ~** quickly. **tener ~** be in a hurry

prisi|ón *f* prison; (*encarcelamiento*) imprisonment. **~onero** *m* prisoner

prism|a *m* prism. **~áticos** *mpl* binoculars

priva|ción *f* deprivation. **~do** *a* (*particular*) private. **~r** *vt* deprive (**de** of); (*prohibir*) prevent (**de** from). ● *vi* be popular. **~tivo** *a* exclusive (**de** to)

privilegi|ado *a* privileged; (*muy bueno*) exceptional. **~o** *m* privilege

pro *prep* for. ● *m* advantage. ● *pref* pro-. **el ~ y el contra** the pros and cons. **en ~ de** on behalf of. **los ~s y los contras** the pros and cons

proa *f* bows

probab|ilidad *f* probability. **~le** *a* probable, likely. **~lemente** *adv* probably

proba|dor *m* fitting-room. **~r** [2] *vt* try; try on ‹*ropa*›; (*demostrar*) prove. ● *vi* try. **~rse** *vpr* try on

probeta *f* test-tube

problem|a *m* problem. **~ático** *a* problematic

procaz *a* insolent

proced|encia *f* origin. **~ente** *a* (*razonable*) reasonable. **~ente de** (coming) from. **~er** *m* conduct. ● *vi* proceed. **~er contra** start legal proceedings against. **~er de** come from. **~imiento** *m* procedure; (*sistema*) process; (*jurid*) proceedings

procesador *m*. **~ de textos** word processor

procesal *a*. **costas ~es** legal costs

procesamiento *m* processing. **~ de textos** word-processing

procesar *vt* prosecute

procesión *f* procession

proceso *m* process; (*jurid*) trial; (*transcurso*) course

proclama *f* proclamation. **~ción** *f* proclamation. **~r** *vt* proclaim

procrea|ción *f* procreation. **~r** *vt* procreate

procura|dor *m* attorney, solicitor. **~r** *vt* try; (*obtener*) get; (*dar*) give

prodigar [12] *vt* lavish. **~se** *vpr* do one's best

prodigio *m* prodigy; (*milagro*) miracle. **~ioso** *a* prodigious
pródigo *a* prodigal
produc|ción *f* production. **~ir** [47] *vt* produce; (*causar*) cause. **~irse** *vpr* (*aparecer*) appear; (*suceder*) happen. **~tivo** *a* productive. **~to** *m* product. **~tor** *m* producer. **~to derivado** by-product. **~tos agrícolas** farm produce. **~tos de belleza** cosmetics. **~tos de consumo** consumer goods
proeza *f* exploit
profan|ación *f* desecration. **~ar** *vt* desecrate. **~o** *a* profane
profecía *f* prophecy
proferir [4] *vt* utter; hurl ‹*insultos etc*›
profes|ar *vt* profess; practise ‹*profesión*›. **~ión** *f* profession. **~ional** *a* professional. **~or** *m* teacher; (*en universidad etc*) lecturer. **~orado** *m* teaching profession; (*conjunto de profesores*) staff
prof|eta *m* prophet. **~ético** *a* prophetic. **~etizar** [10] *vt/i* prophesize
prófugo *a* & *m* fugitive
profund|idad *f* depth. **~o** *a* deep; (*fig*) profound
profus|ión *f* profusion. **~o** *a* profuse. **con ~ión** profusely
progenie *f* progeny
programa *m* programme; (*de ordenador*) program; (*de estudios*) curriculum. **~ción** *f* programming; (*TV etc*) programmes; (*en periódico*) TV guide. **~r** *vt* programme; program ‹*ordenador*›. **~dor** *m* computer programmer
progres|ar *vi* (make) progress. **~ión** *f* progression. **~ista** *a* progressive. **~ivo** *a* progressive. **~o** *m* progress. **hacer ~os** make progress
prohibi|ción *f* prohibition. **~do** *a* forbidden. **~r** *vt* forbid. **~tivo** *a* prohibitive
prójimo *m* fellow man
prole *f* offspring
proletari|ado *m* proletariat. **~o** *a* & *m* proletarian
prol|iferación *f* proliferation. **~iferar** *vi* proliferate. **~ífico** *a* prolific
prolijo *a* long-winded, extensive
prólogo *m* prologue
prolongar [12] *vt* prolong; (*alargar*) lengthen. **~se** *vpr* go on
promedio *m* average
prome|sa *f* promise. **~ter** *vt/i* promise. **~terse** *vpr* ‹*novios*› get engaged. **~térselas muy felices** have high hopes. **~tida** *f* fiancée. **~tido** *a* promised; ‹*novios*› engaged. ● *m* fiancé
prominen|cia *f* prominence. **~te** *a* prominent
promiscu|idad *f* promiscuity. **~o** *a* promiscuous
promoción *f* promotion
promontorio *m* promontory
promo|tor *m* promoter. **~ver** [2] *vt* promote; (*causar*) cause
promulgar [12] *vt* promulgate
pronombre *m* pronoun
pron|osticar [7] *vt* predict. **~óstico** *m* prediction; (*del tiempo*) forecast; (*med*) prognosis
pront|itud *f* quickness. **~o** *a* quick; (*preparado*) ready. ● *adv* quickly; (*dentro de poco*) soon; (*temprano*) early. ● *m* urge. **al ~o** at first. **de ~o** suddenly. **por lo ~o** for the time being; (*al menos*) anyway. **tan ~o como** as soon as
pronuncia|ción *f* pronunciation. **~miento** *m* revolt. **~r** *vt* pronounce; deliver ‹*discurso*›. **~rse** *vpr* be pronounced; (*declarase*) declare o.s.; (*sublevarse*) rise up
propagación *f* propagation
propaganda *f* propaganda; (*anuncios*) advertising
propagar [12] *vt/i* propagate. **~se** *vpr* spread
propano *m* propane
propasarse *vpr* go too far
propens|ión *f* inclination. **~o** *a* inclined
propiamente *adv* exactly
propici|ar *vt* (*provocar*) cause, bring about. **~o** *a* favourable
propie|dad *f* property; (*posesión*) possession. **~tario** *m* owner
propina *f* tip
propio *a* own; (*característico*) typical; (*natural*) natural; (*apropiado*) proper. **de ~** on purpose. **el médico ~** the doctor himself
proponer [34] *vt* propose. **~se** *vpr* propose
proporci|ón *f* proportion. **~onado** *a* proportioned. **~onal** *a* proportional. **~onar** *vt* proportion; (*facilitar*) provide
proposición *f* proposition
propósito *m* intention. **a ~** (*adrede*) on purpose; (*de paso*) incidentally.

a ~ de with regard to. **de ~** on purpose
propuesta *f* proposal
propuls|ar *vt* propel; (*fig*) promote. **~ión** *f* propulsion. **~ión a chorro** jet propulsion
prórroga *f* extension
prorrogar [12] *vt* extend
prorrumpir *vi* burst out
prosa *f* prose. **~ico** *a* prosaic
proscri|bir (*pp* **proscrito**) *vt* banish; (*prohibido*) ban. **~to** *a* banned. ● *m* exile; (*persona*) outlaw
prosecución *f* continuation
proseguir [5 & 13] *vt/i* continue
prospección *f* prospecting
prospecto *m* prospectus
prosper|ar *vi* prosper. **~idad** *f* prosperity; (*éxito*) success
próspero *a* prosperous. **¡P~ Año Nuevo!** Happy New Year!
prostit|ución *f* prostitution. **~uta** *f* prostitute
protagonista *m & f* protagonist
prote|cción *f* protection. **~ctor** *a* protective. ● *m* protector; (*patrocinador*) patron. **~ger** [14] *vt* protect. **~gida** *f* protegée. **~gido** *a* protected. ● *m* protegé
proteína *f* protein
protesta *f* protest; (*declaración*) protestation
protestante *a & m & f* (*relig*) Protestant
protestar *vt/i* protest
protocolo *m* protocol
protuberan|cia *f* protuberance. **~te** *a* protuberant
provecho *m* benefit. **¡buen ~!** enjoy your meal! **de ~** useful. **en ~ de** to the benefit of. **sacar ~ de** benefit from
proveer [18] (*pp* **proveído** *y* **provisto**) *vt* supply, provide
provenir [53] *vi* come (**de** from)
proverbi|al *a* proverbial. **~o** *m* proverb
providencia *f* providence. **~l** *a* providential
provincia *f* province. **~l** *a*, **~no** *a* provincial
provisi|ón *f* provision; (*medida*) measure. **~onal** *a* provisional
provisto *a* provided (**de** with)
provoca|ción *f* provocation. **~r** [7] *vt* provoke; (*causar*) cause. **~tivo** *a* provocative
próximamente *adv* soon
proximidad *f* proximity
próximo *a* next; (*cerca*) near
proyec|ción *f* projection. **~tar** *vt* hurl; cast ‹*luz*›; show ‹*película*›. **~til** *m* missile. **~to** *m* plan. **~to de ley** bill. **~tor** *m* projector. **en ~to** planned
pruden|cia *f* prudence. **~nte** *a* prudent, sensible
prueba *f* proof; (*examen*) test; (*de ropa*) fitting. **a ~** on trial. **a ~ de** proof against. **a ~ de agua** waterproof. **en ~ de** in proof of. **poner a ~** test
pruebo *vb véase* **probar**
psicoan|álisis *f* psychoanalysis. **~alista** *m & f* psychoanalyst. **~alizar** [10] *vt* psychoanalyse
psicodélico *a* psychedelic
psic|ología *f* psychology. **~ológico** *a* psychological. **~ólogo** *m* psychologist
psicópata *m & f* psychopath
psicosis *f* psychosis
psique *f* psyche
psiqui|atra *m & f* psychiatrist. **~atría** *f* psychiatry. **~átrico** *a* psychiatric
psíquico *a* psychic
ptas, pts *abrev* (*pesetas*) pesetas
púa *f* sharp point; (*bot*) thorn; (*de erizo*) quill; (*de peine*) tooth; (*mus*) plectrum
pubertad *f* puberty
publica|ción *f* publication. **~r** [7] *vt* publish; (*anunciar*) announce
publici|dad *f* publicity; (*com*) advertising. **~tario** *a* advertising
público *a* public. ● *m* public; (*de espectáculo etc*) audience. **dar al ~** publish
puchero *m* cooking pot; (*guisado*) stew. **hacer ~s** (*fig, fam*) pout
pude *vb véase* **poder**
púdico *a* modest
pudiente *a* rich
pudín *m* pudding
pudor *m* modesty. **~oso** *a* modest
pudrir (*pp* **podrido**) *vt* rot; (*fig, molestar*) annoy. **~se** *vpr* rot
puebl|ecito *m* small village. **~o** *m* town; (*aldea*) village; (*nación*) nation, people
puedo *vb véase* **poder**
puente *m* bridge; (*fig, fam*) long weekend. **~ colgante** suspension bridge. **~ levadizo** drawbridge. **hacer ~** (*fam*) have a long weekend
puerco *a* filthy; (*grosero*) coarse. ● *m* pig. **~ espín** porcupine

pueril *a* childish
puerro *m* leek
puerta *f* door; (*en deportes*) goal; (*de ciudad*) gate. ~ **principal** main entrance. **a** ~ **cerrada** behind closed doors
puerto *m* port; (*fig*, *refugio*) refuge; (*entre montañas*) pass. ~ **franco** free port
Puerto Rico *m* Puerto Rico
puertorriqueño *a* & *m* Puerto Rican
pues *adv* (*entonces*) then; (*bueno*) well. ● *conj* since
puest|a *f* setting; (*en juegos*) bet. **~a de sol** sunset. **~a en escena** staging. **~a en marcha** starting. **~o** *a* put; (*vestido*) dressed. ● *m* place; (*empleo*) position, job; (*en mercado etc*) stall. ● *conj*. **~o que** since. **~o de socorro** first aid post
pugna *f* fight. **~r** *vt* fight
puja *f* effort; (*en subasta*) bid. **~r** *vt* struggle; (*en subasta*) bid
pulcro *a* neat
pulga *f* flea; (*de juego*) tiddly-wink. **tener malas ~s** be bad-tempered
pulga|da *f* inch. **~r** *m* thumb; (*del pie*) big toe
puli|do *a* neat. **~mentar** *vt* polish. **~mento** *m* polishing; (*substancia*) polish. **~r** *vt* polish; (*suavizar*) smooth
pulm|ón *m* lung. **~onar** *a* pulmonary. **~onía** *f* pneumonia
pulpa *f* pulp
pulpería *f* (*LAm*) grocer's shop (*Brit*), grocery store (*Amer*)
púlpito *m* pulpit
pulpo *m* octopus
pulque *m* (*Mex*) pulque, alcoholic Mexican drink
pulsa|ción *f* pulsation. **~dor** *a* pulsating. ● *m* button. **~r** *vt* (*mus*) play
pulsera *f* bracelet; (*de reloj*) strap
pulso *m* pulse; (*muñeca*) wrist; (*firmeza*) steady hand; (*fuerza*) strength; (*fig*, *tacto*) tact. **tomar el ~ a uno** take s.o.'s pulse
pulular *vi* teem with
pulveriza|dor *m* (*de perfume*) atomizer. **~r** [10] *vt* pulverize; atomize ‹*líquido*›
pulla *f* cutting remark
pum *int* bang!
puma *m* puma
puna *f* puna, high plateau
punitivo *a* punitive
punta *f* point; (*extremo*) tip; (*clavo*) (small) nail. **estar de ~** be in a bad mood. **estar de ~ con uno** be at odds with s.o. **ponerse de ~ con uno** fall out with s.o.. **sacar ~ a** sharpen; (*fig*) find fault with
puntada *f* stitch
puntal *m* prop, support
puntapié *m* kick
puntear *vt* mark; (*mus*) pluck
puntera *f* toe
puntería *f* aim; (*destreza*) markmanship
puntiagudo *a* sharp, pointed
puntilla *f* (*encaje*) lace. **de ~s** on tiptoe
punto *m* point; (*señal*) dot; (*de examen*) mark; (*lugar*) spot, place; (*de taxis*) stand; (*momento*) moment; (*punto final*) full stop (*Brit*), period (*Amer*); (*puntada*) stitch; (*de tela*) mesh. **~ de admiración** exclamation mark. **~ de arranque** starting point. **~ de exclamación** exclamation mark. **~ de interrogación** question mark. **~ de vista** point of view. **~ final** full stop. **~ muerto** (*auto*) neutral (gear). **~ y aparte** full stop, new paragraph (*Brit*), period, new paragraph (*Amer*). **~ y coma** semicolon. **a ~** on time; (*listo*) ready. **a ~ de** on the point of. **de ~** knitted. **dos ~s** colon. **en ~** exactly. **hacer ~** knit. **hasta cierto ~** to a certain extent
puntuación *f* punctuation; (*en deportes*, *acción*) scoring; (*en deportes*, *número de puntos*) score
puntual *a* punctual; (*exacto*) accurate. **~idad** *f* punctuality; (*exactitud*) accuracy
puntuar [21] *vt* punctuate. ● *vi* score
punza|da *f* prick; (*dolor*) pain; (*fig*) pang. **~nte** *a* sharp. **~r** [10] *vt* prick
puñado *m* handful. **a ~s** by the handful
puñal *m* dagger. **~ada** *f* stab
puñ|etazo *m* punch. **~o** *m* fist; (*de ropa*) cuff; (*mango*) handle. **de su ~o (y letra)** in his own handwriting
pupa *f* spot; (*en los labios*) cold sore. **hacer ~** hurt. **hacerse ~** hurt o.s.
pupila *f* pupil
pupitre *m* desk
puquío *m* (*Arg*) spring
puré *m* purée; (*sopa*) thick soup. **~ de patatas** mashed potato
pureza *f* purity
purga *f* purge. **~r** [12] *vt* purge. **~torio** *m* purgatory

purifica|ción *f* purification. **~r** [7] *vt* purify
purista *m & f* purist
puritano *a* puritanical. ● *m* puritan
puro *a* pure; ‹*cielo*› clear; (*fig*) simple. ● *m* cigar. **de ~** so. **de pura casualidad** by sheer chance
púrpura *f* purple
purpúreo *a* purple
pus *m* pus
puse *vb véase* **poner**
pusilánime *a* cowardly
pústula *f* spot
puta *f* whore
putrefacción *f* putrefaction
pútrido *a* rotten, putrid

Q

que *pron rel* (*personas, sujeto*) who; (*personas, complemento*) whom; (*cosas*) which, that. ● *conj* that. **¡~ tengan Vds buen viaje!** have a good journey! **¡que venga!** let him come! **~ venga o no venga** whether he comes or not. **a que** I bet. **creo que tiene razón** I think (that) he is right. **de ~** from which. **yo ~ tú** if I were you
qué *a* (*con sustantivo*) what; (*con a o adv*) how. ● *pron* what. **¡~ bonito!** how nice. **¿en ~ piensas?** what are you thinking about?
quebra|da *f* gorge; (*paso*) pass. **~dizo** *a* fragile. **~do** *a* broken; (*com*) bankrupt. ● *m* (*math*) fraction. **~dura** *f* fracture; (*hondonada*) gorge. **~ntar** *vt* break; (*debilitar*) weaken. **~nto** *m* (*pérdida*) loss; (*daño*) damage. **~r** [1] *vt* break. ● *vi* break; (*com*) go bankrupt. **~rse** *vpr* break
quechua *a & m & f* Quechuan
queda *f* curfew
quedar *vi* stay, remain; (*estar*) be; (*faltar, sobrar*) be left. **~ bien** come off well. **~se** *vpr* stay. **~ con** arrange to meet. **~ en** agree to. **~ en nada** come to nothing. **~ por** (+ *infinitivo*) remain to be (+ *pp*)
quehacer *m* job. **~es domésticos** household chores
quej|a *f* complaint; (*de dolor*) moan. **~arse** *vpr* complain (**de** about); (*gemir*) moan. **~ido** *m* moan. **~oso** *a* complaining
quema|do *a* burnt; (*fig, fam*) bitter. **~dor** *m* burner. **~dura** *f* burn. **~r** *vt* burn; (*prender fuego a*) set fire to. ● *vi* burn. **~rse** *vpr* burn o.s.; (*consumirse*) burn up; (*con el sol*) get sunburnt. **~rropa** *adv*. **a ~rropa** point-blank
quena *f* Indian flute
quepo *vb véase* **caber**
queque *m* (*Mex*) cake
querella *f* (*riña*) quarrel, dispute; (*jurid*) charge
quer|er [35] *vt* want; (*amar*) love; (*necesitar*) need. **~er decir** mean. **~ido** *a* dear; (*amado*) loved. ● *m* darling; (*amante*) lover. **como quiera que** since; (*de cualquier modo*) however. **cuando quiera que** whenever. **donde quiera** wherever. **¿quieres darme ese libro?** would you pass me that book? **quiere llover** it's trying to rain. **¿quieres un helado?** would you like an ice-cream? **quisiera ir a la playa** I'd like to go to the beach. **sin ~er** without meaning to
queroseno *m* kerosene
querubín *m* cherub
ques|adilla *f* cheesecake; (*Mex, empanadilla*) pie. **~o** *m* cheese. **~o de bola** Edam cheese
quiá *int* never!, surely not!
quicio *m* frame. **sacar de ~ a uno** infuriate s.o.
quiebra *f* break; (*fig*) collapse; (*com*) bankruptcy
quiebro *m* dodge
quien *pron rel* (*sujeto*) who; (*complemento*) whom
quién *pron interrogativo* (*sujeto*) who; (*tras preposición*) whom. **¿de ~?** whose. **¿de ~ son estos libros?** whose are these books?
quienquiera *pron* whoever
quiero *vb véase* **querer**
quiet|o *a* still; (*inmóvil*) motionless; ‹*carácter etc*› calm. **~ud** *f* stillness
quijada *f* jaw
quilate *m* carat
quilla *f* keel
quimera *f* (*fig*) illusion
químic|a *f* chemistry. **~o** *a* chemical. ● *m* chemist
quincalla *f* hardware; (*de adorno*) trinket
quince *a & m* fifteen. **~ días** a fortnight. **~na** *f* fortnight. **~nal** *a* fortnightly
quincuagésimo *a* fiftieth

quiniela *f* pools coupon. **~s** *fpl* (football) pools
quinientos *a & m* five hundred
quinino *m* quinine
quinqué *m* oil-lamp; (*fig, fam*) shrewdness
quinquenio *m* (period of) five years
quinta *f* (*casa*) villa
quintaesencia *f* quintessence
quintal *m* a hundred kilograms
quinteto *m* quintet
quinto *a & m* fifth
quiosco *m* kiosk; (*en jardín*) summerhouse; (*en parque etc*) bandstand
quirúrgico *a* surgical
quise *vb véase* **querer**
quisque *pron.* **cada ~** (*fam*) (absolutely) everybody
quisquill|a *f* trifle; (*camarón*) shrimp. **~oso** *a* irritable; (*chinchorrero*) fussy
quita|manchas *m invar* stain remover. **~nieves** *m invar* snow plough. **~r** *vt* remove, take away; take off ‹*ropa*›; (*robar*) steal. **~ndo** (*a excepción de, fam*) apart from. **~rse** *vpr* be removed; take off ‹*ropa*›. **~rse de** (*no hacerlo más*) stop. **~rse de en medio** get out of the way. **~sol** *m invar* sunshade
Quito *m* Quito
quizá(s) *adv* perhaps
quórum *m* quorum

R

rábano *m* radish. **~ picante** horseradish. **me importa un ~** I couldn't care less
rabi|a *f* rabies; (*fig*) rage. **~ar** *vi* (*de dolor*) be in great pain; (*estar enfadado*) be furious; (*fig, tener ganas, fam*) long. **~ar por algo** long for sth. **~ar por hacer algo** long to do sth. **~eta** *f* tantrum. **dar ~a** infuriate
rabino *m* Rabbi
rabioso *a* rabid; (*furioso*) furious; ‹*dolor etc*› violent
rabo *m* tail
racial *a* racial
racimo *m* bunch
raciocinio *m* reason; (*razonamiento*) reasoning
ración *f* share, ration; (*de comida*) portion
racional *a* rational. **~izar** [10] *vt* rationalize
racionar *vt* (*limitar*) ration; (*repartir*) ration out
racis|mo *m* racism. **~ta** *a* racist
racha *f* gust of wind; (*fig*) spate
radar *m* radar
radiación *f* radiation
radiactiv|idad *f* radioactivity. **~o** *a* radioactive
radiador *m* radiator
radial *a* radial
radiante *a* radiant
radical *a & m & f* radical
radicar [7] *vi* (*estar*) be. **~ en** (*fig*) lie in
radio *m* radius; (*de rueda*) spoke; (*elemento metálico*) radium. ● *f* radio
radioactiv|idad *f* radioactivity. **~o** *a* radioactive
radio|difusión *f* broadcasting. **~emisora** *f* radio station. **~escucha** *m & f* listener
radiografía *f* radiography
radi|ología *f* radiology. **~ólogo** *m* radiologist
radioterapia *f* radiotherapy
radioyente *m & f* listener
raer [36] *vt* scrape off
ráfaga *f* (*de viento*) gust; (*de luz*) flash; (*de ametralladora*) burst
rafia *f* raffia
raído *a* threadbare
raigambre *f* roots; (*fig*) tradition
raíz *f* root. **a ~ de** immediately after. **echar raíces** (*fig*) settle
raja *f* split; (*culin*) slice. **~r** *vt* split. **~rse** *vpr* split; (*fig*) back out
rajatabla. a ~ vigorously
ralea *f* sort
ralo *a* sparse
ralla|dor *m* grater. **~r** *vt* grate
rama *f* branch. **~je** *m* branches. **~l** *m* branch. **en ~** raw
rambla *f* gully; (*avenida*) avenue
ramera *f* prostitute
ramifica|ción *f* ramification. **~rse** [7] *vpr* branch out
ramilla *f* twig
ramillete *m* bunch
ramo *m* branch; (*de flores*) bouquet
rampa *f* ramp, slope
ramplón *a* vulgar
rana *f* frog. **ancas** *fpl* **de ~** frogs' legs. **no ser ~** not be stupid
rancio *a* rancid; ‹*vino*› old; (*fig*) ancient

ranch|ero *m* cook; (*LAm, jefe de rancho*) farmer. **~o** *m* (*LAm*) ranch, farm
rango *m* rank
ranúnculo *m* buttercup
ranura *f* groove; (*para moneda*) slot
rapar *vt* shave; crop ‹*pelo*›
rapaz *a* rapacious; ‹*ave*› of prey. ● *m* bird of prey
rapidez *f* speed
rápido *a* fast, quick. ● *adv* quickly. ● *m* (*tren*) express. **~s** *mpl* rapids
rapiña *f* robbery. **ave** *f* **de ~** bird of prey
rapsodia *f* rhapsody
rapt|ar *vt* kidnap. **~o** *m* kidnapping; (*de ira etc*) fit; (*éxtasis*) ecstasy
raqueta *f* racquet
raramente *adv* seldom, rarely
rarefacción *f* rarefaction
rar|eza *f* rarity; (*cosa rara*) oddity. **~o** *a* rare; (*extraño*) odd. **es ~o que** it is strange that. **¡qué ~o!** how strange!
ras *m*. **a ~ de** level with
rasar *vt* level; (*rozar*) graze
rasca|cielos *m invar* skyscraper. **~dura** *f* scratch. **~r** [7] *vt* scratch; (*raspar*) scrape
rasgar [12] *vt* tear
rasgo *m* stroke. **~s** *mpl* (*facciones*) features
rasguear *vt* strum; (*fig, escribir*) write
rasguñ|ar *vt* scratch. **~o** *m* scratch
raso *a* (*llano*) flat; (*liso*) smooth; ‹*cielo*› clear; ‹*cucharada etc*› level; ‹*vuelo etc*› low. ● *m* satin. **al ~** in the open air. **soldado** *m* **~** private
raspa *f* (*de pescado*) backbone
raspa|dura *f* scratch; (*acción*) scratching. **~r** *vt* scratch; (*rozar*) scrape
rastr|a *f* rake. **a ~as** dragging. **~ear** *vt* track. **~eo** *m* dragging. **~ero** *a* creeping; ‹*vuelo*› low. **~illar** *vt* rake. **~illo** *m* rake. **~o** *m* rake; (*huella*) track; (*señal*) sign. **el R~o** the flea market in Madrid. **ni ~o** not a trace
rata *f* rat
rate|ar *vt* steal. **~ría** *f* pilfering. **~ro** *m* petty thief
ratifica|ción *f* ratification. **~r** [7] *vt* ratify
rato *m* moment, short time. **~s libres** spare time. **a ~s** at times. **hace un ~** a moment ago. **¡hasta otro ~!** (*fam*) see you soon! **pasar mal ~** have a rough time
rat|ón *m* mouse. **~onera** *f* mousetrap; (*madriguera*) mouse hole
raud|al *m* torrent; (*fig*) floods. **~o** *a* swift
raya *f* line; (*lista*) stripe; (*de pelo*) parting. **~r** *vt* rule. ● *vi* border (**con** on). **a ~s** striped. **pasar de la ~** go too far
rayo *m* ray; (*descarga eléctrica*) lightning. **~s X** X-rays
raza *f* race; (*de animal*) breed. **de ~** ‹*caballo*› thoroughbred; ‹*perro*› pedigree
raz|ón *f* reason. **a ~ón de** at the rate of. **perder la ~ón** go out of one's mind. **tener ~ón** be right. **~onable** *a* reasonable. **~onamiento** *m* reasoning. **~onar** *vt* reason out. ● *vi* reason
re *m* D; (*solfa*) re
reac|ción *f* reaction. **~cionario** *a & m* reactionary. **~ción en cadena** chain reaction. **~tor** *m* reactor; (*avión*) jet
real *a* real; (*de rey etc*) royal. ● *m* real, old Spanish coin
realce *m* relief; (*fig*) splendour
realidad *f* reality; (*verdad*) truth. **en ~** in fact
realis|mo *m* realism. **~ta** *a* realistic. ● *m & f* realist; (*monárquico*) royalist
realiza|ción *f* fulfilment. **~r** [10] *vt* carry out; make ‹*viaje*›; achieve ‹*meta*›; (*vender*) sell. **~rse** *vpr* ‹*plan etc*› be carried out; ‹*sueño, predicción etc*› come true; ‹*persona*› fulfil o.s.
realzar [10] *vt* (*fig*) enhance
reanima|ción *f* revival. **~r** *vt* revive. **~rse** *vpr* revive
reanudar *vt* resume; renew ‹*amistad*›
reaparecer [11] *vi* reappear
rearm|ar *vt* rearm. **~e** *m* rearmament
reavivar *vt* revive
rebaja *f* reduction. **~do** *a* ‹*precio*› reduced. **~r** *vt* lower. **en ~s** in the sale
rebanada *f* slice
rebaño *m* herd; (*de ovejas*) flock
rebasar *vt* exceed; (*dejar atrás*) leave behind
rebatir *vt* refute
rebel|arse *vpr* rebel. **~de** *a* rebellious. ● *m* rebel. **~día** *f* rebelliousness. **~ión** *f* rebellion
reblandecer [11] *vt* soften

rebosa|nte *a* overflowing. **~r** *vi* overflow; (*abundar*) abound
rebot|ar *vt* bounce; (*rechazar*) repel. ● *vi* bounce; ‹*bala*› ricochet. **~e** *m* bounce, rebound. **de ~e** on the rebound
rebozar [10] *vt* wrap up; (*culin*) coat in batter
rebullir [22] *vi* stir
rebusca|do *a* affected. **~r** [7] *vt* search thoroughly
rebuznar *vi* bray
recabar *vt* claim
recado *m* errand; (*mensaje*) message. **dejar ~** leave a message
reca|er [29] *vi* fall back; (*med*) relapse; (*fig*) fall. **~ída** *f* relapse
recalcar [7] *vt* squeeze; (*fig*) stress
recalcitrante *a* recalcitrant
recalentar [1] *vt* (*de nuevo*) reheat; (*demasiado*) overheat
recamar *vt* embroider
recámara *f* small room; (*de arma de fuego*) chamber; (*LAm, dormitorio*) bedroom
recambio *m* change; (*de pluma etc*) refill. **~s** *mpl* spare parts. **de ~** spare
recapitula|ción *f* summing up. **~r** *vt* sum up
recarg|ar [12] *vt* overload; (*aumentar*) increase; recharge ‹*batería*›. **~o** *m* increase
recat|ado *a* modest. **~ar** *vt* hide. **~arse** *vpr* hide o.s. away; (*actuar discretamente*) act discreetly. **~o** *m* prudence; (*modestia*) modesty. **sin ~arse, sin ~o** openly
recauda|ción *f* (*cantidad*) takings. **~dor** *m* tax collector. **~r** *vt* collect
recel|ar *vt/i* suspect. **~o** *m* distrust; (*temor*) fear. **~oso** *a* suspicious
recepci|ón *f* reception. **~onista** *m & f* receptionist
receptáculo *m* receptacle
recept|ivo *a* receptive. **~or** *m* receiver
recesión *f* recession
receta *f* recipe; (*med*) prescription
recib|imiento *m* (*acogida*) welcome. **~ir** *vt* receive; (*acoger*) welcome. ● *vi* entertain. **~irse** *vpr* graduate. **~o** *m* receipt. **acusar ~o** acknowledge receipt
reci|én *adv* recently; ‹*casado, nacido etc*› newly. **~ente** *a* recent; (*culin*) fresh
recinto *m* enclosure
recio *a* strong; ‹*voz*› loud. ● *adv* hard; (*en voz alta*) loudly
recipiente *m* (*persona*) recipient; (*cosa*) receptacle
recíproco *a* reciprocal. **a la recíproca** vice versa
recita|l *m* recital; (*de poesías*) reading. **~r** *vt* recite
reclama|ción *f* claim; (*queja*) complaint. **~r** *vt* claim. ● *vi* appeal
reclinar *vi* lean. **~se** *vpr* lean
reclu|ir [17] *vt* shut away. **~sión** *f* seclusion; (*cárcel*) prison. **~so** *m* prisoner
recluta *m* recruit. ● *f* recruitment. **~miento** *m* recruitment; (*conjunto de reclutas*) recruits. **~r** *vt* recruit
recobrar *vt* recover. **~se** *vpr* recover
recodo *m* bend
recog|er [14] *vt* collect; pick up ‹*cosa caída*›; (*cosechar*) harvest; (*dar asilo*) shelter. **~erse** *vpr* withdraw; (*ir a casa*) go home; (*acostarse*) go to bed. **~ida** *f* collection; (*cosecha*) harvest. **~ido** *a* withdrawn; (*pequeño*) small
recolección *f* harvest
recomenda|ción *f* recommendation. **~r** [1] *vt* recommend; (*encomendar*) entrust
recomenzar [1 & 10] *vt/i* start again
recompensa *f* reward. **~r** *vt* reward
recomponer [34] *vt* mend
reconcilia|ción *f* reconciliation. **~r** *vt* reconcile. **~rse** *vpr* be reconciled
recóndito *a* hidden
reconoc|er [11] *vt* recognize; (*admitir*) acknowledge; (*examinar*) examine. **~imiento** *m* recognition; (*admisión*) acknowledgement; (*agradecimiento*) gratitude; (*examen*) examination
reconozco *vb véase* **reconocer**
reconquista *f* reconquest. **~r** *vt* reconquer; (*fig*) win back
reconsiderar *vt* reconsider
reconstitu|ir [17] *vt* reconstitute. **~yente** *m* tonic
reconstru|cción *f* reconstruction. **~ir** [17] *vt* reconstruct
récord /'rekor/ *m* record. **batir un ~** break a record
recordar [2] *vt* remember; (*hacer acordar*) remind; (*Lam, despertar*) wake up. ● *vi* remember. **que yo recuerde** as far as I remember. **si mal no recuerdo** if I remember rightly

recorr|er *vt* tour ‹*país*›; (*pasar por*) travel through; cover ‹*distancia*›; (*registrar*) look over. **~ido** *m* journey; (*itinerario*) route

recort|ado *a* jagged. **~ar** *vt* cut (out). **~e** *m* cutting (out); (*de periódico etc*) cutting

recoser *vt* mend

recostar [2] *vt* lean. **~se** *vpr* lie back

recoveco *m* bend; (*rincón*) nook

recre|ación *f* recreation. **~ar** *vt* recreate; (*divertir*) entertain. **~arse** *vpr* amuse o.s. **~ativo** *a* recreational. **~o** *m* recreation; (*escol*) break

recrimina|ción *f* recrimination. **~r** *vt* reproach

recrudecer [11] *vi* increase, worsen, get worse

recta *f* straight line

rect|angular *a* rectangular; ‹*triángulo*› right-angled. **~ángulo** *a* rectangular; ‹*triángulo*› right-angled. ● *m* rectangle

rectifica|ción *f* rectification. **~r** [7] *vt* rectify

rect|itud *f* straightness; (*fig*) honesty. **~o** *a* straight; (*fig, justo*) fair; (*fig, honrado*) honest. ● *m* rectum. **todo ~o** straight on

rector *a* governing. ● *m* rector

recuadro *m* (*en periódico*) box

recubrir [*pp* **recubierto**] *vt* cover

recuerdo *m* memory; (*regalo*) souvenir. ● *vb véase* **recordar**. **~s** *mpl* (*saludos*) regards

recupera|ción *f* recovery. **~r** *vt* recover. **~rse** *vpr* recover. **~r el tiempo perdido** make up for lost time

recur|rir *vi*. **~rir a** resort to ‹*cosa*›; turn to ‹*persona*›. **~so** *m* resort; (*medio*) resource; (*jurid*) appeal. **~sos** *mpl* resources

recusar *vt* refuse

rechaz|ar [10] *vt* repel; reflect ‹*luz*›; (*no aceptar*) refuse; (*negar*) deny. **~o** *m*. **de ~o** on the rebound; (*fig*) consequently

rechifla *f* booing; (*burla*) derision

rechinar *vi* squeak; ‹*madera etc*› creak; ‹*dientes*› grind

rechistar *vt* murmur. **sin ~** without saying a word

rechoncho *a* stout

red *f* network; (*malla*) net; (*para equipaje*) luggage rack; (*fig, engaño*) trap

redac|ción *f* editing; (*conjunto de redactores*) editorial staff; (*oficina*) editorial office; (*escol, univ*) essay. **~tar** *vt* write. **~tor** *m* writer; (*de periódico*) editor

redada *f* casting; (*de policía*) raid

redecilla *f* small net; (*para el pelo*) hairnet

rededor *m*. **al ~, en ~** around

reden|ción *f* redemption. **~tor** *a* redeeming

redil *f* sheepfold

redimir *vt* redeem

rédito *m* interest

redoblar *vt* redouble; (*doblar*) bend back

redoma *f* flask

redomado *a* sly

redond|a *f* (*de imprenta*) roman (type); (*mus*) semibreve (*Brit*), whole note (*Amer*). **~amente** *adv* (*categóricamente*) flatly. **~ear** *vt* round off. **~el** *m* circle; (*de plaza de toros*) arena. **~o** *a* round; (*completo*) complete. ● *m* circle. **a la ~a** around. **en ~o** round; (*categóricamente*) flatly

reduc|ción *f* reduction. **~ido** *a* reduced; (*limitado*) limited; (*pequeño*) small; ‹*precio*› low. **~ir** [47] *vt* reduce. **~irse** *vpr* be reduced; (*fig*) amount

reduje *vb véase* **reducir**

redundan|cia *f* redundancy. **~te** *a* redundant

reduplicar [7] *vt* (*aumentar*) redouble

reduzco *vb véase* **reducir**

reedificar [7] *vt* reconstruct

reembols|ar *vt* reimburse. **~o** *m* repayment. **contra ~o** cash on delivery

reemplaz|ar [10] *vt* replace. **~o** *m* replacement

reemprender *vt* start again

reenviar [20] *vt*, **reexpedir** [5] *vt* forward

referencia *f* reference; (*información*) report. **con ~ a** with reference to. **hacer ~ a** refer to

referéndum *m* (*pl* **referéndums**) referendum

referir [4] *vt* tell; (*remitir*) refer. **~se** *vpr* refer. **por lo que se refiere a** as regards

refiero *vb véase* **referir**

refilón. **de ~** obliquely

refin|amiento *m* refinement. **~ar** *vt* refine. **~ería** *f* refinery

reflector *m* reflector; (*proyector*) searchlight

reflej|ar *vt* reflect. **~o** *a* reflected; (*med*) reflex. ● *m* reflection; (*med*) reflex; (*en el pelo*) highlights

reflexi|ón *f* reflection. **~onar** *vi* reflect. **~vo** *a* ‹*persona*› thoughtful; (*gram*) reflexive. **con ~ón** on reflection. **sin ~ón** without thinking

reflujo *m* ebb

reforma *f* reform. **~s** *fpl* (*reparaciones*) repairs. **~r** *vt* reform. **~rse** *vpr* reform

reforzar [2 & 10] *vt* reinforce

refrac|ción *f* refraction. **~tar** *vt* refract. **~tario** *a* heat-resistant

refrán *m* saying

refregar [1 & 12] *vt* rub

refrenar *vt* rein in ‹*caballo*›; (*fig*) restrain

refrendar *vt* endorse

refresc|ar [7] *vt* refresh; (*enfriar*) cool. ● *vi* get cooler. **~arse** *vpr* refresh o.s.; (*salir*) go out for a walk. **~o** *m* cold drink. **~os** *mpl* refreshments

refrigera|ción *f* refrigeration; (*aire acondicionado*) air-conditioning. **~r** *vt* refrigerate. **~dor** *m*, **~dora** *f* refrigerator

refuerzo *m* reinforcement

refugi|ado *m* refugee. **~arse** *vpr* take refuge. **~o** *m* refuge, shelter

refulgir [14] *vi* shine

refundir *vt* (*fig*) revise, rehash

refunfuñar *vi* grumble

refutar *vt* refute

regadera *f* watering-can; (*Mex, ducha*) shower

regala|damente *adv* very well. **~do** *a* as a present, free; (*cómodo*) comfortable. **~r** *vt* give; (*agasajar*) treat very well. **~rse** *vpr* indulge o.s.

regaliz *m* liquorice

regalo *m* present, gift; (*placer*) joy; (*comodidad*) comfort

regañ|adientes. a ~adientes reluctantly. **~ar** *vt* scold. ● *vi* moan; (*dos personas*) quarrel. **~o** *m* (*reprensión*) scolding

regar [1 & 12] *vt* water

regata *f* regatta

regate *m* dodge; (*en deportes*) dribbling. **~ar** *vt* haggle over; (*economizar*) economize on. ● *vi* haggle; (*en deportes*) dribble. **~o** *m* haggling; (*en deportes*) dribbling

regazo *m* lap

regencia *f* regency

regenerar *vt* regenerate

regente *m & f* regent; (*director*) manager

régimen *m* (*pl* **regímenes**) rule; (*pol*) regime; (*med*) diet. **~ alimenticio** diet

regimiento *m* regiment

regio *a* royal

regi|ón *f* region. **~onal** *a* regional

regir [5 & 14] *vt* rule; govern ‹*país*›; run ‹*colegio, empresa*›. ● *vi* apply, be in force

registr|ado *a* registered. **~ador** *m* recorder; (*persona*) registrar. **~ar** *vt* register; (*grabar*) record; (*examinar*) search. **~arse** *vpr* register; (*darse*) be reported. **~o** *m* (*acción de registrar*) registration; (*libro*) register; (*cosa anotada*) entry; (*inspección*) search. **~o civil** (*oficina*) register office

regla *f* ruler; (*norma*) rule; (*menstruación*) period, menstruation. **~mentación** *f* regulation. **~mentar** *vt* regulate. **~mentario** *a* obligatory. **~mento** *m* regulations. **en ~** in order. **por ~ general** as a rule

regocij|ar *vt* delight. **~arse** *vpr* be delighted. **~o** *m* delight. **~os** *mpl* festivities

regode|arse *vpr* be delighted. **~o** *m* delight

regordete *a* chubby

regres|ar *vi* return. **~ión** *f* regression. **~ivo** *a* backward. **~o** *m* return

reguer|a *f* irrigation ditch. **~o** *m* irrigation ditch; (*señal*) trail

regula|dor *m* control. **~r** *a* regular; (*mediano*) average; (*no bueno*) so-so. ● *vt* regulate; (*controlar*) control. **~ridad** *f* regularity. **con ~ridad** regularly. **por lo ~r** as a rule

rehabilita|ción *f* rehabilitation; (*en un empleo etc*) reinstatement. **~r** *vt* rehabilitate; (*al empleo etc*) reinstate

rehacer [31] *vt* redo; (*repetir*) repeat; (*reparar*) repair. **~se** *vpr* recover

rehén *m* hostage

rehogar [12] *vt* sauté

rehuir [17] *vt* avoid

rehusar *vt/i* refuse

reimpr|esión *f* reprinting. **~imir** (*pp* **reimpreso**) *vt* reprint

reina *f* queen. **~do** *m* reign. **~nte** *a* ruling; (*fig*) prevailing. **~r** *vi* reign; (*fig*) prevail

reincidir *vi* relapse, repeat an offence
reino *m* kingdom. **R~ Unido** United Kingdom
reinstaurar *vt* restore
reintegr|ar *vt* reinstate ‹*persona*›; refund ‹*cantidad*›. **~arse** *vpr* return. **~o** *m* refund
reír [51] *vi* laugh. **~se** *vpr* laugh. **~se de** laugh at. **echarse a ~** burst out laughing
reivindica|ción *f* claim. **~r** [7] *vt* claim; (*restaurar*) restore
rej|a *f* grille, grating. **~illa** *f* grille, grating; (*red*) luggage rack; (*de mimbre*) wickerwork. **entre ~as** behind bars
rejuvenecer [11] *vt/i* rejuvenate. **~se** *vpr* be rejuvenated
relaci|ón *f* relation(ship); (*relato*) tale; (*lista*) list. **~onado** *a* concerning. **~onar** *vt* relate (**con** to). **~onarse** *vpr* be connected. **bien ~onado** well-connected. **con ~ón a**, **en ~ón a** in relation to. **hacer ~ón a** refer to
relaja|ción *f* relaxation; (*aflojamiento*) slackening. **~do** *a* loose. **~r** *vt* relax; (*aflojar*) slacken. **~rse** *vpr* relax
relamerse *vpr* lick one's lips
relamido *a* overdressed
rel|ámpago *m* (flash of) lightning. **~ampaguear** *vi* thunder; (*fig*) sparkle
relatar *vt* tell, relate
relativ|idad *f* relativity. **~o** *a* relative. **en lo ~o a** in relation to
relato *m* tale; (*informe*) report
relegar [12] *vt* relegate. **~ al olvido** forget about
relev|ante *a* outstanding. **~ar** *vt* relieve; (*substituir*) replace. **~o** *m* relief. **carrera** *f* **de ~os** relay race
relieve *m* relief; (*fig*) importance. **de ~** important. **poner de ~** emphasize
religi|ón *f* religion. **~osa** *f* nun. **~oso** *a* religious. ● *m* monk
relinch|ar *vi* neigh. **~o** *m* neigh
reliquia *f* relic
reloj *m* clock; (*de bolsillo o pulsera*) watch. **~ de caja** grandfather clock. **~ de pulsera** wrist-watch. **~ de sol** sundial. **~ despertador** alarm clock. **~ería** *f* watchmaker's (shop). **~ero** *m* watchmaker
reluci|ente *a* shining. **~r** [11] *vi* shine; (*destellar*) sparkle
relumbrar *vi* shine
rellano *m* landing
rellen|ar *vt* refill; (*culin*) stuff; fill in ‹*formulario*›. **~o** *a* full up; (*culin*) stuffed. ● *m* filling; (*culin*) stuffing
remach|ar *vt* rivet; (*fig*) drive home. **~e** *m* rivet
remangar [12] *vt* roll up
remanso *m* pool; (*fig*) haven
remar *vi* row
remat|ado *a* (*total*) complete; ‹*niño*› very naughty. **~ar** *vt* finish off; (*agotar*) use up; (*com*) sell off cheap. **~e** *m* end; (*fig*) finishing touch. **de ~e** completely
remedar *vt* imitate
remedi|ar *vt* remedy; (*ayudar*) help; (*poner fin a*) put a stop to; (*fig, resolver*) solve. **~o** *m* remedy; (*fig*) solution. **como último ~o** as a last resort. **no hay más ~o** there's no other way. **no tener más ~o** have no choice
remedo *m* imitation
rem|endar [1] *vt* repair. **~iendo** *m* patch; (*fig, mejora*) improvement
remilg|ado *a* fussy; (*afectado*) affected. **~o** *m* fussiness; (*afectación*) affectation
reminiscencia *f* reminiscence
remirar *vt* look again at
remisión *f* sending; (*referencia*) reference; (*perdón*) forgiveness
remiso *a* remiss
remit|e *m* sender's name and address. **~ente** *m* sender. **~ir** *vt* send; (*referir*) refer. ● *vi* diminish
remo *m* oar
remoj|ar *vt* soak; (*fig, fam*) celebrate. **~o** *m* soaking. **poner a ~o** soak
remolacha *f* beetroot. **~ azucarera** sugar beet
remolcar [7] *vt* tow
remolino *m* swirl; (*de aire etc*) whirl; (*de gente*) throng
remolque *m* towing; (*cabo*) towrope; (*vehículo*) trailer. **a ~** on tow. **dar ~ a** tow
remontar *vt* mend. **~se** *vpr* soar; (*con tiempo*) go back to
rémora *f* (*fig*) hindrance
remord|er [2] (*fig*) worry. **~imiento** *m* remorse. **tener ~imientos** feel remorse
remoto *a* remote
remover [2] *vt* move; stir ‹*líquido*›; turn over ‹*tierra*›; (*quitar*) remove; (*fig, activar*) revive

remozar [10] *vt* rejuvenate ‹*persona*›; renovate ‹*edificio etc*›

remunera|ción *f* remuneration. **~r** *vt* remunerate

renac|er [11] *vi* be reborn; (*fig*) revive. **~imiento** *m* rebirth. **R~** Renaissance

renacuajo *m* tadpole; (*fig*) tiddler

rencilla *f* quarrel

rencor *m* bitterness. **~oso** *a* (*estar*) resentful; (*ser*) spiteful. **guardar ~ a** have a grudge against

rendi|ción *f* surrender. **~do** *a* submissive; (*agotado*) exhausted

rendija *f* crack

rendi|miento *m* efficiency; (*com*) yield. **~r** [5] *vt* yield; (*vencer*) defeat; (*agotar*) exhaust; pay ‹*homenaje*›. ● *vi* pay; (*producir*) produce. **~rse** *vpr* surrender

renega|do *a & m* renegade. **~r** [1 & 12] *vt* deny. ● *vi* grumble. **~r de** renounce ‹*fe etc*›; disown ‹*personas*›

RENFE *abrev* (*Red Nacional de los Ferrocarriles Españoles*) Spanish National Railways

renglón *m* line; (*com*) item. **a ~ seguido** straight away

reno *m* reindeer

renombr|ado *a* renowned. **~e** *m* renown

renova|ción *f* renewal; (*de edificio*) renovation; (*de cuarto*) decorating. **~r** *vt* renew; renovate ‹*edificio*›; decorate ‹*cuarto*›

rent|a *f* income; (*alquiler*) rent; (*deuda*) national debt. **~able** *a* profitable. **~ar** *vt* produce, yield; (*LAm, alquilar*) rent, hire. **~a vitalicia** (life) annuity. **~ista** *m & f* person of independent means

renuncia *f* renunciation. **~r** *vi*. **~r a** renounce, give up

reñi|do *a* hard-fought. **~r** [5 & 22] *vt* tell off. ● *vi* quarrel. **estar ~do con** be incompatible with ‹*cosas*›; be on bad terms with ‹*personas*›

reo *m & f* culprit; (*jurid*) accused. **~ de Estado** person accused of treason. **~ de muerte** prisoner sentenced to death

reojo. mirar de ~ look out of the corner of one's eye at; (*fig*) look askance at

reorganizar [10] *vt* reorganize

repanchigarse [12] *vpr*, **repantigarse** [12] *vpr* sprawl out

repar|ación *f* repair; (*acción*) repairing; (*fig, compensación*) reparation. **~ar** *vt* repair; (*fig*) make amends for; (*notar*) notice. ● *vi*. **~ar en** notice; (*hacer caso de*) pay attention to. **~o** *m* fault; (*objeción*) objection. **poner ~os** raise objections

repart|ición *f* division. **~idor** *m* delivery man. **~imiento** *m* distribution. **~ir** *vt* distribute, share out; deliver ‹*cartas, leche etc*›; hand out ‹*folleto, premio*›. **~o** *m* distribution; (*de cartas, leche etc*› delivery; (*actores*) cast

repas|ar *vt* go over; check ‹*cuenta*›; revise ‹*texto*›; (*leer a la ligera*) glance through; (*coser*) mend. ● *vi* go back. **~o** *m* revision; (*de ropa*) mending. **dar un ~o** look through

repatria|ción *f* repatriation. **~r** *vt* repatriate

repecho *m* steep slope

repele|nte *a* repulsive. **~r** *vt* repel

repensar [1] *vt* reconsider

repent|e. de ~ suddenly. **~ino** *a* sudden

repercu|sión *f* repercussion. **~tir** *vi* reverberate; (*fig*) have repercussions (**en** on)

repertorio *m* repertoire; (*lista*) index

repeti|ción *f* repetition; (*mus*) repeat. **~damente** *adv* repeatedly. **~r** [5] *vt* repeat; (*imitar*) copy; ● *vi*. **~r de** have a second helping of. **¡que se repita!** encore!

repi|car [7] *vt* ring ‹*campanas*›. **~que** *m* peal

repisa *f* shelf. **~ de chimenea** mantlepiece

repito *vb véase* **repetir**

replegarse [1 & 12] *vpr* withdraw

repleto *a* full up

réplica *a* answer; (*copia*) replica

replicar [7] *vi* answer

repliegue *m* crease; (*mil*) withdrawal

repollo *m* cabbage

reponer [34] *vt* replace; revive ‹*obra de teatro*›; (*contestar*) reply. **~se** *vpr* recover

report|aje *m* report. **~ero** *m* reporter

repos|ado *a* quiet; (*sin prisa*) unhurried. **~ar** *vi* rest. **~arse** *vpr* settle. **~o** *m* rest

repost|ar *vt* replenish; refuel ‹*avión*›; fill up ‹*coche etc*›. **~ería** *f* cake shop

repren|der *vt* reprimand. **~sible** *a* reprehensible

represalia *f* reprisal. **tomar ~s** retaliate

representa|ción *f* representation; (*en el teatro*) performance. **en ~ción de** representing. **~nte** *m* representative; (*actor*) actor. ● *f* representative; (*actriz*) actress. **~r** *vt* represent; perform ‹*obra de teatro*›; play ‹*papel*›; (*aparentar*) look. **~rse** *vpr* imagine. **~tivo** *a* representative

represi|ón *f* repression. **~vo** *a* repressive

reprimenda *f* reprimand

reprimir *vt* supress. **~se** *vpr* stop o.s.

reprobar [2] *vt* condemn; reproach ‹*persona*›

réprobo *a* & *m* reprobate

reproch|ar *vt* reproach. **~e** *m* reproach

reproduc|ción *f* reproduction. **~ir** [47] *vt* reproduce. **~tor** *a* reproductive

reptil *m* reptile

rep|ública *f* republic. **~ublicano** *a* & *m* republican

repudiar *vt* repudiate

repuesto *m* store; (*auto*) spare (part). **de ~** in reserve

repugna|ncia *f* disgust. **~nte** *a* repugnant. **~r** *vt* disgust

repujar *vt* emboss

repuls|a *f* rebuff. **~ión** *f* repulsion. **~ivo** *a* repulsive

reputa|ción *f* reputation. **~do** *a* reputable. **~r** *vt* consider

requebrar [1] *vt* flatter

requemar *vt* scorch; (*culin*) burn; tan ‹*piel*›

requeri|miento *m* request; (*jurid*) summons. **~r** [4] *vt* need; (*pedir*) ask

requesón *m* cottage cheese

requete... *pref* extremely

requiebro *m* compliment

réquiem *m* (*pl* **réquiems**) *m* requiem

requis|a *f* inspection; (*mil*) requisition. **~ar** *vt* requisition. **~ito** *m* requirement

res *f* animal. **~ lanar** sheep. **~ vacuna** (*vaca*) cow; (*toro*) bull; (*buey*) ox. **carne de ~** (*Mex*) beef

resabido *a* well-known; ‹*persona*› pedantic

resabio *m* (unpleasant) after-taste; (*vicio*) bad habit

resaca *f* undercurrent; (*después de beber alcohol*) hangover

resaltar *vi* stand out. **hacer ~** emphasize

resarcir [9] *vt* repay; (*compensar*) compensate. **~se** *vpr* make up for

resbal|adizo *a* slippery. **~ar** *vi* slip; (*auto*) skid; ‹*líquido*› trickle. **~arse** *vpr* slip; (*auto*) skid; ‹*líquido*› trickle. **~ón** *m* slip; (*de vehículo*) skid

rescat|ar *vt* ransom; (*recuperar*) recapture; (*fig*) recover. **~e** *m* ransom; (*recuperación*) recapture; (*salvamento*) rescue

rescindir *vt* cancel

rescoldo *m* embers

resecar [7] *vt* dry up; (*med*) remove. **~se** *vpr* dry up

resenti|do *a* resentful. **~miento** *m* resentment. **~rse** *vpr* feel the effects; (*debilitarse*) be weakened; (*ofenderse*) take offence (**de** at)

reseña *f* account; (*en periódico*) report, review. **~r** *vt* describe; (*en periódico*) report on, review

resero *m* (*Arg*) herdsman

reserva *f* reservation; (*provisión*) reserve(s). **~ción** *f* reservation. **~do** *a* reserved. **~r** *vt* reserve; (*guardar*) keep, save. **~rse** *vpr* save o.s. **a ~ de** except for. **a ~ de que** unless. **de ~** in reserve

resfria|do *m* cold; (*enfriamiento*) chill. **~r** *vt*. **~r a uno** give s.o. a cold. **~rse** *vpr* catch a cold; (*fig*) cool off

resguard|ar *vt* protect. **~arse** *vpr* protect o.s.; (*fig*) take care. **~o** *m* protection; (*garantía*) guarantee; (*recibo*) receipt

resid|encia *f* residence; (*univ*) hall of residence, dormitory (*Amer*); (*de ancianos etc*) home. **~encial** *a* residential. **~ente** *a* & *m* & *f* resident. **~ir** *vi* reside; (*fig*) lie

residu|al *a* residual. **~o** *m* remainder. **~os** *mpl* waste

resigna|ción *f* resignation. **~damente** *adv* with resignation. **~r** *vt* resign. **~rse** *vpr* resign o.s. (**a**, **con** to)

resina *f* resin

resist|encia *f* resistence. **~ente** *a* resistent. **~ir** *vt* resist; (*soportar*) bear. ● *vi* resist. **oponer ~encia a** resist

resma *f* ream

resobado *a* trite

resol|ución *f* resolution; (*solución*) solution; (*decisión*) decision. **~ver**

[2] (*pp* **resuelto**) resolve; solve ‹*problema etc*›. **~verse** *vpr* be solved; (*resultar bien*) work out; (*decidirse*) make up one's mind
resollar [2] *vi* breathe heavily. **sin ~** without saying a word
resona|ncia *f* resonance. **~nte** *a* resonant; (*fig*) resounding. **~r** [2] *vi* resound. **tener ~ncia** cause a stir
resopl|ar *vi* puff; (*por enfado*) snort; (*por cansancio*) pant. **~ido** *m* heavy breathing; (*de enfado*) snort; (*de cansancio*) panting
resorte *m* spring. **tocar (todos los) ~s** (*fig*) pull strings
respald|ar *vt* back; (*escribir*) endorse. **~arse** *vpr* lean back. **~o** *m* back
respect|ar *vi* concern. **~ivo** *a* respective. **~o** *m* respect. **al ~o** on the matter. **(con) ~o a** as regards. **en/por lo que ~ a** as regards
respet|able *a* respectable. ● *m* audience. **~ar** *vt* respect. **~o** *m* respect. **~uoso** *a* respectful. **de ~o** best. **faltar al ~o a** be disrespectful to. **hacerse ~ar** command respect
respingo *m* start
respir|ación *f* breathing; (*med*) respiration; (*ventilación*) ventilation. **~ador** *a* respiratory. **~ar** *vi* breathe; (*fig*) breathe a sigh of relief. **no ~ar** (*no hablar*) not say a word. **~o** *m* breathing; (*fig*) rest
resplend|ecer [11] *vi* shine. **~eciente** *a* shining. **~or** *m* brilliance; (*de llamas*) glow
responder *vi* answer; (*replicar*) answer back; (*fig*) reply, respond. **~ de** answer for
responsab|ilidad *f* responsibility. **~le** *a* responsible. **hacerse ~le de** assume responsibilty for
respuesta *f* reply, answer
resquebra|dura *f* crack. **~jar** *vt* crack. **~jarse** *vpr* crack
resquemor *m* (*fig*) uneasiness
resquicio *m* crack; (*fig*) possibility
resta *f* subtraction
restablecer [11] *vt* restore. **~se** *vpr* recover
restallar *vi* crack
restante *a* remaining. **lo ~** the rest
restar *vt* take away; (*substraer*) subtract. ● *vi* be left
restaura|ción *f* restoration. **~nte** *m* restaurant. **~r** *vt* restore
restitu|ción *f* restitution. **~ir** [17] *vt* return; (*restaurar*) restore
resto *m* rest, remainder; (*en matemática*) remainder. **~s** *mpl* remains; (*de comida*) leftovers
restorán *m* restaurant
restregar [1 & 12] *vt* rub
restri|cción *f* restriction. **~ngir** [14] *vt* restrict, limit
resucitar *vt* resuscitate; (*fig*) revive. ● *vi* return to life
resuelto *a* resolute
resuello *m* breath; (*respiración*) breathing
resulta|do *m* result. **~r** *vi* result; (*salir*) turn out; (*ser*) be; (*ocurrir*) happen; (*costar*) come to
resum|en *m* summary. **~ir** *vt* summarize; (*recapitular*) sum up; (*abreviar*) abridge. **en ~en** in short
resur|gir [14] *vi* reappear; (*fig*) revive. **~gimiento** *m* resurgence. **~rección** *f* resurrection
retaguardia *f* (*mil*) rearguard
retahíla *f* string
retal *m* remnant
retama *f*, **retamo** *m* (*LAm*) broom
retar *vt* challenge
retardar *vt* slow down; (*demorar*) delay
retazo *m* remnant; (*fig*) piece, bit
retemblar [1] *vi* shake
rete... *pref* extremely
reten|ción *f* retention. **~er** [40] *vt* keep; (*en la memoria*) retain; (*no dar*) withhold
reticencia *f* insinuation; (*reserva*) reticence, reluctance
retina *f* retina
retintín *m* ringing. **con ~** (*fig*) sarcastically
retir|ada *f* withdrawal. **~ado** *a* secluded; (*jubilado*) retired. **~ar** *vt* move away; (*quitar*) remove; withdraw ‹*dinero*›; (*jubilar*) pension off. **~arse** *vpr* draw back; (*mil*) withdraw; (*jubilarse*) retire; (*acostarse*) go to bed. **~o** *m* retirement; (*pensión*) pension; (*lugar apartado*) retreat
reto *m* challenge
retocar [7] *vt* retouch
retoño *m* shoot
retoque *m* (*acción*) retouching; (*efecto*) finishing touch
retorc|er [2 & 9] *vt* twist; wring ‹*ropa*›. **~erse** *vpr* get twisted up; (*de dolor*) writhe. **~imiento** *m* twisting; (*de ropa*) wringing
retóric|a *f* rhetoric; (*grandilocuencia*) grandiloquence. **~o** *m* rhetorical

retorn|ar *vt/i* return. **~o** *m* return
retortijón *m* twist; (*de tripas*) stomach cramp
retoz|ar [10] *vi* romp, frolic. **~ón** *a* playful
retractar *vt* retract. **~se** *vpr* retract
retra|er [41] *vt* retract. **~erse** *vpr* withdraw. **~ído** *a* retiring
retransmitir *vt* relay
retras|ado *a* behind; ‹*reloj*› slow; (*poco desarrollado*) backward; (*anticuado*) old-fashioned; (*med*) mentally retarded. **~ar** *vt* delay; put back ‹*reloj*›; (*retardar*) slow down. ● *vi* fall behind; ‹*reloj*› be slow. **~arse** *vpr* be behind; ‹*reloj*› be slow. **~o** *m* delay; (*poco desarrollo*) backwardness; (*de reloj*) slowness. **~os** *mpl* arrears. **con 5 minutos de ~o** 5 minutes late. **traer ~o** be late
retrat|ar *vt* paint a portrait of; (*foto*) photograph; (*fig*) protray. **~ista** *m & f* portrait painter. **~o** *m* portrait; (*fig, descripción*) description. **ser el vivo ~o de** be the living image of
retreparse *vpr* lean back
retreta *f* retreat
retrete *m* toilet
retribu|ción *f* payment. **~ir** [17] *vt* pay
retroce|der *vi* move back; (*fig*) back down. **~so** *m* backward movement; (*de arma de fuego*) recoil; (*med*) relapse
retrógrado *a & m* (*pol*) reactionary
retropropulsión *f* jet propulsion
retrospectivo *a* retrospective
retrovisor *m* rear-view mirror
retumbar *vt* echo; ‹*trueno etc*› boom
reuma *m*, **reúma** *m* rheumatism
reum|ático *a* rheumatic. **~atismo** *m* rheumatism
reuni|ón *f* meeting; (*entre amigos*) reunion. **~r** [23] *vt* join together; (*recoger*) gather (together). **~rse** *vpr* join together; ‹*personas*› meet
rev|álida *f* final exam. **~alidar** *vt* confirm; (*escol*) take an exam in
revancha *f* revenge. **tomar la ~** get one's own back
revela|ción *f* revelation. **~do** *m* developing. **~dor** *a* revealing. **~r** *vt* reveal; (*foto*) develop
revent|ar [1] *vi* burst; (*tener ganas*) be dying to. **~arse** *vpr* burst. **~ón** *m* burst; (*auto*) puncture
reverbera|ción *f* (*de luz*) reflection; (*de sonido*) reverberation. **~r** *vi* ‹*luz*› be reflected; ‹*sonido*› reverberate
reveren|cia *f* reverence; (*muestra de respeto*) bow; (*muestra de respeto de mujer*) curtsy. **~ciar** *vt* revere. **~do** *a* respected; (*relig*) reverend. **~te** *a* reverent
revers|ible *a* reversible. **~o** *m* reverse
revertir [4] *vi* revert
revés *m* wrong side; (*desgracia*) misfortune; (*en deportes*) backhand. **al ~** the other way round; (*con lo de arriba abajo*) upside down; (*con lo de dentro fuera*) inside out
revesti|miento *m* coating. **~r** [5] *vt* cover; put on ‹*ropa*›; (*fig*) take on
revis|ar *vt* check; overhaul ‹*mecanismo*›; service ‹*coche etc*›. **~ión** *f* check(ing); (*inspección*) inspection; (*de coche etc*) service. **~or** *m* inspector
revist|a *f* magazine; (*inspección*) inspection; (*artículo*) review; (*espectáculo*) revue. **~ero** *m* critic; (*mueble*) magazine rack. **pasar ~a a** inspect
revivir *vi* come to life again
revocar [7] *vt* revoke; whitewash ‹*pared*›
revolcar [2 & 7] *vt* knock over. **~se** *vpr* roll
revolotear *vi* flutter
revoltijo *m*, **revoltillo** *m* mess. **~ de huevos** scrambled eggs
revoltoso *a* rebellious; ‹*niño*› naughty
revoluci|ón *f* revolution. **~onar** *vt* revolutionize. **~onario** *a & m* revolutionary
revolver [2, *pp* **revuelto**] *vt* mix; stir ‹*líquido*›; (*desordenar*) mess up; (*pol*) stir up. **~se** *vpr* turn round. **~se contra** turn on
revólver *m* revolver
revoque *m* (*con cal*) whitewashing
revuelo *m* fluttering; (*fig*) stir
revuelt|a *f* turn; (*de calle etc*) bend; (*motín*) revolt; (*conmoción*) disturbance. **~o** *a* mixed up; ‹*líquido*› cloudy; ‹*mar*› rough; ‹*tiempo*› unsettled; ‹*huevos*› scrambled
rey *m* king. **~es** *mpl* king and queen
reyerta *f* quarrel
rezagarse [12] *vpr* fall behind
rez|ar [10] *vt* say. ● *vi* pray; (*decir*) say. **~o** *m* praying; (*oración*) prayer
rezongar [12] *vi* grumble

rezumar *vt/i* ooze
ría *f* estuary
riachuelo *m* stream
riada *f* flood
ribera *f* bank
ribete *m* border; (*fig*) embellishment
ricino *m*. **aceite de ~** castor oil
rico *a* rich; (*culin*, *fam*) delicious. ● *m* rich person
rid|ículo *a* ridiculous. **~iculizar** [10] *vt* ridicule
riego *m* watering; (*irrigación*) irrigation
riel *m* rail
rienda *f* rein
riesgo *m* risk. **a ~ de** at the risk of. **correr (el) ~ de** run the risk of
rifa *f* raffle. **~r** *vt* raffle. **~rse** *vpr* (*fam*) quarrel over
rifle *m* rifle
rigidez *f* rigidity; (*fig*) inflexibility
rígido *a* rigid; (*fig*) inflexible
rig|or *m* strictness; (*exactitud*) exactness; (*de clima*) severity. **~uroso** *a* rigorous. **de ~or** compulsory. **en ~or** strictly speaking
rima *f* rhyme. **~r** *vt/i* rhyme
rimbombante *a* resounding; ‹*lenguaje*› pompous; (*fig*, *ostentoso*) showy
rimel *m* mascara
rincón *m* corner
rinoceronte *m* rhinoceros
riña *f* quarrel; (*pelea*) fight
riñ|ón *m* kidney. **~onada** *f* loin; (*guiso*) kidney stew
río *m* river; (*fig*) stream. ● *vb véase* **reír**. **~ abajo** downstream. **~ arriba** upstream
rioja *m* Rioja wine
riqueza *f* wealth; (*fig*) richness. **~s** *fpl* riches
riquísimo *a* delicious
risa *f* laugh. **desternillarse de ~** split one's sides laughing. **la ~** laughter
risco *m* cliff
ris|ible *a* laughable. **~otada** *f* guffaw
ristra *f* string
risueño *a* smiling; (*fig*) happy
rítmico *a* rhythmic(al)
ritmo *m* rhythm; (*fig*) rate
rit|o *m* rite; (*fig*) ritual. **~ual** *a & m* ritual. **de ~ual** customary
rival *a & m & f* rival. **~idad** *f* rivalry. **~izar** [10] *vi* rival
riz|ado *a* curly. **~ar** [10] *vt* curl; ripple ‹*agua*›. **~o** *m* curl; (*en agua*) ripple. **~oso** *a* curly
róbalo *m* bass
robar *vt* steal ‹*cosa*›; rob ‹*persona*›; (*raptar*) kidnap
roble *m* oak (tree)
roblón *m* rivet
robo *m* theft; (*fig*, *estafa*) robbery
robot (*pl* **robots**) *m* robot
robust|ez *f* strength. **~o** *a* strong
roca *f* rock
roce *m* rubbing; (*toque ligero*) touch; (*señal*) mark; (*fig*, *entre personas*) contact
rociar [20] *vt* spray
rocín *m* nag
rocío *m* dew
rodaballo *m* turbot
rodado *m* (*Arg*, *vehículo*) vehicle
rodaja *f* disc; (*culin*) slice
roda|je *m* (*de película*) shooting; (*de coche*) running in. **~r** [2] *vt* shoot ‹*película*›; run in ‹*coche*›; (*recorrer*) travel. ● *vi* roll; ‹*coche*› run; (*hacer una película*) shoot
rode|ar *vt* surround. **~arse** *vpr* surround o.s. (**de** with). **~o** *m* long way round; (*de ganado*) round-up. **andar con ~os** beat about the bush. **sin ~os** plainly
rodill|a *f* knee. **~era** *f* knee-pad. **de ~as** kneeling
rodillo *m* roller; (*culin*) rolling-pin
rododendro *m* rhododendron
rodrigón *m* stake
roe|dor *m* rodent. **~r** [37] *vt* gnaw
rogar [2 & 12] *vt/i* ask; (*relig*) pray. **se ruega a los Sres pasajeros...** passengers are requested.... **se ruega no fumar** please do not smoke
roj|ete *m* rouge. **~ez** *f* redness. **~izo** *a* reddish. **~o** *a & m* red. **ponerse ~o** blush
roll|izo *a* round; ‹*persona*› plump. **~o** *m* roll; (*de cuerda*) coil; (*culin*, *rodillo*) rolling-pin; (*fig*, *pesadez*, *fam*) bore
romance *a* Romance. ● *m* Romance language; (*poema*) romance. **hablar en ~** speak plainly
rom|ánico *a* Romanesque; ‹*lengua*› Romance. **~ano** *a & m* Roman. **a la ~ana** (*culin*) (deep-)fried in batter
rom|anticismo *m* romanticism. **~ántico** *a* romantic
romería *f* pilgrimage
romero *m* rosemary
romo *a* blunt; ‹*nariz*› snub; (*fig*, *torpe*) dull
rompe|cabezas *m invar* puzzle; (*con tacos de madera*) jigsaw (puzzle).

~nueces *m invar* nutcrackers. **~olas** *m invar* breakwater

romp|er (*pp* **roto**) *vt* break; break off ‹*relaciones etc*›. ● *vi* break; ‹*sol*› break through. **~erse** *vpr* break. **~er a** burst out. **~imiento** *m* (*de relaciones etc*) breaking off

ron *m* rum

ronc|ar [7] *vi* snore. **~o** *a* hoarse

roncha *f* lump; (*culin*) slice

ronda *f* round; (*patrulla*) patrol; (*carretera*) ring road. **~lla** *f* group of serenaders; (*invención*) story. **~r** *vt/i* patrol

rondón. de ~ unannounced

ronquedad *f*, **ronquera** *f* hoarseness

ronquido *m* snore

ronronear *vi* purr

ronzal *m* halter

roñ|a *f* (*suciedad*) grime. **~oso** *a* dirty; (*oxidado*) rusty; (*tacaño*) mean

rop|a *f* clothes, clothing. **~a blanca** linen; (*ropa interior*) underwear. **~a de cama** bedclothes. **~a hecha** ready-made clothes. **~a interior** underwear. **~aje** *m* robes; (*excesivo*) heavy clothing. **~ero** *m* wardrobe

ros|a *a invar* pink. ● *f* rose; (*color*) pink. **~áceo** *a* pink. **~ado** *a* rosy. ● *m* (*vino*) rosé. **~al** *m* rose-bush

rosario *m* rosary; (*fig*) series

rosbif *m* roast beef

rosc|a *f* coil; (*de tornillo*) thread; (*de pan*) roll. **~o** *m* roll

rosetón *m* rosette

rosquilla *f* doughnut; (*oruga*) grub

rostro *m* face

rota|ción *f* rotation. **~tivo** *a* rotary

roto *a* broken

rótula *f* kneecap

rotulador *m* felt-tip pen

rótulo *m* sign; (*etiqueta*) label

rotundo *a* emphatic

rotura *f* break

roturar *vt* plough

roza *f* groove. **~dura** *f* scratch

rozagante *a* showy

rozar [10] *vt* rub against; (*ligeramente*) brush against; (*ensuciar*) dirty; (*fig*) touch on. **~se** *vpr* rub; (*con otras personas*) mix

Rte. *abrev* (*Remite*(*nte*)) sender

rúa *f* (small) street

rubéola *f* German measles

rubí *m* ruby

rubicundo *a* ruddy

rubio *a* ‹*pelo*› fair; ‹*persona*› fair-haired; ‹*tabaco*› Virginian

rubor *m* blush; (*fig*) shame. **~izado** *a* blushing; (*fig*) ashamed. **~izar** [10] *vt* make blush. **~izarse** *vpr* blush

rúbrica *f* red mark; (*de firma*) flourish; (*título*) heading

rudeza *f* roughness

rudiment|al *a* rudimentary. **~os** *mpl* rudiments

rudo *a* rough; (*sencillo*) simple

rueda *f* wheel; (*de mueble*) castor; (*de personas*) ring; (*culin*) slice. **~ de prensa** press conference

ruedo *m* edge; (*redondel*) arena

ruego *m* request; (*súplica*) entreaty. ● *vb véase* **rogar**

rufi|án *m* pimp; (*granuja*) villain. **~anesco** *a* roguish

rugby *m* Rugby

rugi|do *m* roar. **~r** [14] *vi* roar

ruibarbo *m* rhubarb

ruido *m* noise; (*alboroto*) din; (*escándalo*) commotion. **~so** *a* noisy; (*fig*) sensational

ruin *a* despicable; (*tacaño*) mean

ruina *f* ruin; (*colapso*) collapse

ruindad *f* meanness

ruinoso *a* ruinous

ruiseñor *m* nightingale

ruleta *f* roulette

rulo *m* (*culin*) rolling-pin; (*del pelo*) curler

Rumania *f* Romania

rumano *a* & *m* Romanian

rumba *f* rumba

rumbo *m* direction; (*fig*) course; (*fig, generosidad*) lavishness. **~so** *a* lavish. **con ~ a** in the direction of. **hacer ~ a** head for

rumia|nte *a* & *m* ruminant. **~r** *vt* chew; (*fig*) chew over. ● *vi* ruminate

rumor *m* rumour; (*ruido*) murmur. **~earse** *vpr* be rumoured. **~oso** *a* murmuring

runr|ún *m* rumour; (*ruido*) murmur. **~unearse** *vpr* be rumoured

ruptura *f* break; (*de relaciones etc*) breaking off

rural *a* rural

Rusia *f* Russia

ruso *a* & *m* Russian

rústico *a* rural; (*de carácter*) coarse. **en rústica** paperback

ruta *f* route; (*camino*) road; (*fig*) course

rutilante *a* shining

rutina *f* routine. **~rio** *a* routine

S

S.A. *abrev* (*Sociedad Anónima*) Ltd, Limited, plc, Public Limited Company
sábado *m* Saturday
sabana *f* (*esp LAm*) savannah
sábana *f* sheet
sabandija *f* bug
sabañón *m* chilblain
sabático *a* sabbatical
sab|elotodo *m & f invar* know-all (*fam*). **~er** [38] *vt* know; (*ser capaz de*) be able to, know how to; (*enterarse de*) learn. ● *vi*. **~er a** taste of. **~er** *m* knowledge. **~ido** *a* well-known. **~iduría** *f* wisdom; (*conocimientos*) knowledge. **a ~er si** I wonder if. **¡haberlo ~ido!** if only I'd known! **hacer ~er** let know. **no sé cuántos** what's-his-name. **para que lo sepas** let me tell you. **¡qué sé yo!** how should I know? **que yo sepa** as far as I know. **¿~es nadar?** can you swim? **un no sé qué** a certain sth. **¡yo qué sé!** how should I know?
sabiendas. **a ~** knowingly; (*a propósito*) on purpose
sabio *a* learned; (*prudente*) wise
sabor *m* taste, flavour; (*fig*) flavour. **~ear** *vt* taste; (*fig*) savour
sabot|aje *m* sabotage. **~eador** *m* saboteur. **~ear** *vt* sabotage
sabroso *a* tasty; (*fig, substancioso*) meaty
sabueso *m* (*perro*) bloodhound; (*fig, detective*) detective
saca|corchos *m invar* corkscrew. **~puntas** *m invar* pencil-sharpener
sacar [7] *vt* take out; put out ‹*parte del cuerpo*›; (*quitar*) remove; take ‹*foto*›; win ‹*premio*›; get ‹*billete, entrada etc*›; withdraw ‹*dinero*›; reach ‹*solución*›; draw ‹*conclusión*›; make ‹*copia*›. **~ adelante** bring up ‹*niño*›; carry on ‹*negocio*›
sacarina *f* saccharin
sacerdo|cio *m* priesthood. **~tal** *a* priestly. **~te** *m* priest
saciar *vt* satisfy
saco *m* bag; (*anat*) sac; (*LAm, chaqueta*) jacket; (*de mentiras*) pack. **~ de dormir** sleeping-bag
sacramento *m* sacrament
sacrific|ar [7] *vt* sacrifice. **~arse** *vpr* sacrifice o.s. **~io** *m* sacrifice
sacr|ilegio *m* sacrilege. **~ílego** *a* sacrilegious
sacro *a* sacred, holy. **~santo** *a* sacrosanct
sacudi|da *f* shake; (*movimiento brusco*) jolt, jerk; (*fig*) shock. **~da eléctrica** electric shock. **~r** *vt* shake; (*golpear*) beat; (*ahuyentar*) chase away. **~rse** *vpr* shake off; (*fig*) get rid of
sádico *a* sadistic. ● *m* sadist
sadismo *m* sadism
saeta *f* arrow; (*de reloj*) hand
safari *m* safari
sagaz *a* shrewd
Sagitario *m* Sagittarius
sagrado *a* sacred, holy. ● *m* sanctuary
Sahara *m*, **Sáhara** /'saxara/ *m* Sahara
sainete *m* short comedy
sal *f* salt
sala *f* room; (*en teatro*) house. **~ de espectáculos** concert hall, auditorium. **~ de espera** waiting-room. **~ de estar** living-room. **~ de fiestas** nightclub
sala|do *a* salty; ‹*agua del mar*› salt; (*vivo*) lively; (*encantador*) cute; (*fig*) witty. **~r** *vt* salt
salario *m* wages
salazón *f* (*carne*) salted meat; (*pescado*) salted fish
salchich|a *f* (pork) sausage. **~ón** *m* salami
sald|ar *vt* pay ‹*cuenta*›; (*vender*) sell off; (*fig*) settle. **~o** *m* balance; (*venta*) sale; (*lo que queda*) remnant
salero *m* salt-cellar
salgo *vb véase* **salir**
sali|da *f* departure; (*puerta*) exit, way out; (*de gas, de líquido*) leak; (*de astro*) rising; (*com, posibilidad de venta*) opening; (*chiste*) witty remark; (*fig*) way out. **~da de emergencia** emergency exit. **~ente** *a* projecting; (*fig*) outstanding. **~r** [52] *vi* leave; (*de casa etc*) go out; ‹*revista etc*› be published; (*resultar*) turn out; ‹*astro*› rise; (*aparecer*) appear. **~rse** *vpr* leave; ‹*recipiente, líquido etc*› leak. **~r adelante** get by. **~rse con la suya** get one's own way
saliva *f* saliva
salmo *m* psalm
salm|ón *m* salmon. **~onete** *m* red mullet
salmuera *f* brine
salón *m* lounge, sitting-room. **~ de actos** assembly hall. **~ de fiestas** dancehall

salpica|dero *m* (*auto*) dashboard. **~dura** *f* splash; (*acción*) splashing. **~r** [7] *vt* splash; (*fig*) sprinkle

sals|a *f* sauce; (*para carne asada*) gravy; (*fig*) spice. **~a verde** parsley sauce. **~era** *f* sauce-boat

salt|amontes *m invar* grasshopper. **~ar** *vt* jump (over); (*fig*) miss out. ● *vi* jump; (*romperse*) break; ‹*líquido*› spurt out; (*desprenderse*) come off; ‹*pelota*› bounce; (*estallar*) explode. **~eador** *m* highwayman. **~ear** *vt* rob; (*culin*) sauté. ● *vi* skip through

saltimbanqui *m* acrobat

salt|o *m* jump; (*al agua*) dive. **~o de agua** waterfall. **~ón** *a* ‹*ojos*› bulging. ● *m* grasshopper. **a ~os** by jumping; (*fig*) by leaps and bounds. **de un ~o** with one jump

salud *f* health; (*fig*) welfare. ● *int* cheers! **~able** *a* healthy

salud|ar *vt* greet, say hello to; (*mil*) salute. **~o** *m* greeting; (*mil*) salute. **~os** *mpl* best wishes. **le ~a atentamente** (*en cartas*) yours faithfully

salva *f* salvo; (*de aplausos*) thunders

salvación *f* salvation

salvado *m* bran

Salvador *m*. **El ~** El Salvador

salvaguardia *f* safeguard

salvaje *a* ‹*planta, animal*› wild; (*primitivo*) savage. ● *m & f* savage

salvamanteles *m invar* table-mat

salva|mento *m* rescue. **~r** *vt* save, rescue; (*atraversar*) cross; (*recorrer*) travel; (*fig*) overcome. **~rse** *vpr* save o.s. **~vidas** *m invar* lifebelt. **chaleco** *m* **~vidas** life-jacket

salvia *f* sage

salvo *a* safe. ● *adv & prep* except (for). **~ que** unless. **~conducto** *m* safe-conduct. **a ~** out of danger. **poner a ~** put in a safe place

samba *f* samba

San *a* Saint, St. **~ Miguel** St Michael

sana|r *vt* cure. ● *vi* recover. **~torio** *m* sanatorium

sanci|ón *f* sanction. **~onar** *vt* sanction

sancocho *m* (*LAm*) stew

sandalia *f* sandal

sándalo *m* sandalwood

sandía *f* water melon

sandwich /'sambitʃ/ *m* (*pl* **sandwichs, sandwiches**) sandwich

sanear *vt* drain

sangr|ante *a* bleeding; (*fig*) flagrant. **~ar** *vt/i* bleed. **~e** *f* blood. **a ~e fría** in cold blood

sangría *f* (*bebida*) sangria

sangriento *a* bloody

sangu|ijuela *f* leech. **~íneo** *a* blood

san|idad *f* health. **~itario** *a* sanitary. **~o** *a* healthy; (*seguro*) sound. **~o y salvo** safe and sound. **cortar por lo ~o** settle things once and for all

santiamén *m*. **en un ~** in an instant

sant|idad *f* sanctity. **~ificar** [7] *vt* sanctify. **~iguar** [15] *vt* make the sign of the cross over. **~iguarse** *vpr* cross o.s. **~o** *a* holy; (*delante de nombre*) Saint, St. ● *m* saint; (*día*) saint's day, name day. **~uario** *m* sanctuary. **~urrón** *a* sanctimonious, hypocritical

sañ|a *f* fury; (*crueldad*) cruelty. **~oso** *a*, **~udo** *a* furious

sapo *m* toad; (*bicho, fam*) small animal, creature

saque *m* (*en tenis*) service; (*en fútbol*) throw-in; (*inicial en fútbol*) kick-off

saque|ar *vt* loot. **~o** *m* looting

sarampión *m* measles

sarape *m* (*Mex*) blanket

sarc|asmo *m* sarcasm. **~ástico** *a* sarcastic

sardana *f* Catalonian dance

sardina *f* sardine

sardo *a & m* Sardinian

sardónico *a* sardonic

sargento *m* sergeant

sarmiento *m* vine shoot

sarpullido *m* rash

sarta *f* string

sartén *f* frying-pan (*Brit*), fry-pan (*Amer*)

sastre *m* tailor. **~ría** *f* tailoring; (*tienda*) tailor's (shop)

Satanás *m* Satan

satánico *a* satanic

satélite *m* satellite

satinado *a* shiny

sátira *f* satire

satírico *a* satirical. ● *m* satirist

satisf|acción *f* satisfaction. **~acer** [31] *vt* satisfy; (*pagar*) pay; (*gustar*) please; meet ‹*gastos, requisitos*›. **~acerse** *vpr* satisfy o.s.; (*vengarse*) take revenge. **~actorio** *a* satisfactory. **~echo** *a* satisfied. **~echo de sí mismo** smug

satura|ción *f* saturation. **~r** *vt* saturate

Saturno *m* Saturn

sauce *m* willow. **~ llorón** weeping willow

saúco *m* elder
savia *f* sap
sauna *f* sauna
saxofón *m*, **saxófono** *m* saxophone
saz|ón *f* ripeness; (*culin*) seasoning. **~onado** *a* ripe; (*culin*) seasoned. **~onar** *vt* ripen; (*culin*) season. **en ~ón** in season
se *pron* (*él*) him; (*ella*) her; (*Vd*) you; (*reflexivo, él*) himself; (*reflexivo, ella*) herself; (*reflexivo, ello*) itself; (*reflexivo, uno*) oneself; (*reflexivo, Vd*) yourself; (*reflexivo, ellos, ellas*) themselves; (*reflexivo, Vds*) yourselves; (*recíproco*) (to) each other. **~ dice** people say, they say, it is said (**que** that). **~ habla español** Spanish spoken
sé *vb véase* **saber** *y* **ser**
sea *vb véase* **ser**
sebo *m* tallow; (*culin*) suet
seca|dor *m* drier; (*de pelo*) hair-drier. **~nte** *a* drying. ● *m* blotting-paper. **~r** [7] *vt* dry. **~rse** *vpr* dry; ‹*río etc*› dry up; ‹*persona*› dry o.s.
sección *f* section
seco *a* dry; ‹*frutos, flores*› dried; (*flaco*) thin; ‹*respuesta*› curt; (*escueto*) plain. **a secas** just. **en ~** (*bruscamente*) suddenly. **lavar en ~** dry-clean
secre|ción *f* secretion. **~tar** *vt* secrete
secretar|ía *f* secretariat. **~io** *m* secretary
secreto *a & m* secret
secta *f* sect. **~rio** *a* sectarian
sector *m* sector
secuela *f* consequence
secuencia *f* sequence
secuestr|ar *vt* confiscate; kidnap ‹*persona*›; hijack ‹*avión*›. **~o** *m* seizure; (*de persona*) kidnapping; (*de avión*) hijack(ing)
secular *a* secular
secundar *vt* second, help. **~io** *a* secondary
sed *f* thirst. ● *vb véase* **ser**. **tener ~** be thirsty. **tener ~ de** (*fig*) be hungry for
seda *f* silk
sedante *a & m*, **sedativo** *a & m* sedative
sede *f* seat; (*relig*) see
sedentario *a* sedentary
sedici|ón *f* sedition. **~oso** *a* seditious
sediento *a* thirsty
sediment|ar *vi* deposit. **~arse** *vpr* settle. **~o** *m* sediment
seduc|ción *f* seduction. **~ir** [47] *vt* seduce; (*atraer*) attract. **~tor** *a* seductive. ● *m* seducer
sega|dor *m* harvester. **~dora** *f* harvester, mower. **~r** [1 & 12] *vt* reap
seglar *a* secular. ● *m* layman
segmento *m* segment
segoviano *m* person from Segovia
segrega|ción *f* segregation. **~r** [12] *vt* segregate
segui|da *f*. **en ~da** immediately. **~do** *a* continuous; (*en plural*) consecutive. ● *adv* straight; (*después*) after. **todo ~do** straight ahead. **~dor** *a* following. ● *m* follower. **~r** [5 & 13] *vt* follow (*continuar*) continue
según *prep* according to. ● *adv* it depends; (*a medida que*) as
segundo *a* second. ● *m* second; (*culin*) second course
segur|amente *adv* certainly; (*muy probablemente*) surely. **~idad** *f* safety; (*certeza*) certainty; (*aplomo*) confidence. **~idad en sí mismo** self-confidence. **~idad social** social security. **~o** *a* safe; (*cierto*) certain, sure; (*firme*) secure; (*de fiar*) reliable. ● *adv* for certain. ● *m* insurance; (*dispositivo de seguridad*) safety device. **~o de sí mismo** self-confident. **~o de terceros** third-party insurance
seis *a & m* six. **~cientos** *a & m* six hundred
seísmo *m* earthquake
selec|ción *f* selection. **~cionar** *vt* select, choose. **~tivo** *a* selective. **~to** *a* selected; (*fig*) choice
selva *f* forest; (*jungla*) jungle
sell|ar *vt* stamp; (*cerrar*) seal. **~o** *m* stamp; (*en documento oficial*) seal; (*fig, distintivo*) hallmark
semáforo *m* semaphore; (*auto*) traffic lights; (*rail*) signal
semana *f* week. **~l** *a* weekly. **~rio** *a & m* weekly. **S~ Santa** Holy Week
semántic|a *f* semantics. **~o** *a* semantic
semblante *m* face; (*fig*) look
sembrar [1] *vt* sow; (*fig*) scatter
semeja|nte *a* similar; (*tal*) such. ● *m* fellow man; (*cosa*) equal. **~nza** *f* similarity. **~r** *vi* seem. **~rse** *vpr* look alike. **a ~nza de** like. **tener ~nza con** resemble

semen *m* semen. **~tal** *a* stud. ● *m* stud animal

semestr|al *a* half-yearly. **~e** *m* six months

semibreve *m* semibreve (*Brit*), whole note (*Amer*)

semic|ircular *a* semicircular. **~írculo** *m* semicircle

semicorchea *f* semiquaver (*Brit*), sixteenth note (*Amer*)

semifinal *f* semifinal

semill|a *f* seed. **~ero** *m* nursery; (*fig*) hotbed

seminario *m* (*univ*) seminar; (*relig*) seminary

sem|ita *a* Semitic. ● *m* Semite. **~ítico** *a* Semitic

sémola *f* semolina

senado *m* senate; (*fig*) assembly. **~r** *m* senator

sencill|ez *f* simplicity. **~o** *a* simple; (*uno solo*) single

senda *f*, **sendero** *m* path

sendos *apl* each

seno *m* bosom. **~ materno** womb

sensaci|ón *f* sensation. **~onal** *a* sensational

sensat|ez *f* good sense. **~o** *a* sensible

sensi|bilidad *f* sensibility. **~ble** *a* sensitive; (*notable*) notable; (*lamentable*) lamentable. **~tivo** *a* ‹*órgano*› sense

sensual *a* sensual. **~idad** *f* sensuality

senta|do *a* sitting (down). **dar algo por ~do** take something for granted. **~r** [1] *vt* place; (*establecer*) establish. ● *vi* suit; (*de medidas*) fit; ‹*comida*› agree with. **~rse** *vpr* sit (down); ‹*sedimento*› settle

sentencia *f* saying; (*jurid*) sentence. **~r** *vt* sentence

sentido *a* deeply felt; (*sincero*) sincere; (*sensible*) sensitive. ● *m* sense; (*dirección*) direction. **~ común** common sense. **~ del humor** sense of humour. **~ único** one-way. **doble ~** double meaning. **no tener ~** not make sense. **perder el ~** faint. **sin ~** unconscious; ‹*cosa*› senseless

sentim|ental *a* sentimental. **~iento** *m* feeling; (*sentido*) sense; (*pesar*) regret

sentir [4] *vt* feel; (*oír*) hear; (*lamentar*) be sorry for. ● *vi* feel; (*lamentarse*) be sorry. ● *m* (*opinión*) opinion. **~se** *vpr* feel. **lo siento** I'm sorry

seña *f* sign. **~s** *fpl* (*dirección*) address; (*descripción*) description

señal *f* sign; (*rail etc*) signal; (*telefónico*) tone; (*com*) deposit. **~ado** *a* notable. **~ar** *vt* signal; (*poner señales en*) mark; (*apuntar*) point out; ‹*manecilla, aguja*› point to; (*determinar*) fix. **~arse** *vpr* stand out. **dar ~es de** show signs of. **en ~ de** as a token of

señero *a* alone; (*sin par*) unique

señor *m* man; (*caballero*) gentleman; (*delante de nombre propio*) Mr; (*tratamiento directo*) sir. **~a** *f* lady, woman; (*delante de nombre propio*) Mrs; (*esposa*) wife; (*tratamiento directo*) madam. **~ial** *a* ‹*casa*› stately. **~ita** *f* young lady; (*delante de nombre propio*) Miss; (*tratamiento directo*) miss. **~ito** *m* young gentleman. **el ~ alcalde** the mayor. **el ~** Mr. **muy ~ mío** Dear Sir. **¡no ~!** certainly not! **ser ~ de** be master of, control

señuelo *m* lure

sepa *vb véase* **saber**

separa|ción *f* separation. **~do** *a* separate. **~r** *vt* separate; (*apartar*) move away; (*de empleo*) dismiss. **~rse** *vpr* separate; ‹*amigos*› part. **~tista** *a & m & f* separatist. **por ~do** separately

septentrional *a* north(ern)

séptico *a* septic

septiembre *m* September

séptimo *a* seventh

sepulcro *m* sepulchre

sepult|ar *vt* bury. **~ura** *f* burial; (*tumba*) grave. **~urero** *m* gravedigger

sequ|edad *f* dryness. **~ía** *f* drought

séquito *m* entourage; (*fig*) aftermath

ser [39] *vi* be. ● *m* being. **~ de** be made of; (*provenir de*) come from; (*pertenecer a*) belong to. **~ humano** human being. **a no ~ que** unless. **¡así sea!** so be it! **es más** what is more. **lo que sea** anything. **no sea que, no vaya a ~ que** in case. **o sea** in other words. **sea lo que fuere** be that as it may. **sea... sea** either... or. **siendo así que** since. **soy yo** it's me

seren|ar *vt* calm down. **~arse** *vpr* calm down; ‹*tiempo*› clear up. **~ata** *f* serenade. **~idad** *f* serenity. **~o** *a* ‹*cielo*› clear; ‹*tiempo*› fine; (*fig*) calm. ● *m* night watchman. **al ~o** in the open

seri|al *m* serial. **~e** *f* series. **fuera de ~e** (*fig, extraordinario*) special. **producción** *f* **en ~** mass production
seri|edad *f* seriousness. **~o** *a* serious; (*confiable*) reliable. **en ~o** seriously. **poco ~o** frivolous
sermón *m* sermon
serp|enteante *a* winding. **~entear** *vi* wind. **~iente** *f* snake. **~iente de cascabel** rattlesnake
serrano *a* mountain; ‹*jamón*› cured
serr|ar [1] *vt* saw. **~ín** *m* sawdust. **~ucho** *m* (hand)saw
servi|cial *a* helpful. **~cio** *m* service; (*conjunto*) set; (*aseo*) toilet. **~cio a domicilio** delivery service. **~dor** *m* servant. **~dumbre** *f* servitude; (*criados*) servants, staff. **~l** *a* servile. **su (seguro) ~dor** (*en cartas*) yours faithfully
servilleta *f* serviette, (table) napkin
servir [5] *vt* serve; (*ayudar*) help; (*en restaurante*) wait on. ● *vi* serve; (*ser útil*) be of use. **~se** *vpr* help o.s. **~se de** use. **no ~ de nada** be useless. **para ~le** at your service. **sírvase sentarse** please sit down
sesear *vi* pronounce the Spanish *c* as an *s*
sesent|a *a* & *m* sixty. **~ón** *a* & *m* sixty-year-old
seseo *m* pronunciation of the Spanish *c* as an *s*
sesg|ado *a* slanting. **~o** *m* slant; (*fig, rumbo*) turn
sesión *f* session; (*en el cine*) showing; (*en el teatro*) performance
ses|o *m* brain; (*fig*) brains. **~udo** *a* inteligent; (*sensato*) sensible
seta *f* mushroom
sete|cientos *a* & *m* seven hundred. **~nta** *a* & *m* seventy. **~ntón** *a* & *m* seventy-year-old
setiembre *m* September
seto *m* fence; (*de plantas*) hedge. **~ vivo** hedge
seudo... *pref* pseudo...
seudónimo *m* pseudonym
sever|idad *f* severity. **~o** *a* severe; ‹*disciplina, profesor etc*› strict
Sevilla *f* Seville
sevillan|as *fpl* popular dance from Seville. **~o** *m* person from Seville
sexo *m* sex
sext|eto *m* sextet. **~o** *a* sixth
sexual *a* sexual. **~idad** *f* sexuality
si *m* (*mus*) B; (*solfa*) te. ● *conj* if; (*dubitativo*) whether. **~ no** or else. **por ~ (acaso)** in case
sí *pron reflexivo* (*él*) himself; (*ella*) herself; (*ello*) itself; (*uno*) oneself; (*Vd*) yourself; (*ellos, ellas*) themselves; (*Vds*) yourselves; (*recíproco*) each other
sí *adv* yes. ● *m* consent
Siamés *a* & *m* Siamese
Sicilia *f* Sicily
sida *m* Aids
siderurgia *f* iron and steel industry
sidra *f* cider
siega *f* harvesting; (*época*) harvest time
siembra *f* sowing; (*época*) sowing time
siempre *adv* always. **~ que** if. **como ~** as usual. **de ~** (*acostumbrado*) usual. **lo de ~** the same old story. **para ~** for ever
sien *f* temple
siento *vb véase* **sentar** *y* **sentir**
sierra *f* saw; (*cordillera*) mountain range
siervo *m* slave
siesta *f* siesta
siete *a* & *m* seven
sífilis *f* syphilis
sifón *m* U-bend; (*de soda*) syphon
sigilo *m* secrecy
sigla *f* initials, abbreviation
siglo *m* century; (*época*) time, age; (*fig, mucho tiempo, fam*) ages; (*fig, mundo*) world
significa|ción *f* meaning; (*importancia*) significance. **~do** *a* (*conocido*) well-known. ● *m* meaning. **~r** [7] *vt* mean; (*expresar*) express. **~rse** *vpr* stand out. **~tivo** *a* significant
signo *m* sign. **~ de admiración** exclamation mark. **~ de interrogación** question mark
sigo *vb véase* **seguir**
siguiente *a* following, next. **lo ~** the following
sílaba *f* syllable
silb|ar *vt/i* whistle. **~ato** *m*, **~ido** *m* whistle
silenci|ador *m* silencer. **~ar** *vt* hush up. **~o** *m* silence. **~oso** *a* silent
sílfide *f* sylph
silicio *m* silicon
silo *m* silo
silueta *f* silhouette; (*dibujo*) outline
silvestre *a* wild
sill|a *f* chair; (*de montar*) saddle; (*relig*) see. **~a de ruedas** wheelchair. **~ín** *m* saddle. **~ón** *m* armchair

simb|ólico *a* symbolic(al). **~olismo** *m* symbolism. **~olizar** [10] *vt* symbolize
símbolo *m* symbol
sim|etría *f* symmetry. **~étrico** *a* symmetric(al)
simiente *f* seed
similar *a* similar
simp|atía *f* liking; (*cariño*) affection; (*fig, amigo*) friend. **~ático** *a* nice, likeable; (*amable*) kind. **~atizante** *m & f* sympathizer. **~atizar** [10] *vi* get on (well together). **me es ~ático** I like
simpl|e *a* simple; (*mero*) mere. **~eza** *f* simplicity; (*tontería*) stupid thing; (*insignificancia*) trifle. **~icidad** *f* simplicity. **~ificar** [7] *vt* simplify. **~ón** *m* simpleton
simposio *m* symposium
simula|ción *f* simulation. **~r** *vt* feign
simultáneo *a* simultaneous
sin *prep* without. **~ que** without
sinagoga *f* synagogue
sincer|idad *f* sincerity. **~o** *a* sincere
síncopa *f* (*mus*) syncopation
sincopar *vt* syncopate
sincronizar [10] *vt* synchronize
sindica|l *a* (trade-)union. **~lista** *m & f* trade-unionist. **~to** *m* trade union
síndrome *m* syndrome
sinfín *m* endless number
sinf|onía *f* symphony. **~ónico** *a* symphonic
singular *a* singular; (*excepcional*) exceptional. **~izar** [10] *vt* single out. **~izarse** *vpr* stand out
siniestro *a* sinister; (*desgraciado*) unlucky. ● *m* disaster
sinnúmero *m* endless number
sino *m* fate. ● *conj* but; (*salvo*) except
sínodo *m* synod
sinónimo *a* synonymous. ● *m* synonym
sinrazón *f* wrong
sintaxis *f* syntax
síntesis *f invar* synthesis
sint|ético *a* synthetic. **~etizar** [10] *vt* synthesize; (*resumir*) summarize
síntoma *f* sympton
sintomático *a* symptomatic
sinton|ía *f* (*en la radio*) signature tune. **~izar** [10] *vt* (*con la radio*) tune (in)
sinuoso *a* winding
sinvergüenza *m & f* scoundrel
sionis|mo *m* Zionism. **~ta** *m & f* Zionist
siquiera *conj* even if. ● *adv* at least. **ni ~** not even
sirena *f* siren
Siria *f* Syria
sirio *a & m* Syrian
siroco *m* sirocco
sirvienta *f*, **sirviente** *m* servant
sirvo *vb véase* **servir**
sise|ar *vt/i* hiss. **~o** *m* hissing
sísmico *a* seismic
sismo *m* earthquake
sistem|a *m* system. **~ático** *a* systematic. **por ~a** as a rule
sitiar *vt* besiege; (*fig*) surround
sitio *m* place; (*espacio*) space; (*mil*) siege. **en cualquier ~** anywhere
situa|ción *f* position. **~r** [21] *vt* situate; (*poner*) put; (*depositar*) deposit. **~rse** *vpr* be successful, establish o.s.
slip /es'lip/ *m* (*pl* **slips** /es'lip/) underpants, briefs
slogan /es'logan/ *m* (*pl* **slogans** /es'logan/) slogan
smoking /es'mokin/ *m* (*pl* **smokings** /es'mokin/) dinner jacket (*Brit*), tuxedo (*Amer*)
sobaco *m* armpit
sobar *vt* handle; knead ‹*masa*›
soberan|ía *f* sovereignty. **~o** *a* sovereign; (*fig*) supreme. ● *m* sovereign
soberbi|a *f* pride; (*altanería*) arrogance. **~o** *a* proud; (*altivo*) arrogant
soborn|ar *vt* bribe. **~o** *m* bribe
sobra *f* surplus. **~s** *fpl* leftovers. **~do** *a* more than enough. **~nte** *a* surplus. **~r** *vi* be left over; (*estorbar*) be in the way. **de ~** more than enough
sobrasada *f* Majorcan sausage
sobre *prep* on; (*encima de*) on top of; (*más o menos*) about; (*por encima de*) above; (*sin tocar*) over; (*además de*) on top of. ● *m* envelope. **~cargar** [12] *vt* overload. **~coger** [14] *vt* startle. **~cogerse** *vpr* be startled. **~cubierta** *f* dust cover. **~dicho** *a* aforementioned. **~entender** [1] *vt* understand, infer. **~entendido** *a* implicit. **~humano** *a* superhuman. **~llevar** *vt* bear. **~mesa** *f*. **de ~mesa** after-dinner. **~natural** *a* supernatural. **~nombre** *m* nickname. **~pasar** *vt* exceed. **~poner** [34] *vt* superimpose; (*fig, anteponer*) put before. **~ponerse** *vpr* overcome. **~pujar** *vt* surpass. **~saliente** *a* (*fig*) outstanding. ● *m* excellent mark. **~salir** [52] *vi* stick out;

(*fig*) stand out. **~saltar** *vt* startle. **~salto** *m* fright. **~sueldo** *m* bonus. **~todo** *m* overall; (*abrigo*) overcoat. **~ todo** above all, especially. **~venir** [53] *vi* happen. **~viviente** *a* surviving. ● *m & f* survivor. **~vivir** *vi* survive. **~volar** *vt* fly over

sobriedad *f* restraint

sobrin|a *f* niece. **~o** *m* nephew

sobrio *a* moderate, sober

socarr|ón *a* sarcastic; (*taimado*) sly. **~onería** *f* sarcasm

socavar *vt* undermine

soci|able *a* sociable. **~al** *a* social. **~aldemocracia** *f* social democracy. **~aldemócrata** *m & f* social democrat. **~alismo** *m* socialsim. **~alista** *a & m & f* socialist. **~alizar** [10] *vt* nationalize. **~edad** *f* society; (*com*) company. **~edad anónima** limited company. **~o** *m* member; (*com*) partner. **~ología** *f* sociology. **~ólogo** *m* sociologist

socorr|er *vt* help. **~o** *m* help

soda *f* (*bebida*) soda (water)

sodio *m* sodium

sofá *m* sofa, settee

sofistica|ción *f* sophistication. **~do** *a* sophisticated. **~r** [7] *vt* adulterate

sofoca|ción *f* suffocation. **~nte** *a* (*fig*) stifling. **~r** [7] *vt* suffocate; (*fig*) stifle. **~rse** *vpr* suffocate; (*ruborizarse*) blush

soga *f* rope

soja *f* soya (bean)

sojuzgar [12] *vt* subdue

sol *m* sun; (*luz solar*) sunlight; (*mus*) G; (*solfa*) soh. **al ~** in the sun. **día** *m* **de ~** sunny day. **hace ~, hay ~** it is sunny. **tomar el ~** sunbathe

solamente *adv* only

solapa *f* lapel; (*de bolsillo etc*) flap. **~do** *a* sly. **~r** *vt/i* overlap

solar *a* solar. ● *m* plot

solariego *a* ‹*casa*› ancestral

solaz *m* relaxation

soldado *m* soldier. **~ raso** private

solda|dor *m* welder; (*utensilio*) soldering iron. **~r** [2] *vt* weld, solder

solea|do *a* sunny. **~r** *vt* put in the sun

soledad *f* solitude; (*aislamiento*) loneliness

solemn|e *a* solemn. **~idad** *f* solemnity; (*ceremonia*) ceremony

soler [2] *vi* be in the habit of. **suele despertarse a las 6** he usually wakes up at 6 o'clock

sol|icitar *vt* request; apply for ‹*empleo*›; attract ‹*atención*›. **~ícito** *a* solicitous. **~icitud** *f* (*atención*) concern; (*petición*) request; (*para un puesto*) application

solidaridad *f* solidarity

solid|ez *f* solidity; (*de color*) fastness. **~ificar** [7] *vt* solidify. **~ificarse** *vpr* solidify

sólido *a* solid; ‹*color*› fast; (*robusto*) strong. ● *m* solid

soliloquio *m* soliloquy

solista *m & f* soloist

solitario *a* solitary; (*aislado*) lonely. ● *m* recluse; (*juego, diamante*) solitaire

solo *a* (*sin compañía*) alone; (*aislado*) lonely; (*único*) only; (*mus*) solo; ‹*café*› black. ● *m* solo; (*juego*) solitaire. **a solas** alone

sólo *adv* only. **~ que** only. **aunque ~ sea** even if it is only. **con ~ que** if; (*con tal que*) as long as. **no ~... sino también** not only... but also... **tan ~** only

solomillo *m* sirloin

solsticio *m* solstice

soltar [2] *vt* let go of; (*dejar caer*) drop; (*dejar salir, decir*) let out; give ‹*golpe etc*›. **~se** *vpr* come undone; (*librarse*) break loose

solter|a *f* single woman. **~o** *a* single. ● *m* bachelor. **apellido** *m* **de ~a** maiden name

soltura *f* looseness; (*agilidad*) agility; (*en hablar*) ease, fluency

solu|ble *a* soluble. **~ción** *f* solution. **~cionar** *vt* solve; settle ‹*huelga, asunto*›

solvent|ar *vt* resolve; settle ‹*deuda*›. **~e** *a & m* solvent

sollo *m* sturgeon

solloz|ar [10] *vi* sob. **~o** *m* sob

sombr|a *f* shade; (*imagen oscura*) shadow. **~eado** *a* shady. **a la ~a** in the shade

sombrero *m* hat. **~ hongo** bowler hat

sombrío *a* sombre

somero *a* shallow

someter *vt* subdue; subject ‹*persona*›; (*presentar*) submit. **~se** *vpr* give in

somn|oliento *a* sleepy. **~ífero** *m* sleeping-pill

somos *vb véase* **ser**

son *m* sound. ● *vb véase* **ser**

sonámbulo *m* sleepwalker

sonar [2] *vt* blow; ring ‹*timbre*›. ● *vi* sound; ‹*timbre, teléfono etc*› ring; ‹*reloj*› strike; (*pronunciarse*) be pronounced; (*mus*) play; (*fig, ser conocido*) be familiar. **~se** *vpr* blow one's nose. **~ a** sound like
sonata *f* sonata
sonde|ar *vt* sound; (*fig*) sound out. **~o** *m* sounding; (*fig*) poll
soneto *m* sonnet
sónico *a* sonic
sonido *m* sound
sonoro *a* sonorous; (*ruidoso*) loud
sonr|eír [51] *vi* smile. **~eírse** *vpr* smile. **~iente** *a* smiling. **~isa** *f* smile
sonroj|ar *vt* make blush. **~arse** *vpr* blush. **~o** *m* blush
sonrosado *a* rosy, pink
sonsacar [7] *vt* wheedle out
soñ|ado *a* dream. **~ador** *m* dreamer. **~ar** [2] *vi* dream (**con** of). **¡ni ~arlo!** not likely! **(que) ni ~ado** marvellous
sopa *f* soup
sopesar *vt* (*fig*) weigh up
sopl|ar *vt* blow; blow out ‹*vela*›; blow off ‹*polvo*›; (*inflar*) blow up. ● *vi* blow. **~ete** *m* blowlamp. **~o** *m* puff; (*fig, momento*) moment
soporífero *a* soporific. ● *m* sleeping-pill
soport|al *m* porch. **~ales** *mpl* arcade. **~ar** *vt* support; (*fig*) bear. **~e** *m* support
soprano *f* soprano
sor *f* sister
sorb|er *vt* suck; sip ‹*bebida*›; (*absorber*) absorb. **~ete** *m* sorbet, water-ice. **~o** *m* swallow; (*pequeña cantidad*) sip
sord|amente *adv* silently, dully. **~era** *f* deafness
sórdido *a* squalid; (*tacaño*) mean
sordo *a* deaf; (*silencioso*) quiet. ● *m* deaf person. **~mudo** *a* deaf and dumb. **a la sorda, a sordas** on the quiet. **hacerse el ~** turn a deaf ear
sorna *f* sarcasm. **con ~** sarcastically
soroche *m* (*LAm*) mountain sickness
sorpre|ndente *a* surprising. **~nder** *vt* surprise; (*coger desprevenido*) catch. **~sa** *f* surprise
sorte|ar *vt* draw lots for; (*rifar*) raffle; (*fig*) avoid. ● *vi* draw lots; (*con moneda*) toss up. **~o** *m* draw; (*rifa*) raffle; (*fig*) avoidance
sortija *f* ring; (*de pelo*) ringlet
sortilegio *m* witchcraft; (*fig*) spell
sos|egado *a* calm. **~egar** [1 & 12] *vt* calm. ● *vi* rest. **~iego** *m* calmness. **con ~iego** calmly
soslayo. al ~, de ~ sideways
soso *a* tasteless; (*fig*) dull
sospech|a *f* suspicion. **~ar** *vt/i* suspect. **~oso** *a* suspicious. ● *m* suspect
sost|én *m* support; (*prenda femenina*) bra (*fam*), brassière. **~ener** [40] *vt* support; (*sujetar*) hold; (*mantener*) maintain; (*alimentar*) sustain. **~enerse** *vpr* support o.s.; (*continuar*) remain. **~enido** *a* sustained; (*mus*) sharp. ● *m* (*mus*) sharp
sota *f* (*de naipes*) jack
sótano *m* basement
sotavento *m* lee
soto *m* grove; (*matorral*) thicket
soviético *a* (*historia*) Soviet
soy *vb véase* **ser**
Sr *abrev* (*Señor*) Mr. **~a** *abrev* (*Señora*) Mrs. **~ta** *abrev* (*Señorita*) Miss
su *a* (*de él*) his; (*de ella*) her; (*de ello*) its; (*de uno*) one's; (*de Vd*) your; (*de ellos, de ellas*) their; (*de Vds*) your
suav|e *a* smooth; (*fig*) gentle; ‹*color, sonido*› soft. **~idad** *f* smoothness, softness. **~izar** [10] *vt* smooth, soften
subalimentado *a* underfed
subalterno *a* secondary; ‹*persona*› auxiliary
subarrendar [1] *vt* sublet
subasta *f* auction; (*oferta*) tender. **~r** *vt* auction
sub|campeón *m* runner-up. **~consciencia** *f* subconscious. **~consciente** *a* & *m* subconscious. **~continente** *m* subcontinent. **~desarrollado** *a* under-developed. **~director** *m* assistant manager
súbdito *m* subject
sub|dividir *vt* subdivide. **~estimar** *vt* underestimate. **~gerente** *m & f* assistant manager
subi|da *f* ascent; (*aumento*) rise; (*pendiente*) slope. **~do** *a* ‹*precio*› high; ‹*color*› bright; ‹*olor*› strong. **~r** *vt* go up; (*poner*) put; (*llevar*) take up; (*aumentar*) increase. ● *vi* go up. **~r a** get into ‹*coche*›; get on ‹*autobús, avión, barco, tren*›; (*aumentar*) increase. **~rse** *vpr* climb up. **~rse a** get on ‹*tren etc*›
súbito *a* sudden. ● *adv* suddenly. **de ~** suddenly

subjetivo *a* subjective
subjuntivo *a & m* subjunctive
subleva|ción *f* uprising. **~r** *vt* incite to rebellion. **~rse** *vpr* rebel
sublim|ar *vt* sublimate. **~e** *a* sublime
submarino *a* underwater. ● *m* submarine
subordinado *a & m* subordinate
subrayar *vt* underline
subrepticio *a* surreptitious
subsanar *vt* remedy; overcome ‹*dificultad*›
subscri|bir *vt* (*pp* **subscrito**) sign. **~birse** *vpr* subscribe. **~pción** *f* subscription
subsidi|ario *a* subsidiary. **~o** *m* subsidy. **~o de paro** unemployment benefit
subsiguiente *a* subsequent
subsist|encia *f* subsistence. **~ir** *vi* subsist; (*perdurar*) survive
substanci|a *f* substance. **~al** *a* important. **~oso** *a* substantial
substantivo *m* noun
substitu|ción *f* substitution. **~ir** [17] *vt/i* substitute. **~to** *a & m* substitute
substraer [41] *vt* take away
subterfugio *m* subterfuge
subterráneo *a* underground. ● *m* (*bodega*) cellar; (*conducto*) underground passage
subtítulo *m* subtitle
suburb|ano *a* suburban. ● *m* suburban train. **~io** *m* suburb; (*en barrio pobre*) slum
subvenci|ón *f* grant. **~onar** *vt* subsidize
subver|sión *f* subversion. **~sivo** *a* subversive. **~tir** [4] *vt* subvert
subyugar [12] *vt* subjugate; (*fig*) subdue
succión *f* suction
suce|der *vi* happen; (*seguir*) follow; (*substituir*) succeed. **~dido** *m* event. **lo ~dido** what happened. **~sión** *f* succession. **~sivo** *a* successive; (*consecutivo*) consecutive. **~so** *m* event; (*incidente*) incident. **~sor** *m* successor. **en lo ~sivo** in future. **lo que ~de es que** the trouble is that. **¿qué ~de?** what's the matter?
suciedad *f* dirt; (*estado*) dirtiness
sucinto *a* concise; ‹*prenda*› scanty
sucio *a* dirty; (*vil*) mean; ‹*conciencia*› guilty. **en ~** in rough
sucre *m* (*unidad monetaria del Ecuador*) sucre
suculento *a* succulent
sucumbir *vi* succumb
sucursal *f* branch (office)
Sudáfrica *m & f* South Africa
sudafricano *a & m* South African
Sudamérica *f* South America
sudamericano *a & m* South American
sudar *vt* work hard for. ● *vi* sweat
sud|este *m* south-east; (*viento*) south-east wind. **~oeste** *m* south-west; (*viento*) south-west wind
sudor *m* sweat
Suecia *f* Sweden
sueco *a* Swedish. ● *m* (*persona*) Swede; (*lengua*) Swedish. **hacerse el ~** pretend not to hear
suegr|a *f* mother-in-law. **~o** *m* father-in-law. **mis ~os** my in-laws
suela *f* sole
sueldo *m* salary
suelo *m* ground; (*dentro de edificio*) floor; (*tierra*) land. ● *vb véase* **soler**
suelto *a* loose; (*libre*) free; (*sin pareja*) odd; ‹*lenguaje*› fluent. ● *m* (*en periódico*) item; (*dinero*) change
sueño *m* sleep; (*ilusión*) dream. **tener ~** be sleepy
suero *m* serum; (*de leche*) whey
suerte *f* luck; (*destino*) fate; (*azar*) chance. **de otra ~** otherwise. **de ~ que** so. **echar ~s** draw lots. **por ~** fortunately. **tener ~** be lucky
suéter *m* jersey
suficien|cia *f* sufficiency; (*presunción*) smugness; (*aptitud*) suitability. **~te** *a* sufficient; (*presumido*) smug. **~temente** *adv* enough
sufijo *m* suffix
sufragio *m* (*voto*) vote
sufri|do *a* ‹*persona*› long-suffering; ‹*tela*› hard-wearing. **~miento** *m* suffering. **~r** *vt* suffer; (*experimentar*) undergo; (*soportar*) bear. ● *vi* suffer
suge|rencia *f* suggestion. **~rir** [4] *vt* suggest. **~stión** *f* suggestion. **~stionable** *a* impressionable. **~stionar** *vt* influence. **~stivo** *a* (*estimulante*) stimulating; (*atractivo*) attractive
suicid|a *a* suicidal. ● *m & f* suicide; (*fig*) maniac. **~arse** *vpr* commit suicide. **~io** *m* suicide
Suiza *f* Switzerland
suizo *a* Swiss. ● *m* Swiss; (*bollo*) bun

suje|ción *f* subjection. **~tador** *m* fastener; (*de pelo, papeles etc*) clip; (*prenda femenina*) bra (*fam*), brassière. **~tapapeles** *m invar* paper-clip. **~tar** *vt* fasten; (*agarrar*) hold; (*fig*) restrain. **~tarse** *vr* subject o.s.; (*ajustarse*) conform. **~to** *a* fastened; (*susceptible*) subject. ● *m* individual

sulfamida *f* sulpha (drug)

sulfúrico *a* sulphuric

sult|án *m* sultan. **~ana** *f* sultana

suma *f* sum; (*total*) total. **en ~** in short. **~mente** *adv* extremely. **~r** *vt* add (up); (*fig*) gather. ● *vi* add up. **~rse** *vpr*. **~rse a** join in

sumario *a* brief. ● *m* summary; (*jurid*) indictment

sumergi|ble *m* submarine. ● *a* submersible. **~r** [14] *vt* submerge

sumidero *m* drain

suministr|ar *vt* supply. **~o** *m* supply; (*acción*) supplying

sumir *vt* sink; (*fig*) plunge

sumis|ión *f* submission. **~o** *a* submissive

sumo *a* greatest; (*supremo*) supreme. **a lo ~** at the most

suntuoso *a* sumptuous

supe *vb véase* **saber**

superar *vt* surpass; (*vencer*) overcome; (*dejar atrás*) get past. **~se** *vpr* excel o.s.

supercherría *f* swindle

superestructura *f* superstructure

superfici|al *a* superficial. **~e** *f* surface; (*extensión*) area. **de ~e** surface

superfluo *a* superfluous

superhombre *m* superman

superintendente *m* superintendent

superior *a* superior; (*más alto*) higher; (*mejor*) better; ‹*piso*› upper. ● *m* superior. **~idad** *f* superiority

superlativo *a* & *m* superlative

supermercado *m* supermarket

supersónico *a* supersonic

supersticí|ón *f* superstition. **~oso** *a* superstitious

supervis|ión *f* supervision. **~or** *m* supervisor

superviviente *a* surviving. ● *m* & *f* survivor

suplantar *vt* supplant

suplement|ario *a* supplementary. **~o** *m* supplement

suplente *a* & *m* & *f* substitute

súplica *f* entreaty; (*petición*) request

suplicar [7] *vt* beg

suplicio *m* torture

suplir *vt* make up for; (*reemplazar*) replace

supo|ner [34] *vt* suppose; (*significar*) mean; (*costar*) cost. **~sición** *f* supposition

supositorio *m* suppository

suprem|acía *f* supremacy. **~o** *a* supreme; ‹*momento etc*› critical

supr|esión *f* suppression. **~imir** *vt* suppress; (*omitir*) omit

supuesto *a* supposed. ● *m* assumption. **~ que** if. **¡por ~!** of course!

sur *m* south; (*viento*) south wind

surc|ar [7] *vt* plough. **~o** *m* furrow; (*de rueda*) rut; (*en la piel*) wrinkle

surgir [14] *vi* spring up; (*elevarse*) loom up; (*aparecer*) appear; ‹*dificultad, oportunidad*› arise, crop up

surrealis|mo *m* surrealism. **~ta** *a* & *m* & *f* surrealist

surti|do *a* well-stocked; (*variado*) assorted. ● *m* assortment, selection. **~dor** *m* (*de gasolina*) petrol pump (*Brit*), gas pump (*Amer*). **~r** *vt* supply; have ‹*efecto*›. **~rse** *vpr* provide o.s. (**de** with)

susceptib|ilidad *f* susceptibility; (*sensibilidad*) sensitivity. **~le** *a* susceptible; (*sensible*) sensitive

suscitar *vt* provoke; arouse ‹*curiosidad, interés, sospechas*›

suscr... *véase* **subscr...**

susodicho *a* aforementioned

suspen|der *vt* hang (up); (*interrumpir*) suspend; (*univ etc*) fail. **~derse** *vpr* stop. **~sión** *f* suspension. **~so** *a* hanging; (*pasmado*) amazed; (*univ etc*) failed. ● *m* fail. **en ~so** pending

suspicaz *a* suspicious

suspir|ar *vi* sigh. **~o** *m* sigh

sust... *véase* **subst...**

sustent|ación *f* support. **~ar** *vt* support; (*alimentar*) sustain; (*mantener*) maintain. **~o** *m* support; (*alimento*) sustenance

susto *m* fright. **caerse del ~** be frightened to death

susurr|ar *vi* ‹*persona*› whisper; ‹*agua*› murmur; ‹*hojas*› rustle. **~o** *m* (*de persona*) whisper; (*de agua*) murmur; (*de hojas*) rustle

sutil *a* fine; (*fig*) subtle. **~eza** *f* fineness; (*fig*) subtlety

suyo *a* & *pron* (*de él*) his; (*de ella*) hers; (*de ello*) its; (*de uno*) one's; (*de Vd*) yours; (*de ellos, de ellas*) theirs;

(*de Vds*) yours. **un amigo ~** a friend of his, a friend of theirs, etc

T

taba *f* (*anat*) ankle-bone; (*juego*) jacks
tabac|alera *f* (state) tobacconist. **~alero** *a* tobacco. **~o** *m* tobacco; (*cigarillos*) cigarettes; (*rapé*) snuff
tabalear *vi* drum (with one's fingers)
Tabasco *m* Tabasco (**P**)
tabern|a *f* bar. **~ero** *m* barman; (*dueño*) landlord
tabernáculo *m* tabernacle
tabique *m* (thin) wall
tabl|a *f* plank; (*de piedra etc*) slab; (*estante*) shelf; (*de vestido*) pleat; (*lista*) list; (*índice*) index; (*en matemática etc*) table. **~ado** *m* platform; (*en el teatro*) stage. **~ao** *m* place where flamenco shows are held. **~as reales** backgammon. **~ero** *m* board. **~ero de mandos** dashboard. **hacer ~a rasa de** disregard
tableta *f* tablet; (*de chocolate*) bar
tabl|illa *f* small board. **~ón** *m* plank. **~ón de anuncios** notice board (*esp Brit*), bulletin board (*Amer*)
tabú *m* taboo
tabular *vt* tabulate
taburete *m* stool
tacaño *a* mean
tacita *f* small cup
tácito *a* tacit
taciturno *a* taciturn; (*triste*) miserable
taco *m* plug; (*LAm, tacón*) heel; (*de billar*) cue; (*de billetes*) book; (*fig, lío, fam*) mess; (*Mex, culin*) filled tortilla
tacógrafo *m* tachograph
tacón *m* heel
táctic|a *f* tactics. **~o** *a* tactical
táctil *a* tactile
tacto *m* touch; (*fig*) tact
tacuara *f* (*Arg*) bamboo
tacurú *m* (small) ant
tacha *f* fault; (*clavo*) tack. **poner ~s a** find fault with. **sin ~** flawless
tachar *vt* (*borrar*) rub out; (*con raya*) cross out. **~ de** accuse of
tafia *f* (*LAm*) rum
tafilete *m* morocco
tahúr *m* card-sharp
Tailandia *f* Thailand
tailandés *a & m* Thai
taimado *a* sly
taj|ada *f* slice. **~ante** *a* sharp. **~o** *m* slash; (*fig, trabajo, fam*) job; (*culin*) chopping block. **sacar ~ada** profit
Tajo *m* Tagus
tal *a* such; (*ante sustantivo en singular*) such a. ● *pron* (*persona*) someone; (*cosa*) such a thing. ● *adv* so; (*de tal manera*) in such a way. **~ como** the way. **~ cual** (*tal como*) the way; (*regular*) fair. **~ para cual** (*fam*) two of a kind. **con ~ que** as long as. **¿qué ~?** how are you? **un ~** a certain
taladr|ar *vt* drill. **~o** *m* drill; (*agujero*) drill hole
talante *m* mood. **de buen ~** willingly
talar *vt* fell; (*fig*) destroy
talco *m* talcum powder
talcualillo *a* (*fam*) so so
talega *f*, **talego** *m* sack
talento *m* talent
TALGO *m* high-speed train
talismán *m* talisman
tal|ón *m* heel; (*recibo*) counterfoil; (*cheque*) cheque. **~onario** *m* receipt book; (*de cheques*) cheque book
talla *f* carving; (*grabado*) engraving; (*de piedra preciosa*) cutting; (*estatura*) height; (*medida*) size; (*palo*) measuring stick; (*Arg, charla*) gossip. **~do** *a* carved. ● *m* carving. **~dor** *m* engraver
tallarín *m* noodle
talle *m* waist; (*figura*) figure; (*medida*) size
taller *m* workshop; (*de pintor etc*) studio
tallo *m* stem, stalk
tamal *m* (*LAm*) tamale
tamaño *a* (*tan grande*) so big a; (*tan pequeño*) so small a. ● *m* size. **de ~ natural** life-size
tambalearse *vpr* ‹*persona*› stagger; ‹*cosa*› wobble
también *adv* also, too
tambor *m* drum. **~ del freno** brake drum. **~ilear** *vi* drum
Támesis *m* Thames
tamiz *m* sieve. **~ar** [10] *vt* sieve
tampoco *adv* nor, neither, not either
tampón *m* tampon; (*para entintar*) ink-pad
tan *adv* so. **tan... ~** as... as

tanda *f* group; (*capa*) layer; (*de obreros*) shift
tangente *a & f* tangent
Tánger *m* Tangier
tangible *a* tangible
tango *m* tango
tanque *m* tank; (*camión, barco*) tanker
tante|ar *vt* estimate; (*ensayar*) test; (*fig*) weigh up. ● *vi* score. **~o** *m* estimate; (*prueba*) test; (*en deportes*) score
tanto *a* (*en singular*) so much; (*en plural*) so many; (*comparación en singular*) as much; (*comparación en plural*) as many. ● *pron* so much; (*en plural*) so many. ● *adv* so much; (*tiempo*) so long. ● *m* certain amount; (*punto*) point; (*gol*) goal. **~ como** as well as; (*cantidad*) as much as. **~ más... cuanto que** all the more... because. **~ si... como si** whether... or. **a ~s de** sometime in. **en ~, entre ~** meanwhile. **en ~ que** while. **entre ~** meanwhile. **estar al ~ de** be up to date with. **hasta ~ que** until. **no es para ~** it's not as bad as all that. **otro ~** the same; (*el doble*) as much again. **por (lo) ~** so. **un ~** *adv* somewhat
tañer [22] *vt* play
tapa *f* lid; (*de botella*) top; (*de libro*) cover. **~s** *fpl* savoury snacks
tapacubos *m invar* hub-cap
tapa|dera *f* cover, lid; (*fig*) cover. **~r** *vt* cover; (*abrigar*) wrap up; (*obturar*) plug; put the top on ‹*botella*›
taparrabo(s) *m invar* loincloth; (*bañador*) swimming-trunks
tapete *m* (*de mesa*) table cover; (*alfombra*) rug
tapia *f* wall. **~r** *vt* enclose
tapicería *f* tapestry; (*de muebles*) upholstery
tapioca *f* tapioca
tapiz *m* tapestry. **~ar** [10] *vt* hang with tapestries; upholster ‹*muebles*›
tap|ón *m* stopper; (*corcho*) cork; (*med*) tampon; (*tec*) plug. **~onazo** *m* pop
taqu|igrafía *f* shorthand. **~ígrafo** *m* shorthand writer
taquill|a *f* ticket office; (*archivador*) filing cabinet; (*fig, dinero*) takings. **~ero** *m* clerk, ticket seller. ● *a* box-office
tara *f* (*peso*) tare; (*defecto*) defect
taracea *f* marquetry
tarántula *f* tarantula
tararear *vt/i* hum
tarda|nza *f* delay. **~r** *vi* take; (*mucho tiempo*) take a long time. **a más ~r** at the latest. **sin ~r** without delay
tard|e *adv* late. ● *f* (*antes del atardecer*) afternoon; (*después del atardecer*) evening. **~e o temprano** sooner or later. **~ío** *a* late. **de ~e en ~e** from time to time. **por la ~e** in the afternoon
tardo *a* (*torpe*) slow
tarea *f* task, job
tarifa *f* rate, tariff
tarima *f* platform
tarjeta *f* card. **~ de crédito** credit card. **~ postal** postcard
tarro *m* jar
tarta *f* cake; (*torta*) tart. **~ helada** ice-cream gateau
tartamud|ear *vi* stammer. **~o** *a* stammering. ● *m* stammerer. **es ~o** he stammers
tártaro *m* tartar
tarugo *m* chunk
tasa *f* valuation; (*precio*) fixed price; (*índice*) rate. **~r** *vt* fix a price for; (*limitar*) ration; (*evaluar*) value
tasca *f* bar
tatarabuel|a *f* great-great-grandmother. **~o** *m* great-great-grandfather
tatua|je *m* (*acción*) tattooing; (*dibujo*) tattoo. **~r** [21] *vt* tattoo
taurino *a* bullfighting
Tauro *m* Taurus
tauromaquia *f* bullfighting
tax|i *m* taxi. **~ímetro** *m* taxi meter. **~ista** *m & f* taxi-driver
tayuyá *m* (*Arg*) water melon
taz|a *f* cup. **~ón** *m* bowl
te *pron* (*acusativo*) you; (*dativo*) (to) you; (*reflexivo*) (to) yourself
té *m* tea. **dar el ~** bore
tea *f* torch
teatr|al *a* theatre; (*exagerado*) theatrical. **~alizar** [10] *vt* dramatize. **~o** *m* theatre; (*literatura*) drama. **obra** *f* **~al** play
tebeo *m* comic
teca *f* teak
tecla *f* key. **~do** *m* keyboard. **tocar la ~, tocar una ~** pull strings
técnica *f* technique
tecn|icismo *m* technicality
técnico *a* technical. ● *m* technician
tecnol|ogía *f* technology. **~ógico** *a* technological

tecolote *m* (*Mex*) owl
tecomate *m* (*Mex*) earthenware cup
tech|ado *m* roof. **~ar** *vt* roof. **~o** *m* (*interior*) ceiling; (*exterior*) roof. **~umbre** *f* roofing. **bajo ~ado** indoors
teja *f* tile. **~do** *m* roof. **a toca ~** cash
teje|dor *m* weaver. **~r** *vt* weave; (*hacer punto*) knit
tejemaneje *m* (*fam*) fuss; (*intriga*) scheming
tejido *m* material; (*anat, fig*) tissue. **~s** *mpl* textiles
tejón *m* badger
tela *f* material; (*de araña*) web; (*en líquido*) skin
telar *m* loom. **~es** *mpl* textile mill
telaraña *f* spider's web, cobweb
tele *f* (*fam*) television
tele|comunicación *f* telecommunication. **~diario** *m* television news. **~dirigido** *a* remote-controlled. **~férico** *m* cable-car; (*tren*) cable-railway
tel|efonear *vt/i* telephone. **~efónico** *a* telephone. **~efonista** *m & f* telephonist. **~éfono** *m* telephone. **al ~éfono** on the phone
tel|egrafía *f* telegraphy. **~egrafiar** [20] *vt* telegraph. **~egráfico** *a* telegraphic. **~égrafo** *m* telegraph
telegrama *m* telegram
telenovela *f* television soap opera
teleobjetivo *m* telephoto lens
telep|atía *f* telepathy. **~ático** *a* telepathic
telesc|ópico *a* telescopic. **~opio** *m* telescope
telesilla *m* ski-lift, chair-lift
telespectador *m* viewer
telesquí *m* ski-lift
televi|dente *m & f* viewer. **~sar** *vt* televise. **~sión** *f* television. **~sor** *m* television (set)
télex *m* telex
telón *m* curtain. **~ de acero** (*historia*) Iron Curtain
tema *m* subject; (*mus*) theme
tembl|ar [1] *vi* shake; (*de miedo*) tremble; (*de frío*) shiver; (*fig*) shudder. **~or** *m* shaking; (*de miedo*) trembling; (*de frío*) shivering. **~or de tierra** earthquake. **~oroso** *a* trembling
temer *vt* be afraid (of). ● *vi* be afraid. **~se** *vpr* be afraid
temerario *a* reckless
tem|eroso *a* frightened. **~ible** *a* fearsome. **~or** *m* fear
témpano *m* floe
temperamento *m* temperament
temperatura *f* temperature
temperie *f* weather
tempest|ad *f* storm. **~uoso** *a* stormy. **levantar ~ades** (*fig*) cause a storm
templ|ado *a* moderate; (*tibio*) warm; ‹*clima, tiempo*› mild; (*valiente*) courageous; (*listo*) bright. **~anza** *f* moderation; (*de clima o tiempo*) mildness. **~ar** *vt* temper; (*calentar*) warm; (*mus*) tune. **~e** *m* tempering; (*temperatura*) temperature; (*humor*) mood
templ|ete *m* niche; (*pabellón*) pavilion. **~o** *m* temple
tempora|da *f* time; (*época*) season. **~l** *a* temporary. ● *m* (*tempestad*) storm; (*período de lluvia*) rainy spell
tempran|ero *a* ‹*frutos*› early. **~o** *a & adv* early. **ser ~ero** be an early riser
tena|cidad *f* tenacity
tenacillas *fpl* tongs
tenaz *a* tenacious
tenaza *f*, **tenazas** *fpl* pliers; (*para arrancar clavos*) pincers; (*para el fuego, culin*) tongs
tende|ncia *f* tendency. **~nte** *a*. **~nte a** aimed at. **~r** [1] *vt* spread (out); hang out ‹*ropa a secar*›; (*colocar*) lay. ● *vi* have a tendency (**a** to). **~rse** *vpr* stretch out
tender|ete *m* stall. **~o** *m* shopkeeper
tendido *a* spread out; ‹*ropa*› hung out; ‹*persona*› stretched out. ● *m* (*en plaza de toros*) front rows. **~s** *mpl* (*ropa lavada*) washing
tendón *m* tendon
tenebroso *a* gloomy; (*turbio*) shady
tenedor *m* fork; (*poseedor*) holder
tener [40] *vt* have (got); (*agarrar*) hold; be ‹*años, calor, celos, cuidado, frío, ganas, hambre, miedo, razón, sed etc*›. **¡ten cuidado!** be careful! **tengo calor** I'm hot. **tiene 3 años** he's 3 (years old). **~se** *vpr* stand up; (*considerarse*) consider o.s., think o.s. **~ al corriente**, **~ al día** keep up to date. **~ 2 cm de largo** be 2 cms long. **~ a uno por** consider s.o. **~ que** have (got) to. **tenemos que comprar pan** we've got to buy some bread. **¡ahí tienes!** there you are! **no ~ nada que ver con** have nothing to do with. **¿qué tienes?** what's the

matter (with you)? ¡**tenga!** here you are!
tengo *vb véase* **tener**
teniente *m* lieutenant. ~ **de alcalde** deputy mayor
tenis *m* tennis. ~**ta** *m & f* tennis player
tenor *m* sense; (*mus*) tenor. **a este** ~ in this fashion
tens|ión *f* tension; (*presión*) pressure; (*arterial*) blood pressure; (*elec*) voltage; (*de persona*) tenseness. ~**o** *a* tense
tentación *f* temptation
tentáculo *m* tentacle
tenta|dor *a* tempting. ~**r** [1] *vt* feel; (*seducir*) tempt
tentativa *f* attempt
tenue *a* thin; ‹*luz, voz*› faint
teñi|do *m* dye. ~**r** [5 & 22] *vt* dye; (*fig*) tinge (**de** with). ~**rse** *vpr* dye one's hair
te|ología *f* theology. ~**ológico** *a* theological. ~**ólogo** *m* theologian
teorema *m* theorem
te|oría *f* theory. ~**órico** *a* theoretical
tepache *m* (*Mex*) (alcoholic) drink
tequila *f* tequila
TER *m* high-speed train
terap|éutico *a* therapeutic. ~**ia** *f* therapy
tercer *a véase* **tercero**. ~**a** *f* (*auto*) third (gear). ~**o** *a* (*delante de nombre masculino en singular* **tercer**) third. ● *m* third party
terceto *m* trio
terciar *vi* mediate. ~ **en** join in. ~**se** *vpr* occur
tercio *m* third
terciopelo *m* velvet
terco *a* obstinate
tergiversar *vt* distort
terma|l *a* thermal. ~**s** *fpl* thermal baths
termes *m invar* termite
térmico *a* thermal
termina|ción *f* ending; (*conclusión*) conclusion. ~**l** *a & m* terminal. ~**nte** *a* categorical. ~**r** *vt* finish, end. ~**rse** *vpr* come to an end. ~**r por** end up
término *m* end; (*palabra*) term; (*plazo*) period. ~ **medio** average. ~ **municipal** municipal district. **dar** ~ **a** finish off. **en último** ~ as a last resort. **estar en buenos** ~**s con** be on good terms with. **llevar a** ~ carry out. **poner** ~ **a** put an end to. **primer** ~ foreground
terminología *f* terminology
termita *f* termite
termo *m* Thermos flask (P), flask
termómetro *m* thermometer
termo|nuclear *a* thermonuclear. ~**sifón** *m* boiler. ~**stato** *m* thermostat
terner|a *f* (*carne*) veal. ~**o** *m* calf
ternura *f* tenderness
terquedad *f* stubbornness
terracota *f* terracotta
terrado *m* flat roof
terraplén *m* embankment
terrateniente *m & f* landowner
terraza *f* terrace; (*terrado*) flat roof
terremoto *m* earthquake
terre|no *a* earthly. ● *m* land; (*solar*) plot; (*fig*) field. ~**stre** *a* earthly; (*mil*) ground
terr|ible *a* terrible. ~**iblemente** *adv* awfully. ~**ífico** *a* terrifying
territori|al *a* territorial. ~**o** *m* territory
terrón *m* (*de tierra*) clod; (*culin*) lump
terror *m* terror. ~**ífico** *a* terrifying. ~**ismo** *m* terrorism. ~**ista** *m & f* terrorist
terr|oso *a* earthy; (*color*) brown. ~**uño** *m* land; (*patria*) native land
terso *a* polished; ‹*piel*› smooth
tertulia *f* social gathering, get-together (*fam*). ~**r** *vi* (*LAm*) get together. **estar de** ~ chat. **hacer** ~ get together
tesi|na *f* dissertation. ~**s** *f inv* thesis; (*opinión*) theory
tesón *m* perseverance
tesor|ería *f* treasury. ~**ero** *m* treasurer. ~**o** *m* treasure; (*tesorería*) treasury; (*libro*) thesaurus
testa *f* (*fam*) head. ~**ferro** *m* figurehead
testa|mento *m* will. **T**~**mento** (*relig*) Testament. ~**r** *vi* make a will
testarudo *a* stubborn
testículo *m* testicle
testi|ficar [7] *vt/i* testify. ~**go** *m* witness. ~**go de vista**, ~**go ocular**, ~**go presencial** eyewitness. ~**monio** *m* testimony
teta *f* nipple; (*de biberón*) teat
tétanos *m* tetanus
tetera *f* (*para el té*) teapot; (*Mex, biberón*) feeding-bottle
tetilla *f* nipple; (*de biberón*) teat
tétrico *a* gloomy

textil *a & m* textile
text|o *m* text. **~ual** *a* textual
textura *f* texture
teyú *m* (*Arg*) iguana
tez *f* complexion
ti *pron* you
tía *f* aunt; (*fam*) woman
tiara *f* tiara
tibio *a* lukewarm. **ponerle ~ a uno** insult s.o.
tiburón *m* shark
tic *m* tic
tiempo *m* time; (*atmosférico*) weather; (*mus*) tempo; (*gram*) tense; (*en deportes*) half. **a su ~** in due course. **a ~** in time. **¿cuánto ~?** how long? **hace buen ~** the weather is fine. **hace ~** some time ago. **mucho ~** a long time. **perder el ~** waste time. **¿qué ~ hace?** what is the weather like?
tienda *f* shop; (*de campaña*) tent. **~ de comestibles**, **~ de ultramarinos** grocer's (shop) (*Brit*), grocery store (*Amer*)
tiene *vb véase* **tener**
tienta. **a ~s** gropingly. **andar a ~s** grope one's way
tiento *m* touch; (*de ciego*) blind person's stick; (*fig*) tact
tierno *a* tender; (*joven*) young
tierra *f* land; (*planeta*, *elec*) earth; (*suelo*) ground; (*geol*) soil, earth. **caer por ~** (*fig*) crumble. **por ~** overland, by land
tieso *a* stiff; (*firme*) firm; (*engreído*) conceited; (*orgulloso*) proud
tiesto *m* flowerpot
tifoideo *a* typhoid
tifón *m* typhoon
tifus *m* typhus; (*fiebre tifoidea*) typhoid (fever); (*en el teatro*) people with complimentary tickets
tigre *m* tiger
tijera *f*, **tijeras** *fpl* scissors; (*de jardín*) shears
tijeret|a *f* (*insecto*) earwig; (*bot*) tendril. **~ear** *vt* snip
tila *f* lime(-tree); (*infusión*) lime tea
tild|ar *vt*. **~ar de** (*fig*) call. **~e** *m* tilde
tilín *m* tinkle. **hacer ~** appeal
tilingo *a* (*Arg*, *Mex*) silly
tilma *f* (*Mex*) poncho
tilo *m* lime(-tree)
timar *vt* swindle
timbal *m* drum; (*culin*) timbale, meat pie
timbiriche *m* (*Mex*) (alcoholic) drink
timbr|ar *vt* stamp. **~e** *m* (*sello*) stamp; (*elec*) bell; (*sonido*) timbre. **tocar el ~e** ring the bell
timidez *f* shyness
tímido *a* shy
timo *m* swindle
timón *m* rudder; (*fig*) helm
tímpano *m* kettledrum; (*anat*) eardrum. **~s** *mpl* (*mus*) timpani
tina *f* tub. **~ja** *f* large earthenware jar
tinglado *m* (*fig*) intrigue
tinieblas *fpl* darkness; (*fig*) confusion
tino *f* (*habilidad*) skill; (*moderación*) moderation; (*tacto*) tact
tint|a *f* ink. **~e** *m* dyeing; (*color*) dye; (*fig*) tinge. **~ero** *m* ink-well. **de buena ~a** on good authority
tint|ín *m* tinkle; (*de vasos*) chink, clink. **~inear** *vi* tinkle; ‹*vasos*› chink, clink
tinto *a* ‹*vino*› red
tintorería *f* dyeing; (*tienda*) dry cleaner's
tintura *f* dyeing; (*color*) dye; (*noción superficial*) smattering
tío *m* uncle; (*fam*) man. **~s** *mpl* uncle and aunt
tiovivo *m* merry-go-round
típico *a* typical
tipo *m* type; (*persona*, *fam*) person; (*figura de mujer*) figure; (*figura de hombre*) build; (*com*) rate
tip|ografía *f* typography. **~ográfico** *a* typographic(al). **~ógrafo** *m* printer
típula *f* crane-fly, daddy-long-legs
tique *m*, **tíquet** *m* ticket
tiquete *m* (*LAm*) ticket
tira *f* strip. **la ~ de** lots of
tirabuzón *m* corkscrew; (*de pelo*) ringlet
tirad|a *f* distance; (*serie*) series; (*de libros etc*) edition. **~o** *a* (*barato*) very cheap; (*fácil*, *fam*) very easy. **~or** *m* (*asa*) handle; (*juguete*) catapult (*Brit*), slingshot (*Amer*). **de una ~a** at one go
tiran|ía *f* tyranny. **~izar** [10] *vt* tyrannize. **~o** *a* tyrannical. ● *m* tyrant
tirante *a* tight; (*fig*) tense; ‹*relaciones*› strained. ● *m* shoulder strap. **~s** *mpl* braces (*esp Brit*), suspenders (*Amer*)
tirar *vt* throw; (*desechar*) throw away; (*derribar*) knock over; give ‹*golpe*, *coz etc*›; (*imprimir*) print. ● *vi* (*disparar*) shoot. **~se** *vpr*

throw o.s.; (*tumbarse*) lie down. ~ **a** tend to (be); (*parecerse a*) resemble. ~ **de** pull; (*atraer*) attract. **a todo** ~ at the most. **ir tirando** get by
tirita *f* sticking-plaster, plaster (*Brit*)
tirit|ar *vi* shiver. **~ón** *m* shiver
tiro *m* throw; (*disparo*) shot; (*alcance*) range. ~ **a gol** shot at goal. **a** ~ within range. **errar el** ~ miss. **pegarse un** ~ shoot o.s.
tiroides *m* thyroid (gland)
tirón *m* tug. **de un** ~ in one go
tirote|ar *vt* shoot at. **~o** *m* shooting
tisana *f* herb tea
tisis *f* tuberculosis
tisú *m* (*pl* **tisus**) tissue
títere *m* puppet. ~ **de guante** glove puppet. **~s** *mpl* puppet show
titilar *vi* quiver; ‹*estrella*› twinkle
titiritero *m* puppeteer; (*acróbata*) acrobat; (*malabarista*) juggler
titube|ante *a* shaky; (*fig*) hesistant. **~ar** *vi* stagger; ‹*cosa*› be unstable; (*fig*) hesitate. **~o** *m* hesitation
titula|do *a* ‹*libro*› entitled; ‹*persona*› qualified. **~r** *m* headline; (*persona*) holder. ● *vt* call. **~rse** *vpr* be called
título *m* title; (*persona*) titled person; (*académico*) qualification; (*univ*) degree; (*de periódico etc*) headline; (*derecho*) right. **a** ~ **de** as, by way of
tiza *f* chalk
tiz|nar *vt* dirty. **~ne** *m* soot. **~ón** *m* half-burnt stick; (*fig*) stain
toall|a *f* towel. **~ero** *m* towel-rail
tobillo *m* ankle
tobogán *m* slide; (*para la nieve*) toboggan
tocadiscos *m invar* record-player
toca|do *a* (*con sombrero*) wearing. ● *m* hat. **~dor** *m* dressing-table. **~dor de señoras** ladies' room. **~nte** *a* touching. **~r** [7] *vt* touch; (*mus*) play; ring ‹*timbre*›; (*mencionar*) touch on; ‹*barco*› stop at. ● *vi* knock; (*corresponder a uno*) be one's turn. **~rse** *vpr* touch each other; (*cubrir la cabeza*) cover one's head. **en lo que** ~ **a**, **en lo ~nte a** as for. **estar ~do (de la cabeza)** be mad. **te** ~ **a ti** it's your turn
tocateja. a ~ cash
tocayo *m* namesake
tocino *m* bacon
tocólogo *m* obstetrician
todavía *adv* still, yet. ~ **no** not yet
todo *a* all; (*entero*) the whole; (*cada*) every. ● *adv* completely, all. ● *m* whole. ● *pron* everything, all; (*en plural*) everyone. ~ **el día** all day. ~ **el mundo** everyone. ~ **el que** anyone who. ~ **incluido** all in. ~ **lo contrario** quite the opposite. ~ **lo que** anything which. **~s los días** every day. **~s los dos** both (of them). **~s los tres** all three. **ante** ~ above all. **a** ~ **esto** meanwhile. **con** ~ still, however. **del** ~ completely. **en** ~ **el mundo** anywhere. **estar en** ~ be on the ball. **es** ~ **uno** it's all the same. **nosotros** **~s** all of us. **sobre** ~ above all
toldo *m* sunshade
tolera|ncia *f* tolerance. **~nte** *a* tolerant. **~r** *vt* tolerate
tolondro *m* (*chichón*) lump
toma *f* taking; (*med*) dose; (*de agua*) outlet; (*elec*) socket; (*elec, clavija*) plug. ● *int* well!, fancy that! ~ **de corriente** power point. **~dura** *f*. **~dura de pelo** hoax. **~r** *vt* take; catch ‹*autobús, tren etc*›; (*beber*) drink, have; (*comer*) eat, have. ● *vi* take; (*dirigirse*) go. **~rse** *vpr* take; (*beber*) drink, have; (*comer*) eat, have. **~r a bien** take well. **~r a mal** take badly. **~r en serio** take seriously. **~rla con uno** pick on s.o. **~r nota** take note. **~r por** take for. ~ **y daca** give and take. **¿qué va a ~r?** what would you like?
tomate *m* tomato
tomavistas *m invar* cine-camera
tómbola *f* tombola
tomillo *m* thyme
tomo *m* volume
ton. sin ~ **ni son** without rhyme or reason
tonada *f*, **tonadilla** *f* tune
tonel *m* barrel. **~ada** *f* ton. **~aje** *m* tonnage
tónic|a *f* tonic water; (*mus*) tonic. **~o** *a* tonic; ‹*sílaba*› stressed. ● *m* tonic
tonificar [7] *vt* invigorate
tono *m* tone; (*mus, modo*) key; (*color*) shade
tont|ería *f* silliness; (*cosa*) silly thing; (*dicho*) silly remark. **~o** *a* silly. ● *m* fool, idiot; (*payaso*) clown. **dejarse de ~erías** stop wasting time. **hacer el ~o** act the fool. **hacerse el ~o** feign ignorance
topacio *m* topaz

topar *vt* ‹*animal*› butt; ‹*persona*› bump into; (*fig*) run into. ● *vi*. **~ con** run into

tope *a* maximum. ● *m* end; (*de tren*) buffer. **hasta los ~s** crammed full. **ir a ~** go flat out

tópico *a* topical. ● *m* cliché

topo *m* mole

topogr|afía *f* topography. **~áfico** *a* topographical

toque *m* touch; (*sonido*) sound; (*de campana*) peal; (*de reloj*) stroke; (*fig*) crux. **~ de queda** curfew. **~tear** *vt* keep fingering, fiddle with. **dar el último ~** put the finishing touches

toquilla *f* shawl

tórax *m* thorax

torbellino *m* whirlwind; (*de polvo*) cloud of dust; (*fig*) whirl

torcer [2 & 9] *vt* twist; (*doblar*) bend; wring out ‹*ropa*›. ● *vi* turn. **~se** *vpr* twist; (*fig, desviarse*) go astray; (*fig, frustrarse*) go wrong

tordo *a* dapple grey. ● *m* thrush

tore|ar *vt* fight; (*evitar*) dodge; (*entretener*) put off. ● *vi* fight (bulls). **~o** *m* bullfighting. **~ro** *m* bullfighter

torment|a *f* storm. **~o** *m* torture. **~oso** *a* stormy

tornado *m* tornado

tornar *vt* return

tornasolado *a* irridescent

torneo *m* tournament

tornillo *m* screw

torniquete *m* (*entrada*) turnstile

torno *m* lathe; (*de alfarero*) wheel. **en ~ a** around

toro *m* bull. **~s** *mpl* bullfighting. **ir a los ~s** go to a bullfight

toronja *f* grapefruit

torpe *a* clumsy; (*estúpido*) stupid

torped|ero *m* torpedo-boat. **~o** *m* torpedo

torpeza *f* clumsiness; (*de inteligencia*) slowness

torpor *m* torpor

torrado *m* toasted chick-pea

torre *f* tower; (*en ajedrez*) castle, rook

torrefac|ción *f* roasting. **~to** *a* roasted

torren|cial *a* torrential. **~te** *m* torrent; (*circulatorio*) bloodstream; (*fig*) flood

tórrido *a* torrid

torrija *f* French toast

torsión *f* twisting

torso *m* torso

torta *f* tart; (*bollo, fam*) cake; (*golpe*) slap, punch; (*Mex, bocadillo*) sandwich. **~zo** *m* slap, punch. **no entender ni ~** not understand a word of it. **pegarse un ~zo** have a bad accident

tortícolis *f* stiff neck

tortilla *f* omelette; (*Mex, de maiz*) tortilla, maize cake. **~ francesa** plain omelette

tórtola *f* turtle-dove

tortuga *f* tortoise; (*de mar*) turtle

tortuoso *a* winding; (*fig*) devious

tortura *f* torture. **~r** *vt* torture

torvo *a* grim

tos *f* cough. **~ ferina** whooping cough

tosco *a* crude; ‹*persona*› coarse

toser *vi* cough

tósigo *m* poison

tosquedad *f* crudeness; (*de persona*) coarseness

tost|ada *f* toast. **~ado** *a* ‹*pan*› toasted; ‹*café*› roasted; ‹*persona*› tanned; (*marrón*) brown. **~ar** *vt* toast ‹*pan*›; roast ‹*café*›; tan ‹*piel*›. **~ón** *m* (*pan*) crouton; (*lata*) bore

total *a* total. ● *adv* after all. ● *m* total; (*totalidad*) whole. **~idad** *f* whole. **~itario** *a* totalitarian. **~izar** [10] *vt* total. **~ que** so, to cut a long story short

tóxico *a* toxic

toxicómano *m* drug addict

toxina *f* toxin

tozudo *a* stubborn

traba *f* bond; (*fig, obstáculo*) obstacle. **poner ~s a** hinder

trabaj|ador *a* hard-working. ● *m* worker. **~ar** *vt* work (**de** as); knead ‹*masa*›; (*estudiar*) work at; ‹*actor*› act. ● *vi* work. **~o** *m* work. **~os** *mpl* hardships. **~os forzados** hard labour. **~oso** *a* hard. **costar ~o** be difficult. **¿en qué ~as?** what work do you do?

trabalenguas *m invar* tongue-twister

traba|r *vt* (*sujetar*) fasten; (*unir*) join; (*empezar*) start; (*culin*) thicken. **~rse** *vpr* get tangled up. **trabársele la lengua** get tongue-tied. **~zón** *f* joining; (*fig*) connection

trabucar [7] *vt* mix up

trácala *f* (*Mex*) trick

tracción *f* traction

tractor *m* tractor

tradici|ón *f* tradition. **~onal** *a* traditional. **~onalista** *m & f* traditionalist

traduc|ción *f* translation. **~ir** [47] *vt* translate (**al** into). **~tor** *m* translator

traer [41] *vt* bring; (*llevar*) carry; (*atraer*) attract. **traérselas** be difficult

trafica|nte *m & f* dealer. **~r** [7] *vi* deal

tráfico *m* traffic; (*com*) trade

traga|deras *fpl* (*fam*) throat. **tener buenas ~deras** (*ser crédulo*) swallow anything; (*ser tolerante*) be easygoing. **~luz** *m* skylight. **~perras** *f invar* slot-machine. **~r** [12] *vt* swallow; (*comer mucho*) devour; (*absorber*) absorb; (*fig*) swallow up. **no (poder) ~r** not be able to stand. **~rse** *vpr* swallow; (*fig*) swallow up

tragedia *f* tragedy

trágico *a* tragic. ● *m* tragedian

trag|o *m* swallow, gulp; (*pequeña porción*) sip; (*fig, disgusto*) blow. **~ón** *a* greedy. ● *m* glutton. **echar(se) un ~o** have a drink

trai|ción *f* treachery; (*pol*) treason. **~cionar** *vt* betray. **~cionero** *a* treacherous. **~dor** *a* treacherous. ● *m* traitor

traigo *vb véase* **traer**

traje *m* dress; (*de hombre*) suit. ● *vb véase* **traer**. **~ de baño** swimming-costume. **~ de ceremonia**, **~ de etiqueta**, **~ de noche** evening dress

traj|ín *m* (*transporte*) haulage; (*jaleo, fam*) bustle. **~inar** *vt* transport. ● *vi* bustle about

trama *f* weft; (*fig*) link; (*fig, argumento*) plot. **~r** *vt* weave; (*fig*) plot

tramitar *vt* negotiate

trámite *m* step. **~s** *mpl* procedure. **en ~** in hand

tramo *m* (*parte*) section; (*de escalera*) flight

tramp|a *f* trap; (*puerta*) trapdoor; (*fig*) trick. **~illa** *f* trapdoor. **hacer ~a** cheat

trampolín *m* trampoline; (*fig, de piscina*) springboard

tramposo *a* cheating. ● *m* cheat

tranca *f* stick; (*de puerta*) bar

trance *m* moment; (*hipnótico etc*) trance. **a todo ~** at all costs

tranco *m* stride

tranquil|idad *f* (peace and) quiet; (*de espíritu*) peace of mind. **~izar** [10] *vt* reassure. **~o** *a* quiet; ‹*conciencia*› clear; ‹*mar*› calm; (*despreocupado*) thoughtless. **estáte ~o** don't worry

trans... *pref* (*véase también* **tras...**) trans...

transacción *f* transaction; (*acuerdo*) compromise

transatlántico *a* transatlantic. ● *m* (ocean) liner

transbord|ador *m* ferry. **~ar** *vt* transfer. **~arse** *vpr* change. **~o** *m* transfer. **hacer ~o** change (**en** at)

transcri|bir (*pp* **transcrito**) *vt* transcribe. **~pción** *f* transcription

transcur|rir *vi* pass. **~so** *m* course

transeúnte *a* temporary. ● *m & f* passer-by

transfer|encia *f* transfer. **~ir** [4] *vt* transfer

transfigurar *vt* transfigure

transforma|ción *f* transformation. **~dor** *m* transformer. **~r** *vt* transform

transfusión *f* transfusion. **hacer una ~** give a blood transfusion

transgre|dir *vt* transgress. **~sión** *f* transgression

transición *f* transition

transido *a* overcome

transigir [14] *vi* give in, compromise

transistor *m* transistor; (*radio*) radio

transita|ble *a* passable. **~r** *vi* go

transitivo *a* transitive

tránsito *m* transit; (*tráfico*) traffic

transitorio *a* transitory

translúcido *a* translucent

transmi|sión *f* transmission; (*radio, TV*) broadcast. **~sor** *m* transmitter. **~sora** *f* broadcasting station. **~tir** *vt* transmit; (*radio, TV*) broadcast; (*fig*) pass on

transparen|cia *f* transparency. **~tar** *vt* show. **~te** *a* transparent

transpira|ción *f* perspiration. **~r** *vi* transpire; (*sudar*) sweat

transponer [34] *vt* move. ● *vi* disappear round ‹*esquina etc*›; disappear behind ‹*montaña etc*›. **~se** *vpr* disappear

transport|ar *vt* transport. **~e** *m* transport. **empresa** *f* **de ~es** removals company

transversal *a* transverse; ‹*calle*› side

tranvía *m* tram

trapacería *f* swindle

trapear *vt* (*LAm*) mop

trapecio *m* trapeze; (*math*) trapezium

trapiche *m* (*para azúcar*) mill; (*para aceitunas*) press
trapicheo *m* fiddle
trapisonda *f* (*jaleo, fam*) row; (*enredo, fam*) plot
trapo *m* rag; (*para limpiar*) cloth. **~s** *mpl* (*fam*) clothes. **a todo ~** out of control
tráquea *f* windpipe, trachea
traquete|ar *vt* bang, rattle. **~o** *m* banging, rattle
tras *prep* after; (*detrás*) behind; (*encima de*) as well as
tras... *pref* (*véase también* **trans...**) trans...
trascende|ncia *f* importance. **~ntal** *a* transcendental; (*importante*) important. **~r** [1] *vi* (*oler*) smell (**a** of); (*saberse*) become known; (*extenderse*) spread
trasegar [1 & 12] *vt* move around
trasero *a* back, rear. ● *m* (*anat*) bottom
trasgo *m* goblin
traslad|ar *vt* move; (*aplazar*) postpone; (*traducir*) translate; (*copiar*) copy. **~o** *m* transfer; (*copia*) copy; (*mudanza*) removal. **dar ~o** send a copy
trasl|úcido *a* translucent. **~ucirse** [11] *vpr* be translucent; (*dejarse ver*) show through; (*fig, revelarse*) be revealed. **~uz** *m*. **al ~uz** against the light
trasmano *m*. **a ~** out of reach; (*fig*) out of the way
trasnochar *vt* (*acostarse tarde*) go to bed late; (*no acostarse*) stay up all night; (*no dormir*) be unable to sleep; (*pernoctar*) spend the night
traspas|ar *vt* pierce; (*transferir*) transfer; (*pasar el límite*) go beyond. **~o** *m* transfer. **se ~a** for sale
traspié *m* trip; (*fig*) slip. **dar un ~** stumble; (*fig*) slip up
trasplant|ar *vt* transplant. **~e** *m* transplanting; (*med*) transplant
trastada *f* stupid thing; (*jugada*) dirty trick, practical joke
traste *m* fret. **dar al ~ con** ruin. **ir al ~** fall through
trastero *m* storeroom
trastienda *f* back room; (*fig*) shrewdness
trasto *m* piece of furniture; (*cosa inútil*) piece of junk; (*persona*) useless person, dead loss (*fam*)
trastorn|ado *a* mad. **~ar** *vt* upset; (*volver loco*) drive mad; (*fig, gustar mucho, fam*) delight. **~arse** *vpr* get upset; (*volverse loco*) go mad. **~o** *m* (*incl med*) upset; (*pol*) disturbance; (*fig*) confusion
trastrocar [2 & 7] *vt* change round
trat|able *a* friendly. **~ado** *m* treatise; (*acuerdo*) treaty. **~amiento** *m* treatment; (*título*) title. **~ante** *m* & *f* dealer. **~ar** *vt* (*incl med*) treat; deal with ‹*asunto etc*›; (*com*) deal; (*manejar*) handle; (*de tú, de Vd*) address (**de** as); (*llamar*) call. ● *vi* deal (with). **~ar con** have to do with; know ‹*persona*›; (*com*) deal in. **~ar de** be about; (*intentar*) try. **~o** *m* treatment; (*acuerdo*) agreement; (*título*) title; (*relación*) relationship. **¡~o hecho!** agreed! **~os** *mpl* dealings. **¿de qué se ~a?** what's it about?
traum|a *m* trauma. **~ático** *a* traumatic
través *m* (*inclinación*) slant. **a ~ de** through; (*de un lado a otro*) across. **de ~** across; (*de lado*) sideways. **mirar de ~** look askance at
travesaño *m* crosspiece
travesía *f* crossing; (*calle*) side-street
trav|esura *f* prank. **~ieso** *a* ‹*niño*› mischievous, naughty
trayecto *m* road; (*tramo*) stretch; (*ruta*) route; (*viaje*) journey. **~ria** *f* trajectory; (*fig*) course
traz|a *f* plan; (*aspecto*) look, appearance; (*habilidad*) skill. **~ado** *a*. **bien ~ado** good-looking. **mal ~ado** unattractive. ● *m* plan. **~ar** [10] *vt* draw; (*bosquejar*) sketch. **~o** *m* line
trébol *m* clover. **~es** *mpl* (*en naipes*) clubs
trece *a* & *m* thirteen
trecho *m* stretch; (*distancia*) distance; (*tiempo*) while. **a ~s** in places. **de ~ en ~** at intervals
tregua *f* truce; (*fig*) respite
treinta *a* & *m* thirty
tremendo *a* terrible; (*extraordinario*) terrific
trementina *f* turpentine
tren *m* train; (*equipaje*) luggage. **~ de aterrizaje** landing gear. **~ de vida** lifestyle
tren|cilla *f* braid. **~za** *f* braid; (*de pelo*) plait. **~zar** [10] *vt* plait
trepa|dor *a* climbing. **~r** *vt*/*i* climb
tres *a* & *m* three. **~cientos** *a* & *m* three hundred. **~illo** *m* three-piece suite; (*mus*) triplet
treta *f* trick

tri|angular *a* triangular. **~ángulo** *m* triangle
trib|al *a* tribal. **~u** *f* tribe
tribulación *f* tribulation
tribuna *f* platform; (*de espectadores*) stand
tribunal *m* court; (*de examen etc*) board; (*fig*) tribunal
tribut|ar *vt* pay. **~o** *m* tribute; (*impuesto*) tax
triciclo *m* tricycle
tricolor *a* three-coloured
tricornio *a* three-cornered. ● *m* three-cornered hat
tricotar *vt/i* knit
tridimensional *a* three-dimensional
tridente *m* trident
trigésimo *a* thirtieth
trig|al *m* wheat field. **~o** *m* wheat
trigonometría *f* trigonometry
trigueño *a* olive-skinned; ‹*pelo*› dark blonde
trilogía *f* trilogy
trilla|do *a* (*fig, manoseado*) trite; (*fig, conocido*) well-known. **~r** *vt* thresh
trimestr|al *a* quarterly. **~e** *m* quarter; (*escol, univ*) term
trin|ar *vi* warble. **estar que trina** be furious
trinchar *vt* carve
trinchera *f* ditch; (*mil*) trench; (*rail*) cutting; (*abrigo*) trench coat
trineo *m* sledge
trinidad *f* trinity
Trinidad *f* Trinidad
trino *m* warble
trío *m* trio
tripa *f* intestine; (*culin*) tripe; (*fig, vientre*) tummy, belly. **~s** *fpl* (*de máquina etc*) parts, workings. **me duele la ~** I've got tummy-ache. **revolver las ~s** turn one's stomach
tripicallos *mpl* tripe
tripl|e *a* triple. ● *m*. **el ~e (de)** three times as much (as). **~icado** *a*. **por ~icado** in triplicate. **~icar** [7] *vt* treble
trípode *m* tripod
tríptico *m* triptych
tripula|ción *f* crew. **~nte** *m & f* member of the crew. **~r** *vt* man
triquitraque *m* (*ruido*) clatter
tris *m* crack; (*de papel etc*) ripping noise. **estar en un ~** be on the point of
triste *a* sad; ‹*paisaje, tiempo etc*› gloomy; (*fig, insignificante*) miserable. **~za** *f* sadness
tritón *m* newt
triturar *vt* crush
triunf|al *a* triumphal. **~ante** *a* triumphant. **~ar** *vi* triumph (**de, sobre** over). **~o** *m* triumph
triunvirato *m* triumvirate
trivial *a* trivial
triza *f* piece. **hacer algo ~s** smash sth to pieces
trocar [2 & 7] *vt* (ex)change
trocear *vt* cut up, chop
trocito *m* small piece
trocha *f* narrow path; (*atajo*) short cut
trofeo *m* trophy
tromba *f* waterspout. **~ de agua** heavy downpour
trombón *m* trombone; (*músico*) trombonist
trombosis *f invar* thrombosis
trompa *f* horn; (*de orquesta*) French horn; (*de elefante*) trunk; (*hocico*) snout; (*juguete*) (spinning) top; (*anat*) tube. ● *m* horn player. **coger una ~** (*fam*) get drunk
trompada *f*, **trompazo** *m* bump
trompet|a *f* trumpet; (*músico*) trumpeter, trumpet player; (*clarín*) bugle. **~illa** *f* ear-trumpet
trompicar [7] *vi* trip
trompo *m* (*juguete*) (spinning) top
trona|da *f* thunder storm. **~r** *vt* (*Mex*) shoot. ● *vi* thunder
tronco *m* trunk. **dormir como un ~** sleep like a log
tronchar *vt* bring down; (*fig*) cut short. **~se de risa** laugh a lot
trono *m* throne
trop|a *f* troops. **~el** *m* mob. **ser de ~a** be in the army
tropero *m* (*Arg, vaquero*) cowboy
tropez|ar [1 & 10] *vi* trip; (*fig*) slip up. **~ar con** run into. **~ón** *m* stumble; (*fig*) slip
tropical *a* tropical
trópico *a* tropical. ● *m* tropic
tropiezo *m* slip; (*desgracia*) mishap
trot|ar *vi* trot. **~e** *m* trot; (*fig*) toing and froing. **al ~e** trotting; (*de prisa*) in a rush. **de mucho ~e** hard-wearing
trozo *m* piece, bit. **a ~s** in bits
truco *m* knack; (*ardid*) trick. **coger el ~** get the knack
trucha *f* trout
trueno *m* thunder; (*estampido*) bang
trueque *m* exchange. **aun a ~ de** even at the expense of
trufa *f* truffle. **~r** *vt* stuff with truffles

truhán *m* rogue; (*gracioso*) jester
truncar [7] *vt* truncate; (*fig*) cut short
tu *a* your
tú *pron* you
tuba *f* tuba
tubérculo *m* tuber
tuberculosis *f* tuberculosis
tub|ería *f* pipes; (*oleoducto etc*) pipeline. **~o** *m* tube. **~o de ensayo** test tube. **~o de escape** (*auto*) exhaust (pipe). **~ular** *a* tubular
tuerca *f* nut
tuerto *a* one-eyed, blind in one eye. • *m* one-eyed person
tuétano *m* marrow; (*fig*) heart. **hasta los ~s** completely
tufo *m* fumes; (*olor*) bad smell
tugurio *m* hovel, slum
tul *m* tulle
tulipán *m* tulip
tulli|do *a* paralysed. **~r** [22] *vt* cripple
tumba *f* grave, tomb
tumb|ar *vt* knock down, knock over; (*fig, en examen, fam*) fail; (*pasmar, fam*) overwhelm. **~arse** *vpr* lie down. **~o** *m* jolt. **dar un ~o** tumble. **~ona** *f* settee; (*sillón*) armchair; (*de lona*) deckchair
tumefacción *f* swelling
tumido *a* swollen
tumor *m* tumour
tumulto *m* turmoil; (*pol*) riot
tuna *f* prickly pear; (*de estudiantes*) student band
tunante *m & f* rogue
túnel *m* tunnel
Túnez *m* (*ciudad*) Tunis; (*país*) Tunisia
túnica *f* tunic
Tunicia *f* Tunisia
tupé *m* toupee; (*fig*) nerve
tupido *a* thick
turba *f* peat; (*muchedumbre*) mob
turba|ción *f* disturbance, upset; (*confusión*) confusion. **~do** *a* upset
turbante *m* turban
turbar *vt* upset; (*molestar*) disturb. **~se** *vpr* be upset
turbina *f* turbine
turbi|o *a* cloudy; ‹*vista*› blurred; ‹*asunto etc*› unclear. **~ón** *m* squall
turbulen|cia *f* turbulence; (*disturbio*) disturbance. **~te** *a* turbulent; ‹*persona*› restless
turco *a* Turkish. • *m* Turk; (*lengua*) Turkish
tur|ismo *m* tourism; (*coche*) car. **~ista** *m & f* tourist. **~ístico** *a* tourist. **oficina** *f* **de ~ismo** tourist office
turn|arse *vpr* take turns (**para** to). **~o** *m* turn; (*de trabajo*) shift. **por ~o** in turn
turquesa *f* turquoise
Turquía *f* Turkey
turrón *m* nougat
turulato *a* (*fam*) stunned
tutear *vt* address as *tú*. **~se** *vpr* be on familiar terms
tutela *f* (*jurid*) guardianship; (*fig*) protection
tuteo *m* use of the familiar *tú*
tutor *m* guardian; (*escol*) form master
tuve *vb véase* **tener**
tuyo *a & pron* yours. **un amigo ~** a friend of yours

U

u *conj* or
ubicuidad *f* ubiquity
ubre *f* udder
ucraniano *a & m* Ukranian
Ud *abrev* (*Usted*) you
uf *int* phew!; (*de repugnancia*) ugh!
ufan|arse *vpr* be proud (**con, de** of); (*jactarse*) boast (**con, de** about). **~o** *a* proud
ujier *m* usher
úlcera *f* ulcer
ulterior *a* later; ‹*lugar*› further. **~mente** *adv* later, subsequently
últimamente *adv* (*recientemente*) recently; (*al final*) finally; (*en último caso*) as a last resort
ultim|ar *vt* complete. **~átum** *m* ultimatum
último *a* last; (*más reciente*) latest; (*más lejano*) furthest; (*más alto*) top; (*más bajo*) bottom; (*fig, extremo*) extreme. **estar en las últimas** be on one's last legs; (*sin dinero*) be down to one's last penny. **por ~** finally. **ser lo ~** (*muy bueno*) be marvellous; (*muy malo*) be awful. **vestido a la última** dressed in the latest fashion
ultra *a* ultra, extreme
ultraj|ante *a* outrageous. **~e** *m* outrage
ultramar *m* overseas countries. **de ~, en ~** overseas

ultramarino *a* overseas. **~s** *mpl* groceries. **tienda de ~s** grocer's (shop) (*Brit*), grocery store (*Amer*)
ultranza a ~ (*con decisión*) decisively; (*extremo*) extreme
ultra|sónico *a* ultrasonic. **~violeta** *a invar* ultraviolet
ulular *vi* howl; ‹*búho*› hoot
umbilical *a* umbilical
umbral *m* threshold
umbrío *a*, **umbroso** *a* shady
un *art indef m* (*pl* **unos**) a. ● *a* one. **~os** *a pl* some
una *art indef f* a. **la ~** one o'clock
un|ánime *a* unanimous. **~animidad** *f* unanimity
undécimo *a* eleventh
ung|ir [14] *vt* anoint. **~üento** *m* ointment
únic|amente *adv* only. **~o** *a* only; (*fig, incomparable*) unique
unicornio *m* unicorn
unid|ad *f* unit; (*cualidad*) unity. **~o** *a* united
unifica|ción *f* unification. **~r** [7] *vt* unite, unify
uniform|ar *vt* standardize; (*poner uniforme a*) put into uniform. **~e** *a & m* uniform. **~idad** *f* uniformity
uni|génito *a* only. **~lateral** *a* unilateral
uni|ón *f* union; (*cualidad*) unity; (*tec*) joint. **~r** *vt* join; mix ‹*líquidos*›. **~rse** *vpr* join together
unísono *m* unison. **al ~** in unison
unitario *a* unitary
universal *a* universal
universi|dad *f* university. **U~dad a Distancia** Open University. **~tario** *a* university
universo *m* universe
uno *a* one; (*en plural*) some. ● *pron* one; (*alguien*) someone, somebody. ● *m* one. **~ a otro** each other. **~ y otro** both. **(los) ~s... (los) otros** some... others
untar *vt* grease; (*med*) rub; (*fig, sobornar, fam*) bribe
uña *f* nail; (*de animal*) claw; (*casco*) hoof
upa *int* up!
uranio *m* uranium
Urano *m* Uranus
urban|idad *f* politeness. **~ismo** *m* town planning. **~ístico** *a* urban. **~ización** *f* development. **~izar** [10] *vt* civilize; develop ‹*terreno*›. **~o** *a* urban
urbe *f* big city
urdimbre *f* warp
urdir *vt* (*fig*) plot
urg|encia *f* urgency; (*emergencia*) emergency; (*necesidad*) urgent need. **~ente** *a* urgent. **~ir** [14] *vi* be urgent. **carta** *f* **~ente** express letter
urinario *m* urinal
urna *f* urn; (*pol*) ballot box
urraca *f* magpie
URSS *abrev* (*historia*) (*Unión de Repúblicas Socialistas Soviéticas*) USSR, Union of Soviet Socialist Republics
Uruguay *m*. **el ~** Uruguay
uruguayo *a & m* Uruguayan
us|ado *a* used; ‹*ropa etc*› worn. **~anza** *f* usage, custom. **~ar** *vt* use; (*llevar*) wear. **~o** *m* use; (*costumbre*) usage, custom. **al ~o** (*de moda*) in fashion; (*a la manera de*) in the style of. **de ~o externo** for external use
usted *pron* you
usual *a* usual
usuario *a* user
usur|a *f* usury. **~ero** *m* usurer
usurpar *vt* usurp
usuta *f* (*Arg*) sandal
utensilio *m* tool; (*de cocina*) utensil. **~s** *mpl* equipment
útero *m* womb
útil *a* useful. **~es** *mpl* implements
utili|dad *f* usefulness. **~tario** *a* utilitarian; ‹*coche*› utility. **~zación** *f* use, utilization. **~zar** [10] *vt* use, utilize
uva *f* grape. **~ pasa** raisin. **mala ~** bad mood

V

vaca *f* cow; (*carne*) beef
vacaciones *fpl* holiday(s). **estar de ~** be on holiday. **ir de ~** go on holiday
vaca|nte *a* vacant. ● *f* vacancy. **~r** [7] *vi* fall vacant
vaci|ar [20] *vt* empty; (*ahuecar*) hollow out; (*en molde*) cast; (*afilar*) sharpen. **~edad** *f* emptiness; (*tontería*) silly thing, frivolity
vacila|ción *f* hesitation. **~nte** *a* unsteady; (*fig*) hesitant. **~r** *vi* sway; (*dudar*) hesitate; (*fam*) tease
vacío *a* empty; (*vanidoso*) vain. ● *m* empty space; (*estado*) emptiness; (*en física*) vacuum; (*fig*) void

vacuidad *f* emptiness; (*tontería*) silly thing, frivolity
vacuna *f* vaccine. **~ción** *f* vaccination. **~r** *vt* vaccinate
vacuno *a* bovine
vacuo *a* empty
vade *m* folder
vad|ear *vt* ford. **~o** *m* ford
vaga|bundear *vi* wander. **~bundo** *a* vagrant; ‹*perro*› stray. ● *m* tramp. **~r** [12] *vi* wander (about)
vagina *f* vagina
vago *a* vague; (*holgazán*) idle; ‹*foto*› blurred. ● *m* idler
vag|ón *m* carriage; (*de mercancías*) truck, wagon. **~ón restaurante** dining-car. **~oneta** *f* truck
vahído *m* dizzy spell
vaho *m* breath; (*vapor*) steam. **~s** *mpl* inhalation
vaina *f* sheath; (*bot*) pod
vainilla *f* vanilla
vaivén *m* swaying; (*de tráfico*) coming and going; (*fig*, *de suerte*) change. **vaivenes** *mpl* (*fig*) ups and downs
vajilla *f* dishes, crockery. **lavar la ~** wash up
vale *m* voucher; (*pagaré*) IOU. **~dero** *a* valid
valenciano *a* from Valencia
valent|ía *f* courage; (*acción*) brave deed. **~ón** *m* braggart
valer [42] *vt* be worth; (*costar*) cost; (*fig*, *significar*) mean. ● *vi* be worth; (*costar*) cost; (*servir*) be of use; (*ser valedero*) be valid; (*estar permitido*) be allowed. ● *m* worth. **~ la pena** be worthwhile, be worth it. **¿cuánto vale?** how much is it?. **no ~ para nada** be useless. **¡vale!** all right!, OK! (*fam*). **¿vale?** all right?, OK? (*fam*)
valeroso *a* courageous
valgo *vb véase* **valer**
valía *f* worth
validez *f* validity. **dar ~ a** validate
válido *a* valid
valiente *a* brave; (*valentón*) boastful; (*en sentido irónico*) fine. ● *m* brave person; (*valentón*) braggart
valija *f* case; (*de correos*) mailbag. **~ diplomática** diplomatic bag
val|ioso *a* valuable. **~or** *m* value, worth; (*descaro*, *fam*) nerve. **~ores** *mpl* securities. **~oración** *f* valuation. **~orar** *vt* value. **conceder ~or a** attach importance to. **objetos** *mpl* **de ~or** valuables. **sin ~or** worthless
vals *m invar* waltz
válvula *f* valve
valla *f* fence; (*fig*) barrier
valle *m* valley
vampiro *m* vampire
vanagloriarse [20 *o regular*] *vpr* boast
vanamente *adv* uselessly, in vain
vandalismo *m* vandalism
vándalo *m* vandal
vanguardia *f* vanguard. **de ~** (*en arte*, *música etc*) avant-garde
vanid|ad *f* vanity. **~oso** *a* vain
vano *a* vain; (*inútil*) useless. **en ~** in vain
vapor *m* steam; (*gas*) vapour; (*naut*) steamer. **~izador** *m* spray. **~izar** [10] vaporize. **al ~** (*culin*) steamed
vaquer|ía *f* dairy. **~o** *m* cow-herd, cowboy. **~os** *mpl* jeans
vara *f* stick; (*de autoridad*) staff; (*medida*) yard
varar *vi* run aground
varia|ble *a* & *f* variable. **~ción** *f* variation. **~nte** *f* version. **~ntes** *fpl* hors d'oeuvres. **~r** [20] *vt* change; (*dar variedad a*) vary. ● *vi* vary; (*cambiar*) change
varice *f* varicose vein
varicela *f* chickenpox
varicoso *a* having varicose veins
variedad *f* variety
varilla *f* stick; (*de metal*) rod
vario *a* varied; (*en plural*) several
varita *f* wand
variz *f* varicose vein
var|ón *a* male. ● *m* man; (*niño*) boy. **~onil** *a* manly
vasc|o *a* & *m* Basque. **~ongado** *a* Basque. **~uence** *a* & *m* Basque. **las V~ongadas** the Basque provinces
vasectomía *f* vasectomy
vaselina *f* Vaseline (P), petroleum jelly
vasija *f* pot, container
vaso *m* glass; (*anat*) vessel
vástago *m* shoot; (*descendiente*) descendant; (*varilla*) rod
vasto *a* vast
Vaticano *m* Vatican
vaticin|ar *vt* prophesy. **~io** *m* prophesy
vatio *m* watt
vaya *vb véase* **ir**
Vd *abrev* (*Usted*) you
vecin|dad *f* neighbourhood, vicinity; (*vecinos*) neighbours. **~dario** *m*

inhabitants, neighbourhood. **~o** *a* neighbouring; (*de al lado*) next-door. ● *m* neighbour
veda|do *m* preserve. **~do de caza** game preserve. **~r** *vt* prohibit
vega *f* fertile plain
vegeta|ción *f* vegetation. **~l** *a* vegetable. ● *m* plant, vegetable. **~r** *vi* grow; ‹*persona*› vegetate. **~riano** *a & m* vegetarian
vehemente *a* vehement
vehículo *m* vehicle
veinte *a & m* twenty. **~na** *f* score
veinti|cinco *a & m* twenty-five. **~cuatro** *a & m* twenty-four. **~dós** *a & m* twenty-two. **~nueve** *a & m* twenty-nine; **~ocho** *a & m* twenty-eight. **~séis** *a & m* twenty-six. **~siete** *a & m* twenty-seven. **~trés** *a & m* twenty-three. **~ún** *a* twenty-one. **~uno** *a & m* (*delante de nombre masculino* **veintún**) twenty-one
vejar *vt* humiliate; (*molestar*) vex
vejez *f* old age
vejiga *f* bladder; (*med*) blister
vela *f* (*naut*) sail; (*de cera*) candle; (*falta de sueño*) sleeplessness; (*vigilia*) vigil. **pasar la noche en ~** have a sleepless night
velada *f* evening party
vela|do *a* veiled; (*foto*) blurred. **~r** *vt* watch over; (*encubrir*) veil; (*foto*) blur. ● *vi* stay awake, not sleep. **~r por** look after. **~rse** *vpr* (*foto*) blur
velero *m* sailing-ship
veleta *f* weather vane
velo *m* veil
veloc|idad *f* speed; (*auto etc*) gear. **~ímetro** *m* speedometer. **~ista** *m & f* sprinter. **a toda ~idad** at full speed
velódromo *m* cycle-track
veloz *a* fast, quick
vell|o *m* down. **~ón** *m* fleece. **~udo** *a* hairy
vena *f* vein; (*en madera*) grain. **estar de/en ~** be in the mood
venado *m* deer; (*culin*) venison
vencedor *a* winning. ● *m* winner
vencejo *m* (*pájaro*) swift
venc|er [9] *vt* beat; (*superar*) overcome. ● *vi* win; ‹*plazo*› expire. **~erse** *vpr* collapse; ‹*persona*› control o.s. **~ido** *a* beaten; (*com, atrasado*) in arrears. **darse por ~ido** give up. **los ~idos** *mpl* (*en deportes etc*) the losers
venda *f* bandage. **~je** *m* dressing. **~r** *vt* bandage
vendaval *m* gale
vende|dor *a* selling. ● *m* seller, salesman. **~dor ambulante** pedlar. **~r** *vt* sell. **~rse** *vpr* sell. **~rse caro** play hard to get. **se ~** for sale
vendimia *f* grape harvest; (*de vino*) vintage, year
Venecia *f* Venice
veneciano *a* Venetian
veneno *m* poison; (*fig, malevolencia*) spite. **~so** *a* poisonous
venera *f* scallop shell
venera|ble *a* venerable. **~ción** *f* reverence. **~r** *vt* revere
venéreo *a* venereal
venero *m* (*yacimiento*) seam; (*de agua*) spring; (*fig*) source
venezolano *a & m* Venezuelan
Venezuela *f* Venezuela
venga|nza *f* revenge. **~r** [12] *vt* avenge. **~rse** *vpr* take revenge (**de, por** for) (**de, en** on). **~tivo** *a* vindictive
vengo *vb véase* **venir**
venia *f* (*permiso*) permission
venial *a* venial
veni|da *f* arrival; (*vuelta*) return. **~dero** *a* coming. **~r** [53] *vi* come; (*estar, ser*) be. **~r a para** come to. **~r bien** suit. **la semana que viene** next week. **¡venga!** come on!
venta *f* sale; (*posada*) inn. **en ~** for sale
ventaj|a *f* advantage. **~oso** *a* advantageous
ventan|a *f* window; (*de la nariz*) nostril. **~illa** *f* window
ventarrón *m* (*fam*) strong wind
ventear *vt* (*olfatear*) sniff
ventero *m* innkeeper
ventila|ción *f* ventilation. **~dor** *m* fan. **~r** *vt* air
vent|isca *f* blizzard. **~olera** *f* gust of wind. **~osa** *f* sucker. **~osidad** *f* wind, flatulence. **~oso** *a* windy
ventrílocuo *m* ventriloquist
ventrudo *a* pot-bellied
ventur|a *f* happiness; (*suerte*) luck. **~oso** *a* happy, lucky. **a la ~a** at random. **echar la buena ~a a uno** tell s.o.'s fortune. **por ~a** by chance; (*afortunadamente*) fortunately
Venus *f* Venus
ver [43] *vt* see; watch ‹*televisión*›. ● *vi* see. **~se** *vpr* see o.s.; (*encontrarse*) find o.s.; ‹*dos personas*› meet. **a mi (modo de) ~** in my view. **a ~** let's see. **de buen ~** good-looking. **dejarse ~** show. **¡habráse**

visto! did you ever! **no poder ~** not be able to stand. **no tener nada que ~ con** have nothing to do with. **¡para que veas!** so there! **vamos a ~** let's see. **ya lo veo** that's obvious. **ya ~ás** you'll see. **ya ~emos** we'll see
vera *f* edge; (*de río*) bank
veracruzano *a* from Veracruz
veran|eante *m & f* tourist, holiday-maker. **~ear** *vi* spend one's holiday. **~eo** *m* (summer) holiday. **~iego** *a* summer. **~o** *m* summer. **casa** *f* **de ~eo** summer-holiday home. **ir de ~eo** go on holiday. **lugar** *m* **de ~eo** holiday resort
veras *fpl*. **de ~** really
veraz *a* truthful
verbal *a* verbal
verbena *f* (*bot*) verbena; (*fiesta*) fair; (*baile*) dance
verbo *m* verb. **~so** *a* verbose
verdad *f* truth. **¿~?** isn't it?, aren't they?, won't it? etc. **~eramente** *adv* really. **~ero** *a* true; (*fig*) real. **a decir ~** to tell the truth. **de ~** really. **la pura ~** the plain truth. **si bien es ~ que** although
verd|e *a* green; ‹*fruta etc*› unripe; ‹*chiste etc*› dirty, blue. ● *m* green; (*hierba*) grass. **~or** *m* greenness
verdugo *m* executioner; (*fig*) tyrant
verdu|lería *f* greengrocer's (shop). **~lero** *m* greengrocer. **~ra** *f* (green) vegetable(s)
vereda *f* path; (*LAm, acera*) pavement (*Brit*), sidewalk (*Amer*)
veredicto *m* verdict
vergel *m* large garden; (*huerto*) orchard
verg|onzoso *a* shameful; (*tímido*) shy. **~üenza** *f* shame; (*timidez*) shyness. **¡es una ~üenza!** it's a disgrace! **me da ~üenza** I'm ashamed; (*tímido*) I'm shy about. **tener ~üenza** be ashamed; (*tímido*) be shy
verídico *a* true
verifica|ción *f* verification. **~r** [7] *vt* check. **~rse** *vpr* take place; (*resultar verdad*) come true
verja *f* grating; (*cerca*) railings; (*puerta*) iron gate
vermú *m*, **vermut** *m* vermouth
vernáculo *a* vernacular
verosímil *a* likely; ‹*relato etc*› credible
verraco *m* boar
verruga *f* wart
versado *a* versed
versar *vi* turn. **~ sobre** be about
versátil *a* versatile; (*fig*) fickle
versión *f* version; (*traducción*) translation
verso *m* verse; (*línea*) line
vértebra *f* vertebra
verte|dero *m* rubbish tip; (*desaguadero*) drain. **~dor** *m* drain. **~r** [1] *vt* pour; (*derramar*) spill. ● *vi* flow
vertical *a & f* vertical
vértice *f* vertex
vertiente *f* slope
vertiginoso *a* dizzy
vértigo *m* dizziness; (*med*) vertigo. **de ~** (*fam*) amazing
vesania *f* rage; (*med*) insanity
vesícula *f* blister. **~ biliar** gall-bladder
vespertino *a* evening
vestíbulo *m* hall; (*de hotel, teatro etc*) foyer
vestido *m* (*de mujer*) dress; (*ropa*) clothes
vestigio *m* trace. **~s** *mpl* remains
vest|imenta *f* clothing. **~ir** [5] *vt* (*ponerse*) put on; (*llevar*) wear; dress ‹*niño etc*›. ● *vi* dress; (*llevar*) wear. **~irse** *vpr* get dressed; (*llevar*) wear. **~uario** *m* wardrobe; (*cuarto*) dressing-room
Vesuvio *m* Vesuvius
vetar *vt* veto
veterano *a* veteran
veterinari|a *f* veterinary science. **~o** *a* veterinary. ● *m* vet (*fam*), veterinary surgeon (*Brit*), veterinarian (*Amer*)
veto *m* veto. **poner el ~ a** veto
vetusto *a* ancient
vez *f* time; (*turno*) turn. **a la ~** at the same time; (*de una vez*) in one go. **alguna que otra ~** from time to time. **alguna ~** sometimes; (*en preguntas*) ever. **algunas veces** sometimes. **a su ~** in (his) turn. **a veces** sometimes. **cada ~ más** more and more. **de una ~** in one go. **de una ~ para siempre** once and for all. **de ~ en cuando** from time to time. **dos veces** twice. **2 veces 4** 2 times 4. **en ~ de** instead of. **érase una ~, había una ~** once upon a time. **muchas veces** often. **otra ~** again. **pocas veces, rara ~** rarely. **repetidas veces** again and again. **tal ~** perhaps. **una ~ (que)** once
vía *f* road; (*rail*) line; (*anat*) tract; (*fig*) way. ● *prep* via. **~ aérea** by air.

~ de comunicación *f* means of communication. **~ férrea** railway (*Brit*), railroad (*Amer*). **~ rápida** fast lane. **estar en ~s de** be in the process of

viab|ilidad *f* viability. **~le** *a* viable

viaducto *m* viaduct

viaj|ante *m & f* commercial traveller. **~ar** *vi* travel. **~e** *m* journey; (*corto*) trip. **~e de novios** honeymoon. **~ero** *m* traveller; (*pasajero*) passenger. **¡buen ~e!** have a good journey!

víbora *f* viper

vibra|ción *f* vibration. **~nte** *a* vibrant. **~r** *vt/i* vibrate

vicario *m* vicar

vice... *pref* vice-...

viceversa *adv* vice versa

vici|ado *a* corrupt; ‹*aire*› stale. **~ar** *vt* corrupt; (*estropear*) spoil. **~o** *m* vice; (*mala costumbre*) bad habit. **~oso** *a* dissolute; ‹*círculo*› vicious

vicisitud *f* vicissitude

víctima *f* victim; (*de un accidente*) casualty

victori|a *f* victory. **~oso** *a* victorious

vid *f* vine

vida *f* life; (*duración*) lifetime. **¡~ mía!** my darling! **de por ~** for life. **en mi ~** never (in my life). **en ~ de** during the lifetime of. **estar en ~** be alive

vídeo *m* video recorder

video|cinta *f* videotape. **~juego** *m* video game

vidriar *vt* glaze

vidri|era *f* stained glass window; (*puerta*) glass door; (*LAm, escaparate*) shop window. **~ería** *f* glass works. **~ero** *m* glazier. **~o** *m* glass. **~oso** *a* glassy

vieira *f* scallop

viejo *a* old. ● *m* old person

Viena *f* Vienna

viene *vb véase* **venir**

viento *m* wind. **hacer ~** be windy

vientre *f* belly; (*matriz*) womb; (*intestino*) bowels. **llevar un niño en el ~** be pregnant

viernes *m* Friday. **V~ Santo** Good Friday

viga *f* beam; (*de metal*) girder

vigen|cia *f* validity. **~te** *a* valid; ‹*ley*› in force. **entrar en ~cia** come into force

vigésimo *a* twentieth

vigía *f* (*torre*) watch-tower; (*persona*) lookout

vigil|ancia *f* vigilance. **~ante** *a* vigilant. ● *m* watchman, supervisor. **~ar** *vt* keep an eye on. ● *vi* be vigilant; ‹*vigía etc*› keep watch. **~ia** *f* vigil; (*relig*) fasting

vigor *m* vigour; (*vigencia*) force. **~oso** *a* vigorous. **entrar en ~** come into force

vil *a* vile. **~eza** *f* vileness; (*acción*) vile deed

vilipendiar *vt* abuse

vilo. en ~ in the air

villa *f* town; (*casa*) villa. **la V~** Madrid

villancico *m* (Christmas) carol

villano *a* rustic; (*grosero*) coarse

vinagre *m* vinegar. **~ra** *f* vinegar bottle. **~ras** *fpl* cruet. **~ta** *f* vinaigrette (sauce)

vincular *vt* bind

vínculo *m* bond

vindicar [7] *vt* avenge; (*justificar*) vindicate

vine *vb véase* **venir**

vinicult|or *m* wine-grower. **~ura** *f* wine growing

vino *m* wine. **~ de Jerez** sherry. **~ de la casa** house wine. **~ de mesa** table wine

viña *f*, **viñedo** *m* vineyard

viola *f* viola; (*músico*) viola player

violación *f* violation; (*de una mujer*) rape

violado *a & m* violet

violar *vt* violate; break ‹*ley*›; rape ‹*mujer*›

violen|cia *f* violence; (*fuerza*) force; (*embarazo*) embarrassment. **~tar** *vt* force; break into ‹*casa etc*›. **~tarse** *vpr* force o.s. **~to** *a* violent; (*fig*) awkward. **hacer ~cia a** force

violeta *a invar & f* violet

viol|ín *m* violin; (*músico*) violinist. **~inista** *m & f* violinist. **~ón** *m* double bass; (*músico*) double-bass player. **~onc(h)elista** *m & f* cellist. **~onc(h)elo** *m* cello

vira|je *m* turn. **~r** *vt* turn. ● *vi* turn; (*fig*) change direction

virg|en *a & f* virgin. **~inal** *a* virginal. **~inidad** *f* virginity

Virgo *m* Virgo

viril *a* virile. **~idad** *f* virility

virtual *a* virtual

virtud *f* virtue; (*capacidad*) ability. **en ~ de** by virtue of

virtuoso *a* virtuous. ● *m* virtuoso

viruela *f* smallpox. **picado de ~s** pock-marked
virulé. a la ~ (*fam*) crooked; (*estropeado*) damaged
virulento *a* virulent
virus *m invar* virus
visa|do *m* visa. **~r** *vt* endorse
vísceras *fpl* entrails
viscos|a *f* viscose. **~o** *a* viscous
visera *f* visor; (*de gorra*) peak
visib|ilidad *f* visibility. **~le** *a* visible
visig|odo *a* Visigothic. ● *m* Visigoth. **~ótico** *a* Visigothic
visillo *m* (*cortina*) net curtain
visi|ón *f* vision; (*vista*) sight. **~onario** *a* & *m* visionary
visita *f* visit; (*persona*) visitor. **~ de cumplido** courtesy call. **~nte** *m* & *f* visitor. **~r** *vt* visit. **tener ~** have visitors
vislumbr|ar *vt* glimpse. **~e** *f* glimpse; (*resplandor, fig*) glimmer
viso *m* sheen; (*aspecto*) appearance
visón *m* mink
visor *m* viewfinder
víspera *f* day before, eve
vista *f* sight, vision; (*aspecto, mirada*) look; (*panorama*) view. **apartar la ~** look away; (*fig*) turn a blind eye. **a primera ~, a simple ~** at first sight. **clavar la ~ en** stare at. **con ~s a** with a view to. **en ~ de** in view of, considering. **estar a la ~** be obvious. **hacer la ~ gorda** turn a blind eye. **perder de ~** lose sight of. **tener a la ~** have in front of one. **volver la ~ atrás** look back
vistazo *m* glance. **dar/echar un ~ a** glance at
visto *a* seen; (*corriente*) common; (*considerado*) considered. ● *vb véase* **vestir**. **~ bueno** passed. **~ que** since. **bien ~** acceptable. **está ~ que** it's obvious that. **lo nunca ~** an unheard-of thing. **mal ~** unacceptable. **por lo ~** apparently
vistoso *a* colourful, bright
visual *a* visual. ● *f* glance. **echar una ~ a** have a look at
vital *a* vital. **~icio** *a* life. ● *m* (life) annuity. **~idad** *f* vitality
vitamina *f* vitamin
viticult|or *m* wine-grower. **~ura** *f* wine growing
vitorear *vt* cheer
vítreo *a* vitreous
vitrina *f* showcase
vituper|ar *vt* censure. **~io** *m* censure. **~ios** *mpl* abuse

viud|a *f* widow. **~ez** *f* widowhood. **~o** *a* widowed. ● *m* widower
viva *m* cheer
vivacidad *f* liveliness
vivamente *adv* vividly; (*sinceramente*) sincerely
vivaz *a* (*bot*) perennial; (*vivo*) lively
víveres *mpl* supplies
vivero *m* nursery; (*fig*) hotbed
viveza *f* vividness; (*de inteligencia*) sharpness; (*de carácter*) liveliness
vivido *a* true
vívido *a* vivid
vivienda *f* housing; (*casa*) house; (*piso*) flat
viviente *a* living
vivificar [7] *vt* (*animar*) enliven
vivir *vt* live through. ● *vi* live. ● *m* life. **~ de** live on. **de mal ~** dissolute. **¡viva!** hurray! **¡viva el rey!** long live the king!
vivisección *f* vivisection
vivo *a* alive; (*viviente*) living; ‹*color*› bright; (*listo*) clever; (*fig*) lively. **a lo ~, al ~** vividly
Vizcaya *f* Biscay
vizconde *m* viscount. **~sa** *f* viscountess
vocab|lo *m* word. **~ulario** *m* vocabulary
vocación *f* vocation
vocal *a* vocal. ● *f* vowel. ● *m* & *f* member. **~ista** *m* & *f* vocalist
voce|ar *vt* call ‹*mercancías*›; (*fig*) proclaim. ● *vi* shout. **~río** *m* shouting
vociferar *vi* shout
vodka *m* & *f* vodka
vola|da *f* flight. **~dor** *a* flying. ● *m* rocket. **~ndas. en ~ndas** in the air; (*fig, rápidamente*) very quickly. **~nte** *a* flying. ● *m* (*auto*) steering-wheel; (*nota*) note; (*rehilete*) shuttlecock; (*tec*) flywheel. **~r** [2] *vt* blow up. ● *vi* fly; (*desaparecer, fam*) disappear
volátil *a* volatile
volcán *m* volcano. **~ico** *a* volcanic
vol|car [2 & 7] *vt* knock over; (*adrede*) empty out. ● *vi* overturn. **~carse** *vpr* fall over; ‹*vehículo*› overturn; (*fig*) do one's utmost. **~carse en** throw o.s. into
vol(e)ibol *m* volleyball
volquete *m* tipper, dump truck
voltaje *m* voltage
volte|ar *vt* turn over; (*en el aire*) toss; ring ‹*campanas*›. **~reta** *f* somersault

voltio *m* volt
voluble *a* (*fig*) fickle
volum|en *m* volume; (*importancia*) importance. **~inoso** *a* voluminous
voluntad *f* will; (*fuerza de voluntad*) will-power; (*deseo*) wish; (*intención*) intention. **buena ~** goodwill. **mala ~** ill will
voluntario *a* voluntary. ● *m* volunteer. **~so** *a* willing; (*obstinado*) wilful
voluptuoso *a* voluptuous
volver [2, *pp* **vuelto**] *vt* turn; (*de arriba a abajo*) turn over; (*devolver*) restore. ● *vi* return; (*fig*) revert. **~se** *vpr* turn round; (*regresar*) return; (*hacerse*) become. **~ a hacer algo** do sth again. **~ en sí** come round
vomit|ar *vt* bring up. ● *vi* be sick, vomit. **~ivo** *m* emetic. ● *a* disgusting
vómito *m* vomit; (*acción*) vomiting
vorágine *f* maelstrom
voraz *a* voracious
vos *pron* (*LAm*) you
vosotros *pron* you; (*reflexivo*) yourselves. **el libro de ~** your book
vot|ación *f* voting; (*voto*) vote. **~ante** *m & f* voter. **~ar** *vt* vote for. ● *vi* vote. **~o** *m* vote; (*relig*) vow; (*maldición*) curse. **hacer ~os por** hope for
voy *vb véase* **ir**
voz *f* voice; (*grito*) shout; (*rumor*) rumour; (*palabra*) word. **~ pública** public opinion. **aclarar la ~** clear one's throat. **a media ~** softly. **a una ~** unanimously. **dar voces** shout. **en ~ alta** loudly
vuelco *m* upset. **el corazón me dio un ~** my heart missed a beat
vuelo *m* flight; (*acción*) flying; (*de ropa*) flare. **al ~** in flight; (*fig*) in passing
vuelta *f* turn; (*curva*) bend; (*paseo*) walk; (*revolución*) revolution; (*regreso*) return; (*dinero*) change. **a la ~** on one's return; (*de página*) over the page. **a la ~ de la esquina** round the corner. **dar la ~ al mundo** go round the world. **dar una ~** go for a walk. **estar de ~** be back. **¡hasta la ~!** see you soon!
vuelvo *vb véase* **volver**
vuestro *a* your. ● *pron* yours. **un amigo ~** a friend of yours
vulg|ar *a* vulgar; ‹*persona*› common. **~aridad** *f* ordinariness; (*trivialidad*) triviality; (*grosería*) vulgarity. **~arizar** [10] *vt* popularize. **~o** *m* common people
vulnerab|ilidad *f* vulnerability. **~le** *a* vulnerable

wáter *m* toilet
whisky /'wiski/ *m* whisky

X

xenofobia *f* xenophobia
xilófono *m* xylophone

Y

y *conj* and
ya *adv* already; (*ahora*) now; (*luego*) later; (*en seguida*) immediately; (*pronto*) soon. ● *int* of course! **~ no** no longer. **~ que** since. **¡~, ~!** oh yes!, all right!
yacaré *m* (*LAm*) alligator
yac|er [44] *vi* lie. **~imiento** *m* deposit; (*de petróleo*) oilfield
yanqui *m & f* American, Yank(ee)
yate *m* yacht
yegua *f* mare
yeísmo *m* pronunciation of the Spanish *ll* like the Spanish *y*
yelmo *m* helmet
yema *f* (*bot*) bud; (*de huevo*) yolk; (*golosina*) sweet. **~ del dedo** fingertip
yergo *vb véase* **erguir**
yermo *a* uninhabited; (*no cultivable*) barren. ● *m* wasteland
yerno *m* son-in-law
yerro *m* mistake. ● *vb véase* **errar**
yerto *a* stiff
yeso *m* gypsum; (*arquit*) plaster. **~ mate** plaster of Paris
yo *pron* I. ● *m* ego. **~ mismo** I myself. **soy ~** it's me
yodo *m* iodine
yoga *m* yoga
yogur *m* yog(h)urt
York. de ~ ‹*jamón*› cooked
yuca *f* yucca
Yucatán *m* Yucatán
yugo *m* yoke

Yugoslavia *f* Yugoslavia
yugoslavo *a & m* Yugoslav
yunque *m* anvil
yunta *f* yoke
yuxtaponer [34] *vt* juxtapose
yuyo *m* (*Arg*) weed

Z

zafarse *vpr* escape; get out of ‹*obligación etc*›
zafarrancho *m* (*confusión*) mess; (*riña*) quarrel
zafio *a* coarse
zafiro *m* sapphire
zaga *f* rear. **no ir en ~** not be inferior
zaguán *m* hall
zaherir [4] *vt* hurt one's feelings
zahorí *m* clairvoyant; (*de agua*) water diviner
zaino *a* ‹*caballo*› chestnut; ‹*vaca*› black
zalamer|ía *f* flattery. **~o** *a* flattering. ● *m* flatterer
zamarra *f* (*piel*) sheepskin; (*prenda*) sheepskin jacket
zamarrear *vt* shake
zamba *f* (*esp LAm*) South American dance; (*samba*) samba
zambulli|da *f* dive. **~r** [22] *vt* plunge. **~rse** *vpr* dive
zamparse *vpr* fall; (*comer*) gobble up
zanahoria *f* carrot
zancad|a *f* stride. **~illa** *f* trip. **echar la ~illa a uno, poner la ~illa a uno** trip s.o. up
zanc|o *m* stilt. **~udo** *a* long-legged. ● *m* (*LAm*) mosquito
zanganear *vi* idle
zángano *m* drone; (*persona*) idler
zangolotear *vt* fiddle with. ● *vi* rattle; ‹*persona*› fidget
zanja *f* ditch. **~r** *vt* (*fig*) settle
zapapico *m* pickaxe
zapat|ear *vt/i* tap with one's feet. **~ería** *f* shoe shop; (*arte*) shoemaking. **~ero** *m* shoemaker; (*el que remienda zapatos*) cobbler. **~illa** *f* slipper. **~illas deportivas** trainers. **~o** *m* shoe
zaragata *f* turmoil
Zaragoza *f* Saragossa
zarand|a *f* sieve. **~ear** *vt* sieve; (*sacudir*) shake
zarcillo *m* earring
zarpa *f* claw, paw
zarpar *vi* weigh anchor
zarza *f* bramble. **~mora** *f* blackberry
zarzuela *f* musical, operetta
zascandil *m* scatterbrain
zenit *m* zenith
zigzag *m* zigzag. **~uear** *vi* zigzag
zinc *m* zinc
zipizape *m* (*fam*) row
zócalo *m* skirting-board; (*pedestal*) plinth
zodiaco *m*, **zodíaco** *m* zodiac
zona *f* zone; (*área*) area
zoo *m* zoo. **~logía** *f* zoology. **~lógico** *a* zoological
zoólogo *m* zoologist
zopenco *a* stupid. ● *m* idiot
zoquete *m* (*de madera*) block; (*persona*) blockhead
zorr|a *f* fox; (*hembra*) vixen. **~o** *m* fox
zozobra *f* (*fig*) anxiety. **~r** *vi* be shipwrecked; (*fig*) be ruined
zueco *m* clog
zulú *a & m* Zulu
zumb|ar *vt* (*fam*) give ‹*golpe etc*›. ● *vi* buzz. **~ido** *m* buzzing
zumo *m* juice
zurci|do *m* darning. **~r** [9] *vt* darn
zurdo *a* left-handed; ‹*mano*› left
zurrar *vt* (*fig, dar golpes, fam*) beat up
zurriago *m* whip
zutano *m* so-and-so

ENGLISH-SPANISH
INGLÉS-ESPAÑOL

A

a /ə, eɪ/ *indef art* (*before vowel* **an**) un *m*; una *f*
aback /ə'bæk/ *adv*. **be taken ~** quedar desconcertado
abacus /'æbəkəs/ *n* ábaco *m*
abandon /ə'bændən/ *vt* abandonar. • *n* abandono *m*, desenfado *m*. **~ed** *a* abandonado; ‹*behaviour*› perdido. **~ment** *n* abandono *m*
abase /ə'beɪs/ *vt* degradar. **~ment** *n* degradación *f*
abashed /ə'bæʃt/ *a* confuso
abate /ə'beɪt/ *vt* disminuir. • *vi* disminuir; ‹*storm etc*› calmarse. **~ment** *n* disminución *f*
abattoir /'æbətwɑ:(r)/ *n* matadero *m*
abbess /'æbis/ *n* abadesa *f*
abbey /'æbɪ/ *n* abadía *f*
abbot /'æbət/ *n* abad *m*
abbreviat|e /ə'bri:vɪeɪt/ *vt* abreviar. **~ion** /-'eɪʃn/ *n* abreviatura *f*; (*act*) abreviación *f*
ABC /'eɪbi:'si:/ *n* abecé *m*, abecedario *m*
abdicat|e /'æbdɪkeɪt/ *vt/i* abdicar. **~ion** /-'eɪʃn/ *n* abdicación *f*
abdom|en /'æbdəmən/ *n* abdomen *m*. **~inal** /-'dɒmɪnl/ *a* abdominal
abduct /æb'dʌkt/ *vt* secuestrar. **~ion** /-ʃn/ *n* secuestro *m*. **~or** *n* secuestrador *m*
aberration /æbə'reɪʃn/ *n* aberración *f*
abet /ə'bet/ *vt* (*pt* **abetted**) (*jurid*) ser cómplice de
abeyance /ə'beɪəns/ *n*. **in ~** en suspenso
abhor /əb'hɔ:(r)/ *vt* (*pt* **abhorred**) aborrecer. **~rence** /-'hɒrəns/ *n* aborrecimiento *m*; (*thing*) abominación *f*. **~rent** /-'hɒrənt/ *a* aborrecible
abide /ə'baɪd/ *vt* (*pt* **abided**) soportar. • *vi* (*old use*, *pt* **abode**) morar. **~ by** atenerse a; cumplir ‹*promise*›
abiding /ə'baɪdɪŋ/ *a* duradero, permanente
ability /ə'bɪlətɪ/ *n* capacidad *f*; (*cleverness*) habilidad *f*
abject /'æbdʒekt/ *a* (*wretched*) miserable; (*vile*) abyecto
ablaze /ə'bleɪz/ *a* en llamas
able /'eɪbl/ *a* (**-er**, **-est**) capaz. **be ~** poder; (*know how to*) saber
ablutions /ə'blu:ʃnz/ *npl* ablución *f*
ably /'eɪblɪ/ *adv* hábilmente
abnormal /æb'nɔ:ml/ *a* anormal. **~ity** /-'mælətɪ/ *n* anormalidad *f*
aboard /ə'bɔ:d/ *adv* a bordo. • *prep* a bordo de
abode /ə'bəʊd/ *see* **abide**. • *n* (*old use*) domicilio *m*
abolish /ə'bɒlɪʃ/ *vt* suprimir, abolir
abolition /æbə'lɪʃn/ *n* supresión *f*, abolición *f*
abominable /ə'bɒmɪnəbl/ *a* abominable
abominat|e /ə'bɒmɪneɪt/ *vt* abominar. **~ion** /-'neɪʃn/ *n* abominación *f*
aborigin|al /æbə'rɪdʒənl/ *a* & *n* aborigen (*m* & *f*), indígena (*m* & *f*). **~es** /-i:z/ *npl* aborígenes *mpl*
abort /ə'bɔ:t/ *vt* hacer abortar. • *vi* abortar. **~ion** /-ʃn/ *n* aborto *m* provocado; (*fig*) aborto *m*. **~ionist** *n* abortista *m* & *f*. **~ive** *a* abortivo; (*fig*) fracasado
abound /ə'baʊnd/ *vi* abundar (**in** de, en)
about /ə'baʊt/ *adv* (*approximately*) alrededor de; (*here and there*) por todas partes; (*in existence*) por aquí. **~ here** por aquí. **be ~ to** estar a punto de. **be up and ~** estar levantado. • *prep* sobre; (*around*) alrededor de; (*somewhere in*) en. **talk ~** hablar de. **~-face** *n* (*fig*) cambio *m* rotundo. **~-turn** *n* (*fig*) cambio *m* rotundo
above /ə'bʌv/ *adv* arriba. • *prep* encima de; (*more than*) más de. **~ all** sobre todo. **~-board** *a* honrado.

● *adv* abiertamente. **~-mentioned** *a* susodicho

abrasi|on /ə'breɪʒn/ *n* abrasión *f*. **~ve** /ə'breɪsɪv/ *a & n* abrasivo (*m*); (*fig*) agresivo, brusco

abreast /ə'brest/ *adv* de frente. **keep ~ of** mantenerse al corriente de

abridge /ə'brɪdʒ/ *vt* abreviar. **~ment** *n* abreviación *f*; (*abstract*) resumen *m*

abroad /ə'brɔ:d/ *adv* (*be*) en el extranjero; (*go*) al extranjero; (*far and wide*) por todas partes

abrupt /ə'brʌpt/ *a* brusco. **~ly** *adv* (*suddenly*) repentinamente; (*curtly*) bruscamente. **~ness** *n* brusquedad *f*

abscess /'æbsɪs/ *n* absceso *m*

abscond /əb'skɒnd/ *vi* fugarse

absen|ce /'æbsəns/ *n* ausencia *f*; (*lack*) falta *f*. **~t** /'æbsənt/ *a* ausente. /æb'sent/ *vr*. **~ o.s.** ausentarse. **~tly** *adv* distraídamente. **~t-minded** *a* distraído. **~t-mindedness** *n* distracción *f*, despiste *m*

absentee /æbsən'ti:/ *n* ausente *m & f*. **~ism** *n* absentismo *m*

absinthe /'æbsɪnθ/ *n* ajenjo *m*

absolute /'æbsəlu:t/ *a* absoluto. **~ly** *adv* absolutamente

absolution /æbsə'lu:ʃn/ *n* absolución *f*

absolve /əb'zɒlv/ *vt* (*from sin*) absolver; (*from obligation*) liberar

absor|b /əb'zɔ:b/ *vt* absorber. **~bent** *a* absorbente. **~ption** *n* absorción *f*

abstain /əb'steɪn/ *vi* abstenerse (**from** de)

abstemious /əb'sti:mɪəs/ *a* abstemio

abstention /əb'stenʃn/ *n* abstención *f*

abstinen|ce /'æbstɪnəns/ *n* abstinencia *f*. **~t** *a* abstinente

abstract /'æbstrækt/ *a* abstracto. ● *n* (*quality*) abstracto *m*; (*summary*) resumen *m*. /əb'strækt/ *vt* extraer; (*summarize*) resumir. **~ion** /-ʃn/ *n* abstracción *f*

abstruse /əb'stru:s/ *a* abstruso

absurd /əb'sɜ:d/ *a* absurdo. **~ity** *n* absurdo *m*, disparate *m*

abundan|ce /ə'bʌndəns/ *n* abundancia *f*. **~t** *a* abundante

abuse /ə'bju:z/ *vt* (*misuse*) abusar de; (*ill-treat*) maltratar; (*insult*) insultar. /ə'bju:s/ *n* abuso *m*; (*insults*) insultos *mpl*

abusive /ə'bju:sɪv/ *a* injurioso

abut /ə'bʌt/ *vi* (*pt* **abutted**) confinar (**on** con)

abysmal /ə'bɪzməl/ *a* abismal; (*bad, fam*) pésimo; (*fig*) profundo

abyss /ə'bɪs/ *n* abismo *m*

acacia /ə'keɪʃə/ *n* acacia *f*

academic /ækə'demik/ *a* académico; (*pej*) teórico. ● *n* universitario *m*, catedrático *m*. **~ian** /-də'mɪʃn/ *n* académico *m*

academy /ə'kædəmɪ/ *n* academia *f*. **~ of music** conservatorio *m*

accede /ək'si:d/ *vi*. **~ to** acceder a ‹*request*›; tomar posesión de ‹*office*›. **~ to the throne** subir al trono

accelerat|e /ək'seləreɪt/ *vt* acelerar. **~ion** /-'reɪʃn/ *n* aceleración *f*. **~or** *n* acelerador *m*

accent /'æksənt/ *n* acento *m*. /æk'sent/ *vt* acentuar

accentuate /ək'sentʃʊeɪt/ *vt* acentuar

accept /ək'sept/ *vt* aceptar. **~able** *a* aceptable. **~ance** *n* aceptación *f*; (*approval*) aprobación *f*

access /'ækses/ *n* accceso *m*. **~ibility** /-ɪ'bɪlətɪ/ *n* accesibilidad *f*. **~ible** /ək'sesəbl/ *a* accesible; ‹*person*› tratable

accession /æk'seʃn/ *n* (*to power, throne etc*) ascenso *m*; (*thing added*) adquisición *f*

accessory /ək'sesərɪ/ *a* accesorio. ● *n* accesorio *m*, complemento *m*; (*jurid*) cómplice *m & f*

accident /'æksɪdənt/ *n* accidente *m*; (*chance*) casualidad *f*. **by ~** por accidente, por descuido, sin querer; (*by chance*) por casualidad. **~al** /-'dentl/ *a* accidental, fortuito. **~ally** /-'dentəlɪ/ *adv* por accidente, por descuido, sin querer; (*by chance*) por casualidad

acclaim /ə'kleɪm/ *vt* aclamar. ● *n* aclamación *f*

acclimatiz|ation /əklaɪmətaɪ'zeɪʃn/ *n* aclimatación *f*. **~e** /ə'klaɪmətaɪz/ *vt* aclimatar. ● *vi* aclimatarse

accolade /'ækəleɪd/ *n* (*of knight*) acolada *f*; (*praise*) encomio *m*

accommodat|e /ə'kɒmədeɪt/ *vt* (*give hospitality to*) alojar; (*adapt*) acomodar; (*supply*) proveer; (*oblige*) complacer. **~ing** *a* complaciente. **~ion** /-'deɪʃn/ *n* alojamiento *m*; (*rooms*) habitaciones *fpl*

accompan|iment /ə'kʌmpənɪmənt/ *n* acompañamiento *m*. **~ist** *n* acompañante *m & f*. **~y** /ə'kʌmpənɪ/ *vt* acompañar

accomplice /ə'kʌmplɪs/ *n* cómplice *m & f*

accomplish /ə'kʌmplɪʃ/ *vt* (*complete*) acabar; (*achieve*) realizar; (*carry out*) llevar a cabo. **~ed** *a* consumado. **~ment** *n* realización *f*; (*ability*) talento *m*; (*thing achieved*) triunfo *m*, logro *m*

accord /ə'kɔ:d/ *vi* concordar. ● *vt* conceder. ● *n* acuerdo *m*; (*harmony*) armonía *f*. **of one's own ~** espontáneamente. **~ance** *n*. **in ~ance with** de acuerdo con

according /ə'kɔ:dɪŋ/ *adv*. **~ to** según. **~ly** *adv* en conformidad; (*therefore*) por consiguiente

accordion /ə'kɔ:dɪən/ *n* acordeón *m*

accost /ə'kɒst/ *vt* abordar

account /ə'kaʊnt/ *n* cuenta *f*; (*description*) relato *m*; (*importance*) importancia *f*. **on ~ of** a causa de. **on no ~** de ninguna manera. **on this ~** por eso. **take into ~** tener en cuenta. ● *vt* considerar. **~ for** dar cuenta de, explicar

accountab|ility /əkaʊntə'bɪlətɪ/ *n* responsabilidad *f*. **~le** *a* responsable (**for** de)

accountan|cy /ə'kaʊntənsɪ/ *n* contabilidad *f*. **~t** *n* contable *m & f*

accoutrements /ə'ku:trəmənts/ *npl* equipo *m*

accredited /ə'kredɪtɪd/ *a* acreditado; (*authorized*) autorizado

accrue /ə'kru:/ *vi* acumularse

accumulat|e /ə'kju:mjʊleɪt/ *vt* acumular. ● *vi* acumularse. **~ion** /-'leɪʃn/ *n* acumulación *f*. **~or** *n* (*elec*) acumulador *m*

accura|cy /'ækjərəsɪ/ *n* exactitud *f*, precisión *f*. **~te** *a* exacto, preciso

accus|ation /ækju:'zeɪʃn/ *n* acusación *f*. **~e** *vt* acusar

accustom /ə'kʌstəm/ *vt* acostumbrar. **~ed** *a* acostumbrado. **get ~ed (to)** acostumbrarse (a)

ace /eɪs/ *n* as *m*

acetate /'æsɪteɪt/ *n* acetato *m*

ache /eɪk/ *n* dolor *m*. ● *vi* doler. **my leg ~s** me duele la pierna

achieve /ə'tʃi:v/ *vt* realizar; lograr ‹*success*›. **~ment** *n* realización *f*; (*feat*) éxito *m*; (*thing achieved*) proeza *f*, logro *m*

acid /'æsɪd/ *a & n* ácido (*m*). **~ity** /ə'sɪdətɪ/ *n* acidez *f*

acknowledge /ək'nɒlɪdʒ/ *vt* reconocer. **~ receipt of** acusar recibo de. **~ment** *n* reconocimiento *m*; (*com*) acuse *m* de recibo

acme /'ækmɪ/ *n* cima *f*

acne /'æknɪ/ *n* acné *m*

acorn /'eɪkɔ:n/ *n* bellota *f*

acoustic /ə'ku:stɪk/ *a* acústico. **~s** *npl* acústica *f*

acquaint /ə'kweɪnt/ *vt*. **~ s.o. with** poner a uno al corriente de. **be ~ed with** conocer ‹*person*›; saber ‹*fact*›. **~ance** *n* conocimiento *m*; (*person*) conocido *m*

acquiesce /ækwɪ'es/ *vi* consentir (**in** en). **~nce** *n* aquiescencia *f*, consentimiento *m*

acqui|re /ə'kwaɪə(r)/ *vt* adquirir; aprender ‹*language*›. **~re a taste for** tomar gusto a. **~sition** /ækwɪ'zɪʃn/ *n* adquisición *f*. **~sitive** /-'kwɪzətɪv/ *a* codicioso

acquit /ə'kwɪt/ *vt* (*pt* **acquitted**) absolver; **~ o.s. well** defenderse bien, tener éxito. **~tal** *n* absolución *f*

acre /'eɪkə(r)/ *n* acre *m*. **~age** *n* superficie *f* (en acres)

acrid /'ækrɪd/ *a* acre

acrimon|ious /ækrɪ'məʊnɪəs/ *a* cáustico, mordaz. **~y** /'ækrɪmənɪ/ *n* acrimonia *f*, acritud *f*

acrobat /'ækrəbæt/ *n* acróbata *m & f*. **~ic** /-'bætɪk/ *a* acrobático. **~ics** /-'bætɪks/ *npl* acrobacia *f*

acronym /'ækrənɪm/ *n* acrónimo *m*, siglas *fpl*

across /ə'krɒs/ *adv & prep* (*side to side*) de un lado al otro; (*on other side*) del otro lado de; (*crosswise*) a través. **go** *or* **walk ~** atravesar

act /ækt/ *n* acto *m*; (*action*) acción *f*; (*in variety show*) número *m*; (*decree*) decreto *m*. ● *vt* hacer ‹*part, role*›. ● *vi* actuar; (*pretend*) fingir; (*function*) funcionar. **~ as** actuar de. **~ for** representar. **~ing** *a* interino. ● *n* (*of play*) representación *f*; (*by actor*) interpretación *f*; (*profession*) profesión *f* de actor

action /'ækʃn/ *n* acción *f*; (*jurid*) demanda *f*; (*plot*) argumento *m*. **out of ~** (*on sign*) no funciona. **put out of ~** inutilizar. **take ~** tomar medidas

activate /'æktɪveɪt/ *vt* activar

activ|e /'æktɪv/ *a* activo; (*energetic*) enérgico; ‹*volcano*› en actividad. **~ity** /-'tɪvətɪ/ *n* actividad *f*

act|or /'æktə(r)/ *n* actor *m*. **~ress** *n* actriz *f*

actual /'æktʃʊəl/ *a* verdadero. **~ity** /-'ælətɪ/ *n* realidad *f*. **~ly** *adv* en realidad, efectivamente; (*even*) incluso

actuary /'æktʃʊərɪ/ *n* actuario *m*

actuate /'æktjʊeɪt/ *vt* accionar, impulsar

acumen /'ækjʊmen/ *n* perspicacia *f*

acupunctur|e /'ækjʊpʌŋktʃə(r)/ *n* acupuntura *f*. **~ist** *n* acupunturista *m & f*

acute /ə'kju:t/ *a* agudo. **~ly** *adv* agudamente. **~ness** *n* agudeza *f*

ad /æd/ *n* (*fam*) anuncio *m*

AD /eɪ'di:/ *abbr* (*Anno Domini*) d.J.C.

adamant /'ædəmənt/ *a* inflexible

Adam's apple /'ædəmz'æpl/ *n* nuez *f* (de Adán)

adapt /ə'dæpt/ *vt* adaptar. ● *vi* adaptarse

adaptab|ility /ədæptə'bɪlətɪ/ *n* adaptabilidad *f*. **~le** /ə'dæptəbl/ *a* adaptable

adaptation /ædæp'teɪʃn/ *n* adaptación *f*; (*of book etc*) versión *f*

adaptor /ə'dæptə(r)/ *n* (*elec*) adaptador *m*

add /æd/ *vt* añadir. ● *vi* sumar. **~ up** sumar; (*fig*) tener sentido. **~ up to** equivaler a

adder /'ædə(r)/ *n* víbora *f*

addict /'ædɪkt/ *n* adicto *m*; (*fig*) entusiasta *m & f*. **~ed** /ə'dɪktɪd/ *a*. **~ed to** adicto a; (*fig*) fanático de. **~ion** /-ʃn/ *n* (*med*) dependencia *f*; (*fig*) afición *f*. **~ive** *a* que crea dependencia

adding machine /'ædɪŋməʃi:n/ *n* máquina *f* de sumar, sumadora *f*

addition /ə'dɪʃn/ *n* suma *f*. **in ~** además. **~al** /-ʃənl/ *a* suplementario

additive /'ædɪtɪv/ *a & n* aditivo (*m*)

address /ə'dres/ *n* señas *fpl*, dirección *f*; (*speech*) discurso *m*. ● *vt* poner la dirección; (*speak to*) dirigirse a. **~ee** /ædre'si:/ *n* destinatario *m*

adenoids /'ædɪnɔɪdz/ *npl* vegetaciones *fpl* adenoideas

adept /'ædept/ *a & n* experto (*m*)

adequa|cy /'ædɪkwəsɪ/ *n* suficiencia *f*. **~te** *a* suficiente, adecuado. **~tely** *adv* suficientemente, adecuadamente

adhere /əd'hɪə(r)/ *vi* adherirse **(to** a); observar ‹*rule*›. **~nce** /-rəns/ *n* adhesión *f*; (*to rules*) observancia *f*

adhesion /əd'hi:ʒn/ *n* adherencia *f*

adhesive /əd'hi:sɪv/ *a & n* adhesivo (*m*)

ad infinitum /ædɪnfɪ'naɪtəm/ *adv* hasta el infinito

adjacent /ə'dʒeɪsnt/ *a* contiguo

adjective /'ædʒɪktɪv/ *n* adjetivo *m*

adjoin /ə'dʒɔɪn/ *vt* lindar con. **~ing** *a* contiguo

adjourn /ə'dʒɜ:n/ *vt* aplazar; suspender ‹*meeting etc*›. ● *vi* suspenderse. **~ to** trasladarse a

adjudicate /ə'dʒu:dɪkeɪt/ *vt* juzgar. ● *vi* actuar como juez

adjust /ə'dʒʌst/ *vt* ajustar ‹*machine*›; (*arrange*) arreglar. ● *vi*. **~ (to)** adaptarse (a). **~able** *a* ajustable. **~ment** *n* adaptación *f*; (*tec*) ajuste *m*

ad lib /æd'lɪb/ *a* improvisado. ● *vi* (*pt* **-libbed**) (*fam*) improvisar

administer /əd'mɪnɪstə(r)/ *vt* administrar, dar, proporcionar

administrat|ion /ədmɪnɪ'streɪʃn/ *n* administración *f*. **~or** *n* administrador *m*

admirable /'ædmərəbl/ *a* admirable

admiral /'ædmərəl/ *n* almirante *m*

admiration /ædmə'reɪʃn/ *n* admiración *f*

admire /əd'maɪə(r)/ *vt* admirar. **~r** /-'maɪərə(r)/ *n* admirador *m*; (*suitor*) enamorado *m*

admissible /əd'mɪsəbl/ *a* admisible

admission /əd'mɪʃn/ *n* admisión *f*; (*entry*) entrada *f*

admit /əd'mɪt/ *vt* (*pt* **admitted**) dejar entrar; (*acknowledge*) admitir, reconocer. **~ to** confesar. **be ~ted** (*to hospital etc*) ingresar. **~tance** *n* entrada *f*. **~tedly** *adv* es verdad que

admoni|sh /əd'mɒnɪʃ/ *vt* reprender; (*advise*) aconsejar. **~tion** /-'nɪʃn/ *n* reprensión *f*

ado /ə'du:/ *n* alboroto m; (*trouble*) dificultad *f*. **without more ~** en seguida, sin más

adolescen|ce /ædə'lesns/ *n* adolescencia *f*. **~t** *a & n* adolescente (*m & f*)

adopt /ə'dɒpt/ *vt* adoptar. **~ed** *a* ‹*child*› adoptivo. **~ion** /-ʃn/ *n* adopción *f*. **~ive** *a* adoptivo

ador|able /ədɔ:rəbl/ *a* adorable. **~ation** /ædə'reɪʃn/ *n* adoración *f*. **~e** /ə'dɔ:(r)/ *vt* adorar

adorn /ə'dɔ:n/ *vt* adornar. **~ment** *n* adorno *m*

adrenalin /ə'drenəlɪn/ *n* adrenalina *f*
adrift /ə'drɪft/ *a & adv* a la deriva
adroit /ə'drɔɪt/ *a* diestro
adulation /ædjʊ'leɪʃn/ *n* adulación *f*
adult /'ædʌlt/ *a & n* adulto (*m*)
adulterat|ion /ədʌltə'reɪʃn/ *n* adulteración *f*. **~e** /ə'dʌltəreɪt/ *vt* adulterar
adulter|er /ə'dʌltərə(r)/ *n* adúltero *m*. **~ess** *n* adúltera *f*. **~ous** *a* adúltero. **~y** *n* adulterio *m*
advance /əd'vɑ:ns/ *vt* adelantar. ● *vi* adelantarse. ● *n* adelanto *m*. **in ~** con anticipación, por adelantado. **~d** *a* avanzado; ‹*studies*› superior. **~ment** *n* adelanto *m*; (*in job*) promoción *f*
advantage /əd'vɑ:ntɪdʒ/ *n* ventaja *f*. **take ~ of** aprovecharse de; abusar de ‹*person*›. **~ous** /ædvən'teɪdʒəs/ *a* ventajoso
advent /'ædvənt/ *n* venida *f*. **A~** *n* adviento *m*
adventur|e /əd'ventʃə(r)/ *n* aventura *f*. **~er** *n* aventurero *m*. **~ous** *a* ‹*persona*› aventurero; ‹*cosa*› arriesgado; (*fig, bold*) llamativo
adverb /'ædvɜ:b/ *n* adverbio *m*
adversary /'ædvəsərɪ/ *n* adversario *m*
advers|e /'ædvɜ:s/ *a* adverso, contrario, desfavorable. **~ity** /əd'vɜ:sətɪ/ *n* infortunio *m*
advert /'ædvɜ:t/ *n* (*fam*) anuncio *m*. **~ise** /'ædvətaɪz/ *vt* anunciar. ● *vi* hacer publicidad; (*seek, sell*) poner un anuncio. **~isement** /əd'vɜ:tɪsmənt/ *n* anuncio *m*. **~iser** /-ə(r)/ *n* anunciante *m & f*
advice /əd'vaɪs/ *n* consejo *m*; (*report*) informe *m*
advis|able /əd'vaɪzəbl/ *a* aconsejable. **~e** *vt* aconsejar; (*inform*) avisar. **~e against** aconsejar en contra de. **~er** *n* consejero *m*; (*consultant*) asesor *m*. **~ory** *a* consultivo
advocate /'ædvəkət/ *n* defensor *m*; (*jurid*) abogado *m*. /'ædvəkeɪt/ *vt* recomendar
aegis /'i:dʒɪs/ *n* égida *f*. **under the ~ of** bajo la tutela de, patrocinado por
aeon /'i:ən/ *n* eternidad *f*
aerial /'eərɪəl/ *a* aéreo. ● *n* antena *f*
aerobatics /eərə'bætɪks/ *npl* acrobacia *f* aérea
aerobics /eə'rɒbɪks/ *npl* aeróbica *f*
aerodrome /'eərədrəʊm/ *n* aeródromo *m*
aerodynamic /eərəʊdaɪ'næmɪk/ *a* aerodinámico
aeroplane /'eərəpleɪn/ *n* avión *m*
aerosol /'eərəsɒl/ *n* aerosol *m*
aesthetic /i:s'θetɪk/ *a* estético
afar /ə'fɑ:(r)/ *adv* lejos
affable /'æfəbl/ *a* afable
affair /ə'feə(r)/ *n* asunto *m*. **(love) ~** aventura *f*, amorío *m*. **~s** *npl* (*business*) negocios *mpl*
affect /ə'fekt/ *vt* afectar; (*pretend*) fingir
affect|ation /æfek'teɪʃn/ *n* afectación *f*. **~ed** *a* afectado, amanerado
affection /ə'fekʃn/ *n* cariño *m*; (*disease*) afección *f*. **~ate** /-ʃənət/ *a* cariñoso
affiliat|e /ə'fɪlɪeɪt/ *vt* afiliar. **~ion** /-'eɪʃn/ *n* afiliación *f*
affinity /ə'fɪnətɪ/ *n* afinidad *f*
affirm /ə'fɜ:m/ *vt* afirmar. **~ation** /æfə'meɪʃn/ *n* afirmación *f*
affirmative /ə'fɜ:mətɪv/ *a* afirmativo. ● *n* respuesta *f* afirmativa
affix /ə'fɪks/ *vt* sujetar; añadir ‹*signature*›; pegar ‹*stamp*›
afflict /ə'flɪkt/ *vt* afligir. **~ion** /-ʃn/ *n* aflicción *f*, pena *f*
affluen|ce /'æflʊəns/ *n* riqueza *f*. **~t** *a* rico. ● *n* (*geog*) afluente *m*
afford /ə'fɔ:d/ *vt* permitirse; (*provide*) dar
affray /ə'freɪ/ *n* reyerta *f*
affront /ə'frʌnt/ *n* afrenta *f*, ofensa *f*. ● *vt* afrentar, ofender
afield /ə'fi:ld/ *adv*. **far ~** muy lejos
aflame /ə'fleɪm/ *adv & a* en llamas
afloat /ə'fləʊt/ *adv* a flote
afoot /ə'fʊt/ *adv*. **sth is ~** se está tramando algo
aforesaid /ə'fɔ:sed/ *a* susodicho
afraid /ə'freɪd/ *a*. **be ~** tener miedo (**of** a); (*be sorry*) sentir, lamentar
afresh /ə'freʃ/ *adv* de nuevo
Africa /'æfrɪkə/ *n* África *f*. **~n** *a & n* africano (*m*)
after /'ɑ:ftə(r)/ *adv* después; (*behind*) detrás. ● *prep* después de; (*behind*) detrás de. **be ~** (*seek*) buscar, andar en busca de. ● *conj* después de que. ● *a* posterior
afterbirth /'ɑ:ftəbɜ:θ/ *n* placenta *f*
after-effect /'ɑ:ftərɪfekt/ *n* consecuencia *f*, efecto *m* secundario
aftermath /'ɑ:ftəmæθ/ *n* secuelas *fpl*
afternoon /ɑ:ftə'nu:n/ *n* tarde *f*
aftershave /'ɑ:ftəʃeɪv/ *n* loción *f* para después del afeitado

afterthought /ˈɑːftəθɔːt/ *n* ocurrencia *f* tardía
afterwards /ˈɑːftəwədz/ *adv* después
again /əˈgen/ *adv* otra vez; (*besides*) además. **~ and ~** una y otra vez
against /əˈgenst/ *prep* contra, en contra de
age /eɪdʒ/ *n* edad *f*. **of ~** mayor de edad. **under ~** menor de edad. ● *vt/i* (*pres p* **ageing**) envejecer. **~d** /ˈeɪdʒd/ *a* de ... años. **~d 10** de 10 años, que tiene 10 años. **~d** /ˈeɪdʒɪd/ *a* viejo, anciano. **~less** *a* siempre joven; (*eternal*) eterno, inmemorial. **~s** (*fam*) siglos *mpl*
agency /ˈeɪdʒənsɪ/ *n* agencia *f*, organismo *m*, oficina *f*; (*means*) mediación *f*
agenda /əˈdʒendə/ *npl* orden *m* del día
agent /ˈeɪdʒənt/ *n* agente *m & f*; (*representative*) representante *m & f*
agglomeration /əglɒməˈreɪʃn/ *n* aglomeración *f*
aggravat|e /ˈægrəveɪt/ *vt* agravar; (*irritate, fam*) irritar. **~ion** /-ˈveɪʃn/ *n* agravación *f*; (*irritation, fam*) irritación *f*
aggregate /ˈægrɪgət/ *a* total. ● *n* conjunto *m*. /ˈægrɪgeɪt/ *vt* agregar. ● *vi* ascender a
aggress|ion /əˈgreʃn/ *n* agresión *f*. **~ive** *a* agresivo. **~iveness** *n* agresividad *f*. **~or** *n* agresor *m*
aggrieved /əˈgriːvd/ *a* apenado, ofendido
aghast /əˈgɑːst/ *a* horrorizado
agil|e /ˈædʒaɪl/ *a* ágil. **~ity** /əˈdʒɪlətɪ/ *n* agilidad *f*
agitat|e /ˈædʒɪteɪt/ *vt* agitar. **~ion** /-ˈteɪʃn/ *n* agitación *f*, excitación *f*. **~or** *n* agitador *m*
agnostic /ægˈnɒstɪk/ *a & n* agnóstico (*m*). **~ism** /-sɪzəm/ *n* agnosticismo *m*
ago /əˈgəʊ/ *adv* hace. **a long time ~** hace mucho tiempo. **3 days ~** hace 3 días
agog /əˈgɒg/ *a* ansioso
agon|ize /ˈægənaɪz/ *vi* atormentarse. **~izing** *a* atroz, angustioso, doloroso. **~y** *n* dolor *m* (agudo); (*mental*) angustia *f*
agree /əˈgriː/ *vt* acordar. ● *vi* estar de acuerdo; (*of figures*) concordar; (*get on*) entenderse. **~ with** (*of food etc*) sentar bien a. **~able** /əˈgriːəbl/ *a* agradable. **be ~able** (*willing*) estar de acuerdo. **~d** *a* ‹*time, place*› convenido. **~ment** /əˈgriːmənt/ *n* acuerdo *m*. **in ~ment** de acuerdo
agricultur|al /ægrɪˈkʌltʃərəl/ *a* agrícola. **~e** /ˈægrɪkʌltʃə(r)/ *n* agricultura *f*
aground /əˈgraʊnd/ *adv*. **run ~** (*of ship*) varar, encallar
ahead /əˈhed/ *adv* delante; (*of time*) antes de. **be ~** ir delante
aid /eɪd/ *vt* ayudar. ● *n* ayuda *f*. **in ~ of** a beneficio de
aide /eɪd/ *n* (*Amer*) ayudante *m & f*
AIDS /eɪdz/ *n* (*med*) SIDA *m*
ail /eɪl/ *vt* afligir. **~ing** *a* enfermo. **~ment** *n* enfermedad *f*
aim /eɪm/ *vt* apuntar; (*fig*) dirigir. ● *vi* apuntar; (*fig*) pretender. ● *n* puntería *f*; (*fig*) propósito *m*. **~less** *a*, **~lessly** *adv* sin objeto, sin rumbo
air /eə(r)/ *n* aire *m*. **be on the ~** estar en el aire. **put on ~s** darse aires. ● *vt* airear. ● *a* ‹*base etc*› aéreo. **~borne** *a* en el aire; (*mil*) aerotransportado. **~-conditioned** *a* climatizado, con aire acondicionado. **~craft** /ˈeəkrɑːft/ *n* (*pl invar*) avión *m*. **~field** /ˈeəfiːld/ *n* aeródromo *m*. **A~ Force** fuerzas *fpl* aéreas. **~gun** /ˈeəgʌn/ *n* escopeta *f* de aire comprimido. **~lift** /ˈeəlɪft/ *n* puente *m* aéreo. **~line** /ˈeəlaɪn/ *n* línea *f* aérea. **~lock** /ˈeəlɒk/ *n* (*in pipe*) burbuja *f* de aire; (*chamber*) esclusa *f* de aire. **~ mail** *n* correo *m* aéreo. **~man** /ˈeəmən/ (*pl* **-men**) *n* aviador *m*. **~port** /ˈeəpɔːt/ *n* aeropuerto *m*. **~tight** /ˈeətaɪt/ *a* hermético. **~worthy** /ˈeəwɜːðɪ/ *a* en condiciones de vuelo. **~y** /ˈeərɪ/ *a* (**-ier**, **-iest**) aireado; (*manner*) ligero
aisle /aɪl/ *n* nave *f* lateral; (*gangway*) pasillo *m*
ajar /əˈdʒɑː(r)/ *adv & a* entreabierto
akin /əˈkɪn/ *a* semejante (**a** to)
alabaster /ˈæləbɑːstə(r)/ *n* alabastro *m*
alacrity /əˈlækrətɪ/ *n* prontitud *f*
alarm /əˈlɑːm/ *n* alarma *f*; (*clock*) despertador *m*. ● *vt* asustar. **~ist** *n* alarmista *m & f*
alas /əˈlæs/ *int* ¡ay!, ¡ay de mí!
albatross /ˈælbətrɒs/ *n* albatros *m*
albino /ælˈbiːnəʊ/ *a & n* albino (*m*)
album /ˈælbəm/ *n* álbum *m*
alchem|ist /ˈælkəmɪst/ *n* alquimista *m & f*. **~y** *n* alquimia *f*
alcohol /ˈælkəhɒl/ *n* alcohol *m*. **~ic** /-ˈhɒlɪk/ *a & n* alcohólico (*m*). **~ism** *n* alcoholismo *m*

alcove /ˈælkəʊv/ *n* nicho *m*
ale /eɪl/ *n* cerveza *f*
alert /əˈlɜːt/ *a* vivo; (*watchful*) vigilante. ● *n* alerta *f*. **on the ~** alerta. ● *vt* avisar. **~ness** *n* vigilancia *f*
algebra /ˈældʒɪbrə/ *n* álgebra *f*
Algeria /ælˈdʒɪərɪə/ *n* Argelia *f*. **~n** *a & n* argelino (*m*)
alias /ˈeɪlɪəs/ *n* (*pl* **-ases**) alias *m invar*. ● *adv* alias
alibi /ˈælɪbaɪ/ (*pl* **-is**) coartada *f*
alien /ˈeɪlɪən/ *n* extranjero *m*. ● *a* ajeno
alienat|e /ˈeɪlɪəneɪt/ *vt* enajenar. **~ion** /-ˈneɪʃn/ *n* enajenación *f*
alight[1] /əˈlaɪt/ *vi* bajar; ‹*bird*› posarse
alight[2] /əˈlaɪt/ *a* ardiendo; ‹*light*› encendido
align /əˈlaɪn/ *vt* alinear. **~ment** *n* alineación *f*
alike /əˈlaɪk/ *a* parecido, semejante. **look** *or* **be ~** parecerse. ● *adv* de la misma manera
alimony /ˈælɪmənɪ/ *n* pensión *f* alimenticia
alive /əˈlaɪv/ *a* vivo. **~ to** sensible a. **~ with** lleno de
alkali /ˈælkəlaɪ/ *n* (*pl* **-is**) álcali *m*. **~ne** *a* alcalino
all /ɔːl/ *a & pron* todo. **~ but one** todos excepto uno. **~ of it** todo. ● *adv* completamente. **~ but** casi. **~ in** (*fam*) rendido. **~ of a sudden** de pronto. **~ over** (*finished*) acabado; (*everywhere*) por todas partes. **~ right!** ¡vale! **be ~ for** estar a favor de. **not at ~** de ninguna manera; (*after thanks!*) ¡no hay de qué!
allay /əˈleɪ/ *vt* aliviar ‹*pain*›; aquietar ‹*fears etc*›
all-clear /ɔːlˈklɪə(r)/ *n* fin *m* de (la) alarma
allegation /ælɪˈgeɪʃn/ *n* alegato *m*
allege /əˈledʒ/ *vt* alegar. **~dly** /-ɪdlɪ/ *adv* según se dice, supuestamente
allegiance /əˈliːdʒəns/ *n* lealtad *f*
allegor|ical /ælɪˈgɒrɪkl/ *a* alegórico. **~y** /ˈælɪgərɪ/ *n* alegoría *f*
allerg|ic /əˈlɜːdʒɪk/ *a* alérgico. **~y** /ˈælədʒɪ/ *n* alergia *f*
alleviat|e /əˈliːvɪeɪt/ *vt* aliviar. **~ion** /-ˈeɪʃn/ *n* alivio *m*
alley /ˈælɪ/ (*pl* **-eys**) *n* callejuela *f*; (*for bowling*) bolera *f*
alliance /əˈlaɪəns/ *n* alianza *f*
allied /ˈælaɪd/ *a* aliado
alligator /ˈælɪgeɪtə(r)/ *n* caimán *m*
allocat|e /ˈæləkeɪt/ *vt* asignar; (*share out*) repartir. **~ion** /-ˈkeɪʃn/ *n* asignación *f*; (*share*) ración *f*; (*distribution*) reparto *m*
allot /əˈlɒt/ *vt* (*pt* **allotted**) asignar. **~ment** *n* asignación *f*; (*share*) ración *f*; (*land*) parcela *f*
all-out /ɔːlˈaʊt/ *a* máximo
allow /əˈlaʊ/ *vt* permitir; (*grant*) conceder; (*reckon on*) prever; (*agree*) admitir. **~ for** tener en cuenta. **~ance** /əˈlaʊəns/ *n* concesión *f*; (*pension*) pensión *f*; (*com*) rebaja *f*. **make ~ances for** ser indulgente con; (*take into account*) tener en cuenta
alloy /ˈælɔɪ/ *n* aleación *f*. /əˈlɔɪ/ *vt* alear
all-round /ɔːlˈraʊnd/ *a* completo
allude /əˈluːd/ *vi* aludir
allure /əˈlʊə(r)/ *vt* atraer. ● *n* atractivo *m*
allusion /əˈluːʒn/ *n* alusión *f*
ally /ˈælaɪ/ *n* aliado *m*. /əˈlaɪ/ *vt* aliarse
almanac /ˈɔːlmənæk/ *n* almanaque *m*
almighty /ɔːlˈmaɪtɪ/ *a* todopoderoso; (*big, fam*) enorme. ● *n*. **the A~** el Todopoderoso *m*
almond /ˈɑːmənd/ *n* almendra *f*; (*tree*) almendro (*m*)
almost /ˈɔːlməʊst/ *adv* casi
alms /ɑːmz/ *n* limosna *f*
alone /əˈləʊn/ *a* solo. ● *adv* sólo, solamente
along /əˈlɒŋ/ *prep* por, a lo largo de. ● *adv*. **~ with** junto con. **all ~** todo el tiempo. **come ~** venga
alongside /əlɒŋˈsaɪd/ *adv* (*naut*) al costado. ● *prep* al lado de
aloof /əˈluːf/ *adv* apartado. ● *a* reservado. **~ness** *n* reserva *f*
aloud /əˈlaʊd/ *adv* en voz alta
alphabet /ˈælfəbet/ *n* alfabeto *m*. **~ical** /-ˈbetɪkl/ *a* alfabético
alpine /ˈælpaɪn/ *a* alpino
Alps /ælps/ *npl*. **the ~** los Alpes *mpl*
already /ɔːlˈredɪ/ *adv* ya
Alsatian /ælˈseɪʃn/ *n* (*geog*) alsaciano *m*; (*dog*) pastor *m* alemán
also /ˈɔːlsəʊ/ *adv* también; (*moreover*) además
altar /ˈɔːltə(r)/ *n* altar *m*
alter /ˈɔːltə(r)/ *vt* cambiar. ● *vi* cambiarse. **~ation** /-ˈreɪʃn/ *n* modificación *f*; (*to garment*) arreglo *m*
alternate /ɔːlˈtɜːnət/ *a* alterno. /ˈɔːltəneɪt/ *vt/i* alternar. **~ly** *adv* alternativamente

alternative /ɔ:l'tɜ:nətɪv/ *a* alternativo. ● *n* alternativa *f*. **~ly** *adv* en cambio, por otra parte

although /ɔ:l'ðəʊ/ *conj* aunque

altitude /'æltɪtju:d/ *n* altitud *f*

altogether /ɔ:ltə'geðə(r)/ *adv* completamente; (*on the whole*) en total

altruis|m /'æltru:ɪzəm/ *n* altruismo *m*. **~t** /'æltru:ɪst/ *n* altruista *m & f*. **~tic** /-'ɪstɪk/ *a* altruista

aluminium /æljʊ'mɪnɪəm/ *n* aluminio *m*

always /'ɔ:lweɪz/ *adv* siempre

am /æm/ *see* **be**

a.m. /'eɪem/ *abbr* (*ante meridiem*) de la mañana

amalgamate /ə'mælgəmeɪt/ *vt* amalgamar. ● *vi* amalgamarse

amass /ə'mæs/ *vt* amontonar

amateur /'æmətə(r)/ *n* aficionado *m*. ● *a* no profesional; (*in sports*) amateur. **~ish** *a* (*pej*) torpe, chapucero

amaz|e /ə'meɪz/ *vt* asombrar. **~ed** *a* asombrado, estupefacto. **be ~ed at** quedarse asombrado de, asombrarse de. **~ement** *n* asombro *m*. **~ingly** *adv* extaordinariamente

ambassador /æm'bæsədə(r)/ *n* embajador *m*

amber /'æmbə(r)/ *n* ámbar *m*; (*auto*) luz *f* amarilla

ambidextrous /æmbɪ'dekstrəs/ *a* ambidextro

ambience /'æmbɪəns/ *n* ambiente *m*

ambigu|ity /æmbɪ'gju:ətɪ/ *n* ambigüedad *f*. **~ous** /æm'bɪgjʊəs/ *a* ambiguo

ambit /'æmbɪt/ *n* ámbito *m*

ambiti|on /æm'bɪʃn/ *n* ambición *f*. **~ous** *a* ambicioso

ambivalen|ce /æm'bɪvələns/ *n* ambivalencia *f*. **~t** *a* ambivalente

amble /'æmbl/ *vi* andar despacio, andar sin prisa

ambulance /'æmbjʊləns/ *n* ambulancia *f*

ambush /'æmbʊʃ/ *n* emboscada *f*. ● *vt* tender una emboscada a

amen /ɑ:'men/ *int* amén

amenable /ə'mi:nəbl/ *a*. **~ to** (*responsive*) sensible a, flexible a

amend /ə'mend/ *vt* enmendar. **~ment** *n* enmienda *f*. **~s** *npl*. **make ~s** reparar

amenities /ə'mi:nətɪz/ *npl* atractivos *mpl*, comodidades *fpl*, instalaciones *fpl*

America /ə'merɪkə/ *n* América; (*North America*) Estados *mpl* Unidos. **~n** *a & n* americano (*m*); (*North American*) estadounidense (*m & f*). **~nism** *n* americanismo *m*. **~nize** *vt* americanizar

amethyst /'æmɪθɪst/ *n* amatista *f*

amiable /'eɪmɪəbl/ *a* simpático

amicabl|e /'æmɪkəbl/ *a* amistoso. **~y** *adv* amistosamente

amid(st) /ə'mɪd(st)/ *prep* entre, en medio de

amiss /ə'mɪs/ *a* malo. ● *adv* mal. **sth ~** algo que no va bien. **take sth ~** llevar algo a mal

ammonia /ə'məʊnɪə/ *n* amoníaco *m*, amoniaco *m*

ammunition /æmjʊ'nɪʃn/ *n* municiones *fpl*

amnesia /æm'ni:zɪə/ *n* amnesia *f*

amnesty /'æmnəstɪ/ *n* amnistía *f*

amok /ə'mɒk/ *adv*. **run ~** volverse loco

among(st) /ə'mʌŋ(st)/ *prep* entre

amoral /eɪ'mɒrəl/ *a* amoral

amorous /'æmərəs/ *a* amoroso

amorphous /ə'mɔ:fəs/ *a* amorfo

amount /ə'maʊnt/ *n* cantidad *f*; (*total*) total *m*, suma *f*. ● *vi*. **~ to** sumar; (*fig*) equivaler a, significar

amp(ere) /'amp(eə(r))/ *n* amperio *m*

amphibi|an /æm'fɪbɪən/ *n* anfibio *m*. **~ous** *a* anfibio

amphitheatre /'æmfɪθɪətə(r)/ *n* anfiteatro *m*

ampl|e /'æmpl/ *a* (**-er**, **-est**) amplio; (*enough*) suficiente; (*plentiful*) abundante. **~y** *adv* ampliamente, bastante

amplif|ier /'æmplɪfaɪə(r)/ *n* amplificador *m*. **~y** *vt* amplificar

amputat|e /'æmpjʊteɪt/ *vt* amputar. **~ion** /-'teɪʃn/ *n* amputación *f*

amus|e /ə'mju:z/ *vt* divertir. **~ement** *n* diversión *f*. **~ing** *a* divertido

an /ən, æn/ *see* **a**

anachronism /ə'nækrənɪzəm/ *n* anacronismo *m*

anaemi|a /ə'ni:mɪə/ *n* anemia *f*. **~c** *a* anémico

anaesthe|sia /ænɪs'θi:zɪə/ *n* anestesia *f*. **~tic** /ænɪs'θetɪk/ *n* anestésico *m*. **~tist** /ə'ni:sθɪtɪst/ *n* anestesista *m & f*

anagram /'ænəgræm/ *n* anagrama *m*

analogy /ə'nælədʒɪ/ *n* analogía *f*

analys|e /'ænəlaɪz/ *vt* analizar. **~is** /ə'næləsɪs/ *n* (*pl* **-yses** /-si:z/) *n* análisis *m*. **~t** /'ænəlɪst/ *n* analista *m & f*

analytic(al) /ænə'lɪtɪk(əl)/ *a* analítico

anarch|ist /'ænəkɪst/ *n* anarquista *m & f*. **~y** *n* anarquía *f*

anathema /ə'næθəmə/ *n* anatema *m*

anatom|ical /ænə'tɒmɪkl/ *a* anatómico. **~y** /ə'nætəmɪ/ *n* anatomía *f*

ancest|or /'ænsestə(r)/ *n* antepasado *m*. **~ral** /-'sestrəl/ *a* ancestral. **~ry** /'ænsestrɪ/ *n* ascendencia *f*

anchor /'æŋkə(r)/ *n* ancla *f*. ● *vt* anclar; (*fig*) sujetar. ● *vi* anclar

anchovy /'æntʃəvɪ/ *n* (*fresh*) boquerón *m*; (*tinned*) anchoa *f*

ancient /'eɪnʃənt/ *a* antiguo, viejo

ancillary /æn'sɪlərɪ/ *a* auxiliar

and /ənd, ænd/ *conj* y; (*before* i- *and* hi-) e. **go ~ see him** vete a verle. **more ~ more** siempre más, cada vez más. **try ~ come** ven si puedes, trata de venir

Andalusia /ændə'lu:zjə/ *f* Andalucía *f*

anecdote /'ænɪkdəʊt/ *n* anécdota *f*

anew /ə'nju:/ *adv* de nuevo

angel /'eɪndʒl/ *n* ángel *m*. **~ic** /æn'dʒelɪk/ *a* angélico

anger /'æŋgə(r)/ *n* ira *f*. ● *vt* enojar

angle[1] /'æŋgl/ *n* ángulo *m*; (*fig*) punto *m* de vista

angle[2] /'æŋgl/ *vi* pescar con caña. **~ for** (*fig*) buscar. **~r** /-ə(r)/ *n* pescador *m*

Anglican /'æŋglɪkən/ *a & n* anglicano (*m*)

Anglo-... /'æŋgləʊ/ *pref* anglo...

Anglo-Saxon /'æŋgləʊ'sæksn/ *a & n* anglosajón (*m*)

angr|ily /'æŋgrɪlɪ/ *adv* con enojo. **~y** /'æŋgrɪ/ *a* (**-ier**, **-iest**) enojado. **get ~y** enfadarse

anguish /'æŋgwɪʃ/ *n* angustia *f*

angular /'æŋgjʊlə(r)/ *a* angular; ‹*face*› anguloso

animal /'ænɪməl/ *a & n* animal (*m*)

animat|e /'ænɪmət/ *a* vivo. /'ænɪmeɪt/ *vt* animar. **~ion** /-'meɪʃn/ *n* animación *f*

animosity /ænɪ'mɒsətɪ/ *n* animosidad *f*

aniseed /'ænɪsi:d/ *n* anís *m*

ankle /'æŋkl/ *n* tobillo *m*. **~ sock** escarpín *m*, calcetín *m*

annals /'ænlz/ *npl* anales *mpl*

annex /ə'neks/ *vt* anexionar. **~ation** /ænek'seɪʃn/ *n* anexión *f*

annexe /'æneks/ *n* anexo *m*, dependencia *f*

annihilat|e /ə'naɪəleɪt/ *vt* aniquilar. **~ion** /-'leɪʃn/ *n* aniquilación *f*

anniversary /ænɪ'vɜ:sərɪ/ *n* aniversario *m*

annotat|e /'ænəteɪt/ *vt* anotar. **~ion** /-'teɪʃn/ *n* anotación *f*

announce /ə'naʊns/ *vt* anunciar, comunicar. **~ment** *n* anuncio *m*, aviso *m*, declaración *f*. **~r** /-e(r)/ *n* (*radio, TV*) locutor *m*

annoy /ə'nɔɪ/ *vt* molestar. **~ance** *n* disgusto *m*. **~ed** *a* enfadado. **~ing** *a* molesto

annual /'ænjʊəl/ *a* anual. ● *n* anuario *m*. **~ly** *adv* cada año

annuity /ə'nju:ətɪ/ *n* anualidad *f*. **life ~** renta *f* vitalicia

annul /ə'nʌl/ *vt* (*pt* **annulled**) anular. **~ment** *n* anulación *f*

anoint /ə'nɔɪnt/ *vt* ungir

anomal|ous /ə'nɒmələs/ *a* anómalo. **~y** *n* anomalía *f*

anon /ə'nɒn/ *adv* (*old use*) dentro de poco

anonymous /ə'nɒnɪməs/ *a* anónimo

anorak /'ænəræk/ *n* anorac *m*

another /ə'nʌðə(r)/ *a & pron* otro (*m*). **~ 10 minutes** 10 minutos más. **in ~ way** de otra manera. **one ~** unos a otros

answer /'ɑ:nsə(r)/ *n* respuesta *f*; (*solution*) solución *f*. ● *vt* contestar a; escuchar, oír ‹*prayer*›. **~ the door** abrir la puerta. ● *vi* contestar. **~ back** replicar. **~ for** ser responsable de. **~able** *a* responsable. **~ing-machine** *n* contestador *m* automático

ant /ænt/ *n* hormiga *f*

antagoni|sm /æn'tægənɪzəm/ *n* antagonismo *m*. **~stic** /-'nɪstɪk/ *a* antagónico, opuesto. **~ze** /æn'tægənaɪz/ *vt* provocar la enemistad de

Antarctic /æn'tɑ:ktɪk/ *a* antártico. ● *n* Antártico *m*

ante-... /'æntɪ/ *pref* ante...

antecedent /æntɪ'si:dnt/ *n* antecedente *m*

antelope /'æntɪləʊp/ *n* antílope *m*

antenatal /'æntɪneɪtl/ *a* prenatal

antenna /æn'tenə/ *n* antena *f*

anthem /'ænθəm/ *n* himno *m*

anthill /'ænthɪl/ *n* hormiguero *m*

anthology /æn'θɒlədʒɪ/ *n* antología *f*

anthropolog|ist /ænθrə'pɒlədʒɪst/ *n* antropológo *m*. **~y** *n* antropología *f*

anti-... /'æntɪ/ *pref* anti... **~aircraft** *a* antiaéreo

antibiotic /æntɪbaɪ'ɒtɪk/ *a & n* antibiótico (*m*)

antibody /'æntɪbɒdɪ/ *n* anticuerpo *m*

antic /'æntɪk/ *n* payasada *f*, travesura *f*

anticipat|e /æn'tɪsɪpeɪt/ *vt* anticiparse a; (*foresee*) prever; (*forestall*) prevenir. **~ion** /-'peɪʃn/ *n* anticipación *f*; (*expectation*) esperanza *f*

anticlimax /æntɪ'klaɪmæks/ *n* decepción *f*

anticlockwise /æntɪ'klɒkwaɪz/ *adv & a* en sentido contrario al de las agujas del reloj, hacia la izquierda

anticyclone /æntɪ'saɪkləʊn/ *n* anticiclón *m*

antidote /'æntɪdəʊt/ *m* antídoto *m*

antifreeze /'æntɪfri:z/ *n* anticongelante *m*

antipathy /æn'tɪpəθɪ/ *n* antipatía *f*

antiquarian /æntɪ'kweərɪən/ *a & n* anticuario (*m*)

antiquated /'æntɪkweɪtɪd/ *a* anticuado

antique /æn'ti:k/ *a* antiguo. ● *n* antigüedad *f*. **~ dealer** anticuario *m*. **~ shop** tienda *f* de antigüedades

antiquity /æn'tɪkwətɪ/ *n* antigüedad *f*

anti-Semitic /æntɪsɪ'mɪtɪk/ *a* antisemítico

antiseptic /æntɪ'septɪk/ *a & n* antiséptico (*m*)

antisocial /æntɪ'səʊʃl/ *a* antisocial

antithesis /æn'tɪθəsɪs/ *n* (*pl* **-eses** /-si:z/) antítesis *f*

antler /'æntlər/ *n* cornamenta *f*

anus /'eɪnəs/ *n* ano *m*

anvil /'ænvɪl/ *n* yunque *m*

anxiety /æŋ'zaɪətɪ/ *n* ansiedad *f*; (*worry*) inquietud *f*; (*eagerness*) anhelo *m*

anxious /'æŋkʃəs/ *a* inquieto; (*eager*) deseoso. **~ly** *adv* con inquietud; (*eagerly*) con impaciencia

any /'enɪ/ *a* algún *m*; (*negative*) ningún *m*; (*whatever*) cualquier; (*every*) todo. **at ~ moment** en cualquier momento. **have you ~ wine?** ¿tienes vino? ● *pron* alguno; (*negative*) ninguno. **have we ~?** ¿tenemos algunos? **not ~** ninguno. ● *adv* (*a little*) un poco, algo. **is it ~ better?** ¿está algo mejor? **it isn't ~ good** no sirve para nada

anybody /'enɪbɒdɪ/ *pron* alguien; (*after negative*) nadie. **~ can do it** cualquiera sabe hacerlo, cualquiera puede hacerlo

anyhow /'enɪhaʊ/ *adv* de todas formas; (*in spite of all*) a pesar de todo; (*badly*) de cualquier modo

anyone /'enɪwʌn/ *pron* alguien; (*after negative*) nadie

anything /'enɪθɪŋ/ *pron* algo; (*whatever*) cualquier cosa; (*after negative*) nada. **~ but** todo menos

anyway /'enɪweɪ/ *adv* de todas formas

anywhere /'enɪweə(r)/ *adv* en cualquier parte; (*after negative*) en ningún sitio; (*everywhere*) en todas partes. **~ else** en cualquier otro lugar. **~ you go** dondequiera que vayas

apace /ə'peɪs/ *adv* rápidamente

apart /ə'pɑ:t/ *adv* aparte; (*separated*) apartado, separado. **~ from** aparte de. **come ~** romperse. **take ~** desmontar

apartheid /ə'pɑ:theɪt/ *n* segregación *f* racial, apartheid *m*

apartment /ə'pɑ:tmənt/ *n* (*Amer*) apartamento *m*

apath|etic /æpə'θetɪk/ *a* apático, indiferente. **~y** /'æpəθɪ/ *n* apatía *f*

ape /eɪp/ *n* mono *m*. ● *vt* imitar

aperient /ə'pɪərɪənt/ *a & n* laxante (*m*)

aperitif /ə'perətɪf/ *n* aperitivo *m*

aperture /'æpətʃʊə(r)/ *n* abertura *f*

apex /'eɪpeks/ *n* ápice *m*

aphorism /'æfərɪzəm/ *n* aforismo *m*

aphrodisiac /æfrə'dɪzɪæk/ *a & n* afrodisíaco (*m*), afrodisiaco (*m*)

apiece /ə'pi:s/ *adv* cada uno

aplomb /ə'plɒm/ *n* aplomo *m*

apolog|etic /əpɒlə'dʒetɪk/ *a* lleno de disculpas. **be ~etic** disculparse. **~ize** /ə'pɒlədʒaɪz/ *vi* disculparse (**for** de). **~y** /ə'pɒlədʒɪ/ *n* disculpa *f*; (*poor specimen*) birria *f*

apople|ctic /æpə'plektɪk/ *a* apoplético. **~xy** /'æpəpleksɪ/ *n* apoplejía *f*

apostle /ə'pɒsl/ *n* apóstol *m*

apostrophe /ə'pɒstrəfɪ/ *n* (*punctuation mark*) apóstrofo *m*

appal /ə'pɔ:l/ *vt* (*pt* **appalled**) horrorizar. **~ling** *a* espantoso

apparatus /æpə'reɪtəs/ *n* aparato *m*

apparel /ə'pærəl/ *n* ropa *f*, indumentaria *f*

apparent /ə'pærənt/ *a* aparente; (*clear*) evidente. **~ly** *adv* por lo visto

apparition /æpə'rɪʃn/ *n* aparición *f*

appeal /ə'pi:l/ *vi* apelar; (*attract*) atraer. ● *n* llamamiento *m*; (*attraction*) atractivo *m*; (*jurid*) apelación *f*. **~ing** *a* atrayente

appear /ə'pɪə(r)/ *vi* aparecer; (*arrive*) llegar; (*seem*) parecer; (*on stage*) actuar. **~ance** *n* aparición *f*; (*aspect*) aspecto *m*

appease /ə'pi:z/ *vt* aplacar; (*pacify*) apaciguar

append /ə'pend/ *vt* adjuntar. **~age** /ə'pendɪdʒ/ *n* añadidura *f*

appendicitis /əpendɪ'saɪtɪs/ *n* apendicitis *f*

appendix /ə'pendɪks/ *n* (*pl* **-ices** /-si:z/) (*of book*) apéndice *m*. (*pl* **-ixes**) (*anat*) apéndice *m*

appertain /æpə'teɪn/ *vi* relacionarse (**to** con)

appetite /'æpɪtaɪt/ *n* apetito *m*

appetiz|er /'æpɪtaɪzə(r)/ *n* aperitivo *m*. **~ing** *a* apetitoso

applau|d /ə'plɔ:d/ *vt/i* aplaudir. **~se** *n* aplausos *mpl*

apple /'æpl/ *n* manzana *f*. **~-tree** *n* manzano *m*

appliance /ə'plaɪəns/ *n* aparato *m*. **electrical ~** electrodoméstico *m*

applicable /'æplɪkəbl/ *a* aplicable; (*relevant*) pertinente

applicant /'æplɪkənt/ *n* candidato *m*, solicitante *m & f*

application /æplɪ'keɪʃn/ *n* aplicación *f*; (*request*) solicitud *f*. **~ form** formulario *m* (de solicitud)

appl|ied /ə'plaɪd/ *a* aplicado. **~y** /ə'plaɪ/ *vt* aplicar. ● *vi* aplicarse; (*ask*) dirigirse. **~y for** solicitar ‹*job etc*›

appoint /ə'pɔɪnt/ *vt* nombrar; (*fix*) señalar. **~ment** *n* cita *f*; (*job*) empleo *m*

apportion /ə'pɔ:ʃn/ *vt* repartir

apposite /'æpəzɪt/ *a* apropiado

apprais|al /ə'preɪzl/ *n* evaluación *f*. **~e** *vt* evaluar

appreciable /ə'pri:ʃəbl/ *a* sensible; (*considerable*) considerable

appreciat|e /ə'pri:ʃɪeɪt/ *vt* apreciar; (*understand*) comprender; (*be grateful for*) agradecer. ● *vi* (*increase value*) aumentar en valor. **~ion** /-'eɪʃn/ *n* aprecio *m*; (*gratitude*) agradecimiento *m*. **~ive** /ə'pri:ʃɪətɪv/ *a* (*grateful*) agradecido

apprehen|d /æprɪ'hend/ *vt* detener; (*understand*) comprender. **~sion** /-ʃn/ *n* detención *f*; (*fear*) recelo *m*

apprehensive /æprɪ'hensɪv/ *a* aprensivo

apprentice /ə'prentɪs/ *n* aprendiz *m*. ● *vt* poner de aprendiz. **~ship** *n* aprendizaje *m*

approach /ə'prəʊtʃ/ *vt* acercarse a. ● *vi* acercarse. ● *n* acercamiento *m*; (*to problem*) enfoque *m*; (*access*) acceso *m*. **make ~es to** dirigirse a. **~able** *a* accesible

approbation /æprə'beɪʃn/ *n* aprobación *f*

appropriate /ə'prəʊprɪət/ *a* apropiado. /ə'prəʊprɪeɪt/ *vt* apropiarse de. **~ly** *adv* apropiadamente

approval /ə'pru:vl/ *n* aprobación *f*. **on ~** a prueba

approv|e /ə'pru:v/ *vt/i* aprobar. **~ingly** *adv* con aprobación

approximat|e /ə'prɒksɪmət/ *a* aproximado. /ə'prɒksɪmeɪt/ *vt* aproximarse a. **~ely** *adv* aproximadamente. **~ion** /-'meɪʃn/ *n* aproximación *f*

apricot /'eɪprɪkɒt/ *n* albaricoque *m*, chabacano *m* (*Mex*). **~-tree** *n* albaricoquero *m*, chabacano *m* (*Mex*)

April /'eɪprəl/ *n* abril *m*. **~ fool!** ¡inocentón!

apron /'eɪprən/ *n* delantal *m*

apropos /'æprəpəʊ/ *adv* a propósito

apse /æps/ *n* ábside *m*

apt /æpt/ *a* apropiado; ‹*pupil*› listo. **be ~ to** tener tendencia a

aptitude /'æptɪtju:d/ *n* aptitud *f*

aptly /'æptlɪ/ *adv* acertadamente

aqualung /'ækwəlʌŋ/ *n* pulmón *m* acuático

aquarium /ə'kweərɪəm/ *n* (*pl* **-ums**) acuario *m*

Aquarius /ə'kweərɪəs/ *n* Acuario *m*

aquatic /ə'kwætɪk/ *a* acuático

aqueduct /'ækwɪdʌkt/ *n* acueducto *m*

aquiline /'ækwɪlaɪn/ *a* aquilino

Arab /'ærəb/ *a & n* árabe *m*. **~ian** /ə'reɪbɪən/ *a* árabe. **~ic** /'ærəbɪk/ *a & n* árabe (*m*). **~ic numerals** números *mpl* arábigos

arable /'ærəbl/ *a* cultivable

arbiter /'ɑ:bɪtə(r)/ *n* árbitro *m*

arbitrary /'ɑ:bɪtrərɪ/ *a* arbitrario

arbitrat|e /'ɑ:bɪtreɪt/ *vi* arbitrar. **~ion** /-'treɪʃn/ *n* arbitraje *m*. **~or** *n* árbitro *m*

arc /ɑ:k/ *n* arco *m*

arcade /ɑ:'keɪd/ *n* arcada f; (*around square*) soportales *mpl*; (*shops*)

galería *f*. **amusement ~** galería *f* de atracciones
arcane /ɑ:'keɪn/ *a* misterioso
arch[1] /ɑ:tʃ/ *n* arco *m*. ● *vt* arquear. ● *vi* arquearse
arch[2] /ɑ:tʃ/ *a* malicioso
archaeolog|ical /ɑ:kɪə'lɒdʒɪkl/ *a* arqueológico. **~ist** /ɑ:kɪ'ɒlədʒist/ *n* arqueólogo *m*. **~y** /ɑ:kɪ'ɒlədʒɪ/ *n* arqueología *f*
archaic /ɑ:'keɪɪk/ *a* arcaico
archbishop /ɑ:tʃ'bɪʃəp/ *n* arzobispo *m*
arch-enemy /ɑ:tʃ'enəmɪ/ *n* enemigo *m* jurado
archer /'ɑ:tʃə(r)/ *n* arquero *m*. **~y** *n* tiro *m* al arco
archetype /'ɑ:kɪtaɪp/ *n* arquetipo *m*
archipelago /ɑ:kɪ'peləgəʊ/ *n* (*pl* **-os**) archipiélago *m*
architect /'ɑ:kɪtekt/ *n* arquitecto *m*. **~ure** /'ɑ:kɪtektʃə(r)/ *n* arquitectura *f*. **~ural** /-'tektʃərəl/ *a* arquitectónico
archiv|es /'ɑ:kaɪvz/ *npl* archivo *m*. **~ist** /-ɪvɪst/ *n* archivero *m*
archway /'ɑ:tʃweɪ/ *n* arco *m*
Arctic /'ɑ:ktɪk/ *a* ártico. ● *n* Ártico *m*
arctic /'ɑ:ktɪk/ *a* glacial
ardent /'ɑ:dənt/ *a* ardiente, fervoroso, apasionado. **~ly** *adv* ardientemente
ardour /'ɑ:də(r)/ *n* ardor *m*, fervor *m*, pasión *f*
arduous /'ɑ:djʊəs/ *a* arduo
are /ɑ:(r)/ *see* **be**
area /'eərɪə/ *n* (*surface*) superficie *f*; (*region*) zona *f*; (*fig*) campo *m*
arena /ə'ri:nə/ *n* arena *f*; (*in circus*) pista *f*; (*in bullring*) ruedo *m*
aren't /ɑ:nt/ = **are not**
Argentin|a /ɑ:dʒən'ti:nə/ *n* Argentina *f*. **~ian** /-'tɪnɪən/ *a* & *n* argentino (*m*)
arguable /'ɑ:gjʊəbl/ *a* discutible
argue /'ɑ:gju:/ *vi* discutir; (*reason*) razonar
argument /'ɑ:gjʊmənt/ *n* disputa *f*; (*reasoning*) argumento *m*. **~ative** /-'mentətɪv/ *a* discutidor
arid /'ærɪd/ *a* árido
Aries /'eəri:z/ *n* Aries *m*
arise /ə'raɪz/ *vi* (*pt* **arose**, *pp* **arisen**) levantarse; (*fig*) surgir. **~ from** resultar de
aristocra|cy /ærɪ'stɒkrəsɪ/ *n* aristocracia *f*. **~t** /'ærɪstəkræt/ *n* aristócrata *m* & *f*. **~tic** /-'krætɪk/ *a* aristocrático
arithmetic /ə'rɪθmətɪk/ *n* aritmética *f*
ark /ɑ:k/ *n* (*relig*) arca *f*
arm[1] /ɑ:m/ *n* brazo *m*. **~ in ~** cogidos del brazo
arm[2] /ɑ:m/ *n*. **~s** *npl* armas *fpl*. ● *vt* armar
armada /ɑ:'mɑ:də/ *n* armada *f*
armament /'ɑ:məmənt/ *n* armamento *m*
armchair /'ɑ:mtʃeə(r)/ *n* sillón *m*
armed robbery /ɑ:md'rɒbərɪ/ *n* robo *m* a mano armada
armful /'ɑ:mfʊl/ *n* brazada *f*
armistice /'ɑ:mɪstɪs/ *n* armisticio *m*
armlet /'ɑ:mlɪt/ *n* brazalete *m*
armour /'ɑ:mə(r)/ *n* armadura *f*. **~ed** *a* blindado
armoury /'ɑ:mərɪ/ *n* arsenal *m*
armpit /'ɑ:mpɪt/ *n* sobaco *m*, axila *f*
army /'ɑ:mɪ/ *n* ejército *m*
aroma /ə'rəʊmə/ *n* aroma *m*. **~tic** /ærə'mætɪk/ *a* aromático
arose /ə'rəʊz/ *see* **arise**
around /ə'raʊnd/ *adv* alrededor; (*near*) cerca. **all ~** por todas partes. ● *prep* alrededor de; (*with time*) a eso de
arouse /ə'raʊz/ *vt* despertar
arpeggio /ɑ:'pedʒɪəʊ/ *n* arpegio *m*
arrange /ə'reɪndʒ/ *vt* arreglar; (*fix*) fijar. **~ment** *n* arreglo *m*; (*agreement*) acuerdo *m*; (*pl*, *plans*) preparativos *mpl*
array /ə'reɪ/ *vt* (*dress*) ataviar; (*mil*) formar. ● *n* atavío *m*; (*mil*) orden *m*; (*fig*) colección *f*, conjunto *m*
arrears /ə'rɪəz/ *npl* atrasos *mpl*. **in ~** atrasado en pagos
arrest /ə'rest/ *vt* detener; llamar ‹*attention*›. ● *n* detención *f*. **under ~** detenido
arriv|al /ə'raɪvl/ *n* llegada *f*. **new ~al** recien llegado *m*. **~e** /ə'raɪv/ *vi* llegar
arrogan|ce /'ærəgəns/ *n* arrogancia *f*. **~t** *a* arrogante. **~tly** *adv* con arrogancia
arrow /'ærəʊ/ *n* flecha *f*
arsenal /'ɑ:sənl/ *n* arsenal *m*
arsenic /'ɑ:snɪk/ *n* arsénico *m*
arson /'ɑ:sn/ *n* incendio *m* provocado. **~ist** *n* incendiario *m*
art[1] /ɑ:t/ *n* arte *m*. **A~s** *npl* (*Univ*) Filosofía y Letras *fpl*. **fine ~s** bellas artes *fpl*
art[2] /ɑ:t/ (*old use, with* **thou**) = **are**
artefact /'ɑ:tɪfækt/ *n* artefacto *m*
arterial /ɑ:'tɪərɪəl/ *a* arterial. **~ road** *n* carretera *f* nacional
artery /'ɑ:tərɪ/ *n* arteria *f*

artesian /ɑ:'ti:zjən/ *a*. ~ **well** pozo *m* artesiano

artful /'ɑ:tfʊl/ *a* astuto. ~**ness** *n* astucia *f*

art gallery /'ɑ:tgælərɪ/ *n* museo *m* de pinturas, pinacoteca *f*, galería *f* de arte

arthriti|c /ɑ:'θrɪtɪk/ *a* artrítico. ~**s** /ɑ:'θraɪtɪs/ *n* artritis *f*

artichoke /'ɑ:tɪtʃəʊk/ *n* alcachofa *f*. **Jerusalem** ~ pataca *f*

article /'ɑ:tɪkl/ *n* artículo *m*. ~ **of clothing** prenda *f* de vestir. **leading** ~ artículo de fondo

articulat|e /ɑ:'tɪkjʊlət/ *a* articulado; ‹*person*› elocuente. /ɑ:'tɪkjʊleɪt/ *vt/i* articular. ~**ed lorry** *n* camión *m* con remolque. ~**ion** /-'leɪʃn/ *n* articulación *f*

artifice /'ɑ:tɪfɪs/ *n* artificio *m*

artificial /ɑ:tɪ'fɪʃl/ *a* artificial; ‹*hair etc*› postizo

artillery /ɑ:'tɪlərɪ/ *n* artillería *f*

artisan /ɑ:tɪ'zæn/ *n* artesano *m*

artist /'ɑ:tɪst/ *n* artista *m & f*

artiste /ɑ:'ti:st/ *n* (*in theatre*) artista *m & f*

artist|ic /ɑ:'tɪstɪk/ *a* artístico. ~**ry** *n* arte *m*, habilidad *f*

artless /'ɑ:tlɪs/ *a* ingenuo

arty /'ɑ:tɪ/ *a* (*fam*) que se las da de artista

as /æz, əz/ *adv & conj* como; (*since*) ya que; (*while*) mientras. ~ **big** ~ tan grande como. ~ **far** ~ (*distance*) hasta; (*qualitative*) en cuanto a. ~ **far** ~ **I know** que yo sepa. ~ **if** como si. ~ **long** ~ mientras. ~ **much** ~ tanto como. ~ **soon** ~ tan pronto como. ~ **well** también

asbestos /æz'bestɒs/ *n* amianto *m*, asbesto *m*

ascen|d /ə'send/ *vt/i* subir. ~**t** /ə'sent/ *n* subida *f*

ascertain /æsə'teɪn/ *vt* averiguar

ascetic /ə'setɪk/ *a* ascético. ● *n* asceta *m & f*

ascribe /ə'skraɪb/ *vt* atribuir

ash[1] /æʃ/ *n* ceniza *f*

ash[2] /æʃ/ *n*. ~**(-tree)** fresno *m*

ashamed /ə'ʃeɪmd/ *a* avergonzado. **be** ~ avergonzarse

ashen /'æʃn/ *a* ceniciento

ashore /ə'ʃɔ:(r)/ *adv* a tierra. **go** ~ desembarcar

ash: ~**tray** /'æʃtreɪ/ *n* cenicero *m*. **A**~ **Wednesday** *n* Miércoles *m* de Ceniza

Asia /'eɪʃə/ *n* Asia *f*. ~**n** *a & n* asiático (*m*). ~**tic** /-ɪ'ætɪk/ *a* asiático

aside /ə'saɪd/ *adv* a un lado. ● *n* (*in theatre*) aparte *m*

asinine /'æsɪnaɪn/ *a* estúpido

ask /ɑ:sk/ *vt* pedir; preguntar ‹*question*›; (*invite*) invitar. ~ **about** enterarse de. ~ **after** pedir noticias de. ~ **for help** pedir ayuda. ~ **for trouble** buscarse problemas. ~ **s.o. in** invitar a uno a pasar

askance /ə'skæns/ *adv*. **look** ~ **at** mirar de soslayo

askew /ə'skju:/ *adv & a* ladeado

asleep /ə'sli:p/ *adv & a* dormido. **fall** ~ dormirse, quedar dormido

asparagus /ə'spærəgəs/ *n* espárrago *m*

aspect /'æspekt/ *n* aspecto *m*; (*of house etc*) orientación *f*

aspersions /ə'spɜ:ʃnz/ *npl*. **cast** ~ **on** difamar

asphalt /'æsfælt/ *n* asfalto *m*. ● *vt* asfaltar

asphyxia /æs'fɪksɪə/ *n* asfixia *f*. ~**te** /əs'fɪksɪeɪt/ *vt* asfixiar. ~**tion** /-'eɪʃn/ *n* asfixia *f*

aspic /'æspɪk/ *n* gelatina *f*

aspir|ation /æspə'reɪʃn/ *n* aspiración *f*. ~**e** /əs'paɪə(r)/ *vi* aspirar

aspirin /'æsprɪn/ *n* aspirina *f*

ass /æs/ *n* asno *m*; (*fig, fam*) imbécil *m*

assail /ə'seɪl/ *vt* asaltar. ~**ant** *n* asaltador *m*

assassin /ə'sæsɪn/ *n* asesino *m*. ~**ate** /ə'sæsɪneɪt/ *vt* asesinar. ~**ation** /-'eɪʃn/ *n* asesinato *m*

assault /ə'sɔ:lt/ *n* (*mil*) ataque *m*; (*jurid*) atentado *m*. ● *vt* asaltar

assemblage /ə'semblɪdʒ/ *n* (*of things*) colección *f*; (*of people*) reunión *f*; (*mec*) montaje *m*

assemble /ə'sembl/ *vt* reunir; (*mec*) montar. ● *vi* reunirse

assembly /ə'semblɪ/ *n* reunión *f*; (*pol etc*) asamblea *f*. ~ **line** *n* línea *f* de montaje

assent /ə'sent/ *n* asentimiento *m*. ● *vi* asentir

assert /ə'sɜ:t/ *vt* afirmar; hacer valer ‹*one's rights*›. ~**ion** /-ʃn/ *n* afirmación *f*. ~**ive** *a* positivo, firme

assess /ə'ses/ *vt* valorar; (*determine*) determinar; fijar ‹*tax etc*›. ~**ment** *n* valoración *f*

asset /'æset/ *n* (*advantage*) ventaja *f*; (*pl, com*) bienes *mpl*

assiduous /ə'sɪdjʊəs/ *a* asiduo

assign /ə'saɪn/ *vt* asignar; (appoint) nombrar
assignation /æsɪg'neɪʃn/ *n* asignación *f*; (*meeting*) cita *f*
assignment /ə'saɪnmənt/ *n* asignación *f*, misión *f*; (*task*) tarea *f*
assimilat|e /ə'sɪmɪleɪt/ *vt* asimilar. ● *vi* asimilarse. **~ion** /-'eɪʃn/ *n* asimilación *f*
assist /ə'sɪst/ *vt/i* ayudar. **~ance** *n* ayuda *f*. **~ant** /ə'sɪstənt/ *n* ayudante *m & f*; (*shop*) dependienta *f*, dependiente *m*. ● *a* auxiliar, adjunto
associat|e /ə'səʊʃɪeɪt/ *vt* asociar. ● *vi* asociarse. /ə'səʊʃɪət/ *a* asociado. ● *n* colega *m & f*; (*com*) socio *m*. **~ion** /-'eɪʃn/ *n* asociación *f*. **A~ion football** *n* fútbol *m*
assort|ed /ə'sɔ:tɪd/ *a* surtido. **~ment** *n* surtido *m*
assume /ə'sju:m/ *vt* suponer; tomar ‹*power, attitude*›; asumir ‹*role, burden*›
assumption /ə'sʌmpʃn/ *n* suposición *f*. **the A~** la Asunción *f*
assur|ance /ə'ʃʊərəns/ *n* seguridad *f*; (*insurance*) seguro *m*. **~e** /ə'ʃʊə(r)/ *vt* asegurar. **~ed** *a* seguro. **~edly** /-rɪdlɪ/ *adv* seguramente
asterisk /'æstərɪsk/ *n* asterisco *m*
astern /ə'stɜ:n/ *adv* a popa
asthma /'æsmə/ *n* asma *f*. **~tic** /-'mætɪk/ *a & n* asmático (*m*)
astonish /ə'stɒnɪʃ/ *vt* asombrar. **~ing** *a* asombroso. **~ment** *n* asombro *m*
astound /ə'staʊnd/ *vt* asombrar
astray /ə'streɪ/ *adv & a*. **go ~** extraviarse. **lead ~** llevar por mal camino
astride /ə'straɪd/ *adv* a horcajadas. ● *prep* a horcajadas sobre
astringent /ə'strɪndʒənt/ *a* astringente; (*fig*) austero. ● *n* astringente *m*
astrolog|er /ə'strɒlədʒə(r)/ *n* astrólogo *m*. **~y** *n* astrología *f*
astronaut /'æstrənɔ:t/ *n* astronauta *m & f*
astronom|er /ə'strɒnəmə(r)/ *n* astrónomo *m*. **~ical** /æstrə'nɒmɪkl/ *a* astronómico. **~y** /ə'strɒnəmɪ/ *n* astronomía *f*
astute /ə'stju:t/ *a* astuto. **~ness** *n* astucia *f*
asunder /ə'sʌndə(r)/ *adv* en pedazos; (*in two*) en dos
asylum /ə'saɪləm/ *n* asilo *m*. **lunatic ~** manicomio *m*
at /ət, æt/ *prep* a. **~ home** en casa. **~ night** por la noche. **~ Robert's** en casa de Roberto. **~ once** en seguida; (*simultaneously*) a la vez. **~ sea** en el mar. **~ the station** en la estación. **~ times** a veces. **not ~ all** nada; (*after thanks*) ¡de nada!
ate /et/ *see* **eat**
atheis|m /'əɪθɪzəm/ *n* ateísmo *m*. **~t** /'əɪθɪɪst/ *n* ateo *m*
athlet|e /'æθli:t/ *n* atleta *m & f*. **~ic** /-'letɪk/ *a* atlético. **~ics** /-'letɪks/ *npl* atletismo *m*
Atlantic /ət'læntɪk/ *a & n* atlántico (*m*). ● *n*. **~ (Ocean)** (Océano *m*) Atlántico *m*
atlas /'ætləs/ *n* atlas *m*
atmospher|e /'ætməsfɪə(r)/ *n* atmósfera *f*; (*fig*) ambiente *m*. **~ic** /-'ferɪk/ *a* atmosférico. **~ics** /-'ferɪks/ *npl* parásitos *mpl*
atom /'ætəm/ *n* átomo *m*. **~ic** /ə'tɒmɪk/ *a* atómico
atomize /'ætəmaɪz/ *vt* atomizar. **~r** /'ætəmaɪzə(r)/ *n* atomizador *m*
atone /ə'təʊn/ *vi*. **~ for** expiar. **~ment** *n* expiación *f*
atroci|ous /ə'trəʊʃəs/ *a* atroz. **~ty** /ə'trɒsətɪ/ *n* atrocidad *f*
atrophy /'ætrəfɪ/ *n* atrofia *f*
attach /ə'tætʃ/ *vt* sujetar; adjuntar ‹*document etc*›. **be ~ed to** (*be fond of*) tener cariño a
attaché /ə'tæʃeɪ/ *n* agregado *m*. **~ case** maletín *m*
attachment /ə'tætʃmənt/ *n* (*affection*) cariño *m*; (*tool*) accesorio *m*
attack /ə'tæk/ *n* ataque *m*. ● *vt/i* atacar. **~er** *n* agresor *m*
attain /ə'teɪn/ *vt* conseguir. **~able** *a* alcanzable. **~ment** *n* logro *m*. **~ments** *npl* conocimientos *mpl*, talento *m*
attempt /ə'tempt/ *vt* intentar. ● *n* tentativa *f*; (*attack*) atentado *m*
attend /ə'tend/ *vt* asistir a; (*escort*) acompañar. ● *vi* prestar atención. **~ to** (*look after*) ocuparse de. **~ance** *n* asistencia *f*; (*people present*) concurrencia *f*. **~ant** /ə'tendənt/ *a* concomitante. ● *n* encargado *m*; (*servant*) sirviente *m*
attention /ə'tenʃn/ *n* atención *f*. **~!** (*mil*) ¡firmes! **pay ~** prestar atención
attentive /ə'tentɪv/ *a* atento. **~ness** *n* atención *f*
attenuate /ə'tenjʊeɪt/ *vt* atenuar

attest /ə'test/ *vt* atestiguar. ● *vi* dar testimonio. **~ation** /æte'steɪʃn/ *n* testimonio *m*
attic /'ætɪk/ *n* desván *m*
attire /ə'taɪə(r)/ *n* atavío *m*. ● *vt* vestir
attitude /'ætɪtju:d/ *n* postura *f*
attorney /ə'tɜ:nɪ/ *n* (*pl* **-eys**) apoderado *m*; (*Amer*) abogado *m*
attract /ə'trækt/ *vt* atraer. **~ion** /-ʃn/ *n* atracción *f*; (*charm*) atractivo *m*
attractive /ə'træktɪv/ *a* atractivo; (*interesting*) atrayente. **~ness** *n* atractivo *m*
attribute /ə'trɪbju:t/ *vt* atribuir. /'ætrɪbju:t/ *n* atributo *m*
attrition /ə'trɪʃn/ *n* desgaste *m*
aubergine /'əʊbəʒi:n/ *n* berenjena *f*
auburn /'ɔ:bən/ *a* castaño
auction /'ɔ:kʃn/ *n* subasta *f*. ● *vt* subastar. **~eer** /-ə'nɪə(r)/ *n* subastador *m*
audaci|ous /ɔ:'deɪʃəs/ *a* audaz. **~ty** /-æsətɪ/ *n* audacia *f*
audible /'ɔ:dəbl/ *a* audible
audience /'ɔ:dɪəns/ *n* (*interview*) audiencia *f*; (*teatro*, *radio*) público *m*
audio-visual /ɔ:dɪəʊ'vɪʒʊəl/ *a* audiovisual
audit /'ɔ:dɪt/ *n* revisión *f* de cuentas. ● *vt* revisar
audition /ɔ:'dɪʃn/ *n* audición *f*. ● *vt* dar audición a
auditor /'ɔ:dɪtə(r)/ *n* interventor *m* de cuentas
auditorium /ɔ:dɪ'tɔ:rɪəm/ *n* sala *f*, auditorio *m*
augment /ɔ:g'ment/ *vt* aumentar
augur /'ɔ:gə(r)/ *vt* augurar. **it ~s well** es de buen agüero
august /ɔ:'gʌst/ *a* augusto
August /'ɔ:gəst/ *n* agosto *m*
aunt /ɑ:nt/ *n* tía *f*
au pair /əʊ'peə(r)/ *n* chica *f* au pair
aura /'ɔ:rə/ *n* atmósfera *f*, halo *m*
auspices /'ɔ:spɪsɪz/ *npl* auspicios *mpl*
auspicious /ɔ:'spɪʃəs/ *a* propicio
auster|e /ɔ:'stɪə(r)/ *a* austero. **~ity** /-erətɪ/ *n* austeridad *f*
Australia /ɒ'streɪlɪə/ *n* Australia *f*. **~n** *a & n* australiano (*m*)
Austria /'ɒstrɪə/ *n* Austria *f*. **~n** *a & n* austríaco (*m*)
authentic /ɔ:'θentɪk/ *a* auténtico. **~ate** /ɔ:'θentɪkeɪt/ *vt* autenticar. **~ity** /-ən'tɪsətɪ/ *n* autenticidad *f*
author /'ɔ:θə(r)/ *n* autor *m*. **~ess** *n* autora *f*
authoritarian /ɔ:θɒrɪ'teərɪən/ *a* autoritario
authoritative /ɔ:'θɒrɪtətɪv/ *a* autorizado; (*manner*) autoritario
authority /ɔ:'θɒrətɪ/ *n* autoridad *f*; (*permission*) autorización *f*
authoriz|ation /ɔ:θəraɪ'zeɪʃn/ *n* autorización *f*. **~e** /'ɔ:θəraɪz/ *vt* autorizar
authorship /'ɔ:θəʃɪp/ *n* profesión *f* de autor; (*origin*) paternidad *f* literaria
autistic /ɔ:'tɪstɪk/ *a* autista
autobiography /ɔ:təʊbaɪ'ɒgrəfɪ/ *n* autobiografía *f*
autocra|cy /ɔ:'tɒkrəsɪ/ *n* autocracia *f*. **~t** /'ɔ:təkræt/ *n* autócrata *m & f*. **~tic** /-'krætɪk/ *a* autocrático
autograph /'ɔ:təgrɑ:f/ *n* autógrafo *m*. ● *vt* firmar
automat|e /'ɔ:təmeɪt/ *vt* automatizar. **~ic** /ɔ:tə'mætɪk/ *a* automático. **~ion** /-'meɪʃn/ *n* automatización *f*. **~on** /ɔ:'tɒmətən/ *n* autómata *m*
automobile /'ɔ:təməbi:l/ *n* (*Amer*) coche *m*, automóvil *m*
autonom|ous /ɔ:'tɒnəməs/ *a* autónomo. **~y** *n* autonomía *f*
autopsy /'ɔ:tɒpsɪ/ *n* autopsia *f*
autumn /'ɔ:təm/ *n* otoño *m*. **~al** /-'tʌmnəl/ *a* de otoño, otoñal
auxiliary /ɔ:g'zɪlɪərɪ/ *a* auxiliar. ● *n* asistente *m*; (*verb*) verbo *m* auxiliar; (*pl*, *troops*) tropas *fpl* auxiliares
avail /ə'veɪl/ *vt/i* servir. **~ o.s. of** aprovecharse de. ● *n* ventaja *f*. **to no ~** inútil
availab|ility /əveɪlə'bɪlətɪ/ *n* disponibilidad *f*. **~le** /ə'veɪləbl/ *a* disponible
avalanche /'ævəlɑ:nʃ/ *n* avalancha *f*
avaric|e /'ævərɪs/ *n* avaricia *f*. **~ious** /-'rɪʃəs/ *a* avaro
avenge /ə'vendʒ/ *vt* vengar
avenue /'ævənju:/ *n* avenida *f*; (*fig*) vía *f*
average /'ævərɪdʒ/ *n* promedio *m*. **on ~** por término medio. ● *a* medio. ● *vt* calcular el promedio de. ● *vi* alcanzar un promedio de
avers|e /ə'vɜ:s/ *a* enemigo (**to** de). **be ~e to** sentir repugnancia por, no gustarle. **~ion** /-ʃn/ *n* repugnancia *f*

avert /ə'vɜ:t/ *vt* (*turn away*) apartar; (*ward off*) desviar

aviary /'eɪvɪərɪ/ *n* pajarera *f*

aviation /eɪvɪ'eɪʃn/ *n* aviación *f*

aviator /'eɪvɪeɪtə(r)/ *n* (*old use*) aviador *m*

avid /'ævɪd/ *a* ávido. **~ity** /-'vɪdətɪ/ *n* avidez *f*

avocado /ævə'kɑ:dəʊ/ *n* (*pl* **-os**) aguacate *m*

avoid /ə'vɔɪd/ *vt* evitar. **~able** *a* evitable. **~ance** *n* el evitar *m*

avuncular /ə'vʌŋkjʊlə(r)/ *a* de tío

await /ə'weɪt/ *vt* esperar

awake /ə'weɪk/ *vt/i* (*pt* **awoke**, *pp* **awoken**) despertar. ● *a* despierto. **wide ~** completamente despierto; (*fig*) despabilado. **~n** /ə'weɪkən/ *vt/i* despertar. **~ning** *n* el despertar *m*

award /ə'wɔ:d/ *vt* otorgar; (*jurid*) adjudicar. ● *n* premio *m*; (*jurid*) adjudicación *f*; (*scholarship*) beca *f*

aware /ə'weə(r)/ *a* consciente. **are you ~ that?** ¿te das cuenta de que? **~ness** *n* conciencia *f*

awash /ə'wɒʃ/ *a* inundado

away /ə'weɪ/ *adv* (*absent*) fuera; (*far*) lejos; (*persistently*) sin parar. ● *a & n*. **~ (match)** partido *m* fuera de casa

awe /ɔ:/ *n* temor *m*. **~some** *a* imponente. **~struck** *a* atemorizado

awful /'ɔ:fʊl/ *a* terrible, malísimo. **~ly** *adv* terriblemente

awhile /ə'waɪl/ *adv* un rato

awkward /'ɔ:kwəd/ *a* difícil; (*inconvenient*) inoportuno; (*clumsy*) desmañado; (*embarrassed*) incómodo. **~ly** *adv* con dificultad; (*clumsily*) de manera torpe. **~ness** *n* dificultad *f*; (*discomfort*) molestia *f*; (*clumsiness*) torpeza *f*

awning /'ɔ:nɪŋ/ *n* toldo *m*

awoke, awoken /ə'wəʊk, ə'wəʊkən/ *see* **awake**

awry /ə'raɪ/ *adv & a* ladeado. **go ~** salir mal

axe /æks/ *n* hacha *f*. ● *vt* (*pres p* **axing**) cortar con hacha; (*fig*) recortar

axiom /'æksɪəm/ *n* axioma *m*

axis /'æksɪs/ *n* (*pl* **axes** /-i:z/) eje *m*

axle /'æksl/ *n* eje *m*

ay(e) /aɪ/ *adv & n* sí (*m*)

B

BA *abbr see* **bachelor**

babble /'bæbl/ *vi* balbucir; (*chatter*) parlotear; (*of stream*) murmullar. ● *n* balbuceo *m*; (*chatter*) parloteo *m*; (*of stream*) murmullo *m*

baboon /bə'bu:n/ *n* mandril *m*

baby /'beɪbɪ/ *n* niño *m*, bebé *m*; (*Amer*, *sl*) chica *f*. **~ish** /'beɪbɪɪʃ/ *a* infantil. **~-sit** *vi* cuidar a los niños, hacer de canguro. **~sitter** *n* persona *f* que cuida a los niños, canguro *m*

bachelor /'bætʃələ(r)/ *n* soltero *m*. **B~ of Arts (BA)** licenciado *m* en filosofía y letras. **B~ of Science (BSc)** licenciado *m* en ciencias

back /bæk/ *n* espalda *f*; (*of car*) parte *f* trasera; (*of chair*) respaldo *m*; (*of cloth*) revés *m*; (*of house*) parte *f* de atrás; (*of animal, book*) lomo *m*; (*of hand, document*) dorso *m*; (*football*) defensa *m & f*. **~ of beyond** en el quinto pino. ● *a* trasero; (*taxes*) atrasado. ● *adv* atrás; (*returned*) de vuelta. ● *vt* apoyar; (*betting*) apostar a; dar marcha atrás a ‹*car*›. ● *vi* retroceder; ‹*car*› dar marcha atrás. **~ down** *vi* volverse atrás. **~ out** *vi* retirarse. **~ up** *vi* (*auto*) retroceder. **~ache** /'bækeɪk/ *n* dolor *m* de espalda. **~-bencher** *n* (*pol*) diputado *m* sin poder ministerial. **~biting** /'bækbaɪtɪŋ/ *n* maledicencia *f*. **~bone** /'bækbəʊn/ *n* columna *f* vertebral; (*fig*) pilar *m*. **~chat** /'bæktʃæt/ *n* impertinencias *fpl*. **~date** /bæk'deɪt/ *vt* antedatar. **~er** /'bækə(r)/ *n* partidario *m*; (*com*) financiador *m*. **~fire** /bæk'faɪə(r)/ *vi* (*auto*) petardear; (*fig*) fallar, salir el tiro por la culata. **~gammon** /bæk'gæmən/ *n* backgamon *m*. **~ground** /'bækgraʊnd/ *n* fondo *m*; (*environment*) antecedentes *mpl*. **~hand** /'bækhænd/ *n* (*sport*) revés *m*. **~handed** *a* dado con el dorso de la mano; (*fig*) equívoco, ambiguo. **~hander** *n* (*sport*) revés *m*; (*fig*) ataque *m* indirecto; (*bribe, sl*) soborno *m*. **~ing** /'bækɪŋ/ *n* apoyo *m*. **~lash** /'bæklæʃ/ *n* reacción *f*. **~log** /'bæklɒg/ *n* atrasos *mpl*. **~side** /bæk'saɪd/ *n* (*fam*) trasero *m*. **~stage** /bæk'steɪdʒ/ *a* de bastidores. ● *adv* entre bastidores. **~stroke** /'bækstrəʊk/ *n* (*tennis etc*) revés *m*; (*swimming*) braza *f* de espaldas. **~-up** *n* apoyo *m*. **~ward** /'bækwəd/ *a* ‹*step etc*› hacia atrás;

(*retarded*) atrasado. **~wards** /'bækwədz/ *adv* hacia atrás; (*fall*) de espaldas; (*back to front*) al revés. **go ~wards and forwards** ir de acá para allá. **~water** /'bækwɔ:tə(r)/ *n* agua *f* estancada; (*fig*) lugar *m* apartado

bacon /'beɪkən/ *n* tocino *m*

bacteria /bæk'tɪərɪə/ *npl* bacterias *fpl*. **~l** *a* bacteriano

bad /bæd/ *a* (**worse**, **worst**) malo; (*serious*) grave; (*harmful*) nocivo; ‹*language*› indecente. **feel ~** sentirse mal

bade /beɪd/ *see* **bid**

badge /bædʒ/ *n* distintivo *m*, chapa *f*

badger /'bædʒə(r)/ *n* tejón *m*. ● *vt* acosar

bad: **~ly** *adv* mal. **want ~ly** desear muchísimo. **~ly off** mal de dinero. **~-mannered** *a* mal educado

badminton /'bædmɪntən/ *n* bádminton *m*

bad-tempered /bæd'tempəd/ *a* (*always*) de mal genio; (*temporarily*) de mal humor

baffle /'bæfl/ *vt* desconcertar

bag /bæg/ *n* bolsa *f*; (*handbag*) bolso *m*. ● *vt* (*pt* **bagged**) ensacar; (*take*) coger (*not LAm*), agarrar (*LAm*). **~s** *npl* (*luggage*) equipaje *m*. **~s of** (*fam*) montones de

baggage /'bægɪdʒ/ *n* equipaje *m*

baggy /'bægɪ/ *a* ‹*clothes*› holgado

bagpipes /'bægpaɪps/ *npl* gaita *f*

Bahamas /bə'hɑ:məz/ *npl*. **the ~** las Bahamas *fpl*

bail[1] /beɪl/ *n* caución *f*, fianza *f*. ● *vt* poner en libertad bajo fianza. **~ s.o. out** obtener la libertad de uno bajo fianza

bail[2] /beɪl/ *n* (*cricket*) travesaño *m*

bail[3] /beɪl/ *vt* (*naut*) achicar

bailiff /'beɪlɪf/ *n* alguacil *m*; (*estate*) administrador *m*

bait /beɪt/ *n* cebo *m*. ● *vt* cebar; (*torment*) atormentar

bak|e /beɪk/ *vt* cocer al horno. ● *vi* cocerse. **~er** *n* panadero *m*. **~ery** /'beɪkərɪ/ *n* panadería *f*. **~ing** *n* cocción *f*; (*batch*) hornada *f*. **~ing-powder** *n* levadura *f* en polvo

balance /'bæləns/ *n* equilibrio *m*; (*com*) balance *m*; (*sum*) saldo *m*; (*scales*) balanza *f*; (*remainder*) resto *m*. ● *vt* equilibrar; (*com*) saldar; nivelar ‹*budget*›. ● *vi* equilibrarse; (*com*) saldarse. **~d** *a* equilibrado

balcony /'bælkənɪ/ *n* balcón *m*

bald /bɔ:ld/ *a* (**-er**, **-est**) calvo; ‹*tyre*› desgastado

balderdash /'bɔ:ldədæʃ/ *n* tonterías *fpl*

bald: **~ly** *adv* escuetamente. **~ness** *n* calvicie *f*

bale /beɪl/ *n* bala *f*, fardo *m*. ● *vi*. **~ out** lanzarse en paracaídas

Balearic /bælɪ'ærɪk/ *a*. **~ Islands** Islas *fpl* Baleares

baleful /'beɪlfʊl/ *a* funesto

balk /bɔ:k/ *vt* frustrar. ● *vi*. **~ (at)** resistirse (a)

ball[1] /bɔ:l/ *n* bola *f*; (*tennis etc*) pelota *f*; (*football etc*) balón *m*; (*of yarn*) ovillo *m*

ball[2] /bɔ:l/ (*dance*) baile *m*

ballad /'bæləd/ *n* balada *f*

ballast /'bæləst/ *n* lastre *m*

ball: **~-bearing** *n* cojinete *m* de bolas. **~-cock** *n* llave *f* de bola

ballerina /bælə'ri:nə/ *f* bailarina *f*

ballet /'bæleɪ/ *n* ballet *m*

ballistic /bə'lɪstɪk/ *a* balístico. **~s** *n* balística *f*

balloon /bə'lu:n/ *n* globo *m*

balloonist /bə'lu:nɪst/ *n* aeronauta *m & f*

ballot /'bælət/ *n* votación *f*. **~ (-paper)** *n* papeleta *f*. **~-box** *n* urna *f*

ball-point /'bɔ:lpɔɪnt/ *n*. **~ (pen)** bolígrafo *m*

ballroom /'bɔ:lru:m/ *n* salón *m* de baile

ballyhoo /bælɪ'hu:/ *n* (*publicity*) publicidad *f* sensacionalista; (*uproar*) jaleo *m*

balm /bɑ:m/ *n* bálsamo *m*. **~y** *a* (*mild*) suave; (*sl*) chiflado

baloney /bə'ləʊnɪ/ *n* (*sl*) tonterías *fpl*

balsam /'bɔ:lsəm/ *n* bálsamo *m*

balustrade /bælə'streɪd/ *n* barandilla *f*

bamboo /bæm'bu:/ *n* bambú *m*

bamboozle /bæm'bu:zl/ *vt* engatusar

ban /bæn/ *vt* (*pt* **banned**) prohibir. **~ from** excluir de. ● *n* prohibición *f*

banal /bə'nɑ:l/ *a* banal. **~ity** /-æləti/ *n* banalidad *f*

banana /bə'nɑ:nə/ *n* plátano *m*, banana *f* (*LAm*). **~-tree** plátano *m*, banano *m*

band[1] /bænd/ *n* banda *f*

band[2] /bænd/ *n* (*mus*) orquesta *f*; (*military, brass*) banda *f*. ● *vi*. **~ together** juntarse

bandage /ˈbændɪdʒ/ *n* venda *f*. ● *vt* vendar

b & b *abbr* (*bed and breakfast*) cama *f* y desayuno

bandit /ˈbændɪt/ *n* bandido *m*

bandstand /ˈbændstænd/ *n* quiosco *m* de música

bandwagon /ˈbændwægən/ *n*. **jump on the ~** (*fig*) subirse al carro

bandy[1] /ˈbændɪ/ *a* (**-ier**, **-iest**) patizambo

bandy[2] /ˈbændɪ/ *vt*. **~ about** repetir. **be bandied about** estar en boca de todos

bandy-legged /ˈbændɪlegd/ *a* patizambo

bane /beɪn/ *n* (*fig*) perdición *f*. **~ful** *a* funesto

bang /bæŋ/ *n* (*noise*) ruido *m*; (*blow*) golpe *m*; (*of gun*) estampido *m*; (*of door*) golpe *m*. ● *vt/i* golpear. ● *adv* exactamente. ● *int* ¡pum!

banger /ˈbæŋə(r)/ *n* petardo *m*; (*culin, sl*) salchicha *f*

bangle /ˈbæŋgl/ *n* brazalete *m*

banish /ˈbænɪʃ/ *vt* desterrar

banisters /ˈbænɪstəz/ *npl* barandilla *f*

banjo /ˈbændʒəʊ/ *n* (*pl* **-os**) banjo *m*

bank[1] /bæŋk/ *n* (*of river*) orilla *f*. ● *vt* cubrir ‹*fire*›. ● *vi* (*aviat*) ladearse

bank[2] /bæŋk/ *n* banco *m*. ● *vt* depositar. **~ on** *vt* contar con. **~ with** tener una cuenta con. **~er** *n* banquero *m*. **~ holiday** *n* día *m* festivo, fiesta *f*. **~ing** *n* (*com*) banca *f*. **~note** /ˈbæŋknəʊt/ *n* billete *m* de banco

bankrupt /ˈbæŋkrʌpt/ *a* & *n* quebrado (*m*). ● *vt* hacer quebrar. **~cy** *n* bancarrota *f*, quiebra *f*

banner /ˈbænə(r)/ *n* bandera *f*; (*in demonstration*) pancarta *f*

banns /bænz/ *npl* amonestaciones *fpl*

banquet /ˈbæŋkwɪt/ *n* banquete *m*

bantamweight /ˈbæntəmweɪt/ *n* peso *m* gallo

banter /ˈbæntə(r)/ *n* chanza *f*. ● *vi* chancearse

bap /bæp/ *n* panecillo *m* blando

baptism /ˈbæptɪzəm/ *n* bautismo *m*; (*act*) bautizo *m*

Baptist /ˈbæptɪst/ *n* bautista *m* & *f*

baptize /bæpˈtaɪz/ *vt* bautizar

bar /bɑ:(r)/ *n* barra *f*; (*on window*) reja *f*; (*of chocolate*) tableta *f*; (*of soap*) pastilla *f*; (*pub*) bar *m*; (*mus*) compás *m*; (*jurid*) abogacía *f*; (*fig*) obstáculo *m*. ● *vt* (*pt* **barred**) atrancar ‹*door*›; (*exclude*) excluir; (*prohibit*) prohibir. ● *prep* excepto

barbar|ian /bɑ:ˈbeərɪən/ *a* & *n* bárbaro (*m*). **~ic** /bɑ:ˈbærɪk/ *a* bárbaro. **~ity** /-ətɪ/ *n* barbaridad *f*. **~ous** *a* /ˈbɑ:bərəs/ *a* bárbaro

barbecue /ˈbɑ:bɪkju:/ *n* barbacoa *f*. ● *vt* asar a la parilla

barbed /bɑ:bd/ *a*. **~ wire** alambre *m* de espinas

barber /ˈbɑ:bə(r)/ *n* peluquero *m*, barbero *m*

barbiturate /bɑ:ˈbɪtjʊrət/ *n* barbitúrico *m*

bare /beə(r)/ *a* (**-er**, **est**) desnudo; ‹*room*› con pocos muebles; (*mere*) simple; (*empty*) vacío. ● *vt* desnudar; (*uncover*) descubrir. **~ one's teeth** mostrar los dientes. **~back** /ˈbeəbæk/ *adv* a pelo. **~faced** /ˈbeəfeɪst/ *a* descarado. **~foot** *a* descalzo. **~headed** /ˈbeəhedɪd/ *a* descubierto. **~ly** *adv* apenas. **~ness** *n* desnudez *f*

bargain /ˈbɑ:gɪn/ *n* (*agreement*) pacto *m*; (*good buy*) ganga *f*. ● *vi* negociar; (*haggle*) regatear. **~ for** esperar, contar con

barge /bɑ:dʒ/ *n* barcaza *f*. ● *vi*. **~ in** irrumpir

baritone /ˈbærɪtəʊn/ *n* barítono *m*

barium /ˈbeərɪəm/ *n* bario *m*

bark[1] /bɑ:k/ *n* (*of dog*) ladrido *m*. ● *vi* ladrar

bark[2] /bɑ:k/ (*of tree*) corteza *f*

barley /ˈbɑ:lɪ/ *n* cebada *f*. **~-water** *n* hordiate *m*

bar: **~maid** /ˈbɑ:meɪd/ *n* camarera *f*. **~man** /ˈbɑ:mən/ *n* (*pl* **-men**) camarero *m*

barmy /ˈbɑ:mɪ/ *a* (*sl*) chiflado

barn /bɑ:n/ *n* granero *m*

barometer /bəˈrɒmɪtə(r)/ *n* barómetro *m*

baron /ˈbærən/ *n* barón *m*. **~ess** *n* baronesa *f*

baroque /bəˈrɒk/ *a* & *n* barroco (*m*)

barracks /ˈbærəks/ *npl* cuartel *m*

barrage /ˈbærɑ:ʒ/ *n* (*mil*) barrera *f*; (*dam*) presa *f*; (*of questions*) bombardeo *m*

barrel /ˈbærəl/ *n* tonel *m*; (*of gun*) cañón *m*. **~-organ** *n* organillo *m*

barren /ˈbærən/ *a* estéril. **~ness** *n* esterilidad *f*, aridez *f*

barricade /bærɪˈkeɪd/ *n* barricada *f*. ● *vt* cerrar con barricadas

barrier /ˈbærɪə(r)/ *n* barrera *f*

barring /'bɑ:rɪŋ/ *prep* salvo
barrister /'bærɪstə(r)/ *n* abogado *m*
barrow /'bærəʊ/ *n* carro *m*; (*wheelbarrow*) carretilla *f*
barter /'bɑ:tə(r)/ *n* trueque *m*. ● *vt* trocar
base /beɪs/ *n* base *f*. ● *vt* basar. ● *a* vil
baseball /'beɪsbɔ:l/ *n* béisbol *m*
baseless /'beɪslɪs/ *a* infundado
basement /'beɪsmənt/ *n* sótano *m*
bash /bæʃ/ *vt* golpear. ● *n* golpe *m*. **have a ~** (*sl*) probar
bashful /'bæʃfl/ *a* tímido
basic /'beɪsɪk/ *a* básico, fundamental. **~ally** *adv* fundamentalmente
basil /'bæzl/ *n* albahaca *f*
basilica /bə'zɪlɪkə/ *n* basílica *f*
basin /'beɪsn/ *n* (*for washing*) palangana *f*; (*for food*) cuenco *m*; (*geog*) cuenca *f*
basis /'beɪsɪs/ *n* (*pl* **bases** /-si:z/) base *f*
bask /bɑ:sk/ *vi* asolearse; (*fig*) gozar (**in** de)
basket /'bɑ:skɪt/ *n* cesta *f*; (*big*) cesto *m*. **~ball** /'bɑ:skɪtbɔ:l/ *n* baloncesto *m*
Basque /bɑ:sk/ *a* & *n* vasco (*m*). **~ Country** *n* País *m* Vasco. **~ Provinces** *npl* Vascongadas *fpl*
bass[1] /beɪs/ *a* bajo. ● *n* (*mus*) bajo *m*
bass[2] /bæs/ *n* (*marine fish*) róbalo *m*; (*freshwater fish*) perca *f*
bassoon /bə'su:n/ *n* fagot *m*
bastard /'bɑ:stəd/ *a* & *n* bastardo (*m*). **you ~!** (*fam*) ¡cabrón!
baste /beɪst/ *vt* (*sew*) hilvanar; (*culin*) lard(e)ar
bastion /'bæstɪən/ *n* baluarte *m*
bat[1] /bæt/ *n* bate *m*; (*for table tennis*) raqueta *f*. **off one's own ~** por sí solo. ● *vt* (*pt* **batted**) golpear. ● *vi* batear
bat[2] /bæt/ *n* (*mammal*) murciélago *m*
bat[3] /bæt/ *vt*. **without ~ting an eyelid** sin pestañear
batch /bætʃ/ *n* (*of people*) grupo *m*; (*of papers*) lío *m*; (*of goods*) remesa *f*; (*of bread*) hornada *f*
bated /'beɪtɪd/ *a*. **with ~ breath** con aliento entrecortado
bath /bɑ:θ/ *n* (*pl* **-s** /bɑ:ðz/) baño *m*; (*tub*) bañera *f*; (*pl*, *swimming pool*) piscina *f*. ● *vt* bañar. ● *vi* bañarse
bathe /beɪð/ *vt* bañar. ● *vi* bañarse. ● *n* baño *m*. **~r** /-ə(r)/ *n* bañista *m* & *f*
bathing /'beɪðɪŋ/ *n* baños *mpl*. **~-costume** *n* traje *m* de baño
bathroom /'bɑ:θrʊm/ *n* cuarto *m* de baño
batman /'bætmən/ *n* (*pl* **-men**) (*mil*) ordenanza *f*
baton /'bætən/ *n* (*mil*) bastón *m*; (*mus*) batuta *f*
batsman /'bætsmən/ *n* (*pl* **-men**) bateador *m*
battalion /bə'tælɪən/ *n* batallón *m*
batter[1] /'bætə(r)/ *vt* apalear
batter[2] /'bætə(r)/ *n* batido *m* para rebozar, albardilla *f*
batter: **~ed** *a* ‹*car etc*› estropeado; ‹*wife etc*› golpeado. **~ing** *n* (*fam*) bombardeo *m*
battery /'bætərɪ/ *n* (*mil*, *auto*) batería *f*; (*of torch*, *radio*) pila *f*
battle /'bætl/ *n* batalla *f*; (*fig*) lucha *f*. ● *vi* luchar. **~axe** /'bætlæks/ *n* (*woman*, *fam*) arpía *f*. **~field** /'bætlfi:ld/ *n* campo *m* de batalla. **~ments** /'bætlmənts/ *npl* almenas *fpl*. **~ship** /'bætlʃɪp/ *n* acorazado *m*
batty /'bætɪ/ *a* (*sl*) chiflado
baulk /bɔ:lk/ *vt* frustrar. ● *vi*. **~ (at)** resistirse (a)
bawd|iness /'bɔ:dɪnəs/ *n* obscenidad *f*. **~y** /'bɔ:dɪ/ *a* (**-ier**, **-iest**) obsceno, verde
bawl /bɔ:l/ *vt/i* gritar
bay[1] /beɪ/ *n* (*geog*) bahía *f*
bay[2] /beɪ/ *n* (*bot*) laurel *m*
bay[3] /beɪ/ *n* (*of dog*) ladrido *m*. **keep at ~** mantener a raya. ● *vi* ladrar
bayonet /'beɪənet/ *n* bayoneta *f*
bay window /beɪ'wɪndəʊ/ *n* ventana *f* salediza
bazaar /bə'zɑ:(r)/ *n* bazar *m*
BC /bi:'si:/ *abbr* (*before Christ*) a. de C., antes de Cristo
be /bi:/ *vi* (*pres* **am**, **are**, **is**; *pt* **was**, **were**; *pp* **been**) (*position or temporary*) estar; (*permanent*) ser. **~ cold/hot, etc** tener frío/calor, etc. **~ reading/singing, etc** (*aux*) leer/cantar, etc. **~ that as it may** sea como fuere. **he is 30** (*age*) tiene 30 años. **he is to come** (*must*) tiene que venir. **how are you?** ¿cómo estás? **how much is it?** ¿cuánto vale?, ¿cuánto es? **have been to** haber estado en. **it is cold/hot, etc** (*weather*) hace frío/calor, etc
beach /bi:tʃ/ *n* playa *f*
beachcomber /'bi:tʃkəʊmə(r)/ *n* raquero *m*
beacon /'bi:kən/ *n* faro *m*

bead /bi:d/ *n* cuenta *f*; (*of glass*) abalorio *m*
beak /bi:k/ *n* pico *m*
beaker /'bi:kə(r)/ *n* jarra *f*, vaso *m*
beam /bi:m/ *n* viga *f*; (*of light*) rayo *m*; (*naut*) bao *m*. ● *vt* emitir. ● *vi* irradiar; (*smile*) sonreír. **~-ends** *npl*. **be on one's ~-ends** no tener más dinero. **~ing** *a* radiante
bean /bi:n/ *n* judía; (*broad bean*) haba *f*; (*of coffee*) grano *m*
beano /'bi:nəʊ/ *n* (*pl* **-os**) (*fam*) juerga *f*
bear[1] /beə(r)/ *vt* (*pt* **bore**, *pp* **borne**) llevar; parir ‹*niño*›; (*endure*) soportar. **~ right** torcer a la derecha. **~ in mind** tener en cuenta. **~ with** tener paciencia con
bear[2] /beə(r)/ *n* oso *m*
bearable /'beərəbl/ *a* soportable
beard /bɪəd/ *n* barba *f*. **~ed** *a* barbudo
bearer /'beərə(r)/ *n* portador *m*; (*of passport*) poseedor *m*
bearing /'beərɪŋ/ *n* comportamiento *m*; (*relevance*) relación *f*; (*mec*) cojinete *m*. **get one's ~s** orientarse
beast /bi:st/ *n* bestia *f*; (*person*) bruto *m*. **~ly** /'bi:stlɪ/ *a* (**-ier**, **-iest**) bestial; (*fam*) horrible
beat /bi:t/ *vt* (*pt* **beat**, *pp* **beaten**) golpear; (*culin*) batir; (*defeat*) derrotar; (*better*) sobrepasar; (*baffle*) dejar perplejo. **~ a retreat** (*mil*) batirse en retirada. **~ it** (*sl*) largarse. ● *vi* ‹*heart*› latir. ● *n* latido *m*; (*mus*) ritmo *m*; (*of policeman*) ronda *f*. **~ up** dar una paliza a; (*culin*) batir. **~er** *n* batidor *m*. **~ing** *n* paliza *f*
beautician /bju:'tɪʃn/ *n* esteticista *m* & *f*
beautiful /'bju:tɪfl/ *a* hermoso. **~ly** *adv* maravillosamente
beautify /'bju:tɪfaɪ/ *vt* embellecer
beauty /'bju:tɪ/ *n* belleza *f*. **~ parlour** *n* salón *m* de belleza. **~ spot** (*on face*) lunar *m*; (*site*) lugar *m* pintoresco
beaver /'bi:və(r)/ *n* castor *m*
became /bɪ'keɪm/ *see* **become**
because /bɪ'kɒz/ *conj* porque. ● *adv*. **~ of** a causa de
beck /bek/ *n*. **be at the ~ and call of** estar a disposición de
beckon /'bekən/ *vt/i*. **~ (to)** hacer señas (a)
become /bɪ'kʌm/ *vt* (*pt* **became**, *pp* **become**) ‹*clothes*› sentar bien. ● *vi* hacerse, llegar a ser, volverse, convertirse en. **what has ~ of her?** ¿qué es de ella?
becoming /bɪ'kʌmɪŋ/ *a* ‹*clothes*› favorecedor
bed /bed/ *n* cama *f*; (*layer*) estrato *m*; (*of sea, river*) fondo *m*; (*of flowers*) macizo *m*. ● *vi* (*pt* **bedded**). **~ down** acostarse. **~ and breakfast (b & b)** cama y desayuno. **~bug** /'bedbʌg/ *n* chinche *f*. **~clothes** /'bedkləʊðz/ *npl*, **~ding** *n* ropa *f* de cama
bedevil /bɪ'devl/ *vt* (*pt* **bedevilled**) (*torment*) atormentar
bedlam /'bedləm/ *n* confusión *f*, manicomio *m*
bed: **~pan** /'bedpæn/ *n* orinal *m* de cama. **~post** /'bedpəʊst/ *n* columna *f* de la cama
bedraggled /bɪ'drægld/ *a* sucio
bed: **~ridden** /'bedrɪdn/ *a* encamado. **~room** /'bedrʊm/ *n* dormitorio *m*, habitación *f*. **~side** /'bedsaɪd/ *n* cabecera *f*. **~-sitting-room** /bed'sɪtɪŋru:m/ *n* salón *m* con cama, estudio *m*. **~spread** /'bedspred/ *n* colcha *f*. **~time** /'bedtaɪm/ *n* hora *f* de acostarse
bee /bi:/ *n* abeja *f*. **make a ~-line for** ir en línea recta hacia
beech /bi:tʃ/ *n* haya *f*
beef /bi:f/ *n* carne *f* de vaca, carne *f* de res (*LAm*). ● *vi* (*sl*) quejarse. **~burger** /'bi:fbɜ:gə(r)/ *n* hamburguesa *f*
beefeater /'bi:fi:tə(r)/ *n* alabardero *m* de la torre de Londres
beefsteak /bi:f'steɪk/ *n* filete *m*, bistec *m*, bife *m* (*Arg*)
beefy /'bi:fɪ/ *a* (**-ier**, **-iest**) musculoso
beehive /'bi:haɪv/ *n* colmena *f*
been /bi:n/ *see* **be**
beer /bɪə(r)/ *n* cerveza *f*
beet /bi:t/ *n* remolacha *f*
beetle /'bi:tl/ *n* escarabajo *m*
beetroot /'bi:tru:t/ *n invar* remolacha *f*
befall /bɪ'fɔ:l/ *vt* (*pt* **befell**, *pp* **befallen**) acontecer a. ● *vi* acontecer
befit /bɪ'fɪt/ *vt* (*pt* **befitted**) convenir a
before /bɪ'fɔ:(r)/ *prep* (*time*) antes de; (*place*) delante de. **~ leaving** antes de marcharse. ● *adv* (*place*) delante; (*time*) antes. **a week ~** una semana antes. **the week ~** la semana anterior. ● *conj* (*time*) antes de que. **~ he leaves** antes de que se

vaya. **~hand** /bɪ'fɔ:hænd/ *adv* de antemano

befriend /bɪ'frend/ *vt* ofrecer amistad a

beg /beg/ *vt/i* (*pt* **begged**) mendigar; (*entreat*) suplicar; (*ask*) pedir. **~ s.o.'s pardon** pedir perdón a uno. **I ~ your pardon!** ¡perdone Vd! **I ~ your pardon?** ¿cómo? **it's going ~ging** no lo quiere nadie

began /bɪ'gæn/ *see* **begin**

beget /bɪ'get/ *vt* (*pt* **begot**, *pp* **begotten**, *pres p* **begetting**) engendrar

beggar /'begə(r)/ *n* mendigo *m*; (*sl*) individuo *m*, tío *m* (*fam*)

begin /bɪ'gɪn/ *vt/i* (*pt* **began**, *pp* **begun**, *pres p* **beginning**) comenzar, empezar. **~ner** *n* principiante *m & f*. **~ning** *n* principio *m*

begot, begotten /bɪ'gɒt, bɪ'gɒtn/ *see* **beget**

begrudge /bɪ'grʌdʒ/ *vt* envidiar; (*give*) dar de mala gana

beguile /bɪ'gaɪl/ *vt* engañar, seducir; (*entertain*) entretener

begun /bɪ'gʌn/ *see* **begin**

behalf /bɪ'hɑ:f/ *n*. **on ~ of** de parte de, en nombre de

behav|e /bɪ'heɪv/ *vi* comportarse, portarse. **~ (o.s.)** portarse bien. **~iour** /bɪ'heɪvjə(r)/ *n* comportamiento *m*

behead /bɪ'hed/ *vt* decapitar

beheld /bɪ'held/ *see* **behold**

behind /bɪ'haɪnd/ *prep* detrás de. ● *adv* detrás; (*late*) atrasado. ● *n* (*fam*) trasero *m*

behold /bɪ'həʊld/ *vt* (*pt* **beheld**) (*old use*) mirar, contemplar

beholden /bɪ'həʊldən/ *a* agradecido

being /'bi:ɪŋ/ *n* ser *m*. **come into ~** nacer

belated /bɪ'leɪtɪd/ *a* tardío

belch /beltʃ/ *vi* eructar. ● *vt*. **~ out** arrojar ‹*smoke*›

belfry /'belfrɪ/ *n* campanario *m*

Belgi|an /'beldʒən/ *a & n* belga (*m & f*). **~um** /'beldʒəm/ *n* Bélgica *f*

belie /bɪ'laɪ/ *vt* desmentir

belie|f /bɪ'li:f/ *n* (*trust*) fe *f*; (*opinion*) creencia *f*. **~ve** /bɪ'li:v/ *vt/i* creer. **make ~ve** fingir. **~ver** /-ə(r)/ *n* creyente *m & f*; (*supporter*) partidario *m*

belittle /bɪ'lɪtl/ *vt* empequeñecer; (*fig*) despreciar

bell /bel/ *n* campana *f*; (*on door*) timbre *m*

belligerent /bɪ'lɪdʒərənt/ *a & n* beligerante (*m & f*)

bellow /'beləʊ/ *vt* gritar. ● *vi* bramar

bellows /'beləʊz/ *npl* fuelle *m*

belly /'belɪ/ *n* vientre *m*. **~ful** /'belɪfʊl/ *n* panzada *f*. **have a ~ful of** (*sl*) estar harto de

belong /bɪ'lɒŋ/ *vi* pertenecer; (*club*) ser socio (**to** de)

belongings /bɪ'lɒŋɪŋz/ *npl* pertenencias *fpl*. **personal ~** efectos *mpl* personales

beloved /bɪ'lʌvɪd/ *a & n* querido (*m*)

below /bɪ'ləʊ/ *prep* debajo de; (*fig*) inferior a. ● *adv* abajo

belt /belt/ *n* cinturón *m*; (*area*) zona *f*. ● *vt* (*fig*) rodear; (*sl*) pegar

bemused /bɪ'mju:zd/ *a* perplejo

bench /bentʃ/ *n* banco *m*. **the B~** (*jurid*) la magistratura *f*

bend /bend/ *vt* (*pt & pp* **bent**) doblar; torcer ‹*arm, leg*›. ● *vi* doblarse; ‹*road*› torcerse. ● *n* curva *f*. **~ down/over** inclinarse

beneath /bɪ'ni:θ/ *prep* debajo de; (*fig*) inferior a. ● *adv* abajo

benediction /benɪ'dɪkʃn/ *n* bendición *f*

benefactor /'benɪfæktə(r)/ *n* bienhechor *m*, benefactor *m*

beneficial /benɪ'fɪʃl/ *a* provechoso

beneficiary /benɪ'fɪʃərɪ/ *a & n* beneficiario (*m*)

benefit /'benɪfɪt/ *n* provecho *m*, ventaja *f*; (*allowance*) subsidio *m*; (*financial gain*) beneficio *m*. ● *vt* (*pt* **benefited**, *pres p* **benefiting**) aprovechar. ● *vi* aprovecharse

benevolen|ce /bɪ'nevələns/ *n* benevolencia *f*. **~t** *a* benévolo

benign /bɪ'naɪn/ *a* benigno

bent /bent/ *see* **bend**. ● *n* inclinación *f*. ● *a* encorvado; (*sl*) corrompido

bequeath /bɪ'kwi:ð/ *vt* legar

bequest /bɪ'kwest/ *n* legado *m*

bereave|d /bɪ'ri:vd/ *n*. **the ~d** la familia *f* del difunto. **~ment** *n* pérdida *f*; (*mourning*) luto *m*

bereft /bɪ'reft/ *a*. **~ of** privado de

beret /'bereɪ/ *n* boina *f*

Bermuda /bə'mju:də/ *n* Islas *fpl* Bermudas

berry /'berɪ/ *n* baya *f*

berserk /bə'sɜ:k/ *a*. **go ~** volverse loco, perder los estribos

berth /bɜ:θ/ *n* litera *f*; (*anchorage*) amarradero *m*. **give a wide ~ to** evitar. ● *vi* atracar

beseech /bɪ'si:tʃ/ *vt* (*pt* **besought**) suplicar

beset /bɪ'set/ *vt* (*pt* **beset**, *pres p* **besetting**) acosar

beside /bɪ'saɪd/ *prep* al lado de. **be ~ o.s.** estar fuera de sí

besides /bɪ'saɪdz/ *prep* además de; (*except*) excepto. ● *adv* además

besiege /bɪ'si:dʒ/ *vt* asediar; (*fig*) acosar

besought /bɪ'sɔ:t/ *see* **beseech**

bespoke /bɪ'spəʊk/ *a* ‹*tailor*› que confecciona a la medida

best /best/ *a* (el) mejor. **the ~ thing is to...** lo mejor es... ● *adv* (lo) mejor. **like ~** preferir. ● *n* lo mejor. **at ~** a lo más. **do one's ~** hacer todo lo posible. **make the ~ of** contentarse con. **~ man** *n* padrino *m* (de boda)

bestow /bɪ'stəʊ/ *vt* conceder

bestseller /best'selə(r)/ *n* éxito *m* de librería, bestseller *m*

bet /bet/ *n* apuesta *f*. ● *vt/i* (*pt* **bet** *or* **betted**) apostar

betray /bɪ'treɪ/ *vt* traicionar. **~al** *n* traición *f*

betroth|al /bɪ'trəʊðəl/ *n* esponsales *mpl*. **~ed** *a* prometido

better /'betə(r)/ *a & adv* mejor. **~ off** en mejores condiciones; (*richer*) más rico. **get ~** mejorar. **all the ~** tanto mejor. **I'd ~** más vale que. **the ~ part of** la mayor parte de. **the sooner the ~** cuanto antes mejor. ● *vt* mejorar; (*beat*) sobrepasar. ● *n* superior *m*. **get the ~ of** vencer a. **one's ~s** sus superiores *mpl*

between /bɪ'twi:n/ *prep* entre. ● *adv* en medio

beverage /'bevərɪdʒ/ *n* bebida *f*

bevy /bevɪ/ *n* grupo *m*

beware /bɪ'weə(r)/ *vi* tener cuidado. ● *int* ¡cuidado!

bewilder /bɪ'wɪldə(r)/ *vt* desconcertar. **~ment** *n* aturdimiento *m*

bewitch /bɪ'wɪtʃ/ *vt* hechizar

beyond /bɪ'jɒnd/ *prep* más allá de; (*fig*) fuera de. **~ doubt** sin lugar a duda. **~ reason** irrazonable. ● *adv* más allá

bias /'baɪəs/ *n* predisposición *f*; (*prejudice*) prejuicio *m*; (*sewing*) sesgo *m*. ● *vt* (*pt* **biased**) influir en. **~ed** *a* parcial

bib /bɪb/ *n* babero *m*

Bible /'baɪbl/ *n* Biblia *f*

biblical /'bɪblɪkl/ *a* bíblico

bibliography /bɪblɪ'ɒgrəfɪ/ *n* bibliografía *f*

biceps /'baɪseps/ *n* bíceps *m*

bicker /'bɪkə(r)/ *vi* altercar

bicycle /'baɪsɪkl/ *n* bicicleta *f*. ● *vi* ir en bicicleta

bid /bɪd/ *n* (*offer*) oferta *f*; (*attempt*) tentativa *f*. ● *vi* hacer una oferta. ● *vt* (*pt* **bid**, *pres p* **bidding**) ofrecer; (*pt* **bid**, *pp* **bidden**, *pres p* **bidding**) mandar; dar ‹*welcome, good-day etc*›. **~der** *n* postor *m*. **~ding** *n* (*at auction*) ofertas *fpl*; (*order*) mandato *m*

bide /baɪd/ *vt*. **~ one's time** esperar el momento oportuno

biennial /baɪ'enɪəl/ *a* bienal. ● *n* (*event*) bienal *f*; (*bot*) planta *f* bienal

bifocals /baɪ'fəʊklz/ *npl* gafas *fpl* bifocales, anteojos *mpl* bifocales (*LAm*)

big /bɪg/ *a* (**bigger**, **biggest**) grande; (*generous*, *sl*) generoso. ● *adv*. **talk ~** fanfarronear

bigam|ist /'bɪgəmɪst/ *n* bígamo *m*. **~ous** *a* bígamo. **~y** *n* bigamia *f*

big-headed /bɪg'hedɪd/ *a* engreído

bigot /'bɪgət/ *n* fanático *m*. **~ed** *a* fanático. **~ry** *n* fanatismo *m*

bigwig /'bɪgwɪg/ *n* (*fam*) pez *m* gordo

bike /baɪk/ *n* (*fam*) bicicleta *f*, bici *f* (*fam*)

bikini /bɪ'ki:nɪ/ *n* (*pl* **-is**) biquini *m*, bikini *m*

bilberry /'bɪlbərɪ/ *n* arándano *m*

bile /baɪl/ *n* bilis *f*

bilingual /baɪ'lɪŋgwəl/ *a* bilingüe

bilious /'bɪlɪəs/ *a* (*med*) bilioso

bill[1] /bɪl/ *n* cuenta *f*; (*invoice*) factura *f*; (*notice*) cartel *m*; (*Amer*, *banknote*) billete *m*; (*pol*) proyecto *m* de ley. ● *vt* pasar la factura; (*in theatre*) anunciar

bill[2] /bɪl/ *n* (*of bird*) pico *m*

billet /'bɪlɪt/ *n* (*mil*) alojamiento *m*. ● *vt* alojar

billiards /'bɪlɪədz/ *n* billar *m*

billion /'bɪlɪən/ *n* billón *m*; (*Amer*) mil millones *mpl*

billy-goat /'bɪlɪgəʊt/ *n* macho *m* cabrío

bin /bɪn/ *n* recipiente *m*; (*for rubbish*) cubo *m*; (*for waste paper*) papelera *f*

bind /baɪnd/ *vt* (*pt* **bound**) atar; encuadernar ‹*book*›; (*jurid*) obligar. ● *n* (*sl*) lata *f*. **~ing**

/ˈbaɪndɪŋ/ *n* (*of books*) encuadernación *f*; (*braid*) ribete *m*
binge /bɪndʒ/ *n* (*sl*) (*of food*) comilona *f*; (*of drink*) borrachera *f*. **go on a ~** ir de juerga
bingo /ˈbɪŋgəʊ/ *n* bingo *m*
binoculars /bɪˈnɒkjʊləz/ *npl* prismáticos *mpl*
biochemistry /baɪəʊˈkemɪstrɪ/ *n* bioquímica *f*
biograph|er /baɪˈɒgrəfə(r)/ *n* biógrafo m. **~y** *n* biografía *f*
biolog|ical /baɪəˈlɒdʒɪkl/ *a* biologíco. **~ist** *n* biólogo *m*. **~** /baɪˈɒlədʒɪ/ *n* biología *f*
biped /ˈbaɪped/ *n* bípedo *m*
birch /bɜːtʃ/ *n* (*tree*) abedul *m*; (*whip*) férula *f*
bird /bɜːd/ *n* ave *f*; (*small*) pájaro *m*; (*fam*) tipo *m*; (*girl, sl*) chica *f*
Biro /ˈbaɪərəʊ/ *n* (*pl* **-os**) (*P*) bolígrafo *m*, biromen *m* (*Arg*)
birth /bɜːθ/ *n* nacimiento *m*. **~certificate** *n* partida *f* de nacimiento. **~-control** *n* control *m* de la natalidad. **~day** /ˈbɜːθdeɪ/ *n* cumpleaños *m invar*. **~mark** /ˈbɜːθmɑːk/ *n* marca *f* de nacimiento. **~-rate** *n* natalidad *f*. **~right** /ˈbɜːθraɪt/ *n* derechos *mpl* de nacimiento
biscuit /ˈbɪskɪt/ *n* galleta *f*
bisect /baɪˈsekt/ *vt* bisecar
bishop /ˈbɪʃəp/ *n* obispo *m*
bit[1] /bɪt/ *n* trozo *m*; (*quantity*) poco *m*
bit[2] /bɪt/ *see* **bite**
bit[3] /bɪt/ *n* (*of horse*) bocado *m*; (*mec*) broca *f*
bitch /bɪtʃ/ *n* perra *f*; (*woman, fam*) mujer *f* maligna, bruja *f* (*fam*). • *vi* (*fam*) quejarse (**about** de). **~y** *a* malintencionado
bit|e /baɪt/ *vt/i* (*pt* **bit**, *pp* **bitten**) morder. **~e one's nails** morderse las uñas. • *n* mordisco *m*; (*mouthful*) bocado *m*; (*of insect etc*) picadura *f*. **~ing** /ˈbaɪtɪŋ/ *a* mordaz
bitter /ˈbɪtə(r)/ *a* amargo; (*of weather*) glacial. **to the ~ end** hasta el final. • *n* cerveza *f* amarga. **~ly** *adv* amargamente. **it's ~ly cold** hace un frío glacial. **~ness** *n* amargor *m*; (*resentment*) amargura *f*
bizarre /bɪˈzɑː(r)/ *a* extraño
blab /blæb/ *vi* (*pt* **blabbed**) chismear
black /blæk/ *a* (**-er**, **-est**) negro. **~ and blue** amoratado. • *n* negro *m*. • *vt* ennegrecer; limpiar ‹*shoes*›. **~ out** desmayarse; (*make dark*) apagar las luces de
blackball /ˈblækbɔːl/ *vt* votar en contra de
blackberry /ˈblækbərɪ/ *n* zarzamora *f*
blackbird /ˈblækbɜːd/ *n* mirlo *m*
blackboard /ˈblækbɔːd/ *n* pizarra *f*
blackcurrant /blækˈkʌrənt/ *n* casis *f*
blacken /ˈblækən/ *vt* ennegrecer. • *vi* ennegrecerse
blackguard /ˈblægɑːd/ *n* canalla *m*
blackleg /ˈblækleg/ *n* esquirol *m*
blacklist /ˈblæklɪst/ *vt* poner en la lista negra
blackmail /ˈblækmeɪl/ *n* chantaje *m*. • *vt* chantajear. **~er** *n* chantajista *m & f*
black-out /ˈblækaʊt/ *n* apagón *m*; (*med*) desmayo *m*; (*of news*) censura *f*
blacksmith /ˈblæksmɪθ/ *n* herrero *m*
bladder /ˈblædə(r)/ *n* vejiga *f*
blade /bleɪd/ *n* hoja *f*; (*razor-blade*) cuchilla *f*. **~ of grass** brizna *f* de hierba
blame /bleɪm/ *vt* echar la culpa a. **be to ~** tener la culpa. • *n* culpa *f*. **~less** *a* inocente
bland /blænd/ *a* (**-er**, **-est**) suave
blandishments /ˈblændɪʃmənts/ *npl* halagos *mpl*
blank /blæŋk/ *a* en blanco; ‹*cartridge*› sin bala; (*fig*) vacío. **~ verse** *n* verso *m* suelto. • *n* blanco *m*
blanket /ˈblæŋkɪt/ *n* manta *f*; (*fig*) capa *f*. • *vt* (*pt* **blanketed**) (*fig*) cubrir (**in**, **with** de)
blare /bleə(r)/ *vi* sonar muy fuerte. • *n* estrépito *m*
blarney /ˈblɑːnɪ/ *n* coba *f*. • *vt* dar coba
blasé /ˈblɑːzeɪ/ *a* hastiado
blasphem|e /blæsˈfiːm/ *vt/i* blasfemar. **~er** *n* blasfemador *m*. **~ous** /ˈblæsfəməs/ *a* blasfemo. **~y** /ˈblæsfəmɪ/ *n* blasfemia *f*
blast /blɑːst/ *n* explosión *f*; (*gust*) ráfaga *f*; (*sound*) toque *m*. • *vt* volar. **~ed** *a* maldito. **~-furnace** *n* alto horno *m*. **~-off** *n* (*of missile*) despegue *m*
blatant /ˈbleɪtnt/ *a* patente; (*shameless*) descarado
blaze /bleɪz/ *n* llamarada *f*; (*of light*) resplandor *m*; (*fig*) arranque *m*. • *vi* arder en llamas; (*fig*) brillar. **~ a trail** abrir un camino
blazer /ˈbleɪzə(r)/ *n* chaqueta *f*

bleach /bli:tʃ/ *n* lejía *f*; (*for hair*) decolorante *m*. ● *vt* blanquear; decolorar ‹*hair*›. ● *vi* blanquearse
bleak /bli:k/ *a* (**-er**, **-est**) desolado; (*fig*) sombrío
bleary /ˈblɪərɪ/ *a* ‹*eyes*› nublado; (*indistinct*) indistinto
bleat /bli:t/ *n* balido *m*. ● *vi* balar
bleed /bli:d/ *vt/i* (*pt* **bled**) sangrar
bleep /bli:p/ *n* pitido *m*. **~er** *n* busca *m*, buscapersonas *m*
blemish /ˈblemɪʃ/ *n* tacha *f*
blend /blend/ *n* mezcla *f*. ● *vt* mezclar. ● *vi* combinarse
bless /bles/ *vt* bendecir. **~ you!** (*on sneezing*) ¡Jesús! **~ed** *a* bendito. **be ~ed with** estar dotado de. **~ing** *n* bendición *f*; (*advantage*) ventaja *f*
blew /blu:/ *see* **blow**[1]
blight /blaɪt/ *n* añublo *m*, tizón *m*; (*fig*) plaga *f*. ● *vt* añublar, atizonar; (*fig*) destrozar
blighter /ˈblaɪtə(r)/ *n* (*sl*) tío *m* (*fam*), sinvergüenza *m*
blind /blaɪnd/ *a* ciego. **~ alley** *n* callejón *m* sin salida. ● *n* persiana *f*; (*fig*) pretexto *m*. ● *vt* cegar. **~fold** /ˈblaɪndfəʊld/ *a* & *adv* con los ojos vendados. ● *n* venda *f*. ● *vt* vendar los ojos. **~ly** *adv* a ciegas. **~ness** *n* ceguera *f*
blink /blɪŋk/ *vi* parpadear; (*of light*) centellear
blinkers /ˈblɪŋkəz/ *npl* anteojeras *fpl*; (*auto*) intermitente *m*
bliss /blɪs/ *n* felicidad *f*. **~ful** *a* feliz. **~fully** *adv* felizmente; (*completely*) completamente
blister /ˈblɪstə(r)/ *n* ampolla *f*. ● *vi* formarse ampollas
blithe /blaɪð/ *a* alegre
blitz /blɪts/ *n* bombardeo *m* aéreo. ● *vt* bombardear
blizzard /ˈblɪzəd/ *n* ventisca *f*
bloated /ˈbləʊtɪd/ *a* hinchado (**with** de)
bloater /ˈbləʊtə(r)/ *n* arenque *m* ahumado
blob /blɒb/ *n* gota *f*; (*stain*) mancha *f*
bloc /blɒk/ *n* (*pol*) bloque *m*
block /blɒk/ *n* bloque *m*; (*of wood*) zoquete *m*; (*of buildings*) manzana *f*, cuadra *f* (*LAm*); (*in pipe*) obstrucción *f*. **in ~ letters** en letra de imprenta. **traffic ~** embotellamiento *m*. ● *vt* obstruir. **~ade** /blɒˈkeɪd/ *n* bloqueo *m*. ● *vt* bloquear. **~age** *n* obstrucción *f*
blockhead /ˈblɒkhed/ *n* (*fam*) zopenco *m*
bloke /bləʊk/ *n* (*fam*) tío *m* (*fam*), tipo *m*
blond /blɒnd/ *a* & *n* rubio (*m*). **~e** *a* & *n* rubia (*f*)
blood /blʌd/ *n* sangre *f*. **~ count** *n* recuento *m* sanguíneo. **~-curdling** *a* horripilante
bloodhound /ˈblʌdhaʊnd/ *n* sabueso *m*
blood: **~ pressure** *n* tensión *f* arterial. **high ~ pressure** hipertensión *f*. **~shed** /ˈblʌdʃed/ *n* efusión *f* de sangre, derramamiento *m* de sangre, matanza *f*. **~shot** /ˈblʌdʃɒt/ *a* sanguinolento; ‹*eye*› inyectado de sangre. **~stream** /ˈblʌdstri:m/ *n* sangre *f*
bloodthirsty /ˈblʌdθɜ:stɪ/ *a* sanguinario
bloody /ˈblʌdɪ/ *a* (**-ier**, **-iest**) sangriento; (*stained*) ensangrentado; (*sl*) maldito. **~y-minded** *a* (*fam*) terco
bloom /blu:m/ *n* flor *f*. ● *vi* florecer
bloomer /ˈblu:mə(r)/ *n* (*sl*) metedura *f* de pata
blooming *a* floreciente; (*fam*) maldito
blossom /ˈblɒsəm/ *n* flor *f*. ● *vi* florecer. **~ out (into)** (*fig*) llegar a ser
blot /blɒt/ *n* borrón *m*. ● *vt* (*pt* **blotted**) manchar; (*dry*) secar. **~ out** oscurecer
blotch /blɒtʃ/ *n* mancha *f*. **~y** *a* lleno de manchas
blotter /ˈblɒtə(r)/ *n*, **blotting-paper** /ˈblɒtɪŋpeɪpə(r)/ *n* papel *m* secante
blouse /blaʊz/ *n* blusa *f*
blow[1] /bləʊ/ *vt* (*pt* **blew**, *pp* **blown**) soplar; fundir ‹*fuse*›; tocar ‹*trumpet*›. ● *vi* soplar; ‹*fuse*› fundirse; (*sound*) sonar. ● *n* (*puff*) soplo *m*. **~ down** *vt* derribar. **~ out** apagar ‹*candle*›. **~ over** pasar. **~ up** *vt* inflar; (*explode*) volar; (*photo*) ampliar. ● *vi* (*explode*) estallar; (*burst*) reventar
blow[2] /bləʊ/ *n* (*incl fig*) golpe *m*
blow-dry /ˈbləʊdraɪ/ *vt* secar con secador
blowlamp /ˈbləʊlæmp/ *n* soplete *m*
blow: **~-out** *n* (*of tyre*) reventón *m*. **~-up** *n* (*photo*) ampliación *f*
blowzy /ˈblaʊzɪ/ *a* desaliñado
blubber /ˈblʌbə(r)/ *n* grasa *f* de ballena

bludgeon /'blʌdʒən/ *n* cachiporra *f*. ● *vt* aporrear
blue /blu:/ *a* (**-er**, **-est**) azul; ‹*joke*› verde. ● *n* azul *m*. **out of the ~** totalmente inesperado. **~s** *npl*. **have the ~s** tener tristeza
bluebell /'blu:bel/ *n* campanilla *f*
bluebottle /'blu:bɒtl/ *n* moscarda *f*
blueprint /'blu:prɪnt/ *n* ferroprusiato *m*; (*fig*, *plan*) anteproyecto *m*
bluff /blʌf/ *a* ‹*person*› brusco. ● *n* (*poker*) farol *m*. ● *vt* engañar. ● *vi* (*poker*) tirarse un farol
blunder /'blʌndə(r)/ *vi* cometer un error. ● *n* metedura *f* de pata
blunt /blʌnt/ *a* desafilado; ‹*person*› directo, abrupto. ● *vt* desafilar. **~ly** *adv* francamente. **~ness** *n* embotadura *f*; (*fig*) franqueza *f*, brusquedad *f*
blur /blɜ:(r)/ *n* impresión *f* indistinta. ● *vt* (*pt* **blurred**) hacer borroso
blurb /blɜ:b/ *n* resumen *m* publicitario
blurt /blɜ:t/ *vt*. **~ out** dejar escapar
blush /blʌʃ/ *vi* ruborizarse. ● *n* sonrojo *m*
bluster /'blʌstə(r)/ *vi* ‹*weather*› bramar; ‹*person*› fanfarronear. **~y** *a* tempestuoso
boar /bɔ:(r)/ *n* verraco *m*
board /bɔ:d/ *n* tabla *f*, tablero *m*; (*for notices*) tablón *m*; (*food*) pensión *f*; (*admin*) junta *f*. **~ and lodging** casa y comida. **above ~** correcto. **full ~** pensión *f* completa. **go by the ~** ser abandonado. ● *vt* alojar; (*naut*) embarcar en. ● *vi* alojarse (**with** en casa de); (*at school*) ser interno. **~er** *n* huésped *m*; (*schol*) interno *m*. **~ing-house** *n* casa *f* de huéspedes, pensión *f*. **~ing-school** *n* internado *m*
boast /bəʊst/ *vt* enorgullecerse de. ● *vi* jactarse. ● *n* jactancia *f*. **~er** *n* jactancioso *m*. **~ful** *a* jactancioso
boat /bəʊt/ *n* barco *m*; (*large*) navío *m*; (*small*) barca *f*
boater /'bəʊtə(r)/ *n* (*hat*) canotié *m*
boatswain /'bəʊsn/ *n* contramaestre *m*
bob[1] /bɒb/ *vi* (*pt* **bobbed**) menearse, subir y bajar. **~ up** presentarse súbitamente
bob[2] /bɒb/ *n invar* (*sl*) chelín *m*
bobbin /'bɒbɪn/ *n* carrete *m*; (*in sewing machine*) canilla *f*
bobby /'bɒbɪ/ *n* (*fam*) policía *m*, poli *m* (*fam*)
bobsleigh /'bɒbsleɪ/ *n* bob(sleigh) *m*
bode /bəʊd/ *vi* presagiar. **~ well**/**ill** ser de buen/mal agüero
bodice /'bɒdɪs/ *n* corpiño *m*
bodily /'bɒdɪlɪ/ *a* físico, corporal. ● *adv* físicamente; (*in person*) en persona
body /'bɒdɪ/ *n* cuerpo *m*. **~guard** /'bɒdɪgɑ:d/ *n* guardaespaldas *m invar*. **~work** *n* carrocería *f*
boffin /'bɒfɪn/ *n* (*sl*) científico *m*
bog /bɒg/ *n* ciénaga *f*. ● *vt* (*pt* **bogged**). **get ~ged down** empantanarse
bogey /'bəʊgɪ/ *n* duende *m*; (*nuisance*) pesadilla *f*
boggle /'bɒgl/ *vi* sobresaltarse. **the mind ~s** ¡no es posible!
bogus /'bəʊgəs/ *a* falso
bogy /'bəʊgɪ/ *n* duende *m*; (*nuisance*) pesadilla *f*
boil[1] /bɔɪl/ *vt*/*i* hervir. **be ~ing hot** estar ardiendo; ‹*weather*› hacer mucho calor. **~ away** evaporarse. **~ down to** reducirse a. **~ over** rebosar
boil[2] /bɔɪl/ *n* furúnculo *m*
boiled /'bɔɪld/ *a* hervido; ‹*egg*› pasado por agua
boiler /'bɔɪlə(r)/ *n* caldera *f*. **~ suit** *n* mono *m*
boisterous /'bɔɪstərəs/ *a* ruidoso, bullicioso
bold /bəʊld/ *a* (**-er**, **-est**) audaz. **~ness** *n* audacia *f*
Bolivia /bə'lɪvɪə/ *n* Bolivia *f*. **~n** *a* & *n* boliviano (*m*)
bollard /'bɒləd/ *n* (*naut*) noray *m*; (*Brit*, *auto*) poste *m*
bolster /'bəʊlstə(r)/ *n* cabezal *m*. ● *vt*. **~ up** sostener
bolt /bəʊlt/ *n* cerrojo *m*; (*for nut*) perno *m*; (*lightning*) rayo *m*; (*leap*) fuga *f*. ● *vt* echar el cerrojo a ‹*door*›; engullir ‹*food*›. ● *vi* fugarse. ● *adv*. **~ upright** rígido
bomb /bɒm/ *n* bomba *f*. ● *vt* bombardear. **~ard** /bɒm'bɑ:d/ *vt* bombardear
bombastic /bɒm'bæstɪk/ *a* ampuloso
bomb: **~er** /'bɒmə(r)/ *n* bombardero *m*. **~ing** *n* bombardeo *m*. **~shell** *n* bomba *f*
bonanza /bə'nænzə/ *n* bonanza *f*
bond /bɒnd/ *n* (*agreement*) obligación *f*; (*link*) lazo *m*; (*com*) bono *m*

bondage /ˈbɒndɪdʒ/ *n* esclavitud *f*

bone /bəʊn/ *n* hueso *m*; (*of fish*) espina *f*. ● *vt* deshuesar. **~-dry** *a* completamente seco. **~ idle** *a* holgazán

bonfire /ˈbɒnfaɪə(r)/ *n* hoguera *f*

bonnet /ˈbɒnɪt/ *n* gorra *f*; (*auto*) capó *m*, tapa *f* del motor (*Mex*)

bonny /ˈbɒnɪ/ *a* (**-ier, -iest**) bonito

bonus /ˈbəʊnəs/ *n* prima *f*; (*fig*) plus *m*

bony /ˈbəʊnɪ/ *a* (**-ier, -iest**) huesudo; ‹*fish*› lleno de espinas

boo /buː/ *int* ¡bu! ● *vt/i* abuchear

boob /buːb/ *n* (*mistake, sl*) metedura *f* de pata. ● *vi* (*sl*) meter la pata

booby /ˈbuːbɪ/ *n* bobo *m*. **~ trap** trampa *f*; (*mil*) trampa *f* explosiva

book /bʊk/ *n* libro *m*; (*of cheques etc*) talonario *m*; (*notebook*) libreta *f*; (*exercise book*) cuaderno *m*; (*pl, com*) cuentas *fpl*. ● *vt* (*enter*) registrar; (*reserve*) reservar. ● *vi* reservar. **~able** *a* que se puede reservar. **~case** /ˈbʊkkeɪs/ *n* estantería *f*, librería *f*. **~ing-office** (*in theatre*) taquilla *f*; (*rail*) despacho *m* de billetes. **~let** /ˈbʊklɪt/ *n* folleto *m*

bookkeeping /ˈbʊkkiːpɪŋ/ *n* contabilidad *f*

bookmaker /ˈbʊkmeɪkə(r)/ *n* corredor *m* de apuestas

book: **~mark** /ˈbʊkmɑː(r)k/ *n* señal *f*. **~seller** /ˈbʊkselə(r)/ *n* librero *m*. **~shop** /ˈbʊkʃɒp/ *n* librería *f*. **~stall** /ˈbʊkstɔːl/ *n* quiosco *m* de libros. **~worm** /ˈbʊkwɜːm/ *n* (*fig*) ratón *m* de biblioteca

boom /buːm/ *vi* retumbar; (*fig*) prosperar. ● *n* estampido *m*; (*com*) auge *m*

boon /buːn/ *n* beneficio *m*

boor /bʊə(r)/ *n* patán *m*. **~ish** *a* grosero

boost /buːst/ *vt* estimular; reforzar ‹*morale*›; aumentar ‹*price*›; (*publicize*) hacer publicidad por. ● *n* empuje *m*. **~er** *n* (*med*) revacunación *f*

boot /buːt/ *n* bota *f*; (*auto*) maletero *m*, baúl *m* (*LAm*). **get the ~** (*sl*) ser despedido

booth /buːð/ *n* cabina *f*; (*at fair*) puesto *m*

booty /ˈbuːtɪ/ *n* botín *m*

booze /buːz/ *vi* (*fam*) beber mucho. ● *n* (*fam*) alcohol *m*; (*spree*) borrachera *f*

border /ˈbɔːdə(r)/ *n* borde *m*; (*frontier*) frontera *f*; (*in garden*) arriate *m*. ● *vi*. **~ on** lindar con

borderline /ˈbɔːdəlaɪn/ *n* línea *f* divisoria. **~ case** *n* caso *m* dudoso

bore[1] /bɔː(r)/ *vt* (*tec*) taladrar. ● *vi* taladrar

bore[2] /bɔː(r)/ *vt* (*annoy*) aburrir. ● *n* (*person*) pelmazo *m*; (*thing*) lata *f*

bore[3] /bɔː(r)/ *see* **bear**[1]

boredom /ˈbɔːdəm/ *n* aburrimiento *m*

boring /ˈbɔːrɪŋ/ *a* aburrido, pesado

born /bɔːn/ *a* nato. **be ~** nacer

borne /bɔːn/ *see* **bear**[1]

borough /ˈbʌrə/ *n* municipio *m*

borrow /ˈbɒrəʊ/ *vt* pedir prestado

Borstal /ˈbɔːstl/ *n* reformatorio *m*

bosh /bɒʃ/ *int & n* (*sl*) tonterías (*fpl*)

bosom /ˈbʊzəm/ *n* seno *m*. **~ friend** *n* amigo *m* íntimo

boss /bɒs/ *n* (*fam*) jefe *m*. ● *vt*. **~ (about)** (*fam*) dar órdenes a. **~y** /ˈbɒsɪ/ *a* mandón

botan|ical /bəˈtænɪkl/ *a* botánico. **~ist** /ˈbɒtənɪst/ *n* botánico *m*. **~y** /ˈbɒtənɪ/ *n* botánica *f*

botch /bɒtʃ/ *vt* chapucear. ● *n* chapuza *f*

both /bəʊθ/ *a & pron* ambos (*mpl*), los dos (*mpl*). ● *adv* al mismo tiempo, a la vez

bother /ˈbɒðə(r)/ *vt* molestar; (*worry*) preocupar. **~ it!** *int* ¡caramba! ● *vi* molestarse. **~ about** preocuparse de. **~ doing** tenerse la molestia de hacer. ● *n* molestia *f*

bottle /ˈbɒtl/ *n* botella; (*for baby*) biberón *m*. ● *vt* embotellar. **~ up** (*fig*) reprimir. **~neck** /ˈbɒtlnek/ *n* (*traffic jam*) embotellamiento *m*. **~-opener** *n* destapador *m*, abrebotellas *m invar*; (*corkscrew*) sacacorchos *m invar*

bottom /ˈbɒtəm/ *n* fondo *m*; (*of hill*) pie *m*; (*buttocks*) trasero *m*. ● *a* último, inferior. **~less** *a* sin fondo

bough /baʊ/ *n* rama *f*

bought /bɔːt/ *see* **buy**

boulder /ˈbəʊldə(r)/ *n* canto *m*

boulevard /ˈbuːləvɑːd/ *n* bulevar *m*

bounc|e /baʊns/ *vt* hacer rebotar. ● *vi* rebotar; ‹*person*› saltar; ‹*cheque, sl*› ser rechazado. ● *n* rebote *m*. **~ing** /ˈbaʊnsɪŋ/ *a* robusto

bound[1] /baʊnd/ *vi* saltar. ● *n* salto *m*

bound[2] /baʊnd/ *n*. **out of ~s** zona *f* prohibida

bound[3] /baʊnd/ *a*. **be ~ for** dirigirse a

bound[4] /baʊnd/ *see* **bind**. **~ to** obligado a; (*certain*) seguro de

boundary /'baʊndərɪ/ *n* límite *m*

boundless /'baʊndləs/ *a* ilimitado

bountiful /'baʊntɪfl/ *a* abundante

bouquet /bʊ'keɪ/ *n* ramo *m*; (*perfume*) aroma *m*; (*of wine*) buqué *m*, nariz *f*

bout /baʊt/ *n* período *m*; (*med*) ataque *m*; (*sport*) encuentro *m*

bow[1] /bəʊ/ *n* (*weapon, mus*) arco *m*; (*knot*) lazo *m*

bow[2] /baʊ/ *n* reverencia *f*. ● *vi* inclinarse. ● *vt* inclinar

bow[3] /baʊ/ *n* (*naut*) proa *f*

bowels /'baʊəlz/ *npl* intestinos *mpl*; (*fig*) entrañas *fpl*

bowl[1] /bəʊl/ *n* cuenco *m*; (*for washing*) palangana *f*; (*of pipe*) cazoleta *f*

bowl[2] /bəʊl/ *n* (*ball*) bola *f*. ● *vt* (*cricket*) arrojar. ● *vi* (*cricket*) arrojar la pelota. **~ over** derribar

bow-legged /bəʊ'legɪd/ *a* estevado

bowler[1] /'bəʊlə(r)/ *n* (*cricket*) lanzador *m*

bowler[2] /'bəʊlə(r)/ *n*. **~ (hat)** hongo *m*, bombín *m*

bowling /'bəʊlɪŋ/ *n* bolos *mpl*

bow-tie /bəʊ'taɪ/ *n* corbata *f* de lazo, pajarita *f*

box[1] /bɒks/ *n* caja *f*; (*for jewels etc*) estuche *m*; (*in theatre*) palco *m*

box[2] /bɒks/ *vt* boxear contra. **~ s.o.'s ears** dar una manotada a uno. ● *vi* boxear. **~er** *n* boxeador *m*. **~ing** *n* boxeo *m*

box: **B~ing Day** *n* el 26 de diciembre. **~-office** *n* taquilla *f*. **~-room** *n* trastero *m*

boy /bɔɪ/ *n* chico *m*, muchacho *m*; (*young*) niño *m*

boycott /'bɔɪkɒt/ *vt* boicotear. ● *n* boicoteo *m*

boy: **~-friend** *n* novio *m*. **~hood** *n* niñez *f*. **~ish** *a* de muchacho; (*childish*) infantil

bra /brɑ:/ *n* sostén *m*, sujetador *m*

brace /breɪs/ *n* abrazadera *f*; (*dental*) aparato *m*. ● *vt* asegurar. **~ o.s.** prepararse. **~s** *npl* tirantes *mpl*

bracelet /'breɪslɪt/ *n* pulsera *f*

bracing /'breɪsɪŋ/ *a* vigorizante

bracken /'brækən/ *n* helecho *m*

bracket /'brækɪt/ *n* soporte *m*; (*group*) categoría *f*; (*typ*) paréntesis *m invar*. **square ~s** corchetes *mpl*. ● *vt* poner entre paréntesis; (*join together*) agrupar

brag /bræg/ *vi* (*pt* **bragged**) jactarse (**about** de)

braid /breɪd/ *n* galón *m*; (*of hair*) trenza *f*

brain /breɪn/ *n* cerebro *m*. ● *vt* romper la cabeza

brain-child /'breɪntʃaɪld/ *n* invento *m*

brain: **~ drain** (*fam*) fuga *f* de cerebros. **~less** *a* estúpido. **~s** *npl* (*fig*) inteligencia *f*

brainstorm /'breɪnstɔ:m/ *n* ataque *m* de locura; (*Amer, brainwave*) idea *f* genial

brainwash /'breɪnwɒʃ/ *vt* lavar el cerebro

brainwave /'breɪnweɪv/ *n* idea *f* genial

brainy /'breɪnɪ/ *a* (**-ier**, **-iest**) inteligente

braise /breɪz/ *vt* cocer a fuego lento

brake /breɪk/ *n* freno *m*. **disc ~** freno de disco. **hand ~** freno de mano. ● *vt/i* frenar. **~ fluid** *n* líquido *m* de freno. **~ lining** *n* forro *m* del freno. **~ shoe** *n* zapata *f* del freno

bramble /bræmbl/ *n* zarza *f*

bran /bræn/ *n* salvado *m*

branch /brɑ:ntʃ/ *n* rama *f*; (*of road*) bifurcación *f*; (*com*) sucursal *m*; (*fig*) ramo *m*. ● *vi*. **~ off** bifurcarse. **~ out** ramificarse

brand /brænd/ *n* marca *f*; (*iron*) hierro *m*. ● *vt* marcar; (*reputation*) tildar de

brandish /'brændɪʃ/ *vt* blandir

brand-new /brænd'nju:/ *a* flamante

brandy /'brændɪ/ *n* coñac *m*

brash /bræʃ/ *a* descarado

brass /brɑ:s/ *n* latón *m*. **get down to ~ tacks** (*fig*) ir al grano. **top ~** (*sl*) peces *mpl* gordos. **~y** *a* (**-ier**, **-iest**) descarado

brassière /'bræsjeə(r)/ *n* sostén *m*, sujetador *m*

brat /bræt/ *n* (*pej*) mocoso *m*

bravado /brə'vɑ:dəʊ/ *n* bravata *f*

brave /breɪv/ *a* (**-er**, **-est**) valiente. ● *n* (*Red Indian*) guerrero *m* indio. ● *vt* afrontar. **~ry** /-ərɪ/ *n* valentía *f*, valor *m*

brawl /brɔ:l/ *n* alboroto *m*. ● *vi* pelearse

brawn /brɔ:n/ *n* músculo *m*; (*strength*) fuerza *f* muscular. **~y** *a* musculoso

bray /breɪ/ *n* rebuzno *m.* ● *vi* rebuznar
brazen /'breɪzn/ *a* descarado
brazier /'breɪzɪə(r)/ *n* brasero *m*
Brazil /brə'zɪl/ *n* el Brasil *m.* **~ian** *a* & *n* brasileño (*m*)
breach /bri:tʃ/ *n* violación *f*; (*of contract*) incumplimiento *m*; (*gap*) brecha *f.* ● *vt* abrir una brecha en
bread /bred/ *n* pan *m.* **loaf of ~** pan. **~crumbs** /'bredkrʌmz/ *npl* migajas *fpl*; (*culin*) pan rallado. **~line** *n.* **on the ~line** en la miseria
breadth /bredθ/ *n* anchura *f*
bread-winner /'bredwɪnə(r)/ *n* sostén *m* de la familia, cabeza *f* de familia
break /breɪk/ *vt* (*pt* **broke**, *pp* **broken**) romper; quebrantar ‹*law*›; batir ‹*record*›; comunicar ‹*news*›; interrumpir ‹*journey*›. ● *vi* romperse; ‹*news*› divulgarse. ● *n* ruptura *f*; (*interval*) intervalo *m*; (*chance, fam*) oportunidad *f*; (*in weather*) cambio *m.* **~ away** escapar. **~ down** *vt* derribar; analizar ‹*figures*›. ● *vi* estropearse; (*auto*) averiarse; (*med*) sufrir un colapso; (*cry*) deshacerse en lágrimas. **~ into** forzar ‹*house etc*›; (*start doing*) ponerse a. **~ off** interrumpirse. **~ out** ‹*war, disease*› estallar; (*run away*) escaparse. **~ up** romperse; ‹*schools*› terminar. **~able** *a* frágil. **~age** *n* rotura *f*
breakdown /'breɪkdaʊn/ *n* (*tec*) falla *f*; (*med*) colapso *m*, crisis *f* nerviosa; (*of figures*) análisis *f*
breaker /'breɪkə(r)/ *n* (*wave*) cachón *m*
breakfast /'brekfəst/ *n* desayuno *m*
breakthrough /'breɪkθru:/ *n* adelanto *m*
breakwater /'breɪkwɔ:tə(r)/ *n* rompeolas *m invar*
breast /brest/ *n* pecho *m*; (*of chicken etc*) pechuga *f.* **~-stroke** *n* braza *f* de pecho
breath /breθ/ *n* aliento *m*, respiración *f.* **out of ~** sin aliento. **under one's ~** a media voz. **~alyser** /'breθəlaɪzə(r)/ *n* alcoholímetro *m*
breath|e /bri:ð/ *vt/i* respirar. **~er** /'bri:ðə(r)/ *n* descanso *m*, pausa *f.* **~ing** *n* respiración *f*
breathtaking /'breθteɪkɪŋ/ *a* impresionante
bred /bred/ *see* **breed**
breeches /'brɪtʃɪz/ *npl* calzones *mpl*
breed /bri:d/ *vt/i* (*pt* **bred**) reproducirse; (*fig*) engendrar. ● *n* raza *f.* **~er** *n* criador *m.* **~ing** *n* cría *f*; (*manners*) educación *f*
breez|e /bri:z/ *n* brisa *f.* **~y** *a* de mucho viento; ‹*person*› despreocupado. **it is ~y** hace viento
Breton /'bretən/ *a* & *n* bretón (*m*)
brew /bru:/ *vt* hacer. ● *vi* fermentar; ‹*tea*› reposar; (*fig*) prepararse. ● *n* infusión *f.* **~er** *n* cervecero *m.* **~ery** *n* fábrica *f* de cerveza, cervecería *f*
bribe /braɪb/ *n* soborno *m.* ● *vt* sobornar. **~ry** /-ərɪ/ *n* soborno *m*
brick /brɪk/ *n* ladrillo *m.* ● *vt.* **~ up** tapar con ladrillos. **~layer** /'brɪkleɪə(r)/ *n* albañil *m*
bridal /braɪdl/ *a* nupcial
bride /braɪd/ *m* novia *f.* **~groom** /'braɪdgrʊm/ *n* novio *m.* **~smaid** /'braɪdzmeɪd/ *n* dama *f* de honor
bridge[1] /brɪdʒ/ *n* puente *m*; (*of nose*) caballete *m.* ● *vt* tender un puente sobre. **~ a gap** llenar un vacío
bridge[2] /brɪdʒ/ *n* (*cards*) bridge *m*
bridle /'braɪdl/ *n* brida *f.* ● *vt* embridar. **~-path** *n* camino *m* de herradura
brief /bri:f/ *a* (**-er**, **-est**) breve. ● *n* (*jurid*) escrito *m.* ● *vt* dar instrucciones a. **~case** /'bri:fkeɪs/ *n* maletín *m.* **~ly** *adv* brevemente. **~s** *npl* (*man's*) calzoncillos *mpl*; (*woman's*) bragas *fpl*
brigad|e /brɪ'geɪd/ *n* brigada *f.* **~ier** /-ə'dɪə(r)/ *n* general *m* de brigada
bright /braɪt/ *a* (**-er**, **-est**) brillante, claro; (*clever*) listo; (*cheerful*) alegre. **~en** /'braɪtn/ *vt* aclarar; hacer más alegre ‹*house etc*›. ● *vi* ‹*weather*› aclararse; ‹*face*› animarse. **~ly** *adv* brillantemente. **~ness** *n* claridad *f*
brillian|ce /'brɪljəns/ *n* brillantez *f*, brillo *m.* **~t** *a* brillante
brim /brɪm/ *n* borde *m*; (*of hat*) ala *f.* ● *vi* (*pt* **brimmed**). **~ over** desbordarse
brine /braɪn/ *n* salmuera *f*
bring /brɪŋ/ *vt* (*pt* **brought**) traer ‹*thing*›; conducir ‹*person, vehicle*›. **~ about** causar. **~ back** devolver. **~ down** derribar; rebajar ‹*price*›. **~ off** lograr. **~ on** causar. **~ out** sacar; lanzar ‹*product*›; publicar ‹*book*›. **~ round/to** hacer volver en sí ‹*unconscious person*›. **~ up** (*med*) vomitar; educar ‹*children*›; plantear ‹*question*›

brink /brɪŋk/ *n* borde *m*
brisk /brɪsk/ *a* (**-er**, **-est**) enérgico, vivo. **~ness** *n* energía *f*
bristl|e /'brɪsl/ *n* cerda *f*. ● *vi* erizarse. **~ing with** erizado de
Brit|ain /'brɪtən/ *n* Gran Bretaña *f*. **~ish** /'brɪtɪʃ/ *a* británico. **the ~ish** los británicos. **~on** /'brɪtən/ *n* británico *m*
Brittany /'brɪtənɪ/ *n* Bretaña *f*
brittle /'brɪtl/ *a* frágil, quebradizo
broach /brəʊtʃ/ *vt* abordar ‹*subject*›; espitar ‹*cask*›
broad /brɔ:d/ *a* (**-er**, **-est**) ancho. **in ~ daylight** en pleno día. **~ bean** *n* haba *f*
broadcast /'brɔ:dkɑ:st/ *n* emisión *f*. ● *vt* (*pt* **broadcast**) emitir. ● *vi* hablar por la radio. **~ing** *a* de radiodifusión. ● *n* radio-difusión *f*
broad: **~en** /'brɔ:dn/ *vt* ensanchar. ● *vi* ensancharse. **~ly** *adv* en general. **~-minded** *a* de miras amplias, tolerante, liberal
brocade /brə'keɪd/ *n* brocado *m*
broccoli /'brɒkəlɪ/ *n invar* brécol *m*
brochure /'brəʊʃə(r)/ *n* folleto *m*
brogue /brəʊg/ *n* abarca *f*; (*accent*) acento *m* regional
broke /brəʊk/ *see* **break**. ● *a* (*sl*) sin blanca
broken /'brəʊkən/ *see* **break**. ● *a*. **~ English** inglés *m* chapurreado. **~-hearted** *a* con el corazón destrozado
broker /'brəʊkə(r)/ *n* corredor *m*
brolly /'brɒlɪ/ *n* (*fam*) paraguas *m invar*
bronchitis /brɒŋ'kaɪtɪs/ *n* bronquitis *f*
bronze /brɒnz/ *n* bronce *m*. ● *vt* broncear. ● *vi* broncearse
brooch /brəʊtʃ/ *n* broche *m*
brood /bru:d/ *n* cría *f*; (*joc*) prole *m*. ● *vi* empollar; (*fig*) meditar. **~y** *a* contemplativo
brook[1] /brʊk/ *n* arroyo *m*
brook[2] /brʊk/ *vt* soportar
broom /bru:m/ *n* hiniesta *f*; (*brush*) escoba *f*. **~stick** /'bru:mstɪk/ *n* palo *m* de escoba
broth /brɒθ/ *n* caldo *m*
brothel /'brɒθl/ *n* burdel *m*
brother /'brʌðə(r)/ *n* hermano *m*. **~hood** *n* fraternidad *f*, (*relig*) hermandad *f*. **~-in-law** *n* cuñado *m*. **~ly** *a* fraternal
brought /brɔ:t/ *see* **bring**
brow /braʊ/ *n* frente *f*; (*of hill*) cima *f*
browbeat /'braʊbi:t/ *vt* (*pt* **-beat**, *pp* **-beaten**) intimidar
brown /braʊn/ *a* (**-er**, **-est**) marrón; ‹*skin*› moreno; ‹*hair*› castaño. ● *n* marrón *m*. ● *vt* poner moreno; (*culin*) dorar. ● *vi* ponerse moreno; (*culin*) dorarse. **be ~ed off** (*sl*) estar hasta la coronilla
Brownie /'braʊnɪ/ *n* niña *f* exploradora
browse /braʊz/ *vi* (*in a shop*) curiosear; ‹*animal*› pacer
bruise /bru:z/ *n* magulladura *f*. ● *vt* magullar; machucar ‹*fruit*›. ● *vi* magullarse; ‹*fruit*› machacarse
brunch /brʌntʃ/ *n* (*fam*) desayuno *m* tardío
brunette /bru:'net/ *n* morena *f*
brunt /brʌnt/ *n*. **the ~ of** lo más fuerte de
brush /brʌʃ/ *n* cepillo *m*; (*large*) escoba; (*for decorating*) brocha *f*; (*artist's*) pincel; (*skirmish*) escaramuza *f*. ● *vt* cepillar. **~ against** rozar. **~ aside** rechazar. **~ off** (*rebuff*) desairar. **~ up (on)** refrescar
brusque /bru:sk/ *a* brusco. **~ly** *adv* bruscamente
Brussels /'brʌslz/ *n* Bruselas *f*. **~ sprout** col *m* de Bruselas
brutal /'bru:tl/ *a* brutal. **~ity** /-'tælətɪ/ *n* brutalidad *f*
brute /bru:t/ *n* bestia *f*. **~ force** fuerza *f* bruta
BSc *abbr see* **bachelor**
bubble /'bʌbl/ *n* burbuja *f*. ● *vi* burbujear. **~ over** desbordarse
bubbly /'bʌblɪ/ *a* burbujeante. ● *n* (*fam*) champaña *m*, champán *m* (*fam*)
buck[1] /bʌk/ *a* macho. ● *n* (*deer*) ciervo *m*. ● *vi* (*of horse*) corcovear. **~ up** (*hurry, sl*) darse prisa; (*cheer up, sl*) animarse
buck[2] /bʌk/ (*Amer, sl*) dólar *m*
buck[3] /bʌk/ *n*. **pass the ~ to s.o.** echarle a uno el muerto
bucket /'bʌkɪt/ *n* cubo *m*
buckle /'bʌkl/ *n* hebilla *f*. ● *vt* abrochar. ● *vi* torcerse. **~ down to** dedicarse con empeño a
bud /bʌd/ *n* brote *m*. ● *vi* (*pt* **budded**) brotar.
Buddhis|m /'bʊdɪzəm/ *n* budismo *m*. **~t** /'bʊdɪst/ *a* & *n* budista (*m* & *f*)
budding /'bʌdɪŋ/ *a* (*fig*) en ciernes

buddy /ˈbʌdɪ/ *n* (*fam*) compañero *m*, amigote *m* (*fam*)
budge /bʌdʒ/ *vt* mover. ● *vi* moverse
budgerigar /ˈbʌdʒərɪgɑ:(r)/ *n* periquito *m*
budget /ˈbʌdʒɪt/ *n* presupuesto *m*. ● *vi* (*pt* **budgeted**) presupuestar
buff /bʌf/ *n* (*colour*) color *m* de ante; (*fam*) aficionado *m*. ● *vt* pulir
buffalo /ˈbʌfələʊ/ *n* (*pl* **-oes** *or* **-o**) búfalo *m*
buffer /ˈbʌfə(r)/ *n* parachoques *m invar*. **~ state** *n* estado *m* tapón
buffet /ˈbʊfeɪ/ *n* (*meal, counter*) bufé *m*. /ˈbʌfɪt/ *n* golpe *m*; (*slap*) bofetada *f*. ● *vt* (*pt* **buffeted**) golpear
buffoon /bəˈfu:n/ *n* payaso *m*, bufón *m*
bug /bʌg/ *n* bicho *m*; (*germ, sl*) microbio *m*; (*device, sl*) micrófono *m* oculto. ● *vt* (*pt* **bugged**) ocultar un micrófono en; intervenir ‹*telephone*›; (*Amer, sl*) molestar
bugbear /ˈbʌgbeə(r)/ *n* pesadilla *f*
buggy /ˈbʌgɪ/ *n*. **baby ~** (*esp Amer*) cochecito *m* de niño
bugle /ˈbju:gl/ *n* corneta *f*
build /bɪld/ *vt*/*i* (*pt* **built**) construir. **~ up** *vt* urbanizar; (*increase*) aumentar. ● *n* (*of person*) figura *f*, tipo *m*. **~er** *n* constructor *m*. **~-up** *n* aumento *m*; (*of gas etc*) acumulación *f*; (*fig*) propaganda *f*
built /bɪlt/ *see* **build**. **~-in** *a* empotrado. **~-up area** *n* zona *f* urbanizada
bulb /bʌlb/ *n* bulbo *m*; (*elec*) bombilla *f*. **~ous** *a* bulboso
Bulgaria /bʌlˈgeərɪə/ *n* Bulgaria *f*. **~n** *a* & *n* búlgaro (*m*)
bulg|e /bʌldʒ/ *n* protuberancia *f*. ● *vi* pandearse; (*jut out*) sobresalir. **~ing** *a* abultado; ‹*eyes*› saltón
bulk /bʌlk/ *n* bulto *m*, volumen *m*. **in ~** a granel; (*loose*) suelto. **the ~ of** la mayor parte de. **~y** *a* voluminoso
bull /bʊl/ *n* toro *m*
bulldog /ˈbʊldɒg/ *n* buldog *m*
bulldozer /ˈbʊldəʊzə(r)/ *n* oruga *f* aplanadora, bulldozer *m*
bullet /ˈbʊlɪt/ *n* bala *f*
bulletin /ˈbʊlətɪn/ *n* anuncio *m*; (*journal*) boletín *m*
bullet-proof /ˈbʊlɪtpru:f/ *a* a prueba de balas
bullfight /ˈbʊlfaɪt/ *n* corrida *f* (de toros). **~er** *n* torero *m*
bullion /ˈbʊljən/ *n* (*gold*) oro *m* en barras; (*silver*) plata *f* en barras
bull: **~ring** /ˈbʊlrɪŋ/ *n* plaza *f* de toros. **~'s-eye** *n* centro *m* del blanco, diana *f*
bully /ˈbʊlɪ/ *n* matón *m*. ● *vt* intimidar. **~ing** *n* intimidación *f*
bum[1] /bʌm/ *n* (*bottom, sl*) trasero *m*
bum[2] /bʌm/ *n* (*Amer, sl*) holgazán *m*
bumble-bee /ˈbʌmblbi:/ *n* abejorro *m*
bump /bʌmp/ *vt* chocar contra. ● *vi* dar sacudidas. ● *n* choque *m*; (*swelling*) chichón *m*. **~ into** chocar contra; (*meet*) encontrar
bumper /ˈbʌmpə(r)/ *n* parachoques *m invar*. ● *a* abundante. **~ edition** *n* edición *f* especial
bumpkin /ˈbʌmpkɪn/ *n* patán *m*, paleto *m* (*fam*)
bumptious /ˈbʌmpʃəs/ *a* presuntuoso
bun /bʌn/ *n* bollo *m*; (*hair*) moño *m*
bunch /bʌntʃ/ *n* manojo *m*; (*of people*) grupo *m*; (*of bananas, grapes*) racimo *m*, (*of flowers*) ramo *m*
bundle /ˈbʌndl/ *n* bulto *m*; (*of papers*) legajo *m*; (*of nerves*) manojo *m*. ● *vt*. **~ up** atar
bung /bʌŋ/ *n* tapón *m*. ● *vt* tapar; (*sl*) tirar
bungalow /ˈbʌŋgələʊ/ *n* casa *f* de un solo piso, chalé *m*, bungalow *m*
bungle /ˈbʌŋgl/ *vt* chapucear
bunion /ˈbʌnjən/ *n* juanete *m*
bunk /bʌŋk/ *n* litera *f*
bunker /ˈbʌŋkə(r)/ *n* carbonera *f*; (*golf*) obstáculo *m*; (*mil*) refugio *m*, búnker *m*
bunkum /ˈbʌŋkəm/ *n* tonterías *fpl*
bunny /ˈbʌnɪ/ *n* conejito *m*
buoy /bɔɪ/ *n* boya *f*. ● *vt*. **~ up** hacer flotar; (*fig*) animar
buoyan|cy /ˈbɔɪənsɪ/ *n* flotabilidad *f*; (*fig*) optimismo *m*. **~t** /ˈbɔɪənt/ *a* boyante; (*fig*) alegre
burden /ˈbɜ:dn/ *n* carga *f*. ● *vt* cargar (**with** de). **~some** *a* pesado
bureau /ˈbjʊərəʊ/ *n* (*pl* **-eaux** /-əʊz/) escritorio *m*; (*office*) oficina *f*
bureaucra|cy /bjʊəˈrɒkrəsɪ/ *n* burocracia *f*. **~t** /ˈbjʊərəkræt/ *n* burócrata *m* & *f*. **~tic** /-ˈkrætɪk/ *a* burocrático
burgeon /ˈbɜ:dʒən/ *vi* brotar; (*fig*) crecer
burgl|ar /ˈbɜ:glə(r)/ *n* ladrón *m*. **~ary** *n* robo *m* con allanamiento de

morada. **~e** /'bɜ:gl/ *vt* robar con allanamiento

Burgundy /'bɜ:gəndɪ/ *n* Borgoña *f*; (*wine*) vino *m* de Borgoña

burial /'berɪəl/ *n* entierro *m*

burlesque /bɜ:'lesk/ *n* burlesco *m*

burly /'bɜ:lɪ/ *a* (**-ier**, **-iest**) corpulento

Burm|a /'bɜ:mə/ Birmania *f*. **~ese** /-'mi:z/ *a & n* birmano (*m*)

burn /bɜ:n/ *vt* (*pt* **burned** *or* **burnt**) quemar. ● *vi* quemarse. **~ down** *vt* destruir con fuego. ● *n* quemadura *f*. **~er** *n* quemador *m*. **~ing** *a* ardiente; ‹*food*› que quema; ‹*question*› candente

burnish /'bɜ:nɪʃ/ *vt* lustrar, pulir

burnt /bɜ:nt/ *see* **burn**

burp /bɜ:p/ *n* (*fam*) eructo *m*. ● *vi* (*fam*) eructar

burr /bɜ:(r)/ *n* (*bot*) erizo *m*

burrow /'bʌrəʊ/ *n* madriguera *f*. ● *vt* excavar

bursar /'bɜ:sə(r)/ *n* tesorero *m*. **~y** /'bɜ:sərɪ/ *n* beca *f*

burst /bɜ:st/ *vt* (*pt* **burst**) reventar. ● *vi* reventarse; ‹*tyre*› pincharse. ● *n* reventón *m*; (*mil*) ráfaga *f*; (*fig*) explosión *f*. **~ of laughter** carcajada *f*

bury /'berɪ/ *vt* enterrar; (*hide*) ocultar

bus /bʌs/ *n* (*pl* **buses**) autobús *m*, camión *m* (*Mex*). ● *vi* (*pt* **bussed**) ir en autobús

bush /bʊʃ/ *n* arbusto *m*; (*land*) monte *m*. **~y** *a* espeso

busily /'bɪzɪlɪ/ *adv* afanosamente

business /'bɪznɪs/ *n* negocio *m*; (*com*) negocios *mpl*; (*profession*) ocupación *f*; (*fig*) asunto *m*. **mind one's own ~** ocuparse de sus propios asuntos. **~-like** *a* práctico, serio. **~man** *n* hombre *m* de negocios

busker /'bʌskə(r)/ *n* músico *m* ambulante

bus-stop /'bʌsstɒp/ *n* parada *f* de autobús

bust[1] /bʌst/ *n* busto *m*; (*chest*) pecho *m*

bust[2] /bʌst/ *vt* (*pt* **busted** *or* **bust**) (*sl*) romper. ● *vi* romperse. ● *a* roto. **go ~** (*sl*) quebrar

bustle /'bʌsl/ *vi* apresurarse. ● *n* bullicio *m*

bust-up /'bʌstʌp/ *n* (*sl*) riña *f*

busy /'bɪzɪ/ *a* (**-ier**, **-iest**) ocupado; ‹*street*› concurrido. ● *vt*. **~ o.s. with** ocuparse de

busybody /'bɪzɪbɒdɪ/ *n* entrometido *m*

but /bʌt/ *conj* pero; (*after negative*) sino. ● *prep* menos. **~ for** si no fuera por. **last ~ one** penúltimo. ● *adv* solamente

butane /'bju:teɪn/ *n* butano *m*

butcher /'bʊtʃə(r)/ *n* carnicero *m*. ● *vt* matar; (*fig*) hacer una carnicería con. **~y** *n* carnicería *f*, matanza *f*

butler /'bʌtlə(r)/ *n* mayordomo *m*

butt /bʌt/ *n* (*of gun*) culata *f*; (*of cigarette*) colilla *f*; (*target*) blanco *m*. ● *vi* topar. **~ in** interrumpir

butter /'bʌtə(r)/ *n* mantequilla *f*. ● *vt* untar con mantequilla. **~ up** *vt* (*fam*) lisonjear, dar jabón a. **~-bean** *n* judía *f*

buttercup /'bʌtəkʌp/ *n* ranúnculo *m*

butter-fingers /'bʌtəfɪŋgəz/ *n* manazas *m invar*, torpe *m*

butterfly /'bʌtəflaɪ/ *n* mariposa *f*

buttock /'bʌtək/ *n* nalga *f*

button /'bʌtn/ *n* botón *m*. ● *vt* abotonar. ● *vi* abotonarse. **~hole** /'bʌtnhəʊl/ *n* ojal *m*. ● *vt* (*fig*) detener

buttress /'bʌtrɪs/ *n* contrafuerte *m*. ● *vt* apoyar

buxom /'bʌksəm/ *a* ‹*woman*› rollizo

buy /baɪ/ *vt* (*pt* **bought**) comprar. ● *n* compra *f*. **~er** *n* comprador *m*

buzz /bʌz/ *n* zumbido *m*; (*phone call, fam*) llamada *f*. ● *vi* zumbar. **~ off** (*sl*) largarse. **~er** *n* timbre *m*

by /baɪ/ *prep* por; (*near*) cerca de; (*before*) antes de; (*according to*) según. **~ and large** en conjunto, en general. **~ car** en coche. **~ oneself** por sí solo

bye-bye /'baɪbaɪ/ *int* (*fam*) ¡adiós!

by-election /'baɪɪlekʃn/ *n* elección *f* parcial

bygone /'baɪgɒn/ *a* pasado

by-law /'baɪlɔ:/ *n* reglamento *m* (local)

bypass /'baɪpɑ:s/ *n* carretera *f* de circunvalación. ● *vt* evitar

by-product /'baɪprɒdʌkt/ *n* subproducto *m*

bystander /'baɪstændə(r)/ *n* espectador *m*

byword /'baɪwɜ:d/ *n* sinónimo *m*. **be a ~ for** ser conocido por

C

cab /kæb/ *n* taxi *m*; (*of lorry, train*) cabina *f*
cabaret /'kæbəreɪ/ *n* espectáculo *m*
cabbage /'kæbɪdʒ/ *n* col *m*, repollo *m*
cabin /'kæbɪn/ *n* cabaña *f*; (*in ship*) camarote *m*; (*in plane*) cabina *f*
cabinet /'kæbɪnɪt/ *n* (*cupboard*) armario *m*; (*for display*) vitrina *f*. **C~** (*pol*) gabinete *m*. **~-maker** *n* ebanista *m & f*
cable /'keɪbl/ *n* cable *m*. ● *vt* cablegrafiar. **~ railway** *n* funicular *m*
cache /kæʃ/ *n* (*place*) escondrijo *m*; (*things*) reservas *fpl* escondidas. ● *vt* ocultar
cackle /'kækl/ *n* (*of hen*) cacareo *m*; (*laugh*) risotada *f*. ● *vi* cacarear; (*laugh*) reírse a carcajadas
cacophon|ous /kə'kɒfənəs/ *a* cacofónico. **~y** *n* cacofonía *f*
cactus /'kæktəs/ *n* (*pl* **-ti** /-taɪ/) cacto *m*
cad /kæd/ *n* sinvergüenza m. **~dish** *a* desvergonzado
caddie /'kædɪ/ *n* (*golf*) portador *m* de palos
caddy /'kædɪ/ *n* cajita *f*
cadence /'keɪdəns/ *n* cadencia *f*
cadet /kə'det/ *n* cadete *m*
cadge /kædʒ/ *vt/i* gorronear. **~r** /-ə(r)/ *n* gorrón *m*
Caesarean /sɪ'zeərɪən/ *a* cesáreo. **~ section** *n* cesárea *f*
café /'kæfeɪ/ *n* cafetería *f*
cafeteria /kæfɪ'tɪərɪə/ *n* autoservicio *m*
caffeine /'kæfi:n/ *n* cafeína *f*
cage /keɪdʒ/ *n* jaula *f*. ● *vt* enjaular
cagey /'keɪdʒɪ/ *a* (*fam*) evasivo
Cairo /'kaɪərəʊ/ *n* el Cairo *m*
cajole /kə'dʒəʊl/ *vt* engatusar. **~ry** *n* engatusamiento *m*
cake /keɪk/ *n* pastel *m*, tarta *f*; (*sponge*) bizcocho *m*. **~ of soap** pastilla *f* de jabón. **~d** *a* incrustado
calamit|ous /kə'læmɪtəs/ *a* desastroso. **~y** /kə'læmətɪ/ *n* calamidad *f*
calcium /'kælsɪəm/ *n* calcio *m*
calculat|e /'kælkjʊleɪt/ *vt/i* calcular; (*Amer*) suponer. **~ing** *a* calculador. **~ion** /-'leɪʃn/ *n* cálculo *m*. **~or** *n* calculadora *f*
calculus /'kælkjʊləs/ *n* (*pl* **-li**) cálculo *m*
calendar /'kælɪndə(r)/ *n* calendario *m*
calf[1] /kɑ:f/ *n* (*pl* **calves**) ternero *m*
calf[2] /kɑ:f/ *n* (*pl* **calves**) (*of leg*) pantorrilla *f*
calibre /'kælɪbə(r)/ *n* calibre *m*
calico /'kælɪkəʊ/ *n* calicó *m*
call /kɔ:l/ *vt/i* llamar. ● *n* llamada *f*; (*shout*) grito *m*; (*visit*) visita *f*. **be on ~** estar de guardia. **long distance ~** conferencia *f*. **~ back** *vt* hacer volver; (*on phone*) volver a llamar. ● *vi* volver; (*on phone*) volver a llamar. **~ for** pedir; (*fetch*) ir a buscar. **~ off** cancelar. **~ on** visitar. **~ out** dar voces. **~ together** convocar. **~ up** (*mil*) llamar al servicio militar; (*phone*) llamar. **~-box** *n* cabina *f* telefónica. **~er** *n* visita *f*; (*phone*) el que llama *m*. **~ing** *n* vocación *f*
callous /'kæləs/ *a* insensible, cruel. **~ness** *n* crueldad *f*
callow /'kæləʊ/ *a* (**-er**, **-est**) inexperto
calm /kɑ:m/ *a* (**-er**, **-est**) tranquilo; ‹*weather*› calmoso. ● *n* tranquilidad *f*, calma *f*. ● *vt* calmar. ● *vi* calmarse. **~ness** *n* tranquilidad *f*, calma *f*
calorie /'kælərɪ/ *n* caloría *f*
camber /'kæmbə(r)/ *n* curvatura *f*
came /keɪm/ *see* **come**
camel /'kæml/ *n* camello *m*
camellia /kə'mi:ljə/ *n* camelia *f*
cameo /'kæmɪəʊ/ *n* (*pl* **-os**) camafeo *m*
camera /'kæmərə/ *n* máquina *f* (fotográfica); (*TV*) cámara *f*. **~man** *n* (*pl* **-men**) operador *m*, cámara *m*
camouflage /'kæməflɑ:ʒ/ *n* camuflaje *m*. ● *vt* encubrir; (*mil*) camuflar
camp[1] /kæmp/ *n* campamento *m*. ● *vi* acamparse
camp[2] /kæmp/ *a* (*affected*) amanerado
campaign /kæm'peɪn/ *n* campaña *f*. ● *vi* hacer campaña
camp: **~-bed** *n* catre *m* de tijera. **~er** *n* campista *m & f*; (*vehicle*) caravana *f*. **~ing** *n* camping *m*. **go ~ing** hacer camping. **~site** /'kæmpsaɪt/ *n* camping *m*
campus /'kæmpəs/ *n* (*pl* **-puses**) ciudad *f* universitaria
can[1] /kæn/ *v aux* (*pt* **could**) (*be able to*) poder; (*know how to*) saber. **~not** (*neg*), **~'t** (*neg, fam*). **I ~not/~'t go** no puedo ir

can[2] /kæn/ *n* lata *f*. ● *vt* (*pt* **canned**) enlatar. **~ned music** música *f* grabada

Canad|a /'kænədə/ *n* el Canadá *m*. **~ian** /kə'neɪdɪən/ *a* & *n* canadiense (*m* & *f*)

canal /kə'næl/ *n* canal *m*

canary /kə'neərɪ/ *n* canario *m*

cancel /'kænsl/ *vt/i* (*pt* **cancelled**) anular; cancelar ‹*contract etc*›; suspender ‹*appointment etc*›; (*delete*) tachar. **~lation** /-'leɪʃn/ *n* cancelación *f*

cancer /'kænsə(r)/ *n* cáncer *m*. **C~** *n* (*Astr*) Cáncer *m*. **~ous** *a* canceroso

candid /'kændɪd/ *a* franco

candida|cy /'cændɪdəsɪ/ *n* candidatura *f*. **~te** /'kændɪdeɪt/ *n* candidato *m*

candle /'kændl/ *n* vela *f*. **~stick** /'kændlstɪk/ *n* candelero *m*

candour /'kændə(r)/ *n* franqueza *f*

candy /'kændɪ/ *n* (*Amer*) caramelo *m*. **~-floss** *n* algodón *m* de azúcar

cane /keɪn/ *n* caña *f*; (*for baskets*) mimbre *m*; (*stick*) bastón *m*. ● *vt* (*strike*) castigar con palmeta

canine /'keɪnaɪn/ *a* canino

canister /'kænɪstə(r)/ *n* bote *m*

cannabis /'kænəbɪs/ *n* cáñamo *m* índico, hachís *m*, mariguana *f*

cannibal /'kænɪbl/ *n* caníbal *m*. **~ism** *n* canibalismo *m*

cannon /'kænən/ *n invar* cañón *m*. **~ shot** cañonazo *m*

cannot /'kænət/ *see* **can**[1]

canny /'kænɪ/ *a* astuto

canoe /kə'nu:/ *n* canoa *f*, piragua *f*. ● *vi* ir en canoa. **~ist** *n* piragüista *m* & *f*

canon /'kænən/ *n* canon *m*; (*person*) canónigo *m*. **~ize** /'kænənaɪz/ *vt* canonizar

can-opener /'kænəʊpnə(r)/ *n* abrelatas *m invar*

canopy /'kænəpɪ/ *n* dosel *m*; (*of parachute*) casquete *m*

cant /kænt/ *n* jerga *f*

can't /kɑ:nt/ *see* **can**[1]

cantankerous /kæn'tæŋkərəs/ *a* malhumorado

canteen /kæn'ti:n/ *n* cantina *f*; (*of cutlery*) juego *m*; (*flask*) cantimplora *f*

canter /'kæntə(r)/ *n* medio galope *m*. ●.*vi* ir a medio galope

canvas /'kænvəs/ *n* lona *f*; (*artist's*) lienzo *m*

canvass /'kænvəs/ *vi* hacer campaña, solicitar votos. **~ing** *n* solicitación *f* (de votos)

canyon /'kænjən/ *n* cañón *m*

cap /kæp/ *n* gorra *f*; (*lid*) tapa *f*; (*of cartridge*) cápsula *f*; (*academic*) birrete *m*; (*of pen*) capuchón *m*; (*mec*) casquete *m*. ● *vt* (*pt* **capped**) tapar, poner cápsula a; (*outdo*) superar

capab|ility /keɪpə'bɪlətɪ/ *n* capacidad *f*. **~le** /'keɪpəbl/ *a* capaz. **~ly** *adv* competentemente

capacity /kə'pæsətɪ/ *n* capacidad *f*; (*function*) calidad *f*

cape[1] /keɪp/ *n* (*cloak*) capa *f*

cape[2] /keɪp/ *n* (*geog*) cabo *m*

caper[1] /'keɪpə(r)/ *vi* brincar. ● *n* salto *m*; (*fig*) travesura *f*

caper[2] /'keɪpə(r)/ *n* (*culin*) alcaparra *f*

capital /'kæpɪtl/ *a* capital. **~ letter** *n* mayúscula *f*. ● *n* (*town*) capital *f*; (*money*) capital *m*

capitalis|m /'kæpɪtəlɪzəm/ *n* capitalismo *m*. **~t** *a* & *n* capitalista (*m* & *f*)

capitalize /'kæpɪtəlaɪz/ *vt* capitalizar; (*typ*) escribir con mayúsculas. **~ on** aprovechar

capitulat|e /kə'pɪtʃʊleɪt/ *vi* capitular. **~ion** /-'leɪʃn/ *n* capitulación *f*

capon /'keɪpən/ *n* capón *m*

capricious /kə'prɪʃəs/ *a* caprichoso

Capricorn /'kæprɪkɔ:n/ *n* Capricornio *m*

capsicum /'kæpsɪkəm/ *n* pimiento *m*

capsize /kæp'saɪz/ *vt* hacer zozobrar. ● *vi* zozobrar

capsule /'kæpsju:l/ *n* cápsula *f*

captain /'kæptɪn/ *n* capitán *m*. ● *vt* capitanear

caption /'kæpʃn/ *n* (*heading*) título *m*; (*of cartoon etc*) leyenda *f*

captivate /'kæptɪveɪt/ *vt* encantar

captiv|e /'kæptɪv/ *a* & *n* cautivo (*m*). **~ity** /-'tɪvətɪ/ *n* cautiverio *m*, cautividad *f*

capture /'kæptʃə(r)/ *vt* prender; llamar ‹*attention*›; (*mil*) tomar. ● *n* apresamiento *m*; (*mil*) toma *f*

car /kɑ:(r)/ *n* coche *m*, carro *m* (*LAm*)

carafe /kə'ræf/ *n* jarro *m*, garrafa *f*

caramel /'kærəmel/ *n* azúcar *m* quemado; (*sweet*) caramelo *m*

carat /'kærət/ *n* quilate *m*

caravan /'kærəvæn/ *n* caravana *f*

carbohydrate /kɑ:bəʊ'haɪdreɪt/ *n* hidrato *m* de carbono

carbon /'kɑ:bən/ *n* carbono *m*; (*paper*) carbón *m*. **~ copy** copia *f* al carbón
carburettor /kɑ:bjʊ'retə(r)/ *n* carburador *m*
carcass /'kɑ:kəs/ *n* cadáver *m*, esqueleto *m*
card /kɑ:d/ *n* tarjeta *f*; (*for games*) carta *f*; (*membership*) carnet *m*; (*records*) ficha *f*
cardboard /'kɑ:dbɔ:d/ *n* cartón *m*
cardiac /'kɑ:dɪæk/ *a* cardíaco
cardigan /'kɑ:dɪgən/ *n* chaqueta *f* de punto, rebeca *f*
cardinal /'kɑ:dɪnəl/ *a* cardinal. ● *n* cardenal *m*
card-index /'kɑ:dɪndeks/ *n* fichero *m*
care /keə(r)/ *n* cuidado *m*; (*worry*) preocupación *f*; (*protection*) cargo *m*. **~ of** a cuidado de, en casa de. **take ~ of** cuidar de ‹*person*›; ocuparse de ‹*matter*›. ● *vi* interesarse. **I don't ~** me es igual. **~ about** interesarse por. **~ for** cuidar de; (*like*) querer
career /kə'rɪə(r)/ *n* carrera *f*. ● *vi* correr a toda velocidad
carefree /'keəfri:/ *a* despreocupado
careful /'keəfʊl/ *a* cuidadoso; (*cautious*) prudente. **~ly** *adv* con cuidado
careless /'keəlɪs/ *a* negligente; (*not worried*) indiferente. **~ly** *adv* descuidadamente. **~ness** *n* descuido *m*
caress /kə'res/ *n* caricia *f*. ● *vt* acariciar
caretaker /'keəteɪkə(r)/ *n* vigilante *m*; (*of flats etc*) portero *m*
car-ferry /'kɑ:ferɪ/ *n* transbordador *m* de coches
cargo /'kɑ:gəʊ/ *n* (*pl* **-oes**) carga *f*
Caribbean /kærɪ'bi:ən/ *a* caribe. **~ Sea** *n* mar *m* Caribe
caricature /'kærɪkətʃʊə(r)/ *n* caricatura *f*. ● *vt* caricaturizar
carnage /'kɑ:nɪdʒ/ *n* carnicería *f*, matanza *f*
carnal /'kɑ:nl/ *a* carnal
carnation /kɑ:'neɪʃn/ *n* clavel *m*
carnival /'kɑ:nɪvl/ *n* carnaval *m*
carol /'kærəl/ *n* villancico *m*
carouse /kə'raʊz/ *vi* correrse una juerga
carousel /kærə'sel/ *n* tiovivo *m*
carp[1] /kɑ:p/ *n invar* carpa *f*
carp[2] /kɑ:p/ *vi*. **~ at** quejarse de
car park /'kɑ:pɑ:k/ *n* aparcamiento *m*
carpent|er /'kɑ:pɪntə(r)/ *n* carpintero *m*. **~ry** *n* carpintería *f*
carpet /'kɑ:pɪt/ *n* alfombra *f*. **be on the ~** (*fam*) recibir un rapapolvo; (*under consideration*) estar sobre el tapete. ● *vt* alfombrar. **~-sweeper** *n* escoba *f* mecánica
carriage /'kærɪdʒ/ *n* coche *m*; (*mec*) carro *m*; (*transport*) transporte *m*; (*cost, bearing*) porte *m*
carriageway /'kærɪdʒweɪ/ *n* calzada *f*, carretera *f*
carrier /'kærɪə(r)/ *n* transportista *m* & *f*; (*company*) empresa *f* de transportes; (*med*) portador *m*. **~-bag** bolsa *f*
carrot /'kærət/ *n* zanahoria *f*
carry /'kærɪ/ *vt* llevar; transportar ‹*goods*›; (*involve*) llevar consigo, implicar. ● *vi* ‹*sounds*› llegar, oírse. **~ off** llevarse. **~ on** continuar; (*complain, fam*) quejarse. **~ out** realizar; cumplir ‹*promise, threat*›. **~-cot** *n* capazo *m*
cart /kɑ:t/ *n* carro *m*. ● *vt* acarrear; (*carry, fam*) llevar
cartilage /'kɑ:tɪlɪdʒ/ *n* cartílago *m*
carton /'kɑ:tən/ *n* caja *f* (de cartón)
cartoon /kɑ:'tu:n/ *n* caricatura *f*, chiste *m*; (*strip*) historieta *f*; (*film*) dibujos *mpl* animados. **~ist** *n* caricaturista *m* & *f*
cartridge /'kɑ:trɪdʒ/ *n* cartucho *m*
carve /kɑ:v/ *vt* tallar; trinchar ‹*meat*›
cascade /kæs'keɪd/ *n* cascada *f*. ● *vi* caer en cascadas
case /keɪs/ *n* caso *m*; (*jurid*) proceso *m*; (*crate*) cajón *m*; (*box*) caja *f*; (*suitcase*) maleta *f*. **in any ~** en todo caso. **in ~ he comes** por si viene. **in ~ of** en caso de. **lower ~** caja *f* baja, minúscula *f*. **upper ~** caja *f* alta, mayúscula *f*
cash /kæʃ/ *n* dinero *m* efectivo. **pay (in) ~** pagar al contado. ● *vt* cobrar. **~ in (on)** aprovecharse de. **~ desk** *n* caja *f*
cashew /'kæʃu:/ *n* anacardo *m*
cashier /kæ'ʃɪə(r)/ *n* cajero *m*
cashmere /kæʃ'mɪə(r)/ *n* casimir *m*, cachemir *m*
casino /kə'si:nəʊ/ *n* (*pl* **-os**) casino *m*
cask /kɑ:sk/ *n* barril *m*
casket /'kɑ:skɪt/ *n* cajita *f*
casserole /'kæsərəʊl/ *n* cacerola *f*; (*stew*) cazuela *f*
cassette /kə'set/ *n* casete *m*
cast /kɑ:st/ *vt* (*pt* **cast**) arrojar; fundir ‹*metal*›; dar ‹*vote*›; (*in theatre*)

repartir. ● *n* lanzamiento *m*; (*in play*) reparto *m*; (*mould*) molde *m*
castanets /kæstə'nets/ *npl* castañuelas *fpl*
castaway /'kɑ:stəweɪ/ *n* náufrago *m*
caste /kɑ:st/ *n* casta *f*
cast: ~ **iron** *n* hierro *m* fundido. ~**-iron** *a* de hierro fundido; (*fig*) sólido
castle /'kɑ:sl/ *n* castillo *m*; (*chess*) torre *f*
cast-offs /'kɑ:stɒfs/ *npl* desechos *mpl*
castor /'kɑ:stə(r)/ *n* ruedecilla *f*
castor oil /kɑ:stər'ɔɪl/ *n* aceite *m* de ricino
castor sugar /'kɑ:stəʃʊgə(r)/ *n* azúcar *m* extrafino
castrat|e /kæ'streɪt/ *vt* castrar. ~**ion** /-ʃn/ *n* castración *f*
casual /'kæʒʊəl/ *a* casual; ‹*meeting*› fortuito; ‹*work*› ocasional; ‹*attitude*› despreocupado; ‹*clothes*› informal, de sport. ~**ly** *adv* de paso
casualt|y /'kæʒʊəltɪ/ *n* accidente *m*; (*injured*) víctima *f*, herido *m*; (*dead*) víctima *f*, muerto *m*. ~**ies** *npl* (*mil*) bajas *fpl*
cat /kæt/ *n* gato *m*
cataclysm /'kætəklɪzəm/ *n* cataclismo *m*
catacomb /'kætəku:m/ *n* catacumba *f*
catalogue /'kætəlɒg/ *n* catálogo *m*. ● *vt* catalogar
catalyst /'kætəlɪst/ *n* catalizador *m*
catamaran /kætəmə'ræn/ *n* catamarán *m*
catapult /'kætəpʌlt/ *n* catapulta *f*; (*child's*) tirador *m*, tirachinos *m invar*
cataract /'kætərækt/ *n* catarata *f*
catarrh /kə'tɑ:(r)/ *n* catarro *m*
catastroph|e /kə'tæstrəfɪ/ *n* catástrofe *m*. ~**ic** /kætə'strɒfɪk/ *a* catastrófico
catch /kætʃ/ *vt* (*pt* **caught**) coger (*not LAm*), agarrar; (*grab*) asir; tomar ‹*train, bus*›; (*unawares*) sorprender; (*understand*) comprender; contraer ‹*disease*›. ~ **a cold** resfriarse. ~ **sight of** avistar. ● *vi* (*get stuck*) engancharse; ‹*fire*› prenderse. ● *n* cogida *f*; (*of fish*) pesca *f*; (*on door*) pestillo *m*; (*on window*) cerradura *f*. ~ **on** (*fam*) hacerse popular. ~ **up** poner al día. ~ **up with** alcanzar; ponerse al corriente de ‹*news etc*›
catching /'kætʃɪŋ/ *a* contagioso
catchment /'kætʃmənt/ *n*. ~ **area** *n* zona *f* de captación
catch-phrase /'kætʃfreɪz/ *n* eslogan *m*
catchword /'kætʃwɜ:d/ *n* eslogan *m*, consigna *f*
catchy /'kætʃɪ/ *a* pegadizo
catechism /'kætɪkɪzəm/ *n* catecismo *m*
categorical /kætɪ'gɒrɪkl/ *a* categórico
category /'kætɪgərɪ/ *n* categoría *f*
cater /'keɪtə(r)/ *vi* proveer comida a. ~ **for** proveer a ‹*needs*›. ~**er** *n* proveedor *m*
caterpillar /'kætəpɪlə(r)/ *n* oruga *f*
cathedral /kə'θi:drəl/ *n* catedral *f*
catholic /'kæθəlɪk/ *a* universal. **C**~ *a* & *n* católico (*m*). **C**~**ism** /kə'θɒlɪsɪzəm/ *n* catolicismo *m*
catnap /'kætnæp/ *n* sueñecito *m*
cat's eyes /'kætsaɪz/ *npl* catafotos *mpl*
cattle /'kætl/ *npl* ganado *m* (vacuno)
cat|ty /'kætɪ/ *a* malicioso. ~**walk** /'kætwɔ:k/ *n* pasarela *f*
caucus /'kɔ:kəs/ *n* comité *m* electoral
caught /kɔ:t/ *see* **catch**
cauldron /'kɔ:ldrən/ *n* caldera *f*
cauliflower /'kɒlɪflaʊə(r)/ *n* coliflor *f*
cause /kɔ:z/ *n* causa *f*, motivo *m*. ● *vt* causar
causeway /'kɔ:zweɪ/ *n* calzada *f* elevada, carretera *f* elevada
caustic /'kɔ:stɪk/ *a* & *n* cáustico (*m*)
cauterize /'kɔ:təraɪz/ *vt* cauterizar
caution /'kɔ:ʃn/ *n* cautela *f*; (*warning*) advertencia *f*. ● *vt* advertir; (*jurid*) amonestar
cautious /'kɔ:ʃəs/ *a* cauteloso, prudente. ~**ly** *adv* con precaución, cautelosamente
cavalcade /kævəl'keɪd/ *n* cabalgata *f*
cavalier /kævə'lɪə(r)/ *a* arrogante
cavalry /'kævəlrɪ/ *n* caballería *f*
cave /keɪv/ *n* cueva *f*. ● *vi*. ~ **in** hundirse. ~**-man** *n* (*pl* **-men**) troglodita *m*
cavern /'kævən/ *n* caverna *f*, cueva *f*
caviare /'kævɪɑ:(r)/ *n* caviar *m*
caving /'keɪvɪŋ/ *n* espeleología *f*
cavity /'kævətɪ/ *n* cavidad *f*; (*in tooth*) caries *f*
cavort /kə'vɔ:t/ *vi* brincar
cease /si:s/ *vt/i* cesar. ● *n*. **without** ~ sin cesar. ~**-fire** *n* tregua *f*, alto *m* el fuego. ~**less** *a* incesante
cedar /'si:də(r)/ *n* cedro *m*

cede /si:d/ *vt* ceder
cedilla /sɪ'dɪlə/ *n* cedilla *f*
ceiling /'si:lɪŋ/ *n* techo *m*
celebrat|e /'selɪbreɪt/ *vt* celebrar. ● *vi* divertirse. **~ed** /'selɪbreɪtɪd/ *a* célebre. **~ion** /-'breɪʃn/ *n* celebración *f*; (*party*) fiesta *f*
celebrity /sɪ'lebrətɪ/ *n* celebridad *f*
celery /'selərɪ/ *n* apio *m*
celestial /sɪ'lestjəl/ *a* celestial
celiba|cy /'selɪbəsɪ/ *n* celibato *m*. **~te** /'selɪbət/ *a* & *n* célibe (*m* & *f*)
cell /sel/ *n* celda *f*; (*biol*) célula *f*; (*elec*) pila *f*
cellar /'selə(r)/ *n* sótano *m*; (*for wine*) bodega *f*
cell|ist /'tʃelɪst/ *n* violonc(h)elo *m* & *f*, violonc(h)elista *m* & *f*. **~o** /'tʃeləʊ/ *n* (*pl* **-os**) violonc(h)elo *m*
Cellophane /'seləfeɪn/ *n* (*P*) celofán *m* (*P*)
cellular /'seljʊlə(r)/ *a* celular
celluloid /'seljʊlɔɪd/ *n* celuloide *m*
cellulose /'seljʊləʊs/ *n* celulosa *f*
Celt /kelt/ *n* celta *m* & *f*. **~ic** *a* céltico
cement /sɪ'ment/ *n* cemento *m*. ● *vt* cementar; (*fig*) consolidar
cemetery /'semətrɪ/ *n* cementerio *m*
cenotaph /'senətɑ:f/ *n* cenotafio *m*
censor /'sensə(r)/ *n* censor *m*. ● *vt* censurar. **~ship** *n* censura *f*
censure /'senʃə(r)/ *n* censura *f*. ● *vt* censurar
census /'sensəs/ *n* censo *m*
cent /sent/ *n* centavo *m*
centenary /sen'ti:nərɪ/ *n* centenario *m*
centigrade /'sentɪgreɪd/ *a* centígrado
centilitre /'sentɪli:tə(r)/ *n* centilitro *m*
centimetre /'sentɪmi:tə(r)/ *n* centímetro *m*
centipede /'sentɪpi:d/ *n* ciempiés *m invar*
central /'sentrəl/ *a* central; (*of town*) céntrico. **~ heating** *n* calefacción *f* central. **~ize** *vt* centralizar. **~ly** *adv* (*situated*) en el centro
centre /'sentə(r)/ *n* centro *m*. ● *vt* (*pt* **centred**) *vi* concentrarse
centrifugal /sen'trɪfjʊgəl/ *a* centrífugo
century /'sentʃərɪ/ *n* siglo *m*
ceramic /sɪ'ræmɪk/ *a* cerámico. **~s** *npl* cerámica *f*
cereal /'sɪərɪəl/ *n* cereal *m*
cerebral /'serɪbrəl/ *a* cerebral
ceremon|ial /serɪ'məʊnɪəl/ *a* & *n* ceremonial (*m*). **~ious** /-'məʊnɪəs/ *a* ceremonioso. **~y** /'serɪmənɪ/ *n* ceremonia *f*
certain /'sɜ:tn/ *a* cierto. **for ~** seguro. **make ~ of** asegurarse de. **~ly** *adv* desde luego. **~ty** *n* certeza *f*
certificate /sə'tɪfɪkət/ *n* certificado *m*; (*of birth, death etc*) partida *f*
certify /'sɜ:tɪfaɪ/ *vt* certificar
cessation /se'seɪʃən/ *n* cesación *f*
cesspit /'sespɪt/ *n*, **cesspool** /'sespu:l/ *n* pozo *m* negro; (*fam*) sentina *f*
chafe /tʃeɪf/ *vt* rozar. ● *vi* rozarse; (*fig*) irritarse
chaff /tʃæf/ *vt* zumbarse de
chaffinch /'tʃæfɪntʃ/ *n* pinzón *m*
chagrin /'ʃægrɪn/ *n* disgusto *m*
chain /tʃeɪn/ *n* cadena *f*. ● *vt* encadenar. **~ reaction** *n* reacción *f* en cadena. **~-smoker** *n* fumador *m* que siempre tiene un cigarillo encendido. **~ store** *n* sucursal *m*
chair /tʃeə(r)/ *n* silla *f*; (*univ*) cátedra *f*. ● *vt* presidir. **~-lift** *n* telesilla *m*
chairman /'tʃeəmən/ *n* (*pl* **-men**) presidente *m*
chalet /'ʃæleɪ/ *n* chalé *m*
chalice /'tʃælɪs/ *n* cáliz *m*
chalk /tʃɔ:k/ *n* creta *f*; (*stick*) tiza *f*. **~y** *a* cretáceo
challeng|e /'tʃælɪndʒ/ *n* desafío *m*; (*fig*) reto *m*. ● *vt* desafiar; (*question*) poner en duda. **~ing** *a* estimulante
chamber /'tʃeɪmbə(r)/ *n* (*old use*) cámara *f*. **~maid** /'tʃeɪmbəmeɪd/ *n* camarera *f*. **~-pot** *n* orinal *m*. **~s** *npl* despacho *m*, bufete *m*
chameleon /kə'mi:ljən/ *n* camaleón *m*
chamois /'ʃæmɪ/ *n* gamuza *f*
champagne /ʃæm'peɪn/ *n* champaña *m*, champán *m* (*fam*)
champion /'tʃæmpɪən/ *n* campeón *m*. ● *vt* defender. **~ship** *n* campeonato *m*
chance /tʃɑ:ns/ *n* casualidad *f*; (*likelihood*) probabilidad *f*; (*opportunity*) oportunidad *f*; (*risk*) riesgo *m*. **by ~** por casualidad. ● *a* fortuito. ● *vt* arriesgar. ● *vi* suceder. **~ upon** tropezar con
chancellor /'tʃɑ:nsələ(r)/ *n* canciller *m*; (*univ*) rector *m*. **C~ of the Exchequer** Ministro *m* de Hacienda
chancy /'tʃɑ:nsɪ/ *a* arriesgado; (*uncertain*) incierto

chandelier /ʃændəˈlɪə(r)/ *n* araña *f* (de luces)

change /tʃeɪndʒ/ *vt* cambiar; (*substitute*) reemplazar. **~ one's mind** cambiar de idea. ● *vi* cambiarse. ● *n* cambio *m*; (*small coins*) suelto *m*. **~ of life** menopausia *f*. **~able** *a* cambiable; ‹*weather*› variable. **~-over** *n* cambio *m*

channel /ˈtʃænl/ *n* canal *m*; (*fig*) medio *m*. **the C~ Islands** *npl* las islas *fpl* Anglonormandas. **the (English) C~** el canal de la Mancha. ● *vt* (*pt* **channelled**) acanalar; (*fig*) encauzar

chant /tʃɑːnt/ *n* canto *m*. ● *vt/i* cantar; (*fig*) salmodiar

chao|s /ˈkeɪɒs/ *n* caos *m*, desorden *m*. **~tic** /-ˈɒtɪk/ *a* caótico, desordenado

chap[1] /tʃæp/ *n* (*crack*) grieta *f*. ● *vt* (*pt* **chapped**) agrietar. ● *vi* agrietarse

chap[2] /tʃæp/ *n* (*fam*) hombre *m*, tío *m* (*fam*)

chapel /ˈtʃæpl/ *n* capilla *f*

chaperon /ˈʃæpərəʊn/ *n* acompañanta *f*. ● *vt* acompañar

chaplain /ˈtʃæplɪn/ *n* capellán *m*

chapter /ˈtʃæptə(r)/ *n* capítulo *m*

char[1] /tʃɑː(r)/ *vt* (*pt* **charred**) carbonizar

char[2] /tʃɑː(r)/ *n* asistenta *f*

character /ˈkærəktə(r)/ *n* carácter *m*; (*in play*) personaje *m*. **in ~** característico

characteristic /kærəktəˈrɪstɪk/ *a* característico. **~ally** *adv* típicamente

characterize /ˈkærəktəraɪz/ *vt* caracterizar

charade /ʃəˈrɑːd/ *n* charada *f*, farsa *f*

charcoal /ˈtʃɑːkəʊl/ *n* carbón *m* vegetal; (*for drawing*) carboncillo *m*

charge /tʃɑːdʒ/ *n* precio *m*; (*elec, mil*) carga *f*; (*jurid*) acusación *f*; (*task, custody*) encargo *m*; (*responsibility*) responsabilidad *f*. **in ~ of** responsable de, encargado de. **take ~ of** encargarse de. ● *vt* pedir; (*elec, mil*) cargar; (*jurid*) acusar; (*entrust*) encargar. ● *vi* cargar; (*money*) cobrar. **~able** *a* a cargo (de)

chariot /ˈtʃærɪət/ *n* carro *m*

charisma /kəˈrɪzmə/ *n* carisma *m*. **~tic** /-ˈmætɪk/ *a* carismático

charitable /ˈtʃærɪtəbl/ *a* caritativo

charity /ˈtʃærɪtɪ/ *n* caridad *f*; (*society*) institución *f* benéfica

charlatan /ˈʃɑːlətən/ *n* charlatán *m*

charm /tʃɑːm/ *n* encanto *m*; (*spell*) hechizo *m*; (*on bracelet*) dije *m*, amuleto *m*. ● *vt* encantar. **~ing** *a* encantador

chart /tʃɑːt/ *n* (*naut*) carta *f* de marear; (*table*) tabla *f*. ● *vt* poner en una carta de marear

charter /ˈtʃɑːtə(r)/ *n* carta *f*. ● *vt* conceder carta a, estatuir; alquilar ‹*bus, train*›; fletar ‹*plane, ship*›. **~ed accountant** *n* contador *m* titulado. **~ flight** *n* vuelo *m* charter

charwoman /ˈtʃɑːwʊmən/ *n* (*pl* **-women**) asistenta *f*

chary /ˈtʃeərɪ/ *a* cauteloso

chase /tʃeɪs/ *vt* perseguir. ● *vi* correr. ● *n* persecución *f*. **~ away**, **~ off** ahuyentar

chasm /ˈkæzəm/ *n* abismo *m*

chassis /ˈʃæsɪ/ *n* chasis *m*

chaste /tʃeɪst/ *a* casto

chastise /tʃæsˈtaɪz/ *vt* castigar

chastity /ˈtʃæstətɪ/ *n* castidad *f*

chat /tʃæt/ *n* charla *f*. **have a ~** charlar. ● *vi* (*pt* **chatted**) charlar

chattels /ˈtʃætlz/ *n* bienes *mpl* muebles

chatter /ˈtʃætə(r)/ *n* charla *f*. ● *vi* charlar. **his teeth are ~ing** le castañetean los dientes. **~box** /ˈtʃætəbɒks/ *n* parlanchín *m*

chatty *a* hablador; ‹*style*› familiar

chauffeur /ˈʃəʊfə(r)/ *n* chófer *m*

chauvinis|m /ˈʃəʊvɪnɪzəm/ *n* patriotería *f*; (*male*) machismo *m*. **~t** /ˈʃəʊvɪnɪst/ *n* patriotero *m*; (*male*) machista *m & f*

cheap /tʃiːp/ *a* (**-er**, **-est**) barato; (*poor quality*) de baja calidad; ‹*rate*› económico. **~en** /ˈtʃiːpən/ *vt* abaratar. **~(ly)** *adv* barato, a bajo precio. **~ness** *n* baratura *f*

cheat /ˈtʃiːt/ *vt* defraudar; (*deceive*) engañar. ● *vi* (*at cards*) hacer trampas. ● *n* trampa *f*; (*person*) tramposo *m*

check[1] /tʃek/ *vt* comprobar; (*examine*) inspeccionar; (*curb*) detener; (*chess*) dar jaque a. ● *vi* comprobar. ● *n* comprobación *f*; (*of tickets*) control *m*; (*curb*) freno *m*; (*chess*) jaque *m*; (*bill, Amer*) cuenta *f*. **~ in** registrarse; (*at airport*) facturar el equipaje. **~ out** pagar la cuenta y marcharse. **~ up** comprobar. **~ up on** investigar

check[2] /tʃek/ *n* (*pattern*) cuadro *m*. **~ed** *a* a cuadros

checkmate /ˈtʃekmeɪt/ *n* jaque *m* mate. ● *vt* dar mate a
check-up /ˈtʃekʌp/ *n* examen *m*
cheek /tʃi:k/ *n* mejilla *f*; (*fig*) descaro *m*. **~-bone** *n* pómulo *m*. **~y** *a* descarado
cheep /tʃi:p/ *vi* piar
cheer /tʃɪə(r)/ *n* alegría *f*; (*applause*) viva *m*. ● *vt* alegrar; (*applaud*) aplaudir. ● *vi* alegrarse; (*applaud*) aplaudir. **~ up!** ¡anímate! **~ful** *a* alegre. **~fulness** *n* alegría *f*
cheerio /tʃɪərɪˈəʊ/ *int* (*fam*) ¡adiós!, ¡hasta luego!
cheer: **~less** /ˈtʃɪəlɪs/ *a* triste. **~s!** ¡salud!
cheese /tʃi:z/ *n* queso *m*
cheetah /ˈtʃi:tə/ *n* guepardo *m*
chef /ʃef/ *n* cocinero *m*
chemical /ˈkemɪkl/ *a* químico. ● *n* producto *m* químico
chemist /ˈkemɪst/ *n* farmacéutico *m*; (*scientist*) químico *m*. **~ry** *n* química *f*. **~'s (shop)** *n* farmacia *f*
cheque /tʃek/ *n* cheque *m*, talón *m*. **~-book** *n* talonario *m*
chequered /ˈtʃekəd/ *a* a cuadros; (*fig*) con altibajos
cherish /ˈtʃerɪʃ/ *vt* cuidar; (*love*) querer; abrigar ‹*hope*›
cherry /ˈtʃerɪ/ *n* cereza *f*. **~-tree** *n* cerezo *m*
cherub /ˈtʃerəb/ *n* (*pl* **-im**) (*angel*) querubín *m*
chess /tʃes/ *n* ajedrez *m*. **~-board** *n* tablero *m* de ajedrez
chest /tʃest/ *n* pecho *m*; (*box*) cofre *m*, cajón *m*. **~ of drawers** *n* cómoda *f*
chestnut /ˈtʃesnʌt/ *n* castaña *f*. **~-tree** *n* castaño *m*
chew /tʃu:/ *vt* masticar; (*fig*) rumiar. **~ing-gum** *n* chicle *m*
chic /ʃi:k/ *a* elegante. ● *n* elegancia *f*
chick /tʃɪk/ *n* polluelo *m*. **~en** /ˈtʃɪkɪn/ *n* pollo *m*. ● *a* (*sl*) cobarde. ● *vi*. **~en out** (*sl*) retirarse. **~en-pox** *n* varicela *f*
chicory /ˈtʃɪkərɪ/ *n* (*in coffee*) achicoria *f*; (*in salad*) escarola *f*
chide /tʃaɪd/ *vt* (*pt* **chided**) reprender
chief /tʃi:f/ *n* jefe *m*. ● *a* principal. **~ly** *adv* principalmente
chilblain /ˈtʃɪlbleɪn/ *n* sabañón *m*
child /tʃaɪld/ *n* (*pl* **children** /ˈtʃɪldrən/) niño *m*; (*offspring*) hijo *m*. **~birth** /ˈtʃaɪldbɜ:θ/ *n* parto *m*. **~hood** *n* niñez *f*. **~ish** *a* infantil. **~less** *a* sin hijos. **~like** *a* inocente, infantil
Chile /ˈtʃɪlɪ/ *n* Chile *m*. **~an** *a & n* chileno (*m*)
chill /tʃɪl/ *n* frío *m*; (*illness*) resfriado *m*. ● *a* frío. ● *vt* enfriar; refrigerar ‹*food*›
chilli /ˈtʃɪlɪ/ *n* (*pl* **-ies**) chile *m*
chilly /ˈtʃɪlɪ/ *a* frío
chime /tʃaɪm/ *n* carillón *m*. ● *vt* tocar ‹*bells*›; dar ‹*hours*›. ● *vi* repicar
chimney /ˈtʃɪmnɪ/ *n* (*pl* **-eys**) chimenea *f*. **~-pot** *n* cañón *m* de chimenea. **~-sweep** *n* deshollinador *m*
chimpanzee /tʃɪmpænˈzi:/ *n* chimpancé *m*
chin /tʃɪn/ *n* barbilla *f*
china /ˈtʃaɪnə/ *n* porcelana *f*
Chin|a /ˈtʃaɪnə/ *n* China *f*. **~ese** /-ˈni:z/ *a & n* chino (*m*)
chink[1] /tʃɪŋk/ *n* (*crack*) grieta *f*
chink[2] /tʃɪŋk/ *n* (*sound*) tintín *m*. ● *vt* hacer tintinear. ● *vi* tintinear
chip /tʃɪp/ *n* pedacito *m*; (*splinter*) astilla *f*; (*culin*) patata *f* frita; (*gambling*) ficha *f*. **have a ~ on one's shoulder** guardar rencor. ● *vt* (*pt* **chipped**) desportillar. ● *vi* desportillarse. **~ in** (*fam*) interrumpir; (*with money*) contribuir
chiropodist /kɪˈrɒpədɪst/ *n* callista *m & f*
chirp /tʃɜ:p/ *n* pío *m*. ● *vi* piar
chirpy /ˈtʃɜ:pɪ/ *a* alegre
chisel /ˈtʃɪzl/ *n* formón *m*. ● *vt* (*pt* **chiselled**) cincelar
chit /tʃɪt/ *n* vale *m*, nota *f*
chit-chat /ˈtʃɪttʃæt/ *n* cháchara *f*
chivalr|ous *a* /ˈʃɪvəlrəs/ *a* caballeroso. **~y** /ˈʃɪvəlrɪ/ *n* caballerosidad *f*
chive /tʃaɪv/ *n* cebollino *m*
chlorine /ˈklɔ:ri:n/ *n* cloro *m*
chock /tʃɒk/ *n* calzo *m*. **~-a-block** *a*, **~-full** *a* atestado
chocolate /ˈtʃɒklɪt/ *n* chocolate *m*; (*individual sweet*) bombón *m*
choice /tʃɔɪs/ *n* elección *f*; (*preference*) preferencia *f*. ● *a* escogido
choir /ˈkwaɪə(r)/ *n* coro *m*. **~boy** /ˈkwaɪəbɔɪ/ *n* niño *m* de coro
choke /tʃəʊk/ *vt* sofocar. ● *vi* sofocarse. ● *n* (*auto*) estrangulador *m*, estárter *m*
cholera /ˈkɒlərə/ *n* cólera *m*
cholesterol /kəˈlestərɒl/ *n* colesterol *m*

choose /tʃu:z/ *vt/i* (*pt* **chose,** *pp* **chosen**) elegir. **~y** /'tʃu:zɪ/ *a* (*fam*) exigente

chop /tʃɒp/ *vt* (*pt* **chopped**) cortar. ● *n* (*culin*) chuleta *f*. **~ down** talar. **~ off** cortar. **~per** *n* hacha *f*; (*butcher's*) cuchilla *f*; (*sl*) helicóptero *m*

choppy /'tʃɒpɪ/ *a* picado

chopstick /'tʃɒpstɪk/ *n* palillo *m* (chino)

choral /'kɔ:rəl/ *a* coral

chord /kɔ:d/ *n* cuerda *f*; (*mus*) acorde *m*

chore /tʃɔ:(r)/ *n* tarea *f*, faena *f*. **household ~s** *npl* faenas *fpl* domésticas

choreographer /kɒrɪ'ɒgrəfə(r)/ *n* coreógrafo *m*

chorister /'kɒrɪstə(r)/ *n* (*singer*) corista *m & f*

chortle /'tʃɔ:tl/ *n* risita *f* alegre. ● *vi* reírse alegremente

chorus /'kɔ:rəs/ *n* coro *m*; (*of song*) estribillo *m*

chose, chosen /tʃəʊz, 'tʃəʊzn/ *see* **choose**

Christ /kraɪst/ *n* Cristo *m*

christen /'krɪsn/ *vt* bautizar. **~ing** *n* bautizo *m*

Christian /'krɪstjən/ *a & n* cristiano (*m*). **~ name** *n* nombre *m* de pila

Christmas /'krɪsməs/ *n* Navidad *f*; (*period*) Navidades *fpl*. ● *a* de Navidad, navideño. **~-box** *n* aguinaldo *m*. **~ day** *n* día *m* de Navidad. **~ Eve** *n* Nochebuena *f*. **Father ~** *n* Papá *m* Noel. **Happy ~!** ¡Felices Pascuas!

chrom|e /krəʊm/ *n* cromo *m*. **~ium** /'krəʊmɪəm/ *n* cromo *m*. **~ium plating** *n* cromado *m*

chromosome /'krəʊməsəʊm/ *n* cromosoma *m*

chronic /'krɒnɪk/ *a* crónico; (*bad, fam*) terrible

chronicle /'krɒnɪkl/ *n* crónica *f*. ● *vt* historiar

chronolog|ical /krɒnə'lɒdʒɪkl/ *a* cronológico. **~y** /krə'nɒlədʒɪ/ *n* cronología *f*

chrysanthemum /krɪ'sænθəməm/ *n* crisantemo *m*

chubby /'tʃʌbɪ/ *a* (**-ier, -iest**) regordete; ‹*face*› mofletudo

chuck /tʃʌk/ *vt* (*fam*) arrojar. **~ out** tirar

chuckle /'tʃʌkl/ *n* risa *f* ahogada. ● *vi* reírse entre dientes

chuffed /tʃʌft/ *a* (*sl*) contento

chug /tʃʌg/ *vi* (*pt* **chugged**) (*of motor*) traquetear

chum /tʃʌm/ *n* amigo *m*, compinche *m*. **~my** *a*. **be ~my** ‹*2 people*› ser muy amigos. **be ~my with** ser muy amigo de

chump /tʃʌmp/ *n* (*sl*) tonto *m*. **~ chop** *n* chuleta *f*

chunk /tʃʌŋk/ *n* trozo *m* grueso. **~y** /tʃʌŋkɪ/ *a* macizo

church /'tʃɜ:tʃ/ *n* iglesia *f*. **~yard** /'tʃɜ:tʃjɑ:d/ *n* cementerio *m*

churlish /'tʃɜ:lɪʃ/ *a* grosero

churn /'tʃɜ:n/ *n* (*for milk*) lechera *f*, cántara *f*; (*for butter*) mantequera *f*. ● *vt* agitar. **~ out** producir en profusión

chute /ʃu:t/ *n* tobogán *m*

chutney /'tʃʌtnɪ/ *n* (*pl* **-eys**) condimento *m* agridulce

cider /'saɪdə(r)/ *n* sidra *f*

cigar /sɪ'gɑ:(r)/ *n* puro *m*

cigarette /sɪgə'ret/ *n* cigarillo *m*. **~-holder** *n* boquilla *f*

cine-camera /'sɪnɪkæmərə/ *n* cámara *f*, tomavistas *m invar*

cinema /'sɪnəmə/ *n* cine *m*

cinnamon /'sɪnəmən/ *n* canela *f*

cipher /'saɪfə(r)/ *n* (*math, fig*) cero *m*; (*secret system*) cifra *f*

circle /'sɜ:kl/ *n* círculo *m*; (*in theatre*) anfiteatro *m*. ● *vt* girar alrededor de. ● *vi* dar vueltas

circuit /'sɜ:kɪt/ *n* circuito *m*; (*chain*) cadena *f*

circuitous /sɜ:'kju:ɪtəs/ *a* indirecto

circular /'sɜ:kjʊlə(r)/ *a & n* circular (*f*)

circularize /'sɜ:kjʊləraɪz/ *vt* enviar circulares a

circulat|e /'sɜ:kjʊleɪt/ *vt* hacer circular. ● *vi* circular. **~ion** /-'leɪʃn/ *n* circulación *f*; (*of journals*) tirada *f*

circumcis|e /'sɜ:kəmsaɪz/ *vt* circuncidar. **~ion** /-'sɪʒn/ *n* circuncisión *f*

circumference /sə'kʌmfərəns/ *n* circunferencia *f*

circumflex /'sɜ:kəmfleks/ *a & n* circunflejo (*m*)

circumspect /'sɜ:kəmspekt/ *a* circunspecto

circumstance /'sɜ:kəmstəns/ *n* circunstancia *f*. **~s** (*means*) *npl* situación *f* económica

circus /'sɜ:kəs/ *n* circo *m*

cistern /'sɪstən/ *n* depósito *m*; (*of WC*) cisterna *f*

citadel /'sɪtədl/ *n* ciudadela *f*

citation /saɪ'teɪʃn/ *n* citación *f*
cite /saɪt/ *vt* citar
citizen /'sɪtɪzn/ *n* ciudadano *m*; (*inhabitant*) habitante *m & f*. **~ship** *n* ciudadanía *f*
citrus /'sɪtrəs/ *n*. **~ fruits** cítricos *mpl*
city /'sɪtɪ/ *n* ciudad *f*; **the C~** el centro *m* financiero de Londres
civic /'sɪvɪk/ *a* cívico. **~s** *npl* cívica *f*
civil /'sɪvl/ *a* civil, cortés
civilian /sɪ'vɪlɪən/ *a & n* civil (*m & f*). **~ clothes** *npl* traje *m* de paisano
civility /sɪ'vɪlətɪ/ *n* cortesía *f*
civiliz|ation /sɪvɪlaɪ'zeɪʃn/ *n* civilización *f*. **~e** /'sɪvəlaɪz/ *vt* civilizar.
civil: **~ servant** *n* funcionario *m*. **~ service** *n* administración *f* pública
civvies /'sɪvɪz/ *npl*. **in ~** (*sl*) en traje *m* de paisano
clad /klæd/ *see* **clothe**
claim /kleɪm/ *vt* reclamar; (*assert*) pretender. ● *n* reclamación *f*; (*right*) derecho *m*; (*jurid*) demanda *f*. **~ant** *n* demandante *m & f*; (*to throne*) pretendiente *m*
clairvoyant /kleə'vɔɪənt/ *n* clarividente *m & f*
clam /klæm/ *n* almeja *f*
clamber /'klæmbə(r)/ *vi* trepar a gatas
clammy /'klæmɪ/ *a* (**-ier**, **-iest**) húmedo
clamour /'klæmə(r)/ *n* clamor *m*. ● *vi*. **~ for** pedir a voces
clamp /klæmp/ *n* abrazadera *f*; (*auto*) cepo *m*. ● *vt* sujetar con abrazadera. **~ down on** reprimir
clan /klæn/ *n* clan *m*
clandestine /klæn'destɪn/ *a* clandestino
clang /klæŋ/ *n* sonido *m* metálico
clanger /'klæŋə(r)/ *n* (*sl*) metedura *f* de pata
clap /klæp/ *vt* (*pt* **clapped**) aplaudir; batir ‹*hands*›. ● *vi* aplaudir. ● *n* palmada *f*; (*of thunder*) trueno *m*
claptrap /'klæptræp/ *n* charlatanería *f*, tonterías *fpl*
claret /'klærət/ *n* clarete *m*
clarif|ication /klærɪfɪ'keɪʃn/ *n* aclaración *f*. **~y** /'klærɪfaɪ/ *vt* aclarar. ● *vi* aclararse
clarinet /klærɪ'net/ *n* clarinete *m*
clarity /'klærətɪ/ *n* claridad *f*
clash /klæʃ/ *n* choque *m*; (*noise*) estruendo *m*; (*contrast*) contraste *m*; (*fig*) conflicto *m*. ● *vt* golpear. ● *vi* encontrarse; ‹*dates*› coincidir; ‹*opinions*› estar en desacuerdo; ‹*colours*› desentonar
clasp /klɑ:sp/ *n* cierre *m*. ● *vt* agarrar; apretar ‹*hand*›; (*fasten*) abrochar
class /klɑ:s/ *n* clase *f*. **evening ~** *n* clase nocturna. ● *vt* clasificar
classic /'klæsɪk/ *a & n* clásico (*m*). **~al** *a* clásico. **~s** *npl* estudios *mpl* clásicos
classif|ication /klæsɪfɪ'keɪʃn/ *n* clasificación *f*. **~y** /'klæsɪfaɪ/ *vt* clasificar
classroom /'klɑ:sru:m/ *n* aula *f*
classy /'klɑ:sɪ/ *a* (*sl*) elegante
clatter /'klætə(r)/ *n* estrépito *m*. ● *vi* hacer ruido
clause /klɔ:z/ *n* cláusula *f*; (*gram*) oración *f*
claustrophobia /klɔ:strə'fəʊbɪə/ *n* claustrofobia *f*
claw /klɔ:/ *n* garra *f*; (*of cat*) uña *f*; (*of crab*) pinza *f*; (*device*) garfio *m*. ● *vt* arañar
clay /kleɪ/ *n* arcilla *f*
clean /kli:n/ *a* (**-er**, **-est**) limpio; ‹*stroke*› neto. ● *adv* completamente. ● *vt* limpiar. ● *vi* hacer la limpieza. **~ up** hacer la limpieza. **~-cut** *a* bien definido. **~er** *n* mujer *f* de la limpieza. **~liness** /'klenlɪnɪs/ *n* limpieza *f*
cleans|e /klenz/ *vt* limpiar; (*fig*) purificar. **~ing cream** *n* crema *f* desmaquilladora
clear /klɪə(r)/ *a* (**-er**, **-est**) claro; (*transparent*) transparente; (*without obstacles*) libre; ‹*profit*› neto; ‹*sky*› despejado. **keep ~ of** evitar. ● *adv* claramente. ● *vt* despejar; liquidar ‹*goods*›; (*jurid*) absolver; (*jump over*) saltar por encima de; quitar ‹*table*›. ● *vi* ‹*weather*› despejarse; ‹*fog*› disolverse. **~ off** *vi* (*sl*), **~ out** *vi* (*sl*) largarse. **~ up** *vt* (*tidy*) poner en orden; aclarar ‹*mystery*›; ● *vi* ‹*weather*› despejarse
clearance /'klɪərəns/ *n* espacio *m* libre; (*removal of obstructions*) despeje *m*; (*authorization*) permiso *m*; (*by customs*) despacho *m*; (*by security*) acreditación *f*. **~ sale** *n* liquidación *f*
clearing /'klɪərɪŋ/ *n* claro *m*
clearly /'klɪəlɪ/ *adv* evidentemente
clearway /'klɪəweɪ/ *n* carretera *f* en la que no se permite parar
cleavage /'kli:vɪdʒ/ *n* escote *m*; (*fig*) división *f*
cleave /kli:v/ *vt* (*pt* **cleaved, clove** *or* **cleft;** *pp* **cloven** *or* **cleft**) hender. ● *vi* henderse

clef /klef/ *n* (*mus*) clave *f*
cleft /kleft/ *see* **cleave**
clemen|cy /ˈklemənsɪ/ *n* clemencia *f*. **~t** *a* clemente
clench /klentʃ/ *vt* apretar
clergy /ˈklɜːdʒɪ/ *n* clero *m*. **~man** *n* (*pl* **-men**) clérigo *m*
cleric /ˈklerɪk/ *n* clérigo *m*. **~al** *a* clerical; (*of clerks*) de oficina
clerk /klɑːk/ *n* empleado *m*; (*jurid*) escribano *m*
clever /ˈklevə(r)/ *a* (**-er**, **-est**) listo; (*skilful*) hábil. **~ly** *adv* inteligentemente; (*with skill*) hábilmente. **~ness** *n* inteligencia *f*
cliché /ˈkliːʃeɪ/ *n* tópico *m*, frase *f* hecha
click /klɪk/ *n* golpecito *m*. ● *vi* chascar; (*sl*) llevarse bien
client /ˈklaɪənt/ *n* cliente *m* & *f*
clientele /kliːənˈtel/ *n* clientela *f*
cliff /klɪf/ *n* acantilado *m*
climat|e /ˈklaɪmɪt/ *n* clima *m*. **~ic** /-ˈmætɪk/ *a* climático
climax /ˈklaɪmæks/ *n* punto *m* culminante
climb /klaɪm/ *vt* subir ‹*stairs*›; trepar ‹*tree*›; escalar ‹*mountain*›. ● *vi* subir. ● *n* subida *f*. **~ down** bajar; (*fig*) volverse atrás, rajarse. **~er** *n* (*sport*) alpinista *m* & *f*; (*plant*) trepadora *f*
clinch /klɪntʃ/ *vt* cerrar ‹*deal*›
cling /klɪŋ/ *vi* (*pt* **clung**) agarrarse; (*stick*) pegarse
clinic /ˈklɪnɪk/ *n* clínica *f*. **~al** /ˈklɪnɪkl/ *a* clínico
clink /klɪŋk/ *n* sonido *m* metálico. ● *vt* hacer tintinear. ● *vi* tintinear
clinker /ˈklɪŋkə(r)/ *n* escoria *f*
clip[1] /klɪp/ *n* (*for paper*) sujetapapeles *m invar*; (*for hair*) horquilla *f*. ● *vt* (*pt* **clipped**) (*join*) sujetar
clip[2] /klɪp/ *n* (*with scissors*) tijeretada *f*; (*blow, fam*) golpe *m*. ● *vt* (*pt* **clipped**) (*cut*) cortar; (*fam*) golpear. **~pers** /ˈklɪpəz/ *npl* (*for hair*) maquinilla *f* para cortar el pelo; (*for nails*) cortauñas *m invar*. **~ping** *n* recorte *m*
clique /kliːk/ *n* pandilla *f*
cloak /kləʊk/ *n* capa *f*. **~room** /ˈkləʊkruːm/ *n* guardarropa *m*; (*toilet*) servicios *mpl*
clobber /ˈklɒbə(r)/ *n* (*sl*) trastos *mpl*. ● *vt* (*sl*) dar una paliza a
clock /klɒk/ *n* reloj *m*. **grandfather ~** reloj de caja. ● *vi*. **~ in** fichar, registrar la llegada. **~wise** /ˈklɒkwaɪz/ *a* & *adv* en el sentido de las agujas del reloj, a la derecha. **~work** /ˈklɒkwɜːk/ *n* mecanismo *m* de relojería. **like ~work** con precisión
clod /klɒd/ *n* terrón *m*
clog /klɒg/ *n* zueco *m*. ● *vt* (*pt* **clogged**) atascar. ● *vi* atascarse
cloister /ˈklɔɪstə(r)/ *n* claustro *m*
close[1] /kləʊs/ *a* (**-er**, **-est**) cercano; (*together*) apretado; ‹*friend*› íntimo; ‹*weather*› bochornoso; ‹*link etc*› estrecho; ‹*game, battle*› reñido. **have a ~ shave** (*fig*) escaparse de milagro. ● *adv* cerca. ● *n* recinto *m*
close[2] /kləʊz/ *vt* cerrar. ● *vi* cerrarse; (*end*) terminar. ● *n* fin *m*. **~d shop** *n* empresa *f* que emplea solamente a miembros del sindicato
close: **~ly** *adv* de cerca; (*with attention*) atentamente; (*exactly*) exactamente. **~ness** *n* proximidad *f*; (*togetherness*) intimidad *f*
closet /ˈklɒzɪt/ *n* (*Amer*) armario *m*
close-up /ˈkləʊsʌp/ *n* (*cinema etc*) primer plano *m*
closure /ˈkləʊʒə(r)/ *n* cierre *m*
clot /klɒt/ *n* (*culin*) grumo *m*; (*med*) coágulo *m*; (*sl*) tonto *m*. ● *vi* (*pt* **clotted**) cuajarse
cloth /klɒθ/ *n* tela *f*; (*duster*) trapo *m*; (*table-cloth*) mantel *m*
cloth|e /kləʊð/ *vt* (*pt* **clothed** *or* **clad**) vestir. **~es** /kləʊðz/ *npl*, **~ing** *n* ropa *f*
cloud /klaʊd/ *n* nube *f*. ● *vi* nublarse. **~burst** /ˈklaʊdbɜːst/ *n* chaparrón *m*. **~y** *a* (**-ier**, **-iest**) nublado; ‹*liquid*› turbio
clout /klaʊt/ *n* bofetada *f*. ● *vt* abofetear
clove[1] /kləʊv/ *n* clavo *m*
clove[2] /kləʊv/ *n*. **~ of garlic** *n* diente *m* de ajo
clove[3] /kləʊv/ *see* **cleave**
clover /ˈkləʊvə(r)/ *n* trébol *m*
clown /klaʊn/ *n* payaso *m*. ● *vi* hacer el payaso
cloy /klɔɪ/ *vt* empalagar
club /klʌb/ *n* club *m*; (*weapon*) porra *f*; (*at cards*) trébol *m*. ● *vt* (*pt* **clubbed**) aporrear. ● *vi*. **~ together** reunirse, pagar a escote
cluck /klʌk/ *vi* cloquear
clue /kluː/ *n* pista *f*; (*in crosswords*) indicación *f*. **not to have a ~** no tener la menor idea

clump /klʌmp/ *n* grupo *m*. ● *vt* agrupar. ● *vi* pisar fuertemente

clums|iness /'klʌmzɪnɪs/ *n* torpeza *f*. **~y** /'klʌmzɪ/ *a* (**-ier**, **-iest**) torpe

clung /klʌŋ/ *see* **cling**

cluster /'klʌstə(r)/ *n* grupo *m*. ● *vi* agruparse

clutch /klʌtʃ/ *vt* agarrar. ● *n* (*auto*) embrague *m*

clutter /'klʌtə(r)/ *n* desorden *m*. ● *vt* llenar desordenadamente

coach /kəʊtʃ/ *n* autocar *m*; (*of train*) vagón *m*; (*horse-drawn*) coche *m*; (*sport*) entrenador *m*. ● *vt* dar clases particulares; (*sport*) entrenar

coagulate /kəʊ'ægjʊleɪt/ *vt* coagular. ● *vi* coagularse

coal /kəʊl/ *n* carbón *m*. **~field** /'kəʊlfi:ld/ *n* yacimiento *m* de carbón

coalition /kəʊə'lɪʃn/ *n* coalición *f*

coarse /kɔ:s/ *a* (**-er**, **-est**) grosero; ‹*material*› basto. **~ness** *n* grosería *f*; (*texture*) basteza *f*

coast /kəʊst/ *n* costa *f*. ● *vi* (*with cycle*) deslizarse cuesta abajo; (*with car*) ir en punto muerto. **~al** *a* costero. **~er** /'kəʊstə(r)/ *n* (*ship*) barco *m* de cabotaje; (*for glass*) posavasos *m invar*. **~guard** /'kəʊstgɑ:d/ *n* guardacostas *m invar*. **~line** /'kəʊstlaɪn/ *n* litoral *m*

coat /kəʊt/ *n* abrigo *m*; (*jacket*) chaqueta *f*; (*of animal*) pelo *m*; (*of paint*) mano *f*. ● *vt* cubrir, revestir. **~ing** *n* capa *f*. **~ of arms** *n* escudo *m* de armas

coax /kəʊks/ *vt* engatusar

cob /kɒb/ *n* (*of corn*) mazorca *f*

cobble[1] /'kɒbl/ *n* guijarro *m*, adoquín *m*. ● *vt* empedrar con guijarros, adoquinar

cobble[2] /'kɒbl/ *vt* (*mend*) remendar. **~r** /'kɒblə(r)/ *n* (*old use*) remendón *m*

cobweb /'kɒbweb/ *n* telaraña *f*

cocaine /kə'keɪn/ *n* cocaína *f*

cock /kɒk/ *n* gallo *m*; (*mec*) grifo m; (*of gun*) martillo *m*. ● *vt* amartillar ‹*gun*›; aguzar ‹*ears*›. **~-and-bull story** *n* patraña *f*. **~erel** /'kɒkərəl/ *n* gallo *m*. **~-eyed** *a* (*sl*) torcido

cockle /'kɒkl/ *n* berberecho *m*

cockney /'kɒknɪ/ *a & n* (*pl* **-eys**) londinense (*m & f*) (del este de Londres)

cockpit /'kɒkpɪt/ *n* (*in aircraft*) cabina *f* del piloto

cockroach /'kɒkrəʊtʃ/ *n* cucaracha *f*

cocksure /kɒk'ʃʊə(r)/ *a* presuntuoso

cocktail /'kɒkteɪl/ *n* cóctel *m*. **fruit ~** macedonia *f* de frutas

cock-up /'kɒkʌp/ *n* (*sl*) lío *m*

cocky /'kɒkɪ/ *a* (**-ier**, **-iest**) engreído

cocoa /'kəʊkəʊ/ *n* cacao *m*; (*drink*) chocolate *m*

coconut /'kəʊkənʌt/ *n* coco *m*

cocoon /kə'ku:n/ *n* capullo *m*

cod /kɒd/ *n* (*pl* **cod**) bacalao *m*, abadejo *m*

coddle /'kɒdl/ *vt* mimar; (*culin*) cocer a fuego lento

code /kəʊd/ *n* código *m*; (*secret*) cifra *f*

codify /'kəʊdɪfaɪ/ *vt* codificar

cod-liver oil /'kɒdlɪvə(r)ɒɪl/ *n* aceite *m* de hígado de bacalao

coeducational /kəʊedʒʊ'keɪʃənl/ *a* mixto

coerc|e /kəʊ'ɜ:s/ *vt* obligar. **~ion** /-ʃn/ *n* coacción *f*

coexist /kəʊɪg'zɪst/ *vi* coexistir. **~ence** *n* coexistencia *f*

coffee /'kɒfɪ/ *n* café *m*. **~-mill** *n* molinillo *m* de café. **~-pot** *n* cafetera *f*

coffer /'kɒfə(r)/ *n* cofre *m*

coffin /'kɒfɪn/ *n* ataúd *m*

cog /kɒg/ *n* diente *m*; (*fig*) pieza *f*

cogent /'kəʊdʒənt/ *a* convincente

cohabit /kəʊ'hæbɪt/ *vi* cohabitar

coherent /kəʊ'hɪərənt/ *a* coherente

coil /kɔɪl/ *vt* enrollar. ● *n* rollo *m*; (*one ring*) vuelta *f*

coin /kɔɪn/ *n* moneda *f*. ● *vt* acuñar. **~age** *n* sistema *m* monetario

coincide /kəʊɪn'saɪd/ *vi* coincidir

coinciden|ce /kəʊ'ɪnsɪdəns/ *n* casualidad *f*. **~tal** /-'dentl/ *a* casual; (*coinciding*) coincidente

coke /kəʊk/ *n* (*coal*) coque *m*

colander /'kʌləndə(r)/ *n* colador *m*

cold /kəʊld/ *a* (**-er**, **-est**) frío. **be ~** tener frío. **it is ~** hace frío. ● *n* frío *m*; (*med*) resfriado *m*. **have a ~** estar constipado. **~-blooded** *a* insensible. **~ cream** *n* crema *f*. **~ feet** (*fig*) mieditis *f*. **~ness** *n* frialdad *f*. **~-shoulder** *vt* tratar con frialdad. **~ sore** *n* herpes *m* labial. **~ storage** *n* conservación *f* en frigorífico

coleslaw /'kəʊlslɔ:/ *n* ensalada *f* de col

colic /'kɒlɪk/ *n* cólico *m*

collaborat|e /kə'læbəreɪt/ *vi* colaborar. **~ion** /-'reɪʃn/ *n* colaboración *f*. **~or** *n* colaborador *m*

collage /'kɒlɑ:ʒ/ *n* collage *m*
collaps|e /kə'læps/ *vi* derrumbarse; (*med*) sufrir un colapso. ● *n* derrumbamiento *m*; (*med*) colapso *m*. **~ible** /kə'læpsəbl/ *a* plegable
collar /'kɒlə(r)/ *n* cuello *m*; (*for animals*) collar *m*. ● *vt* (*fam*) hurtar. **~-bone** *n* clavícula *f*
colleague /'kɒli:g/ *n* colega *m & f*
collect /kə'lekt/ *vt* reunir; (*hobby*) coleccionar; (*pick up*) recoger; recaudar ‹*rent*›. ● *vi* ‹*people*› reunirse; ‹*things*› acumularse. **~ed** /kə'lektɪd/ *a* reunido; ‹*person*› tranquilo. **~ion** /-ʃn/ *n* colección *f*; (*in church*) colecta *f*; (*of post*) recogida *f*. **~ive** /kə'lektɪv/ *a* colectivo. **~or** *n* coleccionista *m & f*; (*of taxes*) recaudador *m*
college /'kɒlɪdʒ/ *n* colegio *m*; (*of art, music etc*) escuela *f*; (*univ*) colegio *m* mayor
collide /kə'laɪd/ *vi* chocar
colliery /'kɒlɪərɪ/ *n* mina *f* de carbón
collision /kə'lɪʒn/ *n* choque *m*
colloquial /kə'ləʊkwɪəl/ *a* familiar. **~ism** *n* expresión *f* familiar
collusion /kə'lu:ʒn/ *n* connivencia *f*
colon /'kəʊlən/ *n* (*gram*) dos puntos *mpl*; (*med*) colon *m*
colonel /'kɜ:nl/ *n* coronel *m*
colon|ial /kə'ləʊnɪəl/ *a* colonial. **~ize** /'kɒlənaɪz/ *vt* colonizar. **~y** /'kɒlənɪ/ *n* colonia *f*
colossal /kə'lɒsl/ *a* colosal
colour /'kʌlə(r)/ *n* color *m*. **off ~** (*fig*) indispuesto. ● *a* de color(es), en color(es). ● *vt* colorar; (*dye*) teñir. ● *vi* (*blush*) sonrojarse. **~ bar** *n* barrera *f* racial. **~-blind** *a* daltoniano. **~ed** /'kʌləd/ *a* de color. **~ful** *a* lleno de color; (*fig*) pintoresco. **~less** *a* incoloro. **~s** *npl* (*flag*) bandera *f*
colt /kəʊlt/ *n* potro *m*
column /'kɒləm/ *n* columna *f*. **~ist** /'kɒləmnɪst/ *n* columnista *m & f*
coma /'kəʊmə/ *n* coma *m*
comb /kəʊm/ *n* peine *m*. ● *vt* peinar; (*search*) registrar
combat /'kɒmbæt/ *n* combate *m*. ● *vt* (*pt* **combated**) combatir. **~ant** /-ətənt/ *n* combatiente *m & f*
combination /kɒmbɪ'neɪʃn/ *n* combinación *f*
combine /kəm'baɪn/ *vt* combinar. ● *vi* combinarse. /'kɒmbaɪn/ *n* asociación *f*. **~harvester** *n* cosechadora *f*
combustion /kəm'bʌstʃən/ *n* combustión *f*
come /kʌm/ *vi* (*pt* **came**, *pp* **come**) venir; (*occur*) pasar. **~ about** ocurrir. **~ across** encontrarse con ‹*person*›; encontrar ‹*object*›. **~ apart** deshacerse. **~ away** marcharse. **~ back** volver. **~ by** obtener; (*pass*) pasar. **~ down** bajar. **~ in** entrar. **~ in for** recibir. **~ into** heredar ‹*money*›. **~ off** desprenderse; (*succeed*) tener éxito. **~ off it!** (*fam*) ¡no me vengas con eso! **~ out** salir; (*result*) resultar. **~ round** (*after fainting*) volver en sí; (*be converted*) cambiar de idea. **~ to** llegar a ‹*decision etc*›. **~ up** subir; (*fig*) salir. **~ up with** proponer ‹*idea*›
comeback /'kʌmbæk/ *n* retorno *m*; (*retort*) réplica *f*
comedian /kə'mi:dɪən/ *n* cómico *m*
comedown /'kʌmdaʊn/ *n* revés *m*
comedy /'kɒmədɪ/ *n* comedia *f*
comely /'kʌmlɪ/ *a* (**-ier**, **-iest**) (*old use*) bonito
comet /'kɒmɪt/ *n* cometa *m*
comeuppance /kʌm'ʌpəns/ *n* (*Amer*) merecido *m*
comf|ort /'kʌmfət/ *n* bienestar *m*; (*consolation*) consuelo *m*. ● *vt* consolar. **~ortable** *a* cómodo; (*wealthy*) holgado. **~y** /'kʌmfɪ/ *a* (*fam*) cómodo
comic /'kɒmɪk/ *a* cómico. ● *n* cómico *m*; (*periodical*) tebeo *m*. **~al** *a* cómico. **~ strip** *n* historieta *f*
coming /'kʌmɪŋ/ *n* llegada *f*. ● *a* próximo; ‹*week, month etc*› que viene. **~ and going** ir y venir
comma /'kɒmə/ *n* coma *f*
command /kə'mɑ:nd/ *n* orden *f*; (*mastery*) dominio *m*. ● *vt* mandar; (*deserve*) merecer
commandeer /kɒmən'dɪə(r)/ *vt* requisar
commander /kə'mɑ:ndə(r)/ *n* comandante *m*
commanding /kə'mɑ:ndɪŋ/ *a* imponente
commandment /kə'mɑ:ndmənt/ *n* mandamiento *m*
commando /kə'mɑ:ndəʊ/ *n* (*pl* **-os**) comando *m*
commemorat|e /kə'meməreɪt/ *vt* conmemorar. **~ion** /-'reɪʃn/ *n* conmemoración *f*. **~ive** /-ətɪv/ *a* conmemorativo
commence /kə'mens/ *vt/i* empezar. **~ment** *n* principio *m*

commend /kə'mend/ *vt* alabar; (*entrust*) encomendar. **~able** *a* loable. **~ation** /kɒmen'deɪʃn/ *n* elogio *m*

commensurate /kə'menʃərət/ *a* proporcionado

comment /'kɒment/ *n* observación *f*. ● *vi* hacer observaciones

commentary /'kɒməntrɪ/ *n* comentario *m*; (*radio, TV*) reportaje *m*

commentat|e /'kɒmənteɪt/ *vi* narrar. **~or** *n* (*radio, TV*) locutor *m*

commerc|e /'kɒmɜ:s/ *n* comercio *m*. **~ial** /kə'mɜ:ʃl/ *a* comercial. ● *n* anuncio *m*. **~ialize** *vt* comercializar

commiserat|e /kə'mɪzəreɪt/ *vt* compadecer. ● *vi* compadecerse (**with** de). **~ion** /-'reɪʃn/ *n* conmiseración *f*

commission /kə'mɪʃn/ *n* comisión *f*. **out of ~** fuera de servicio. ● *vt* encargar; (*mil*) nombrar

commissionaire /kəmɪʃə'neə(r)/ *n* portero *m*

commissioner /kə'mɪʃənə(r)/ *n* comisario *m*; (*of police*) jefe *m*

commit /kə'mɪt/ *vt* (*pt* **committed**) cometer; (*entrust*) confiar. **~ o.s.** comprometerse. **~ to memory** aprender de memoria. **~ment** *n* compromiso *m*

committee /kə'mɪtɪ/ *n* comité *m*

commodity /kə'mɒdətɪ/ *n* producto *m*, artículo *m*

common /'kɒmən/ *a* (**-er, -est**) común; (*usual*) corriente; (*vulgar*) ordinario. ● *n* ejido *m*

commoner /'kɒmənə(r)/ *n* plebeyo *m*

common: **~ law** *n* derecho *m* consuetudinario. **~ly** *adv* comúnmente. **C~ Market** *n* Mercado *m* Común

commonplace /'kɒmənpleɪs/ *a* banal. ● *n* banalidad *f*

common: **~-room** *n* sala *f* común, salón *m* común. **~ sense** *n* sentido *m* común

Commonwealth /'kɒmənwelθ/ *n*. **the ~** la Mancomunidad *f* Británica

commotion /kə'məʊʃn/ *n* confusión *f*

communal /'kɒmjʊnl/ *a* comunal

commune[1] /'kɒmju:n/ *n* comuna *f*

commune[2] /kə'mju:n/ *vi* comunicarse

communicat|e /kə'mju:nɪkeɪt/ *vt* comunicar. ● *vi* comunicarse. **~ion** /-'keɪʃn/ *n* comunicación *f*. **~ive** /-ətɪv/ *a* comunicativo

communion /kə'mju:nɪən/ *n* comunión *f*

communiqué /kə'mju:nɪkeɪ/ *n* comunicado *m*

communis|m /'kɒmjʊnɪsəm/ *n* comunismo *m*. **~t** /'kɒmjʊnɪst/ *n* comunista *m & f*

community /kə'mju:nətɪ/ *n* comunidad *f*. **~ centre** *n* centro *m* social

commute /kə'mju:t/ *vi* viajar diariamente. ● *vt* (*jurid*) conmutar. **~r** /-ə(r)/ *n* viajero *m* diario

compact /kəm'pækt/ *a* compacto. /'kɒmpækt/ *n* (*for powder*) polvera *f*. **~ disc** /'kɒm-/ *n* disco *m* compacto

companion /kəm'pænɪən/ *n* compañero *m*. **~ship** *n* compañerismo *m*

company /'kʌmpənɪ/ *n* compañía *f*; (*guests, fam*) visita *f*; (*com*) sociedad *f*

compar|able /'kɒmpərəbl/ *a* comparable. **~ative** /kəm'pærətɪv/ *a* comparativo; (*fig*) relativo. ● *n* (*gram*) comparativo *m*. **~e** /kəm'peə(r)/ *vt* comparar. ● *vi* poderse comparar. **~ison** /kəm'pærɪsn/ *n* comparación *f*

compartment /kəm'pɑ:tmənt/ *n* compartimiento *m*; (*on train*) departamento *m*

compass /'kʌmpəs/ *n* brújula *f*. **~es** *npl* compás *m*

compassion /kəm'pæʃn/ *n* compasión *f*. **~ate** *a* compasivo

compatib|ility /kəmpætə'bɪlətɪ/ *n* compatibilidad *f*. **~le** /kəm'pætəbl/ *a* compatible

compatriot /kəm'pætrɪət/ *n* compatriota *m & f*

compel /kəm'pel/ *vt* (*pt* **compelled**) obligar. **~ling** *a* irresistible

compendium /kəm'pendɪəm/ *n* compendio *m*

compensat|e /'kɒmpənseɪt/ *vt* compensar; (*for loss*) indemnizar. ● *vi* compensar. **~ion** /-'seɪʃn/ *n* compensación *f*; (*financial*) indemnización *f*

compère /'kɒmpeə(r)/ *n* presentador *m*. ● *vt* presentar

compete /kəm'pi:t/ *vi* competir

competen|ce /'kɒmpətəns/ *n* competencia *f*, aptitud *f*. **~t** /'kɒmpɪtənt/ *a* competente, capaz

competit|ion /kɒmpə'tɪʃn/ *n* (*contest*) concurso *m*; (*com*) competencia *f*. **~ive** /kəm'petətɪv/ *a*

competidor; ‹*price*› competitivo. **~or** /kəm'petɪtə(r)/ *n* competidor *m*; (*in contest*) concursante *m* & *f*
compile /kəm'paɪl/ *vt* compilar. **~r** /-ə(r)/ *n* recopilador *m*, compilador *m*
complacen|cy /kəm'pleɪsənsɪ/ *n* satisfacción *f* de sí mismo. **~t** /kəm'pleɪsnt/ *a* satisfecho de sí mismo
complain /kəm'pleɪn/ *vi*. **~ (about)** quejarse (de). **~ of** (*med*) sufrir de. **~t** /kəm'pleɪnt/ *n* queja *f*; (*med*) enfermedad *f*
complement /'kɒmplɪmənt/ *n* complemento *m*. • *vt* complementar. **~ary** /-'mentrɪ/ *a* complementario
complet|e /kəm'pli:t/ *a* completo; (*finished*) acabado; (*downright*) total. • *vt* acabar; llenar ‹*a form*›. **~ely** *adv* completamente. **~ion** /-ʃn/ *n* conclusión *f*
complex /'kɒmpleks/ *a* complejo. • *n* complejo *m*
complexion /kəm'plekʃn/ *n* tez *f*; (*fig*) aspecto *m*
complexity /kəm'pleksətɪ/ *n* complejidad *f*
complian|ce /kəm'plaɪəns/ *n* sumisión *f*. **in ~ce with** de acuerdo con. **~t** *a* sumiso
complicat|e /'kɒmplɪkeɪt/ *vt* complicar. **~ed** *a* complicado. **~ion** /-'keɪʃn/ *n* complicación *f*
complicity /kəm'plɪsətɪ/ *n* complicidad *f*
compliment /'kɒmplɪmənt/ *n* cumplido *m*; (*amorous*) piropo *m*. • *vt* felicitar. **~ary** /-'mentrɪ/ *a* halagador; (*given free*) de favor. **~s** *npl* saludos *mpl*
comply /kəm'plaɪ/ *vi*. **~ with** conformarse con
component /kəm'pəʊnənt/ *a* & *n* componente (*m*)
compose /kəm'pəʊz/ *vt* componer. **~ o.s.** tranquilizarse. **~d** *a* sereno
compos|er /kəm'pəʊzə(r)/ *n* compositor *m*. **~ition** /kɒmpə'zɪʃn/ *n* composición *f*
compost /'kɒmpɒst/ *n* abono *m*
composure /kəm'pəʊʒə(r)/ *n* serenidad *f*
compound[1] /'kɒmpaʊnd/ *n* compuesto *m*. • *a* compuesto; ‹*fracture*› complicado. /kəm'paʊnd/ *vt* componer; agravar ‹*problem etc*›. • *vi* (*settle*) arreglarse
compound[2] /'kɒmpaʊnd/ *n* (*enclosure*) recinto *m*
comprehen|d /kɒmprɪ'hend/ *vt* comprender. **~sion** /kɒmprɪ'henʃn/ *n* comprensión *f*
comprehensive /kɒmprɪ'hensɪv/ *a* extenso; ‹*insurance*› a todo riesgo. **~ school** *n* instituto *m*
compress /'kɒmpres/ *n* (*med*) compresa *f*. /kəm'pres/ *vt* comprimir; (*fig*) condensar. **~ion** /-ʃn/ *n* compresión *f*
comprise /kəm'praɪz/ *vt* comprender
compromise /'kɒmprəmaɪz/ *n* acuerdo *m*, acomodo *m*, arreglo *m*. • *vt* comprometer. • *vi* llegar a un acuerdo
compuls|ion /kəm'pʌlʃn/ *n* obligación *f*, impulso *m*. **~ive** /kəm'pʌlsɪv/ *a* compulsivo. **~ory** /kəm'pʌlsərɪ/ *a* obligatorio
compunction /kəm'pʌŋkʃn/ *n* remordimiento *m*
computer /kəm'pju:tə(r)/ *n* ordenador *m*. **~ize** *vt* instalar ordenadores en. **be ~ized** tener ordenador
comrade /'kɒmreɪd/ *n* camarada *m* & *f*. **~ship** *n* camaradería *f*
con[1] /kɒn/ *vt* (*pt* **conned**) (*fam*) estafar. • *n* (*fam*) estafa *f*
con[2] /kɒn/ *see* **pro and con**
concave /'kɒŋkeɪv/ *a* cóncavo
conceal /kən'si:l/ *vt* ocultar. **~ment** *n* encubrimiento *m*
concede /kən'si:d/ *vt* conceder
conceit /kən'si:t/ *n* vanidad *f*. **~ed** *a* engreído
conceiv|able /kən'si:vəbl/ *a* concebible. **~ably** *adv*. **may ~ably** es concebible que. **~e** /kən'si:v/ *vt/i* concebir
concentrat|e /'kɒnsəntreɪt/ *vt* concentrar. • *vi* concentrarse. **~ion** /-'treɪʃn/ *n* concentración *f*. **~ion camp** *n* campo *m* de concentración
concept /'kɒnsept/ *n* concepto *m*
conception /kən'sepʃn/ *n* concepción *f*
conceptual /kən'septʃʊəl/ *a* conceptual
concern /kən'sɜ:n/ *n* asunto *m*; (*worry*) preocupación *f*; (*com*) empresa *f*. • *vt* tener que ver con; (*deal with*) tratar de. **as far as I'm ~ed** en cuanto a mí. **be ~ed about** preocuparse por. **~ing** *prep* acerca de

concert /'kɒnsət/ *n* concierto *m*. **in ~** de común acuerdo. **~ed** /kən'sɜ:tɪd/ *a* concertado

concertina /kɒnsə'ti:nə/ *n* concertina *f*

concerto /kən'tʃɜ:təʊ/ *n* (*pl* **-os**) concierto *m*

concession /kən'seʃn/ *n* concesión *f*

conciliat|e /kən'sɪlɪeɪt/ *vt* conciliar. **~ion** /-'eɪʃn/ *n* conciliación *f*

concise /kən'saɪs/ *a* conciso. **~ly** *adv* concisamente. **~ness** *n* concisión *f*

conclu|de /kən'klu:d/ *vt* concluir. ● *vi* concluirse. **~ding** *a* final. **~sion** *n* conclusión *f*

conclusive /kən'klu:sɪv/ *a* decisivo. **~ly** *adv* concluyentemente

concoct /kən'kɒkt/ *vt* confeccionar; (*fig*) inventar. **~ion** /-ʃn/ *n* mezcla *f*; (*drink*) brebaje *m*

concourse /'kɒŋkɔ:s/ *n* (*rail*) vestíbulo *m*

concrete /'kɒŋkri:t/ *n* hormigón *m*. ● *a* concreto. ● *vt* cubrir con hormigón

concur /kən'kɜ:(r)/ *vi* (*pt* **concurred**) estar de acuerdo

concussion /kən'kʌʃn/ *n* conmoción *f* cerebral

condemn /kən'dem/ *vt* condenar. **~ation** /kɒndem'neɪʃn/ *n* condenación *f*, condena *f*; (*censure*) censura *f*

condens|ation /kɒnden'seɪʃn/ *n* condensación *f*. **~e** /kən'dens/ *vt* condensar. ● *vi* condensarse

condescend /kɒndɪ'send/ *vi* dignarse (**to** a). **~ing** *a* superior

condiment /'kɒndɪmənt/ *n* condimento *m*

condition /kən'dɪʃn/ *n* condición *f*. **on ~ that** a condición de que. ● *vt* condicionar. **~al** *a* condicional. **~er** *n* acondicionador *m*; (*for hair*) suavizante *m*

condolences /kən'dəʊlənsɪz/ *npl* pésame *m*

condom /'kɒndɒm/ *n* condón *m*

condone /kən'dəʊn/ *vt* condonar

conducive /kən'dju:sɪv/ *a*. **be ~ to** ser favorable a

conduct /kən'dʌkt/ *vt* conducir; dirigir ‹*orchestra*›. /'kɒndʌkt/ *n* conducta *f*. **~or** /kən'dʌktə(r)/ *n* director *m*; (*of bus*) cobrador *m*. **~ress** *n* cobradora *f*

cone /kəʊn/ *n* cono *m*; (*for ice-cream*) cucurucho *m*

confectioner /kən'fekʃənə(r)/ *n* pastelero *m*. **~y** *n* dulces *mpl*, golosinas *fpl*

confederation /kənfedə'reɪʃn/ *n* confederación *f*

confer /kən'fɜ:(r)/ *vt* (*pt* **conferred**) conferir. ● *vi* consultar

conference /'kɒnfərəns/ *n* congreso *m*

confess /kən'fes/ *vt* confesar. ● *vi* confesarse. **~ion** /-ʃn/ *n* confesión *f*. **~ional** *n* confes(i)onario *m*. **~or** *n* confesor *m*

confetti /kən'fetɪ/ *n* confeti *m*, confetis *mpl*

confide /kən'faɪd/ *vt/i* confiar

confiden|ce /'kɒnfɪdəns/ *n* confianza *f*; (*secret*) confidencia *f*. **~ce trick** *n* estafa *f*, timo *m*. **~t** /'kɒnfɪdənt/ *a* seguro

confidential /kɒnfɪ'denʃl/ *a* confidencial

confine /kən'faɪn/ *vt* confinar; (*limit*) limitar. **~ment** *n* (*imprisonment*) prisión *f*; (*med*) parto *m*

confines /'kɒnfaɪnz/ *npl* confines *mpl*

confirm /kən'fɜ:m/ *vt* confirmar. **~ation** /kɒnfə'meɪʃn/ *n* confirmación *f*. **~ed** *a* inveterado

confiscat|e /'kɒnfɪskeɪt/ *vt* confiscar. **~ion** /-'keɪʃn/ *n* confiscación *f*

conflagration /kɒnflə'greɪʃn/ *n* conflagración *f*

conflict /'kɒnflɪkt/ *n* conflicto *m*. /kən'flɪkt/ *vi* chocar. **~ing** /kən-/ *a* contradictorio

conform /kən'fɔ:m/ *vt* conformar. ● *vi* conformarse. **~ist** *n* conformista *m & f*

confound /kən'faʊnd/ *vt* confundir. **~ed** *a* (*fam*) maldito

confront /kən'frʌnt/ *vt* hacer frente a; (*face*) enfrentarse con. **~ation** /kɒnfrʌn'teɪʃn/ *n* confrontación *f*

confus|e /kən'fju:z/ *vt* confundir. **~ing** *a* desconcertante. **~ion** /-ʒn/ *n* confusión *f*

congeal /kən'dʒi:l/ *vt* coagular. ● *vi* coagularse

congenial /kən'dʒi:nɪəl/ *a* simpático

congenital /kən'dʒenɪtl/ *a* congénito

congest|ed /kən'dʒestɪd/ *a* congestionado. **~ion** /-tʃən/ *n* congestión *f*

congratulat|e /kən'grætjʊleɪt/ *vt* felicitar. **~ions** /-'leɪʃnz/ *npl* felicitaciones *fpl*

congregat|e /'kɒŋgrɪgeɪt/ *vi* congregarse. **~ion** /-'geɪʃn/ *n* asamblea *f*; (*relig*) fieles *mpl*, feligreses *mpl*

congress /'kɒŋgres/ *n* congreso *m*. **C~** (*Amer*) el Congreso

conic(al) /'kɒnɪk(l)/ *a* cónico

conifer /'kɒnɪfə(r)/ *n* conífera *f*

conjecture /kən'dʒektʃə(r)/ *n* conjetura *f*. ● *vt* conjeturar. ● *vi* hacer conjeturas

conjugal /'kɒndʒʊgl/ *a* conyugal

conjugat|e /'kɒndʒʊgeɪt/ *vt* conjugar. **~ion** /-'geɪʃn/ *n* conjugación *f*

conjunction /kən'dʒʌŋkʃn/ *n* conjunción *f*

conjur|e /'kʌndʒə(r)/ *vi* hacer juegos de manos. ● *vt*. **~e up** evocar. **~or** *n* prestidigitador *m*

conk /kɒŋk/ *vi*. **~ out** (*sl*) fallar; ‹*person*› desmayarse

conker /'kɒŋkə(r)/ *n* (*fam*) castaña *f* de Indias

conman /'kɒnmæn/ *n* (*fam*) estafador *m*, timador *m*

connect /kə'nekt/ *vt* juntar; (*elec*) conectar. ● *vi* unirse; (*elec*) conectarse. **~ with** ‹*train*› enlazar con. **~ed** *a* unido; (*related*) relacionado. **be ~ed with** tener que ver con, estar emparentado con

connection /kə'nekʃn/ *n* unión *f*; (*rail*) enlace *m*; (*elec, mec*) conexión *f*; (*fig*) relación *f*. **in ~ with** a propósito de, con respecto a. **~s** *npl* relaciones *fpl*

conniv|ance /kə'naɪvəns/ *n* connivencia *f*. **~e** /kə'naɪv/ *vi*. **~e at** hacer la vista gorda a

connoisseur /kɒnə'sɜ:(r)/ *n* experto *m*

connot|ation /kɒnə'teɪʃn/ *n* connotación *f*. **~e** /kə'nəʊt/ *vt* connotar; (*imply*) implicar

conquer /'kɒŋkə(r)/ *vt* conquistar; (*fig*) vencer. **~or** *n* conquistador *m*

conquest /'kɒŋkwest/ *n* conquista *f*

conscience /'kɒnʃəns/ *n* conciencia *f*

conscientious /kɒnʃɪ'enʃəs/ *a* concienzudo

conscious /'kɒnʃəs/ *a* consciente; (*deliberate*) intencional. **~ly** *adv* a sabiendas. **~ness** *n* consciencia *f*; (*med*) conocimiento *m*

conscript /'kɒnskrɪpt/ *n* recluta *m*. /kən'skrɪpt/ *vt* reclutar. **~ion** /kən'skrɪpʃn/ *n* reclutamiento *m*

consecrat|e /'kɒnsɪkreɪt/ *vt* consagrar. **~ion** /-'kreɪʃn/ *n* consagración *f*

consecutive /kən'sekjʊtɪv/ *a* sucesivo

consensus /kən'sensəs/ *n* consenso *m*

consent /kən'sent/ *vi* consentir. ● *n* consentimiento *m*

consequen|ce /'kɒnsɪkwəns/ *n* consecuencia *f*. **~t** /'kɒnsɪkwənt/ *a* consiguiente. **~tly** *adv* por consiguiente

conservation /kɒnsə'veɪʃn/ *n* conservación *f*, preservación *f*. **~ist** /kɒnsə'veɪʃənɪst/ *n* conservacionista *m & f*

conservative /kən'sɜ:vətɪv/ *a* conservador; (*modest*) prudente, moderado. **C~** *a & n* conservador (*m*)

conservatory /kən'sɜ:vətrɪ/ *n* (*greenhouse*) invernadero *m*

conserve /kən'sɜ:v/ *vt* conservar

consider /kən'sɪdə(r)/ *vt* considerar; (*take into account*) tomar en cuenta. **~able** /kən'sɪdərəbl/ *a* considerable. **~ably** *adv* considerablemente

considerat|e /kən'sɪdərət/ *a* considerado. **~ion** /-'reɪʃn/ *n* consideración *f*

considering /kən'sɪdərɪŋ/ *prep* en vista de

consign /kən'saɪn/ *vt* consignar; (*send*) enviar. **~ment** *n* envío *m*

consist /kən'sɪst/ *vi*. **~ of** consistir en

consistency /kən'sɪstənsɪ/ *n* consistencia *f*; (*fig*) coherencia *f*

consistent /kən'sɪstənt/ *a* coherente; (*unchanging*) constante. **~ with** compatible con. **~ly** *adv* constantemente

consolation /kɒnsə'leɪʃn/ *n* consuelo *m*

console /kən'səʊl/ *vt* consolar

consolidat|e /kən'sɒlɪdeɪt/ *vt* consolidar. ● *vi* consolidarse. **~ion** /-'deɪʃn/ *n* consolidación *f*

consonant /'kɒnsənənt/ *n* consonante *f*

consort /'kɒnsɔ:t/ *n* consorte *m & f*. /kən'sɔ:t/ *vi*. **~ with** asociarse con

consortium /kən'sɔ:tɪəm/ *n* (*pl* **-tia**) consorcio *m*

conspicuous /kən'spɪkjʊəs/ *a* (*easily seen*) visible; (*showy*) llamativo; (*noteworthy*) notable

conspir|acy /kən'spɪrəsɪ/ *n* complot *m*, conspiración *f*. **~e** /kən'spaɪə(r)/ *vi* conspirar

constab|le /'kʌnstəbl/ *n* policía *m*, guardia *m*. **~ulary** /kən'stæbjʊlərɪ/ *n* policía *f*

constant /'kɒnstənt/ *a* constante. **~ly** *adv* constantemente

constellation /kɒnstə'leɪʃn/ *n* constelación *f*

consternation /kɒnstə'neɪʃn/ *n* consternación *f*

constipat|ed /'kɒnstɪpeɪtɪd/ *a* estreñido. **~ion** /-'peɪʃn/ *n* estreñimiento *m*

constituen|cy /kən'stɪtjʊənsɪ/ *n* distrito *m* electoral. **~t** /kən'stɪtjʊənt/ *n* componente *m*; (*pol*) elector *m*

constitut|e /'kɒnstɪtju:t/ *vt* constituir. **~ion** /-'tju:ʃn/ *n* constitución *f*. **~ional** /-'tju:ʃənl/ *a* constitucional. ● *n* paseo *m*

constrain /kən'streɪn/ *vt* forzar, obligar, constreñir. **~t** /kən'streɪnt/ *n* fuerza *f*

constrict /kən'strɪkt/ *vt* apretar. **~ion** /-ʃn/ *n* constricción *f*

construct /kən'strʌkt/ *vt* construir. **~ion** /-ʃn/ *n* construcción *f*. **~ive** /kən'strʌktɪv/ *a* constructivo

construe /kən'stru:/ *vt* interpretar; (*gram*) construir

consul /'kɒnsl/ *n* cónsul *m*. **~ar** /-jʊlə(r)/ *a* consular. **~ate** /-ət/ *n* consulado *m*

consult /kən'sʌlt/ *vt/i* consultar. **~ant** /kən'sʌltənt/ *n* asesor *m*; (*med*) especialista *m & f*; (*tec*) consejero *m* técnico. **~ation** /kɒnsəl'teɪʃn/ *n* consulta *f*

consume /kən'sju:m/ *vt* consumir; (*eat*) comer; (*drink*) beber. **~r** /-ə(r)/ *n* consumidor *m*. ● *a* de consumo. **~rism** /kən'sju:mərɪzəm/ *n* protección *f* del consumidor, consumismo *m*

consummat|e /'kɒnsəmeɪt/ *vt* consumar. **~ion** /-'meɪʃn/ *n* consumación *f*

consumption /kən'sʌmpʃn/ *n* consumo *m*; (*med*) tisis *f*

contact /'kɒntækt/ *n* contacto *m*. ● *vt* ponerse en contacto con

contagious /kən'teɪdʒəs/ *a* contagioso

contain /kən'teɪn/ *vt* contener. **~ o.s.** contenerse. **~er** *n* recipiente *m*; (*com*) contenedor *m*

contaminat|e /kən'tæmɪneɪt/ *vt* contaminar. **~ion** /-'neɪʃn/ *n* contaminación *f*

contemplat|e /'kɒntəmpleɪt/ *vt* contemplar; (*consider*) considerar. **~ion** /-'pleɪʃn/ *n* contemplación *f*

contemporary /kən'tempərərɪ/ *a & n* contemporáneo (*m*)

contempt /kən'tempt/ *n* desprecio *m*. **~ible** *a* despreciable. **~uous** /-tjʊəs/ *a* desdeñoso

contend /kən'tend/ *vt* sostener. ● *vi* contender. **~er** *n* contendiente *m & f*

content[1] /kən'tent/ *a* satisfecho. ● *vt* contentar

content[2] /'kɒntent/ *n* contenido *m*

contented /kən'tentɪd/ *a* satisfecho

contention /kən'tenʃn/ *n* contienda *f*; (*opinion*) opinión *f*, argumento *m*

contentment /kən'tentmənt/ *n* contento *m*

contest /'kɒntest/ *n* (*competition*) concurso *m*; (*fight*) contienda *f*. /kən'test/ *vt* disputar. **~ant** *n* contendiente *m & f*, concursante *m & f*

context /'kɒntekst/ *n* contexto *m*

continent /'kɒntɪnənt/ *n* continente *m*. **the C~** Europa *f*. **~al** /-'nentl/ *a* continental

contingency /kən'tɪndʒənsɪ/ *n* contingencia *f*

contingent /kən'tɪndʒənt/ *a & n* contingente (*m*)

continu|al /kən'tɪnjʊəl/ *a* continuo. **~ance** /kən'tɪnjʊəns/ *n* continuación *f*. **~ation** /-ʊ'eɪʃn/ *n* continuación *f*. **~e** /kən'tɪnju:/ *vt/i* continuar; (*resume*) seguir. **~ed** *a* continuo. **~ity** /kɒntɪ'nju:ətɪ/ *n* continuidad *f*. **~ity girl** (*cinema, TV*) secretaria *f* de rodaje. **~ous** /kən'tɪnjʊəs/ *a* continuo. **~ously** *adv* continuamente

contort /kən'tɔ:t/ *vt* retorcer. **~ion** /-ʃn/ *n* contorsión *f*. **~ionist** /-ʃənɪst/ *n* contorsionista *m & f*

contour /'kɒntʊə(r)/ *n* contorno *m*. **~ line** *n* curva *f* de nivel

contraband /'kɒntrəbænd/ *n* contrabando *m*

contracepti|on /kɒntrə'sepʃn/ *n* contracepción *f*. **~ve** /kɒntrə'septɪv/ *a & n* anticonceptivo (*m*)

contract /'kɒntrækt/ *n* contrato *m*. /kən'trækt/ *vt* contraer. ● *vi* contraerse. **~ion** /kən'trækʃn/ *n* contracción *f*. **~or** /kən'træktə(r)/ *n* contratista *m & f*

contradict /kɒntrə'dɪkt/ *vt* contradecir. **~ion** /-ʃn/ *n* contradicción *f*. **~ory** *a* contradictorio

contraption /kən'træpʃn/ *n* (*fam*) artilugio *m*
contrary /'kɒntrərɪ/ *a* & *n* contrario (*m*). **on the ~** al contrario. ● *adv*. **~ to** contrariamente a. /kən'treərɪ/ *a* terco
contrast /'kɒntrɑ:st/ *n* contraste *m*. /kən'trɑ:st/ *vt* poner en contraste. ● *vi* contrastar. **~ing** *a* contrastante
contraven|e /kɒntrə'vi:n/ *vt* contravenir. **~tion** /-'venʃn/ *n* contravención *f*
contribut|e /kən'trɪbju:t/ *vt/i* contribuir. **~e to** escribir para ‹*newspaper*›. **~ion** /kɒntrɪ'bju:ʃn/ *n* contribución *f*; (*from salary*) cotización *f*. **~or** *n* contribuyente *m* & *f*; (*to newspaper*) colaborador *m*
contrite /'kɒntraɪt/ *a* arrepentido, pesaroso
contriv|ance /kən'traɪvəns/ *n* invención *f*. **~e** /kən'traɪv/ *vt* idear. **~e to** conseguir
control /kən'trəʊl/ *vt* (*pt* **controlled**) controlar. ● *n* control *m*. **~s** *npl* (*mec*) mandos *mpl*
controvers|ial /kɒntrə'vɜ:ʃl/ *a* polémico, discutible. **~y** /'kɒntrəvɜ:sɪ/ *n* controversia *f*
conundrum /kə'nʌndrəm/ *n* adivinanza *f*; (*problem*) enigma *m*
conurbation /kɒnɜ:'beɪʃn/ *n* conurbación *f*
convalesce /kɒnvə'les/ *vi* convalecer. **~nce** *n* convalecencia *f*. **~nt** *a* & *n* convaleciente (*m* & *f*). **~nt home** *n* casa *f* de convalecencia
convector /kən'vektə(r)/ *n* estufa *f* de convección
convene /kən'vi:n/ *vt* convocar. ● *vi* reunirse
convenien|ce /kən'vi:nɪəns/ *n* conveniencia *f*, comodidad *f*. **all modern ~ces** todas las comodidades. **at your ~ce** según le convenga. **~ces** *npl* servicios *mpl*. **~t** /kən'vi:nɪənt/ *a* cómodo; ‹*place*› bien situado; ‹*time*› oportuno. **be ~t** convenir. **~tly** *adv* convenientemente
convent /'kɒnvənt/ *n* convento *m*
convention /kən'venʃn/ *n* convención *f*; (*meeting*) congreso *m*. **~al** *a* convencional
converge /kən'vɜ:dʒ/ *vi* convergir
conversant /kən'vɜ:sənt/ *a*. **~ with** versado en
conversation /kɒnvə'seɪʃn/ *n* conversación *f*. **~al** *a* de la conversación. **~alist** *n* hábil conversador *m*
converse[1] /kən'vɜ:s/ *vi* conversar
converse[2] /'kɒnvɜ:s/ *a* inverso. ● *n* lo contrario. **~ly** *adv* a la inversa
conver|sion /kən'vɜ:ʃn/ *n* conversión *f*. **~t** /kən'vɜ:t/ *vt* convertir. /'kɒnvɜ:t/ *n* converso *m*. **~tible** /kən'vɜ:tɪbl/ *a* convertible. ● *n* (*auto*) descapotable *m*
convex /'kɒnveks/ *a* convexo
convey /kən'veɪ/ *vt* llevar; transportar ‹*goods*›; comunicar ‹*idea, feeling*›. **~ance** *n* transporte *m*. **~or belt** *n* cinta *f* transportadora
convict /kən'vɪkt/ *vt* condenar. /'kɒnvɪkt/ *n* presidiario *m*. **~ion** /kən'vikʃn/ *n* condena *f*; (*belief*) creencia *f*
convinc|e /kən'vɪns/ *vt* convencer. **~ing** *a* convincente
convivial /kən'vɪvɪəl/ *a* alegre
convoke /kən'vəʊk/ *vt* convocar
convoluted /'kɒnvəlu:tɪd/ *a* enrollado; ‹*argument*› complicado
convoy /'kɒnvɔɪ/ *n* convoy *m*
convuls|e /kən'vʌls/ *vt* convulsionar. **be ~ed with laughter** desternillarse de risa. **~ion** /-ʃn/ *n* convulsión *f*
coo /ku:/ *vi* arrullar
cook /kʊk/ *vt* cocinar; (*alter, fam*) falsificar. **~ up** (*fam*) inventar. ● *n* cocinero *m*
cooker /'kʊkə(r)/ *n* cocina *f*
cookery /'kʊkərɪ/ *n* cocina *f*
cookie /'kʊkɪ/ *n* (*Amer*) galleta *f*
cool /ku:l/ *a* (**-er, -est**) fresco; (*calm*) tranquilo; (*unfriendly*) frío. ● *n* fresco *m*; (*sl*) calma *f*. ● *vt* enfriar. ● *vi* enfriarse. **~ down** ‹*person*› calmarse. **~ly** *adv* tranquilamente. **~ness** *n* frescura *f*
coop /ku:p/ *n* gallinero *m*. ● *vt*. **~ up** encerrar
co-operat|e /kəʊ'ɒpəreɪt/ *vi* cooperar. **~ion** /-'reɪʃn/ *n* cooperación *f*
cooperative /kəʊ'ɒpərətɪv/ *a* cooperativo. ● *n* cooperativa *f*
co-opt /kəʊ'ɒpt/ *vt* cooptar
co-ordinat|e /kəʊ'ɔ:dɪneɪt/ *vt* coordinar. **~ion** /-'neɪʃn/ *n* coordinación *f*
cop /kɒp/ *vt* (*pt* **copped**) (*sl*) prender. ● *n* (*sl*) policía *m*

cope /kəʊp/ *vi* (*fam*) arreglárselas. **~ with** enfrentarse con

copious /ˈkəʊpɪəs/ *a* abundante

copper[1] /ˈkɒpə(r)/ *n* cobre *m*; (*coin*) perra *f*. ● *a* de cobre

copper[2] /ˈkɒpə(r)/ *n* (*sl*) policía *m*

coppice /ˈkɒpɪs/ *n*, **copse** /kɒps/ *n* bosquecillo *m*

Coptic /ˈkɒptɪk/ *a* copto

copulat|e /ˈkɒpjʊleɪt/ *vi* copular. **~ion** /-ˈleɪʃn/ *n* cópula *f*

copy /ˈkɒpɪ/ *n* copia *f*; (*typ*) material *m*. ● *vt* copiar

copyright /ˈkɒpɪraɪt/ *n* derechos *mpl* de autor

copy-writer /ˈkɒpɪraɪtə(r)/ *n* redactor *m* de textos publicitarios

coral /ˈkɒrəl/ *n* coral *m*

cord /kɔːd/ *n* cuerda *f*; (*fabric*) pana *f*. **~s** *npl* pantalones *mpl* de pana

cordial /ˈkɔːdɪəl/ *a* & *n* cordial (*m*)

cordon /ˈkɔːdn/ *n* cordón *m*. ● *vt*. **~ off** acordonar

corduroy /ˈkɔːdərɔɪ/ *n* pana *f*

core /kɔː(r)/ *n* (*of apple*) corazón *m*; (*fig*) meollo *m*

cork /kɔːk/ *n* corcho *m*. ● *vt* taponar. **~screw** /ˈkɔːkskruː/ *n* sacacorchos *m invar*

corn[1] /kɔːn/ *n* (*wheat*) trigo *m*; (*Amer*) maíz *m*; (*seed*) grano *m*

corn[2] /kɔːn/ *n* (*hard skin*) callo *m*

corned /kɔːnd/ *a*. **~ beef** *n* carne *f* de vaca en lata

corner /ˈkɔːnə(r)/ *n* ángulo *m*; (*inside*) rincón *m*; (*outside*) esquina *f*; (*football*) saque *m* de esquina. ● *vt* arrinconar; (*com*) acaparar. **~-stone** *n* piedra *f* angular

cornet /ˈkɔːnɪt/ *n* (*mus*) corneta *f*; (*for ice-cream*) cucurucho *m*

cornflakes /ˈkɔːnfleɪks/ *npl* copos *mpl* de maíz

cornflour /ˈkɔːnflaʊə(r)/ *n* harina *f* de maíz

cornice /ˈkɔːnɪs/ *n* cornisa *f*

cornucopia /kɔːnjʊˈkəʊpɪə/ *n* cuerno *m* de la abundancia

Corn|ish /ˈkɔːnɪʃ/ *a* de Cornualles. **~wall** /ˈkɔːnwəl/ *n* Cornualles *m*

corny /ˈkɔːnɪ/ *a* (*trite, fam*) gastado; (*mawkish*) sentimental, sensiblero

corollary /kəˈrɒlərɪ/ *n* corolario *m*

coronary /ˈkɒrənərɪ/ *n* trombosis *f* coronaria

coronation /kɒrəˈneɪʃn/ *n* coronación *f*

coroner /ˈkɒrənə(r)/ *n* juez *m* de primera instancia

corporal[1] /ˈkɔːpərəl/ *n* cabo *m*

corporal[2] /ˈkɔːpərəl/ *a* corporal

corporate /ˈkɔːpərət/ *a* corporativo

corporation /kɔːpəˈreɪʃn/ *n* corporación *f*; (*of town*) ayuntamiento *m*

corps /kɔː(r)/ *n* (*pl* **corps** /kɔːz/) cuerpo *m*

corpse /kɔːps/ *n* cadáver *m*

corpulent /ˈkɔːpjʊlənt/ *a* gordo, corpulento

corpuscle /ˈkɔːpʌsl/ *n* glóbulo *m*

corral /kəˈrɑːl/ *n* (*Amer*) corral *m*

correct /kəˈrekt/ *a* correcto; ‹*time*› exacto. ● *vt* corregir. **~ion** /-ʃn/ *n* corrección *f*

correlat|e /ˈkɒrəleɪt/ *vt* poner en correlación. **~ion** /-ˈleɪʃn/ *n* correlación *f*

correspond /kɒrɪˈspɒnd/ *vi* corresponder; (*write*) escribirse. **~ence** *n* correspondencia *f*. **~ent** *n* corresponsal *m* & *f*

corridor /ˈkɒrɪdɔː(r)/ *n* pasillo *m*

corroborate /kəˈrɒbəreɪt/ *vt* corroborar

corro|de /kəˈrəʊd/ *vt* corroer. ● *vi* corroerse. **~sion** *n* corrosión *f*

corrugated /ˈkɒrəgeɪtɪd/ *a* ondulado. **~ iron** *n* hierro *m* ondulado

corrupt /kəˈrʌpt/ *a* corrompido. ● *vt* corromper. **~ion** /-ʃn/ *n* corrupción *f*

corset /ˈkɔːsɪt/ *n* corsé *m*

Corsica /ˈkɔːsɪkə/ *n* Córcega *f*. **~n** *a* & *n* corso (*m*)

cortège /ˈkɔːteɪʒ/ *n* cortejo *m*

cos /kɒs/ *n* lechuga *f* romana

cosh /kɒʃ/ *n* cachiporra *f*. ● *vt* aporrear

cosiness /ˈkəʊzɪnɪs/ *n* comodidad *f*

cosmetic /kɒzˈmetɪk/ *a* & *n* cosmético (*m*)

cosmic /ˈkɒzmɪk/ *a* cósmico

cosmonaut /ˈkɒzmənɔːt/ *n* cosmonauta *m* & *f*

cosmopolitan /kɒzməˈpɒlɪtən/ *a* & *n* cosmopolita (*m* & *f*)

cosmos /ˈkɒzmɒs/ *n* cosmos *m*

Cossack /ˈkɒsæk/ *a* & *n* cosaco (*m*)

cosset /ˈkɒsɪt/ *vt* (*pt* **cosseted**) mimar

cost /kɒst/ *vi* (*pt* **cost**) costar, valer. ● *vt* (*pt* **costed**) calcular el coste de. ● *n* precio *m*. **at all ~s** cueste lo que cueste. **to one's ~** a sus expensas. **~s** *npl* (*jurid*) costas *fpl*

Costa Rica /kɒstəˈriːkə/ *n* Costa *f* Rica. **~n** *a* & *n* costarricense (*m* & *f*), costarriqueño (*m*)

costly /ˈkɒstlɪ/ *a* (**-ier**, **-iest**) caro, costoso
costume /ˈkɒstjuːm/ *n* traje *m*
cosy /ˈkəʊzɪ/ *a* (**-ier**, **-iest**) cómodo; ‹*place*› acogedor. ● *n* cubierta *f* (de tetera)
cot /kɒt/ *n* cuna *f*
cottage /ˈkɒtɪdʒ/ *n* casita *f* de campo. ~ **cheese** *n* requesón *m*. ~ **industry** *n* industria *f* casera. ~ **pie** *n* carne *f* picada con puré de patatas
cotton /ˈkɒtn/ *n* algodón *m*. ● *vi*. ~ **on** (*sl*) comprender. ~ **wool** *n* algodón hidrófilo
couch /kaʊtʃ/ *n* sofá *m*. ● *vt* expresar
couchette /kuːˈʃet/ *n* litera *f*
cough /kɒf/ *vi* toser. ● *n* tos *f*. ~ **up** (*sl*) pagar. ~ **mixture** *n* jarabe *m* para la tos
could /kʊd, kəd/ *pt of* **can**
couldn't /ˈkʊdnt/ = **could not**
council /ˈkaʊnsl/ *n* consejo *m*; (*of town*) ayuntamiento *m*. ~ **house** *n* vivienda *f* protegida. **~lor** /ˈkaʊnsələ(r)/ *n* concejal *m*
counsel /ˈkaʊnsl/ *n* consejo *m*; (*pl invar*) (*jurid*) abogado *m*. **~lor** *n* consejero *m*
count[1] /kaʊnt/ *n* recuento *m*. ● *vt*/*i* contar
count[2] /kaʊnt/ *n* (*nobleman*) conde *m*
countdown /ˈkaʊntdaʊn/ *n* cuenta *f* atrás
countenance /ˈkaʊntɪnəns/ *n* semblante *m*. ● *vt* aprobar
counter /ˈkaʊntə(r)/ *n* (*in shop etc*) mostrador *m*; (*token*) ficha *f*. ● *adv*. ~ **to** en contra de. ● *a* opuesto. ● *vt* oponerse a; parar ‹*blow*›. ● *vi* contraatacar
counter... /ˈkaʊntə(r)/ *pref* contra...
counteract /kaʊntərˈækt/ *vt* contrarrestar
counter-attack /ˈkaʊntərətæk/ *n* contraataque *m*. ● *vt*/*i* contraatacar
counterbalance /ˈkaʊntəbæləns/ *n* contrapeso *m*. ● *vt*/*i* contrapesar
counterfeit /ˈkaʊntəfɪt/ *a* falsificado. ● *n* falsificación *f*. ● *vt* falsificar
counterfoil /ˈkaʊntəfɔɪl/ *n* talón *m*
counterpart /ˈkaʊntəpɑːt/ *n* equivalente *m*; (*person*) homólogo *m*
counter-productive /ˈkaʊntəprəˈdʌktɪv/ *a* contraproducente
countersign /ˈkaʊntəsaɪn/ *vt* refrendar
countess /ˈkaʊntɪs/ *n* condesa *f*
countless /ˈkaʊntlɪs/ *a* innumerable
countrified /ˈkʌntrɪfaɪd/ *a* rústico
country /ˈkʌntrɪ/ *n* (*native land*) país *m*; (*countryside*) campo *m*. ~ **folk** *n* gente *f* del campo. **go to the** ~ ir al campo; (*pol*) convocar elecciones generales
countryman /ˈkʌntrɪmən/ *n* (*pl* **-men**) campesino *m*; (*of one's own country*) compatriota *m*
countryside /ˈkʌntrɪsaɪd/ *n* campo *m*
county /ˈkaʊntɪ/ *n* condado *m*, provincia *f*
coup /kuː/ *n* golpe *m*
coupé /ˈkuːpeɪ/ *n* cupé *m*
couple /ˈkʌpl/ *n* (*of things*) par *m*; (*of people*) pareja *f*; (*married*) matrimonio *m*. **a** ~ **of** un par de. ● *vt* unir; (*tec*) acoplar. ● *vi* copularse
coupon /ˈkuːpɒn/ *n* cupón *m*
courage /ˈkʌrɪdʒ/ *n* valor *m*. **~ous** /kəˈreɪdʒəs/ *a* valiente. **~ously** *adv* valientemente
courgette /kʊəˈʒet/ *n* calabacín *m*
courier /ˈkʊrɪə(r)/ *n* mensajero *m*; (*for tourists*) guía *m* & *f*
course /kɔːs/ *n* curso *m*; (*behaviour*) conducta *f*; (*aviat, naut*) rumbo *m*; (*culin*) plato *m*; (*for golf*) campo *m*. **in due** ~ a su debido tiempo. **in the** ~ **of** en el transcurso de, durante. **of** ~ desde luego, por supuesto
court /kɔːt/ *n* corte *f*; (*tennis*) pista *f*; (*jurid*) tribunal *m*. ● *vt* cortejar; buscar ‹*danger*›
courteous /ˈkɜːtɪəs/ *a* cortés
courtesan /kɔːtɪˈzæn/ *n* (*old use*) cortesana *f*
courtesy /ˈkɜːtəsɪ/ *n* cortesía *f*
court: **~ier** /ˈkɔːtɪə(r)/ *n* (*old use*) cortesano *m*. ~ **martial** *n* (*pl* **courts martial**) consejo *m* de guerra. **~-martial** *vt* (*pt* **~-martialled**) juzgar en consejo de guerra. **~ship** /ˈkɔːtʃɪp/ *n* cortejo *m*
courtyard /ˈkɔːtjɑːd/ *n* patio *m*
cousin /ˈkʌzn/ *n* primo *m*. **first** ~ primo carnal. **second** ~ primo segundo
cove /kəʊv/ *n* cala *f*
covenant /ˈkʌvənənt/ *n* acuerdo *m*
Coventry /ˈkɒvntrɪ/ *n*. **send to** ~ hacer el vacío
cover /ˈkʌvə(r)/ *vt* cubrir; (*journalism*) hacer un reportaje sobre. ~

up cubrir; (*fig*) ocultar. ● *n* cubierta *f*; (*shelter*) abrigo *m*; (*lid*) tapa *f*; (*for furniture*) funda *f*; (*pretext*) pretexto *m*; (*of magazine*) portada *f*. **~age** /'kʌvərɪdʒ/ *n* reportaje *m*. **~ charge** *n* precio *m* del cubierto. **~ing** *n* cubierta *f*. **~ing letter** *n* carta *f* explicatoria, carta *f* adjunta

covet /'kʌvɪt/ *vt* codiciar

cow /kaʊ/ *n* vaca *f*

coward /'kaʊəd/ *n* cobarde *m*. **~ly** *a* cobarde. **~ice** /'kaʊədɪs/ *n* cobardía *f*

cowboy /'kaʊbɔɪ/ *n* vaquero *m*

cower /'kaʊə(r)/ *vi* encogerse, acobardarse

cowl /kaʊl/ *n* capucha *f*; (*of chimney*) sombrerete *m*

cowshed /'kaʊʃed/ *n* establo *m*

coxswain /'kɒksn/ *n* timonel *m*

coy /kɔɪ/ *a* (**-er**, **-est**) (falsamente) tímido, remilgado

crab[1] /kræb/ *n* cangrejo *m*

crab[2] /kræb/ *vi* (*pt* **crabbed**) quejarse

crab-apple /'kræbæpl/ *n* manzana *f* silvestre

crack /kræk/ *n* grieta *f*; (*noise*) crujido *m*; (*of whip*) chasquido *m*; (*joke, sl*) chiste *m*. ● *a* (*fam*) de primera. ● *vt* agrietar; chasquear ‹*whip, fingers*›; cascar ‹*nut*›; gastar ‹*joke*›; resolver ‹*problem*›. ● *vi* agrietarse. **get ~ing** (*fam*) darse prisa. **~ down on** (*fam*) tomar medidas enérgicas contra. **~ up** *vi* fallar; ‹*person*› volverse loco. **~ed** /krækt/ *a* (*sl*) chiflado

cracker /'krækə(r)/ *n* petardo *m*; (*culin*) galleta *f* (soso); (*culin, Amer*) galleta *f*

crackers /'krækəz/ *a* (*sl*) chiflado

crackl|e /'krækl/ *vi* crepitar. ● *n* crepitación *f*, crujido *m*. **~ing** /'kræklɪŋ/ *n* crepitación *f*, crujido *m*; (*of pork*) chicharrón *m*

crackpot /'krækpɒt/ *n* (*sl*) chiflado *m*

cradle /'kreɪdl/ *n* cuna *f*. ● *vt* acunar

craft /krɑːft/ *n* destreza *f*; (*technique*) arte *f*; (*cunning*) astucia *f*. ● *n invar* (*boat*) barco *m*

craftsman /'krɑːftsmən/ *n* (*pl* **-men**) artesano *m*. **~ship** *n* artesanía *f*

crafty /'krɑːftɪ/ *a* (**-ier**, **-iest**) astuto

crag /kræg/ *n* despeñadero *m*. **~gy** *a* peñascoso

cram /kræm/ *vt* (*pt* **crammed**) rellenar. **~ with** llenar de. ● *vi* (*for exams*) empollar. **~-full** *a* atestado

cramp /kræmp/ *n* calambre *m*

cramped /kræmpt/ *a* apretado

cranberry /'krænbərɪ/ *n* arándano *m*

crane /kreɪn/ *n* grúa *f*; (*bird*) grulla *f*. ● *vt* estirar ‹*neck*›

crank[1] /kræŋk/ *n* manivela *f*

crank[2] /kræŋk/ *n* (*person*) excéntrico *m*. **~y** *a* excéntrico

cranny /'krænɪ/ *n* grieta *f*

crash /kræʃ/ *n* accidente *m*; (*noise*) estruendo *m*; (*collision*) choque *m*; (*com*) quiebra *f*. ● *vt* estrellar. ● *vi* quebrar con estrépito; (*have accident*) tener un accidente; ‹*car etc*› chocar; (*fail*) fracasar. **~ course** *n* curso *m* intensivo. **~-helmet** *n* casco *m* protector. **~-land** *vi* hacer un aterrizaje de emergencia, hacer un aterrizaje forzoso

crass /kræs/ *a* craso, burdo

crate /kreɪt/ *n* cajón *m*. ● *vt* embalar

crater /'kreɪtə(r)/ *n* cráter *m*

cravat /krə'væt/ *n* corbata *f*, fular *m*

crav|e /kreɪv/ *vi*. **~e for** anhelar. **~ing** *n* ansia *f*

crawl /krɔːl/ *vi* andar a gatas; (*move slowly*) avanzar lentamente; (*drag o.s.*) arrastrarse. ● *n* (*swimming*) crol *m*. **at a ~** a paso lento. **~ to** humillarse ante. **~ with** hervir de

crayon /'kreɪən/ *n* lápiz *m* de color

craze /kreɪz/ *n* manía *f*

craz|iness /'kreɪzɪnɪs/ *n* locura *f*. **~y** /'kreɪzɪ/ *a* (**-ier**, **-iest**) loco. **be ~y about** andar loco por. **~y paving** *n* enlosado *m* irregular

creak /kriːk/ *n* crujido *m*; (*of hinge*) chirrido *m*. ● *vi* crujir; ‹*hinge*› chirriar

cream /kriːm/ *n* crema *f*; (*fresh*) nata *f*. ● *a* (*colour*) color de crema. ● *vt* (*remove*) desnatar; (*beat*) batir. **~ cheese** *n* queso *m* de nata. **~y** *a* cremoso

crease /kriːs/ *n* pliegue *m*; (*crumple*) arruga *f*. ● *vt* plegar; (*wrinkle*) arrugar. ● *vi* arrugarse

creat|e /kriː'eɪt/ *vt* crear. **~ion** /-ʃn/ *n* creación *f*. **~ive** *a* creativo. **~or** *n* creador *m*

creature /'kriːtʃə(r)/ *n* criatura *f*, bicho *m*, animal *m*

crèche /kreɪʃ/ *n* guardería *f* infantil

credence /'kriːdns/ *n* creencia *f*, fe *f*

credentials /krɪ'denʃlz/ *npl* credenciales *mpl*

credib|ility /kredə'bɪlətɪ/ *n* credibilidad *f*. **~le** /'kredəbl/ *a* creíble

credit /'kredɪt/ *n* crédito *m*; (*honour*) honor *m*. **take the ~ for** atribuirse el mérito de. ● *vt* (*pt* **credited**) acreditar; (*believe*) creer. ~ **s.o. with** atribuir a uno. **~able** *a* loable. ~ **card** *n* tarjeta *f* de crédito. **~or** *n* acreedor *m*

credulous /'krədjʊləs/ *a* crédulo

creed /kri:d/ *n* credo *m*

creek /kri:k/ *n* ensenada *f*. **up the** ~ (*sl*) en apuros

creep /kri:p/ *vi* (*pt* **crept**) arrastrarse; ‹*plant*› trepar. ● *n* (*sl*) persona *f* desagradable. **~er** *n* enredadera *f*. **~s** /kri:ps/ *npl*. **give s.o. the ~s** dar repugnancia a uno

cremat|e /krɪ'meɪt/ *vt* incinerar. **~ion** /-ʃn/ *n* cremación *f*. **~orium** /kremə'tɔ:rɪəm/ *n* (*pl* **-ia**) crematorio *m*

Creole /'krɪəʊl/ *a* & *n* criollo (*m*)

crêpe /kreɪp/ *n* crespón *m*

crept /krept/ *see* **creep**

crescendo /krɪ'ʃendəʊ/ *n* (*pl* **-os**) crescendo *m*

crescent /'kresnt/ *n* media luna *f*; (*street*) calle *f* en forma de media luna

cress /kres/ *n* berro *m*

crest /krest/ *n* cresta *f*; (*coat of arms*) blasón *m*

Crete /kri:t/ *n* Creta *f*

cretin /'kretɪn/ *n* cretino *m*

crevasse /krɪ'væs/ *n* grieta *f*

crevice /'krevɪs/ *n* grieta *f*

crew[1] /kru:/ *n* tripulación *f*; (*gang*) pandilla *f*

crew[2] /kru:/ *see* **crow**[2]

crew: ~ **cut** *n* corte *m* al rape. ~ **neck** *n* cuello *m* redondo

crib /krɪb/ *n* cuna *f*; (*relig*) belén *m*; (*plagiarism*) plagio *m*. ● *vt/i* (*pt* **cribbed**) plagiar

crick /krɪk/ *n* calambre *m*; (*in neck*) tortícolis *f*

cricket[1] /'krɪkɪt/ *n* criquet *m*

cricket[2] /'krɪkɪt/ *n* (*insect*) grillo *m*

cricketer /'krɪkɪtə(r)/ *n* jugador *m* de criquet

crim|e /kraɪm/ *n* crimen *m*; (*acts*) criminalidad *f*. **~inal** /'krɪmɪnl/ *a* & *n* criminal (*m*)

crimp /krɪmp/ *vt* rizar

crimson /'krɪmzn/ *a* & *n* carmesí (*m*)

cringe /krɪndʒ/ *vi* encogerse; (*fig*) humillarse

crinkle /'krɪŋkl/ *vt* arrugar. ● *vi* arrugarse. ● *n* arruga *f*

crinoline /'krɪnəlɪn/ *n* miriñaque *m*

cripple /'krɪpl/ *n* lisiado *m*, mutilado *m*. ● *vt* lisiar; (*fig*) paralizar

crisis /'kraɪsɪs/ *n* (*pl* **crises** /'kraɪsi:z/) crisis *f*

crisp /krɪsp/ *a* (**-er**, **-est**) (*culin*) crujiente; ‹*air*› vigorizador. **~s** *npl* patatas *fpl* fritas a la inglesa

criss-cross /'krɪskrɒs/ *a* entrecruzado. ● *vt* entrecruzar. ● *vi* entrecruzarse

criterion /kraɪ'tɪərɪən/ *n* (*pl* **-ia**) criterio *m*

critic /'krɪtɪk/ *n* crítico *m*

critical /'krɪtɪkl/ *a* crítico. **~ly** *adv* críticamente; (*ill*) gravemente

critici|sm /'krɪtɪsɪzəm/ *n* crítica *f*. **~ze** /'krɪtɪsaɪz/ *vt/i* criticar

croak /krəʊk/ *n* (*of person*) gruñido *m*; (*of frog*) canto *m*. ● *vi* gruñir; ‹*frog*› croar

crochet /'krəʊʃeɪ/ *n* croché *m*, ganchillo *m*. ● *vt* hacer ganchillo

crock[1] /krɒk/ *n* (*person, fam*) vejancón *m*; (*old car*) cacharro *m*

crock[2] /krɒk/ *n* vasija *f* de loza

crockery /'krɒkərɪ/ *n* loza *f*

crocodile /'krɒkədaɪl/ *n* cocodrilo *m*. ~ **tears** *npl* lágrimas *fpl* de cocodrilo

crocus /'krəʊkəs/ *n* (*pl* **-es**) azafrán *m*

crony /'krəʊnɪ/ *n* amigote *m*

crook /krʊk/ *n* (*fam*) maleante *m* & *f*, estafador *m*, criminal *m*; (*stick*) cayado *m*; (*of arm*) pliegue *m*

crooked /'krʊkɪd/ *a* torcido; (*winding*) tortuoso; (*dishonest*) poco honrado

croon /kru:n/ *vt/i* canturrear

crop /krɒp/ *n* cosecha *f*; (*fig*) montón *m*. ● *vt* (*pt* **cropped**) *vi* cortar. ~ **up** surgir

cropper /'krɒpər/ *n*. **come a** ~ (*fall, fam*) caer; (*fail, fam*) fracasar

croquet /'krəʊkeɪ/ *n* croquet *m*

croquette /krə'ket/ *n* croqueta *f*

cross /krɒs/ *n* cruz *f*; (*of animals*) cruce *m*. ● *vt/i* cruzar; (*oppose*) contrariar. ~ **off** tachar. ~ **o.s.** santiguarse. ~ **out** tachar. ~ **s.o.'s mind** ocurrírsele a uno. ● *a* enfadado. **talk at ~ purposes** hablar sin entenderse

crossbar /'krɒsbɑ:(r)/ *n* travesaño *m*

cross-examine /krɒsɪg'zæmɪn/ *vt* interrogar

cross-eyed /'krɒsaɪd/ *a* bizco

crossfire /'krɒsfaɪə(r)/ *n* fuego *m* cruzado

crossing /'krɒsɪŋ/ *n* (*by boat*) travesía *f*; (*on road*) paso *m* para peatones

crossly /ˈkrɒslɪ/ *adv* con enfado
cross-reference /krɒsˈrefrəns/ *n* referencia *f*
crossroads /ˈkrɒsrəʊdz/ *n* cruce *m* (de carreteras)
cross-section /krɒsˈsekʃn/ *n* sección *f* transversal; (*fig*) muestra *f* representativa
crosswise /ˈkrɒswaɪz/ *adv* al través
crossword /ˈkrɒswɜːd/ *n* crucigrama *m*
crotch /krɒtʃ/ *n* entrepiernas *fpl*
crotchety /ˈkrɒtʃɪtɪ/ *a* de mal genio
crouch /kraʊtʃ/ *vi* agacharse
crow[1] /krəʊ/ *n* cuervo *m*. **as the ~ flies** en línea recta
crow[2] /krəʊ/ *vi* (*pt* **crew**) cacarear
crowbar /ˈkrəʊbɑː(r)/ *n* palanca *f*
crowd /kraʊd/ *n* muchedumbre *f*. ● *vt* amontonar; (*fill*) llenar. ● *vi* amontonarse; (*gather*) reunirse. **~ed** *a* atestado
crown /kraʊn/ *n* corona *f*; (*of hill*) cumbre *f*; (*of head*) coronilla *f*. ● *vt* coronar; poner una corona a ‹*tooth*›. **C~ Court** *n* tribunal *m* regional. **C~ prince** *n* príncipe *m* heredero
crucial /ˈkruːʃl/ *a* crucial
crucifix /ˈkruːsɪfɪks/ *n* crucifijo *m*. **~ion** /-ˈfɪkʃn/ *n* crucifixión *f*
crucify /ˈkruːsɪfaɪ/ *vt* crucificar
crude /kruːd/ *a* (**-er**, **-est**) (*raw*) crudo; (*rough*) tosco; (*vulgar*) ordinario
cruel /krʊəl/ *a* (**crueller**, **cruellest**) cruel. **~ty** *n* crueldad *f*
cruet /ˈkruːɪt/ *n* vinagreras *fpl*
cruise /kruːz/ *n* crucero *m*. ● *vi* hacer un crucero; (*of car*) circular lentamente. **~r** *n* crucero *m*
crumb /krʌm/ *n* migaja *f*
crumble /ˈkrʌmbl/ *vt* desmenuzar. ● *vi* desmenuzarse; (*collapse*) derrumbarse
crummy /ˈkrʌmɪ/ *a* (**-ier**, **-iest**) (*sl*) miserable
crumpet /ˈkrʌmpɪt/ *n* bollo *m* blando
crumple /ˈkrʌmpl/ *vt* arrugar; estrujar ‹*paper*›. ● *vi* arrugarse
crunch /krʌntʃ/ *vt* hacer crujir; (*bite*) ronzar, morder, masticar. ● *n* crujido *m*; (*fig*) momento *m* decisivo
crusade /kruːˈseɪd/ *n* cruzada *f*. **~r** /-ə(r)/ *n* cruzado *m*
crush /krʌʃ/ *vt* aplastar; arrugar ‹*clothes*›; estrujar ‹*paper*›. ● *n* (*crowd*) aglomeración *f*. **have a ~ on** (*sl*) estar perdido por. **orange ~** *n* naranjada *f*
crust /krʌst/ *n* corteza *f*. **~y** *a* ‹*bread*› de corteza dura; ‹*person*› malhumorado
crutch /krʌtʃ/ *n* muleta *f*; (*anat*) entrepiernas *fpl*
crux /krʌks/ *n* (*pl* **cruxes**) punto *m* más importante, quid *m*, busilis *m*
cry /kraɪ/ *n* grito *m*. **be a far ~ from** (*fig*) distar mucho de. ● *vi* llorar; (*call out*) gritar. **~ off** rajarse. **~-baby** *n* llorón *m*
crypt /krɪpt/ *n* cripta *f*
cryptic /ˈkrɪptɪk/ *a* enigmático
crystal /ˈkrɪstl/ *n* cristal *m*. **~lize** *vt* cristalizar. ● *vi* cristalizarse
cub /kʌb/ *n* cachorro *m*. **C~ (Scout)** *n* niño *m* explorador
Cuba /ˈkjuːbə/ *n* Cuba *f*. **~n** *a* & *n* cubano (*m*)
cubby-hole /ˈkʌbɪhəʊl/ *n* casilla *f*; (*room*) chiribitil *m*, cuchitril *m*
cub|e /kjuːb/ *n* cubo *m*. **~ic** *a* cúbico
cubicle /ˈkjuːbɪkl/ *n* cubículo *m*; (*changing room*) caseta *f*
cubis|m /ˈkjuːbɪzm/ *n* cubismo *m*. **~t** *a* & *n* cubista (*m* & *f*)
cuckold /ˈkʌkəʊld/ *n* cornudo *m*
cuckoo /ˈkʊkuː/ *n* cuco *m*, cuclillo *m*
cucumber /ˈkjuːkʌmbə(r)/ *n* pepino *m*
cuddl|e /ˈkʌdl/ *vt* abrazar. ● *vi* abrazarse. ● *n* abrazo *m*. **~y** *a* mimoso
cudgel /ˈkʌdʒl/ *n* porra *f*. ● *vt* (*pt* **cudgelled**) aporrear
cue[1] /kjuː/ *n* indicación *f*; (*in theatre*) pie *m*
cue[2] /kjuː/ *n* (*in billiards*) taco *m*
cuff /kʌf/ *n* puño *m*; (*blow*) bofetada *f*. **speak off the ~** hablar de improviso. ● *vt* abofetear. **~-link** *n* gemelo *m*
cul-de-sac /ˈkʌldəsæk/ *n* callejón *m* sin salida
culinary /ˈkʌlɪnərɪ/ *a* culinario
cull /kʌl/ *vt* coger ‹*flowers*›; entresacar ‹*animals*›
culminat|e /ˈkʌlmɪneɪt/ *vi* culminar. **~ion** /-ˈneɪʃn/ *n* culminación *f*
culottes /kʊˈlɒts/ *npl* falda *f* pantalón
culprit /ˈkʌlprɪt/ *n* culpable *m*
cult /kʌlt/ *n* culto *m*
cultivat|e /ˈkʌltɪveɪt/ *vt* cultivar. **~ion** /-ˈveɪʃn/ *n* cultivo *m*; (*fig*) cultura *f*

cultur|al /'kʌltʃərəl/ *a* cultural. **~e** /'kʌltʃə(r)/ *n* cultura *f*; (*bot etc*) cultivo *m*. **~ed** *a* cultivado; ‹*person*› culto

cumbersome /'kʌmbəsəm/ *a* incómodo; (*heavy*) pesado

cumulative /'kju:mjʊlətɪv/ *a* cumulativo

cunning /'kʌnɪŋ/ *a* astuto. ● *n* astucia *f*

cup /kʌp/ *n* taza *f*; (*prize*) copa *f*

cupboard /'kʌbəd/ *n* armario *m*

Cup Final /kʌp'faɪnl/ *n* final *f* del campeonato

cupful /'kʌpfʊl/ *n* taza *f*

cupidity /kju:'pɪdɪtɪ/ *n* codicia *f*

curable /'kjʊərəbl/ *a* curable

curate /'kjʊərət/ *n* coadjutor *m*

curator /kjʊə'reɪtə(r)/ *n* (*of museum*) conservador *m*

curb /k3:b/ *n* freno *m*. ● *vt* refrenar

curdle /'k3:dl/ *vt* cuajar. ● *vi* cuajarse; ‹*milk*› cortarse

curds /k3:dz/ *npl* cuajada *f*, requesón *m*

cure /kjʊə(r)/ *vt* curar. ● *n* cura *f*

curfew /'k3:fju:/ *n* queda *f*; (*signal*) toque *m* de queda

curio /'kjʊərɪəʊ/ *n* (*pl* **-os**) curiosidad *f*

curio|us /'kjʊərɪəs/ *a* curioso. **~sity** /-'ɒsətɪ/ *n* curiosidad *f*

curl /k3:l/ *vt* rizar ‹*hair*›. **~ o.s. up** acurrucarse. ● *vi* ‹*hair*› rizarse; ‹*paper*› arrollarse. ● *n* rizo *m*. **~er** /'k3:lə(r)/ *n* bigudí *m*, rulo *m*. **~y** /'k3:lɪ/ *a* (**-ier**, **-iest**) rizado

currant /'kʌrənt/ *n* pasa *f* de Corinto

currency /'kʌrənsɪ/ *n* moneda *f*; (*acceptance*) uso *m* (corriente)

current /'kʌrənt/ *a* & *n* corriente (*f*). **~ events** asuntos *mpl* de actualidad. **~ly** *adv* actualmente

curriculum /kə'rɪkjʊləm/ *n* (*pl* **-la**) programa *m* de estudios. **~ vitae** *n* curriculum *m* vitae

curry[1] /'kʌrɪ/ *n* curry *m*

curry[2] /'kʌrɪ/ *vt*. **~ favour with** congraciarse con

curse /k3:s/ *n* maldición *f*; (*oath*) palabrota *f*. ● *vt* maldecir. ● *vi* decir palabrotas

cursory /'k3:sərɪ/ *a* superficial

curt /k3:t/ *a* brusco

curtail /k3:'teɪl/ *vt* abreviar; reducir ‹*expenses*›

curtain /'k3:tn/ *n* cortina *f*; (*in theatre*) telón *m*

curtsy /'k3:tsɪ/ *n* reverencia *f*. ● *vi* hacer una reverencia

curve /k3:v/ *n* curva *f*. ● *vt* encurvar. ● *vi* encorvarse; ‹*road*› torcerse

cushion /'kʊʃn/ *n* cojín *m*. ● *vt* amortiguar ‹*a blow*›; (*fig*) proteger

cushy /'kʊʃɪ/ *a* (**-ier**, **-iest**) (*fam*) fácil

custard /'kʌstəd/ *n* natillas *fpl*

custodian /kʌ'stəʊdɪən/ *n* custodio *m*

custody /'kʌstədɪ/ *n* custodia *f*. **be in ~** (*jurid*) estar detenido

custom /'kʌstəm/ *n* costumbre *f*; (*com*) clientela *f*

customary /'kʌstəmərɪ/ *a* acostumbrado

customer /'kʌstəmə(r)/ *n* cliente *m*

customs /'kʌstəmz/ *npl* aduana *f*. **~ officer** *n* aduanero *m*

cut /kʌt/ *vt/i* (*pt* **cut**, *pres p* **cutting**) cortar; reducir ‹*prices*›. ● *n* corte *m*; (*reduction*) reducción *f*. **~ across** atravesar. **~ back**, **~ down** reducir. **~ in** interrumpir. **~ off** cortar; (*phone*) desconectar; (*fig*) aislar. **~ out** recortar; (*omit*) suprimir. **~ through** atravesar. **~ up** cortar en pedazos. **be ~ up about** (*fig*) afligirse por

cute /kju:t/ *a* (**-er**, **-est**) (*fam*) listo; (*Amer*) mono

cuticle /'kju:tɪkl/ *n* cutícula *f*

cutlery /'kʌtlərɪ/ *n* cubiertos *mpl*

cutlet /'kʌtlɪt/ *n* chuleta *f*

cut-price /'kʌtpraɪs/ *a* a precio reducido

cut-throat /'kʌtθrəʊt/ *a* despiadado

cutting /'kʌtɪŋ/ *a* cortante; ‹*remark*› mordaz. ● *n* (*from newspaper*) recorte *m*; (*of plant*) esqueje *m*

cyanide /'saɪənaɪd/ *n* cianuro *m*

cybernetics /saɪbə'netɪks/ *n* cibernética *f*

cyclamen /'sɪkləmən/ *n* ciclamen *m*

cycle /'saɪkl/ *n* ciclo *m*; (*bicycle*) bicicleta *f*. ● *vi* ir en bicicleta

cyclic(al) /'saɪklɪk(l)/ *a* cíclico

cycli|ng /'saɪklɪŋ/ *n* ciclismo *m*. **~st** *n* ciclista *m & f*

cyclone /'saɪkləʊn/ *n* ciclón *m*

cylind|er /'sɪlɪndə(r)/ *n* cilindro *m*. **~er head** (*auto*) *n* culata *f*. **~rical** /-'lɪndrɪkl/ *a* cilíndrico

cymbal /'sɪmbl/ *n* címbalo *m*

cynic /'sɪnɪk/ *n* cínico *m*. **~al** *a* cínico. **~ism** /-sɪzəm/ *n* cinismo *m*

cypress /'saɪprəs/ *n* ciprés *m*

Cypr|iot /'sɪprɪət/ *a & n* chipriota (*m & f*). **~us** /'saɪprəs/ *n* Chipre *f*
cyst /sɪst/ *n* quiste *m*
czar /zɑ:(r)/ *n* zar *m*
Czech /tʃek/ *a & n* checo (*m*). **the ~ Republic** *n* la república *f* Checa
Czechoslovak /tʃekəʊ'sləʊvæk/ *a & n* (*history*) checoslovaco (*m*). **~ia** /-ə'vækɪə/ *n* (*history*) Checoslovaquia *f*

D

dab /dæb/ *vt* (*pt* **dabbed**) tocar ligeramente. ● *n* toque *m* suave. **a ~ of** un poquito de
dabble /'dæbl/ *vi.* **~ in** meterse (superficialmente) en. **~r** /ə(r)/ *n* aficionado *m*
dad /dæd/ *n* (*fam*) papá *m*. **~dy** *n* (*children's use*) papá *m*. **~dy-long-legs** *n* típula *f*
daffodil /'dæfədɪl/ *n* narciso *m*
daft /dɑ:ft/ *a* (**-er**, **-est**) tonto
dagger /'dægə(r)/ *n* puñal *m*
dahlia /'deɪlɪə/ *n* dalia *f*
daily /'deɪlɪ/ *a* diario. ● *adv* diariamente, cada día. ● *n* diario *m*; (*cleaner, fam*) asistenta *f*
dainty /'deɪntɪ/ *a* (**-ier**, **-iest**) delicado
dairy /'deərɪ/ *n* vaquería *f*; (*shop*) lechería *f*. ● *a* lechero
dais /dei:s/ *n* estrado *m*
daisy /'deɪzɪ/ *n* margarita *f*
dale /deɪl/ *n* valle *m*
dally /'dælɪ/ *vi* tardar; (*waste time*) perder el tiempo
dam /dæm/ *n* presa *f*. ● *vt* (*pt* **dammed**) embalsar
damag|e /'dæmɪdʒ/ *n* daño *m*; (*pl, jurid*) daños *mpl* y perjuicios *mpl*. ● *vt* (*fig*) dañar, estropear. **~ing** *a* perjudicial
damask /'dæməsk/ *n* damasco *m*
dame /deɪm/ *n* (*old use*) dama *f*; (*Amer, sl*) chica *f*
damn /dæm/ *vt* condenar; (*curse*) maldecir. ● *int* ¡córcholis! ● *a* maldito. ● *n*. **I don't care a ~** (no) me importa un comino. **~ation** /-'neɪʃn/ *n* condenación *f*, perdición *f*
damp /dæmp/ *n* humedad *f*. ● *a* (**-er**, **-est**) húmedo. ● *vt* mojar; (*fig*) ahogar. **~er** /'dæmpə(r)/ *n* apagador *m*, sordina *f*; (*fig*) aguafiestas *m invar*. **~ness** *n* humedad *f*
damsel /'dæmzl/ *n* (*old use*) doncella *f*
dance /dɑ:ns/ *vt/i* bailar. ● *n* baile *m*. **~-hall** *n* salón *m* de baile. **~r** /-ə(r)/ *n* bailador *m*; (*professional*) bailarín *m*
dandelion /'dændɪlaɪən/ *n* diente *m* de león
dandruff /'dændrʌf/ *n* caspa *f*
dandy /'dændɪ/ *n* petimetre *m*
Dane /deɪn/ *n* danés *m*
danger /'deɪndʒə(r)/ *n* peligro *m*; (*risk*) riesgo *m*. **~ous** *a* peligroso
dangle /'dæŋgl/ *vt* balancear. ● *vi* suspender, colgar
Danish /'deɪnɪʃ/ *a* danés. ● *m* (*lang*) danés *m*
dank /dæŋk/ *a* (**-er**, **-est**) húmedo, malsano
dare /deə(r)/ *vt* desafiar. ● *vi* atreverse a. **I ~ say** probablemente. ● *n* desafío *m*
daredevil /'deədevl/ *n* atrevido *m*
daring /'deərɪŋ/ *a* atrevido
dark /dɑ:k/ *a* (**-er**, **-est**) oscuro; (*gloomy*) sombrío; ‹*skin, hair*› moreno. ● *n* oscuridad *f*; (*nightfall*) atardecer. **in the ~** a oscuras. **~en** /'dɑ:kən/ *vt* oscurecer. ● *vi* oscurecerse. **~ horse** *n* persona *f* de talentos desconocidos. **~ness** *n* oscuridad *f*. **~-room** *n* cámara *f* oscura
darling /'dɑ:lɪŋ/ *a* querido. ● *n* querido *m*
darn /dɑ:n/ *vt* zurcir
dart /dɑ:t/ *n* dardo *m*. ● *vi* lanzarse; (*run*) precipitarse. **~board** /'dɑ:tbɔ:d/ *n* blanco *m*. **~s** *npl* los dardos *mpl*
dash /dæʃ/ *vi* precipitarse. **~ off** marcharse apresuradamente. **~ out** salir corriendo. ● *vt* lanzar; (*break*) romper; defraudar ‹*hopes*›. ● *n* carrera *f*; (*small amount*) poquito *m*; (*stroke*) raya *f*. **cut a ~** causar sensación
dashboard /'dæʃbɔ:d/ *n* tablero *m* de mandos
dashing /'dæʃɪŋ/ *a* vivo; (*showy*) vistoso
data /'deɪtə/ *npl* datos *mpl*. **~ processing** *n* proceso *m* de datos
date[1] /deɪt/ *n* fecha *f*; (*fam*) cita *f*. **to ~** hasta la fecha. ● *vt* fechar; (*go out with, fam*) salir con. ● *vi* datar; (*be old-fashioned*) quedar anticuado
date[2] /deɪt/ *n* (*fruit*) dátil *m*
dated /'deɪtɪd/ *a* pasado de moda

daub /dɔ:b/ *vt* embadurnar

daughter /'dɔ:tə(r)/ *n* hija *f*. **~-in-law** *n* nuera *f*

daunt /dɔ:nt/ *vt* intimidar

dauntless /'dɔ:ntlɪs/ *a* intrépido

dawdle /'dɔ:dl/ *vi* andar despacio; (*waste time*) perder el tiempo. **~r** /-ə(r)/ *n* rezagado *m*

dawn /dɔ:n/ *n* amanecer *m*. ● *vi* amanecer; (*fig*) nacer. **it ~ed on me that** caí en la cuenta de que, comprendí que

day /deɪ/ *n* día *m*; (*whole day*) jornada *f*; (*period*) época *f*. **~-break** *n* amanecer *m*. **~-dream** *n* ensueño *m*. ● *vi* soñar despierto. **~light** /'deɪlaɪt/ *n* luz *f* del día. **~time** /'deɪtaɪm/ *n* día *m*

daze /deɪz/ *vt* aturdir. ● *n* aturdimiento *m*. **in a ~** aturdido

dazzle /'dæzl/ *vt* deslumbrar

deacon /'di:kən/ *n* diácono *m*

dead /ded/ *a* muerto; (*numb*) entumecido. **~ centre** justo en medio. ● *adv* completamente. **~ beat** rendido. **~ on time** justo a tiempo. **~ slow** muy lento. **stop ~** parar en seco. ● *n* muertos *mpl*. **in the ~ of night** en plena noche. **the ~** los muertos *mpl*. **~en** /'dedn/ *vt* amortiguar ‹*sound, blow*›; calmar ‹*pain*›. **~ end** *n* callejón *m* sin salida. **~ heat** *n* empate *m*

deadline /'dedlaɪn/ *n* fecha *f* tope, fin *m* de plazo

deadlock /'dedlɒk/ *n* punto *m* muerto

deadly /'dedlɪ/ *a* (**-ier**, **-iest**) mortal; (*harmful*) nocivo; (*dreary*) aburrido

deadpan/'dedpæn/ *a* impasible

deaf /def/ *a* (**-er**, **-est**) sordo. **~-aid** *n* audífono *m*. **~en** /'defn/ *vt* ensordecer. **~ening** *a* ensordecedor. **~ mute** *n* sordomudo *m*. **~ness** *n* sordera *f*

deal /di:l/ *n* (*transaction*) negocio *m*; (*agreement*) pacto *m*; (*of cards*) reparto m; (*treatment*) trato *m*; (*amount*) cantidad *f*. **a great ~** muchísimo. ● *vt* (*pt* **dealt**) distribuir; dar ‹*a blow, cards*›. ● *vi*. **~ in** comerciar en. **~ with** tratar con ‹*person*›; tratar de ‹*subject etc*›; ocuparse de ‹*problem etc*›. **~er** *n* comerciante *m*. **~ings** /'di:lɪŋz/ *npl* trato *m*

dean /di:n/ *n* deán *m*; (*univ*) decano *m*

dear /dɪə(r)/ *a* (**-er**, **-est**) querido; (*expensive*) caro. ● *n* querido *m;* (*child*) pequeño *m*. ● *adv* caro. ● *int* ¡Dios mío! **~ me!** ¡Dios mío! **~ly** *adv* tiernamente; (*pay*) caro; (*very much*) muchísimo

dearth /dɜ:θ/ *n* escasez *f*

death /deθ/ *n* muerte *f*. **~ duty** *n* derechos *mpl* reales. **~ly** *a* mortal; ‹*silence*› profundo. ● *adv* como la muerte. **~'s head** *n* calavera *f*. **~-trap** *n* lugar *m* peligroso.

débâcle /deɪ'bɑ:kl/ *n* fracaso *m*, desastre *m*

debar /dɪ'bɑ:(r)/ *vt* (*pt* **debarred**) excluir

debase /dɪ'beɪs/ *vt* degradar

debat|able /dɪ'beɪtəbl/ *a* discutible. **~e** /dɪ'beɪt/ *n* debate *m*. ● *vt* debatir, discutir. ● *vi* discutir; (*consider*) considerar

debauch /dɪ'bɔ:tʃ/ *vt* corromper. **~ery** *n* libertinaje *m*

debilit|ate /dɪ'bɪlɪteɪt/ *vt* debilitar. **~y** /dɪ'bɪlətɪ/ *n* debilidad *f*

debit /'debɪt/ *n* debe *m*. ● *vt*. **~ s.o.'s account** cargar en cuenta a uno

debonair /debə'neə(r)/ *a* alegre

debris /'debri:/ *n* escombros *mpl*

debt /det/ *n* deuda *f*. **be in ~** tener deudas. **~or** *n* deudor *m*

debutante /'debju:tɑ:nt/ *n* (*old use*) debutante *f*

decade /'dekeɪd/ *n* década *f*

decaden|ce /'dekədəns/ *n* decadencia *f*. **~t** /'dekədənt/ *a* decadente

decant /dɪ'kænt/ *vt* decantar. **~er** /ə(r)/ *n* garrafa *f*

decapitate /dɪ'kæpɪteɪt/ *vt* decapitar

decay /dɪ'keɪ/ *vi* decaer; ‹*tooth*› cariarse. ● *n* decadencia *f*; (*of tooth*) caries *f*

deceased /dɪ'si:st/ *a* difunto

deceit /dɪ'si:t/ *n* engaño *m*. **~ful** *a* falso. **~fully** *adv* falsamente

deceive /dɪ'si:v/ *vt* engañar

December /dɪ'sembə(r)/ *n* diciembre *m*

decen|cy /'di:sənsɪ/ *n* decencia *f*. **~t** /'di:snt/ *a* decente; (*good, fam*) bueno; (*kind, fam*) amable. **~tly** *adv* decentemente

decentralize /di:'sentrəlaɪz/ *vt* descentralizar

decepti|on /dɪ'sepʃn/ *n* engaño *m*. **~ve** /dɪ'septɪv/ *a* engañoso

decibel /'desɪbel/ *n* decibel(io) *m*

decide /dɪ'saɪd/ *vt/i* decidir. **~d** /-ɪd/ *a* resuelto; (*unquestionable*) indudable. **~dly** /-ɪdlɪ/ *adv* decididamente; (*unquestionably*) indudablemente

decimal /'desɪml/ *a & n* decimal (*f*). **~ point** *n* coma *f* (decimal)

decimate /'desɪmeɪt/ *vt* diezmar

decipher /dɪ'saɪfə(r)/ *vt* descifrar

decision /dɪ'sɪʒn/ *n* decisión *f*

decisive /dɪ'saɪsɪv/ *a* decisivo; ‹*manner*› decidido. **~ly** *adv* de manera decisiva

deck /dek/ *n* cubierta *f*; (*of cards, Amer*) baraja *f*. **top ~** (*of bus*) imperial *m*. ● *vt* adornar. **~-chair** *n* tumbona *f*

declaim /dɪ'kleɪm/ *vt* declamar

declar|ation /deklə'reɪʃn/ *n* declaración *f*. **~e** /dɪ'kleə(r)/ *vt* declarar

decline /dɪ'klaɪn/ *vt* rehusar; (*gram*) declinar. ● *vi* disminuir; (*deteriorate*) deteriorarse; (*fall*) bajar. ● *n* decadencia *f*; (*decrease*) disminución *f*; (*fall*) baja *f*

decode /di:'kəʊd/ *vt* descifrar

decompos|e /di:kəm'pəʊz/ *vt* descomponer. ● *vi* descomponerse. **~ition** /-ɒmpə'zɪʃn/ *n* descomposición *f*

décor /'deɪkɔ:(r)/ *n* decoración *f*

decorat|e /'dekəreɪt/ *vt* decorar; empapelar y pintar ‹*room*›. **~ion** /-'reɪʃn/ *n* (*act*) decoración *f*; (*ornament*) adorno *m*. **~ive** /-ətɪv/ *a* decorativo. **~or** /'dekəreɪtə(r)/ *n* pintor *m* decorador. **interior ~or** decorador *m* de interiores

decorum /dɪ'kɔ:rəm/ *n* decoro *m*

decoy /'di:kɔɪ/ *n* señuelo *m*. /dɪ'kɔɪ/ *vt* atraer con señuelo

decrease /dɪ'kri:s/ *vt* disminuir. ● *vi* disminuirse. /'di:kri:s/ *n* disminución *f*

decree /dɪ'kri:/ *n* decreto *m*; (*jurid*) sentencia *f*. ● *vt* (*pt* **decreed**) decretar

decrepit /dɪ'krepɪt/ *a* decrépito

decry /dɪ'kraɪ/ *vt* denigrar

dedicat|e /'dedɪkeɪt/ *vt* dedicar. **~ion** /-'keɪʃn/ *n* dedicación *f*; (*in book*) dedicatoria *f*

deduce /dɪ'dju:s/ *vt* deducir

deduct /dɪ'dʌkt/ *vt* deducir. **~ion** /-ʃn/ *n* deducción *f*

deed /di:d/ *n* hecho *m*; (*jurid*) escritura *f*

deem /di:m/ *vt* juzgar, considerar

deep /di:p/ *a* (**-er, est**) *adv* profundo. **get into ~ waters** meterse en honduras. **go off the ~ end** enfadarse. ● *adv* profundamente. **be ~ in thought** estar absorto en sus pensamientos. **~en** /'di:pən/ *vt* profundizar. ● *vi* hacerse más profundo. **~-freeze** *n* congelador *m*. **~ly** *adv* profundamente

deer /dɪə(r)/ *n invar* ciervo *m*

deface /dɪ'feɪs/ *vt* desfigurar

defamation /defə'meɪʃn/ *n* difamación *f*

default /dɪ'fɔ:lt/ *vi* faltar. ● *n*. **by ~** en rebeldía. **in ~ of** en ausencia de

defeat /dɪ'fi:t/ *vt* vencer; (*frustrate*) frustrar. ● *n* derrota *f*; (*of plan etc*) fracaso *m*. **~ism** /dɪ'fi:tɪzm/ *n* derrotismo *m*. **~ist** /dɪ'fi:tɪst/ *n* derrotista *m & f*

defect /'di:fekt/ *n* defecto *m*. /dɪ'fekt/ *vi* desertar. **~ to** pasar a. **~ion** /dɪ'fekʃn/ *n* deserción *f*. **~ive** /dɪ'fektɪv/ *a* defectuoso

defence /dɪ'fens/ *n* defensa *f*. **~less** *a* indefenso

defend /dɪ'fend/ *vt* defender. **~ant** *n* (*jurid*) acusado *m*

defensive /dɪ'fensɪv/ *a* defensivo. ● *n* defensiva *f*

defer /dɪ'fɜ:(r)/ *vt* (*pt* **deferred**) aplazar

deferen|ce /'defərəns/ *n* deferencia *f*. **~tial** /-'renʃl/ *a* deferente

defian|ce /dɪ'faɪəns/ *n* desafío *m*. **in ~ce of** a despecho de. **~t** *a* desafiante. **~tly** *adv* con tono retador

deficien|cy /dɪ'fɪʃənsɪ/ *n* falta *f*. **~t** /dɪ'fɪʃnt/ *a* deficiente. **be ~t in** carecer de

deficit /'defɪsɪt/ *n* déficit *m*

defile /dɪ'faɪl/ *vt* ensuciar; (*fig*) deshonrar

define /dɪ'faɪn/ *vt* definir

definite /'defɪnɪt/ *a* determinado; (*clear*) claro; (*firm*) categórico. **~ly** *adv* claramente; (*certainly*) seguramente

definition /defɪ'nɪʃn/ *n* definición *f*

definitive /dɪ'fɪnətɪv/ *a* definitivo

deflat|e /dɪ'fleɪt/ *vt* desinflar. ● *vi* desinflarse. **~ion** /-ʃn/ *n* (*com*) deflación *f*

deflect /dɪ'flekt/ *vt* desviar. ● *vi* desviarse

deform /dɪ'fɔ:m/ *vt* deformar. **~ed** *a* deforme. **~ity** *n* deformidad *f*

defraud /dɪ'frɔ:d/ *vt* defraudar

defray /dɪ'freɪ/ *vt* pagar

defrost /di:'frɒst/ *vt* descongelar

deft /deft/ *a* (**-er, -est**) hábil. **~ness** *n* destreza *f*

defunct /dɪ'fʌŋkt/ *a* difunto

defuse /di:'fju:z/ *vt* desactivar ‹*bomb*›; (*fig*) calmar

defy /dɪ'faɪ/ *vt* desafiar; (*resist*) resistir

degenerate /dɪ'dʒenəreɪt/ *vi* degenerar. /dɪ'dʒenərət/ *a & n* degenerado (*m*)

degrad|ation /degrə'deɪʃn/ *n* degradación *f*. **~e** /dɪ'greɪd/ *vt* degradar

degree /dɪ'gri:/ *n* grado *m*; (*univ*) licenciatura *f*; (*rank*) rango *m*. **to a certain ~** hasta cierto punto. **to a ~** (*fam*) sumamente

dehydrate /di:'haɪdreɪt/ *vt* deshidratar

de-ice /di:'aɪs/ *vt* descongelar

deign /deɪn/ *vi*. **~ to** dignarse

deity /'di:ɪtɪ/ *n* deidad *f*

deject|ed /dɪ'dʒektɪd/ *a* desanimado. **~ion** /-ʃn/ *n* abatimiento *m*

delay /dɪ'leɪ/ *vt* retardar; (*postpone*) aplazar. ● *vi* demorarse. ● *n* demora *f*

delectable /dɪ'lektəbl/ *a* deleitable

delegat|e /'delɪgeɪt/ *vt* delegar. /'delɪgət/ *n* delegado *m*. **~ion** /-'geɪʃn/ *n* delegación *f*

delet|e /dɪ'li:t/ *vt* tachar. **~ion** /-ʃn/ *n* tachadura *f*

deliberat|e /dɪ'lɪbəreɪt/ *vt/i* deliberar. /dɪ'lɪbərət/ *a* intencionado; ‹*steps etc*› pausado. **~ely** *adv* a propósito. **~ion** /-'reɪʃn/ *n* deliberación *f*

delica|cy /'delɪkəsɪ/ *n* delicadeza *f*; (*food*) manjar *m*; (*sweet food*) golosina *f*. **~te** /'delɪkət/ *a* delicado

delicatessen /delɪkə'tesn/ *n* charcutería *f* fina

delicious /dɪ'lɪʃəs/ *a* delicioso

delight /dɪ'laɪt/ *n* placer *m*. ● *vt* encantar. ● *vi* deleitarse. **~ed** *a* encantado. **~ful** *a* delicioso

delineat|e /dɪ'lɪnɪeɪt/ *vt* delinear. **~ion** /-'eɪʃn/ *n* delineación *f*

delinquen|cy /dɪ'lɪŋkwənsɪ/ *n* delincuencia *f*. **~t** /dɪ'lɪŋkwənt/ *a & n* delincuente (*m & f*)

deliri|ous /dɪ'lɪrɪəs/ *a* delirante. **~um** *n* delirio *m*

deliver /dɪ'lɪvə(r)/ *vt* entregar; (*utter*) pronunciar; (*aim*) lanzar; (*set free*) librar; (*med*) asistir al parto de. **~ance** *n* liberación *f*. **~y** *n* entrega *f*; (*of post*) reparto *m*; (*med*) parto *m*

delta /'deltə/ *n* (*geog*) delta *m*

delude /dɪ'lu:d/ *vt* engañar. **~ o.s.** engañarse

deluge /'delju:dʒ/ *n* diluvio *m*

delusion /dɪ'lu:ʒn/ *n* ilusión *f*

de luxe /dɪ'lʌks/ *a* de lujo

delve /delv/ *vi* cavar. **~ into** (*investigate*) investigar

demagogue /'deməgɒg/ *n* demagogo *m*

demand /dɪ'mɑ:nd/ *vt* exigir. ● *n* petición *f*; (*claim*) reclamación *f*; (*com*) demanda *f*. **in ~** muy popular, muy solicitado. **on ~** a solicitud. **~ing** *a* exigente. **~s** *npl* exigencias *fpl*

demarcation /di:mɑ:'keɪʃn/ *n* demarcación *f*

demean /dɪ'mi:n/ *vt*. **~ o.s.** degradarse. **~our** /dɪ'mi:nə(r)/ *n* conducta *f*

demented /dɪ'mentɪd/ *a* demente

demerara /demə'reərə/ *n*. **~ (sugar)** *n* azúcar *m* moreno

demise /dɪ'maɪz/ *n* fallecimiento *m*

demo /'deməʊ/ *n* (*pl* **-os**) (*fam*) manifestación *f*

demobilize /di:'məʊbəlaɪz/ *vt* desmovilizar

democra|cy /dɪ'mɒkrəsɪ/ *n* democracia *f*. **~t** /'deməkræt/ *n* demócrata *m & f*. **~tic** /-'krætɪk/ *a* democrático

demoli|sh /dɪ'mɒlɪʃ/ *vt* derribar. **~tion** /demə'lɪʃn/ *n* demolición *f*

demon /'di:mən/ *n* demonio *m*

demonstrat|e /'demənstreɪt/ *vt* demostrar. ● *vi* manifestarse, hacer una manifestación. **~ion** /-'streɪʃn/ *n* demostración *f*; (*pol etc*) manifestación *f*

demonstrative /dɪ'mɒnstrətɪv/ *a* demostrativo

demonstrator /'demənstreɪtə(r)/ *n* demostrador *m*: (*pol etc*) manifestante *m & f*

demoralize /dɪ'mɒrəlaɪz/ *vt* desmoralizar

demote /dɪ'məʊt/ *vt* degradar

demure /dɪ'mjʊə(r)/ *a* recatado

den /den/ *n* (*of animal*) guarida *f*, madriguera *f*

denial /dɪ'naɪəl/ *n* denegación *f*; (*statement*) desmentimiento *m*

denigrate /'denɪgreɪt/ *vt* denigrar

denim /'denɪm/ *n* dril *m* (de algodón azul grueso). **~s** *npl* pantalón *m* vaquero

Denmark /'denmɑ:k/ *n* Dinamarca *f*
denomination /dɪnɒmɪ'neɪʃn/ *n* denominación *f*; (*relig*) secta *f*
denote /dɪ'nəʊt/ *vt* denotar
denounce /dɪ'naʊns/ *vt* denunciar
dens|e /dens/ *a* (**-er**, **-est**) espeso; ‹*person*› torpe. **~ely** *adv* densamente. **~ity** *n* densidad *f*
dent /dent/ *n* abolladura *f*. ● *vt* abollar
dental /'dentl/ *a* dental. **~ surgeon** *n* dentista *m & f*
dentist /'dentɪst/ *n* dentista *m & f*. **~ry** *n* odontología *f*
denture /'dentʃə(r)/ *n* dentadura *f* postiza
denude /dɪ'nju:d/ *vt* desnudar; (*fig*) despojar
denunciation /dɪnʌnsɪ'eɪʃn/ *n* denuncia *f*
deny /dɪ'naɪ/ *vt* negar; desmentir ‹*rumour*›; (*disown*) renegar
deodorant /di'əʊdərənt/ *a & n* desodorante (*m*)
depart /dɪ'pɑ:t/ *vi* marcharse; ‹*train etc*› salir. **~ from** apartarse de
department /dɪ'pɑ:tment/ *n* departamento *m*; (*com*) sección *f*. **~ store** *n* grandes almacenes *mpl*
departure /dɪ'pɑ:tʃə(r)/ *n* partida *f*; (*of train etc*) salida *f*. **~ from** (*fig*) desviación *f*
depend /dɪ'pend/ *vi* depender. **~ on** depender de; (*rely*) contar con. **~able** *a* seguro. **~ant** /dɪ'pendənt/ *n* familiar *m & f* dependiente. **~ence** *n* dependencia *f*. **~ent** *a* dependiente. **be ~ent on** depender de
depict /dɪ'pɪkt/ *vt* pintar; (*in words*) describir
deplete /dɪ'pli:t/ *vt* agotar
deplor|able /dɪ'plɔ:rəbl/ *a* lamentable. **~e** /dɪ'plɔ:(r)/ *vt* lamentar
deploy /dɪ'plɔɪ/ *vt* desplegar. ● *vi* desplegarse
depopulate /di:'pɒpjʊleɪt/ *vt* despoblar
deport /dɪ'pɔ:t/ *vt* deportar. **~ation** /di:pɔ:'teɪʃn/ *n* deportación *f*
depose /dɪ'pəʊz/ *vt* deponer
deposit /dɪ'pɒzɪt/ *vt* (*pt* **deposited**) depositar. ● *n* depósito *m*. **~or** *n* depositante *m & f*
depot /'depəʊ/ *n* depósito *m*; (*Amer*) estación *f*
deprav|e /dɪ'preɪv/ *vt* depravar. **~ity** /-'prævətɪ/ *n* depravación *f*
deprecate /'deprɪkeɪt/ *vt* desaprobar
depreciat|e /dɪ'pri:ʃɪeɪt/ *vt* depreciar. ● *vi* depreciarse. **~ion** /-'eɪʃn/ *n* depreciación *f*
depress /dɪ'pres/ *vt* deprimir; (*press down*) apretar. **~ion** /-ʃn/ *n* depresión *f*
depriv|ation /deprɪ'veɪʃn/ *n* privación *f*. **~e** /dɪ'praɪv/ *vt*. **~ of** privar de
depth /depθ/ *n* profundidad *f*. **be out of one's ~** perder pie; (*fig*) meterse en honduras. **in the ~s of** en lo más hondo de
deputation /depjʊ'teɪʃn/ *n* diputación *f*
deputize /'depjʊtaɪz/ *vi*. **~ for** sustituir a
deputy /'depjʊtɪ/ *n* sustituto *m*. **~ chairman** *n* vicepresidente *m*
derail /dɪ'reɪl/ *vt* hacer descarrilar. **~ment** *n* descarrilamiento *m*
deranged /dɪ'reɪndʒd/ *a* ‹*mind*› trastornado
derelict /'derəlɪkt/ *a* abandonado
deri|de /dɪ'raɪd/ *vt* mofarse de. **~sion** /-'rɪʒn/ *n* mofa *f*. **~sive** *a* burlón. **~sory** /dɪ'raɪsərɪ/ *a* mofador; ‹*offer etc*› irrisorio
deriv|ation /derɪ'veɪʃn/ *n* derivación *f*. **~ative** /dɪ'rɪvətɪv/ *a & n* derivado (*m*). **~e** /dɪ'raɪv/ *vt/i* derivar
derogatory /dɪ'rɒgətrɪ/ *a* despectivo
derv /dɜ:v/ *n* gasóleo *m*
descen|d /dɪ'send/ *vt/i* descender, bajar. **~dant** *n* descendiente *m & f*. **~t** /dɪ'sent/ *n* descenso *m*; (*lineage*) descendencia *f*
descri|be /dɪs'kraɪb/ *vt* describir. **~ption** /-'krɪpʃn/ *n* descripción *f*. **~ptive** /-'krɪptɪv/ *a* descriptivo
desecrat|e /'desɪkreɪt/ *vt* profanar. **~ion** /-'kreɪʃn/ *n* profanación *f*
desert[1] /dɪ'zɜ:t/ *vt* abandonar. ● *vi* (*mil*) desertar
desert[2] /'dezət/ *a & n* desierto (*m*)
deserter /dɪ'zɜ:tə(r)/ *n* desertor *m*
deserts /dɪ'zɜ:ts/ *npl* lo merecido. **get one's ~** llevarse su merecido
deserv|e /dɪ'zɜ:v/ *vt* merecer. **~edly** *adv* merecidamente. **~ing** *a* ‹*person*› digno de; ‹*action*› meritorio
design /dɪ'zaɪn/ *n* diseño *m*; (*plan*) proyecto *m*; (*pattern*) modelo *m*; (*aim*) propósito *m*. **have ~s on**

poner la mira en. ● *vt* diseñar; (*plan*) proyectar

designat|e /'dezɪgneɪt/ *vt* designar; (*appoint*) nombrar. **~ion** /-'neɪʃn/ *n* denominación *f*; (*appointment*) nombramiento *m*

designer /dɪ'zaɪnə(r)/ *n* diseñador *m*; (*of clothing*) modisto *m*; (*in theatre*) escenógrafo *m*

desirab|ility /dɪzaɪərə'bɪlətɪ/ *n* conveniencia *f*. **~le** /dɪ'zaɪrəbl/ *a* deseable

desire /dɪ'zaɪə(r)/ *n* deseo *m*. ● *vt* desear

desist /dɪ'zɪst/ *vi* desistir

desk /desk/ *n* escritorio *m*; (*at school*) pupitre *m*; (*in hotel*) recepción *f*; (*com*) caja *f*

desolat|e /'desələt/ *a* desolado; (*uninhabited*) deshabitado. **~ion** /-'leɪʃn/ *n* desolación *f*

despair /dɪ'speə(r)/ *n* desesperación *f*. ● *vi*. **~ of** desesperarse de

desperat|e /'despərət/ *a* desesperado; (*dangerous*) peligroso. **~ely** *adv* desesperadamente. **~ion** /-'reɪʃn/ *n* desesperación *f*

despicable /dɪ'spɪkəbl/ *a* despreciable

despise /dɪ'spaɪz/ *vt* despreciar

despite /dɪ'spaɪt/ *prep* a pesar de

desponden|cy /dɪ'spɒndənsɪ/ *n* abatimiento *m*. **~t** /dɪ'spɒndənt/ *a* desanimado

despot /'despɒt/ *n* déspota *m*

dessert /dɪ'zɜ:t/ *n* postre *m*. **~spoon** *n* cuchara *f* de postre

destination /destɪ'neɪʃn/ *n* destino *m*

destine /'destɪn/ *vt* destinar

destiny /'destɪnɪ/ *n* destino *m*

destitute /'destɪtju:t/ *a* indigente. **~ of** desprovisto de

destroy /dɪ'strɔɪ/ *vt* destruir

destroyer /dɪ'strɔɪə(r)/ *n* (*naut*) destructor *m*

destructi|on /dɪ'strʌkʃn/ *n* destrucción *f*. **~ve** *a* destructivo

desultory /'desəltrɪ/ *a* irregular

detach /dɪ'tætʃ/ *vt* separar. **~able** *a* separable. **~ed** *a* separado. **~ed house** *n* chalet *m*. **~ment** /dɪ'tætʃmənt/ *n* separación *f*; (*mil*) destacamento *m*; (*fig*) indiferencia *f*

detail /'di:teɪl/ *n* detalle *m*. ● *vt* detallar; (*mil*) destacar. **~ed** *a* detallado

detain /dɪ'teɪn/ *vt* detener; (*delay*) retener. **~ee** /di:teɪ'ni:/ *n* detenido *m*

detect /dɪ'tekt/ *vt* percibir; (*discover*) descubrir. **~ion** /-ʃn/ *n* descubrimiento *m*, detección *f*. **~or** *n* detector *m*

detective /dɪ'tektɪv/ *n* detective *m*. **~ story** *n* novela *f* policíaca

detention /dɪ'tenʃn/ *n* detención *f*

deter /dɪ'tɜ:(r)/ *vt* (*pt* **deterred**) disuadir; (*prevent*) impedir

detergent /dɪ'tɜ:dʒənt/ *a* & *n* detergente (*m*)

deteriorat|e /dɪ'tɪərɪəreɪt/ *vi* deteriorarse. **~ion** /-'reɪʃn/ *n* deterioro *m*

determination /dɪtɜ:mɪ'neɪʃn/ *n* determinación *f*

determine /dɪ'tɜ:mɪn/ *vt* determinar; (*decide*) decidir. **~d** *a* determinado; (*resolute*) resuelto

deterrent /dɪ'terənt/ *n* fuerza *f* de disuasión

detest /dɪ'test/ *vt* aborrecer. **~able** *a* odioso

detonat|e /'detəneɪt/ *vt* hacer detonar. ● *vi* detonar. **~ion** /-'neɪʃn/ *n* detonación *f*. **~or** *n* detonador *m*

detour /'di:tʊə(r)/ *n* desviación *f*

detract /dɪ'trækt/ *vi*. **~ from** (*lessen*) disminuir

detriment /'detrɪmənt/ *n* perjuicio *m*. **~al** /-'mentl/ *a* perjudicial

devalu|ation /di:vælju:'eɪʃn/ *n* desvalorización *f*. **~e** /di:'vælju:/ *vt* desvalorizar

devastat|e /'devəsteɪt/ *vt* devastar. **~ing** *a* devastador; (*fig*) arrollador

develop /dɪ'veləp/ *vt* desarrollar; contraer ‹*illness*›; urbanizar ‹*land*›. ● *vi* desarrollarse; (*show*) aparecerse. **~er** *n* (*foto*) revelador *m*. **~ing country** *n* país *m* en vías de desarrollo. **~ment** *n* desarrollo *m*. **(new) ~ment** novedad *f*

deviant /'di:vɪənt/ *a* desviado

deviat|e /'di:vɪeɪt/ *vi* desviarse. **~ion** /-'eɪʃn/ *n* desviación *f*

device /dɪ'vaɪs/ *n* dispositivo *m*; (*scheme*) estratagema *f*

devil /'devl/ *n* diablo *m*. **~ish** *a* diabólico

devious /'di:vɪəs/ *a* tortuoso

devise /dɪ'vaɪz/ *vt* idear

devoid /dɪ'vɔɪd/ *a*. **~ of** desprovisto de

devolution /di:və'lu:ʃn/ *n* descentralización *f*; (*of power*) delegación *f*

devot|e /dɪ'vəʊt/ *vt* dedicar. **~ed** *a* leal. **~edly** *adv* con devoción *f*. **~ee**

/devəˈtiː/ *n* partidario *m*. **~ion** /-ʃn/ *n* dedicación *f*. **~ions** *npl* (*relig*) oraciones *fpl*
devour /dɪˈvaʊə(r)/ *vt* devorar
devout /dɪˈvaʊt/ *a* devoto
dew /djuː/ *n* rocío *m*
dext|erity /dekˈsterətɪ/ *n* destreza *f*. **~(e)rous** /ˈdekstrəs/ *a* diestro
diabet|es /daɪəˈbiːtiːz/ *n* diabetes *f*. **~ic** /-ˈbetɪk/ *a* & *n* diabético (*m*)
diabolical /daɪəˈbɒlɪkl/ *a* diabólico
diadem /ˈdaɪədem/ *n* diadema *f*
diagnos|e /ˈdaɪəgnəʊz/ *vt* diagnosticar. **~is** /daɪəgˈnəʊsɪs/ *n* (*pl* **-oses** /-siːz/) diagnóstico *m*
diagonal /daɪˈægənl/ *a* & *n* diagonal (*f*)
diagram /ˈdaɪəgræm/ *n* diagrama *m*
dial /ˈdaɪəl/ *n* cuadrante *m*; (*on phone*) disco *m*. ● *vt* (*pt* **dialled**) marcar
dialect /ˈdaɪəlekt/ *n* dialecto *m*
dial: **~ling code** *n* prefijo *m*. **~ling tone** *n* señal *f* para marcar
dialogue /ˈdaɪəlɒg/ *n* diálogo *m*
diameter /daɪˈæmɪtə(r)/ *n* diámetro *m*
diamond /ˈdaɪəmənd/ *n* diamante *m*; (*shape*) rombo *m*. **~s** *npl* (*cards*) diamantes *mpl*
diaper /ˈdaɪəpə(r)/ *n* (*Amer*) pañal *m*
diaphanous /daɪˈæfənəs/ *a* diáfano
diaphragm /ˈdaɪəfræm/ *n* diafragma *m*
diarrhoea /daɪəˈrɪə/ *n* diarrea *f*
diary /ˈdaɪərɪ/ *n* diario *m*; (*book*) agenda *f*
diatribe /ˈdaɪətraɪb/ *n* diatriba *f*
dice /daɪs/ *n invar* dado *m*. ● *vt* (*culin*) cortar en cubitos
dicey /ˈdaɪsɪ/ *a* (*sl*) arriesgado
dictat|e /dɪkˈteɪt/ *vt/i* dictar. **~es** /ˈdɪkteɪts/ *npl* dictados *mpl*. **~ion** /dɪkˈteɪʃn/ *n* dictado *m*
dictator /dɪkˈteɪtə(r)/ *n* dictador *m*. **~ship** *n* dictadura *f*
diction /ˈdɪkʃn/ *n* dicción *f*
dictionary /ˈdɪkʃənərɪ/ *n* diccionario *m*
did /dɪd/ *see* **do**
didactic /daɪˈdæktɪk/ *a* didáctico
diddle /ˈdɪdl/ *vt* (*sl*) estafar
didn't /ˈdɪdnt/ = **did not**
die[1] /daɪ/ *vi* (*pres p* **dying**) morir. **be dying to** morirse por. **~ down** disminuir. **~ out** extinguirse
die[2] /daɪ/ *n* (*tec*) cuño *m*
die-hard /ˈdaɪhɑːd/ *n* intransigente *m* & *f*
diesel /ˈdiːzl/ *n* (*fuel*) gasóleo *m*. **~ engine** *n* motor *m* diesel
diet /ˈdaɪət/ *n* alimentación *f*; (*restricted*) régimen *m*. ● *vi* estar a régimen. **~etic** /daɪəˈtetɪk/ *a* dietético. **~itian** *n* dietético *m*
differ /ˈdɪfə(r)/ *vi* ser distinto; (*disagree*) no estar de acuerdo. **~ence** /ˈdɪfrəns/ *n* diferencia *f*; (*disagreement*) desacuerdo *m*. **~ent** /ˈdɪfrənt/ *a* distinto, diferente
differentia|l /dɪfəˈrenʃl/ *a* & *n* diferencial (*f*). **~te** /dɪfəˈrenʃɪeɪt/ *vt* diferenciar. ● *vi* diferenciarse
differently /ˈdɪfrəntlɪ/ *adv* de otra manera
difficult /ˈdɪfɪkəlt/ *a* difícil. **~y** *n* dificultad *f*
diffiden|ce /ˈdɪfɪdəns/ *n* falta *f* de confianza. **~t** /ˈdɪfɪdənt/ *a* que falta confianza
diffus|e /dɪˈfjuːs/ *a* difuso. /dɪˈfjuːz/ *vt* difundir. ● *vi* difundirse. **~ion** /-ʒn/ *n* difusión *f*
dig /dɪg/ *n* (*poke*) empujón *m*; (*poke with elbow*) codazo *m*; (*remark*) indirecta *f*; (*archaeol*) excavación *f*. ● *vt* (*pt* **dug**, *pres p* **digging**) cavar; (*thrust*) empujar. ● *vi* cavar. **~ out** extraer. **~ up** desenterrar. **~s** *npl* (*fam*) alojamiento *m*
digest /ˈdaɪdʒest/ *n* resumen *m*. ● *vt* digerir. **~ible** *a* digerible. **~ion** /-ʃn/ *n* digestión *f*. **~ive** *a* digestivo
digger /ˈdɪgə(r)/ *n* (*mec*) excavadora *f*
digit /ˈdɪdʒɪt/ *n* cifra *f*; (*finger*) dedo *m*. **~al** /ˈdɪdʒɪtl/ *a* digital
dignif|ied /ˈdɪgnɪfaɪd/ *a* solemne. **~y** /ˈdɪgnɪfaɪ/ *vt* dignificar
dignitary /ˈdɪgnɪtərɪ/ *n* dignatario *m*
dignity /ˈdɪgnətɪ/ *n* dignidad *f*
digress /daɪˈgres/ *vi* divagar. **~ from** apartarse de. **~ion** /-ʃn/ *n* digresión *f*
dike /daɪk/ *n* dique *m*
dilapidated /dɪˈlæpɪdeɪtɪd/ *a* ruinoso
dilat|e /daɪˈleɪt/ *vt* dilatar. ● *vi* dilatarse. **~ion** /-ʃn/ *n* dilatación *f*
dilatory /ˈdɪlətərɪ/ *a* dilatorio, lento
dilemma /daɪˈlemə/ *n* dilema *m*
diligen|ce /ˈdɪlɪdʒəns/ *n* diligencia *f*. **~t** /ˈdɪlɪdʒənt/ *a* diligente
dilly-dally /ˈdɪlɪdælɪ/ *vi* (*fam*) perder el tiempo
dilute /daɪˈljuːt/ *vt* diluir
dim /dɪm/ *a* (**dimmer**, **dimmest**) (*weak*) débil; (*dark*) oscuro; (*stupid*,

fam) torpe. ● *vt* (*pt* **dimmed**) amortiguar. ● *vi* apagarse. ~ **the headlights** bajar los faros
dime /daɪm/ *n* (*Amer*) moneda *f* de diez centavos
dimension /daɪ'menʃn/ *n* dimensión *f*
diminish /dɪ'mɪnɪʃ/ *vt*/*i* disminuir
diminutive /dɪ'mɪnjʊtɪv/ *a* diminuto. ● *n* diminutivo *m*
dimness /'dɪmnɪs/ *n* debilidad *f*; (*of room etc*) oscuridad *f*
dimple /'dɪmpl/ *n* hoyuelo *m*
din /dɪn/ *n* jaleo *m*
dine /daɪn/ *vi* cenar. ~**r** /-ə(r)/ *n* comensal *m* & *f*; (*rail*) coche *m* restaurante
dinghy /'dɪŋgɪ/ *n* (*inflatable*) bote *m* neumático
ding|iness /'dɪndʒɪnɪs/ *n* suciedad *f*. ~**y** /'dɪndʒɪ/ *a* (**-ier**, **-iest**) miserable, sucio
dining-room /'daɪnɪŋru:m/ *n* comedor *m*
dinner /'dɪnə(r)/ *n* cena *f*. ~**-jacket** *n* esmoquin *m*. ~ **party** *n* cena *f*
dinosaur /'daɪnəsɔ:(r)/ *n* dinosaurio *m*
dint /dɪnt/ *n*. **by** ~ **of** a fuerza de
diocese /'daɪəsɪs/ *n* diócesis *f*
dip /dɪp/ *vt* (*pt* **dipped**) sumergir. ● *vi* bajar. ~ **into** hojear ‹*book*›. ● *n* (*slope*) inclinación *f*; (*in sea*) baño *m*
diphtheria /dɪf'θɪərɪə/ *n* difteria *f*
diphthong /'dɪfθɒŋ/ *n* diptongo *m*
diploma /dɪ'pləʊmə/ *n* diploma *m*
diplomacy /dɪ'pləʊməsɪ/ *n* diplomacia *f*
diplomat /'dɪpləmæt/ *n* diplomático *m*. ~**ic** /-'mætɪk/ *a* diplomático
dipstick /'dɪpstɪk/ *n* (*auto*) varilla *f* del nivel de aceite
dire /daɪə(r)/ *a* (**-er**, **-est**) terrible; ‹*need, poverty*› extremo
direct /dɪ'rekt/ *a* directo. ● *adv* directamente. ● *vt* dirigir; (*show the way*) indicar
direction /dɪ'rekʃn/ *n* dirección *f*. ~**s** *npl* instrucciones *fpl*
directly /dɪ'rektlɪ/ *adv* directamente; (*at once*) en seguida. ● *conj* (*fam*) en cuanto
director /dɪ'rektə(r)/ *n* director *m*
directory /dɪ'rektərɪ/ *n* guía *f*
dirge /dɜ:dʒ/ *n* canto *m* fúnebre
dirt /dɜ:t/ *n* suciedad *f*. ~**-track** *n* (*sport*) pista *f* de ceniza. ~**y** /'dɜ:tɪ/ *a* (**-ier**, **-iest**) sucio. ~**y trick** *n* mala jugada *f*. ~**y word** *n* palabrota *f*. ● *vt* ensuciar
disability /dɪsə'bɪlətɪ/ *n* invalidez *f*
disable /dɪs'eɪbl/ *vt* incapacitar. ~**d** *a* minusválido
disabuse /dɪsə'bju:z/ *vt* desengañar
disadvantage /dɪsəd'vɑ:ntɪdʒ/ *n* desventaja *f*. ~**d** *a* desventajado
disagree /dɪsə'gri:/ *vi* no estar de acuerdo; ‹*food, climate*› sentar mal a. ~**able** /dɪsə'gri:əbl/ *a* desagradable. ~**ment** *n* desacuerdo *m*; (*quarrel*) riña *f*
disappear /dɪsə'pɪə(r)/ *vi* desaparecer. ~**ance** *n* desaparición *f*
disappoint /dɪsə'pɔɪnt/ *vt* desilusionar, decepcionar. ~**ment** *n* desilusión *f*, decepción *f*
disapprov|al /dɪsə'pru:vl/ *n* desaprobación *f*. ~**e** /dɪsə'pru:v/ *vi*. ~ **of** desaprobar
disarm /dɪs'ɑ:m/ *vt*/*i* desarmar. ~**ament** *n* desarme *m*
disarray /dɪsə'reɪ/ *n* desorden *m*
disast|er /dɪ'zɑ:stə(r)/ *n* desastre *m*. ~**rous** *a* catastrófico
disband /dɪs'bænd/ *vt* disolver. ● *vi* disolverse
disbelief /dɪsbɪ'li:f/ *n* incredulidad *f*
disc /dɪsk/ *n* disco *m*
discard /dɪs'kɑ:d/ *vt* descartar; abandonar ‹*beliefs etc*›
discern /dɪ'sɜ:n/ *vt* percibir. ~**ible** *a* perceptible. ~**ing** *a* perspicaz
discharge /dɪs'tʃɑ:dʒ/ *vt* descargar; cumplir ‹*duty*›; (*dismiss*) despedir; poner en libertad ‹*prisoner*›; (*mil*) licenciar. /'dɪstʃɑ:dʒ/ *n* descarga *f*; (*med*) secreción *f*; (*mil*) licenciamiento *m*; (*dismissal*) despedida *f*
disciple /dɪ'saɪpl/ *n* discípulo *m*
disciplin|arian /dɪsəplɪ'neərɪən/ *n* ordenancista *m* & *f*. ~**ary** *a* disciplinario. ~**e** /'dɪsɪplɪn/ *n* disciplina *f*. ● *vt* disciplinar; (*punish*) castigar
disc jockey /'dɪskdʒɒkɪ/ *n* (*on radio*) pinchadiscos *m* & *f invar*
disclaim /dɪs'kleɪm/ *vt* desconocer. ~**er** *n* renuncia *f*
disclos|e /dɪs'kləʊz/ *vt* revelar. ~**ure** /-ʒə(r)/ *n* revelación *f*
disco /'dɪskəʊ/ *n* (*pl* **-os**) (*fam*) discoteca *f*
discolo|ur /dɪs'kʌlə(r)/ *vt* decolorar. ● *vi* decolorarse. ~**ration** /-'reɪʃn/ *n* decoloración *f*

discomfort /dɪs'kʌmfət/ *n* malestar *m*; (*lack of comfort*) incomodidad *f*
disconcert /dɪskən'sɜ:t/ *vt* desconcertar
disconnect /dɪskə'nekt/ *vt* separar; (*elec*) desconectar
disconsolate /dɪs'kɒnsələt/ *a* desconsolado
discontent /dɪskən'tent/ *n* descontento *m*. **~ed** *a* descontento
discontinue /dɪskən'tɪnju:/ *vt* interrumpir
discord /'dɪskɔ:d/ *n* discordia *f*; (*mus*) disonancia *f*. **~ant** /-'skɔ:dənt/ *a* discorde; (*mus*) disonante
discothèque /'dɪskətek/ *n* discoteca *f*
discount /'dɪskaʊnt/ *n* descuento *m*. /dɪs'kaʊnt/ *vt* hacer caso omiso de; (*com*) descontar
discourage /dɪs'kʌrɪdʒ/ *vt* desanimar; (*dissuade*) disuadir
discourse /'dɪskɔ:s/ *n* discurso *m*
discourteous /dɪs'kɜ:tɪəs/ *a* descortés
discover /dɪs'kʌvə(r)/ *vt* descubrir. **~y** *n* descubrimiento *m*
discredit /dɪs'kredɪt/ *vt* (*pt* **discredited**) desacreditar. • *n* descrédito *m*
discreet /dɪs'kri:t/ *a* discreto. **~ly** *adv* discretamente
discrepancy /dɪ'skrepənsɪ/ *n* discrepancia *f*
discretion /dɪ'skreʃn/ *n* discreción *f*
discriminat|e /dɪs'krɪmɪneɪt/ *vt/i* discriminar. **~e between** distinguir entre. **~ing** *a* perspicaz. **~ion** /-'neɪʃn/ *n* discernimiento *m*; (*bias*) discriminación *f*
discus /'dɪskəs/ *n* disco *m*
discuss /dɪ'skʌs/ *vt* discutir. **~ion** /-ʃn/ *n* discusión *f*
disdain /dɪs'deɪn/ *n* desdén *m*. • *vt* desdeñar. **~ful** *a* desdeñoso
disease /dɪ'zi:z/ *n* enfermedad *f*. **~d** *a* enfermo
disembark /dɪsɪm'bɑ:k/ *vt/i* desembarcar
disembodied /dɪsɪm'bɒdɪd/ *a* incorpóreo
disenchant /dɪsɪn'tʃɑ:nt/ *vt* desencantar. **~ment** *n* desencanto *m*
disengage /dɪsɪn'geɪdʒ/ *vt* soltar. **~ the clutch** desembragar. **~ment** *n* soltura *f*
disentangle /dɪsɪn'tæŋgl/ *vt* desenredar
disfavour /dɪs'feɪvə(r)/ *n* desaprobación *f*. **fall into ~** ‹*person*› caer en desgracia; ‹*custom, word*› caer en desuso
disfigure /dɪs'fɪgə(r)/ *vt* desfigurar
disgorge /dɪs'gɔ:dʒ/ *vt* arrojar; ‹*river*› descargar; (*fig*) restituir
disgrace /dɪs'greɪs/ *n* deshonra *f*; (*disfavour*) desgracia *f*. • *vt* deshonrar. **~ful** *a* vergonzoso
disgruntled /dɪs'grʌntld/ *a* descontento
disguise /dɪs'gaɪz/ *vt* disfrazar. • *n* disfraz *m*. **in ~** disfrazado
disgust /dɪs'gʌst/ *n* repugnancia *f*, asco *m*. • *vt* repugnar, dar asco. **~ing** *a* repugnante, asqueroso
dish /dɪʃ/ *n* plato *m*. • *vt*. **~ out** (*fam*) distribuir. **~ up** servir. **~cloth** /'dɪʃklɒθ/ *n* bayeta *f*
dishearten /dɪs'hɑ:tn/ *vt* desanimar
dishevelled /dɪ'ʃevld/ *a* desaliñado; ‹*hair*› despeinado
dishonest /dɪs'ɒnɪst/ *a* ‹*person*› poco honrado; ‹*means*› fraudulento. **~y** *n* falta *f* de honradez
dishonour /dɪs'ɒnə(r)/ *n* deshonra *f*. • *vt* deshonrar. **~able** *a* deshonroso. **~ably** *adv* deshonrosamente
dishwasher /'dɪʃwɒʃə(r)/ *n* lavaplatos *m & f*
disillusion /dɪsɪ'lu:ʒn/ *vt* desilusionar. **~ment** *n* desilusión
disincentive /dɪsɪn'sentɪv/ *n* freno *m*
disinclined /dɪsɪn'klaɪnd/ *a* poco dispuesto
disinfect /dɪsɪn'fekt/ *vt* desinfectar. **~ant** *n* desinfectante *m*
disinherit /dɪsɪn'herɪt/ *vt* desheredar
disintegrate /dɪs'ɪntɪgreɪt/ *vt* desintegrar. • *vi* desintegrarse
disinterested /dɪs'ɪntrəstɪd/ *a* desinteresado
disjointed /dɪs'dʒɔɪntɪd/ *a* inconexo
disk /dɪsk/ *n* disco *m*
dislike /dɪs'laɪk/ *n* aversión *f*. • *vt* tener aversión a
dislocat|e /'dɪsləkeɪt/ *vt* dislocar(se) ‹*limb*›. **~ion** /-'keɪʃn/ *n* dislocación *f*
dislodge /dɪs'lɒdʒ/ *vt* sacar; (*oust*) desalojar
disloyal /dɪs'lɔɪəl/ *a* desleal. **~ty** *n* deslealtad *f*
dismal /'dɪzməl/ *a* triste; (*bad*) fatal
dismantle /dɪs'mæntl/ *vt* desarmar

dismay /dɪs'meɪ/ *n* consternación *f*. ● *vt* consternar

dismiss /dɪs'mɪs/ *vt* despedir; (*reject*) rechazar. **~al** *n* despedida *f*; (*of idea*) abandono *m*

dismount /dɪs'maʊnt/ *vi* apearse

disobedien|ce /dɪsə'bi:dɪəns/ *n* desobediencia *f*. **~t** /dɪsə'bi:dɪənt/ *a* desobediente

disobey /dɪsə'beɪ/ *vt/i* desobedecer

disorder /dɪs'ɔ:də(r)/ *n* desorden *m*; (*ailment*) trastorno *m*. **~ly** *a* desordenado

disorganize /dɪs'ɔ:gənaɪz/ *vt* desorganizar

disorientate /dɪs'ɔ:rɪənteɪt/ *vt* desorientar

disown /dɪs'əʊn/ *vt* repudiar

disparaging /dɪs'pærɪdʒɪŋ/ *a* despreciativo. **~ly** *adv* con desprecio

disparity /dɪs'pærətɪ/ *n* disparidad *f*

dispassionate /dɪs'pæʃənət/ *a* desapasionado

dispatch /dɪs'pætʃ/ *vt* enviar. ● *n* envío *m*; (*report*) despacho *m*. **~-rider** *n* correo *m*

dispel /dɪs'pel/ *vt* (*pt* **dispelled**) disipar

dispensable /dɪs'pensəbl/ *a* prescindible

dispensary /dɪs'pensərɪ/ *n* farmacia *f*

dispensation /dɪspen'seɪʃn/ *n* distribución *f*; (*relig*) dispensa *f*

dispense /dɪs'pens/ *vt* distribuir; (*med*) preparar; (*relig*) dispensar; administrar ‹*justice*›. **~ with** prescindir de. **~r** /-ə(r)/ *n* (*mec*) distribuidor *m* automático; (*med*) farmacéutico *m*

dispers|al /dɪ'spɜ:sl/ *n* dispersión *f*. **~e** /dɪ'spɜ:s/ *vt* dispersar. ● *vi* dispersarse

dispirited /dɪs'pɪrɪtɪd/ *a* desanimado

displace /dɪs'pleɪs/ *vt* desplazar

display /dɪs'pleɪ/ *vt* mostrar; exhibir ‹*goods*›; manifestar ‹*feelings*›. ● *n* exposición *f*; (*of feelings*) manifestación *f*; (*pej*) ostentación *f*

displeas|e /dɪs'pli:z/ *vt* desagradar. **be ~ed with** estar disgustado con. **~ure** /-'pleʒə(r)/ *n* desagrado *m*

dispos|able /dɪs'pəʊzəbl/ *a* desechable. **~al** *n* (*of waste*) eliminación *f*. **at s.o.'s ~al** a la disposición de uno. **~e** /dɪs'pəʊz/ *vt* disponer. **be well ~ed towards** estar bien dispuesto hacia. ● *vi*. **~e of** deshacerse de

disposition /dɪspə'zɪʃn/ *n* disposición *f*

disproportionate /dɪsprə'pɔ:ʃənət/ *a* desproporcionado

disprove /dɪs'pru:v/ *vt* refutar

dispute /dɪs'pju:t/ *vt* disputar. ● *n* disputa *f*. **in ~** disputado

disqualif|ication /dɪskwɒlɪfɪ'keɪʃn/ *n* descalificación *f*. **~y** /dɪs'kwɒlɪfaɪ/ *vt* incapacitar; (*sport*) descalificar

disquiet /dɪs'kwaɪət/ *n* inquietud *f*

disregard /dɪsrɪ'gɑ:d/ *vt* no hacer caso de. ● *n* indiferencia *f* (**for** a)

disrepair /dɪsrɪ'peə(r)/ *n* mal estado *m*

disreputable /dɪs'repjʊtəbl/ *a* de mala fama

disrepute /dɪsrɪ'pju:t/ *n* discrédito *m*

disrespect /dɪsrɪs'pekt/ *n* falta *f* de respeto

disrobe /dɪs'rəʊb/ *vt* desvestir. ● *vi* desvestirse

disrupt /dɪs'rʌpt/ *vt* interrumpir; trastornar ‹*plans*›. **~ion** /-ʃn/ *n* interrupción *f*; (*disorder*) desorganización *f*. **~ive** *a* desbaratador

dissatisfaction /dɪsætɪs'fækʃn/ *n* descontento *m*

dissatisfied /dɪ'sætɪsfaɪd/ *a* descontento

dissect /dɪ'sekt/ *vt* disecar. **~ion** /-ʃn/ *n* disección *f*

disseminat|e /dɪ'semɪneɪt/ *vt* diseminar. **~ion** /-'neɪʃn/ *n* diseminación *f*

dissent /dɪ'sent/ *vi* disentir. ● *n* disentimiento *m*

dissertation /dɪsə'teɪʃn/ *n* disertación *f*; (*univ*) tesis *f*

disservice /dɪs'sɜ:vɪs/ *n* mal servicio *m*

dissident /'dɪsɪdənt/ *a* & *n* disidente (*m* & *f*)

dissimilar /dɪ'sɪmɪlə(r)/ *a* distinto

dissipate /'dɪsɪpeɪt/ *vt* disipar; (*fig*) desvanecer. **~d** *a* disoluto

dissociate /dɪ'səʊʃɪeɪt/ *vt* disociar

dissolut|e /'dɪsəlu:t/ *a* disoluto. **~ion** /dɪsə'lu:ʃn/ *n* disolución *f*

dissolve /dɪ'zɒlv/ *vt* disolver. ● *vi* disolverse

dissuade /dɪ'sweɪd/ *vt* disuadir

distan|ce /'dɪstəns/ *n* distancia *f*. **from a ~ce** desde lejos. **in the ~ce** a

lo lejos. **~t** /'dɪstənt/ *a* lejano; (*aloof*) frío
distaste /dɪs'teɪst/ *n* aversión *f*. **~ful** *a* desagradable
distemper[1] /dɪ'stempə(r)/ *n* (*paint*) temple *m*. ● *vt* pintar al temple
distemper[2] /dɪ'stempə(r)/ *n* (*of dogs*) moquillo *m*
distend /dɪs'tend/ *vt* dilatar. ● *vi* dilatarse
distil /dɪs'tɪl/ *vt* (*pt* **distilled**) destilar. **~lation** /-'leɪʃn/ *n* destilación *f*. **~lery** /dɪs'tɪlərɪ/ *n* destilería *f*
distinct /dɪs'tɪŋkt/ *a* distinto; (*clear*) claro; (*marked*) marcado. **~ion** /-ʃn/ *n* distinción *f*; (*in exam*) sobresaliente *m*. **~ive** *a* distintivo. **~ly** *adv* claramente
distinguish /dɪs'tɪŋgwɪʃ/ *vt/i* distinguir. **~ed** *a* distinguido
distort /dɪs'tɔ:t/ *vt* torcer. **~ion** /-ʃn/ *n* deformación *f*
distract /dɪs'trækt/ *vt* distraer. **~ed** *a* aturdido. **~ing** *a* molesto. **~ion** /-ʃn/ *n* distracción *f*; (*confusion*) aturdimiento *m*
distraught /dɪs'trɔ:t/ *a* aturdido
distress /dɪs'tres/ *n* angustia *f*; (*poverty*) miseria *f*; (*danger*) peligro *m*. ● *vt* afligir. **~ing** *a* penoso
distribut|e /dɪs'trɪbju:t/ *vt* distribuir. **~ion** /-'bju:ʃn/ *n* distribución *f*. **~or** *n* distribuidor *m*; (*auto*) distribuidor *m* de encendido
district /'dɪstrɪkt/ *n* districto *m*; (*of town*) barrio *m*
distrust /dɪs'trʌst/ *n* desconfianza *f*. ● *vt* desconfiar de
disturb /dɪs'tɜ:b/ *vt* molestar; (*perturb*) inquietar; (*move*) desordenar; (*interrupt*) interrumpir. **~ance** *n* disturbio *m*; (*tumult*) alboroto *m*. **~ed** *a* trastornado. **~ing** *a* inquietante
disused /dɪs'ju:zd/ *a* fuera de uso
ditch /dɪtʃ/ *n* zanja *f*; (*for irrigation*) acequia *f*. ● *vt* (*sl*) abandonar
dither /'dɪðə(r)/ *vi* vacilar
ditto /'dɪtəʊ/ *adv* ídem
divan /dɪ'væn/ *n* diván *m*
dive /daɪv/ *vi* tirarse de cabeza; (*rush*) meterse (precipitadamente); (*underwater*) bucear. ● *n* salto *m*; (*of plane*) picado *m*; (*place, fam*) taberna *f*. **~r** *n* saltador *m*; (*underwater*) buzo *m*
diverge /daɪ'vɜ:dʒ/ *vi* divergir. **~nt** /daɪ'vɜ:dʒənt/ *a* divergente
divers|e /daɪ'vɜ:s/ *a* diverso. **~ify** /daɪ'vɜ:sɪfaɪ/ *vt* diversificar. **~ity** /daɪ'vɜ:sətɪ/ *n* diversidad *f*
diver|sion /daɪ'vɜ:ʃn/ *n* desvío *m*; (*distraction*) diversión *f*. **~t** /daɪ'vɜ:t/ *vt* desviar; (*entertain*) divertir
divest /daɪ'vest/ *vt*. **~ of** despojar de
divide /dɪ'vaɪd/ *vt* dividir. ● *vi* dividirse
dividend /'dɪvɪdend/ *n* dividendo *m*
divine /dɪ'vaɪn/ *a* divino
diving-board /'daɪvɪŋbɔ:d/ *n* trampolín *m*
diving-suit /'daɪvɪŋsu:t/ *n* escafandra *f*
divinity /dɪ'vɪnɪtɪ/ *n* divinidad *f*
division /dɪ'vɪʒn/ *n* división *f*
divorce /dɪ'vɔ:s/ *n* divorcio *m*. ● *vt* divorciarse de; ‹*judge*› divorciar. ● *vi* divorciarse. **~e** /dɪvɔ:'si:/ *n* divorciado *m*
divulge /daɪ'vʌldʒ/ *vt* divulgar
DIY *abbr see* **do-it-yourself**
dizz|iness /'dɪzɪnɪs/ *n* vértigo *m*. **~y** /'dɪzɪ/ *a* (**-ier, -iest**) mareado; ‹*speed*› vertiginoso. **be** *or* **feel ~y** marearse
do /du:/ *vt* (*3 sing pres* **does,** *pt* **did**, *pp* **done**) hacer; (*swindle, sl*) engañar. ● *vi* hacer; (*fare*) ir; (*be suitable*) convenir; (*be enough*) bastar. ● *n* (*pl* **dos** *or* **do's**) (*fam*) fiesta *f*. ● *v aux*. **~ you speak Spanish? Yes I ~** ¿habla Vd español? Sí. **doesn't he?, don't you?** ¿verdad? **~ come in!** (*emphatic*) ¡pase Vd! **~ away with** abolir. **~ in** (*exhaust, fam*) agotar; (*kill, sl*) matar. **~ out** (*clean*) limpiar. **~ up** abotonar ‹*coat etc*›; renovar ‹*house*›. **~ with** tener que ver con; (*need*) necesitar. **~ without** prescindir de. **~ne for** (*fam*) arruinado. **~ne in** (*fam*) agotado. **well ~ne** (*culin*) bien hecho. **well ~ne!** ¡muy bien!
docile /'dəʊsaɪl/ *a* dócil
dock[1] /dɒk/ *n* dique *m*. ● *vt* poner en dique. ● *vi* atracar al muelle
dock[2] /dɒk/ *n* (*jurid*) banquillo *m* de los acusados
dock: **~er** *n* estibador *m*. **~yard** /'dɒkjɑ:d/ *n* astillero *m*
doctor /'dɒktə(r)/ *n* médico *m*, doctor *m*; (*univ*) doctor *m*. ● *vt* castrar ‹*cat*›; (*fig*) adulterar
doctorate /'dɒktərət/ *n* doctorado *m*
doctrine /'dɒktrɪn/ *n* doctrina *f*
document /'dɒkjʊmənt/ *n* documento *m*. **~ary** /-'mentrɪ/ *a* & *n* documental (*m*)

doddering /'dɒdərɪŋ/ *a* chocho
dodge /dɒdʒ/ *vt* esquivar. ● *vi* esquivarse. ● *n* regate *m*; (*fam*) truco *m*
dodgems /'dɒdʒəmz/ *npl* autos *mpl* de choque
dodgy /'dɒdʒɪ/ *a* (**-ier, -iest**) (*awkward*) difícil
does /dʌz/ *see* **do**
doesn't /'dʌznt/ = **does not**
dog /dɒg/ *n* perro *m*. ● *vt* (*pt* **dogged**) perseguir. **~-collar** *n* (*relig, fam*) alzacuello *m*. **~-eared** *a* ‹*book*› sobado
dogged /'dɒgɪd/ *a* obstinado
doghouse /'dɒghaʊs/ *n* (*Amer*) perrera *f*. **in the ~** (*sl*) en desgracia
dogma /'dɒgmə/ *n* dogma *m*. **~tic** /-'mætɪk/ *a* dogmático
dogsbody /'dɒgzbɒdɪ/ *n* (*fam*) burro *m* de carga
doh /dəʊ/ *n* (*mus, first note of any musical scale*) do *m*
doily /'dɔɪlɪ/ *n* tapete *m*
doings /'du:ɪŋz/ *npl* (*fam*) actividades *fpl*
do-it-yourself /du:ɪtjɔ:'self/ (*abbr* **DIY**) *n* bricolaje *m*. **~ enthusiast** *n* manitas *m*
doldrums /'dɒldrəmz/ *npl*. **be in the ~** estar abatido
dole /dəʊl/ *vt*. **~ out** distribuir. ● *n* (*fam*) subsidio *m* de paro. **on the ~** (*fam*) parado
doleful /'dəʊlfl/ *a* triste
doll /dɒl/ *n* muñeca *f*. ● *vt*. **~ up** (*fam*) emperejilar
dollar /'dɒlə(r)/ *n* dólar *m*
dollop /'dɒləp/ *n* (*fam*) masa *f*
dolphin /'dɒlfɪn/ *n* delfín *m*
domain /dəʊ'meɪn/ *n* dominio *m*; (*fig*) campo *m*
dome /dəʊm/ *n* cúpula *f*. **~d** *a* abovedado
domestic /də'mestɪk/ *a* doméstico; ‹*trade, flights, etc*› nacional
domesticated *a* ‹*animal*› domesticado
domesticity /dɒme'stɪsətɪ/ *n* domesticidad *f*
domestic: **~ science** *n* economía *f* doméstica. **~ servant** *n* doméstico *m*
dominant /'dɒmɪnənt/ *a* dominante
dominat|e /'dɒmɪneɪt/ *vt/i* dominar. **~ion** /-'neɪʃn/ *n* dominación *f*
domineer /dɒmɪ'nɪə(r)/ *vi* tiranizar
Dominican Republic /dəmɪnɪkən rɪ'pʌblɪk/ *n* República *f* Dominicana
dominion /də'mɪnjən/ *n* dominio *m*
domino /'dɒmɪnəʊ/ *n* (*pl* **~es**) ficha *f* de dominó. **~es** *npl* (*game*) dominó *m*
don[1] /dɒn/ *n* profesor *m*
don[2] /dɒn/ *vt* (*pt* **donned**) ponerse
donat|e /dəʊ'neɪt/ *vt* donar. **~ion** /-ʃn/ *n* donativo *m*
done /dʌn/ *see* **do**
donkey /'dɒŋkɪ/ *n* burro *m*. **~-work** *n* trabajo *m* penoso
donor /'dəʊnə(r)/ *n* donante *m & f*
don't /dəʊnt/ = **do not**
doodle /'du:dl/ *vi* garrapatear
doom /du:m/ *n* destino *m*; (*death*) muerte *f*. ● *vt*. **be ~ed to** ser condenado a
doomsday /'du:mzdeɪ/ *n* día *m* del juicio final
door /dɔ:(r)/ *n* puerta *f*. **~man** /'dɔ:mən/ *n* (*pl* **-men**) portero *m*. **~mat** /'dɔ:mæt/ *n* felpudo *m*. **~step** /'dɔ:step/ *n* peldaño *m*. **~way** /'dɔ:weɪ/ *n* entrada *f*
dope /dəʊp/ *n* (*fam*) droga *f*; (*idiot, sl*) imbécil *m*. ● *vt* (*fam*) drogar. **~y** *a* (*sl*) torpe
dormant /'dɔ:mənt/ *a* inactivo
dormer /'dɔ:mə(r)/ *n*. **~ (window)** buhardilla *f*
dormitory /'dɔ:mɪtrɪ/ *n* dormitorio *m*
dormouse /'dɔ:maʊs/ *n* (*pl* **-mice**) lirón *m*
dos|age /'dəʊsɪdʒ/ *n* dosis *f*. **~e** /dəʊs/ *n* dosis *f*
doss /dɒs/ *vi* (*sl*) dormir. **~-house** *n* refugio *m*
dot /dɒt/ *n* punto *m*. **on the ~** en punto. ● *vt* (*pt* **dotted**) salpicar. **be ~ted with** estar salpicado de
dote /dəʊt/ *vi*. **~ on** adorar
dotted line /dɒtɪd'laɪn/ *n* línea *f* de puntos
dotty /'dɒtɪ/ *a* (**-ier, -iest**) (*fam*) chiflado
double /'dʌbl/ *a* doble. ● *adv* doble, dos veces. ● *n* doble *m*; (*person*) doble *m & f*. **at the ~** corriendo. ● *vt* doblar; redoblar ‹*efforts etc*›. ● *vi* doblarse. **~-bass** *n* contrabajo *m*. **~ bed** *n* cama *f* de matrimonio. **~-breasted** *a* cruzado. **~ chin** *n* papada *f*. **~-cross** *vt* traicionar. **~-dealing** *n* doblez *m & f*. **~-decker** *n* autobús *m* de dos pisos. **~ Dutch** *n* galimatías

m. **~-jointed** *a* con articulaciones dobles. **~s** *npl* (*tennis*) doble *m*
doubt /daʊt/ *n* duda *f*. ● *vt* dudar; (*distrust*) dudar de, desconfiar de. **~ful** *a* dudoso. **~less** *adv* sin duda
doubly /'dʌblɪ/ *adv* doblemente
dough /dəʊ/ *n* masa *f*; (*money, sl*) dinero *m*, pasta *f* (*sl*)
doughnut /'dəʊnʌt/ *n* buñuelo *m*
douse /daʊs/ *vt* mojar; apagar ‹*fire*›
dove /dʌv/ *n* paloma *f*
dowager /'daʊədʒə(r)/ *n* viuda *f* (con bienes o título del marido)
dowdy /'daʊdɪ/ *a* (**-ier, -iest**) poco atractivo
down[1] /daʊn/ *adv* abajo. **~ with** abajo. **come ~** bajar. **go ~** bajar; ‹*sun*› ponerse. ● *prep* abajo. ● *a* (*sad*) triste. ● *vt* derribar; (*drink, fam*) beber
down[2] /daʊn/ *n* (*feathers*) plumón *m*
down-and-out /'daʊnənd'aʊt/ *n* vagabundo *m*
downcast /'daʊnkɑ:st/ *a* abatido
downfall /'daʊnfɔ:l/ *n* caída *f*; (*fig*) perdición *f*
downgrade /daʊn'greɪd/ *vt* degradar
down-hearted /daʊn'hɑ:tɪd/ *a* abatido
downhill /daʊn'hɪl/ *adv* cuesta abajo
down payment /'daʊnpeɪmənt/ *n* depósito *m*
downpour /'daʊnpɔ:(r)/ *n* aguacero *m*
downright /'daʊnraɪt/ *a* completo; (*honest*) franco. ● *adv* completamente
downs /daʊnz/ *npl* colinas *fpl*
downstairs /daʊn'steəz/ *adv* abajo. /'daʊnsteəz/ *a* de abajo
downstream /'daʊnstri:m/ *adv* río abajo
down-to-earth /daʊntʊ'ɜ:θ/ *a* práctico
downtrodden /'daʊntrɒdn/ *a* oprimido
down: **~ under** en las antípodas; (*in Australia*) en Australia. **~ward** /'daʊnwəd/ *a* & *adv*, **~wards** *adv* hacia abajo
dowry /'daʊərɪ/ *n* dote *f*
doze /dəʊz/ *vi* dormitar. **~ off** dormirse, dar una cabezada. ● *n* sueño *m* ligero
dozen /'dʌzn/ *n* docena *f*. **~s of** (*fam*) miles de, muchos

Dr *abbr* (*Doctor*) Dr, Doctor *m*. **~ Broadley** (el) Doctor Broadley
drab /dræb/ *a* monótono
draft /drɑ:ft/ *n* borrador *m*; (*outline*) bosquejo *m*; (*com*) letra *f* de cambio; (*Amer, mil*) reclutamiento *m*; (*Amer, of air*) corriente *f* de aire. ● *vt* bosquejar; (*mil*) destacar; (*Amer, conscript*) reclutar
drag /dræg/ *vt* (*pt* **dragged**) arrastrar; rastrear ‹*river*›. ● *vi* arrastrarse por el suelo. ● *n* (*fam*) lata *f*. **in ~** (*man, sl*) vestido de mujer
dragon /'drægən/ *n* dragón *m*
dragon-fly /'drægənflaɪ/ *n* libélula *f*
drain /dreɪn/ *vt* desaguar; apurar ‹*tank, glass*›; (*fig*) agotar. ● *vi* escurrirse. ● *n* desaguadero *m*. **be a ~ on** agotar. **~ing-board** *n* escurridero *m*
drama /'drɑ:mə/ *n* drama *m*; (*art*) arte *m* teatral. **~tic** /drə'mætɪk/ *a* dramático. **~tist** /'dræmətɪst/ *n* dramaturgo *m*. **~tize** /'dræmətaɪz/ *vt* adaptar al teatro; (*fig*) dramatizar
drank /dræŋk/ *see* **drink**
drape /dreɪp/ *vt* cubrir; (*hang*) colgar. **~s** *npl* (*Amer*) cortinas *fpl*
drastic /'dræstɪk/ *a* drástico
draught /drɑ:ft/ *n* corriente *f* de aire. **~ beer** *n* cerveza *f* de barril. **~s** *n pl* (*game*) juego *m* de damas
draughtsman /'drɑ:ftsmən/ *n* (*pl* **-men**) diseñador *m*
draughty /'drɑ:ftɪ/ *a* lleno de corrientes de aire
draw /drɔ:/ *vt* (*pt* **drew**, *pp* **drawn**) tirar; (*attract*) atraer; dibujar ‹*picture*›; trazar ‹*line*›; retirar ‹*money*›. **~ the line at** trazar el límite. ● *vi* (*sport*) empatar; dibujar ‹*pictures*›; (*in lottery*) sortear. ● *n* (*sport*) empate *m*; (*in lottery*) sorteo *m*. **~ in** ‹*days*› acortarse. **~ out** sacar ‹*money*›. **~ up** pararse; redactar ‹*document*›; acercar ‹*chair*›
drawback /'drɔ:bæk/ *n* desventaja *f*
drawbridge /'drɔ:brɪdʒ/ *n* puente *m* levadizo
drawer /drɔ:(r)/ *n* cajón *m*. **~s** /drɔ:z/ *npl* calzoncillos *mpl*; (*women's*) bragas *fpl*
drawing /'drɔ:ɪŋ/ *n* dibujo *m*. **~-pin** *n* chinche *m*, chincheta *f*
drawing-room /'drɔ:ɪŋru:m/ *n* salón *m*
drawl /drɔ:l/ *n* habla *f* lenta
drawn /drɔ:n/ *see* **draw**. ● *a* ‹*face*› ojeroso

dread /dred/ *n* terror *m*. ● *vt* temer. **~ful** /ˈdredfl/ *a* terrible. **~fully** *adv* terriblemente

dream /dri:m/ *n* sueño *m*. ● *vt/i* (*pt* **dreamed** *or* **dreamt**) soñar. ● *a* ideal. **~ up** idear. **~er** *n* soñador *m*. **~y** *a* soñador

drear|iness /ˈdrɪərɪnɪs/ *n* tristeza *f*; (*monotony*) monotonía *f*. **~y** /ˈdrɪərɪ/ *a* (**-ier, -iest**) triste; (*boring*) monótono

dredge[1] /dredʒ/ *n* draga *f*. ● *vt* dragar

dredge[2] /dredʒ/ *n* (*culin*) espolvorear

dredger[1] /ˈdredʒə(r)/ *n* draga *f*

dredger[2] /ˈdredʒə(r)/ *n* (*for sugar*) espolvoreador *m*

dregs /dregz/ *npl* heces *fpl*; (*fig*) hez *f*

drench /drentʃ/ *vt* empapar

dress /dres/ *n* vestido *m*; (*clothing*) ropa *f*. ● *vt* vestir; (*decorate*) adornar; (*med*) vendar; (*culin*) aderezar, aliñar. ● *vi* vestirse. **~ circle** *n* primer palco *m*

dresser[1] /ˈdresə(r)/ *n* (*furniture*) aparador *m*

dresser[2] /ˈdresə(r)/ *n* (*in theatre*) camarero *m*

dressing /ˈdresɪŋ/ *n* (*sauce*) aliño *m*; (*bandage*) vendaje *m*. **~-case** *n* neceser *m*. **~-down** *n* rapapolvo *m*, reprensión *f*. **~-gown** *n* bata *f*. **~-room** *n* tocador *m*; (*in theatre*) camarín *m*. **~-table** *n* tocador *m*

dressmak|er /ˈdresmeɪkə(r)/ *n* modista *m & f*. **~ing** *n* costura *f*

dress rehearsal /ˈdresrɪhɜ:sl/ *n* ensayo *m* general

dressy /ˈdresɪ/ *a* (**-ier, -iest**) elegante

drew /dru:/ *see* **draw**

dribble /ˈdrɪbl/ *vi* gotear; ‹*baby*› babear; (*in football*) regatear

dribs and drabs /drɪbznˈdræbz/ *npl*. **in ~** poco a poco, en cantidades pequeñas

drie|d /draɪd/ *a* ‹*food*› seco; ‹*fruit*› paso. **~r** /ˈdraɪə(r)/ *n* secador *m*

drift /drɪft/ *vi* ir a la deriva; ‹*snow*› amontonarse. ● *n* (*movement*) dirección *f*; (*of snow*) montón *m*; (*meaning*) significado *m*. **~er** *n* persona *f* sin rumbo. **~wood** /ˈdrɪftwʊd/ *n* madera *f* flotante

drill /drɪl/ *n* (*tool*) taladro *m*; (*training*) ejercicio *m*; (*fig*) lo normal. ● *vt* taladrar, perforar; (*train*) entrenar. ● *vi* entrenarse

drily /ˈdraɪlɪ/ *adv* secamente

drink /drɪŋk/ *vt/i* (*pt* **drank**, *pp* **drunk**) beber. ● *n* bebida *f*. **~able** *a* bebible; ‹*water*› potable. **~er** *n* bebedor *m*. **~ing-water** *n* agua *f* potable

drip /drɪp/ *vi* (*pt* **dripped**) gotear. ● *n* gota *f*; (*med*) goteo *m* intravenoso; (*person, sl*) mentecato *m*. **~-dry** *a* que no necesita plancharse

dripping /ˈdrɪpɪŋ/ *n* (*culin*) pringue *m*

drive /draɪv/ *vt* (*pt* **drove**, *pp* **driven**) empujar; conducir, manejar (*LAm*) ‹*car etc*›. **~ in** clavar ‹*nail*›. **~ s.o. mad** volver loco a uno. ● *vi* conducir. **~ in** (*in car*) entrar en coche. ● *n* paseo *m*; (*road*) calle *f*; (*private road*) camino *m* de entrada; (*fig*) energía *f*; (*pol*) campaña *f*. **~ at** querer decir. **~r** /ˈdraɪvə(r)/ *n* conductor *m*, chófer *m* (*LAm*)

drivel /ˈdrɪvl/ *n* tonterías *fpl*

driving /ˈdraɪvɪŋ/ *n* conducción *f*. **~-licence** *n* carné *m* de conducir. **~ school** *n* autoescuela *f*

drizzl|e /ˈdrɪzl/ *n* llovizna *f*. ● *vi* lloviznar. **~y** *a* lloviznoso

dromedary /ˈdrɒmədərɪ/ *n* dromedario *m*

drone /drəʊn/ *n* (*noise*) zumbido *m*; (*bee*) zángano *m*. ● *vi* zumbar; (*fig*) hablar en voz monótona; (*idle, fam*) holgazanear

drool /dru:l/ *vi* babear

droop /dru:p/ *vt* inclinar. ● *vi* inclinarse; ‹*flowers*› marchitarse

drop /drɒp/ *n* gota *f*; (*fall*) caída *f*; (*decrease*) baja *f*; (*of cliff*) precipicio *m*. ● *vt* (*pt* **dropped**) dejar caer; (*lower*) bajar. ● *vi* caer. **~ in on** pasar por casa de. **~ off** (*sleep*) dormirse. **~ out** retirarse; ‹*student*› abandonar los estudios. **~-out** *n* marginado *m*

droppings /ˈdrɒpɪŋz/ *npl* excremento *m*

dross /drɒs/ *n* escoria *f*

drought /draʊt/ *n* sequía *f*

drove[1] /drəʊv/ *see* **drive**

drove[2] /drəʊv/ *n* manada *f*

drown /draʊn/ *vt* ahogar. ● *vi* ahogarse

drowsy /ˈdraʊzɪ/ *a* soñoliento

drudge /drʌdʒ/ *n* esclavo *m* del trabajo. **~ry** /-ərɪ/ *n* trabajo *m* pesado

drug /drʌg/ *n* droga *f*; (*med*) medicamento *m*. ● *vt* (*pt* **drugged**) drogar. **~ addict** *n* toxicómano *m*

drugstore /'drʌgstɔ:(r)/ *n* (*Amer*) farmacia *f* (que vende otros artículos también)
drum /drʌm/ *n* tambor *m*; (*for oil*) bidón *m*. ● *vi* (*pt* **drummed**) tocar el tambor. ● *vt*. ~ **into s.o.** inculcar en la mente de uno. ~**mer** *n* tambor *m*; (*in group*) batería *f*. ~**s** *npl* batería *f*. ~**stick** /'drʌmstɪk/ *n* baqueta *f*; (*culin*) pierna *f* (de pollo)
drunk /drʌŋk/ *see* **drink**. ● *a* borracho. **get** ~ emborracharse. ~**ard** *n* borracho *m*. ~**en** *a* borracho. ~**enness** *n* embriaguez *f*
dry /draɪ/ *a* (**drier, driest**) seco. ● *vt* secar. ● *vi* secarse. ~ **up** (*fam*) secar los platos. ~**-clean** *vt* limpiar en seco. ~**-cleaner** *n* tintorero *m*. ~**cleaner's** (*shop*) tintorería *f*. ~**ness** *n* sequedad *f*
dual /'dju:əl/ *a* doble. ~ **carriageway** *n* autovía *f*, carretera *f* de doble calzada. ~**-purpose** *a* de doble uso
dub /dʌb/ *vt* (*pt* **dubbed**) doblar ‹*film*›; (*nickname*) apodar
dubious /'dju:bɪəs/ *a* dudoso; ‹*person*› sospechoso
duchess /'dʌtʃɪs/ *n* duquesa *f*
duck[1] /dʌk/ *n* pato *m*
duck[2] /dʌk/ *vt* sumergir; bajar ‹*head etc*›. ● *vi* agacharse
duckling /'dʌklɪŋ/ *n* patito *m*
duct /dʌkt/ *n* conducto *m*
dud /dʌd/ *a* inútil; ‹*cheque*› sin fondos; ‹*coin*› falso
due /dju:/ *a* debido; (*expected*) esperado. ~ **to** debido a. ● *adv*. ~ **north** *n* derecho hacia el norte. ~**s** *npl* derechos *mpl*
duel /'dju:əl/ *n* duelo *m*
duet /dju:'et/ *n* dúo *m*
duffle /'dʌfl/ *a*. ~ **bag** *n* bolsa *f* de lona. ~**-coat** *n* trenca *f*
dug /dʌg/ *see* **dig**
duke /dju:k/ *n* duque *m*
dull /dʌl/ *a* (**-er, -est**) ‹*weather*› gris; ‹*colour*› apagado; ‹*person, play, etc*› pesado; ‹*sound*› sordo; (*stupid*) torpe. ● *vt* aliviar ‹*pain*›; entorpecer ‹*mind*›
duly /'dju:lɪ/ *adv* debidamente
dumb /dʌm/ *a* (**-er, -est**) mudo; (*fam*) estúpido
dumbfound /dʌm'faʊnd/ *vt* pasmar
dummy /'dʌmɪ/ *n* muñeco *m*; (*of tailor*) maniquí *m*; (*of baby*) chupete *m*. ● *a* falso. ~ **run** *n* prueba *f*
dump /dʌmp/ *vt* descargar; (*fam*) deshacerse de. ● *n* vertedero *m*; (*mil*) depósito *m*; (*fam*) lugar *m* desagradable. **be down in the** ~**s** estar deprimido
dumpling /'dʌmplɪŋ/ *n* bola *f* de masa hervida
dumpy /'dʌmpɪ/ *a* (**-ier, -iest**) regordete
dunce /dʌns/ *n* burro *m*
dung /dʌŋ/ *n* excremento *m*; (*manure*) estiércol *m*
dungarees /dʌŋgə'ri:z/ *npl* mono *m*, peto *m*
dungeon /'dʌndʒən/ *n* calabozo *m*
dunk /dʌŋk/ *vt* remojar
duo /'dju:əʊ/ *n* dúo *m*
dupe /dju:p/ *vt* engañar. ● *n* inocentón *m*
duplicat|e /'dju:plɪkət/ *a* & *n* duplicado (*m*). /'dju:plɪkeɪt/ *vt* duplicar; (*on machine*) reproducir. ~**or** *n* multicopista *f*
duplicity /dju:'plɪsətɪ/ *n* doblez *f*
durable /'djʊərəbl/ *a* resistente; (*enduring*) duradero
duration /djʊ'reɪʃn/ *n* duración *f*
duress /djʊ'res/ *n* coacción *f*
during /'djʊərɪŋ/ *prep* durante
dusk /dʌsk/ *n* crepúsculo *m*
dusky /'dʌskɪ/ *a* (**-ier, -iest**) oscuro
dust /dʌst/ *n* polvo *m*. ● *vt* quitar el polvo a; (*sprinkle*) espolvorear
dustbin /'dʌstbɪn/ *n* cubo *m* de la basura
dust-cover /'dʌstkʌvə(r)/ *n* sobrecubierta *f*
duster /'dʌstə(r)/ *n* trapo *m*
dust-jacket /'dʌstdʒækɪt/ *n* sobrecubierta *f*
dustman /'dʌstmən/ *n* (*pl* **-men**) basurero *m*
dustpan /'dʌstpæn/ *n* recogedor *m*
dusty /'dʌstɪ/ *a* (**-ier, -iest**) polvoriento
Dutch /dʌtʃ/ *a* & *n* holandés (*m*). **go** ~ pagar a escote. ~**man** *m* holandés *m*. ~**woman** *n* holandesa *f*
dutiful /'dju:tɪfl/ *a* obediente
duty /'dju:tɪ/ *n* deber *m*; (*tax*) derechos *mpl* de aduana. **on** ~ de servicio. ~**-free** *a* libre de impuestos
duvet /'dju:veɪ/ *n* edredón *m*
dwarf /dwɔ:f/ *n* (*pl* **-s**) enano *m*. ● *vt* empequeñecer
dwell /dwel/ *vi* (*pt* **dwelt**) morar. ~ **on** dilatarse. ~**er** *n* habitante *m* & *f*. ~**ing** *n* morada *f*
dwindle /'dwɪndl/ *vi* disminuir

dye /daɪ/ *vt* (*pres p* **dyeing**) teñir. ● *n* tinte *m*
dying /'daɪɪŋ/ *see* **die**
dynamic /daɪ'næmɪk/ *a* dinámico. **~s** *npl* dinámica *f*
dynamite /'daɪnəmaɪt/ *n* dinamita *f*. ● *vt* dinamitar
dynamo /'daɪnəməʊ/ *n* dinamo *f*, dínamo *f*
dynasty /'dɪnəstɪ/ *n* dinastía *f*
dysentery /'dɪsəntrɪ/ *n* disentería *f*
dyslexia /dɪs'leksɪə/ *n* dislexia *f*

E

each /i:tʃ/ *a* cada. ● *pron* cada uno. **~ one** cada uno. **~ other** uno a otro, el uno al otro. **they love ~ other** se aman
eager /'i:gə(r)/ *a* impaciente; (*enthusiastic*) ávido. **~ly** *adv* con impaciencia. **~ness** *n* impaciencia *f*, ansia *f*
eagle /'i:gl/ *n* águila *f*
ear[1] /ɪə(r)/ *n* oído *m*; (*outer*) oreja *f*
ear[2] /ɪə(r)/ *n* (*of corn*) espiga *f*
ear: **~ache** /'ɪəreɪk/ *n* dolor *m* de oído. **~-drum** *n* tímpano *m*
earl /3:l/ *n* conde *m*
early /'3:lɪ/ *a* (**-ier, -iest**) temprano; (*before expected time*) prematuro. **in the ~ spring** a principios de la primavera. ● *adv* temprano; (*ahead of time*) con anticipación
earmark /'ɪəmɑ:k/ *vt*. **~ for** destinar a
earn /3:n/ *vt* ganar; (*deserve*) merecer
earnest /'3:nɪst/ *a* serio. **in ~** en serio
earnings /'3:nɪŋz/ *npl* ingresos *mpl*; (*com*) ganancias *fpl*
ear: **~phones** /'ɪəfəʊnz/ *npl* auricular *m*. **~-ring** *n* pendiente *m*
earshot /'ɪəʃɒt/ *n*. **within ~** al alcance del oído
earth /3:θ/ *n* tierra *f*. ● *vt* (*elec*) conectar a tierra. **~ly** *a* terrenal
earthenware /'3:θnweə(r)/ *n* loza *f* de barro
earthquake /'3:θkweɪk/ *n* terremoto *m*
earthy /'3:θɪ/ *a* terroso; (*coarse*) grosero
earwig /'ɪəwɪg/ *n* tijereta *f*
ease /i:z/ *n* facilidad *f*; (*comfort*) tranquilidad *f*. **at ~** a gusto; (*mil*) en posición de descanso. **ill at ~** molesto. **with ~** fácilmente. ● *vt* calmar; aliviar ‹*pain*›; tranquilizar ‹*mind*›; (*loosen*) aflojar. ● *vi* calmarse; (*lessen*) disminuir
easel /'i:zl/ *n* caballete *m*
east /i:st/ *n* este *m*, oriente *m*. ● *a* del este, oriental. ● *adv* hacia el este.
Easter /'i:stə(r)/ *n* Semana *f* Santa; (*relig*) Pascua *f* de Resurrección. **~ egg** *n* huevo *m* de Pascua
east: **~erly** *a* este; ‹*wind*› del este. **~ern** *a* del este, oriental. **~ward** *adv*, **~wards** *adv* hacia el este
easy /'i:zɪ/ *a* (**-ier**, **-iest**) fácil; (*relaxed*) tranquilo. **go ~ on** (*fam*) tener cuidado con. **take it ~** no preocuparse. ● *int* ¡despacio! **~ chair** *n* sillón *m*. **~-going** *a* acomodadizo
eat /i:t/ *vt/i* (*pt* **ate**, *pp* **eaten**) comer. **~ into** corroer. **~able** *a* comestible. **~er** *n* comedor *m*
eau-de-Cologne /əʊdəkə'ləʊn/ *n* agua *f* de colonia
eaves /i:vz/ *npl* alero *m*
eavesdrop /'i:vzdrɒp/ *vi* (*pt* **-dropped**) escuchar a escondidas
ebb /eb/ *n* reflujo *m*. ● *vi* bajar; (*fig*) decaer
ebony /'ebənɪ/ *n* ébano *m*
ebullient /ɪ'bʌlɪənt/ *a* exuberante
EC /i:'si:/ *abbr* (*European Community*) CE (Comunidad *f* Europea)
eccentric /ɪk'sentrɪk/ *a* & *n* excéntrico (*m*). **~ity** /eksen'trɪsətɪ/ *n* excentricidad *f*
ecclesiastical /ɪkli:zɪ'æstɪkl/ *a* eclesiástico
echelon /'eʃəlɒn/ *n* escalón *m*
echo /'ekəʊ/ *n* (*pl* **-oes**) eco *m*. ● *vt* (*pt* **echoed**, *pres p* **echoing**) repetir; (*imitate*) imitar. ● *vi* hacer eco
eclectic /ɪk'lektɪk/ *a* & *n* ecléctico (*m*)
eclipse /ɪ'klɪps/ *n* eclipse *m*. ● *vt* eclipsar
ecology /ɪ'kɒlədʒɪ/ *n* ecología *f*
econom|ic /i:kə'nɒmɪk/ *a* económico. **~ical** *a* económico. **~ics** *n* economía *f*. **~ist** /ɪ'kɒnəmɪst/ *n* economista *m* & *f*. **~ize** /ɪ'kɒnəmaɪz/ *vi* economizar. **~y** /ɪ'kɒnəmɪ/ *n* economía *f*
ecsta|sy /'ekstəsɪ/ *n* éxtasis *f*. **~tic** /ɪk'stætɪk/ *a* extático. **~tically** *adv* con éxtasis
Ecuador /'ekwədɔ:(r)/ *n* el Ecuador *m*

ecumenical /i:kju:'menɪkl/ *a* ecuménico

eddy /'edɪ/ *n* remolino *m*

edge /edʒ/ *n* borde *m*, margen *m*; (*of knife*) filo *m*; (*of town*) afueras *fpl*. **have the ~ on** (*fam*) llevar la ventaja a. **on ~** nervioso. ● *vt* ribetear; (*move*) mover poco a poco. ● *vi* avanzar cautelosamente. **~ways** *adv* de lado

edging /'edʒɪŋ/ *n* borde *m*; (*sewing*) ribete *m*

edgy /'edʒɪ/ *a* nervioso

edible /'edɪbl/ *a* comestible

edict /'i:dɪkt/ *n* edicto *m*

edifice /'edɪfɪs/ *n* edificio *m*

edify /'edɪfaɪ/ *vt* edificar

edit /'edɪt/ *vt* dirigir ‹*newspaper*›; preparar una edición de ‹*text*›; (*write*) redactar; montar ‹*film*›. **~ed by** a cargo de. **~ion** /ɪ'dɪʃn/ *n* edición *f*. **~or** /'edɪtə(r)/ *n* (*of newspaper*) director *m*; (*of text*) redactor *m*. **~orial** /edɪ'tɔ:rɪəl/ *a* editorial. ● *n* artículo *m* de fondo. **~or in chief** *n* jefe *m* de redacción

educat|e /'edʒʊkeɪt/ *vt* instruir, educar. **~ed** *a* culto. **~ion** /-'keɪʃn/ *n* enseñanza *f*; (*culture*) cultura *f*; (*upbringing*) educación *f*. **~ional** /-'keɪʃənl/ *a* instructivo

EEC /i:i:'si:/ *abbr* (*European Economic Community*) CEE (Comunidad *f* Económica Europea)

eel /i:l/ *n* anguila *f*

eerie /'ɪərɪ/ *a* (**-ier, -iest**) misterioso

efface /ɪ'feɪs/ *vt* borrar

effect /ɪ'fekt/ *n* efecto *m*. **in ~** efectivamente. **take ~** entrar en vigor. ● *vt* efectuar

effective /ɪ'fektɪv/ *a* eficaz; (*striking*) impresionante; (*mil*) efectivo. **~ly** *adv* eficazmente. **~ness** *n* eficacia *f*

effeminate /ɪ'femɪnət/ *a* afeminado

effervescent /efə'vesnt/ *a* efervescente

effete /ɪ'fi:t/ *a* agotado

efficien|cy /ɪ'fɪʃənsɪ/ *n* eficiencia *f*; (*mec*) rendimiento *m*. **~t** /ɪ'fɪʃnt/ *a* eficiente. **~tly** *adv* eficientemente

effigy /'efɪdʒɪ/ *n* efigie *f*

effort /'efət/ *n* esfuerzo *m*. **~less** *a* fácil

effrontery /ɪ'frʌntərɪ/ *n* descaro *m*

effusive /ɪ'fju:sɪv/ *a* efusivo

e.g. /i:'dʒi:/ *abbr* (*exempli gratia*) p.ej., por ejemplo

egalitarian /ɪgælɪ'teərɪən/ *a & n* igualitario (*m*)

egg[1] /eg/ *n* huevo *m*

egg[2] /eg/ *vt*. **~ on** (*fam*) incitar

egg-cup /'egkʌp/ *n* huevera *f*

egg-plant /'egplɑ:nt/ *n* berenjena *f*

eggshell /'egʃel/ *n* cáscara *f* de huevo

ego /'i:gəʊ/ *n* (*pl* **-os**) yo *m*. **~ism** *n* egoísmo *m*. **~ist** *n* egoísta *m & f*. **~centric** /i:gəʊ'sentrɪk/ *a* egocéntrico. **~tism** *n* egotismo *m*. **~tist** *n* egotista *m & f*

Egypt /'i:dʒɪpt/ *n* Egipto *m*. **~ian** /ɪ'dʒɪpʃn/ *a & n* egipcio (*m*)

eh /eɪ/ *int* (*fam*) ¡eh!

eiderdown /'aɪdədaʊn/ *n* edredón *m*

eight /eɪt/ *a & n* ocho (*m*)

eighteen /eɪ'ti:n/ *a & n* dieciocho (*m*). **~th** *a & n* decimoctavo (*m*)

eighth /eɪtθ/ *a & n* octavo (*m*)

eight|ieth /'eɪtɪəθ/ *a & n* ochenta (*m*), octogésimo (*m*). **~y** /'eɪtɪ/ *a & n* ochenta (*m*)

either /'aɪðə(r)/ *a* cualquiera de los dos; (*negative*) ninguno de los dos; (*each*) cada. ● *pron* uno u otro; (*with negative*) ni uno ni otro. ● *adv* (*negative*) tampoco. ● *conj* o. **~ he or** o él o; (*with negative*) ni él ni

ejaculate /ɪ'dʒækjʊleɪt/ *vt/i* (*exclaim*) exclamar

eject /ɪ'dʒekt/ *vt* expulsar, echar

eke /i:k/ *vt*. **~ out** hacer bastar; (*increase*) complementar

elaborate /ɪ'læbərət/ *a* complicado. /ɪ'læbəreɪt/ *vt* elaborar. ● *vi* explicarse

elapse /ɪ'læps/ *vi* (*of time*) transcurrir

elastic /ɪ'læstɪk/ *a & n* elástico (*m*). **~ band** *n* goma *f* (elástica)

elasticity /ɪlæ'stɪsətɪ/ *n* elasticidad *f*

elat|ed /ɪ'leɪtɪd/ *a* regocijado. **~ion** /-ʃn/ *n* regocijo *m*

elbow /'elbəʊ/ *n* codo *m*

elder[1] /'eldə(r)/ *a & n* mayor (*m*)

elder[2] /'eldə(r)/ *n* (*tree*) saúco *m*

elderly /'eldəlɪ/ *a* mayor, anciano

eldest /'eldɪst/ *a & n* el mayor (*m*)

elect /ɪ'lekt/ *vt* elegir. **~ to do** decidir hacer. ● *a* electo. **~ion** /-ʃn/ *n* elección *f*

elector /ɪ'lektə(r)/ *n* elector *m*. **~al** *a* electoral. **~ate** *n* electorado *m*

electric /ɪ'lektrɪk/ *a* eléctrico. **~al** *a* eléctrico. **~ blanket** *n* manta *f* eléctrica. **~ian** /ɪlek'trɪʃn/ *n* electricista

m & f. **~ity** /ɪlek'trɪsətɪ/ *n* electricidad *f*
electrify /ɪ'lektrɪfaɪ/ *vt* electrificar; (*fig*) electrizar
electrocute /ɪ'lektrəkju:t/ *vt* electrocutar
electrolysis /ɪlek'trɒlɪsɪs/ *n* electrólisis *f*
electron /ɪ'lektrɒn/ *n* electrón *m*
electronic /ɪlek'trɒnɪk/ *a* electrónico. **~s** *n* electrónica *f*
elegan|ce /'elɪgəns/ *n* elegancia *f.* **~t** /'elɪgənt/ *a* elegante. **~tly** *adv* elegantemente
element /'elɪmənt/ *n* elemento *m.* **~ary** /-'mentrɪ/ *a* elemental
elephant /'elɪfənt/ *n* elefante *m*
elevat|e /'elɪveɪt/ *vt* elevar. **~ion** /-'veɪʃn/ *n* elevación *f.* **~or** /'elɪveɪtə(r)/ *n* (*Amer*) ascensor *m*
eleven /ɪ'levn/ *a & n* once (*m*). **~th** *a & n* undécimo (*m*)
elf /elf/ *n* (*pl* **elves**) duende *m*
elicit /ɪ'lɪsɪt/ *vt* sacar
eligible /'elɪdʒəbl/ *a* elegible. **be ~ for** tener derecho a
eliminat|e /ɪ'lɪmɪneɪt/ *vt* eliminar. **~ion** /-'neɪʃn/ *n* eliminación *f*
élite /eɪ'li:t/ *n* elite *f*, élite *m*
elixir /ɪ'lɪksɪə(r)/ *n* elixir *m*
ellip|se /ɪ'lɪps/ *n* elipse *f.* **~tical** *a* elíptico
elm /elm/ *n* olmo *m*
elocution /elə'kju:ʃn/ *n* elocución *f*
elongate /'i:lɒŋgeɪt/ *vt* alargar
elope /ɪ'ləʊp/ *vi* fugarse con el amante. **~ment** *n* fuga *f*
eloquen|ce /'eləkwəns/ *n* elocuencia *f.* **~t** /'eləkwənt/ *a* elocuente. **~tly** *adv* con elocuencia
El Salvador /el'sælvədɔ:(r)/ *n* El Salvador *m*
else /els/ *adv* más. **everybody ~** todos los demás. **nobody ~** ningún otro, nadie más. **nothing ~** nada más. **or ~** o bien. **somewhere ~** en otra parte
elsewhere /els'weə(r)/ *adv* en otra parte
elucidate /ɪ'lu:sɪdeɪt/ *vt* aclarar
elude /ɪ'lu:d/ *vt* eludir
elusive /ɪ'lu:sɪv/ *a* esquivo
emaciated /ɪ'meɪʃɪeɪtɪd/ *a* esquelético
emanate /'eməneɪt/ *vi* emanar
emancipat|e /ɪ'mænsɪpeɪt/ *vt* emancipar. **~ion** /-'peɪʃn/ *n* emancipación *f*
embalm /ɪm'bɑ:m/ *vt* embalsamar
embankment /ɪm'bæŋkmənt/ *n* terraplén *m*; (*of river*) dique *m*
embargo /ɪm'bɑ:gəʊ/ *n* (*pl* **-oes**) prohibición *f*
embark /ɪm'bɑ:k/ *vt* embarcar. ● *vi* embarcarse. **~ on** (*fig*) emprender. **~ation** /embɑ:'keɪʃn/ *n* (*of people*) embarco *m*; (*of goods*) embarque *m*
embarrass /ɪm'bærəs/ *vt* desconcertar; (*shame*) dar vergüenza. **~ment** *n* desconcierto *m*; (*shame*) vergüenza *f*
embassy /'embəsɪ/ *n* embajada *f*
embed /ɪm'bed/ *vt* (*pt* **embedded**) embutir; (*fig*) fijar
embellish /ɪm'belɪʃ/ *vt* embellecer. **~ment** *n* embellecimiento *m*
embers /'embəz/ *npl* ascua *f*
embezzle /ɪm'bezl/ *vt* desfalcar. **~ment** *n* desfalco *m*
embitter /ɪm'bɪtə(r)/ *vt* amargar
emblem /'embləm/ *n* emblema *m*
embod|iment /ɪm'bɒdɪmənt/ *n* encarnación *f.* **~y** /ɪm'bɒdɪ/ *vt* encarnar; (*include*) incluir
emboss /ɪm'bɒs/ *vt* grabar en relieve, repujar. **~ed** *a* en relieve, repujado
embrace /ɪm'breɪs/ *vt* abrazar; (*fig*) abarcar. ● *vi* abrazarse. ● *n* abrazo *m*
embroider /ɪm'brɔɪdə(r)/ *vt* bordar. **~y** *n* bordado *m*
embroil /ɪm'brɔɪl/ *vt* enredar
embryo /'embrɪəʊ/ *n* (*pl* **-os**) embrión *m.* **~nic** /-'ɒnɪk/ *a* embrionario
emend /ɪ'mend/ *vt* enmendar
emerald /'emərəld/ *n* esmeralda *f*
emerge /ɪ'mɜ:dʒ/ *vi* salir. **~nce** /-əns/ *n* aparición *f*
emergency /ɪ'mɜ:dʒənsɪ/ *n* emergencia *f.* **in an ~** en caso de emergencia. **~ exit** *n* salida *f* de emergencia
emery /'emərɪ/ *n* esmeril *m.* **~-board** *n* lima *f* de uñas
emigrant /'emɪgrənt/ *n* emigrante *m & f*
emigrat|e /'emɪgreɪt/ *vi* emigrar. **~ion** /-'greɪʃn/ *n* emigración *f*
eminen|ce /'emɪnəns/ *n* eminencia *f.* **~t** /'emɪnənt/ *a* eminente. **~tly** *adv* eminentemente
emissary /'emɪsərɪ/ *n* emisario *m*
emission /ɪ'mɪʃn/ *n* emisión *f*
emit /ɪ'mɪt/ *vt* (*pt* **emitted**) emitir
emollient /ɪ'mɒlɪənt/ *a & n* emoliente (*m*)

emoti|on /ɪ'məʊʃn/ *n* emoción *f*. **~onal** *a* emocional; ‹*person*› emotivo; (*moving*) conmovedor. **~ve** /ɪ'məʊtɪv/ *a* emotivo

empathy /'empəθɪ/ *n* empatía *f*

emperor /'empərə(r)/ *n* emperador *m*

emphasi|s /'emfəsɪs/ *n* (*pl* **~ses** /-si:z/) énfasis *m*. **~ze** /'emfəsaɪz/ *vt* subrayar; (*single out*) destacar

emphatic /ɪm'fætɪk/ *a* categórico; (*resolute*) decidido

empire /'empaɪə(r)/ *n* imperio *m*

empirical /ɪm'pɪrɪkl/ *a* empírico

employ /ɪm'plɔɪ/ *vt* emplear. **~ee** /emplɔɪ'i:/ *n* empleado *m*. **~er** *n* patrón *m*. **~ment** *n* empleo *m*. **~ment agency** *n* agencia *f* de colocaciones

empower /ɪm'paʊə(r)/ *vt* autorizar (**to do** a hacer)

empress /'emprɪs/ *n* emperatriz *f*

empt|ies /'emptɪz/ *npl* envases *mpl*. **~iness** *n* vacío *m*. **~y** /'emptɪ/ *a* vacío; ‹*promise*› vano. **on an ~y stomach** con el estómago vacío. ● *vt* vaciar. ● *vi* vaciarse

emulate /'emjʊleɪt/ *vt* emular

emulsion /ɪ'mʌlʃn/ *n* emulsión *f*

enable /ɪ'neɪbl/ *vt*. **~ s.o. to** permitir a uno

enact /ɪ'nækt/ *vt* (*jurid*) decretar; (*in theatre*) representar

enamel /ɪ'næml/ *n* esmalte *m*. ● *vt* (*pt* **enamelled**) esmaltar

enamoured /ɪ'næməd/ *a*. **be ~ of** estar enamorado de

encampment /ɪn'kæmpmənt/ *n* campamento *m*

encase /ɪn'keɪs/ *vt* encerrar

enchant /ɪn'tʃɑ:nt/ *vt* encantar. **~ing** *a* encantador. **~ment** *n* encanto *m*

encircle /ɪn'sɜ:kl/ *vt* rodear

enclave /'enkleɪv/ *n* enclave *m*

enclos|e /ɪn'kləʊz/ *vt* cercar ‹*land*›; (*with letter*) adjuntar; (*in receptacle*) encerrar. **~ed** *a* ‹*space*› encerrado; (*com*) adjunto. **~ure** /ɪn'kləʊʒə(r)/ *n* cercamiento *m*; (*area*) recinto *m*; (*com*) documento *m* adjunto

encompass /ɪn'kʌmpəs/ *vt* cercar; (*include*) incluir, abarcar

encore /'ɒŋkɔ:(r)/ *int* ¡bis! ● *n* bis *m*, repetición *f*

encounter /ɪn'kaʊntə(r)/ *vt* encontrar. ● *n* encuentro *m*

encourage /ɪn'kʌrɪdʒ/ *vt* animar; (*stimulate*) estimular. **~ment** *n* estímulo *m*

encroach /ɪn'krəʊtʃ/ *vi*. **~ on** invadir ‹*land*›; quitar ‹*time*›. **~ment** *n* usurpación *f*

encumb|er /ɪn'kʌmbə(r)/ *vt* (*hamper*) estorbar; (*burden*) cargar. **be ~ered with** estar cargado de. **~rance** *n* estorbo *m*; (*burden*) carga *f*

encyclical /ɪn'sɪklɪkl/ *n* encíclica *f*

encyclopaedi|a /ɪnsaɪklə'pi:dɪə/ *n* enciclopedia *f*. **~c** *a* enciclopédico

end /end/ *n* fin *m*; (*furthest point*) extremo *m*. **in the ~** por fin. **make ~s meet** poder llegar a fin de mes. **no ~** (*fam*) muy. **no ~ of** muchísimos. **on ~** de pie; (*consecutive*) seguido. ● *vt/i* terminar, acabar

endanger /ɪn'deɪndʒə(r)/ *vt* arriesgar

endear|ing /ɪn'dɪərɪŋ/ *a* simpático. **~ment** *n* palabra *f* cariñosa

endeavour /ɪn'devə(r)/ *n* tentativa *f*. ● *vi*. **~ to** esforzarse por

ending /'endɪŋ/ *n* fin *m*

endive /'endɪv/ *n* escarola *f*, endibia *f*

endless /'endlɪs/ *a* interminable; ‹*patience*› infinito

endorse /ɪn'dɔ:s/ *vt* endosar; (*fig*) aprobar. **~ment** *n* endoso *m*; (*fig*) aprobación *f*; (*auto*) nota *f* de inhabilitación

endow /ɪn'daʊ/ *vt* dotar

endur|able /ɪn'djʊərəbl/ *a* aguantable. **~ance** *n* resistencia *f*. **~e** /ɪn'djʊə(r)/ *vt* aguantar. ● *vi* durar. **~ing** *a* perdurable

enemy /'enəmɪ/ *n & a* enemigo (*m*)

energ|etic /enə'dʒetɪk/ *a* enérgico. **~y** /'enədʒɪ/ *n* energía *f*

enervat|e /'enə:veɪt/ *vt* debilitar. **~ing** *a* debilitante

enfold /ɪn'fəʊld/ *vt* envolver; (*in arms*) abrazar

enforce /ɪn'fɔ:s/ *vt* aplicar; (*impose*) imponer; hacer cumplir ‹*law*›. **~d** *a* forzado

engage /ɪn'geɪdʒ/ *vt* emplear ‹*staff*›; (*reserve*) reservar; ocupar ‹*attention*›; (*mec*) hacer engranar. ● *vi* (*mec*) engranar. **~d** *a* prometido; (*busy*) ocupado. **get ~d** prometerse. **~ment** *n* compromiso *m*; (*undertaking*) obligación *f*

engaging /ɪn'geɪdʒɪŋ/ *a* atractivo

engender /ɪn'dʒendə(r)/ *vt* engendrar

engine /'endʒɪn/ *n* motor *m*; (*of train*) locomotora *f*. **~-driver** *n* maquinista *m*

engineer /endʒɪ'nɪə(r)/ *n* ingeniero *m*; (*mechanic*) mecánico *m*. • *vt* (*contrive, fam*) lograr. **~ing** *n* ingeniería *f*

England /'ɪŋglənd/ *n* Inglaterra *f*

English /'ɪŋglɪʃ/ *a* inglés. • *n* (*lang*) inglés *m*; (*people*) ingleses *mpl*. **~man** *n* inglés *m*. **~woman** *n* inglesa *f*. **the ~ Channel** *n* el canal *m* de la Mancha

engrav|e /ɪn'greɪv/ *vt* grabar. **~ing** *n* grabado *m*

engrossed /ɪn'grəʊst/ *a* absorto

engulf /ɪn'gʌlf/ *vt* tragar(se)

enhance /ɪn'hɑ:ns/ *vt* aumentar

enigma /ɪ'nɪgmə/ *n* enigma *m*. **~tic** /enɪg'mætɪk/ *a* enigmático

enjoy /ɪn'dʒɔɪ/ *vt* gozar de. **~ o.s.** divertirse. **I ~ reading** me gusta la lectura. **~able** *a* agradable. **~ment** *n* placer *m*

enlarge /ɪn'lɑ:dʒ/ *vt* agrandar; (*foto*) ampliar. • *vi* agrandarse. **~ upon** extenderse sobre. **~ment** *n* (*foto*) ampliación *f*

enlighten /ɪn'laɪtn/ *vt* aclarar; (*inform*) informar. **~ment** *n* aclaración *f*. **the E~ment** el siglo *m* de la luces

enlist /ɪn'lɪst/ *vt* alistar; (*fig*) conseguir. • *vi* alistarse

enliven /ɪn'laɪvn/ *vt* animar

enmity /'enmətɪ/ *n* enemistad *f*

ennoble /ɪ'nəʊbl/ *vt* ennoblecer

enorm|ity /ɪ'nɔ:mətɪ/ *n* enormidad *f*. **~ous** /ɪ'nɔ:məs/ *a* enorme

enough /ɪ'nʌf/ *a & adv* bastante. • *n* bastante *m*, suficiente *m*. • *int* ¡basta!

enquir|e /ɪn'kwaɪə(r)/ *vt/i* preguntar. **~e about** informarse de. **~y** *n* pregunta *f*; (*investigation*) investigación *f*

enrage /ɪn'reɪdʒ/ *vt* enfurecer

enrapture /ɪn'ræptʃə(r)/ *vt* extasiar

enrich /ɪn'rɪtʃ/ *vt* enriquecer

enrol /ɪn'rəʊl/ *vt* (*pt* **enrolled**) inscribir; matricular ‹*student*›. • *vi* inscribirse; ‹*student*› matricularse. **~ment** *n* inscripción *f*; (*of student*) matrícula *f*

ensconce /ɪn'skɒns/ *vt*. **~ o.s.** arrellanarse

ensemble /ɒn'sɒmbl/ *n* conjunto *m*

enshrine /ɪn'ʃraɪn/ *vt* encerrar

ensign /'ensaɪn/ *n* enseña *f*

enslave /ɪn'sleɪv/ *vt* esclavizar

ensue /ɪn'sju:/ *vi* resultar, seguirse

ensure /ɪn'ʃʊə(r)/ *vt* asegurar

entail /ɪn'teɪl/ *vt* suponer; acarrear ‹*trouble etc*›

entangle /ɪn'tæŋgl/ *vt* enredar. **~ment** *n* enredo *m*; (*mil*) alambrada *f*

enter /'entə(r)/ *vt* entrar en; (*write*) escribir; matricular ‹*school etc*›; hacerse socio de ‹*club*›. • *vi* entrar

enterprise /'entəpraɪz/ *n* empresa *f*; (*fig*) iniciativa *f*

enterprising /'entəpraɪzɪŋ/ *a* emprendedor

entertain /entə'teɪn/ *vt* divertir; recibir ‹*guests*›; abrigar ‹*ideas, hopes*›; (*consider*) considerar. **~ment** *n* diversión *f*; (*performance*) espectáculo *m*; (*reception*) recepción *f*

enthral /ɪn'θrɔ:l/ *vt* (*pt* **enthralled**) cautivar

enthuse /ɪn'θju:z/ *vi*. **~ over** entusiasmarse por

enthusias|m /ɪn'θju:zɪæzəm/ *n* entusiasmo *m*. **~tic** /-'æstɪk/ *a* entusiasta; ‹*thing*› entusiástico. **~tically** /-'æstɪklɪ/ *adv* con entusiasmo. **~t** /ɪn'θju:zɪæst/ *n* entusiasta *m & f*

entice /ɪn'taɪs/ *vt* atraer. **~ment** *n* atracción *f*

entire /ɪn'taɪə(r)/ *a* entero. **~ly** *adv* completamente. **~ty** /ɪn'taɪərətɪ/ *n*. **in its ~ty** en su totalidad

entitle /ɪn'taɪtl/ *vt* titular; (*give a right*) dar derecho a. **be ~d to** tener derecho a. **~ment** *n* derecho *m*

entity /'entətɪ/ *n* entidad *f*

entomb /ɪn'tu:m/ *vt* sepultar

entrails /'entreɪlz/ *npl* entrañas *fpl*

entrance[1] /'entrəns/ *n* entrada *f*; (*right to enter*) admisión *f*

entrance[2] /ɪn'trɑ:ns/ *vt* encantar

entrant /'entrənt/ *n* participante *m & f*; (*in exam*) candidato *m*

entreat /ɪn'tri:t/ *vt* suplicar. **~y** *n* súplica *f*

entrench /ɪn'trentʃ/ *vt* atrincherar

entrust /ɪn'trʌst/ *vt* confiar

entry /'entrɪ/ *n* entrada *f*; (*of street*) bocacalle *f*; (*note*) apunte *m*

entwine /ɪn'twaɪn/ *vt* entrelazar

enumerate /ɪ'nju:məreɪt/ *vt* enumerar

enunciate /ɪ'nʌnsɪeɪt/ *vt* pronunciar; (*state*) enunciar

envelop /ɪn'veləp/ *vt* (*pt* **enveloped**) envolver

envelope /'envələʊp/ *n* sobre *m*

enviable /'envɪəbl/ *a* envidiable

envious /'envɪəs/ *a* envidioso. **~ly** *adv* con envidia

environment /ɪn'vaɪərənmənt/ *n* medio *m* ambiente. **~al** /-'mentl/ *a* ambiental

envisage /ɪn'vɪzɪdʒ/ *vt* prever; (*imagine*) imaginar

envoy /'envɔɪ/ *n* enviado *m*

envy /'envɪ/ *n* envidia *f*. ● *vt* envidiar

enzyme /'enzaɪm/ *n* enzima *f*

epaulette /'epəʊlet/ *n* charretera *f*

ephemeral /ɪ'femərəl/ *a* efímero

epic /'epɪk/ *n* épica *f*. ● *a* épico

epicentre /'epɪsentə(r)/ *n* epicentro *m*

epicure /'epɪkjʊə(r)/ *n* sibarita *m* & *f*; (*gourmet*) gastrónomo *m*

epidemic /epɪ'demɪk/ *n* epidemia *f*. ● *a* epidémico

epilep|sy /'epɪlepsɪ/ *n* epilepsia *f*. **~tic** /-'leptɪk/ *a* & *n* epiléptico (*m*)

epilogue /'epɪlɒg/ *n* epílogo *m*

episode /'epɪsəʊd/ *n* episodio *m*

epistle /ɪ'pɪsl/ *n* epístola *f*

epitaph /'epɪtɑ:f/ *n* epitafio *m*

epithet /'epɪθet/ *n* epíteto *m*

epitom|e /ɪ'pɪtəmɪ/ *n* epítome *m*, personificación *f*. **~ize** *vt* epitomar, personificar, ser la personificación de

epoch /'i:pɒk/ *n* época *f*. **~-making** *a* que hace época

equal /'i:kwəl/ *a* & *n* igual (*m* & *f*). **~ to** (*a task*) a la altura de. ● *vt* (*pt* **equalled**) ser igual a; (*math*) ser. **~ity** /ɪ'kwɒlətɪ/ *n* igualdad *f*. **~ize** /'i:kwəlaɪz/ *vt*/*i* igualar. **~izer** /-ə(r)/ *n* (*sport*) tanto *m* de empate. **~ly** *adv* igualmente

equanimity /ekwə'nɪmətɪ/ *n* ecuanimidad *f*

equate /ɪ'kweɪt/ *vt* igualar

equation /ɪ'kweɪʒn/ *n* ecuación *f*

equator /ɪ'kweɪtə(r)/ *n* ecuador *m*. **~ial** /ekwə'tɔ:rɪəl/ *a* ecuatorial

equestrian /ɪ'kwestrɪən/ *a* ecuestre

equilateral /i:kwɪ'lætərl/ *a* equilátero

equilibrium /i:kwɪ'lɪbrɪəm/ *n* equilibrio *m*

equinox /'i:kwɪnɒks/ *n* equinoccio *m*

equip /ɪ'kwɪp/ *vt* (*pt* **equipped**) equipar. **~ment** *n* equipo *m*

equitable /'ekwɪtəbl/ *a* equitativo

equity /'ekwətɪ/ *n* equidad *f*; (*pl*, *com*) acciones *fpl* ordinarias

equivalen|ce /ɪ'kwɪvələns/ *n* equivalencia *f*. **~t** /ɪ'kwɪvələnt/ *a* & *n* equivalente (*m*)

equivocal /ɪ'kwɪvəkl/ *a* equívoco

era /'ɪərə/ *n* era *f*

eradicate /ɪ'rædɪkeɪt/ *vt* extirpar

erase /ɪ'reɪz/ *vt* borrar. **~r** /-ə(r)/ *n* borrador *m*

erect /ɪ'rekt/ *a* erguido. ● *vt* levantar. **~ion** /-ʃn/ *n* erección *f*, montaje *m*

ermine /'з:mɪn/ *n* armiño *m*

ero|de /ɪ'rəʊd/ *vt* desgastar. **~sion** /-ʒn/ *n* desgaste *m*

erotic /ɪ'rɒtɪk/ *a* erótico. **~ism** /-sɪzəm/ *n* erotismo *m*

err /з:(r)/ *vi* errar; (*sin*) pecar

errand /'erənd/ *n* recado *m*

erratic /ɪ'rætɪk/ *a* irregular; ‹*person*› voluble

erroneous /ɪ'rəʊnɪəs/ *a* erróneo

error /'erə(r)/ *n* error *m*

erudit|e /'eru:daɪt/ *a* erudito. **~ion** /-'dɪʃn/ *n* erudición *f*

erupt /ɪ'rʌpt/ *vi* estar en erupción; (*fig*) estallar. **~ion** /-ʃn/ *n* erupción *f*

escalat|e /'eskəleɪt/ *vt* intensificar. ● *vi* intensificarse. **~ion** /-'leɪʃn/ *n* intensificación *f*

escalator /'eskəleɪtə(r)/ *n* escalera *f* mecánica

escapade /eskə'peɪd/ *n* aventura *f*

escap|e /ɪ'skeɪp/ *vi* escaparse. ● *vt* evitar. ● *n* fuga *f*; (*avoidance*) evasión *f*. **have a narrow ~e** escapar por un pelo. **~ism** /ɪ'skeɪpɪzəm/ *n* escapismo *m*

escarpment /ɪs'kɑ:pmənt/ *n* escarpa *f*

escort /'eskɔ:t/ *n* acompañante *m*; (*mil*) escolta *f*. /ɪ'skɔ:t/ *vt* acompañar; (*mil*) escoltar

Eskimo /'eskɪməʊ/ *n* (*pl* **-os, -o**) esquimal (*m* & *f*)

especial /ɪ'speʃl/ *a* especial. **~ly** *adv* especialmente

espionage /'espɪənɑ:ʒ/ *n* espionaje *m*

esplanade /esplə'neɪd/ *n* paseo *m* marítimo

Esq. /ɪ'skwaɪə(r)/ *abbr* (*Esquire*) (*in address*). **E. Ashton, ~** Sr. D. E. Ashton

essay /'eseɪ/ *n* ensayo *m*; (*at school*) composición *f*

essence /'esns/ *n* esencia *f*. **in ~** esencialmente

essential /ɪ'senʃl/ *a* esencial. ● *n* lo esencial. **~ly** *adv* esencialmente

establish /ɪ'stæblɪʃ/ *vt* establecer; (*prove*) probar. **~ment** *n* establecimiento *m*. **the E~ment** los que mandan, el sistema *m*
estate /ɪ'steɪt/ *n* finca *f*; (*possessions*) bienes *mpl*. **~ agent** *n* agente *m* inmobiliario. **~ car** *n* furgoneta *f*
esteem /ɪ'sti:m/ *vt* estimar. ● *n* estimación *f*, estima *f*
estimat|e /'estɪmət/ *n* cálculo *m*; (*com*) presupuesto *m*. /'estɪmeɪt/ *vt* calcular. **~ion** /-'meɪʃn/ *n* estima *f*, estimación *f*; (*opinion*) opinión *f*
estranged /ɪs'treɪndʒd/ *a* alejado
estuary /'estʃʊərɪ/ *n* estuario *m*
etc. /et'setrə/ *abbr* (*et cetera*) etc., etcétera
etching /'etʃɪŋ/ *n* aguafuerte *m*
eternal /ɪ'tɜ:nl/ *a* eterno
eternity /ɪ'tɜ:nətɪ/ *n* eternidad *f*
ether /'i:θə(r)/ *n* éter *m*
ethereal /ɪ'θɪərɪəl/ *a* etéreo
ethic /'eθɪk/ *n* ética *f*. **~s** *npl* ética *f*. **~al** *a* ético
ethnic /'eθnɪk/ *a* étnico
ethos /'i:θɒs/ *n* carácter *m* distintivo
etiquette /'etɪket/ *n* etiqueta *f*
etymology /etɪ'mɒlədʒɪ/ *n* etimología *f*
eucalyptus /ju:kə'lɪptəs/ *n* (*pl* **-tuses**) eucalipto *m*
eulogy /'ju:lədʒɪ/ *n* encomio *m*
euphemism /'ju:fəmɪzəm/ *n* eufemismo *m*
euphoria /ju:'fɔ:rɪə/ *n* euforia *f*
Europe /'jʊərəp/ *n* Europa *f*. **~an** /-'pɪən/ *a* & *n* europeo (*m*)
euthanasia /ju:θə'neɪzɪə/ *n* eutanasia *f*
evacuat|e /ɪ'vækjʊeɪt/ *vt* evacuar; desocupar ‹*building*›. **~ion** /-'eɪʃn/ *n* evacuación *f*
evade /ɪ'veɪd/ *vt* evadir
evaluate /ɪ'væljʊeɪt/ *vt* evaluar
evangeli|cal /i:væn'dʒelɪkl/ *a* evangélico. **~st** /ɪ'vændʒəlɪst/ *n* evangelista *m & f*
evaporat|e /ɪ'væpəreɪt/ *vi* evaporarse. **~ion** /-'reɪʃn/ *n* evaporación *f*
evasion /ɪ'veɪʒn/ *n* evasión *f*
evasive /ɪ'veɪsɪv/ *a* evasivo
eve /i:v/ *n* víspera *f*
even /'i:vn/ *a* regular; (*flat*) llano; ‹*surface*› liso; ‹*amount*› igual; ‹*number*› par. **get ~ with** desquitarse con. ● *vt* nivelar. **~ up** igualar. ● *adv* aun, hasta, incluso. **~ if** aunque. **~ so** aun así. **not ~** ni siquiera
evening /'i:vnɪŋ/ *n* tarde *f*; (*after dark*) noche *f*. **~ class** *n* clase *f* nocturna. **~ dress** *n* (*man's*) traje *m* de etiqueta; (*woman's*) traje *m* de noche
evensong /'i:vənsɒŋ/ *n* vísperas *fpl*
event /ɪ'vent/ *n* acontecimiento *m*; (*sport*) prueba *f*. **in the ~ of** en caso de. **~ful** *a* lleno de acontecimientos
eventual /ɪ'ventʃʊəl/ *a* final, definitivo. **~ity** /-'ælətɪ/ *n* eventualidad *f*. **~ly** *adv* finalmente
ever /'evə(r)/ *adv* jamás, nunca; (*at all times*) siempre. **~ after** desde entonces. **~ since** desde entonces. ● *conj* después de que. **~ so** (*fam*) muy. **for ~** para siempre. **hardly ~** casi nunca
evergreen /'evəgri:n/ *a* de hoja perenne. ● *n* árbol *m* de hoja perenne
everlasting /'evəlɑ:stɪŋ/ *a* eterno
every /'evrɪ/ *a* cada, todo. **~ child** todos los niños. **~ one** cada uno. **~ other day** cada dos días
everybody /'evrɪbɒdɪ/ *pron* todo el mundo
everyday /'evrɪdeɪ/ *a* todos los días
everyone /'evrɪwʌn/ *pron* todo el mundo. **~ else** todos los demás
everything /'evrɪθɪŋ/ *pron* todo
everywhere /'evrɪweə(r)/ *adv* en todas partes
evict /ɪ'vɪkt/ *vt* desahuciar. **~ion** /-ʃn/ *n* desahucio *m*
eviden|ce /'evɪdəns/ *n* evidencia *f*; (*proof*) pruebas *fpl*; (*jurid*) testimonio *m*. **~ce of** señales de. **in ~ce** visible. **~t** /'evɪdənt/ *a* evidente. **~tly** *adv* evidentemente
evil /'i:vl/ *a* malo. ● *n* mal *m*, maldad *f*
evocative /ɪ'vɒkətɪv/ *a* evocador
evoke /ɪ'vəʊk/ *vt* evocar
evolution /i:və'lu:ʃn/ *n* evolución *f*
evolve /ɪ'vɒlv/ *vt* desarrollar. ● *vi* desarrollarse, evolucionar
ewe /ju:/ *n* oveja *f*
ex... /eks/ *pref* ex...
exacerbate /ɪg'zæsəbeɪt/ *vt* exacerbar
exact /ɪg'zækt/ *a* exacto. ● *vt* exigir (**from** a). **~ing** *a* exigente. **~itude** *n* exactitud *f*. **~ly** *adv* exactamente
exaggerat|e /ɪg'zædʒəreɪt/ *vt* exagerar. **~ion** /-'reɪʃn/ *n* exageración *f*
exalt /ɪg'zɔ:lt/ *vt* exaltar

exam /ɪg'zæm/ *n* (*fam*) examen *m*. **~ination** /ɪgzæmɪ'neɪʃn/ *n* examen *m*. **~ine** /ɪg'zæmɪn/ *vt* examinar; interrogar ‹*witness*›. **~iner** /-ə(r)/ *n* examinador *m*

example /ɪg'zɑ:mpl/ *n* ejemplo *m*. **make an ~ of** infligir castigo ejemplar a

exasperat|e /ɪg'zæspəreɪt/ *vt* exasperar. **~ion** /-'reɪʃn/ *n* exasperación *f*

excavat|e /'ekskəveɪt/ *vt* excavar. **~ion** /-'veɪʃn/ *n* excavación *f*

exceed /ɪk'si:d/ *vt* exceder. **~ingly** *adv* extremadamente

excel /ɪk'sel/ *vi* (*pt* **excelled**) sobresalir. ● *vt* superar

excellen|ce /'eksələns/ *n* excelencia *f*. **~t** /'eksələnt/ *a* excelente. **~tly** *adv* excelentemente

except /ɪk'sept/ *prep* excepto, con excepción de. **~ for** con excepción de. ● *vt* exceptuar. **~ing** *prep* con excepción de

exception /ɪk'sepʃən/ *n* excepción *f*. **take ~ to** ofenderse por. **~al** /ɪk'sepʃənl/ *a* excepcional. **~ally** *adv* excepcionalmente

excerpt /'eksɜ:pt/ *n* extracto *m*

excess /ɪk'ses/ *n* exceso *m*. /'ekses/ *a* excedente. **~ fare** *n* suplemento *m*. **~ luggage** *n* exceso *m* de equipaje

excessive /ɪk'sesɪv/ *a* excesivo. **~ly** *adv* excesivamente

exchange /ɪk'stʃeɪndʒ/ *vt* cambiar. ● *n* cambio *m*. **(telephone) ~** central *f* telefónica

exchequer /ɪks'tʃekə(r)/ *n* (*pol*) erario *m*, hacienda *f*

excise[1] /'eksaɪz/ *n* impuestos *mpl* indirectos

excise[2] /ek'saɪz/ *vt* quitar

excit|able /ɪk'saɪtəbl/ *a* excitable. **~e** /ɪk'saɪt/ *vt* emocionar; (*stimulate*) excitar. **~ed** *a* entusiasmado. **~ement** *n* emoción *f*; (*enthusiasm*) entusiasmo *m*. **~ing** *a* emocionante

excla|im /ɪk'skleɪm/ *vi* exclamar. **~mation** /ekskləˈmeɪʃn/ *n* exclamación *f*. **~mation mark** *n* signo *m* de admiración *f*, punto *m* de exclamación

exclu|de /ɪk'sklu:d/ *vt* excluir. **~sion** /-ʒən/ *n* exclusión *f*

exclusive /ɪk'sklu:sɪv/ *a* exclusivo; ‹*club*› selecto. **~ of** excluyendo. **~ly** *adv* exclusivamente

excomunicate /ekskə'mju:nɪkeɪt/ *vt* excomulgar

excrement /'ekskrɪmənt/ *n* excremento *m*

excruciating /ɪk'skru:ʃɪeɪtɪŋ/ *a* atroz, insoportable

excursion /ɪk'skɜ:ʃn/ *n* excursión *f*

excus|able *a* /ɪk'skju:zəbl/ *a* perdonable. **~e** /ɪk'skju:z/ *vt* perdonar. **~e from** dispensar de. **~e me!** ¡perdón! /ɪk'skju:s/ *n* excusa *f*

ex-directory /eksdɪ'rektərɪ/ *a* que no está en la guía telefónica

execrable /'eksɪkrəbl/ *a* execrable

execut|e /'eksɪkju:t/ *vt* ejecutar. **~ion** /eksɪ'kju:ʃn/ *n* ejecución *f*. **~ioner** *n* verdugo *m*

executive /ɪg'zekjʊtɪv/ *a & n* ejecutivo (*m*)

executor /ɪg'zekjʊtə(r)/ *n* (*jurid*) testamentario *m*

exemplary /ɪg'zemplərɪ/ *a* ejemplar

exemplify /ɪg'zemplɪfaɪ/ *vt* ilustrar

exempt /ɪg'zempt/ *a* exento. ● *vt* dispensar. **~ion** /-ʃn/ *n* exención *f*

exercise /'eksəsaɪz/ *n* ejercicio *m*. ● *vt* ejercer. ● *vi* hacer ejercicios. **~ book** *n* cuaderno *m*

exert /ɪg'zɜ:t/ *vt* ejercer. **~ o.s.** esforzarse. **~ion** /-ʃn/ *n* esfuerzo *m*

exhal|ation /ekshə'leɪʃn/ *n* exhalación *f*. **~e** /eks'heɪl/ *vt/i* exhalar

exhaust /ɪg'zɔ:st/ *vt* agotar. ● *n* (*auto*) tubo *m* de escape. **~ed** *a* agotado. **~ion** /-stʃən/ *n* agotamiento *m*. **~ive** /ɪg'zɔ:stɪv/ *a* exhaustivo

exhibit /ɪg'zɪbɪt/ *vt* exponer; (*jurid*) exhibir; (*fig*) mostrar. ● *n* objeto *m* expuesto; (*jurid*) documento *m*

exhibition /eksɪ'bɪʃn/ *n* exposición *f*; (*act of showing*) demostración *f*; (*univ*) beca *f*. **~ist** *n* exhibicionista *m & f*

exhibitor /ɪg'zɪbɪtə(r)/ *n* expositor *m*

exhilarat|e /ɪg'zɪləreɪt/ *vt* alegrar. **~ion** /-'reɪʃn/ *n* regocijo *m*

exhort /ɪg'zɔ:t/ *vt* exhortar

exile /'eksaɪl/ *n* exilio *m*; (*person*) exiliado *m*. ● *vt* desterrar

exist /ɪg'zɪst/ *vi* existir. **~ence** *n* existencia *f*. **in ~ence** existente

existentialism /egzɪs'tenʃəlɪzəm/ *n* existencialismo *m*

exit /'eksɪt/ *n* salida *f*

exodus /'eksədəs/ *n* éxodo *m*

exonerate /ɪg'zɒnəreɪt/ *vt* disculpar

exorbitant /ɪg'zɔ:bɪtənt/ *a* exorbitante

exorcis|e /'eksɔ:saɪz/ *vt* exorcizar. **~m** /-sɪzəm/ *n* exorcismo *m*
exotic /ɪg'zɒtɪk/ *a* exótico
expand /ɪk'spænd/ *vt* extender; dilatar ‹*metal*›; (*develop*) desarrollar. ● *vi* extenderse; (*develop*) desarrollarse; ‹*metal*› dilatarse
expanse /ɪk'spæns/ *n* extensión *f*
expansion /ɪk'spænʃn/ *n* extensión *f*; (*of metal*) dilatación *f*
expansive /ɪk'spænsɪv/ *a* expansivo
expatriate /eks'pætrɪət/ *a* & *n* expatriado (*m*)
expect /ɪk'spekt/ *vt* esperar; (*suppose*) suponer; (*demand*) contar con. **I ~ so** supongo que sí
expectan|cy /ɪk'spektənsɪ/ *n* esperanza *f*. **life ~cy** esperanza *f* de vida. **~t** /ɪk'spektənt/ *a* expectante. **~t mother** *n* futura madre *f*
expectation /ekspek'teɪʃn/ *n* esperanza *f*
expedien|cy /ɪk'spi:dɪənsɪ/ *n* conveniencia *f*. **~t** /ɪk'spi:dɪənt/ *a* conveniente
expedite /'ekspɪdaɪt/ *vt* acelerar
expedition /ekspɪ'dɪʃn/ *n* expedición *f*. **~ary** *a* expedicionario
expel /ɪk'spel/ *vt* (*pt* **expelled**) expulsar
expend /ɪk'spend/ *vt* gastar. **~able** *a* prescindible
expenditure /ɪk'spendɪtʃə(r)/ *n* gastos *mpl*
expens|e /ɪk'spens/ *n* gasto *m*; (*fig*) costa *f*. **at s.o.'s ~e** a costa de uno. **~ive** /ɪk'spensɪv/ *a* caro. **~ively** *adv* costosamente
experience /ɪk'spɪərɪəns/ *n* experiencia. ● *vt* experimentar. **~d** *a* experto
experiment /ɪk'sperɪmənt/ *n* experimento *m*. ● *vi* experimentar. **~al** /-'mentl/ *a* experimental
expert /'ekspɜ:t/ *a* & *n* experto (*m*). **~ise** /ekspɜ:'ti:z/ *n* pericia *f*. **~ly** *adv* hábilmente
expir|e /ɪk'spaɪə(r)/ *vi* expirar. **~y** *n* expiración *f*
expla|in /ɪk'spleɪn/ *vt* explicar. **~nation** /eksplə'neɪʃn/ *n* explicación *f*. **~natory** /ɪks'plænətərɪ/ *a* explicativo
expletive /ɪk'spli:tɪv/ *n* palabrota *f*
explicit /ɪk'splɪsɪt/ *a* explícito
explode /ɪk'spləʊd/ *vt* hacer explotar; (*tec*) explosionar. ● *vi* estallar
exploit /'eksplɔɪt/ *n* hazaña *f*. /ɪk'splɔɪt/ *vt* explotar. **~ation** /eksplɔɪ'teɪʃn/ *n* explotación *f*
explor|ation /eksplə'reɪʃn/ *n* exploración *f*. **~atory** /ɪk'splɒrətrɪ/ *a* exploratorio. **~e** /ɪk'splɔ:(r)/ *vt* explorar. **~er** *n* explorador *m*
explosi|on /ɪk'spləʊʒn/ *n* explosión *f*. **~ve** *a* & *n* explosivo (*m*)
exponent /ɪk'spəʊnənt/ *n* exponente *m*
export /ɪk'spɔ:t/ *vt* exportar. /'ekspɔ:t/ *n* exportación *f*. **~er** /ɪks'pɔ:tə(r)/ exportador *m*
expos|e /ɪk'spəʊz/ *vt* exponer; (*reveal*) descubrir. **~ure** /-ʒə(r)/ *n* exposición *f*. **die of ~ure** morir de frío
expound /ɪk'spaʊnd/ *vt* exponer
express[1] /ɪk'spres/ *vt* expresar
express[2] /ɪk'spres/ *a* expreso; ‹*letter*› urgente. ● *adv* (*by express post*) por correo urgente. ● *n* (*train*) rápido *m*, expreso *m*
expression /ɪk'spreʃn/ *n* expresión *f*
expressive /ɪk'spresɪv/ *a* expresivo
expressly /ɪk'spreslɪ/ *adv* expresamente
expulsion /ɪk'spʌlʃn/ *n* expulsión *f*
expurgate /'ekspəgeɪt/ *vt* expurgar
exquisite /'ekskwɪzɪt/ *a* exquisito. **~ly** *adv* primorosamente
ex-serviceman /eks'sɜ:vɪsmən/ *n* (*pl* **-men**) excombatiente *m*
extant /ek'stænt/ *a* existente
extempore /ek'stempərɪ/ *a* improvisado. ● *adv* de improviso
exten|d /ɪk'stend/ *vt* extender; (*prolong*) prolongar; ensanchar ‹*house*›. ● *vi* extenderse. **~sion** *n* extensión *f*; (*of road, time*) prolongación *f*; (*building*) anejo *m*; (*com*) prórroga *f*
extensive /ɪk'stensɪv/ *a* extenso. **~ly** *adv* extensamente
extent /ɪk'stent/ *n* extensión *f*; (*fig*) alcance. **to a certain ~** hasta cierto punto
extenuate /ɪk'stenjʊeɪt/ *vt* atenuar
exterior /ɪk'stɪərɪə(r)/ *a* & *n* exterior (*m*)
exterminat|e /ɪk'stɜ:mɪneɪt/ *vt* exterminar. **~ion** /-'neɪʃn/ *n* exterminio *m*
external /ɪk'stɜ:nl/ *a* externo. **~ly** *adv* externamente
extinct /ɪk'stɪŋkt/ *a* extinto. **~ion** /-ʃn/ *n* extinción *f*
extinguish /ɪk'stɪŋgwɪʃ/ *vt* extinguir. **~er** *n* extintor *m*
extol /ɪk'stəʊl/ *vt* (*pt* **extolled**) alabar

extort /ɪk'stɔ:t/ *vt* sacar por la fuerza. **~ion** /-ʃn/ *n* exacción *f*. **~ionate** /ɪk'stɔ:ʃənət/ *a* exorbitante

extra /'ekstrə/ *a* suplementario. ● *adv* extraordinariamente. ● *n* suplemento *m*; (*cinema*) extra *m* & *f*

extract /'ekstrækt/ *n* extracto *m*. /ɪk'strækt/ *vt* extraer; (*fig*) arrancar. **~ion** /-ʃn/ *n* extracción *f*; (*lineage*) origen *m*

extradit|e /'ekstrədaɪt/ *vt* extraditar. **~ion** /-'dɪʃn/ *n* extradición *f*

extramarital /ekstrə'mærɪtl/ *a* fuera del matrimonio

extramural /ekstrə'mjʊərəl/ *a* fuera del recinto universitario; (*for external students*) para estudiantes externos

extraordinary /ɪk'strɔ:dnrɪ/ *a* extraordinario

extra-sensory /ekstrə'sensərɪ/ *a* extrasensorial

extravagan|ce /ɪk'strævəgəns/ *n* prodigalidad *f*, extravagancia *f*. **~t** /ɪk'strævəgənt/ *a* pródigo, extravagante

extrem|e /ɪk'stri:m/ *a* & *n* extremo (*m*). **~ely** *adv* extremadamente. **~ist** *n* extremista *m* & *f*. **~ity** /ɪk'stremətɪ/ *n* extremidad *f*

extricate /'ekstrɪkeɪt/ *vt* desenredar, librar

extrovert /'ekstrəvɜ:t/ *n* extrovertido *m*

exuberan|ce /ɪg'zju:bərəns/ *n* exuberancia *f*. **~t** /ɪg'zju:bərənt/ *a* exuberante

exude /ɪg'zju:d/ *vt* rezumar

exult /ɪg'zʌlt/ *vi* exultar

eye /aɪ/ *n* ojo *m*. **keep an ~ on** no perder de vista. **see ~ to ~** estar de acuerdo con. ● *vt* (*pt* **eyed**, *pres p* **eyeing**) mirar. **~ball** /'aɪbɔ:l/ *n* globo *m* del ojo. **~brow** /'aɪbraʊ/ *n* ceja *f*. **~ful** /'aɪfʊl/ *n* (*fam*) espectáculo *m* sorprendente. **~lash** /'aɪlæʃ/ *n* pestaña *f*. **~let** /'aɪlɪt/ *n* ojete *m*. **~lid** /'aɪlɪd/ *n* párpado *m*. **~-opener** *n* (*fam*) revelación *f*. **~-shadow** *n* sombra *f* de ojos, sombreador *m*. **~sight** /'aɪsaɪt/ *n* vista *f*. **~sore** /'aɪsɔ:(r)/ *n* (*fig*, *fam*) monstruosidad *f*, horror *m*. **~witness** /'aɪwɪtnɪs/ *n* testigo *m* ocular

F

fable /'feɪbl/ *n* fábula *f*

fabric /'fæbrɪk/ *n* tejido *m*, tela *f*

fabrication /fæbrɪ'keɪʃn/ *n* invención *f*

fabulous /'fæbjʊləs/ *a* fabuloso

façade /fə'sɑ:d/ *n* fachada *f*

face /feɪs/ *n* cara *f*, rostro *m*; (*of watch*) esfera *f*; (*aspect*) aspecto *m*. **~ down(wards)** boca abajo. **~ up(wards)** boca arriba. **in the ~ of** frente a. **lose ~** quedar mal. **pull ~s** hacer muecas. ● *vt* mirar hacia; ‹*house*› dar a; (*confront*) enfrentarse con. ● *vi* volverse. **~ up to** enfrentarse con. **~ flannel** *n* paño *m* (para lavarse la cara). **~less** *a* anónimo. **~-lift** *n* cirugía *f* estética en la cara

facet /'fæsɪt/ *n* faceta *f*

facetious /fə'si:ʃəs/ *a* chistoso, gracioso

facial /'feɪʃl/ *a* facial. ● *n* masaje *m* facial

facile /'fæsaɪl/ *a* fácil

facilitate /fə'sɪlɪteɪt/ *vt* facilitar

facility /fə'sɪlɪtɪ/ *n* facilidad *f*

facing /'feɪsɪŋ/ *n* revestimiento *m*. **~s** *npl* (*on clothes*) vueltas *fpl*

facsimile /fæk'sɪmɪlɪ/ *n* facsímile *m*

fact /fækt/ *n* hecho *m*. **as a matter of ~, in ~** en realidad, a decir verdad

faction /'fækʃn/ *n* facción *f*

factor /'fæktə(r)/ *n* factor *m*

factory /'fæktərɪ/ *n* fábrica *f*

factual /'fæktʃʊəl/ *a* basado en hechos, factual

faculty /'fækəltɪ/ *n* facultad *f*

fad /fæd/ *n* manía *f*, capricho *m*

fade /feɪd/ *vi* ‹*colour*› descolorarse; ‹*flowers*› marchitarse; ‹*light*› apagarse; ‹*memory*, *sound*› desvanecerse

faeces /'fi:si:z/ *npl* excrementos *mpl*

fag[1] /fæg/ *n* (*chore*, *fam*) faena *f*; (*cigarette*, *sl*) cigarillo *m*, pitillo *m*

fag[2] /fæg/ *n* (*homosexual*, *Amer*, *sl*) marica *m*

fagged /fægd/ *a*. **~ (out)** rendido

fah /fɑ/ *n* (*mus*, *fourth note of any musical scale*) fa *m*

fail /feɪl/ *vi* fallar; (*run short*) acabarse. **he ~ed to arrive** no llegó. ● *vt* no aprobar ‹*exam*›; suspender ‹*candidate*›; (*disappoint*) fallar. **~ s.o.** ‹*words etc*› faltarle a uno. ● *n*. **without ~** sin falta

failing /'feɪlɪŋ/ *n* defecto *m*. ● *prep* a falta de

failure /ˈfeɪljə(r)/ *n* fracaso *m*; (*person*) fracasado *m*; (*med*) ataque *m*; (*mec*) fallo *m*. **~ to do** dejar *m* de hacer

faint /feɪnt/ *a* (**-er, -est**) (*weak*) débil; (*indistinct*) indistinto. **feel ~** estar mareado. **the ~est idea** la más remota idea. ● *vi* desmayarse. ● *n* desmayo *m*. **~-hearted** *a* pusilánime, cobarde. **~ly** *adv* (*weakly*) débilmente; (*indistinctly*) indistintamente. **~ness** *n* debilidad *f*

fair[1] /feə(r)/ *a* (**-er, -est**) (*just*) justo; ‹*weather*› bueno; ‹*amount*› razonable; ‹*hair*› rubio; ‹*skin*› blanco. **~ play** *n* juego *m* limpio. ● *adv* limpio

fair[2] /feə(r)/ *n* feria *f*

fair: **~ly** *adv* (*justly*) justamente; (*rather*) bastante. **~ness** *n* justicia *f*

fairy /ˈfeərɪ/ *n* hada *f*. **~land** *n* país *m* de las hadas. **~ story**, **~-tale** cuento *m* de hadas

fait accompli /feɪtəˈkɒmpli:/ *n* hecho *m* consumado

faith /feɪθ/ *n* (*trust*) confianza *f*; (*relig*) fe *f*. **~ful** *a* fiel. **~fully** *adv* fielmente. **~fulness** *n* fidelidad *f*. **~-healing** *n* curación *f* por la fe

fake /feɪk/ *n* falsificación *f*; (*person*) impostor *m*. ● *a* falso. ● *vt* falsificar; (*pretend*) fingir

fakir /ˈfeɪkɪə(r)/ *n* faquir *m*

falcon /ˈfɔ:lkən/ *n* halcón *m*

Falkland /ˈfɔ:lklənd/ *n*. **the ~ Islands** *npl* las islas *fpl* Malvinas

fall /fɔ:l/ *vi* (*pt* **fell**, *pp* **fallen**) caer. ● *n* caída *f*; (*autumn*, *Amer*) otoño *m*; (*in price*) baja *f*. **~ back on** recurrir a. **~ down** (*fall*) caer; (*be unsuccessful*) fracasar. **~ for** (*fam*) enamorarse de ‹*person*›; (*fam*) dejarse engañar por ‹*trick*›. **~ in** (*mil*) formar filas. **~ off** (*diminish*) disminuir. **~ out** (*quarrel*) reñir (**with** con); (*drop out*) caer. **~ over** caer(se). **~ over sth** tropezar con algo. **~ short** ser insuficiente. **~ through** fracasar

fallacy /ˈfæləsɪ/ *n* error *m*

fallible /ˈfælɪbl/ *a* falible

fallout /ˈfɔ:laʊt/ *n* lluvia *f* radiactiva

fallow /ˈfæləʊ/ *a* en barbecho

false /fɔ:ls/ *a* falso. **~hood** *n* mentira *f*. **~ly** *adv* falsamente. **~ness** *n* falsedad *f*

falsetto /fɔ:lˈsetəʊ/ *n* (*pl* **-os**) falsete *m*

falsify /ˈfɔ:lsɪfaɪ/ *vt* falsificar

falter /ˈfɔ:ltə(r)/ *vi* vacilar

fame /feɪm/ *n* fama *f*. **~d** *a* famoso

familiar /fəˈmɪlɪə(r)/ *a* familiar. **be ~ with** conocer. **~ity** /-ˈærətɪ/ *n* familiaridad *f*. **~ize** *vt* familiarizar

family /ˈfæməlɪ/ *n* familia *f*. ● *a* de (la) familia, familiar

famine /ˈfæmɪn/ *n* hambre *f*, hambruna *f* (*Amer*)

famished /ˈfæmɪʃt/ *a* hambriento

famous /ˈfeɪməs/ *a* famoso. **~ly** *adv* (*fam*) a las mil maravillas

fan[1] /fæn/ *n* abanico *m*; (*mec*) ventilador *m*. ● *vt* (*pt* **fanned**) abanicar; soplar ‹*fire*›. ● *vi*. **~ out** desparramarse en forma de abanico

fan[2] /fæn/ *n* (*of person*) admirador *m*; (*enthusiast*) aficionado *m*, entusiasta *m & f*

fanatic /fəˈnætɪk/ *n* fanático *m*. **~al** *a* fanático. **~ism** /-sɪzəm/ *n* fanatismo *m*

fan belt /ˈfænbelt/ *n* correa *f* de ventilador

fancier /ˈfænsɪə(r)/ *n* aficionado *m*

fanciful /ˈfænsɪfl/ *a* (*imaginative*) imaginativo; (*unreal*) imaginario

fancy /ˈfænsɪ/ *n* fantasía *f*; (*liking*) gusto *m*. **take a ~ to** tomar cariño a ‹*person*›; aficionarse a ‹*thing*›. ● *a* de lujo; (*extravagant*) excesivo. ● *vt* (*imagine*) imaginar; (*believe*) creer; (*want, fam*) apetecer a. **~ dress** *n* disfraz *m*

fanfare /ˈfænfeə(r)/ *n* fanfarria *f*

fang /fæŋ/ *n* (*of animal*) colmillo *m*; (*of snake*) diente *m*

fanlight /ˈfænlaɪt/ *n* montante *m*

fantasize /ˈfæntəsaɪz/ *vi* fantasear

fantastic /fænˈtæstɪk/ *a* fantástico

fantasy /ˈfæntəsɪ/ *n* fantasía *f*

far /fɑ:(r)/ *adv* lejos; (*much*) mucho. **as ~ as** hasta. **as ~ as I know** que yo sepa. **by ~** con mucho. ● *a* (**further, furthest** *or* **farther, farthest**) lejano

far-away /ˈfɑ:rəweɪ/ *a* lejano

farc|e /fɑ:s/ *n* farsa *f*. **~ical** *a* ridículo

fare /feə(r)/ *n* (*for transport*) tarifa *f*; (*food*) comida *f*. ● *vi* irle. **how did you ~?** ¿qué tal te fue?

Far East /fɑ:(r)ˈi:st/ *n* Extremo/Lejano Oriente *m*

farewell /feəˈwel/ *int & n* adiós (*m*)

far-fetched /fɑ:ˈfetʃt/ *a* improbable

farm /fɑ:m/ *n* granja *f*. ● *vt* cultivar. **~ out** arrendar. ● *vi* ser agricultor. **~er** *n* agricultor *m*. **~house** *n* granja *f*. **~ing** *n* agricultura *f*. **~yard** *n* corral *m*

far: **~-off** *a* lejano. **~-reaching** *a* trascendental. **~-seeing** *a* clarividente. **~-sighted** *a* hipermétrope; (*fig*) clarividente
farther, **farthest** /'fɑːðə(r), 'fɑːðəst/ *see* **far**
fascinat|e /'fæsɪneɪt/ *vt* fascinar. **~ion** /-'neɪʃn/ *n* fascinación *f*
fascis|m /'fæʃɪzəm/ *n* fascismo *m*. **~t** /'fæʃɪst/ *a & n* fascista (*m & f*)
fashion /'fæʃn/ *n* (*manner*) manera *f*; (*vogue*) moda *f*. **~able** *a* de moda
fast[1] /fɑːst/ *a* (**-er, -est**) rápido; ‹*clock*› adelantado; (*secure*) fijo; ‹*colours*› sólido. ● *adv* rápidamente; (*securely*) firmemente. **~ asleep** profundamente dormido
fast[2] /fɑːst/ *vi* ayunar. ● *n* ayuno *m*
fasten /'fɑːsn/ *vt/i* sujetar; cerrar ‹*windows, doors*›; abrochar ‹*belt etc*›. **~er** *n*, **~ing** *n* (*on box, window*) cierre *m*; (*on door*) cerrojo *m*
fastidious /fə'stɪdɪəs/ *a* exigente, minucioso
fat /fæt/ *n* grasa *f*. ● *a* (**fatter, fattest**) gordo; ‹*meat*› que tiene mucha grasa; (*thick*) grueso. **a ~ lot of** (*sl*) muy poco
fatal /'feɪtl/ *a* mortal; (*fateful*) fatídico
fatalis|m /'feɪtəlɪzəm/ *n* fatalismo *m*. **~t** *n* fatalista *m & f*
fatality /fə'tælətɪ/ *n* calamidad *f*; (*death*) muerte *f*
fatally /'feɪtəlɪ/ *adv* mortalmente; (*by fate*) fatalmente
fate /feɪt/ *n* destino *m*; (*one's lot*) suerte *f*. **~d** *a* predestinado. **~ful** *a* fatídico
fat-head /'fæthed/ *n* imbécil *m*
father /'fɑːðə(r)/ *n* padre *m*. **~hood** *m* paternidad *f*. **~-in-law** *m* (*pl* **fathers-in-law**) *m* suegro *m*. **~ly** *a* paternal
fathom /'fæðəm/ *n* braza *f*. ● *vt*. **~ (out)** comprender
fatigue /fə'tiːg/ *n* fatiga *f*. ● *vt* fatigar
fat: **~ness** *n* gordura *f*. **~ten** *vt/i* engordar. **~tening** *a* que engorda. **~ty** *a* graso. ● *n* (*fam*) gordinflón *m*
fatuous /'fætjʊəs/ *a* fatuo
faucet /'fɔːsɪt/ *n* (*Amer*) grifo *m*
fault /fɔːlt/ *n* defecto *m*; (*blame*) culpa *f*; (*tennis*) falta *f*; (*geol*) falla *f*. **at ~** culpable. ● *vt* criticar. **~less** *a* impecable. **~y** *a* defectuoso
fauna /'fɔːnə/ *n* fauna *f*
faux pas /fəʊ'pɑː/ (*pl* **faux pas** /fəʊ'pɑː/) *n* metedura *f* de pata, paso *m* en falso

favour /'feɪvə(r)/ *n* favor *m*. ● *vt* favorecer; (*support*) estar a favor de; (*prefer*) preferir. **~able** *a* favorable. **~ably** *adv* favorablemente
favourit|e /'feɪvərɪt/ *a & n* preferido (*m*). **~ism** *n* favoritismo *m*
fawn[1] /fɔːn/ *n* cervato *m*. ● *a* color de cervato, beige, beis
fawn[2] /fɔːn/ *vi*. **~ on** adular
fax /fæks/ *n* telefacsímil *m*, fax *m*
fear /fɪə(r)/ *n* miedo *m*. ● *vt* temer. **~ful** *a* (*frightening*) espantoso; (*frightened*) temeroso. **~less** *a* intrépido. **~lessness** *n* intrepidez *f*. **~some** *a* espantoso
feasib|ility /fiːzə'bɪlətɪ/ *n* viabilidad *f*. **~le** /'fiːzəbl/ *a* factible; (*likely*) posible
feast /fiːst/ *n* (*relig*) fiesta *f*; (*meal*) banquete *m*, comilona *f*. ● *vt* banquetear, festejar. **~ on** regalarse con
feat /fiːt/ *n* hazaña *f*
feather /'feðə(r)/ *n* pluma *f*. ● *vt*. **~ one's nest** hacer su agosto. **~-brained** *a* tonto. **~weight** *n* peso *m* pluma
feature /'fiːtʃə(r)/ *n* (*on face*) facción *f*; (*characteristic*) característica *f*; (*in newspaper*) artículo *m*; **~ (film)** película *f* principal, largometraje *m*. ● *vt* presentar; (*give prominence to*) destacar. ● *vi* figurar
February /'februərɪ/ *n* febrero *m*
feckless /'feklɪs/ *a* inepto; (*irresponsible*) irreflexivo
fed /fed/ *see* **feed**. ● *a*. **~ up** (*sl*) harto (**with** de)
federal /'fedərəl/ *a* federal
federation /fedə'reɪʃn/ *n* federación *f*
fee /fiː/ *n* (*professional*) honorarios *mpl*; (*enrolment*) derechos *mpl*; (*club*) cuota *f*
feeble /'fiːbl/ *a* (**-er, -est**) débil. **~-minded** *a* imbécil
feed /fiːd/ *vt* (*pt* **fed**) dar de comer a; (*supply*) alimentar. ● *vi* comer. ● *n* (*for animals*) pienso *m*; (*for babies*) comida *f*. **~back** *n* reacciones *fpl*, comentarios *mpl*
feel /fiːl/ *vt* (*pt* **felt**) sentir; (*touch*) tocar; (*think*) parecerle. **do you ~ it's a good idea?** te parece buena idea? **I ~ it is necessary** me parece necesario. **~ as if** tener la impresión de que. **~ hot/hungry** tener calor/hambre. **~ like** (*want, fam*)

tener ganas de. ~ **up to** sentirse capaz de
feeler /'fi:lə(r)/ *n* (*of insects*) antena *f*. **put out a** ~ (*fig*) hacer un sondeo
feeling /'fi:lɪŋ/ *n* sentimiento *m*; (*physical*) sensación *f*
feet /fi:t/ *see* **foot**
feign /feɪn/ *vt* fingir
feint /feɪnt/ *n* finta *f*
felicitous /fə'lɪsɪtəs/ *a* feliz, oportuno
feline /'fi:laɪn/ *a* felino
fell[1] /fel/ *see* **fall**
fell[2] /fel/ *vt* derribar
fellow /'feləʊ/ *n* (*fam*) tipo *m*; (*comrade*) compañero *m*; (*society*) socio *m*. ~**-countryman** *n* compatriota *m* & *f*. ~ **passenger/traveller** *n* compañero *m* de viaje. ~**ship** *n* compañerismo *m*; (*group*) asociación *f*
felony /'felənɪ/ *n* crimen *m*
felt[1] /felt/ *n* fieltro *m*
felt[2] /felt/ *see* **feel**
female /'fi:meɪl/ *a* hembra; ‹*voice, sex etc*› femenino. ● *n* mujer *f*; (*animal*) hembra *f*
femini|ne /'femənɪn/ *a* & *n* femenino (*m*). ~**nity** /-'nɪnətɪ/ *n* feminidad *f*. ~**st** *n* feminista *m* & *f*
fenc|e /fens/ *n* cerca *f*; (*person, sl*) perista *m* & *f* (*fam*). ● *vt*. ~**e (in)** encerrar, cercar. ● *vi* (*sport*) practicar la esgrima. ~**er** *n* esgrimidor *m*. ~**ing** *n* (*sport*) esgrima *f*
fend /fend/ *vi*. ~ **for o.s.** valerse por sí mismo. ● *vt*. ~ **off** defenderse de
fender /'fendə(r)/ *n* guardafuego *m*; (*mudguard, Amer*) guardabarros *m invar*; (*naut*) defensa *f*
fennel /'fenl/ *n* hinojo *m*
ferment /'fɜ:ment/ *n* fermento *m*; (*fig*) agitación *f*. /fə'ment/ *vt/i* fermentar. ~**ation** /-'teɪʃn/ *n* fermentación *f*
fern /fɜ:n/ *n* helecho *m*
feroci|ous /fə'rəʊʃəs/ *a* feroz. ~**ty** /fə'rɒsətɪ/ *n* ferocidad *f*
ferret /'ferɪt/ *n* hurón *m*. ● *vi* (*pt* **ferreted**) huronear. ● *vt*. ~ **out** descubrir
ferry /'ferɪ/ *n* ferry *m*. ● *vt* transportar
fertil|e /'fɜ:taɪl/ *a* fértil; (*biol*) fecundo. ~**ity** /-'tɪlətɪ/ *n* fertilidad *f*; (*biol*) fecundidad *f*
fertilize /'fɜ:təlaɪz/ *vt* abonar; (*biol*) fecundar. ~**r** *n* abono *m*
fervent /'fɜ:vənt/ *a* ferviente
fervour /'fɜ:və(r)/ *n* fervor *m*
fester /'festə(r)/ *vi* enconarse
festival /'festəvl/ *n* fiesta *f*; (*of arts*) festival *m*
festive /'festɪv/ *a* festivo. ~ **season** *n* temporada *f* de fiestas
festivity /fe'stɪvətɪ/ *n* festividad *f*
festoon /fe'stu:n/ *vi*. ~ **with** adornar de
fetch /fetʃ/ *vt* (*go for*) ir a buscar; (*bring*) traer; (*be sold for*) venderse por
fetching /'fetʃɪŋ/ *a* atractivo
fête /feɪt/ *n* fiesta *f*. ● *vt* festejar
fetid /'fetɪd/ *a* fétido
fetish /'fetɪʃ/ *n* fetiche *m*; (*psych*) obsesión *f*
fetter /'fetə(r)/ *vt* encadenar. ~**s** *npl* grilletes *mpl*
fettle /'fetl/ *n* condición *f*
feud /fju:d/ *n* enemistad *f* (inveterada)
feudal /fju:dl/ *a* feudal. ~**ism** *n* feudalismo m
fever /'fi:və(r)/ *n* fiebre *f*. ~**ish** *a* febril
few /fju:/ *a* pocos. ● *n* pocos *mpl*. **a** ~ unos (pocos). **a good** ~, **quite a** ~ (*fam*) muchos. ~**er** *a* & *n* menos. ~**est** *a* & *n* el menor número de
fiancé /fɪ'ɒnseɪ/ *n* novio *m*. ~**e** /fɪ'ɒnseɪ/ *n* novia *f*
fiasco /fɪ'æskəʊ/ *n* (*pl* **-os**) fiasco *m*
fib /fɪb/ *n* mentirijilla *f*. ~**ber** *n* mentiroso *m*
fibre /'faɪbə(r)/ *n* fibra *f*. ~**glass** *n* fibra *f* de vidrio
fickle /'fɪkl/ *a* inconstante
fiction /'fɪkʃn/ *n* ficción *f*. **(works of)** ~ novelas *fpl*. ~**al** *a* novelesco
fictitious /fɪk'tɪʃəs/ *a* ficticio
fiddle /'fɪdl/ *n* (*fam*) violín *m*; (*swindle, sl*) trampa *f*. ● *vt* (*sl*) falsificar. ~ **with** juguetear con, toquetear, manosear. ~**r** *n* (*fam*) violinista *m* & *f*; (*cheat, sl*) tramposo *m*
fidelity /fɪ'delətɪ/ *n* fidelidad *f*
fidget /'fɪdʒɪt/ *vi* (*pt* **fidgeted**) moverse, ponerse nervioso. ~ **with** juguetear con. ● *n* azogado *m*. ~**y** *a* azogado
field /fi:ld/ *n* campo *m*. ~ **day** *n* gran ocasión *f*. ~ **glasses** *npl* gemelos *mpl*. **F**~ **Marshal** *n* mariscal *m* de campo, capitán *m* general. ~**work** *n* investigaciones *fpl* en el terreno
fiend /fi:nd/ *n* demonio *m*. ~**ish** *a* diabólico

fierce /fɪəs/ *a* (**-er, -est**) feroz; ‹*attack*› violento. **~ness** *n* ferocidad *f*, violencia *f*
fiery /'faɪərɪ/ *a* (**-ier, -iest**) ardiente
fifteen /fɪf'ti:n/ *a & n* quince (*m*). **~th** *a & n* quince (*m*), decimoquinto (*m*). ● *n* (*fraction*) quinzavo *m*
fifth /fɪfθ/ *a & n* quinto (*m*). **~ column** *n* quinta columna *f*
fift|ieth /'fɪftɪəθ/ *a & n* cincuenta (*m*). **~y** *a & n* cincuenta (*m*). **~y-~y** mitad y mitad, a medias. **a ~y-~y chance** una posibilidad *f* de cada dos
fig /fɪg/ *n* higo *m*
fight /faɪt/ *vt/i* (*pt* **fought**) luchar; (*quarrel*) disputar. **~ shy of** evitar. ● *n* lucha *f*; (*quarrel*) disputa *f*; (*mil*) combate *m*. **~ back** defenderse. **~ off** rechazar ‹*attack*›; luchar contra ‹*illness*›. **~er** *n* luchador *m*; (*mil*) combatiente *m & f*; (*aircraft*) avión *m* de caza. **~ing** *n* luchas *fpl*
figment /'fɪgmənt/ *n* invención *f*
figurative /'fɪgjʊrətɪv/ *a* figurado
figure /'fɪgə(r)/ *n* (*number*) cifra *f*; (*diagram*) figura *f*; (*shape*) forma *f*; (*of woman*) tipo *m*. ● *vt* imaginar. ● *vi* figurar. **that ~s** (*Amer, fam*) es lógico. **~ out** explicarse. **~head** *n* testaferro *m*, mascarón *m* de proa. **~ of speech** *n* tropo *m*, figura *f*. **~s** *npl* (*arithmetic*) aritmética *f*
filament /'fɪləmənt/ *n* filamento *m*
filch /fɪltʃ/ *vt* hurtar
file[1] /faɪl/ *n* carpeta *f*; (*set of papers*) expediente *m*. ● *vt* archivar ‹*papers*›
file[2] /faɪl/ *n* (*row*) fila *f*. ● *vi*. **~ in** entrar en fila. **~ past** desfilar ante
file[3] /faɪl/ *n* (*tool*) lima *f*. ● *vt* limar
filings /'faɪlɪŋz/ *npl* limaduras *fpl*
fill /fɪl/ *vt* llenar. ● *vi* llenarse. **~ in** rellenar ‹*form*›. **~ out** (*get fatter*) engordar. **~ up** (*auto*) llenar, repostar. ● *n*. **eat one's ~** hartarse de comer. **have had one's ~ of** estar harto de
fillet /'fɪlɪt/ *n* filete *m*. ● *vt* (*pt* **filleted**) cortar en filetes
filling /'fɪlɪŋ/ *n* (*in tooth*) empaste *m*. **~ station** *n* estación *f* de servicio
film /fɪlm/ *n* película *f*. ● *vt* filmar. **~ star** *n* estrella *f* de cine. **~-strip** *n* tira *f* de película
filter /'fɪltə(r)/ *n* filtro *m*. ● *vt* filtrar. ● *vi* filtrarse. **~-tipped** *a* con filtro
filth /fɪlθ/ *n* inmundicia *f*. **~iness** *n* inmundicia *f*. **~y** *a* inmundo
fin /fɪn/ *n* aleta *f*
final /'faɪnl/ *a* último; (*conclusive*) decisivo. ● *n* (*sport*) final *f*. **~s** *npl* (*schol*) exámenes *mpl* de fin de curso
finale /fɪ'nɑ:lɪ/ *n* final *m*
final: **~ist** *n* finalista *m & f*. **~ize** *vt* concluir. **~ly** *adv* (*lastly*) finalmente, por fin; (*once and for all*) definitivamente
financ|e /'faɪnæns/ *n* finanzas *fpl*. ● *vt* financiar. **~ial** /faɪ'nænʃl/ *a* financiero. **~ially** *adv* económicamente. **~ier** /faɪ'nænsɪə(r)/ *n* financiero *m*
finch /fɪntʃ/ *n* pinzón *m*
find /faɪnd/ *vt* (*pt* **found**) encontrar. **~ out** enterarse de. **~er** *n* el *m* que encuentra, descubridor *m*. **~ings** *npl* resultados *mpl*
fine[1] /faɪn/ *a* (**-er, -est**) fino; (*excellent*) excelente. ● *adv* muy bien; (*small*) en trozos pequeños
fine[2] /faɪn/ *n* multa *f*. ● *vt* multar
fine: **~ arts** *npl* bellas artes *fpl*. **~ly** *adv* (*admirably*) espléndidamente; (*cut*) en trozos pequeños. **~ry** /'faɪnərɪ/ *n* galas *fpl*
finesse /fɪ'nes/ *n* tino *m*
finger /'fɪŋgə(r)/ *n* dedo *m*. ● *vt* tocar. **~-nail** *n* uña *f*. **~print** *n* huella *f* dactilar. **~-stall** *n* dedil *m*. **~tip** *n* punta *f* del dedo
finicking /'fɪnɪkɪŋ/ *a*, **finicky** /'fɪnɪkɪ/ *a* melindroso
finish /'fɪnɪʃ/ *vt/i* terminar. **~ doing** terminar de hacer. **~ up doing** terminar por hacer. ● *n* fin *m*; (*of race*) llegada *f*, meta *f*; (*appearance*) acabado *m*
finite /'faɪnaɪt/ *a* finito
Fin|land /'fɪnlənd/ *n* Finlandia *f*. **~n** *n* finlandés *m*. **~nish** *a & n* finlandés (*m*)
fiord /fjɔ:d/ *n* fiordo *m*
fir /fɜ:(r)/ *n* abeto *m*
fire /faɪə(r)/ *n* fuego *m*; (*conflagration*) incendio *m*. ● *vt* disparar ‹*bullet etc*›; (*dismiss*) despedir; (*fig*) excitar, enardecer, inflamar. ● *vi* tirar. **~arm** *n* arma *f* de fuego. **~ brigade** *n* cuerpo *m* de bomberos. **~cracker** *n* (*Amer*) petardo *m*. **~ department** *n* (*Amer*) cuerpo *m* de bomberos. **~-engine** *n* coche *m* de bomberos. **~-escape** *n* escalera *f* de incendios. **~light** *n*

lumbre *f.* **~man** *n* bombero *m.* **~place** *n* chimenea *f.* **~side** *n* hogar *m.* **~ station** *n* parque *m* de bomberos. **~wood** *n* leña *f.* **~work** *n* fuego *m* artificial

firing-squad /'faɪərɪŋskwɒd/ *n* pelotón *m* de ejecución

firm[1] /fɜ:m/ *n* empresa *f*

firm[2] /fɜ:m/ *a* (**-er, -est**) firme. **~ly** *adv* firmemente. **~ness** *n* firmeza *f*

first /fɜ:st/ *a* primero. **at ~ hand** directamente. **at ~ sight** a primera vista. ● *n* primero *m.* ● *adv* primero; (*first time*) por primera vez. **~ of all** ante todo. **~ aid** *n* primeros auxilios *mpl.* **~-born** *a* primogénito. **~-class** *a* de primera clase. **~ floor** *n* primer piso *m*; (*Amer*) planta *f* baja. **F~ Lady** *n* (*Amer*) Primera Dama *f.* **~ly** *adv* en primer lugar. **~ name** *n* nombre *m* de pila. **~-rate** *a* excelente

fiscal /'fɪskl/ *a* fiscal

fish /fɪʃ/ *n* (*usually invar*) (*alive in water*) pez *m*; (*food*) pescado *m.* ● *vi* pescar. **~ for** pescar. **~ out** (*take out, fam*) sacar. **go ~ing** ir de pesca. **~erman** /'fɪʃəmən/ *n* pescador *m.* **~ing** *n* pesca *f.* **~ing-rod** *n* caña *f* de pesca. **~monger** *n* pescadero *m.* **~-shop** *n* pescadería *f.* **~y** *a* ‹*smell*› a pescado; (*questionable, fam*) sospechoso

fission /'fɪʃn/ *n* fisión *f*

fist /fɪst/ *n* puño *m*

fit[1] /fɪt/ *a* (**fitter**, **fittest**) conveniente; (*healthy*) sano; (*good enough*) adecuado; (*able*) capaz. ● *n* (*of clothes*) corte *m.* ● *vt* (*pt* **fitted**) (*adapt*) adaptar; (*be the right size for*) sentar bien a; (*install*) colocar. ● *vi* encajar; (*in certain space*) caber; ‹*clothes*› sentar. **~ out** equipar. **~ up** equipar

fit[2] /fɪt/ *n* ataque *m*

fitful /'fɪtfl/ *a* irregular

fitment /'fɪtmənt/ *n* mueble *m*

fitness /'fɪtnɪs/ *n* (*buena*) salud *f*; (*of remark*) conveniencia *f*

fitting /'fɪtɪŋ/ *a* apropiado. ● *n* (*of clothes*) prueba *f.* **~s** /'fɪtɪŋz/ *npl* (*in house*) accesorios *mpl*

five /faɪv/ *a* & *n* cinco (*m*). **~r** /'faɪvə(r)/ *n* (*fam*) billete *m* de cinco libras

fix /fɪks/ *vt* (*make firm, attach, decide*) fijar; (*mend, deal with*) arreglar. ● *n.* **in a ~** en un aprieto. **~ation** /-eɪʃn/ *n* fijación *f.* **~ed** *a* fijo

fixture /'fɪkstʃə(r) *n* (*sport*) partido *m.* **~s** (*in house*) accesorios *mpl*

fizz /fɪz/ *vi* burbujear. ● *n* efervescencia *f.* **~le** /fɪzl/ *vi* burbujear. **~le out** fracasar. **~y** *a* efervescente; ‹*water*› con gas

flab /flæb/ *n* (*fam*) flaccidez *f*

flabbergast /'flæbəgɑ:st/ *vt* pasmar

flabby /'flaæbɪ/ *a* flojo

flag /flæg/ *n* bandera *f.* ● *vt* (*pt* **flagged**). **~ down** hacer señales de parada a. ● *vi* (*pt* **flagged**) (*weaken*) flaquear; ‹*interest*› decaer; ‹*conversation*› languidecer

flagon /'flægən/ *n* botella *f* grande, jarro *m*

flag-pole /'flægpəʊl/ *n* asta *f* de bandera

flagrant /'fleɪgrənt/ *a* (*glaring*) flagrante; (*scandalous*) escandaloso

flagstone /'flægstəʊn/ *n* losa *f*

flair /fleə(r)/ *n* don *m* (**for** de)

flak|e /fleɪk/ *n* copo *m*; (*of paint, metal*) escama *f.* ● *vi* desconcharse. **~e out** (*fam*) caer rendido. **~y** *a* escamoso

flamboyant /flæm'bɔɪənt/ *a* ‹*clothes*› vistoso; ‹*manner*› extravagante

flame /fleɪm/ *n* llama *f.* ● *vi* llamear

flamingo /flə'mɪŋgəʊ/ *n* (*pl* **-o(e)s**) flamenco *m*

flammable /'flæməbl/ *a* inflamable

flan /flæn/ *n* tartaleta *f*, tarteleta *f*

flank /flænk/ *n* (*of animal*) ijada *f*, flanco *m*; (*of person*) costado *m*; (*of mountain*) falda *f*; (*mil*) flanco *m*

flannel /'flænl/ *n* franela *f* (de lana); (*for face*) paño *m* (para lavarse la cara). **~ette** *n* franela *f* (de algodón), muletón *m*

flap /flæp/ *vi* (*pt* **flapped**) ondear; ‹*wings*› aletear; (*become agitated, fam*) ponerse nervioso. ● *vt* sacudir; batir ‹*wings*›. ● *n* (*of pocket*) cartera *f*; (*of table*) ala *f.* **get into a ~** ponerse nervioso

flare /fleə(r)/ ● *n* llamarada *f*; (*mil*) bengala *f*; (*in skirt*) vuelo *m.* ● *vi.* **~ up** llamear; ‹*fighting*› estallar; ‹*person*› encolerizarse. **~d** *a* ‹*skirt*› acampanado

flash /flæʃ/ ● *vi* brillar; (*on and off*) destellar. ● *vt* despedir; (*aim torch*) dirigir; (*flaunt*) hacer ostentación de. **~ past** pasar como un rayo. ● *n* relámpago *m*; (*of news, camera*)

flash *m*. **~back** *n* escena *f* retrospectiva. **~light** *n* (*torch*) linterna *f*
flashy /'flæʃɪ/ *a* ostentoso
flask /flɑ:sk/ *n* frasco *m*; (*vacuum flask*) termo *m*
flat[1] /flæt/ *a* (**flatter**, **flattest**) llano; ‹*tyre*› desinflado; ‹*refusal*› categórico; ‹*fare, rate*› fijo; (*mus*) desafinado. ● *adv*. **~ out** (*at top speed*) a toda velocidad
flat[2] /flæt/ *n* (*rooms*) piso *m*, apartamento *m*; ‹*tyre*› (*fam*) pinchazo *m*; (*mus*) bemol *m*
flat: **~ly** *adv* categóricamente. **~ness** *n* llanura *f*. **~ten** /'flætn/ *vt* allanar, aplanar. ● *vi* allanarse, aplanarse
flatter /flætə(r)/ *vt* adular. **~er** *n* adulador *m*. **~ing** *a* ‹*person*› lisonjero; ‹*clothes*› favorecedor. **~y** *n* adulación *f*
flatulence /'flætjʊləns/ *n* flatulencia *f*
flaunt /flɔ:nt/ *vt* hacer ostentación de
flautist /'flɔ:tɪst/ *n* flautista *m & f*
flavour /'fleɪvə(r)/ *n* sabor *m*. ● *vt* condimentar. **~ing** *n* condimento *m*
flaw /flɔ:/ *n* defecto *m*. **~less** *a* perfecto
flax /flæks/ *n* lino *m*. **~en** *a* de lino; ‹*hair*› rubio
flea /fli:/ *n* pulga *f*
fleck /flek/ *n* mancha *f*, pinta *f*
fled /fled/ *see* **flee**
fledged /fledʒd/ *a*. **fully ~** ‹*doctor etc*› hecho y derecho; ‹*member*› de pleno derecho
fledg(e)ling /'fledʒlɪŋ/ *n* pájaro *m* volantón
flee /fli:/ *vi* (*pt* **fled**) huir. ● *vt* huir de
fleece /fli:s/ *n* vellón *m*. ● *vt* (*rob*) desplumar
fleet /fli:t/ *n* (*naut, aviat*) flota *f*; (*of cars*) parque *m*
fleeting /'fli:tɪŋ/ *a* fugaz
Flemish /'flemɪʃ/ *a & n* flamenco (*m*)
flesh /fleʃ/ *n* carne *f*. **in the ~** en persona. **one's own ~ and blood** los de su sangre. **~y** *a* ‹*fruit*› carnoso
flew /flu:/ *see* **fly**[1]
flex /fleks/ *vt* doblar; flexionar ‹*muscle*›. ● *n* (*elec*) cable *m*, flexible *m*
flexib|ility /fleksə'bɪlətɪ/ *n* flexibilidad *f*. **~le** /'fleksəbl/ *a* flexible
flexitime /fleksɪ'taɪm/ *n* horario *m* flexible
flick /flɪk/ *n* golpecito *m*. ● *vt* dar un golpecito a. **~ through** hojear
flicker /'flɪkə(r)/ *vi* temblar; ‹*light*› parpadear. ● *n* temblor *m*; (*of hope*) resquicio *m*; (*of light*) parpadeo *m*
flick: **~-knife** *n* navaja *f* de muelle. **~s** *npl* cine *m*
flier /'flaɪə(r)/ *n* aviador *m*; (*circular, Amer*) prospecto *m*, folleto *m*
flies /flaɪz/ *npl* (*on trousers, fam*) bragueta *f*
flight /flaɪt/ *n* vuelo *m*; (*fleeing*) huida *f*, fuga *f*. **~ of stairs** tramo *m* de escalera *f*. **put to ~** poner en fuga. **take (to) ~** darse a la fuga. **~-deck** *n* cubierta *f* de vuelo
flighty /'flaɪtɪ/ *a* (**-ier, -iest**) frívolo
flimsy /'flɪmzɪ/ *a* (**-ier**, **-iest**) flojo, débil, poco substancioso
flinch /flɪntʃ/ *vi* (*draw back*) retroceder (**from** ante). **without ~ing** (*without wincing*) sin pestañear
fling /flɪŋ/ *vt* (*pt* **flung**) arrojar. ● *n*. **have a ~** echar una cana al aire
flint /flɪnt/ *n* pedernal *m*; (*for lighter*) piedra *f*
flip /flɪp/ *vt* (*pt* **flipped**) dar un golpecito a. **~ through** hojear. ● *n* golpecito *m*. **~ side** *n* otra cara *f*
flippant /'flɪpənt/ *a* poco serio; (*disrespectful*) irrespetuoso
flipper /'flɪpə(r)/ *n* aleta *f*
flirt /flɜ:t/ *vi* coquetear. ● *n* (*woman*) coqueta *f*; (*man*) mariposón *m*, coqueto *m*. **~ation** /-'teɪʃn/ *n* coqueteo *m*
flit /flɪt/ *vi* (*pt* **flitted**) revolotear
float /fləʊt/ *vi* flotar. ● *vt* hacer flotar. ● *n* flotador *m*; (*on fishing line*) corcho *m*; (*cart*) carroza *f*
flock /flɒk/ *n* (*of birds*) bandada *f*; (*of sheep*) rebaño *m*; (*of people*) muchedumbre *f*, multitud *f*. ● *vi* congregarse
flog /flɒg/ *vt* (*pt* **flogged**) (*beat*) azotar; (*sell, sl*) vender
flood /flʌd/ *n* inundación *f*; (*fig*) torrente *m*. ● *vt* inundar. ● *vi* ‹*building etc*› inundarse; ‹*river*› desbordar
floodlight /'flʌdlaɪt/ *n* foco *m*. ● *vt* (*pt* **floodlit**) iluminar (con focos)
floor /flɔ:(r)/ *n* suelo *m*; (*storey*) piso *m*; (*for dancing*) pista *f*. ● *vt* (*knock down*) derribar; (*baffle*) confundir
flop /flɒp/ *vi* (*pt* **flopped**) dejarse caer pesadamente; (*fail, sl*)

fracasar. ● *n* (*sl*) fracaso *m*. **~py** *a* flojo
flora /'flɔ:rə/ *n* flora *f*
floral /'flɔ:rəl/ *a* floral
florid /'flɒrɪd/ *a* florido
florist /'flɒrɪst/ *n* florista *m* & *f*
flounce /flaʊns/ *n* volante *m*
flounder[1] /'flaʊndə(r)/ *vi* avanzar con dificultad, no saber qué hacer
flounder[2] /'flaʊndə(r)/ *n* (*fish*) platija *f*
flour /flaʊə(r)/ *n* harina *f*
flourish /'flʌrɪʃ/ *vi* prosperar. ● *vt* blandir. ● *n* ademán *m* elegante; (*in handwriting*) rasgo *m*. **~ing** *a* próspero
floury /'flaʊərɪ/ *a* harinoso
flout /flaʊt/ *vt* burlarse de
flow /fləʊ/ *vi* correr; (*hang loosely*) caer. **~ into** ‹*river*› desembocar en. ● *n* flujo *m*; (*jet*) chorro *m*; (*stream*) corriente *f*; (*of words, tears*) torrente *m*. **~ chart** *n* organigrama *m*
flower /'flaʊə(r)/ *n* flor *f*. **~-bed** *n* macizo *m* de flores. **~ed** *a* floreado, de flores. **~y** *a* florido
flown /fləʊn/ *see* **fly**[1]
flu /flu:/ *n* (*fam*) gripe *f*
fluctuat|e /'flʌktjʊeɪt/ *vi* fluctuar. **~ion** /-eɪʃn/ *n* fluctuación *f*
flue /flu:/ *n* humero *m*
fluen|cy /'flu:ənsɪ/ *n* facilidad *f*. **~t** *a* ‹*style*› fluido; ‹*speaker*› elocuente. **be ~t (in a language)** hablar (un idioma) con soltura. **~tly** *adv* con fluidez; (*lang*) con soltura
fluff /flʌf/ *n* pelusa *f*. **~y** *a* (**-ier**, **-iest**) velloso
fluid /'flu:id/ *a* & *n* fluido (*m*)
fluke /flu:k/ *n* (*stroke of luck*) chiripa *f*
flung /flʌŋ/ *see* **fling**
flunk /flʌŋk/ *vt* (*Amer*, *fam*) ser suspendido en ‹*exam*›; suspender ‹*person*›. ● *vi* (*fam*) ser suspendido
fluorescent /flʊə'resnt/ *a* fluorescente
fluoride /flʊəraɪd/ *n* fluoruro *m*
flurry /'flʌrɪ/ *n* (*squall*) ráfaga *f*; (*fig*) agitación *f*
flush[1] /flʌʃ/ *vi* ruborizarse. ● *vt* limpiar con agua. **~ the toilet** tirar de la cadena. ● *n* (*blush*) rubor *m*; (*fig*) emoción *f*
flush[2] /flʌʃ/ *a*. **~ (with)** a nivel (con)
flush[3] /flʌʃ/ *vt*/*i*. **~ out** (*drive out*) echar fuera
fluster /'flʌstə(r)/ *vt* poner nervioso
flute /flu:t/ *n* flauta *f*
flutter /'flʌtə(r)/ *vi* ondear; ‹*bird*› revolotear. ● *n* (*of wings*) revoloteo *m*; (*fig*) agitación *f*
flux /flʌks/ *n* flujo *m*. **be in a state of ~** estar siempre cambiando
fly[1] /flaɪ/ *vi* (*pt* **flew**, *pp* **flown**) volar; ‹*passenger*› ir en avión; ‹*flag*› flotar; (*rush*) correr. ● *vt* pilotar ‹*aircraft*›; transportar en avión ‹*passengers, goods*›; izar ‹*flag*›. ● *n* (*of trousers*) bragueta *f*
fly[2] /flaɪ/ *n* mosca *f*
flyer /'flaɪə(r)/ *n* aviador *m*; (*circular, Amer*) prospecto *m*, folleto *m*
flying /'flaɪɪŋ/ *a* volante; (*hasty*) relámpago *invar*. ● *n* (*activity*) aviación *f*. **~ visit** *n* visita *f* relámpago
fly: **~leaf** *n* guarda *f*. **~over** *n* paso *m* elevado. **~weight** *n* peso *m* mosca
foal /fəʊl/ *n* potro *m*
foam /fəʊm/ *n* espuma *f*. **~(rubber)** *n* goma *f* espuma. ● *vi* espumar
fob /fɒb/ *vt* (*pt* **fobbed**). **~ off on s.o.** (*palm off*) encajar a uno
focal /'fəʊkl/ *a* focal
focus /'fəʊkəs/ *n* (*pl* **-cuses** *or* **-ci** /-saɪ/) foco *m*; (*fig*) centro *m*. **in ~** enfocado. **out of ~** desenfocado. ● *vt*/*i* (*pt* **focused**) enfocar(se); (*fig*) concentrar
fodder /'fɒdə(r)/ *n* forraje *m*
foe /fəʊ/ *n* enemigo *m*
foetus /'fi:təs/ *n* (*pl* **-tuses**) feto *m*
fog /fɒg/ *n* niebla *f*. ● *vt* (*pt* **fogged**) envolver en niebla; (*photo*) velar. ● *vi*. **~ (up)** empañarse; (*photo*) velarse
fog(e)y /fəʊgɪ/ *n*. **be an old ~** estar chapado a la antigua
foggy /'fɒgɪ/ *a* (**-ier**, **-iest**) nebuloso. **it is ~** hay niebla
foghorn /'fɒghɔ:n/ *n* sirena *f* de niebla
foible /'fɔɪbl/ *n* punto *m* débil
foil[1] /fɔɪl/ *vt* (*thwart*) frustrar
foil[2] /fɔɪl/ *n* papel *m* de plata; (*fig*) contraste *m*
foist /fɔɪst/ *vt* encajar (on a)
fold[1] /fəʊld/ *vt* doblar; cruzar ‹*arms*›. ● *vi* doblarse; (*fail*) fracasar. ● *n* pliegue *m*
fold[2] /fəʊld/ *n* (*for sheep*) redil *m*
folder /'fəʊldə(r)/ *n* (*file*) carpeta *f*; (*leaflet*) folleto *m*
folding /'fəʊldɪŋ/ *a* plegable
foliage /'fəʊlɪɪdʒ/ *n* follaje *m*

folk /fəʊk/ *n* gente *f*. ● *a* popular. **~lore** *n* folklore *m*. **~s** *npl* (*one's relatives*) familia *f*

follow /ˈfɒləʊ/ *vt/i* seguir. **~ up** seguir; (*investigate further*) investigar. **~er** *n* seguidor *m*. **~ing** *n* partidarios *mpl*. ● *a* siguiente. ● *prep* después de

folly /ˈfɒlɪ/ *n* locura *f*

foment /fəˈment/ *vt* fomentar

fond /fɒnd/ *a* (**-er**, **-est**) (*loving*) cariñoso; ‹*hope*› vivo. **be ~ of s.o.** tener(le) cariño a uno. **be ~ of sth** ser aficionado a algo

fondle /ˈfɒndl/ *vt* acariciar

fondness /ˈfɒndnɪs/ *n* cariño *m*; (*for things*) afición *f*

font /fɒnt/ *n* pila *f* bautismal

food /fu:d/ *n* alimento *m*, comida *f*. **~ processor** *n* robot *m* de cocina, batidora *f*

fool /fu:l/ *n* tonto *m*. ● *vt* engañar. ● *vi* hacer el tonto

foolhardy /ˈfu:lhɑ:dɪ/ *a* temerario

foolish /ˈfu:lɪʃ/ *a* tonto. **~ly** *adv* tontamente. **~ness** *n* tontería *f*

foolproof /ˈfu:lpru:f/ *a* infalible, a toda prueba, a prueba de tontos

foot /fʊt/ *n* (*pl* **feet**) pie *m*; (*measure*) pie *m* (*=30,48 cm*); (*of animal, furniture*) pata *f*. **get under s.o.'s feet** estorbar a uno. **on ~** a pie. **on/to one's feet** de pie. **put one's ~ in it** meter la pata. ● *vt* pagar ‹*bill*›. **~ it** ir andando

footage /ˈfʊtɪdʒ/ *n* (*of film*) secuencia *f*

football /ˈfʊtbɔ:l/ *n* (*ball*) balón *m*; (*game*) fútbol *m*. **~er** *n* futbolista *m & f*

footbridge /ˈfʊtbrɪdʒ/ *n* puente *m* para peatones

foothills /ˈfʊthɪlz/ *npl* estribaciones *fpl*

foothold /ˈfʊthəʊld/ *n* punto *m* de apoyo *m*

footing /ˈfʊtɪŋ/ *n* pie *m*

footlights /ˈfʊtlaɪts/ *npl* candilejas *fpl*

footloose /ˈfʊtlu:s/ *a* libre

footman /ˈfʊtmən/ *n* lacayo *m*

footnote /ˈfʊtnəʊt/ *n* nota *f* (al pie de la página)

foot: **~path** *n* (*in country*) senda *f*; (*in town*) acera *f*, vereda *f* (*Arg*), banqueta *f* (*Mex*). **~print** *n* huella *f*. **~sore** *a*. **be ~sore** tener los pies doloridos. **~step** *n* paso *m*. **~stool** *n* escabel *m*. **~wear** *n* calzado *m*

for /fɔ:(r)/, *unstressed* /fə(r)/ *prep* (*expressing purpose*) para; (*on behalf of*) por; (*in spite of*) a pesar de; (*during*) durante; (*in favour of*) a favor de. **he has been in Madrid ~ two months** hace dos meses que está en Madrid. ● *conj* ya que

forage /ˈfɒrɪdʒ/ *vi* forrajear. ● *n* forraje *m*

foray /ˈfɒreɪ/ *n* incursión *f*

forbade /fəˈbæd/ *see* **forbid**

forbear /fɔ:ˈbeər/ *vt/i* (*pt* **forbore**, *pp* **forborne**) contenerse. **~ance** *n* paciencia *f*

forbid /fəˈbɪd/ *vt* (*pt* **forbade**, *pp* **forbidden**) prohibir (**s.o. to do** a uno hacer). **~ s.o. sth** prohibir algo a uno

forbidding /fəˈbɪdɪŋ/ *a* imponente

force /fɔ:s/ *n* fuerza *f*. **come into ~** entrar en vigor. **the ~s** las fuerzas *fpl* armadas. ● *vt* forzar. **~ on** imponer a. **~d** *a* forzado. **~-feed** *vt* alimentar a la fuerza. **~ful** /ˈfɔ:sfʊl/ *a* enérgico

forceps /ˈfɔ:seps/ *n invar* tenazas *fpl*; (*for obstetric use*) fórceps *m invar*; (*for dental use*) gatillo *m*

forcibl|e /ˈfɔ:səbl/ *a* a la fuerza. **~y** *adv* a la fuerza

ford /fɔ:d/ *n* vado *m*, botadero *m* (*Mex*). ● *vt* vadear

fore /fɔ:(r)/ *a* anterior. ● *n*. **come to the ~** hacerse evidente

forearm /ˈfɔ:rɑ:m/ *n* antebrazo *m*

foreboding /fɔ:ˈbəʊdɪŋ/ *n* presentimiento *m*

forecast /ˈfɔ:kɑ:st/ *vt* (*pt* **forecast**) pronosticar. ● *n* pronóstico *m*

forecourt /ˈfɔ:kɔ:t/ *n* patio *m*

forefathers /ˈfɔ:fɑ:ðəz/ *npl* antepasados *mpl*

forefinger /ˈfɔ:fɪŋgə(r)/ *n* (dedo *m*) índice *m*

forefront /ˈfɔ:frʌnt/ *n* vanguardia *f*. **in the ~** a/en vanguardia, en primer plano

foregone /ˈfɔ:gɒn/ *a*. **~ conclusion** resultado *m* previsto

foreground /ˈfɔ:graʊnd/ *n* primer plano *m*

forehead /ˈfɒrɪd/ *n* frente *f*

foreign /ˈfɒrən/ *a* extranjero; ‹*trade*› exterior; ‹*travel*› al extranjero, en el extranjero. **~er** *n* extranjero *m*. **F~ Secretary** *n* ministro *m* de Asuntos Exteriores

foreman /ˈfɔ:mən/ *n* capataz *m*, caporal *m*

foremost /ˈfɔːməʊst/ *a* primero. ● *adv.* **first and ~** ante todo

forensic /fəˈrensɪk/ *a* forense

forerunner /ˈfɔːrʌnə(r)/ *n* precursor *m*

foresee /fɔːˈsiː/ *vt* (*pt* **-saw**, *pp* **-seen**) prever. **~able** *a* previsible

foreshadow /fɔːˈʃædəʊ/ *vt* presagiar

foresight /ˈfɔːsaɪt/ *n* previsión *f*

forest /ˈfɒrɪst/ *n* bosque *m*

forestall /fɔːˈstɔːl/ *vt* anticiparse a

forestry /ˈfɒrɪstrɪ/ *n* silvicultura *f*

foretaste /ˈfɔːteɪst/ *n* anticipación *f*

foretell /fɔːˈtel/ *vt* (*pt* **foretold**) predecir

forever /fəˈrevə(r)/ *adv* para siempre

forewarn /fɔːˈwɔːn/ *vt* prevenir

foreword /ˈfɔːwɜːd/ *n* prefacio *m*

forfeit /ˈfɔːfɪt/ *n* (*penalty*) pena *f*; (*in game*) prenda *f*; (*fine*) multa *f*. ● *vt* perder

forgave /fəˈgeɪv/ *see* **forgive**

forge[1] /fɔːdʒ/ *n* fragua *f*. ● *vt* fraguar; (*copy*) falsificar

forge[2] /fɔːdʒ/ *vi* avanzar. **~ahead** adelantarse rápidamente

forge: ~r /ˈfɔːdʒə(r)/ *n* falsificador *m*. **~ry** *n* falsificación *f*

forget /fəˈget/ *vt* (*pt* **forgot**, *pp* **forgotten**) olvidar. **~ o.s.** propasarse, extralimitarse. ● *vi* olvidar(se). **I forgot** se me olvidó. **~ful** *a* olvidadizo. **~ful of** olvidando. **~-me-not** *n* nomeolvides *f invar*

forgive /fəˈgɪv/ *vt* (*pt* **forgave**, *pp* **forgiven**) perdonar. **~ness** *n* perdón *m*

forgo /fɔːˈgəʊ/ *vt* (*pt* **forwent**, *pp* **forgone**) renunciar a

fork /fɔːk/ *n* tenedor *m*; (*for digging*) horca *f*; (*in road*) bifurcación *f*. ● *vi* ‹*road*› bifurcarse. **~ out** (*sl*) aflojar la bolsa (*fam*), pagar. **~ed** *a* ahorquillado; ‹*road*› bifurcado. **~-lift truck** *n* carretilla *f* elevadora

forlorn /fəˈlɔːn/ *a* (*hopeless*) desesperado; (*abandoned*) abandonado. **~ hope** *n* empresa *f* desesperada

form /fɔːm/ *n* forma *f*; (*document*) impreso *m*, formulario *m*; (*schol*) clase *f*. ● *vt* formar. ● *vi* formarse

formal /ˈfɔːml/ *a* formal; ‹*person*› formalista; ‹*dress*› de etiqueta. **~ity** /-ˈmælətɪ/ *n* formalidad *f*. **~ly** *adv* oficialmente

format /ˈfɔːmæt/ *n* formato *m*

formation /fɔːˈmeɪʃn/ *n* formación *f*

formative /ˈfɔːmətɪv/ *a* formativo

former /ˈfɔːmə(r)/ *a* anterior; (*first of two*) primero. **~ly** *adv* antes

formidable /ˈfɔːmɪdəbl/ *a* formidable

formless /ˈfɔːmlɪs/ *a* informe

formula /ˈfɔːmjʊlə/ *n* (*pl* **-ae** /-iː/ *or* **-as**) fórmula *f*

formulate /ˈfɔːmjʊleɪt/ *vt* formular

fornicat|e /ˈfɔːnɪkeɪt/ *vi* fornicar. **~ion** /-ˈkeɪʃn/ *n* fornicación *f*

forsake /fəˈseɪk/ *vt* (*pt* **forsook**, *pp* **forsaken**) abandonar

fort /fɔːt/ *n* (*mil*) fuerte *m*

forte /ˈfɔːteɪ/ *n* (*talent*) fuerte *m*

forth /fɔːθ/ *adv* en adelante. **and so ~** y así sucesivamente. **go back and ~** ir y venir

forthcoming /fɔːθˈkʌmɪŋ/ *a* próximo, venidero; (*sociable, fam*) comunicativo

forthright /ˈfɔːθraɪt/ *a* directo

forthwith /fɔːθˈwɪθ/ *adv* inmediatamente

fortieth /ˈfɔːtɪɪθ/ *a* cuarenta, cuadragésimo. ● *n* cuadragésima parte *f*

fortif|ication /fɔːtɪfɪˈkeɪʃn/ *n* fortificación *f*. **~y** /ˈfɔːtɪfaɪ/ *vt* fortificar

fortitude /ˈfɔːtɪtjuːd/ *n* valor *m*

fortnight /ˈfɔːtnaɪt/ *n* quince días *mpl*, quincena *f*. **~ly** *a* bimensual. ● *adv* cada quince días

fortress /ˈfɔːtrɪs/ *n* fortaleza *f*

fortuitous /fɔːˈtjuːɪtəs/ *a* fortuito

fortunate /ˈfɔːtʃənət/ *a* afortunado. **be ~** tener suerte. **~ly** *adv* afortunadamente

fortune /ˈfɔːtʃuːn/ *n* fortuna *f*. **have the good ~ to** tener la suerte de. **~-teller** *n* adivino *m*

forty /ˈfɔːtɪ/ *a* & *n* cuarenta (*m*). **~ winks** un sueñecito *m*

forum /ˈfɔːrəm/ *n* foro *m*

forward /ˈfɔːwəd/ *a* delantero; (*advanced*) precoz; (*pert*) impertinente. ● *n* (*sport*) delantero *m*. ● *adv* adelante. **come ~** presentarse. **go ~** avanzar. ● *vt* hacer seguir ‹*letter*›; enviar ‹*goods*›; (*fig*) favorecer. **~ness** *n* precocidad *f*

forwards /ˈfɔːwədz/ *adv* adelante

fossil /ˈfɒsl/ *a* & *n* fósil (*m*)

foster /ˈfɒstə(r)/ *vt* (*promote*) fomentar; criar ‹*child*›. **~-child** *n* hijo *m* adoptivo. **~-mother** *n* madre *f* adoptiva

fought /fɔːt/ *see* **fight**

foul /faʊl/ *a* (**-er, -est**) ‹*smell, weather*› asqueroso; (*dirty*) sucio; ‹*language*› obsceno; ‹*air*› viciado. **~ play** *n* jugada *f* sucia; (*crime*) delito *m*. ● *n* (*sport*) falta *f*. ● *vt* ensuciar; manchar ‹*reputation*›. **~-mouthed** *a* obsceno

found[1] /faʊnd/ *see* **find**

found[2] /faʊnd/ *vt* fundar

found[3] /faʊnd/ *vt* (*tec*) fundir

foundation /faʊn'deɪʃn/ *n* fundación *f*; (*basis*) fundamento. **~s** *npl* (*archit*) cimientos *mpl*

founder[1] /'faʊndə(r)/ *n* fundador *m*

founder[2] /'faʊndə(r)/ *vi* ‹*ship*› hundirse

foundry /'faʊndrɪ/ *n* fundición *f*

fountain /'faʊntɪn/ *n* fuente *f*. **~-pen** *n* estilográfica *f*

four /fɔ:(r)/ *a & n* cuatro (*m*). **~fold** *a* cuádruple. ● *adv* cuatro veces. **~-poster** *n* cama *f* con cuatro columnas

foursome /'fɔ:səm/ *n* grupo *m* de cuatro personas

fourteen /'fɔ:ti:n/ *a & n* catorce (*m*). **~th** *a & n* catorce (*m*), decimocuarto (*m*). ● *n* (*fraction*) catorceavo *m*

fourth /fɔ:θ/ *a & n* cuarto (*m*)

fowl /faʊl/ *n* ave *f*

fox /fɒks/ *n* zorro *m*, zorra *f*. ● *vt* (*baffle*) dejar perplejo; (*deceive*) engañar

foyer /'fɔɪeɪ/ *n* (*hall*) vestíbulo *m*

fraction /'frækʃn/ *n* fracción *f*

fractious /'frækʃəs/ *a* díscolo

fracture /'fræktʃə(r)/ *n* fractura *f*. ● *vt* fracturar. ● *vi* fracturarse

fragile /'frædʒaɪl/ *a* frágil

fragment /'frægmənt/ *n* fragmento *m*. **~ary** *a* fragmentario

fragran|ce /'freɪgrəns/ *n* fragancia *f*. **~t** *a* fragante

frail /freɪl/ *a* (**-er, -est**) frágil

frame /freɪm/ *n* (*of picture, door, window*) marco *m*; (*of spectacles*) montura *f*; (*fig, structure*) estructura *f*; (*temporary state*) estado *m*. **~ of mind** estado *m* de ánimo. ● *vt* enmarcar; (*fig*) formular; (*jurid, sl*) incriminar falsamente. **~-up** *n* (*sl*) complot *m*

framework /'freɪmwɜ:k/ *n* estructura *f*; (*context*) marco *m*

France /frɑ:ns/ *n* Francia *f*

franchise /'fræntʃaɪz/ *n* (*pol*) derecho *m* a votar; (*com*) concesión *f*

Franco... /'fræŋkəʊ/ *pref* franco...

frank /fræŋk/ *a* sincero. ● *vt* franquear. **~ly** *adv* sinceramente. **~ness** *n* sinceridad *f*

frantic /'fræntɪk/ *a* frenético. **~ with** loco de

fraternal /frə'tɜ:nl/ *a* fraternal

fraternity /frə'tɜ:nɪtɪ/ *n* fraternidad *f*; (*club*) asociación *f*

fraternize /'frætənaɪz/ *vi* fraternizar

fraud /frɔ:d/ *n* (*deception*) fraude *m*; (*person*) impostor *m*. **~ulent** *a* fraudulento

fraught /frɔ:t/ *a* (*tense*) tenso. **~ with** cargado de

fray[1] /freɪ/ *vt* desgastar. ● *vi* deshilacharse

fray[2] /freɪ/ *n* riña *f*

freak /fri:k/ *n* (*caprice*) capricho *m*; (*monster*) monstruo *m*; (*person*) chalado *m*. ● *a* anormal. **~ish** *a* anormal

freckle /'frekl/ *n* peca *f*. **~d** *a* pecoso

free /fri:/ *a* (**freer** /'fri:ə(r)/, **freest** /'fri:ɪst/) libre; (*gratis*) gratis; (*lavish*) generoso. **~ kick** *n* golpe *m* franco. **~ of charge** gratis. **~ speech** *n* libertad *f* de expresión. **give a ~ hand** dar carta blanca. ● *vt* (*pt* **freed**) (*set at liberty*) poner en libertad; (*relieve from*) liberar (**from**/**of** de); (*untangle*) desenredar; (*loosen*) soltar

freedom /'fri:dəm/ *n* libertad *f*

freehold /'fri:həʊld/ *n* propiedad *f* absoluta

freelance /'fri:lɑ:ns/ *a* independiente

freely /'fri:lɪ/ *adv* libremente

Freemason /'fri:meɪsn/ *n* masón *m*. **~ry** *n* masonería *f*

free-range /'fri:reɪndʒ/ *a* ‹*eggs*› de granja

freesia /'fri:zjə/ *n* fresia *f*

freeway /'fri:weɪ/ *n* (*Amer*) autopista *f*

freez|e /'fri:z/ *vt* (*pt* **froze**, *pp* **frozen**) helar; congelar ‹*food, wages*›. ● *vi* helarse, congelarse; (*become motionless*) quedarse inmóvil. ● *n* helada *f*; (*of wages, prices*) congelación *f*. **~er** *n* congelador *m*. **~ing** *a* glacial. ● *n* congelación *f*. **below ~ing** bajo cero

freight /freɪt/ *n* (*goods*) mercancías *fpl*; (*hire of ship etc*) flete *m*. **~er** *n* (*ship*) buque *m* de carga

French /frentʃ/ *a* francés. ● *n* (*lang*) francés *m*. **~man** *n* francés *m*. **~-speaking** *a* francófono. **~ window** *n* puertaventana *f*. **~woman** *f* francesa *f*

frenz|ied /ˈfrenzɪd/ *a* frenético. **~y** *n* frenesí *m*
frequency /ˈfriːkwənsɪ/ *n* frecuencia *f*
frequent /frɪˈkwent/ *vt* frecuentar. /ˈfriːkwənt/ *a* frecuente. **~ly** *adv* frecuentemente
fresco /ˈfreskəʊ/ *n* (*pl* **-o(e)s**) fresco *m*
fresh /freʃ/ *a* (**-er**, **-est**) fresco; (*different, additional*) nuevo; (*cheeky*) fresco, descarado; ‹*water*› dulce. **~en** *vi* refrescar. **~en up** ‹*person*› refrescarse. **~ly** *adv* recientemente. **~man** *n* estudiante *m* de primer año. **~ness** *n* frescura *f*
fret /fret/ *vi* (*pt* **fretted**) inquietarse. **~ful** *a* (*discontented*) quejoso; (*irritable*) irritable
Freudian /ˈfrɔɪdjən/ *a* freudiano
friar /ˈfraɪə(r)/ *n* fraile *m*
friction /ˈfrɪkʃn/ *n* fricción *f*
Friday /ˈfraɪdeɪ/ *n* viernes *m*. **Good ~** Viernes Santo
fridge /frɪdʒ/ *n* (*fam*) nevera *f*, refrigerador *m*, refrigeradora *f*
fried /fraɪd/ *see* **fry**. ● *a* frito
friend /frend/ *n* amigo *m*. **~liness** /ˈfrendlɪnɪs/ *n* simpatía *f*. **~ly** *a* (**-ier**, **-iest**) simpático. **F~ly Society** *n* mutualidad *f*. **~ship** /ˈfrendʃɪp/ *n* amistad *f*
frieze /friːz/ *n* friso *m*
frigate /ˈfrɪgət/ *n* fragata *f*
fright /fraɪt/ *n* susto *m*; (*person*) espantajo *m*; (*thing*) horror *m*
frighten /ˈfraɪtn/ *vt* asustar. **~ off** ahuyentar. **~ed** *a* asustado. **be ~ed** tener miedo (**of** de)
frightful /ˈfraɪtfl/ *a* espantoso, horrible. **~ly** *adv* terriblemente
frigid /ˈfrɪdʒɪd/ *a* frío; (*psych*) frígido. **~ity** /-ˈdʒɪdətɪ/ *n* frigidez *f*
frill /frɪl/ *n* volante *m*. **~s** *npl* (*fig*) adornos *mpl*. **with no ~s** sencillo
fringe /frɪndʒ/ *n* (*sewing*) fleco *m*; (*ornamental border*) franja *f*; (*of hair*) flequillo *m*; (*of area*) periferia *f*; (*of society*) margen *m*. **~ benefits** *npl* beneficios *mpl* suplementarios. **~ theatre** *n* teatro *m* de vanguardia
frisk /frɪsk/ *vt* (*search*) cachear
frisky /ˈfrɪskɪ/ *a* (**-ier**, **-iest**) retozón; ‹*horse*› fogoso
fritter[1] /ˈfrɪtə(r)/ *vt*. **~ away** desperdiciar
fritter[2] /ˈfrɪtə(r)/ *n* buñuelo *m*
frivol|ity /frɪˈvɒlətɪ/ *n* frivolidad *f*. **~ous** /ˈfrɪvələs/ *a* frívolo
frizzy /ˈfrɪzɪ/ *a* crespo
fro /frəʊ/ *see* **to and fro**
frock /frɒk/ *n* vestido *m*; (*of monk*) hábito *m*
frog /frɒg/ *n* rana *f*. **have a ~ in one's throat** tener carraspera
frogman /ˈfrɒgmən/ *n* hombre *m* rana
frolic /ˈfrɒlɪk/ *vi* (*pt* **frolicked**) retozar. ● *n* broma *f*
from /frɒm/, *unstressed* /frəm/ *prep* de; (*with time, prices, etc*) a partir de; (*habit, conviction*) por; (*according to*) según. **take ~** (*away from*) quitar a
front /frʌnt/ *n* parte *f* delantera; (*of building*) fachada *f*; (*of clothes*) delantera *f*; (*mil, pol*) frente *f*; (*of book*) principio *m*; (*fig, appearance*) apariencia *f*; (*sea front*) paseo *m* marítimo. **in ~ of** delante de. **put a bold ~ on** hacer de tripas corazón, mostrar firmeza. ● *a* delantero; (*first*) primero. **~age** *n* fachada *f*. **~al** *a* frontal; ‹*attack*› de frente. **~ door** *n* puerta *f* principal. **~ page** *n* (*of newspaper*) primera plana *f*
frontier /ˈfrʌntɪə(r)/ *n* frontera *f*
frost /frɒst/ *n* (*freezing*) helada *f*; (*frozen dew*) escarcha *f*. **~-bite** *n* congelación *f*. **~-bitten** *a* congelado. **~ed** *a* ‹*glass*› esmerilado
frosting /ˈfrɒstɪŋ/ *n* (*icing, Amer*) azúcar *m* glaseado
frosty *a* ‹*weather*› de helada; ‹*window*› escarchado; (*fig*) glacial
froth /frɒθ/ *n* espuma *f*. ● *vi* espumar. **~y** *a* espumoso
frown /fraʊn/ *vi* fruncir el entrecejo. **~ on** desaprobar. ● *n* ceño *m*
froze /frəʊz/, **frozen** /ˈfrəʊzn/ *see* **freeze**
frugal /ˈfruːgl/ *a* frugal. **~ly** *adv* frugalmente
fruit /fruːt/ *n* (*bot, on tree, fig*) fruto *m*; (*as food*) fruta *f*. **~erer** *n* frutero *m*. **~ful** /ˈfruːtfl/ *a* fértil; (*fig*) fructífero. **~less** *a* infructuoso. **~ machine** *n* (máquina *f*) tragaperras *m*. **~ salad** *n* macedonia *f* de frutas. **~y** /ˈfruːtɪ/ *a* ‹*taste*› que sabe a fruta
fruition /fruːˈɪʃn/ *n*. **come to ~** realizarse
frump /frʌmp/ *n* espantajo *m*
frustrat|e /frʌˈstreɪt/ *vt* frustrar. **~ion** /-ʃn/ *n* frustración *f*; (*disappointment*) decepción *f*
fry[1] /fraɪ/ *vt* (*pt* **fried**) freír. ● *vi* freírse

fry[2] /fraɪ/ *n* (*pl* **fry**). **small ~** gente *f* de poca monta
frying-pan /'fraɪɪŋpæn/ *n* sartén *f*
fuchsia /'fju:ʃə/ *n* fucsia *f*
fuddy-duddy /'fʌdɪdʌdɪ/ *n*. **be a ~** (*sl*) estar chapado a la antigua
fudge /fʌdʒ/ *n* dulce *m* de azúcar
fuel /'fju:əl/ *n* combustible *m*; (*for car engine*) carburante *m*; (*fig*) pábulo *m*. ● *vt* (*pt* **fuelled**) alimentar de combustible
fugitive /'fju:dʒɪtɪv/ *a* & *n* fugitivo (*m*)
fugue /fju:g/ *n* (*mus*) fuga *f*
fulfil /fʊl'fɪl/ *vt* (*pt* **fulfilled**) cumplir (con) ‹*promise, obligation*›; satisfacer ‹*condition*›; realizar ‹*hopes, plans*›; llevar a cabo ‹*task*›. **~ment** *n* (*of promise, obligation*) cumplimiento *m*; (*of conditions*) satisfacción *f*; (*of hopes, plans*) realización *f*; (*of task*) ejecución *f*
full /fʊl/ *a* (**-er**, **-est**) lleno; ‹*bus, hotel*› completo; ‹*skirt*› amplio; ‹*account*› detallado. **at ~ speed** a máxima velocidad. **be ~ (up)** (*with food*) no poder más. **in ~ swing** en plena marcha. ● *n*. **in ~** sin quitar nada. **to the ~** completamente. **write in ~** escribir con todas las letras. **~ back** *n* (*sport*) defensa *m* & *f*. **~-blooded** *a* vigoroso. **~ moon** *n* plenilunio *m*. **~-scale** *a* ‹*drawing*› de tamaño natural; (*fig*) amplio. **~ stop** *n* punto *m*; (*at end of paragraph, fig*) punto *m* final. **~ time** *a* de jornada completa. **~y** *adv* completamente
fulsome /'fʊlsəm/ *a* excesivo
fumble /'fʌmbl/ *vi* buscar (torpemente)
fume /fju:m/ *vi* humear; (*fig, be furious*) estar furioso. **~s** *npl* humo *m*
fumigate /'fju:mɪgeɪt/ *vt* fumigar
fun /fʌn/ *n* (*amusement*) diversión *f*; (*merriment*) alegría *f*. **for ~** en broma. **have ~** divertirse. **make ~ of** burlarse de
function /'fʌŋkʃn/ *n* (*purpose, duty*) función *f*; (*reception*) recepción *f*. ● *vi* funcionar. **~al** *a* funcional
fund /fʌnd/ *n* fondo *m*. ● *vt* proveer fondos para
fundamental /fʌndə'mentl/ *a* fundamental
funeral /'fju:nərəl/ *n* funeral *m*, funerales *mpl*. ● *a* fúnebre
fun-fair /'fʌnfeə(r)/ *n* parque *m* de atracciones
fungus /'fʌŋgəs/ *n* (*pl* **-gi** /-gaɪ/) hongo *m*
funicular /fju:'nɪkjʊlə(r)/ *n* funicular *m*
funk /fʌŋk/ *m* (*fear, sl*) miedo *m*; (*state of depression, Amer, sl*) depresión *f*. **be in a (blue) ~** tener (mucho) miedo; (*Amer*) estar (muy) deprimido. ● *vi* rajarse
funnel /'fʌnl/ *n* (*for pouring*) embudo *m*; (*of ship*) chimenea *f*
funn|ily /'fʌnɪlɪ/ *adv* graciosamente; (*oddly*) curiosamente. **~y** *a* (**-ier**, **-iest**) divertido, gracioso; (*odd*) curioso, raro. **~y-bone** *n* cóndilo *m* del húmero. **~y business** *n* engaño *m*
fur /fɜ:(r)/ *n* pelo *m*; (*pelt*) piel *f*; (*in kettle*) sarro *m*
furbish /'fɜ:bɪʃ/ *vt* pulir; (*renovate*) renovar
furious /'fjʊərɪəs/ *a* furioso. **~ly** *adv* furiosamente
furnace /'fɜ:nɪs/ *n* horno *m*
furnish /'fɜ:nɪʃ/ *vt* (*with furniture*) amueblar; (*supply*) proveer. **~ings** *npl* muebles *mpl*, mobiliario *m*
furniture /'fɜ:nɪtʃə(r)/ *n* muebles *mpl*, mobiliario *m*
furrier /'fʌrɪə(r)/ *n* peletero *m*
furrow /'fʌrəʊ/ *n* surco *m*
furry /'fɜ:rɪ/ *a* peludo
furthe|r /'fɜ:ðə(r)/ *a* más lejano; (*additional*) nuevo. ● *adv* más lejos; (*more*) además. ● *vt* fomentar. **~rmore** *adv* además. **~rmost** *a* más lejano. **~st** *a* más lejano. ● *adv* más lejos
furtive /'fɜ:tɪv/ *a* furtivo
fury /'fjʊərɪ/ *n* furia *f*
fuse[1] /fju:z/ *vt* (*melt*) fundir; (*fig, unite*) fusionar. **~ the lights** fundir los plomos. ● *vi* fundirse; (*fig*) fusionarse. ● *n* fusible *m*, plomo *m*
fuse[2] /fju:z/ *n* (*of bomb*) mecha *f*
fuse-box /'fju:zbɒks/ *n* caja *f* de fusibles
fuselage /'fju:zəlɑ:ʒ/ *n* fuselaje *m*
fusion /'fju:ʒn/ *n* fusión *f*
fuss /fʌs/ *n* (*commotion*) jaleo *m*. **kick up a ~** armar un lío, armar una bronca, protestar. **make a ~ of** tratar con mucha atención. **~y** *a* (**-ier**, **-iest**) (*finicky*) remilgado; (*demanding*) exigente; (*ornate*) recargado
fusty /'fʌstɪ/ *a* (**-ier**, **-iest**) que huele a cerrado

futile /'fju:taɪl/ *a* inútil, vano
future /'fju:tʃə(r) *a* futuro. ● *n* futuro *m*, porvenir *m*; (*gram*) futuro *m*. **in ~** en lo sucesivo, de ahora en adelante
futuristic /fju:tʃə'rɪstɪk/ *a* futurista
fuzz /fʌz/ *n* (*fluff*) pelusa *f*; (*police, sl*) policía *f*, poli *f* (*fam*)
fuzzy /'fʌzɪ/ *a* ‹*hair*› crespo; ‹*photograph*› borroso

G

gab /gæb/ *n* charla *f*. **have the gift of the ~** tener un pico de oro
gabardine /gæbə'di:n/ *n* gabardina *f*
gabble /'gæbl/ *vt* decir atropelladamente. ● *vi* hablar atropelladamente. ● *n* torrente *m* de palabras
gable /'geɪbl/ *n* aguilón *m*
gad /gæd/ *vi* (*pt* **gadded**). **~ about** callejear
gadget /'gædʒɪt/ *n* chisme *m*
Gaelic /'geɪlɪk/ *a & n* gaélico (*m*)
gaffe /gæf/ *n* plancha *f*, metedura *f* de pata
gag /gæg/ *n* mordaza *f*; (*joke*) chiste *m*. ● *vt* (*pt* **gagged**) amordazar
gaga /'gɑ:gɑ:/ *a* (*sl*) chocho
gaiety /'geɪətɪ/ *n* alegría *f*
gaily /'geɪlɪ/ *adv* alegremente
gain /geɪn/ *vt* ganar; (*acquire*) adquirir; (*obtain*) conseguir. ● *vi* ‹*clock*› adelantar. ● *n* ganancia *f*; (*increase*) aumento *m*. **~ful** *a* lucrativo
gainsay /geɪn'seɪ/ *vt* (*pt* **gainsaid**) (*formal*) negar
gait /geɪt/ *n* modo *m* de andar
gala /'gɑ:lə/ *n* fiesta *f*; (*sport*) competición *f*
galaxy /'gæləksɪ/ *n* galaxia *f*
gale /geɪl/ *n* vendaval *m*; (*storm*) tempestad *f*
gall /gɔ:l/ *n* bilis *f*; (*fig*) hiel *f*; (*impudence*) descaro *m*
gallant /'gælənt/ *a* (*brave*) valiente; (*chivalrous*) galante. **~ry** *n* valor *m*
gall-bladder /'gɔ:lblædə(r)/ *n* vesícula *f* biliar
galleon /'gælɪən/ *n* galeón *m*
gallery /'gælərɪ/ *n* galería *f*
galley /'gælɪ/ *n* (*ship*) galera *f*; (*ship's kitchen*) cocina *f*. **~ (proof)** *n* (*typ*) galerada *f*
Gallic /'gælɪk/ *a* gálico. **~ism** *n* galicismo *m*
gallivant /'gælɪvænt/ *vi* (*fam*) callejear
gallon /'gælən/ *n* galón *m* (*imperial = 4,546l; Amer = 3,785l*)
gallop /'gæləp/ *n* galope *m*. ● *vi* (*pt* **galloped**) galopar
gallows /'gæləʊz/ *n* horca *f*
galore /gə'lɔ:(r)/ *adv* en abundancia
galosh /gə'lɒʃ/ *n* chanclo *m*
galvanize /'gælvənaɪz/ *vt* galvanizar
gambit /'gæmbɪt/ *n* (*in chess*) gambito *m*; (*fig*) táctica *f*
gambl|e /'gæmbl/ *vt/i* jugar. **~e on** contar con. ● *n* (*venture*) empresa *f* arriesgada; (*bet*) jugada *f*; (*risk*) riesgo *m*. **~er** *n* jugador *m*. **~ing** *n* juego *m*
game[1] /geɪm/ *n* juego *m*; (*match*) partido *m*; (*animals, birds*) caza *f*. ● *a* valiente. **~ for** listo para
game[2] /geɪm/ *a* (*lame*) cojo
gamekeeper /'geɪmki:pə(r)/ *n* guardabosque *m*
gammon /'gæmən/ *n* jamón *m* ahumado
gamut /'gæmət/ *n* gama *f*
gamy /'geɪmɪ/ *a* manido
gander /'gændə(r)/ *n* ganso *m*
gang /gæŋ/ *n* pandilla *f*; (*of workmen*) equipo *m*. ● *vi*. **~ up** unirse (**on** contra)
gangling /'gæŋglɪŋ/ *a* larguirucho
gangrene /'gæŋgri:n/ *n* gangrena *f*
gangster /'gæŋstə(r)/ *n* bandido *m*, gangster *m*
gangway /'gæŋweɪ/ *n* pasillo *m*; (*of ship*) pasarela *f*
gaol /dʒeɪl/ *n* cárcel *f*. **~bird** *n* criminal *m* empedernido. **~er** *n* carcelero *m*
gap /gæp/ *n* vacío *m*; (*breach*) brecha *f*; (*in time*) intervalo *m*; (*deficiency*) laguna *f*; (*difference*) diferencia *f*
gap|e /'geɪp/ *vi* quedarse boquiabierto; (*be wide open*) estar muy abierto. **~ing** *a* abierto; (*person*) boquiabierto
garage /'gærɑ:ʒ/ *n* garaje *m*; (*petrol station*) gasolinera *f*; (*for repairs*) taller *m*. ● *vt* dejar en (el) garaje
garb /gɑ:b/ *n* vestido *m*
garbage /'gɑ:bɪdʒ/ *n* basura *f*
garble /'gɑ:bl/ *vt* mutilar
garden /'gɑ:dn/ *n* (*of flowers*) jardín *m*; (*of vegetables/fruit*) huerto *m*. ● *vi* trabajar en el jardín/huerto. **~er** *n* jardinero/hortelano *m*. **~ing** *n* jardinería/horticultura *f*

gargantuan /gɑ:ˈgæntjʊən/ *a* gigantesco
gargle /ˈgɑ:gl/ *vi* hacer gárgaras. *n* gargarismo *m*
gargoyle /ˈgɑ:gɔɪl/ *n* gárgola *f*
garish /ˈgeərɪʃ/ *a* chillón
garland /ˈgɑ:lənd/ *n* guirnalda *f*
garlic /ˈgɑ:lɪk/ *n* ajo *m*
garment /ˈgɑ:mənt/ *n* prenda *f* (de vestir)
garnet /ˈgɑ:nɪt/ *n* granate *m*
garnish /ˈgɑ:nɪʃ/ *vt* aderezar. ● *n* aderezo *m*
garret /ˈgærət/ *n* guardilla *f*, buhardilla *f*
garrison /ˈgærɪsn/ *n* guarnición *f*
garrulous /ˈgærələs/ *a* hablador
garter /ˈgɑ:tə(r)/ *n* liga *f*
gas /gæs/ *n* (*pl* **gases**) gas *m*; (*med*) anestésico *m*; (*petrol, Amer, fam*) gasolina *f*. ● *vt* (*pt* **gassed**) asfixiar con gas. ● *vi* (*fam*) charlar. **~ fire** *n* estufa *f* de gas
gash /gæʃ/ *n* cuchillada *f*. ● *vt* acuchillar
gasket /ˈgæskɪt/ *n* junta *f*
gas: **~ mask** *n* careta *f* antigás *a invar*. **~ meter** *n* contador *m* de gas
gasoline /ˈgæsəli:n/ *n* (*petrol, Amer*) gasolina *f*
gasometer /gæˈsɒmɪtə(r)/ *n* gasómetro *m*
gasp /gɑ:sp/ *vi* jadear; (*with surprise*) quedarse boquiabierto. ● *n* jadeo *m*
gas: **~ ring** *n* hornillo *m* de gas. **~ station** *n* (*Amer*) gasolinera *f*
gastric /ˈgæstrɪk/ *a* gástrico
gastronomy /gæˈstrɒnəmɪ/ *n* gastronomía *f*
gate /geɪt/ *n* puerta *f*; (*of metal*) verja *f*; (*barrier*) barrera *f*
gateau /ˈgætəʊ/ *n* (*pl* **gateaux**) tarta *f*
gate: **~crasher** *n* intruso *m* (que ha entrado sin ser invitado o sin pagar). **~way** *n* puerta f
gather /ˈgæðə(r)/ *vt* reunir ‹*people, things*›; (*accumulate*) acumular; (*pick up*) recoger; recoger ‹*flowers*›; (*fig, infer*) deducir; (*sewing*) fruncir. **~ speed** acelerar. ● *vi* ‹*people*› reunirse; ‹*things*› acumularse. **~ing** *n* reunión *f*
gauche /gəʊʃ/ *a* torpe
gaudy /ˈgɔ:dɪ/ *a* (**-ier**, **-iest**) chillón
gauge /geɪdʒ/ *n* (*measurement*) medida *f*; (*rail*) entrevía *f*; (*instrument*) indicador *m*. ● *vt* medir; (*fig*) estimar
gaunt /gɔ:nt/ *a* macilento; (*grim*) lúgubre
gauntlet /ˈgɔ:ntlɪt/ *n*. **run the ~ of** estar sometido a
gauze /gɔ:z/ *n* gasa *f*
gave /geɪv/ *see* **give**
gawk /gɔ:k/ *vi*. **~ at** mirar como un tonto
gawky /ˈgɔ:kɪ/ *a* (**-ier**, **-iest**) torpe
gawp /gɔ:p/ *vi*. **~ at** mirar como un tonto
gay /geɪ/ *a* (**-er**, **-est**) (*joyful*) alegre; (*homosexual, fam*) homosexual, gay (*fam*)
gaze /geɪz/ *vi*. **~ (at)** mirar (fijamente). ● *n* mirada *f* (fija)
gazelle /gəˈzel/ *n* gacela *f*
gazette /gəˈzet/ *n* boletín *m* oficial, gaceta *f*
gazump /gəˈzʌmp/ *vt* aceptar un precio más elevado de otro comprador
GB *abbr see* **Great Britain**
gear /gɪə(r)/ *n* equipo *m*; (*tec*) engranaje *m*; (*auto*) marcha *f*. **in ~** engranado. **out of ~** desengranado. ● *vt* adaptar. **~box** *n* (*auto*) caja *f* de cambios
geese /gi:s/ *see* **goose**
geezer /ˈgi:zə(r)/ *n* (*sl*) tipo *m*
gelatine /ˈdʒeləti:n/ *n* gelatina *f*
gelignite /ˈdʒelɪgnaɪt/ *n* gelignita *f*
gem /dʒem/ *n* piedra *f* preciosa
Gemini /ˈdʒemɪnaɪ/ *n* (*astr*) Gemelos *mpl*, Géminis *mpl*
gen /dʒen/ *n* (*sl*) información *f*
gender /ˈdʒendə(r)/ *n* género *m*
gene /dʒi:n/ *n* gene *m*
genealogy /dʒi:nɪˈælədʒɪ/ *n* genealogía *f*
general /ˈdʒenərəl/ *a* general. ● *n* general *m*. **in ~** generalmente. **~ election** *n* elecciones *fpl* generales
generaliz|ation /dʒenərəlaɪˈzeɪʃn/ *n* generalización *f*. **~e** *vt/i* generalizar
generally /ˈdʒenərəlɪ/ *adv* generalmente
general practitioner /ˈdʒenərəl prækˈtɪʃənə(r)/ *n* médico *m* de cabecera
generate /ˈdʒenəreɪt/ *vt* producir; (*elec*) generar
generation /dzenəˈreɪʃn/ *n* generación *f*
generator /ˈdʒenəreɪtə(r)/ *n* (*elec*) generador *m*
genero|sity /dʒenəˈrɒsətɪ/ *n* generosidad *f*. **~us** /ˈdʒenərəs/ *a* generoso; (*plentiful*) abundante

genetic /dʒɪ'netɪk/ *a* genético. **~s** *n* genética *f*

Geneva /dʒɪ'ni:və/ *n* Ginebra *f*

genial /'dʒi:nɪəl/ *a* simpático, afable; ‹*climate*› suave, templado

genital /'dʒenɪtl/ *a* genital. **~s** *npl* genitales *mpl*

genitive /'dʒenɪtɪv/ *a & n* genitivo (*m*)

genius /'dʒi:nɪəs/ *n* (*pl* **-uses**) genio *m*

genocide /'dʒenəsaɪd/ *n* genocidio *m*

genre /ʒɑ:ŋr/ *n* género *m*

gent /dʒent/ *n* (*sl*) señor *m*. **~s** *n* aseo *m* de caballeros

genteel /dʒen'ti:l/ *a* distinguido; (*excessively refined*) cursi

gentle /'dʒentl/ *a* (**-er**, **-est**) (*mild, kind*) amable, dulce; (*slight*) ligero; ‹*hint*› discreto

gentlefolk /'dʒentlfəʊk/ *npl* gente *f* de buena familia

gentleman /'dʒentlmən/ *n* señor *m*; (*well-bred*) caballero *m*

gentleness /'dʒentlnɪs/ *n* amabilidad *f*

gentlewoman /'dʒentlwʊmən/ *n* señora *f* (de buena familia)

gently /'dʒentlɪ/ *adv* amablemente; (*slowly*) despacio

gentry /'dʒentrɪ/ *npl* pequeña aristocracia *f*

genuflect /'dʒenju:flekt/ *vi* doblar la rodilla

genuine /'dʒenjʊɪn/ *a* verdadero; ‹*person*› sincero

geograph|er /dʒɪ'ɒgrəfə(r)/ *n* geógrafo *m*. **~ical** /dʒɪə'græfɪkl/ *a* geográfico. **~y** /dʒɪ'ɒgrəfɪ/ *n* geografía *f*

geolog|ical /dʒɪə'lɒdʒɪkl/ *a* geológico. **~ist** *n* geólogo *m*. **~y** /dʒɪ'ɒlədʒɪ/ *n* geología *f*

geometr|ic(al) /dʒɪə'metrɪk(l)/ *a* geométrico. **~y** /dʒɪ'ɒmətrɪ/ *n* geometría *f*

geranium /dʒə'reɪnɪəm/ *n* geranio *m*

geriatrics /dʒerɪ'ætrɪks/ *n* geriatría *f*

germ /dʒɜ:m/ *n* (*rudiment, seed*) germen *m*; (*med*) microbio *m*

German /'dʒɜ:mən/ *a & n* alemán (*m*). **~ic** /dʒə'mænɪk/ *a* germánico. **~ measles** *n* rubéola *f*. **~ shepherd (dog)** *n* (perro *m*) pastor *m* alemán. **~y** *n* Alemania *f*

germicide /'dʒɜ:mɪsaɪd/ *n* germicida *m*

germinate /'dʒɜ:mɪneɪt/ *vi* germinar. • *vt* hacer germinar

gerrymander /'dʒerɪmændə(r)/ *n* falsificación *f* electoral

gestation /dʒe'steɪʃn/ *n* gestación *f*

gesticulate /dʒe'stɪkjʊleɪt/ *vi* hacer ademanes, gesticular

gesture /'dʒestʃə(r)/ *n* ademán *m*; (*fig*) gesto *m*

get /get/ *vt* (*pt & pp* **got**, *pp Amer* **gotten**, *pres p* **getting**) obtener, tener; (*catch*) coger (*not LAm*), agarrar (*esp LAm*); (*buy*) comprar; (*find*) encontrar; (*fetch*) buscar, traer; (*understand, sl*) comprender, caer (*fam*). **~ s.o. to do sth** conseguir que uno haga algo. • *vi* (*go*) ir; (*become*) hacerse; (*start to*) empezar a; (*manage*) conseguir. **~ married** casarse. **~ ready** prepararse. **~ about** ‹*person*› salir mucho; (*after illness*) levantarse. **~ along** (*manage*) ir tirando; (*progress*) hacer progresos. **~ along with** llevarse bien con. **~ at** (*reach*) llegar a; (*imply*) querer decir. **~ away** salir; (*escape*) escaparse. **~ back** *vi* volver. • *vt* (*recover*) recobrar. **~ by** (*manage*) ir tirando; (*pass*) pasar. **~ down** bajar; (*depress*) deprimir. **~ in** entrar; subir ‹*vehicle*›; (*arrive*) llegar. **~ off** bajar de ‹*train, car etc*›; (*leave*) irse; (*jurid*) salir absuelto. **~ on** (*progress*) hacer progresos; (*succeed*) tener éxito. **~ on with** (*be on good terms with*) llevarse bien con; (*continue*) seguir. **~ out** ‹*person*› salir; (*take out*) sacar. **~ out of** (*fig*) librarse de. **~ over** reponerse de ‹*illness*›. **~ round** soslayar ‹*difficulty etc*›; engatusar ‹*person*›. **~ through** (*pass*) pasar; (*finish*) terminar; (*on phone*) comunicar con. **~ up** levantarse; (*climb*) subir; (*organize*) preparar. **~away** *n* huida *f*. **~-up** *n* traje *m*

geyser /'gi:zə(r)/ *n* calentador *m* de agua; (*geog*) géiser *m*

Ghana /'gɑ:nə/ *n* Ghana *f*

ghastly /'gɑ:stlɪ/ *a* (**-ier**, **-iest**) horrible; (*pale*) pálido

gherkin /'gɜ:kɪn/ *n* pepinillo *m*

ghetto /'getəʊ/ *n* (*pl* **-os**) (*Jewish quarter*) judería *f*; (*ethnic settlement*) barrio *m* pobre habitado por un grupo étnico

ghost /gəʊst/ *n* fantasma *m*. **~ly** *a* espectral

ghoulish /'gu:lɪʃ/ *a* macabro

giant /'dʒaɪənt/ *n* gigante *m*. • *a* gigantesco

gibberish /ˈdʒibərɪʃ/ *n* jerigonza *f*

gibe /dʒaɪb/ *n* mofa *f*

giblets /ˈdʒɪblɪts/ *npl* menudillos *mpl*

Gibraltar /dʒɪˈbrɔːltə(r)/ *n* Gibraltar *m*

gidd|iness /ˈgɪdɪnɪs/ *n* vértigo *m*. **~y** *a* (**-ier**, **-iest**) mareado; ‹*speed*› vertiginoso. **be**/**feel** **~y** estar/sentirse mareado

gift /gɪft/ *n* regalo *m*; (*ability*) don *m*. **~ed** *a* dotado de talento. **~-wrap** *vt* envolver para regalo

gig /gɪg/ *n* (*fam*) concierto *m*

gigantic /dʒaɪˈgæntɪk/ *a* gigantesco

giggle /ˈgɪgl/ *vi* reírse tontamente. ● *n* risita *f*. **the ~s** la risa *f* tonta

gild /gɪld/ *vt* dorar

gills /gɪlz/ *npl* agallas *fpl*

gilt /gɪlt/ *a* dorado. **~-edged** *a* (*com*) de máxima garantía

gimmick /ˈgɪmɪk/ *n* truco *m*

gin / dʒɪn/ *n* ginebra *f*

ginger /ˈdʒɪndʒə(r)/ *n* jengibre *m*. ● *a* rojizo. ● *vt*. **~ up** animar. **~ ale** *n*, **~ beer** *n* cerveza *f* de jengibre. **~bread** *n* pan *m* de jengibre

gingerly /ˈdʒɪndʒəlɪ/ *adv* cautelosamente

gingham /ˈgɪŋəm/ *n* guinga *f*

gipsy /ˈdʒɪpsɪ/ *n* gitano *m*

giraffe /dʒɪˈrɑːf/ *n* jirafa *f*

girder /ˈgɜːdə(r)/ *n* viga *f*

girdle /ˈgɜːdl/ *n* (*belt*) cinturón *m*; (*corset*) corsé *m*

girl /gɜːl/ *n* chica *f*, muchacha *f*; (*child*) niña *f*. **~-friend** *n* amiga *f*; (*of boy*) novia *f*. **~hood** *n* (*up to adolescence*) niñez *f*; (*adolescence*) juventud *f*. **~ish** *a* de niña; ‹*boy*› afeminado

giro /ˈdʒaɪrəʊ/ *n* (*pl* **-os**) giro *m* (bancario)

girth /gɜːθ/ *n* circunferencia *f*

gist /dʒɪst/ *n* lo esencial *invar*

give /gɪv/ *vt* (*pt* **gave**, *pp* **given**) dar; (*deliver*) entregar; regalar ‹*present*›; prestar ‹*aid, attention*›; (*grant*) conceder; (*yield*) ceder; (*devote*) dedicar. **~ o.s. to** darse a. ● *vi* dar; (*yield*) ceder; (*stretch*) estirarse. ● *n* elasticidad *f*. **~ away** regalar; descubrir ‹*secret*›. **~ back** devolver. **~ in** (*yield*) rendirse. **~ off** emitir. **~ o.s. up** entregarse (a). **~ out** distribuir; (*announce*) anunciar; (*become used up*) agotarse. **~ over** (*devote*) dedicar; (*stop, fam*) dejar (de). **~ up** (*renounce*) renunciar a; (*yield*) ceder

given /ˈgɪvn/ *see* **give**. ● *a* dado. **~ name** *n* nombre *m* de pila

glacier /ˈglæsɪə(r)/ *n* glaciar *m*

glad /glæd/ *a* contento. **~den** *vt* alegrar

glade /gleɪd/ *n* claro *m*

gladiator /ˈglædɪeɪtə(r)/ *n* gladiador *m*

gladiolus /glædɪˈəʊləs/ *n* (*pl* **-li** /-laɪ/) estoque *m*, gladiolo *m*, gladíolo *m*

gladly /ˈglædlɪ/ *adv* alegremente; (*willingly*) con mucho gusto

glamo|rize /ˈglæməraɪz/ *vt* embellecer. **~rous** *a* atractivo. **~ur** *n* encanto *m*

glance /glɑːns/ *n* ojeada *f*. ● *vi*. **~ at** dar un vistazo a

gland /glænd/ *n* glándula *f*

glar|e /gleə(r)/ *vi* deslumbrar; (*stare angrily*) mirar airadamente. ● *n* deslumbramiento *m*; (*stare, fig*) mirada *f* airada. **~ing** *a* deslumbrador; (*obvious*) manifiesto

glass /glɑːs/ *n* (*material*) vidrio *m*; (*without stem or for wine*) vaso *m*; (*with stem*) copa *f*; (*for beer*) caña *f*; (*mirror*) espejo *m*. **~es** *npl* (*spectacles*) gafas *fpl*, anteojos (*LAm*) *mpl*. **~y** *a* vítreo

glaze /gleɪz/ *vt* poner cristales a ‹*windows, doors*›; vidriar ‹*pottery*›. ● *n* barniz *m*; (*for pottery*) esmalte *m*. **~d** *a* ‹*object*› vidriado; ‹*eye*› vidrioso

gleam /gliːm/ *n* destello *m*. ● *vi* destellar

glean /gliːn/ *vt* espigar

glee /gliː/ *n* regocijo *m*. **~ club** *n* orfeón *m*. **~ful** *a* regocijado

glen /glen/ *n* cañada *f*

glib /glɪb/ *a* de mucha labia; ‹*reply*› fácil. **~ly** *adv* con poca sinceridad

glid|e /glaɪd/ *vi* deslizarse; ‹*plane*› planear. **~er** *n* planeador *m*. **~ing** *n* planeo *m*

glimmer /ˈglɪmə(r)/ *n* destello *m*. ● *vi* destellar

glimpse /glɪmps/ *n* vislumbre *f*. **catch a ~ of** vislumbrar. ● *vt* vislumbrar

glint /glɪnt/ *n* destello *m*. ● *vi* destellar

glisten /ˈglɪsn/ *vi* brillar

glitter /ˈglɪtə(r)/ *vi* brillar. ● *n* brillo *m*

gloat /gləʊt/ *vi*. **~ on**/**over** regodearse

global /gləʊbl/ *a* (*world-wide*) mundial; (*all-embracing*) global

globe /gləʊb/ *n* globo *m*

globule /ˈglɒbjuːl/ *n* glóbulo *m*

gloom /gluːm/ *n* oscuridad *f*; (*sadness, fig*) tristeza *f*. **~y** *a* (**-ier**, **-iest**) triste; (*pessimistic*) pesimista

glorify /ˈglɔːrɪfaɪ/ *vt* glorificar

glorious /ˈglɔːrɪəs/ *a* espléndido; ‹*deed, hero etc*› glorioso

glory /ˈglɔːrɪ/ *n* gloria *f*; (*beauty*) esplendor *m*. ● *vi*. **~ in** enorgullecerse de. **~-hole** *n* (*untidy room*) leonera *f*

gloss /glɒs/ *n* lustre *m*. ● *a* brillante. ● *vi*. **~ over** (*make light of*) minimizar; (*cover up*) encubrir

glossary /ˈglɒsərɪ/ *n* glosario *m*

glossy /ˈglɒsɪ/ *a* brillante

glove /glʌv/ *n* guante *m*. **~ compartment** *n* (*auto*) guantera *f*, gaveta *f*. **~d** *a* enguantado

glow /gləʊ/ *vi* brillar; (*with health*) rebosar de; (*with passion*) enardecerse. ● *n* incandescencia *f*; (*of cheeks*) rubor *m*

glower /ˈglaʊə(r)/ *vi*. **~ (at)** mirar airadamente

glowing /ˈgləʊɪŋ/ *a* incandescente; ‹*account*› entusiasta; ‹*complexion*› rojo; (*with health*) rebosante de

glucose /ˈgluːkəʊs/ *n* glucosa *f*

glue /gluː/ *n* cola *f*. ● *vt* (*pres p* **gluing**) pegar

glum /glʌm/ *a* (**glummer**, **glummest**) triste

glut /glʌt/ *n* superabundancia *f*

glutton /ˈglʌtn/ *n* glotón *m*. **~ous** *a* glotón. **~y** *n* glotonería *f*

glycerine /ˈglɪsəriːn/ *n* glicerina *f*

gnarled /nɑːld/ *a* nudoso

gnash /næʃ/ *vt*. **~ one's teeth** rechinar los dientes

gnat /næt/ *n* mosquito *m*

gnaw /nɔː/ *vt/i* roer

gnome /nəʊm/ *n* gnomo *m*

go /gəʊ/ *vi* (*pt* **went**, *pp* **gone**) ir; (*leave*) irse; (*work*) funcionar; (*become*) hacerse; (*be sold*) venderse; (*vanish*) desaparecer. **~ ahead!** ¡adelante! **~ bad** pasarse. **~ riding** montar a caballo. **~ shopping** ir de compras. **be ~ing to do** ir a hacer. ● *n* (*pl* **goes**) (*energy*) energía *f*. **be on the ~** trabajar sin cesar. **have a ~** intentar. **it's your ~** te toca a ti. **make a ~ of** tener éxito en. **~ across** cruzar. **~ away** irse. **~ back** volver. **~ back on** faltar a ‹*promise etc*›. **~ by** pasar. **~ down** bajar; ‹*sun*› ponerse. **~ for** buscar, traer; (*like*) gustar; (*attack, sl*) atacar. **~ in** entrar. **~ in for** presentarse para ‹*exam*›. **~ off** (*leave*) irse; (*go bad*) pasarse; (*explode*) estallar. **~ on** seguir; (*happen*) pasar. **~ out** salir; ‹*light, fire*› apagarse. **~ over** (*check*) examinar. **~ round** (*be enough*) ser bastante. **~ through** (*suffer*) sufrir; (*check*) examinar. **~ under** hundirse. **~ up** subir. **~ without** pasarse sin

goad /gəʊd/ *vt* aguijonear

go-ahead /ˈgəʊəhed/ *n* luz *f* verde. ● *a* dinámico

goal /gəʊl/ *n* fin *m*, objeto *m*; (*sport*) gol *m*. **~ie** *n* (*fam*) portero *m*. **~keeper** *n* portero *m*. **~-post** *n* poste *m* (de la portería)

goat /gəʊt/ *n* cabra *f*

goatee /gəʊˈtiː/ *n* perilla *f*, barbas *fpl* de chivo

gobble /ˈgɒbl/ *vt* engullir

go-between /ˈgəʊbɪtwiːn/ *n* intermediario *m*

goblet /ˈgɒblɪt/ *n* copa *f*

goblin /ˈgɒblɪn/ *n* duende *m*

God /gɒd/ *n* Dios *m*. **~-forsaken** *a* olvidado de Dios

god /gɒd/ *n* dios *m*. **~child** *n* ahijado *m*. **~-daughter** *n* ahijada *f*. **~dess** /ˈgɒdɪs/ *n* diosa *f*. **~father** *n* padrino *m*. **~ly** *a* devoto. **~mother** *n* madrina *f*. **~send** *n* beneficio *m* inesperado. **~son** *n* ahijado *m*

go-getter /gəʊˈgetə(r)/ *n* persona *f* ambiciosa

goggle /ˈgɒgl/ *vi*. **~ (at)** mirar con los ojos desmesuradamente abiertos

goggles /ˈgɒglz/ *npl* gafas *fpl* protectoras

going /ˈgəʊɪŋ/ *n* camino *m*; (*racing*) (estado *m* del) terreno *m*. **it is slow/hard ~** es lento/difícil. ● *a* ‹*price*› actual; ‹*concern*› en funcionamiento. **~s-on** *npl* actividades *fpl* anormales, tejemaneje *m*

gold /gəʊld/ *n* oro *m*. ● *a* de oro. **~en** /ˈgəʊldən/ *a* de oro; (*in colour*) dorado; ‹*opportunity*› único. **~en wedding** *n* bodas *fpl* de oro. **~fish** *n invar* pez *m* de colores, carpa *f* dorada. **~-mine** *n* mina *f* de oro; (*fig*) fuente *f* de gran riqueza. **~-plated** *a* chapado en oro. **~smith** *n* orfebre *m*

golf /gɒlf/ *n* golf *m*. **~-course** *n* campo *m* de golf. **~er** *n* jugador *m* de golf
golly /'gɒlɪ/ *int* ¡caramba!
golosh /gə'lɒʃ/ *n* chanclo *m*
gondol|a /'gɒndələ/ *n* góndola *f*. **~ier** /gɒndə'lɪə(r)/ *n* gondolero *m*
gone /gɒn/ *see* **go**. ● *a* pasado. **~ six o'clock** después de las seis
gong /gɒŋ/ *n* gong(o) *m*
good /gʊd/ *a* (**better**, **best**) bueno, (*before masculine singular noun*) buen. **~ afternoon!** ¡buenas tardes! **~ evening!** (*before dark*) ¡buenas tardes!; (*after dark*) ¡buenas noches! **G~ Friday** *n* Viernes *m* Santo. **~ morning!** ¡buenos días! **~ name** *n* (buena) reputación *f*. **~ night!** ¡buenas noches! **a ~ deal** bastante. **as ~ as** (*almost*) casi. **be ~ with** entender. **do ~** hacer bien. **feel ~** sentirse bien. **have a ~ time** divertirse. **it is ~ for you** le sentará bien. ● *n* bien *m*. **for ~** para siempre. **it is no ~ shouting**/**etc** es inútil gritar/etc.
goodbye /gʊd'baɪ/ *int* ¡adiós! ● *n* adiós *m*. **say ~ to** despedirse de
good: **~-for-nothing** *a* & *n* inútil (*m*). **~-looking** *a* guapo
goodness /'gʊdnɪs/ *n* bondad *f*. **~!**, **~ gracious!**, **~ me!**, **my ~!** ¡Dios mío!
goods /gʊdz/ *npl* (*merchandise*) mercancías *fpl*
goodwill /gʊd'wɪl/ *n* buena voluntad *f*
goody / 'gʊdɪ/ *n* (*culin, fam*) golosina *f*; (*in film*) bueno *m*. **~-goody** *n* mojigato *m*
gooey /'gu:ɪ/ *a* (**gooier**, **gooiest**) (*sl*) pegajoso; (*fig*) sentimental
goof /gu:f/ *vi* (*Amer*, *blunder*) cometer una pifia. **~y** *a* (*sl*) necio
goose /gu:s/ *n* (*pl* **geese**) oca *f*
gooseberry /'gʊzbərɪ/ *n* uva *f* espina, grosella *f*
goose-flesh /'gu:sfleʃ/ *n*, **goose-pimples** /'gu:spɪmplz/ *n* carne *f* de gallina
gore /gɔ:(r)/ *n* sangre *f*. ● *vt* cornear
gorge /gɔ:dʒ/ *n* (*geog*) garganta *f*. ● *vt*. **~ o.s.** hartarse (**on** de)
gorgeous /'gɔ:dʒəs/ *a* magnífico
gorilla /gə'rɪlə/ *n* gorila *m*
gormless /'gɔ:mlɪs/ *a* (*sl*) idiota
gorse /gɔ:s/ *n* aulaga *f*
gory /'gɔ:rɪ/ *a* (**-ier**, **-iest**) (*covered in blood*) ensangrentado; (*horrific, fig*) horrible
gosh /gɒʃ/ *int* ¡caramba!
go-slow /gəʊ'sləʊ/ *n* huelga *f* de celo
gospel /'gɒspl/ *n* evangelio *m*
gossip /'gɒsɪp/ *n* (*idle chatter*) charla *f*; (*tittle-tattle*) comadreo *m*; (*person*) chismoso *m*. ● *vi* (*pt* **gossiped**) (*chatter*) charlar; (*repeat scandal*) comadrear. **~y** *a* chismoso
got /gɒt/ *see* **get**. **have ~** tener. **have ~ to do** tener que hacer
Gothic /'gɒθɪk/ *a* (*archit*) gótico; ‹*people*› godo
gouge /gaʊdʒ/ *vt*. **~ out** arrancar
gourmet /'gʊəmeɪ/ *n* gastrónomo *m*
gout /gaʊt/ *n* (*med*) gota *f*
govern /'gʌvn/ *vt*/*i* gobernar
governess /'gʌvənɪs/ *n* institutriz *f*
government /'gʌvənmənt/ *n* gobierno *m*. **~al** /gʌvən'mentl/ *a* gubernamental
governor /'gʌvənə(r)/ *n* gobernador *m*
gown /gaʊn/ *n* vestido *m*; (*of judge, teacher*) toga *f*
GP *abbr see* **general practitioner**
grab /græb/ *vt* (*pt* **grabbed**) agarrar
grace /greɪs/ *n* gracia *f*. **~ful** *a* elegante
gracious /'greɪʃəs/ *a* (*kind*) amable; (*elegant*) elegante
gradation /grə'deɪʃn/ *n* gradación *f*
grade /greɪd/ *n* clase *f*, categoría *f*; (*of goods*) clase *f*, calidad *f*; (*on scale*) grado *m*; (*school mark*) nota *f*; (*class, Amer*) curso *m*. **~ school** *n* (*Amer*) escuela *f* primaria. ● *vt* clasificar; (*schol*) calificar
gradient /'greɪdɪənt/ *n* (*slope*) pendiente *f*
gradual /'grædʒʊəl/ *a* gradual. **~ly** *adv* gradualmente
graduat|e /'grædjʊət/ *n* (*univ*) licenciado. ● *vi* /'grædjʊeɪt/ licenciarse. ● *vt* graduar. **~ion** /-'eɪʃn/ *n* entrega *f* de títulos
graffiti /grə'fi:tɪ/ *npl* pintada *f*
graft[1] /grɑ:ft/ *n* (*med, bot*) injerto *m*. ● *vt* injertar
graft[2] /grɑ:ft/ *n* (*bribery, fam*) corrupción *f*
grain /greɪn/ *n* grano *m*
gram /græm/ *n* gramo *m*
gramma|r /'græmə(r)/ *n* gramática *f*. **~tical** /grə'mætɪkl/ *a* gramatical
gramophone /'græməfəʊn/ *n* tocadiscos *m invar*
grand /grænd/ *a* (**-er**, **-est**) magnífico; (*excellent, fam*) estupendo. **~child** *n* nieto *m*. **~daughter** *n* nieta *f*

grandeur /'grændʒə(r)/ *n* grandiosidad *f*

grandfather /'grændfɑ:ðə(r)/ *n* abuelo *m*

grandiose /'grændɪəʊs/ *a* grandioso

grand: **~mother** *n* abuela *f*. **~parents** *npl* abuelos *mpl*. **~ piano** *n* piano *m* de cola. **~son** *n* nieto *m*

grandstand /'grænstænd/ *n* tribuna *f*

granite /'grænɪt/ *n* granito *m*

granny /'grænɪ/ *n* (*fam*) abuela *f*, nana *f* (*fam*)

grant /grɑ:nt/ *vt* conceder; (*give*) donar; (*admit*) admitir (**that** que). **take for ~ed** dar por sentado. ● *n* concesión *f*; (*univ*) beca *f*

granulated /'grænjʊleɪtɪd/ *a*. **~ sugar** *n* azúcar *m* granulado

granule /'grænu:l/ *n* gránulo *m*

grape /greɪp/ *n* uva *f*

grapefruit /'greɪpfru:t/ *n invar* toronja *f*, pomelo *m*

graph /grɑ:f/ *n* gráfica *f*

graphic /'græfɪk/ *a* gráfico

grapple /'græpl/ *vi*. **~ with** intentar vencer

grasp /grɑ:sp/ *vt* agarrar. ● *n* (*hold*) agarro *m*; (*strength of hand*) apretón *m*; (*reach*) alcance *m*; (*fig*) comprensión *f*

grasping /'grɑ:spɪŋ/ *a* avaro

grass /grɑ:s/ *n* hierba *f*. **~hopper** *n* saltamontes *m invar*. **~land** *n* pradera *f*. **~ roots** *npl* base *f* popular. ● *a* popular. **~y** *a* cubierto de hierba

grate /greɪt/ *n* (*fireplace*) parrilla *f*. ● *vt* rallar. **~ one's teeth** hacer rechinar los dientes. ● *vi* rechinar

grateful /'greɪtfl/ *a* agradecido. **~ly** *adv* con gratitud

grater /'greɪtə(r)/ *n* rallador *m*

gratif|ied /'grætɪfaɪd/ *a* contento. **~y** *vt* satisfacer; (*please*) agradar a. **~ying** *a* agradable

grating /'greɪtɪŋ/ *n* reja *f*

gratis /'grɑ:tɪs/ *a* & *adv* gratis (*a invar*)

gratitude /'grætɪtju:d/ *n* gratitud *f*

gratuitous /grə'tju:ɪtəs/ *a* gratuito

gratuity /grə'tju:ətɪ/ *n* (*tip*) propina *f*; (*gift of money*) gratificación *f*

grave[1] /greɪv/ *n* sepultura *f*

grave[2] /greɪv/ *a* (**-er**, **-est**) (*serious*) serio. /grɑ:v/ *a*. **~ accent** *n* acento *m* grave

grave-digger /'greɪvdɪgə(r)/ *n* sepulturero *m*

gravel /'grævl/ *n* grava *f*

gravely /'greɪvlɪ/ *a* (*seriously*) seriamente

grave: **~stone** *n* lápida *f*. **~yard** *n* cementerio *m*

gravitat|e /'grævɪteɪt/ *vi* gravitar. **~ion** / -'teɪʃn/ *n* gravitación *f*

gravity /'grævətɪ/ *n* gravedad *f*

gravy /'greɪvɪ/ *n* salsa *f*

graze[1] /greɪz/ *vt*/*i* (*eat*) pacer

graze[2] /greɪz/ *vt* (*touch*) rozar; (*scrape*) raspar. ● *n* rozadura *f*

greas|e /gri:s/ *n* grasa *f*. ● *vt* engrasar. **~e-paint** *n* maquillaje *m*. **~e-proof paper** *n* papel *m* a prueba de grasa, apergaminado *m*. **~y** *a* grasiento

great /greɪt/ *a* (**-er**, **-est**) grande, (*before singular noun*) gran; (*very good, fam*) estupendo. **G~ Britain** *n* Gran Bretaña *f*. **~-grandfather** *n* bisabuelo *m*. **~-grandmother** *n* bisabuela *f*. **~ly** /'greɪtlɪ/ *adv* (*very*) muy; (*much*) mucho. **~ness** *n* grandeza *f*

Greece /gri:s/ *n* Grecia *f*

greed /gri:d/ *n* avaricia *f*; (*for food*) glotonería *f*. **~y** *a* avaro; (*for food*) glotón

Greek /gri:k/ *a* & *n* griego (*m*)

green /gri:n/ *a* (**-er**, **-est**) verde; (*fig*) crédulo. ● *n* verde *m*; (*grass*) césped *m*. **~ belt** *n* zona *f* verde. **~ery** *n* verdor *m*. **~ fingers** *npl* habilidad *f* con las plantas

greengage /'gri:ngeɪdʒ/ *n* (*plum*) claudia *f*

greengrocer /'gri:ngrəʊsə(r)/ *n* verdulero *m*

greenhouse /'gri:nhaʊs/ *n* invernadero *m*

green: **~ light** *n* luz *f* verde. **~s** *npl* verduras *fpl*

Greenwich Mean Time /grenɪtʃ'mi:ntaɪm/ *n* hora *f* media de Greenwich

greet /gri:t/ *vt* saludar; (*receive*) recibir. **~ing** *n* saludo *m*. **~ings** *npl* (*in letter*) recuerdos *mpl*

gregarious /grɪ'geərɪəs/ *a* gregario

grenade /grɪ'neɪd/ *n* granada *f*

grew /gru:/ *see* **grow**

grey /greɪ/ *a* & *n* (**-er**, **-est**) gris (*m*). ● *vi* ‹*hair*› encanecer

greyhound /'greɪhaʊnd/ *n* galgo *m*

grid /grɪd/ *n* reja *f*; (*network, elec*) red *f*; (*culin*) parrilla *f*; (*on map*) cuadrícula *f*

grief /gri:f/ *n* dolor *m*. **come to ~** ‹*person*› sufrir un accidente; (*fail*) fracasar

grievance /'gri:vns/ *n* queja *f*

grieve /gri:v/ *vt* afligir. ● *vi* afligirse. **~ for** llorar

grievous /'gri:vəs/ *a* doloroso; (*serious*) grave

grill /grɪl/ *n* (*cooking device*) parrilla *f*; (*food*) parrillada *f*, asado *m*, asada *f*. ● *vt* asar a la parrilla; (*interrogate*) interrogar

grille /grɪl/ *n* rejilla *f*

grim /grɪm/ *a* (**grimmer**, **grimmest**) severo

grimace /'grɪməs/ *n* mueca *f*. ● *vi* hacer muecas

grim|e /graɪm/ *n* mugre *f*. **~y** *a* mugriento

grin /grɪn/ *vt* (*pt* **grinned**) sonreír. ● *n* sonrisa *f* (abierta)

grind /graɪnd/ *vt* (*pt* **ground**) moler ‹*coffee, corn etc*›; (*pulverize*) pulverizar; (*sharpen*) afilar. **~ one's teeth** hacer rechinar los dientes. ● *n* faena *f*

grip /grɪp/ *vt* (*pt* **gripped**) agarrar; (*interest*) captar la atención de. ● *n* (*hold*) agarro *m*; (*strength of hand*) apretón *m*. **come to ~s** encararse (**with** a/con)

gripe /graɪp/ *n*. **~s** *npl* (*med*) cólico *m*

grisly /'grɪzlɪ/ *a* (**-ier**, **-iest**) horrible

gristle /'grɪsl/ *n* cartílago *m*

grit /grɪt/ *n* arena *f*; (*fig*) valor *m*, aguante *m*. ● *vt* (*pt* **gritted**) echar arena en ‹*road*›. **~ one's teeth** (*fig*) acorazarse

grizzle /'grɪzl/ *vi* lloriquear

groan /grəʊn/ *vi* gemir. ● *n* gemido *m*

grocer /'grəʊsə(r)/ *n* tendero *m*. **~ies** *npl* comestibles *mpl*. **~y** *n* tienda *f* de comestibles

grog /grɒg/ *n* grog *m*

groggy /'grɒgɪ/ *a* (*weak*) débil; (*unsteady*) inseguro; (*ill*) malucho

groin /grɔɪn/ *n* ingle *f*

groom /gru:m/ *n* mozo *m* de caballos; (*bridegroom*) novio *m*. ● *vt* almohazar ‹*horses*›; (*fig*) preparar. **well-~ed** *a* bien arreglado

groove /gru:v/ *n* ranura *f*; (*in record*) surco *m*

grope /grəʊp/ *vi* (*find one's way*) moverse a tientas. **~ for** buscar a tientas

gross /grəʊs/ *a* (**-er**, **-est**) (*coarse*) grosero; (*com*) bruto; (*fat*) grueso; (*flagrant*) grave. ● *n invar* gruesa *f*. **~ly** *adv* groseramente; (*very*) enormemente

grotesque /grəʊ'tesk/ *a* grotesco

grotto /'grɒtəʊ/ *n* (*pl* **-oes**) gruta *f*

grotty /'grɒtɪ/ *a* (*sl*) desagradable; (*dirty*) sucio

grouch /graʊtʃ/ *vi* (*grumble, fam*) rezongar

ground[1] /graʊnd/ *n* suelo *m*; (*area*) terreno *m*; (*reason*) razón *f*; (*elec, Amer*) toma *f* de tierra. ● *vt* varar ‹*ship*›; prohibir despegar ‹*aircraft*›. **~s** *npl* jardines *mpl*; (*sediment*) poso *m*

ground[2] /graʊnd/ *see* **grind**

ground: **~ floor** *n* planta *f* baja. **~ rent** *n* alquiler *m* del terreno

grounding /'graʊndɪŋ/ *n* base *f*, conocimientos *mpl* (**in** de)

groundless /'graʊndlɪs/ *a* infundado

ground: **~sheet** *n* tela *f* impermeable. **~swell** *n* mar *m* de fondo. **~work** *n* trabajo *m* preparatorio

group /gru:p/ *n* grupo *m*. ● *vt* agrupar. ● *vi* agruparse

grouse[1] /graʊs/ *n invar* (*bird*) urogallo *m*. **red ~** lagópodo *m* escocés

grouse[2] /graʊs/ *vi* (*grumble, fam*) rezongar

grove /grəʊv/ *n* arboleda *f*. **lemon ~** *n* limonar *m*. **olive ~** *n* olivar *m*. **orange ~** *n* naranjal *m*. **pine ~** *n* pinar *m*

grovel /'grɒvl/ *vi* (*pt* **grovelled**) arrastrarse, humillarse. **~ling** *a* servil

grow /grəʊ/ *vi* (*pt* **grew**, *pp* **grown**) crecer; ‹*cultivated plant*› cultivarse; (*become*) volverse, ponerse. ● *vt* cultivar. **~ up** hacerse mayor. **~er** *n* cultivador *m*

growl /graʊl/ *vi* gruñir. ● *n* gruñido *m*

grown /grəʊn/ *see* **grow**. ● *a* adulto. **~-up** *a* & *n* adulto (*m*)

growth /grəʊθ/ *n* crecimiento *m*; (*increase*) aumento *m*; (*development*) desarrollo *m*; (*med*) tumor *m*

grub /grʌb/ *n* (*larva*) larva *f*; (*food, sl*) comida *f*

grubby /'grʌbɪ/ *a* (**-ier**, **-iest**) mugriento

grudg|e /grʌdʒ/ *vt* dar de mala gana; (*envy*) envidiar. **~e doing** molestarle hacer. **he ~ed paying** le molestó pagar. ● *n* rencor *m*. **bear/have a ~e against s.o.** guardar rencor a alguien. **~ingly** *adv* de mala gana

gruelling /'gru:əlɪŋ/ *a* agotador

gruesome /'gru:səm/ *a* horrible

gruff /grʌf/ *a* (**-er**, **-est**) ‹*manners*› brusco; ‹*voice*› ronco

grumble /'grʌmbl/ *vi* rezongar

grumpy /'grʌmpɪ/ *a* (**-ier**, **-iest**) malhumorado

grunt /grʌnt/ *vi* gruñir. ● *n* gruñido *m*

guarant|ee /gærən'ti:/ *n* garantía *f*. ● *vt* garantizar. **~or** *n* garante *m & f*

guard /gɑ:d/ *vt* proteger; (*watch*) vigilar. ● *vi*. **~ against** guardar de. ● *n* (*vigilance, mil group*) guardia *f*; (*person*) guardia *m*; (*on train*) jefe *m* de tren

guarded /'gɑ:dɪd/ *a* cauteloso

guardian /'gɑ:dɪən/ *n* guardián *m*; (*of orphan*) tutor *m*

guer(r)illa /gə'rɪlə/ *n* guerrillero *m*. **~ warfare** *n* guerra *f* de guerrillas

guess /ges/ *vt/i* adivinar; (*suppose, Amer*) creer. ● *n* conjetura *f*. **~work** *n* conjetura(s) *f(pl)*

guest /gest/ *n* invitado *m*; (*in hotel*) huésped *m*. **~house** *n* casa *f* de huéspedes

guffaw /gʌ'fɔ:/ *n* carcajada *f*. ● *vi* reírse a carcajadas

guidance /'gaɪdəns/ *n* (*advice*) consejos *mpl*; (*information*) información *f*

guide /gaɪd/ *n* (*person*) guía *m & f*; (*book*) guía *f*. **Girl G~** exploradora *f*, guía *f* (*fam*). ● *vt* guiar. **~book** *n* guía *f*. **~d missile** *n* proyectil *m* teledirigido. **~-lines** *npl* pauta *f*

guild /gɪld/ *n* gremio *m*

guile /gaɪl/ *n* astucia *f*

guillotine /'gɪləti:n/ *n* guillotina *f*

guilt /gɪlt/ *n* culpabilidad *f*. **~y** *a* culpable

guinea-pig /'gɪnɪpɪg/ *n* (*including fig*) cobaya *f*

guise /gaɪz/ *n* (*external appearance*) apariencia *f*; (*style*) manera *f*

guitar /gɪ'ta:(r)/ *n* guitarra *f*. **~ist** *n* guitarrista *m & f*

gulf /gʌlf/ *n* (*part of sea*) golfo *m*; (*hollow*) abismo *m*

gull /gʌl/ *n* gaviota *f*

gullet /'gʌlɪt/ *n* esófago *m*

gullible /'gʌləbl/ *a* crédulo

gully /'gʌlɪ/ *n* (*ravine*) barranco *m*

gulp /gʌlp/ *vt*. **~ down** tragarse de prisa. ● *vi* tragar; (*from fear etc*) sentir dificultad para tragar. ● *n* trago *m*

gum[1] /gʌm/ *n* goma *f*; (*for chewing*) chicle *m*. ● *vt* (*pt* **gummed**) engomar

gum[2] /gʌm/ *n* (*anat*) encía *f*. **~boil** /'gʌmbɔɪl/ *n* flemón *m*

gumboot /'gʌmbu:t/ *n* bota *f* de agua

gumption /'gʌmpʃn/ *n* (*fam*) iniciativa *f*; (*common sense*) sentido *m* común

gun /gʌn/ *n* (*pistol*) pistola *f*; (*rifle*) fusil *m*; (*large*) cañón *m*. ● *vt* (*pt* **gunned**). **~ down** abatir a tiros. **~fire** *n* tiros *mpl*

gunge /gʌndʒ/ *n* (*sl*) materia *f* sucia (y pegajosa)

gun: **~man** /'gʌnmən/ *n* pistolero *m*. **~ner** /'gʌnə(r)/ *n* artillero *m*. **~powder** *n* pólvora *f*. **~shot** *n* disparo *m*

gurgle /'gɜ:gl/ *n* (*of liquid*) gorgoteo *m*; (*of baby*) gorjeo *m*. ● *vi* ‹*liquid*› gorgotear; ‹*baby*› gorjear

guru /'gʊru:/ *n* (*pl* **-us**) mentor *m*

gush /gʌʃ/ *vi*. **~ (out)** salir a borbotones. ● *n* (*of liquid*) chorro *m*; (*fig*) torrente *m*. **~ing** *a* efusivo

gusset /'gʌsɪt/ *n* escudete *m*

gust /gʌst/ *n* ráfaga *f*; (*of smoke*) bocanada *f*

gusto /'gʌstəʊ/ *n* entusiasmo *m*

gusty /'gʌstɪ/ *a* borrascoso

gut /gʌt/ *n* tripa *f*, intestino *m*. ● *vt* (*pt* **gutted**) destripar; ‹*fire*› destruir. **~s** *npl* tripas *fpl*; (*courage, fam*) valor *m*

gutter /'gʌtə(r)/ *n* (*on roof*) canalón *m*; (*in street*) cuneta *f*; (*slum, fig*) arroyo *m*. **~snipe** *n* golfillo *m*

guttural /'gʌtərəl/ *a* gutural

guy /gaɪ/ *n* (*man, fam*) hombre *m*, tío *m* (*fam*)

guzzle /'gʌzl/ *vt/i* soplarse, tragarse

gym /dʒɪm/ *n* (*gymnasium, fam*) gimnasio *m*; (*gymnastics, fam*) gimnasia *f*

gymkhana /dʒɪmkɑ:nə/ *n* gincana *f*, gymkhana *f*

gymnasium /dʒɪm'neɪzɪəm/ *n* gimnasio *m*

gymnast /'dʒɪmnæst/ *n* gimnasta *m & f*. **~ics** *npl* gimnasia *f*

gym-slip /'dʒɪmslɪp/ *n* túnica *f* (de gimnasia)

gynaecolog|ist /gaɪnɪ'kɒlədʒɪst/ *n* ginecólogo *m*. **~y** *n* ginecología *f*

gypsy /'dʒɪpsɪ/ *n* gitano *m*

gyrate /dʒaɪəˈreɪt/ *vi* girar
gyroscope /ˈdʒaɪərəskəʊp/ *n* giroscopio *m*

H

haberdashery /hæbəˈdæʃərɪ/ *n* mercería *f*
habit /ˈhæbɪt/ *n* costumbre *f*; (*costume, relig*) hábito *m*. **be in the ~ of** (+ *gerund*) tener la costumbre de (+ *infintive*), soler (+ *infinitive*). **get into the ~ of** (+ *gerund*) acostumbrarse a (+ *infinitive*)
habitable /ˈhæbɪtəbl/ *a* habitable
habitat /ˈhæbɪtæt/ *n* hábitat *m*
habitation /hæbɪˈteɪʃn/ *n* habitación *f*
habitual /həˈbɪtjʊəl/ *a* habitual; ‹*smoker, liar*› inveterado. **~ly** *adv* de costumbre
hack /hæk/ *n* (*old horse*) jamelgo *m*; (*writer*) escritorzuelo *m*. ● *vt* cortar. **~ to pieces** cortar en pedazos
hackney /ˈhæknɪ/ *a*. **~ carriage** *n* coche *m* de alquiler, taxi *m*
hackneyed /ˈhæknɪd/ *a* manido
had /hæd/ *see* **have**
haddock /ˈhædək/ *n invar* eglefino *m*. **smoked ~** *n* eglefino *m* ahumado
haemorrhage /ˈhemərɪdʒ/ *n* hemorragia *f*
haemorrhoids /ˈhemərɔɪdz/ *npl* hemorroides *fpl*, almorranas *fpl*
hag /hæg/ *n* bruja *f*
haggard /ˈhægəd/ *a* ojeroso
haggle /ˈhægl/ *vi* regatear
Hague /heɪg/ *n*. **The ~** La Haya *f*
hail[1] /heɪl/ *n* granizo *m*. ● *vi* granizar
hail[2] /heɪl/ *vt* (*greet*) saludar; llamar ‹*taxi*›. ● *vi*. **~ from** venir de
hailstone /ˈheɪlstəʊn/ *n* grano *m* de granizo
hair /heə(r)/ *n* pelo *m*. **~brush** *n* cepillo *m* para el pelo. **~cut** *n* corte *m* de pelo. **have a ~cut** cortarse el pelo. **~do** *n* (*fam*) peinado *m*. **~dresser** *n* peluquero *m*. **~dresser's (shop)** *n* peluquería *f*. **~-dryer** *n* secador *m*. **~pin** *n* horquilla *f*. **~pin bend** *n* curva *f* cerrada. **~-raising** *a* espeluznante. **~-style** *n* peinado *m*
hairy /ˈheərɪ/ *a* (**-ier**, **-iest**) peludo; (*terrifying, sl*) espeluznante
hake /heɪk/ *n invar* merluza *f*
halcyon /ˈhælsɪən/ *a* sereno. **~ days** *npl* época *f* feliz
hale /heɪl/ *a* robusto
half /hɑːf/ *n* (*pl* **halves**) mitad *f*. ● *a* medio. **~ a dozen** media docena *f*. **~ an hour** media hora *f*. ● *adv* medio, a medias. **~-back** *n* (*sport*) medio *m*. **~-caste** *a* & *n* **mestizo** (*m*). **~-hearted** *a* poco entusiasta. **~-term** *n* vacaciones *fpl* de medio trimestre. **~-time** *n* (*sport*) descanso *m*. **~way** *a* medio. ● *adv* a medio camino. **~-wit** *n* imbécil *m* & *f*. **at ~-mast** a media asta
halibut /ˈhælɪbət/ *n invar* hipogloso *m*, halibut *m*
hall /hɔːl/ *n* (*room*) sala *f*; (*mansion*) casa *f* solariega; (*entrance*) vestíbulo *m*. **~ of residence** *n* colegio *m* mayor
hallelujah /hælɪˈluːjə/ *int* & *n* aleluya (*f*)
hallmark /ˈhɔːlmɑːk/ *n* (*on gold etc*) contraste *m*; (*fig*) sello *m* (distintivo)
hallo /həˈləʊ/ *int* = **hello**
hallow /ˈhæləʊ/ *vt* santificar. **H~e'en** *n* víspera *f* de Todos los Santos
hallucination /həluːsɪˈneɪʃn/ *n* alucinación *f*
halo /ˈheɪləʊ/ *n* (*pl* **-oes**) aureola *f*
halt /hɔːlt/ *n* alto *m*. ● *vt* parar. ● *vi* pararse
halve /hɑːv/ *vt* dividir por mitad
ham /hæm/ *n* jamón *m*; (*theatre, sl*) racionista *m* & *f*
hamburger /ˈhæmbɜːgə(r)/ *n* hamburguesa *f*
hamlet /ˈhæmlɪt/ *n* aldea *f*, caserío *m*
hammer /ˈhæmə(r)/ *n* martillo *m*. ● *vt* martill(e)ar; (*defeat, fam*) machacar
hammock /ˈhæmək/ *n* hamaca *f*
hamper[1] /ˈhæmpə(r)/ *n* cesta *f*
hamper[2] /ˈhæmpə(r)/ *vt* estorbar, poner trabas
hamster /ˈhæmstə(r)/ *n* hámster *m*
hand /ˈhænd/ *n* (*including cards*) mano *f*; (*of clock*) manecilla *f*; (*writing*) escritura *f*, letra *f*; (*worker*) obrero *m*. **at ~** a mano. **by ~** a mano. **lend a ~** echar una mano. **on ~** a mano. **on one's ~s** (*fig*) en (las) manos de uno. **on the one ~... on the other ~** por un lado... por otro.

out of ~ fuera de control. **to ~** a mano. ● *vt* dar. **~ down** pasar. **~ in** entregar. **~ over** entregar. **~ out** distribuir. **~bag** *n* bolso *m*, cartera *f* (*LAm*). **~book** *n* (*manual*) manual *m*; (*guidebook*) guía *f*. **~cuffs** *npl* esposas *fpl*. **~ful** /'hændfʊl/ *n* puñado *m*; (*person, fam*) persona *f* difícil. **~-luggage** *n* equipaje *m* de mano. **~-out** *n* folleto *m*; (*money*) limosna *f*

handicap /'hændɪkæp/ *n* desventaja *f*; (*sport*) handicap *m*. ● *vt* (*pt* **handicapped**) imponer impedimentos a

handicraft /'hændɪkrɑ:ft/ *n* artesanía *f*

handiwork /'hændɪwɜ:k/ *n* obra *f*, trabajo *m* manual

handkerchief /'hæŋkətʃɪf/ *n* (*pl* **-fs**) pañuelo *m*

handle /'hændl/ *n* (*of door etc*) tirador *m*; (*of implement*) mango *m*; (*of cup, bag, basket etc*) asa *f*. ● *vt* manejar; (*touch*) tocar; (*control*) controlar

handlebar /'hændlbɑ:(r)/ *n* (*on bicycle*) manillar *m*

handshake /'hændʃeɪk/ *n* apretón *m* de manos

handsome /'hænsəm/ *a* (*good-looking*) guapo; (*generous*) generoso; (*large*) considerable

handwriting /'hændraɪtɪŋ/ *n* escritura *f*, letra *f*

handy /'hændɪ/ *a* (**-ier**, **-iest**) (*useful*) cómodo; ‹*person*› diestro; (*near*) a mano. **~man** *n* hombre *m* habilidoso

hang /hæŋ/ *vt* (*pt* **hung**) colgar; (*pt* **hanged**) (*capital punishment*) ahorcar. ● *vi* colgar; ‹*hair*› caer. ● *n*. **get the ~ of sth** coger el truco de algo. **~ about** holgazanear. **~ on** (*hold out*) resistir; (*wait, sl*) esperar. **~ out** *vi* tender; (*live, sl*) vivir. **~ up** (*telephone*) colgar

hangar /'hæŋə(r)/ *n* hangar *m*

hanger /'hæŋə(r)/ *n* (*for clothes*) percha *f*. **~-on** *n* parásito *m*, pegote *m*

hang-gliding /'hæŋglaɪdɪŋ/ *n* vuelo *m* libre

hangman /'hæŋmən/ *n* verdugo *m*

hangover /'hæŋəʊvə(r)/ *n* (*after drinking*) resaca *f*

hang-up /'hæŋʌp/ *n* (*sl*) complejo *m*

hanker /'hæŋkə(r)/ *vi*. **~ after** anhelar. **~ing** *n* anhelo *m*

hanky-panky /'hæŋkɪpæŋkɪ/ *n* (*trickery, sl*) trucos *mpl*

haphazard /hæp'hæzəd/ *a* fortuito. **~ly** *adv* al azar

hapless /'hæplɪs/ *a* desafortunado

happen /'hæpən/ *vi* pasar, suceder, ocurrir. **if he ~s to come** si acaso viene. **~ing** *n* acontecimiento *m*

happ|ily /'hæpɪlɪ/ *adv* felizmente; (*fortunately*) afortunadamente. **~iness** *n* felicidad *f*. **~y** *a* (**-ier**, **-iest**) feliz. **~y-go-lucky** *a* despreocupado. **~y medium** *n* término *m* medio

harangue /hə'ræŋ/ *n* arenga *f*. ● *vt* arengar

harass /'hærəs/ *vt* acosar. **~ment** *n* tormento *m*

harbour /'hɑ:bə(r)/ *n* puerto *m*. ● *vt* encubrir ‹*criminal*›; abrigar ‹*feelings*›

hard /hɑ:d/ *a* (**-er**, **-est**) duro; (*difficult*) difícil. **~ of hearing** duro de oído. ● *adv* mucho; (*pull*) fuerte. **~ by** (muy) cerca. **~ done by** tratado injustamente. **~ up** (*fam*) sin un cuarto. **~board** *n* chapa *f* de madera, tabla *f*. **~-boiled egg** *n* huevo *m* duro. **~en** /'hɑ:dn/ *vt* endurecer. ● *vi* endurecerse. **~-headed** *a* realista

hardly /'hɑ:dlɪ/ *adv* apenas. **~ ever** casi nunca

hardness /'hɑ:dnɪs/ *n* dureza *f*

hardship /'hɑ:dʃɪp/ *n* apuro *m*

hard: **~ shoulder** *n* arcén *m*. **~ware** *n* ferretería *f*; ‹*computer*› hardware *m*. **~-working** *a* trabajador

hardy /'hɑ:dɪ/ *a* (**-ier**, **-iest**) (*bold*) audaz; (*robust*) robusto; (*bot*) resistente

hare /heə(r)/ *n* liebre *f*. **~-brained** *a* aturdido

harem /'hɑ:ri:m/ *n* harén *m*

haricot /'hærɪkəʊ/ *n*. **~ bean** alubia *f*, judía *f*

hark /hɑ:k/ *vi* escuchar. **~ back to** volver a

harlot /'hɑ:lət/ *n* prostituta *f*

harm /hɑ:m/ *n* daño *m*. **there is no ~ in** (+ *gerund*) no hay ningún mal en (+ *infinitive*). ● *vt* hacer daño a ‹*person*›; dañar ‹*thing*›; perjudicar ‹*interests*›. **~ful** *a* perjudical. **~less** *a* inofensivo

harmonica /hɑ:'mɒnɪkə/ *n* armónica *f*

harmon|ious /hɑ:'məʊnɪəs/ *a* armonioso. **~ize** *vt/i* armonizar. **~y** *n* armonía *f*

harness /'hɑ:nɪs/ *n* (*for horses*) guarniciones *fpl*; (*for children*) andadores *mpl*. ● *vt* poner guarniciones a ‹*horse*›; (*fig*) aprovechar

harp /hɑ:p/ *n* arpa *f*. ● *vi*. ~ **on (about)** machacar. **~ist** /'hɑ:pɪst/ *n* arpista *m & f*

harpoon /hɑ:'pu:n/ *n* arpón *m*

harpsichord /'hɑ:psɪkɔ:d/ *n* clavicémbalo *m*, clave *m*

harrowing /'hærəʊɪŋ/ *a* desgarrador

harsh /hɑ:ʃ/ *a* (**-er**, **-est**) duro, severo; ‹*taste, sound*› áspero. **~ly** *adv* severamente. **~ness** *n* severidad *f*

harvest /'hɑ:vɪst/ *n* cosecha *f*. ● *vt* cosechar. **~er** *n* (*person*) segador; (*machine*) cosechadora *f*

has /hæz/ *see* **have**

hash /hæʃ/ *n* picadillo *m*. **make a ~ of sth** hacer algo con los pies, estropear algo

hashish /'hæʃi:ʃ/ *n* hachís *m*

hassle /'hæsl/ *n* (*quarrel*) pelea *f*; (*difficulty*) problema *m*, dificultad *f*; (*bother, fam*) pena *f*, follón *m*, lío *m*. ● *vt* (*harass*) acosar, dar la lata

haste /heɪst/ *n* prisa *f*. **in ~** de prisa. **make ~** darse prisa

hasten /'heɪsn/ *vt* apresurar. ● *vi* apresurarse, darse prisa

hast|ily /'heɪstɪlɪ/ *adv* de prisa. **~y** *a* (**-ier**, **-iest**) precipitado; (*rash*) irreflexivo

hat /hæt/ *n* sombrero *m*. **a ~ trick** *n* tres victorias *fpl* consecutivas

hatch[1] /hætʃ/ *n* (*for food*) ventanilla *f*; (*naut*) escotilla *f*

hatch[2] /hætʃ/ *vt* empollar ‹*eggs*›; tramar ‹*plot*›. ● *vi* salir del cascarón

hatchback /'hætʃbæk/ *n* (coche *m*) cincopuertas *m invar*, coche *m* con puerta trasera

hatchet /'hætʃɪt/ *n* hacha *f*

hate /heɪt/ *n* odio *m*. ● *vt* odiar. **~ful** *a* odioso

hatred /'heɪtrɪd/ *n* odio *m*

haughty /'hɔ:tɪ/ *a* (**-ier**, **-iest**) altivo

haul /hɔ:l/ *vt* arrastrar; transportar ‹*goods*›. ● *n* (*catch*) redada *f*; (*stolen goods*) botín *m*; (*journey*) recorrido *m*. **~age** *n* transporte *m*. **~ier** *n* transportista *m & f*

haunch /hɔ:ntʃ/ *n* anca *f*

haunt /hɔ:nt/ *vt* frecuentar. ● *n* sitio *m* preferido. **~ed house** *n* casa *f* frecuentada por fantasmas

Havana /hə'vænə/ *n* La Habana *f*

have /hæv/ *vt* (*3 sing pres tense* **has**, *pt* **had**) tener; (*eat, drink*) tomar. **~ it out with** resolver el asunto. **~ sth done** hacer hacer algo. **~ to do** tener que hacer. ● *v aux* haber. **~ just done** acabar de hacer. ● *n*. **the ~s and ~-nots** los ricos *mpl* y los pobres *mpl*

haven /'heɪvn/ *n* puerto *m*; (*refuge*) refugio *m*

haversack /'hævəsæk/ *n* mochila *f*

havoc /'hævək/ *n* estragos *mpl*

haw /hɔ:/ *see* **hum**

hawk[1] /hɔ:k/ *n* halcón *m*

hawk[2] /hɔ:k/ *vt* vender por las calles. **~er** *n* vendedor *m* ambulante

hawthorn /'hɔ:θɔ:n/ *n* espino *m* (blanco)

hay /heɪ/ *n* heno *m*. **~ fever** *n* fiebre *f* del heno. **~stack** *n* almiar *m*

haywire /'heɪwaɪə(r)/ *a*. **go ~** ‹*plans*› desorganizarse; ‹*machine*› estropearse

hazard /'hæzəd/ *n* riesgo *m*. ● *vt* arriesgar; aventurar ‹*guess*›. **~ous** *a* arriesgado

haze /heɪz/ *n* neblina *f*

hazel /'heɪzl/ *n* avellano *m*. **~-nut** *n* avellana *f*

hazy /'heɪzɪ/ *a* (**-ier**, **-iest**) nebuloso

he /hi:/ *pron* él. ● *n* (*animal*) macho *m*; (*man*) varón *m*

head /hed/ *n* cabeza *f*; (*leader*) jefe *m*; (*of beer*) espuma *f*. **~s or tails** cara o cruz. ● *a* principal. **~ waiter** *n* jefe *m* de comedor. ● *vt* encabezar. **~ the ball** dar un cabezazo. **~ for** dirigirse a. **~ache** *n* dolor *m* de cabeza. **~-dress** *n* tocado *m*. **~er** *n* (*football*) cabezazo *m*. **~ first** *adv* de cabeza. **~gear** *n* tocado *m*

heading /'hedɪŋ/ *n* título *m*, encabezamiento *m*

headlamp /'hedlæmp/ *n* faro *m*

headland /'hedlənd/ *n* promontorio *m*

headlight /'hedlaɪt/ *n* faro *m*

headline /'hedlaɪn/ *n* titular *m*

headlong /'hedlɒŋ/ *adv* de cabeza; (*precipitately*) precipitadamente

head: **~master** *n* director *m*. **~mistress** *n* directora *f*. **~-on** *a & adv* de frente. **~phone** *n* auricular *m*, audífono *m* (*LAm*)

headquarters /hed'kwɔ:təz/ *n* (*of organization*) sede *f*; (*of business*) oficina *f* central; (*mil*) cuartel *m* general

headstrong /'hedstrɒŋ/ *a* testarudo
headway /'hedweɪ/ *n* progreso *m*. **make ~** hacer progresos
heady /'hedɪ/ *a* (**-ier**, **-iest**) (*impetuous*) impetuoso; (*intoxicating*) embriagador
heal /hi:l/ *vt* curar. ● *vi* ‹*wound*› cicatrizarse; (*fig*) curarse
health /helθ/ *n* salud *f*. **~y** *a* sano
heap /hi:p/ *n* montón *m*. ● *vt* amontonar. **~s of** (*fam*) montones de, muchísimos
hear /hɪə(r)/ *vt*/*i* (*pt* **heard** /hɜ:d/) oír. **~, ~!** ¡bravo! **not ~ of** (*refuse to allow*) no querer oír. **~ about** oir hablar de. **~ from** recibir noticias de. **~ of** oir hablar de
hearing /'hɪərɪŋ/ *n* oído *m*; (*of witness*) audición *f*. **~-aid** *n* audífono *m*
hearsay /'hɪəseɪ/ *n* rumores *mpl*. **from ~** según los rumores
hearse /hɜ:s/ *n* coche *m* fúnebre
heart / hɑ:t/ *n* corazón *m*. **at ~** en el fondo. **by ~** de memoria. **lose ~** descorozonarse. **~ache** *n* pena *f*. **~ attack** *n* ataque *m* al corazón. **~-break** *n* pena *f*. **~-breaking** *a* desgarrador. **~-broken** *a*. **be ~-broken** partírsele el corazón
heartburn /'hɑ:tbɜ:n/ *n* acedía *f*
hearten /'hɑ:tn/ *vt* animar
heartfelt /'hɑ:tfelt/ *a* sincero
hearth /hɑ:θ/ *n* hogar *m*
heartily /'hɑ:tɪlɪ/ *adv* de buena gana; (*sincerely*) sinceramente
heart: **~less** *a* cruel. **~-searching** *n* examen *m* de conciencia. **~-to-~** *a* abierto
hearty /'hɑ:tɪ/ *a* (*sincere*) sincero; ‹*meal*› abundante
heat /hi:t/ *n* calor *m*; (*contest*) eliminatoria *f*. ● *vt* calentar. ● *vi* calentarse. **~ed** *a* (*fig*) acalorado. **~er** /'hi:tə(r)/ *n* calentador *m*
heath /hi:θ/ *n* brezal *m*, descampado *m*, terreno *m* baldío
heathen /'hi:ðn/ *n* & *a* pagano (*m*)
heather /'heðə(r)/ *n* brezo *m*
heat: **~ing** *n* calefacción *f*. **~-stroke** *n* insolación *f*. **~wave** *n* ola *f* de calor
heave /hi:v/ *vt* (*lift*) levantar; exhalar ‹*sigh*›; (*throw*, *fam*) lanzar. ● *vi* (*retch*) sentir náuseas
heaven /'hevn/ *n* cielo *m*. **~ly** *a* celestial; (*astronomy*) celeste; (*excellent*, *fam*) divino
heav|ily /'hevɪlɪ/ *adv* pesadamente; (*smoke*, *drink*) mucho. **~y** *a* (**-ier**, **-iest**) pesado; ‹*sea*› grueso; ‹*traffic*› denso; ‹*work*› duro. **~yweight** *n* peso *m* pesado
Hebrew /'hi:bru:/ *a* & *n* hebreo (*m*)
heckle /'hekl/ *vt* interrumpir ‹*speaker*›
hectic /'hektɪk/ *a* febril
hedge /hedʒ/ *n* seto *m* vivo. ● *vt* rodear con seto vivo. ● *vi* escaparse por la tangente
hedgehog /'hedʒhɒg/ *n* erizo *m*
heed /hi:d/ *vt* hacer caso de. ● *n* atención *f*. **pay ~ to** hacer caso de. **~less** *a* desatento
heel /hi:l/ *n* talón *m*; (*of shoe*) tacón *m*. **down at ~**, **down at the ~s** (*Amer*) desharrapado
hefty /'heftɪ/ *a* (**-ier**, **-iest**) (*sturdy*) fuerte; (*heavy*) pesado
heifer /'hefə(r)/ *n* novilla *f*
height /haɪt/ *n* altura *f*; (*of person*) estatura *f*; (*of fame*, *glory*) cumbre *f*; (*of joy*, *folly*, *pain*) colmo *m*
heighten /'haɪtn/ *vt* (*raise*) elevar; (*fig*) aumentar
heinous /'heɪnəs/ *a* atroz
heir /eə(r)/ *n* heredero *m*. **~ess** *n* heredera *f*. **~loom** /'eəlu:m/ *n* reliquia *f* heredada
held /held/ *see* **hold**[1]
helicopter /'helɪkɒptə(r)/ *n* helicóptero *m*
heliport /'helɪpɔ:t/ *n* helipuerto *m*
hell /hel/ *n* infierno *m*. **~-bent** *a* resuelto. **~ish** *a* infernal
hello /hə'ləʊ/ *int* ¡hola!; (*telephone*, *caller*) ¡oiga!, ¡bueno! (*Mex*), ¡hola! (*Arg*); (*telephone*, *person answering*) ¡diga!, ¡bueno! (*Mex*), ¡hola! (*Arg*); (*surprise*) ¡vaya! **say ~ to** saludar
helm /helm/ *n* (*of ship*) timón *m*
helmet /'helmɪt/ *n* casco *m*
help /help/ *vt*/*i* ayudar. **he cannot ~ laughing** no puede menos de reír. **~ o.s. to** servirse. **it cannot be ~ed** no hay más remedio. ● *n* ayuda *f*; (*charwoman*) asistenta *f*. **~er** *n* ayudante *m*. **~ful** *a* útil; ‹*person*› amable
helping /'helpɪŋ/ *n* porción *f*
helpless /'helplɪs/ *a* (*unable to manage*) incapaz; (*powerless*) impotente
helter-skelter /heltə'skeltə(r)/ *n* tobogán *m*. ● *adv* atropelladamente
hem /hem/ *n* dobladillo *m*. ● *vt* (*pt* **hemmed**) hacer un dobladillo. **~ in** encerrar

hemisphere /'hemɪsfɪə(r)/ *n* hemisferio *m*
hemp /hemp/ *n* (*plant*) cáñamo *m*; (*hashish*) hachís *m*
hen /hen/ *n* gallina *f*
hence /hens/ *adv* de aquí. **~forth** *adv* de ahora en adelante
henchman /'hentʃmən/ *n* secuaz *m*
henna /'henə/ *n* alheña *f*
hen-party /'henpɑ:tɪ/ *n* (*fam*) reunión *f* de mujeres
henpecked /'henpekt/ *a* dominado por su mujer
her /hɜ:(r)/ *pron* (*accusative*) la; (*dative*) le; (*after prep*) ella. **I know ~** la conozco. ● *a* su, sus *pl*
herald /'herəld/ *vt* anunciar
heraldry /'herəldrɪ/ *n* heráldica *f*
herb /hɜ:b/ *n* hierba *f*. **~s** *npl* hierbas *fpl* finas
herbaceous /hɜ:'beɪʃəs/ *a* herbáceo
herbalist /'hɜ:bəlɪst/ *n* herbolario *m*
herculean /hɜ:kjʊ'li:ən/ *a* hercúleo
herd /hɜ:d/ *n* rebaño *m*. ● *vt*. **~ together** reunir
here /hɪə(r)/ *adv* aquí. **~!** (*take this*) ¡tenga! **~abouts** *adv* por aquí. **~after** *adv* en el futuro. **~by** *adv* por este medio; (*in letter*) por la presente
heredit|ary /hɪ'redɪtərɪ/ *a* hereditario. **~y** /hɪ'redətɪ/ *n* herencia *f*
here|sy /'herəsɪ/ *n* herejía *f*. **~tic** *n* hereje *m* & *f*
herewith /hɪə'wɪð/ *adv* adjunto
heritage /'herɪtɪdʒ/ *n* herencia *f*; (*fig*) patrimonio *m*
hermetic /hɜ:'metɪk/ *a* hermético
hermit /'hɜ:mɪt/ *n* ermitaño *m*
hernia /'hɜ:nɪə/ *n* hernia *f*
hero /'hɪərəʊ/ *n* (*pl* **-oes**) héroe *m*. **~ic** *a* heroico
heroin /'herəʊɪn/ *n* heroína *f*
hero: **~ine** /'herəʊɪn/ *n* heroína *f*. **~ism** /'herəʊɪzm/ *n* heroismo *m*
heron /'herən/ *n* garza *f* real
herring /'herɪŋ/ *n* arenque *m*
hers /hɜ:z/ *poss pron* suyo *m*, suya *f*, suyos *mpl*, suyas *fpl*, de ella
herself /hɜ:'self/ *pron* ella misma; (*reflexive*) se; (*after prep*) sí
hesitant /'hezɪtənt/ *a* vacilante
hesitat|e /'hezɪteɪt/ *vi* vacilar. **~ion** /-'teɪʃn/ *n* vacilación *f*
hessian /'hesɪən/ *n* arpillera *f*
het /het/ *a*. **~ up** (*sl*) nervioso
heterogeneous /hetərəʊ'dʒi:nɪəs/ *a* heterogéneo
heterosexual /hetərəʊ'seksjʊəl/ *a* heterosexual
hew /hju:/ *vt* (*pp* **hewn**) cortar; (*cut into shape*) tallar
hexagon /'heksəgən/ *n* hexágono *m*. **~al** /-'ægənl/ *a* hexagonal
hey /heɪ/ *int* ¡eh!
heyday /heɪdeɪ/ *n* apogeo *m*
hi /haɪ/ *int* (*fam*) ¡hola!
hiatus /haɪ'eɪtəs/ *n* (*pl* **-tuses**) hiato *m*
hibernat|e /'haɪbəneɪt/ *vi* hibernar. **~ion** *n* hibernación *f*
hibiscus /hɪ'bɪskəs/ *n* hibisco *m*
hiccup /'hɪkʌp/ *n* hipo *m*. **have (the) ~s** tener hipo. ● *vi* tener hipo
hide[1] /haɪd/ *vt* (*pt* **hid**, *pp* **hidden**) esconder. ● *vi* esconderse
hide[2] /haɪd/ *n* piel *f*, cuero *m*
hideous /'hɪdɪəs/ *a* (*dreadful*) horrible; (*ugly*) feo
hide-out /'haɪdaʊt/ *n* escondrijo *m*
hiding[1] /'haɪdɪŋ/ *n* (*thrashing*) paliza *f*
hiding[2] /'haɪdɪŋ/ *n*. **go into ~** esconderse
hierarchy /'haɪərɑ:kɪ/ *n* jerarquía *f*
hieroglyph /'haɪərəglɪf/ *n* jeroglífico *m*
hi-fi /'haɪfaɪ/ *a* de alta fidelidad. ● *n* (equipo *m* de) alta fidelidad (*f*)
higgledy-piggledy /hɪgldɪ'pɪgldɪ/ *adv* en desorden
high /haɪ/ *a* (**-er**, **-est**) alto; ‹*price*› elevado; ‹*number*, *speed*› grande; ‹*wind*› fuerte; (*intoxicated*, *fam*) ebrio; ‹*voice*› agudo; ‹*meat*› manido. **in the ~ season** en plena temporada. ● *n* alto nivel *m*. **a (new) ~** un récord *m*. ● *adv* alto
highbrow /'haɪbraʊ/ *a* & *n* intelectual (*m* & *f*)
higher education /haɪər edʒʊ'keɪʃn/ *n* enseñanza *f* superior
high-falutin /haɪfə'lu:tɪn/ *a* pomposo
high-handed /haɪ'hændɪd/ *a* despótico
high jump /'haɪdʒʌmp/ *n* salto *m* de altura
highlight /'haɪlaɪt/ *n* punto *m* culminante. ● *vt* destacar
highly /'haɪlɪ/ *adv* muy; ‹*paid*› muy bien. **~ strung** *a* nervioso
highness /'haɪnɪs/ *n* (*title*) alteza *f*
high: **~-rise building** *n* rascacielos *m*. **~ school** *n* instituto *m*. **~-speed** *a* de gran velocidad. **~ spot** *n* (*fam*) punto *m* culminante. **~ street** *n*

calle *f* mayor. **~-strung** *a* (*Amer*) nervioso. **~ tea** *n* merienda *f* substanciosa

highway /'haɪweɪ/ *n* carretera *f*. **~man** *n* salteador *m* de caminos

hijack /'haɪdʒæk/ *vt* secuestrar. ● *n* secuestro *m*. **~er** *n* secuestrador

hike /haɪk/ *n* caminata *f*. ● *vi* darse la caminata. **~r** *n* excursionista *m* & *f*

hilarious /hɪ'leərɪəs/ *a* (*funny*) muy divertido

hill /hɪl/ *n* colina *f*; (*slope*) cuesta *f*. **~-billy** *n* rústico *m*. **~side** *n* ladera *f*. **~y** *a* montuoso

hilt /hɪlt/ *n* (*of sword*) puño *m*. **to the ~** totalmente

him /hɪm/ *pron* le, lo; (*after prep*) él. **I know ~** le/lo conozco

himself /hɪm'self/ *pron* él mismo; (*reflexive*) se

hind /haɪnd/ *a* trasero

hinder /'hɪndə(r)/ *vt* estorbar; (*prevent*) impedir

hindrance /'hɪndrəns/ *n* obstáculo *m*

hindsight /'haɪnsaɪt/ *n*. **with ~** retrospectivamente

Hindu /hɪn'du:/ *n* & *a* hindú (*m* & *f*). **~ism** *n* hinduismo *m*

hinge /hɪndʒ/ *n* bisagra *f*. ● *vi*. **~ on** (*depend on*) depender de

hint /hɪnt/ *n* indirecta *f*; (*advice*) consejo *m*. ● *vt* dar a entender. ● *vi* soltar una indirecta. **~ at** hacer alusión a

hinterland /'hɪntəlænd/ *n* interior *m*

hip /hɪp/ *n* cadera *f*

hippie /'hɪpɪ/ *n* hippie *m* & *f*

hippopotamus /hɪpə'pɒtəməs/ *n* (*pl* **-muses** *or* **-mi**) hipopótamo *m*

hire /haɪə(r)/ *vt* alquilar ‹*thing*›; contratar ‹*person*›. ● *n* alquiler *m*. **~-purchase** *n* compra *f* a plazos

hirsute /'hɜ:sju:t/ *a* hirsuto

his /hɪz/ *a* su, sus *pl*. ● *poss pron* el suyo *m*, la suya *f*, los suyos *mpl*, las suyas *fpl*

Hispan|ic /hɪ'spænɪk/ *a* hispánico. **~ist** /'hɪspənɪst/ *n* hispanista *m* & *f*. **~o...** *pref* hispano...

hiss /hɪs/ *n* silbido. ● *vt*/*i* silbar

histor|ian /hɪ'stɔ:rɪən/ *n* historiador *m*. **~ic(al)** /hɪ'stɒrɪkl/ *a* histórico. **~y** /'hɪstərɪ/ *n* historia *f*. **make ~y** pasar a la historia

histrionic /hɪstrɪ'ɒnɪk/ *a* histriónico

hit /hɪt/ *vt* (*pt* **hit**, *pres p* **hitting**) golpear; (*collide with*) chocar con; (*find*) dar con; (*affect*) afectar. **~ it off with** hacer buenas migas con. ● *n* (*blow*) golpe *m*; (*fig*) éxito *m*. **~ on** *vi* encontrar, dar con

hitch /hɪtʃ/ *vt* (*fasten*) atar. ● *n* (*snag*) problema *m*. **~ a lift**, **~-hike** *vi* hacer autostop, hacer dedo (*Arg*), pedir aventón (*Mex*). **~-hiker** *n* autostopista *m* & *f*

hither /'hɪðə(r)/ *adv* acá. **~ and thither** acá y allá

hitherto /'hɪðətu:/ *adv* hasta ahora

hit-or-miss /'hɪtɔ:'mɪs/ *a* (*fam*) a la buena de Dios, a ojo

hive /haɪv/ *n* colmena *f*. ● *vt*. **~off** separar; (*industry*) desnacionalizar

hoard /hɔ:d/ *vt* acumular. ● *n* provisión *f*; (*of money*) tesoro *m*

hoarding /'hɔ:dɪŋ/ *n* cartelera *f*, valla *f* publicitaria

hoar-frost /'hɔ:frɒst/ *n* escarcha *f*

hoarse /hɔ:s/ *a* (**-er**, **-est**) ronco. **~ness** *n* (*of voice*) ronquera *f*; (*of sound*) ronquedad *f*

hoax /həʊks/ *n* engaño *m*. ● *vt* engañar

hob /hɒb/ *n* repisa *f*; (*of cooker*) fogón *m*

hobble /'hɒbl/ *vi* cojear

hobby /'hɒbɪ/ *n* pasatiempo *m*

hobby-horse /'hɒbɪhɔ:s/ *n* (*toy*) caballito *m* (de niño); (*fixation*) caballo *m* de batalla

hobnail /'hɒbneɪl/ *n* clavo *m*

hob-nob /'hɒbnɒb/ *vi* (*pt* **hob-nobbed**). **~ with** codearse con

hock[1] /hɒk/ *n* vino *m* del Rin

hock[2] /hɒk/ *vt* (*pawn*, *sl*) empeñar

hockey /'hɒkɪ/ *n* hockey *m*

hodgepodge /'hɒdʒpɒdʒ/ *n* mezcolanza *f*

hoe /həʊ/ *n* azada *f*. ● *vt* (*pres p* **hoeing**) azadonar

hog / hɒg/ *n* cerdo *m*. ● *vt* (*pt* **hogged**) (*fam*) acaparar

hoist /hɔɪst/ *vt* levantar; izar ‹*flag*›. ● *n* montacargas *m invar*

hold[1] /həʊld/ *vt* (*pt* **held**) tener; (*grasp*) coger (*not LAm*), agarrar; (*contain*) contener; mantener ‹*interest*›; (*believe*) creer; contener ‹*breath*›. **~ one's tongue** callarse. ● *vi* mantenerse. ● *n* asidero *m*; (*influence*) influencia *f*. **get ~ of** agarrar; (*fig*, *acquire*) adquirir. **~ back** (*contain*) contener; (*conceal*) ocultar. **~ on** (*stand firm*) resistir; (*wait*) esperar. **~ on to** (*keep*) guardar; (*cling to*) agarrarse a. **~**

out *vt* (*offer*) ofrecer. ● *vi* (*resist*) resistir. ~ **over** aplazar. ~ **up** (*support*) sostener; (*delay*) retrasar; (*rob*) atracar. ~ **with** aprobar

hold[2] /həʊld/ *n* (*of ship*) bodega *f*

holdall /'həʊldɔ:l/ *n* bolsa *f* (de viaje)

holder /'həʊldə(r)/ *n* tenedor *m*; (*of post*) titular *m*; (*for object*) soporte *m*

holding /'həʊldɪŋ/ *n* (*land*) propiedad *f*

hold-up /'həʊldʌp/ *n* atraco *m*

hole /həʊl/ *n* agujero *m*; (*in ground*) hoyo *m*; (*in road*) bache *m*. ● *vt* agujerear

holiday /'hɒlɪdeɪ/ *n* vacaciones *fpl*; (*public*) fiesta *f*. ● *vi* pasar las vacaciones. ~**-maker** *n* veraneante *m*

holiness /'həʊlɪnɪs/ *n* santidad *f*

Holland /'hɒlənd/ *n* Holanda *f*

hollow /'hɒləʊ/ *a* & *n* hueco (*m*). ● *vt* ahuecar

holly /'hɒlɪ/ *n* acebo *m*. ~**hock** *n* malva *f* real

holocaust /'hɒləkɔ:st/ *n* holocausto *m*

holster /'həʊlstə(r)/ *n* pistolera *f*

holy /'həʊlɪ/ *a* (**-ier**, **-iest**) santo, sagrado. **H~ Ghost** *n*, **H~ Spirit** *n* Espíritu *m* Santo. ~ **water** *n* agua *f* bendita

homage /'hɒmɪdʒ/ *n* homenaje *m*

home /həʊm/ *n* casa *f*; (*institution*) asilo *m*; (*for soldiers*) hogar *m*; (*native land*) patria *f*. **feel at ~ with** sentirse como en su casa. ● *a* casera, de casa; (*of family*) de familia; (*pol*) interior; ‹*match*› de casa. ● *adv*. **(at)** ~ en casa. **H~ Counties** *npl* región *f* alrededor de Londres. ~**land** *n* patria *f*. ~**less** *a* sin hogar. ~**ly** /'həʊmlɪ/ *a* (**-ier**, **-iest**) casero; (*ugly*) feo. **H~ Office** *n* Ministerio *m* del Interior. **H~ Secretary** *n* Ministro *m* del Interior. ~**sick** *a*. **be ~sick** tener morriña. ~ **town** *n* ciudad *f* natal. ~ **truths** *npl* las verdades *fpl* del barquero, las cuatro verdades *fpl*. ~**ward** /'həʊmwəd/ *a* ‹*journey*› de vuelta. ● *adv* hacia casa. ~**work** *n* deberes *mpl*

homicide /'hɒmɪsaɪd/ *n* homicidio *m*

homoeopath|ic /həʊmɪəʊ'pæθɪk/ *a* homeopático. ~**y** /-'ɒpəθɪ/ *n* homeopatía *f*

homogeneous /həʊməʊ'dʒi:nɪəs/ *a* homogéneo

homosexual /həʊməʊ'seksjʊəl/ *a* & *n* homosexual (*m*)

hone /həʊn/ *vt* afilar

honest /'ɒnɪst/ *a* honrado; (*frank*) sincero. ~**ly** *adv* honradamente. ~**y** *n* honradez *f*

honey /'hʌnɪ/ *n* miel *f*; (*person, fam*) cielo *m*, cariño *m*. ~**comb** /'hʌnɪkəʊm/ *n* panal *m*

honeymoon /'hʌnɪmu:n/ *n* luna *f* de miel

honeysuckle /'hʌnɪsʌkl/ *n* madreselva *f*

honk /hɒŋk/ *vi* tocar la bocina

honorary /'ɒnərərɪ/ *a* honorario

honour /'ɒnə(r)/ *n* honor *m*. ● *vt* honrar. ~**able** *a* honorable

hood /hʊd/ *n* capucha *f*; (*car roof*) capota *f*; (*car bonnet*) capó *m*

hoodlum /'hu:dləm/ *n* gamberro *m*, matón *m*

hoodwink /'hʊdwɪŋk/ *vt* engañar

hoof /hu:f/ *n* (*pl* **hoofs** *or* **hooves**) casco *m*

hook /hʊk/ *n* gancho *m*; (*on garment*) corchete *m*; (*for fishing*) anzuelo *m*. **by ~ or by crook** por fas o por nefas, por las buenas o por las malas. **get s.o. off the ~** sacar a uno de un apuro. **off the ~** ‹*telephone*› descolgado. ● *vt* enganchar. ● *vi* engancharse

hooked /hʊkt/ *a* ganchudo. ~ **on** (*sl*) adicto a

hooker /'hʊkə(r)/ *n* (*rugby*) talonador *m*; (*Amer*, *sl*) prostituta *f*

hookey /'hʊkɪ/ *n*. **play ~** (*Amer*, *sl*) hacer novillos

hooligan /'hu:lɪgən/ *n* gamberro *m*

hoop /hu:p/ *n* aro *m*

hooray /hʊ'reɪ/ *int* & *n* ¡viva! (*m*)

hoot /hu:t/ *n* (*of horn*) bocinazo *m*; (*of owl*) ululato *m*. ● *vi* tocar la bocina; ‹*owl*› ulular

hooter /'hu:tə(r)/ *n* (*of car*) bocina *f*; (*of factory*) sirena *f*

Hoover /'hu:və(r)/ *n* (*P*) aspiradora *f*. ● *vt* pasar la aspiradora

hop[1] /hɒp/ *vi* (*pt* **hopped**) saltar a la pata coja. ~ **in** (*fam*) subir. ~ **it** (*sl*) largarse. ~ **out** (*fam*) bajar. ● *n* salto *m*; (*flight*) etapa *f*

hop[2] /hɒp/ *n*. ~**(s)** lúpulo *m*

hope /həʊp/ *n* esperanza *f*. ● *vt/i* esperar. ~ **for** esperar. ~**ful** *a* esperanzador. ~**fully** *adv* con optimismo; (*it is hoped*) se espera. ~**less** *a* desesperado. ~**lessly** *adv* sin esperanza

hopscotch /'hɒpskɒtʃ/ *n* tejo *m*

horde /hɔ:d/ *n* horda *f*

horizon /hə'raɪzn/ *n* horizonte *m*
horizontal /hɒrɪ'zɒntl/ *a* horizontal. **~ly** *adv* horizontalmente
hormone /'hɔ:məʊn/ *n* hormona *f*
horn /hɔ:n/ *n* cuerno *m*; (*of car*) bocina *f*; (*mus*) trompa *f*. ● *vt*. **~ in** (*sl*) entrometerse. **~ed** *a* con cuernos
hornet /'hɔ:nɪt/ *n* avispón *m*
horny /'hɔ:nɪ/ *a* ‹*hands*› calloso
horoscope /'hɒrəskəʊp/ *n* horóscopo *m*
horri|ble /'hɒrəbl/ *a* horrible. **~d** /'hɒrɪd/ *a* horrible
horrif|ic /hə'rɪfɪk/ *a* horroroso. **~y** /'hɒrɪfaɪ/ *vt* horrorizar
horror /'hɒrə(r)/ *n* horror *m*. **~ film** *n* película *f* de miedo
hors-d'oevre /ɔ:'dɜ:vr/ *n* entremés *m*
horse /hɔ:s/ *n* caballo *m*. **~back** *n*. **on ~back** a caballo
horse chestnut /hɔ:s'tʃesnʌt/ *n* castaña *f* de Indias
horse: **~man** *n* jinete *m*. **~play** *n* payasadas *fpl*. **~power** *n* (*unit*) caballo *m* (de fuerza). **~-racing** *n* carreras *fpl* de caballos
horseradish /'hɔ:srædɪʃ/ *n* rábano *m* picante
horse: **~ sense** *n* (*fam*) sentido *m* común. **~shoe** /'hɔ:sʃu:/ *n* herradura *f*
horsy /'hɔ:sɪ/ *a* ‹*face etc*› caballuno
horticultur|al /hɔ:tɪ'kʌltʃərəl/ *a* hortícola. **~e** /'hɔ:tɪkʌltʃə(r)/ *n* horticultura *f*
hose /həʊz/ *n* (*tube*) manga *f*. ● *vt* (*water*) regar con una manga; (*clean*) limpiar con una manga. **~-pipe** *n* manga *f*
hosiery /'həʊzɪərɪ/ *n* calcetería *f*
hospice /'hɒspɪs/ *n* hospicio *m*
hospitabl|e /hɒ'spɪtəbl/ *a* hospitalario. **~y** *adv* con hospitalidad
hospital /'hɒspɪtl/ *n* hospital *m*
hospitality /hɒspɪ'tælətɪ/ *n* hospitalidad *f*
host[1] /həʊst/ *n*. **a ~ of** un montón de
host[2] /həʊst/ *n* (*master of house*) huésped *m*, anfitrión *m*
host[3] /həʊst/ *n* (*relig*) hostia *f*
hostage /'hɒstɪdʒ/ *n* rehén *m*
hostel /'hɒstl/ *n* (*for students*) residencia *f*. **youth ~** albergue *m* juvenil
hostess /'həʊstɪs/ *n* huéspeda *f*, anfitriona *f*
hostil|e /'hɒstaɪl/ *a* hostil. **~ity** *n* hostilidad *f*
hot /hɒt/ *a* (**hotter**, **hottest**) caliente; (*culin*) picante; ‹*news*› de última hora. **be/feel ~** tener calor. **in ~ water** (*fam*) en un apuro. **it is ~** hace calor. ● *vt/i*. **~ up** (*fam*) calentarse
hotbed /'hɒtbed/ *n* (*fig*) semillero *m*
hotchpotch /'hɒtʃpɒtʃ/ *n* mezcolanza *f*
hot dog /hɒt'dɒg/ *n* perrito *m* caliente
hotel /həʊ'tel/ *n* hotel *m*. **~ier** *n* hotelero *m*
hot: **~head** *n* impetuoso *m*. **~-headed** *a* impetuoso. **~-house** *n* invernadero *m*. **~ line** *n* teléfono *m* rojo. **~plate** *n* calentador *m*. **~-water bottle** *n* bolsa *f* de agua caliente
hound /haʊnd/ *n* perro *m* de caza. ● *vt* perseguir
hour /aʊə(r)/ *n* hora *f*. **~ly** *a & adv* cada hora. **~ly pay** *n* sueldo *m* por hora. **paid ~ly** pagado por hora
house /haʊs/ *n* (*pl* **-s** /'haʊzɪz/) casa *f*; (*theatre building*) sala *f*; (*theatre audience*) público *m*; (*pol*) cámara *f*. /haʊz/ *vt* alojar; (*keep*) guardar. **~boat** *n* casa *f* flotante. **~breaking** *n* robo *m* de casa. **~hold** /'haʊshəʊld/ *n* casa *f*, familia *f*. **~holder** *n* dueño *m* de una casa; (*head of household*) cabeza *f* de familia. **~keeper** *n* ama *f* de llaves. **~keeping** *n* gobierno *m* de la casa. **~maid** *n* criada *f*, mucama *f* (*LAm*). **H~ of Commons** *n* Cámara *f* de los Comunes. **~-proud** *a* meticuloso. **~-warming** *n* inauguración *f* de una casa. **~wife** /'haʊswaɪf/ *n* ama *f* de casa. **~work** *n* quehaceres *mpl* domésticos
housing /'haʊzɪŋ/ *n* alojamiento *m*. **~ estate** *n* urbanización *f*
hovel /'hɒvl/ *n* casucha *f*
hover /'hɒvə(r)/ *vi* ‹*bird, threat etc*› cernerse; (*loiter*) rondar. **~craft** *n* aerodeslizador *m*
how /haʊ/ *adv* cómo. **~ about a walk?** ¿qué le parece si damos un paseo? **~ are you?** ¿cómo está Vd? **~ do you do?** (*in introduction*) mucho gusto. **~ long?** ¿cuánto tiempo? **~ many?** ¿cuántos? **~ much?** ¿cuánto? **~ often?** ¿cuántas veces? **and ~!** ¡y cómo!
however /haʊ'evə(r)/ *adv* (*with verb*) de cualquier manera que (+ *subjunctive*); (*with adjective or adverb*) por... que (+ *subjunctive*);

(*nevertheless*) no obstante, sin embargo. ~ **much it rains** por mucho que llueva
howl /haʊl/ *n* aullido. ● *vi* aullar
howler /ˈhaʊlə(r)/ *n* (*fam*) plancha *f*
HP *abbr see* **hire-purchase**
hp *abbr see* **horsepower**
hub /hʌb/ *n* (*of wheel*) cubo *m*; (*fig*) centro *m*
hubbub /ˈhʌbʌb/ *n* barahúnda *f*
hub-cap /ˈhʌbkæp/ *n* tapacubos *m invar*
huddle /ˈhʌdl/ *vi* apiñarse
hue[1] /hju:/ *n* (*colour*) color *m*
hue[2] /hju:/ *n*. ~ **and cry** clamor *m*
huff /hʌf/ *n*. **in a** ~ enojado
hug /hʌg/ *vt* (*pt* **hugged**) abrazar; (*keep close to*) no apartarse de. ● *n* abrazo *m*
huge /hju:dʒ/ *a* enorme. ~**ly** *adv* enormemente
hulk /hʌlk/ *n* (*of ship*) barco *m* viejo; (*person*) armatoste *m*
hull /hʌl/ *n* (*of ship*) casco *m*
hullabaloo /hʌləbəˈlu:/ *n* tumulto *m*
hullo /həˈləʊ/ *int* = **hello**
hum /hʌm/ *vt/i* (*pt* **hummed**) ‹*person*› canturrear; ‹*insect, engine*› zumbar. ● *n* zumbido *m*. ~ **(or hem) and haw (or ha)** vacilar
human /ˈhju:mən/ *a & n* humano (*m*). ~ **being** *n* ser *m* humano
humane /hju:ˈmeɪn/ *a* humano
humanism /ˈhju:mənɪzəm/ *n* humanismo *m*
humanitarian /hju:mænɪˈteərɪən/ *a* humanitario
humanity /hju:ˈmænətɪ/ *n* humanidad *f*
humbl|e /ˈhʌmbl/ *a* (**-er**, **-est**) humilde. ● *vt* humillar. ~**y** *adv* humildemente
humbug /ˈhʌmbʌg/ *n* (*false talk*) charlatanería *f*; (*person*) charlatán *m*; (*sweet*) caramelo *m* de menta
humdrum /ˈhʌmdrʌm/ *a* monótono
humid /ˈhju:mɪd/ *a* húmedo. ~**ifier** *n* humedecedor *m*. ~**ity** /hju:ˈmɪdətɪ/ *n* humedad *f*
humiliat|e /hju:ˈmɪlɪeɪt/ *vt* humillar. ~**ion** /-ˈeɪʃn/ *n* humillación *f*
humility /hju:ˈmɪlətɪ/ *n* humildad *f*
humorist /ˈhju:mərɪst/ *n* humorista *m & f*
humo|rous /ˈhju:mərəs/ *a* divertido. ~**rously** *adv* con gracia. ~**ur** *n* humorismo *m*; (*mood*) humor *m*. **sense of** ~**ur** *n* sentido *m* del humor
hump /hʌmp/ *n* montecillo *m*; (*of the spine*) joroba *f*. **the** ~ (*sl*) malhumor *m*. ● *vt* encorvarse; (*hoist up*) llevar al hombro
hunch /hʌntʃ/ *vt* encorvar. ~**ed up** encorvado. ● *n* presentimiento *m*; (*lump*) joroba *f*. ~**back** /ˈhʌntʃbæk/ *n* jorobado *m*
hundred /ˈhʌndrəd/ *a* ciento, (*before noun*) cien. ● *n* ciento *m*. ~**fold** *a* céntuplo. ● *adv* cien veces. ~**s of** centenares de. ~**th** *a* centésimo. ● *n* centésimo *m*, centésima parte *f*
hundredweight /ˈhʌndrədweɪt/ *n* 50,8kg; (*Amer*) 45,36kg
hung /hʌŋ/ *see* **hang**
Hungar|ian /hʌŋˈgeərɪən/ *a & n* húngaro (*m*). ~**y** /ˈhʌŋgərɪ/ *n* Hungría *f*
hunger /ˈhʌŋgə(r)/ *n* hambre *f*. ● *vi*. ~ **for** tener hambre de. ~**-strike** *n* huelga *f* de hambre
hungr|ily /ˈhʌŋgrəlɪ/ *adv* ávidamente. ~**y** *a* (**-ier**, **-iest**) hambriento. **be** ~**y** tener hambre
hunk /hʌŋk/ *n* (buen) pedazo *m*
hunt /hʌnt/ *vt/i* cazar. ~ **for** buscar. ● *n* caza *f*. ~**er** *n* cazador *m*. ~**ing** *n* caza *f*
hurdle /ˈhɜ:dl/ *n* (*sport*) valla *f*; (*fig*) obstáculo *m*
hurdy-gurdy /ˈhɜ:dɪgɜ:dɪ/ *n* organillo *m*
hurl /hɜ:l/ *vt* lanzar
hurly-burly /ˈhɜ:lɪbɜ:lɪ/ *n* tumulto *m*
hurrah /hʊˈrɑ:/, **hurray** /hʊˈreɪ/ *int & n* ¡viva! (*m*)
hurricane /ˈhʌrɪkən/ *n* huracán *m*
hurried /ˈhʌrɪd/ *a* apresurado. ~**ly** *adv* apresuradamente
hurry /ˈhʌrɪ/ *vi* apresurarse, darse prisa. ● *vt* apresurar, dar prisa a. ● *n* prisa *f*. **be in a** ~ tener prisa
hurt /hɜ:t/ *vt/i* (*pt* **hurt**) herir. ● *n* (*injury*) herida *f*; (*harm*) daño *m*. ~**ful** *a* hiriente; (*harmful*) dañoso
hurtle /ˈhɜ:tl/ *vt* lanzar. ● *vi*. ~ **along** mover rápidamente
husband /ˈhʌzbənd/ *n* marido *m*
hush /hʌʃ/ *vt* acallar. ● *n* silencio *m*. ~ **up** ocultar ‹*affair*›. ~**-**~ *a* (*fam*) muy secreto
husk /hʌsk/ *n* cáscara *f*
husky /ˈhʌskɪ/ *a* (**-ier**, **-iest**) (*hoarse*) ronco; (*burly*) fornido
hussy /ˈhʌsɪ/ *n* desvergonzada *f*
hustle /ˈhʌsl/ *vt* (*jostle*) empujar. ● *vi* (*hurry*) darse prisa. ● *n* empuje *m*. ~ **and bustle** *n* bullicio *m*
hut /hʌt/ *n* cabaña *f*

hutch /hʌtʃ/ *n* conejera *f*
hyacinth /ˈhaɪəsɪnθ/ *n* jacinto *m*
hybrid /ˈhaɪbrɪd/ *a & n* híbrido (*m*)
hydrangea /haɪˈdreɪndʒə/ *n* hortensia *f*
hydrant /ˈhaɪdrənt/ *n*. **(fire)** ~ *n* boca *f* de riego
hydraulic /haɪˈdrɔ:lɪk/ *a* hidráulico
hydroelectric /haɪdrəʊɪˈlektrɪk/ *a* hidroeléctrico
hydrofoil /ˈhaɪdrəfɔɪl/ *n* aerodeslizador *m*
hydrogen /ˈhaɪdrədʒən/ *n* hidrógeno *m*. ~ **bomb** *n* bomba *f* de hidrógeno. ~ **peroxide** *n* peróxido *m* de hidrógeno
hyena /haɪˈi:nə/ *n* hiena *f*
hygien|e /ˈhaɪdʒi:n/ *n* higiene *f*. **~ic** *a* higiénico
hymn /hɪm/ *n* himno *m*
hyper... /ˈhaɪpə(r)/ *pref* hiper...
hypermarket /ˈhaɪpəmɑ:kɪt/ *n* hipermercado *m*
hyphen /ˈhaɪfn/ *n* guión *m*. **~ate** *vt* escribir con guión
hypno|sis /hɪpˈnəʊsɪs/ *n* hipnosis *f*. **~tic** /-ˈnɒtɪk/ *a* hipnótico. **~tism** /hɪpnəˈtɪzəm/ *n* hipnotismo *m*. **~tist** *n* hipnotista *m & f*. **~tize** *vt* hipnotizar
hypochondriac /haɪpəˈkɒndrɪæk/ *n* hipocondríaco *m*
hypocrisy /hɪˈpɒkrəsɪ/ *n* hipocresía *f*
hypocrit|e /ˈhɪpəkrɪt/ *n* hipócrita *m & f*. **~ical** *a* hipócrita
hypodermic /haɪpəˈdɜ:mɪk/ *a* hipodérmico. ● *n* jeringa *f* hipodérmica
hypothe|sis /haɪˈpɒθəsɪs/ *n* (*pl* **-theses** /-si:z/) hipótesis *f*. **~tical** /-əˈθetɪkl/ *a* hipotético
hysteri|a /hɪˈstɪərɪə/ *n* histerismo *m*. **~cal** /-ˈterɪkl/ *a* histérico. **~cs** /hɪˈsterɪks/ *npl* histerismo *m*. **have ~cs** ponerse histérico; (*laugh*) morir de risa

I

I /aɪ/ *pron* yo
ice /aɪs/ *n* hielo *m*. ● *vt* helar; glasear ‹*cake*›. ● *vi*. ~ **(up)** helarse. **~berg** *n* iceberg *m*, témpano *m*. **~-cream** *n* helado *m*. **~-cube** *n* cubito *m* de hielo. ~ **hockey** *n* hockey *m* sobre hielo
Iceland /ˈaɪslənd/ *n* Islandia *f*. **~er** *n* islandés *m*. **~ic** /-ˈlændɪk/ *a* islandés
ice lolly /aɪsˈlɒlɪ/ polo *m*, paleta *f* (*LAm*)
icicle /ˈaɪsɪkl/ *n* carámbano *m*
icing /ˈaɪsɪŋ/ *n* (*sugar*) azúcar *m* glaseado
icon /ˈaɪkɒn/ *n* icono *m*
icy /ˈaɪsɪ/ *a* (**-ier**, **-iest**) glacial
idea /aiˈdɪə/ *n* idea *f*
ideal /aiˈdɪəl/ *a* ideal. ● *n* ideal *m*. **~ism** *n* idealismo *m*. **~ist** *n* idealista *m & f*. **~istic** /-ˈlɪstɪk/ *a* idealista. **~ize** *vt* idealizar. **~ly** *adv* idealmente
identical /aiˈdentɪkl/ *a* idéntico
identif|ication /aɪdentɪfɪˈkeɪʃn/ *n* identificación *f*. **~y** /aɪˈdentɪfaɪ/ *vt* identificar. ● *vi*. **~y with** identificarse con
identikit /aɪˈdentɪkɪt/ *n* retrato-robot *m*
identity /aɪˈdentɪtɪ/ *n* identidad *f*
ideolog|ical /aɪdɪəˈlɒdʒɪkl/ *a* ideológico. **~y** /aɪdɪˈɒlədʒɪ/ *n* ideología *f*
idiocy /ˈɪdɪəsɪ/ *n* idiotez *f*
idiom /ˈɪdɪəm/ *n* locución *f*. **~atic** /-ˈmætɪk/ *a* idiomático
idiosyncrasy /ɪdɪəʊˈsɪnkrəsɪ/ *n* idiosincrasia *f*
idiot /ˈɪdɪət/ *n* idiota *m & f*. **~ic** /-ˈɒtɪk/ *a* idiota
idle /ˈaɪdl/ *a* (**-er**, **-est**) ocioso; (*lazy*) holgazán; (*out of work*) desocupado; ‹*machine*› parado. ● *vi* ‹*engine*› marchar en vacío. ● *vt*. ~ **away** perder. **~ness** *n* ociosidad *f*. **~r** /-ə(r)/ *n* ocioso *m*
idol /ˈaɪdl/ *n* ídolo *m*. **~ize** *vt* idolatrar
idyllic /ɪˈdɪlɪk/ *a* idílico
i.e. /aɪˈi:/ *abbr* (*id est*) es decir
if /ɪf/ *conj* si
igloo /ˈiglu:/ *n* iglú *m*
ignite /ɪgˈnaɪt/ *vt* encender. ● *vi* encenderse
ignition /ɪgˈnɪʃn/ *n* ignición *f*; (*auto*) encendido *m*. ~ **(switch)** *n* contacto *m*
ignoramus /ɪgnəˈreɪməs/ *n* (*pl* **-muses**) ignorante
ignoran|ce /ˈɪgnərəns/ *n* ignorancia *f*. **~t** *a* ignorante. **~tly** *adv* por ignorancia
ignore /ɪgˈnɔ:(r)/ *vt* no hacer caso de
ilk /ɪlk/ *n* ralea *f*
ill /ɪl/ *a* enfermo; (*bad*) malo. ~ **will** *n* mala voluntad *f*. ● *adv* mal. ~ **at**

ease inquieto. ● *n* mal *m*. **~-advised** *a* imprudente. **~-bred** *a* mal educado

illegal /ɪ'li:gl/ *a* ilegal

illegible /ɪ'ledʒəbl/ *a* ilegible

illegitima|cy /ɪlɪ'dʒɪtɪməsɪ/ *n* ilegitimidad *f*. **~te** *a* ilegítimo

ill: **~-fated** *a* malogrado. **~-gotten** *a* mal adquirido

illitera|cy /ɪ'lɪtərəsɪ/ *n* analfabetismo *m*. **~te** *a & n* analfabeto (*m*)

ill: **~-natured** *a* poco afable. **~ness** *n* enfermedad *f*

illogical /ɪ'lɒdʒɪkl/ *a* ilógico

ill: **~-starred** *a* malogrado. **~-treat** *vt* maltratar

illuminat|e /ɪ'lu:mɪneɪt/ *vt* iluminar. **~ion** /-'neɪʃn/ *n* iluminación *f*

illus|ion /ɪ'lu:ʒn/ *n* ilusión *f*. **~sory** *a* ilusorio

illustrat|e /'ɪləstreɪt/ *vt* ilustrar. **~ion** *n* (*example*) ejemplo *m*; (*picture in book*) grabado *m*, lámina *f*. **~ive** *a* ilustrativo

illustrious /ɪ'lʌstrɪəs/ *a* ilustre

image /'ɪmɪdʒ/ *n* imagen *f*. **~ry** *n* imágenes *fpl*

imagin|able /ɪ'mædʒɪnəbl/ *a* imaginable. **~ary** *a* imaginario. **~ation** /-'neɪʃn/ *n* imaginación *f*. **~ative** *a* imaginativo. **~e** *vt* imaginar(se)

imbalance /ɪm'bæləns/ *n* desequilibrio *m*

imbecil|e /'ɪmbəsi:l/ *a & n* imbécil (*m & f*). **~ity** /-'sɪlətɪ/ *n* imbecilidad *f*

imbibe /ɪm'baɪb/ *vt* embeber; (*drink*) beber

imbue /ɪm'bju:/ *vt* empapar (**with** de)

imitat|e /'ɪmɪteɪt/ *vt* imitar. **~ion** /-'teɪʃn/ *n* imitación *f*. **~or** *n* imitador *m*

immaculate /ɪ'mækjʊlət/ *a* inmaculado

immaterial /ɪmə'tɪərɪəl/ *a* inmaterial; (*unimportant*) insignificante

immature /ɪmə'tjʊə(r)/ *a* inmaduro

immediate /ɪ'mi:dɪət/ *a* inmediato. **~ly** *adv* inmediatamente. **~ly you hear me** en cuanto me oigas. ● *conj* en cuanto (+ *subj*)

immens|e /ɪ'mens/ *a* inmenso. **~ely** *adv* inmensamente; (*very much*, *fam*) muchísimo. **~ity** *n* inmensidad *f*

immers|e /ɪ'mɜ:s/ *vt* sumergir. **~ion** /ɪ'mɜ:ʃn/ *n* inmersión *f*. **~ion heater** *n* calentador *m* de inmersión

immigra|nt /'ɪmɪgrənt/ *a & n* inmigrante (*m & f*). **~te** *vi* inmigrar. **~tion** /-'greɪʃn/ *n* inmigración *f*

imminen|ce /'ɪmɪnəns/ *n* inminencia *f*. **~t** *a* inminente

immobil|e /ɪ'məʊbaɪl/ *a* inmóvil. **~ize** /-bɪlaɪz/ *vt* inmovilizar

immoderate /ɪ'mɒdərət/ *a* inmoderado

immodest /ɪ'mɒdɪst/ *a* inmodesto

immoral /ɪ'mɒrəl/ *a* inmoral. **~ity** /ɪmə'rælətɪ/ *n* inmoralidad *f*

immortal /ɪ'mɔ:tl/ *a* inmortal. **~ity** /-'tælətɪ/ *n* inmortalidad *f*. **~ize** *vt* inmortalizar

immun|e /ɪ'mju:n/ *a* inmune (**from**, **to** a, contra). **~ity** *n* inmunidad *f*. **~ization** /ɪmjʊnaɪ'zeɪʃn/ *n* inmunización *f*. **~ize** *vt* inmunizar

imp /ɪmp/ *n* diablillo *m*

impact /'ɪmpækt/ *n* impacto *m*

impair /ɪm'peə(r)/ *vt* perjudicar

impale /ɪm'peɪl/ *vt* empalar

impart /ɪm'pɑ:t/ *vt* comunicar

impartial /ɪm'pɑ:ʃl/ *a* imparcial. **~ity** /-ɪ'ælətɪ/ *n* imparcialidad *f*

impassable /ɪm'pɑ:səbl/ *a* ‹*barrier etc*› infranqueable; ‹*road*› impracticable

impasse /æm'pɑ:s/ *n* callejón *m* sin salida

impassioned /ɪm'pæʃnd/ *a* apasionado

impassive /ɪm'pæsɪv/ *a* impasible

impatien|ce /ɪm'peɪʃəns/ *n* impaciencia *f*. **~t** *a* impaciente. **~tly** *adv* con impaciencia

impeach /ɪm'pi:tʃ/ *vt* acusar

impeccable /ɪm'pekəbl/ *a* impecable

impede /ɪm'pi:d/ *vt* estorbar

impediment /ɪm'pedɪmənt/ *n* obstáculo *m*. **(speech) ~** *n* defecto *m* del habla

impel /ɪm'pel/ *vt* (*pt* **impelled**) impeler

impending /ɪm'pendɪŋ/ *a* inminente

impenetrable /ɪm'penɪtrəbl/ *a* impenetrable

imperative /ɪm'perətɪv/ *a* imprescindible. ● *n* (*gram*) imperativo *m*

imperceptible /ɪmpə'septəbl/ *a* imperceptible

imperfect /ɪm'pɜ:fɪkt/ *a* imperfecto. **~ion** /ə-'fekʃn/ *n* imperfección *f*

imperial /ɪm'pɪərɪəl/ *a* imperial. **~ism** *n* imperialismo *m*

imperil /ɪm'perəl/ *vt* (*pt* **imperilled**) poner en peligro
imperious /ɪm'pɪərɪəs/ *a* imperioso
impersonal /ɪm'pɜ:sənl/ *a* impersonal
impersonat|e /ɪm'pɜ:səneɪt/ *vt* hacerse pasar por; (*mimic*) imitar. **~ion** /-'neɪʃn/ *n* imitación *f*. **~or** *n* imitador *m*
impertinen|ce /ɪm'pɜ:tɪnəns/ *n* impertinencia *f*. **~t** *a* impertinente. **~tly** *adv* impertinentemente
impervious /ɪm'pɜ:vɪəs/ *a*. **~ to** impermeable a; (*fig*) insensible a
impetuous /ɪm'petjʊəs/ *a* impetuoso
impetus /'ɪmpɪtəs/ *n* ímpetu *m*
impinge /ɪm'pɪndʒ/ *vi*. **~ on** afectar a
impish /'ɪmpɪʃ/ *a* travieso
implacable /ɪm'plækəbl/ *a* implacable
implant /ɪm'plɑ:nt/ *vt* implantar
implement /'ɪmplɪmənt/ *n* herramienta *f*. /'ɪmplɪment/ *vt* realizar
implicat|e /'ɪmplɪkeɪt/ *vt* implicar. **~ion** /-'keɪʃn/ *n* implicación *f*
implicit /ɪm'plɪsɪt/ *a* (*implied*) implícito; (*unquestioning*) absoluto
implied /ɪm'plaɪd/ *a* implícito
implore /ɪm'plɔ:(r)/ *vt* implorar
imply /ɪm'plaɪ/ *vt* implicar; (*mean*) querer decir; (*insinuate*) dar a entender
impolite /ɪmpə'laɪt/ *a* mal educado
imponderable /ɪm'pɒndərəbl/ *a & n* imponderable (*m*)
import /ɪm'pɔ:t/ *vt* importar. /'ɪmpɔ:t/ *n* (*article*) importación *f*; (*meaning*) significación *f*
importan|ce /ɪm'pɔ:təns/ *n* importancia *f*. **~t** *a* importante
importation /ɪmpɔ:'teɪʃn/ *n* importación *f*
importer /ɪm'pɔ:tə(r)/ *n* importador *m*
impose /ɪm'pəʊz/ *vt* imponer. ● *vi*. **~ on** abusar de la amabilidad de
imposing /ɪm'pəʊzɪŋ/ *a* imponente
imposition /ɪmpə'zɪʃn/ *n* imposición *f*; (*fig*) molestia *f*
impossib|ility /ɪmpɒsə'bɪlətɪ/ *n* imposibilidad *f*. **~le** *a* imposible
impostor /ɪm'pɒstə(r)/ *n* impostor *m*
impoten|ce /'ɪmpətəns/ *n* impotencia *f*. **~t** *a* impotente
impound /ɪm'paʊnd/ *vt* confiscar
impoverish /ɪm'pɒvərɪʃ/ *vt* empobrecer
impracticable /ɪm'præktɪkəbl/ *a* impracticable
impractical /ɪm'præktɪkl/ *a* poco práctico
imprecise /ɪmprɪ'saɪs/ *a* impreciso
impregnable /ɪm'pregnəbl/ *a* inexpugnable
impregnate /'ɪmpregneɪt/ *vt* impregnar (**with** de)
impresario /ɪmprɪ'sɑ:rɪəʊ/ *n* (*pl* **-os**) empresario *m*
impress /ɪm'pres/ *vt* impresionar; (*imprint*) imprimir. **~ on s.o.** hacer entender a uno
impression /ɪm'preʃn/ *n* impresión *f*. **~able** *a* impresionable
impressive /ɪm'presɪv/ *a* impresionante
imprint /'ɪmprɪnt/ *n* impresión *f*. /ɪm'prɪnt/ *vt* imprimir
imprison /ɪm'prɪzn/ *vt* encarcelar. **~ment** *n* encarcelamiento *m*
improbab|ility /ɪmprɒbə'bɪlətɪ/ *n* improbabilidad *f*. **~le** *a* improbable
impromptu /ɪm'prɒmptju:/ *a* improvisado. ● *adv* de improviso
improper /ɪm'prɒpə(r)/ *a* impropio; (*incorrect*) incorrecto
impropriety /ɪmprə'praɪətɪ/ *n* inconveniencia *f*
improve /ɪm'pru:v/ *vt* mejorar. ● *vi* mejorar(se). **~ment** *n* mejora *f*
improvis|ation /ɪmprəvaɪ'zeɪʃn/ *n* improvisación *f*. **~e** *vt/i* improvisar
imprudent /ɪm'pru:dənt/ *a* imprudente
impuden|ce /'ɪmpjʊdəns/ *n* insolencia *f*. **~t** *a* insolente
impulse /'ɪmpʌls/ *n* impulso *m*. **on ~** sin reflexionar
impulsive /ɪm'pʌlsɪv/ *a* irreflexivo. **~ly** *adv* sin reflexionar
impunity /ɪm'pju:nətɪ/ *n* impunidad *f*. **with ~** impunemente
impur|e /ɪm'pjʊə(r)/ *a* impuro. **~ity** *n* impureza *f*
impute /ɪm'pu:t/ *vt* imputar
in /ɪn/ *prep* en, dentro de. **~ a firm manner** de una manera terminante. **~ an hour('s time)** dentro de una hora. **~ doing** al hacer. **~ so far as** en cuanto que. **~ the evening** por la tarde. **~ the main** por la mayor parte. **~ the rain** bajo la lluvia. **~ the sun** al sol. **one ~ ten** uno de cada diez. **the best ~** el mejor de. ● *adv* (*inside*) dentro; (*at home*) en

casa; (*in fashion*) de moda. ● *n*. **the ~s and outs of** los detalles *mpl* de
inability /ɪnə'bɪlətɪ/ *n* incapacidad *f*
inaccessible /ɪnæk'sesəbl/ *a* inaccesible
inaccura|cy /ɪn'ækjʊrəsɪ/ *n* inexactitud *f*. **~te** *a* inexacto
inaction /ɪn'ækʃn/ *n* inacción *f*
inactiv|e /ɪn'æktɪv/ *a* inactivo. **~ity** /-'tɪvətɪ/ *n* inactividad *f*
inadequa|cy /ɪn'ædɪkwəsɪ/ *a* insuficiencia *f*. **~te** *a* insuficiente
inadmissible /ɪnəd'mɪsəbl/ *a* inadmisible
inadvertently /ɪnəd'vɜ:təntlɪ/ *adv* por descuido
inadvisable /ɪnəd'vaɪzəbl/ *a* no aconsejable
inane /ɪ'neɪn/ *a* estúpido
inanimate /ɪn'ænɪmət/ *a* inanimado
inappropriate /ɪnə'prəʊpriət/ *a* inoportuno
inarticulate /ɪnɑ:'tɪkjʊlət/ *a* incapaz de expresarse claramente
inasmuch as /ɪnəz'mʌtʃəz/ *adv* ya que
inattentive /ɪnə'tentɪv/ *a* desatento
inaudible /ɪn'ɔ:dəbl/ *a* inaudible
inaugural /ɪ'nɔ:gjʊrəl/ *a* inaugural
inaugurat|e /ɪ'nɔ:gjʊreɪt/ *vt* inaugurar. **~ion** /-'reɪʃn/ *n* inauguración *f*
inauspicious /ɪnɔ:'spɪʃəs/ *a* poco propicio
inborn /'ɪnbɔ:n/ *a* innato
inbred /ɪn'bred/ *a* (*inborn*) innato
incalculable /ɪn'kælkjʊləbl/ *a* incalculable
incapab|ility /ɪnkeɪpə'bɪlətɪ/ *n* incapacidad *f*. **~le** *a* incapaz
incapacit|ate /ɪnkə'pæsɪteɪt/ *vt* incapacitar. **~y** *n* incapacidad *f*
incarcerat|e /ɪn'kɑ:səreɪt/ *vt* encarcelar. **~ion** /-'reɪʃn/ *n* encarcelamiento *m*
incarnat|e /ɪn'kɑ:nət/ *a* encarnado. **~ion** /-'neɪʃn/ *n* encarnación *f*
incautious /ɪn'kɔ:ʃəs/ *a* incauto. **~ly** *adv* incautamente
incendiary /ɪn'sendɪərɪ/ *a* incendiario. ● *n* (*person*) incendiario *m*; (*bomb*) bomba *f* incendiaria
incense[1] /'ɪnsens/ *n* incienso *m*
incense[2] /ɪn'sens/ *vt* enfurecer
incentive /ɪn'sentɪv/ *n* incentivo *m*; (*payment*) prima *f* de incentivo
inception /ɪn'sepʃn/ *n* principio *m*
incertitude /ɪn'sɜ:tɪtju:d/ *n* incertidumbre *f*
incessant /ɪn'sesnt/ *a* incesante. **~ly** *adv* sin cesar
incest /'ɪnsest/ *n* incesto *m*. **~uous** /-'sestjʊəs/ *a* incestuoso
inch /ɪntʃ/ *n* pulgada *f* (= *2,54cm*). ● *vi* avanzar palmo a palmo
incidence /'ɪnsɪdəns/ *n* frecuencia *f*
incident /'ɪnsɪdənt/ *n* incidente *m*
incidental /ɪnsɪ'dentl/ *a* fortuito. **~ly** *adv* incidentemente; (*by the way*) a propósito
incinerat|e /ɪn'sɪnəreɪt/ *vt* incinerar. **~or** *n* incinerador *m*
incipient /ɪn'sɪpɪənt/ *a* incipiente
incision /ɪn'sɪʒn/ *n* incisión *f*
incisive /ɪn'saɪsɪv/ *a* incisivo
incite /ɪn'saɪt/ *vt* incitar. **~ment** *n* incitación *f*
inclement /ɪn'klemənt/ *a* inclemente
inclination /ɪnklɪ'neɪʃn/ *n* inclinación *f*
incline[1] /ɪn'klaɪn/ *vt* inclinar. ● *vi* inclinarse. **be ~d to** tener tendencia a
incline[2] /'ɪnklaɪn/ *n* cuesta *f*
inclu|de /ɪn'klu:d/ *vt* incluir. **~ding** *prep* incluso. **~sion** /-ʒn/ *n* inclusión *f*
inclusive /ɪn'klu:sɪv/ *a* inclusivo. **be ~ of** incluir. ● *adv* inclusive
incognito /ɪnkɒg'ni:təʊ/ *adv* de incógnito
incoherent /ɪnkəʊ'hɪərənt/ *a* incoherente
income /'ɪnkʌm/ *n* ingresos *mpl*. **~ tax** *n* impuesto *m* sobre la renta
incoming /'ɪnkʌmɪŋ/ *a* ‹*tide*› ascendente; ‹*tenant etc*› nuevo
incomparable /ɪn'kɒmpərəbl/ *a* incomparable
incompatible /ɪnkəm'pætəbl/ *a* incompatible
incompeten|ce /ɪn'kɒmpɪtəns/ *n* incompetencia *f*. **~t** *a* incompetente
incomplete /ɪnkəm'pli:t/ *a* incompleto
incomprehensible /ɪnkɒmprɪ'hensəbl/ *a* incomprensible
inconceivable /ɪnkən'si:vəbl/ *a* inconcebible
inconclusive /ɪnkən'klu:sɪv/ *a* poco concluyente
incongruous /ɪn'kɒŋgrʊəs/ *a* incongruente
inconsequential /ɪnkɒnsɪ'kwenʃl/ *a* sin importancia

inconsiderate /ɪnkən'sɪdərət/ *a* desconsiderado

inconsisten|cy /ɪnkən'sɪstənsɪ/ *n* inconsecuencia *f.* **~t** *a* inconsecuente. **be ~t with** no concordar con

inconspicuous /ɪnkən'spɪkjʊəs/ *a* que no llama la atención. **~ly** *adv* sin llamar la atención

incontinen|ce /ɪn'kɒntɪnəns/ *a* incontinencia *f.* **~t** *a* incontinente

inconvenien|ce /ɪnkən'vi:nɪəns/ *a* incomodidad *f*; (*drawback*) inconveniente m. **~t** *a* incómodo; ‹*time*› inoportuno

incorporat|e /ɪn'kɔ:pəreɪt/ *vt* incorporar; (*include*) incluir. **~ion** /-'reɪʃn/ *n* incorporación *f*

incorrect /ɪnkə'rekt/ *a* incorrecto

incorrigible /ɪn'kɒrɪdʒəbl/ *a* incorregible

incorruptible /ɪnkə'rʌptəbl/ *a* incorruptible

increase /'ɪnkri:s/ *n* aumento *m* (**in, of** de). /ɪn'kri:s/ *vt/i* aumentar

increasing /ɪn'kri:sɪŋ/ *a* creciente. **~ly** *adv* cada vez más

incredible /ɪn'kredəbl/ *a* increíble

incredulous /ɪn'kredjʊləs/ *a* incrédulo

increment /'ɪnkrɪmənt/ *n* aumento *m*

incriminat|e /ɪn'krɪmɪneɪt/ *vt* acriminar. **~ing** *a* acriminador

incubat|e /'ɪŋkjʊbeɪt/ *vt* incubar. **~ion** /-'beɪʃn/ *n* incubación *f.* **~or** *n* incubadora *f*

inculcate /'ɪnkʌlkeɪt/ *vt* inculcar

incumbent /ɪn'kʌmbənt/ *n* titular. ● *a.* **be ~ on** incumbir a

incur /ɪn'kɜ:(r)/ *vt* (*pt* **incurred**) incurrir en; contraer ‹*debts*›

incurable /ɪn'kjʊərəbl/ *a* incurable

incursion /ɪn'kɜ:ʃn/ *n* incursión *f*

indebted /ɪn'detɪd/ *a.* **~ to s.o.** estar en deuda con uno

indecen|cy /ɪn'di:snsɪ/ *n* indecencia *f.* **~t** *a* indecente

indecisi|on /ɪndɪ'sɪʒn/ *n* indecisión *f.* **~ve** /ɪndɪ'saɪsɪv/ *a* indeciso

indeed /ɪn'dɪ:d/ *adv* en efecto; (*really?*) ¿de veras?

indefatigable /ɪndɪ'fætɪgəbl/ *a* incansable

indefinable /ɪndɪ'faɪnəbl/ *a* indefinible

indefinite /ɪn'defɪnət/ *a* indefinido. **~ly** *adv* indefinidamente

indelible /ɪn'delɪbl/ *a* indeleble

indemni|fy /ɪn'demnɪfaɪ/ *vt* indemnizar. **~ty** /-ətɪ/ *n* indemnización *f*

indent /ɪn'dent/ *vt* endentar ‹*text*›. **~ation** /-'teɪʃn/ *n* mella *f*

independen|ce /ɪndɪ'pendəns/ *n* independencia *f.* **~t** *a* independiente. **~tly** *adv* independientemente. **~tly of** independientemente de

indescribable /ɪndɪ'skraɪbəbl/ *a* indescriptible

indestructible /ɪndɪ'strʌktəbl/ *a* indestructible

indeterminate /ɪndɪ'tɜ:mɪnət/ *a* indeterminado

index /'ɪndeks/ *n* (*pl* **indexes**) índice *m.* ● *vt* poner índice a; (*enter in the/an index*) poner en el/un índice. **~ finger** *n* (dedo *m*) índice *m.* **~-linked** *a* indexado

India /'ɪndɪə/ *n* la India *f.* **~n** *a* & *n* indio (*m*). **~n summer** *n* veranillo *m* de San Martín

indicat|e /'ɪndɪkeɪt/ *vt* indicar. **~ion** /-'keɪʃn/ *n* indicación *f.* **~ive** /ɪn'dɪkətɪv/ *a* & *n* indicativo (*m*). **~or** /'ɪndɪkeɪtə(r)/ *n* indicador *m*

indict /ɪn'daɪt/ *vt* acusar. **~ment** *n* acusación *f*

indifferen|ce /ɪn'dɪfrəns/ *n* indiferencia *f.* **~t** *a* indiferente; (*not good*) mediocre

indigenous /ɪn'dɪdʒɪnəs/ *a* indígena

indigesti|ble /ɪndɪ'dʒestəbl/ *a* indigesto. **~on** /-tʃən/ *n* indigestión *f*

indigna|nt /ɪn'dɪgnənt/ *a* indignado. **~tion** /-'neɪʃn/ *n* indignación *f*

indignity /ɪn'dɪgnətɪ/ *n* indignidad *f*

indigo /'ɪndɪgəʊ/ *n* añil (*m*)

indirect /ɪndɪ'rekt/ *a* indirecto. **~ly** *adv* indirectamente

indiscre|et /ɪndɪ'skri:t/ *a* indiscreto. **~tion** /-'kreʃn/ *n* indiscreción *f*

indiscriminate /ɪndɪ'skrɪmɪnət/ *a* indistinto. **~ly** *adv* indistintamente

indispensable /ɪndɪ'spensəbl/ *a* imprescindible

indispos|ed /ɪndɪ'spəʊzd/ *a* indispuesto. **~ition** /-ə'zɪʃn/ *n* indisposición *f*

indisputable /ɪndɪ'spju:təbl/ *a* indiscutible

indissoluble /ɪndɪ'sɒljʊbl/ *a* indisoluble

indistinct /ɪndɪ'stɪŋkt/ *a* indistinto

indistinguishable /ɪndɪ'stɪŋgwɪʃəbl/ *a* indistinguible

individual /ɪndɪ'vɪdjʊəl/ *a* individual. ● *n* individuo *m.* **~ist** *n* individualista *m* & *f.* **~ity** *n*

individualidad *f.* **~ly** *adv* individualmente
indivisible /ɪndɪ'vɪzəbl/ *a* indivisible
Indo-China /ɪndəʊ'tʃaɪnə/ *n* Indochina *f*
indoctrinat|e /ɪn'dɒktrɪneɪt/ *vt* adoctrinar. **~ion** /-'neɪʃn/ *n* adoctrinamiento *m*
indolen|ce /'ɪndələns/ *n* indolencia *f.* **~t** *a* indolente
indomitable /ɪn'dɒmɪtəbl/ *a* indomable
Indonesia /ɪndəʊ'ni:zɪə/ *n* Indonesia *f.* **~n** *a & n* indonesio (*m*)
indoor /'ɪndɔ:(r)/ *a* interior; ‹*clothes etc*› de casa; (*covered*) cubierto. **~s** *adv* dentro; (*at home*) en casa
induce /ɪn'dju:s/ *vt* inducir; (*cause*) provocar. **~ment** *n* incentivo *m*
induct /ɪn'dʌkt/ *vt* instalar; (*mil, Amer*) incorporar
indulge /ɪn'dʌldʒ/ *vt* satisfacer ‹*desires*›; complacer ‹*person*›. ● *vi.* **~ in** entregarse a. **~nce** /ɪn'dʌldʒəns/ *n* (*of desires*) satisfacción *f*; (*relig*) indulgencia *f.* **~nt** *a* indulgente
industrial /ɪn'dʌstrɪəl/ *a* industrial; ‹*unrest*› laboral. **~ist** *n* industrial *m & f.* **~ized** *a* industrializado
industrious /ɪn'dʌstrɪəs/ *a* trabajador
industry /'ɪndəstrɪ/ *n* industria *f*; (*zeal*) aplicación *f*
inebriated /ɪ'ni:brɪeɪtɪd/ *a* borracho
inedible /ɪn'edɪbl/ *a* incomible
ineffable /ɪn'efəbl/ *a* inefable
ineffective /ɪnɪ'fektɪv/ *a* ineficaz; ‹*person*› incapaz
ineffectual /ɪnɪ'fektjʊəl/ *a* ineficaz
inefficien|cy /ɪnɪ'fɪʃnsɪ/ *n* ineficacia *f*; (of *person*) incompetencia *f.* **~t** *a* ineficaz; ‹*person*› incompetente
ineligible /ɪn'elɪdʒəbl/ *a* inelegible. **be ~ for** no tener derecho a
inept /ɪ'nept/ *a* inepto
inequality /ɪnɪ'kwɒlətɪ/ *n* desigualdad *f*
inert /ɪ'nɜ:t/ *a* inerte
inertia /ɪ'nɜ:ʃə/ *n* inercia *f*
inescapable /ɪnɪ'skeɪpəbl/ *a* ineludible
inestimable /ɪn'estɪməbl/ *a* inestimable
inevitabl|e /ɪn'evɪtəbl/ *a* inevitable. **~ly** *adv* inevitablemente
inexact /ɪnɪg'zækt/ *a* inexacto
inexcusable /ɪnɪk'skju:səbl/ *a* imperdonable
inexhaustible /ɪnɪg'zɔ:stəbl/ *a* inagotable
inexorable /ɪn'eksərəbl/ *a* inexorable
inexpensive /ɪnɪk'spensɪv/ *a* económico, barato
inexperience /ɪnɪk'spɪərɪəns/ *n* falta *f* de experiencia. **~d** *a* inexperto
inexplicable /ɪnɪk'splɪkəbl/ *a* inexplicable
inextricable /ɪnɪk'strɪkəbl/ *a* inextricable
infallib|ility /ɪn'fæləbɪlətɪ/ *n* infalibilidad *f.* **~le** *a* infalible
infam|ous /'ɪnfəməs/ *a* infame. **~y** *n* infamia *f*
infan|cy /'ɪnfənsɪ/ *n* infancia *f.* **~t** *n* niño *m.* **~tile** /'ɪnfəntaɪl/ *a* infantil
infantry /'ɪnfəntrɪ/ *n* infantería *f*
infatuat|ed /ɪn'fætjʊeɪtɪd/ *a.* **be ~ed with** encapricharse por. **~ion** /-'eɪʃn/ *n* encaprichamiento *m*
infect /ɪn'fekt/ *vt* infectar; (*fig*) contagiar. **~ s.o. with** contagiar a uno. **~ion** /-'fekʃn/ *n* infección *f*; (*fig*) contagio *m.* **~ious** /ɪn'fekʃəs/ *a* contagioso
infer /ɪn'fɜ:(r)/ *vt* (*pt* **inferred**) deducir. **~ence** /'ɪnfərəns/ *n* deducción *f*
inferior /ɪn'fɪərɪə(r)/ *a* inferior. ● *n* inferior *m & f.* **~ity** /-'ɒrətɪ/ *n* inferioridad *f*
infernal /ɪn'fɜ:nl/ *a* infernal. **~ly** *adv* (*fam*) atrozmente
inferno /ɪn'fɜ:nəʊ/ *n* (*pl* **-os**) infierno *m*
infertil|e /ɪn'fɜ:taɪl/ *a* estéril. **~ity** /-'tɪlətɪ/ *n* esterilidad *f*
infest /ɪn'fest/ *vt* infestar. **~ation** /-'steɪʃn/ *n* infestación *f*
infidelity /ɪnfɪ'delətɪ/ *n* infidelidad *f*
infighting /'ɪnfaɪtɪŋ/ *n* lucha *f* cuerpo a cuerpo; (*fig*) riñas *fpl* (internas)
infiltrat|e /ɪnfɪl'treɪt/ *vt* infiltrar. ● *vi* infiltrarse. **~ion** /-'treɪʃn/ *n* infiltración *f*
infinite /'ɪnfɪnət/ *a* infinito. **~ly** *adv* infinitamente
infinitesimal /ɪnfɪnɪ'tesɪml/ *a* infinitesimal
infinitive /ɪn'fɪnətɪv/ *n* infinitivo *m*
infinity /ɪn'fɪnətɪ/ *n* (*infinite distance*) infinito *m*; (*infinite quantity*) infinidad *f*
infirm /ɪn'fɜ:m/ *a* enfermizo
infirmary /ɪn'fɜ:mərɪ/ *n* hospital *m*; (*sick bay*) enfermería *f*

infirmity /ɪn'fɜ:mətɪ/ *n* enfermedad *f*; (*weakness*) debilidad *f*
inflam|e /ɪn'fleɪm/ *vt* inflamar. **~mable** /ɪn'flæməbl/ *a* inflamable. **~mation** /-ə'meɪʃn/ *n* inflamación *f*. **~matory** /ɪn'flæmətərɪ/ *a* inflamatorio
inflate /ɪn'fleɪt/ *vt* inflar
inflation /ɪn'fleɪʃn/ *n* inflación *f*. **~ary** *a* inflacionario
inflection /ɪn'flekʃn/ *n* inflexión *f*
inflexible /ɪn'fleksəbl/ *a* inflexible
inflict /ɪn'flɪkt/ *vt* infligir (**on** a)
inflow /'ɪnfləʊ/ *n* afluencia *f*
influence /'ɪnflʊəns/ *n* influencia *f*. **under the ~** (*drunk, fam*) borracho. • *vt* influir, influenciar (*esp LAm*)
influential /ɪnflʊ'enʃl/ *a* influyente
influenza /ɪnflʊ'enzə/ *n* gripe *f*
influx /'ɪnflʌks/ *n* afluencia *f*
inform /ɪn'fɔ:m/ *vt* informar. **keep ~ed** tener al corriente
informal /ɪn'fɔ:ml/ *a* (*simple*) sencillo, sin ceremonia; (*unofficial*) oficioso. **~ity** /'mælətɪ/ *n* falta *f* de ceremonia. **~ly** *adv* sin ceremonia
inform|ant /ɪn'fɔ:mənt/ *n* informador *m*. **~ation** /ɪnfə'meɪʃn/ *n* información *f*. **~ative** /ɪn'fɔ:mətɪv/ *a* informativo. **~er** /ɪn'fɔ:mə(r)/ *n* denunciante *m*
infra-red /ɪnfrə'red/ *a* infrarrojo
infrequent /ɪn'fri:kwənt/ *a* poco frecuente. **~ly** *adv* raramente
infringe /ɪn'frɪndʒ/ *vt* infringir. **~ on** usurpar. **~ment** *n* infracción *f*
infuriate /ɪn'fjʊərɪeɪt/ *vt* enfurecer
infus|e /ɪn'fju:z/ *vt* infundir. **~ion** /-ʒn/ *n* infusión *f*
ingen|ious /ɪn'dʒi:nɪəs/ *a* ingenioso. **~uity** /ɪndʒɪ'nju:ətɪ/ *n* ingeniosidad *f*
ingenuous /ɪn'dʒenjʊəs/ *a* ingenuo
ingest /ɪn'dʒest/ *vt* ingerir
ingot /'ɪŋgət/ *n* lingote *m*
ingrained /ɪn'greɪnd/ *a* arraigado
ingratiate /ɪn'greɪʃɪeɪt/ *vt*. **~ o.s. with** congraciarse con
ingratitude /ɪn'grætɪtju:d/ *n* ingratitud *f*
ingredient /ɪn'gri:dɪənt/ *n* ingrediente *m*
ingrowing /'ɪngrəʊɪŋ/ *a*. **~ nail** *n* uñero *m*, uña *f* encarnada
inhabit /ɪn'hæbɪt/ *vt* habitar. **~able** *a* habitable. **~ant** *n* habitante *m*
inhale /ɪn'heɪl/ *vt* aspirar. • *vi* (*tobacco*) aspirar el humo
inherent /ɪn'hɪərənt/ *a* inherente. **~ly** *adv* intrínsecamente
inherit /ɪn'herɪt/ *vt* heredar. **~ance** *n* herencia *f*
inhibit /ɪn'hɪbɪt/ *vt* inhibir. **be ~ed** tener inhibiciones. **~ion** /-'bɪʃn/ *n* inhibición *f*
inhospitable /ɪnhə'spɪtəbl/ *a* ‹*place*› inhóspito; ‹*person*› inhospitalario
inhuman /ɪn'hju:mən/ *a* inhumano. **~e** /ɪnhju:'meɪn/ *a* inhumano. **~ity** /ɪnhju:'mænətɪ/ *n* inhumanidad *f*
inimical /ɪ'nɪmɪkl/ *a* hostil
inimitable /ɪ'nɪmɪtəbl/ *a* inimitable
iniquit|ous /ɪ'nɪkwɪtəs/ *a* inicuo. **~y** /-ətɪ/ *n* iniquidad *f*
initial /ɪ'nɪʃl/ *n* inicial *f*. • *vt* (*pt* **initialled**) firmar con iniciales. **he ~led the document** firmó el documento con sus iniciales. • *a* inicial. **~ly** *adv* al principio
initiat|e /ɪ'nɪʃɪeɪt/ *vt* iniciar; promover ‹*scheme etc*›. **~ion** /-'eɪʃn/ *n* iniciación *f*
initiative /ɪ'nɪʃətɪv/ *n* iniciativa *f*
inject /ɪn'dʒekt/ *vt* inyectar; (*fig*) injertar ‹*new element*›. **~ion** /-ʃn/ *n* inyección *f*
injunction /ɪn'dʒʌŋkʃn/ *n* (*court order*) entredicho *m*
injur|e /'ɪndʒə(r)/ *vt* (*wound*) herir; (*fig, damage*) perjudicar. **~y** /'ɪndʒərɪ/ *n* herida *f*; (*damage*) perjuicio *m*
injustice /ɪn'dʒʌstɪs/ *n* injusticia *f*
ink /ɪŋk/ *n* tinta *f*
inkling /'ɪŋklɪŋ/ *n* atisbo *m*
ink: **~-well** *n* tintero *m*. **~y** *a* manchado de tinta
inland /'ɪnlənd/ *a* interior. • *adv* tierra adentro. **I~ Revenue** *n* Hacienda *f*
in-laws /'ɪnlɔ:z/ *npl* parientes *mpl* políticos
inlay /ɪn'leɪ/ *vt* (*pt* **inlaid**) taracear, incrustar. /'ɪnleɪ/ *n* taracea *f*, incrustación *f*
inlet /'ɪnlet/ *n* ensenada *f*; (*tec*) entrada *f*
inmate /'ɪnmeɪt/ *n* (*of asylum*) internado *m*; (*of prison*) preso *m*
inn /ɪn/ *n* posada *f*
innards /'ɪnədz/ *npl* tripas *fpl*
innate /ɪ'neɪt/ *a* innato
inner /'ɪnə(r)/ *a* interior; (*fig*) íntimo. **~most** *a* más íntimo. **~ tube** *n* cámara *f* de aire, llanta *f* (*LAm*)
innings /'ɪnɪŋz/ *n invar* turno *m*
innkeeper /'ɪnki:pə(r)/ *n* posadero *m*

innocen|ce /'ɪnəsns/ *n* inocencia *f*. **~t** *a & n* inocente (*m & f*)
innocuous /ɪ'nɒkjʊəs/ *a* inocuo
innovat|e /'ɪnəveɪt/ *vi* innovar. **~ion** /-'veɪʃn/ *n* innovación *f*. **~or** *n* innovador *m*
innuendo /ɪnju:'endəʊ/ *n* (*pl* **-oes**) insinuación *f*
innumerable /ɪ'nju:mərəbl/ *a* innumerable
inoculat|e /ɪ'nɒkjʊleɪt/ *vt* inocular. **~ion** /-'leɪʃn/ *n* inoculación *f*
inoffensive /ɪnə'fensɪv/ *a* inofensivo
inoperative /ɪn'ɒpərətɪv/ *a* inoperante
inopportune /ɪn'ɒpətju:n/ *a* inoportuno
inordinate /ɪ'nɔ:dɪnət/ *a* excesivo. **~ly** *adv* excesivamente
in-patient /'ɪnpeɪʃnt/ *n* paciente *m* interno
input /'ɪnpʊt/ *n* (*data*) datos *mpl*; (*comput process*) entrada *f*, input *m*; (*elec*) energía *f*
inquest /'ɪnkwest/ *n* investigación *f* judicial
inquir|e /ɪn'kwaɪə(r)/ *vi* preguntar. **~y** *n* (*question*) pregunta *f*; (*investigation*) investigación *f*
inquisition /ɪnkwɪ'zɪʃn/ *n* inquisición *f*
inquisitive /ɪn'kwɪzətɪv/ *a* inquisitivo
inroad /'ɪnrəʊd/ *n* incursión *f*
inrush /'ɪnrʌʃ/ *n* irrupción *f*
insan|e /ɪn'seɪn/ *a* loco. **~ity** /-'sænətɪ/ *n* locura *f*
insanitary /ɪn'sænɪtərɪ/ *a* insalubre
insatiable /ɪn'seɪʃəbl/ *a* insaciable
inscri|be /ɪn'skraɪb/ *vt* inscribir; dedicar ‹*book*›. **~ption** /-ɪpʃn/ *n* inscripción *f*; (*in book*) dedicatoria *f*
inscrutable /ɪn'skru:təbl/ *a* inescrutable
insect /'ɪnsekt/ *n* insecto *m*. **~icide** /ɪn'sektɪsaɪd/ *n* insecticida *f*
insecur|e /ɪnsɪ'kjʊə(r)/ *a* inseguro. **~ity** *n* inseguridad *f*
insemination /ɪnsemɪ'neɪʃn/ *n* inseminación *f*
insensible /ɪn'sensəbl/ *a* insensible; (*unconscious*) sin conocimiento
insensitive /ɪn'sensətɪv/ *a* insensible
inseparable /ɪn'sepərəbl/ *a* inseparable
insert /'ɪnsɜ:t/ *n* materia *f* insertada. /ɪn'sɜ:t/ *vt* insertar. **~ion** /-ʃ:ɪ/ *n* inserción *f*
inshore /ɪn'ʃɔ:(r)/ *a* costero
inside /ɪn'saɪd/ *n* interior *m*. **~ out** al revés; (*thoroughly*) a fondo. ● *a* interior. ● *adv* dentro. ● *prep* dentro de. **~s** *npl* tripas *fpl*
insidious /ɪn'sɪdɪəs/ *a* insidioso
insight /'ɪnsaɪt/ *n* (*perception*) penetración *f*, revelación *f*
insignia /ɪn'sɪgnɪə/ *npl* insignias *fpl*
insignificant /ɪnsɪg'nɪfɪkənt/ *a* insignificante
insincer|e /ɪnsɪn'sɪə(r)/ *a* poco sincero. **~ity** /-'serətɪ/ *n* falta *f* de sinceridad *f*
insinuat|e /ɪn'sɪnjʊeɪt/ *vt* insinuar. **~ion** /-'eɪʃn/ *n* insinuación *f*
insipid /ɪn'sɪpɪd/ *a* insípido
insist /ɪn'sɪst/ *vt/i* insistir. **~ on** insistir en; (*demand*) exigir
insisten|ce /ɪn'sɪstəns/ *n* insistencia *f*. **~t** *a* insistente. **~tly** *adv* con insistencia
insolen|ce /'ɪnsələns/ *n* insolencia *f*. **~t** *a* insolente
insoluble /ɪn'sɒljʊbl/ *a* insoluble
insolvent /ɪn'sɒlvənt/ *a* insolvente
insomnia /ɪn'sɒmnɪə/ *n* insomnio *m*. **~c** /-ɪæk/ *n* insomne *m & f*
inspect /ɪn'spekt/ *vt* inspeccionar; revisar ‹*ticket*›. **~ion** /-ʃn/ *n* inspección *f*. **~or** *n* inspector *m*; (*on train, bus*) revisor *m*
inspir|ation /ɪnspə'reɪʃn/ *n* inspiración *f*. **~e** /ɪn'spaɪə(r)/ *vt* inspirar
instability /ɪnstə'bɪlətɪ/ *n* inestabilidad *f*
install /ɪn'stɔ:l/ *vt* instalar. **~ation** /-ə'leɪʃn/ *n* instalación *f*
instalment /ɪn'stɔ:lmənt/ *n* (*payment*) plazo *m*; (*of serial*) entrega *f*
instance /'ɪnstəns/ *n* ejemplo *m*; (*case*) caso *m*. **for ~** por ejemplo. **in the first ~** en primer lugar
instant /'ɪnstənt/ *a* inmediato; ‹*food*› instantáneo. ● *n* instante *m*. **~aneous** /ɪnstən'teɪnɪəs/ *a* instantáneo. **~ly** /'ɪnstəntlɪ/ *adv* inmediatamente
instead /ɪn'sted/ *adv* en cambio. **~ of doing** en vez de hacer. **~ of s.o.** en lugar de uno
instep /'ɪnstep/ *n* empeine *m*
instigat|e /'ɪnstɪgeɪt/ *vt* instigar. **~ion** /-'geɪʃn/ *n* instigación *f*. **~or** *n* instigador *m*
instil /ɪn'stɪl/ *vt* (*pt* **instilled**) infundir
instinct /'ɪnstɪŋkt/ *n* instinto *m*. **~ive** /ɪn'stɪŋktɪv/ *a* instintivo

institut|e /ˈɪnstɪtjuːt/ *n* instituto *m*. • *vt* instituir; iniciar ‹*enquiry etc*›. **~ion** /-ˈtjuːʃn/ *n* institución *f*

instruct /ɪnˈstrʌkt/ *vt* instruir; (*order*) mandar. **~ s.o. in sth** enseñar algo a uno. **~ion** /-ʃn/ *n* instrucción *f*. **~ions** /-ʃnz/ *npl* (*for use*) modo *m* de empleo. **~ive** *a* instructivo

instrument /ˈɪnstrəmənt/ *n* instrumento *m*. **~al** /ɪnstrəˈmentl/ *a* instrumental. **be ~al in** contribuir a. **~alist** *n* instrumentalista *m & f*

insubordinat|e /ɪnsəˈbɔːdɪnət/ *a* insubordinado. **~ion** /-ˈneɪʃn/ *n* insubordinación *f*

insufferable /ɪnˈsʌfərəbl/ *a* insufrible, insoportable

insufficient /ɪnsəˈfɪʃnt/ *a* insuficiente. **~ly** *adv* insuficientemente

insular /ˈɪnsjʊlə(r)/ *a* insular; (*narrow-minded*) de miras estrechas

insulat|e /ˈɪnsjʊleɪt/ *vt* aislar. **~ing tape** *n* cinta *f* aisladora/aislante. **~ion** /-ˈleɪʃn/ *n* aislamiento *m*

insulin /ˈɪnsjʊlɪn/ *n* insulina *f*

insult /ɪnˈsʌlt/ *vt* insultar. /ˈɪnsʌlt/ *n* insulto *m*

insuperable /ɪnˈsjuːpərəbl/ *a* insuperable

insur|ance /ɪnˈʃʊərəns/ *n* seguro *m*. **~e** *vt* asegurar. **~e that** asegurarse de que

insurgent /ɪnˈsɜːdʒənt/ *a & n* insurrecto (*m*)

insurmountable /ɪnsəˈmaʊntəbl/ *a* insuperable

insurrection /ɪnsəˈrekʃn/ *n* insurrección *f*

intact /ɪnˈtækt/ *a* intacto

intake /ˈɪnteɪk/ *n* (*quantity*) número *m*; (*mec*) admisión *f*; (*of food*) consumo *m*

intangible /ɪnˈtændʒəbl/ *a* intangible

integral /ˈɪntɪgrəl/ *a* íntegro. **be an ~ part of** ser parte integrante de

integrat|e /ˈɪntɪgreɪt/ *vt* integrar. • *vi* integrarse. **~ion** /-ˈgreɪʃn/ *n* integración *f*

integrity /ɪnˈtegrətɪ/ *n* integridad *f*

intellect /ˈɪntəlekt/ *n* intelecto *m*. **~ual** *a & n* intelectual (*m*)

intelligen|ce /ɪnˈtelɪdʒəns/ *n* inteligencia *f*; (*information*) información *f*. **~t** *a* inteligente. **~tly** *adv* inteligentemente. **~tsia** /ɪntelɪˈdʒentsɪə/ *n* intelectualidad *f*

intelligible /ɪnˈtelɪdʒəbl/ *a* inteligible

intemperance /ɪnˈtempərəns/ *n* inmoderación *f*

intend /ɪnˈtend/ *vt* destinar. **~ to do** tener la intención de hacer. **~ed** *a* intencionado. • *n* (*future spouse*) novio *m*

intense /ɪnˈtens/ *a* intenso; ‹*person*› apasionado. **~ly** *adv* intensamente; (*very*) sumamente

intensif|ication /ɪntensɪfɪˈkeɪʃn/ *n* intensificación *f*. **~y** /-faɪ/ *vt* intensificar

intensity /ɪnˈtensətɪ/ *n* intensidad *f*

intensive /ɪnˈtensɪv/ *a* intensivo. **~ care** *n* asistencia *f* intensiva, cuidados *mpl* intensivos

intent /ɪnˈtent/ *n* propósito *m*. • *a* atento. **~ on** absorto en. **~ on doing** resuelto a hacer

intention /ɪnˈtenʃn/ *n* intención *f*. **~al** *a* intencional

intently /ɪnˈtentlɪ/ *adv* atentamente

inter /ɪnˈtɜː(r)/ *vt* (*pt* **interred**) enterrar

inter... /ˈɪntə(r)/ *pref* inter..., entre...

interact /ɪntərˈækt/ *vi* obrar recíprocamente. **~ion** /-ʃn/ *n* interacción *f*

intercede /ɪntəˈsiːd/ *vi* interceder

intercept /ɪntəˈsept/ *vt* interceptar. **~ion** /-ʃn/ *n* interceptación *f*; (*in geometry*) intersección *f*

interchange /ˈɪntətʃeɪndʒ/ *n* (*road junction*) cruce *m*. **~able** /-ˈtʃeɪndʒəbl/ *a* intercambiable

intercom /ˈɪntəkɒm/ *n* intercomunicador *m*

interconnected /ɪntəkəˈnektɪd/ *a* relacionado

intercourse /ˈɪntəkɔːs/ *n* trato *m*; (*sexual*) trato *m* sexual

interest /ˈɪntrest/ *n* interés *m*; (*advantage*) ventaja *f*. • *vt* interesar. **~ed** *a* interesado. **be ~ed in** interesarse por. **~ing** *a* interesante

interfere /ɪntəˈfɪə(r)/ *vi* entrometerse. **~ in** entrometerse en. **~ with** entrometerse en, interferir en; interferir ‹*radio*›. **~nce** *n* interferencia *f*

interim *a* provisional. • *n*. **in the ~** entre tanto

interior /ɪnˈtɪərɪə(r)/ *a & n* interior (*m*)

interjection /ɪntəˈdʒekʃn/ *n* interjección *f*
interlock /ɪntəˈlɒk/ *vt/i* (*tec*) engranar
interloper /ˈɪntələʊpə(r)/ *n* intruso *m*
interlude /ˈɪntəlu:d/ *n* intervalo *m*; (*theatre, music*) interludio *m*
intermarr|iage /ɪntəˈmærɪdʒ/ *n* matrimonio *m* entre personas de distintas razas. **~y** *vi* casarse (con personas de distintas razas)
intermediary /ɪntəˈmi:dɪərɪ/ *a & n* intermediario (*m*)
intermediate /ɪntəˈmi:dɪət/ *a* intermedio
interminable /ɪnˈtɜ:mɪnəbl/ *a* interminable
intermission /ɪntəˈmɪʃn/ *n* pausa *f*; (*theatre*) descanso *m*
intermittent /ɪntəˈmɪtnt/ *a* intermitente. **~ly** *adv* con discontinuidad
intern /ɪnˈtɜ:n/ *vt* internar. /ˈɪntɜ:n/ *n* (*doctor, Amer*) interno *m*
internal /ɪnˈtɜ:nl/ *a* interior. **~ly** *adv* interiormente
international /ɪntəˈnæʃənl/ *a & n* internacional (*m*)
internee /ˌɪntɜ:ˈni:/ *n* internado *m*
internment /ɪnˈtɜ:nmənt/ *n* internamiento *m*
interplay /ˈɪntəpleɪ/ *n* interacción *f*
interpolate /ɪnˈtɜ:pəleɪt/ *vt* interpolar
interpret /ɪnˈtɜ:prɪt/ *vt/i* interpretar. **~ation** /-ˈteɪʃn/ *n* interpretación *f*. **~er** *n* intérprete *m & f*
interrelated /ɪntərɪˈleɪtɪd/ *a* interrelacionado
interrogat|e /ɪnˈterəgeɪt/ *vt* interrogar. **~ion** /-ˈgeɪʃn/ *n* interrogación *f*; (*session of questions*) interrogatorio *m*
interrogative /ɪntəˈrɒgətɪv/ *a & n* interrogativo (*m*)
interrupt /ɪntəˈrʌpt/ *vt* interrumpir. **~ion** /-ʃn/ *n* interrupción *f*
intersect /ɪntəˈsekt/ *vt* cruzar. ● *vi* ‹*roads*› cruzarse; (*geometry*) intersecarse. **~ion** /-ʃn/ *n* (*roads*) cruce *m*; (*geometry*) intersección *f*
interspersed /ɪntəˈspɜ:st/ *a* disperso. **~ with** salpicado de
intertwine /ɪntəˈtwaɪn/ *vt* entrelazar. ● *vi* entrelazarse
interval /ˈɪntəvl/ *n* intervalo *m*; (*theatre*) descanso *m*. **at ~s** a intervalos
interven|e /ɪntəˈvi:n/ *vi* intervenir. **~tion** /-ˈvenʃn/ *n* intervención *f*
interview /ˈɪntəvju:/ *n* entrevista *f*. ● *vt* entrevistarse con. **~er** *n* entrevistador *m*
intestin|al /ɪnteˈstaɪnl/ *a* intestinal. **~e** /ɪnˈtestɪn/ *n* intestino *m*
intimacy /ˈɪntɪməsɪ/ *n* intimidad *f*
intimate[1] /ˈɪntɪmət/ *a* íntimo
intimate[2] /ˈɪntɪmeɪt/ *vt* (*state*) anunciar; (*imply*) dar a entender
intimately /ˈɪntɪmətlɪ/ *adv* íntimamente
intimidat|e /ɪnˈtɪmɪdeɪt/ *vt* intimidar. **~ion** /-ˈdeɪʃn/ *n* intimidación *f*
into /ˈɪntu:/, *unstressed* /ˈɪntə/ *prep* en; (*translate*) a
intolerable /ɪnˈtɒlərəbl/ *a* intolerable
intoleran|ce /ɪnˈtɒlərəns/ *n* intolerancia *f*. **~t** *a* intolerante
intonation /ɪntəˈneɪʃn/ *n* entonación *f*
intoxicat|e /ɪnˈtɒksɪkeɪt/ *vt* embriagar; (*med*) intoxicar. **~ed** *a* ebrio. **~ion** /-ˈkeɪʃn/ *n* embriaguez *f*; (*med*) intoxicación *f*
intra... /ˈɪntrə/ *pref* intra...
intractable /ɪnˈtræktəbl/ *a* ‹*person*› intratable; ‹*thing*› muy difícil
intransigent /ɪnˈtrænsɪdʒənt/ *a* intransigente
intransitive /ɪnˈtrænsɪtɪv/ *a* intransitivo
intravenous /ɪntrəˈvi:nəs/ *a* intravenoso
intrepid /ɪnˈtrepɪd/ *a* intrépido
intrica|cy /ˈɪntrɪkəsɪ/ *n* complejidad *f*. **~te** *a* complejo
intrigu|e /ɪnˈtri:g/ *vt/i* intrigar. ● *n* intriga *f*. **~ing** *a* intrigante
intrinsic /ɪnˈtrɪnsɪk/ *a* intrínseco. **~ally** *adv* intrínsecamente
introduc|e /ɪntrəˈdju:s/ *vt* introducir; presentar ‹*person*›. **~tion** /ɪntrəˈdʌkʃn/ *n* introducción *f*; (*to person*) presentación *f*. **~tory** /-tərɪ/ *a* preliminar
introspective /ɪntrəˈspektɪv/ *a* introspectivo
introvert /ˈɪntrəvɜ:t/ *n* introvertido *m*
intru|de /ɪnˈtru:d/ *vi* entrometerse; (*disturb*) molestar. **~der** *n* intruso *m*. **~sion** *n* intrusión *f*
intuiti|on /ɪntju:ˈɪʃn/ *n* intuición *f*. **~ve** /ɪnˈtju:ɪtɪv/ *a* intuitivo

inundat|e /ˈɪnʌndeɪt/ *vt* inundar. **~ion** /-ˈdeɪʃn/ *n* inundación *f*

invade /ɪnˈveɪd/ *vt* invadir. **~r** /-ə(r)/ *n* invasor *m*

invalid[1] /ˈɪnvəlɪd/ *n* enfermo *m*, inválido *m*

invalid[2] /ɪnˈvælɪd/ *a* nulo. **~ate** *vt* invalidar

invaluable /ɪnˈvæljʊəbl/ *a* inestimable

invariabl|e /ɪnˈveərɪəbl/ *a* invariable. **~y** *adv* invariablemente

invasion /ɪnˈveɪʒn/ *n* invasión *f*

invective /ɪnˈvektɪv/ *n* invectiva *f*

inveigh /ɪnˈveɪ/ *vi* dirigir invectivas (**against** contra)

inveigle /ɪnˈveɪgl/ *vt* engatusar, persuadir

invent /ɪnˈvent/ *vt* inventar. **~ion** /-ˈvenʃn/ *n* invención *f*. **~ive** *a* inventivo. **~or** *n* inventor *m*

inventory /ˈɪnvəntərɪ/ *n* inventario *m*

invers|e /ɪnˈvɜːs/ *a & n* inverso (*m*). **~ely** *adv* inversamente. **~ion** /ɪnˈvɜːʃn/ *n* inversión *f*

invert /ɪnˈvɜːt/ *vt* invertir. **~ed commas** *npl* comillas *fpl*

invest /ɪnˈvest/ *vt* invertir. ● *vi*. **~ in** hacer una inversión *f*

investigat|e /ɪnˈvestɪgeɪt/ *vt* investigar. **~ion** /-ˈgeɪʃn/ *n* investigación *f*. **under ~ion** sometido a examen. **~or** *n* investigador *m*

inveterate /ɪnˈvetərət/ *a* inveterado

invidious /ɪnˈvɪdɪəs/ *a* (*hateful*) odioso; (*unfair*) injusto

invigilat|e /ɪnˈvɪdʒɪleɪt/ *vi* vigilar. **~or** *n* celador *m*

invigorate /ɪnˈvɪgəreɪt/ *vt* vigorizar; (*stimulate*) estimular

invincible /ɪnˈvɪnsɪbl/ *a* invencible

invisible /ɪnˈvɪzəbl/ *a* invisible

invit|ation /ɪnvɪˈteɪʃn/ *n* invitación *f*. **~e** /ɪnˈvaɪt/ *vt* invitar; (*ask for*) pedir. **~ing** *a* atrayente

invoice /ˈɪnvɔɪs/ *n* factura *f*. ● *vt* facturar

invoke /ɪnˈvəʊk/ *vt* invocar

involuntary /ɪnˈvɒləntərɪ/ *a* involuntario

involve /ɪnˈvɒlv/ *vt* enredar. **~d** *a* (*complex*) complicado. **~d in** embrollado en. **~ment** *n* enredo *m*

invulnerable /ɪnˈvʌlnərəbl/ *a* invulnerable

inward /ˈɪnwəd/ *a* interior. ● *adv* interiormente. **~s** *adv* hacia/para dentro

iodine /ˈaɪədiːn/ *n* yodo *m*

iota /aɪˈəʊtə/ *n* (*amount*) pizca *f*

IOU /aɪəʊˈjuː/ *abbr* (*I owe you*) pagaré *m*

IQ /aɪˈkjuː/ *abbr* (*intelligence quotient*) cociente *m* intelectual

Iran /ɪˈrɑːn/ *n* Irán *m*. **~ian** /ɪˈreɪnɪən/ *a & n* iraní (*m*)

Iraq /ɪˈrɑːk/ *n* Irak *m*. **~i** *a & n* iraquí (*m*)

irascible /ɪˈræsəbl/ *a* irascible

irate /aɪˈreɪt/ *a* colérico

ire /aɪə(r)/ *n* ira *f*

Ireland /ˈaɪələnd/ *n* Irlanda *f*

iris /ˈaɪərɪs/ *n* (*anat*) iris *m*; (*bot*) lirio *m*

Irish /ˈaɪərɪʃ/ *a* irlandés. ● *n* (*lang*) irlandés *m*. **~man** *n* irlandés *m*. **~woman** *n* irlandesa *f*

irk /ɜːk/ *vt* fastidiar. **~some** *a* fastidioso

iron /ˈaɪən/ *n* hierro *m*; (*appliance*) plancha *f*. ● *a* de hierro. ● *vt* planchar. **~ out** allanar. **I~ Curtain** *n* telón *m* de acero

ironic(al) /aɪˈrɒnɪk(l)/ *a* irónico

ironing-board /ˈaɪənɪŋˈbɔːd/ *n* tabla *f* de planchar

ironmonger /ˈaɪənmʌŋgə(r)/ *n* ferretero *m*. **~y** *n* ferretería *f*

ironwork /ˈaɪənwɜːk/ *n* herraje *m*

irony /ˈaɪərənɪ/ *n* ironía *f*

irrational /ɪˈræʃənl/ *a* irracional

irreconcilable /ɪrekənˈsaɪləbl/ *a* irreconciliable

irrefutable /ɪrɪˈfjuːtəbl/ *a* irrefutable

irregular /ɪˈregjʊlə(r)/ *a* irregular. **~ity** /-ˈlærətɪ/ *n* irregularidad *f*

irrelevan|ce /ɪˈreləvəns/ *n* inoportunidad *f*, impertinencia *f*. **~t** *a* no pertinente

irreparable /ɪˈrepərəbl/ *a* irreparable

irreplaceable /ɪrɪˈpleɪsəbl/ *a* irreemplazable

irrepressible /ɪrɪˈpresəbl/ *a* irreprimible

irresistible /ɪrɪˈzɪstəbl/ *a* irresistible

irresolute /ɪˈrezəluːt/ *a* irresoluto, indeciso

irrespective /ɪrɪˈspektɪv/ *a*. **~ of** sin tomar en cuenta

irresponsible /ɪrɪˈspɒnsəbl/ *a* irresponsable

irretrievable /ɪrɪˈtriːvəbl/ *a* irrecuperable

irreverent /ɪˈrevərənt/ *a* irreverente

irreversible /ɪrɪ'vɜ:səbl/ *a* irreversible; ‹*decision*› irrevocable
irrevocable /ɪ'revəkəbl/ *a* irrevocable
irrigat|e /'ɪrɪgeɪt/ *vt* regar; (*med*) irrigar. **~ion** /-'geɪʃn/ *n* riego *m*; (*med*) irrigación *f*
irritable /'ɪrɪtəbl/ *a* irritable
irritat|e /'ɪrɪteɪt/ *vt* irritar. **~ion** /-'teɪʃn/ *n* irritación *f*
is /ɪz/ *see* **be**
Islam /'ɪzlɑ:m/ *n* Islam *m*. **~ic** /ɪz'læmɪk/ *a* islámico
island /'aɪlənd/ *n* isla *f*. **traffic ~** *n* refugio *m* (en la calle). **~er** *n* isleño *m*
isle /aɪl/ *n* isla *f*
isolat|e /'aɪsəleɪt/ *vt* aislar. **~ion** /-'leɪʃn/ *n* aislamiento *m*
isotope /'aɪsətəʊp/ *n* isotopo *m*
Israel /'ɪzreɪl/ *n* Israel *m*. **~i** /ɪz'reɪlɪ/ *a & n* israelí (*m*)
issue /'ɪʃu:/ *n* asunto *m*; (*outcome*) resultado *m*; (*of magazine etc*) número *m*; (*of stamps*) emisión *f*; (*offspring*) descendencia *f*. **at ~** en cuestión. **take ~ with** oponerse a. ● *vt* distribuir; emitir ‹*stamps etc*›; publicar ‹*book*›. ● *vi*. **~ from** salir de
isthmus /'ɪsməs/ *n* istmo *m*
it /ɪt/ *pron* (*subject*) el, ella, ello; (*direct object*) lo, la; (*indirect object*) le; (*after preposition*) él, ella, ello. **~ is hot** hace calor. **~ is me** soy yo. **far from ~** ni mucho menos. **that's ~** eso es. **who is ~?** ¿quién es?
italic /ɪ'tælɪk/ *a* bastardillo *m*. **~s** *npl* (letra *f*) bastardilla *f*
ital|ian /ɪ'tæljən/ *a & n* italiano (*m*). **I~y** /'ɪtəlɪ/ *n* Italia f
itch /ɪtʃ/ *n* picazón *f*. ● *vi* picar. **I'm ~ing to** rabio por. **my arm ~es** me pica el brazo. **~y** *a* que pica
item /'aɪtəm/ *n* artículo *m*; (*on agenda*) asunto *m*. **news ~** *n* noticia *f*. **~ize** *vt* detallar
itinerant /aɪ'tɪnərənt/ *a* ambulante
itinerary /aɪ'tɪnərərɪ/ *n* itinerario *m*
its /ɪts/ *a* su, sus (*pl*). ● *pron* (el) suyo *m*, (la) suya *f*, (los) suyos *mpl*, (las) suyas *fpl*
it's /ɪts/ = **it is, it has**
itself /ɪt'self/ *pron* él mismo, ella misma, ello mismo; (*reflexive*) se; (*after prep*) sí mismo, sí misma
ivory /'aɪvərɪ/ *n* marfil *m*. **~ tower** *n* torre *f* de marfil
ivy /'aɪvɪ/ *n* hiedra *f*

J

jab /dʒæb/ *vt* (*pt* **jabbed**) pinchar; (*thrust*) hurgonear. ● *n* pinchazo *m*
jabber /'dʒæbə(r)/ *vi* barbullar. ● *n* farfulla *f*
jack /dʒæk/ *n* (*mec*) gato *m*; (*cards*) sota *f*. ● *vt*. **~ up** alzar con gato
jackal /'dʒækl/ *n* chacal *m*
jackass /'dʒækæs/ *n* burro *m*
jackdaw /'dʒækdɔ:/ *n* grajilla *f*
jacket /'dʒækɪt/ *n* chaqueta *f*, saco *m* (*LAm*); (*of book*) sobrecubierta *f*, camisa *f*
jack-knife /'dʒæknaɪf/ *n* navaja *f*
jackpot /'dʒækpɒt/ *n* premio *m* gordo. **hit the ~** sacar el premio gordo
jade /dʒeɪd/ *n* (*stone*) jade *m*
jaded /'dʒeɪdɪd/ *a* cansado
jagged /'dʒægɪd/ *a* dentado
jaguar /'dʒægjʊə(r)/ *n* jaguar *m*
jail /dʒeɪl/ *n* cárcel *m*. **~bird** *n* criminal *m* emperdernido. **~er** *n* carcelero *m*
jalopy /dʒə'lɒpɪ/ *n* cacharro *m*
jam[1] /dʒæm/ *vt* (*pt* **jammed**) interferir con ‹*radio*›; ‹*traffic*› embotellar; ‹*people*› agolparse en. ● *vi* obstruirse; ‹*mechanism etc*› atascarse. ● *n* (*of people*) agolpamiento *m*; (*of traffic*) embotellamiento *m*; (*situation, fam*) apuro *m*
jam[2] /dʒæm/ *n* mermelada *f*
Jamaica /dʒə'meɪkə/ *n* Jamaica *f*
jamboree /dʒæmbə'ri:/ *n* reunión *f*
jam-packed /'dʒæm'pækt/ *a* atestado
jangle /'dʒæŋgl/ *n* sonido *m* metálico (y áspero). ● *vt/i* sonar discordemente
janitor /'dʒænɪtə(r)/ *n* portero *m*
January /'dʒænjʊərɪ/ *n* enero *m*
Japan /dʒə'pæn/ *n* el Japón *m*. **~ese** /dʒæpə'ni:z/ *a & n* japonés (*m*)
jar[1] /dʒɑ:(r)/ *n* tarro *m*, frasco *m*
jar[2] /dʒɑ:(r)/ *vi* (*pt* **jarred**) ‹*sound*› sonar mal; ‹*colours*› chillar. ● *vt* sacudir
jar[3] /dʒɑ:(r)/ *n*. **on the ~** (*ajar*) entreabierto
jargon /'dʒɑ:gən/ *n* jerga *f*
jarring /'dʒɑ:rɪŋ/ *a* discorde
jasmine /'dʒæsmɪn/ *n* jazmín *m*
jaundice /'dʒɔ:ndɪs/ *n* ictericia *f*. **~d** *a* (*envious*) envidioso; (*bitter*) amargado
jaunt /dʒɔ:nt/ *n* excursión *f*

jaunty /'dʒɔ:ntɪ/ *a* (**-ier**, **-iest**) garboso

javelin /'dʒævəlɪn/ *n* jabalina *f*

jaw /dʒɔ:/ *n* mandíbula *f*. ● *vi* (*talk lengthily, sl*) hablar por los codos

jay /dʒeɪ/ *n* arrendajo *m*. **~-walk** *vi* cruzar la calle descuidadamente

jazz /dʒæz/ *n* jazz *m*. ● *vt*. **~ up** animar. **~y** *a* chillón

jealous /dʒeləs/ *a* celoso. **~y** *n* celos *mpl*

jeans /dʒi:nz/ *npl* (pantalones *mpl*) vaqueros *mpl*

jeep /dʒi:p/ *n* jeep *m*

jeer /dʒɪə(r)/ *vt/i*. **~ at** mofarse de, befar; (*boo*) abuchear. ● *n* mofa *f*; (*boo*) abucheo *m*

jell /dʒel/ *vi* cuajar. **~ied** *a* en gelatina

jelly /dʒelɪ/ *n* jalea *f*. **~fish** *n* medusa *f*

jeopard|ize /'dʒepədaɪz/ *vt* arriesgar. **~y** *n* peligro *m*

jerk /dʒɜ:k/ *n* sacudida *f*; (*fool, sl*) idiota *m* & *f*. ● *vt* sacudir. **~ily** *adv* a sacudidads. **~y** *a* espasmódico

jersey /'dʒɜ:zɪ/ *n* (*pl* **-eys**) jersey *m*

jest /dʒest/ *n* broma *f*. ● *vi* bromear. **~er** *n* bufón *m*

Jesus /'dʒi:zəs/ *n* Jesús *m*

jet[1] /dʒet/ *n* (*stream*) chorro *m*; (*plane*) yet *m*, avión *m* de propulsión por reacción

jet[2] /dʒet/ *n* (*mineral*) azabache *m*. **~-black** *a* de azabache, como el azabache

jet: **~ lag** *n* cansancio *m* retardado después de un vuelo largo. **have ~ lag** estar desfasado. **~-propelled** *a* (de propulsión) a reacción

jettison /'dʒetɪsn/ *vt* echar al mar; (*fig, discard*) deshacerse de

jetty /'dʒetɪ/ *n* muelle *m*

Jew /dʒu:/ *n* judío *m*

jewel /'dʒu:əl/ *n* joya *f*. **~led** *a* enjoyado. **~ler** *n* joyero *m*. **~lery** *n* joyas *fpl*

Jew: **~ess** *n* judía *f*. **~ish** *a* judío. **~ry** /'dʒʊərɪ/ *n* los judíos *mpl*

jib[1] /dʒɪb/ *n* (*sail*) foque *m*

jib[2] /dʒɪb/ *vi* (*pt* **jibbed**) rehusar. **~ at** oponerse a.

jiffy /'dʒɪfɪ/ *n* momentito *m*. **do sth in a ~** hacer algo en un santiamén

jig /dʒɪg/ *n* (*dance*) giga *f*

jiggle /'dʒɪgl/ *vt* zangolotear

jigsaw /'dʒɪgsɔ:/ *n* rompecabezas *m invar*

jilt /dʒɪlt/ *vt* plantar, dejar plantado

jingle /'dʒɪŋgl/ *vt* hacer sonar. ● *vi* tintinear. ● *n* tintineo *m*; (*advert*) anuncio *m* cantado

jinx /dʒɪŋks/ *n* (*person*) gafe *m*; (*spell*) maleficio *m*

jitter|s /'dʒɪtəz/ *npl*. **have the ~s** estar nervioso. **~y** /-ərɪ/ *a* nervioso. **be ~y** estar nervioso

job /dʒɒb/ *n* trabajo *m*; (*post*) empleo *m*, puesto *m*. **have a ~ doing** costar trabajo hacer. **it is a good ~ that** menos mal que. **~centre** *n* bolsa *f* de trabajo. **~less** *a* sin trabajo.

jockey /'dʒɒkɪ/ *n* jockey *m*. ● *vi* (*manoevre*) maniobrar (**for** para)

jocular /'dʒɒkjʊlə(r)/ *a* jocoso

jog /dʒɒg/ *vt* (*pt* **jogged**) empujar; refrescar ‹*memory*›. ● *vi* hacer footing. **~ging** *n* jogging *m*

join /dʒɔɪn/ *vt* unir, juntar; hacerse socio de ‹*club*›; hacerse miembro de ‹*political group*›; alistarse en ‹*army*›; reunirse con ‹*another person*›. ● *vi* ‹*roads etc*› empalmar; ‹*rivers*› confluir. **~ in** participar (en). **~ up** (*mil*) alistarse. ● *n* juntura

joiner /'dʒɔɪnə(r)/ *n* carpintero *m*

joint /dʒɔɪnt/ *a* común. **~ author** *n* coautor *m*. ● *n* (*join*) juntura *f*; (*anat*) articulación *f*; (*culin*) asado *m*; (*place, sl*) garito *m*; (*marijuana, sl*) cigarillo *m* de marijuana. **out of ~** descoyuntado. **~ly** *adv* conjuntamente

joist /dʒɔɪst/ *n* viga *f*

jok|e /dʒəʊk/ *n* broma *f*; (*funny story*) chiste *m*. ● *vi* bromear. **~er** *n* bromista *m* & *f*; (*cards*) comodín *m*. **~ingly** *adv* en broma

joll|ification /dʒɒlɪfɪ'keɪʃn/ *n* jolgorio *m*. **~ity** *n* jolgorio *m*. **~y** *a* (**-ier**, **-iest**) alegre. ● *adv* (*fam*) muy

jolt /dʒɒlt/ *vt* sacudir. ● *vt* ‹*vehicle*› traquetear. ● *n* sacudida *f*

Jordan /'dʒɔ:dən/ *n* Jordania *f*. **~ian** *a* & *n* /-'deɪnɪən/ jordano (*m*)

jostle /'dʒɒsl/ *vt/i* empujar(se)

jot /dʒɒt/ *n* pizca *f*. ● *vt* (*pt* **jotted**) apuntar. **~ter** *n* bloc *m*

journal /'dʒɜ:nl/ *n* (*diary*) diario *m*; (*newspaper*) periódico *m*; (*magazine*) revista *f*. **~ese** /dʒɜ:nə'li:z/ *n* jerga *f* periodística. **~ism** *n* periodismo *m*. **~ist** *n* periodista *m* & *f*

journey /'dʒɜ:nɪ/ *n* viaje *m*. ● *vi* viajar

jovial /'dʒəʊvɪəl/ *a* jovial

jowl /dʒaʊl/ *n* (*jaw*) quijada *f*; (*cheek*) mejilla *f*. **cheek by ~** muy cerca

joy /dʒɔɪ/ *n* alegría *f*. **~ful** *a* alegre. **~ride** *n* paseo *m* en coche sin permiso del dueño. **~ous** *a* alegre

jubila|nt /ˈdʒu:bɪlənt/ *a* jubiloso. **~tion** /-ˈleɪʃn/ *n* júbilo *m*

jubilee /ˈdʒu:bɪli:/ *n* aniversario *m* especial

Judaism /ˈdʒu:deɪɪzəm/ *n* judaísmo *m*

judder /ˈdʒʌdə(r)/ *vi* vibrar. ● *n* vibración *f*

judge /dʒʌdʒ/ *n* juez *m*. ● *vt* juzgar. **~ment** *n* juicio *m*

judicia|l /dʒu:ˈdɪʃl/ *a* judicial. **~ry** *n* magistratura *f*

judicious /dʒu:ˈdɪʃəs/ *a* juicioso

judo /ˈdʒu:dəʊ/ *n* judo *m*

jug /dʒʌg/ *n* jarra *f*

juggernaut /ˈdʒʌgənɔ:t/ *n* (*lorry*) camión *m* grande

juggle /ˈdʒʌgl/ *vt/i* hacer juegos malabares (con). **~r** *n* malabarista *m & f*

juic|e /dʒu:s/ *n* jugo *m*, zumo *m*. **~y** *a* jugoso, zumoso; ‹*story etc*› (*fam*) picante

juke-box /ˈdʒu:kbɒks/ *n* tocadiscos *m invar* tragaperras

July /dʒu:ˈlaɪ/ *n* julio

jumble /ˈdʒʌmbl/ *vt* mezclar. ● *n* (*muddle*) revoltijo *m*. **~ sale** *n* venta *f* de objetos usados, mercadillo *m*

jumbo /ˈdʒʌmbəʊ/ *a*. **~ jet** *n* jumbo *m*

jump /dʒʌmp/ *vt/i* saltar. **~ the gun** obrar prematuramente. **~ the queue** colarse. ● *vi* saltar; (*start*) asustarse; ‹*prices*› alzarse. **~ at** apresurarse a aprovechar. ● *n* salto *m*; (*start*) susto *m*; (*increase*) aumento *m*

jumper /ˈdʒʌmpə(r)/ *n* jersey *m*; (*dress, Amer*) mandil *m*, falda *f* con peto

jumpy /ˈdʒʌmpɪ/ *a* nervioso

junction /ˈdʒʌŋkʃn/ *n* juntura *f*; (*of roads*) cruce *m*, entronque *m* (*LAm*); (*rail*) empalme *m*, entronque *m* (*LAm*)

juncture /ˈdʒʌŋktʃə(r)/ *n* momento *m*; (*state of affairs*) coyuntura *f*

June /dʒu:n/ *n* junio *m*

jungle /ˈdʒʌŋgl/ *n* selva *f*

junior /ˈdʒu:nɪə(r)/ *a* (*in age*) más joven (**to** que); (*in rank*) subalterno. ● *n* menor *m*. **~ school** *n* escuela *f*

junk /dʒʌŋk/ *n* trastos *mpl* viejos. ● *vt* (*fam*) tirar

junkie /ˈdʒʌŋkɪ/ *n* (*sl*) drogadicto *m*

junk shop /ˈdʒʌŋkʃɒp/ *n* tienda *f* de trastos viejos

junta /ˈdʒʌntə/ *n* junta *f*

jurisdiction /dʒʊərɪsˈdɪkʃn/ *n* jurisdicción *f*

jurisprudence /dʒʊərɪsˈpru:dəns/ *n* jurisprudencia *f*

juror /ˈdʒʊərə(r)/ *n* jurado *m*

jury /ˈdʒʊərɪ/ *n* jurado *m*

just /dʒʌst/ *a* (*fair*) justo. ● *adv* exactamente; (*slightly*) apenas; (*only*) sólo, solamente. **~ as tall** tan alto (**as** como). **~ listen!** ¡escucha! **he has ~ left** acaba de marcharse

justice /ˈdʒʌstɪs/ *n* justicia *f*. **J~ of the Peace** juez *m* de paz

justif|iable /dʒʌstɪˈfaɪəbl/ *a* justificable. **~iably** *adv* con razón. **~ication** /dʒʌstɪfɪˈkeɪʃn/ *n* justificación *f*. **~y** /ˈdʒʌstɪfaɪ/ *vt* justificar

justly /ˈdʒʌstlɪ/ *adv* con justicia

jut /dʒʌt/ *vi* (*pt* **jutted**). **~ out** sobresalir

juvenile /ˈdʒu:vənaɪl/ *a* juvenil; (*childish*) infantil. ● *n* joven *m & f*. **~ court** *n* tribunal *m* de menores

juxtapose /dʒʌkstəˈpəʊz/ *vt* yuxtaponer

K

kaleidoscope /kəˈlaɪdəskəʊp/ *n* calidoscopio *m*

kangaroo /kæŋgəˈru:/ *n* canguro *m*

kapok /ˈkeɪpɒk/ *n* miraguano *m*

karate /kəˈrɑ:tɪ/ *n* karate *m*

kebab /kɪˈbæb/ *n* broqueta *f*

keel /ki:l/ *n* (*of ship*) quilla *f*. ● *vi*. **~ over** volcarse

keen /ki:n/ *a* (**-er, -est**) ‹*interest, feeling*› vivo; ‹*wind, mind, analysis*› penetrante; ‹*edge*› afilado; ‹*appetite*› bueno; ‹*eyesight*› agudo; (*eager*) entusiasta. **be ~ on** gustarle a uno. **he's ~ on Shostakovich** le gusta Shostakovich. **~ly** *adv* vivamente; (*enthusiastically*) con entusiasmo. **~ness** *n* intensidad *f*; (*enthusiasm*) entusiasmo *m*.

keep /ki:p/ *vt* (*pt* **kept**) guardar; cumplir ‹*promise*›; tener ‹*shop, animals*›; mantener ‹*family*›; observar ‹*rule*›; (*celebrate*) celebrar; (*delay*) detener; (*prevent*) impedir. ● *vi* ‹*food*› conservarse; (*remain*) quedarse. ● *n* subsistencia *f*; (*of castle*) torreón *m*. **for ~s** (*fam*) para siempre. **~ back** *vt* retener. ● *vi* no acercarse. **~ in** no dejar salir. **~ in with** mantenerse en buenas relaciones con. **~ out** no dejar entrar. **~ up** mantener. **~ up (with)** estar al día (en). **~er** *n* guarda *m*

keeping /ˈki:pɪŋ/ *n* cuidado *m*. **in ~ with** de acuerdo con

keepsake /ˈki:pseɪk/ *n* recuerdo *m*

keg /keg/ *n* barrilete *m*

kennel /ˈkenl/ *n* perrera *f*

Kenya /ˈkenjə/ *n* Kenia *f*

kept /kept/ *see* **keep**

kerb /kɜ:b/ *n* bordillo *m*

kerfuffle /kəˈfʌfl/ *n* (*fuss, fam*) lío *m*

kernel /ˈkɜ:nl/ *n* almendra *f*; (*fig*) meollo *m*

kerosene /ˈkerəsi:n/ *n* queroseno *m*

ketchup /ˈketʃʌp/ *n* salsa *f* de tomate

kettle /ˈketl/ *n* hervidor *m*

key /ki:/ *n* llave *f*; (*of typewriter, piano etc*) tecla *f*. ● *a* clave. ● *vt*. **~ up** excitar. **~board** *n* teclado *m*. **~hole** *n* ojo *m* de la cerradura. **~note** *n* (*mus*) tónica *f*; (*speech*) idea *f* fundamental. **~-ring** *n* llavero *m*. **~stone** *n* piedra *f* clave

khaki /ˈkɑ:kɪ/ *a* caqui

kibbutz /kɪˈbʊts/ *n* (*pl* **-im** /-i:m/ *or* **-es**) kibbutz *m*

kick /kɪk/ *vt* dar una patada a; ‹*animals*› tirar una coz a. ● *vi* dar patadas; ‹*firearm*› dar culatazo. ● *n* patada *f*; (*of animal*) coz *f*; (*of firearm*) culatazo *m*; (*thrill, fam*) placer *m*. **~ out** (*fam*) echar a patadas. **~ up** armar ‹*fuss etc*›. **~back** *n* culatazo *m*; (*payment*) soborno *m*. **~-off** *n* (*sport*) saque *m* inicial

kid /kɪd/ *n* (*young goat*) cabrito *m*; (*leather*) cabritilla *f*; (*child, sl*) chaval *m*. ● *vt* (*pt* **kidded**) tomar el pelo a. ● *vi* bromear

kidnap /ˈkɪdnæp/ *vt* (*pt* **kidnapped**) secuestrar. **~ping** *n* secuestro *m*

kidney /ˈkɪdnɪ/ *n* riñón *m*. ● *a* renal

kill /kɪl/ *vt* matar; (*fig*) acabar con. ● *n* matanza *f*; (*in hunt*) pieza(s) *f*(*pl*). **~er** *n* matador *m*; (*murderer*) asesino *m*. **~ing** *n* matanza *f*; (*murder*) asesinato *m*. ● *a* (*funny, fam*) para morirse de risa; (*tiring, fam*) agotador. **~joy** *n* aguafiestas *m & f invar*

kiln /kɪln/ *n* horno *m*

kilo /ˈki:ləʊ/ *n* (*pl* **-os**) kilo *m*

kilogram(me) /ˈkɪləgræm/ *n* kilogramo *m*

kilohertz /ˈkɪləhɜ:ts/ *n* kilohercio *m*

kilometre /ˈkɪləmi:tə(r)/ *n* kilómetro *m*

kilowatt /ˈkɪləwɒt/ *n* kilovatio *m*

kilt /kɪlt/ *n* falda *f* escocesa

kin /kɪn/ *n* parientes *mpl*. **next of ~** pariente *m* más próximo, parientes *mpl* más próximos

kind[1] /kaɪnd/ *n* clase *f*. **~ of** (*somewhat, fam*) un poco. **in ~** en especie. **be two of a ~** ser tal para cual

kind[2] /kaɪnd/ *a* amable

kindergarten /ˈkɪndəgɑ:tn/ *n* escuela *f* de párvulos

kind-hearted /kaɪndˈhɑ:tɪd/ *a* bondadoso

kindle /ˈkɪndl/ *vt/i* encender(se)

kind: **~liness** *n* bondad *f*. **~ly** *a* (**-ier, -iest**) bondadoso. ● *adv* bondadosamente; (*please*) haga el favor de. **~ness** *n* bondad *f*

kindred /ˈkɪndrɪd/ *a* emparentado. **~ spirits** *npl* almas *fpl* afines

kinetic /kɪˈnetɪk/ *a* cinético

king /kɪŋ/ *n* rey *m*

kingdom /ˈkɪŋdəm/ *n* reino *m*

kingpin /ˈkɪŋpɪn/ *n* (*person*) persona *f* clave; (*thing*) piedra *f* angular

king-size(d) /ˈkɪŋsaɪz(d)/ *a* extraordinariamente grande

kink /kɪŋk/ *n* (*in rope*) retorcimiento *m*; (*fig*) manía *f*. **~y** *a* (*fam*) pervertido

kiosk /ˈki:ɒsk/ *n* quiosco *m*. **telephone ~** cabina *f* telefónica

kip /kɪp/ *n* (*sl*) sueño *m*. ● *vi* (*pt* **kipped**) dormir

kipper /ˈkɪpə(r)/ *n* arenque *m* ahumado

kiss /kɪs/ *n* beso *m*. ● *vt/i* besar(se)

kit /kɪt/ *n* avíos *mpl*; (*tools*) herramientos *mpl*. ● *vt* (*pt* **kitted**). **~ out** equipar de. **~bag** *n* mochila *f*

kitchen /ˈkɪtʃɪn/ *n* cocina *f*. **~ette** /kɪtʃɪˈnet/ *n* cocina *f* pequeña. **~ garden** *n* huerto *m*

kite /kaɪt/ *n* (*toy*) cometa *f*

kith /kɪθ/ *n*. **~ and kin** amigos *mpl* y parientes *mpl*

kitten /ˈkɪtn/ *n* gatito *m*

kitty /ˈkɪtɪ/ *n* (*fund*) fondo *m* común

kleptomaniac /kleptəʊˈmeɪnɪæk/ *n* cleptómano *m*

knack /næk/ *n* truco *m*

knapsack /ˈnæpsæk/ *n* mochila *f*

knave /neɪv/ *n* (*cards*) sota *f*

knead /ni:d/ *vt* amasar

knee /ni:/ *n* rodilla *f*. **~cap** *n* rótula *f*

kneel /ni:l/ *vi* (*pt* **knelt**). **~ (down)** arrodillarse
knees-up /'ni:zʌp/ *n* (*fam*) baile *m*
knell /nel/ *n* toque *m* de difuntos
knelt /nelt/ *see* **kneel**
knew /nju:/ *see* **know**
knickerbockers /'nɪkəbɒkəz/ *npl* pantalón *m* bombacho
knickers /'nɪkəz/ *npl* bragas *fpl*
knick-knack /'nɪknæk/ *n* chuchería *f*
knife /naɪf/ *n* (*pl* **knives**) cuchillo *m*. ● *vt* acuchillar
knight /naɪt/ *n* caballero *m*; (*chess*) caballo *m*. ● *vt* conceder el título de Sir a. **~hood** *n* título *m* de Sir
knit /nɪt/ *vt* (*pt* **knitted** *or* **knit**) tejer. ● *vi* hacer punto. **~ one's brow** fruncir el ceño. **~ting** *n* labor *f* de punto. **~wear** *n* artículos *mpl* de punto
knob /nɒb/ *n* botón *m*; (*of door, drawer etc*) tirador *m*. **~bly** *a* nudoso
knock /nɒk/ *vt* golpear; (*criticize*) criticar. ● *vi* golpear; (*at door*) llamar. ● *n* golpe *m*. **~ about** *vt* maltratar. ● *vi* rodar. **~ down** derribar; atropellar ‹*person*›; rebajar ‹*prices*›. **~ off** *vt* hacer caer; (*complete quickly, fam*) despachar; (*steal, sl*) birlar. ● *vi* (*finish work, fam*) terminar, salir del trabajo. **~ out** (*by blow*) dejar sin conocimiento; (*eliminate*) eliminar; (*tire*) agotar. **~ over** tirar; atropellar ‹*person*›. **~ up** preparar de prisa ‹*meal etc*›. **~-down** *a* ‹*price*› de saldo. **~er** *n* aldaba *f*. **~-kneed** *a* patizambo. **~out** *n* (*boxing*) knockout *m*
knot /nɒt/ *n* nudo *m*. ● *vt* (*pt* **knotted**) anudar. **~ty** /'nɒtɪ/ *a* nudoso
know /nəʊ/ *vt* (*pt* **knew**) saber; (*be acquainted with*) conocer. ● *vi* saber. ● *n*. **be in the ~** estar al tanto. **~ about** entender de ‹*cars etc*›. **~ of** saber de. **~-all** *n*, **~-it-all** (*Amer*) *n* sabelotodo *m & f*. **~-how** *n* habilidad *f*. **~ingly** *adv* deliberadamente
knowledge /'nɒlɪdʒ/ *n* conocimiento *m*; (*learning*) conocimientos *mpl*. **~able** *a* informado
known /nəʊn/ *see* **know**. ● *a* conocido
knuckle /'nʌkl/ *n* nudillo *m*. ● *vi*. **~ under** someterse
Koran /kə'rɑ:n/ *n* Corán *m*, Alcorán *m*
Korea /kə'rɪə/ *n* Corea *f*
kosher /'kəʊʃə(r)/ *a* preparado según la ley judía
kowtow /kaʊ'taʊ/ *vi* humillarse (**to** ante)
kudos /'kju:dɒs/ *n* prestigio *m*

L

lab /læb/ *n* (*fam*) laboratorio *m*
label /'leɪbl/ *n* etiqueta *f*. ● *vt* (*pt* **labelled**) poner etiqueta a; (*fig, describe as*) describir como
laboratory /lə'bɒrətərɪ/ *n* laboratorio *m*
laborious /lə'bɔ:rɪəs/ *a* penoso
labour /'leɪbə(r)/ *n* trabajo *m*; (*workers*) mano *f* de obra. **in ~** de parto. ● *vi* trabajar. ● *vt* insistir en
Labour /'leɪbə(r)/ *n* el partido *m* laborista. ● *a* laborista
laboured /'leɪbəd/ *a* penoso
labourer /'leɪbərə(r)/ *n* obrero *m*; (*on farm*) labriego *m*
labyrinth /'læbərɪnθ/ *n* laberinto *m*
lace /leɪs/ *n* encaje *m*; (*of shoe*) cordón *m*, agujeta *f* (*Mex*). ● *vt* (*fasten*) atar. **~ with** echar a ‹*a drink*›
lacerate /'læsəreɪt/ *vt* lacerar
lack /læk/ *n* falta *f*. **for ~ of** por falta de. ● *vt* faltarle a uno. **he ~s money** carece de dinero. **be ~ing** faltar
lackadaisical /lækə'deɪzɪkl/ *a* indolente, apático
lackey /'lækɪ/ *n* lacayo *m*
laconic /lə'kɒnɪk/ *a* lacónico
lacquer /'lækə(r)/ *n* laca *f*
lad /læd/ *n* muchacho *m*
ladder /'lædə(r)/ *n* escalera *f* (de mano); (*in stocking*) carrera *f*. ● *vt* hacer una carrera en. ● *vi* hacerse una carrera
laden /'leɪdn/ *a* cargado (**with** de)
ladle /'leɪdl/ *n* cucharón *m*
lady /'leɪdɪ/ *n* señora *f*. **young ~** señorita *f*. **~bird** *n*, **~bug** *n* (*Amer* mariquita *f*. **~ friend** *n* amiga *f*. **~-in-waiting** *n* dama *f* de honor. **~like** *a* distinguido. **~ship** *n* Señora *f*
lag[1] /læg/ *vi* (*pt* **lagged**). **~ (behind)** retrasarse. ● *n* (*interval*) intervalo *m*
lag[2] /læg/ *vt* (*pt* **lagged**) revestir ‹*pipes*›
lager /'lɑ:gə(r)/ *n* cerveza *f* dorada
laggard /'lægəd/ *n* holgazán *m*

lagging /'lægɪŋ/ *n* revestimiento *m* calorífugo
lagoon /lə'gu:n/ *n* laguna *f*
lah /lɑ:/ *n* (*mus, sixth note of any musical scale*) la *m*
laid /leɪd/ *see* **lay**[1]
lain /leɪn/ *see* **lie**[1]
lair /leə(r)/ *n* guarida *f*
laity /'leɪətɪ/ *n* laicado *m*
lake /leɪk/ *n* lago *m*
lamb /læm/ *n* cordero *m*. **~swool** *n* lana *f* de cordero
lame /leɪm/ *a* (**-er**, **-est**) cojo; ‹*excuse*› poco convincente. **~ly** *adv* (*argue*) con poca convicción *f*
lament /lə'ment/ *n* lamento *m*. ● *vt/i* lamentarse (de). **~able** /'læməntəbl/ *a* lamentable
laminated /'læmɪneɪtɪd/ *a* laminado
lamp /læmp/ *n* lámpara *f*. **~post** *n* farol *m*. **~shade** *n* pantalla *f*
lance /lɑ:ns/ *n* lanza *f*. ● *vt* (*med*) abrir con lanceta. **~-corporal** *n* cabo *m* interino
lancet /'lɑ:nsɪt/ *n* lanceta *f*
land /lænd/ *n* tierra *f*; (*country*) país *m*; (*plot*) terreno *m*. ● *a* terrestre; ‹*breeze*› de tierra; ‹*policy, reform*› agrario. ● *vt* desembarcar; (*obtain*) conseguir; dar ‹*blow*›; (*put*) meter. ● *vi* (*from ship*) desembarcar; ‹*aircraft*› aterrizar; (*fall*) caer. **~ up** ir a parar
landed /'lændɪd/ *a* hacendado
landing /'lændɪŋ/ *n* desembarque *m*; (*aviat*) aterrizaje *m*; (*top of stairs*) descanso *m*. **~-stage** *n* desembarcadero *m*
landlady /'lændleɪdɪ/ *n* propietaria *f*; (*of inn*) patrona *f*
land-locked /'lændlɒkt/ *a* rodeado de tierra
landlord /'lændlɔ:d/ *n* propietario *m*; (*of inn*) patrón *m*
land: **~mark** *n* punto *m* destacado. **~scape** /'lændskeɪp/ *n* paisaje *m*. ● *vt* ajardinar. **~slide** *n* desprendimiento *m* de tierras; (*pol*) victoria *f* arrolladora
lane /leɪn/ *n* (*path, road*) camino *m*; (*strip of road*) carril *m*; (*aviat*) ruta *f*
language /'længwɪdʒ/ *n* idioma *m*; (*speech, style*) lenguaje *m*
langu|id /'læŋgwɪd/ *a* lánguido. **~ish** /'læŋgwɪʃ/ *vi* languidecer. **~or** /'læŋgə(r)/ *n* languidez *f*
lank /læŋk/ *a* larguirucho; ‹*hair*› lacio. **~y** /'læŋkɪ/ *a* (**-ier**, **-iest**) larguirucho
lantern /'læntən/ *n* linterna *f*
lap[1] /læp/ *n* regazo *m*
lap[2] /læp/ *n* (*sport*) vuelta *f*. ● *vt/i* (*pt* **lapped**). **~ over** traslapar(se)
lap[3] /læp/ *vt* (*pt* **lapped**). **~ up** beber a lengüetazos; (*fig*) aceptar con entusiasmo. ● *vi* ‹*waves*› chapotear
lapel /lə'pel/ *n* solapa *f*
lapse /læps/ *vi* (*decline*) degradarse; (*expire*) caducar; ‹*time*› transcurrir. **~ into** recaer en. ● *n* error *m*; (*of time*) intervalo *m*
larceny /'lɑ:sənɪ/ *n* robo *m*
lard /lɑ:d/ *n* manteca *f* de cerdo
larder /'lɑ:də(r)/ *n* despensa *f*
large /lɑ:dʒ/ *a* (**-er**, **-est**) grande, (*before singular noun*) gran. ● *n*. **at ~** en libertad. **~ly** *adv* en gran parte. **~ness** *n* (gran) tamaño *m*
largesse /lɑ:'ʒes/ *n* generosidad *f*
lark[1] /lɑ:k/ *n* alondra *f*
lark[2] /lɑ:k/ *n* broma *f*; (*bit of fun*) travesura *f*. ● *vi* andar de juerga
larva /'lɑ:və/ *n* (*pl* **-vae** /-vi:/) larva *f*
laryn|gitis /lærɪn'dʒaɪtɪs/ *n* laringitis *f*. **~x** /'lærɪŋks/ *n* laringe *f*
lascivious /lə'sɪvɪəs/ *a* lascivo
laser /'leɪzə(r)/ *n* láser *m*
lash /læʃ/ *vt* azotar. **~ out** (*spend*) gastar. **~ out against** atacar. ● *n* latigazo *m*; (*eyelash*) pestaña *f*
lashings /'læʃɪŋz/ *npl*. **~ of** (*cream etc, sl*) montones de
lass /læs/ *n* muchacha *f*
lassitude /'læsɪtju:d/ *n* lasitud *f*
lasso /læ'su:/ *n* (*pl* **-os**) lazo *m*
last[1] /lɑ:st/ *a* último; ‹*week etc*› pasado. **~ Monday** *n* el lunes pasado. **have the ~ word** decir la última palabra. **the ~ straw** *n* el colmo *m*. ● *adv* por último; (*most recently*) la última vez. **he came ~** llegó el último. ● *n* último *m*; (*remainder*) lo que queda. **~ but one** penúltimo. **at (long) ~** en fin.
last[2] /lɑ:st/ *vi* durar. **~ out** sobrevivir
last[3] /lɑ:st/ *n* horma *f*
lasting /'lɑ:stɪŋ/ *a* duradero
last: **~ly** *adv* por último. **~ night** *n* anoche *m*
latch /lætʃ/ *n* picaporte *m*
late /leɪt/ *a* (**-er**, **-est**) (*not on time*) tarde; (*recent*) reciente; (*former*) antiguo, ex; ‹*fruit*› tardío; ‹*hour*› avanzado; (*deceased*) difunto. **in ~ July** a fines de julio. **the ~ Dr Phillips** el difunto Dr. Phillips. ● *adv* tarde. **of ~** últimamente. **~ly** *adv* últimamente. **~ness** *n* (*delay*) retraso *m*; (*of hour*) lo avanzado

latent /'leɪtnt/ *a* latente
lateral /'lætərəl/ *a* lateral
latest /'leɪtɪst/ *a* último. **at the ~** a más tardar
lathe /leɪð/ *n* torno *m*
lather /'lɑ:ðə(r)/ *n* espuma *f*. ● *vt* enjabonar. ● *vi* hacer espuma
Latin /'lætɪn/ *n* (*lang*) latín *m*. ● *a* latino
latitude /'lætɪtju:d/ *n* latitud *m*
latrine /lə'tri:n/ *n* letrina *f*
latter /'lætə(r)/ *a* último; (*of two*) segundo. ● *n*. **the ~** éste *m*, ésta *f*, éstos *mpl*, éstas *fpl*. **~-day** *a* moderno. **~ly** *adv* últimamente
lattice /'lætɪs/ *n* enrejado *m*
laudable /'lɔ:dəbl/ *a* laudable
laugh /lɑ:f/ *vi* reír(se) (**at** de). ● *n* risa *f*. **~able** *a* ridículo. **~ing-stock** *n* hazmerreír *m invar*. **~ter** /'lɑ:ftə(r)/ *n* (*act*) risa *f*; (*sound of laughs*) risas *fpl*
launch[1] /lɔ:ntʃ/ *vt* lanzar. ● *n* lanzamiento *m*. **~ (out) into** lanzarse a
launch[2] /lɔ:ntʃ/ *n* (*boat*) lancha *f*
launching pad /'lɔ:ntʃɪŋpæd/ *n* plataforma *f* de lanzamiento
laund|er /'lɔ:ndə(r)/ *vt* lavar (y planchar). **~erette** *n* lavandería *f* automática. **~ress** *n* lavandera *f*. **~ry** /'lɔ:ndrɪ/ *n* (*place*) lavandería *f*; (*dirty clothes*) ropa *f* sucia; (*clean clothes*) colada *f*
laurel /'lɒrəl/ *n* laurel *m*
lava /'lɑ:və/ *n* lava *f*
lavatory /'lævətərɪ/ *n* retrete *m*. **public ~** servicios *mpl*
lavender /'lævəndə(r)/ *n* lavanda *f*
lavish /'lævɪʃ/ *a* ‹*person*› pródigo; (*plentiful*) abundante; (*lush*) suntuoso. ● *vt* prodigar. **~ly** *adv* profusamente
law /lɔ:/ *n* ley *f*; (*profession, subject of study*) derecho *m*. **~-abiding** *a* observante de la ley. **~ and order** *n* orden *m* público. **~ court** *n* tribunal *m*. **~ful** *a* (*permitted by law*) lícito; (*recognized by law*) legítimo. **~fully** *adv* legalmente. **~less** *a* sin leyes
lawn /lɔ:n/ *n* césped *m*. **~-mower** *n* cortacésped *f*. **~ tennis** *n* tenis *m* (sobre hierba)
lawsuit /'lɔ:su:t/ *n* pleito *m*
lawyer /'lɔɪə(r)/ *n* abogado *m*
lax /læks/ *a* descuidado; ‹*morals etc*› laxo
laxative /'læksətɪv/ *n* laxante *m*
laxity /'læksətɪ/ *n* descuido *m*
lay[1] /leɪ/ *vt* (*pt* **laid**) poner ‹*incl table, eggs*›; tender ‹*trap*›; formar ‹*plan*›. **~ hands on** echar mano a. **~ hold of** agarrar. **~ waste** asolar. **~ aside** dejar a un lado. **~ down** dejar a un lado; imponer ‹*condition*›. **~ into** (*sl*) dar una paliza a. **~ off** *vt* despedir ‹*worker*›; ● *vi* (*fam*) terminar. **~ on** (*provide*) proveer. **~ out** (*design*) disponer; (*display*) exponer; desembolsar ‹*money*›. **~ up** (*store*) guardar; obligar a guardar cama ‹*person*›
lay[2] /leɪ/ *a* (*non-clerical*) laico; ‹*opinion etc*› profano
lay[3] /leɪ/ *see* **lie**
layabout /'leɪəbaʊt/ *n* holgazán *m*
lay-by /'leɪbaɪ/ *n* apartadero *m*
layer /'leɪə(r)/ *n* capa *f*
layette /leɪ'et/ *n* canastilla *f*
layman /'leɪmən/ *n* lego *m*
lay-off /'leɪɒf/ *n* paro *m* forzoso
layout /'leɪaʊt/ *n* disposición *f*
laze /leɪz/ *vi* holgazanear; (*relax*) descansar
laz|iness /'leɪzɪnɪs/ *n* pereza *f*. **~y** *a* perezoso. **~y-bones** *n* holgazán *m*
lb. *abbr* (*pound*) libra *f*
lead[1] /li:d/ *vt* (*pt* **led**) conducir; dirigir ‹*team*›; llevar ‹*life*›; (*induce*) inducir a. ● *vi* (*go first*) ir delante; ‹*road*› ir, conducir; (*in cards*) salir. ● *n* mando *m*; (*clue*) pista *f*; (*leash*) correa *f*; (*in theatre*) primer papel *m*; (*wire*) cable *m*; (*example*) ejemplo *m*. **in the ~** en cabeza. **~ away** llevar. **~ up to** preparar el terreno para
lead[2] /led/ *n* plomo *m*; (*of pencil*) mina *f*. **~en** /'ledn/ *a* de plomo
leader /'li:də(r)/ *n* jefe *m*; (*leading article*) editorial *m*. **~ship** *n* dirección *f*
leading /'li:dɪŋ/ *a* principal; (*in front*) delantero. **~ article** *n* editorial *m*
leaf /li:f/ *n* (*pl* **leaves**) hoja *f*. ● *vi*. **~ through** hojear
leaflet /'li:flɪt/ *n* folleto *m*
leafy /'li:fɪ/ *a* frondoso
league /li:g/ *n* liga *f*. **be in ~ with** conchabarse con
leak /li:k/ *n* (*hole*) agujero *m*; (*of gas, liquid*) escape *m*; (*of information*) filtración *f*; (*in roof*) gotera *f*; (*in boat*) vía *f* de agua. ● *vi* ‹*receptacle, gas, liquid*› salirse; ‹*information*› filtrarse; (*drip*) gotear; ‹*boat*› hacer agua. ● *vt* dejar escapar; filtrar ‹*in-*

formation›. **~age** *n* = **leak**. **~y** *a* ‹*receptacle*› agujereado; ‹*roof*› que tiene goteras; ‹*boat*› que hace agua

lean[1] /li:n/ *vt* (*pt* **leaned** *or* **leant** /lent/) apoyar. ● *vi* inclinarse. **~ against** apoyarse en. **~ on** apoyarse en. **~out** asomarse (**of** a). **~ over** inclinarse

lean[2] /li:n/ *a* (**-er**, **-est**) magro. ● *n* carne *f* magra

leaning /ˈli:nɪŋ/ *a* inclinado. ● *n* inclinación *f*

leanness /ˈli:nnɪs/ *n* (*of meat*) magrez *f*; (*of person*) flaqueza *f*

lean-to /ˈli:ntu:/ *n* colgadizo *m*

leap /li:p/ *vi* (*pt* **leaped** *or* **leapt** /lept/) saltar. ● *n* salto *m*. **~-frog** *n* salto *m*, saltacabrilla *f*. ● *vi* (*pt* **-frogged**) jugar a saltacabrilla. **~ year** *n* año *m* bisiesto

learn /lɜ:n/ *vt/i* (*pt* **learned** *or* **learnt**) aprender (**to do** a hacer). **~ed** /ˈlɜ:nɪd/ *a* culto. **~er** /ˈlɜ:nə(r)/ *n* principiante *m*; (*apprentice*) aprendiz *m*; (*student*) estudiante *m & f*. **~ing** *n* saber *m*

lease /li:s/ *n* arriendo *m*. ● *vt* arrendar

leash /li:ʃ/ *n* correa *f*

least /li:st/ *a*. **the ~** (*smallest amount of*) mínimo; (*slightest*) menor; (*smallest*) más pequeño. ● *n* lo menos. **at ~** por lo menos. **not in the ~** en absoluto. ● *adv* menos

leather /ˈleðə(r)/ *n* piel *f*, cuero *m*

leave /li:v/ *vt* (*pt* **left**) dejar; (*depart from*) marcharse de. **~ alone** dejar de tocar ‹*thing*›; dejar en paz ‹*person*›. **be left (over)** quedar. ● *vi* marcharse; ‹*train*› salir. ● *n* permiso *m*. **on ~** (*mil*) de permiso. **take one's ~ of** despedirse de. **~ out** omitir

leavings /ˈli:vɪŋz/ *npl* restos *mpl*

Leban|on /ˈlebənən/ *n* el Líbano *m*. **~ese** /-ˈni:z/ *a & n* libanés (*m*)

lecher /ˈletʃə(r)/ *n* libertino *m*. **~ous** *a* lascivo. **~y** *n* lascivia *f*

lectern /ˈlektɜ:n/ *n* atril *m*; (*in church*) facistol *m*

lecture /ˈlektʃə(r)/ *n* conferencia *f*; (*univ*) clase *f*; (*rebuke*) sermón *m*. ● *vt/i* dar una conferencia (a); (*univ*) dar clases (a); (*rebuke*) sermonear. **~r** *n* conferenciante *m*; (*univ*) profesor *m*

led /led/ *see* **lead**[1]

ledge /ledʒ/ *n* repisa *f*; (*of window*) antepecho *m*

ledger /ˈledʒə(r)/ *n* libro *m* mayor

lee /li:/ *n* sotavento *m*; (*fig*) abrigo *m*

leech /li:tʃ/ *n* sanguijuela *f*

leek /li:k/ *n* puerro *m*

leer /ˈlɪə(r)/ *vi*. **~ (at)** mirar impúdicamente. ● *n* mirada *f* impúdica

leeway /ˈli:weɪ/ *n* deriva *f*; (*fig, freedom of action*) libertad *f* de acción. **make up ~** recuperar los atrasos

left[1] /left/ *a* izquierdo. ● *adv* a la izquierda. ● *n* izquierda *f*

left[2] /left/ *see* **leave**

left: **~-hand** *a* izquierdo. **~-handed** *a* zurdo. **~ist** *n* izquierdista *m & f*. **~ luggage** *n* consigna *f*. **~-overs** *npl* restos *mpl*

left-wing /leftˈwɪŋ/ *a* izquierdista

leg /leg/ *n* pierna *f*; (*of animal, furniture*) pata *f*; (*of pork*) pernil *m*; (*of lamb*) pierna *f*; (*of journey*) etapa *f*. **on its last ~s** en las últimas

legacy /ˈlegəsɪ/ *n* herencia *f*

legal /ˈli:gl/ *a* (*permitted by law*) lícito; (*recognized by law*) legítimo; ‹*affairs etc*› jurídico. **~ aid** *n* abogacía *f* de pobres. **~ity** /-ˈgælətɪ/ *n* legalidad *f*. **~ize** *vt* legalizar. **~ly** *adv* legalmente

legation /lɪˈgeɪʃn/ *n* legación *f*

legend /ˈledʒənd/ *n* leyenda *f*. **~ary** *a* legendario

leggings /ˈlegɪŋz/ *npl* polainas *fpl*

legib|ility /ˈledʒəbɪlətɪ/ *n* legibilidad *f*. **~le** *a* legible. **~ly** *a* legiblemente

legion /ˈli:dʒən/ *n* legión *f*

legislat|e /ˈledʒɪsleɪt/ *vi* legislar. **~ion** /-ˈleɪʃn/ *n* legislación *f*. **~ive** *a* legislativo. **~ure** /-eɪtʃə(r)/ *n* cuerpo *m* legislativo

legitima|cy /lɪˈdʒɪtɪməsɪ/ *f* legitimidad *f*. **~te** *a* legítimo

leisure /ˈleʒə(r)/ *n* ocio *m*. **at one's ~** cuando tenga tiempo. **~ly** *adv* sin prisa

lemon /ˈlemən/ *n* limón *m*. **~ade** /leməˈneɪd/ *n* (*fizzy*) gaseosa *f* (de limón); (*still*) limonada *f*

lend /lend/ *vt* (*pt* **lent**) prestar. **~ itself to** prestarse a. **~er** *n* prestador *m*; (*moneylender*) prestamista *m & f*. **~ing** *n* préstamo *m*. **~ing library** *n* biblioteca *f* de préstamo

length /leŋθ/ *n* largo *m*; (*in time*) duración *f*; (*of cloth*) largo *m*; (*of road*) tramo *m*. **at ~** (*at last*) por fin. **at (great) ~** detalladamente. **~en**

/'leŋθən/ *vt* alargar. • *vi* alargarse. **~ways** *adv* a lo largo. **~y** *a* largo

lenien|cy /'li:nɪənsɪ/ *n* indulgencia *f*. **~t** *a* indulgente. **~tly** *adv* con indulgencia

lens /lens/ *n* lente *f*. **contact ~es** *npl* lentillas *fpl*

lent /lent/ *see* **lend**

Lent /lent/ *n* cuaresma *f*

lentil /'lentl/ *n* (*bean*) lenteja *f*

Leo /'li:əʊ/ *n* (*astr*) Leo *m*

leopard /'lepəd/ *n* leopardo *m*

leotard /'li:ətɑ:d/ *n* leotardo *m*

lep|er /'lepə(r)/ *n* leproso *m*. **~rosy** /'leprəsɪ/ *n* lepra *f*

lesbian /'lezbɪən/ *n* lesbiana *f*. • *a* lesbiano

lesion /'li:ʒn/ *n* lesión *f*

less /les/ *a* (*in quantity*) menos; (*in size*) menor. • *adv & prep* menos. **~ than** menos que; (*with numbers*) menos de. • *n* menor *m*. **~ and ~** cada vez menos. **none the ~** sin embargo. **~en** /'lesn/ *vt/i* disminuir. **~er** /'lesə(r)/ *a* menor

lesson /'lesn/ *n* clase *f*

lest /lest/ *conj* por miedo de que

let /let/ *vt* (*pt* **let**, *pres p* **letting**) dejar; (*lease*) alquilar. **~ me do it** déjame hacerlo. • *v aux*. **~'s go!** ¡vamos!, ¡vámonos! **~'s see** (vamos) a ver. **~'s talk/drink** hablemos/bebamos. • *n* alquiler *m*. **~ down** bajar; (*deflate*) desinflar; (*fig*) defraudar. **~ go** soltar. **~ in** dejar entrar. **~ off** disparar ‹*gun*›; (*cause to explode*) hacer explotar; hacer estallar ‹*firework*›; (*excuse*) perdonar. **~ off steam** (*fig*) desfogarse. **~ on** (*sl*) revelar. **~ o.s. in for** meterse en. **~ out** dejar salir. **~ through** dejar pasar. **~ up** disminuir. **~-down** *n* desilusión *f*

lethal /'li:θl/ *a* ‹*dose, wound*› mortal; ‹*weapon*› mortífero

letharg|ic /lɪ'tɑ:dʒɪk/ *a* letárgico. **~y** /'leθədʒɪ/ *n* letargo *m*

letter /'letə(r)/ *n* (*of alphabet*) letra *f*; (*written message*) carta *f*. **~-bomb** *n* carta *f* explosiva. **~-box** *n* buzón *m*. **~-head** *n* membrete *m*. **~ing** *n* letras *fpl*

lettuce /'letɪs/ *n* lechuga *f*

let-up /'letʌp/ *n* (*fam*) descanso *m*

leukaemia /lu:'ki:mɪə/ *n* leucemia *f*

level /'levl/ *a* (*flat*) llano; (*on surface*) horizontal; (*in height*) a nivel; (*in score*) igual; ‹*spoonful*› raso. • *n* nivel *m*. **be on the ~** (*fam*) ser honrado. • *vt* (*pt* **levelled**) nivelar; (*aim*) apuntar. **~ crossing** *n* paso *m* a nivel. **~-headed** *a* juicioso

lever /'li:və(r)/ *n* palanca *f*. • *vt* apalancar. **~age** /'li:vərɪdʒ/ *n* apalancamiento *m*

levity /'levətɪ/ *n* ligereza *f*

levy /'levɪ/ *vt* exigir ‹*tax*›. • *n* impuesto *m*

lewd /lu:d/ *a* (**-er**, **-est**) lascivo

lexicography /leksɪ'kɒgrəfɪ/ *n* lexicografía *f*

lexicon /'leksɪkən/ *n* léxico *m*

liable /'laɪəbl/ *a*. **be ~ to do** tener tendencia a hacer. **~ for** responsable de. **~ to** susceptible de; expuesto a ‹*fine*›

liability /laɪə'bɪlətɪ/ *n* responsabilidad *f*; (*disadvantage, fam*) inconveniente *m*. **liabilities** *npl* (*debts*) deudas *fpl*

liais|e /lɪ'eɪz/ *vi* hacer un enlace, enlazar. **~on** /lɪ'eɪzɒn/ *n* enlace *m*; (*love affair*) lío *m*

liar /'laɪə(r)/ *n* mentiroso *m*

libel /'laɪbl/ *n* libelo *m*. • *vt* (*pt* **libelled**) difamar (por escrito)

Liberal /'lɪbərəl/ *a & n* liberal (*m & f*)

liberal /'lɪbərəl/ *a* liberal; (*generous*) generoso; (*tolerant*) tolerante. **~ly** *adv* liberalmente; (*generously*) generosamente; (*tolerantly*) tolerantemente

liberat|e /'lɪbəreɪt/ *vt* liberar. **~ion** /-'reɪʃn/ *n* liberación *f*

libertine /'lɪbəti:n/ *n* libertino *m*

liberty /'lɪbətɪ/ *n* libertad *f*. **be at ~ to** estar autorizado para. **take liberties** tomarse libertades. **take the ~ of** tomarse la libertad de

libido /lɪ'bi:dəʊ/ *n* (*pl* **-os**) libido *m*

Libra /'li:brə/ *n* (*astr*) Libra *f*

librar|ian /laɪ'breərɪən/ *n* bibliotecario *m*. **~y** /'laɪbrərɪ/ *n* biblioteca *f*

libretto /lɪ'bretəʊ/ *n* (*pl* **-os**) libreto *m*

Libya /'lɪbɪə/ *n* Libia *f*. **~n** *a & n* libio (*m*)

lice /laɪs/ *see* **louse**

licence /'laɪsns/ *n* licencia *f*, permiso *m*; (*fig, liberty*) libertad *f*. **~ plate** *n* (placa *f* de) matrícula *f*. **driving ~** carné *m* de conducir

license /'laɪsns/ *vt* autorizar

licentious /laɪ'senʃəs/ *a* licencioso

lichen /'laɪkən/ *n* liquen *m*

lick /lɪk/ *vt* lamer; (*defeat, sl*) dar una paliza a. **~ one's chops** relamerse. ● *n* lametón *m*

licorice /ˈlɪkərɪs/ *n* (*Amer*) regaliz *m*

lid /lɪd/ *n* tapa *f*; (*of pan*) cobertera *f*

lido /ˈli:dəʊ/ *n* (*pl* **-os**) piscina *f*

lie[1] /laɪ/ *vi* (*pt* **lay**, *pp* **lain**, *pres p* **lying**) echarse; (*state*) estar echado; (*remain*) quedarse; (*be*) estar, encontrarse; (*in grave*) yacer. **be lying** estar echado. **~ down** acostarse. **~ low** quedarse escondido

lie[2] /laɪ/ *n* mentira *f*. ● *vi* (*pt* **lied**, *pres p* **lying**) mentir. **give the ~ to** desmentir

lie-in /laɪˈɪn/ *n*. **have a ~-in** quedarse en la cama

lieu /lju:/ *n*. **in ~ of** en lugar de

lieutenant /lefˈtenənt/ *n* (*mil*) teniente *m*

life /laɪf/ *n* (*pl* **lives**) vida *f*. **~belt** *n* cinturón *m* salvavidas. **~boat** *n* lancha *f* de salvamento; (*on ship*) bote *m* salvavidas. **~buoy** *n* boya *f* salvavidas. **~ cycle** *n* ciclo *m* vital. **~-guard** *n* bañero *m*. **~-jacket** *n* chaleco *m* salvavidas. **~less** *a* sin vida. **~like** *a* natural. **~line** *n* cuerda *f* salvavidas; (*fig*) cordón *m* umbilical. **~long** *a* de toda la vida. **~-size(d)** *a* de tamaño natural. **~time** *n* vida *f*

lift /lɪft/ *vt* levantar; (*steal, fam*) robar. ● *vi* ‹*fog*› disiparse. ● *n* ascensor *m*, elevador *m* (*LAm*). **give a ~ to s.o.** llevar a uno en su coche, dar aventón a uno (*LAm*). **~-off** *n* (*aviat*) despegue *m*

ligament /ˈlɪgəmənt/ *n* ligamento *m*

light[1] /laɪt/ *n* luz *f*; (*lamp*) lámpara *f*, luz *f*; (*flame*) fuego *m*; (*headlight*) faro *m*. **bring to ~** sacar a luz. **come to ~** salir a luz. **have you got a ~?** ¿tienes fuego? **the ~s** *npl* (*auto, traffic signals*) el semáforo *m*. ● *a* claro. ● *vt* (*pt* **lit** *or* **lighted**) encender; (*illuminate*) alumbrar. **~ up** *vt/i* iluminar(se)

light[2] /laɪt/ *a* (**-er**, **-est**) (*not heavy*) ligero

lighten[1] /ˈlaɪtn/ *vt* (*make less heavy*) aligerar

lighten[2] /ˈlaɪtn/ *vt* (*give light to*) iluminar; (*make brighter*) aclarar

lighter /ˈlaɪtə(r)/ *n* (*for cigarettes*) mechero *m*

light-fingered /laɪtˈfɪŋgəd/ *a* largo de uñas

light-headed /laɪtˈhedɪd/ *a* (*dizzy*) mareado; (*frivolous*) casquivano

light-hearted /laɪtˈhɑ:tɪd/ *a* alegre

lighthouse /ˈlaɪthaʊs/ *n* faro *m*

lighting /ˈlaɪtɪŋ/ *n* (*system*) alumbrado *m*; (*act*) iluminación *f*

light: **~ly** *adv* ligeramente. **~ness** *n* ligereza *f*

lightning /ˈlaɪtnɪŋ/ *n* relámpago *m*. ● *a* relámpago

lightweight /ˈlaɪtweɪt/ *a* ligero. ● *n* (*boxing*) peso *m* ligero

light-year /ˈlaɪtjɪə(r)/ *n* año *m* luz

like[1] /laɪk/ *a* parecido. ● *prep* como. ● *conj* (*fam*) como. ● *n* igual. **the ~s of you** la gente como tú

like[2] /laɪk/ *vt* gustarle (a uno). **I ~ chocolate** me gusta el chocolate. **I should ~** quisiera. **they ~ swimming** (a ellos) les gusta nadar. **would you ~?** ¿quieres? **~able** *a* simpático. **~s** *npl* gustos *mpl*

likelihood /ˈlaɪklɪhʊd/ *n* probabilidad *f*

likely *a* (**-ier**, **-iest**) probable. **he is ~ to come** es probable que venga. ● *adv* probablemente. **not ~!** ¡ni hablar!

like-minded /laɪkˈmaɪndɪd/ *a*. **be ~** tener las mismas opiniones

liken /ˈlaɪkən/ *vt* comparar

likeness /ˈlaɪknɪs/ *n* parecido *m*. **be a good ~** parecerse mucho

likewise /ˈlaɪkwaɪz/ *adv* (*also*) también; (*the same way*) lo mismo

liking /ˈlaɪkɪŋ/ *n* (*for thing*) afición *f*; (*for person*) simpatía *f*

lilac /ˈlaɪlək/ *n* lila *f*. ● *a* color de lila

lilt /lɪlt/ *n* ritmo *m*

lily /ˈlɪlɪ/ *n* lirio *m*. **~ of the valley** lirio *m* de los valles

limb /lɪm/ *n* miembro *m*. **out on a ~** aislado

limber /ˈlɪmbə(r)/ *vi*. **~ up** hacer ejercicios preliminares

limbo /ˈlɪmbəʊ/ *n* limbo *m*. **be in ~** (*forgotten*) estar olvidado

lime[1] /laɪm/ *n* (*white substance*) cal *f*

lime[2] /laɪm/ *n* (*fruit*) lima *f*

lime[3] /laɪm/ *n*. **~(-tree)** (*linden tree*) tilo *m*

limelight /ˈlaɪmlaɪt/ *n*. **be in the ~** estar muy a la vista

limerick /ˈlɪmərɪk/ *n* quintilla *f* humorística

limestone /ˈlaɪmstəʊn/ *n* caliza *f*

limit /ˈlɪmɪt/ *n* límite *m*. ● *vt* limitar. **~ation** /-ˈteɪʃn/ *n* limitación *f*. **~ed**

a limitado. **~ed company** *n* sociedad *f* anónima
limousine /ˈlɪməzi:n/ *n* limusina *f*
limp[1] /lɪmp/ *vi* cojear. ● *n* cojera *f*. **have a ~** cojear
limp[2] /lɪmp/ *a* (**-er**, **-est**) flojo
limpid /ˈlɪmpɪd/ *a* límpido
linctus /ˈlɪŋktəs/ *n* jarabe *m* (para la tos)
line[1] /laɪn/ *n* línea *f*; (*track*) vía *f*; (*wrinkle*) arruga *f*; (*row*) fila *f*; (*of poem*) verso *m*; (*rope*) cuerda *f*; (*of goods*) surtido *m*; (*queue, Amer*) cola *f*. **in ~ with** de acuerdo con. ● *vt* (*on paper etc*) rayar; bordear ‹*streets etc*›. **~ up** alinearse; (*in queue*) hacer cola
line[2] /laɪn/ *vt* forrar; (*fill*) llenar
lineage /ˈlɪnɪɪdʒ/ *n* linaje *m*
linear /ˈlɪnɪə(r)/ *a* lineal
linen /ˈlɪnɪn/ *n* (*sheets etc*) ropa *f* blanca; (*material*) lino *m*
liner /ˈlaɪnə(r)/ *n* transatlántico *m*
linesman /ˈlaɪnzmən/ *n* (*football*) juez *m* de línea
linger /ˈlɪŋgə(r)/ *vi* tarder en marcharse; ‹*smells etc*› persistir. **~ over** dilatarse en
lingerie /ˈlænʒərɪ/ *n* ropa *f* interior, lencería *f*
lingo /ˈlɪŋgəʊ/ *n* (*pl* **-os**) idioma *m*; (*specialized vocabulary*) jerga *f*
linguist /ˈlɪŋgwɪst/ *n* (*specialist in languages*) polígiota *m* & *f*; (*specialist in linguistics*) lingüista *m* & *f*. **~ic** /lɪŋˈgwɪstɪk/ *a* lingüístico. **~ics** *n* lingüística *f*
lining /ˈlaɪnɪŋ/ *n* forro *m*; (*auto, of brakes*) guarnición *f*
link /lɪŋk/ *n* (*of chain*) eslabón *m*; (*fig*) lazo *m*. ● *vt* eslabonar; (*fig*) enlazar. **~ up with** reunirse con. **~age** *n* enlace *m*
links /lɪŋks/ *n invar* campo *m* de golf
lino /ˈlaɪnəʊ/ *n* (*pl* **-os**) linóleo *m*. **~leum** /lɪˈnəʊlɪəm/ *n* linóleo *m*
lint /lɪnt/ *n* (*med*) hilas *fpl*; (*fluff*) pelusa *f*
lion /ˈlaɪən/ *n* león *m*. **the ~'s share** la parte *f* del león. **~ess** *n* leona *f*
lionize /ˈlaɪənaɪz/ *vt* tratar como una celebridad
lip /lɪp/ *n* labio *m*; (*edge*) borde *m*. **pay ~ service to** aprobar de boquilla. **stiff upper ~** *n* imperturbabilidad *f*. **~-read** *vt/i* leer en los labios. **~salve** *n* crema *f* para los labios. **~stick** *n* lápiz *m* de labios.
liquefy /ˈlɪkwɪfaɪ/ *vt/i* licuar(se)
liqueur /lɪˈkjʊə(r)/ *n* licor *m*
liquid /ˈlɪkwɪd/ *a* & *n* líquido (*m*)
liquidat|e /ˈlɪkwɪdeɪt/ *vt* liquidar. **~ion** /-ˈdeɪʃn/ *n* liquidación *f*
liquidize /ˈlikwɪdaɪz/ *vt* licuar. **~r** *n* licuadora *f*
liquor /ˈlɪkə(r)/ *n* bebida *f* alcohólica
liquorice /ˈlɪkərɪs/ *n* regaliz *m*
lira /ˈlɪərə/ *n* (*pl* **lire** /ˈlɪəreɪ/ *or* **liras**) lira *f*
lisle /laɪl/ *n* hilo *m* de Escocia
lisp /lɪsp/ *n* ceceo *m*. **speak with a ~** cecear. ● *vi* cecear
lissom /ˈlɪsəm/ *a* flexible, ágil
list[1] /lɪst/ *n* lista *f*. ● *vt* hacer una lista de; (*enter in a list*) inscribir
list[2] /lɪst/ *vi* ‹*ship*› escorar
listen /ˈlɪsn/ *vi* escuchar. **~ in (to)** escuchar. **~ to** escuchar. **~er** *n* oyente *m* & *f*
listless /ˈlɪstlɪs/ *a* apático
lit /lɪt/ *see* **light**[1]
litany /ˈlɪtənɪ/ *n* letanía *f*
literacy /ˈlɪtərəsɪ/ *n* capacidad *f* de leer y escribir
literal /ˈlɪtərəl/ *a* literal; (*fig*) prosaico. **~ly** *adv* al pie de la letra, literalmente
literary /ˈlɪtərərɪ/ *a* literario
literate /ˈlɪtərət/ *a* que sabe leer y escribir
literature /ˈlɪtərətʃə(r)/ *n* literatura *f*; (*fig*) impresos *mpl*
lithe /laɪð/ *a* ágil
lithograph /ˈlɪθəgrɑ:f/ *n* litografía *f*
litigation /lɪtɪˈgeɪʃn/ *n* litigio *m*
litre /ˈli:tə(r)/ *n* litro *m*
litter /ˈlɪtə(r)/ *n* basura *f*; (*of animals*) camada *f*. ● *vt* ensuciar; (*scatter*) esparcir. **~ed with** lleno de. **~-bin** *n* papelera *f*
little /ˈlɪtl/ *a* pequeño; (*not much*) poco de. ● *n* poco *m*. **a ~** un poco. **a ~ water** un poco de agua. ● *adv* poco. **~ by ~** poco a poco. **~ finger** *n* meñique *m*
liturgy /ˈlɪtədʒɪ/ *n* liturgia *f*
live[1] /lɪv/ *vt/i* vivir. **~ down** lograr borrar. **~ it up** echar una cana al aire. **~ on** (*feed o.s. on*) vivir de; (*continue*) perdurar. **~ up to** vivir de acuerdo con; cumplir ‹*a promise*›
live[2] /laɪv/ *a* vivo; ‹*wire*› con corriente; ‹*broadcast*› en directo. **be a ~ wire** ser una persona enérgica
livelihood /ˈlaɪvlɪhʊd/ *n* sustento *m*
livel|iness /ˈlaɪvlɪnɪs/ *n* vivacidad *f*. **~y** *a* (**-ier**, **-iest**) vivo

liven /'laɪvn/ *vt/i*. ~ **up** animar(se); (*cheer up*) alegrar(se)
liver /'lɪvə(r)/ *n* hígado *m*
livery /'lɪvərɪ/ *n* librea *f*
livestock /'laɪvstɒk/ *n* ganado *m*
livid /'lɪvɪd/ *a* lívido; (*angry, fam*) furioso
living /'lɪvɪŋ/ *a* vivo. ● *n* vida *f*. ~**-room** *n* cuarto *m* de estar, cuarto *m* de estancia (*LAm*)
lizard /'lɪzəd/ *n* lagartija *f*; (*big*) lagarto *m*
llama /'lɑːmə/ *n* llama *f*
load /ləʊd/ *n* (*incl elec*) carga *f*; (*quantity*) cantidad *f*; (*weight, strain*) peso *m*. ● *vt* cargar. ~**ed** *a* ‹*incl dice*› cargado; (*wealthy, sl*) muy rico. ~**s of** (*fam*) montones de
loaf[1] /ləʊf/ *n* (*pl* **loaves**) pan *m*; (*stick of bread*) barra *f*
loaf[2] /ləʊf/ *vi*. ~ **(about)** holgazanear. ~**er** *n* holgazán *m*
loam /ləʊm/ *n* marga *f*
loan /ləʊn/ *n* préstamo *m*. **on** ~ prestado. ● *vt* prestar
loath /ləʊθ/ *a* poco dispuesto (**to** a)
loath|e /ləʊð/ *vt* odiar. ~**ing** *n* odio *m* (**of** a). ~**some** *a* odioso
lobby /'lɒbɪ/ *n* vestíbulo *m*; (*pol*) grupo *m* de presión. ● *vt* hacer presión sobre
lobe /ləʊb/ *n* lóbulo *m*
lobster /'lɒbstə(r)/ *n* langosta *f*
local /'ləʊkl/ *a* local. ● *n* (*pub, fam*) bar *m*. **the** ~**s** los vecinos *mpl*
locale /ləʊ'kɑːl/ *n* escenario *m*
local government /ləʊkl-'gʌvənmənt/ *n* gobierno *m* municipal
locality /ləʊ'kælətɪ/ *n* localidad *f*
localized /'ləʊkəlaɪzd/ *a* localizado
locally /'ləʊkəlɪ/ *adv* localmente; (*nearby*) en la localidad
locate /ləʊ'keɪt/ *vt* (*situate*) situar; (*find*) encontrar
location /ləʊ'keɪʃn/ *n* colocación *f*; (*place*) situación *f*. **on** ~ fuera del estudio. **to film on** ~ **in Andalusia** rodar en Andalucía
lock[1] /lɒk/ *n* (*of door etc*) cerradura *f*; (*on canal*) esclusa *f*. ● *vt/i* cerrar(se) con llave. ~ **in** encerrar. ~ **out** cerrar la puerta a. ~ **up** encerrar
lock[2] /lɒk/ *n* (*of hair*) mechón *m*. ~**s** *npl* pelo *m*
locker /'lɒkə(r)/ *n* armario *m*
locket /'lɒkɪt/ *n* medallón *m*
lock-out /'lɒkaʊt/ *n* lock-out *m*
locksmith /'lɒksmɪθ/ *n* cerrajero *m*
locomotion /ləʊkə'məʊʃn/ *n* locomoción *f*
locomotive /ləʊkə'məʊtɪv/ *n* locomotora *f*
locum /'ləʊkəm/ *n* interino *m*
locust /'ləʊkəst/ *n* langosta *f*
lodge /lɒdʒ/ *n* (*in park*) casa *f* del guarda; (*of porter*) portería *f*. ● *vt* alojar; presentar ‹*complaint*›; depositar ‹*money*›. ● *vi* alojarse. ~**r** /-ə(r)/ *n* huésped *m*
lodgings /'lɒdʒɪŋz/ *n* alojamiento *m*; (*room*) habitación *f*
loft /lɒft/ *n* desván *m*
lofty /'lɒftɪ/ *a* (**-ier**, **-iest**) elevado; (*haughty*) altanero
log /lɒg/ *n* (*of wood*) leño *m*; (*naut*) cuaderno *m* de bitácora. **sleep like a** ~ dormir como un lirón. ● *vt* (*pt* **logged**) apuntar; (*travel*) recorrer
logarithm /'lɒgərɪðəm/ *n* logaritmo *m*
log-book /'lɒgbʊk/ *n* cuaderno *m* de bitácora; (*aviat*) diario *m* de vuelo
loggerheads /'lɒgəhedz/ *npl*. **be at** ~ **with** estar a matar con
logic /'lɒdʒɪk/ *a* lógica *f*. ~**al** *a* lógico. ~**ally** *adv* lógicamente
logistics /lə'dʒɪstɪks/ *n* logística *f*
logo /'ləʊgəʊ/ *n* (*pl* **-os**) logotipo *m*
loin /lɔɪn/ *n* (*culin*) solomillo *m*. ~**s** *npl* ijadas *fpl*
loiter /'lɔɪtə(r)/ *vi* holgazanear
loll /lɒl/ *vi* repantigarse
loll|ipop /'lɒlɪpɒp/ *n* (*boiled sweet*) pirulí *m*. ~**y** *n* (*iced*) polo *m*; (*money, sl*) dinero *m*
London /'lʌndən/ *n* Londres *m*. ● *a* londinense. ~**er** *n* londinense *m & f*
lone /ləʊn/ *a* solitario. ~**ly** /'ləʊnlɪ/ *a* (**-ier**, **-iest**) solitario. **feel** ~**ly** sentirse muy solo. ~**r** /'ləʊnə(r)/ *n* solitario *m*. ~**some** *a* solitario
long[1] /lɒŋ/ *a* (**-er**, **-est**) largo. **a** ~ **time** mucho tiempo. **how** ~ **is it?** ¿cuánto tiene de largo? **in the** ~ **run** a la larga. ● *adv* largo/mucho tiempo. **as** ~ **as** (*while*) mientras; (*provided that*) con tal que (+ *subjunctive*). **before** ~ dentro de poco. **so** ~! ¡hasta luego! **so** ~ **as** (*provided that*) con tal que (+ *subjunctive*)
long[2] /lɒŋ/ *vi*. ~ **for** anhelar
long-distance /lɒŋ'dɪstəns/ *a* de larga distancia. ~ **(tele)phone call** *n* conferencia *f*
longer /'lɒŋgə(r)/ *adv*. **no** ~**er** ya no

longevity /lɒn'dʒevətɪ/ *n* longevidad *f*

long: ~ **face** *n* cara *f* triste. ~**hand** *n* escritura *f* a mano. ~ **johns** *npl* (*fam*) calzoncillos *mpl* largos. ~ **jump** *n* salto *m* de longitud

longing /'lɒŋɪŋ/ *n* anhelo *m*, ansia *f*

longitude /'lɒŋgɪtju:d/ *n* longitud *f*

long: ~**-playing record** *n* elepé *m*. ~**-range** *a* de gran alcance. ~**-sighted** *a* présbita. ~**-standing** *a* de mucho tiempo. ~**-suffering** *a* sufrido. ~**-term** *a* a largo plazo. ~ **wave** *n* onda *f* larga. ~**-winded** *a* ‹*speaker etc*› prolijo

loo /lu:/ *n* (*fam*) servicios *mpl*

look /lʊk/ *vt* mirar; (*seem*) parecer; representar ‹*age*›. ● *vi* mirar; (*seem*) parecer; (*search*) buscar. ● *n* mirada *f*; (*appearance*) aspecto *m*. ~ **after** ocuparse de; cuidar ‹*person*›. ~ **at** mirar. ~ **down on** despreciar. ~ **for** buscar. ~ **forward to** esperar con ansia. ~ **in on** pasar por casa de. ~ **into** investigar. ~ **like** (*resemble*) parecerse a. ~ **on to** ‹*room, window*› dar a. ~ **out** tener cuidado. ~ **out for** buscar; (*watch*) tener cuidado con. ~ **round** volver la cabeza. ~ **through** hojear. ~ **up** buscar ‹*word*›; (*visit*) ir a ver. ~ **up to** respetar. ~**er-on** *n* espectador *m*. ~**ing-glass** *n* espejo *m*. ~**-out** *n* (*mil*) atalaya *f*; (*person*) vigía *m*. ~**s** *npl* belleza *f*. **good** ~**s** *mpl* belleza *f*

loom[1] /lu:m/ *n* telar *m*

loom[2] /lu:m/ *vi* aparecerse

loony /'lu:nɪ/ *a* & *n* (*sl*) chiflado (*m*) (*fam*), loco (*m*). ~ **bin** *n* (*sl*) manicomio *m*

loop /lu:p/ *n* lazo *m*. ● *vt* hacer presilla con

loophole /'lu:phəʊl/ *n* (*in rule*) escapatoria *f*

loose /lu:s/ *a* (**-er**, **-est**) (*untied*) suelto; (*not tight*) flojo; (*inexact*) vago; (*immoral*) inmoral; (*not packed*) suelto. **be at a** ~ **end**, **be at** ~ **ends** (*Amer*) no tener nada que hacer. ~**ly** *adv* sueltamente; (*roughly*) aproximadamente. ~**n** /'lu:sn/ *vt* (*slacken*) aflojar; (*untie*) desatar

loot /lu:t/ *n* botín *m*. ● *vt* saquear. ~**er** *n* saqueador *m*. ~**ing** *n* saqueo *m*

lop /lɒp/ *vt* (*pt* **lopped**). ~ **off** cortar

lop-sided /lɒp'saɪdɪd/ *a* ladeado

loquacious /ləʊ'kweɪʃəs/ *a* locuaz

lord /lɔ:d/ *n* señor *m*; (*British title*) lord *m*. **(good) L~!** ¡Dios mío! **the L~** el Señor *m*. **the (House of) L~s** la Cámara *f* de los Lores. ~**ly** señorial; (*haughty*) altivo. ~**ship** *n* señoría *f*

lore /lɔ:(r)/ *n* tradiciones *fpl*

lorgnette /lɔ:'njet/ *n* impertinentes *mpl*

lorry /'lɒrɪ/ *n* camión *m*

lose /lu:z/ *vt*/*i* (*pt* **lost**) perder. ~**r** *n* perdedor *m*

loss /lɒs/ *n* pérdida *f*. **be at a** ~ estar perplejo. **be at a** ~ **for words** no encontrar palabras. **be at a** ~ **to** no saber cómo

lost /lɒst/ *see* **lose**. ● *a* perdido. ~ **property** *n*, ~ **and found** (*Amer*) *n* oficina *f* de objetos perdidos. **get** ~ perderse

lot /lɒt/ *n* (*fate*) suerte *f*; (*at auction*) lote *m*; (*land*) solar *m*. **a** ~ **(of)** muchos. **quite a** ~ **of** (*fam*) bastante. ~**s (of)** (*fam*) muchos. **the** ~ todos *mpl*

lotion /'ləʊʃn/ *n* loción *f*

lottery /'lɒtərɪ/ *n* lotería *f*

lotto /'lɒtəʊ/ *n* lotería *f*

lotus /'ləʊtəs/ *n* (*pl* **-uses**) loto *m*

loud /laʊd/ *a* (**-er**, **-est**) fuerte; (*noisy*) ruidoso; (*gaudy*) chillón. **out** ~ en voz alta. ~ **hailer** *n* megáfono *m*. ~**ly** *adv* (*speak etc*) en voz alta; (*noisily*) ruidosamente. ~**speaker** *n* altavoz *m*

lounge /laʊndʒ/ *vi* repantigarse. ● *n* salón *m*. ~ **suit** *n* traje *m* de calle

louse /laʊs/ *n* (*pl* **lice**) piojo *m*

lousy /'laʊzɪ/ *a* (**-ier**, **-iest**) piojoso; (*bad, sl*) malísimo

lout /laʊt/ *n* patán *m*

lovable /'lʌvəbl/ *a* adorable

love /lʌv/ *n* amor *m*; (*tennis*) cero *m*. **be in** ~ **with** estar enamorado de. **fall in** ~ **with** enamorarse de. ● *vt* querer ‹*person*›; gustarle mucho a uno, encantarle a uno ‹*things*›. **I** ~ **milk** me encanta la leche. ~ **affair** *n* amores *mpl*

lovely /'lʌvlɪ/ *a* (**-ier**, **-iest**) hermoso; (*delightful, fam*) precioso. **have a** ~ **time** divertirse

lover /'lʌvə(r)/ *n* amante *m* & *f*

lovesick /'lʌvsɪk/ *a* atortolado

loving /'lʌvɪŋ/ *a* cariñoso

low[1] /ləʊ/ *a* & *adv* (**-er**, **-est**) bajo. ● *n* (*low pressure*) área *f* de baja presión

low[2] /ləʊ/ *vi* mugir

lowbrow /ˈləʊbraʊ/ *a* poco culto
low-cut /ˈləʊkʌt/ *a* escotado
low-down /ˈləʊdaʊn/ *a* bajo. ● *n* (*sl*) informes *mpl*
lower /ˈləʊə(r)/ *a & adv see* **low**². ● *vt* bajar. ~ **o.s.** envilecerse
low-key /ˈləʊˈkiː/ *a* moderado
lowlands /ˈləʊləndz/ *npl* tierra *f* baja
lowly /ˈləʊlɪ/ *a* (**-ier**, **-iest**) humilde
loyal /ˈlɔɪəl/ *a* leal. ~**ly** *adv* lealmente. ~**ty** *n* lealtad *f*
lozenge /ˈlɒzɪŋdʒ/ *n* (*shape*) rombo *m*; (*tablet*) pastilla *f*
LP /elˈpiː/ *abbr* (*long-playing record*) elepé *m*
Ltd /ˈlɪmɪtɪd/ *abbr* (*Limited*) S.A., Sociedad Anónima
lubrica|nt /ˈluːbrɪkənt/ *n* lubricante *m*. ~**te** /-ˈkeɪt/ *vt* lubricar. ~**tion** /-ˈkeɪʃn/ *n* lubricación *f*
lucid /ˈluːsɪd/ *a* lúcido. ~**ity** /-ˈsɪdətɪ/ *n* lucidez *f*
luck /lʌk/ *n* suerte *f*. **bad** ~ *n* mala suerte *f*. ~**ily** /ˈlʌkɪlɪ/ *adv* afortunadamente. ~**y** *a* (**-ier**, **-iest**) afortunado
lucrative /ˈluːkrətɪv/ *a* lucrativo
lucre /ˈluːkə(r)/ *n* (*pej*) dinero *m*. **filthy** ~ vil metal *m*
ludicrous /ˈluːdɪkrəs/ *a* ridículo
lug /lʌg/ *vt* (*pt* **lugged**) arrastrar
luggage /ˈlʌgɪdʒ/ *n* equipaje *m*. ~**-rack** *n* rejilla *f*. ~**-van** *n* furgón *m*
lugubrious /luːˈguːbrɪəs/ *a* lúgubre
lukewarm /ˈluːkwɔːm/ *a* tibio
lull /lʌl/ *vt* (*soothe, send to sleep*) adormecer; (*calm*) calmar. ● *n* periodo *m* de calma
lullaby /ˈlʌləbaɪ/ *n* canción *f* de cuna
lumbago /lʌmˈbeɪgəʊ/ *n* lumbago *m*
lumber /ˈlʌmbə(r)/ *n* trastos *mpl* viejos; (*wood*) maderos *mpl*. ● *vt*. ~ **s.o. with** hacer que uno cargue con. ~**jack** *n* leñador *m*
luminous /ˈluːmɪnəs/ *a* luminoso
lump¹ /ˈlʌmp/ *n* protuberancia *f*; (*in liquid*) grumo *m*; (*of sugar*) terrón *m*; (*in throat*) nudo *m*. ● *vt*. ~ **together** agrupar
lump² /lʌmp/ *vt*. ~ **it** (*fam*) aguantarlo
lump: ~ **sum** *n* suma *f* global. ~**y** *a* ‹*sauce*› grumoso; (*bumpy*) cubierto de protuberancias
lunacy /ˈluːnəsɪ/ *n* locura *f*
lunar /ˈluːnə(r)/ *a* lunar
lunatic /ˈluːnətɪk/ *n* loco *m*
lunch /lʌntʃ/ *n* comida *f*, almuerzo *m*. ● *vi* comer
luncheon /ˈlʌntʃən/ *n* comida *f*, almuerzo *m*. ~ **meat** *n* carne *f* en lata. ~ **voucher** *n* vale *m* de comida
lung /lʌŋ/ *n* pulmón *m*
lunge /lʌndʒ/ *n* arremetida *f*
lurch¹ /lɜːtʃ/ *vi* tambalearse
lurch² /lɜːtʃ/ *n*. **leave in the** ~ dejar en la estacada
lure /ljʊə(r)/ *vt* atraer. ● *n* (*attraction*) atractivo *m*
lurid /ˈljʊərɪd/ *a* chillón; (*shocking*) espeluznante
lurk /lɜːk/ *vi* esconderse; (*in ambush*) estar al acecho; (*prowl*) rondar
luscious /ˈlʌʃəs/ *a* delicioso
lush /lʌʃ/ *a* exuberante. ● *n* (*Amer, sl*) borracho *m*
lust /lʌst/ *n* lujuria *f*; (*fig*) ansia *f*. ● *vi*. ~ **after** codiciar. ~**ful** *a* lujurioso
lustre /ˈlʌstə(r)/ *n* lustre *m*
lusty /ˈlʌstɪ/ *a* (**-ier, -iest**) fuerte
lute /luːt/ *n* laúd *m*
Luxemburg /ˈlʌksəmbɜːg/ *n* Luxemburgo *m*
luxuriant /lʌgˈzjʊərɪənt/ *a* exuberante
luxur|ious /lʌgˈzjʊərɪəs/ *a* lujoso. ~**y** /ˈlʌkʃərɪ/ *n* lujo *m*. ● *a* de lujo
lye /laɪ/ *n* lejía *f*
lying /ˈlaɪɪŋ/ *see* **lie**¹, **lie**². ● *n* mentiras *fpl*
lynch /lɪntʃ/ *vt* linchar
lynx /lɪŋks/ *n* lince *m*
lyre /ˈlaɪə(r)/ *n* lira *f*
lyric /ˈlɪrɪk/ *a* lírico. ~**al** *a* lírico. ~**ism** /-sɪzəm/ *n* lirismo *m*. ~**s** *npl* letra *f*

M

MA *abbr* (*Master of Arts*) Master *m*, grado *m* universitario entre el de licenciado y doctor
mac /mæk/ *n* (*fam*) impermeable *m*
macabre /məˈkɑːbrə/ *a* macabro
macaroni /mækəˈrəʊnɪ/ *n* macarrones *mpl*
macaroon /mækəˈruːn/ *n* mostachón *m*
mace¹ /meɪs/ *n* (*staff*) maza *f*
mace² /meɪs/ *n* (*spice*) macis *f*
Mach /mɑːk/ *n*. ~ **(number)** *n* (número *m* de) Mach (*m*)
machiavellian /mækɪəˈvelɪən/ *a* maquiavélico

machinations /mækɪ'neɪʃnz/ *npl* maquinaciones *fpl*
machine /mə'ʃi:n/ *n* máquina *f.* • *vt* (*sew*) coser a máquina; (*tec*) trabajar a máquina. **~-gun** *n* ametralladora *f.* **~ry** /mə'ʃi:nərɪ/ *n* maquinaria *f*; (*working parts, fig*) mecanismo *m.* **~ tool** *n* máquina *f* herramienta
machinist /mə'ʃi:nɪst/ *n* maquinista *m & f*
mach|ismo /mæ'tʃɪzməʊ/ *n* machismo *m.* **~o** *a* macho
mackerel /'mækrəl/ *n invar* (*fish*) caballa *f*
mackintosh /'mækɪntɒʃ/ *n* impermeable *m*
macrobiotic /mækrəʊbaɪ'ɒtɪk/ *a* macrobiótico
mad /mæd/ *a* (**madder, maddest**) loco; (*foolish*) insensato; ‹*dog*› rabioso; (*angry, fam*) furioso. **be ~ about** estar loco por. **like ~** como un loco; (*a lot*) muchísimo
Madagascar /mædə'gæskə(r)/ *n* Madagascar *m*
madam /'mædəm/ *n* señora *f*; (*unmarried*) señorita *f*
madcap /'mædkæp/ *a* atolondrado. • *n* locuelo *m*
madden /'mædn/ *vt* (*make mad*) enloquecer; (*make angry*) enfurecer
made /meɪd/ *see* **make**. **~ to measure** hecho a la medida
Madeira /mə'dɪərə/ *n* (*wine*) vino *m* de Madera
mad: **~house** *n* manicomio *m.* **~ly** *adv* (*interested, in love etc*) locamente; (*frantically*) como un loco. **~man** *n* loco *m.* **~ness** *n* locura *f*
madonna /mə'dɒnə/ *n* Virgen *f* María
madrigal /'mædrɪgl/ *n* madrigal *m*
maelstrom /'meɪlstrəm/ *n* remolino *m*
maestro /'maɪstrəʊ/ *n* (*pl* **maestri** /-stri:/ *or* **os**) maestro *m*
Mafia /'mæfɪə/ *n* mafia *f*
magazine /mægə'zi:n/ *n* revista *f*; (*of gun*) recámara *f*
magenta /mə'dʒentə/ *a* rojo purpúreo
maggot /'mægət/ *n* gusano *m.* **~y** *a* agusanado
Magi /'meɪdʒaɪ/ *npl.* **the ~** los Reyes *mpl* Magos
magic /'mædʒɪk/ *n* magia *f.* • *a* mágico. **~al** *a* mágico. **~ian** /mə'dʒɪʃn/ *n* mago *m*
magisterial /mædʒɪ'stɪərɪəl/ *a* magistral; (*imperious*) autoritario
magistrate /'mædʒɪstreɪt/ *n* magistrado *m*, juez *m*
magnanim|ity /mægnə'nɪmətɪ/ *n* magnanimidad *f.* **~ous** /-'nænɪməs/ *a* magnánimo
magnate /'mægneɪt/ *n* magnate *m*
magnesia /mæg'ni:ʒə/ *n* magnesia *f*
magnet /'mægnɪt/ *n* imán *m.* **~ic** /-'netɪk/ *a* magnético. **~ism** *n* magnetismo *m.* **~ize** *vt* magnetizar
magnificen|ce /mæg'nɪfɪsns/ *a* magnificencia *f.* **~t** *a* magnífico
magnif|ication /mægnɪfɪ'keɪʃn/ *n* aumento *m.* **~ier** /-'faɪə(r)/ *n* lupa *f*, lente *f* de aumento. **~y** /-'faɪ/ *vt* aumentar. **~ying-glass** *n* lupa *f*, lente *f* de aumento
magnitude /'mægnɪtju:d/ *n* magnitud *f*
magnolia /mæg'nəʊlɪə/ *n* magnolia *f*
magnum /'mægnəm/ *n* botella *f* de litro y medio
magpie /'mægpaɪ/ *n* urraca *f*
mahogany /mə'hɒgənɪ/ *n* caoba *f*
maid /meɪd/ *n* (*servant*) criada *f*; (*girl, old use*) doncella *f.* **old ~** solterona *f*
maiden /'meɪdn/ *n* doncella *f.* • *a* ‹*aunt*› soltera; ‹*voyage*› inaugural. **~hood** *n* doncellez *f*, virginidad *f*, soltería *f.* **~ly** *adv* virginal. **~ name** *n* apellido *m* de soltera
mail[1] /meɪl/ *n* correo *m*; (*letters*) cartas *fpl.* • *a* postal, de correos. • *vt* (*post*) echar al correo; (*send*) enviar por correo
mail[2] /meɪl/ *n* (*armour*) (cota *f* de) malla *f*
mail: **~ing list** *n* lista *f* de direcciones. **~man** *n* (*Amer*) cartero *m.* **~ order** *n* venta *f* por correo
maim /meɪm/ *vt* mutilar
main /meɪn/ *n.* **(waterugas) ~** cañería *f* principal. **in the ~** en su mayor parte. **the ~s** *npl* (*elec*) la red *f* eléctrica. • *a* principal. **a ~ road** *n* una carretera *f.* **~land** *n* continente *m.* **~ly** *adv* principalmente. **~spring** *n* muelle *m* real; (*fig, motive*) móvil *m* principal. **~stay** *n* sostén *m.* **~stream** *n* corriente *f* principal. **~ street** *n* calle *f* principal
maintain /meɪn'teɪn/ *vt* mantener
maintenance /'meɪntənəns/ *n* mantenimiento *m*; (*allowance*) pensión *f* alimenticia

maisonette /meɪzə'net/ *n* (*small house*) casita *f*; (*part of house*) dúplex *m*
maize /meɪz/ *n* maíz *m*
majestic /mə'dʒestɪk/ *a* majestuoso
majesty /'mædʒəstɪ/ *n* majestad *f*
major /'meɪdʒə(r)/ *a* mayor. **a ~ road** una calle *f* prioritaria. ● *n* comandante *m*. ● *vi*. **~ in** (*univ, Amer*) especializarse en
Majorca /mə'jɔ:kə/ *n* Mallorca *f*
majority /mə'dʒɒrətɪ/ *n* mayoría *f*. **the ~ of people** la mayoría *f* de la gente. ● *a* mayoritario
make /meɪk/ *vt/i* (*pt* **made**) hacer; (*manufacture*) fabricar; ganar ‹*money*›; tomar ‹*decision*›; llegar a ‹*destination*›. **~ s.o. do sth** obligar a uno a hacer algo. **be made of** estar hecho de. **I cannot ~ anything of it** no me lo explico. **I ~ it two o'clock** yo tengo las dos. ● *n* fabricación *f*; (*brand*) marca *f*. **~ as if to** estar a punto de. **~ believe** fingir. **~ do** (*manage*) arreglarse. **~ do with** (*content o.s.*) contentarse con. **~ for** dirigirse a. **~ good** *vi* tener éxito. ● *vt* compensar; (*repair*) reparar. **~ it** llegar; (*succeed*) tener éxito. **~ it up** (*become reconciled*) hacer las paces. **~ much of** dar mucha importancia a. **~ off** escaparse (**with** con). **~ out** *vt* distinguir; (*understand*) entender; (*draw up*) extender; (*assert*) dar a entender. ● *vi* arreglárselas. **~ over** ceder (**to** a). **~ up** formar; (*prepare*) preparar; inventar ‹*story*›; (*compensate*) compensar. ● *vi* hacer las paces. **~ up (one's face)** maquillarse. **~ up for** compensar; recuperar ‹*time*›. **~ up to** congraciarse con. **~-believe** *a* fingido, simulado. ● *n* ficción *f*
maker /'meɪkə(r)/ *n* fabricante *m* & *f*. **the M~** el Hacedor *m*, el Creador *m*
makeshift /'meɪkʃɪft/ *n* expediente *m*. ● *a* (*temporary*) provisional; (*improvised*) improvisado
make-up /'meɪkʌp/ *n* maquillaje *m*
makeweight /'meɪkweɪt/ *n* complemento *m*
making /'meɪkɪŋ/ *n*. **be the ~ of** ser la causa del éxito de. **he has the ~s of** tiene madera de. **in the ~** en vías de formación
maladjust|ed /mælə'dʒʌstɪd/ *a* inadaptado. **~ment** *n* inadaptación *f*
maladministration /mæləd mɪnɪ'streɪʃn/ *n* mala administración *f*
malady /'mælədɪ/ *n* enfermedad *f*
malaise /mæ'leɪz/ *n* malestar *m*
malaria /mə'leərɪə/ *n* paludismo *m*
Malay /mə'leɪ/ *a* & *n* malayo (*m*). **~sia** *n* Malasia *f*
male /meɪl/ *a* masculino; (*bot, tec*) macho. ● *n* macho *m*; (*man*) varón *m*
malefactor /'mælɪfæktə(r)/ *n* malhechor *m*
malevolen|ce /mə'levəlns/ *n* malevolencia *f*. **~t** *a* malévolo
malform|ation /mælfɔ:'meɪʃn/ *n* malformación *f*. **~ed** *a* deforme
malfunction /mæl'fʌŋkʃn/ *n* funcionamiento *m* defectuoso. ● *vi* funcionar mal
malic|e /'mælɪs/ *n* rencor *m*. **bear s.o. ~e** guardar rencor a uno. **~ious** /mə'lɪʃəs/ *a* malévolo. **~iously** *adv* con malevolencia
malign /mə'laɪn/ *a* maligno. ● *vt* calumniar
malignan|cy /mə'lɪgnənsɪ/ *n* malignidad *f*. **~t** *a* maligno
malinger /mə'lɪŋgə(r)/ *vi* fingirse enfermo. **~er** *n* enfermo *m* fingido
malleable /'mælɪəbl/ *a* maleable
mallet /'mælɪt/ *n* mazo *m*
malnutrition /mælnju:'trɪʃn/ *n* desnutrición *f*
malpractice /mæl'præktɪs/ *n* falta *f* profesional
malt /mɔ:lt/ *n* malta *f*
Malt|a /'mɔ:ltə/ *n* Malta *f*. **~ese** /-'ti:z/ *a* & *n* maltés (*m*)
maltreat /mæl'tri:t/ *vt* maltratar. **~ment** *n* maltrato *m*
malt whisky /mɔ:lt'wɪskɪ/ *n* güisqui *m* de malta
mammal /'mæml/ *n* mamífero *m*
mammoth /'mæməθ/ *n* mamut *m*. ● *a* gigantesco
man /mæn/ *n* (*pl* **men**) hombre *m*; (*in sports team*) jugador *m*; (*chess*) pieza *f*. **~ in the street** hombre *m* de la calle. **~ to ~** de hombre a hombre. ● *vt* (*pt* **manned**) guarnecer (de hombres); tripular ‹*ship*›; servir ‹*guns*›
manacle /'mænəkl/ *n* manilla *f*. ● *vt* poner esposas a
manage /'mænɪdʒ/ *vt* dirigir; llevar ‹*shop, affairs*›; (*handle*) manejar. ● *vi* arreglárselas. **~ to do** lograr

hacer. **~able** *a* manejable. **~ment** *n* dirección *f*

manager /'mænɪdʒə(r)/ *n* director *m*; (*of actor*) empresario *m*. **~ess** /-'res/ *n* directora *f*. **~ial** /-'dʒɪərɪəl/ *a* directivo. **~ial staff** *n* personal *m* dirigente

managing director /mænɪdʒɪŋ daɪ'rektə(r)/ *n* director *m* gerente

mandarin /'mændərɪn/ *n* mandarín *m*; (*orange*) mandarina *f*

mandate /'mændeɪt/ *n* mandato *m*

mandatory /'mændətərɪ/ *a* obligatorio

mane /meɪn/ *n* (*of horse*) crin *f*; (*of lion*) melena *f*

manful /'mænfl/ *a* valiente

manganese /'mæŋgəni:z/ *n* manganeso *m*

manger /'meɪndʒə(r)/ *n* pesebre *m*

mangle[1] /'mæŋgl/ *n* (*for wringing*) exprimidor *m*; (*for smoothing*) máquina *f* de planchar

mangle[2] /'mæŋgl/ *vt* destrozar

mango /'mæŋgəʊ/ *n* (*pl* **-oes**) mango *m*

mangy /'meɪndʒɪ/ *a* sarnoso

man: **~handle** *vt* maltratar. **~hole** *n* registro *m*. **~hole cover** *n* tapa *f* de registro. **~hood** *n* edad *f* viril; (*quality*) virilidad *f*. **~-hour** *n* hora-hombre *f*. **~-hunt** *n* persecución *f*

mania /'meɪnɪə/ *n* manía *f*. **~c** /-ɪæk/ *n* maníaco *m*

manicur|e /'mænɪkjʊə(r)/ *n* manicura *f*. ● *vt* hacer la manicura a ‹*person*›. **~ist** *n* manicuro *m*

manifest /'mænɪfest/ *a* manifiesto. ● *vt* mostrar. **~ation** /-'steɪʃn/ *n* manifestación *f*

manifesto /mænɪ'festəʊ/ *n* (*pl* **-os**) manifiesto *m*

manifold /'mænɪfəʊld/ *a* múltiple

manipulat|e /mə'nɪpjʊleɪt/ *vt* manipular. **~ion** /-'leɪʃn/ *n* manipulación *f*

mankind /mæn'kaɪnd/ *n* la humanidad *f*

man: **~ly** *adv* viril. **~-made** *a* artificial

mannequin /'mænɪkɪn/ *n* maniquí *m*

manner /'mænə(r)/ *n* manera *f*; (*behaviour*) comportamiento *m*; (*kind*) clase *f*. **~ed** *a* amanerado. **bad-~ed** *a* mal educado. **~s** *npl* (*social behaviour*) educación *f*. **have no ~s** no tener educación

mannerism /'mænərɪzəm/ *n* peculiaridad *f*

mannish /'mænɪʃ/ *a* ‹*woman*› hombruna

manoevre /mə'nu:və(r)/ *n* maniobra *f*. ● *vt/i* maniobrar

man-of-war /mænəv'wɔ:(r)/ *n* buque *m* de guerra

manor /'mænə(r)/ *n* casa *f* solariega

manpower /'mænpaʊə(r)/ *n* mano *f* de obra

manservant /'mænsɜ:vənt/ *n* criado *m*

mansion /'mænʃn/ *n* mansión *f*

man: **~-size(d)** *a* grande. **~slaughter** *n* homicidio *m* impremeditado

mantelpiece /'mæntlpi:s/ *n* repisa *f* de chimenea

mantilla /mæn'tɪlə/ *n* mantilla *f*

mantle /'mæntl/ *n* manto *m*

manual /'mænjʊəl/ *a* manual. ● *n* (*handbook*) manual *m*

manufacture /mænjʊ'fæktʃə(r)/ *vt* fabricar. ● *n* fabricación *f*. **~r** /-ə(r)/ *n* fabricante *m*

manure /mə'njʊə(r)/ *n* estiércol *m*

manuscript /'mænjʊskrɪpt/ *n* manuscrito *m*

many /'menɪ/ *a* & *n* muchos (*mpl*). **~ people** mucha gente *f*. **~ a time** muchas veces. **a great/good ~** muchísimos

map /mæp/ *n* mapa *m*; (*of streets etc*) plano *m*. ● *vt* (*pt* **mapped**) levantar un mapa de. **~ out** organizar

maple /'meɪpl/ *n* arce *m*

mar /mɑ:/ *vt* (*pt* **marred**) estropear; aguar ‹*enjoyment*›

marathon /'mærəθən/ *n* maratón *m*

maraud|er /mə'rɔ:də(r)/ *n* merodeador *m*. **~ing** *a* merodeador

marble /'mɑ:bl/ *n* mármol *m*; (*for game*) canica *f*

March /mɑ:tʃ/ *n* marzo *m*

march /mɑ:tʃ/ *vi* (*mil*) marchar. **~ off** irse. ● *vt*. **~ off** (*lead away*) llevarse. ● *n* marcha *f*

marchioness /mɑ:ʃə'nes/ *n* marquesa *f*

march-past /'mɑ:tʃpɑ:st/ *n* desfile *m*

mare /meə(r)/ *n* yegua *f*

margarine /mɑ:dʒə'ri:n/ *n* margarina *f*

margin /'mɑ:dʒɪn/ *n* margen *f*. **~al** *a* marginal. **~al seat** *n* (*pol*) escaño *m* inseguro. **~ally** *adv* muy poco

marguerite /mɑ:gə'ri:t/ *n* margarita *f*

marigold /'mærɪgəʊld/ *n* caléndula *f*

marijuana /mærɪ'hwɑ:nə/ *n* marihuana *f*
marina /mə'ri:nə/ *n* puerto *m* deportivo
marina|de /mærɪ'neɪd/ *n* escabeche *m*. **~te** /'mærɪneɪt/ *vt* escabechar
marine /mə'ri:n/ *a* marino. ● *n* (*sailor*) soldado *m* de infantería de marina; (*shipping*) marina *f*
marionette /mærɪə'net/ *n* marioneta *f*
marital /'mærɪtl/ *a* marital, matrimonial. **~ status** *n* estado *m* civil
maritime /'mærɪtaɪm/ *a* marítimo
marjoram /'mɑ:dʒərəm/ *n* mejorana *f*
mark[1] /mɑ:k/ *n* marca *f*; (*trace*) huella *f*; (*schol*) nota *f*; (*target*) blanco *m*. ● *vt* marcar; poner nota a ‹*exam*›. **~ time** marcar el paso. **~ out** trazar; escoger ‹*person*›
mark[2] /mɑ:k/ *n* (*currency*) marco *m*
marked /mɑ:kt/ *a* marcado. **~ly** /-kɪdlɪ/ *adv* marcadamente
marker /'mɑ:kə(r)/ *n* marcador *m*; (*for book*) registro *m*
market /'mɑ:kɪt/ *n* mercado *m*. **on the ~** en venta. ● *vt* (*sell*) vender; (*launch*) comercializar. **~ garden** *n* huerto *m*. **~ing** *n* marketing *m*
marking /'mɑ:kɪŋ/ *n* (*marks*) marcas *fpl*
marksman /'mɑ:ksmən/ *n* tirador *m*. **~ship** *n* puntería *f*
marmalade /'mɑ:məleɪd/ *n* mermelada *f* de naranja
marmot /'mɑ:mət/ *n* marmota *f*
maroon /mə'ru:n/ *n* granate *m*. ● *a* de color granate
marooned /mə'ru:nd/ *a* abandonado; (*snow-bound etc*) aislado
marquee /mɑ:ki:/ *n* tienda de campaña *f* grande; (*awning*, *Amer*) marquesina *f*
marquetry /'mɑ:kɪtrɪ/ *n* marquetería *f*
marquis /'mɑ:kwɪs/ *n* marqués *m*
marriage /'mærɪdʒ/ *n* matrimonio *m*; (*wedding*) boda *f*. **~able** *a* casadero
married /'mærɪd/ *a* casado; ‹*life*› conjugal
marrow /'mærəʊ/ *n* (*of bone*) tuétano *m*; (*vegetable*) calabacín *m*
marry /'mærɪ/ *vt* casarse con; (*give or unite in marriage*) casar. ● *vi* casarse. **get married** casarse
marsh /mɑ:ʃ/ *n* pantano *m*
marshal /'mɑ:ʃl/ *n* (*mil*) mariscal *m*; (*master of ceremonies*) maestro *m* de ceremonias; (*at sports events*) oficial *m*. ● *vt* (*pt* **marshalled**) ordenar; formar ‹*troops*›
marsh mallow /mɑ:ʃ'mæləʊ/ *n* (*plant*) malvavisco *m*
marshmallow /mɑ:ʃ'mæləʊ/ *n* (*sweet*) caramelo *m* blando
marshy /'mɑ:ʃɪ/ *a* pantanoso
martial /'mɑ:ʃl/ *a* marcial. **~ law** *n* ley *f* marcial
Martian /'mɑ:ʃn/ *a* & *n* marciano (*m*)
martinet /mɑ:tɪ'net/ *n* ordenancista *m* & *f*
martyr /'mɑ:tə(r)/ *n* mártir *m* & *f*. ● *vt* martirizar. **~dom** *n* martirio *m*
marvel /'mɑ:vl/ *n* maravilla *f*. ● *vi* (*pt* **marvelled**) maravillarse (**at** con, de). **~lous** /'mɑ:vələs/ *a* maravilloso
Marxis|m /'mɑ:ksɪzəm/ *n* marxismo *m*. **~t** *a* & *n* marxista (*m* & *f*)
marzipan /'mɑ:zɪpæn/ *n* mazapán *m*
mascara /mæ'skɑ:rə/ *n* rimel *m*
mascot /'mæskɒt/ *n* mascota *f*
masculin|e /'mæskjʊlɪn/ *a* & *n* masculino (*m*). **~ity** /-'lɪnətɪ/ *n* masculinidad *f*
mash /mæʃ/ *n* mezcla *f*; (*potatoes*, *fam*) puré *m* de patatas. ● *vt* (*crush*) machacar; (*mix*) mezclar. **~ed potatoes** *n* puré *m* de patatas
mask /mɑ:sk/ *n* máscara *f*. ● *vt* enmascarar
masochis|m /'mæsəkɪzəm/ *n* masoquismo *m*. **~t** *n* masoquista *m* & *f*
mason /'meɪsn/ *n* (*builder*) albañil *m*
Mason /'meɪsn/ *n*. **~** masón *m*. **~ic** /mə'sɒnɪk/ *a* masónico
masonry /'meɪsnrɪ/ *n* albañilería *f*
masquerade /mɑ:skə'reɪd/ *n* mascarada *f*. ● *vi*. **~ as** hacerse pasar por
mass[1] /mæs/ *n* masa *f*; (*large quantity*) montón *m*. **the ~es** *npl* las masas *fpl*. ● *vt*/*i* agrupar(se)
mass[2] /mæs/ *n* (*relig*) misa *f*. **high ~** misa *f* mayor
massacre /'mæsəkə(r)/ *n* masacre *f*, matanza *f*. ● *vt* masacrar
massage /'mæsɑ:ʒ/ *n* masaje *m*. ● *vt* dar masaje a
masseu|r /mæ'sɜ:(r)/ *n* masajista *m*. **~se** /mæ'sɜ:z/ *n* masajista *f*
massive /'mæsɪv/ *a* masivo; (*heavy*) macizo; (*huge*) enorme
mass: **~ media** *n* medios *mpl* de comunicación. **~-produce** *vt* fabricar en serie

mast /mɑ:st/ *n* mástil *m*; (*for radio, TV*) torre *f*
master /'mɑ:stə(r)/ *n* maestro *m*; (*in secondary school*) profesor *m*; (*of ship*) capitán *m*. ● *vt* dominar. **~-key** *n* llave *f* maestra. **~ly** *a* magistral. **~mind** *n* cerebro *m*. ● *vt* dirigir. **M~ of Arts** master *m*, grado *m* universitario entre el de licenciado y el de doctor
masterpiece /'mɑ:stəpi:s/ *n* obra *f* maestra
master-stroke /'mɑ:stəstrəʊk/ *n* golpe *m* maestro
mastery /'mɑ:stərɪ/ *n* dominio *m*; (*skill*) maestría *f*
masturbat|e /'mæstəbeɪt/ *vi* masturbarse. **~ion** /-'beɪʃn/ *n* masturbación *f*
mat /mæt/ *n* estera *f*; (*at door*) felpudo *m*
match[1] /mætʃ/ *n* (*sport*) partido *m*; (*equal*) igual *m*; (*marriage*) matrimonio *m*; (*s.o. to marry*) partido *m*. ● *vt* emparejar; (*equal*) igualar; ‹*clothes, colours*› hacer juego con. ● *vi* hacer juego
match[2] /mætʃ/ *n* (*of wood*) fósforo *m*; (*of wax*) cerilla *f*. **~box** /'mætʃbɒks/ *n* (*for wooden matches*) caja *f* de fósforos; (*for wax matches*) caja *f* de cerillas
matching /'mætʃɪŋ/ *a* que hace juego
mate[1] /meɪt/ *n* compañero *m*; (*of animals*) macho *m*, hembra *f*; (*assistant*) ayudante *m*. ● *vt/i* acoplar(se)
mate[2] /meɪt/ *n* (*chess*) mate *m*
material /mə'tɪərɪəl/ *n* material *m*; (*cloth*) tela *f*. ● *a* material; (*fig*) importante. **~istic** /-'lɪstɪk/ *a* materialista. **~s** *npl* materiales *mpl*. **raw ~s** *npl* materias *fpl* primas
materialize /mə'tɪərɪəlaɪz/ *vi* materializarse
maternal /mə'tɜ:nl/ *a* maternal; ‹*relation*› materno
maternity /mə'tɜ:nɪtɪ/ *n* maternidad *f*. ● *a* de maternidad. **~ clothes** *npl* vestido *m* pre-mamá. **~ hospital** *n* maternidad *f*
matey /'meɪtɪ/ *a* (*fam*) simpático
mathematic|ian /mæθəmə'tɪʃn/ *n* matemático *m*. **~al** /-'mætɪkl/ *a* matemático. **~s** /-'mætɪks/ *n & npl* matemáticas *fpl*
maths /mæθs/, **math** (*Amer*) *n & npl* matemáticas *fpl*
matinée /'mætɪneɪ/ *n* función *f* de tarde
matriculat|e /mə'trɪkjʊleɪt/ *vt/i* matricular(se). **~ion** /-'leɪʃn/ *n* matriculación *f*
matrimon|ial /mætrɪ'məʊnɪəl/ *a* matrimonial. **~y** /'mætrɪmənɪ/ *n* matrimonio *m*
matrix /'meɪtrɪks/ *n* (*pl* **matrices** /-si:z/) matriz *f*
matron /'meɪtrən/ *n* (*married, elderly*) matrona *f*; (*in school*) ama *f* de llaves; (*former use, in hospital*) enfermera *f* jefe. **~ly** *a* matronil
matt /mæt/ *a* mate
matted /'mætɪd/ *a* enmarañado
matter /'mætə(r)/ *n* (*substance*) materia *f*; (*affair*) asunto *m*; (*pus*) pus *m*. **as a ~ of fact** en realidad. **no ~** no importa. **what is the ~?** ¿qué pasa? ● *vi* importar. **it does not ~** no importa. **~-of-fact** *a* realista
matting /'mætɪŋ/ *n* estera *f*
mattress /'mætrɪs/ *n* colchón *m*
matur|e /mə'tjʊə(r)/ *a* maduro. ● *vt/i* madurar. **~ity** *n* madurez *f*
maul /mɔ:l/ *vt* maltratar
Mauritius /mə'rɪʃəs/ *n* Mauricio *m*
mausoleum /mɔ:sə'lɪəm/ *n* mausoleo *m*
mauve /məʊv/ *a & n* color (*m*) de malva
mawkish /'mɔ:kɪʃ/ *a* empalagoso
maxim /'mæksɪm/ *n* máxima *f*
maxim|ize /'mæksɪmaɪz/ *vt* llevar al máximo. **~um** *a & n* (*pl* **-ima**) máximo (*m*)
may /meɪ/ *v aux* (*pt* **might**) poder. **~ I smoke?** ¿se permite fumar? **~ he be happy** ¡que sea feliz! **he ~/might come** puede que venga. **I ~/might as well stay** más vale quedarme. **it ~/might be true** puede ser verdad
May /meɪ/ *n* mayo *m*. **~ Day** *n* el primero *m* de mayo
maybe /'meɪbɪ/ *adv* quizá(s)
mayhem /'meɪhem/ *n* (*havoc*) alboroto *m*
mayonnaise /meɪə'neɪz/ *n* mayonesa *f*
mayor /meə(r)/ *n* alcalde *m*, alcaldesa *f*. **~ess** *n* alcaldesa *f*
maze /meɪz/ *n* laberinto *m*
me[1] /mi:/ *pron* me; (*after prep*) mí. **he knows ~** me conoce. **it's ~** soy yo
me[2] /mi:/ *n* (*mus, third note of any musical scale*) mi *m*
meadow /'medəʊ/ *n* prado *m*

meagre /'mi:gə(r)/ *a* escaso
meal[1] /mi:l/ *n* comida *f*
meal[2] /mi:l/ *n* (*grain*) harina *f*
mealy-mouthed /mi:lɪ'maʊðd/ *a* hipócrita
mean[1] /mi:n/ *vt* (*pt* **meant**) (*intend*) tener la intención de, querer; (*signify*) querer decir, significar. **~ to do** tener la intención de hacer. **~ well** tener buenas intenciones. **be meant for** estar destinado a
mean[2] /mi:n/ *a* (**-er**, **-est**) (*miserly*) tacaño; (*unkind*) malo; (*poor*) pobre
mean[3] /mi:n/ *a* medio. ● *n* medio *m*; (*average*) promedio *m*
meander /mɪ'ændə(r)/ *vi* ‹*river*› serpentear; ‹*person*› vagar
meaning /'mi:nɪŋ/ *n* sentido *m*. **~ful** *a* significativo. **~less** *a* sin sentido
meanness /'mi:nnɪs/ *n* (*miserliness*) tacañería *f*; (*unkindness*) maldad *f*
means /mi:nz/ *n* medio *m*. **by all ~** por supuesto. **by no ~** de ninguna manera. ● *npl* (*wealth*) recursos *mpl*. **~ test** *n* investigación *f* financial
meant /ment/ *see* **mean**[1]
meantime /'mi:ntaɪm/ *adv* entretanto. **in the ~** entretanto
meanwhile /'mi:nwaɪl/ *adv* entretanto
measles /'mi:zlz/ *n* sarampión *m*
measly /'mi:zlɪ/ *a* (*sl*) miserable
measurable /'meʒərəbl/ *a* mensurable
measure /'meʒə(r)/ *n* medida *f*; (*ruler*) regla *f*. ● *vt*/*i* medir. **~ up to** estar a la altura de. **~d** *a* (*rhythmical*) acompasado; (*carefully considered*) prudente. **~ment** *n* medida *f*
meat /mi:t/ *n* carne *f*. **~y** *a* carnoso; (*fig*) sustancioso
mechanic /mɪ'kænɪk/ *n* mecánico *m*. **~al** /mɪ'kænɪkl/ *a* mecánico. **~s** *n* mecánica *f*
mechani|sm /'mekənɪzəm/ *n* mecanismo *m*. **~ze** *vt* mecanizar
medal /'medl/ *n* medalla *f*
medallion /mɪ'dælɪən/ *n* medallón *m*
medallist /'medəlɪst/ *n* ganador *m* de una medalla. **be a gold ~** ganar una medalla de oro
meddle /'medl/ *vi* entrometerse (**in** en); (*tinker*) tocar. **~ with** (*tinker*) tocar. **~some** *a* entrometido
media /'mi:dɪə/ *see* **medium**. ● *npl*. **the ~** *npl* los medios *mpl* de comunicación
mediat|e /'mi:dɪeɪt/ *vi* mediar. **~ion** /-eɪʃn/ *n* mediación *f*. **~or** *n* mediador *m*
medical /'medɪkl/ *a* médico; ‹*student*› de medicina. ● *n* (*fam*) reconocimiento *m* médico
medicat|ed /'medɪkeɪtɪd/ *a* medicinal. **~ion** /-'keɪʃn/ *n* medicación *f*
medicin|e /'medsɪn/ *n* medicina *f*. **~al** /mɪ'dɪsɪnl/ *a* medicinal
medieval /medɪ'i:vl/ *a* medieval
mediocr|e /mi:dɪ'əʊkə(r)/ *a* mediocre. **~ity** /-'ɒkrətɪ/ *n* mediocridad *f*
meditat|e /'medɪteɪt/ *vt*/*i* meditar. **~ion** /-'teɪʃn/ *n* meditación *f*
Mediterranean /medɪtə'reɪnɪən/ *a* mediterráneo. ● *n*. **the ~** el Mediterráneo *m*
medium /'mi:dɪəm/ *n* (*pl* **media**) medio *m*; (*pl* **mediums**) (*person*) médium *m*. ● *a* mediano
medley /'medlɪ/ *n* popurrí *m*
meek /mi:k/ *a* (**-er**, **-est**) manso
meet /mi:t/ *vt* (*pt* **met**) encontrar; (*bump into s.o.*) encontrarse con; (*see again*) ver; (*fetch*) ir a buscar; (*get to know, be introduced to*) conocer. **~ the bill** pagar la cuenta. ● *vi* encontrarse; (*get to know*) conocerse; (*in session*) reunirse. **~ with** tropezar con ‹*obstacles*›
meeting /'mi:tɪŋ/ *n* reunión *f*; (*accidental between two people*) encuentro *m*; (*arranged between two people*) cita *f*
megalomania /megələʊ'meɪnɪə/ *n* megalomanía *f*
megaphone /'megəfəʊn/ *n* megáfono *m*
melanchol|ic /melən'kɒlɪk/ *a* melancólico. **~y** /'melənkɒlɪ/ *n* melancolía *f*. ● *a* melancólico
mêlée /me'leɪ/ *n* pelea *f* confusa
mellow /'meləʊ/ *a* (**-er**, **-est**) ‹*fruit, person*› maduro; ‹*sound, colour*› dulce. ● *vt*/*i* madurar(se)
melodi|c /mɪ'lɒdɪk/ *a* melódico. **~ous** /mɪ'ləʊdɪəs/ *a* melodioso
melodrama /'melədrɑ:mə/ *n* melodrama *m*. **~tic** /-ə'mætɪk/ *a* melodramático
melody /'melədɪ/ *n* melodía *f*
melon /'melən/ *n* melón *m*
melt /melt/ *vt* (*make liquid*) derretir; fundir ‹*metals*›. ● *vi* (*become liquid*) derretirse; ‹*metals*› fundirse. **~ing-pot** *n* crisol *m*
member /'membə(r)/ *n* miembro *m*. **M~ of Parliament** *n* diputado *m*.

~ship *n* calidad *f* de miembro; (*members*) miembros *mpl*
membrane /'membreɪn/ *n* membrana *f*
memento /mɪ'mentəʊ/ *n* (*pl* **-oes**) recuerdo *m*
memo /'meməʊ/ *n* (*pl* **-os**) (*fam*) nota *f*
memoir /'memwɑ:(r)/ *n* memoria *f*
memorable /'memərəbl/ *a* memorable
memorandum /memə'rændəm/ *n* (*pl* **-ums**) nota *f*
memorial /mɪ'mɔ:rɪəl/ *n* monumento *m*. ● *a* conmemorativo
memorize /'meməraɪz/ *vt* aprender de memoria
memory /'memərɪ/ *n* (*faculty*) memoria *f*; (*thing remembered*) recuerdo *m*. **from ~** de memoria. **in ~ of** en memoria de
men /men/ *see* **man**
menac|e /'menəs/ *n* amenaza *f*; (*nuisance*) pesado *m*. ● *vt* amenazar. **~ingly** *adv* de manera amenazadora
menagerie /mɪ'nædʒərɪ/ *n* casa *f* de fieras
mend /mend/ *vt* reparar; (*darn*) zurcir. **~ one's ways** enmendarse. ● *n* remiendo *m*. **be on the ~** ir mejorando
menfolk /'menfəʊk/ *n* hombres *mpl*
menial /'mi:nɪəl/ *a* servil
meningitis /menɪn'dʒaɪtɪs/ *n* meningitis *f*
menopause /'menəpɔ:z/ *n* menopausia *f*
menstruat|e /'menstrʊeɪt/ *vi* menstruar. **~ion** /-eɪʃn/ *n* menstruación *f*
mental /'mentl/ *a* mental; ‹*hospital*› psiquiátrico
mentality /men'tælətɪ/ *n* mentalidad *f*
menthol /'menθɒl/ *n* mentol *m*. **~ated** *a* mentolado
mention /'menʃn/ *vt* mencionar. **don't ~ it!** ¡no hay de qué! ● *n* mención *f*
mentor /'mentɔ:(r)/ *n* mentor *m*
menu /'menju:/ *n* (*set meal*) menú *m*; (*a la carte*) lista *f* (de platos)
mercantile /'mɜ:kəntaɪl/ *a* mercantil
mercenary /'mɜ:sɪnərɪ/ *a* & n mercenario (*m*)
merchandise /'mɜ:tʃəndaɪz/ *n* mercancias *fpl*
merchant /'mɜ:tʃənt/ *n* comerciante *m*. ● *a* ‹*ship, navy*› mercante. **~ bank** *n* banco *m* mercantil
merci|ful /'mɜ:sɪfl/ *a* misericordioso. **~fully** *adv* (*fortunately, fam*) gracias a Dios. **~less** /'mɜ:sɪlɪs/ *a* despiadado
mercur|ial /mɜ:'kjʊərɪəl/ *a* mercurial; (*fig, active*) vivo. **~y** /'mɜ:kjʊrɪ/ *n* mercurio *m*
mercy /'mɜ:sɪ/ *n* compasión *f*. **at the ~ of** a merced de
mere /mɪə(r)/ *a* simple. **~ly** *adv* simplemente
merest /'mɪərɪst/ *a* mínimo
merge /mɜ:dʒ/ *vt* unir; fusionar ‹*companies*›. ● *vi* unirse; ‹*companies*› fusionarse. **~r** /-ə(r)/ *n* fusión *f*
meridian /mə'rɪdɪən/ *n* meridiano *m*
meringue /mə'ræŋ/ *n* merengue *m*
merit /'merɪt/ *n* mérito *m*. ● *vt* (*pt* **merited**) merecer. **~orious** /-'tɔ:rɪəs/ *a* meritorio
mermaid /'mɜ:meɪd/ *n* sirena *f*
merr|ily /'merəlɪ/ *adv* alegremente. **~iment** /'merɪmənt/ *n* alegría *f*. **~y** /'merɪ/ *a* (**-ier**, **-iest**) alegre. **make ~** divertirse. **~y-go-round** *n* tiovivo *m*. **~y-making** *n* holgorio *m*
mesh /meʃ/ *n* malla *f*; (*network*) red *f*
mesmerize /'mezməraɪz/ *vt* hipnotizar
mess /mes/ *n* desorden *m*; (*dirt*) suciedad *f*; (*mil*) rancho *m*. **make a ~ of** chapucear, estropear. ● *vt*. **~ up** desordenar; (*dirty*) ensuciar. ● *vi*. **~ about** entretenerse. **~ with** (*tinker with*) manosear
message /'mesɪdʒ/ *n* recado *m*
messenger /'mesɪndʒə(r)/ *n* mensajero *m*
Messiah /mɪ'saɪə/ *n* Mesías *m*
Messrs /'mesəz/ *npl*. **~ Smith** los señores *mpl or* Sres. Smith
messy /'mesɪ/ *a* (**-ier**, **-iest**) en desorden; (*dirty*) sucio
met /met/ *see* **meet**
metabolism /mɪ'tæbəlɪzəm/ *n* metabolismo *m*
metal /'metl/ *n* metal. ● *a* de metal. **~lic** /mɪ'tælɪk/ *a* metálico
metallurgy /mɪ'tælədʒɪ/ *n* metalurgia *f*
metamorphosis /metə'mɔ:fəsɪs/ *n* (*pl* **-phoses** /-sɪ:z/) metamorfosis *f*
metaphor /'metəfə(r)/ *n* metáfora *f*. **~ical** /-'fɔrɪkl/ *a* metafórico

mete /mi:t/ *vt*. **~ out** repartir; dar ‹*punishment*›
meteor /'mi:tɪə(r)/ *n* meteoro *m*
meteorite /'mi:tɪəraɪt/ *n* meteorito *m*
meteorolog|ical /mi:tɪərə'lɒdʒɪkl/ *a* meteorológico. **~y** /-'rɒlədʒɪ/ *n* meteorología *f*
meter[1] /'mi:tə(r)/ *n* contador *m*
meter[2] /'mi:tə(r)/ *n* (*Amer*) = **metre**
method /'meθəd/ *n* método *m*
methodical /mɪ'θɒdɪkl/ *a* metódico
Methodist /'meθədɪst/ *a* & *n* metodista (*m* & *f*)
methylated /'meθɪleɪtɪd/ *a*. **~ spirit** *n* alcohol *m* desnaturalizado
meticulous /mɪ'tɪkjʊləs/ *a* meticuloso
metre /'mi:tə(r)/ *n* metro *m*
metric /'metrɪk/ *a* métrico. **~ation** /-'keɪʃn/ *n* cambio *m* al sistema métrico
metropolis /mɪ'trɒpəlɪs/ *n* metrópoli *f*
metropolitan /metrə'pɒlɪtən/ *a* metropolitano
mettle /'metl/ *n* valor *m*
mew /mju:/ *n* maullido *m*. ● *vi* maullar
mews /mju:z/ *npl* casas *fpl* pequeñas (que antes eran caballerizas)
Mexic|an /'meksɪkən/ *a* & *n* mejicano (*m*); (*in Mexico*) mexicano (*m*). **~o** /-kəʊ/ *n* Méjico *m*; (*in Mexico*) México *m*
mezzanine /'metsəni:n/ *n* entresuelo *m*
mi /mi:/ *n* (*mus, third note of any musical scale*) mi *m*
miaow /mi:'aʊ/ *n* & *vi* = **mew**
mice /maɪs/ *see* **mouse**
mickey /'mɪkɪ/ *n*. **take the ~ out of** (*sl*) tomar el pelo a
micro... /'maɪkrəʊ/ *pref* micro...
microbe /'maɪkrəʊb/ *n* microbio *m*
microchip /'maɪkrəʊtʃɪp/ *n* pastilla *f*
microfilm /'maɪkrəʊfɪlm/ *n* microfilme *m*
microphone /'maɪkrəfəʊn/ *n* micrófono *m*
microprocessor /maɪkrəʊ'prəʊsesə(r)/ *n* microprocesador *m*
microscop|e /'maɪkrəskəʊp/ *n* microscopio *m*. **~ic** /-'skɒpɪk/ *a* microscópico
microwave /'maɪkrəʊweɪv/ *n* microonda *f*. **~ oven** *n* horno *m* de microondas
mid /mɪd/ *a*. **in ~ air** en pleno aire. **in ~ March** a mediados de marzo. **in ~ ocean** en medio del océano
midday /mɪd'deɪ/ *n* mediodía *m*
middle /'mɪdl/ *a* de en medio; ‹*quality*› mediano. ● *n* medio *m*. **in the ~ of** en medio de. **~-aged** *a* de mediana edad. **M~ Ages** *npl* Edad *f* Media. **~ class** *n* clase *f* media. **~-class** *a* de la clase media. **M~ East** *n* Oriente *m* Medio. **~man** *n* intermediario *m*
middling /'mɪdlɪŋ/ *a* regular
midge /mɪdʒ/ *n* mosquito *m*
midget /'mɪdʒɪt/ *n* enano *m*. ● *a* minúsculo
Midlands /'mɪdləndz/ *npl* región *f* central de Inglaterra
midnight /'mɪdnaɪt/ *n* medianoche *f*
midriff /'mɪdrɪf/ *n* diafragma *m*; (*fam*) vientre *m*
midst /mɪdst/ *n*. **in our ~** entre nosotros. **in the ~ of** en medio de
midsummer /mɪd'sʌmə(r)/ *n* pleno verano *m*; (*solstice*) solsticio *m* de verano
midway /mɪd'weɪ/ *adv* a medio camino
midwife /'mɪdwaɪf/ *n* comadrona *f*
midwinter /mɪd'wɪntə(r)/ *n* pleno invierno *m*
might[1] /maɪt/ *see* **may**
might[2] /maɪt/ *n* (*strength*) fuerza *f*; (*power*) poder *m*. **~y** *a* (*strong*) fuerte; (*powerful*) poderoso; (*very great, fam*) enorme. ● *adv* (*fam*) muy
migraine /'mi:greɪn/ *n* jaqueca *f*
migrant /'maɪgrənt/ *a* migratorio. ● *n* (*person*) emigrante *m* & *f*
migrat|e /maɪ'greɪt/ *vi* emigrar. **~ion** /-ʃn/ *n* migración *f*
mike /maɪk/ *n* (*fam*) micrófono *m*
mild /maɪld/ *a* (**-er**, **-est**) ‹*person*› apacible; ‹*climate*› templado; (*slight*) ligero; ‹*taste*› suave; ‹*illness*› benigno
mildew /'mɪldju:/ *n* moho *m*
mild: **~ly** *adv* (*slightly*) ligeramente. **~ness** *n* (*of person*) apacibilidad *f*; (*of climate, illness*) benignidad *f*; (*of taste*) suavidad *f*
mile /maɪl/ *n* milla *f*. **~s better** (*fam*) mucho mejor. **~s too big** (*fam*) demasiado grande. **~age** *n* (*loosely*) kilometraje *m*. **~stone** *n* mojón *m*; (*event, stage, fig*) hito *m*
milieu /mɪ'ljɜ:/ *n* ambiente *m*

militant /ˈmɪlɪtənt/ *a & n* militante (*m & f*)
military /ˈmɪlɪtərɪ/ *a* militar
militate /ˈmɪlɪteɪt/ *vi* militar (**against** contra)
militia /mɪˈlɪʃə/ *n* milicia *f*
milk /mɪlk/ *n* leche *f*. ● *a* ‹*product*› lácteo; ‹*chocolate*› con leche. ● *vt* ordeñar ‹*cow*›; (*exploit*) chupar. **~man** *n* repartidor *m* de leche. **~ shake** *n* batido *m* de leche. **~y** *a* lechoso. **M~y Way** *n* Vía *f* Láctea
mill /mɪl/ *n* molino *m*; (*for coffee, pepper*) molinillo *m*; (*factory*) fábrica *f*. ● *vt* moler. ● *vi*. **~ about/around** apiñarse, circular
millennium /mɪˈlenɪəm/ *n* (*pl* **-ia** *or* **-iums**) milenio *m*
miller /ˈmɪlə(r)/ *n* molinero *m*
millet /ˈmɪlɪt/ *n* mijo *m*
milli... /ˈmɪlɪ/ *pref* mili...
milligram(me) /ˈmɪlɪgræm/ *n* miligramo *m*
millimetre /ˈmɪlɪmi:tə(r)/ *n* milímetro *m*
milliner /ˈmɪlɪnə(r)/ *n* sombrerero *m*
million /ˈmɪlɪən/ *n* millón *m*. **a ~ pounds** un millón *m* de libras. **~aire** *n* millonario *m*
millstone /ˈmɪlstəʊn/ *n* muela *f* (de molino); (*fig, burden*) losa *f*
mime /maɪm/ *n* pantomima *f*. ● *vt* hacer en pantomima. ● *vi* actuar de mimo
mimic /ˈmɪmɪk/ *vt* (*pt* **mimicked**) imitar. ● *n* imitador *m*. **~ry** *n* imitación *f*
mimosa /mɪˈməʊzə/ *n* mimosa *f*
minaret /mɪnəˈret/ *n* alminar *m*
mince /mɪns/ *vt* desmenuzar; picar ‹*meat*›. **not to ~ matters/words** no tener pelos en la lengua. ● *n* carne *f* picada. **~meat** *n* conserva *f* de fruta picada. **make ~meat of s.o.** hacer trizas a uno. **~ pie** *n* pastel *m* con frutas picadas. **~r** *n* máquina *f* de picar carne
mind /maɪnd/ *n* mente *f*; (*sanity*) juicio *m*; (*opinion*) parecer *m*; (*intention*) intención *f*. **be on one's ~** preocuparle a uno. ● *vt* (*look after*) cuidar; (*heed*) hacer caso de. **I don't ~** me da igual. **I don't ~ the noise** no me molesta el ruido. **never ~** no te preocupes, no se preocupe. **~er** *n* cuidador *m*. **~ful** *a* atento (**of** a). **~less** *a* estúpido
mine[1] /maɪn/ *poss pron* (el) mío *m*, (la) mía *f*, (los) míos *mpl*, (las) mías *fpl*. **it is ~** es mío
mine[2] /maɪn/ *n* mina *f*. ● *vt* extraer. **~field** *n* campo *m* de minas. **~r** *n* minero *m*
mineral /ˈmɪnərəl/ *a & n* mineral (*m*). **~ (water)** *n* (*fizzy soft drink*) gaseosa *f*. **~ water** *n* (*natural*) agua *f* mineral
minesweeper /ˈmaɪnswi:pə(r)/ *n* (*ship*) dragaminas *m invar*
mingle /ˈmɪŋgl/ *vt*/*i* mezclar(se)
mingy /ˈmɪndʒɪ/ *a* tacaño
mini... /ˈmɪnɪ/ *pref* mini...
miniature /ˈmɪnɪtʃə(r)/ *a & n* miniatura (*f*)
mini: **~bus** *n* microbús *m*. **~cab** *n* taxi *m*
minim /ˈmɪnɪm/ *n* (*mus*) blanca *f*
minim|al /ˈmɪnɪml/ *a* mínimo. **~ize** *vt* minimizar. **~um** *a & n* (*pl* **-ima**) mínimo (*m*)
mining /ˈmaɪnɪŋ/ *n* explotación *f*. ● *a* minero
miniskirt /ˈmɪnɪskɜ:t/ *n* minifalda *f*
minist|er /ˈmɪnɪstə(r)/ *n* ministro *m*; (*relig*) pastor *m*. **~erial** /-ˈstɪərɪəl/ *a* ministerial. **~ry** *n* ministerio *m*
mink /mɪŋk/ *n* visón *m*
minor /ˈmaɪnə(r)/ *a* (*incl mus*) menor; (*of little importance*) sin importancia. ● *n* menor *m & f* de edad
minority /maɪˈnɒrətɪ/ *n* minoría *f*. ● *a* minoritario
minster /ˈmɪnstə(r)/ *n* catedral *f*
minstrel /ˈmɪnstrəl/ *n* juglar *m*
mint[1] /mɪnt/ *n* (*plant*) menta *f*; (*sweet*) caramelo *m* de menta
mint[2] /mɪnt/ *n*. **the M~** *n* casa *f* de la moneda. **a ~** un dineral *m*. ● *vt* acuñar. **in ~ condition** como nuevo
minuet /mɪnjʊˈet/ *n* minué *m*
minus /ˈmaɪnəs/ *prep* menos; (*without, fam*) sin. ● *n* (*sign*) menos *m*. **~ sign** *n* menos *m*
minuscule /ˈmɪnəskju:l/ *a* minúsculo
minute[1] /ˈmɪnɪt/ *n* minuto *m*. **~s** *npl* (*of meeting*) actas *fpl*
minute[2] /maɪˈnju:t/ *a* minúsculo; (*detailed*) minucioso
minx /mɪŋks/ *n* chica *f* descarada
mirac|le /ˈmɪrəkl/ *n* milagro *m*. **~ulous** /mɪˈrækjʊləs/ *a* milagroso
mirage /ˈmɪrɑ:ʒ/ *n* espejismo *m*
mire /ˈmaɪə(r)/ *n* fango *m*
mirror /ˈmɪrə(r)/ *n* espejo *m*. ● *vt* reflejar
mirth /mɜ:θ/ *n* (*merriment*) alegría *f*; (*laughter*) risas *fpl*

misadventure /mɪsəd'ventʃə(r)/ *n* desgracia *f*
misanthropist /mɪ'zænθrəpɪst/ *n* misántropo *m*
misapprehension /mɪsæpri'henʃŋ/ *n* malentendido *m*
misbehav|e /mɪsbɪ'heɪv/ *vi* portarse mal. **~iour** *n* mala conducta *f*
miscalculat|e /mɪs'kælkjʊleɪt/ *vt/i* calcular mal. **~ion** /-'leɪʃn/ *n* desacierto *m*
miscarr|iage /'mɪskærɪdʒ/ *n* aborto *m*. **~iage of justice** *n* error *m* judicial. **~y** *vi* abortar
miscellaneous /mɪsə'leɪnɪəs/ *a* vario
mischief /'mɪstʃɪf/ *n* (*foolish conduct*) travesura *f*; (*harm*) daño *m*. **get into ~** cometer travesuras. **make ~** armar un lío
mischievous /'mɪstʃɪvəs/ *a* travieso; (*malicious*) perjudicial
misconception /mɪskən'sepʃn/ *n* equivocación *f*
misconduct /mɪs'kɒndʌkt/ *n* mala conducta *f*
misconstrue /mɪskən'stru:/ *vt* interpretar mal
misdeed /mɪs'di:d/ *n* fechoría *f*
misdemeanour /mɪsdɪ'mi:nə(r)/ *n* fechoría *f*
misdirect /mɪsdɪ'rekt/ *vt* dirigir mal ‹*person*›
miser /'maɪzə(r)/ *n* avaro *m*
miserable /'mɪzərəbl/ *a* (*sad*) triste; (*wretched*) miserable; ‹*weather*› malo
miserly /'maɪzəlɪ/ *a* avariento
misery /'mɪzərɪ/ *n* (*unhappiness*) tristeza *f*; (*pain*) sufrimiento *m*; (*poverty*) pobreza *f*; (*person, fam*) aguafiestas *m & f*
misfire /mɪs'faɪə(r)/ *vi* fallar
misfit /'mɪsfɪt/ *n* (*person*) inadaptado *m*; (*thing*) cosa *f* mal ajustada
misfortune /mɪs'fɔ:tʃu:n/ *n* desgracia *f*
misgiving /mɪs'gɪvɪŋ/ *n* (*doubt*) duda *f*; (*apprehension*) presentimiento *m*
misguided /mɪs'gaɪdɪd/ *a* equivocado. **be ~** equivocarse
mishap /'mɪshæp/ *n* desgracia *f*
misinform /mɪsɪn'fɔ:m/ *vt* informar mal
misinterpret /mɪsɪn'tɜ:prɪt/ *vt* interpretar mal
misjudge /mɪs'dʒʌdʒ/ *vt* juzgar mal
mislay /mɪs'leɪ/ *vt* (*pt* **mislaid**) extraviar
mislead /mɪs'li:d/ *vt* (*pt* **misled**) engañar. **~ing** *a* engañoso
mismanage /mɪs'mænɪdʒ/ *vt* administrar mal. **~ment** *n* mala administración *f*
misnomer /mɪs'nəʊmə(r)/ *n* nombre *m* equivocado
misplace /mɪs'pleɪs/ *vt* colocar mal; (*lose*) extraviar
misprint /'mɪsprɪnt/ *n* errata *f*
misquote /mɪs'kwəʊt/ *vt* citar mal
misrepresent /mɪsreprɪ'zent/ *vt* describir engañosamente
miss[1] /mɪs/ *vt* (*fail to hit*) errar; (*notice absence of*) echar de menos; perder ‹*train*›. **~ the point** no comprender. ● *n* fallo *m*. **~ out** omitir
miss[2] /mɪs/ *n* (*pl* **misses**) señorita *f*
misshapen /mɪs'ʃeɪpən/ *a* deforme
missile /'mɪsaɪl/ *n* proyectil *m*
missing /'mɪsɪŋ/ *a* ‹*person*› (*absent*) ausente; ‹*person*› (*after disaster*) desaparecido; (*lost*) perdido. **be ~** faltar
mission /'mɪʃn/ *n* misión *f*. **~ary** /'mɪʃənərɪ/ *n* misionero *m*
missive /'mɪsɪv/ *n* misiva *f*
misspell /mɪs'spel/ *vt* (*pt* **misspelt** *or* **misspelled**) escribir mal
mist /mɪst/ *n* neblina *f*; (*at sea*) bruma *f*. ● *vt/i* empañar(se)
mistake /mɪ'steɪk/ *n* error *m*. ● *vt* (*pt* **mistook**, *pp* **mistaken**) equivocarse de; (*misunderstand*) entender mal. **~ for** tomar por. **~n** /-ən/ *a* equivocado. **be ~n** equivocarse. **~nly** *adv* equivocadamente
mistletoe /'mɪsltəʊ/ *n* muérdago *m*
mistreat /mɪs'tri:t/ *vt* maltratar
mistress /'mɪstrɪs/ *n* (*of house*) señora *f*; (*primary school teacher*) maestra *f*; (*secondary school teacher*) profesora *f*; (*lover*) amante *f*
mistrust /mɪs'trʌst/ *vt* desconfiar de. ● *n* desconfianza *f*
misty /'mɪstɪ/ *a* (**-ier, -iest**) nebuloso; ‹*day*› de niebla; ‹*glass*› empañado. **it is ~** hay neblina
misunderstand /mɪsʌndə'stænd/ *vt* (*pt* **-stood**) entender mal. **~ing** *n* malentendido *m*
misuse /mɪs'ju:z/ *vt* emplear mal; abusar de ‹*power etc*›. /mɪs'ju:s/ *n* mal uso *m*; (*unfair use*) abuso *m*
mite /maɪt/ *n* (*insect*) ácaro *m*, garrapata *f*; (*child*) niño *m* pequeño
mitigate /'mɪtɪgeɪt/ *vt* mitigar

mitre /ˈmaɪtə(r)/ *n* (*head-dress*) mitra *f*
mitten /ˈmɪtn/ *n* manopla *f*; (*leaving fingers exposed*) mitón *m*
mix /mɪks/ *vt/i* mezclar(se). **~ up** mezclar; (*confuse*) confundir. **~ with** frecuentar ‹*people*›. ● *n* mezcla *f*
mixed /mɪkst/ *a* ‹*school etc*› mixto; (*assorted*) variado. **be ~ up** estar confuso
mixer /ˈmɪksə(r)/ *n* (*culin*) batidora *f*. **be a good ~** tener don de gentes
mixture /ˈmɪkstʃə(r)/ *n* mezcla *f*
mix-up /ˈmɪksʌp/ *n* lío *m*
moan /məʊn/ *n* gemido *m*. ● *vi* gemir; (*complain*) quejarse (**about** de). **~er** *n* refunfuñador *m*
moat /məʊt/ *n* foso *m*
mob /mɒb/ *n* (*crowd*) muchedumbre *f*; (*gang*) pandilla *f*; (*masses*) populacho *m*. ● *vt* (*pt* **mobbed**) acosar
mobil|e /ˈməʊbaɪl/ *a* móvil. **~e home** *n* caravana *f*. ● *n* móvil *m*. **~ity** /məˈbɪlətɪ/ *n* movilidad *f*
mobiliz|ation /məʊbɪlaɪˈzeɪʃn/ *n* movilización *f*. **~e** /ˈməʊbɪlaɪz/ *vt/i* movilizar
moccasin /ˈmɒkəsɪn/ *n* mocasín *m*
mocha /ˈmɒkə/ *n* moca *m*
mock /mɒk/ *vt* burlarse de. ● *vi* burlarse. ● *a* fingido
mockery /ˈmɒkərɪ/ *n* burla *f*. **a ~ of** una parodia *f* de
mock-up /ˈmɒkʌp/ *n* maqueta *f*
mode /məʊd/ *n* (*way, method*) modo *m*; (*fashion*) moda *f*
model /ˈmɒdl/ *n* modelo *m*; (*mock-up*) maqueta *f*; (*for fashion*) maniquí *m*. ● *a* (*exemplary*) ejemplar; ‹*car etc*› en miniatura. ● *vt* (*pt* **modelled**) modelar; presentar ‹*clothes*›. ● *vi* ser maniquí; (*pose*) posar. **~ling** *n* profesión *f* de maniquí
moderate /ˈmɒdərət/ *a* & *n* moderado (*m*). /ˈmɒdəreɪt/ *vt/i* moderar(se). **~ly** /ˈmɒdərətlɪ/ *adv* (*in moderation*) moderadamente; (*fairly*) medianamente
moderation /mɒdəˈreɪʃn/ *n* moderación *f*. **in ~** con moderación
modern /ˈmɒdn/ *a* moderno. **~ize** *vt* modernizar
modest /ˈmɒdɪst/ *a* modesto. **~y** *n* modestia *f*
modicum /ˈmɒdɪkəm/ *n*. **a ~ of** un poquito *m* de
modif|ication /mɒdɪfɪˈkeɪʃn/ *n* modificación *f*. **~y** /-faɪ/ *vt/i* modificar(se)
modulat|e /ˈmɒdjʊleɪt/ *vt/i* modular. **~ion** /-ˈleɪʃn/ *n* modulación *f*
module /ˈmɒdju:l/ *n* módulo *m*
mogul /ˈməʊgəl/ *n* (*fam*) magnate *m*
mohair /ˈməʊheə(r)/ *n* mohair *m*
moist /mɔɪst/ *a* (**-er**, **-est**) húmedo. **~en** /ˈmɔɪsn/ *vt* humedecer
moistur|e /ˈmɔɪstʃə(r)/ *n* humedad *f*. **~ize** /ˈmɔɪstʃəraɪz/ *vt* humedecer. **~izer** *n* crema *f* hidratante
molar /ˈməʊlə(r)/ *n* muela *f*
molasses /məˈlæsɪz/ *n* melaza *f*
mold /məʊld/ (*Amer*) = **mould**
mole[1] /məʊl/ *n* (*animal*) topo *m*
mole[2] /məʊl/ *n* (*on skin*) lunar *m*
mole[3] /məʊl/ *n* (*breakwater*) malecón *m*
molecule /ˈmɒlɪkju:l/ *n* molécula *f*
molehill /ˈməʊlhɪl/ *n* topera *f*
molest /məˈlest/ *vt* importunar
mollify /ˈmɒlɪfaɪ/ *vt* apaciguar
mollusc /ˈmɒləsk/ *n* molusco *m*
mollycoddle /ˈmɒlɪkɒdl/ *vt* mimar
molten /ˈməʊltən/ *a* fundido
mom /mɒm/ *n* (*Amer*) mamá *f*
moment /ˈməʊmənt/ *n* momento *m*. **~arily** /ˈməʊməntərɪlɪ/ *adv* momentáneamente. **~ary** *a* momentáneo
momentous /məˈmentəs/ *a* importante
momentum /məˈmentəm/ *n* momento *m*; (*speed*) velocidad *f*; (*fig*) ímpetu *m*
Monaco /ˈmɒnəkəʊ/ *n* Mónaco *m*
monarch /ˈmɒnək/ *n* monarca *m*. **~ist** *n* monárquico *m*. **~y** *n* monarquía *f*
monast|ery /ˈmɒnəstərɪ/ *n* monasterio *m*. **~ic** /məˈnæstɪk/ *a* monástico
Monday /ˈmʌndeɪ/ *n* lunes *m*
monetar|ist /ˈmʌnɪtərɪst/ *n* monetarista *m* & *f*. **~y** *a* monetario
money /ˈmʌnɪ/ *n* dinero *m*. **~-box** *n* hucha *f*. **~ed** *a* adinerado. **~-lender** *n* prestamista *m* & *f*. **~ order** *n* giro *m* postal. **~s** *npl* cantidades *fpl* de dinero. **~spinner** *n* mina *f* de dinero
mongol /ˈmɒŋgl/ *n* & *a* (*med*) mongólico (*m*)
mongrel /ˈmʌŋgrəl/ *n* perro *m* mestizo
monitor /ˈmɒnɪtə(r)/ *n* (*pupil*) monitor *m* & *f*; (*tec*) monitor *m*. ● *vt* controlar; escuchar ‹*a broadcast*›

monk /mʌŋk/ *n* monje *m*
monkey /'mʌŋkɪ/ *n* mono *m*. **~-nut** *n* cacahuete *m*, maní *m* (*LAm*). **~-wrench** *n* llave *f* inglesa
mono /'mɒnəʊ/ *a* monofónico
monocle /'mɒnəkl/ *n* monóculo *m*
monogram /'mɒnəgræm/ *n* monograma *m*
monologue /'mɒnəlɒg/ *n* monólogo *m*
monopol|ize /mə'nɒpəlaɪz/ *vt* monopolizar. **~y** *n* monopolio *m*
monosyllab|ic /mɒnəsɪ'læbɪk/ *a* monosilábico. **~le** /-'sɪləbl/ *n* monosílabo *m*
monotone /'mɒnətəʊn/ *n* monotonía *f*. **speak in a ~** hablar con una voz monótona
monoton|ous /mə'nɒtənəs/ *a* monótono. **~y** *n* monotonía *f*
monsoon /mɒn'su:n/ *n* monzón *m*
monster /'mɒnstə(r)/ *n* monstruo *m*
monstrosity /mɒn'strɒsətɪ/ *n* monstruosidad *f*
monstrous /'mɒnstrəs/ *a* monstruoso
montage /mɒn'tɑ:ʒ/ *n* montaje *m*
month /mʌnθ/ *n* mes *m*. **~ly** /'mʌnθlɪ/ *a* mensual. ● *adv* mensualmente. ● *n* (*periodical*) revista *f* mensual
monument /'mɒnjʊmənt/ *n* monumento *m*. **~al** /-'mentl/ *a* monumental
moo /mu:/ *n* mugido *m*. ● *vi* mugir
mooch /mu:tʃ/ *vi* (*sl*) haraganear. ● *vt* (*Amer*, *sl*) birlar
mood /mu:d/ *n* humor *m*. **be in the ~ for** tener ganas de. **in a good/bad ~** de buen/mal humor. **~y** *a* (**-ier**, **-iest**) de humor cambiadizo; (*bad-tempered*) malhumorado
moon /mu:n/ *n* luna *f*. **~light** *n* luz *f* de la luna. **~lighting** *n* (*fam*) pluriempleo *m*. **~lit** *a* iluminado por la luna; ‹*night*› de luna
moor[1] /mʊə(r)/ *n* (*open land*) páramo *m*
moor[2] /mʊə(r)/ *vt* amarrar. **~ings** *npl* (*ropes*) amarras *fpl*; (*place*) amarradero *m*
Moor /mʊə(r)/ *n* moro *m*
moose /mu:s/ *n invar* alce *m*
moot /mu:t/ *a* discutible. ● *vt* proponer ‹*question*›
mop /mɒp/ *n* fregona *f*. **~ of hair** pelambrera *f*. ● *vt* (*pt* **mopped**) fregar. **~ (up)** limpiar
mope /məʊp/ *vi* estar abatido
moped /'məʊped/ *n* ciclomotor *m*
moral /'mɒrəl/ *a* moral. ● *n* moraleja *f*. **~s** *npl* moralidad *f*
morale /mə'rɑ:l/ *n* moral *f*
moral|ist /'mɒrəlɪst/ *n* moralista *m & f*. **~ity** /mə'rælətɪ/ *n* moralidad *f*. **~ize** *vi* moralizar. **~ly** *adv* moralmente
morass /mə'ræs/ *n* (*marsh*) pantano *m*; (*fig*, *entanglement*) embrollo *m*
morbid /'mɔ:bɪd/ *a* morboso
more /mɔ:(r)/ *a & n & adv* más. **~ and ~** cada vez más. **~ or less** más o menos. **once ~** una vez más. **some ~** más
moreover /mɔ:'rəʊvə(r)/ *adv* además
morgue /mɔ:g/ *n* depósito *m* de cadáveres
moribund /'mɒrɪbʌnd/ *a* moribundo
morning /'mɔ:nɪŋ/ *n* mañana *f*; (*early hours*) madrugada *f*. **at 11 o'clock in the ~** a las once de la mañana. **in the ~** por la mañana
Morocc|an /mə'rɒkən/ *a &* n marroquí (*m & f*). **~o** /-kəʊ/ *n* Marruecos *mpl*
moron /'mɔ:rɒn/ *n* imbécil *m & f*
morose /mə'rəʊs/ *a* malhumorado
morphine /'mɔ:fi:n/ *n* morfina *f*
Morse /mɔ:s/ *n* Morse *m*. **~ (code)** *n* alfabeto *m* Morse
morsel /'mɔ:sl/ *n* pedazo *m*; (*mouthful*) bocado *m*
mortal /'mɔ:tl/ *a & n* mortal (*m*). **~ity** /-'tælətɪ/ *n* mortalidad *f*
mortar /'mɔ:tə(r)/ *n* (*all senses*) mortero *m*
mortgage /'mɔ:gɪdʒ/ *n* hipoteca *f*. ● *vt* hipotecar
mortify /'mɔ:tɪfaɪ/ *vt* mortificar
mortuary /'mɔ:tjʊərɪ/ *n* depósito *m* de cadáveres
mosaic /məʊ'zeɪk/ *n* mosaico *m*
Moscow /'mɒskəʊ/ *n* Moscú *m*
Moses /'məʊzɪz/ *a*. **~ basket** *n* moisés *m*
mosque /mɒsk/ *n* mezquita *f*
mosquito /mɒs'ki:təʊ/ *n* (*pl* **-oes**) mosquito *m*
moss /mɒs/ *n* musgo *m*. **~y** *a* musgoso
most /məʊst/ *a* más. **for the ~ part** en su mayor parte. ● *n* la mayoría *f*. **~ of** la mayor parte de. **at ~** a lo más. **make the ~ of** aprovechar al máximo. ● *adv* más; (*very*) muy. **~ly** *adv* principalmente

MOT *abbr* (*Ministry of Transport*). **~ (test)** ITV, inspección *f* técnica de vehículos

motel /məʊ'tel/ *n* motel *m*

moth /mɒθ/ *n* mariposa *f* (nocturna); (*in clothes*) polilla *f*. **~-ball** *n* bola *f* de naftalina. **~-eaten** *a* apolillado

mother /'mʌðə(r)/ *n* madre *f*. ● *vt* cuidar como a un hijo. **~hood** *n* maternidad *f*. **~-in-law** *n* (*pl* **~s-in-law**) suegra *f*. **~land** *n* patria *f*. **~ly** *adv* maternalmente. **~-of-pearl** *n* nácar *m*. **M~'s Day** *n* el día *m* de la Madre. **~-to-be** *n* futura madre *f*. **~ tongue** *n* lengua *f* materna

motif /məʊ'ti:f/ *n* motivo *m*

motion /'məʊʃn/ *n* movimiento *m*; (*proposal*) moción *f*. ● *vt/i*. **~ (to) s.o. to** hacer señas a uno para que. **~less** *a* inmóvil

motivat|e /'məʊtɪveɪt/ *vt* motivar. **~ion** /-'veɪʃn/ *n* motivación *f*

motive /'məʊtɪv/ *n* motivo *m*

motley /'mɒtlɪ/ *a* abigarrado

motor /'məʊtə(r)/ *n* motor *m*; (*car*) coche *m*. ● *a* motor; (*fem*) motora, motriz. ● *vi* ir en coche. **~ bike** *n* (*fam*) motocicleta *f*, moto *f* (*fam*). **~ boat** *n* lancha *f* motora. **~cade** /'məʊtəkeɪd/ *n* (*Amer*) desfile *m* de automóviles. **~ car** *n* coche *m*, automóvil *m*. **~ cycle** *n* motocicleta *f*. **~cyclist** *n* motociclista *m* & *f*. **~ing** *n* automovilismo *m*. **~ist** *n* automovilista *m* & *f*. **~ize** *vt* motorizar. **~way** *n* autopista *f*

mottled /'mɒtld/ *a* abigarrado

motto /'mɒtəʊ/ *n* (*pl* **-oes**) lema *m*

mould[1] /məʊld/ *n* molde *m*. ● *vt* moldear

mould[2] /məʊld/ *n* (*fungus, rot*) moho *m*

moulding /'məʊldɪŋ/ *n* (*on wall etc*) moldura *f*

mouldy /'məʊldɪ/ *a* mohoso

moult /məʊlt/ *vi* mudar

mound /maʊnd/ *n* montículo *m*; (*pile, fig*) montón *m*

mount[1] /maʊnt/ *vt/i* subir. ● *n* montura *f*. **~ up** aumentar

mount[2] /maʊnt/ *n* (*hill*) monte *m*

mountain /'maʊntɪn/ *n* montaña *f*. **~eer** /maʊntɪ'nɪə(r)/ *n* alpinista *m* & *f*. **~eering** *n* alpinismo *m*. **~ous** /'maʊntɪnəs/ *a* montañoso

mourn /mɔ:n/ *vt* llorar. ● *vi* lamentarse. **~ for** llorar la muerte de. **~er** *n* persona *f* que acompaña el cortejo fúnebre. **~ful** *a* triste. **~ing** *n* luto *m*

mouse /maʊs/ *n* (*pl* **mice**) ratón *m*. **~trap** *n* ratonera *f*

mousse /mu:s/ *n* (*dish*) crema *f* batida

moustache /mə'stɑ:ʃ/ *n* bigote *m*

mousy /'maʊsɪ/ *a* ‹*hair*› pardusco; (*fig*) tímido

mouth /maʊð/ *vt* formar con los labios. /maʊθ/ *n* boca *f*. **~ful** *n* bocado *m*. **~-organ** *n* armónica *f*. **~piece** *n* (*mus*) boquilla *f*; (*fig, person*) portavoz *f*, vocero *m* (*LAm*). **~wash** *n* enjuague *m*

movable /'mu:vəbl/ *a* móvil, movible

move /mu:v/ *vt* mover; mudarse de ‹*house*›; (*with emotion*) conmover; (*propose*) proponer. ● *vi* moverse; (*be in motion*) estar en movimiento; (*progress*) hacer progresos; (*take action*) tomar medidas; (*depart*) irse. **~ (out)** irse. ● *n* movimiento *m*; (*in game*) jugada *f*; (*player's turn*) turno *m*; (*removal*) mudanza *f*. **on the ~** en movimiento. **~ along** (hacer) circular. **~ away** alejarse. **~ back** (hacer) retroceder. **~ forward** (hacer) avanzar. **~ in** instalarse. **~ on** (hacer) circular. **~ over** apartarse. **~ment** /'mu:vmənt/ *n* movimiento *m*

movie /'mu:vɪ/ *n* (*Amer*) película *f*. **the ~s** *npl* el cine *m*

moving /'mu:vɪŋ/ *a* en movimiento; (*touching*) conmovedor

mow /məʊ/ *vt* (*pt* **mowed** *or* **mown**) segar. **~ down** derribar. **~er** *n* (*for lawn*) cortacésped *m inv*

MP *abbr see* **Member of Parliament**

Mr /'mɪstə(r)/ *abbr* (*pl* **Messrs**) (*Mister*) señor *m*. **~ Coldbeck** (el) Sr. Coldbeck

Mrs /'mɪsɪz/ *abbr* (*pl* **Mrs**) (*Missis*) señora *f*. **~ Andrews** (la) Sra. Andrews. **the ~ Andrews** (las) Sras. Andrews

Ms /mɪz/ *abbr* (*title of married or unmarried woman*) señora *f*, señorita. **Ms Lawton** (la) Sra. Lawton

much /mʌtʃ/ *a* & *n* mucho (*m*). ● *adv* mucho; (*before pp*) muy. **~ as** por mucho que. **~ the same** más o menos lo mismo. **so ~** tanto. **too ~** demasiado

muck /mʌk/ *n* estiércol *m*; (*dirt, fam*) suciedad *f*. ● *vi*. **~ about** (*sl*) perder el tiempo. **~ about with** (*sl*)

juguetear con. ● *vt*. ~ **up** (*sl*) echar a perder. ~ **in** (*sl*) participar. **~y** *a* sucio
mucus /'mju:kəs/ *n* moco *m*
mud /mʌd/ *n* lodo *m*, barro *m*
muddle /'mʌdl/ *vt* embrollar. ● *vi*. ~ **through** salir del paso. ● *n* desorden *m*; (*mix-up*) lío *m*
muddy /'mʌdɪ/ *a* lodoso; ‹*hands etc*› cubierto de lodo
mudguard /'mʌdgɑ:d/ *n* guardabarros *m invar*
muff /mʌf/ *n* manguito *m*
muffin /'mʌfɪn/ *n* mollete *m*
muffle /'mʌfl/ *vt* tapar; amortiguar ‹*a sound*›. **~r** *n* (*scarf*) bufanda *f*
mug /mʌg/ *n* tazón *m*; (*for beer*) jarra *f*; (*face, sl*) cara *f*, jeta *f* (*sl*); (*fool, sl*) primo *m*. ● *vt* (*pt* **mugged**) asaltar. **~ger** *n* asaltador *m*. **~ging** *n* asalto *m*
muggy /'mʌgɪ/ *a* bochornoso
Muhammadan /mə'hæmɪdən/ *a* & *n* mahometano (*m*)
mule[1] /mju:l/ *n* mula *f*, mulo *m*
mule[2] /mju:l/ *n* (*slipper*) babucha *f*
mull[1] /mʌl/ *vt*. ~ **over** reflexionar sobre
mull[2] /mʌl/ *vt* calentar con especias ‹*wine*›
multi... /'mʌltɪ/ *pref* multi...
multicoloured /mʌltɪ'kʌləd/ *a* multicolor
multifarious /mʌltɪ'feərɪəs/ *a* múltiple
multinational /mʌltɪ'næʃənl/ *a* & *n* multinacional (*f*)
multipl|e /'mʌltɪpl/ *a* & *n* múltiplo (*m*). **~ication** /mʌltɪplɪ'keɪʃn/ *n* multiplicación *f*. **~y** /'mʌltiplaɪ/ *vt/i* multiplicar(se)
multitude /'mʌltɪtju:d/ *n* multitud *f*
mum[1] /mʌm/ *n* (*fam*) mamá *f* (*fam*)
mum[2] /mʌm/ *a*. **keep** ~ (*fam*) guardar silencio
mumble /'mʌmbl/ *vt* decir entre dientes. ● *vi* hablar entre dientes
mummify /'mʌmɪfaɪ/ *vt/i* momificar(se)
mummy[1] /'mʌmɪ/ *n* (*mother, fam*) mamá *f* (*fam*)
mummy[2] /'mʌmɪ/ *n* momia *f*
mumps /mʌmps/ *n* paperas *fpl*
munch /mʌntʃ/ *vt/i* mascar
mundane /mʌn'deɪn/ *a* mundano
municipal /mju:'nɪsɪpl/ *a* municipal. **~ity** /-'pælətɪ/ *n* municipio *m*
munificent /mju:'nɪfɪsənt/ *a* munífico
munitions /mju:'nɪʃnz/ *npl* municiones *fpl*
mural /'mjʊərəl/ *a* & *n* mural (*f*)
murder /'mɜ:də(r)/ *n* asesinato *m*. ● *vt* asesinar. **~er** *n* asesino *m*. **~ess** *n* asesina *f*. **~ous** *a* homicida
murky /'mɜ:kɪ/ *a* (**-ier**, **-iest**) oscuro
murmur /'mɜ:mə(r)/ *n* murmullo *m*. ● *vt/i* murmurar
muscle /'mʌsl/ *n* músculo *m*. ● *vi*. ~ **in** (*Amer*, *sl*) meterse por fuerza en
muscular /'mʌskjʊlə(r)/ *a* muscular; (*having well-developed muscles*) musculoso
muse /mju:z/ *vi* meditar
museum /mju:'zɪəm/ *n* museo *m*
mush /mʌʃ/ *n* pulpa *f*
mushrom /'mʌʃrʊm/ *n* champiñón *m*; (*bot*) seta *f*. ● *vi* (*appear in large numbers*) crecer como hongos
mushy /'mʌʃɪ/ *a* pulposo
music /'mju:zɪk/ *n* música *f*. **~al** *a* musical; ‹*instrument*› de música; (*talented*) que tiene don de música. ● *n* comedia *f* musical. ~ **hall** *n* teatro *m* de variedades. **~ian** /mju:'zɪʃn/ *n* músico *m*
musk /mʌsk/ *n* almizcle *m*
Muslim /'mʊzlɪm/ *a* & *n* musulmán (*m*)
muslin /'mʌzlɪn/ *n* muselina *f*
musquash /'mʌskwɒʃ/ *n* ratón *m* almizclero
mussel /mʌsl/ *n* mejillón *m*
must /mʌst/ *v aux* deber, tener que. **he ~ be old** debe ser viejo. **I ~ have done it** debo haberlo hecho. **you ~ go** debes marcharte. ● *n*. **be a ~** ser imprescindible
mustard /'mʌstəd/ *n* mostaza *f*
muster /'mʌstə(r)/ *vt/i* reunir(se)
musty /'mʌstɪ/ *a* (**-ier**, **-iest**) que huele a cerrado
mutation /mju:'teɪʃn/ *n* mutación *f*
mute /mju:t/ *a* & *n* mudo (*m*). **~d** *a* ‹*sound*› sordo; ‹*criticism*› callado
mutilat|e /'mju:tɪleɪt/ *vt* mutilar. **~ion** /-'leɪʃn/ *n* mutilación *f*
mutin|ous /'mju:tɪnəs/ *a* ‹*sailor etc*› amotinado; (*fig*) rebelde. **~y** *n* motín *m*. ● *vi* amotinarse
mutter /'mʌtə(r)/ *vt/i* murmurar
mutton /'mʌtn/ *n* cordero *m*
mutual /'mju:tʃʊəl/ *a* mutuo; (*common, fam*) común. **~ly** *adv* mutuamente
muzzle /mʌzl/ *n* (*snout*) hocico *m*; (*device*) bozal *m*; (*of gun*) boca *f*. ● *vt* poner el bozal a

my /maɪ/ *a* mi, mis *pl*
myopic /maɪ'ɒpɪk/ *a* miope
myriad /'mɪrɪəd/ *n* miríada *f*
myself /maɪ'self/ *pron* yo mismo *m*, yo misma *f*; (*reflexive*) me; (*after prep*) mí (mismo) *m*, mí (misma) *f*
myster|ious /mɪ'stɪərɪəs/ *a* misterioso. **~y** /'mɪstərɪ/ *n* misterio *m*
mystic /'mɪstɪk/ *a* & *n* místico (*m*). **~al** *a* místico. **~ism** /-sɪzəm/ *n* misticismo *m*
mystif|ication /mɪstɪfɪ'keɪʃn/ *n* confusión *f*. **~y** /-faɪ/ *vt* dejar perplejo
mystique /mɪ'stiːk/ *n* mística *f*
myth /mɪθ/ *n* mito *m*. **~ical** *a* mítico. **~ology** /mɪ'θɒlədʒɪ/ *n* mitología *f*

N

N *abbr* (*north*) norte *m*
nab /næb/ *vt* (*pt* **nabbed**) (*arrest, sl*) coger (*not LAm*), agarrar (*esp LAm*)
nag /næg/ *vt* (*pt* **nagged**) fastidiar; (*scold*) regañar. ● *vi* criticar
nagging /'nægɪŋ/ *a* persistente, regañón
nail /neɪl/ *n* clavo *m*; (*of finger, toe*) uña *f*. **pay on the ~** pagar a tocateja. ● *vt* clavar. **~ polish** *n* esmalte *m* para las uñas
naïve /naɪ'iːv/ *a* ingenuo
naked /'neɪkɪd/ *a* desnudo. **to the ~ eye** a simple vista. **~ly** *adv* desnudamente. **~ness** *n* desnudez *f*
namby-pamby /næmbɪ'pæmbɪ/ *a* & *n* ñoño (*m*)
name /neɪm/ *n* nombre *m*; (*fig*) fama *f*. ● *vt* nombrar; (*fix*) fijar. **be ~d after** llevar el nombre de. **~less** *a* anónimo. **~ly** /'neɪmlɪ/ *adv* a saber. **~sake** /'neɪmseɪk/ *n* (*person*) tocayo *m*
nanny /'nænɪ/ *n* niñera *f*. **~-goat** *n* cabra *f*
nap[1] /næp/ *n* (*sleep*) sueñecito *m*; (*after lunch*) siesta *f*. ● *vi* (*pt* **napped**) echarse un sueño. **catch s.o. ~ping** coger a uno desprevenido
nap[2] /næp/ *n* (*fibres*) lanilla *f*
nape /neɪp/ *n* nuca *f*
napkin /'næpkɪn/ *n* (*at meals*) servilleta *f*; (*for baby*) pañal *m*
nappy /'næpɪ/ *n* pañal *m*
narcotic /nɑː'kɒtɪk/ *a* & *n* narcótico (*m*)
narrat|e /nə'reɪt/ *vt* contar. **~ion** /-ʃn/ *n* narración *f*. **~ive** /'nærətɪv/ *n* relato *m*. **~or** /nə'reɪtə(r)/ *n* narrador *m*
narrow /'nærəʊ/ *a* (**-er**, **-est**) estrecho. **have a ~ escape** escaparse por los pelos. ● *vt* estrechar; (*limit*) limitar. ● *vi* estrecharse. **~ly** *adv* estrechamente; (*just*) por poco. **~-minded** *a* de miras estrechas. **~ness** *n* estrechez *f*
nasal /'neɪzl/ *a* nasal
nast|ily /'nɑːstɪlɪ/ *adv* desagradablemente; (*maliciously*) con malevolencia. **~iness** *n* (*malice*) malevolencia *f*. **~y** *a* /'nɑːstɪ/ (**-ier**, **-iest**) desagradable; (*malicious*) malévolo; ‹*weather*› malo; ‹*taste, smell*› asqueroso; ‹*wound*› grave; ‹*person*› antipático
natal /'neɪtl *a* natal
nation /'neɪʃn/ *n* nación *f*
national /'næʃənl/ *a* nacional. ● *n* súbdito *m*. **~ anthem** *n* himno *m* nacional. **~ism** *n* nacionalismo *m*. **~ity** /næʃə'nælətɪ/ *n* nacionalidad *f*. **~ize** *vt* nacionalizar. **~ly** *adv* a nivel nacional
nationwide /'neɪʃnwaɪd/ *a* nacional
native /'neɪtɪv/ *n* natural *m* & *f*. **be a ~ of** ser natural de. ● *a* nativo; ‹*country, town*› natal; (*inborn*) innato. **~ speaker of Spanish** hispanohablante *m* & *f*. **~ language** *n* lengua *f* materna
Nativity /nə'tɪvətɪ/ *n*. **the ~** la Natividad *f*
NATO /'neɪtəʊ/ *abbr* (*North Atlantic Treaty Organization*) OTAN *f*, Organización *f* del Tratado del Atlántico Norte
natter /'nætə(r)/ *vi* (*fam*) charlar. ● *n* (*fam*) charla *f*
natural /'nætʃərəl/ *a* natural. **~ history** *n* historia *f* natural. **~ist** *n* naturalista *m* & *f*
naturaliz|ation /nætʃərəlaɪ'zeɪʃn/ *n* naturalización *f*. **~e** *vt* naturalizar
naturally /'nætʃərəlɪ/ *adv* (*of course*) naturalmente; (*by nature*) por naturaleza
nature /'neɪtʃə(r)/ *n* naturaleza *f*; (*kind*) género *m*; (*of person*) carácter *m*
naught /nɔːt/ *n* (*old use*) nada *f*; (*maths*) cero *m*
naught|ily /'nɔːtɪlɪ/ *adv* mal. **~y** *a* (**-ier**, **-iest**) malo; ‹*child*› travieso; ‹*joke*› verde

nause|a /'nɔ:zɪə/ *n* náusea *f*. **~ate** *vt* dar náuseas a. **~ous** *a* nauseabundo

nautical /'nɔ:tɪkl/ *a* náutico. **~ mile** *n* milla *f* marina

naval /'neɪvl/ *a* naval; ‹*officer*› de marina

Navarre /nə'vɑ:(r)/ *n* Navarra *f*. **~se** *a* navarro

nave /neɪv/ *n* (*of church*) nave *f*

navel /'neɪvl/ *n* ombligo *m*

navigable /'nævɪgəbl/ *a* navegable

navigat|e /'nævɪgeɪt/ *vt* navegar por ‹*sea etc*›; gobernar ‹*ship*›. ● *vi* navegar. **~ion** *n* navegación *f*. **~or** *n* navegante *m*

navvy /'nævɪ/ *n* peón *m* caminero

navy /'neɪvɪ/ *n* marina *f*. **~ (blue)** azul *m* marino

NE *abbr* (*north-east*) noreste *m*

near /'nɪə(r)/ *adv* cerca. **~ at hand** muy cerca. **~ by** *adv* cerca. **draw ~** acercarse. ● *prep*. **~ (to)** cerca de. ● *a* cercano. ● *vt* acercarse a. **~by** *a* cercano. **N~ East** *n* Oriente *m* Próximo. **~ly** /'nɪəlɪ/ *adv* casi. **not ~ly as pretty as** no es ni con mucho tan guapa como. **~ness** /'nɪənɪs/ *n* proximidad *f*

neat /ni:t/ *a* (**-er**, **-est**) pulcro; ‹*room etc*› bien arreglado; (*clever*) diestro; (*ingenious*) hábil; ‹*whisky, brandy etc*› solo. **~ly** *adv* pulcramente. **~ness** *n* pulcritud *f*

nebulous /'nebjʊləs/ *a* nebuloso

necessar|ies /'nesəsərɪz/ *npl* lo indispensable. **~ily** /nesə'serɪlɪ/ *adv* necesariamente. **~y** *a* necesario, imprescindible

necessit|ate /nə'sesɪteɪt/ *vt* necesitar. **~y** /nɪ'sesətɪ/ *n* necesidad *f*; (*thing*) cosa *f* indispensable

neck /nek/ *n* (*of person, bottle, dress*) cuello *m*; (*of animal*) pescuezo *m*. **~ and ~** parejos. **~lace** /'nekləs/ *n* collar *m*. **~line** *n* escote *m*. **~tie** n corbata *f*

nectar /'nektə(r)/ *n* néctar *m*

nectarine /nektə'ri:n/ *n* nectarina *f*

née /neɪ/ *a* de soltera

need /ni:d/ *n* necesidad *f*. ● *vt* necesitar; (*demand*) exigir. **you ~ not speak** no tienes que hablar

needle /'ni:dl/ *n* aguja *f*. ● *vt* (*annoy, fam*) pinchar

needless /'ni:dlɪs/ *a* innecesario. **~ly** *adv* innecesariamente

needlework /'ni:dlwɜ:k/ *n* costura *f*; (*embroidery*) bordado *m*

needy /'ni:dɪ/ *a* (**-ier**, **-iest**) necesitado

negation /nɪ'geɪʃn/ *n* negación *f*

negative /'negətɪv/ *a* negativo. ● *n* (*of photograph*) negativo *m*; (*word, gram*) negativa *f*. **~ly** *adv* negativamente

neglect /nɪ'glekt/ *vt* descuidar; no cumplir con ‹*duty*›. **~ to do** dejar de hacer. ● *n* descuido *m*, negligencia *f*. **(state of) ~** abandono *m*. **~ful** *a* descuidado

négligé /'neglɪʒeɪ/ *n* bata *f*, salto *m* de cama

negligen|ce /'neglidʒəns/ *n* negligencia *f*, descuido *m*. **~t** *a* descuidado

negligible /'neglɪdʒəbl/ *a* insignificante

negotiable /nɪ'gəʊʃəbl/ *a* negociable

negotiat|e /nɪ'gəʊʃɪeɪt/ *vt/i* negociar. **~ion** /-'eɪʃn/ *n* negociación *f*. **~or** *n* negociador *m*

Negr|ess /'ni:grɪs/ *n* negra *f*. **~o** *n* (*pl* **-oes**) negro *m*. ● *a* negro

neigh /neɪ/ *n* relincho *m*. ● *vi* relinchar

neighbour /'neɪbə(r)/ *n* vecino *m*. **~hood** *n* vecindad *f*, barrio *m*. **in the ~hood of** alrededor de. **~ing** *a* vecino. **~ly** /'neɪbəlɪ/ *a* amable

neither /'naɪðə(r)/ *a & pron* ninguno *m* de los dos, ni el uno *m* ni el otro *m*. ● *adv* ni. **~ big nor small** ni grande ni pequeño. **~ shall I come** no voy yo tampoco. ● *conj* tampoco

neon /'ni:ɒn/ *n* neón *m*. ● *a* ‹*lamp etc*› de neón

nephew /'nevju:/ *n* sobrino *m*

nepotism /'nepətɪzəm/ *m* nepotismo *m*

nerve /nɜ:v/ *n* nervio *m*; (*courage*) valor *m*; (*calm*) sangre *f* fría; (*impudence, fam*) descaro *m*. **~-racking** *a* exasperante. **~s** *npl* (*before exams etc*) nervios *mpl*

nervous /'nɜ:vəs/ *a* nervioso. **be/feel ~** (*afraid*) tener miedo (**of** a). **~ly** *adv* (*tensely*) nerviosamente; (*timidly*) tímidamente. **~ness** *n* nerviosidad *f*; (*fear*) miedo *m*

nervy /'nɜ:vɪ/ *a see* **nervous**; (*Amer, fam*) descarado

nest /nest/ *n* nido *m*. ● *vi* anidar. **~-egg** *n* (*money*) ahorros *mpl*

nestle /'nesl/ *vi* acomodarse. **~ up to** arrimarse a

net /net/ *n* red *f*. ● *vt* (*pt* **netted**) coger (*not LAm*), agarrar (*esp LAm*). ● *a* (*weight etc*) neto
netball /'netbɔ:l/ *n* baloncesto *m*
Netherlands /'neðələndz/ *npl*. **the ~** los Países *mpl* Bajos
netting /'netɪŋ/ *n* (*nets*) redes *fpl*; (*wire*) malla *f*; (*fabric*) tul *m*
nettle /'netl/ *n* ortiga *f*
network /'netwɜ:k/ *n* red *f*
neuralgia /njʊə'rældʒɪə/ *n* neuralgia *f*
neuro|sis /njʊə'rəʊsɪs/ *n* (*pl* **-oses** /-si:z/) neurosis *f*. **~tic** *a & n* neurótico (*m*)
neuter /'nju:tə(r)/ *a & n* neutro (*m*). ● *vt* castrar ‹*animals*›
neutral /'nju:trəl/ *a* neutral; ‹*colour*› neutro; (*elec*) neutro. **~ (gear)** (*auto*) punto *m* muerto. **~ity** /-'trælətɪ/ *n* neutralidad *f*
neutron /'nju:trɒn/ *n* neutrón *m*. **~ bomb** *n* bomba *f* de neutrones
never /nevə(r)/ *adv* nunca, jamás; (*not, fam*) no. **~ again** nunca más. **~ mind** (*don't worry*) no te preocupes, no se preocupe; (*it doesn't matter*) no importa. **he ~ smiles** no sonríe nunca. **I ~ saw him** (*fam*) no le vi. **~-ending** *a* interminable
nevertheless /nevəðə'les/ *adv* sin embargo, no obstante
new /nju:/ *a* (**-er**, **-est**) (*new to owner*) nuevo (*placed before noun*); (*brand new*) nuevo (*placed after noun*). **~-born** *a* recién nacido. **~comer** *n* recién llegado *m*. **~fangled** *a* (*pej*) moderno. **~-laid egg** *n* huevo *m* fresco. **~ly** *adv* nuevamente; (*recently*) recién. **~ly-weds** *npl* recién casados *mpl*. **~ moon** *n* luna *f* nueva. **~ness** *n* novedad *f*
news /nju:z/ *n* noticias *fpl*; (*broadcasting, press*) informaciones *fpl*; (*on TV*) telediario *m*; (*on radio*) diario *m* hablado. **~agent** *n* vendedor *m* de periódicos. **~caster** *n* locutor *m*. **~letter** *n* boletín *m*. **~paper** *n* periódico *m*. **~-reader** *n* locutor *m*. **~reel** *n* noticiario *m*, nodo *m* (*in Spain*)
newt /nju:t/ *n* tritón *m*
new year /nju:'jɪə(r)/ *n* año *m* nuevo. **N~'s Day** *n* día *m* de Año Nuevo. **N~'s Eve** *n* noche *f* vieja
New Zealand /nju:'zi:lənd/ *n* Nueva Zelanda *f*. **~er** *n* neozelandés *m*
next /nekst/ *a* próximo; ‹*week, month etc*› que viene, próximo; (*adjoining*) vecino; (*following*) siguiente. ● *adv* la próxima vez; (*afterwards*) después. ● *n* siguiente *m*. **~ to** junto a. **~ to nothing** casi nada. **~ door** al lado (**to** de). **~-door** de al lado. **~-best** mejor alternativa *f*. **~ of kin** *n* pariente *m* más próximo, parientes *mpl* más próximos
nib /nɪb/ *n* (*of pen*) plumilla *f*
nibble /'nɪbl/ *vt/i* mordisquear. ● *n* mordisco *m*
nice /naɪs/ *a* (**-er**, **-est**) agradable; (*likeable*) simpático; (*kind*) amable; (*pretty*) bonito; ‹*weather*› bueno; (*subtle*) sutil. **~ly** *adv* agradablemente; (*kindly*) amablemente; (*well*) bien
nicety /'naɪsətɪ/ *n* (*precision*) precisión *f*; (*detail*) detalle. **to a ~** exactamente
niche /nɪtʃ, ni:ʃ/ *n* (*recess*) nicho *m*; (*fig*) buena posición *f*
nick /nɪk/ *n* corte *m* pequeño; (*prison, sl*) cárcel *f*. **in the ~ of time** justo a tiempo. ● *vt* (*steal, arrest, sl*) birlar
nickel /'nɪkl/ *n* níquel *m*; (*Amer*) moneda *f* de cinco centavos
nickname /'nɪkneɪm/ *n* apodo *m*; (*short form*) diminutivo *m*. ● *vt* apodar
nicotine /'nɪkəti:n/ *n* nicotina *f*
niece /ni:s/ *n* sobrina *f*
nifty /'nɪftɪ/ *a* (*sl*) (*smart*) elegante
Nigeria /naɪ'dʒɪərɪə/ *n* Nigeria *f*. **~n** *a & n* nigeriano (*m*)
niggardly /'nɪgədlɪ/ *a* ‹*person*› tacaño; ‹*thing*› miserable
niggling /'nɪglɪŋ/ *a* molesto
night /naɪt/ *n* noche *f*; (*evening*) tarde *f*. ● *a* nocturno, de noche. **~-cap** *n* (*hat*) gorro *m* de dormir; (*drink*) bebida *f* (tomada antes de acostarse). **~-club** *n* sala *f* de fiestas, boîte *f*. **~-dress** *n* camisón *m*. **~fall** *n* anochecer *m*. **~-gown** *n* camisón *m*
nightingale /'naɪtɪŋgeɪl/ *n* ruiseñor *m*
night: **~-life** *n* vida *f* nocturna. **~ly** *adv* todas las noches. **~mare** *n* pesadilla *f*. **~-school** *n* escuela *f* nocturna. **~-time** *n* noche *f*. **~-watchman** *n* sereno *m*
nil /nɪl/ *n* nada *f*; (*sport*) cero *m*
nimble /'nɪmbl/ *a* (**-er**, **-est**) ágil
nine /naɪn/ *a & n* nueve (*m*)
nineteen /naɪn'ti:n/ *a & n* diecinueve (*m*). **~th** *a & n* diecinueve (*m*), decimonoveno (*m*)

ninet|ieth /'naɪntɪəθ/ *a* noventa, nonagésimo. **~y** *a & n* noventa (*m*)
ninth /'naɪnθ/ *a & n* noveno (*m*)
nip[1] /nɪp/ *vt* (*pt* **nipped**) (*pinch*) pellizcar; (*bite*) mordisquear. ● *vi* (*rush, sl*) correr. ● *n* (*pinch*) pellizco *m*; (*cold*) frío *m*
nip[2] /nɪp/ *n* (*of drink*) trago *m*
nipper /'nɪpə(r)/ *n* (*sl*) chaval *m*
nipple /'nɪpl/ *n* pezón *m*; (*of baby's bottle*) tetilla *f*
nippy /'nɪpɪ/ *a* (**-ier**, **-iest**) (*nimble, fam*) ágil; (*quick, fam*) rápido; (*chilly, fam*) fresquito
nitrogen /'naɪtrədʒən/ *n* nitrógeno *m*
nitwit /'nɪtwɪt/ *n* (*fam*) imbécil *m & f*
no /nəʊ/ *a* ninguno. **~ entry** prohibido el paso. **~ man's land** *n* tierra *f* de nadie. **~ smoking** se prohibe fumar. **~ way!** (*Amer, fam*) ¡ni hablar! ● *adv* no. ● *n* (*pl* **noes**) no *m*
nobility /nəʊ'bɪlətɪ/ *n* nobleza *f*
noble /nəʊbl/ *a* (**-er**, **-est**) noble. **~man** *n* noble *m*
nobody /'nəʊbədɪ/ *pron* nadie *m*. ● *n* nadie *m*. **~ is there** no hay nadie. **he knows ~** no conoce a nadie
nocturnal /nɒk'tɜ:nl/ *a* nocturno
nod /nɒd/ *vt* (*pt* **nodded**). **~ one's head** asentir con la cabeza. ● *vi* (*in agreement*) asentir con la cabeza; (*in greeting*) saludar; (*be drowsy*) dar cabezadas. ● *n* inclinación *f* de cabeza
nodule /'nɒdju:l/ *n* nódulo *m*
nois|e /nɔɪz/ *n* ruido *m*. **~eless** *a* silencioso. **~ily** /'nɔɪzɪlɪ/ *adv* ruidosamente. **~y** *a* (**-ier, -iest**) ruidoso
nomad /'nəʊmæd/ *n* nómada *m & f*. **~ic** /-'mædɪk/ *a* nómada
nominal /'nɒmɪnl/ *a* nominal
nominat|e /'nɒmɪneɪt/ *vt* nombrar; (*put forward*) proponer. **~ion** /-'neɪʃn/ *n* nombramiento *m*
non-... /nɒn/ pref *no* ...
nonagenarian /nəʊnədʒɪ'neərɪən/ *a & n* nonagenario (*m*), noventón (*m*)
nonchalant /'nɒnʃələnt/ *a* imperturbable
non-commissioned /nɒnkə'mɪʃnd/ *a*. **~ officer** *n* suboficial *m*
non-comittal /nɒnkə'mɪtl/ *a* evasivo
nondescript /'nɒndɪskrɪpt/ *a* inclasificable, anodino
none /nʌn/ *pron* (*person*) nadie, ninguno; (*thing*) ninguno, nada. **~ of** nada de. **~ of us** ninguno de nosotros. **I have ~** no tengo nada. ● *adv* no, de ninguna manera. **he is ~ the happier** no está más contento
nonentity /nɒ'nentətɪ/ *n* nulidad *f*
non-existent /nɒnɪg'zɪstənt/ *a* inexistente
nonplussed /nɒn'plʌst/ *a* perplejo
nonsens|e /'nɒnsns/ *n* tonterías *fpl*, disparates *mpl*. **~ical** /-'sensɪkl/ *a* absurdo
non-smoker /nɒn'sməʊkə(r)/ *n* persona *f* que no fuma; (*rail*) departamento *m* de no fumadores
non-starter /nɒn'stɑ:tə(r)/ *n* (*fam*) proyecto *m* imposible
non-stop /nɒn'stɒp/ *a* ‹*train*› directo; ‹*flight*› sin escalas. ● *adv* sin parar; (*by train*) directamente; (*by air*) sin escalas
noodles /'nu:dlz/ *npl* fideos *mpl*
nook /nʊk/ *n* rincón *m*
noon /nu:n/ *n* mediodía *m*
no-one /'nəʊwʌn/ *pron* nadie. *see* **nobody**
noose /nu:s/ *n* nudo *m* corredizo
nor /nɔ:(r)/ *conj* ni, tampoco. **neither blue ~ red** ni azul ni rojo. **he doesn't play the piano, ~ do I** no sabe tocar el piano, ni yo tampoco
Nordic /'nɔ:dɪk/ *a* nórdico
norm /nɔ:m/ *n* norma *f*; (*normal*) lo normal
normal /'nɔ:ml/ *a* normal. **~cy** *n* (*Amer*) normalidad *f*. **~ity** /-'mælətɪ/ *n* normalidad *f*. **~ly** *adv* normalmente
Norman /'nɔ:mən/ *a & n* normando (*m*)
Normandy /'nɔ:məndɪ/ *n* Normandia *f*
north /nɔ:θ/ *n* norte *m*. ● *a* del norte, norteño. ● *adv* hacia el norte. **N~ America** *n* América *f* del Norte, Norteamérica *f*. **N~ American** *a & n* norteamericano (*m*). **~-east** *n* nordeste *m*. **~erly** /'nɔ:ðəlɪ/ *a* del norte. **~ern** /'nɔ:ðən/ *a* del norte. **~erner** *n* norteño *m*. **N~ Sea** *n* mar *m* del Norte. **~ward** *a* hacia el norte. **~wards** *adv* hacia el norte. **~west** *n* noroeste *m*
Norw|ay /'nɔ:weɪ/ *n* Noruega *f*. **~egian** *a & n* noruego (*m*)
nose /nəʊz/ *n* nariz *f*. ● *vi*. **~ about** curiosear. **~bleed** *n* hemorragia *f* nasal. **~dive** *n* picado *m*
nostalgi|a /nɒ'stældʒə/ *n* nostalgia *f*. **~c** *a* nostálgico

nostril /ˈnɒstrɪl/ *n* nariz *f*; (*of horse*) ollar *m*

nosy /ˈnəʊzɪ/ *a* (**-ier**, **-iest**) (*fam*) entrometido

not /nɒt/ *adv* no. **~ at all** no... nada; (*after thank you*) de nada. **~ yet** aún no. **I do ~ know** no sé. **I suppose ~** supongo que no

notabl|e /ˈnəʊtəbl/ *a* notable. ● *n* (*person*) notabilidad *f*. **~y** /ˈnəʊtəblɪ/ *adv* notablemente

notary /ˈnəʊtərɪ/ *n* notario *m*

notation /nəʊˈteɪʃn/ *n* notación *f*

notch /nɒtʃ/ *n* muesca *f*. ● *vt*. **~ up** apuntar ‹*score etc*›

note /nəʊt/ *n* nota *f*; (*banknote*) billete *m*. **take ~s** tomar apuntes. ● *vt* notar. **~book** *n* libreta *f*. **~d** *a* célebre. **~paper** *n* papel *m* de escribir. **~worthy** *a* notable

nothing /ˈnʌθɪŋ/ *pron* nada. **he eats ~** no come nada. **for ~** (*free*) gratis; (*in vain*) inútilmente. ● *n* nada *f*; (*person*) nulidad *f*; (*thing of no importance*) fruslería *f*; (*zero*) cero *m*. ● *adv* de ninguna manera. **~ big** nada grande. **~ else** nada más. **~ much** poca cosa

notice /ˈnəʊtɪs/ *n* (*attention*) atención *f*; (*advert*) anuncio *m*; (*sign*) letrero *m*; (*poster*) cartel *m*; (*termination of employment*) despido *m*; (*warning*) aviso *m*. **(advance) ~** previo aviso *m*. **~ (of dismissal)** despido *m*. **take ~ of** prestar atención a, hacer caso a ‹*person*›; hacer caso de ‹*thing*›. ● *vt* notar. **~able** *a* evidente. **~ably** *adv* visiblemente. **~-board** *n* tablón *m* de anuncios

notif|ication /nəʊtɪfɪˈkeɪʃn/ *n* aviso *m*, notificación *f*. **~y** *vt* avisar

notion /ˈnəʊʃn/ *n* (*concept*) concepto *m*; (*idea*) idea *f*. **~s** *npl* (*sewing goods etc, Amer*) artículos *mpl* de mercería

notori|ety /nəʊtəˈraɪətɪ/ *n* notoriedad *f*; (*pej*) mala fama *f*. **~ous** /nəʊˈtɔːrɪəs/ *a* notorio. **~ously** *adv* notoriamente

notwithstanding /nɒtwɪθˈstændɪŋ/ *prep* a pesar de. ● *adv* sin embargo

nougat /ˈnuːgɑː/ *n* turrón *m*

nought /nɔːt/ *n* cero *m*

noun /naʊn/ *n* sustantivo *m*, nombre *m*

nourish /ˈnʌrɪʃ/ *vt* alimentar; (*incl fig*) nutrir. **~ment** *n* alimento *m*

novel /ˈnɒvl/ *n* novela *f*. ● *a* nuevo. **~ist** *n* novelista *m* & *f*. **~ty** *n* novedad *f*

November /nəʊˈvembə(r)/ *n* noviembre *m*

novice /ˈnɒvɪs/ *n* principiante *m* & *f*

now /naʊ/ *adv* ahora. **~ and again**, **~ and then** de vez en cuando. **just ~** ahora mismo; (*a moment ago*) hace poco. ● *conj* ahora que

nowadays /ˈnaʊədeɪz/ *adv* hoy (en) día

nowhere /ˈnəʊweə(r)/ *adv* en/por ninguna parte; (*after motion towards*) a ninguna parte

noxious /ˈnɒkʃəs/ *a* nocivo

nozzle /ˈnɒzl/ *n* boquilla *f*; (*tec*) tobera *f*

nuance /ˈnjʊɑːns/ *n* matiz *m*

nuclear /ˈnjuːklɪə(r)/ *a* nuclear

nucleus /ˈnjuːklɪəs/ *n* (*pl* **-lei** /-lɪaɪ/) núcleo *m*

nude /njuːd/ *a* & *n* desnudo (*m*). **in the ~** desnudo

nudge /nʌdʒ/ *vt* dar un codazo a. ● *n* codazo *m*

nudi|sm /ˈnjuːdɪzəm/ *n* desnudismo *m*. **~st** *n* nudista *m* & *f*. **~ty** /ˈnjuːdətɪ/ *n* desnudez *f*

nuisance /ˈnjuːsns/ *n* (*thing, event*) fastidio *m*; (*person*) pesado *m*. **be a ~** dar la lata

null /nʌl/ *a* nulo. **~ify** *vt* anular

numb /nʌm/ *a* entumecido. ● *vt* entumecer

number /ˈnʌmbə(r)/ *n* número *m*. ● *vt* numerar; (*count, include*) contar. **~-plate** *n* matrícula *f*

numeracy /ˈnjuːmərəsɪ/ *n* conocimientos *mpl* de matemáticas

numeral /ˈnjuːmərəl/ *n* número *m*

numerate /ˈnjuːmərət/ *a* que tiene buenos conocimientos de matemáticas

numerical /njuːˈmerɪkl/ *a* numérico

numerous /ˈnjuːmərəs/ *a* numeroso

nun /nʌn/ *n* monja *f*

nurse /nɜːs/ *n* enfermera *f*, enfermero *m*; (*nanny*) niñera *f*. **wet ~** *n* nodriza *f*. ● *vt* cuidar; abrigar ‹*hope etc*›. **~maid** *n* niñera *f*

nursery /ˈnɜːsərɪ/ *n* cuarto *m* de los niños; (*for plants*) vivero *m*. **(day) ~** *n* guardería *f* infantil. **~ rhyme** *n* canción *f* infantil. **~ school** *n* escuela *f* de párvulos

nursing home /ˈnɜːsɪŋhəʊm/ *n* (*for old people*) asilo *m* de ancianos

nurture /ˈnɜːtʃə(r)/ *vt* alimentar

nut /nʌt/ *n* (*walnut, Brazil nut etc*) nuez *f*; (*hazlenut*) avellana *f*; (*peanut*) cacahuete *m*; (*tec*) tuerca *f*;

(*crazy person, sl*) chiflado *m*. **~crackers** *npl* cascanueces *m invar*
nutmeg /'nʌtmeg/ *n* nuez *f* moscada
nutrient /'nju:trɪənt/ *n* alimento *m*
nutrit|ion /nju:'trɪʃn/ *n* nutrición *f*. **~ious** *a* nutritivo
nuts /nʌtz/ *a* (*crazy, sl*) chiflado
nutshell /'nʌtʃel/ *n* cáscara *f* de nuez. **in a ~** en pocas palabras
nuzzle /'nʌzl/ *vt* acariciar con el hocico
NW *abbr* (*north-west*) noroeste *m*
nylon /'naɪlɒn/ *n* nailon *m*. **~s** *npl* medias *fpl* de nailon
nymph /nɪmf/ *n* ninfa *f*

O

oaf /əʊf/ *n* (*pl* **oafs**) zoquete *m*
oak /əʊk/ *n* roble *m*
OAP /əʊeɪ'pi:/ *abbr* (*old-age pensioner*) *n* pensionista *m & f*
oar /ɔ:(r)/ *n* remo *m*. **~sman** /'ɔ:zmən/ *n* (*pl* **-men**) remero *m*
oasis /əʊ'eɪsɪs/ *n* (*pl* **oases** /-si:z/) oasis *m invar*
oath /əʊθ/ *n* juramento *m*; (*swear-word*) palabrota *f*
oat|meal /'əʊtmi:l/ *n* harina *f* de avena. **~s** /əʊts/ *npl* avena *f*
obedien|ce /əʊ'bi:dɪəns/ *n* obediencia *f*. **~t** /əʊ'bi:dɪənt/ *a* obediente. **~tly** *adv* obedientemente
obelisk /'ɒbəlɪsk/ *n* obelisco *m*
obes|e /əʊ'bi:s/ *a* obeso. **~ity** *n* obesidad *f*
obey /əʊ'beɪ/ *vt* obedecer; cumplir ‹*instructions etc*›
obituary /ə'bɪtʃʊərɪ/ *n* necrología *f*
object /'ɒbdʒɪkt/ *n* objeto *m*. /əb'dʒekt/ *vi* oponerse
objection /əb'dʒekʃn/ *n* objeción *f*. **~able** /əb'dʒekʃnəbl/ *a* censurable; (*unpleasant*) desagradable
objective /əb'dʒektɪv/ *a & n* objetivo (*m*). **~ively** *adv* objetivamente
objector /əb'dʒektə(r)/ *n* objetante *m & f*
oblig|ation /ɒblɪ'geɪʃn/ *n* obligación *f*. **be under an ~ation to** tener obligación de. **~atory** /ə'blɪgətrɪ/ *a* obligatorio. **~e** /ə'blaɪdʒ/ *vt* obligar; (*do a small service*) hacer un favor a. **~ed** *a* agradecido. **much ~ed!** ¡muchas gracias! **~ing** *a* atento
oblique /ə'bli:k/ *a* oblicuo
obliterat|e /ə'blɪtəreɪt/ *vt* borrar. **~ion** /-'reɪʃn/ *n* borradura *f*
oblivio|n /ə'blɪvɪən/ *n* olvido *m*. **~us** /ə'blɪvɪəs/ *a* (*unaware*) inconsciente (**to, of** de)
oblong /'ɒblɒŋ/ *a & n* oblongo (*m*)
obnoxious /əb'nɒkʃəs/ *a* odioso
oboe /'əʊbəʊ/ *n* oboe *m*
obscen|e /əb'si:n/ *a* obsceno. **~ity** /-enətɪ/ *n* obscenidad *f*
obscur|e /əb'skjʊə(r)/ *a* oscuro. ● *vt* oscurecer; (*conceal*) esconder; (*confuse*) confundir. **~ity** *n* oscuridad *f*
obsequious /əb'si:kwɪəs/ *a* obsequioso
observan|ce /əb'zɜ:vəns/ *n* observancia *f*. **~t** /əb'zɜ:vənt/ *a* observador
observation /ɒbzə'veɪʃn/ *n* observación *f*
observatory /əb'zɜ:vətrɪ/ *n* observatorio *m*
observe /əb'zɜ:v/ *vt* observar. **~r** *n* observador *m*
obsess /əb'ses/ *vt* obsesionar. **~ion** /-ʃn/ *n* obsesión *f*. **~ive** *a* obsesivo
obsolete /'ɒbsəli:t/ *a* desusado
obstacle /'ɒbstəkl/ *n* obstáculo *m*
obstetrics /əb'stetrɪks/ *n* obstetricia *f*
obstina|cy /'ɒbstɪnəsɪ/ *n* obstinación *f*. **~te** /'ɒbstɪnət/ *a* obstinado. **~tely** *adv* obstinadamente
obstreperous /ɒb'strepərəs/ *a* turbulento, ruidoso, protestón
obstruct /əb'strʌkt/ *vt* obstruir. **~ion** /-ʃn/ *n* obstrucción *f*
obtain /əb'teɪn/ *vt* obtener. ● *vi* prevalecer. **~able** *a* asequible
obtrusive /əb'tru:sɪv/ *a* importuno
obtuse /əb'tju:s/ *a* obtuso
obviate /'ɒbvɪeɪt/ *vt* evitar
obvious /'ɒbvɪəs/ *a* obvio. **~ly** obviamente
occasion /ə'keɪʒn/ *n* ocasión *f*, oportunidad *f*. **on ~** de vez en cuando. ● *vt* ocasionar. **~al** /ə'keɪʒənl/ *a* poco frecuente. **~ally** *adv* de vez en cuando
occult /ɒ'kʌlt/ *a* oculto
occup|ant /'ɒkjʊpənt/ *n* ocupante *m & f*. **~ation** /ɒkjʊ'peɪʃn/ *n* ocupación *f*; (*job*) trabajo *m*, profesión *f*. **~ational** *a* profesional. **~ier** *n* ocupante *m & f*. **~y** /'ɒkjʊpaɪ/ *vt* ocupar
occur /ə'kɜ:(r)/ *vi* (*pt* **occurred**) ocurrir, suceder; (*exist*) encontrarse. **it ~red to me that** se me ocurrió que.

~**rence** /ə'kʌrəns/ *n* suceso *m*, acontecimiento *m*
ocean /'əʊʃn/ *n* océano *m*
o'clock /ə'klɒk/ *adv*. **it is 7 ~** son las siete
octagon /'ɒktəgən/ *n* octágono *m*
octane /'ɒkteɪn/ *n* octano *m*
octave /'ɒktɪv/ *n* octava *f*
October /ɒk'təʊbə(r)/ *n* octubre *m*
octopus /'ɒktəpəs/ *n* (*pl* **-puses**) pulpo *m*
oculist /'ɒkjʊlɪst/ *n* oculista *m & f*
odd /ɒd/ *a* (**-er**, **-est**) extraño, raro; ‹*number*› impar; (*one of pair*) sin pareja; (*occasional*) poco frecuente; (*left over*) sobrante. **fifty-~** unos cincuenta, cincuenta y pico. **the ~ one out** la excepción *f*. ~**ity** *n* (*thing*) curiosidad *f*; (*person*) excéntrico *m*. ~**ly** *adv* extrañamente. ~**ly enough** por extraño que parezca. ~**ment** /'ɒdmənt/ *n* retazo *m*. ~**s** /ɒdz/ *npl* probabilidades *fpl*; (*in betting*) apuesta *f*. ~**s and ends** retazos *mpl*. **at ~s** de punta, de malas
ode /əʊd/ *n* oda *f*
odious /'əʊdɪəs/ *a* odioso
odour /'əʊdə(r)/ *n* olor *m*. ~**less** *a* inodoro
of /əv, ɒv/ *prep* de. **a friend ~ mine** un amigo mío. **how kind ~ you** es Vd muy amable
off /ɒf/ *adv* lejos; ‹*light etc*› apagado; ‹*tap*› cerrado; ‹*food*› pasado. • *prep* de, desde; (*away from*) fuera de; (*distant from*) lejos de. **be better ~** estar mejor. **be ~** marcharse. **day ~** *n* día *m* de asueto, día *m* libre
offal /'ɒfl/ *n* menudos *mpl*, asaduras *fpl*
off: ~**-beat** *a* insólito. ~ **chance** *n* posibilidad *f* remota. ~ **colour** *a* indispuesto
offen|ce /ə'fens/ *n* ofensa *f*; (*illegal act*) delito *m*. **take ~ce** ofenderse. ~**d** /ə'fend/ *vt* ofender. ~**der** *n* delincuente *m & f*. ~**sive** /ə'fensɪv/ *a* ofensivo; (*disgusting*) repugnante. • *n* ofensiva *f*
offer /'ɒfə(r)/ *vt* ofrecer. • *n* oferta *f*. **on ~** en oferta
offhand /ɒf'hænd/ *a* (*casual*) desenvuelto; (*brusque*) descortés. • *adv* de improviso
office /'ɒfɪs/ *n* oficina *f*; (*post*) cargo *m*
officer /'ɒfɪsə(r)/ *n* oficial *m*; (*policeman*) policía *f*, guardia *m*; (*of organization*) director *m*
official /ə'fɪʃl/ *a & n* oficial (*m*). ~**ly** *adv* oficialmente
officiate /ə'fɪʃɪeɪt/ *vi* oficiar. ~ **as** desempeñar las funciones de
officious /ə'fɪʃəs/ *a* oficioso
offing /'ɒfɪŋ/ *n*. **in the ~** en perspectiva
off: ~**-licence** *n* tienda *f* de bebidas alcohólicas. ~**-load** *vt* descargar. ~**-putting** *a* (*disconcerting*, *fam*) desconcertante; (*repellent*) repugnante. ~**set** /'ɒfset/ *vt* (*pt* **-set**, *pres p* **-setting**) contrapesar. ~**shoot** /'ɒfʃu:t/ *n* retoño *m*; (*fig*) ramificación *f*. ~**side** /ɒf'saɪd/ *a* (*sport*) fuera de juego. ~**spring** /'ɒfsprɪŋ/ *n invar* progenie *f*. ~**-stage** *a* entre bastidores. ~**-white** *a* blancuzco, color hueso
often /'ɒfn/ *adv* muchas veces, con frecuencia, a menudo. **how ~?** ¿cuántas veces?
ogle /'əʊgl/ *vt* comerse con los ojos
ogre /'əʊgə(r)/ *n* ogro *m*
oh /əʊ/ *int* ¡oh!, ¡ay!
oil /ɔɪl/ *n* aceite *m*; (*petroleum*) petróleo *m*. • *vt* lubricar. ~**field** /'ɔɪlfi:ld/ *n* yacimiento *m* petrolífero. ~**-painting** *n* pintura *f* al óleo. ~**-rig** /'ɔɪlrɪg/ *n* plataforma *f* de perforación. ~**skins** /'ɔɪlskɪnz/ *npl* chubasquero *m*. ~**y** *a* aceitoso; ‹*food*› grasiento
ointment /'ɔɪntmənt/ *n* ungüento *m*
OK /əʊ'keɪ/ *int* ¡vale!, ¡de acuerdo! • *a* bien; (*satisfactory*) satisfactorio. • *adv* muy bien
old /əʊld/ *a* (**-er**, **-est**) viejo; (*not modern*) anticuado; (*former*) antiguo. **how ~ is she?** ¿cuántos años tiene? **she is ten years ~** tiene diez años. **of ~** de antaño. ~ **age** *n* vejez *f*. ~**-fashioned** *a* anticuado. ~ **maid** *n* solterona *f*. ~**-world** *a* antiguo
oleander /əʊlɪ'ændə(r)/ *n* adelfa *f*
olive /'ɒlɪv/ *n* (*fruit*) aceituna *f*; (*tree*) olivo *m*. • *a* de oliva; (*colour*) aceitunado
Olympic /ə'lɪmpɪk/ *a* olímpico. ~**s** *npl*, ~ **Games** *npl* Juegos *mpl* Olímpicos
omelette /'ɒmlɪt/ *n* tortilla *f*, tortilla *f* de huevos (*Mex*)
om|en /'əʊmen/ *n* agüero *m*. ~**inous** /'ɒmɪnəs/ *a* siniestro
omi|ssion /ə'mɪʃn/ *n* omisión *f*. ~**t** /ə'mɪt/ *vt* (*pt* **omitted**) omitir
omnipotent /ɒm'nɪpətənt/ *a* omnipotente

on /ɒn/ *prep* en, sobre. **~ foot** a pie. **~ Monday** el lunes. **~ Mondays** los lunes. **~ seeing** al ver. **~ the way** de camino. ● *adv* (*light etc*) encendido; (*put on*) puesto, poco natural; (*machine*) en marcha; (*tap*) abierto. **~ and off** de vez en cuando. **~ and ~** sin cesar. **and so ~** y así sucesivamente. **be ~ at** (*fam*) criticar. **go ~** continuar. **later ~** más tarde

once /wʌns/ *adv* una vez; (*formerly*) antes. ● *conj* una vez que. **at ~** en seguida. **~-over** *n* (*fam*) ojeada *f*

oncoming /'ɒnkʌmɪŋ/ *a* que se acerca; ‹*traffic*› que viene en sentido contrario, de frente

one /wʌn/ *a & n* uno (*m*). ● *pron* uno. **~ another** el uno al otro. **~ by ~** uno a uno. **~ never knows** nunca se sabe. **the blue ~** el azul. **this ~** éste. **~-off** *a* (*fam*) único

onerous /'ɒnərəs/ *a* oneroso

one: ~self /wʌn'self/ *pron* (*subject*) uno mismo; (*object*) se; (*after prep*) sí (mismo). **by ~self** solo. **~-sided** *a* unilateral. **~-way** *a* ‹*street*› de dirección única; ‹*ticket*› de ida

onion /'ʌnɪən/ *n* cebolla *f*

onlooker /'ɒnlʊkə(r)/ *n* espectador *m*

only /'əʊnlɪ/ *a* único. **~ son** *n* hijo *m* único. ● *adv* sólo, solamente. **~ just** apenas. **~ too** de veras. ● *conj* pero, sólo que

onset /'ɒnset/ *n* principio *m*; (*attack*) ataque *m*

onslaught /'ɒnslɔ:t/ *n* ataque *m* violento

onus /'əʊnəs/ *n* responsabilidad *f*

onward(s) /'ɒnwəd(z)/ *a & adv* hacia adelante

onyx /'ɒnɪks/ *n* ónice *f*

ooze /u:z/ *vt/i* rezumar

opal /'əʊpl/ *n* ópalo *m*

opaque /əʊ'peɪk/ *a* opaco

open /'əʊpən/ *a* abierto; (*free to all*) público; (*undisguised*) manifiesto; ‹*question*› discutible; ‹*view*› despejado. **~ sea** *n* alta mar *f*. **~ secret** *n* secreto *m* a voces. **O~ University** *n* Universidad *f* a Distancia. **half-~** *a* medio abierto. **in the ~** *n* al aire libre. ● *vt/i* abrir. **~-ended** *a* abierto. **~er** /'əʊpənə(r)/ *n* (*for tins*) abrelatas *m invar*; (*for bottles with caps*) abrebotellas *m invar*; (*corkscrew*) sacacorchos *m invar*. **eye-~er** *n* (*fam*) revelación *f*. **~ing** /'əʊpənɪŋ/ *n* abertura *f*; (*beginning*) principio *m*; (*job*) vacante *m*. **~ly** /'əʊpənlɪ/ *adv* abiertamente. **~-minded** *a* imparcial

opera /'ɒprə/ *n* ópera *f*. **~-glasses** *npl* gemelos *mpl* de teatro

operate /'ɒpəreɪt/ *vt* hacer funcionar. ● *vi* funcionar; ‹*medicine etc*› operar. **~ on** (*med*) operar a

operatic /ɒpə'rætɪk/ *a* operístico

operation /ɒpə'reɪʃn/ *n* operación *f*; (*mec*) funcionamiento *m*. **in ~** en vigor. **~al** /ɒpə'reɪʃnl/ *a* operacional

operative /'ɒpərətɪv/ *a* operativo; ‹*law etc*› en vigor

operator *n* operario *m*; (*telephonist*) telefonista *m & f*

operetta /ɒpə'retə/ *n* opereta *f*

opinion /ə'pɪnɪən/ *n* opinión *f*. **in my ~** a mi parecer. **~ated** *a* dogmático

opium /'əʊpɪəm/ *n* opio *m*

opponent /ə'pəʊnənt/ *n* adversario *m*

opportun|e /'ɒpətju:n/ *a* oportuno. **~ist** /ɒpə'tju:nɪst/ *n* oportunista *m & f*. **~ity** /ɒpə'tju:nətɪ/ *n* oportunidad *f*

oppos|e /ə'pəʊz/ *vt* oponerse a. **~ed to** en contra de. **be ~ed to** oponerse a. **~ing** *a* opuesto

opposite /'ɒpəzɪt/ *a* opuesto; (*facing*) de enfrente. ● *n* contrario *m*. ● *adv* enfrente. ● *prep* enfrente de. **~ number** *n* homólogo *m*

opposition /ɒpə'zɪʃn/ *n* oposición *f*; (*resistence*) resistencia *f*

oppress /ə'pres/ *vt* oprimir. **~ion** /-ʃn/ *n* opresión *f*. **~ive** *a* (*cruel*) opresivo; ‹*heat*› sofocante. **~or** *n* opresor *m*

opt /ɒpt/ *vi*. **~ for** elegir. **~ out** negarse a participar

optic|al /'ɒptɪkl/ *a* óptico. **~ian** /ɒp'tɪʃn/ *n* óptico *m*

optimis|m /'ɒptɪmɪzəm/ *n* optimismo *m*. **~t** /'ɒptɪmɪst/ *n* optimista *m & f*. **~tic** /-'mɪstɪk/ *a* optimista

optimum /'ɒptɪməm/ *n* lo óptimo, lo mejor

option /'ɒpʃn/ *n* opción *f*. **~al** /'ɒpʃənl/ *a* facultativo

opulen|ce /'ɒpjʊləns/ *n* opulencia *f*. **~t** /'ɒpjʊlənt/ *a* opulento

or /ɔ:(r)/ *conj* o; (*before Spanish* o- *and* ho-) u; (*after negative*) ni. **~ else** si no, o bien

oracle /'ɒrəkl/ *n* oráculo *m*

oral /'ɔ:rəl/ *a* oral. ● *n* (*fam*) examen *m* oral
orange /'ɒrɪndʒ/ *n* naranja *f*; (*tree*) naranjo *m*; (*colour*) color *m* naranja. ● *a* de color naranja. **~ade** *n* naranjada *f*
orator /'ɒrətə(r)/ *n* orador *m*
oratorio /ɒrə'tɔ:rɪəʊ/ *n* (*pl* **-os**) oratorio *m*
oratory /'ɒrətrɪ/ *n* oratoria *f*
orb /ɔ:b/ *n* orbe *m*
orbit /'ɔ:bɪt/ *n* órbita *f*. ● *vt* orbitar
orchard /'ɔ:tʃəd/ *n* huerto *m*
orchestra /'ɔ:kɪstrə/ *n* orquesta *f*. **~l** /-'kestrəl/ *a* orquestal. **~te** /'ɔ:kɪstreɪt/ *vt* orquestar
orchid /'ɔ:kɪd/ *n* orquídea *f*
ordain /ɔ:'deɪn/ *vt* ordenar
ordeal /ɔ:'di:l/ *n* prueba *f* dura
order /'ɔ:də(r)/ *n* orden *m*; (*com*) pedido *m*. **in ~ that** para que. **in ~ to** para. ● *vt* (*command*) mandar; (*com*) pedir
orderly /'ɔ:dəlɪ/ *a* ordenado. ● *n* asistente *m* & *f*
ordinary /'ɔ:dɪnrɪ/ *a* corriente; (*average*) medio; (*mediocre*) ordinario
ordination /ɔ:dɪ'neɪʃn/ *n* ordenación *f*
ore /ɔ:(r)/ *n* mineral *m*
organ /'ɔ:gən/ *n* órgano *m*
organic /ɔ:'gænɪk/ *a* orgánico
organism /'ɔ:gənɪzəm/ *n* organismo *m*
organist /'ɔ:gənɪst/ *n* organista *m* & *f*
organiz|ation /ɔ:gənaɪ'zeɪʃn/ *n* organización *f*. **~e** /'ɔ:gənaɪz/ *vt* organizar. **~er** *n* organizador *m*
orgasm /'ɔ:gæzəm/ *n* orgasmo *m*
orgy /'ɔ:dʒɪ/ *n* orgía *f*
Orient /'ɔ:rɪənt/ *n* Oriente *m*. **~al** /-'entl/ *a* & *n* oriental (*m* & *f*)
orientat|e /'ɔ:rɪənteɪt/ *vt* orientar. **~ion** /-'teɪʃn/ *n* orientación *f*
orifice /'ɒrɪfɪs/ *n* orificio *m*
origin /'ɒrɪdʒɪn/ *n* origen *m*. **~al** /ə'rɪdʒənl/ *a* original. **~ality** /-'nælətɪ/ *n* originalidad *f*. **~ally** *adv* originalmente. **~ate** /ə'rɪdʒɪneɪt/ *vi*. **~ate from** provenir de. **~ator** *n* autor *m*
ormolu /'ɔ:məlu:/ *n* similor *m*
ornament /'ɔ:nəmənt/ *n* adorno *m*. **~al** /-'mentl/ *a* de adorno. **~ation** /-en'teɪʃn/ *n* ornamentación *f*
ornate /ɔ:'neɪt/ *a* adornado; ‹*style*› florido
ornithology /ɔ:nɪ'θɒlədʒɪ/ *n* ornitología *f*
orphan /'ɔ:fn/ *n* huérfano *m*. ● *vt* dejar huérfano. **~age** *n* orfanato *m*
orthodox /'ɔ:θədɒks/ *a* ortodoxo. **~y** *n* ortodoxia *f*
orthopaedic /ɔ:θə'pi:dɪk/ *a* ortopédico. **~s** *n* ortopedia *f*
oscillate /'ɒsɪleɪt/ *vi* oscilar
ossify /'ɒsɪfaɪ/ *vt* osificar. ● *vi* osificarse
ostensibl|e /ɒs'tensɪbl/ *a* aparente. **~y** *adv* aparentemente
ostentat|ion /ɒsten'teɪʃn/ *n* ostentación *f*. **~ious** *a* ostentoso
osteopath /'ɒstɪəpæθ/ *n* osteópata *m* & *f*. **~y** /-'ɒpəθɪ/ *n* osteopatía *f*
ostracize /'ɒstrəsaɪz/ *vt* excluir
ostrich /'ɒstrɪtʃ/ *n* avestruz *m*
other /'ʌðə(r)/ *a* & *n* & *pron* otro (*m*). **~ than** de otra manera que. **the ~ one** el otro. **~wise** /'ʌðəwaɪz/ *adv* de otra manera; (*or*) si no
otter /'ɒtə(r)/ *n* nutria *f*
ouch /aʊtʃ/ *int* ¡ay!
ought /ɔ:t/ *v aux* deber. **I ~ to see it** debería verlo. **he ~ to have done it** debería haberlo hecho
ounce /aʊns/ *n* onza *f* (= *28.35 gr.*)
our /'aʊə(r)/ *a* nuestro. **~s** /'aʊəz/ *poss pron* el nuestro, la nuestra, los nuestros, las nuestras. **~selves** /aʊə'selvz/ *pron* (*subject*) nosotros mismos, nosotras mismas; (*reflexive*) nos; (*after prep*) nosotros (mismos), nosotras (mismas)
oust /aʊst/ *vt* expulsar, desalojar
out /aʊt/ *adv* fuera; ‹*light*› apagado; (*in blossom*) en flor; (*in error*) equivocado. **~-and-~** *a* cien por cien. **~ of date** anticuado; (*not valid*) caducado. **~ of doors** fuera. **~ of order** estropeado; (*sign*) no funciona. **~ of pity** por compasión. **~ of place** fuera de lugar; (*fig*) inoportuno. **~ of print** agotado. **~ of sorts** indispuesto. **~ of stock** agotado. **~ of tune** desafinado. **~ of work** parado, desempleado. **be ~** equivocarse. **be ~ of** quedarse sin. **be ~ to** estar resuelto a. **five ~ of six** cinco de cada seis. **made ~ of** hecho de
outbid /aʊt'bɪd/ *vt* (*pt* **-bid**, *pres p* **-bidding**) ofrecer más que
outboard /'aʊtbɔ:d/ *a* fuera borda
outbreak /'aʊtbreɪk/ *n* (*of anger*) arranque *m*; (*of war*) comienzo *m*; (*of disease*) epidemia *f*

outbuilding /'aʊtbɪldɪŋ/ *n* dependencia *f*
outburst /'aʊtbɜ:st/ *n* explosión *f*
outcast /'aʊtkɑ:st/ *n* paria *m & f*
outcome /'aʊtkʌm/ *n* resultado *m*
outcry /'aʊtkraɪ/ *n* protesta *f*
outdated /aʊt'deɪtɪd/ *a* anticuado
outdo /aʊt'du:/ *vt* (*pt* **-did**, *pp* **-done**) superar
outdoor /'aʊtdɔ:(r)/ *a* al aire libre. **~s** /-'dɔ:z/ *adv* al aire libre
outer /'aʊtə(r)/ *a* exterior
outfit /'aʊtfɪt/ *n* equipo *m*; (*clothes*) traje *m*. **~ter** *n* camisero *m*
outgoing /'aʊtgəʊɪŋ/ *a* ‹*minister etc*› saliente; (*sociable*) abierto. **~s** *npl* gastos *mpl*
outgrow /æʊt'grəʊ/ *vt* (*pt* **-grew**, *pp* **-grown**) crecer más que ‹*person*›; hacerse demasiado grande para ‹*clothes*›. **he's ~n his trousers** le quedan pequeños los pantalones
outhouse /'aʊthaʊs/ *n* dependencia *f*
outing /'aʊtɪŋ/ *n* excursión *f*
outlandish /aʊt'lændɪʃ/ *a* extravagante
outlaw /'aʊtlɔ:/ *n* proscrito *m*. ● *vt* proscribir
outlay /'aʊtleɪ/ *n* gastos *mpl*
outlet /'aʊtlet/ *n* salida *f*
outline /'aʊtlaɪn/ *n* contorno *m*; (*summary*) resumen *m*. ● *vt* trazar; (*describe*) dar un resumen de
outlive /aʊt'lɪv/ *vt* sobrevivir a
outlook /'aʊtlʊk/ *n* perspectiva *f*
outlying /'aʊtlaɪɪŋ/ *a* remoto
outmoded /aʊt'məʊdɪd/ *a* anticuado
outnumber /aʊt'nʌmbə(r)/ *vt* sobrepasar en número
outpatient /aʊt'peɪʃnt/ *n* paciente *m* externo
outpost /'aʊtpəʊst/ *n* avanzada *f*
output /'aʊtpʊt/ *n* producción *f*
outrage /'aʊtreɪdʒ/ *n* ultraje *m*. ● *vt* ultrajar. **~ous** /aʊt'reɪdʒəs/ *a* escandaloso, atroz
outright /'aʊtraɪt/ *adv* completamente; (*at once*) inmediatamente; (*frankly*) francamente. ● *a* completo; ‹*refusal*› rotundo
outset /'aʊtset/ *n* principio *m*
outside /'aʊtsaɪd/ *a* & *n* exterior (*m*). /aʊt'saɪd/ *adv* fuera. ● *prep* fuera de. **~r** /aʊt'saɪdə(r)/ *n* forastero *m*; (*in race*) caballo *m* no favorito
outsize /'aʊtsaɪz/ *a* de tamaño extraordinario
outskirts /'aʊtskɜ:ts/ *npl* afueras *fpl*
outspoken /aʊt'spəʊkn/ *a* franco. **be ~** no tener pelos en la lengua
outstanding /aʊt'stændɪŋ/ *a* excepcional; (*not settled*) pendiente; (*conspicuous*) sobresaliente
outstretched /aʊt'stretʃt/ *a* extendido
outstrip /aʊt'strɪp/ *vt* (*pt* **-stripped**) superar
outward /'aʊtwəd/ *a* externo; ‹*journey*› de ida. **~ly** *adv* por fuera, exteriormente. **~(s)** *adv* hacia fuera
outweigh /aʊt'weɪ/ *vt* pesar más que; (*fig*) valer más que
outwit /aʊt'wɪt/ *vt* (*pt* **-witted**) ser más listo que
oval /'əʊvl/ *a* oval(ado). ● *n* óvalo *m*
ovary /'əʊvərɪ/ *n* ovario *m*
ovation /əʊ'veɪʃn/ *n* ovación *f*
oven /'ʌvn/ *n* horno *m*
over /'əʊvə(r)/ *prep* por encima de; (*across*) al otro lado de; (*during*) durante; (*more than*) más de. **~ and above** por encima de. ● *adv* por encima; (*ended*) terminado; (*more*) más; (*in excess*) de sobra. **~ again** otra vez. **~ and ~** una y otra vez. **~ here** por aquí. **~ there** por allí. **all ~** por todas partes
over... /'əʊvə(r)/ *pref* sobre..., super...
overall /əʊvər'ɔ:l/ *a* global; ‹*length, cost*› total. ● *adv* en conjunto. /'əʊvərɔ:l/ *n*, **~s** *npl* mono *m*
overawe /əʊvər'ɔ:/ *vt* intimidar
overbalance /əʊvə'bæləns/ *vt* hacer perder el equilibrio. ● *vi* perder el equilibrio
overbearing /əʊvə'beərɪŋ/ *a* dominante
overboard /'əʊvəbɔ:d/ *adv* al agua
overbook /əʊvə'bʊk/ *vt* aceptar demasiadas reservaciones para
overcast /əʊvə'kɑ:st/ *a* nublado
overcharge /əʊvə'tʃɑ:dʒ/ *vt* (*fill too much*) sobrecargar; (*charge too much*) cobrar demasiado
overcoat /'əʊvəkəʊt/ *n* abrigo *m*
overcome /əʊvə'kʌm/ *vt* (*pt* **-came**, *pp* **-come**) superar, vencer. **be ~ by** estar abrumado de
overcrowded /əʊvə'kraʊdɪd/ *a* atestado (de gente)
overdo /əʊvə'du:/ *vt* (*pt* **-did**, *pp* **-done**) exagerar; (*culin*) cocer demasiado

overdose /'əʊvədəʊs/ *n* sobredosis *f*
overdraft /'əʊvədrɑ:ft/ *n* giro *m* en descubierto
overdraw /əʊvə'drɔ:/ *vt* (*pt* **-drew**, *pp* **-drawn**) girar en descubierto. **be ~n** tener un saldo deudor
overdue /əʊvə'dju:/ *a* retrasado; (*belated*) tardío; ‹*bill*› vencido y no pagado
overestimate /əʊvər'estɪmeɪt/ *vt* sobrestimar
overflow /əʊvə'fləʊ/ *vi* desbordarse. /'əʊvəfləʊ/ *n* (*excess*) exceso *m*; (*outlet*) rebosadero *m*
overgrown /əʊvə'grəʊn/ *a* demasiado grande; ‹*garden*› cubierto de hierbas
overhang /əʊvə'hæŋ/ *vt* (*pt* **-hung**) sobresalir por encima de; (*fig*) amenazar. ● *vi* sobresalir. /'əʊvəhæŋ/ *n* saliente *f*
overhaul /əʊvə'hɔ:l/ *vt* revisar. /'əʊvəhɔ:l/ *n* revisión *f*
overhead /əʊvə'hed/ *adv* por encima. /'əʊvəhed/ *a* de arriba. **~s** *npl* gastos *mpl* generales
overhear /əʊvə'hɪə(r)/ *vt* (*pt* **-heard**) oír por casualidad
overjoyed /əʊvə'dʒɔɪd/ *a* muy contento. **he was ~** rebosaba de alegría
overland /'əʊvəlænd/ *a* terrestre. ● *adv* por tierra
overlap /əʊvə'læp/ *vt* (*pt* **-lapped**) traslapar. ● *vi* traslaparse
overleaf /əʊvə'li:f/ *adv* a la vuelta. **see ~** véase al dorso
overload /əʊvə'ləʊd/ *vt* sobrecargar
overlook /əʊvə'lʊk/ *vt* dominar; ‹*building*› dar a; (*forget*) olvidar; (*oversee*) inspeccionar; (*forgive*) perdonar
overnight /əʊvə'naɪt/ *adv* por la noche, durante la noche; (*fig, instantly*) de la noche a la mañana. **stay ~** pasar la noche. ● *a* de noche
overpass /'əʊvəpɑ:s/ *n* paso *m* a desnivel, paso *m* elevado
overpay /əʊvə'peɪ/ *vt* (*pt* **-paid**) pagar demasiado
overpower /əʊvə'paʊə(r)/ *vt* subyugar; dominar ‹*opponent*›; (*fig*) abrumar. **~ing** *a* abrumador
overpriced /əʊvə'praɪst/ *a* demasiado caro
overrate /əʊvə'reɪt/ *vt* supervalorar
overreach /əʊvə'ri:tʃ/ *vr.* **~ o.s.** extralimitarse
overreact /əʊvərɪ'ækt/ *vi* reaccionar excesivamente
overrid|e /əʊvə'raɪd/ *vt* (*pt* **-rode**, *pp* **-ridden**) pasar por encima de. **~ing** *a* dominante
overripe /'əʊvəraɪp/ *a* pasado, demasiado maduro
overrule /əʊvə'ru:l/ *vt* anular; denegar ‹*claim*›
overrun /əʊvə'rʌn/ *vt* (*pt* **-ran**, *pp* **-run**, *pres p* **-running**) invadir; exceder ‹*limit*›
overseas /əʊvə'si:z/ *a* de ultramar. ● *adv* al extranjero, en ultramar
oversee /əʊvə'si:/ *vt* (*pt* **-saw**, *pp* **-seen**) vigilar. **~r** /'əʊvəsɪə(r)/ *n* supervisor *m*
overshadow /əʊvə'ʃædəʊ/ *vt* (*darken*) sombrear; (*fig*) eclipsar
overshoot /əʊvə'ʃu:t/ *vt* (*pt* **-shot**) excederse. **~ the mark** pasarse de la raya
oversight /'əʊvəsaɪt/ *n* descuido *m*
oversleep /əʊvə'sli:p/ *vi* (*pt* **-slept**) despertarse tarde. **I overslept** se me pegaron las sábanas
overstep /əʊvə'step/ *vt* (*pt* **-stepped**) pasar de. **~ the mark** pasarse de la raya
overt /'əʊvɜ:t/ *a* manifiesto
overtak|e /əʊvə'teɪk/ *vt/i* (*pt* **-took**, *pp* **-taken**) sobrepasar; (*auto*) adelantar. **~ing** *n* adelantamiento *m*
overtax /əʊvə'tæks/ *vt* exigir demasiado
overthrow /əʊvə'θrəʊ/ *vt* (*pt* **-threw**, *pp* **-thrown**) derrocar. /'əʊvəθrəʊ/ *n* derrocamiento *m*
overtime /'əʊvətaɪm/ *n* horas *fpl* extra
overtone /'əʊvətəʊn/ *n* (*fig*) matiz *m*
overture /'əʊvətjʊə(r)/ *n* obertura *f*. **~s** *npl* (*fig*) propuestas *fpl*
overturn /əʊvə'tɜ:n/ *vt/i* volcar
overweight /əʊvə'weɪt/ *a* demasiado pesado. **be ~** pesar demasiado, ser gordo
overwhelm /əʊvə'welm/ *vt* aplastar; (*with emotion*) abrumar. **~ing** *a* aplastante; (*fig*) abrumador
overwork /əʊvə'wɜ:k/ *vt* hacer trabajar demasiado. ● *vi* trabajar demasiado. ● *n* trabajo *m* excesivo
overwrought /əʊvə'rɔ:t/ *a* agotado, muy nervioso
ovulation /ɒvjʊ'leɪʃn/ *n* ovulación *f*
ow|e /əʊ/ *vt* deber. **~ing** *a* debido. **~ing to** a causa de
owl /aʊl/ *n* lechuza *f*, búho *m*
own /əʊn/ *a* propio. **get one's ~ back** (*fam*) vengarse. **hold one's ~**

mantenerse firme, saber defenderse. **on one's ~** por su cuenta. ● *vt* poseer, tener. ● *vi*. **~ up (to)** (*fam*) confesar. **~er** *n* propietario *m*, dueño *m*. **~ership** *n* posesión *f*; (*right*) propiedad *f*

ox /ɒks/ *n* (*pl* **oxen**) buey *m*

oxide /'ɒksaɪd/ *n* óxido *m*

oxygen /'ɒksɪdʒən/ *n* oxígeno *m*

oyster /'ɔɪstə(r)/ *n* ostra *f*

P

p /pi:/ *abbr* (*pence, penny*) penique(s) (*m*(*pl*))

pace /peɪs/ *n* paso *m*. ● *vi*. **~ up and down** pasearse de aquí para allá. **~-maker** *n* (*runner*) el que marca el paso; (*med*) marcapasos *m invar*. **keep ~ with** andar al mismo paso que

Pacific /pə'sɪfɪk/ *a* pacífico. ● *n*. **~ (Ocean)** (Océano *m*) Pacífico *m*

pacif|ist /'pæsɪfɪst/ *n* pacifista *m & f*. **~y** /'pæsɪfaɪ/ *vt* apaciguar

pack /pæk/ *n* fardo *m*; (*of cards*) baraja *f*; (*of hounds*) jauría *f*; (*of wolves*) manada *f*; (*large amount*) montón *m*. ● *vt* empaquetar; hacer ‹*suitcase*›; (*press down*) apretar. ● *vi* hacer la maleta. **~age** /'pækɪdʒ/ *n* paquete *m*. ● *vt* empaquetar. **~age deal** *n* acuerdo *m* global. **~age tour** *n* viaje *m* organizado. **~ed lunch** *n* almuerzo *m* frío. **~ed out** (*fam*) de bote en bote. **~et** /'pækɪt/ *n* paquete *m*. **send ~ing** echar a paseo

pact /pækt/ *n* pacto *m*, acuerdo *m*

pad /pæd/ *n* almohadilla *f*; (*for writing*) bloc *m*; (*for ink*) tampón *m*; (*flat, fam*) piso *m*. ● *vt* (*pt* **padded**) rellenar. **~ding** *n* relleno *m*. ● *vi* andar a pasos quedos. **launching ~** plataforma *f* de lanzamiento

paddle[1] /'pædl/ *n* canalete *m*

paddle[2] /'pædl/ *vi* mojarse los pies

paddle-steamer /'pædlsti:mə(r)/ *n* vapor *m* de ruedas

paddock /'pædək/ *n* recinto *m*; (*field*) prado *m*

paddy /'pædɪ/ *n* arroz *m* con cáscara. **~-field** *n* arrozal *m*

padlock /'pædlɒk/ *n* candado *m*. ● *vt* cerrar con candado

paediatrician /pi:dɪə'trɪʃn/ *n* pediatra *m & f*

pagan /'peɪgən/ *a & n* pagano (*m*)

page[1] /peɪdʒ/ *n* página *f*. ● *vt* paginar

page[2] /peɪdʒ/ (*in hotel*) botones *m invar*. ● *vt* llamar

pageant /'pædʒənt/ *n* espectáculo *m* (histórico). **~ry** *n* boato *m*

pagoda /pə'gəʊdə/ *n* pagoda *f*

paid /peɪd/ *see* **pay**. ● *a*. **put ~ to** (*fam*) acabar con

pail /peɪl/ *n* cubo *m*

pain /peɪn/ *n* dolor *m*. **~ in the neck** (*fam*) ‹*persona*› pesado *m*; ‹*thing*› lata *f*. **be in ~** tener dolores. **~s** *npl* (*effort*) esfuerzos *mpl*. **be at ~s** esmerarse. ● *vt* doler. **~ful** /'peɪnfl/ *a* doloroso; (*laborious*) penoso. **~-killer** *n* calmante *m*. **~less** *a* indoloro. **~staking** /'peɪnzteɪkɪŋ/ *a* esmerado

paint /peɪnt/ *n* pintura *f*. ● *vt*/*i* pintar. **~er** *n* pintor *m*. **~ing** *n* pintura *f*

pair /peə(r)/ *n* par *m*; (*of people*) pareja *f*. **~ of trousers** pantalón *m*, pantalones *mpl*. ● *vi* emparejarse. **~ off** emparejarse

pajamas /pə'dʒɑ:məz/ *npl* pijama *m*

Pakistan /pɑ:kɪ'stɑ:n/ *n* el Pakistán *m*. **~i** *a & n* paquistaní (*m & f*)

pal /pæl/ *n* (*fam*) amigo *m*

palace /'pælɪs/ *n* palacio *m*

palat|able /'pælətəbl/ *a* sabroso; (*fig*) aceptable. **~e** /'pælət/ *n* paladar *m*

palatial /pə'leɪʃl/ *a* suntuoso

palaver /pə'lɑ:və(r)/ *n* (*fam*) lío *m*

pale[1] /peɪl/ *a* (**-er**, **-est**) pálido; ‹*colour*› claro. ● *vi* palidecer

pale[2] /peɪl/ *n* estaca *n*

paleness /'peɪlnɪs/ *n* palidez *f*

Palestin|e /'pælɪstaɪn/ *n* Palestina *f*. **~ian** /-'stɪnɪən/ *a & n* palestino (*m*)

palette /'pælɪt/ *n* paleta *f*. **~-knife** *n* espátula *f*

pall[1] /pɔ:l/ *n* paño *m* mortuorio; (*fig*) capa *f*

pall[2] /pɔ:l/ *vi*. **~ (on)** perder su sabor (para)

pallid /'pælɪd/ *a* pálido

palm /pɑ:m/ *n* palma *f*. ● *vt*. **~ off** encajar (**on** a). **~ist** /'pɑ:mɪst/ *n* quiromántico *m*. **P~ Sunday** *n* Domingo *m* de Ramos

palpable /'pælpəbl/ *a* palpable

palpitat|e /'pælpɪteɪt/ *vi* palpitar. **~ion** /-'teɪʃn/ *n* palpitación *f*

paltry /'pɔ:ltrɪ/ *a* (**-ier**, **-iest**) insignificante

pamper /'pæmpə(r)/ *vt* mimar

pamphlet /'pæmflɪt/ *n* folleto *m*
pan /pæn/ *n* cacerola *f*; (*for frying*) sartén *f*; (*of scales*) platillo *m*; (*of lavatory*) taza *f*
panacea /pænə'sɪə/ *n* panacea *f*
panache /pæ'næʃ/ *n* brío *m*
pancake /'pænkeɪk/ *n* hojuela *f*, crêpe *f*
panda /'pændə/ *n* panda *m*. **~ car** *n* coche *m* de la policía
pandemonium /pændɪ'məʊnɪəm/ *n* pandemonio *m*
pander /'pændə(r)/ *vi*. **~ to** complacer
pane /peɪn/ *n* (*of glass*) vidrio *m*
panel /'pænl/ *n* panel *m*; (*group of people*) jurado *m*. **~ling** *n* paneles *mpl*
pang /pæŋ/ *n* punzada *f*
panic /'pænɪk/ *n* pánico *m*. • *vi* (*pt* **panicked**) ser preso de pánico. **~-stricken** *a* preso de pánico
panoram|a /pænə'rɑ:mə/ *n* panorama *m*. **~ic** /-'ræmɪk/ *a* panorámico
pansy /'pænzɪ/ *n* pensamiento *m*; (*effeminate man, fam*) maricón *m*
pant /pænt/ *vi* jadear
pantechnicon /pæn'teknɪkən/ *n* camión *m* de mudanzas
panther /'pænθə(r)/ *n* pantera *f*
panties /'pæntɪz/ *npl* bragas *fpl*
pantomime /'pæntəmaɪm/ *n* pantomima *f*
pantry /'pæntrɪ/ *n* despensa *f*
pants /pænts/ *npl* (*man's underwear, fam*) calzoncillos *mpl*; (*woman's underwear, fam*) bragas *fpl*; (*trousers, fam*) pantalones *mpl*
papa|cy /'peɪpəsɪ/ *n* papado *m*. **~l** *a* papal
paper /'peɪpə(r)/ *n* papel *m*; (*newspaper*) periódico *m*; (*exam*) examen *m*; (*document*) documento *m*. **on ~** en teoría. • *vt* empapelar, tapizar (*LAm*). **~back** /'peɪpəbæk/ *a* en rústica. • *n* libro *m* en rústica. **~-clip** *n* sujetapapeles *m invar*, clip *m*. **~weight** /'peɪpəweɪt/ *n* pisapapeles *m invar*. **~work** *n* papeleo *m*, trabajo *m* de oficina
papier mâché /pæpɪeɪ'mæʃeɪ/ *n* cartón *m* piedra
par /pɑ:(r)/ *n* par *f*; (*golf*) par *m*. **feel below ~** no estar en forma. **on a ~ with** a la par con
parable /'pærəbl/ *n* parábola *f*
parachut|e /'pærəʃu:t/ *n* paracaídas *m invar*. • *vi* lanzarse en paracaídas. **~ist** *n* paracaidista *m & f*
parade /pə'reɪd/ *n* desfile *m*; (*street*) paseo *m*; (*display*) alarde *m*. • *vi* desfilar. • *vt* hacer alarde de
paradise /'pærədaɪs/ *n* paraíso *m*
paradox /'pærədɒks/ *n* paradoja *f*. **~ical** /-'dɒksɪkl/ *a* paradójico
paraffin /'pærəfɪn/ *n* queroseno *m*
paragon /'pærəgən/ *n* dechado *m*
paragraph /'pærəgrɑ:f/ *n* párrafo *m*
parallel /'pærəlel/ *a* paralelo. • *n* paralelo *m*; (*line*) paralela *f*. • *vt* ser paralelo a
paraly|se /'pærəlaɪz/ *vt* paralizar. **~sis** /pə'ræləsɪs/ *n* (*pl* **-ses** /-si:z/) parálisis *f*. **~tic** /pærə'lɪtɪk/ *a & n* paralítico (*m*)
parameter /pə'ræmɪtə(r)/ *n* parámetro *m*
paramount /'pærəmaʊnt/ *a* supremo
paranoia /pærə'nɔɪə/ *n* paranoia *f*
parapet /'pærəpɪt/ *n* parapeto *m*
paraphernalia /pærəfə'neɪlɪə/ *n* trastos *mpl*
paraphrase /'pærəfreɪz/ *n* paráfrasis *f*. • *vt* parafrasear
paraplegic /pærə'pli:dʒɪk/ *n* parapléjico *m*
parasite /'pærəsaɪt/ *n* parásito *m*
parasol /'pærəsɒl/ *n* sombrilla *f*
paratrooper /'pærətru:pə(r)/ *n* paracaidista *m*
parcel /'pɑ:sl/ *n* paquete *m*
parch /pɑ:tʃ/ *vt* resecar. **be ~ed** tener mucha sed
parchment /'pɑ:tʃmənt/ *n* pergamino *m*
pardon /'pɑ:dn/ *n* perdón *m*; (*jurid*) indulto *m*. **I beg your ~!** ¡perdone Vd! **I beg your ~?** ¿cómo?, ¿mande? (*Mex*). • *vt* perdonar
pare /peə(r)/ *vt* cortar ‹*nails*›; (*peel*) pelar, mondar
parent /'peərənt/ *n* (*father*) padre *m*; (*mother*) madre *f*; (*source*) origen *m*. **~s** *npl* padres *mpl*. **~al** /pə'rentl/ *a* de los padres
parenthesis /pə'renθəsɪs/ *n* (*pl* **-theses** /-si:z/) paréntesis *m invar*
parenthood /'peərənthʊd/ *n* paternidad *f*, maternidad *f*
Paris /'pærɪs/ *n* París *m*
parish /'pærɪʃ/ *n* parroquia *f*; (*municipal*) municipio *m*. **~ioner** /pə'rɪʃənə(r)/ *n* feligrés *m*
Parisian /pə'rɪzɪən/ *a & n* parisino (*m*)
parity /'pærətɪ/ *n* igualdad *f*

park /pɑ:k/ *n* parque *m*. ● *vt/i* aparcar. ~ **oneself** *vr* (*fam*) instalarse

parka /'pɑ:kə/ *n* anorak *m*

parking-meter /'pɑ:kɪŋmi:tə(r)/ *n* parquímetro *m*

parliament /'pɑ:ləmənt/ *n* parlamento *m*. ~**ary** /-'mentrɪ/ *a* parlamentario

parlour /'pɑ:lə(r)/ *n* salón *m*

parochial /pə'rəʊkɪəl/ *a* parroquial; (*fig*) pueblerino

parody /'pærədɪ/ *n* parodia *f*. ● *vt* parodiar

parole /pə'rəʊl/ *n* libertad *f* bajo palabra, libertad *f* provisional. **on** ~ libre bajo palabra. ● *vt* liberar bajo palabra

paroxysm /'pærəksɪzəm/ *n* paroxismo *m*

parquet /'pɑ:keɪ/ *n*. ~ **floor** *n* parqué *m*

parrot /'pærət/ *n* papagayo *m*

parry /'pærɪ/ *vt* parar; (*avoid*) esquivar. ● *n* parada *f*

parsimonious /pɑ:sɪ'məʊnɪəs/ *a* parsimonioso

parsley /'pɑ:slɪ/ *n* perejil *m*

parsnip /'pɑ:snɪp/ *n* pastinaca *f*

parson /'pɑ:sn/ *n* cura *m*, párroco *m*

part /pɑ:t/ *n* parte *f*; (*of machine*) pieza *f*; (*of serial*) entrega *f*; (*in play*) papel *m*; (*side in dispute*) partido *m*. **on the** ~ **of** por parte de. ● *adv* en parte. ● *vt* separar. ~ **with** *vt* separarse de. ● *vi* separarse

partake /pɑ:'teɪk/ *vt* (*pt* **-took**, *pp* **-taken**) participar. ~ **of** compartir

partial /'pɑ:ʃl/ *a* parcial. **be** ~ **to** ser aficionado a. ~**ity** /-ɪ'ælətɪ/ *n* parcialidad *f*. ~**ly** *adv* parcialmente

participa|nt /pɑ:'tɪsɪpənt/ *n* participante *m & f*. ~**te** /pɑ:'tɪsɪpeɪt/ *vi* participar. ~**tion** /-'peɪʃn/ *n* participación *f*

participle /'pɑ:tɪsɪpl/ *n* participio *m*

particle /'pɑ:tɪkl/ *n* partícula *f*

particular /pə'tɪkjʊlə(r)/ *a* particular; (*precise*) meticuloso; (*fastidious*) quisquilloso. ● *n*. **in** ~ especialmente. ~**ly** *adv* especialmente. ~**s** *npl* detalles *mpl*

parting /'pɑ:tɪŋ/ *n* separación *f*; (*in hair*) raya *f*. ● *a* de despedida

partisan /pɑ:tɪ'zæn/ *n* partidario *m*

partition /pɑ:'tɪʃn/ *n* partición *f*; (*wall*) tabique *m*. ● *vt* dividir

partly /'pɑ:tlɪ/ *adv* en parte

partner /'pɑ:tnə(r)/ *n* socio *m*; (*sport*) pareja *f*. ~**ship** *n* asociación *f*; (*com*) sociedad *f*

partridge /'pɑ:trɪdʒ/ *n* perdiz *f*

part-time /pɑ:t'taɪm/ *a & adv* a tiempo parcial

party /'pɑ:tɪ/ *n* reunión *f*, fiesta *f*; (*group*) grupo *m*; (*pol*) partido *m*; (*jurid*) parte *f*. ~ **line** *n* (*telephone*) línea *f* colectiva

pass /pɑ:s/ *vt* pasar; (*in front of*) pasar por delante de; (*overtake*) adelantar; (*approve*) aprobar ‹*exam, bill, law*›; hacer ‹*remark*›; pronunciar ‹*judgement*›. ~ **down** transmitir. ~ **over** pasar por alto de. ~ **round** distribuir. ~ **through** pasar por; (*cross*) atravesar. ~ **up** (*fam*) dejar pasar. ● *vi* pasar; (*in exam*) aprobar. ~ **away** morir. ~ **out** (*fam*) desmayarse. ● *n* (*permit*) permiso *m*; (*in mountains*) puerto *m*, desfiladero *m*; (*sport*) pase *m*; (*in exam*) aprobado *m*. **make a** ~ **at** (*fam*) hacer proposiciones amorosas a. ~**able** /'pɑ:səbl/ *a* pasable; ‹*road*› transitable

passage /'pæsɪdʒ/ *n* paso *m*; (*voyage*) travesía *f*; (*corridor*) pasillo *m*; (*in book*) pasaje *m*

passenger /'pæsɪndʒə(r)/ *n* pasajero *m*

passer-by /pɑ:sə'baɪ/ *n* (*pl* **passers-by**) transeúnte *m & f*

passion /'pæʃn/ *n* pasión *f*. ~**ate** *a* apasionado. ~**ately** *adv* apasionadamente

passive /'pæsɪv/ *a* pasivo. ~**ness** *n* pasividad *f*

passmark /'pɑ:smɑ:k/ *n* aprobado *m*

Passover /'pɑ:səʊvə(r)/ *n* Pascua *f* de los hebreos

passport /'pɑ:spɔ:t/ *n* pasaporte *m*

password /'pɑ:swɜ:d/ *n* contraseña *f*

past /pɑ:st/ *a & n* pasado (*m*). **in times** ~ en tiempos pasados. **the** ~ **week** *n* la semana *f* pasada. ● *prep* por delante de; (*beyond*) más allá de. ● *adv* por delante. **drive** ~ pasar en coche. **go** ~ pasar

paste /peɪst/ *n* pasta *f*; (*adhesive*) engrudo *m*. ● *vt* (*fasten*) pegar; (*cover*) engrudar. ~**board** /'peɪstbɔ:d/ *n* cartón *m*. ~ **jewellery** *n* joyas *fpl* de imitación

pastel /'pæstl/ *a & n* pastel (*m*)

pasteurize /'pæstʃəraɪz/ *vt* pasteurizar

pastiche /pæ'sti:ʃ/ *n* pastiche *m*

pastille /'pæstɪl/ *n* pastilla *f*
pastime /'pɑ:staɪm/ *n* pasatiempo *m*
pastoral /'pɑ:stərəl/ *a* pastoral
pastr|ies *npl* pasteles *mpl*, pastas *fpl*. **~y** /'peɪstrɪ/ *n* pasta *f*
pasture /'pɑ:stʃə(r)/ *n* pasto *m*
pasty[1] /'pæstɪ/ *n* empanada *f*
pasty[2] /'peɪstɪ/ *a* pastoso; (*pale*) pálido
pat[1] /pæt/ *vt* (*pt* **patted**) dar palmaditas en; acariciar ‹*dog etc*›. ● *n* palmadita *f*; (*of butter*) porción *f*
pat[2] /pæt/ *adv* en el momento oportuno
patch /pætʃ/ *n* pedazo *m*; (*period*) período *m*; (*repair*) remiendo *m*; (*piece of ground*) terreno *m*. **not a ~ on** (*fam*) muy inferior a. ● *vt* remendar. **~ up** arreglar. **~work** *n* labor *m* de retazos; (*fig*) mosaico *m*. **~y** *a* desigual
pâté /'pæteɪ/ *n* pasta *f*, paté *m*
patent /'peɪtnt/ *a* patente. ● *n* patente *f*. ● *vt* patentar. **~ leather** *n* charol *m*. **~ly** *adv* evidentemente
patern|al /pə'tɜ:nl/ *a* paterno. **~ity** /pə'tɜ:nətɪ/ *n* paternidad *f*
path /pɑ:θ/ *n* (*pl* **-s** /pɑ:ðz/) sendero *m*; (*sport*) pista *f*; (*of rocket*) trayectoria *f*; (*fig*) camino *m*
pathetic /pə'θetɪk/ *a* patético, lastimoso
pathology /pə'θɒlədʒɪ/ *n* patología *f*
pathos /'peɪθɒs/ *n* patetismo *m*
patien|ce /'peɪʃns/ *n* paciencia *f*. **~t** /'peɪʃnt/ *a* & *n* paciente (*m* & *f*). **~tly** *adv* con paciencia
patio /'pætɪəʊ/ *n* (*pl* **-os**) patio *m*
patriarch /'peɪtrɪɑ:k/ *n* patriarca *m*
patrician /pə'trɪʃn/ *a* & *n* patricio (*m*)
patriot /'pætrɪət/ *n* patriota *m* & *f*. **~ic** /-'ɒtɪk/ *a* patriótico. **~ism** *n* patriotismo *m*
patrol /pə'trəʊl/ *n* patrulla *f*. ● *vt/i* patrullar
patron /'peɪtrən/ *n* (*of the arts etc*) mecenas *m* & *f*; (*customer*) cliente *m* & *f*; (*of charity*) patrocinador *m*. **~age** /'pætrənɪdʒ/ *n* patrocinio *m*; (*of shop etc*) clientela *f*. **~ize** *vt* ser cliente de; (*fig*) tratar con condescendencia
patter[1] /'pætə(r)/ *n* (*of steps*) golpeteo *m*; (*of rain*) tamborileo *m*. ● *vi* correr con pasos ligeros; ‹*rain*› tamborilear
patter[2] /'pætə(r)/ (*speech*) jerga *f*; (*chatter*) parloteo *m*
pattern /'pætn/ *n* diseño *m*; (*model*) modelo *m*; (*sample*) muestra *f*; (*manner*) modo *m*; (*in dressmaking*) patrón *m*
paunch /pɔ:ntʃ/ *n* panza *f*
pauper /'pɔ:pə(r)/ *n* indigente *m* & *f*, pobre *m* & *f*
pause /pɔ:z/ *n* pausa *f*. ● *vi* hacer una pausa
pave /peɪv/ *vt* pavimentar. **~ the way for** preparar el terreno para
pavement /'peɪvmənt/ *n* pavimento *m*; (*at side of road*) acera *f*
pavilion /pə'vɪlɪən/ *n* pabellón *m*
paving-stone /'peɪvɪŋstəʊn/ *n* losa *f*
paw /pɔ:/ *n* pata *f*; (*of cat*) garra *f*. ● *vi* tocar con la pata; ‹*person*› manosear
pawn[1] /pɔ:n/ *n* (*chess*) peón *m*; (*fig*) instrumento *m*
pawn[2] /pɔ:n/ *vt* empeñar. ● *n*. **in ~** en prenda. **~broker** /'pɔ:nbrəʊkə(r)/ *n* prestamista *m* & *f*. **~shop** *n* monte *m* de piedad
pawpaw /'pɔ:pɔ:/ *n* papaya *f*
pay /peɪ/ *vt* (*pt* **paid**) pagar; prestar ‹*attention*›; hacer ‹*compliment, visit*›. **~ back** devolver. **~ cash** pagar al contado. **~ in** ingresar. **~ off** pagar. **~ out** pagar. ● *vi* pagar; (*be profitable*) rendir. ● *n* paga *f*. **in the ~ of** al servicio de. **~able** /'peɪəbl/ *a* pagadero. **~ment** /'peɪmənt/ *n* pago *m*. **~-off** *n* (*sl*) liquidación *f*; (*fig*) ajuste *m* de cuentas. **~roll** /'peɪrəʊl/ *n* nómina *f*. **~ up** pagar
pea /pi:/ *n* guisante *m*
peace /pi:s/ *n* paz *f*. **~ of mind** tranquilidad *f*. **~able** *a* pacífico. **~ful** /'pi:sfl/ *a* tranquilo. **~maker** /'pi:smeɪkə(r)/ *n* pacificador *m*
peach /pi:tʃ/ *n* melocotón *m*, durazno *m* (*LAm*); (*tree*) melocotonero *m*, duraznero *m* (*LAm*)
peacock /'pi:kɒk/ *n* pavo *m* real
peak /pi:k/ *n* cumbre *f*; (*maximum*) máximo *m*. **~ hours** *npl* horas *fpl* punta. **~ed cap** *n* gorra *f* de visera
peaky /'pi:kɪ/ *a* pálido
peal /pi:l/ *n* repique *m*. **~s of laughter** risotadas *fpl*
peanut /'pi:nʌt/ *n* cacahuete *m*, maní *m* (*Mex*). **~s** (*sl*) una bagatela *f*
pear /peə(r)/ *n* pera *f*; (*tree*) peral *m*
pearl /pɜ:l/ *n* perla *f*. **~y** *a* nacarado
peasant /'peznt/ *n* campesino *m*
peat /pi:t/ *n* turba *f*
pebble /'pebl/ *n* guijarro *m*

peck /pek/ *vt* picotear; (*kiss, fam*) dar un besito a. ● *n* picotazo *m*; (*kiss*) besito *m*. **~ish** /ˈpekɪʃ/ *a*. **be ~ish** (*fam*) tener hambre, tener gazuza (*fam*)

peculiar /pɪˈkju:lɪə(r)/ *a* raro; (*special*) especial. **~ity** /-ˈærətɪ/ *n* rareza *f*; (*feature*) particularidad *f*

pedal /ˈpedl/ *n* pedal *m*. ● *vi* pedalear

pedantic /pɪˈdæntɪk/ *a* pedante

peddle /ˈpedl/ *vt* vender por las calles

pedestal /ˈpedɪstl/ *n* pedestal *m*

pedestrian /pɪˈdestrɪən/ *n* peatón *m*. ● *a* de peatones; (*dull*) prosaico. **~ crossing** *n* paso *m* de peatones

pedigree /ˈpedɪgri:/ linaje *m*; (*of animal*) pedigrí *m*. ● *a* ‹*animal*› de raza

pedlar /ˈpedlə(r)/ *n* buhonero *m*, vendedor *m* ambulante

peek /pi:k/ *vi* mirar a hurtadillas

peel /pi:l/ *n* cáscara *f*. ● *vt* pelar ‹*fruit, vegetables*›. ● *vi* pelarse. **~ings** *npl* peladuras *fpl*, monda *f*

peep[1] /pi:p/ *vi* mirar a hurtadillas. ● *n* mirada *f* furtiva

peep[2] /pi:p/ ‹*bird*› piar. ● *n* pío *m*

peep-hole /ˈpi:phəʊl/ *n* mirilla *f*

peer[1] /pɪə(r)/ *vi* mirar. **~ at** escudriñar

peer[2] /pɪə(r)/ *n* par *m*, compañero *m*. **~age** *n* pares *mpl*

peev|ed /pi:vd/ *a* (*sl*) irritado. **~ish** /ˈpi:vɪʃ/ *a* picajoso

peg /peg/ *n* clavija *f*; (*for washing*) pinza *f*; (*hook*) gancho *m*; (*for tent*) estaca *f*. **off the ~** de percha. ● *vt* (*pt* **pegged**) fijar ‹*precios*›. **~ away at** afanarse por

pejorative /pɪˈdʒɒrətɪv/ *a* peyorativo, despectivo

pelican /ˈpelɪkən/ *n* pelícano *m*. **~ crossing** *n* paso *m* de peatones (con semáforo)

pellet /ˈpelɪt/ *n* pelotilla *f*; (*for gun*) perdigón *m*

pelt[1] /pelt/ *n* pellejo *m*

pelt[2] /pelt/ *vt* tirar. ● *vi* llover a cántaros

pelvis /ˈpelvɪs/ *n* pelvis *f*

pen[1] /pen/ *n* (*enclosure*) recinto *m*

pen[2] /pen/ (*for writing*) pluma *f*, estilográfica *f*; (*ball-point*) bolígrafo *m*

penal /ˈpi:nl/ *a* penal. **~ize** *vt* castigar. **~ty** /ˈpenltɪ/ *n* castigo *m*; (*fine*) multa *f*. **~ty kick** *n* (*football*) penalty *m*

penance /ˈpenəns/ *n* penitencia *f*

pence /pens/ *see* **penny**

pencil /ˈpensl/ *n* lápiz *m*. ● *vt* (*pt* **pencilled**) escribir con lápiz. **~-sharpener** *n* sacapuntas *m invar*

pendant /ˈpendənt/ *n* dije *m*, medallón *m*

pending /ˈpendɪŋ/ *a* pendiente. ● *prep* hasta

pendulum /ˈpendjʊləm/ *n* péndulo *m*

penetrat|e /ˈpenɪtreɪt/ *vt/i* penetrar. **~ing** *a* penetrante. **~ion** /-ˈtreɪʃn/ *n* penetración *f*

penguin /ˈpeŋgwɪn/ *n* pingüino *m*

penicillin /penɪˈsɪlɪn/ *n* penicilina *f*

peninsula /pəˈnɪnsjʊlə/ *n* península *f*

penis /ˈpi:nɪs/ *n* pene *m*

peniten|ce /ˈpenɪtəns/ *n* penitencia *f*. **~t** /ˈpenɪtənt/ *a* & *n* penitente (*m* & *f*). **~tiary** /penɪˈtenʃərɪ/ *n* (*Amer*) cárcel *m*

pen: **~knife** /ˈpennaɪf/ *n* (*pl* **penknives**) navaja *f*; (*small*) cortaplumas *m invar*. **~-name** *n* seudónimo *m*

pennant /ˈpenənt/ *n* banderín *m*

penn|iless /ˈpenɪlɪs/ *a* sin un céntimo. **~y** /ˈpenɪ/ *n* (*pl* **pennies** *or* **pence**) penique *m*

pension /ˈpenʃn/ *n* pensión *f*; (*for retirement*) jubilación *f*. ● *vt* pensionar. **~able** *a* con derecho a pensión; ‹*age*› de la jubilación. **~er** *n* jubilado *m*. **~ off** jubilar

pensive /ˈpensɪv/ *a* pensativo

pent-up /pentˈʌp/ *a* reprimido; (*confined*) encerrado

pentagon /ˈpentəgən/ *n* pentágono *m*

Pentecost /ˈpentɪkɒst/ *n* Pentecostés *m*

penthouse /ˈpenthaʊs/ *n* ático *m*

penultimate /penˈʌltɪmət/ *a* penúltimo

penury /ˈpenjʊərɪ/ *n* penuria *f*

peony /ˈpi:ənɪ/ *n* peonía *f*

people /ˈpi:pl/ *npl* gente *f*; (*citizens*) pueblo *m*. **~ say** se dice. **English ~** los ingleses *mpl*. **my ~** (*fam*) mi familia *f*. ● *vt* poblar

pep /pep/ *n* vigor *m*. ● *vt*. **~ up** animar

pepper /ˈpepə(r)/ *n* pimienta *f*; (*vegetable*) pimiento *m*. ● *vt* sazonar con pimienta. **~y** *a* picante. **~corn**

/ˈpepəkɔ:n/ *n* grano *m* de pimienta. **~corn rent** *n* alquiler *m* nominal

peppermint /ˈpepəmɪnt/ *n* menta *f*; (*sweet*) pastilla *f* de menta

pep talk /ˈceptɔ:k/ *n* palabras *fpl* animadoras

per /pɜ:(r)/ *prep* por. **~ annum** al año. **~ cent** por ciento. **~ head** por cabeza, por persona. **ten miles ~ hour** diez millas por hora

perceive /pəˈsi:v/ *vt* percibir; (*notice*) darse cuenta de

percentage /pəˈsentɪdʒ/ *n* porcentaje *m*

percepti|ble /pəˈseptəbl/ *a* perceptible. **~on** /pəˈsepʃn/ *n* percepción *f*. **~ve** *a* perspicaz

perch[1] /pɜ:tʃ/ *n* (*of bird*) percha *f*. ● *vi* posarse

perch[2] /pɜ:tʃ/ (*fish*) perca *f*

percolat|e /ˈpɜ:kəleɪt/ *vt* filtrar. ● *vi* filtrarse. **~or** *n* cafetera *f*

percussion /pəˈkʌʃn/ *n* percusión *f*

peremptory /pəˈremptərɪ/ *a* perentorio

perennial /pəˈrenɪəl/ *a* & *n* perenne (*m*)

perfect /ˈpɜ:fɪkt/ *a* perfecto. /pəˈfekt/ *vt* perfeccionar. **~ion** /pəˈfekʃn/ *n* perfección *f*. **to ~ion** a la perfección. **~ionist** *n* perfeccionista *m* & *f*. **~ly** /ˈpɜ:fɪktlɪ/ *adv* perfectamente

perforat|e /ˈpɜ:fəreɪt/ *vt* perforar. **~ion** /-ˈreɪʃn/ *n* perforación *f*

perform /pəˈfɔ:m/ *vt* hacer, realizar; representar ‹*play*›; desempeñar ‹*role*›; (*mus*) interpretar. **~ an operation** (*med*) operar. **~ance** *n* ejecución *f*; (*of play*) representación *f*; (*of car*) rendimiento *m*; (*fuss, fam*) jaleo *m*. **~er** *n* artista *m* & *f*

perfume /ˈpɜ:fju:m/ *n* perfume *m*

perfunctory /pəˈfʌŋktərɪ/ *a* superficial

perhaps /pəˈhæps/ *adv* quizá(s), tal vez

peril /ˈperəl/ *n* peligro *m*. **~ous** *a* arriesgado, peligroso

perimeter /pəˈrɪmɪtə(r)/ *n* perímetro *m*

period /ˈpɪərɪəd/ *n* período *m*; (*lesson*) clase *f*; (*gram*) punto *m*. ● *a* de (la) época. **~ic** /-ˈɒdɪk/ *a* periódico. **~ical** /pɪərɪˈɒdɪkl/ *n* revista *f*. **~ically** /-ˈɒdɪklɪ/ *adv* periódico

peripher|al /pəˈrɪfərəl/ *a* periférico. **~y** /pəˈrɪfərɪ/ *n* periferia *f*

periscope /ˈperɪskəʊp/ *n* periscopio *m*

perish /ˈperɪʃ/ *vi* perecer; (*rot*) estropearse. **~able** *a* perecedero. **~ing** *a* (*fam*) glacial

perjur|e /ˈpɜ:dʒə(r)/ *vr*. **~e o.s.** perjurarse. **~y** *n* perjurio *m*

perk[1] /pɜ:k/ *n* gaje *m*

perk[2] /pɜ:k/ *vt*/*i*. **~ up** *vt* reanimar. ● *vi* reanimarse. **~y** *a* alegre

perm /pɜ:m/ *n* permanente *f*. ● *vt* hacer una permanente a

permanen|ce /ˈpɜ:mənəns/ *n* permanencia *f*. **~t** /ˈpɜ:mənənt/ *a* permanente. **~tly** *adv* permanentemente

permea|ble /ˈpɜ:mɪəbl/ *a* permeable. **~te** /ˈpɜ:mɪeɪt/ *vt* penetrar; (*soak*) empapar

permissible /pəˈmɪsəbl/ *a* permisible

permission /pəˈmɪʃn/ *n* permiso *m*

permissive /pəˈmɪsɪv/ *a* indulgente. **~ness** *n* tolerancia *f*. **~ society** *n* sociedad *f* permisiva

permit /pəˈmɪt/ *vt* (*pt* **permitted**) permitir. /ˈpɜ:mɪt/ *n* permiso *m*

permutation /pɜ:mju:ˈteɪʃn/ *n* permutación *f*

pernicious /pəˈnɪʃəs/ *a* pernicioso

peroxide /pəˈrɒksaɪd/ *n* peróxido *m*

perpendicular /pɜ:pənˈdɪkjʊlə(r)/ *a* & *n* perpendicular (*f*)

perpetrat|e /ˈpɜ:pɪtreɪt/ *vt* cometer. **~or** *n* autor *m*

perpetua|l /pəˈpetʃʊəl/ *a* perpetuo. **~te** /pəˈpetʃʊeɪt/ *vt* perpetuar. **~tion** /-ˈeɪʃn/ *n* perpetuación *f*

perplex /pəˈpleks/ *vt* dejar perplejo. **~ed** *a* perplejo. **~ing** *a* desconcertante. **~ity** *n* perplejidad *f*

persecut|e /ˈpɜ:sɪkju:t/ *vt* perseguir. **~ion** /-ˈkju:ʃn/ *n* persecución *f*

persever|ance /pɜ:sɪˈvɪərəns/ *n* perseverancia *f*. **~e** /pɜ:sɪˈvɪə(r)/ *vi* perseverar, persistir

Persian /ˈpɜ:ʃn/ *a* persa. **the ~ Gulf** *n* el golfo *m* Pérsico. ● *n* persa (*m* & *f*); (*lang*) persa *m*

persist /pəˈsɪst/ *vi* persistir. **~ence** *n* persistencia *f*. **~ent** *a* persistente; (*continual*) continuo. **~ently** *adv* persistentemente

person /ˈpɜ:sn/ *n* persona *f*

personal /ˈpɜ:sənl/ *a* personal

personality /pɜ:səˈnælətɪ/ *n* personalidad *f*; (*on TV*) personaje *m*

personally /ˈpɜ:sənəlɪ/ *adv* personalmente; (*in person*) en persona

personify /pəˈsɒnɪfaɪ/ *vt* personificar
personnel /pɜːsəˈnel/ *n* personal *m*
perspective /pəˈspektɪv/ *n* perspectiva *f*
perspicacious /pɜːspɪˈkeɪʃəs/ *a* perspicaz
perspir|ation /pɜːspəˈreɪʃn/ *n* sudor *m*. **~e** /pəsˈpaɪə(r)/ *vi* sudar
persua|de /pəˈsweɪd/ *vt* persuadir. **~sion** *n* persuasión *f*. **~sive** /pəˈsweɪsɪv/ *a* persuasivo. **~sively** *adv* de manera persuasiva
pert /pɜːt/ *a* (*saucy*) impertinente; (*lively*) animado
pertain /pəˈteɪn/ *vi*. **~ to** relacionarse con
pertinent /ˈpɜːtɪnənt/ *a* pertinente. **~ly** *adv* pertinentemente
pertly /ˈpɜːtlɪ/ *adv* impertinentemente
perturb /pəˈtɜːb/ *vt* perturbar
Peru /pəˈruː/ *n* el Perú *m*
perus|al /pəˈruːzl/ *n* lectura *f* cuidadosa. **~e** /pəˈruːz/ *vt* leer cuidadosamente
Peruvian /pəˈruːvɪan/ *a* & *n* peruano (*m*)
perva|de /pəˈveɪd/ *vt* difundirse por. **~sive** *a* penetrante
perver|se /pəˈvɜːs/ *a* (*stubborn*) terco; (*wicked*) perverso. **~sity** *n* terquedad *f*; (*wickedness*) perversidad *f*. **~sion** *n* perversión *f*. **~t** /pəˈvɜːt/ *vt* pervertir. /ˈpɜːvɜːt/ *n* pervertido *m*
pessimis|m /ˈpesɪmɪzəm/ *n* pesimismo *m*. **~t** /ˈpesɪmɪst/ *n* pesimista *m* & *f*. **~tic** /-ˈmɪstɪk/ *a* pesimista
pest /pest/ *n* insecto *m* nocivo, plaga *f*; (*person*) pelma *m*; (*thing*) lata *f*
pester /ˈpestə(r)/ *vt* importunar
pesticide /ˈpestɪsaɪd/ *n* pesticida *f*
pet /pet/ *n* animal *m* doméstico; (*favourite*) favorito *m*. ● *a* preferido. ● *vt* (*pt* **petted**) acariciar
petal /ˈpetl/ *n* pétalo *m*
peter /ˈpiːtə(r)/ *vi*. **~ out** ‹*supplies*› agotarse; (*disappear*) desparecer
petite /pəˈtiːt/ *a* (*of woman*) chiquita
petition /pɪˈtɪʃn/ *n* petición *f*. ● *vt* dirigir una petición a
pet name /ˈpetneɪm/ *n* apodo *m* cariñoso
petrify /ˈpetrɪfaɪ/ *vt* petrificar. ● *vi* petrificarse
petrol /ˈpetrəl/ *n* gasolina *f*. **~eum** /pɪˈtrəʊlɪəm/ *n* petróleo *m*. **~ gauge** *n* indicador *m* de nivel de gasolina. **~ pump** *n* (*in car*) bomba *f* de gasolina; (*at garage*) surtidor *m* de gasolina. **~ station** *n* gasolinera *f*. **~ tank** *n* depósito *m* de gasolina
petticoat /ˈpetɪkəʊt/ *n* enaguas *fpl*
pett|iness /ˈpetɪnɪs/ *n* mezquindad *f*. **~y** /ˈpetɪ/ *a* (**-ier**, **-iest**) insignificante; (*mean*) mezquino. **~y cash** *n* dinero *m* para gastos menores. **~y officer** *n* suboficial *m* de marina
petulan|ce /ˈpetjʊləns/ *n* irritabilidad *f*. **~t** /ˈpetjʊlənt/ *a* irritable
pew /pjuː/ *n* banco *m* (de iglesia)
pewter /ˈpjuːtə(r)/ *n* peltre *m*
phallic /ˈfælɪk/ *a* fálico
phantom /ˈfæntəm/ *n* fantasma *m*
pharmaceutical /fɑːməˈsjuːtɪkl/ *a* farmacéutico
pharmac|ist /ˈfɑːməsɪst/ *n* farmacéutico *m*. **~y** /ˈfɑːməsɪ/ *n* farmacia *f*
pharyngitis /færɪnˈdʒaɪtɪs/ *n* faringitis *f*
phase /feɪz/ *n* etapa *f*. ● *vt*. **~ in** introducir progresivamente. **~ out** retirar progresivamente
PhD *abbr* (*Doctor of Philosophy*) *n* Doctor *m* en Filosofía
pheasant /ˈfeznt/ *n* faisán *m*
phenomenal /fɪˈnɒmɪnl/ *a* fenomenal
phenomenon /fɪˈnɒmɪnən/ *n* (*pl* **-ena**) fenómeno *m*
phew /fjuː/ *int* ¡uy!
phial /ˈfaɪəl/ *n* frasco *m*
philanderer /fɪˈlændərə(r)/ *n* mariposón *m*
philanthrop|ic /fɪlənˈθrɒpɪk/ *a* filantrópico. **~ist** /fɪˈlænθrəpɪst/ *n* filántropo *m*
philatel|ist /fɪˈlætəlɪst/ *n* filatelista *m* & *f*. **~y** /fɪˈlætəlɪ/ *n* filatelia *f*
philharmonic /fɪlhɑːˈmɒnɪk/ *a* filarmónico
Philippines /ˈfɪlɪpiːnz/ *npl* Filipinas *fpl*
philistine /ˈfɪlɪstaɪn/ *a* & *n* filisteo (*m*)
philosoph|er /fɪˈlɒsəfə(r)/ *n* filósofo *m*. **~ical** /-əˈsɒfɪkl/ *a* filosófico. **~y** /fɪˈlɒsəfɪ/ *n* filosofía *f*
phlegm /flem/ *n* flema *f*. **~atic** /flegˈmætɪk/ *a* flemático
phobia /ˈfəʊbɪə/ *n* fobia *f*
phone /fəʊn/ *n* (*fam*) teléfono *m*. ● *vt/i* llamar por teléfono. **~ back**

‹*caller*› volver a llamar; ‹*person called*› llamar. ~ **box** *n* cabina *f* telefónica
phonetic /fəˈnetɪk/ *a* fonético. **~s** *n* fonética *f*
phoney /ˈfəʊnɪ/ *a* (**-ier**, **-iest**) (*sl*) falso. ● *n* (*sl*) farsante *m & f*
phosphate /ˈfɒsfeɪt/ *n* fosfato *m*
phosphorus /ˈfɒsfərəs/ *n* fósforo *m*
photo /ˈfəʊtəʊ/ *n* (*pl* **-os**) (*fam*) fotografía *f*, foto *f* (*fam*)
photocopy /ˈfəʊtəʊkɒpɪ/ *n* fotocopia *f*. ● *vt* fotocopiar
photogenic /fəʊtəʊˈdʒenɪk/ *a* fotogénico
photograph /ˈfəʊtəgrɑːf/ *n* fotografía *f*. ● *vt* hacer una fotografía de, sacar fotos de. **~er** /fəˈtɒgrəfə(r)/ *n* fotógrafo *m*. **~ic** /-ˈgræfɪk/ *a* fotográfico **~y** /fəˈtɒgrəfɪ/ *n* fotografía *f*
phrase /freɪz/ *n* frase *f*, locución *f*, expresión *f*. ● *vt* expresar. **~-book** *n* libro *m* de frases
physical /ˈfɪzɪkl/ *a* físico
physician /fɪˈzɪʃn/ *n* médico *m*
physic|ist /ˈfɪzɪsɪst/ *n* físico *m*. **~s** /ˈfɪzɪks/ *n* física *f*
physiology /fɪzɪˈɒlədʒɪ/ *n* fisiología *f*
physiotherap|ist /fɪzɪəʊˈθerəpɪst/ *n* fisioterapeuta *m & f*. **~y** /fɪzɪəʊˈθerəpɪ/ *n* fisioterapia *f*
physique /fɪˈziːk/ *n* constitución *f*; (*appearance*) físico *m*
pian|ist /ˈpɪənɪst/ *n* pianista *m & f*. **~o** /pɪˈænəʊ/ *n* (*pl* **-os**) piano *m*
piccolo /ˈpɪkələʊ/ *n* flautín *m*, píccolo *m*
pick[1] /pɪk/ (*tool*) pico *m*
pick[2] /pɪk/ *vt* escoger; recoger ‹*flowers etc*›; forzar ‹*a lock*›; (*dig*) picar. ~ **a quarrel** buscar camorra. ~ **holes in** criticar. ● *n* (*choice*) selección *f*; (*the best*) lo mejor. ~ **on** *vt* (*nag*) meterse con. ~ **out** *vt* escoger; (*identify*) identificar; destacar ‹*colour*›. ~ **up** *vt* recoger; (*lift*) levantar; (*learn*) aprender; adquirir ‹*habit, etc*›; obtener ‹*information*›; contagiarse de ‹*illness*›. ● *vi* mejorar; (*med*) reponerse
pickaxe /ˈpɪkæks/ *n* pico *m*
picket /ˈpɪkɪt/ *n* (*striker*) huelguista *m & f*; (*group of strikers*) piquete *m*; (*stake*) estaca *f*. ~ **line** *n* piquete *m*. ● *vt* vigilar por piquetes. ● *vi* estar de guardia
pickle /ˈpɪkl/ *n* (*in vinegar*) encurtido *m*; (*in brine*) salmuera *f*. **in a** ~ (*fam*) en un apuro. ● *vt* encurtir. **~s** *npl* encurtido *m*
pick: **~pocket** /ˈpɪkpɒkɪt/ *n* ratero *m*. **~-up** *n* (*sl*) ligue *m*; (*truck*) camioneta *f*; (*stylus-holder*) fonocaptor *m*, brazo *m*
picnic /ˈpɪknɪk/ *n* comida *f* campestre. ● *vi* (*pt* **picnicked**) merendar en el campo
pictorial /pɪkˈtɔːrɪəl/ *a* ilustrado
picture /ˈpɪktʃə(r)/ *n* (*painting*) cuadro *m*; (*photo*) fotografía *f*; (*drawing*) dibujo *m*; (*beautiful thing*) preciosidad *f*; (*film*) película *f*; (*fig*) descripción *f*. **the ~s** *npl* el cine *m*. ● *vt* imaginarse; (*describe*) describir
picturesque /pɪktʃəˈresk/ *a* pintoresco
piddling /ˈpɪdlɪŋ/ *a* (*fam*) insignificante
pidgin /ˈpɪdʒɪn/ *a*. ~ **English** *n* inglés *m* corrompido
pie /paɪ/ *n* empanada *f*; (*sweet*) pastel *m*, tarta *f*
piebald /ˈpaɪbɔːld/ *a* pío
piece /piːs/ *n* pedazo *m*; (*coin*) moneda *f*; (*in game*) pieza *f*. **a ~ of advice** un consejo *m*. **a ~ of news** una noticia *f*. **take to ~s** desmontar. ● *vt*. ~ **together** juntar. **~meal** /ˈpiːsmiːl/ *a* gradual; (*unsystematic*) poco sistemático. —adv poco a poco. **~-work** *n* trabajo *m* a destajo
pier /pɪə(r)/ *n* muelle *m*
pierc|e /pɪəs/ *vt* perforar. **~ing** *a* penetrante
piety /ˈpaɪətɪ/ *n* piedad *f*
piffl|e /ˈpɪfl/ *n* (*sl*) tonterías *fpl*. **~ing** *a* (*sl*) insignificante
pig /pɪg/ *n* cerdo *m*
pigeon /ˈpɪdʒɪn/ *n* paloma *f*; (*culin*) pichón *m*. **~-hole** *n* casilla *f*
pig: **~gy** /ˈpɪgɪ/ *a* (*greedy, fam*) glotón. **~gy-back** *adv* a cuestas. **~gy bank** *n* hucha *f*. **~-headed** *a* terco
pigment /ˈpɪgmənt/ *n* pigmento *m*. **~ation** /-ˈteɪʃn/ *n* pigmentación *f*
pig: **~skin** /ˈpɪgskɪn/ *n* piel *m* de cerdo. **~sty** /ˈpɪgstaɪ/ *n* pocilga *f*
pigtail /ˈpɪgteɪl/ *n* (*plait*) trenza *f*
pike /paɪk/ *n invar* (*fish*) lucio *m*
pilchard /ˈpɪltʃəd/ *n* sardina *f*
pile[1] /paɪl/ *n* (*heap*) montón *m*. ● *vt* amontonar. ~ **it on** exagerar. ● *vi* amontonarse. ~ **up** *vt* amontonar. ● *vi* amontonarse. **~s** /paɪlz/ *npl* (*med*) almorranas *fpl*
pile[2] /paɪl/ *n* (*of fabric*) pelo *m*

pile-up /ˈpaɪlʌp/ *n* accidente *m* múltiple
pilfer /ˈpɪlfə(r)/ *vt/i* hurtar. **~age** *n*, **~ing** *n* hurto *m*
pilgrim /ˈpɪlgrɪm/ *n* peregrino. **~age** *n* peregrinación *f*
pill /pɪl/ *n* píldora *f*
pillage /ˈpɪlɪdʒ/ *n* saqueo *m*. ● *vt* saquear
pillar /ˈpɪlə(r)/ *n* columna *f*. **~-box** *n* buzón *m*
pillion /ˈpɪlɪən/ *n* asiento *m* trasero. **ride ~** ir en el asiento trasero
pillory /ˈpɪlərɪ/ *n* picota *f*
pillow /ˈpɪləʊ/ *n* almohada *f*. **~case** /ˈpɪləʊkeɪs/ *n* funda *f* de almohada
pilot /ˈpaɪlət/ *n* piloto *m*. ● *vt* pilotar. **~-light** *n* fuego *m* piloto
pimp /pɪmp/ *n* alcahuete *m*
pimple /ˈpɪmpl/ *n* grano *m*
pin /pɪn/ *n* alfiler *m*; (*mec*) perno *m*. **~s and needles** hormigueo *m*. ● *vt* (*pt* **pinned**) prender con alfileres; (*hold down*) enclavijar; (*fix*) sujetar. **~ s.o. down** obligar a uno a que se decida. **~ up** fijar
pinafore /ˈpɪnəfɔ:(r)/ *n* delantal *m*. **~ dress** *n* mandil *m*
pincers /ˈpɪnsəz/ *npl* tenazas *fpl*
pinch /pɪntʃ/ *vt* pellizcar; (*steal, sl*) hurtar. ● *vi* ‹*shoe*› apretar. ● *n* pellizco *m*; (*small amount*) pizca *f*. **at a ~** en caso de necesidad
pincushion /ˈpɪnkʊʃn/ *n* acerico *m*
pine[1] /paɪn/ *n* pino *m*
pine[2] /paɪn/ *vi*. **~ away** consumirse. **~ for** suspirar por
pineapple /ˈpaɪnæpl/ *n* piña *f*, ananás *m*
ping /pɪŋ/ *n* sonido *m* agudo. **~-pong** /ˈpɪŋpɒŋ/ *n* pimpón *m*, ping-pong *m*
pinion /ˈpɪnjən/ *vt* maniatar
pink /pɪŋk/ *a & n* color (*m*) de rosa
pinnacle /ˈpɪnəkl/ *n* pináculo *m*
pin: ~point *vt* determinar con precisión *f*. **~stripe** /ˈpɪnstraɪp/ *n* raya *f* fina
pint /paɪnt/ *n* pinta *f* (= *0.57 litre*)
pin-up /ˈpɪnʌp/ *n* (*fam*) fotografía *f* de mujer
pioneer /paɪəˈnɪə(r)/ *n* pionero *m*. ● *vt* ser el primero, promotor de, promover
pious /ˈpaɪəs/ *a* piadoso
pip[1] /pɪp/ *n* (*seed*) pepita *f*
pip[2] /pɪp/ (*time signal*) señal *f*
pip[3] /pɪp/ (*on uniform*) estrella *f*
pipe /paɪp/ *n* tubo *m*; (*mus*) caramillo *m*; (*for smoking*) pipa *f*. ● *vt* conducir por tuberías. **~down** (*fam*) bajar la voz, callarse. **~-cleaner** *n* limpiapipas *m invar*. **~-dream** *n* ilusión *f*. **~line** /ˈpaɪplaɪn/ *n* tubería *f*; (*for oil*) oleoducto *m*. **in the ~line** en preparación *f*. **~r** *n* flautista *m & f*
piping /ˈpaɪpɪŋ/ *n* tubería *f*. **~ hot** muy caliente, hirviendo
piquant /ˈpi:kənt/ *a* picante
pique /pi:k/ *n* resentimiento *m*
pira|cy /ˈpaɪərəsɪ/ *n* piratería *f*. **~te** /ˈpaɪərət/ *n* pirata *m*
pirouette /pɪrʊˈet/ *n* pirueta *f*. ● *vi* piruetear
Pisces /ˈpaɪsi:z/ *n* (*astr*) Piscis *m*
pistol /ˈpɪstl/ *n* pistola *f*
piston /ˈpɪstən/ *n* pistón *m*
pit /pɪt/ *n* foso *m*; (*mine*) mina *f*; (*of stomach*) boca *f*. ● *vt* (*pt* **pitted**) marcar con hoyos; (*fig*) oponer. **~ o.s. against** medirse con
pitch[1] /pɪtʃ/ *n* brea *f*
pitch[2] /pɪtʃ/ (*degree*) grado *m*; (*mus*) tono *m*; (*sport*) campo *m*. ● *vt* lanzar; armar ‹*tent*›. **~ into** (*fam*) atacar. ● *vi* caerse; ‹*ship*› cabecear. **~ in** (*fam*) contribuir. **~ed battle** *n* batalla *f* campal
pitch-black /pɪtʃˈblæk/ *a* oscuro como boca de lobo
pitcher /ˈpɪtʃə(r)/ *n* jarro *m*
pitchfork /ˈpɪtʃfɔ:k/ *n* horca *f*
piteous /ˈpɪtɪəs/ *a* lastimoso
pitfall /ˈpɪtfɔ:l/ *n* trampa *f*
pith /pɪθ/ *n* (*of orange, lemon*) médula *f*; (*fig*) meollo *m*
pithy /ˈpɪθɪ/ *a* (**-ier**, **-iest**) conciso
piti|ful /ˈpɪtɪfl/ *a* lastimoso. **~less** *a* despiadado
pittance /ˈpɪtns/ *n* sueldo *m* irrisorio
pity /ˈpɪtɪ/ *n* piedad *f*; (*regret*) lástima *f*. ● *vt* compadecerse de
pivot /ˈpɪvət/ *n* pivote *m*. ● *vt* montonar sobre un pivote. ● *vi* girar sobre un pivote; (*fig*) depender (**on** de)
pixie /ˈpɪksɪ/ *n* duende *m*
placard /ˈplækɑ:d/ *n* pancarta *f*; (*poster*) cartel *m*
placate /pləˈkeɪt/ *vt* apaciguar
place /pleɪs/ *n* lugar *m*; (*seat*) asiento *m*; (*post*) puesto *m*; (*house, fam*) casa *f*. **take ~** tener lugar. ● *vt* poner, colocar; (*remember*) recordar; (*identify*) identificar. **be**

~d (*in race*) colocarse. **~-mat** *n* salvamanteles *m invar*. **~ment** /'pleɪsmənt/ *n* colocación *f*

placid /'plæsɪd/ *a* plácido

plagiari|sm /'pleɪdʒərɪzm/ *n* plagio *m*. **~ze** /'pleɪdʒəraɪz/ *vt* plagiar

plague /pleɪg/ *n* peste *f*; (*fig*) plaga *f*. ● *vt* atormentar

plaice /pleɪs/ *n invar* platija *f*

plaid /plæd/ *n* tartán *m*

plain /pleɪn/ *a* (**-er**, **-est**) claro; (*simple*) sencillo; (*candid*) franco; (*ugly*) feo. **in ~ clothes** en traje de paisano. ● *adv* claramente. ● *n* llanura *f*. **~ly** *adv* claramente; (*frankly*) francamente; (*simply*) sencillamente. **~ness** *n* claridad *f*; (*simplicity*) sencillez *f*

plaintiff /'pleɪntɪf/ *n* demandante *m & f*

plait /plæt/ *vt* trenzar. ● *n* trenza *f*

plan /plæn/ *n* proyecto *m*; (*map*) plano *m*. ● *vt* (*pt* **planned**) planear, proyectar; (*intend*) proponerse

plane[1] /pleɪn/ *n* (*tree*) plátano *m*

plane[2] /pleɪn/ (*level*) nivel *m*; (*aviat*) avión *m*. ● *a* plano

plane[3] /pleɪn/ (*tool*) cepillo *m*. ● *vt* cepillar

planet /'plænɪt/ *n* planeta *m*. **~ary** *a* planetario

plank /plæŋk/ *n* tabla *f*

planning /'plænɪŋ/ *n* planificación *f*. **family ~** *n* planificación familiar. **town ~** *n* urbanismo *m*

plant /plɑ:nt/ *n* planta *f*; (*mec*) maquinaria *f*; (*factory*) fábrica *f*. ● *vt* plantar; (*place in position*) colocar. **~ation** /plæn'teɪʃn/ *n* plantación *f*

plaque /plæk/ *n* placa *f*

plasma /'plæzmə/ *n* plasma *m*

plaster /'plɑ:stə(r)/ *n* yeso *m*; (*adhesive*) esparadrapo *m*; (*for setting bones*) escayola *f*. **~ of Paris** *n* yeso *m* mate. ● *vt* enyesar; (*med*) escayolar ‹*broken bone*›; (*cover*) cubrir (**with** de). **~ed** *a* (*fam*) borracho

plastic /'plæstɪk/ *a & n* plástico (*m*)

Plasticine /'plæstɪsi:n/ *n* (*P*) pasta *f* de modelar, plastilina *f* (*P*)

plastic surgery /plæstɪk'sɜ:dʒərɪ/ *n* cirugía *f* estética

plate /pleɪt/ *n* plato *m*; (*of metal*) chapa *f*; (*silverware*) vajilla *f* de plata; (*in book*) lámina *f*. ● *vt* (*cover with metal*) chapear

plateau /'plætəʊ/ *n* (*pl* **plateaux**) *n* meseta *f*

plateful /'pleɪtfl/ *n* (*pl* **-fuls**) plato *m*

platform /'plætfɔ:m/ *n* plataforma *f*; (*rail*) andén *m*

platinum /'plætɪnəm/ *n* platino *m*

platitude /'plætɪtju:d/ *n* tópico *m*, perogrullada *f*, lugar *m* común

platonic /plə'tɒnɪk/ *a* platónico

platoon /plə'tu:n/ *n* pelotón *m*

platter /'plætə(r)/ *n* fuente *f*, plato *m* grande

plausible /'plɔ:zəbl/ *a* plausible; ‹*person*› convincente

play /pleɪ/ *vt* jugar; (*act role*) desempeñar el papel de; tocar ‹*instrument*›. **~ safe** no arriesgarse. **~ up to** halagar. ● *vi* jugar. **~ed out** agotado. ● *n* juego *m*; (*drama*) obra *f* de teatro. **~ on words** *n* juego *m* de palabras. **~ down** *vt* minimizar. **~ on** *vt* aprovecharse de. **~ up** *vi* (*fam*) causar problemas. **~-act** *vi* hacer la comedia. **~boy** /'pleɪbɔɪ/ *n* calavera *m*. **~er** *n* jugador *m*; (*mus*) músico *m*. **~ful** /'pleɪfl/ *a* juguetón. **~fully** *adv* jugando; (*jokingly*) en broma. **~ground** /'pleɪgraʊnd/ *n* parque *m* de juegos infantiles; (*in school*) campo *m* de recreo. **~-group** *n* jardín *m* de la infancia. **~ing** /'pleɪɪŋ/ *n* juego *m*. **~ing-card** *n* naipe *m*. **~ing-field** *n* campo *m* de deportes. **~mate** /'pleɪmeɪt/ *n* compañero *m* (de juego). **~-pen** *n* corralito *m*. **~thing** *n* juguete *m*. **~wright** /'pleɪraɪt/ *n* dramaturgo *m*

plc /pi:el'si:/ *abbr* (*public limited company*) S.A., sociedad *f* anónima

plea /pli:/ *n* súplica *f*; (*excuse*) excusa *f*; (*jurid*) defensa *f*

plead /pli:d/ *vt* (*jurid*) alegar; (*as excuse*) pretextar. ● *vi* suplicar; (*jurid*) abogar. **~ with** suplicar

pleasant /'pleznt/ *a* agradable

pleas|e /pli:z/ *int* por favor. ● *vt* agradar, dar gusto a. ● *vi* agradar; (*wish*) querer. **~e o.s.** hacer lo que quiera. **do as you ~e** haz lo que quieras. **~ed** *a* contento. **~ed with** satisfecho de. **~ing** *a* agradable

pleasur|e /'pleʒə(r)/ *n* placer *m*. **~able** *a* agradable

pleat /pli:t/ *n* pliegue *m*. ● *vt* hacer pliegues en

plebiscite /'plebɪsɪt/ *n* plebiscito *m*

plectrum /'plektrəm/ *n* plectro *m*

pledge /pledʒ/ *n* prenda *f*; (*promise*) promesa *f*. ● *vt* empeñar; (*promise*) prometer

plent|iful /'plentɪfl/ *a* abundante. **~y** /'plentɪ/ *n* abundancia *f*. **~y (of)** muchos (de)

pleurisy /'plʊərəsɪ/ *n* pleuresía *f*

pliable /'plaɪəbl/ *a* flexible

pliers /'plaɪəz/ *npl* alicates *mpl*

plight /plaɪt/ *n* situación *f* (difícil)

plimsolls /'plɪmsəlz/ *npl* zapatillas *fpl* de lona

plinth /plɪnθ/ *n* plinto *m*

plod /plɒd/ *vi* (*pt* **plodded**) caminar con paso pesado; (*work hard*) trabajar laboriosamente. **~der** *n* empollón *m*

plonk /plɒŋk/ *n* (*sl*) vino *m* peleón

plop /plɒp/ *n* paf *m*. ● *vi* (*pt* **plopped**) caerse con un paf

plot /plɒt/ *n* complot *m*; (*of novel etc*) argumento *m*; (*piece of land*) parcela *f*. ● *vt* (*pt* **plotted**) tramar; (*mark out*) trazar. ● *vi* conspirar

plough /plaʊ/ *n* arado *m*. ● *vt/i* arar. **~ through** avanzar laboriosamente por

ploy /plɔɪ/ *n* (*fam*) estratagema *f*, truco *m*

pluck /plʌk/ *vt* arrancar; depilarse ‹*eyebrows*›; desplumar ‹*bird*›; recoger ‹*flowers*›. **~ up courage** hacer de tripas corazón. ● *n* valor *m*. **~y** *a* (**-ier**, **-iest**) valiente

plug /plʌg/ *n* tapón *m*; (*elec*) enchufe *m*; (*auto*) bujía *f*. ● *vt* (*pt* **plugged**) tapar; (*advertise, fam*) dar publicidad a. **~ in** (*elec*) enchufar

plum /plʌm/ *n* ciruela *f*; (*tree*) ciruelo *m*

plumage /'plu:mɪdʒ/ *n* plumaje *m*

plumb /plʌm/ *a* vertical. ● *n* plomada *f*. ● *adv* verticalmente; (*exactly*) exactamente. ● *vt* sondar

plumb|er /'plʌmə(r)/ *n* fontanero *m*. **~ing** *n* instalación *f* sanitaria, instalación *f* de cañerías

plume /plu:m/ *n* pluma *f*

plum job /plʌm'dʒɒb/ *n* (*fam*) puesto *m* estupendo

plummet /'plʌmɪt/ *n* plomada *f*. ● *vi* caer a plomo, caer en picado

plump /plʌmp/ *a* (**-er**, **-est**) rechoncho. ● *vt*. **~ for** elegir. **~ness** *n* gordura *f*

plum pudding /plʌm'pʊdɪŋ/ *n* budín *m* de pasas

plunder /'plʌndə(r)/ *n* (*act*) saqueo *m*; (*goods*) botín *m*. ● *vt* saquear

plung|e /plʌndʒ/ *vt* hundir; (*in water*) sumergir. ● *vi* zambullirse; (*fall*) caer. ● *n* salto *m*. **~er** *n* (*for sink*) desatascador *m*; (*mec*) émbolo *m*. **~ing** *a* ‹*neckline*› bajo, escotado

plural /'plʊərəl/ *a* & *n* plural (*m*)

plus /plʌs/ *prep* más. ● *a* positivo. ● *n* signo *m* más; (*fig*) ventaja *f*. **five ~** más de cinco

plush /plʌʃ/ *n* felpa *f*. ● *a* de felpa, afelpado; (*fig*) lujoso. **~y** *a* lujoso

plutocrat /'plu:təkræt/ *n* plutócrata *m* & *f*

plutonium /plu:'təʊnjəm/ *n* plutonio *m*

ply /plaɪ/ *vt* manejar ‹*tool*›; ejercer ‹*trade*›. **~ s.o. with drink** dar continuamente de beber a uno. **~wood** *n* contrachapado *m*

p.m. /pi:'em/ *abbr* (*post meridiem*) de la tarde

pneumatic /nju:'mætɪk/ *a* neumático

pneumonia /nju:'məʊnjə/ *n* pulmonía *f*

PO /pi:'əʊ/ *abbr* (*Post Office*) oficina *f* de correos

poach /pəʊtʃ/ *vt* escalfar ‹*egg*›; cocer ‹*fish etc*›; (*steal*) cazar en vedado. **~er** *n* cazador *m* furtivo

pocket /'pɒkɪt/ *n* bolsillo *m*; (*of air, resistance*) bolsa *f*. **be in ~** salir ganado. **be out of ~** salir perdiendo. ● *vt* poner en el bolsillo. **~-book** *n* (*notebook*) libro *m* de bolsillo; (*purse, Amer*) cartera *f*; (*handbag, Amer*) bolso *m*. **~-money** *n* dinero *m* para los gastos personales

pock-marked /'pɒkmɑ:kt/ *a* ‹*face*› picado de viruelas

pod /pɒd/ *n* vaina *f*

podgy /'pɒdʒɪ/ *a* (**-ier**, **-iest**) rechoncho

poem /'pəʊɪm/ *n* poesía *f*

poet /'pəʊɪt/ *n* poeta *m*. **~ess** *n* poetisa *f*. **~ic** /-'etɪk/ *a*, **~ical** /-'etɪkl/ *a* poético. **P~ Laureate** *n* poeta laureado. **~ry** /'pəʊɪtrɪ/ *n* poesía *f*

poignant /'pɔɪnjənt/ *a* conmovedor

point /pɔɪnt/ *n* punto *m*; (*sharp end*) punta *f*; (*significance*) lo importante; (*elec*) toma *f* de corriente. **good ~s** cualidades *fpl*. **to the ~** pertinente. **up to a ~** hasta cierto punto. **what is the ~?** ¿para qué?, ¿a qué fin? ● *vt* (*aim*) apuntar; (*show*) indicar. **~ out** señalar. ● *vi* señalar. **~-blank** *a* & *adv* a boca de jarro, a quemarropa. **~ed** /'pɔɪntɪd/ *a* puntiagudo; (*fig*) mordaz. **~er** /'pɔɪntə(r)/ *n* indicador *m*; (*dog*) perro *m* de muestra; (*clue, fam*) indicación *f*. **~less** /'pɔɪntlɪs/ *a* inútil

poise /pɔɪz/ *n* equilibrio *m*; (*elegance*) elegancia *f*; (*fig*) aplomo *m*. **~d** *a* en equilibrio. **~d for** listo para

poison /'pɔɪzn/ *n* veneno *m*. ● *vt* envenenar. **~ous** *a* venenoso; ‹*chemical etc*› tóxico

poke /pəʊk/ *vt* empujar; atizar ‹*fire*›. **~ fun at** burlarse de. **~ out** asomar ‹*head*›. ● *vi* hurgar; (*pry*) meterse. **~ about** fisgonear. ● *n* empuje *m*

poker[1] /'pəʊkə(r)/ *n* atizador *m*

poker[2] /'pəʊkə(r)/ (*cards*) póquer *m*. **~-face** *n* cara *f* inmutable

poky /'pəʊkɪ/ *a* (**-ier**, **-iest**) estrecho

Poland /'pəʊlənd/ *n* Polonia *f*

polar /'pəʊlə(r)/ *a* polar. **~ bear** *n* oso *m* blanco

polarize /'pəʊləraɪz/ *vt* polarizar

Pole /pəʊl/ polaco *n*

pole[1] /pəʊl/ *n* palo *m*; (*for flag*) asta *f*

pole[2] /pəʊl/ (*geog*) polo *m*. **~-star** *n* estrella *f* polar

polemic /pə'lemɪk/ *a* polémico. ● *n* polémica *f*

police /pə'li:s/ *n* policía *f*. ● *vt* vigilar. **~man** /pə'li:smən/ *n* (*pl* **-men**) policía *m*, guardia *m*. **~ record** *n* antecedentes *mpl* penales. **~ state** *n* estado *m* policíaco. **~ station** *n* comisaría *f*. **~woman** /-wʊmən/ *n* (*pl* **-women**) mujer *m* policía

policy[1] /'pɒlɪsɪ/ *n* política *f*

policy[2] /'pɒlɪsɪ/ (*insurance*) póliza *f* (de seguros)

polio(myelitis) /'pəʊlɪəʊ(maɪə'laɪtɪs)/ *n* polio(mielitis) *f*

polish /'pɒlɪʃ/ *n* (*for shoes*) betún *m*; (*for floor*) cera *f*; (*for nails*) esmalte *m* de uñas; (*shine*) brillo *m*; (*fig*) finura *f*. **nail ~** esmalte *m* de uñas. ● *vt* pulir; limpiar ‹*shoes*›; encerar ‹*floor*›. **~ off** despachar. **~ed** *a* pulido; ‹*manner*› refinado. **~er** *n* pulidor *m*; (*machine*) pulidora *f*

Polish /'pəʊlɪʃ/ *a* & *n* polaco (*m*)

polite /pə'laɪt/ *a* cortés. **~ly** *adv* cortésmente. **~ness** *n* cortesía *f*

politic|al /pə'lɪtɪkl/ *a* político. **~ian** /pɒlɪ'tɪʃn/ *n* político *m*. **~s** /'pɒlətɪks/ *n* política *f*

polka /'pɒlkə/ *n* polca *f*. **~ dots** *npl* diseño *m* de puntos

poll /pəʊl/ *n* elección *f*; (*survey*) encuesta *f*. ● *vt* obtener ‹*votes*›

pollen /'pɒlən/ *n* polen *m*

polling-booth /'pəʊlɪŋbu:ð/ *n* cabina *f* de votar

pollut|e /pə'lu:t/ *vt* contaminar. **~ion** /-ʃn/ *n* contaminación *f*

polo /'pəʊləʊ/ *n* polo *m*. **~-neck** *n* cuello *m* vuelto

poltergeist /'pɒltəgaɪst/ *n* duende *m*

polyester /pɒlɪ'estə(r)/ *n* poliéster *m*

polygam|ist /pə'lɪgəmɪst/ *n* polígamo *m*. **~ous** *a* polígamo. **~y** /pə'lɪgəmɪ/ *n* poligamia *f*

polyglot /'pɒlɪglɒt/ *a* & *n* políglota (*m* & *f*)

polygon /'pɒlɪgən/ *n* polígono *m*

polyp /'pɒlɪp/ *n* pólipo *m*

polystyrene /pɒlɪ'staɪri:n/ *n* poliestireno *m*

polytechnic /pɒlɪ'teknɪk/ *n* escuela *f* politécnica

polythene /'pɒlɪθi:n/ *n* polietileno *m*. **~ bag** *n* bolsa *f* de plástico

pomegranate /'pɒmɪgrænɪt/ *n* (*fruit*) granada *f*

pommel /'pʌml/ *n* pomo *m*

pomp /pɒmp/ *n* pompa *f*

pompon /'pɒmpɒn/ *n* pompón *m*

pompo|sity /pɒm'pɒsətɪ/ *n* pomposidad *f*. **~us** /'pɒmpəs/ *a* pomposo

poncho /'pɒntʃəʊ/ *n* (*pl* **-os**) poncho *m*

pond /pɒnd/ *n* charca *f*; (*artificial*) estanque *m*

ponder /'pɒndə(r)/ *vt* considerar. ● *vi* reflexionar. **~ous** /'pɒndərəs/ *a* pesado

pong /pɒŋ/ *n* (*sl*) hedor *m*. ● *vi* (*sl*) apestar

pontif|f /'pɒntɪf/ *n* pontífice *m*. **~ical** /-'tɪfɪkl/ *a* pontifical; (*fig*) dogmático. **~icate** /pɒn'tɪfɪkeɪt/ *vi* pontificar

pontoon /pɒn'tu:n/ *n* pontón *m*. **~ bridge** *n* puente *m* de pontones

pony /'pəʊnɪ/ *n* poni *m*. **~-tail** *n* cola *f* de caballo. **~-trekking** *n* excursionismo *m* en poni

poodle /'pu:dl/ *n* perro *m* de lanas, caniche *m*

pool[1] /pu:l/ *n* charca *f*; (*artificial*) estanque *m*. **(swimming-)~** *n* piscina *f*

pool[2] /pu:l/ (*common fund*) fondos *mpl* comunes; (*snooker*) billar *m* americano. ● *vt* aunar. **~s** *npl* quinielas *fpl*

poor /pʊə(r)/ *a* (**-er**, **-est**) pobre; (*not good*) malo. **be in ~ health** estar mal de salud. **~ly** *a* (*fam*) indispuesto. ● *adv* pobremente; (*badly*) mal

pop[1] /pɒp/ *n* ruido *m* seco; (*of bottle*) taponazo *m*. ● *vt* (*pt* **popped**) hacer reventar; (*put*) poner. ~ **in** *vi* entrar; (*visit*) pasar por. ~ **out** *vi* saltar; ‹*person*› salir un rato. ~ **up** *vi* surgir, aparecer

pop[2] /pɒp/ *a* (*popular*) pop *invar*. ● *n* (*fam*) música *f* pop. ~ **art** *n* arte *m* pop

popcorn /ˈpɒpkɔ:n/ *n* palomitas *fpl*

pope /pəʊp/ *n* papa *m*

popgun /ˈpɒpgʌn/ *n* pistola *f* de aire comprimido

poplar /ˈpɒplə(r)/ *n* chopo *m*

poplin /ˈpɒplɪn/ *n* popelina *f*

poppy /ˈpɒpɪ/ *n* amapola *f*

popular /ˈpɒpjʊlə(r)/ *a* popular. **~ity** /-ˈlærətɪ/ *n* popularidad *f*. **~ize** *vt* popularizar

populat|e /ˈpɒpjʊleɪt/ *vt* poblar. **~ion** /-ˈleɪʃn/ *n* población *f*; (*number of inhabitants*) habitantes *mpl*

porcelain /ˈpɔ:səlɪn/ *n* porcelana *f*

porch /pɔ:tʃ/ *n* porche *m*

porcupine /ˈpɔ:kjʊpaɪn/ *n* puerco *m* espín

pore[1] /pɔ:(r)/ *n* poro *m*

pore[2] /pɔ:(r)/ *vi*. ~ **over** estudiar detenidamente

pork /pɔ:k/ *n* cerdo *m*

porn /pɔ:n/ *n* (*fam*) pornografía *f*. **~ographic** /-əˈgræfɪk/ *a* pornográfico. **~ography** /pɔ:ˈnɒgrəfɪ/ *n* pornografía *f*

porous /ˈpɔ:rəs/ *a* poroso

porpoise /ˈpɔ:pəs/ *n* marsopa *f*

porridge /ˈpɒrɪdʒ/ *n* gachas *fpl* de avena

port[1] /pɔ:t/ *n* puerto *m*; (*porthole*) portilla *f*. ~ **of call** puerto de escala

port[2] /pɔ:t/ (*naut, left*) babor *m*. ● *a* de babor

port[3] /pɔ:t/ (*wine*) oporto *m*

portable /ˈpɔ:təbl/ *a* portátil

portal /ˈpɔ:tl/ *n* portal *m*

portent /ˈpɔ:tent/ *n* presagio *m*

porter /ˈpɔ:tə(r)/ *n* portero *m*; (*for luggage*) mozo *m*. **~age** *n* porte *m*

portfolio /pɔ:tˈfəʊljəʊ/ *n* (*pl* **-os**) cartera *f*

porthole /ˈpɔ:thəʊl/ *n* portilla *f*

portico /ˈpɔ:tɪkəʊ/ *n* (*pl* **-oes**) pórtico *m*

portion /ˈpɔ:ʃn/ *n* porción *f*. ● *vt* repartir

portly /ˈpɔ:tlɪ/ *a* (**-ier**, **-iest**) corpulento

portrait /ˈpɔ:trɪt/ *n* retrato *m*

portray /pɔ:ˈtreɪ/ *vt* retratar; (*represent*) representar. **~al** *n* retrato *m*

Portug|al /ˈpɔ:tjʊgl/ *n* Portugal *m*. **~uese** /-ˈgi:z/ *a* & *n* portugués (*m*)

pose /pəʊz/ *n* postura *f*. ● *vt* colocar; hacer ‹*question*›; plantear ‹*problem*›. ● *vi* posar. ~ **as** hacerse pasar por. **~r** /ˈpəʊzə(r)/ *n* pregunta *f* difícil

posh /pɒʃ/ *a* (*sl*) elegante

position /pəˈzɪʃn/ *n* posición *f*; (*job*) puesto *m*; (*status*) rango *m*. ● *vt* colocar

positive /ˈpɒzətɪv/ *a* positivo; (*real*) verdadero; (*certain*) seguro. ● *n* (*foto*) positiva *f*. **~ly** *adv* positivamente

possess /pəˈzes/ *vt* poseer. **~ion** /pəˈzeʃn/ *n* posesión *f*. **take ~ion of** tomar posesión de. **~ions** *npl* posesiones *fpl*; (*jurid*) bienes *mpl*. **~ive** /pəˈzesɪv/ *a* posesivo. **~or** *n* poseedor *m*

possib|ility /pɒsəˈbɪlətɪ/ *n* posibilidad *f*. **~le** /ˈpɒsəbl/ *a* posible. **~ly** *adv* posiblemente

post[1] /pəʊst/ *n* (*pole*) poste *m*. ● *vt* fijar ‹*notice*›

post[2] /pəʊst/ (*place*) puesto *m*

post[3] /pəʊst/ (*mail*) correo *m*. ● *vt* echar ‹*letter*›. **keep s.o. ~ed** tener a uno al corriente

post... /pəʊst/ *pref* post

post: ~age /ˈpəʊstɪdʒ/ *n* franqueo *m*. **~al** /ˈpəʊstl/ *a* postal. **~al order** *n* giro *m* postal. **~-box** *n* buzón *m*. **~card** /ˈpəʊstkɑ:d/ *n* (tarjeta *f*) postal *f*. **~-code** *n* código *m* postal

post-date /pəʊstˈdeɪt/ *vt* poner fecha posterior a

poster /ˈpəʊstə(r)/ *n* cartel *m*

poste restante /pəʊstˈrestɑ:nt/ *n* lista *f* de correos

posteri|or /pɒˈstɪərɪə(r)/ *a* posterior. ● *n* trasero *m*. **~ty** /pɒsˈterətɪ/ *n* posteridad *f*

posthumous /ˈpɒstjʊməs/ *a* póstumo. **~ly** *adv* después de la muerte

post: ~man /ˈpəʊstmən/ *n* (*pl* **-men**) cartero *m*. **~mark** /ˈpəʊstmɑ:k/ *n* matasellos *m invar*. **~master** /ˈpəʊstmɑ:stə(r) *n* administrador *m* de correos. **~mistress** /ˈpəʊstmɪstrɪs/ *n* administradora *f* de correos

post-mortem /ˈpəʊstmɔ:təm/ *n* autopsia *f*

Post Office /ˈpəʊstɒfɪs/ *n* oficina *f* de correos, correos *mpl*

postpone /pəʊst'pəʊn/ *vt* aplazar. **~ment** *n* aplazamiento *m*
postscript /'pəʊstskrɪpt/ *n* posdata *f*
postulant /'pɒstjʊlənt/ *n* postulante *m & f*
postulate /'pɒstjʊleɪt/ *vt* postular
posture /'pɒstʃə(r)/ *n* postura *f*. ● *vi* adoptar una postura
posy /'pəʊzɪ/ *n* ramillete *m*
pot /pɒt/ *n* (*for cooking*) olla *f*; (*for flowers*) tiesto *m*; (*marijuana, sl*) mariguana *f*. **go to ~** (*sl*) echarse a perder. ● *vt* (*pt* **potted**) poner en tiesto
potassium /pə'tæsjəm/ *n* potasio *m*
potato /pə'teɪtəʊ/ *n* (*pl* **-oes**) patata *f*, papa *f* (*LAm*)
pot: **~-belly** *n* barriga *f*. **~-boiler** *n* obra *f* literaria escrita sólo para ganar dinero
poten|cy /'pəʊtənsɪ/ *n* potencia *f*. **~t** /'pəʊtnt/ *a* potente; ‹*drink*› fuerte
potentate /'pəʊtənteɪt/ *n* potentado *m*
potential /pəʊ'tenʃl/ *a & n* potencial (*m*). **~ity** /-ʃɪ'ælətɪ/ *n* potencialidad *f*. **~ly** *adv* potencialmente
pot-hole /'pɒthəʊl/ *n* caverna *f*; (*in road*) bache *m*. **~r** *n* espeleólogo *m*
potion /'pəʊʃn/ *n* poción *f*
pot: **~ luck** *n* lo que haya. **~-shot** *n* tiro *m* al azar. **~ted** /'pɒtɪd/ *see* **pot**. ● *a* ‹*food*› en conserva
potter[1] /'pɒtə(r)/ *n* alfarero *m*
potter[2] /'pɒtə(r)/ *vi* hacer pequeños trabajos agradables, no hacer nada de particular
pottery /'pɒtərɪ/ *n* cerámica *f*
potty /'pɒtɪ/ *a* (**-ier**, **-iest**) (*sl*) chiflado. ● *n* orinal *m*
pouch /paʊtʃ/ *n* bolsa *f* pequeña
pouffe /pu:f/ *n* (*stool*) taburete *m*
poulterer /'pəʊltərə(r)/ *n* pollero *m*
poultice /'pəʊltɪs/ *n* cataplasma *f*
poultry /'pəʊltrɪ/ *n* aves *fpl* de corral
pounce /paʊns/ *vi* saltar, atacar de repente. ● *n* salto *m*, ataque *m* repentino
pound[1] /paʊnd/ *n* (*weight*) libra *f* (= *454g*); (*money*) libra *f* (esterlina)
pound[2] /paʊnd/ *n* (*for cars*) depósito *m*
pound[3] /paʊnd/ *vt* (*crush*) machacar; (*bombard*) bombardear. ● *vi* golpear; ‹*heart*› palpitar; (*walk*) ir con pasos pesados
pour /pɔ:(r)/ *vt* verter. **~ out** servir ‹*drink*›. ● *vi* fluir; (*rain*) llover a cántaros. **~ in** ‹*people*› entrar en tropel. **~ing rain** *n* lluvia *f* torrencial. **~ out** ‹*people*› salir en tropel
pout /paʊt/ *vi* hacer pucheros. ● *n* puchero *m*, mala cara *f*
poverty /'pɒvətɪ/ *n* pobreza *f*
powder /'paʊdə(r)/ *n* polvo *m*; (*cosmetic*) polvos *mpl*. ● *vt* polvorear; (*pulverize*) pulverizar. **~ one's face** ponerse polvos en la cara. **~ed** *a* en polvo. **~y** *a* polvoriento
power /'paʊə(r)/ *n* poder *m*; (*elec*) corriente *f*; (*energy*) energía *f*; (*nation*) potencia *f*. **~ cut** *n* apagón *m*. **~ed** *a* con motor. **~ed by** impulsado por. **~ful** *a* poderoso. **~less** *a* impotente. **~-station** *n* central *f* eléctrica
practicable /'præktɪkəbl/ *a* practicable
practical /'præktɪkl/ *a* práctico. **~ joke** *n* broma *f* pesada. **~ly** *adv* prácticamente
practi|ce /'præktɪs/ *n* práctica *f*; (*custom*) costumbre *f*; (*exercise*) ejercicio *m*; (*sport*) entrenamiento *m*; (*clients*) clientela *f*. **be in ~ce** ‹*doctor, lawyer*› ejercer. **be out of ~ce** no estar en forma. **in ~ce** (*in fact*) en la práctica; (*on form*) en forma. **~se** /'præktɪs/ *vt* hacer ejercicios en; (*put into practice*) poner en práctica; (*sport*) entrenarse en; ejercer ‹*profession*›. ● *vi* ejercitarse; ‹*professional*› ejercer. — **~sed** *a* experto
practitioner /præk'tɪʃənə(r)/ *n* profesional *m & f*. **general ~** médico *m* de cabecera. **medical ~** médico *m*
pragmatic /præg'mætɪk/ *a* pragmático
prairie /'preərɪ/ *n* pradera *f*
praise /preɪz/ *vt* alabar. ● *n* alabanza *f*. **~worthy** *a* loable
pram /præm/ *n* cochecito *m* de niño
prance /prɑ:ns/ *vi* ‹*horse*› hacer cabriolas; ‹*person*› pavonearse
prank /præŋk/ *n* travesura *f*
prattle /prætl/ *vi* parlotear. ● *n* parloteo *m*
prawn /prɔ:n/ *n* gamba *f*
pray /preɪ/ *vi* rezar. **~er** /preə(r)/ *n* oración *f*. **~ for** rogar
pre.. /pri:/ *pref* pre...
preach /pri:tʃ/ *vt/i* predicar. **~er** *n* predicador *m*
preamble /pri:'æmbl/ *n* preámbulo *m*

pre-arrange /pri:ə'reɪndʒ/ *vt* arreglar de antemano. **~ment** *n* arreglo *m* previo

precarious /prɪ'keərɪəs/ *a* precario. **~ly** *adv* precariamente

precaution /prɪ'kɔ:ʃn/ *n* precaución *f*. **~ary** *a* de precaución; (*preventive*) preventivo

precede /prɪ'si:d/ *vt* preceder

preceden|ce /'presɪdəns/ *n* precedencia *f*. **~t** /'presɪdənt/ *n* precedente *m*

preceding /prɪ'si:dɪŋ/ *a* precedente

precept /'pri:sept/ *n* precepto *m*

precinct /'pri:sɪŋkt/ *n* recinto *m*. **pedestrian ~** zona *f* peatonal. **~s** *npl* contornos *mpl*

precious /'preʃəs/ *a* precioso. ● *adv* (*fam*) muy

precipice /'presɪpɪs/ *n* precipicio *m*

precipitat|e /prɪ'sɪpɪteɪt/ *vt* precipitar. /prɪ'sɪpɪtət/ *n* precipitado *m*. ● *a* precipitado. **~ion** /-'teɪʃn/ *n* precipitación *f*

precipitous /prɪ'sɪpɪtəs/ *a* escarpado

précis /'preɪsi:/ *n* (*pl* **précis** /-si:z/) resumen *m*

precis|e /prɪ'saɪs/ *a* preciso; (*careful*) meticuloso. **~ely** *adv* precisamente. **~ion** /-'sɪʒn/ *n* precisión *f*

preclude /prɪ'klu:d/ *vt* (*prevent*) impedir; (*exclude*) excluir

precocious /prɪ'kəʊʃəs/ *a* precoz. **~ly** *adv* precozmente

preconce|ived /pri:kən'si:vd/ *a* preconcebido. **~ption** /-'sepʃn/ *n* preconcepción *f*

precursor /pri:'kɜ:sə(r)/ *n* precursor *m*

predator /'predətə(r)/ *n* animal *m* de rapiña. **~y** *a* de rapiña

predecessor /'pri:dɪsesə(r)/ *n* predecesor *m*, antecesor *m*

predestin|ation /prɪdestɪ'neɪʃn/ *n* predestinación *f*. **~e** /pri:'destɪn/ *vt* predestinar

predicament /prɪ'dɪkəmənt/ *n* apuro *m*

predicat|e /'predɪkət/ *n* predicado *m*. **~ive** /prɪ'dɪkətɪv/ *a* predicativo

predict /prɪ'dɪkt/ *vt* predecir. **~ion** /-ʃn/ *n* predicción *f*

predilection /pri:dɪ'lekʃn/ *n* predilección *f*

predispose /pri:dɪ'spəʊz/ *vt* predisponer

predomina|nt /prɪ'dɒmɪnənt/ *a* predominante. **~te** /prɪ'dɒmɪneɪt/ *vi* predominar

pre-eminent /pri:'emɪnənt/ *a* preeminente

pre-empt /pri:'empt/ *vt* adquirir por adelantado, adelantarse a

preen /pri:n/ *vt* limpiar, arreglar. **~ o.s.** atildarse

prefab /'pri:fæb/ *n* (*fam*) casa *f* prefabricada. **~ricated** /-'fæbrɪkeɪtɪd/ *a* prefabricado

preface /'prefəs/ *n* prólogo *m*

prefect /'pri:fekt/ *n* monitor *m*; (*official*) prefecto *m*

prefer /prɪ'fɜ:(r)/ *vt* (*pt* **preferred**) preferir. **~able** /'prefrəbl/ *a* preferible. **~ence** /'prefrəns/ *n* preferencia *f*. **~ential** /-ə'renʃl/ *a* preferente

prefix /'pri:fɪks/ *n* (*pl* **-ixes**) prefijo *m*

pregnan|cy /'pregnənsɪ/ *n* embarazo *m*. **~t** /'pregnənt/ *a* embarazada

prehistoric /pri:hɪ'stɒrɪk/ *a* prehistórico

prejudge /pri:'dʒʌdʒ/ *vt* prejuzgar

prejudice /'predʒʊdɪs/ *n* prejuicio *m*; (*harm*) perjuicio *m*. ● *vt* predisponer; (*harm*) perjudicar. **~d** *a* parcial

prelate /'prelət/ *n* prelado *m*

preliminar|ies /prɪ'lɪmɪnərɪz/ *npl* preliminares *mpl*. **~y** /prɪ'lɪmɪnərɪ/ *a* preliminar

prelude /'prelju:d/ *n* preludio *m*

pre-marital /pri:'mærɪtl/ *a* prematrimonial

premature /'premətjʊə(r)/ *a* prematuro

premeditated /pri:'medɪteɪtɪd/ *a* premeditado

premier /'premɪə(r)/ *a* primero. ● *n* (*pol*) primer ministro

première /'premɪə(r)/ *n* estreno *m*

premises /'premɪsɪz/ *npl* local *m*. **on the ~** en el local

premiss /'premɪs/ *n* premisa *f*

premium /'pri:mɪəm/ *n* premio *m*. **at a ~** muy solicitado

premonition /pri:mə'nɪʃn/ *n* presentimiento *m*

preoccup|ation /pri:ɒkjʊ'peɪʃn/ *n* preocupación *f*. **~ied** /-'ɒkjʊpaɪd/ *a* preocupado

prep /prep/ *n* deberes *mpl*

preparation /prepə'reɪʃn/ *n* preparación *f*. **~s** *npl* preparativos *mpl*

preparatory /prɪ'pærətrɪ/ *a* preparatorio. ~ **school** *n* escuela *f* primaria privada

prepare /prɪ'peə(r)/ *vt* preparar. ● *vi* prepararse. ~**d to** dispuesto a

prepay /pri:'peɪ/ *vt* (*pt* **-paid**) pagar por adelantado

preponderance /prɪ'pɒndərəns/ *n* preponderancia *f*

preposition /prepə'zɪʃn/ *n* preposición *f*

prepossessing /pri:pə'zesɪŋ/ *a* atractivo

preposterous /prɪ'pɒstərəs/ *a* absurdo

prep school /'prepsku:l/ *n* escuela *f* primaria privada

prerequisite /pri:'rekwɪzɪt/ *n* requisito *m* previo

prerogative /prɪ'rɒgətɪv/ *n* prerrogativa *f*

Presbyterian /prezbɪ'tɪərɪən/ *a* & *n* presbiteriano (*m*)

prescri|be /prɪ'skraɪb/ *vt* prescribir; (*med*) recetar. ~**ption** /-'ɪpʃn/ *n* prescripción *f*; (*med*) receta *f*

presence /'prezns/ *n* presencia *f*; (*attendance*) asistencia *f*. ~ **of mind** presencia *f* de ánimo

present[1] /'preznt/ *a* & *n* presente (*m* & *f*). **at** ~ actualmente. **for the** ~ por ahora

present[2] /'preznt/ *n* (*gift*) regalo *m*

present[3] /prɪ'zent/ *vt* presentar; (*give*) obsequiar. ~ **s.o. with** obsequiar a uno con. ~**able** *a* presentable. ~**ation** /prezn'teɪʃn/ *n* presentación *f*; (*ceremony*) ceremonia *f* de entrega

presently /'prezntlɪ/ *adv* dentro de poco

preserv|ation /prezə'veɪʃn/ *n* conservación *f*. ~**ative** /prɪ'zɜ:vətɪv/ *n* preservativo *m*. ~**e** /prɪ'zɜ:v/ *vt* conservar; (*maintain*) mantener; (*culin*) poner en conserva. ● *n* coto *m*; (*jam*) confitura *f*

preside /prɪ'zaɪd/ *vi* presidir. ~ **over** presidir

presiden|cy /'prezɪdənsɪ/ *n* presidencia *f*. ~**t** /'prezɪdənt/ *n* presidente *m*. ~**tial** /-'denʃl/ *a* presidencial

press /pres/ *vt* apretar; exprimir ‹*fruit etc*›; (*insist on*) insistir en; (*iron*) planchar. **be** ~**ed for** tener poco. ● *vi* apretar; ‹*time*› apremiar; (*fig*) urgir. ~ **on** seguir adelante. ● *n* presión *f*; (*mec, newspapers*) prensa *f*; (*printing*) imprenta *f*. ~ **conference** *n* rueda *f* de prensa. ~ **cutting** *n* recorte *m* de periódico. ~**ing** /'presɪŋ/ *a* urgente. ~**-stud** *n* automático *m*. ~**-up** *n* plancha *f*

pressure /'preʃə(r)/ *n* presión *f*. ● *vt* hacer presión sobre. ~**-cooker** *n* olla *f* a presión. ~ **group** *n* grupo *m* de presión

pressurize /'preʃəraɪz/ *vt* hacer presión sobre

prestig|e /pre'sti:ʒ/ *n* prestigio *m*. ~**ious** /pre'stɪdʒəs/ *a* prestigioso

presum|ably /prɪ'zju:məblɪ/ *adv* presumiblemente, probablemente. ~**e** /prɪ'zju:m/ *vt* presumir. ~**e (up)on** *vi* abusar de. ~**ption** /-'zʌmpʃn/ *n* presunción *f*. ~**ptuous** /prɪ'zʌmptʃʊəs/ *a* presuntuoso

presuppose /pri:sə'pəʊz/ *vt* presuponer

preten|ce /prɪ'tens/ *n* fingimiento *m*; (*claim*) pretensión *f*; (*pretext*) pretexto *m*. ~**d** /prɪ'tend/ *vt/i* fingir. ~**d to** (*lay claim*) pretender

pretentious /prɪ'tenʃəs/ *a* pretencioso

pretext /'pri:tekst/ *n* pretexto *m*

pretty /'prɪtɪ/ *a* (**-ier**, **-iest**) *adv* bonito, lindo (*esp LAm*); ‹*person*› guapo

prevail /prɪ'veɪl/ *vi* predominar; (*win*) prevalecer. ~ **on** persuadir

prevalen|ce /'prevələns/ *n* costumbre *f*. ~**t** /'prevələnt/ *a* extendido

prevaricate /prɪ'værɪkeɪt/ *vi* despistar

prevent /prɪ'vent/ *vt* impedir. ~**able** *a* evitable. ~**ion** /-ʃn/ *n* prevención *f*. ~**ive** *a* preventivo

preview /'pri:vju:/ *n* preestreno *m*, avance *m*

previous /'pri:vɪəs/ *a* anterior. ~ **to** antes de. ~**ly** *adv* anteriormente, antes

pre-war /pri:'wɔ:(r)/ *a* de antes de la guerra

prey /preɪ/ *n* presa *f*; (*fig*) víctima *f*. **bird of** ~ *n* ave *f* de rapiña. ● *vi*. ~ **on** alimentarse de; (*worry*) atormentar

price /praɪs/ *n* precio *m*. ● *vt* fijar el precio de. ~**less** *a* inapreciable; (*amusing, fam*) muy divertido. ~**y** *a* (*fam*) caro

prick /prɪk/ *vt/i* pinchar. ~ **up one's ears** aguzar las orejas. ● *n* pinchazo *m*

prickl|e /'prɪkl/ *n* (*bot*) espina f; (*of animal*) púa *f*; (*sensation*) picor *m*. **~y** *a* espinoso; ‹*animal*› lleno de púas; ‹*person*› quisquilloso

pride /praɪd/ *n* orgullo *m*. **~ of place** *n* puesto *m* de honor. ● *vr*. **~ o.s. on** enorgullecerse de

priest /pri:st/ *n* sacerdote *m*. **~hood** *n* sacerdocio *m*. **~ly** *a* sacerdotal

prig /prɪg/ *n* mojigato *m*. **~gish** *a* mojigato

prim /prɪm/ *a* (**primmer, primmest**) estirado; (*prudish*) gazmoño

primarily /'praɪmərɪlɪ/ *adv* en primer lugar

primary /'praɪmərɪ/ *a* primario; (*chief*) principal. **~ school** *n* escuela *f* primaria

prime[1] /praɪm/ *vt* cebar ‹*gun*›; (*prepare*) preparar; aprestar ‹*surface*›

prime[2] /praɪm/ *a* principal; (*first rate*) excelente. **~ minister** *n* primer ministro *m*. ● *n*. **be in one's ~** estar en la flor de la vida

primer[1] /'praɪmə(r)/ *n* (*of paint*) primera mano *f*

primer[2] /'praɪmə(r)/ (*book*) silabario *m*

primeval /praɪ'mi:vl/ *a* primitivo

primitive /'prɪmɪtɪv/ *a* primitivo

primrose /'prɪmrəʊz/ *n* primavera *f*

prince /prɪns/ *n* príncipe *m*. **~ly** *a* principesco. **~ss** /prɪn'ses/ *n* princesa *f*

principal /'prɪnsəpl/ *a* principal. ● *n* (*of school etc*) director *m*

principality /prɪnsɪ'pælətɪ/ *n* principado *m*

principally /'prɪnsɪpəlɪ/ *adv* principalmente

principle /'prɪnsəpl/ *n* principio *m*. **in ~** en principio. **on ~** por principio

print /prɪnt/ *vt* imprimir; (*write in capitals*) escribir con letras de molde. ● *n* (*of finger, foot*) huella *f*; (*letters*) caracteres *mpl*; (*of design*) estampado *m*; (*picture*) grabado *m*; (*photo*) copia *f*. **in ~** ‹*book*› disponible. **out of ~** agotado. **~ed matter** *n* impresos *mpl*. **~er** /'prɪntə(r)/ *n* impresor *m*; (*machine*) impresora *f*. **~ing** *n* tipografía *f*. **~-out** *n* listado *m*

prior /'praɪə(r)/ *n* prior *m*. ● *a* anterior. **~ to** antes de

priority /praɪ'ɒrətɪ/ *n* prioridad *f*

priory /'praɪərɪ/ *n* priorato *m*

prise /praɪz/ *vt* apalancar. **~ open** abrir por fuerza

prism /'prɪzəm/ *n* prisma *m*

prison /'prɪzn/ *n* cárcel *m*. **~er** *n* prisionero *m*; (*in prison*) preso *m*; (*under arrest*) detenido *m*. **~ officer** *n* carcelero *m*

pristine /'prɪsti:n/ *a* prístino

privacy /'prɪvəsɪ/ *n* intimidad *f*; (*private life*) vida *f* privada. **in ~** en la intimidad

private /'praɪvət/ *a* privado; (*confidential*) personal; ‹*lessons, house*› particular; ‹*ceremony*› en la intimidad. ● *n* soldado *m* raso. **in ~** en privado; (*secretly*) en secreto. **~ eye** *n* (*fam*) detective *m* privado. **~ly** *adv* en privado; (*inwardly*) interiormente

privation /praɪ'veɪʃn/ *n* privación *f*

privet /'prɪvɪt/ *n* alheña *f*

privilege /'prɪvəlɪdʒ/ *n* privilegio *m*. **~d** *a* privilegiado

privy /'prɪvɪ/ *a*. **~ to** al corriente de

prize /praɪz/ *n* premio *m*. ● *a* ‹*idiot etc*› de remate. ● *vt* estimar. **~-fighter** *n* boxeador *m* profesional. **~-giving** *n* reparto *m* de premios. **~winner** *n* premiado *m*

pro /prəʊ/ *n*. **~s and cons** el pro *m* y el contra *m*

probab|ility /prɒbə'bɪlətɪ/ *n* probabilidad *f*. **~le** /'prɒbəbl/ *a* probable. **~ly** *adv* probablemente

probation /prə'beɪʃn/ *n* prueba *f*; (*jurid*) libertad *f* condicional. **~ary** *a* de prueba

probe /prəʊb/ *n* sonda *f*; (*fig*) encuesta *f*. ● *vt* sondar. ● *vi*. **~ into** investigar

problem /'prɒbləm/ *n* problema *m*. ● *a* difícil. **~atic** /-'mætɪk/ *a* problemático

procedure /prə'si:dʒə(r)/ *n* procedimiento *m*

proceed /prə'si:d/ *vi* proceder. **~ing** *n* procedimiento *m*. **~ings** /prə'si:dɪŋz/ *npl* (*report*) actas *fpl*; (*jurid*) proceso *m*

proceeds /'prəʊsi:dz/ *npl* ganancias *fpl*

process /'prəʊses/ *n* proceso *m*. **in ~ of** en vías de. **in the ~ of time** con el tiempo. ● *vt* tratar; revelar ‹*photo*›. **~ion** /prə'seʃn/ *n* desfile *m*

procla|im /prə'kleɪm/ *vt* proclamar. **~mation** /prɒklə'meɪʃn/ *n* proclamación *f*

procrastinate /prəʊ'kræstɪneɪt/ *vi* aplazar, demorar, diferir

procreation /prəʊkrɪ'eɪʃn/ *n* procreación *f*

procure /prə'kjʊə(r)/ *vt* obtener

prod /prɒd/ *vt* (*pt* **prodded**) empujar; (*with elbow*) dar un codazo a. ● *vi* dar con el dedo. ● *n* empuje *m*; (*with elbow*) codazo *m*

prodigal /'prɒdɪgl/ *a* pródigo

prodigious /prə'dɪdʒəs/ *a* prodigioso

prodigy /'prɒdɪdʒɪ/ *n* prodigio *m*

produce /prə'dju:s/ *vt* (*show*) presentar; (*bring out*) sacar; poner en escena ‹*play*›; (*cause*) causar; (*manufacture*) producir. /'prɒdju:s/ *n* productos *mpl*. **~er** /prə'dju:sə(r)/ *n* productor *m*; (*in theatre*) director *m*

product /'prɒdʌkt/ *n* producto *m*. **~ion** /prə'dʌkʃn/ *n* producción *f*; (*of play*) representación *f*

productiv|e /prə'dʌktɪv/ *a* productivo. **~ity** /prɒdʌk'tɪvətɪ/ *n* productividad *f*

profan|e /prə'feɪn/ *a* profano; (*blasphemous*) blasfemo. **~ity** /-'fænətɪ/ *n* profanidad *f*

profess /prə'fes/ *vt* profesar; (*pretend*) pretender

profession /prə'feʃn/ *n* profesión *f*. **~al** *a & n* profesional (*m & f*)

professor /prə'fesə(r)/ *n* catedrático *m*; (*Amer*) profesor *m*

proffer /'prɒfə(r)/ *vt* ofrecer

proficien|cy /prə'fɪʃənsɪ/ *n* competencia *f*. **~t** /prə'fɪʃnt/ *a* competente

profile /'prəʊfaɪl/ *n* perfil *m*

profit /'prɒfɪt/ *n* (*com*) ganancia *f*; (*fig*) provecho *m*. ● *vi*. **~ from** sacar provecho de. **~able** *a* provechoso

profound /prə'faʊnd/ *a* profundo. **~ly** *adv* profundamente

profus|e /prə'fju:s/ *a* profuso. **~ely** *adv* profusamente. **~ion** /-ʒn/ *n* profusión *f*

progeny /'prɒdʒənɪ/ *n* progenie *f*

prognosis /prɒ'gnəʊsɪs/ *n* (*pl* **-oses**) pronóstico *m*

program(|me) /'prəʊgræm/ *n* programa *m*. ● *vt* (*pt* **programmed**) programar. **~mer** *n* programador *m*

progress /'prəʊgres/ *n* progreso *m*, progresos *mpl*; (*development*) desarrollo *m*. **in ~** en curso. /prə'gres/ *vi* hacer progresos; (*develop*) desarrollarse. **~ion** /prə'greʃn/ *n* progresión *f*

progressive /prə'gresɪv/ *a* progresivo; (*reforming*) progresista. **~ly** *adv* progresivamente

prohibit /prə'hɪbɪt/ *vt* prohibir. **~ive** /-bətɪv/ *a* prohibitivo

project /prə'dʒekt/ *vt* proyectar. ● *vi* (*stick out*) sobresalir. /'prɒdʒekt/ *n* proyecto *m*

projectile /prə'dʒektaɪl/ *n* proyectil *m*

projector /prə'dʒektə(r)/ *n* proyector *m*

proletari|an /prəʊlɪ'teərɪən/ *a & n* proletario (*m*). **~at** /prəʊlɪ'teərɪət/ *n* proletariado *m*

prolif|erate /prə'lɪfəreɪt/ *vi* proliferar. **~eration** /-'reɪʃn/ *n* proliferación *f*. **~ic** /prə'lɪfɪk/ *a* prolífico

prologue /'prəʊlɒg/ *n* prólogo *m*

prolong /prə'lɒŋ/ *vt* prolongar

promenade /prɒmə'nɑ:d/ *n* paseo *m*; (*along beach*) paseo *m* marítimo. ● *vt* pasear. ● *vi* pasearse. **~ concert** *n* concierto *m* (que forma parte de un festival de música clásica en Londres, en que no todo el público tiene asientos)

prominen|ce /'prɒmɪnəns/ *n* prominencia *f*; (*fig*) importancia *f*. **~t** /'prɒmɪnənt/ *a* prominente; (*important*) importante; (*conspicuous*) conspicuo

promiscu|ity /prɒmɪ'skju:ətɪ/ *n* libertinaje *m*. **~ous** /prə'mɪskjʊəs/ *a* libertino

promis|e /'prɒmɪs/ *n* promesa *f*. ● *vt/i* prometer. **~ing** *a* prometedor; ‹*person*› que promete

promontory /'prɒməntrɪ/ *n* promontorio *m*

promot|e /prə'məʊt/ *vt* promover. **~ion** /-'məʊʃn/ *n* promoción *f*

prompt /prɒmpt/ *a* pronto; (*punctual*) puntual. ● *adv* en punto. ● *vt* incitar; apuntar ‹*actor*›. **~er** *n* apuntador *m*. **~ly** *adv* puntualmente. **~ness** *n* prontitud *f*

promulgate /'prɒməlgeɪt/ *vt* promulgar

prone /prəʊn/ *a* echado boca abajo. **~ to** propenso a

prong /prɒŋ/ *n* (*of fork*) diente *m*

pronoun /'prəʊnaʊn/ *n* pronombre *m*

pronounc|e /prə'naʊns/ *vt* pronunciar; (*declare*) declarar. **~ement** *n* declaración *f*. **~ed**

/prə'naʊnst/ *a* pronunciado; (*noticeable*) marcado
pronunciation /prənʌnsɪ'eɪʃn/ *n* pronunciación *f*
proof /pru:f/ *n* prueba *f*; (*of alcohol*) graduación *f* normal. ● *a*. ~ **against** a prueba de. ~**-reading** *n* corrección *f* de pruebas
prop[1] /prɒp/ *n* puntal *m*; (*fig*) apoyo *m*. ● *vt* (*pt* **propped**) apoyar. ~ **against** (*lean*) apoyar en
prop[2] /prɒp/ (*in theatre, fam*) accesorio *m*
propaganda /prɒpə'gændə/ *n* propaganda *f*
propagat|e /'prɒpəgeɪt/ *vt* propagar. ● *vi* propagarse. ~**ion** /-'geɪʃn/ *n* propagación *f*
propel /prə'pel/ *vt* (*pt* **propelled**) propulsar. ~**ler** /prə'pelə(r)/ *n* hélice *f*
propensity /prə'pensətɪ/ *n* propensión *f*
proper /'prɒpə(r)/ *a* correcto; (*suitable*) apropiado; (*gram*) propio; (*real, fam*) verdadero. ~**ly** *adv* correctamente
property /'prɒpətɪ/ *n* propiedad *f*; (*things owned*) bienes *mpl*. ● *a* inmobiliario
prophe|cy /'prɒfəsɪ/ *n* profecía *f*. ~**sy** /'prɒfɪsaɪ/ *vt/i* profetizar. ~**t** /'prɒfɪt/ *n* profeta *m*. ~**tic** /prə'fetɪk/ *a* profético
propitious /prə'pɪʃəs/ *a* propicio
proportion /prə'pɔ:ʃn/ *n* proporción *f*. ~**al** *a*, ~**ate** *a* proporcional
propos|al /prə'pəʊzl/ *n* propuesta *f*. ~**al of marriage** oferta *f* de matrimonio. ~**e** /prə'pəʊz/ *vt* proponer. ● *vi* hacer una oferta de matrimonio
proposition /prɒpə'zɪʃn/ *n* proposición *f*; (*project, fam*) asunto *m*
propound /prə'paʊnd/ *vt* proponer
proprietor /prə'praɪətə(r)/ *n* propietario *m*
propriety /prə'praɪətɪ/ *n* decoro *m*
propulsion /prə'pʌlʃn/ *n* propulsión *f*
prosaic /prə'zeɪk/ *a* prosaico
proscribe /prə'skraɪb/ *vt* proscribir
prose /prəʊz/ *n* prosa *f*
prosecut|e /'prɒsɪkju:t/ *vt* procesar; (*carry on*) proseguir. ~**ion** /-'kju:ʃn/ *n* proceso *m*. ~**or** *n* acusador *m*. **Public P~or** fiscal *m*
prospect /'prɒspekt/ *n* vista *f*; (*expectation*) perspectiva *f*. /prə'spekt/ *vi* prospectar
prospective /prə'spektɪv/ *a* probable; (*future*) futuro
prospector /prə'spektə(r)/ *n* prospector *m*, explorador *m*
prospectus /prə'spektəs/ *n* prospecto *m*
prosper /'prɒspə(r)/ *vi* prosperar. ~**ity** /-'sperətɪ/ *n* prosperidad *f*. ~**ous** /'prɒspərəs/ *a* próspero
prostitut|e /'prɒstɪtju:t/ *n* prostituta *f*. ~**ion** /-'tju:ʃn/ *n* prostitución *f*
prostrate /'prɒstreɪt/ *a* echado boca abajo; (*fig*) postrado
protagonist /prə'tægənɪst/ *n* protagonista *m & f*
protect /prə'tekt/ *vt* proteger. ~**ion** /-ʃn/ *n* protección *f*. ~**ive** /prə'tektɪv/ *a* protector. ~**or** *n* protector *m*
protégé /'prɒtɪʒeɪ/ *n* protegido *m*. ~**e** *n* protegida *f*
protein /'prəʊti:n/ *n* proteína *f*
protest /'prəʊtest/ *n* protesta *f*. **under** ~ bajo protesta. /prə'test/ *vt/i* protestar. ~**er** *n* (*demonstrator*) manifestante *m & f*
Protestant /'prɒtɪstənt/ *a & n* protestante (*m & f*)
protocol /'prəʊtəkɒl/ *n* protocolo *m*
prototype /'prəʊtətaɪp/ *n* prototipo *m*
protract /prə'trækt/ *vt* prolongar
protractor /prə'træktə(r)/ *n* transportador *m*
protrude /prə'tru:d/ *vi* sobresalir
protuberance /prə'tju:bərəns/ *n* protuberancia *f*
proud /praʊd/ *a* orgulloso. ~**ly** *adv* orgullosamente
prove /pru:v/ *vt* probar. ● *vi* resultar. ~**n** *a* probado
provenance /'prɒvənəns/ *n* procedencia *f*
proverb /'prɒvɜ:b/ *n* proverbio *m*. ~**ial** /prə'vɜ:bɪəl/ *a* proverbial
provide /prə'vaɪd/ *vt* proveer. ● *vi*. ~ **against** precaverse de. ~ **for** (*allow for*) prever; mantener ‹*person*›. ~**d** /prə'vaɪdɪd/ *conj*. ~ **(that)** con tal que
providen|ce /'prɒvɪdəns/ *n* providencia *f*. ~**t** *a* providente. ~**tial** /prɒvɪ'denʃl/ *a* providencial
providing /prə'vaɪdɪŋ/ *conj*. ~ **that** con tal que
provinc|e /'prɒvɪns/ *n* provincia *f*; (*fig*) competencia *f*. ~**ial** /prə'vɪnʃl/ *a* provincial

provision /prə'vɪʒn/ *n* provisión *f*; (*supply*) suministro *m*; (*stipulation*) condición *f*. **~s** *npl* comestibles *mpl*
provisional /prə'vɪʒənl/ *a* provisional. **~ly** *adv* provisionalmente
proviso /prə'vaɪzəʊ/ *n* (*pl* **-os**) condición *f*
provo|cation /prɒvə'keɪʃn/ *n* provocación *f*. **~cative** /-'vɒkətɪv/ *a* provocador. **~ke** /prə'vəʊk/ *vt* provocar
prow /praʊ/ *n* proa *f*
prowess /'praʊɪs/ *n* habilidad *f*; (*valour*) valor *m*
prowl /praʊl/ *vi* merodear. ● *n* ronda *f*. **be on the ~** merodear. **~er** *n* merodeador *m*
proximity /prɒk'sɪmətɪ/ *n* proximidad *f*
proxy /'prɒksɪ/ *n* poder *m*. **by ~** por poder
prude /pru:d/ *n* mojigato *m*
pruden|ce /'pru:dəns/ *n* prudencia *f*. **~t** /'pru:dənt/ *a* prudente. **~tly** *adv* prudentemente
prudish /'pru:dɪʃ/ *a* mojigato
prune[1] /pru:n/ *n* ciruela *f* pasa
prune[2] /pru:n/ *vt* podar
pry /praɪ/ *vi* entrometerse
psalm /sɑ:m/ *n* salmo *m*
pseudo... /'sju:dəʊ/ *pref* seudo...
pseudonym /'sju:dənɪm/ *n* seudónimo *m*
psychiatr|ic /saɪkɪ'ætrɪk/ *a* psiquiátrico. **~ist** /saɪ'kaɪətrɪst/ *n* psiquiatra *m & f*. **~y** /saɪ'kaɪətrɪ/ *n* psiquiatría *f*
physic /'saɪkɪk/ *a* psíquico
psycho-analys|e /saɪkəʊ'ænəlaɪz/ *vt* psicoanalizar. **~is** /saɪkəʊə'næləsɪs/ *n* psicoanálisis *m*. **~t** /-ɪst/ *n* psicoanalista *m & f*
psycholog|ical /saɪkə'lɒdʒɪkl/ *a* psicológico. **~ist** /saɪ'kɒlədʒɪst/ *n* psicólogo *m*. **~y** /saɪ'kɒlədʒɪ/ *n* psicología *f*
psychopath /'saɪkəpæθ/ *n* psicópata *m & f*
pub /pʌb/ *n* bar *m*
puberty /'pju:bətɪ/ *n* pubertad *f*
pubic /'pju:bɪk/ *a* pubiano, púbico
public /'pʌblɪk/ *a* público
publican /'pʌblɪkən/ *n* tabernero *m*
publication /pʌblɪ'keɪʃn/ *n* publicación *f*
public house /pʌblɪk'haʊs/ *n* bar *m*
publicity /pʌb'lɪsətɪ/ *n* publicidad *f*
publicize /'pʌblɪsaɪz/ *vt* publicar, anunciar
publicly /'pʌblɪklɪ/ *adv* públicamente
public school /pʌblɪk'sku:l/ *n* colegio *m* privado; (*Amer*) instituto *m*
public-spirited /pʌblɪk'spɪrɪtɪd/ *a* cívico
publish /'pʌblɪʃ/ *vt* publicar. **~er** *n* editor *m*. **~ing** *n* publicación *f*
puck /pʌk/ *n* (*ice hockey*) disco *m*
pucker /'pʌkə(r)/ *vt* arrugar. ● *vi* arrugarse
pudding /'pʊdɪŋ/ *n* postre *m*; (*steamed*) budín *m*
puddle /'pʌdl/ *n* charco *m*
pudgy /'pʌdʒɪ/ *a* (**-ier**, **-iest**) rechoncho
puerile /'pjʊəraɪl/ *a* pueril
puff /pʌf/ *n* soplo *m*; (*for powder*) borla *f*. ● *vt/i* soplar. **~ at** chupar ‹*pipe*›. **~ out** apagar ‹*candle*›; (*swell up*) hinchar. **~ed** *a* (*out of breath*) sin aliento. **~ pastry** *n* hojaldre *m*. **~y** /'pʌfɪ/ *a* hinchado
pugnacious /pʌg'neɪʃəs/ *a* belicoso
pug-nosed /'pʌgnəʊzd/ *a* chato
pull /pʊl/ *vt* tirar de; sacar ‹*tooth*›; torcer ‹*muscle*›. **~ a face** hacer una mueca. **~ a fast one** hacer una mala jugada. **~ down** derribar ‹*building*›. **~ off** quitarse; (*fig*) lograr. **~ one's weight** poner de su parte. **~ out** sacar. **~ s.o.'s leg** tomarle el pelo a uno. **~ up** (*uproot*) desarraigar; (*reprimand*) reprender. ● *vi* tirar (**at** de). **~ away** (*auto*) alejarse. **~ back** retirarse. **~ in** (*enter*) entrar; (*auto*) parar. **~ o.s. together** tranquilizarse. **~ out** (*auto*) salirse. **~ through** recobrar la salud. **~ up** (*auto*) parar. ● *n* tirón *m*; (*fig*) atracción *f*; (*influence*) influencia *f*. **give a ~** tirar
pulley /'pʊlɪ/ *n* polea *f*
pullover /'pʊləʊvə(r)/ *n* jersey *m*
pulp /pʌlp/ *n* pulpa *f*; (*for paper*) pasta *f*
pulpit /'pʊlpɪt/ *n* púlpito *m*
pulsate /'pʌlseɪt/ *vi* pulsar
pulse /pʌls/ *n* (*med*) pulso *m*
pulverize /'pʌlvəraɪz/ *vt* pulverizar
pumice /'pʌmɪs/ *n* piedra *f* pómez
pummel /'pʌml/ *vt* (*pt* **pummelled**) aporrear
pump[1] /pʌmp/ *n* bomba *f*; ● *vt* sacar con una bomba; (*fig*) sonsacar. **~ up** inflar
pump[2] /pʌmp/ (*plimsoll*) zapatilla *f* de lona; (*dancing shoe*) escarpín *m*
pumpkin /'pʌmpkɪn/ *n* calabaza *f*

pun /pʌn/ *n* juego *m* de palabras
punch[1] /pʌntʃ/ *vt* dar un puñetazo a; (*perforate*) perforar; hacer ‹*hole*›. ● *n* puñetazo *m*; (*vigour, sl*) empuje *m*; (*device*) punzón *m*
punch[2] /pʌntʃ/ (*drink*) ponche *m*
punch: **~-drunk** *a* aturdido a golpes. **~ line** *n* gracia *f*. **~-up** *n* riña *f*
punctilious /pʌŋk'tɪlɪəs/ *a* meticuloso
punctual /'pʌŋktʃʊəl/ *a* puntual. **~ity** /-'ælətɪ/ *n* puntualidad *f*. **~ly** *adv* puntualmente
punctuat|e /'pʌŋkʃʊeɪt/ *vt* puntuar. **~ion** /-'eɪʃn/ *n* puntuación *f*
puncture /'pʌŋktʃə(r)/ *n* (*in tyre*) pinchazo *m*. ● *vt* pinchar. ● *vi* pincharse
pundit /'pʌndɪt/ *n* experto *m*
pungen|cy /'pʌndʒənsɪ/ *n* acritud *f*; (*fig*) mordacidad *f*. **~t** /'pʌndʒənt/ *a* acre; ‹*remark*› mordaz
punish /'pʌnɪʃ/ *vt* castigar. **~able** *a* castigable. **~ment** *n* castigo *m*
punitive /'pju:nɪtɪv/ *a* punitivo
punk /pʌŋk/ *a* ‹*music, person*› punk
punnet /'pʌnɪt/ *n* canastilla *f*
punt[1] /pʌnt/ *n* (*boat*) batea *f*
punt[2] /pʌnt/ *vi* apostar. **~er** *n* apostante *m & f*
puny /'pju:nɪ/ *a* (**-ier, -iest**) diminuto; (*weak*) débil; (*petty*) insignificante
pup /pʌp/ *n* cachorro *m*
pupil[1] /'pju:pl/ *n* alumno *m*
pupil[2] /'pju:pl/ (*of eye*) pupila *f*
puppet /'pʌpɪt/ *n* títere *m*
puppy /'pʌpɪ/ *n* cachorro *m*
purchase /'pɜ:tʃəs/ *vt* comprar. ● *n* compra *f*. **~r** *n* comprador *m*
pur|e /'pjʊə(r)/ *a* (**-er, -est**) puro. **~ely** *adv* puramente. **~ity** *n* pureza *f*
purée /'pjʊəreɪ/ *n* puré *m*
purgatory /'pɜ:gətrɪ/ *n* purgatorio *m*
purge /pɜ:dʒ/ *vt* purgar. ● *n* purga *f*
purif|ication /pjʊərɪfɪ'keɪʃn/ *n* purificación *f*. **~y** /'pjʊərɪfaɪ/ *vt* purificar
purist /'pjʊərɪst/ *n* purista *m & f*
puritan /'pjʊərɪtən/ *n* puritano *m*. **~ical** /-'tænɪkl/ *a* puritano
purl /pɜ:l/ *n* (*knitting*) punto *m* del revés
purple /'pɜ:pl/ *a* purpúreo, morado. ● *n* púrpura *f*
purport /pə'pɔ:t/ *vt*. **~ to be** pretender ser
purpose /'pɜ:pəs/ *n* propósito *m*; (*determination*) resolución *f*. **on ~** a propósito. **to no ~** en vano. **~-built** *a* construido especialmente. **~ful** *a* (*resolute*) resuelto. **~ly** *adv* a propósito
purr /pɜ:(r)/ *vi* ronronear
purse /pɜ:s/ *n* monedero *m*; (*Amer*) bolso *m*, cartera *f* (*LAm*). ● *vt* fruncir
pursu|e /pə'sju:/ *vt* perseguir, seguir. **~er** *n* perseguidor *m*. **~it** /pə'sju:t/ *n* persecución *f*; (*fig*) ocupación *f*
purveyor /pə'veɪə(r)/ *n* proveedor *m*
pus /pʌs/ *n* pus *m*
push /pʊʃ/ *vt* empujar; apretar ‹*button*›. ● *vi* empujar. ● *n* empuje *m*; (*effort*) esfuerzo *m*; (*drive*) dinamismo *m*. **at a ~** en caso de necesidad. **get the ~** (*sl*) ser despedido. **~ aside** *vt* apartar. **~ back** *vt* hacer retroceder. **~ off** *vi* (*sl*) marcharse. **~ on** *vi* seguir adelante. **~ up** *vt* levantar. **~-button telephone** *n* teléfono *m* de teclas. **~-chair** *n* sillita *f* con ruedas. **~ing** /'pʊʃɪŋ/ *a* ambicioso. **~-over** *n* (*fam*) cosa *f* muy fácil, pan comido. **~y** *a* (*pej*) ambicioso
puss /pʊs/ *n* minino *m*
put /pʊt/ *vt* (*pt* **put**, *pres p* **putting**) poner; (*express*) expresar; (*say*) decir; (*estimate*) estimar; hacer ‹*question*›. **~ across** comunicar; (*deceive*) engañar. **~ aside** poner aparte. **~ away** guardar. **~ back** devolver; retrasar ‹*clock*›. **~ by** guardar; ahorrar ‹*money*›. **~ down** depositar; (*suppress*) suprimir; (*write*) apuntar; (*kill*) sacrificar. **~ forward** avanzar. **~ in** introducir; (*submit*) presentar. **~ in for** pedir. **~ off** aplazar; (*disconcert*) desconcertar. **~ on** (*wear*) ponerse; cobrar ‹*speed*›; encender ‹*light*›. **~ one's foot down** mantenerse firme. **~ out** (*extinguish*) apagar; (*inconvenience*) incomodar; extender ‹*hand*›; (*disconcert*) desconcertar. **~ to sea** hacerse a la mar. **~ through** (*phone*) poner. **~ up** levantar; subir ‹*price*›; alojar ‹*guest*›. **~ up with** soportar. **stay ~** (*fam*) no moverse
putrefy /'pju:trɪfaɪ/ *vi* pudrirse
putt /pʌt/ *n* (*golf*) golpe *m* suave
putty /'pʌtɪ/ *n* masilla *f*
put-up /'pʊtʌp/ *a*. **~ job** *n* confabulación *f*

puzzl|e /'pʌzl/ *n* enigma *m*; (*game*) rompecabezas *m invar*. ● *vt* dejar perplejo. ● *vi* calentarse los sesos. **~ing** *a* incomprensible; (*odd*) curioso
pygmy /'pɪgmɪ/ *n* pigmeo *m*
pyjamas /pə'dʒɑ:məz/ *npl* pijama *m*
pylon /'paɪlɒn/ *n* pilón *m*
pyramid /'pɪrəmɪd/ *n* pirámide *f*
python /'paɪθn/ *n* pitón *m*

Q

quack[1] /kwæk/ *n* (*of duck*) graznido *m*
quack[2] /kwæk/ (*person*) charlatán *m*. **~ doctor** *n* curandero *m*
quadrangle /'kwɒdræŋgl/ *n* cuadrilátero *m*; (*court*) patio *m*
quadruped /'kwɒdrʊped/ *n* cuadrúpedo *m*
quadruple /'kwɒdrʊpl/ *a & n* cuádruplo (*m*). ● *vt* cuadruplicar. **~t** /-plət/ *n* cuatrillizo *m*
quagmire /'kwægmaɪə(r)/ *n* ciénaga *f*; (*fig*) atolladero *m*
quail /kweɪl/ *n* codorniz *f*
quaint /kweɪnt/ *a* (**-er**, **-est**) pintoresco; (*odd*) curioso
quake /kweɪk/ *vi* temblar. ● *n* (*fam*) terremoto *m*
Quaker /'kweɪkə(r)/ *n* cuáquero (*m*)
qualification /kwɒlɪfɪ'keɪʃn/ *n* título *m*; (*requirement*) requisito *m*; (*ability*) capacidad *f*; (*fig*) reserva *f*
qualif|ied /'kwɒlɪfaɪd/ *a* cualificado; (*limited*) limitado; (*with degree, diploma*) titulado. **~y** /'kwɒlɪfaɪ/ *vt* calificar; (*limit*) limitar. ● *vi* sacar el título; (*sport*) clasificarse; (*fig*) llenar los requisitos
qualitative /'kwɒlɪtətɪv/ *a* cualitativo
quality /'kwɒlɪtɪ/ *n* calidad *f*; (*attribute*) cualidad *f*
qualm /kwɑ:m/ *n* escrúpulo *m*
quandary /'kwɒndrɪ/ *n*. **in a ~** en un dilema
quantitative /'kwɒntɪtətɪv/ *a* cuantitativo
quantity /'kwɒntɪtɪ/ *n* cantidad *f*
quarantine /'kwɒrənti:n/ *n* cuarentena *f*
quarrel /'kwɒrəl/ *n* riña *f*. ● *vi* (*pt* **quarrelled**) reñir. **~some** *a* pendenciero
quarry[1] /'kwɒrɪ/ *n* (*excavation*) cantera *f*
quarry[2] /'kwɒrɪ/ *n* (*animal*) presa *f*
quart /kwɔ:t/ *n* (poco más de un) litro *m*
quarter /'kwɔ:tə(r)/ *n* cuarto *m*; (*of year*) trimestre *m*; (*district*) barrio *m*. **from all ~s** de todas partes. ● *vt* dividir en cuartos; (*mil*) acuartelar. **~s** *npl* alojamiento *m*
quartermaster /'kwɔ:təmɑ:stə(r)/ *n* intendente *m*
quarter: **~-final** *n* cuarto *m* de final. **~ly** *a* trimestral. ● *adv* cada tres meses
quartet /kwɔ:'tet/ *n* cuarteto *m*
quartz /kwɔ:ts/ *n* cuarzo *m*. ● *a* ‹*watch etc*› de cuarzo
quash /kwɒʃ/ *vt* anular
quasi.. /'kweɪsaɪ/ *pref* cuasi...
quaver /'kweɪvə(r)/ *vi* temblar. ● *n* (*mus*) corchea *f*
quay /ki:/ *n* muelle *m*
queasy /'kwi:zɪ/ *a* ‹*stomach*› delicado
queen /kwi:n/ *n* reina *f*. **~ mother** *n* reina *f* madre
queer /kwɪə(r)/ *a* (**-er**, **-est**) extraño; (*dubious*) sospechoso; (*ill*) indispuesto. ● *n* (*sl*) homosexual *m*
quell /kwel/ *vt* reprimir
quench /kwentʃ/ *vt* apagar; sofocar ‹*desire*›
querulous /'kwerʊləs/ *a* quejumbroso
query /'kwɪərɪ/ *n* pregunta *f*. ● *vt* preguntar; (*doubt*) poner en duda
quest /kwest/ *n* busca *f*
question /'kwestʃən/ *n* pregunta *f*; (*for discussion*) cuestión *f*. **in ~** en cuestión. **out of the ~** imposible. **without ~** sin duda. ● *vt* preguntar; ‹*police etc*› interrogar; (*doubt*) poner en duda. **~able** /'kwestʃənəbl/ *a* discutible. **~ mark** *n* signo *m* de interrogación. **~naire** /kwestʃə'neə(r)/ *n* cuestionario *m*
queue /kju:/ *n* cola *f*. ● *vi* (*pres p* **queuing**) hacer cola
quibble /'kwɪbl/ *vi* discutir; (*split hairs*) sutilizar
quick /kwɪk/ *a* (**-er**, **-est**) rápido. **be ~!** ¡date prisa! ● *adv* rápidamente. ● *n*. **to the ~** en lo vivo. **~en** /'kwɪkən/ *vt* acelerar. ● *vi* acelerarse. **~ly** *adv* rápidamente. **~sand** /'kwɪksænd/ *n* arena *f* movediza. **~-tempered** *a* irascible

quid /kwɪd/ *n invar* (*sl*) libra *f* (esterlina)

quiet /'kwaɪət/ *a* (**-er**, **-est**) tranquilo; (*silent*) callado; (*discreet*) discreto. ● *n* tranquilidad *f*. **on the ~** a escondidas. **~en** /'kwaɪətn/ *vt* calmar. ● *vi* calmarse. **~ly** *adv* tranquilamente; (*silently*) silenciosamente; (*discreetly*) discretamente. **~ness** *n* tranquilidad *f*

quill /kwɪl/ *n* pluma *f*

quilt /kwɪlt/ *n* edredón *m*. ● *vt* acolchar

quince /kwɪns/ *n* membrillo *m*

quinine /kwɪ'ni:n/ *n* quinina *f*

quintessence /kwɪn'tesns/ *n* quintaesencia *f*

quintet /kwɪn'tet/ *n* quinteto *m*

quintuplet /'kwɪntju:plət/ *n* quintillizo *m*

quip /kwɪp/ *n* ocurrencia *f*

quirk /kwɜ:k/ *n* peculiaridad *f*

quit /kwɪt/ *vt* (*pt* **quitted**) dejar. ● *vi* abandonar; (*leave*) marcharse; (*resign*) dimitir. **~ doing** (*cease, Amer*) dejar de hacer

quite /kwaɪt/ *adv* bastante; (*completely*) totalmente; (*really*) verdaderamente. **~ (so)!** ¡claro! **~ a few** bastante

quits /kwɪts/ *a* a la par. **call it ~** darlo por terminado

quiver /'kwɪvə(r)/ *vi* temblar

quixotic /kwɪk'sɒtɪk/ *a* quijotesco

quiz /kwɪz/ *n* (*pl* **quizzes**) serie *f* de preguntas; (*game*) concurso *m*. ● *vt* (*pt* **quizzed**) interrogar. **~zical** /'kwɪzɪkl/ *a* burlón

quorum /'kwɔ:rəm/ *n* quórum *m*

quota /'kwəʊtə/ *n* cuota *f*

quot|ation /kwəʊ'teɪʃn/ *n* cita *f*; (*price*) presupuesto *m*. **~ation marks** *npl* comillas *fpl*. **~e** /kwəʊt/ *vt* citar; (*com*) cotizar. ● *n* (*fam*) cita *f*; (*price*) presupuesto *m*. **in ~es** *npl* entre comillas

quotient /'kwəʊʃnt/ *n* cociente *m*

R

rabbi /'ræbaɪ/ *n* rabino *m*

rabbit /'ræbɪt/ *n* conejo *m*

rabble /'ræbl/ *n* gentío *m*. **the ~** (*pej*) el populacho *m*

rabi|d /'ræbɪd/ *a* feroz; ‹*dog*› rabioso. **~es** /'reɪbi:z/ *n* rabia *f*

race[1] /reɪs/ *n* carrera *f*. ● *vt* hacer correr ‹*horse*›; acelerar ‹*engine*›. ● *vi* (*run*) correr, ir corriendo; (*rush*) ir de prisa

race[2] /reɪs/ (*group*) raza *f*

race: **~course** /'reɪskɔ:s/ *n* hipódromo *m*. **~horse** /'reɪshɔ:s/ *n* caballo *m* de carreras. **~riots** /'reɪsraɪəts/ *npl* disturbios *mpl* raciales. **~-track** /'reɪstræk/ *n* hipódromo *m*

racial /'reɪʃl/ *a* racial. **~ism** /-ɪzəm/ *n* racismo *m*

racing /'reɪsɪŋ/ *n* carreras *fpl*. **~ car** *n* coche *m* de carreras

racis|m /'reɪsɪzəm/ *n* racismo *m*. **~t** /'reɪsɪst/ *a & n* racista (*m & f*)

rack[1] /ræk/ *n* (*shelf*) estante *m*; (*for luggage*) rejilla *f*; (*for plates*) escurreplatos *m invar*. ● *vt*. **~ one's brains** devanarse los sesos

rack[2] /ræk/ *n*. **go to ~ and ruin** quedarse en la ruina

racket[1] /'rækɪt/ *n* (*for sports*) raqueta

racket[2] /'rækɪt/ (*din*) alboroto *m*; (*swindle*) estafa *f*. **~eer** /-ə'tɪə(r)/ *n* estafador *m*

raconteur /rækɒn'tɜ:/ *n* anecdotista *m & f*

racy /'reɪsɪ/ *a* (**-ier**, **-iest**) vivo

radar /'reɪdɑ:(r)/ *n* radar *m*

radian|ce /'reɪdɪəns/ *n* resplandor *m*. **~t** /'reɪdɪənt/ *a* radiante. **~tly** *adv* con resplandor

radiat|e /'reɪdɪeɪt/ *vt* irradiar. ● *vi* divergir. **~ion** /-'eɪʃn/ *n* radiación *f*. **~or** /'reɪdɪeɪtə(r)/ *n* radiador *m*

radical /'rædɪkl/ *a & n* radical (*m*)

radio /'reɪdɪəʊ/ *n* (*pl* **-os**) radio *f*. ● *vt* transmitir por radio

radioactiv|e /reɪdɪəʊ'æktɪv/ *a* radiactivo. **~ity** /-'tɪvətɪ/ *n* radiactividad *f*

radiograph|er /reɪdɪ'ɒgrəfə(r)/ *n* radiógrafo *m*. **~y** *n* radiografía *f*

radish /'rædɪʃ/ *n* rábano *m*

radius /'reɪdɪəs/ *n* (*pl* **-dii** /-dɪaɪ/) radio *m*

raffish /'ræfɪʃ/ *a* disoluto

raffle /'ræfl/ *n* rifa *f*

raft /rɑ:ft/ *n* balsa *f*

rafter /'rɑ:ftə(r)/ *n* cabrio *m*

rag[1] /ræg/ *n* andrajo *m*; (*for wiping*) trapo *m*; (*newspaper*) periodicucho *m*. **in ~s** ‹*person*› andrajoso; ‹*clothes*› hecho jirones

rag[2] /ræg/ *n* (*univ*) festival *m* estudiantil; (*prank, fam*) broma *f* pesada. ● *vt* (*pt* **ragged**) (*sl*) tomar el pelo a

ragamuffin /'rægəmʌfɪn/ *n* granuja *m*, golfo *m*

rage /reɪdʒ/ *n* rabia *f*; (*fashion*) moda *f*. ● *vi* estar furioso; ‹*storm*› bramar

ragged /'rægɪd/ *a* ‹person› andrajoso; ‹*clothes*› hecho jirones; ‹*edge*› mellado

raid /reɪd/ *n* (*mil*) incursión *f*; (*by police, etc*) redada *f*; (*by thieves*) asalto *m*. ● *vt* (*mil*) atacar; ‹*police*› hacer una redada en; ‹*thieves*› asaltar. **~er** *n* invasor *m*; (*thief*) ladrón *m*

rail[1] /reɪl/ *n* barandilla *f*; (*for train*) riel *m*; (*rod*) barra *f*. **by ~** por ferrocarril

rail[2] /reɪl/ *vi*. **~ against**, **~ at** insultar

railing /'reɪlɪŋ/ *n* barandilla *f*; (*fence*) verja *f*

rail|road /'reɪlrəʊd/ *n* (*Amer*), **~way** /'reɪlweɪ/ *n* ferrocarril *m*. **~wayman** *n* (*pl* **-men**) ferroviario *m*. **~way station** *n* estación *f* de ferrocarril

rain /reɪn/ *n* lluvia *f*. ● *vi* llover. **~bow** /'reɪnbəʊ/ *n* arco *m* iris. **~coat** /'reɪnkəʊt/ *n* impermeable *m*. **~fall** /'reɪnfɔ:l/ *n* precipitación *f*. **~-water** *n* agua *f* de lluvia. **~y** /'reɪnɪ/ *a* (**-ier**, **-iest**) lluvioso

raise /reɪz/ *vt* levantar; (*breed*) criar; obtener ‹*money etc*›; hacer ‹*question*›; plantear ‹*problem*›; subir ‹*price*›. **~ one's glass to** brindar por. **~ one's hat** descubrirse. ● *n* (*Amer*) aumento *m*

raisin /'reɪzn/ *n* (uva *f*) pasa *f*

rake[1] /reɪk/ *n* rastrillo *m*. ● *vt* rastrillar; (*search*) buscar en. **~ up** remover

rake[2] /reɪk/ *n* (*man*) calavera *m*

rake-off /'reɪkɒf/ *n* (*fam*) comisión *f*

rally /'rælɪ/ *vt* reunir; (*revive*) reanimar. ● *vi* reunirse; (*in sickness*) recuperarse. ● *n* reunión *f*; (*recovery*) recuperación *f*; (*auto*) rallye *m*

ram /ræm/ *n* carnero *m*. ● *vt* (*pt* **rammed**) (*thrust*) meter por la fuerza; (*crash into*) chocar con

rambl|e /'ræmbl/ *n* excursión *f* a pie. ● *vi* ir de paseo; (*in speech*) divagar. **~e on** divagar. **~er** *n* excursionista *m & f*. **~ing** *a* ‹*speech*› divagador

ramification /ræmɪfɪ'keɪʃn/ *n* ramificación *f*

ramp /ræmp/ *n* rampa *f*

rampage /ræm'peɪdʒ/ *vi* alborotarse. /'ræmpeɪdʒ/ *n*. **go on the ~** alborotarse

rampant /'ræmpənt/ *a*. **be ~** ‹*disease etc*› estar extendido

rampart /'ræmpɑ:t/ *n* muralla *f*

ramshackle /'ræmʃækl/ *a* desvencijado

ran /ræn/ *see* **run**

ranch /rɑ:ntʃ/ *n* hacienda *f*

rancid /'rænsɪd/ *a* rancio

rancour /'ræŋkə(r)/ *n* rencor *m*

random /'rændəm/ *a* hecho al azar; (*chance*) fortuito. ● *n*. **at ~** al azar

randy /'rændɪ/ *a* (**-ier**, **-iest**) lujurioso, cachondo (*fam*)

rang /ræŋ/ *see* **ring**[2]

range /reɪndʒ/ *n* alcance *m*; (*distance*) distancia *f*; (*series*) serie *f*; (*of mountains*) cordillera *f*; (*extent*) extensión *f*; (*com*) surtido *m*; (*open area*) dehesa *f*; (*stove*) cocina *f* económica. ● *vi* extenderse; (*vary*) variar

ranger /'reɪndʒə(r)/ *n* guardabosque *m*

rank[1] /ræŋk/ *n* posición *f*, categoría *f*; (*row*) fila *f*; (*for taxis*) parada *f*. **the ~ and file** la masa *f*. ● *vt* clasificar. ● *vi* clasificarse. **~s** *npl* soldados *mpl* rasos

rank[2] /ræŋk/ *a* (**-er**, **-est**) exuberante; (*smell*) fétido; (*fig*) completo

rankle /ræŋkl/ *vi* (*fig*) causar rencor

ransack /'rænsæk/ *vt* registrar; (*pillage*) saquear

ransom /'rænsəm/ *n* rescate *m*. **hold s.o. to ~** exigir rescate por uno; (*fig*) hacer chantaje a uno. ● *vt* rescatar; (*redeem*) redimir

rant /rænt/ *vi* vociferar

rap /ræp/ *n* golpe *m* seco. ● *vt/i* (*pt* **rapped**) golpear

rapacious /rə'peɪʃs/ *a* rapaz

rape /reɪp/ *vt* violar. ● *n* violación *f*

rapid /'ræpɪd/ *a* rápido. **~ity** /rə'pɪdətɪ/ *n* rapidez *f*. **~s** /'ræpɪdz/ *npl* rápido *m*

rapist /'reɪpɪst/ *n* violador *m*

rapport /ræ'pɔ:(r)/ *n* armonía *f*, relación *f*

rapt /ræpt/ *a* ‹*attention*› profundo. **~ in** absorto en

raptur|e /'ræptʃə(r)/ *n* éxtasis *m*. **~ous** *a* extático

rare[1] /reə(r)/ *a* (**-er**, **-est**) raro

rare[2] /reə(r)/ *a* (*culin*) poco hecho

rarefied /'reərɪfaɪd/ *a* enrarecido

rarely /'reəlɪ/ *adv* raramente
rarity /'reərətɪ/ *n* rareza *f*
raring /'reərɪŋ/ *a* (*fam*). **~ to** impaciente por
rascal /'rɑ:skl/ *n* tunante *m & f*
rash[1] /ræʃ/ *a* (**-er**, **-est**) imprudente, precipitado
rash[2] /ræʃ/ *n* erupción *f*
rasher /'ræʃə(r)/ *n* loncha *f*
rash|ly /'ræʃlɪ/ *adv* imprudentemente, a la ligera. **~ness** *n* imprudencia *f*
rasp /rɑ:sp/ *n* (*file*) escofina *f*
raspberry /'rɑ:zbrɪ/ *n* frambuesa *f*
rasping /'rɑ:spɪŋ/ *a* áspero
rat /ræt/ *n* rata *f*. ● *vi* (*pt* **ratted**). **~ on** (*desert*) desertar; (*inform on*) denunciar, chivarse
rate /reɪt/ *n* (*ratio*) proporción *f*; (*speed*) velocidad *f*; (*price*) precio *m*; (*of interest*) tipo *m*. **at any ~** de todas formas. **at the ~ of** (*on the basis of*) a razón de. **at this ~** así. ● *vt* valorar; (*consider*) considerar; (*deserve, Amer*) merecer. ● *vi* ser considerado. **~able value** *n* valor *m* imponible. **~payer** /'reɪtpeɪə(r)/ *n* contribuyente *m & f*. **~s** *npl* (*taxes*) impuestos *mpl* municipales
rather /'rɑ:ðə(r)/ *adv* mejor dicho; (*fairly*) bastante; (*a little*) un poco. ● *int* claro. **I would ~ not** prefiero no
ratif|ication /rætɪfɪ'keɪʃn/ *n* ratificación *f*. **~y** /'rætɪfaɪ/ *vt* ratificar
rating /'reɪtɪŋ/ *n* clasificación *f*; (*sailor*) marinero *m*; (*number*, *TV*) índice *m*
ratio /'reɪʃɪəʊ/ *n* (*pl* **-os**) proporción *f*
ration /'ræʃn/ *n* ración *f*. ● *vt* racionar
rational /'ræʃənəl/ *a* racional. **~ize** /'ræʃənəlaɪz/ *vt* racionalizar
rat race /'rætreɪs/ *n* lucha *f* incesante para triunfar
rattle /rætl/ *vi* traquetear. ● *vt* (*shake*) agitar; (*sl*) desconcertar. ● *n* traqueteo *m*; (*toy*) sonajero *m*. **~ off** (*fig*) decir de corrida
rattlesnake /'rætlsneɪk/ *n* serpiente *f* de cascabel
ratty /'rætɪ/ *a* (**-ier**, **-iest**) (*sl*) irritable
raucous /'rɔ:kəs/ *a* estridente
ravage /'rævɪdʒ/ *vt* estragar. **~s** /'rævɪdʒɪz/ *npl* estragos *mpl*
rave /reɪv/ *vi* delirar; (*in anger*) enfurecerse. **~ about** entusiasmarse por
raven /'reɪvn/ *n* cuervo *m*. ● *a* ‹*hair*› negro
ravenous /'rævənəs/ *a* voraz; ‹*person*› hambriento. **be ~** morirse de hambre
ravine /rə'vi:n/ *n* barranco *m*
raving /'reɪvɪŋ/ *a*. **~ mad** loco de atar. **~s** *npl* divagaciones *fpl*
ravish /'rævɪʃ/ *vt* (*rape*) violar. **~ing** *a* (*enchanting*) encantador
raw /rɔ:/ *a* (**-er**, **-est**) crudo; (*not processed*) bruto; ‹*wound*› en carne viva; (*inexperienced*) inexperto; ‹*weather*› crudo. **~ deal** *n* tratamiento *m* injusto, injusticia *f*. **~ materials** *npl* materias *fpl* primas
ray /reɪ/ *n* rayo *m*
raze /reɪz/ *vt* arrasar
razor /'reɪzə(r)/ *n* navaja *f* de afeitar; (*electric*) maquinilla *f* de afeitar
Rd *abbr* (*Road*) C/, Calle *f*
re[1] /ri:/ *prep* con referencia a. ● *pref* re...
re[2] /reɪ/ *n* (*mus, second note of any musical scale*) re *m*
reach /ri:tʃ/ *vt* alcanzar; (*extend*) extender; (*arrive at*) llegar a; (*achieve*) lograr; (*hand over*) pasar, dar. ● *vi* extenderse. ● *n* alcance *m*; (*of river*) tramo *m* recto. **within ~ of** al alcance de; (*close to*) a corta distancia de
react /rɪ'ækt/ *vi* reaccionar. **~ion** /rɪ'ækʃn/ *n* reacción *f*. **~ionary** *a & n* reaccionario (*m*)
reactor /rɪ'æktə(r)/ *n* reactor *m*
read /ri:d/ *vt* (*pt* **read** /red/) leer; (*study*) estudiar; (*interpret*) interpretar. ● *vi* leer; ‹*instrument*› indicar. ● *n* (*fam*) lectura *f*. **~ out** *vt* leer en voz alta. **~able** *a* interesante, agradable; (*clear*) legible. **~er** /'ri:də(r)/ *n* lector *m*. **~ership** *n* lectores *m*
readi|ly /'redɪlɪ/ *adv* (*willingly*) de buena gana; (*easily*) fácilmente. **~ness** /'redɪnɪs/ *n* prontitud *f*. **in ~ness** preparado, listo
reading /'ri:dɪŋ/ *n* lectura *f*
readjust /ri:ə'dʒʌst/ *vt* reajustar. ● *vi* readaptarse (**to** a)
ready /'redɪ/ *a* (**-ier**, **-iest**) listo, preparado; (*quick*) pronto. **~-made** *a* confeccionado. **~ money** *n* dinero *m* contante. **~ reckoner** *n* baremo *m*. **get ~** preparase
real /rɪəl/ *a* verdadero. ● *adv* (*Amer, fam*) verdaderamente. **~ estate** *n* bienes *mpl* raíces

realis|m /'rɪəlɪzəm/ *n* realismo *m*. **~t** /'rɪəlɪst/ *n* realista *m* & *f*. **~tic** /-'lɪstɪk/ *a* realista. **~tically** /-'lɪstɪklɪ/ *adv* de manera realista
reality /rɪ'ælətɪ/ *n* realidad *f*
realiz|ation /rɪəlaɪ'zeɪʃn/ *n* comprensión *f*; (*com*) realización *f*. **~e** /'rɪəlaɪz/ *vt* darse cuenta de; (*fulfil, com*) realizar
really /'rɪəlɪ/ *adv* verdaderamente
realm /relm/ *n* reino *m*
ream /ri:m/ *n* resma *f*
reap /ri:p/ *vt* segar; (*fig*) cosechar
re: **~appear** /ri:ə'pɪə(r)/ *vi* reaparecer. **~appraisal** /ri:ə'preɪzl/ *n* revaluación *f*
rear[1] /rɪə(r)/ *n* parte *f* de atrás. ● *a* posterior, trasero
rear[2] /rɪə(r)/ *vt* (*bring up, breed*) criar. **~ one's head** levantar la cabeza. ● *vi* ‹*horse*› encabritarse. **~ up** ‹*horse*› encabritarse
rear: **~-admiral** *n* contraalmirante *m*. **~guard** /'rɪəgɑ:d/ *n* retaguardia *f*
re: **~arm** /ri:'ɑ:m/ *vt* rearmar. ● *vi* rearmarse. **~arrange** /ri:ə'reɪndʒ/ *vt* arreglar de otra manera
reason /'ri:zn/ *n* razón *f*, motivo *m*. **within ~** dentro de lo razonable. ● *vi* razonar
reasonable /'ri:zənəbl/ *a* razonable
reasoning /'ri:znɪŋ/ *n* razonamiento *m*
reassur|ance /ri:ə'ʃʊərəns/ *n* promesa *f* tranquilizadora; (*guarantee*) garantía *f*. **~e** /ri:ə'ʃʊə(r)/ *vt* tranquilizar
rebate /'ri:beɪt/ *n* reembolso *m*; (*discount*) rebaja *f*
rebel /'rebl/ *n* rebelde *m* & *f*. /rɪ'bel/ *vi* (*pt* **rebelled**) rebelarse. **~lion** *n* rebelión *f*. **~lious** *a* rebelde
rebound /rɪ'baʊnd/ *vi* rebotar; (*fig*) recaer. /'ri:baʊnd/ *n* rebote *m*. **on the ~** (*fig*) por reacción
rebuff /rɪ'bʌf/ *vt* rechazar. ● *n* desaire *m*
rebuild /ri:'bɪld/ *vt* (*pt* **rebuilt**) reconstruir
rebuke /rɪ'bju:k/ *vt* reprender. ● *n* reprensión *f*
rebuttal /rɪ'bʌtl/ *n* refutación *f*
recall /rɪ'kɔ:l/ *vt* (*call s.o. back*) llamar; (*remember*) recordar. ● *n* llamada *f*
recant /rɪ'kænt/ *vi* retractarse
recap /'ri:kæp/ *vt/i* (*pt* **recapped**) (*fam*) resumir. ● *n* (*fam*) resumen *m*
recapitulat|e /ri:kə'pɪtʃʊleɪt/ *vt/i* resumir. **~ion** /-'leɪʃn/ *n* resumen *m*
recapture /ri:'kæptʃə(r)/ *vt* recobrar; (*recall*) hacer revivir
reced|e /rɪ'si:d/ *vi* retroceder. **~ing** *a* ‹*forehead*› huidizo
receipt /rɪ'si:t/ *n* recibo *m*. **~s** *npl* (*com*) ingresos *mpl*
receive /rɪ'si:v/ *vt* recibir. **~r** /-ə(r)/ *n* (*of stolen goods*) perista *m* & *f*; (*of phone*) auricular *m*
recent /'ri:snt/ *a* reciente. **~ly** *adv* recientemente
receptacle /rɪ'septəkl/ *n* recipiente *m*
reception /rɪ'sepʃn/ *n* recepción *f*; (*welcome*) acogida *f*. **~ist** *n* recepcionista *m* & *f*
receptive /rɪ'septɪv/ *a* receptivo
recess /rɪ'ses/ *n* hueco *m*; (*holiday*) vacaciones *fpl*; (*fig*) parte *f* recóndita
recession /rɪ'seʃn/ *n* recesión *f*
recharge /ri:'tʃɑ:dʒ/ *vt* cargar de nuevo, recargar
recipe /'resəpɪ/ *n* receta *f*
recipient /rɪ'sɪpɪənt/ *n* recipiente *m* & *f*; (*of letter*) destinatario *m*
reciprocal /rɪ'sɪprəkl/ *a* recíproco
reciprocate /rɪ'sɪprəkeɪt/ *vt* corresponder a
recital /rɪ'saɪtl/ *n* (*mus*) recital *m*
recite /rɪ'saɪt/ *vt* recitar; (*list*) enumerar
reckless /'reklɪs/ *a* imprudente. **~ly** *adv* imprudentemente. **~ness** *n* imprudencia *f*
reckon /'rekən/ *vt/i* calcular; (*consider*) considerar; (*think*) pensar. **~ on** (*rely*) contar con. **~ing** *n* cálculo *m*
reclaim /rɪ'kleɪm/ *vt* reclamar; recuperar ‹*land*›
reclin|e /rɪ'klaɪn/ *vi* recostarse. **~ing** *a* acostado; ‹*seat*› reclinable
recluse /rɪ'klu:s/ *n* solitario *m*
recogni|tion /rekəg'nɪʃn/ *n* reconocimiento *m*. **beyond ~tion** irreconocible. **~ze** /'rekəgnaɪz/ *vt* reconocer
recoil /rɪ'kɔɪl/ *vi* retroceder. ● *n* (*of gun*) culatazo *m*
recollect /rekə'lekt/ *vt* recordar. **~ion** /-ʃn/ *n* recuerdo *m*
recommend /rekə'mend/ *vt* recomendar. **~ation** /-'deɪʃn/ *n* recomendación *f*

recompense /ˈrekəmpens/ *vt* recompensar. ● *n* recompensa *f*

reconcil|e /ˈrekənsaɪl/ *vt* reconciliar ‹*people*›; conciliar ‹*facts*›. **~e o.s.** resignarse (**to** a). **~iation** /-sɪlɪˈeɪʃn/ *n* reconciliación *f*

recondition /riːkənˈdɪʃn/ *vt* reacondicionar, arreglar

reconnaissance /rɪˈkɒnɪsns/ *n* reconocimiento *m*

reconnoitre /rekəˈnɔɪtə(r)/ *vt* (*pres p* **-tring**) (*mil*) reconocer. ● *vi* hacer un reconocimiento

re: **~consider** /riːkənˈsɪdə(r)/ *vt* volver a considerar. **~construct** /riːkənˈstrʌkt/ *vt* reconstruir. **~construction** /-ʃn/ *n* reconstrucción *f*

record /rɪˈkɔːd/ *vt* (*in register*) registrar; (*in diary*) apuntar; (*mus*) grabar. /ˈrekɔːd/ *n* (*file*) documentación *f*, expediente *m*; (*mus*) disco *m*; (*sport*) récord *m*. **off the ~** en confianza. **~er** /rɪˈkɔːdə(r)/ *n* registrador *m*; (*mus*) flauta *f* dulce. **~ing** *n* grabación *f*. **~-player** *n* tocadiscos *m invar*

recount /rɪˈkaʊnt/ *vt* contar, relatar, referir

re-count /riːˈkaʊnt/ *vt* recontar. /ˈriːkaʊnt/ *n* (*pol*) recuento *m*

recoup /rɪˈkuːp/ *vt* recuperar

recourse /rɪˈkɔːs/ *n* recurso *m*. **have ~ to** recurrir a

recover /rɪˈkʌvə(r)/ *vt* recuperar. ● *vi* reponerse. **~y** *n* recuperación *f*

recreation /rekrɪˈeɪʃn/ *n* recreo *m*. **~al** *a* de recreo

recrimination /rɪkrɪmɪˈneɪʃn/ *n* recriminación *f*

recruit /rɪˈkruːt/ *n* recluta *m*. ● *vt* reclutar. **~ment** *n* reclutamiento *m*

rectang|le /ˈrektæŋgl/ *n* rectángulo *m*. **~ular** /-ˈtæŋgjʊlə(r)/ *a* rectangular

rectif|ication /rektɪfɪˈkeɪʃn/ *n* rectificación *f*. **~y** /ˈrektɪfaɪ/ *vt* rectificar

rector /ˈrektə(r)/ *n* párroco *m*; (*of college*) rector *m*. **~y** *n* rectoría *f*

recumbent /rɪˈkʌmbənt/ *a* recostado

recuperat|e /rɪˈkuːpəreɪt/ *vt* recuperar. ● *vi* reponerse. **~ion** /-ˈreɪʃn/ *n* recuperación *f*

recur /rɪˈkɜː(r)/ *vi* (*pt* **recurred**) repetirse. **~rence** /rɪˈkʌrns/ *n* repetición *f*. **~rent** /rɪˈkʌrənt/ *a* repetido

recycle /riːˈsaɪkl/ *vt* reciclar

red /red/ *a* (**redder**, **reddest**) rojo. ● *n* rojo. **in the ~** ‹*account*› en descubierto. **~breast** /ˈredbrest/ *n* petirrojo *m*. **~brick** /ˈredbrɪk/ *a* ‹*univ*› de reciente fundación. **~den** /ˈredn/ *vt* enrojecer. ● *vi* enrojecerse. **~dish** *a* rojizo

redecorate /riːˈdekəreɪt/ *vt* pintar de nuevo

rede|em /rɪˈdiːm/ *vt* redimir. **~eming quality** *n* cualidad *f* compensadora. **~mption** /-ˈdempʃn/ *n* redención *f*

redeploy /riːdɪˈplɔɪ/ *vt* disponer de otra manera; (*mil*) cambiar de frente

red: **~-handed** *a* en flagrante. **~ herring** *n* (*fig*) pista *f* falsa. **~-hot** *a* al rojo; ‹*news*› de última hora

Red Indian /redˈɪndjən/ *n* piel *m* & *f* roja

redirect /riːdaɪˈrekt/ *vt* reexpedir

red: **~-letter day** *n* día *m* señalado, día *m* memorable. **~ light** *n* luz *f* roja. **~ness** *n* rojez *f*

redo /riːˈduː/ *vt* (*pt* **redid**, *pp* **redone**) rehacer

redouble /rɪˈdʌbl/ *vt* redoblar

redress /rɪˈdres/ *vt* reparar. ● *n* reparación *f*

red tape /redˈteɪp/ *n* (*fig*) papeleo *m*

reduc|e /rɪˈdjuːs/ *vt* reducir. ● *vi* reducirse; (*slim*) adelgazar. **~tion** /ˈdʌkʃn/ *n* reducción *f*

redundan|cy /rɪˈdʌndənsɪ/ *n* superfluidad *f*; (*unemployment*) desempleo *m*. **~t** /rɪˈdʌndənt/ superfluo. **be made ~t** perder su empleo

reed /riːd/ *n* caña *f*; (*mus*) lengüeta *f*

reef /riːf/ *n* arrecife *m*

reek /riːk/ *n* mal olor *m*. ● *vi*. **~ (of)** apestar a

reel /riːl/ *n* carrete *m*. ● *vi* dar vueltas; (*stagger*) tambalearse. ● *vt*. **~ off** (*fig*) enumerar

refectory /rɪˈfektərɪ/ *n* refectorio *m*

refer /rɪˈfɜː(r)/ *vt* (*pt* **referred**) remitir. ● *vi* referirse. **~ to** referirse a; (*consult*) consultar

referee /refəˈriː/ *n* árbitro *m*; (*for job*) referencia *f*. ● *vi* (*pt* **refereed**) arbitrar

reference /ˈrefrəns/ *n* referencia *f*. **~ book** *n* libro *m* de consulta. **in ~ to, with ~ to** en cuanto a; (*com*) respecto a

referendum /refəˈrendəm/ *n* (*pl* **-ums**) referéndum *m*

refill /riːˈfɪl/ *vt* rellenar. /ˈriːfɪl/ *n* recambio *m*

refine /rɪ'faɪn/ *vt* refinar. **~d** *a* refinado. **~ment** *n* refinamiento *m*; (*tec*) refinación *f*. **~ry** /-ərɪ/ *n* refinería *f*

reflect /rɪ'flekt/ *vt* reflejar. ● *vi* reflejar; (*think*) reflexionar. **~ upon** perjudicar. **~ion** /-ʃn/ *n* reflexión *f*; (*image*) reflejo *m*. **~ive** /rɪ'flektɪv/ *a* reflector; (*thoughtful*) pensativo. **~or** *n* reflector *m*

reflex /'ri:fleks/ *a* & *n* reflejo (*m*)

reflexive /rɪ'fleksɪv/ *a* (*gram*) reflexivo

reform /rɪ'fɔ:m/ *vt* reformar. ● *vi* reformarse. ● *n* reforma *f*. **~er** *n* reformador *m*

refract /rɪ'frækt/ *vt* refractar

refrain[1] /rɪ'freɪn/ *n* estribillo *m*

refrain[2] /rɪ'freɪn/ *vi* abstenerse (**from** de)

refresh /rɪ'freʃ/ *vt* refrescar. **~er** /rɪ'freʃə(r)/ *a* ‹*course*› de repaso. **~ing** *a* refrescante. **~ments** *npl* (*food and drink*) refrigerio *m*

refrigerat|e /rɪ'frɪdʒəreɪt/ *vt* refrigerar. **~or** *n* nevera *f*, refrigeradora *f* (*LAm*)

refuel /ri:'fju:əl/ *vt/i* (*pt* **refuelled**) repostar

refuge /'refju:dʒ/ *n* refugio *m*. **take ~** refugiarse. **~e** /refjʊ'dʒi:/ *n* refugiado *m*

refund /rɪ'fʌnd/ *vt* reembolsar. /'ri:fʌnd/ *n* reembolso *m*

refurbish /ri:'fɜ:bɪʃ/ *vt* renovar

refusal /rɪ'fju:zl/ *n* negativa *f*

refuse[1] /rɪ'fju:z/ *vt* rehusar. ● *vi* negarse

refuse[2] /'refju:s/ *n* basura *f*

refute /rɪ'fju:t/ *vt* refutar

regain /rɪ'geɪn/ *vt* recobrar

regal /'ri:gl/ *a* real

regale /rɪ'geɪl/ *vt* festejar

regalia /rɪ'geɪlɪə/ *npl* insignias *fpl*

regard /rɪ'gɑ:d/ *vt* mirar; (*consider*) considerar. **as ~s** en cuanto a. ● *n* mirada *f*; (*care*) atención *f*; (*esteem*) respeto *m*. **~ing** *prep* en cuanto a. **~less** /rɪ'gɑ:dlɪs/ *adv* a pesar de todo. **~less of** sin tener en cuenta. **~s** *npl* saludos *mpl*. **kind ~s** *npl* recuerdos *mpl*

regatta /rɪ'gætə/ *n* regata *f*

regency /'ri:dʒənsɪ/ *n* regencia *f*

regenerate /rɪ'dʒenəreɪt/ *vt* regenerar

regent /'ri:dʒənt/ *n* regente *m* & *f*

regime /reɪ'ʒi:m/ *n* régimen *m*

regiment /'redʒɪmənt/ *n* regimiento *m*. **~al** /-'mentl/ *a* del regimiento. **~ation** /-en'teɪʃn/ *n* reglamentación *f* rígida

region /'ri:dʒən/ *n* región *f*. **in the ~ of** alrededor de. **~al** *a* regional

register /'redʒɪstə(r)/ *n* registro *m*. ● *vt* registrar; matricular ‹*vehicle*›; declarar ‹*birth*›; certificar ‹*letter*›; facturar ‹*luggage*›; (*indicate*) indicar; (*express*) expresar. ● *vi* (*enrol*) inscribirse; (*fig*) producir impresión. **~ office** *n* registro *m* civil

registrar /redʒɪ'strɑ:(r)/ *n* secretario *m* del registro civil; (*univ*) secretario *m* general

registration /redʒɪ'streɪʃn/ *n* registración *f*; (*in register*) inscripción *f*; (*of vehicle*) matrícula *f*

registry /'redʒɪstrɪ/ *n*. **~ office** *n* registro *m* civil

regression /rɪ'greʃn/ *n* regresión *f*

regret /rɪ'gret/ *n* pesar *m*. ● *vt* (*pt* **regretted**) lamentar. **I ~ that** siento (que). **~fully** *adv* con pesar. **~table** *a* lamentable. **~tably** *adv* lamentablemente

regular /'regjʊlə(r)/ *a* regular; (*usual*) habitual. ● *n* (*fam*) cliente *m* habitual. **~ity** /-'lærətɪ/ *n* regularidad *f*. **~ly** *adv* regularmente

regulat|e /'regjʊleɪt/ *vt* regular. **~ion** /-'leɪʃn/ *n* arreglo *m*; (*rule*) regla *f*

rehabilitat|e /ri:hə'bɪlɪteɪt/ *vt* rehabilitar. **~ion** /-'teɪʃn/ *n* rehabilitación *f*

rehash /ri:'hæʃ/ *vt* volver a presentar. /'ri:hæʃ/ *n* refrito *m*

rehears|al /rɪ'hɜ:sl/ *n* ensayo *m*. **~e** /rɪ'hɜ:s/ *vt* ensayar

reign /reɪn/ *n* reinado *m*. ● *vi* reinar

reimburse /ri:ɪm'bɜ:s/ *vt* reembolsar

reins /reɪnz/ *npl* riendas *fpl*

reindeer /'reɪndɪə(r)/ *n invar* reno *m*

reinforce /ri:ɪn'fɔ:s/ *vt* reforzar. **~ment** *n* refuerzo *m*

reinstate /ri:ɪn'steɪt/ *vt* reintegrar

reiterate /ri:'ɪtəreɪt/ *vt* reiterar

reject /rɪ'dʒekt/ *vt* rechazar. /'ri:dʒekt/ *n* producto *m* defectuoso. **~ion** /'dʒekʃn/ *n* rechazamiento *m*, rechazo *m*

rejoic|e /rɪ'dʒɔɪs/ *vi* regocijarse. **~ing** *n* regocijo *m*

rejoin /rɪ'dʒɔɪn/ *vt* reunirse con; (*answer*) replicar. **~der** /rɪ'dʒɔɪndə(r)/ *n* réplica *f*

rejuvenate /rɪ'dʒu:vəneɪt/ *vt* rejuvenecer

rekindle /ri:'kɪndl/ *vt* reavivar

relapse /rɪ'læps/ *n* recaída *f*. ● *vi* recaer; (*into crime*) reincidir

relate /rɪ'leɪt/ *vt* contar; (*connect*) relacionar. ● *vi* relacionarse (**to** con). **~d** *a* emparentado; ‹*ideas etc*› relacionado

relation /rɪ'leɪʃn/ *n* relación *f*; (*person*) pariente *m & f*. **~ship** *n* relación *f*; (*blood tie*) parentesco *m*; (*affair*) relaciones *fpl*

relative /'relətɪv/ *n* pariente *m & f*. ● *a* relativo. **~ly** *adv* relativamente

relax /rɪ'læks/ *vt* relajar. ● *vi* relajarse. **~ation** /ri:læk'seɪʃn/ *n* relajación *f*; (*rest*) descanso *m*; (*recreation*) recreo *m*. **~ing** *a* relajante

relay /'ri:leɪ/ *n* relevo *m*. **~ (race)** *n* carrera *f* de relevos. /rɪ'leɪ/ *vt* retransmitir

release /rɪ'li:s/ *vt* soltar; poner en libertad ‹*prisoner*›; lanzar ‹*bomb*›; estrenar ‹*film*›; (*mec*) desenganchar; publicar ‹*news*›; emitir ‹*smoke*›. ● *n* liberación *f*; (*of film*) estreno *m*; (*record*) disco *m* nuevo

relegate /'relɪgeɪt/ *vt* relegar

relent /rɪ'lent/ *vi* ceder. **~less** *a* implacable; (*continuous*) incesante

relevan|ce /'reləvəns/ *n* pertinencia *f*. **~t** /'reləvənt/ *a* pertinente

reliab|ility /rɪlaɪə'bɪlətɪ/ *n* fiabilidad *f*. **~le** /rɪ'laɪəbl/ *a* seguro; ‹*person*› de fiar; (*com*) serio

relian|ce /rɪ'laɪəns/ *n* dependencia *f*; (*trust*) confianza *f*. **~t** *a* confiado

relic /'relɪk/ *n* reliquia *f*. **~s** *npl* restos *mpl*

relie|f /rɪ'li:f/ *n* alivio *m*; (*assistance*) socorro *m*; (*outline*) relieve *m*. **~ve** /rɪ'li:v/ *vt* aliviar; (*take over from*) relevar

religio|n /rɪ'lɪdʒən/ *n* religión *f*. **~us** /rɪ'lɪdʒəs/ *a* religioso

relinquish /rɪ'lɪnkwɪʃ/ *vt* abandonar, renunciar

relish /'relɪʃ/ *n* gusto *m*; (*culin*) salsa *f*. ● *vt* saborear. **I don't ~ the idea** no me gusta la idea

relocate /ri:ləʊ'keɪt/ *vt* colocar de nuevo

reluctan|ce /rɪ'lʌktəns/ *n* desgana *f*. **~t** /rɪ'lʌktənt/ *a* mal dispuesto. **be ~t to** no tener ganas de. **~tly** *adv* de mala gana

rely /rɪ'laɪ/ *vi*. **~ on** contar con; (*trust*) fiarse de; (*depend*) depender

remain /rɪ'meɪn/ *vi* quedar. **~der** /rɪ'meɪndə(r)/ *n* resto *m*. **~s** *npl* restos *mpl*; (*left-overs*) sobras *fpl*

remand /rɪ'mɑ:nd/ *vt*. **~ in custody** mantener bajo custodia. ● *n*. **on ~** bajo custodia

remark /rɪ'mɑ:k/ *n* observación *f*. ● *vt* observar. **~able** *a* notable

remarry /ri:'mærɪ/ *vi* volver a casarse

remedial /rɪ'mi:dɪəl/ *a* remediador

remedy /'remədɪ/ *n* remedio *m*. ● *vt* remediar

rememb|er /rɪ'membə(r)/ *vt* acordarse de. ● *vi* acordarse. **~rance** *n* recuerdo *m*

remind /rɪ'maɪnd/ *vt* recordar. **~er** *n* recordatorio *m*; (*letter*) notificación *f*

reminisce /remɪ'nɪs/ *vi* recordar el pasado. **~nces** *npl* recuerdos *mpl*. **~nt** /remɪ'nɪsnt/ *a*. **be ~nt of** recordar

remiss /rɪ'mɪs/ *a* negligente

remission /rɪ'mɪʃn/ *n* remisión *f*; (*of sentence*) reducción *f* de condena

remit /rɪ'mɪt/ *vt* (*pt* **remitted**) perdonar; enviar ‹*money*›. ● *vi* moderarse. **~tance** *n* remesa *f*

remnant /'remnənt/ *n* resto *m*; (*of cloth*) retazo *m*; (*trace*) vestigio *m*

remonstrate /'remənstreɪt/ *vi* protestar

remorse /rɪ'mɔ:s/ *n* remordimiento *m*. **~ful** *a* lleno de remordimiento. **~less** *a* implacable

remote /rɪ'məʊt/ *a* remoto; (*slight*) leve; ‹*person*› distante. **~ control** *n* mando *m* a distancia. **~ly** *adv* remotamente. **~ness** *n* lejanía *f*; (*isolation*) aislamiento *m*, alejamiento *m*; (*fig*) improbabilidad *f*

remov|able /rɪ'mu:vəbl/ *a* movible; (*detachable*) de quita y pon, separable. **~al** *n* eliminación *f*; (*from house*) mudanza *f*. **~e** /rɪ'mu:v/ *vt* quitar; (*dismiss*) despedir; (*get rid of*) eliminar; (*do away with*) suprimir

remunerat|e /rɪ'mju:nəreɪt/ *vt* remunerar. **~ion** /-'reɪʃn/ *n* remuneración *f*. **~ive** *a* remunerador

Renaissance /rə'neɪsəns/ *n* Renacimiento *m*

rend /rend/ *vt* (*pt* **rent**) rasgar

render /'rendə(r)/ *vt* rendir; (*com*) presentar; (*mus*) interpretar; prestar ‹*help etc*›. **~ing** *n* (*mus*) interpretación *f*

rendezvous /'rɒndɪvu:/ *n* (*pl* **-vous** /-vu:z/) cita *f*

renegade /'renɪgeɪd/ *n* renegado

renew /rɪ'nju:/ *vt* renovar; (*resume*) reanudar. **~able** *a* renovable. **~al** *n* renovación *f*

renounce /rɪ'naʊns/ *vt* renunciar a; (*disown*) repudiar

renovat|e /'renəveɪt/ *vt* renovar. **~ion** /-'veɪʃn/ *n* renovación *f*

renown /rɪ'naʊn/ *n* fama *f*. **~ed** *a* célebre

rent[1] /rent/ *n* alquiler *m*. ● *vt* alquilar

rent[2] /rent/ *see* **rend**

rental /rentl/ *n* alquiler *m*

renunciation /rɪnʌnsɪ'eɪʃn/ *n* renuncia *f*

reopen /ri:'əʊpən/ *vt* reabrir. ● *vi* reabrirse. **~ing** *n* reapertura *f*

reorganize /ri:'ɔ:gənaɪz/ *vt* reorganizar

rep[1] /rep/ *n* (*com, fam*) representante *m* & *f*

rep[2] /rep/ (*theatre, fam*) teatro *m* de repertorio

repair /rɪ'peə(r)/ *vt* reparar; remendar ‹*clothes, shoes*›. ● *n* reparación *f*; (*patch*) remiendo *m*. **in good ~** en buen estado

repartee /repɑ:'ti:/ *n* ocurrencias *fpl*

repatriat|e /ri:'pætrɪeɪt/ *vt* repatriar. **~ion** /-'eɪʃn/ *n* repatriación *f*

repay /ri:'peɪ/ *vt* (*pt* **repaid**) reembolsar; pagar ‹*debt*›; (*reward*) recompensar. **~ment** *n* reembolso *m*, pago *m*

repeal /rɪ'pi:l/ *vt* abrogar. ● *n* abrogación *f*

repeat /rɪ'pi:t/ *vt* repetir. ● *vi* repetir(se). ● *n* repetición *f*. **~edly** /rɪ'pi:tɪdlɪ/ *adv* repetidas veces

repel /rɪ'pel/ *vt* (*pt* **repelled**) repeler. **~lent** *a* repelente

repent /rɪ'pent/ *vi* arrepentirse. **~ance** *n* arrepentimiento *m*. **~ant** *a* arrepentido

repercussion /ri:pə'kʌʃn/ *n* repercusión *f*

reperto|ire /'repətwɑ:(r)/ *n* repertorio *m*. **~ry** /'repətrɪ/ *n* repertorio *m*. **~ry (theatre)** *n* teatro *m* de repertorio

repetit|ion /repɪ'tɪʃn/ *n* repetición *f*. **~ious** /-'tɪʃəs/ *a*, **~ive** /rɪ'petətɪv/ *a* que se repite; (*dull*) monótono

replace /rɪ'pleɪs/ *vt* reponer; (*take the place of*) sustituir. **~ment** *n* sustitución *f*; (*person*) sustituto *m*. **~ment part** *n* recambio *m*

replay /'ri:pleɪ/ *n* (*sport*) repetición *f* del partido; (*recording*) repetición *f* inmediata

replenish /rɪ'plenɪʃ/ *vt* reponer; (*refill*) rellenar

replete /rɪ'pli:t/ *a* repleto

replica /'replɪkə/ *n* copia *f*

reply /rɪ'plaɪ/ *vt/i* contestar. ● *n* respuesta *f*

report /rɪ'pɔ:t/ *vt* anunciar; (*denounce*) denunciar. ● *vi* presentar un informe; (*present o.s.*) presentarse. ● *n* informe *m*; (*schol*) boletín *m*; (*rumour*) rumor *m*; (*newspaper*) reportaje *m*; (*sound*) estallido *m*. **~age** /repɔ:'tɑ:ʒ/ *n* reportaje *m*. **~edly** *adv* según se dice. **~er** /rɪ'pɔ:tə(r)/ *n* reportero *m*, informador *m*

repose /rɪ'pəʊz/ *n* reposo *m*

repository /rɪ'pɒzɪtrɪ/ *n* depósito *m*

repossess /ri:pə'zes/ *vt* recuperar

reprehen|d /reprɪ'hend/ *vt* reprender. **~sible** /-səbl/ *a* reprensible

represent /reprɪ'zent/ *vt* representar. **~ation** /-'teɪʃn/ *n* representación *f*. **~ative** /reprɪ'zentətɪv/ *a* representativo. ● *n* representante *m* & *f*

repress /rɪ'pres/ *vt* reprimir. **~ion** /-ʃn/ *n* represión *f*. **~ive** *a* represivo

reprieve /rɪ'pri:v/ *n* indulto *m*; (*fig*) respiro *m*. ● *vt* indultar; (*fig*) aliviar

reprimand /'reprɪmɑ:nd/ *vt* reprender. ● *n* reprensión *f*

reprint /'ri:prɪnt/ *n* reimpresión *f*; (*offprint*) tirada *f* aparte. /ri:'prɪnt/ *vt* reimprimir

reprisal /rɪ'praɪzl/ *n* represalia *f*

reproach /rɪ'prəʊtʃ/ *vt* reprochar. ● *n* reproche *m*. **~ful** *a* de reproche, reprobador. **~fully** *adv* con reproche

reprobate /'reprəbeɪt/ *n* malvado *m*; (*relig*) réprobo *m*

reproduc|e /ri:prə'dju:s/ *vt* reproducir. ● *vi* reproducirse. **~tion** /-'dʌkʃn/ *n* reproducción *f*. **~tive** /-'dʌktɪv/ *a* reproductor

reprove /rɪ'pru:v/ *vt* reprender

reptile /'reptaɪl/ *n* reptil *m*

republic /rɪ'pʌblɪk/ *n* república *f*. **~an** *a & n* republicano (*m*)
repudiate /rɪ'pju:dɪeɪt/ *vt* repudiar; (*refuse to recognize*) negarse a reconocer
repugnan|ce /rɪ'pʌgnəns/ *n* repugnancia *f*. **~t** /rɪ'pʌgnənt/ *a* repugnante
repuls|e /rɪ'pʌls/ *vt* rechazar, repulsar. **~ion** /-ʃn/ *n* repulsión *f*. **~ive** *a* repulsivo
reputable /'repjʊtəbl/ *a* acreditado, de confianza, honroso
reputation /repjʊ'teɪʃn/ *n* reputación *f*
repute /rɪ'pju:t/ *n* reputación *f*. **~d** /-ɪd/ *a* supuesto. **~dly** *adv* según se dice
request /rɪ'kwest/ *n* petición *f*. ● *vt* pedir. **~ stop** *n* parada *f* discrecional
require /rɪ'kwaɪə(r)/ *vt* requerir; (*need*) necesitar; (*demand*) exigir. **~d** *a* necesario. **~ment** *n* requisito *m*
requisite /'rekwɪzɪt/ *a* necesario. ● *n* requisito *m*
requisition /rekwɪ'zɪʃn/ *n* requisición *f*. ● *vt* requisar
resale /'ri:seɪl/ *n* reventa *f*
rescind /rɪ'sɪnd/ *vt* rescindir
rescue /'reskju:/ *vt* salvar. ● *n* salvamento *m*. **~r** /-ə(r)/ *n* salvador *m*
research /rɪ'sɜ:tʃ/ *n* investigación *f*. ● *vt* investigar. **~er** *n* investigador *m*
resembl|ance /rɪ'zembləns/ *n* parecido *m*. **~e** /rɪ'zembl/ *vt* parecerse a
resent /rɪ'zent/ *vt* resentirse por. **~ful** *a* resentido. **~ment** *n* resentimiento *m*
reservation /rezə'veɪʃn/ *n* reserva *f*; (*booking*) reservación *f*
reserve /rɪ'zɜ:v/ *vt* reservar. ● *n* reserva *f*; (*in sports*) suplente *m & f*. **~d** *a* reservado
reservist /rɪ'zɜ:vɪst/ *n* reservista *m & f*
reservoir /'rezəvwɑ:(r)/ *n* embalse *m*; (*tank*) depósito *m*
reshape /ri:'ʃeɪp/ *vt* formar de nuevo, reorganizar
reshuffle /ri:'ʃʌfl/ *vt* (*pol*) reorganizar. ● *n* (*pol*) reorganización *f*
reside /rɪ'zaɪd/ *vi* residir
residen|ce /'rezɪdəns/ *n* residencia *f*. **~ce permit** *n* permiso *m* de residencia. **be in ~ce** ‹*doctor etc*› interno. **~t** /'rezɪdənt/ *a & n* residente (*m & f*). **~tial** /rezɪ'denʃl/ *a* residencial
residue /'rezɪdju:/ *n* residuo *m*
resign /rɪ'zaɪn/ *vt/i* dimitir. **~ o.s. to** resignarse a. **~ation** /rezɪg'neɪʃn/ *n* resignación *f*; (*from job*) dimisión *f*. **~ed** *a* resignado
resilien|ce /rɪ'zɪlɪəns/ *n* elasticidad *f*; (*of person*) resistencia *f*. **~t** /rɪ'zɪlɪənt/ *a* elástico; ‹*person*› resistente
resin /'rezɪn/ *n* resina *f*
resist /rɪ'zɪst/ *vt* resistir. ● *vi* resistirse. **~ance** *n* resistencia *f*. **~ant** *a* resistente
resolut|e /'rezəlu:t/ *a* resuelto. **~ion** /-'lu:ʃn/ *n* resolución *f*
resolve /rɪ'zɒlv/ *vt* resolver. **~ to do** resolverse a hacer. ● *n* resolución *f*. **~d** *a* resuelto
resonan|ce /'rezənəns/ *n* resonancia *f*. **~t** /'rezənənt/ *a* resonante
resort /rɪ'zɔ:t/ *vi*. **~ to** recurrir a. ● *n* recurso *m*; (*place*) lugar *m* turístico. **in the last ~** como último recurso
resound /rɪ'zaʊnd/ *vi* resonar. **~ing** *a* resonante
resource /rɪ'sɔ:s/ *n* recurso *m*. **~ful** *a* ingenioso. **~fulness** *n* ingeniosidad *f*
respect /rɪ'spekt/ *n* (*esteem*) respeto *m*; (*aspect*) respecto *m*. **with ~ to** con respecto a. ● *vt* respetar
respectab|ility /rɪspektə'bɪlətɪ/ *n* respetabilidad *f*. **~le** /rɪ'spektəbl/ *a* respetable. **~ly** *adv* respetablemente
respectful /rɪ'spektfl/ *a* respetuoso
respective /rɪ'spektɪv/ *a* respectivo. **~ly** *adv* respectivamente
respiration /respə'reɪʃn/ *n* respiración *f*
respite /'respaɪt/ *n* respiro *m*, tregua *f*
resplendent /rɪ'splendənt/ *a* resplandeciente
respon|d /rɪ'spɒnd/ *vi* responder. **~se** /rɪ'spɒns/ *n* respuesta *f*; (*reaction*) reacción *f*
responsib|ility /rɪspɒnsə'bɪlətɪ/ *n* responsabilidad *f*. **~le** /rɪ'spɒnsəbl/ *a* responsable; ‹*job*› de responsabilidad. **~ly** *adv* con formalidad
responsive /rɪ'spɒnsɪv/ *a* que reacciona bien. **~ to** sensible a
rest[1] /rest/ *vt* descansar; (*lean*) apoyar; (*place*) poner, colocar. ● *vi*

descansar; (*lean*) apoyarse. ● *n* descanso *m*; (*mus*) pausa *f*

rest[2] /rest/ *n* (*remainder*) resto *m*, lo demás; (*people*) los demás, los otros *mpl*. ● *vi* (*remain*) quedar

restaurant /'restərɒnt/ *n* restaurante *m*

restful /'restfl/ *a* sosegado

restitution /restɪ'tju:ʃn/ *n* restitución *f*

restive /'restɪv/ *a* inquieto

restless /'restlɪs/ *a* inquieto. **~ly** *adv* inquietamente. **~ness** *n* inquietud *f*

restor|ation /restə'reɪʃn/ *n* restauración *f*. **~e** /rɪ'stɔ:(r)/ *vt* restablecer; restaurar ‹*building*›; (*put back in position*) reponer; (*return*) devolver

restrain /rɪ'streɪn/ *vt* contener. **~ o.s.** contenerse. **~ed** *a* (*moderate*) moderado; (*in control of self*) comedido. **~t** *n* restricción *f*; (*moderation*) moderación *f*

restrict /rɪ'strɪkt/ *vt* restringir. **~ion** /-ʃn/ *n* restricción *f*. **~ive** /rɪ'strɪktɪv/ *a* restrictivo

result /rɪ'zʌlt/ *n* resultado *m*. ● *vi*. **~ from** resultar de. **~ in** dar como resultado

resume /rɪ'zju:m/ *vt* reanudar. ● *vi* continuar

résumé /'rezjʊmeɪ/ *n* resumen *m*

resumption /rɪ'zʌmpʃn/ *n* continuación *f*

resurgence /rɪ'sɜ:dʒəns/ *n* resurgimiento *m*

resurrect /rezə'rekt/ *vt* resucitar. **~ion** /-ʃn/ *n* resurrección *f*

resuscitat|e /rɪ'sʌsɪteɪt/ *vt* resucitar. **~ion** /-'teɪʃn/ *n* resucitación *f*

retail /'ri:teɪl/ *n* venta *f* al por menor. ● *a & adv* al por menor. ● *vt* vender al por menor. ● *vi* venderse al por menor. **~er** *n* minorista *m & f*

retain /rɪ'teɪn/ *vt* retener; (*keep*) conservar

retainer /rɪ'teɪnə(r)/ *n* (*fee*) anticipo *m*

retaliat|e /rɪ'tælɪeɪt/ *vi* desquitarse. **~ion** /-'eɪʃn/ *n* represalias *fpl*

retarded /rɪ'tɑ:dɪd/ *a* retrasado

retentive /rɪ'tentɪv/ *a* ‹*memory*› bueno

rethink /ri:'θɪŋk/ *vt* (*pt* **rethought**) considerar de nuevo

reticen|ce /'retɪsns/ *n* reserva *f*. **~t** /'retɪsnt/ *a* reservado, callado

retina /'retɪnə/ *n* retina *f*

retinue /'retɪnju:/ *n* séquito *m*

retir|e /rɪ'taɪə(r)/ *vi* (*from work*) jubilarse; (*withdraw*) retirarse; (*go to bed*) acostarse. ● *vt* jubilar. **~ed** *a* jubilado. **~ement** *n* jubilación *f*. **~ing** /rɪ'taɪərɪŋ/ *a* reservado

retort /rɪ'tɔ:t/ *vt/i* replicar. ● *n* réplica *f*

retrace /ri:'treɪs/ *vt* repasar. **~ one's steps** volver sobre sus pasos

retract /rɪ'trækt/ *vt* retirar. ● *vi* retractarse

retrain /ri:'treɪn/ *vt* reciclar, reeducar

retreat /rɪ'tri:t/ *vi* retirarse. ● *n* retirada *f*; (*place*) refugio *m*

retrial /ri:'traɪəl/ *n* nuevo proceso *m*

retribution /retrɪ'bju:ʃn/ *n* justo *m* castigo

retriev|al /rɪ'tri:vl/ *n* recuperación *f*. **~e** /rɪ'tri:v/ *vt* (*recover*) recuperar; (*save*) salvar; (*put right*) reparar. **~er** *n* (*dog*) perro *m* cobrador

retrograde /'retrəgreɪd/ *a* retrógrado

retrospect /'retrəspekt/ *n* retrospección *f*. **in ~** retrospectivamente. **~ive** /-'spektɪv/ *a* retrospectivo

return /rɪ'tɜ:n/ *vi* volver; (*reappear*) reaparecer. ● *vt* devolver; (*com*) declarar; (*pol*) elegir. ● *n* vuelta *f*; (*com*) ganancia *f*; (*restitution*) devolución *f*. **~ of income** *n* declaración *f* de ingresos. **in ~ for** a cambio de. **many happy ~s!** ¡feliz cumpleaños! **~ing** /rɪ'tɜ:nɪŋ/ *a*. **~ing officer** *n* escrutador *m*. **~ match** *n* partido *m* de desquite. **~ ticket** *n* billete *m* de ida y vuelta. **~s** *npl* (*com*) ingresos *mpl*

reunion /ri:'ju:nɪən/ *n* reunión *f*

reunite /ri:ju:'naɪt/ *vt* reunir

rev /rev/ *n* (*auto, fam*) revolución *f*. ● *vt/i*. **~ (up)** (*pt* **revved**) (*auto, fam*) acelerar(se)

revamp /ri:'væmp/ *vt* renovar

reveal /rɪ'vi:l/ *vt* revelar. **~ing** *a* revelador

revel /'revl/ *vi* (*pt* **revelled**) jaranear. **~ in** deleitarse en. **~ry** *n* juerga *f*

revelation /revə'leɪʃn/ *n* revelación *f*

revenge /rɪ'vendʒ/ *n* venganza *f*; (*sport*) desquite *m*. **take ~** vengarse. ● *vt* vengar. **~ful** *a* vindicativo, vengativo

revenue /'revənju:/ *n* ingresos *mpl*

reverberate /rɪ'vɜ:bəreɪt/ *vi* ‹*light*› reverberar; ‹*sound*› resonar
revere /rɪ'vɪə(r)/ *vt* venerar
reverence /'revərəns/ *n* reverencia *f*
reverend /'revərənd/ *a* reverendo
reverent /'revərənt/ *a* reverente
reverie /'revərɪ/ *n* ensueño *m*
revers /rɪ'vɪə/ *n* (*pl* **revers** /rɪ'vɪəz/) *n* solapa *f*
revers|al /rɪ'vɜ:sl/ *n* inversión *f*. **~e** /rɪ'vɜ:s/ *a* inverso. ● *n* contrario *m*; (*back*) revés *m*; (*auto*) marcha *f* atrás. ● *vt* invertir; anular ‹*decision*›; (*auto*) dar marcha atrás a. ● *vi* (*auto*) dar marcha atrás
revert /rɪ'vɜ:t/ *vi*. **~ to** volver a
review /rɪ'vju:/ *n* repaso *m*; (*mil*) revista *f*; (*of book, play, etc*) crítica *f*. ● *vt* analizar ‹*situation*›; reseñar ‹*book, play, etc*›. **~er** *n* crítico *m*
revile /rɪ'vaɪl/ *vt* injuriar
revis|e /rɪ'vaɪz/ *vt* revisar; (*schol*) repasar. **~ion** /-ɪʒn/ *n* revisión *f*; (*schol*) repaso *m*
reviv|al /rɪ'vaɪvl/ *n* restablecimiento *m*; (*of faith*) despertar *m*; (*of play*) reestreno *m*. **~e** /rɪ'vaɪv/ *vt* restablecer; resucitar ‹*person*›. ● *vi* restablecerse; ‹*person*› volver en sí
revoke /rɪ'vəʊk/ *vt* revocar
revolt /rɪ'vəʊlt/ *vi* sublevarse. ● *vt* dar asco a. ● *n* sublevación *f*
revolting /rɪ'vəʊltɪŋ/ *a* asqueroso
revolution /revə'lu:ʃn/ *n* revolución *f*. **~ary** *a* & *n* revolucionario (*m*). **~ize** *vt* revolucionar
revolve /rɪ'vɒlv/ *vi* girar
revolver /rɪ'vɒlvə(r)/ *n* revólver *m*
revolving /rɪ'vɒlvɪŋ/ *a* giratorio
revue /rɪ'vju:/ *n* revista *f*
revulsion /rɪ'vʌlʃn/ *n* asco *m*
reward /rɪ'wɔ:d/ *n* recompensa *f*. ● *vt* recompensar. **~ing** *a* remunerador; (*worthwhile*) que vale la pena
rewrite /ri:'raɪt/ *vt* (*pt* **rewrote**, *pp* **rewritten**) escribir de nuevo; (*change*) redactar de nuevo
rhapsody /'ræpsədɪ/ *n* rapsodia *f*
rhetoric /'retərɪk/ *n* retórica *f*. **~al** /rɪ'tɒrɪkl/ *a* retórico
rheumati|c /ru:'mætɪk/ *a* reumático. **~sm** /'ru:mətɪzəm/ *n* reumatismo *m*
rhinoceros /raɪ'nɒsərəs/ *n* (*pl* **-oses**) rinoceronte *m*
rhubarb /'ru:bɑ:b/ *n* ruibarbo *m*
rhyme /raɪm/ *n* rima *f*; (*poem*) poesía *f*. ● *vt/i* rimar
rhythm /'rɪðəm/ *n* ritmo *m*. **~ic(al)** /'rɪðmɪk(l)/ *a* rítmico
rib /rɪb/ *n* costilla *f*. —**vt** (*pt* **ribbed**) (*fam*) tomar el pelo a
ribald /'rɪbld/ *a* obsceno, verde
ribbon /'rɪbən/ *n* cinta *f*
rice /raɪs/ *n* arroz *m*. **~ pudding** *n* arroz con leche
rich /rɪtʃ/ *a* (**-er, -est**) rico. ● *n* ricos *mpl*. **~es** *npl* riquezas *fpl*. **~ly** *adv* ricamente. **~ness** *n* riqueza *f*
rickety /'rɪkətɪ/ *a* (*shaky*) cojo, desvencijado
ricochet /'rɪkəʃeɪ/ *n* rebote *m*. ● *vi* rebotar
rid /rɪd/ *vt* (*pt* **rid**, *pres p* **ridding**) librar (**of** de). **get ~ of** deshacerse de. **~dance** /'rɪdns/ *n*. **good ~dance!** ¡qué alivio!
ridden /'rɪdn/ *see* **ride**. ● *a* (*infested*) infestado. **~ by** (*oppressed*) agobiado de
riddle[1] /'rɪdl/ *n* acertijo *m*
riddle[2] /'ridl/ *vt* acribillar. **be ~d with** estar lleno de
ride /raɪd/ *vi* (*pt* **rode**, *pp* **ridden**) (*on horseback*) montar; (*go*) ir (en bicicleta, a caballo etc). **take s.o. for a ~** (*fam*) engañarle a uno. ● *vt* montar a ‹*horse*›; ir en ‹*bicycle*›; recorrer ‹*distance*›. ● *n* (*on horse*) cabalgata *f*; (*in car*) paseo *m* en coche. **~r** /-ə(r)/ *n* (*on horse*) jinete *m*; (*cyclist*) ciclista *m* & *f*; (*in document*) cláusula *f* adicional
ridge /rɪdʒ/ *n* línea *f*, arruga *f*; (*of mountain*) cresta *f*; (*of roof*) caballete *m*
ridicul|e /'rɪdɪkju:l/ *n* irrisión *f*. ● *vt* ridiculizar. **~ous** /rɪ'dɪkjʊləs/ *a* ridículo
riding /'raɪdɪŋ/ *n* equitación *f*
rife /raɪf/ *a* difundido. **~ with** lleno de
riff-raff /'rɪfræf/ *n* gentuza *f*
rifle[1] /'raɪfl/ *n* fusil *m*
rifle[2] /'raɪfl/ *vt* saquear
rifle-range /'raɪflreɪndʒ/ *n* campo *m* de tiro
rift /rɪft/ *n* grieta *f*; (*fig*) ruptura *f*
rig[1] /rɪg/ *vt* (*pt* **rigged**) aparejar. ● *n* (*at sea*) plataforma *f* de perforación. **~ up** *vt* improvisar
rig[2] /rɪg/ *vt* (*pej*) amañar
right /raɪt/ *a* (*correct, fair*) exacto, justo; (*morally*) bueno; (*not left*) derecho; (*suitable*) adecuado. ● *n* (*entitlement*) derecho *m*; (*not left*) derecha *f*; (*not evil*) bien *m*. **~ of**

way *n* (*auto*) prioridad *f*. **be in the ~** tener razón. **on the ~** a la derecha. **put ~** rectificar. • *vt* enderezar; (*fig*) corregir. • *adv* a la derecha; (*directly*) derecho; (*completely*) completamente; (*well*) bien. **~ away** *adv* inmediatamente. **~ angle** *n* ángulo *m* recto

righteous /ˈraɪtʃəs/ *a* recto; ‹*cause*› justo

right: **~ful** /ˈraɪtfl/ *a* legítimo. **~fully** *adv* legítimamente. **~-hand man** *n* brazo *m* derecho. **~ly** *adv* justamente. **~ wing** *a* (*pol*) *n* derechista

rigid /ˈrɪdʒɪd/ *a* rígido. **~ity** /-ˈdʒɪdətɪ/ *n* rigidez *f*

rigmarole /ˈrɪgmərəʊl/ *n* galimatías *m invar*

rig|orous /ˈrɪgərəs/ *a* riguroso. **~our** /ˈrɪgə(r)/ *n* rigor *m*

rig-out /ˈrɪgaʊt/ *n* (*fam*) atavío *m*

rile /raɪl/ *vt* (*fam*) irritar

rim /rɪm/ *n* borde *m*; (*of wheel*) llanta *f*; (*of glasses*) montura *f*. **~med** *a* bordeado

rind /raɪnd/ *n* corteza *f*; (*of fruit*) cáscara *f*

ring[1] /rɪŋ/ *n* (*circle*) círculo *m*; (*circle of metal etc*) aro *m*; (*on finger*) anillo *m*; (*on finger with stone*) sortija *f*; (*boxing*) cuadrilátero *m*; (*bullring*) ruedo *m*, redondel *m*, plaza *f*; (*for circus*) pista *f*; • *vt* rodear

ring[2] /rɪŋ/ *n* (*of bell*) toque *m*; (*tinkle*) tintineo *m*; (*telephone call*) llamada *f*. • *vt* (*pt* **rang**, *pp* **rung**) hacer sonar; (*telephone*) llamar por teléfono. **~ the bell** tocar el timbre. • *v* sonar. **~ back** *vt/i* volver a llamar. **~ off** *vi* colgar. **~ up** *vt* llamar por teléfono

ring: **~leader** /ˈrɪŋli:də(r)/ *n* cabecilla *f*. **~ road** *n* carretera *f* de circunvalación

rink /rɪŋk/ *n* pista *f*

rinse /rɪns/ *vt* enjuagar. • *n* aclarado *m*; (*of dishes*) enjuague *m*; (*for hair*) reflejo *m*

riot /ˈraɪət/ *n* disturbio *m*; (*of colours*) profusión *f*. **run ~** desenfrenarse. • *vi* amotinarse. **~er** *n* amotinador *m*. **~ous** *a* tumultuoso

rip /rɪp/ *vt* (*pt* **ripped**) rasgar. • *vi* rasgarse. **let ~** (*fig*) soltar. • *n* rasgadura *f*. **~ off** *vt* (*sl*) robar. **~-cord** *n* (*of parachute*) cuerda *f* de abertura

ripe /raɪp/ *a* (**-er**, **-est**) maduro. **~n** /ˈraɪpən/ *vt/i* madurar. **~ness** *n* madurez *f*

rip-off /ˈrɪpɒf/ *n* (*sl*) timo *m*

ripple /ˈrɪpl/ *n* rizo *m*; (*sound*) murmullo *m*. • *vt* rizar. • *vi* rizarse

rise /raɪz/ *vi* (*pt* **rose**, *pp* **risen**) levantarse; (*rebel*) sublevarse; ‹*river*› crecer; ‹*prices*› subir. • *n* subida *f*; (*land*) altura *f*; (*increase*) aumento *m*; (*to power*) ascenso *m*. **give ~ to** ocasionar. **~r** /-ə(r)/ *n*. **early ~r** *n* madrugador *m*

rising /ˈraɪzɪŋ/ *n* (*revolt*) sublevación *f*. • *a* ‹*sun*› naciente. **~ generation** *n* nueva generación *f*

risk /rɪsk/ *n* riesgo *m*. • *vt* arriesgar. **~y** *a* (**-ier**, **-iest**) arriesgado

risqué /ˈri:skeɪ/ *a* subido de color

rissole /ˈrɪsəʊl/ *n* croqueta *f*

rite /raɪt/ *n* rito *m*

ritual /ˈrɪtʃʊəl/ *a* & *n* ritual (*m*)

rival /ˈraɪvl/ *a* & *n* rival (*m*). • *vt* (*pt* **rivalled**) rivalizar con. **~ry** *n* rivalidad *f*

river /ˈrɪvə(r)/ *n* río *m*

rivet /ˈrɪvɪt/ *n* remache *m*. • *vt* remachar. **~ing** *a* fascinante

Riviera /rɪvɪˈerə/ *n*. **the (French) ~** la Costa *f* Azul. **the (Italian) ~** la Riviera *f* (Italiana)

rivulet /ˈrɪvjʊlɪt/ *n* riachuelo *m*

road /rəʊd/ *n* (*in town*) calle *f*; (*between towns*) carretera *f*; (*way*) camino *m*. **on the ~** en camino. **~-hog** *n* conductor *m* descortés. **~-house** *n* albergue *m*. **~-map** *n* mapa *m* de carreteras. **~side** /ˈrəʊdsaɪd/ *n* borde *m* de la carretera. **~ sign** *n* señal *f* de tráfico. **~way** /ˈrəʊdweɪ/ *n* calzada *f*. **~-works** *npl* obras *fpl*. **~worthy** /ˈrəʊdwɜ:ðɪ/ *a* ‹*vehicle*› seguro

roam /rəʊm/ *vi* vagar

roar /rɔ:(r)/ *n* rugido *m*; (*laughter*) carcajada *f*. • *vt/i* rugir. **~ past** ‹*vehicles*› pasar con estruendo. **~ with laughter** reírse a carcajadas. **~ing** /ˈrɔ:rɪŋ/ *a* ‹*trade etc*› activo

roast /rəʊst/ *vt* asar; tostar ‹*coffee*›. • *vi* asarse; ‹*person*, *coffee*› tostarse. • *a* & *n* asado (*m*). **~ beef** *n* rosbif *m*

rob /rɒb/ *vt* (*pt* **robbed**) robar; asaltar ‹*bank*›. **~ of** privar de. **~ber** *n* ladrón *m*; (*of bank*) atracador *m*. **~bery** *n* robo *m*

robe /rəʊb/ *n* manto *m*; (*univ etc*) toga *f*. **bath-~** *n* albornoz *m*

robin /ˈrɒbɪn/ *n* petirrojo *m*

robot /ˈrəʊbɒt/ *n* robot *m*, autómata *m*
robust /rəʊˈbʌst/ *a* robusto
rock[1] /rɒk/ *n* roca *f*; (*boulder*) peñasco *m*; (*sweet*) caramelo *m* en forma de barra; (*of Gibraltar*) peñón *m*. **on the ~s** ‹*drink*› con hielo; (*fig*) arruinado. **be on the ~s** ‹*marriage etc*› andar mal
rock[2] /rɒk/ *vt* mecer; (*shake*) sacudir. ● *vi* mecerse; (*shake*) sacudirse. ● *n* (*mus*) música *f* rock
rock: **~-bottom** *a* (*fam*) bajísimo. **~ery** /ˈrɒkərɪ/ *n* cuadro *m* alpino, rocalla *f*
rocket /ˈrɒkɪt/ *n* cohete *m*
rock: **~ing-chair** *n* mecedora *f*. **~ing-horse** *n* caballo *m* de balancín. **~y** /ˈrɒkɪ/ *a* (**-ier**, **-iest**) rocoso; (*fig, shaky*) bamboleante
rod /rɒd/ *n* vara *f*; (*for fishing*) caña *f*; (*metal*) barra *f*
rode /rəʊd/ *see* **ride**
rodent /ˈrəʊdnt/ *n* roedor *m*
rodeo /rəˈdeɪəʊ/ *n* (*pl* **-os**) rodeo *m*
roe[1] /rəʊ/ *n* (*fish eggs*) hueva *f*
roe[2] /rəʊ/ (*pl* **roe**, *or* **roes**) (*deer*) corzo *m*
rogu|e /rəʊg/ *n* pícaro *m*. **~ish** *a* picaresco
role /rəʊl/ *n* papel *m*
roll /rəʊl/ *vt* hacer rodar; (*roll up*) enrollar; (*flatten lawn*) allanar; aplanar ‹*pastry*›. ● *vi* rodar; ‹*ship*› balancearse; (*on floor*) revolcarse. **be ~ing (in money)** (*fam*) nadar (en dinero). ● *n* rollo *m*; (*of ship*) balanceo *m*; (*of drum*) redoble *m*; (*of thunder*) retumbo *m*; (*bread*) panecillo *m*; (*list*) lista *f*. **~ over** *vi* (*turn over*) dar una vuelta. **~ up** *vt* enrollar; arremangar ‹*sleeve*›. ● *vi* (*fam*) llegar. **~-call** *n* lista *f*
roller /ˈrəʊlə(r)/ *n* rodillo *m*; (*wheel*) rueda *f*; (*for hair*) rulo *m*, bigudí *m*. **~-coaster** *n* montaña *f* rusa. **~-skate** *n* patín *m* de ruedas
rollicking /ˈrɒlɪkɪŋ/ *a* alegre
rolling /ˈrəʊlɪŋ/ *a* ondulado. **~-pin** *n* rodillo *m*
Roman /ˈrəʊmən/ *a* & *n* romano (*m*). **~ Catholic** *a* & *n* católico (*m*) (romano)
romance /rəʊˈmæns/ *n* novela *f* romántica; (*love*) amor *m*; (*affair*) aventura *f*
Romania /rəʊˈmeɪnɪə/ *n* Rumania *f*. **~n** *a* & *n* rumano (*m*)
romantic /rəʊˈmæntɪk/ *a* romántico. **~ism** *n* romanticismo *m*
Rome /ˈrəʊm/ *n* Roma *f*
romp /rɒmp/ *vi* retozar. ● *n* retozo *m*
rompers /ˈrɒmpəz/ *npl* pelele *m*
roof /ru:f/ *n* techo *m*, tejado *m*; (*of mouth*) paladar *m*. ● *vt* techar. **~-garden** *n* jardín *m* en la azotea. **~-rack** *n* baca *f*. **~-top** *n* tejado *m*
rook[1] /rʊk/ *n* grajo *m*
rook[2] /rʊk/ (*in chess*) torre *f*
room /ru:m/ *n* cuarto *m*, habitación *f*; (*bedroom*) dormitorio *m*; (*space*) sitio *m*; (*large hall*) sala *f*. **~y** *a* espacioso; ‹*clothes*› holgado
roost /ru:st/ *n* percha *f*. ● *vi* descansar. **~er** *n* gallo *m*
root[1] /ru:t/ *n* raíz *f*. **take ~** echar raíces. ● *vt* hacer arraigar. ● *vi* echar raíces, arraigarse
root[2] /ru:t/ *vt*/*i*. **~ about** *vi* hurgar. **~ for** *vi* (*Amer*, *sl*) alentar. **~ out** *vt* extirpar
rootless /ˈru:tlɪs/ *a* desarraigado
rope /rəʊp/ *n* cuerda *f*. **know the ~s** estar al corriente. ● *vt* atar. **~ in** *vt* agarrar
rosary /ˈrəʊzərɪ/ *n* (*relig*) rosario *m*
rose[1] /rəʊz/ *n* rosa *f*; (*nozzle*) roseta *f*
rose[2] /rəʊz/ *see* **rise**
rosé /ˈrəʊzeɪ/ *n* (vino *m*) rosado *m*
rosette /rəʊˈzet/ *n* escarapela *f*
roster /ˈrɒstə(r)/ *n* lista *f*
rostrum /ˈrɒstrəm/ *n* tribuna *f*
rosy /ˈrəʊzɪ/ *a* (**-ier**, **-iest**) rosado; ‹*skin*› sonrosado
rot /rɒt/ *vt* (*pt* **rotted**) pudrir. ● *vi* pudrirse. ● *n* putrefacción *f*; (*sl*) tonterías *fpl*
rota /ˈrəʊtə/ *n* lista *f*
rotary /ˈrəʊtərɪ/ *a* giratorio, rotativo
rotat|e /rəʊˈteɪt/ *vt* girar; (*change round*) alternar. ● *vi* girar; (*change round*) alternarse. **~ion** /-ʃn/ *n* rotación *f*
rote /rəʊt/ *n*. **by ~** maquinalmente, de memoria
rotten /ˈrɒtn/ *a* podrido; (*fam*) desagradable
rotund /rəʊˈtʌnd/ *a* redondo; ‹*person*› regordete
rouge /ru:ʒ/ *n* colorete *m*
rough /rʌf/ *a* (**-er**, **-est**) áspero; ‹*person*› tosco; (*bad*) malo; ‹*ground*› accidentado; (*violent*) brutal; (*aproximate*) aproximado; ‹*diamond*› bruto. ● *adv* duro. **~ copy** *n*, **~ draft** *n* borrador *m*. ● *n*

(*ruffian*) matón *m*. ● *vt*. ~ **it** vivir sin comodidades. ~ **out** *vt* esbozar

roughage /ˈrʌfɪdʒ/ *n* alimento *m* indigesto, afrecho *m*; (*for animals*) forraje *m*

rough: ~**-and-ready** *a* improvisado. ~**-and-tumble** *n* riña *f*. ~**ly** *adv* toscamente; (*more or less*) más o menos. ~**ness** *n* aspereza *f*; (*lack of manners*) incultura *f*; (*crudeness*) tosquedad *f*

roulette /ru:ˈlet/ *n* ruleta *f*

round /raʊnd/ *a* (**-er**, **-est**) redondo. ● *n* círculo *m*; (*slice*) tajada *f*; (*of visits, drinks*) ronda *f*; (*of competition*) vuelta *f*; (*boxing*) asalto *m*.● *prep* alrededor de. ● *adv* alrededor. ~ **about** (*approximately*) aproximadamente. **come** ~ **to**, **go** ~ **to** (*a friend etc*) pasar por casa de. ● *vt* redondear; doblar ‹*corner*›. ~ **off** *vt* terminar. ~ **up** *vt* reunir; redondear ‹*price*›

roundabout /ˈraʊndəbaʊt/ *n* tiovivo *m*; (*for traffic*) glorieta *f*. ● *a* indirecto

rounders /ˈraʊndəz/ *n* juego *m* parecido al béisbol

round: ~**ly** *adv* (*bluntly*) francamente. ~ **trip** *n* viaje *m* de ida y vuelta. ~**-up** *n* reunión *f*; (*of suspects*) redada *f*

rous|e /raʊz/ *vt* despertar. ~**ing** *a* excitante

rout /raʊt/ *n* derrota *f*. ● *vt* derrotar

route /ru:t/ *n* ruta *f*; (*naut, aviat*) rumbo *m*; (*of bus*) línea *f*

routine /ru:ˈti:n/ *n* rutina *f*. ● *a* rutinario

rov|e /rəʊv/ *vt/i* vagar (por). ~**ing** *a* errante

row[1] /rəʊ/ *n* fila *f*

row[2] /rəʊ/ *n* (*in boat*) paseo *m* en bote (de remos). ● *vi* remar

row[3] /raʊ/ *n* (*noise, fam*) ruido *m*; (*quarrel*) pelea *f*. ● *vi* (*fam*) pelearse

rowdy /ˈraʊdɪ/ *a* (**-ier**, **-iest**) *n* ruidoso

rowing /ˈrəʊɪŋ/ *n* remo *m*. ~**-boat** *n* bote *m* de remos

royal /ˈrɔɪəl/ *a* real. ~**ist** *a* & *n* monárquico (*m*). ~**ly** *adv* magníficamente. ~**ty** /ˈrɔɪəltɪ/ *n* familia *f* real; (*payment*) derechos *mpl* de autor

rub /rʌb/ *vt* (*pt* **rubbed**) frotar. ~ **it in** insistir en algo. ● *n* frotamiento *m*. ~ **off on s.o.** *vi* pegársele a uno. ~ **out** *vt* borrar

rubber /ˈrʌbə(r)/ *n* goma *f*. ~ **band** *n* goma *f* (elástica). ~ **stamp** *n* sello *m* de goma. ~**-stamp** *vt* (*fig*) aprobar maquinalmente. ~**y** *a* parecido al caucho

rubbish /ˈrʌbɪʃ/ *n* basura *f*; (*junk*) trastos *mpl*; (*fig*) tonterías *fpl*. ~**y** *a* sin valor

rubble /ˈrʌbl/ *n* escombros; (*small*) cascajo *m*

ruby /ˈru:bɪ/ *n* rubí *m*

rucksack /ˈrʌksæk/ *n* mochila *f*

rudder /ˈrʌdə(r)/ *n* timón *m*

ruddy /ˈrʌdɪ/ *a* (**-ier**, **-iest**) rubicundo; (*sl*) maldito

rude /ru:d/ *a* (**-er**, **-est**) descortés, mal educado; (*improper*) indecente; (*brusque*) brusco. ~**ly** *adv* con descortesía. ~**ness** *n* descortesía *f*

rudiment /ˈru:dɪmənt/ *n* rudimento *m*. ~**ary** /-ˈmentrɪ/ *a* rudimentario

rueful /ˈru:fl/ *a* triste

ruffian /ˈrʌfɪən/ *n* rufián *m*

ruffle /ˈrʌfl/ *vt* despeinar ‹*hair*›; arrugar ‹*clothes*›. ● *n* (*frill*) volante *m*, fruncido *m*

rug /rʌg/ *n* tapete *m*; (*blanket*) manta *f*

Rugby /ˈrʌgbɪ/ *n*. ~ **(football)** *n* rugby *m*

rugged /ˈrʌgɪd/ *a* desigual; (*landscape*) accidentado; (*fig*) duro

ruin /ˈru:ɪn/ *n* ruina *f*. ● *vt* arruinar. ~**ous** *a* ruinoso

rule /ru:l/ *n* regla *f*; (*custom*) costumbre *f*; (*pol*) dominio *m*. **as a** ~ por regla general. ● *vt* gobernar; (*master*) dominar; (*jurid*) decretar; (*decide*) decidir. ~ **out** *vt* descartar. ~**d paper** *n* papel *m* rayado

ruler /ˈru:lə(r)/ *n* (*sovereign*) soberano *m*; (*leader*) gobernante *m* & *f*; (*measure*) regla *f*

ruling /ˈru:lɪŋ/ *a* ‹*class*› dirigente. ● *n* decisión *f*

rum /rʌm/ *n* ron *m*

rumble /rʌmbl/ *vi* retumbar; ‹*stomach*› hacer ruidos. ● *n* retumbo *m*; (*of stomach*) ruido *m*

ruminant /ˈru:mɪnənt/ *a* & *n* rumiante (*m*)

rummage /ˈrʌmɪdʒ/ *vi* hurgar

rumour /ˈru:mə(r)/ *n* rumor *m*. ● *vt*. **it is** ~**ed that** se dice que

rump /rʌmp/ *n* (*of horse*) grupa *f*; (*of fowl*) rabadilla *f*. ~ **steak** *n* filete *m*

rumpus /ˈrʌmpəs/ *n* (*fam*) jaleo *m*

run /rʌn/ *vi* (*pt* **ran**, *pp* **run**, *pres p* **running**) correr; (*flow*) fluir; (*pass*) pasar; (*function*) funcionar; (*melt*) derretirse; ‹*bus etc*› circular; ‹*play*› representarse (continuamente); ‹*colours*› correrse; (*in election*) presentarse. ● *vt* tener ‹*house*›; (*control*) dirigir; correr ‹*risk*›; (*drive*) conducir; (*pass*) pasar; (*present*) presentar; forzar ‹*blockade*›. ~ **a temperature** tener fiebre. ● *n* corrida *f*, carrera *f*; (*journey*) viaje *m*; (*outing*) paseo *m*, excursión *f*; (*distance travelled*) recorrido *m*; (*ladder*) carrera *f*; (*ski*) pista *f*; (*series*) serie *f*. **at a** ~ corriendo. **have the** ~ **of** tener a su disposición. **in the long** ~ a la larga. **on the** ~ de fuga. ~ **across** *vt* toparse con ‹*friend*›. ~ **away** *vi* escaparse. ~ **down** *vi* bajar corriendo; ‹*clock*› quedarse sin cuerda. ● *vt* (*auto*) atropellar; (*belittle*) denigrar. ~ **in** *vt* rodar ‹*vehicle*›. ● *vi* entrar corriendo. ~ **into** *vt* toparse con ‹*friend*›; (*hit*) chocar con. ~ **off** *vt* tirar ‹*copies etc*›. ~ **out** *vi* salir corriendo; ‹*liquid*› salirse; (*fig*) agotarse. ~ **out of** quedar sin. ~ **over** *vt* (*auto*) atropellar. ~ **through** *vt* traspasar; (*revise*) repasar. ~ **up** *vt* hacerse ‹*bill*›. ● *vi* subir corriendo. ~ **up against** tropezar con ‹*difficulties*›. ~**away** /ˈrʌnəweɪ/ *a* fugitivo; ‹*success*› decisivo; ‹*inflation*› galopante. ● *n* fugitivo *m*. ~ **down** *a* ‹*person*› agotado. ~**-down** *n* informe *m* detallado

rung[1] /rʌŋ/ *n* (*of ladder*) peldaño *m*

rung[2] /rʌŋ/ *see* **ring**

run: ~**ner** /ˈrʌnə(r)/ *n* corredor *m*; (*on sledge*) patín *m*. ~**ner bean** *n* judía *f* escarlata. ~**ner-up** *n* subcampeón *m*, segundo *m*. ~**ning** /ˈrʌnɪŋ/ *n* (*race*) carrera *f*. **be in the** ~**ning** tener posibilidades de ganar. ● *a* en marcha; ‹*water*› corriente; ‹*commentary*› en directo. **four times** ~**ning** cuatro veces seguidas. ~**ny** /ˈrʌnɪ/ *a* líquido; ‹*nose*› que moquea. ~**-of-the-mill** *a* ordinario. ~**-up** *n* período *m* que precede. ~**way** /ˈrʌnweɪ/ *n* pista *f*

rupture /ˈrʌptʃə(r)/ *n* ruptura *f*; (*med*) hernia *f*. ● *vt*/*i* quebrarse

rural /ˈrʊərəl/ *a* rural

ruse /ru:z/ *n* ardid *m*

rush[1] /rʌʃ/ *n* (*haste*) prisa *f*; (*crush*) bullicio *m*. ● *vi* precipitarse. ● *vt* apresurar; (*mil*) asaltar

rush[2] /rʌʃ/ *n* (*plant*) junco *m*

rush-hour /ˈrʌʃaʊə(r)/ *n* hora *f* punta

rusk /rʌsk/ *n* galleta *f*, tostada *f*

russet /ˈrʌsɪt/ *a* rojizo. ● *n* (*apple*) manzana *f* rojiza

Russia /ˈrʌʃə/ *n* Rusia *f*. ~**n** *a* & *n* ruso (*m*)

rust /rʌst/ *n* orín *m*. ● *vt* oxidar. ● *vi* oxidarse

rustic /ˈrʌstɪk/ *a* rústico

rustle /ˈrʌsl/ *vt* hacer susurrar; (*Amer*) robar. ~ **up** (*fam*) preparar. ● *vi* susurrar

rust: ~**-proof** *a* inoxidable. ~**y** *a* (**-ier**, **-iest**) oxidado

rut /rʌt/ *n* surco *m*. **in a** ~ en la rutina de siempre

ruthless /ˈru:θlɪs/ *a* despiadado. ~**ness** *n* crueldad *f*

rye /raɪ/ *n* centeno *m*

S

S *abbr* (*south*) sur *m*

sabbath /ˈsæbəθ/ *n* día *m* de descanso; (*Christian*) domingo *m*; (*Jewish*) sábado *m*

sabbatical /səˈbætɪkl/ *a* sabático

sabot|age /ˈsæbətɑ:ʒ/ *n* sabotaje *m*. ● *vt* sabotear. ~**eur** /-ˈtɜ:(r)/ *n* saboteador *m*

saccharin /ˈsækərɪn/ *n* sacarina *f*

sachet /ˈsæʃeɪ/ *n* bolsita *f*

sack[1] /sæk/ *n* saco *m*. **get the** ~ (*fam*) ser despedido. ● *vt* (*fam*) despedir. ~**ing** *n* arpillera *f*; (*fam*) despido *m*

sack[2] /sæk/ *vt* (*plunder*) saquear

sacrament /ˈsækrəmənt/ *n* sacramento *m*

sacred /ˈseɪkrɪd/ *a* sagrado

sacrifice /ˈsækrɪfaɪs/ *n* sacrificio *m*. ● *vt* sacrificar

sacrileg|e /ˈsækrɪlɪdʒ/ *n* sacrilegio *m*. ~**ious** /-ˈlɪdʒəs/ *a* sacrílego

sacrosanct /ˈsækrəʊsæŋkt/ *a* sacrosanto

sad /sæd/ *a* (**sadder**, **saddest**) triste. ~**den** /ˈsædn/ *vt* entristecer

saddle /ˈsædl/ *n* silla *f*. **be in the** ~ (*fig*) tener las riendas. ● *vt* ensillar ‹*horse*›. ~ **s.o. with** (*fig*) cargar a uno con. ~**-bag** *n* alforja *f*

sad: ~**ly** *adv* tristemente; (*fig*) desgraciadamente. ~**ness** *n* tristeza *f*

sadis|m /ˈseɪdɪzəm/ *n* sadismo *m*. ~**t** /ˈseɪdɪst/ *n* sádico *m*. ~**tic** /səˈdɪstɪk/ *a* sádico

safari /sə'fɑːrɪ/ *n* safari *m*

safe /seɪf/ *a* (**-er**, **-est**) seguro; (*out of danger*) salvo; (*cautious*) prudente. **~ and sound** sano y salvo. ● *n* caja *f* fuerte. **~ deposit** *n* caja *f* de seguridad. **~guard** /'seɪfgɑːd/ *n* salvaguardia *f*. ● *vt* salvaguardar. **~ly** *adv* sin peligro; (*in safe place*) en lugar seguro. **~ty** /'seɪftɪ/ *n* seguridad *f*. **~ty belt** *n* cinturón *m* de seguridad. **~ty-pin** *n* imperdible *m*. **~ty-valve** *n* válvula *f* de seguridad

saffron /'sæfrən/ *n* azafrán *m*

sag /sæg/ *vi* (*pt* **sagged**) hundirse; (*give*) aflojarse

saga /'sɑːgə/ *n* saga *f*

sage[1] /seɪdʒ/ *n* (*wise person*) sabio *m*. ● *a* sabio

sage[2] /seɪdʒ/ *n* (*herb*) salvia *f*

sagging /'sægɪŋ/ *a* hundido; (*fig*) decaído

Sagittarius /sædʒɪ'teərɪəs/ *n* (*astr*) Sagitario *m*

sago /'seɪgəʊ/ *n* sagú *m*

said /sed/ *see* **say**

sail /seɪl/ *n* vela *f*; (*trip*) paseo *m* (en barco). ● *vi* navegar; (*leave*) partir; (*sport*) practicar la vela; (*fig*) deslizarse. ● *vt* manejar ‹*boat*›. **~ing** *n* (*sport*) vela *f*. **~ing-boat** *n*, **~ing-ship** *n* barco *m* de vela. **~or** /'seɪlə(r)/ *n* marinero *m*

saint /seɪnt, *before name* sənt/ *n* santo *m*. **~ly** *a* santo

sake /seɪk/ *n*. **for the ~ of** por, por el amor de

salacious /sə'leɪʃəs/ *a* salaz

salad /'sæləd/ *n* ensalada *f*. **~ bowl** *n* ensaladera *f*. **~ cream** *n* mayonesa *f*. **~-dressing** *n* aliño *m*

salar|ied /'sælərɪd/ *a* asalariado. **~y** /'sælərɪ/ *n* sueldo *m*

sale /seɪl/ *n* venta *f*; (*at reduced prices*) liquidación *f*. **for ~** (*sign*) se vende. **on ~** en venta. **~able** /'seɪləbl/ *a* vendible. **~sman** /'seɪlzmən/ *n* (*pl* **-men**) vendedor *m*; (*in shop*) dependiente *m*; (*traveller*) viajante *m*. **~swoman** *n* (*pl* **-women**) vendedora *f*; (*in shop*) dependienta *f*

salient /'seɪlɪənt/ *a* saliente, destacado

saliva /sə'laɪvə/ *n* saliva *f*

sallow /'sæləʊ/ *a* (**-er**, **-est**) amarillento

salmon /'sæmən/ *n invar* salmón *m*. **~ trout** *n* trucha *f* salmonada

salon /'sælɒn/ *n* salón *m*

saloon /sə'luːn/ *n* (*on ship*) salón *m*; (*Amer*, *bar*) bar *m*; (*auto*) turismo *m*

salt /sɔːlt/ *n* sal *f*. ● *a* salado. ● *vt* salar. **~-cellar** *n* salero *m*. **~y** *a* salado

salutary /'sæljʊtrɪ/ *a* saludable

salute /sə'luːt/ *n* saludo *m*. ● *vt* saludar. ● *vi* hacer un saludo

salvage /'sælvɪdʒ/ *n* salvamento *m*; (*goods*) objetos *mpl* salvados. ● *vt* salvar

salvation /sæl'veɪʃn/ *n* salvación *f*

salve /sælv/ *n* ungüento *m*

salver /'sælvə(r)/ *n* bandeja *f*

salvo /'sælvəʊ/ *n* (*pl* **-os**) salva *f*

same /seɪm/ *a* igual (**as** que); (*before noun*) mismo (**as** que). **at the ~ time** al mismo tiempo. ● *pron*. **the ~** el mismo, la misma, los mismos, las mismas. **do the ~ as** hacer como. ● *adv*. **the ~** de la misma manera. **all the ~** de todas formas

sample /'sɑːmpl/ *n* muestra *f*. ● *vt* probar ‹*food*›

sanatorium /sænə'tɔːrɪəm/ *n* (*pl* **-ums**) sanatorio *m*

sanctify /'sæŋktɪfaɪ/ *vt* santificar

sanctimonious /sæŋktɪ'məʊnɪəs/ *a* beato

sanction /'sæŋkʃn/ *n* sanción *f*. ● *vt* sancionar

sanctity /'sæŋktətɪ/ *n* santidad *f*

sanctuary /'sæŋktʃʊərɪ/ *n* (*relig*) santuario *m*; (*for wildlife*) reserva *f*; (*refuge*) asilo *m*

sand /sænd/ *n* arena *f*. ● *vt* enarenar. **~s** *npl* (*beach*) playa *f*

sandal /'sændl/ *n* sandalia *f*

sand: **~castle** *n* castillo *m* de arena. **~paper** /'sændpeɪpə(r)/ *n* papel *m* de lija. ● *vt* lijar. **~storm** /'sændstɔːm/ *n* tempestad *f* de arena

sandwich /'sænwɪdʒ/ *n* bocadillo *m*, sandwich *m*. ● *vt*. **~ed between** intercalado

sandy /'sændɪ/ *a* arenoso

sane /seɪn/ *a* (**-er**, **-est**) ‹*person*› cuerdo; ‹*judgement*, *policy*› razonable. **~ly** *adv* sensatamente

sang /sæŋ/ *see* **sing**

sanitary /'sænɪtrɪ/ *a* higiénico; ‹*system etc*› sanitario. **~ towel** *n*, **~ napkin** *n* (*Amer*) compresa *f* (higiénica)

sanitation /sænɪ'teɪʃn/ *n* higiene *f*; (*drainage*) sistema *m* sanitario

sanity /'sænɪtɪ/ *n* cordura *f*; (*fig*) sensatez *f*

sank /sæŋk/ *see* **sink**

Santa Claus /'sæntəklɔ:z/ *n* Papá *m* Noel

sap /sæp/ *n* (*in plants*) savia *f*. ● *vt* (*pt* **sapped**) agotar

sapling /'sæplɪŋ/ *n* árbol *m* joven

sapphire /'sæfaɪə(r)/ *n* zafiro *m*

sarcas|m /'sɑ:kæzəm/ *n* sarcasmo *m*. **~tic** /-'kæstɪk/ *a* sarcástico

sardine /sɑ:'di:n/ *n* sardina *f*

Sardinia /sɑ:'dɪnɪə/ *n* Cerdeña *f*. **~n** *a* & *n* sardo (*m*)

sardonic /sɑ:'dɒnɪk/ *a* sardónico

sash /sæʃ/ *n* (*over shoulder*) banda *f*; (*round waist*) fajín *m*. **~-window** *n* ventana *f* de guillotina

sat /sæt/ *see* **sit**

satanic /sə'tænɪk/ *a* satánico

satchel /'sætʃl/ *n* cartera *f*

satellite /'sætəlaɪt/ *n* & *a* satélite (*m*)

satiate /'seɪʃɪeɪt/ *vt* saciar

satin /'sætɪn/ *n* raso *m*. ● *a* de raso; (*like satin*) satinado

satir|e /'sætaɪə(r)/ *n* sátira *f*. **~ical** /sə'tɪrɪkl/ *a* satírico. **~ist** /'sætərɪst/ *n* satírico *m*. **~ize** /'sætəraɪz/ *vt* satirizar

satisfaction /sætɪs'fækʃn/ *n* satisfacción *f*

satisfactor|ily /sætɪs'fæktərɪlɪ/ *adv* satisfactoriamente. **~y** /sætɪs'fæktərɪ/ *a* satisfactorio

satisfy /'sætɪsfaɪ/ *vt* satisfacer; (*convince*) convencer. **~ing** *a* satisfactorio

satsuma /sæt'su:mə/ *n* mandarina *f*

saturat|e /'sætʃəreɪt/ *vt* saturar, empapar. **~ed** *a* saturado, empapado. **~ion** /-'reɪʃn/ *n* saturación *f*

Saturday /'sætədeɪ/ *n* sábado *m*

sauce /sɔ:s/ *n* salsa *f*; (*cheek*) descaro *m*. **~pan** /'sɔ:spən/ *n* cazo *m*

saucer /'sɔ:sə(r)/ *n* platillo *m*

saucy /'sɔ:sɪ/ *a* (**-ier**, **-iest**) descarado

Saudi Arabia /saʊdɪə'reɪbɪə/ *n* Arabia *f* Saudí

sauna /'sɔ:nə/ *n* sauna *f*

saunter /'sɔ:ntə(r)/ *vi* deambular, pasearse

sausage /'sɒsɪdʒ/ *n* salchicha *f*

savage /'sævɪdʒ/ *a* salvaje; (*fierce*) feroz; (*furious*, *fam*) rabioso. ● *n* salvaje *m* & *f*. ● *vt* atacar. **~ry** *n* ferocidad *f*

sav|e /seɪv/ *vt* salvar; ahorrar ‹*money*, *time*›; (*prevent*) evitar. ● *n* (*football*) parada *f*. ● *prep* salvo, con excepción de. **~er** *n* ahorrador *m*. **~ing** *n* ahorro *m*. **~ings** *npl* ahorros *mpl*

saviour /'seɪvɪə(r)/ *n* salvador *m*

savour /'seɪvə(r)/ *n* sabor *m*. ● *vt* saborear. **~y** *a* (*appetizing*) sabroso; (*not sweet*) no dulce. ● *n* aperitivo *m* (no dulce)

saw[1] /sɔ:/ *see* **see**[1]

saw[2] /sɔ:/ *n* sierra *f*. ● *vt* (*pt* **sawed**, *pp* **sawn**) serrar. **~dust** /'sɔ:dʌst/ *n* serrín *m*. **~n** /sɔ:n/ *see* **saw**

saxophone /'sæksəfəʊn/ *n* saxófono *m*

say /seɪ/ *vt/i* (*pt* **said** /sed/) decir; rezar ‹*prayer*›. **I ~!** ¡no me digas! ● *n*. **have a ~** expresar una opinión; (*in decision*) tener voz en capítulo. **have no ~** no tener ni voz ni voto. **~ing** /'seɪɪŋ/ *n* refrán *m*

scab /skæb/ *n* costra *f*; (*blackleg*, *fam*) esquirol *m*

scaffold /'skæfəʊld/ *n* (*gallows*) cadalso *m*, patíbulo *m*. **~ing** /'skæfəldɪŋ/ *n* (*for workmen*) andamio *m*

scald /skɔ:ld/ *vt* escaldar; calentar ‹*milk etc*›. ● *n* escaldadura *f*

scale[1] /skeɪl/ *n* escala *f*

scale[2] /skeɪl/ *n* (*of fish*) escama *f*

scale[3] /skeɪl/ *vt* (*climb*) escalar. **~ down** *vt* reducir (proporcionalmente)

scales /skeɪlz/ *npl* (*for weighing*) balanza *f*, peso *m*

scallop /'skɒləp/ *n* venera *f*; (*on dress*) festón *m*

scalp /skælp/ *n* cuero *m* cabelludo. ● *vt* quitar el cuero cabelludo a

scalpel /'skælpəl/ *n* escalpelo *m*

scamp /skæmp/ *n* bribón *m*

scamper /'skæmpə(r)/ *vi*. **~ away** marcharse corriendo

scampi /'skæmpɪ/ *npl* gambas *fpl* grandes

scan /skæn/ *vt* (*pt* **scanned**) escudriñar; (*quickly*) echar un vistazo a; ‹*radar*› explorar. ● *vi* ‹*poetry*› estar bien medido

scandal /'skændl/ *n* escándalo *m*; (*gossip*) chismorreo *m*. **~ize** /'skændəlaɪz/ *vt* escandalizar. **~ous** *a* escandaloso

Scandinavia /skændɪ'neɪvɪə/ *n* Escandinavia *f*. **~n** *a* & *n* escandinavo (*m*)

scant /skænt/ *a* escaso. **~ily** *adv* insuficientemente. **~y** /'skæntɪ/ *a* (**-ier**, **-iest**) escaso

scapegoat /'skeɪpgəʊt/ *n* cabeza *f* de turco

scar /skɑ:(r)/ *n* cicatriz *f*. ● *vt* (*pt* **scarred**) dejar una cicatriz en. ● *vi* cicatrizarse

scarc|e /skeəs/ *a* (**-er**, **-est**) escaso. **make o.s. ~e** (*fam*) mantenerse lejos. **~ely** /'skeəslɪ/ *adv* apenas. **~ity** *n* escasez *f*

scare /'skeə(r)/ *vt* asustar. **be ~d** tener miedo. ● *n* susto *m*. **~crow** /'skeəkrəʊ/ *n* espantapájaros *m invar*. **~monger** /'skeəmʌŋgə(r)/ *n* alarmista *m & f*

scarf /skɑ:f/ *n* (*pl* **scarves**) bufanda *f*; (*over head*) pañuelo *m*

scarlet /'skɑ:lət/ *a* escarlata *f*. **~ fever** *n* escarlatina *f*

scary /'skeərɪ/ *a* (**-ier**, **-iest**) que da miedo

scathing /'skeɪðɪŋ/ *a* mordaz

scatter /'skætə(r)/ *vt* (*throw*) esparcir; (*disperse*) dispersar. ● *vi* dispersarse. **~-brained** *a* atolondrado. **~ed** *a* disperso; (*occasional*) esporádico

scatty /'skætɪ/ *a* (**-ier**, **-iest**) (*sl*) atolondrado

scavenge /'skævɪndʒ/ *vi* buscar (en la basura). **~r** /-ə(r)/ *n* (*vagrant*) persona *f* que busca objetos en la basura

scenario /sɪ'nɑ:rɪəʊ/ *n* (*pl* **-os**) argumento; (*of film*) guión *m*

scen|e /si:n/ *n* escena *f*; (*sight*) vista *f*; (*fuss*) lío *m*. **behind the ~es** entre bastidores. **~ery** /'si:nərɪ/ *n* paisaje *m*; (*in theatre*) decorado *m*. **~ic** /'si:nɪk/ *a* pintoresco

scent /sent/ *n* olor *m*; (*perfume*) perfume *m*; (*trail*) pista *f*. ● *vt* presentir; (*make fragrant*) perfumar

sceptic /'skeptɪk/ *n* escéptico *m*. **~al** *a* escéptico. **~ism** /-sɪzəm/ *n* escepticismo *m*

sceptre /'septə(r)/ *n* cetro *m*

schedule /'ʃedju:l, 'skedju:l/ *n* programa *f*; (*timetable*) horario *m*. **behind ~** con retraso. **on ~** sin retraso. ● *vt* proyectar. **~d flight** *n* vuelo *m* regular

scheme /ski:m/ *n* proyecto *m*; (*plot*) intriga *f*. ● *vi* hacer proyectos; (*pej*) intrigar. **~r** *n* intrigante *m & f*

schism /'sɪzəm/ *n* cisma *m*

schizophrenic /skɪtsə'frenɪk/ *a & n* esquizofrénico (*m*)

scholar /'skɒlə(r)/ *n* erudito *m*. **~ly** *a* erudito. **~ship** *n* erudición *f*; (*grant*) beca *f*

scholastic /skə'læstɪk/ *a* escolar

school /sku:l/ *n* escuela *f*; (*of univ*) facultad *f*. ● *a* ‹*age, holidays, year*› escolar. ● *vt* enseñar; (*discipline*) disciplinar. **~boy** /'sku:lbɔɪ/ *n* colegial *m*. **~girl** /-gɜ:l/ *n* colegiala *f*. **~ing** *n* instrucción *f*. **~master** /'sku:lmɑ:stə(r)/ *n* (*primary*) maestro *m*; (*secondary*) profesor *m*. **~-mistress** *n* (*primary*) maestra *f*; (*secondary*) profesora *f*. **~-teacher** *n* (*primary*) maestro *m*; (*secondary*) profesor *m*

schooner /'sku:nə(r)/ *n* goleta *f*; (*glass*) vaso *m* grande

sciatica /saɪ'ætɪkə/ *n* ciática *f*

scien|ce /'saɪəns/ *n* ciencia *f*. **~ce fiction** *n* ciencia *f* ficción. **~tific** /-'tɪfɪk/ *a* científico. **~tist** /'saɪəntɪst/ *n* científico *m*

scintillate /'sɪntɪleɪt/ *vi* centellear

scissors /'sɪsəz/ *npl* tijeras *fpl*

sclerosis /sklə'rəʊsɪs/ *n* esclerosis *f*

scoff /skɒf/ *vt* (*sl*) zamparse. ● *vi*. **~ at** mofarse de

scold /skəʊld/ *vt* regañar. **~ing** *n* regaño *m*

scone /skɒn/ *n* (tipo *m* de) bollo *m*

scoop /sku:p/ *n* paleta *f*; (*news*) noticia *f* exclusiva. ● *vt*. **~ out** excavar. **~ up** recoger

scoot /sku:t/ *vi* (*fam*) largarse corriendo. **~er** /'sku:tə(r)/ *n* escúter *m*; (*for child*) patinete *m*

scope /skəʊp/ *n* alcance *m*; (*opportunity*) oportunidad *f*

scorch /skɔ:tʃ/ *vt* chamuscar. **~er** *n* (*fam*) día *m* de mucho calor. **~ing** *a* (*fam*) de mucho calor

score /skɔ:(r)/ *n* tanteo *m*; (*mus*) partitura *f*; (*twenty*) veintena *f*; (*reason*) motivo *m*. **on that ~** en cuanto a eso. ● *vt* marcar; (*slash*) rayar; (*mus*) instrumentar; conseguir ‹*success*›. ● *vi* marcar un tanto; (*keep score*) tantear. **~ over s.o.** aventajar a. **~r** /-ə(r)/ *n* tanteador *m*

scorn /skɔ:n/ *n* desdén m. ● *vt* desdeñar. **~ful** *a* desdeñoso. **~fully** *adv* desdeñosamente

Scorpio /'skɔ:pɪəʊ/ *n* (*astr*) Escorpión *m*

scorpion /'skɔ:pɪən/ *n* escorpión *m*

Scot /skɒt/ *n* escocés *m*. **~ch** /skɒtʃ/ *a* escocés. ● *n* güisqui *m*

scotch /skɒtʃ/ *vt* frustrar; (*suppress*) suprimir

scot-free /skɒt'fri:/ *a* impune; (*gratis*) sin pagar

Scot: **~land** /'skɒtlənd/ *n* Escocia *f*. **~s** *a* escocés. **~sman** *n* escocés *m*. **~swoman** *n* escocesa *f*. **~tish** *a* escocés

scoundrel /'skaʊndrəl/ *n* canalla *f*

scour /'skaʊə(r)/ *vt* estregar; (*search*) registrar. **~er** *n* estropajo *m*

scourge /skɜ:dʒ/ *n* azote *m*

scout /skaʊt/ *n* explorador *m*. **Boy S~** explorador *m*. ● *vi*. **~ (for)** buscar

scowl /skaʊl/ *n* ceño *m*. ● *vi* fruncir el entrecejo

scraggy /'skrægɪ/ *a* (**-ier**, **-iest**) descarnado

scram /skræm/ *vi* (*sl*) largarse

scramble /'skræmbl/ *vi* (*clamber*) gatear. **~ for** pelearse para obtener. ● *vt* revolver ‹*eggs*›. ● *n* (*difficult climb*) subida *f* difícil; (*struggle*) lucha *f*

scrap /skræp/ *n* pedacito *m*; (*fight*, *fam*) pelea *f*. ● *vt* (*pt* **scrapped**) desechar. **~-book** *n* álbum *m* de recortes. **~s** *npl* sobras *fpl*

scrape /skreɪp/ *n* raspadura *f*; (*fig*) apuro *m*. ● *vt* raspar; (*graze*) arañar; (*rub*) frotar. ● *vi*. **~ through** lograr pasar; aprobar por los pelos ‹*exam*›. **~ together** reunir. **~r** /-ə(r)/ *n* raspador *m*

scrap: **~ heap** *n* montón *m* de deshechos. **~-iron** *n* chatarra *f*

scrappy /'skræpɪ/ *a* fragmentario, pobre, de mala calidad

scratch /skrætʃ/ *vt* rayar; (*with nail etc*) arañar; rascar ‹*itch*›. ● *vi* arañar. ● *n* raya *f*; (*from nail etc*) arañazo *m*. **start from ~** empezar sin nada, empezar desde el principio. **up to ~** al nivel requerido

scrawl /skrɔ:l/ *n* garrapato *m*. ● *vt/i* garrapatear

scrawny /'skrɔ:nɪ/ *a* (**-ier**, **-iest**) descarnado

scream /skri:m/ *vt/i* gritar. ● *n* grito *m*

screech /skri:tʃ/ *vi* gritar; ‹*brakes etc*› chirriar. ● *n* grito *m*; (*of brakes etc*) chirrido *m*

screen /skri:n/ *n* pantalla *f*; (*folding*) biombo *m*. ● *vt* (*hide*) ocultar; (*protect*) proteger; proyectar ‹*film*›; seleccionar ‹*candidates*›

screw /skru:/ *n* tornillo *m*. ● *vt* atornillar. **~driver** /'skru:draɪvə(r)/ *n* destornillador *m*. **~ up** atornillar; entornar ‹*eyes*›; torcer ‹*face*›; (*ruin*, *sl*) arruinar. **~y** /'skru:ɪ/ *a* (**-ier**, **-iest**) (*sl*) chiflado

scribble /'skrɪbl/ *vt/i* garrapatear. ● *n* garrapato *m*

scribe /skraɪb/ *n* copista *m* & *f*

script /skrɪpt/ *n* escritura *f*; (*of film etc*) guión *m*

Scriptures /'skrɪptʃəz/ *npl* Sagradas Escrituras *fpl*

script-writer /'skrɪptraɪtə(r)/ *n* guionista *m* & *f*

scroll /skrəʊl/ *n* rollo *m* (de pergamino)

scrounge /skraʊndʒ/ *vt/i* obtener de gorra; (*steal*) birlar. **~r** /-ə(r)/ *n* gorrón *m*

scrub /skrʌb/ *n* (*land*) maleza *f*; (*clean*) fregado *m*. ● *vt/i* (*pt* **scrubbed**) fregar

scruff /skrʌf/ *n*. **the ~ of the neck** el cogote *m*

scruffy /'skrʌfɪ/ *a* (**-ier**, **-iest**) desaliñado

scrum /skrʌm/ *n*, **scrummage** /'skrʌmɪdʒ/ *n* (*Rugby*) melée *f*

scrup|le /'skru:pl/ *n* escrúpulo *m*. **~ulous** /'skru:pjʊləs/ *a* escrupuloso. **~ulously** *adv* escrupulosamente

scrutin|ize /'skru:tɪnaɪz/ *vt* escudriñar. **~y** /'skru:tɪnɪ/ *n* examen *m* minucioso

scuff /skʌf/ *vt* arañar ‹*shoes*›

scuffle /'skʌfl/ *n* pelea *f*

scullery /'skʌlərɪ/ *n* trascocina *f*

sculpt /skʌlpt/ *vt/i* esculpir. **~or** *n* escultor *m*. **~ure** /-tʃə(r)/ *n* escultura *f*. ● *vt/i* esculpir

scum /skʌm/ *n* espuma *f*; (*people*, *pej*) escoria *f*

scurf /skɜ:f/ *n* caspa *f*

scurrilous /'skʌrɪləs/ *a* grosero

scurry /'skʌrɪ/ *vi* correr

scurvy /'skɜ:vɪ/ *n* escorbuto *m*

scuttle[1] /'skʌtl/ *n* cubo *m* del carbón

scuttle[2] /'skʌtl/ *vt* barrenar ‹*ship*›

scuttle[3] /'skʌtl/ *vi*. **~ away** correr, irse de prisa

scythe /saɪð/ *n* guadaña *f*

SE *abbr* (*south-east*) sudeste *m*

sea /si:/ *n* mar *m*. **at ~** en el mar; (*fig*) confuso. **by ~** por mar. **~board** /'si:bɔ:d/ *n* litoral *m*. **~farer** /'si:feərə(r)/ *n* marinero *m*. **~food** /'si:fu:d/ *n* mariscos *mpl*. **~gull** /'si:gʌl/ *n* gaviota *f*. **~-horse** *n* caballito *m* de mar, hipocampo *m*

seal[1] /si:l/ *n* sello *m*. ● *vt* sellar. **~ off** acordonar ‹*area*›

seal[2] /si:l/ (*animal*) foca *f*
sea level /'si:levl/ *n* nivel *m* del mar
sealing-wax /'si:lɪŋwæks/ *n* lacre *m*
sea lion /'si:laɪən/ *n* león *m* marino
seam /si:m/ *n* costura *f*; (*of coal*) veta *f*
seaman /'si:mən/ *n* (*pl* **-men**) marinero *m*
seamy /'si:mɪ/ *a*. **the ~ side** *n* el lado *m* sórdido, el revés *m*
seance /'seɪɑ:ns/ *n* sesión *f* de espiritismo
sea: **~plane** /'si:pleɪn/ *n* hidroavión *f*. **~port** /'si:pɔ:t/ *n* puerto *m* de mar
search /sɜ:tʃ/ *vt* registrar; (*examine*) examinar. ● *vi* buscar. ● *n* (*for sth*) búsqueda *f*; (*of sth*) registro *m*. **in ~ of** en busca de. **~ for** buscar. **~ing** *a* penetrante. **~-party** *n* equipo *m* de salvamento. **~light** /'sɜ:tʃlaɪt/ *n* reflector *m*
sea: **~scape** /'si:skeɪp/ *n* marina *f*. **~shore** *n* orilla *f* del mar. **~sick** /'si:sɪk/ *a* mareado. **be ~sick** marearse. **~side** /'si:saɪd/ *n* playa *f*
season /'si:zn/ *n* estación *f*; (*period*) temporada *f*. ● *vt* (*culin*) sazonar; secar ‹*wood*›. **~able** *a* propio de la estación. **~al** *a* estacional. **~ed** /'si:znd/ *a* (*fig*) experto. **~ing** *n* condimento *m*. **~-ticket** *n* billete *m* de abono
seat /si:t/ *n* asiento *m*; (*place*) lugar *m*; (*of trousers*) fondillos *mpl*; (*bottom*) trasero *m*. **take a ~** sentarse. ● *vt* sentar; (*have seats for*) tener asientos para. **~-belt** *n* cinturón *m* de seguridad
sea: **~-urchin** *n* erizo *m* de mar. **~weed** /'si:wi:d/ *n* alga *f*. **~worthy** /'si:wɜ:ðɪ/ *a* en estado de navegar
secateurs /'sekətɜ:z/ *npl* tijeras *fpl* de podar
sece|de /sɪ'si:d/ *vi* separase. **~ssion** /-eʃn/ *n* secesión *f*
seclu|de /sɪ'klu:d/ *vt* aislar. **~ded** *a* aislado. **~sion** /-ʒn/ *n* aislamiento *m*
second[1] /'sekənd/ *a* & *n* segundo (*m*). **on ~ thoughts** pensándolo bien. ● *adv* (*in race etc*) en segundo lugar. ● *vt* apoyar. **~s** *npl* (*goods*) artículos *mpl* de segunda calidad; (*more food, fam*) otra porción *f*
second[2] /sɪ'kɒnd/ *vt* (*transfer*) trasladar temporalmente
secondary /'sekəndrɪ/ *a* secundario. **~ school** *n* instituto *m*
second: **~-best** *a* segundo. **~-class** *a* de segunda clase. **~-hand** *a* de segunda mano. **~ly** *adv* en segundo lugar. **~-rate** *a* mediocre
secre|cy /'si:krəsɪ/ *n* secreto *m*. **~t** /'si:krɪt/ *a* & *n* secreto (*m*). **in ~t** en secreto
secretar|ial /sekrə'teərɪəl/ *a* de secretario. **~iat** /sekrə'teərɪət/ *n* secretaría *f*. **~y** /'sekrətrɪ/ *n* secretario *m*. **S~y of State** ministro *m*: (*Amer*) Ministro *m* de Asuntos Exteriores
secret|e /sɪ'kri:t/ *vt* (*med*) secretar. **~ion** /-ʃn/ *n* secreción *f*
secretive /'si:krɪtɪv/ *a* reservado
secretly /'si:krɪtlɪ/ *adv* en secreto
sect /sekt/ *n* secta *f*. **~arian** /-'teərɪən/ *a* sectario
section /'sekʃn/ *n* sección *f*; (*part*) parte *f*
sector /'sektə(r)/ *n* sector *m*
secular /'sekjʊlə(r)/ *a* seglar
secur|e /sɪ'kjʊə(r)/ *a* seguro; (*fixed*) fijo. ● *vt* asegurar; (*obtain*) obtener. **~ely** *adv* seguramente. **~ity** /sɪ'kjʊərətɪ/ *n* seguridad *f*; (*for loan*) garantía *f*, fianza *f*
sedate /sɪ'deɪt/ *a* sosegado
sedat|ion /sɪ'deɪʃn/ *n* sedación *f*. **~ive** /'sedətɪv/ *a* & *n* sedante (*m*)
sedentary /'sedəntrɪ/ *a* sedentario
sediment /'sedɪmənt/ *n* sedimento *m*
seduc|e /sɪ'dju:s/ *vt* seducir. **~er** /-ə(r)/ *n* seductor *m*. **~tion** /sɪ'dʌkʃn/ *n* seducción *f*. **~tive** /-tɪv/ *a* seductor
see[1] /si:/ ● *vt* (*pt* **saw**, *pp* **seen**) ver; (*understand*) comprender; (*notice*) notar; (*escort*) acompañar. **~ing that** visto que. **~ you later!** ¡hasta luego! ● *vi* ver; (*understand*) comprender. **~ about** ocuparse de. **~ off** despedirse de. **~ through** llevar a cabo; descubrir el juego de ‹*person*›. **~ to** ocuparse de
see[2] /si:/ *n* diócesis *f*
seed /si:d/ *n* semilla *f*; (*fig*) germen *m*; (*tennis*) preseleccionado *m*. **~ling** *n* plantón *m*. **go to ~** granar; (*fig*) echarse a perder. **~y** /'si:dɪ/ *a* (**-ier**, **-iest**) sórdido
seek /si:k/ *vt* (*pt* **sought**) buscar. **~ out** buscar
seem /si:m/ *vi* parecer. **~ingly** *adv* aparentemente
seemly /'si:mlɪ/ *a* (**-ier**, **-iest**) correcto

seen /si:n/ *see* **see**[1]
seep /si:p/ *vi* filtrarse. **~age** *n* filtración *f*
see-saw /'si:sɔ:/ *n* balancín *m*
seethe /si:ð/ *vi* (*fig*) hervir. **be seething with anger** estar furioso
see-through /'si:θru:/ *a* transparente
segment /'segmənt/ *n* segmento *m*; (*of orange*) gajo *m*
segregat|e /'segrɪgeɪt/ *vt* segregar. **~ion** /-'geɪʃn/ *n* segregación *f*
seiz|e /si:z/ *vt* agarrar; (*jurid*) incautarse de. **~e on** *vi* valerse de. **~e up** *vi* (*tec*) agarrotarse. **~ure** /'si:ʒə(r)/ *n* incautación *f*; (*med*) ataque *m*
seldom /'seldəm/ *adv* raramente
select /sɪ'lekt/ *vt* escoger; (*sport*) seleccionar. ● *a* selecto; (*exclusive*) exclusivo. **~ion** /-ʃn/ *n* selección *f*. **~ive** *a* selectivo
self /self/ *n* (*pl* **selves**) sí mismo. **~-addressed** *a* con su propia dirección. **~-assurance** *n* confianza *f* en sí mismo. **~-assured** *a* seguro de sí mismo. **~-catering** *a* con facilidades para cocinar. **~-centred** *a* egocéntrico. **~-confidence** *n* confianza *f* en sí mismo. **~-confident** *a* seguro de sí mismo. **~-conscious** *a* cohibido. **~-contained** *a* independiente. **~-control** *n* dominio *m* de sí mismo. **~-defence** *n* defensa *f* propia. **~-denial** *n* abnegación *f*. **~-employed** *a* que trabaja por cuenta propia. **~-esteem** *n* amor *m* propio. **~-evident** *a* evidente. **~-government** *n* autonomía *f*. **~-important** *a* presumido. **~-indulgent** *a* inmoderado. **~-interest** *n* interés *m* propio. **~ish** /'selfɪʃ/ *a* egoísta. **~ishness** *n* egoísmo *m*. **~less** /'selflɪs/ *a* desinteresado. **~-made** *a* rico por su propio esfuerzo. **~-opinionated** *a* intransigente; (*arrogant*) engreído. **~-pity** *n* compasión *f* de sí mismo. **~-portrait** *n* autorretrato *m*. **~-possessed** *a* dueño de sí mismo. **~-reliant** *a* independiente. **~-respect** *n* amor *m* propio. **~-righteous** *a* santurrón. **~-sacrifice** *n* abnegación *f*. **~-satisfied** *a* satisfecho de sí mismo. **~-seeking** *a* egoísta. **~-service** *a* & *n* autoservicio (*m*). **~-styled** *a* sedicente, llamado. **~-sufficient** *a* independiente. **~-willed** *a* terco
sell /sel/ *vt* (*pt* **sold**) vender. **be sold on** (*fam*) entusiasmarse por. **be sold out** estar agotado. ● *vi* venderse. **~-by date** *n* fecha *f* de caducidad. **~ off** *vt* liquidar. **~ up** *vt* vender todo. **~er** *n* vendedor *m*
Sellotape /'seləteɪp/ *n* (*P*) (papel *m*) celo *m*, cinta *f* adhesiva
sell-out /'selaʊt/ *n* (*betrayal, fam*) traición *f*
semantic /sɪ'mæntɪk/ *a* semántico. **~s** *n* semántica *f*
semaphore /'seməfɔ:(r)/ *n* semáforo *m*
semblance /'sembləns/ *n* apariencia *f*
semen /'si:mən/ *n* semen *m*
semester /sɪ'mestə(r)/ *n* (*Amer*) semestre *m*
semi... /'semɪ/ *pref* semi...
semi|breve /'semɪbri:v/ *n* semibreve *f*, redonda *f*. **~circle** /'semɪsɜ:kl/ *n* semicírculo *m*. **~circular** /-'sɜ:kjʊlə(r)/ *a* semicircular. **~colon** /semɪ'kəʊlən/ *n* punto *m* y coma. **~-detached** /semɪdɪ'tætʃt/ *a* ‹*house*› adosado. **~final** /semɪ'faɪnl/ *n* semifinal *f*
seminar /'semɪnɑ:(r)/ *n* seminario *m*
seminary /'semɪnərɪ/ *n* (*college*) seminario *m*
semiquaver /'semɪkweɪvə(r)/ *n* (*mus*) semicorchea *f*
Semit|e /'si:maɪt/ *n* semita *m* & *f*. **~ic** /sɪ'mɪtɪk/ *a* semítico
semolina /semə'li:nə/ *n* sémola *f*
senat|e /'senɪt/ *n* senado *m*. **~or** /-ətə(r)/ *n* senador *m*
send /send/ *vt/i* (*pt* **sent**) enviar. **~ away** despedir. **~ away for** pedir (por correo). **~ for** enviar a buscar. **~ off for** pedir (por correo). **~ up** (*fam*) parodiar. **~er** *n* remitente *m*. **~-off** *n* despedida *f*
senil|e /'si:naɪl/ *a* senil. **~ity** /sɪ'nɪlətɪ/ *n* senilidad *f*
senior /'si:nɪə(r)/ *a* mayor; (*in rank*) superior; ‹*partner etc*› principal. ● *n* mayor *m* & *f*. **~ citizen** *n* jubilado *m*. **~ity** /-'ɒrətɪ/ *n* antigüedad *f*
sensation /sen'seɪʃn/ *n* sensación *f*. **~al** *a* sensacional
sense /sens/ *n* sentido *m*; (*common sense*) juicio *m*; (*feeling*) sensación *f*. **make ~** *vt* tener sentido. **make ~ of** comprender. **~less** *a* insensato; (*med*) sin sentido
sensibilities /sensɪ'bɪlətɪz/ *npl* susceptibilidad *f*. **~ibility** /sensɪ'bɪlətɪ/ *n* sensibilidad *f*

sensible /'sensəbl/ *a* sensato; ‹*clothing*› práctico

sensitiv|e /'sensɪtɪv/ *a* sensible; (*touchy*) susceptible. **~ity** /-'tɪvətɪ/ *n* sensibilidad *f*

sensory /'sensərɪ/ *a* sensorio

sensual /'senʃʊəl/ *a* sensual. **~ity** /-'æləti/ *n* sensualidad *f*

sensuous /'sensʊəs/ *a* sensual

sent /sent/ *see* **send**

sentence /'sentəns/ *n* frase *f*; (*jurid*) sentencia *f*; (*punishment*) condena *f*. ● *vt*. **~ to** condenar a

sentiment /'sentɪmənt/ *n* sentimiento *m*; (*opinion*) opinión *f*. **~al** /sentɪ'mentl/ *a* sentimental. **~ality** /-'tæləti/ *n* sentimentalismo *m*

sentry /'sentrɪ/ *n* centinela *f*

separable /'sepərəbl/ *a* separable

separate[1] /'sepərət/ *a* separado; (*independent*) independiente. **~ly** *adv* por separado. **~s** *npl* coordinados *mpl*

separat|e[2] /'sepəreɪt/ *vt* separar. ● *vi* separarse. **~ion** /-'reɪʃn/ *n* separación *f*. **~ist** /'sepərətɪst/ *n* separatista *m & f*

September /sep'tembə(r)/ *n* se(p)tiembre *m*

septic /'septɪk/ *a* séptico. **~ tank** *n* fosa *f* séptica

sequel /'si:kwəl/ *n* continuación *f*; (*consequence*) consecuencia *f*

sequence /'si:kwəns/ *n* sucesión *f*; (*of film*) secuencia *f*

sequin /'si:kwɪn/ *n* lentejuela *f*

serenade /serə'neɪd/ *n* serenata *f*. ● *vt* dar serenata a

seren|e /sɪ'ri:n/ *a* sereno. **~ity** /-enətɪ/ *n* serenidad *f*

sergeant /'sɑ:dʒənt/ *n* sargento *m*

serial /'sɪərɪəl/ *n* serial *m*. ● *a* de serie. **~ize** *vt* publicar por entregas

series /'sɪəri:z/ *n* serie *f*

serious /'sɪərɪəs/ *a* serio. **~ly** *adv* seriamente; (*ill*) gravemente. **take ~ly** tomar en serio. **~ness** *n* seriedad *f*

sermon /'sɜ:mən/ *n* sermón *m*

serpent /'sɜ:pənt/ *n* serpiente *f*

serrated /sɪ'reɪtɪd/ *a* serrado

serum /'sɪərəm/ *n* (*pl* **-a**) suero *m*

servant /'sɜ:vənt/ *n* criado *m*; (*fig*) servidor *m*

serve /sɜ:v/ *vt* servir; (*in the army etc*) prestar servicio; cumplir ‹*sentence*›. **~ as** servir de. **~ its purpose** servir para el caso. **it ~s you right** ¡bien te lo mereces! ¡te está bien merecido! ● *vi* servir. ● *n* (*in tennis*) saque *m*

service /'sɜ:vɪs/ *n* servicio *m*; (*maintenance*) revisión *f*. **of ~ to** útil a. ● *vt* revisar ‹*car etc*›. **~able** /'sɜ:vɪsəbl/ *a* práctico; (*durable*) duradero. **~ charge** *n* servicio *m*. **~man** /'sɜ:vɪsmən/ *n* (*pl* **-men**) militar *m*. **~s** *npl* (*mil*) fuerzas *fpl* armadas. **~ station** *n* estación *f* de servicio

serviette /sɜ:vɪ'et/ *n* servilleta *f*

servile /'sɜ:vaɪl/ *a* servil

session /'seʃn/ *n* sesión *f*; (*univ*) curso *m*

set /set/ *vt* (*pt* **set**, *pres p* **setting**) poner; poner en hora ‹*clock etc*›; fijar ‹*limit etc*›; (*typ*) componer. **~ fire to** pegar fuego a. **~ free** *vt* poner en libertad. ● *vi* ‹*sun*› ponerse; ‹*jelly*› cuajarse. ● *n* serie *f*; (*of cutlery etc*) juego *m*; (*tennis*) set *m*; (*TV, radio*) aparato *m*; (*of hair*) marcado *m*; (*in theatre*) decorado *m*; (*of people*) círculo *m*. ● *a* fijo. **be ~ on** estar resuelto a. **~ about** *vi* empezar a. **~ back** *vt* (*delay*) retardar; (*cost, sl*) costar. **~ off** *vi* salir. ● *vt* (*make start*) poner en marcha; hacer estallar ‹*bomb*›. **~ out** *vi* (*declare*) declarar; (*leave*) salir. **~ sail** salir. **~ the table** poner la mesa. **~ up** *vt* establecer. **~-back** *n* revés *m*. **~ square** *n* escuadra *f* de dibujar

settee /se'ti:/ *n* sofá *m*

setting /'setɪŋ/ *n* (*of sun*) puesta *f*; (*of jewel*) engaste *m*; (*in theatre*) escenario *m*; (*typ*) composición *f*. **~-lotion** *n* fijador *m*

settle /'setl/ *vt* (*arrange*) arreglar; (*pay*) pagar; fijar ‹*date*›; calmar ‹*nerves*›. ● *vi* (*come to rest*) posarse; (*live*) instalarse. **~ down** calmarse; (*become orderly*) sentar la cabeza. **~ for** aceptar. **~ up** ajustar cuentas. **~ment** /'setlmənt/ *n* establecimiento *m*; (*agreement*) acuerdo *m*; (*com*) liquidación *f*; (*place*) colonia *f*. **~r** /-ə(r)/ *n* colonizador *m*

set: **~-to** *n* pelea *f*. **~-up** *n* (*fam*) sistema *m*

seven /'sevn/ *a & n* siete (*m*). **~teen** /sevn'ti:n/ *a & n* diecisiete (*m*). **~teenth** *a & n* decimoséptimo (*m*). **~th** *a & n* séptimo (*m*). **~tieth** *a & n* setenta (*m*), septuagésimo (*m*). **~ty** /'sevntɪ/ *a & n* setenta (*m*)

sever /'sevə(r)/ *vt* cortar; (*fig*) romper
several /'sevrəl/ *a & pron* varios
severance /'sevərəns/ *n* (*breaking off*) ruptura *f*
sever|e /sɪ'vɪə(r)/ *a* (**-er**, **-est**) severo; (*violent*) violento; (*serious*) grave; ‹*weather*› riguroso. **~ely** *adv* severamente; (*seriously*) gravemente. **~ity** /-'verətɪ/ *n* severidad *f*; (*violence*) violencia *f*; (*seriousness*) gravedad *f*
sew /səʊ/ *vt/i* (*pt* **sewed**, *pp* **sewn**, *or* **sewed**) coser
sew|age /'su:ɪdʒ/ *n* aguas *fpl* residuales. **~er** /'su:ə(r)/ *n* cloaca *f*
sewing /'səʊɪŋ/ *n* costura *f*. **~-machine** *n* máquina *f* de coser
sewn /səʊn/ *see* **sew**
sex /seks/ *n* sexo *m*. **have ~** tener relaciones sexuales. ● *a* sexual. **~ist** /'seksɪst/ *a & n* sexista (*m & f*)
sextet /seks'tet/ *n* sexteto *m*
sexual /'sekʃʊəl/ *a* sexual. **~ intercourse** *n* relaciones *fpl* sexuales. **~ity** /-'ælətɪ/ *n* sexualidad *f*
sexy /'seksɪ/ *a* (**-ier**, **-iest**) excitante, sexy, provocativo
shabb|ily /'ʃæbɪlɪ/ *adv* pobremente; (*act*) mezquinamente. **~iness** *n* pobreza *f*; (*meanness*) mezquindad *f*. **~y** /'ʃæbɪ/ *a* (**-ier**, **-iest**) ‹*clothes*› gastado; ‹*person*› pobremente vestido; (*mean*) mezquino
shack /ʃæk/ *n* choza *f*
shackles /'ʃæklz/ *npl* grillos *mpl*, grilletes *mpl*
shade /ʃeɪd/ *n* sombra *f*; (*of colour*) matiz *m*; (*for lamp*) pantalla *f*. **a ~ better** un poquito mejor. ● *vt* dar sombra a
shadow /'ʃædəʊ/ *n* sombra *f*. **S~ Cabinet** *n* gobierno *m* en la sombra. ● *vt* (*follow*) seguir. **~y** *a* (*fig*) vago
shady /'ʃeɪdɪ/ *a* (**-ier**, **-iest**) sombreado; (*fig*) dudoso
shaft /ʃɑ:ft/ *n* (*of arrow*) astil *m*; (*mec*) eje *m*; (*of light*) rayo *m*; (*of lift, mine*) pozo *m*
shaggy /'ʃægɪ/ *a* (**-ier**, **-iest**) peludo
shak|e /ʃeɪk/ *vt* (*pt* **shook**, *pp* **shaken**) sacudir; agitar ‹*bottle*›; (*shock*) desconcertar. **~e hands with** estrechar la mano a. ● *vi* temblar. **~e off** *vi* deshacerse de. ● *n* sacudida *f*. **~e-up** *n* reorganización *f*. **~y** /'ʃeɪkɪ/ *a* (**-ier**, **-iest**) tembloroso; ‹*table etc*› inestable; (*unreliable*) incierto

shall /ʃæl/ *v, aux* (*first person in future tense*). **I ~ go** iré. **we ~ see** veremos
shallot /ʃə'lɒt/ *n* chalote *m*
shallow /'ʃæləʊ/ *a* (**-er**, **-est**) poco profundo; (*fig*) superficial
sham /ʃæm/ *n* farsa *f*; (*person*) impostor *m*. ● *a* falso; (*affected*) fingido. ● *vt* (*pt* **shammed**) fingir
shambles /'ʃæmblz/ *npl* (*mess, fam*) desorden *m* total
shame /ʃeɪm/ *n* vergüenza *f*. **what a ~!** ¡qué lástima! ● *vt* avergonzar. **~faced** /'ʃeɪmfeɪst/ *a* avergonzado. **~ful** *a* vergonzoso. **~fully** *adv* vergonzosamente. **~less** *a* desvergonzado
shampoo /ʃæm'pu:/ *n* champú *m*. ● *vt* lavar
shamrock /'ʃæmrɒk/ *n* trébol *m*
shandy /'ʃændɪ/ *n* cerveza *f* con gaseosa, clara *f*
shan't /ʃɑ:nt/ = **shall not**
shanty /'ʃæntɪ/ *n* chabola *f*. **~ town** *n* chabolas *fpl*
shape /ʃeɪp/ *n* forma *f*. ● *vt* formar; determinar ‹*future*›. ● *vi* formarse. **~ up** prometer. **~less** *a* informe. **~ly** /'ʃeɪplɪ/ *a* (**-ier**, **-iest**) bien proporcionado
share /ʃeə(r)/ *n* porción *f*; (*com*) acción *f*. **go ~s** compartir. ● *vt* compartir; (*divide*) dividir. ● *vi* participar. **~ in** participar en. **~holder** /'ʃeəhəʊldə(r)/ *n* accionista *m & f*. **~-out** *n* reparto *m*
shark /ʃɑ:k/ *n* tiburón *m*; (*fig*) estafador *m*
sharp /ʃɑ:p/ *a* (**-er**, **-est**) ‹*knife etc*› afilado; ‹*pin etc*› puntiagudo; ‹*pain, sound*› agudo; ‹*taste*› acre; (*sudden, harsh*) brusco; (*well defined*) marcado; (*dishonest*) poco escrupuloso; (*clever*) listo. ● *adv* en punto. **at seven o'clock ~** a las siete en punto. ● *n* (*mus*) sostenido *m*. **~en** /'ʃɑ:pn/ *vt* afilar; sacar punta a ‹*pencil*›. **~ener** *n* (*mec*) afilador *m*; (*for pencils*) sacapuntas *m invar*. **~ly** *adv* bruscamente
shatter /'ʃætə(r)/ *vt* hacer añicos; (*upset*) perturbar. ● *vi* hacerse añicos. **~ed** *a* (*exhausted*) agotado
shav|e /ʃeɪv/ *vt* afeitar. ● *vi* afeitarse. ● *n* afeitado *m*. **have a ~e** afeitarse. **~en** *a* ‹*face*› afeitado; ‹*head*› rapado. **~er** *n* maquinilla *f* (de afeitar). **~ing-brush** *n* brocha *f* de

afietar. **~ing-cream** *n* crema *f* de afeitar

shawl /ʃɔ:l/ *n* chal *m*

she /ʃi:/ *pron* ella. ● *n* hembra *f*

sheaf /ʃi:f/ *n* (*pl* **sheaves**) gavilla *f*

shear /ʃɪə(r)/ *vt* (*pp* **shorn**, *or* **sheared**) esquilar. **~s** /ʃɪəz/ *npl* tijeras *fpl* grandes

sheath /ʃi:θ/ *n* (*pl* **-s** /ʃi:ðz/) vaina *f*; (*contraceptive*) condón *m*. **~e** /ʃi:ð/ *vt* envainar

shed[1] /ʃed/ *n* cobertizo *m*

shed[2] /ʃed/ *vt* (*pt* **shed**, *pres p* **shedding**) perder; derramar ‹*tears*›; despojarse de ‹*clothes*›. **~ light on** aclarar

sheen /ʃi:n/ *n* lustre *m*

sheep /ʃi:p/ *n invar* oveja *f*. **~-dog** *n* perro *m* pastor. **~ish** /ˈʃi:pɪʃ/ *a* vergonzoso. **~ishly** *adv* tímidamente. **~skin** /ˈʃi:pskɪn/ *n* piel *f* de carnero, zamarra *f*

sheer /ʃɪə(r)/ *a* puro; (*steep*) perpendicular; ‹*fabric*› muy fino. ● *adv* a pico

sheet /ʃi:t/ *n* sábana *f*; (*of paper*) hoja *f*; (*of glass*) lámina *f*; (*of ice*) capa *f*

sheikh /ʃeɪk/ *n* jeque *m*

shelf /ʃelf/ *n* (*pl* **shelves**) estante *m*. **be on the ~** quedarse para vestir santos

shell /ʃel/ *n* concha *f*; (*of egg*) cáscara *f*; (*of building*) casco *m*; (*explosive*) proyectil *m*. ● *vt* desgranar ‹*peas etc*›; (*mil*) bombardear. **~fish** /ˈʃelfɪʃ/ *n invar* (*crustacean*) crustáceo *m*; (*mollusc*) marisco *m*

shelter /ˈʃeltə(r)/ *n* refugio *m*, abrigo *m*. ● *vt* abrigar; (*protect*) proteger; (*give lodging to*) dar asilo a. ● *vi* abrigarse. **~ed** *a* ‹*spot*› abrigado; ‹*life etc*› protegido

shelv|e /ʃelv/ *vt* (*fig*) dar carpetazo a. **~ing** /ˈʃelvɪŋ/ *n* estantería *f*

shepherd /ˈʃepəd/ *n* pastor *m*. ● *vt* guiar. **~ess** /-ˈdes/ *n* pastora *f*. **~'s pie** *n* carne *f* picada con puré de patatas

sherbet /ˈʃɜ:bət/ *n* (*Amer*, *water-ice*) sorbete *m*

sheriff /ˈʃerɪf/ *n* alguacil *m*, sheriff *m*

sherry /ˈʃerɪ/ *n* (vino *m* de) jerez *m*

shield /ʃi:ld/ *n* escudo *m*. ● *vt* proteger

shift /ʃɪft/ *vt* cambiar; cambiar de sitio ‹*furniture etc*›; echar ‹*blame etc*›. ● *n* cambio *m*; (*work*) turno *m*; (*workers*) tanda *f*. **make ~** arreglárselas. **~less** /ˈʃɪftlɪs/ *a* holgazán

shifty /ˈʃɪftɪ/ *a* (**-ier**, **-iest**) taimado

shilling /ˈʃɪlɪŋ/ *n* chelín *m*

shilly-shally /ˈʃɪlɪʃælɪ/ *vi* titubear

shimmer /ˈʃɪmə(r)/ *vi* rielar, relucir. ● *n* luz *f* trémula

shin /ʃɪn/ *n* espinilla *f*

shine /ʃaɪn/ *vi* (*pt* **shone**) brillar. ● *vt* sacar brillo a. **~ on** dirigir ‹*torch*›. ● *n* brillo *m*

shingle /ˈʃɪŋgl/ *n* (*pebbles*) guijarros *mpl*

shingles /ˈʃɪŋglz/ *npl* (*med*) herpes *mpl* & *fpl*

shiny /ˈʃaɪnɪ/ *a* (**-ier**, **-iest**) brillante

ship /ʃɪp/ *n* buque *m*, barco *m*. ● *vt* (*pt* **shipped**) transportar; (*send*) enviar; (*load*) embarcar. **~building** /ˈʃɪpbɪldɪŋ/ *n* construcción *f* naval. **~ment** *n* envío *m*. **~per** *n* expedidor *m*. **~ping** *n* envío *m*; (*ships*) barcos *mpl*. **~shape** /ˈʃɪpʃeɪp/ *adv* & *a* en buen orden, en regla. **~wreck** /ˈʃɪprek/ *n* naufragio *m*. **~wrecked** *a* naufragado. **be ~wrecked** naufragar. **~yard** /ˈʃɪpjɑ:d/ *n* astillero *m*

shirk /ʃɜ:k/ *vt* esquivar. **~er** *n* gandul *m*

shirt /ʃɜ:t/ *n* camisa *f*. **in ~-sleeves** en mangas de camisa. **~y** /ˈʃɜ:tɪ/ *a* (*sl*) enfadado

shiver /ˈʃɪvə(r)/ *vi* temblar. ● *n* escalofrío *m*

shoal /ʃəʊl/ *n* banco *m*

shock /ʃɒk/ *n* sacudida *f*; (*fig*) susto *m*; (*elec*) descarga *f*; (*med*) choque *m*. ● *vt* escandalizar. **~ing** *a* escandaloso; (*fam*) espantoso. **~ingly** *adv* terriblemente

shod /ʃɒd/ *see* **shoe**

shodd|ily /ˈʃɒdɪlɪ/ *adv* mal. **~y** /ˈʃɒdɪ/ *a* (**-ier**, **-iest**) mal hecho, de pacotilla

shoe /ʃu:/ *n* zapato *m*; (*of horse*) herradura *f*. ● *vt* (*pt* **shod**, *pres p* **shoeing**) herrar ‹*horse*›. **be well shod** estar bien calzado. **~horn** /ˈʃu:hɔ:n/ *n* calzador *m*. **~-lace** *n* cordón *m* de zapato. **~maker** /ˈʃu:meɪkə(r)/ *n* zapatero *m*. **~ polish** *n* betún *m*. **~-string** *n*. **on a ~-string** con poco dinero. **~-tree** *n* horma *f*

shone /ʃɒn/ *see* **shine**

shoo /ʃu:/ *vt* ahuyentar

shook /ʃʊk/ *see* **shake**

shoot /ʃu:t/ *vt* (*pt* **shot**) disparar; rodar ‹*film*›. ● *vi* (*hunt*) cazar. ● *n* (*bot*) retoño *m*; (*hunt*) cacería *f*. ~ **down** *vt* derribar. ~ **out** *vi* (*rush*) salir disparado. ~ **up** ‹*prices*› subir de repente; (*grow*) crecer. ~**ing-range** *n* campo *m* de tiro

shop /ʃɒp/ *n* tienda *f*; (*work-shop*) taller *m*. **talk** ~ hablar de su trabajo. ● *vi* (*pt* **shopping**) hacer compras. ~ **around** buscar el mejor precio. **go** ~**ping** ir de compras. ~ **assistant** *n* dependiente *m*. ~**keeper** /ˈʃɒpkiːpə(r)/ *n* tendero *m*. ~**-lifter** *n* ratero *m* (de tiendas). ~**-lifting** *n* ratería *f* (de tiendas). ~**per** *n* comprador *m*. ~**ping** /ˈʃɒpɪŋ/ *n* compras *fpl*. ~**ping bag** *n* bolsa *f* de la compra. ~**ping centre** *n* centro *m* comercial. ~ **steward** *n* enlace *m* sindical. ~**-window** *n* escaparate *m*

shore /ʃɔː(r)/ *n* orilla *f*

shorn /ʃɔːn/ *see* **shear**

short /ʃɔːt/ *a* (**-er**, **-est**) corto; (*not lasting*) breve; ‹*person*› bajo; (*curt*) brusco. **a** ~ **time ago** hace poco. **be** ~ **of** necesitar. **Mick is** ~ **for Michael** Mick es el diminutivo de Michael. ● *adv* (*stop*) en seco. ~ **of doing** a menos que no hagamos. ● *n*. **in** ~ en resumen. ~**age** /ˈʃɔːtɪdʒ/ *n* escasez *f*. ~**bread** /ˈʃɔːtbred/ *n* galleta *f* de mantequilla. ~**-change** *vt* estafar, engañar. ~ **circuit** *n* cortocircuito *m*. ~**coming** /ˈʃɔːtkʌmɪŋ/ *n* deficiencia *f*. ~ **cut** *n* atajo *m*. ~**en** /ˈʃɔːtn/ *vt* acortar. ~**hand** /ˈʃɔːthænd/ *n* taquigrafía *f*. ~**hand typist** *n* taquimecanógrafo *m*, taquimeca *f* (*fam*). ~**-lived** *a* efímero. ~**ly** /ˈʃɔːtlɪ/ *adv* dentro de poco. ~**s** *npl* pantalón *m* corto. ~**-sighted** *a* miope. ~**tempered** *a* de mal genio

shot /ʃɒt/ *see* **shoot**. ● *n* tiro *m*; (*person*) tirador *m*; (*photo*) foto *f*; (*injection*) inyección *f*. **like a** ~ como una bala; (*willingly*) de buena gana. ~**-gun** *n* escopeta *f*

should /ʃʊd, ʃəd/ *v, aux*. **I** ~ **go** debería ir. **I** ~ **have seen him** debiera haberlo visto. **I** ~ **like** me gustaría. **if he** ~ **come** si viniese

shoulder /ˈʃəʊldə(r)/ *n* hombro *m*. ● *vt* cargar con ‹*responsibility*›; llevar a hombros ‹*burden*›. ~**-blade** *n* omóplato *m*. ~**-strap** *n* correa *f* del hombro; (*of bra etc*) tirante *m*

shout /ʃaʊt/ *n* grito *m*. ● *vt/i* gritar. ~ **at s.o.** gritarle a uno. ~ **down** hacer callar a gritos

shove /ʃʌv/ *n* empujón *m*. ● *vt* empujar; (*put, fam*) poner. ● *vi* empujar. ~ **off** *vi* (*fam*) largarse

shovel /ˈʃʌvl/ *n* pala *f*. ● *vt* (*pt* **shovelled**) mover con la pala

show /ʃəʊ/ *vt* (*pt* **showed**, *pp* **shown**) mostrar; (*put on display*) exponer; poner ‹*film*›. ● *vi* (*be visible*) verse. ● *n* demostración *f*; (*exhibition*) exposición *f*; (*ostentation*) pompa *f*; (*in theatre*) espectáculo *m*; (*in cinema*) sesión *f*. **on** ~ expuesto. ~ **off** *vt* lucir; (*pej*) ostentar. ● *vi* presumir. ~ **up** *vi* destacar; (*be present*) presentarse. ● *vt* (*unmask*) desenmascarar. ~**-case** *n* vitrina *f*. ~**-down** *n* confrontación *f*

shower /ˈʃaʊə(r)/ *n* chaparrón *m*; (*of blows etc*) lluvia *f*; (*for washing*) ducha *f*. **have a** ~ ducharse. ● *vi* ducharse. ● *vt*. ~ **with** colmar de. ~**proof** /ˈʃaʊəpruːf/ *a* impermeable. ~**y** *a* lluvioso

show: ~**-jumping** *n* concurso *m* hípico. ~**manship** /ˈʃəʊmənʃɪp/ *n* teatralidad *f*, arte *f* de presentar espectáculos

shown /ʃəʊn/ *see* **show**

show: ~**-off** *n* fanfarrón *m*. ~**-place** *n* lugar *m* de interés turístico. ~**room** /ˈʃəʊruːm/ *n* sala *f* de exposición *f*

showy /ˈʃəʊɪ/ *a* (**-ier**, **-iest**) llamativo; ‹*person*› ostentoso

shrank /ʃræŋk/ *see* **shrink**

shrapnel /ˈʃræpnəl/ *n* metralla *f*

shred /ʃred/ *n* pedazo *m*; (*fig*) pizca *f*. ● *vt* (*pt* **shredded**) hacer tiras; (*culin*) cortar en tiras. ~**der** *n* desfibradora *f*, trituradora *f*

shrew /ʃruː/ *n* musaraña *f*; (*woman*) arpía *f*

shrewd /ʃruːd/ *a* (**-er, -est**) astuto. ~**ness** *n* astucia *f*

shriek /ʃriːk/ *n* chillido *m*. ● *vt/i* chillar

shrift /ʃrɪft/ *n*. **give s.o. short** ~ despachar a uno con brusquedad

shrill /ʃrɪl/ *a* agudo

shrimp /ʃrɪmp/ *n* camarón *m*

shrine /ʃraɪn/ *n* (*place*) lugar *m* santo; (*tomb*) sepulcro *m*

shrink /ʃrɪŋk/ *vt* (*pt* **shrank,** *pp* **shrunk**) encoger. ● *vi* encogerse; (*draw back*) retirarse; (*lessen*) disminuir. ~**age** *n* encogimiento *m*

shrivel /ˈʃrɪvl/ *vi* (*pt* **shrivelled**) (*dry up*) secarse; (*become wrinkled*) arrugarse

shroud /ʃraʊd/ *n* sudario *m*; (*fig*) velo *m*. ● *vt* (*veil*) velar
Shrove /ʃrəʊv/ *n*. ~ **Tuesday** *n* martes *m* de carnaval
shrub /ʃrʌb/ *n* arbusto *m*
shrug /ʃrʌg/ *vt* (*pt* **shrugged**) encogerse de hombros. ● *n* encogimiento *m* de hombros
shrunk /ʃrʌŋk/ *see* **shrink**
shrunken /'ʃrʌnkən/ *a* encogido
shudder /'ʃʌdə(r)/ *vi* estremecerse. ● *n* estremecimiento *m*
shuffle /'ʃʌfl/ *vi* arrastrar los pies. ● *vt* barajar ‹*cards*›. ● *n* arrastramiento *m* de los pies; (*of cards*) barajadura *f*
shun /ʃʌn/ *vt* (*pt* **shunned**) evitar
shunt /ʃʌnt/ *vt* apartar, desviar
shush /ʃʊʃ/ *int* ¡chitón!
shut /ʃʌt/ *vt* (*pt* **shut**, *pres p* **shutting**) cerrar. ● *vi* cerrarse. ~ **down** cerrar. ~ **up** *vt* cerrar; (*fam*) hacer callar. ● *vi* callarse. ~**-down** *n* cierre *m*. ~**ter** /'ʃʌtə(r)/ *n* contraventana *f*; (*photo*) obturador *m*
shuttle /'ʃʌtl/ *n* lanzadera *f*; (*train*) tren *m* de enlace. ● *vt* transportar. ● *vi* ir y venir. ~**cock** /'ʃʌtlkɒk/ *n* volante *m*. ~ **service** *n* servicio *m* de enlace
shy /ʃaɪ/ *a* (**-er**, **-est**) tímido. ● *vi* (*pt* **shied**) asustarse. ~ **away from** huir. ~**ness** *n* timidez *f*
Siamese /saɪə'mi:z/ *a* siamés
sibling /'sɪblɪŋ/ *n* hermano *m*, hermana *f*
Sicil|ian /sɪ'sɪljən/ *a* & *n* siciliano (*m*). ~**y** /'sɪsɪlɪ/ *n* Sicilia *f*
sick /sɪk/ *a* enfermo; ‹*humour*› negro; (*fed up*, *fam*) harto. **be** ~ (*vomit*) vomitar. **be** ~ **of** (*fig*) estar harto de. **feel** ~ sentir náuseas. ~**en** /'sɪkən/ *vt* dar asco. ● *vi* caer enfermo. **be** ~**ening for** incubar
sickle /'sɪkl/ *n* hoz *f*
sick: ~**ly** /'sɪklɪ/ *a* (**-ier**, **-iest**) enfermizo; ‹*taste*, *smell etc*› nauseabundo. ~**ness** /'sɪknɪs/ *n* enfermedad *f*. ~**-room** *n* cuarto *m* del enfermo
side /saɪd/ *n* lado *m*; (*of river*) orilla *f*; (*of hill*) ladera *f*; (*team*) equipo *m*; (*fig*) parte *f*. ~ **by** ~ uno al lado del otro. **on the** ~ (*sideline*) como actividad secundaria; (*secretly*) a escondidas. ● *a* lateral. ● *vi*. ~ **with** tomar el partido de. ~**board** /'saɪdbɔ:d/ *n* aparador *m*. ~**boards** *npl*, ~**burns** *npl* (*sl*) patillas *fpl*. ~**-car** *n* sidecar *m*. ~**-effect** *n* efecto *m* secundario. ~**light** /'saɪdlaɪt/ *n* luz *f* de posición. ~**line** /'saɪdlaɪn/ *n* actividad *f* secundaria. ~**long** /-lɒŋ/ *a* & *adv* de soslayo. ~**-road** *n* calle *f* secundaria. ~**-saddle** *n* silla *f* de mujer. **ride** ~**-saddle** *adv* a mujeriegas. ~**-show** *n* atracción *f* secundaria. ~**-step** *vt* evitar. ~**-track** *vt* desviar del asunto. ~**walk** /'saɪdwɔ:k/ *n* (*Amer*) acera *f*, vereda *f* (*LAm*). ~**ways** /'saɪdweɪz/ *a* & *adv* de lado. ~**-whiskers** *npl* patillas *fpl*
siding /'saɪdɪŋ/ *n* apartadero *m*
sidle /'saɪdl/ *vi* avanzar furtivamente. ~ **up to** acercarse furtivamente
siege /si:dʒ/ *n* sitio *m*, cerco *m*
siesta /sɪ'estə/ *n* siesta *f*
sieve /sɪv/ *n* cernedor *m*. ● *vt* cerner
sift /sɪft/ *vt* cerner. ● *vi*. ~ **through** examinar
sigh /saɪ/ *n* suspiro. ● *vi* suspirar
sight /saɪt/ *n* vista *f*; (*spectacle*) espectáculo *m*; (*on gun*) mira *f*. **at (first)** ~ a primera vista. **catch** ~ **of** vislumbrar. **lose** ~ **of** perder de vista. **on** ~ a primera vista. **within** ~ **of** (*near*) cerca de. ● *vt* ver, divisar. ~**-seeing** /'saɪtsi:ɪŋ/ *n* visita *f* turística. ~**seer** /-ə(r)/ *n* turista *m* & *f*
sign /saɪn/ *n* señal *f*. ● *vt* firmar. ~ **on**, ~ **up** *vt* inscribir. ● *vi* inscribirse
signal /'sɪgnəl/ *n* señal *f*. ● *vt* (*pt* **signalled**) comunicar; hacer señas a ‹*person*›. ~**-box** *n* casilla *f* del guardavía. ~**man** /'sɪgnəlmən/ *n* (*pl* **-men**) guardavía *f*
signatory /'sɪgnətrɪ/ *n* firmante *m* & *f*
signature /'sɪgnətʃə(r)/ *n* firma *f*. ~ **tune** *n* sintonía *f*
signet-ring /'sɪgnɪtrɪŋ/ *n* anillo *m* de sello
significan|ce /sɪg'nɪfɪkəns/ *n* significado *m*. ~**t** /sɪg'nɪfɪkənt/ *a* significativo; (*important*) importante. ~**tly** *adv* significativamente
signify /'sɪgnɪfaɪ/ *vt* significar. ● *vi* (*matter*) importar, tener importancia
signpost /'saɪnpəʊst/ *n* poste *m* indicador
silen|ce /'saɪləns/ *n* silencio *m*. ● *vt* hacer callar. ~**cer** /-ə(r)/ *n* silenciador *m*. ~**t** /'saɪlənt/ *a* silencioso;

‹*film*› mudo. **~tly** *adv* silenciosamente

silhouette /sɪlu:'et/ *n* silueta *f*. ● *vt*. **be ~d** perfilarse, destacarse (**against** contra)

silicon /'sɪlɪkən/ *n* silicio *m*. **~ chip** *n* pastilla *f* de silicio

silk /sɪlk/ *n* seda *f*. **~en** *a*, **~y** *a* (*of silk*) de seda; (*like silk*) sedoso. **~worm** *n* gusano *m* de seda

sill /sɪl/ *n* antepecho *m*; (*of window*) alféizar *m*; (*of door*) umbral *m*

silly /'sɪlɪ/ *a* (**-ier**, **-iest**) tonto. ● *n*. **~-billy** (*fam*) tonto *m*

silo /'saɪləʊ/ *n* (*pl* **-os**) silo *m*

silt /sɪlt/ *n* sedimento *m*

silver /'sɪlvə(r)/ *n* plata *f*. ● *a* de plata. **~ plated** *a* bañado en plata, plateado. **~side** /'sɪlvəsaɪd/ *n* (*culin*) contra *f*. **~smith** /'sɪlvəsmɪθ/ *n* platero *m*. **~ware** /'sɪlvəweə(r)/ *n* plata *f*. **~ wedding** *n* bodas *fpl* de plata. **~y** *a* plateado; ‹*sound*› argentino

simil|ar /'sɪmɪlə(r)/ *a* parecido. **~arity** /-ɪ'lærətɪ/ *n* parecido *m*. **~arly** *adv* de igual manera

simile /'sɪmɪlɪ/ *n* símil *m*

simmer /'sɪmə(r)/ *vt/i* hervir a fuego lento; (*fig*) hervir. **~ down** calmarse

simpl|e /'sɪmpl/ *a* (**-er**, **-est**) sencillo; ‹*person*› ingenuo. **~e-minded** *a* ingenuo. **~eton** /'sɪmpltən/ *n* simplón *m*. **~icity** /-'plɪsetɪ/ *n* secillez *f*. **~ification** /-ɪ'keɪʃn/ *n* simplificación *f*. **~ify** /'sɪmplɪfaɪ/ *vt* simplificar. **~y** *adv* sencillamente; (*absolutely*) absolutamente

simulat|e /'sɪmjʊleɪt/ *vt* simular. **~ion** /-'leɪʃn/ *n* simulación *f*

simultaneous /sɪml'teɪnɪəs/ *a* simultáneo. **~ly** *adv* simultáneamente

sin /sɪn/ *n* pecado *m*. ● *vi* (*pt* **sinned**) pecar

since /sɪns/ *prep* desde. ● *adv* desde entonces. ● *conj* desde que; (*because*) ya que

sincer|e /sɪn'sɪə(r)/ *a* sincero. **~ely** *adv* sinceramente. **~ity** /-'serətɪ/ *n* sinceridad *f*

sinew /'sɪnju:/ *n* tendón *m*. **~s** *npl* músculos *mpl*

sinful /'sɪnfl/ *a* pecaminoso; (*shocking*) escandaloso

sing /sɪŋ/ *vt/i* (*pt* **sang**, *pp* **sung**) cantar

singe /sɪndʒ/ *vt* (*pres p* **singeing**) chamuscar

singer /'sɪŋə(r)/ *n* cantante *m* & *f*

singl|e /'sɪŋgl/ *a* único; (*not double*) sencillo; (*unmarried*) soltero; ‹*bed, room*› individual. ● *n* (*tennis*) juego *m* individual; (*ticket*) billete *m* sencillo. ● *vt*. **~e out** escoger; (*distinguish*) distinguir. **~e-handed** *a* & *adv* sin ayuda. **~e-minded** *a* resuelto

singlet /'sɪŋglɪt/ *n* camiseta *f*

singly /'sɪŋglɪ/ *adv* uno a uno

singsong /'sɪŋsɒŋ/ *a* monótono. ● *n*. **have a ~** cantar juntos

singular /'sɪŋgjʊlə(r)/ *n* singular *f*. ● *a* singular; (*uncommon*) raro; ‹*noun*› en singular. **~ly** *adv* singularmente

sinister /'sɪnɪstə(r)/ *a* siniestro

sink /sɪŋk/ *vt* (*pt* **sank**, *pp* **sunk**) hundir; perforar ‹*well*›; invertir ‹*money*›. ● *vi* hundirse; ‹*patient*› debilitarse. ● *n* fregadero *m*. **~ in** *vi* penetrar

sinner /'sɪnə(r)/ *n* pecador *m*

sinuous /'sɪnjʊəs/ *a* sinuoso

sinus /'saɪnəs/ *n* (*pl* **-uses**) seno *m*

sip /sɪp/ *n* sorbo *m*. ● *vt* (*pt* **sipped**) sorber

siphon /'saɪfən/ *n* sifón *m*. *vt*. **~ out** sacar con sifón

sir /sɜ:(r)/ *n* señor *m*. **S~** *n* (*title*) sir *m*

siren /'saɪərən/ *n* sirena *f*

sirloin /'sɜ:lɔɪn/ *n* solomillo *m*, lomo *m* bajo

sirocco /sɪ'rɒkəʊ/ *n* siroco *m*

sissy /'sɪsɪ/ *n* hombre *m* afeminado, marica *m*, mariquita *m*; (*coward*) gallina *m* & *f*

sister /'sɪstə(r)/ *n* hermana *f*; (*nurse*) enfermera *f* jefe. **S~ Mary** Sor María. **~-in-law** *n* (*pl* **~s-in-law**) cuñada *f*. **~ly** *a* de hermana; (*like sister*) como hermana

sit /sɪt/ *vt* (*pt* **sat**, *pres p* **sitting**) sentar. ● *vi* sentarse; ‹*committee etc*› reunirse. **be ~ting** estar sentado. **~ back** *vi* (*fig*) relajarse. **~ down** *vi* sentarse. **~ for** *vi* presentarse a ‹*exam*›; posar para ‹*portrait*›. **~ up** *vi* enderezarse; (*stay awake*) velar. **~-in** *n* ocupación *f*

site /saɪt/ *n* sitio *m*. **building ~** *n* solar *m*. ● *vt* situar

sit: ~ting *n* sesión *f*; (*in restaurant*) turno *m*. **~ting-room** *n* cuarto *m* de estar

situat|e /'sɪtjʊeɪt/ *vt* situar. **~ed** *a* situado. **~ion** /-'eɪʃn/ *n* situación *f*; (*job*) puesto *m*

six /sɪks/ *a* & *n* seis (*m*). **~teen** /sɪk'sti:n/ *a* & *n* dieciséis (*m*). **~teenth** *a* & *n* decimosexto (*m*). **~th** *a* & *n* sexto (*m*). **~tieth** *a* & *n* sesenta (*m*), sexagésimo (*m*). **~ty** /'sɪkstɪ/ *a* & *n* sesenta (*m*)

size /saɪz/ *n* tamaño *m*; (*of clothes*) talla *f*; (*of shoes*) número *m*; (*extent*) magnitud *f*. ● *vt*. **~ up** (*fam*) juzgar. **~able** *a* bastante grande

sizzle /'sɪzl/ *vi* crepitar

skate[1] /skeɪt/ *n* patín *m*. ● *vi* patinar. **~board** /'skeɪtbɔ:d/ *n* monopatín *m*. **~r** *n* patinador *m*

skate[2] /skeɪt/ *n invar* (*fish*) raya *f*

skating /'skeɪtɪŋ/ *n* patinaje *m*. **~-rink** *n* pista *f* de patinaje

skein /skeɪn/ *n* madeja *f*

skelet|al /'skelɪtl/ *a* esquelético. **~on** /'skelɪtn/ *n* esqueleto *m*. **~on staff** *n* personal *m* reducido

sketch /sketʃ/ *n* esbozo *m*; (*drawing*) dibujo *m*; (*in theatre*) pieza *f* corta y divertida. ● *vt* esbozar. ● *vi* dibujar. **~y** /'sketʃɪ/ *a* (**-ier**, **-iest**) incompleto

skew /skju:/ *n*. **on the ~** sesgado

skewer /'skju:ə(r)/ *n* broqueta *f*

ski /ski:/ *n* (*pl* **skis**) esquí *m*. ● *vi* (*pt* **skied**, *pres p* **skiing**) esquiar. **go ~ing** ir a esquiar

skid /skɪd/ *vi* (*pt* **skidded**) patinar. ● *n* patinazo *m*

ski: **~er** *n* esquiador *m*. **~ing** *n* esquí *m*

skilful /'skɪlfl/ *a* diestro

ski-lift /'ski:lɪft/ *n* telesquí *m*

skill /skɪl/ *n* destreza *f*, habilidad *f*. **~ed** *a* hábil; ‹*worker*› cualificado

skim /skɪm/ *vt* (*pt* **skimmed**) espumar; desnatar ‹*milk*›; (*glide over*) rozar. **~ over** *vt* rasar. **~ through** *vi* hojear

skimp /skɪmp/ *vt* escatimar. **~y** /'skɪmpɪ/ *a* (**-ier**, **-iest**) insuficiente; ‹*skirt, dress*› corto

skin /skɪn/ *n* piel *f*. ● *vt* (*pt* **skinned**) despellejar; pelar (*fruit*). **~-deep** *a* superficial. **~-diving** *n* natación *f* submarina. **~flint** /'skɪnflɪnt/ *n* tacaño *m*. **~ny** /'skɪnɪ/ *a* (**-ier**, **-iest**) flaco

skint /skɪnt/ *a* (*sl*) sin una perra

skip[1] /skɪp/ *vi* (*pt* **skipped**) *vi* saltar; (*with rope*) saltar a la comba. ● *vt* saltarse. ● *n* salto *m*

skip[2] /skɪp/ *n* (*container*) cuba *f*

skipper /'skɪpə(r)/ *n* capitán *m*

skipping-rope /'skɪpɪŋrəʊp/ *n* comba *f*

skirmish /'skɜ:mɪʃ/ *n* escaramuza *f*

skirt /skɜ:t/ *n* falda *f*. ● *vt* rodear; (*go round*) ladear

skirting-board /'skɜ:tɪŋbɔ:d/ *n* rodapié *m*, zócalo *m*

skit /skɪt/ *n* pieza *f* satírica

skittish /'skɪtɪʃ/ *a* juguetón; ‹*horse*› nervioso

skittle /'skɪtl/ *n* bolo *m*

skive /skaɪv/ *vi* (*sl*) gandulear

skivvy /'skɪvɪ/ *n* (*fam*) criada *f*

skulk /skʌlk/ *vi* avanzar furtivamente; (*hide*) esconderse

skull /skʌl/ *n* cráneo *m*; (*remains*) calavera *f*. **~-cap** *n* casquete *m*

skunk /skʌŋk/ *n* mofeta *f*; (*person*) canalla *f*

sky /skaɪ/ *n* cielo *m*. **~-blue** *a* & *n* azul (*m*) celeste. **~jack** /'skaɪdʒæk/ *vt* secuestrar. **~jacker** *n* secuestrador *m*. **~light** /'skaɪlaɪt/ *n* tragaluz *m*. **~scraper** /'skaɪskreɪpə(r)/ *n* rascacielos *m invar*

slab /slæb/ *n* bloque *m*; (*of stone*) losa *f*; (*of chocolate*) tableta *f*

slack /slæk/ *a* (**-er**, **-est**) flojo; ‹*person*› negligente; ‹*period*› de poca actividad. ● *n* (*of rope*) parte *f* floja. ● *vt* aflojar. ● *vi* aflojarse; ‹*person*› descansar. **~en** /'slækən/ *vt* aflojar. ● *vi* aflojarse; ‹*person*› descansar. **~en (off)** *vt* aflojar. **~ off** (*fam*) aflojar

slacks /slæks/ *npl* pantalones *mpl*

slag /slæg/ *n* escoria *f*

slain /sleɪn/ *see* **slay**

slake /sleɪk/ *vt* apagar

slam /slæm/ *vt* (*pt* **slammed**) golpear; (*throw*) arrojar; (*criticize*, *sl*) criticar. **~ the door** dar un portazo. ● *vi* cerrarse de golpe. ● *n* golpe *m*; (*of door*) portazo *m*

slander /'slɑ:ndə(r)/ *n* calumnia *f*. ● *vt* difamar. **~ous** *a* calumnioso

slang /slæŋ/ *n* jerga *f*, argot *m*. **~y** *a* vulgar

slant /slɑ:nt/ *vt* inclinar; presentar con parcialidad ‹*news*›. ● *n* inclinación *f*; (*point of view*) punto *m* de vista

slap /slæp/ *vt* (*pt* **slapped**) abofetear; (*on the back*) dar una palmada; (*put*) arrojar. ● *n* bofetada *f*; (*on back*) palmada *f*. ● *adv* de lleno. **~dash**

/'slæpdæʃ/ *a* descuidado. **~-happy** *a* (*fam*) despreocupado; (*dazed, fam*) aturdido. **~stick** /'slæpstɪk/ *n* payasada *f*. **~-up** *a* (*sl*) de primera categoría

slash /slæʃ/ *vt* acuchillar; (*fig*) reducir radicalmente. ● *n* cuchillada *f*

slat /slæt/ *n* tablilla *f*

slate /sleɪt/ *n* pizarra *f*. ● *vt* (*fam*) criticar

slaughter /'slɔːtə(r)/ *vt* masacrar; matar ‹*animal*›. ● *n* carnicería *f*; (*of animals*) matanza *f*. **~house** /'slɔːtəhaʊs/ *n* matadero *m*

Slav /slɑːv/ *a* & *n* eslavo (*m*)

slav|e /sleɪv/ *n* esclavo *m*. ● *vi* trabajar como un negro. **~e-driver** *n* negrero *m*. **~ery** /-ərɪ/ *n* esclavitud *f*. **~ish** /'sleɪvɪʃ/ *a* servil

Slavonic /slə'vɒnɪk/ *a* eslavo

slay /sleɪ/ *vt* (*pt* **slew**, *pp* **slain**) matar

sleazy /'sliːzɪ/ *a* (**-ier**, **-iest**) (*fam*) sórdido

sledge /sledʒ/ *n* trineo *m*. **~-hammer** *n* almádena *f*

sleek /sliːk/ *a* (**-er**, **-est**) liso, brillante; (*elegant*) elegante

sleep /sliːp/ *n* sueño *m*. **go to ~** dormirse. ● *vi* (*pt* **slept**) dormir. ● *vt* poder alojar. **~er** *n* durmiente *m* & *f*; (*on track*) traviesa *f*; (*berth*) coche-cama *m*. **~ily** *adv* soñolientamente. **~ing-bag** *n* saco *m* de dormir. **~ing-pill** *n* somnífero *m*. **~less** *a* insomne. **~lessness** *n* insomnio *m*. **~-walker** *n* sonámbulo *m*. **~y** /'sliːpɪ/ *a* (**-ier**, **-iest**) soñoliento. **be ~y** tener sueño

sleet /sliːt/ *n* aguanieve *f*. ● *vi* caer aguanieve

sleeve /sliːv/ *n* manga *f*; (*for record*) funda *f*. **up one's ~** en reserva. **~less** *a* sin mangas

sleigh /sleɪ/ *n* trineo *m*

sleight /slaɪt/ *n*. **~ of hand** prestidigitación *f*

slender /'slendə(r)/ *a* delgado; (*fig*) escaso

slept /slept/ *see* **sleep**

sleuth /sluːθ/ *n* investigador *m*

slew[1] /sluː/ *see* **slay**

slew[2] /sluː/ *vi* (*turn*) girar

slice /slaɪs/ *n* lonja *f*; (*of bread*) rebanada *f*; (*of sth round*) rodaja *f*; (*implement*) paleta *f*. ● *vt* cortar; rebanar ‹*bread*›

slick /slɪk/ *a* liso; (*cunning*) astuto. ● *n*. **(oil)-~** capa *f* de aceite

slid|e /slaɪd/ *vt* (*pt* **slid**) deslizar. ● *vi* resbalar. **~e over** pasar por alto de. ● *n* resbalón *m*; (*in playground*) tobogán *m*; (*for hair*) pasador *m*; (*photo*) diapositiva *f*; (*fig, fall*) baja *f*. **~e-rule** *n* regla *f* de cálculo. **~ing** *a* corredizo. **~ing scale** *n* escala *f* móvil

slight /slaɪt/ *a* (**-er**, **-est**) ligero; (*slender*) delgado. ● *vt* ofender. ● *n* desaire *m*. **~est** *a* mínimo. **not in the ~est** en absoluto. **~ly** *adv* un poco

slim /slɪm/ *a* (**slimmer**, **slimmest**) delgado. ● *vi* (*pt* **slimmed**) adelgazar

slime /slaɪm/ *n* légamo *m*, lodo *m*, fango *m*

slimness /'slɪmnɪs/ *n* delgadez *f*

slimy /'slaɪmɪ/ *a* legamoso, fangoso, viscoso; (*fig*) rastrero

sling /slɪŋ/ *n* honda *f*; (*toy*) tirador; (*med*) cabestrillo *m*. ● *vt* (*pt* **slung**) lanzar

slip /slɪp/ *vt* (*pt* **slipped**) deslizar. **~ s.o.'s mind** olvidársele a uno. ● *vi* deslizarse. ● *n* resbalón *m*; (*mistake*) error *m*; (*petticoat*) combinación *f*; (*paper*) trozo *m*. **~ of the tongue** *n* lapsus *m* linguae. **give the ~ to** zafarse de, dar esquinazo a. **~ away** *vi* escabullirse. **~ into** *vi* ponerse ‹*clothes*›. **~ up** *vi* (*fam*) equivocarse

slipper /'slɪpə(r)/ *n* zapatilla *f*

slippery /'slɪpərɪ/ *a* resbaladizo

slip: **~-road** *n* rampa *f* de acceso. **~shod** /'slɪpʃɒd/ *a* descuidado. **~-up** *n* (*fam*) error *m*

slit /slɪt/ *n* raja *f*; (*cut*) corte *m*. ● *vt* (*pt* **slit**, *pres p* **slitting**) rajar; (*cut*) cortar

slither /'slɪðə(r)/ *vi* deslizarse

sliver /'slɪvə(r)/ *n* trocito *m*; (*splinter*) astilla *f*

slobber /'slɒbə(r)/ *vi* babear

slog /slɒg/ *vt* (*pt* **slogged**) golpear. ● *vi* trabajar como un negro. ● *n* golpetazo *m*; (*hard work*) trabajo *m* penoso

slogan /'sləʊgən/ *n* eslogan *m*

slop /slɒp/ *vt* (*pt* **slopped**) derramar. ● *vi* derramarse. **~s** *npl* (*fam*) agua *f* sucia

slop|e /sləʊp/ *vi* inclinarse. ● *vt* inclinar. ● *n* declive *m*, pendiente *m*. **~ing** *a* inclinado

sloppy /'slɒpɪ/ *a* (**-ier**, **-iest**) (*wet*) mojado; ‹*food*› líquido; ‹*work*› descuidado; ‹*person*› desaliñado; (*fig*) sentimental

slosh /slɒʃ/ *vi* (*fam*) chapotear. ● *vt* (*hit, sl*) pegar

slot /slɒt/ *n* ranura *f*. ● *vt* (*pt* **slotted**) encajar

sloth /sləʊθ/ *n* pereza *f*

slot-machine /ˈslɒtməʃiːn/ *n* distribuidor *m* automático; (*for gambling*) máquina *f* tragaperras

slouch /slaʊtʃ/ *vi* andar cargado de espaldas; (*in chair*) repanchigarse

Slovak /ˈsləʊvæk/ *a* & *n* eslovaco (*m*). **~ia** /sləʊˈvækɪə/ *n* Eslovaquia *f*

slovenl|iness /ˈslʌvnlɪnɪs/ *n* despreocupación *f*. **~y** /ˈslʌvnlɪ/ *a* descuidado

slow /sləʊ/ *a* (**-er**, **-est**) lento. **be ~** ‹*clock*› estar atrasado. **in ~ motion** a cámara lenta. ● *adv* despacio. ● *vt* retardar. ● *vi* ir más despacio. **~ down**, **~ up** *vt* retardar. ● *vi* ir más despacio. **~coach** /ˈsləʊkəʊtʃ/ *n* tardón *m*. **~ly** *adv* despacio. **~ness** *n* lentitud *f*

sludge /slʌdʒ/ *n* fango *m*; (*sediment*) sedimento *m*

slug /slʌg/ *n* babosa *f*; (*bullet*) posta *f*. **~gish** /ˈslʌgɪʃ/ *a* lento

sluice /sluːs/ *n* (*gate*) compuerta *f*; (*channel*) canal *m*

slum /slʌm/ *n* tugurio *m*

slumber /ˈslʌmbə(r)/ *n* sueño *m*. ● *vi* dormir

slump /slʌmp/ *n* baja *f* repentina; (*in business*) depresión *f*. ● *vi* bajar repentinamente; (*flop down*) dejarse caer pesadamente; (*collapse*) desplomarse

slung /slʌŋ/ *see* **sling**

slur /slɜː(r)/ *vt/i* (*pt* **slurred**) articular mal. ● *n* dicción *f* defectuosa; (*discredit*) calumnia *f*

slush /slʌʃ/ *n* nieve *f* medio derretida; (*fig*) sentimentalismo *m*. **~ fund** *n* fondos *mpl* secretos para fines deshonestos. **~y** *a* ‹*road*› cubierto de nieve medio derretida

slut /slʌt/ *n* mujer *f* desaseada

sly /slaɪ/ *a* (**slyer**, **slyest**) (*crafty*) astuto; (*secretive*) furtivo. ● *n*. **on the ~** a escondidas. **~ly** *adv* astutamente

smack[1] /smæk/ *n* golpe *m*; (*on face*) bofetada *f*. ● *adv* (*fam*) de lleno. ● *vt* pegar

smack[2] /smæk/ *vi*. **~ of** saber a; (*fig*) oler a

small /smɔːl/ *a* (**-er**, **-est**) pequeño. ● *n*. **the ~ of the back** la región *f* lumbar. **~ ads** *npl* anuncios *mpl* por palabras. **~ change** *n* cambio *m*. **~holding** /ˈsmɔːlhəʊldɪŋ/ *n* parcela *f*. **~pox** /ˈsmɔːlpɒks/ *n* viruela *f*. **~ talk** *n* charla *f*. **~-time** *a* (*fam*) de poca monta

smarmy /ˈsmɑːmɪ/ *a* (**-ier**, **-iest**) (*fam*) zalamero

smart /smɑːt/ *a* (**-er**, **-est**) elegante; (*clever*) inteligente; (*brisk*) rápido. ● *vi* escocer. **~en** /ˈsmɑːtn/ *vt* arreglar. ● *vi* arreglarse. **~en up** *vi* arreglarse. **~ly** *adv* elegantemente; (*quickly*) rápidamente. **~ness** *n* elegancia *f*

smash /smæʃ/ *vt* romper; (*into little pieces*) hacer pedazos; batir ‹*record*›. ● *vi* romperse; (*collide*) chocar (**into** con). ● *n* (*noise*) estruendo *m*; (*collision*) choque *m*; (*com*) quiebra *f*. **~ing** /ˈsmæʃɪŋ/ *a* (*fam*) estupendo

smattering /ˈsmætərɪŋ/ *n* conocimientos *mpl* superficiales

smear /smɪə(r)/ *vt* untar (**with** de); (*stain*) manchar (**with** de); (*fig*) difamar. ● *n* mancha *f*; (*med*) frotis *m*

smell /smel/ *n* olor *m*; (*sense*) olfato *m*. ● *vt/i* (*pt* **smelt**) oler. **~y** *a* maloliente

smelt[1] /smelt/ *see* **smell**

smelt[2] /smelt/ *vt* fundir

smile /smaɪl/ *n* sonrisa *f*. ● *vi* sonreír(se)

smirk /smɜːk/ *n* sonrisa *f* afectada

smite /smaɪt/ *vt* (*pt* **smote**, *pp* **smitten**) golpear

smith /smɪθ/ *n* herrero *m*

smithereens /smɪðəˈriːnz/ *npl* añicos *mpl*. **smash to ~** hacer añicos

smitten /ˈsmɪtn/ *see* **smite**. ● *a* encaprichado (**with** por)

smock /smɒk/ *n* blusa *f*, bata *f*

smog /smɒg/ *n* niebla *f* con humo

smok|e /sməʊk/ *n* humo *m*. ● *vt/i* fumar. **~eless** *a* sin humo. **~er** /-ə(r)/ *n* fumador *m*. **~e-screen** *n* cortina *f* de humo. **~y** *a* ‹*room*› lleno de humo

smooth /smuːð/ *a* (**-er**, **-est**) liso; ‹*sound*, *movement*› suave; ‹*sea*› tranquilo; ‹*manners*› zalamero. ● *vt* alisar; (*fig*) allanar. **~ly** *adv* suavemente

smote /sməʊt/ *see* **smite**

smother /ˈsmʌðə(r)/ *vt* sofocar; (*cover*) cubrir

smoulder /ˈsməʊldə(r)/ *vi* arder sin llama; (*fig*) arder

smudge /smʌdʒ/ *n* borrón *m*, mancha *f*. ● *vt* tiznar. ● *vi* tiznarse

smug /smʌg/ *a* (**smugger**, **smuggest**) satisfecho de sí mismo

smuggl|e /ˈsmʌgl/ *vt* pasar de contrabando. **~er** *n* contrabandista *m* & *f*. **~ing** *n* contrabando *m*

smug: **~ly** *adv* con suficiencia. **~ness** *n* suficiencia *f*

smut /smʌt/ *n* tizne *m*; (*mark*) tiznajo *m*. **~ty** *a* (**-ier**, **-iest**) tiznado; (*fig*) obsceno

snack /snæk/ *n* tentempié *m*. **~-bar** *n* cafetería *f*

snag /snæg/ *n* problema *m*; (*in cloth*) rasgón *m*

snail /sneɪl/ *n* caracol *m*. **~'s pace** *n* paso *m* de tortuga

snake /sneɪk/ *n* serpiente *f*

snap /snæp/ *vt* (*pt* **snapped**) (*break*) romper; castañetear ‹*fingers*›. ● *vi* romperse; ‹*dog*› intentar morder; (*say*) contestar bruscamente; ‹*whip*› chasquear. **~ at** ‹*dog*› intentar morder; (*say*) contestar bruscamente. ● *n* chasquido *m*; (*photo*) foto *f*. ● *a* instantáneo. **~ up** *vt* agarrar. **~py** /ˈsnæpɪ/ *a* (**-ier**, **-iest**) (*fam*) rápido. **make it ~py!** (*fam*) ¡date prisa! **~shot** /ˈsnæpʃɒt/ *n* foto *f*

snare /sneə(r)/ *n* trampa *f*

snarl /snɑ:l/ *vi* gruñir. ● *n* gruñido *m*

snatch /snætʃ/ *vt* agarrar; (*steal*) robar. ● *n* arrebatamiento *m*; (*short part*) trocito *m*; (*theft*) robo *m*

sneak /sni:k/ ● *n* soplón *m*. ● *vi*. **~ in** entrar furtivamente. **~ out** salir furtivamente

sneakers /ˈsni:kəz/ *npl* zapatillas *fpl* de lona

sneak|ing /ˈsni:kɪŋ/ *a* furtivo. **~y** *a* furtivo

sneer /snɪə(r)/ *n* sonrisa *f* de desprecio. ● *vi* sonreír con desprecio. **~ at** hablar con desprecio a

sneeze /sni:z/ *n* estornudo *m*. ● *vi* estornudar

snide /snaɪd/ *a* (*fam*) despreciativo

sniff /snɪf/ *vt* oler. ● *vi* aspirar por la nariz. ● *n* aspiración *f*

snigger /ˈsnɪgə(r)/ *n* risa *f* disimulada. ● *vi* reír disimuladamente

snip /snɪp/ *vt* (*pt* **snipped**) tijeretear. ● *n* tijeretada *f*; (*bargain*, *sl*) ganga *f*

snipe /snaɪp/ *vi* disparar desde un escondite. **~r** /ə(r)/ *n* tirador *m* emboscado, francotirador *m*

snippet /ˈsnɪpɪt/ *n* retazo *m*

snivel /ˈsnɪvl/ *vi* (*pt* **snivelled**) lloriquear. **~ling** *a* llorón

snob /snɒb/ *n* esnob *m*. **~bery** *n* esnobismo *m*. **~bish** *a* esnob

snooker /ˈsnu:kə(r)/ *n* billar *m*

snoop /snu:p/ *vi* (*fam*) curiosear

snooty /ˈsnu:tɪ/ *a* (*fam*) desdeñoso

snooze /snu:z/ *n* sueñecito *m*. ● *vi* echarse un sueñecito

snore /snɔ:(r)/ *n* ronquido *m*. ● *vi* roncar

snorkel /ˈsnɔ:kl/ *n* tubo *m* respiratorio

snort /snɔ:t/ *n* bufido *m*. ● *vi* bufar

snout /snaʊt/ *n* hocico *m*

snow /snəʊ/ *n* nieve *f*. ● *vi* nevar. **be ~ed under with** estar inundado por. **~ball** /ˈsnəʊbɔ:l/ *n* bola *f* de nieve. **~-drift** *n* nieve amontonada. **~drop** /ˈsnəʊdrɒp/ *n* campanilla *f* de invierno. **~fall** /ˈsnəʊfɔ:l/ *n* nevada *f*. **~flake** /ˈsnəʊfleɪk/ *n* copo *m* de nieve. **~man** /ˈsnəʊmæn/ *n* (*pl* **-men**) muñeco *m* de nieve. **~-plough** *n* quitanieves *m invar*. **~storm** /ˈsnəʊstɔ:m/ *n* nevasca *f*. **~y** *a* ‹*place*› de nieves abundantes; ‹*weather*› con nevadas seguidas

snub /snʌb/ *vt* (*pt* **snubbed**) desairar. ● *n* desaire *m*. **~-nosed** /ˈsnʌbnəʊzd/ *a* chato

snuff /snʌf/ *n* rapé *m*. ● *vt* despabilar ‹*candle*›. **~ out** apagar ‹*candle*›

snuffle /ˈsnʌfl/ *vi* respirar ruidosamente

snug /snʌg/ *a* (**snugger**, **snuggest**) cómodo; (*tight*) ajustado

snuggle /ˈsnʌgl/ *vi* acomodarse

so /səʊ/ *adv* (*before a or adv*) tan; (*thus*) así. ● *conj* así que. **~ am I** yo tambien. **~ as to** para. **~ far** *adv* (*time*) hasta ahora; (*place*) hasta aquí. **~ far as I know** que yo sepa. **~ long!** (*fam*) ¡hasta luego! **~ much** tanto. **~ that** *conj* para que. **and ~ forth**, **and ~ on** y así sucesivamente. **if ~** si es así. **I think ~** creo que sí. **or ~** más o menos

soak /səʊk/ *vt* remojar. ● *vi* remojarse. **~ in** penetrar. **~ up** absorber. **~ing** *a* empapado. ● *n* remojón *m*

so-and-so /ˈsəʊənsəʊ/ *n* fulano *m*

soap /səʊp/ *n* jabón *m*. ● *vt* enjabonar. ~ **powder** *n* jabón en polvo. ~**y** *a* jabonoso

soar /sɔ:(r)/ *vi* elevarse; ‹*price etc*› ponerse por las nubes

sob /sɒb/ *n* sollozo *m*. ● *vi* (*pt* **sobbed**) sollozar

sober /'səʊbə(r)/ *a* sobrio; ‹*colour*› discreto

so-called /'səʊkɔ:ld/ *a* llamado, supuesto

soccer /'sɒkə(r)/ *n* (*fam*) fútbol *m*

sociable /'səʊʃəbl/ *a* sociable

social /'səʊʃl/ *a* social; (*sociable*) sociable. ● *n* reunión *f*. ~**ism** /-zəm/ *n* socialismo *m*. ~**ist** /'səʊʃəlɪst/ *a* & *n* socialista *m* & *f*. ~**ize** /'səʊʃəlaɪz/ *vt* socializar. ~**ly** *adv* socialmente. ~ **security** *n* seguridad *f* social. ~ **worker** *n* asistente *m* social

society /sə'saɪətɪ/ *n* sociedad *f*

sociolog|ical /səʊsɪə'lɒdʒɪkl/ *a* sociológico. ~**ist** *n* sociólogo *m*. ~**y** /səʊsɪ'ɒlədʒɪ/ *n* sociología *f*

sock[1] /sɒk/ *n* calcetín *m*

sock[2] /sɒk/ *vt* (*sl*) pegar

socket /'sɒkɪt/ *n* hueco *m*; (*of eye*) cuenca *f*; (*wall plug*) enchufe *m*; (*for bulb*) portalámparas *m invar*, casquillo *m*

soda /'səʊdə/ *n* sosa *f*; (*water*) soda *f*. ~**-water** *n* soda *f*

sodden /'sɒdn/ *a* empapado

sodium /'səʊdɪəm/ *n* sodio *m*

sofa /'səʊfə/ *n* sofá *m*

soft /sɒft/ *a* (**-er**, **-est**) blando; ‹*sound, colour*› suave; (*gentle*) dulce, tierno; (*silly*) estúpido. ~ **drink** *n* bebida *f* no alcohólica. ~ **spot** *n* debilidad *f*. ~**en** /'sɒfn/ *vt* ablandar; (*fig*) suavizar. ● *vi* ablandarse; (*fig*) suavizarse. ~**ly** *adv* dulcemente. ~**ness** *n* blandura *f*; (*fig*) dulzura *f*. ~**ware** /'sɒftweə(r)/ *n* programación *f*, software *m*

soggy /'sɒgɪ/ *a* (**-ier**, **-iest**) empapado

soh /səʊ/ *n* (*mus, fifth note of any musical scale*) sol *m*

soil[1] /sɔɪl/ *n* suelo *m*

soil[2] /sɔɪl/ *vt* ensuciar. ● *vi* ensuciarse

solace /'sɒləs/ *n* consuelo *m*

solar /'səʊlə(r)/ *a* solar. ~**ium** /sə'leərɪəm/ *n* (*pl* **-a**) solario *m*

sold /səʊld/ *see* **sell**

solder /'sɒldə(r)/ *n* soldadura *f*. ● *vt* soldar

soldier /'səʊldʒə(r)/ *n* soldado *m*. ● *vi*. ~ **on** (*fam*) perseverar

sole[1] /səʊl/ *n* (*of foot*) planta *f*; (*of shoe*) suela *f*

sole[2] /səʊl/ (*fish*) lenguado *m*

sole[3] /səʊl/ *a* único, solo. ~**ly** *adv* únicamente

solemn /'sɒləm/ *a* solemne. ~**ity** /sə'lemnətɪ/ *n* solemnidad *f*. ~**ly** *adv* solemnemente

solicit /sə'lɪsɪt/ *vt* solicitar. ● *vi* importunar

solicitor /sə'lɪsɪtə(r)/ *n* abogado *m*; (*notary*) notario *m*

solicitous /sə'lɪsɪtəs/ *a* solícito

solid /'sɒlɪd/ *a* sólido; ‹*gold etc*› macizo; (*unanimous*) unánime; ‹*meal*› sustancioso. ● *n* sólido *m*. ~**arity** /sɒlɪ'dærətɪ/ *n* solidaridad *f*. ~**ify** /sə'lɪdɪfaɪ/ *vt* solidificar. ● *vi* solidificarse. ~**ity** /sə'lɪdətɪ/ *n* solidez *f*. ~**ly** *adv* sólidamente. ~**s** *npl* alimentos *mpl* sólidos

soliloquy /sə'lɪləkwɪ/ *n* soliloquio *m*

solitaire /sɒlɪ'teə(r)/ *n* solitario *m*

solitary /'sɒlɪtrɪ/ *a* solitario

solitude /'sɒlɪtju:d/ *n* soledad *f*

solo /'səʊləʊ/ *n* (*pl* **-os**) (*mus*) solo *m*. ~**ist** *n* solista *m* & *f*

solstice /'sɒlstɪs/ *n* solsticio *m*

soluble /'sɒljʊbl/ *a* soluble

solution /sə'lu:ʃn/ *n* solución *f*

solvable *a* soluble

solve /sɒlv/ *vt* resolver

solvent /'sɒlvənt/ *a* & *n* solvente (*m*)

sombre /'sɒmbə(r)/ *a* sombrío

some /sʌm/ *a* alguno; (*a little*) un poco de. ~ **day** algún día. ~ **two hours** unas dos horas. **will you have ~ wine?** ¿quieres vino? ● *pron* algunos; (*a little*) un poco. ~ **of us** algunos de nosotros. **I want ~** quiero un poco. ● *adv* (*approximately*) unos. ~**body** /'sʌmbədɪ/ *pron* alguien. ● *n* personaje *m*. ~**how** /'sʌmhaʊ/ *adv* de algún modo. ~**how or other** de una manera u otra. ~**one** /'sʌmwʌn/ *pron* alguien. ● *n* personaje *m*

somersault /'sʌməsɔ:lt/ *n* salto *m* mortal. ● *vi* dar un salto mortal

some: ~**thing** /'sʌmθɪŋ/ *pron* algo *m*. ~**thing like** algo como; (*approximately*) cerca de. ~**time** /'sʌmtaɪm/ *a* ex. ● *adv* algún día; (*in past*) durante. ~**time last summer** *a* (durante) el verano pasado. ~**times** /'sʌmtaɪmz/ *adv* de vez en cuando, a veces. ~**what** /'sʌmwɒt/ *adv* algo, un poco. ~**where** /'sʌmweə(r)/ *adv* en alguna parte

son /sʌn/ *n* hijo *m*
sonata /səˈnɑːtə/ *n* sonata *f*
song /sɒŋ/ *n* canción *f*. **sell for a ~** vender muy barato. **~-book** *n* cancionero *m*
sonic /ˈsɒnɪk/ *a* sónico
son-in-law /ˈsʌnɪnlɔː/ *n* (*pl* **sons-in-law**) yerno *m*
sonnet /ˈsɒnɪt/ *n* soneto *m*
sonny /ˈsʌnɪ/ *n* (*fam*) hijo *m*
soon /suːn/ *adv* (**-er**, **-est**) pronto; (*in a short time*) dentro de poco; (*early*) temprano. **~ after** poco después. **~er or later** tarde o temprano. **as ~ as** en cuanto; **as ~ as possible** lo antes posible. **I would ~er not go** prefiero no ir
soot /sʊt/ *n* hollín *m*
sooth|e /suːð/ *vt* calmar. **~ing** *a* calmante
sooty /ˈsʊtɪ/ *a* cubierto de hollín
sophisticated /səˈfɪstɪkeɪtɪd/ *a* sofisticado; (*complex*) complejo
soporific /sɒpəˈrɪfɪk/ *a* soporífero
sopping /ˈsɒpɪŋ/ *a*. **~ (wet)** empapado
soppy /ˈsɒpɪ/ *a* (**-ier**, **-iest**) (*fam*) sentimental; (*silly, fam*) tonto
soprano /səˈprɑːnəʊ/ *n* (*pl* **-os**) (*voice*) soprano *m*; (*singer*) soprano *f*
sorcerer /ˈsɔːsərə(r)/ *n* hechicero *m*
sordid /ˈsɔːdɪd/ *a* sórdido
sore /ˈsɔː(r)/ *a* (**-er**, **-est**) que duele, dolorido; (*distressed*) penoso; (*vexed*) enojado. ● *n* llaga *f*. **~ly** /ˈsɔːlɪ/ *adv* gravemente. **~ throat** *n* dolor *m* de garganta. **I've got a ~ throat** me duele la garganta
sorrow /ˈsɒrəʊ/ *n* pena *f*, tristeza *f*. **~ful** *a* triste
sorry /ˈsɒrɪ/ *a* (**-ier**, **-ier**) arrepentido; (*wretched*) lamentable; (*sad*) triste. **be ~** sentirlo; (*repent*) arrepentirse. **be ~ for s.o.** (*pity*) compadecerse de uno. **~!** ¡perdón!, ¡perdone!
sort /sɔːt/ *n* clase *f*; (*person, fam*) tipo *m*. **be out of ~s** estar indispuesto; (*irritable*) estar de mal humor. ● *vt* clasificar. **~ out** (*choose*) escoger; (*separate*) separar; resolver ‹*problem*›
so-so /ˈsəʊsəʊ/ *a* & *adv* regular
soufflé /ˈsuːfleɪ/ *n* suflé *m*
sought /sɔːt/ *see* **seek**
soul /səʊl/ *n* alma *f*. **~ful** /ˈsəʊlfl/ *a* sentimental
sound[1] /saʊnd/ *n* sonido *m*; ruido *m*. ● *vt* sonar; (*test*) sondar. ● *vi* sonar; (*seem*) parecer (**as if** que)
sound[2] /saʊnd/ *a* (**-er**, **-est**) sano; ‹*argument etc*› lógico; (*secure*) seguro. **~ asleep** profundamente dormido
sound[3] /saʊnd/ (*strait*) estrecho *m*
sound barrier /ˈsaʊndbærɪə(r)/ *n* barrera *f* del sonido
soundly /ˈsaʊndlɪ/ *adv* sólidamente; (*asleep*) profundamente
sound: **~-proof** *a* insonorizado. **~-track** *n* banda *f* sonora
soup /suːp/ *n* sopa *f*. **in the ~** (*sl*) en apuros
sour /ˈsaʊə(r)/ *a* (**-er**, **-est**) agrio; ‹*cream, milk*› cortado. ● *vt* agriar. ● *vi* agriarse
source /sɔːs/ *n* fuente *f*
south /saʊθ/ *n* sur *m*. ● *a* del sur. ● *adv* hacia el sur. **S~ Africa** *n* Africa *f* del Sur. **S~ America** *n* América *f* (del Sur), Sudamérica *f*. **S~ American** *a* & *n* sudamericano (*m*). **~-east** *n* sudeste *m*. **~erly** /ˈsʌðəlɪ/ *a* sur; ‹*wind*› del sur. **~ern** /ˈsʌðən/ *a* del sur, meridional. **~erner** *n* meridional *m*. **~ward** *a* sur; ● *adv* hacia el sur. **~wards** *adv* hacia el sur. **~-west** *n* sudoeste *m*
souvenir /suːvəˈnɪə(r)/ *n* recuerdo *m*
sovereign /ˈsɒvrɪn/ *n* & *a* soberano (*m*). **~ty** *n* soberanía *f*
Soviet /ˈsəʊvɪət/ *a* (*history*) soviético. **the ~ Union** *n* la Unión *f* Soviética
sow[1] /səʊ/ *vt* (*pt* **sowed**, *pp* **sowed** *or* **sown**) sembrar
sow[2] /saʊ/ *n* cerda *f*
soya /ˈsɔɪə/ *n*. **~ bean** *n* soja *f*
spa /spɑː/ *n* balneario *m*
space /speɪs/ *n* espacio *m*; (*room*) sitio *m*; (*period*) período *m*. ● *a* ‹*research etc*› espacial. ● *vt* espaciar. **~ out** espaciar. **~craft** /ˈspeɪskrɑːft/ *n*, **~ship** *n* nave *f* espacial. **~suit** *n* traje *m* espacial
spacious /ˈspeɪʃəs/ *a* espacioso
spade /speɪd/ *n* pala *f*. **~s** *npl* (*cards*) picos *mpl*, picas *fpl*; (*in Spanish pack*) espadas *fpl*. **~work** /ˈspeɪdwɜːk/ *n* trabajo *m* preparatorio
spaghetti /spəˈgetɪ/ *n* espaguetis *mpl*
Spain /speɪn/ *n* España *f*
span[1] /spæn/ *n* (*of arch*) luz *f*; (*of time*) espacio *m*; (*of wings*) envergadura *f*. ● *vt* (*pt* **spanned**) extenderse sobre
span[2] /spæn/ *see* **spick**
Spaniard /ˈspænjəd/ *n* español *m*

spaniel /'spænjəl/ *n* perro *m* de aguas

Spanish /'spænɪʃ/ *a & n* español (*m*)

spank /spæŋk/ *vt* dar un azote a. **~ing** *n* azote *m*

spanner /'spænə(r)/ *n* llave *f*

spar /spɑ:(r)/ *vi* (*pt* **sparred**) entrenarse en el boxeo; (*argue*) disputar

spare /speə(r)/ *vt* salvar; (*do without*) prescindir de; (*afford to give*) dar; (*use with restraint*) escatimar. ● *a* de reserva; (*surplus*) sobrante; ‹*person*› enjuto; ‹*meal etc*› frugal. **~ (part)** *n* repuesto *m*. **~ time** *n* tiempo *m* libre. **~ tyre** *n* neumático *m* de repuesto

sparing /'speərɪŋ/ *a* frugal. **~ly** *adv* frugalmente

spark /spɑ:k/ *n* chispa *f*. ● *vt*. **~ off** (*initiate*) provocar. **~ing-plug** *n* (*auto*) bujía *f*

sparkl|e /'spɑ:kl/ *vi* centellear. ● *n* centelleo *m*. **~ing** *a* centelleante; ‹*wine*› espumoso

sparrow /'spærəʊ/ *n* gorrión *m*

sparse /spɑ:s/ *a* escaso; ‹*population*› poco denso. **~ly** *adv* escasamente

spartan /'spɑ:tn/ *a* espartano

spasm /'spæzəm/ *n* espasmo *m*; (*of cough*) acceso *m*. **~odic** /spæz'mɒdɪk/ *a* espasmódico

spastic /'spæstɪk/ *n* víctima *f* de parálisis cerebral

spat /spæt/ *see* **spit**

spate /speɪt/ *n* avalancha *f*

spatial /'speɪʃl/ *a* espacial

spatter /'spætə(r)/ *vt* salpicar (**with** de)

spatula /'spætjʊlə/ *n* espátula *f*

spawn /spɔ:n/ *n* hueva *f*. ● *vt* engendrar. ● *vi* desovar

speak /spi:k/ *vt/i* (*pt* **spoke**, *pp* **spoken**) hablar. **~ for** *vi* hablar en nombre de. **~ up** *vi* hablar más fuerte. **~er** /'spi:kə(r)/ *n* (*in public*) orador *m*; (*loudspeaker*) altavoz *m*. **be a Spanish ~er** hablar español

spear /spɪə(r)/ *n* lanza *f*. **~head** /'spɪəhed/ *n* punta *f* de lanza. ● *vt* (*lead*) encabezar. **~mint** /'spɪəmɪnt/ *n* menta *f* verde

spec /spek/ *n*. **on ~** (*fam*) por si acaso

special /'speʃl/ *a* especial. **~ist** /'speʃəlɪst/ *n* especialista *m & f*. **~ity** /-ɪ'ælətɪ/ *n* especialidad *f*. **~ization** /-'zeɪʃn/ *n* especialización *f*. **~ize** /'speʃəlaɪz/ *vi* especializarse. **~ized** *a* especializado. **~ty** *n* especialidad *f*. **~ly** *adv* especialmente

species /'spi:ʃi:z/ *n* especie *f*

specif|ic /spə'sɪfɪk/ *a* específico. **~ically** *adv* específicamente. **~ication** /-ɪ'keɪʃn/ *n* especificación *f*; (*details*) descripción *f*. **~y** /'spesɪfaɪ/ *vt* especificar

specimen /'spesɪmɪn/ *n* muestra *f*

speck /spek/ *n* manchita *f*; (*particle*) partícula *f*

speckled /'spekld/ *a* moteado

specs /speks/ *npl* (*fam*) gafas *fpl*, anteojos *mpl* (*LAm*)

spectac|le /'spektəkl/ *n* espectáculo *m*. **~les** *npl* gafas *fpl*, anteojos *mpl* (*LAm*). **~ular** /spek'tækjʊlə(r)/ *a* espectacular

spectator /spek'teɪtə(r)/ *n* espectador *m*

spectre /'spektə(r)/ *n* espectro *m*

spectrum /'spektrəm/ *n* (*pl* **-tra**) espectro *m*; (*of ideas*) gama *f*

speculat|e /'spekjʊleɪt/ *vi* especular. **~ion** /-'leɪʃn/ *n* especulación *f*. **~ive** /-lətɪv/ *a* especulativo. **~or** *n* especulador *m*

sped /sped/ *see* **speed**

speech /spi:tʃ/ *n* (*faculty*) habla *f*; (*address*) discurso *m*. **~less** *a* mudo

speed /spi:d/ *n* velocidad *f*; (*rapidity*) rapidez *f*; (*haste*) prisa *f*. ● *vi* (*pt* **sped**) apresurarse. (*pt* **speeded**) (*drive too fast*) ir a una velocidad excesiva. **~ up** *vt* acelerar. ● *vi* acelerarse. **~boat** /'spi:dbəʊt/ *n* lancha *f* motora. **~ily** *adv* rápidamente. **~ing** *n* exceso *m* de velocidad. **~ometer** /spi:'dɒmɪtə(r)/ *n* velocímetro *m*. **~way** /'spi:dweɪ/ *n* pista *f*; (*Amer*) autopista *f*. **~y** /'spi:dɪ/ *a* (**-ier**, **-iest**) rápido

spell[1] /spel/ *n* (*magic*) hechizo *m*

spell[2] /spel/ *vt/i* (*pt* **spelled** *or* **spelt**) escribir; (*mean*) significar. **~ out** *vt* deletrear; (*fig*) explicar. **~ing** *n* ortografía *f*

spell[3] /spel/ (*period*) período *m*

spellbound /'spelbaʊnd/ *a* hechizado

spelt /spelt/ *see* **spell**[2]

spend /spend/ *vt* (*pt* **spent**) gastar; pasar ‹*time etc*›; dedicar ‹*care etc*›. ● *vi* gastar dinero. **~thrift** /'spendθrɪft/ *n* derrochador *m*

spent /spent/ *see* **spend**

sperm /spɜ:m/ *n* (*pl* **sperms** *or* **sperm**) esperma *f*

spew /spju:/ *vt/i* vomitar

spher|e /sfɪə(r)/ *n* esfera *f*. **~ical** /'sferɪkl/ *a* esférico
sphinx /sfɪŋks/ *n* esfinge *f*
spice /spaɪs/ *n* especia *f*; (*fig*) sabor *m*
spick /spɪk/ *a*. **~ and span** impecable
spicy /'spaɪsɪ/ *a* picante
spider /'spaɪdə(r)/ *n* araña *f*
spik|e /spaɪk/ *n* (*of metal etc*) punta *f*. **~y** *a* puntiagudo; ‹*person*› quisquilloso
spill /spɪl/ *vt* (*pt* **spilled** *or* **spilt**) derramar. ● *vi* derramarse. **~ over** desbordarse
spin /spɪn/ *vt* (*pt* **spun**, *pres p* **spinning**) hacer girar; hilar ‹*wool etc*›. ● *vi* girar. ● *n* vuelta *f*; (*short drive*) paseo *m*
spinach /'spɪnɪdʒ/ *n* espinacas *fpl*
spinal /'spaɪnl/ *a* espinal. **~ cord** *n* médula *f* espinal
spindl|e /'spɪndl/ *n* (*for spinning*) huso *m*. **~y** *a* larguirucho
spin-drier /spɪn'draɪə(r)/ *n* secador *m* centrífugo
spine /spaɪn/ *n* columna *f* vertebral; (*of book*) lomo *m*. **~less** *a* (*fig*) sin carácter
spinning /'spɪnɪŋ/ *n* hilado *m*. **~-top** *n* trompa *f*, peonza *f*. **~-wheel** *n* rueca *f*
spin-off /'spɪnɒf/ *n* beneficio *m* incidental; (*by-product*) subproducto *m*
spinster /'spɪnstə(r)/ *n* soltera *f*; (*old maid, fam*) solterona *f*
spiral /'spaɪərəl/ *a* espiral, helicoidal. ● *n* hélice *f*. ● *vi* (*pt* **spiralled**) moverse en espiral. **~ staircase** *n* escalera *f* de caracol
spire /'spaɪə(r)/ *n* (*archit*) aguja *f*
spirit /'spɪrɪt/ *n* espíritu *m*; (*boldness*) valor *m*. **in low ~s** abatido. ● *vt*. **~ away** hacer desaparecer. **~ed** /'spɪrɪtɪd/ *a* animado, fogoso. **~-lamp** *n* lamparilla *f* de alcohol. **~-level** *n* nivel *m* de aire. **~s** *npl* (*drinks*) bebidas *fpl* alcohólicas
spiritual /'spɪrɪtjʊəl/ *a* espiritual. ● *n* canción *f* religiosa de los negros. **~ualism** /-zəm/ *n* espiritismo *m*. **~ualist** /'spɪrɪtjʊəlɪst/ *n* espiritista *m & f*
spit[1] /spɪt/ *vt* (*pt* **spat** *or* **spit**, *pres p* **spitting**) escupir. ● *vi* escupir; (*rain*) lloviznar. ● *n* esputo *m*; (*spittle*) saliva *f*
spit[2] /spɪt/ (*for roasting*) asador *m*
spite /spaɪt/ *n* rencor *m*. **in ~ of** a pesar de. ● *vt* fastidiar. **~ful** *a* rencoroso. **~fully** *adv* con rencor
spitting image /spɪtɪŋ'ɪmɪdʒ/ *n* vivo retrato *m*
spittle /spɪtl/ *n* saliva *f*
splash /splæʃ/ *vt* salpicar. ● *vi* esparcirse; ‹*person*› chapotear. ● *n* salpicadura *f*; (*sound*) chapoteo *m*; (*of colour*) mancha *f*; (*drop, fam*) gota *f*. **~ about** *vi* chapotear. **~ down** *vi* ‹*spacecraft*› amerizar
spleen /spli:n/ *n* bazo *m*; (*fig*) esplín *m*
splendid /'splendɪd/ *a* espléndido
splendour /'splendə(r)/ *n* esplendor *m*
splint /splɪnt/ *n* tablilla *f*
splinter /'splɪntə(r)/ *n* astilla *f*. ● *vi* astillarse. **~ group** *n* grupo *m* disidente
split /splɪt/ *vt* (*pt* **split**, *pres p* **splitting**) hender, rajar; (*tear*) rajar; (*divide*) dividir; (*share*) repartir. **~ one's sides** caerse de risa. ● *vi* partirse; (*divide*) dividirse. **~ on s.o.** (*sl*) traicionar. ● *n* hendidura *f*; (*tear*) desgarrón *m*; (*quarrel*) ruptura *f*; (*pol*) escisión *f*. **~ up** *vi* separarse. **~ second** *n* fracción *f* de segundo
splurge /splɜ:dʒ/ *vi* (*fam*) derrochar
splutter /'splʌtə(r)/ *vi* chisporrotear; ‹*person*› farfullar. ● *n* chisporroteo *m*; (*speech*) farfulla *f*
spoil /spɔɪl/ *vt* (*pt* **spoilt** *or* **spoiled**) estropear, echar a perder; (*ruin*) arruinar; (*indulge*) mimar. ● *n* botín *m*. **~s** *npl* botín *m*. **~-sport** *n* aguafiestas *m invar*
spoke[1] /spəʊk/ *see* **speak**
spoke[2] /spəʊk/ *n* (*of wheel*) radio *m*
spoken /spəʊkən/ *see* **speak**
spokesman /'spəʊksmən/ *n* (*pl* **-men**) portavoz *m*
spong|e /spʌndʒ/ *n* esponja *f*. ● *vt* limpiar con una esponja. ● *vi*. **~e on** vivir a costa de. **~e-cake** *n* bizcocho *m*. **~er** /-ə(r)/ *n* gorrón *m*. **~y** *a* esponjoso
sponsor /'spɒnsə(r)/ *n* patrocinador *m*; (*surety*) garante *m*. ● *vt* patrocinar. **~ship** *n* patrocinio *m*
spontane|ity /spɒntə'neɪɪtɪ/ *n* espontaneidad *f*. **~ous** /spɒn'teɪnjəs/ *a* espontáneo. **~ously** *adv* espontáneamente
spoof /spu:f/ *n* (*sl*) parodia *f*
spooky /'spu:kɪ/ *a* (**-ier**, **-iest**) (*fam*) escalofriante

spool /spu:l/ *n* carrete *m*; (*of sewing-machine*) canilla *f*

spoon /spu:n/ *n* cuchara *f*. **~-fed** *a* (*fig*) mimado. **~-feed** *vt* (*pt* **-fed**) dar de comer con cuchara. **~ful** *n* (*pl* **-fuls**) cucharada *f*

sporadic /spəˈrædɪk/ *a* esporádico

sport /spɔ:t/ *n* deporte *m*; (*amusement*) pasatiempo *m*; (*person, fam*) persona *f* alegre, buen chico *m*, buena chica *f*. **be a good ~** ser buen perdedor. ● *vt* lucir. **~ing** *a* deportivo. **~ing chance** *n* probabilidad *f* de éxito. **~s car** *n* coche *m* deportivo. **~s coat** *n* chaqueta *f* de sport. **~sman** /ˈspɔ:tsmən/ *n*, (*pl* **-men**), **~swoman** /ˈspɔ:tswʊmən/ *n* (*pl* **-women**) deportista *m & f*

spot /spɒt/ *n* mancha *f*; (*pimple*) grano *m*; (*place*) lugar *m*; (*in pattern*) punto *m*; (*drop*) gota *f*; (*a little, fam*) poquito *m*. **in a ~** (*fam*) en un apuro. **on the ~** en el lugar; (*without delay*) en el acto. ● *vt* (*pt* **spotted**) manchar; (*notice, fam*) observar, ver. **~ check** *n* control *m* hecho al azar. **~less** *a* inmaculado. **~light** /ˈspɒtlaɪt/ *n* reflector *m*. **~ted** *a* moteado; ‹*cloth*› a puntos. **~ty** *a* (**-ier**, **-iest**) manchado; ‹*skin*› con granos

spouse /spaʊz/ *n* cónyuge *m & f*

spout /spaʊt/ *n* pico *m*; (*jet*) chorro *m*. **up the ~** (*ruined, sl*) perdido. ● *vi* chorrear

sprain /spreɪn/ *vt* torcer. ● *n* torcedura *f*

sprang /spræŋ/ *see* **spring**

sprat /spræt/ *n* espadín *m*

sprawl /sprɔ:l/ *vi* ‹*person*› repanchigarse; ‹*city etc*› extenderse

spray /spreɪ/ *n* (*of flowers*) ramo *m*; (*water*) rociada *f*; (*from sea*) espuma *f*; (*device*) pulverizador *m*. ● *vt* rociar. **~-gun** *n* pistola *f* pulverizadora

spread /spred/ *vt* (*pt* **spread**) (*stretch, extend*) extender; untar ‹*jam etc*›; difundir ‹*idea, news*›. ● *vi* extenderse; ‹*disease*› propagarse; ‹*idea, news*› difundirse. ● *n* extensión *f*; (*paste*) pasta *f*; (*of disease*) propagación *f*; (*feast, fam*) comilona *f*. **~-eagled** *a* con los brazos y piernas extendidos

spree /spri:/ *n*. **go on a ~** (*have fun, fam*) ir de juerga

sprig /sprɪg/ *n* ramito *m*

sprightly /ˈspraɪtlɪ/ *a* (**-ier**, **-iest**) vivo

spring /sprɪŋ/ *n* (*season*) primavera *f*; (*device*) muelle *m*; (*elasticity*) elasticidad *f*; (*water*) manantial *m*. ● *a* de primavera. ● *vt* (*pt* **sprang**, *pp* **sprung**) hacer inesperadamente. ● *vi* saltar; (*issue*) brotar. **~ from** *vi* provenir de. **~ up** *vi* surgir. **~-board** *n* trampolín *m*. **~time** *n* primavera *f*. **~y** *a* (**-ier**, **-iest**) elástico

sprinkl|e /ˈsprɪŋkl/ *vt* salpicar; (*with liquid*) rociar. ● *n* salpicadura *f*; (*of liquid*) rociada *f*. **~ed with** salpicado de. **~er** /-ə(r)/ *n* regadera *f*. **~ing** /ˈsprɪŋklɪŋ/ *n* (*fig, amount*) poco *m*

sprint /sprɪnt/ *n* carrera *f*. ● *vi* correr. **~er** *n* corredor *m*

sprite /spraɪt/ *n* duende *m*, hada *f*

sprout /spraʊt/ *vi* brotar. ● *n* brote *m*. **(Brussels) ~s** *npl* coles *fpl* de Bruselas

spruce /spru:s/ *a* elegante

sprung /sprʌŋ/ *see* **spring**. ● *a* de muelles

spry /spraɪ/ *a* (**spryer**, **spryest**) vivo

spud /spʌd/ *n* (*sl*) patata *f*, papa *f* (*LAm*)

spun /spʌn/ *see* **spin**

spur /spɜ:(r)/ *n* espuela *f*; (*stimulus*) estímulo *m*. **on the ~ of the moment** impulsivamente. ● *vt* (*pt* **spurred**). **~ (on)** espolear; (*fig*) estimular

spurious /ˈspjʊərɪəs/ *a* falso. **~ly** *adv* falsamente

spurn /spɜ:n/ *vt* despreciar; (*reject*) rechazar

spurt /spɜ:t/ *vi* chorrear; (*make sudden effort*) hacer un esfuerzo repentino. ● *n* chorro *m*; (*effort*) esfuerzo *m* repentino

spy /spaɪ/ *n* espía *m & f*. ● *vt* divisar. ● *vi* espiar. **~ out** *vt* reconocer. **~ing** *n* espionaje *m*

squabble /ˈskwɒbl/ *n* riña *f*. ● *vi* reñir

squad /skwɒd/ *n* (*mil*) pelotón *m*; (*of police*) brigada *f*; (*sport*) equipo *m*

squadron /ˈskwɒdrən/ *n* (*mil*) escuadrón *m*; (*naut, aviat*) escuadrilla *f*

squalid /ˈskwɒlɪd/ *a* asqueroso; (*wretched*) miserable

squall /skwɔ:l/ *n* turbión *m*. ● *vi* chillar. **~y** *a* borrascoso

squalor /ˈskwɒlə(r)/ *n* miseria *f*

squander /ˈskwɒndə(r)/ *vt* derrochar

square /skweə(r)/ *n* cuadrado *m*; (*open space in town*) plaza *f*; (*for drawing*) escuadra *f*. ● *a* cuadrado; (*not owing*) sin deudas, iguales; (*honest*) honrado; ‹*meal*› satisfactorio; (*old-fashioned, sl*) chapado a la antigua. **all ~** iguales. ● *vt* (*settle*) arreglar; (*math*) cuadrar. ● *vi* (*agree*) cuadrar. **~ up to** enfrentarse con. **~ly** *adv* directamente

squash /skwɒʃ/ *vt* aplastar; (*suppress*) suprimir. ● *n* apiñamiento *m*; (*drink*) zumo *m*; (*sport*) squash *m*. **~y** *a* blando

squat /skwɒt/ *vi* (*pt* **squatted**) ponerse en cuclillas; (*occupy illegally*) ocupar sin derecho. ● *n* casa *f* ocupada sin derecho. ● *a* (*dumpy*) achaparrado. **~ter** /-ə(r)/ *n* ocupante *m* & *f* ilegal

squawk /skwɔ:k/ *n* graznido *m*. ● *vi* graznar

squeak /skwi:k/ *n* chillido *m*; (*of door etc*) chirrido *m*. ● *vi* chillar; ‹*door etc*› chirriar. **~y** *a* chirriador

squeal /skwi:l/ *n* chillido *m*. ● *vi* chillar. **~ on** (*inform on, sl*) denunciar

squeamish /'skwi:mɪʃ/ *a* delicado; (*scrupulous*) escrupuloso. **be ~ about snakes** tener horror a las serpientes

squeeze /skwi:z/ *vt* apretar; exprimir ‹*lemon etc*›; (*extort*) extorsionar (**from** de). ● *vi* (*force one's way*) abrirse paso. ● *n* estrujón *m*; (*of hand*) apretón *m*. **credit ~** *n* restricción *f* de crédito

squelch /skweltʃ/ *vi* chapotear. ● *n* chapoteo *m*

squib /skwɪb/ *n* (*firework*) buscapiés *m invar*

squid /skwɪd/ *n* calamar *m*

squiggle /'skwɪgl/ *n* garabato *m*

squint /skwɪnt/ *vi* ser bizco; (*look sideways*) mirar de soslayo. ● *n* estrabismo *m*

squire /'skwaɪə(r)/ *n* terrateniente *m*

squirm /skwɜ:m/ *vi* retorcerse

squirrel /'skwɪrəl/ *n* ardilla *f*

squirt /skwɜ:t/ *vt* arrojar a chorros. ● *vi* salir a chorros. ● *n* chorro *m*

St *abbr* (*saint*) /sənt/ S, San(to); (*street*) C/, Calle *f*

stab /stæb/ *vt* (*pt* **stabbed**) apuñalar. ● *n* puñalada *f*; (*pain*) punzada *f*; (*attempt, fam*) tentativa *f*

stabili|ty /stə'bɪlətɪ/ *n* estabilidad *f*. **~ze** /'steɪbɪlaɪz/ *vt* estabilizar. **~zer** /-ə(r)/ *n* estabilizador *m*

stable[1] /'steɪbl/ *a* (**-er**, **-est**) estable

stable[2] /'steɪbl/ *n* cuadra *f*. ● *vt* poner en una cuadra. **~-boy** *n* mozo *m* de cuadra

stack /stæk/ *n* montón *m*. ● *vt* amontonar

stadium /'steɪdjəm/ *n* estadio *m*

staff /stɑ:f/ *n* (*stick*) palo *m*; (*employees*) personal *m*; (*mil*) estado *m* mayor; (*in school*) profesorado *m*. ● *vt* proveer de personal

stag /stæg/ *n* ciervo *m*. **~-party** *n* reunión *f* de hombres, fiesta *f* de despedida de soltero

stage /steɪdʒ/ *n* (*in theatre*) escena *f*; (*phase*) etapa *f*; (*platform*) plataforma *f*. **go on the ~** hacerse actor. ● *vt* representar; (*arrange*) organizar. **~-coach** *n* (*hist*) diligencia *f*. **~ fright** *n* miedo *m* al público. **~-manager** *n* director *m* de escena. **~ whisper** *n* aparte *m*

stagger /'stægə(r)/ *vi* tambalearse. ● *vt* asombrar; escalonar ‹*holidays etc*›. ● *n* tambaleo *m*. **~ing** *a* asombroso

stagna|nt /'stægnənt/ *a* estancado. **~te** /stæg'neɪt/ *vi* estancarse. **~tion** /-ʃn/ *n* estancamiento *m*

staid /steɪd/ *a* serio, formal

stain /steɪn/ *vt* manchar; (*colour*) teñir. ● *n* mancha *f*; (*liquid*) tinte *m*. **~ed glass window** *n* vidriera *f* de colores. **~less** /'steɪnlɪs/ *a* inmaculado. **~less steel** *n* acero *m* inoxidable. **~ remover** *n* quitamanchas *m invar*

stair /steə(r)/ *n* escalón *m*. **~s** *npl* escalera *f*. **flight of ~s** tramo *m* de escalera. **~case** /'steəkeɪs/ *n*, **~way** *n* escalera *f*

stake /steɪk/ *n* estaca *f*; (*for execution*) hoguera *f*; (*wager*) apuesta *f*; (*com*) intereses *mpl*. **at ~** en juego. ● *vt* estacar; (*wager*) apostar. **~ a claim** reclamar

stalactite /'stæləktaɪt/ *n* estalactita *f*

stalagmite /'stæləgmaɪt/ *n* estalagmita *f*

stale /steɪl/ *a* (**-er**, **-est**) no fresco; ‹*bread*› duro; ‹*smell*› viciado; ‹*news*› viejo; (*uninteresting*) gastado. **~mate** /'steɪlmeɪt/ *n* (*chess*) ahogado *m*; (*deadlock*) punto *m* muerto

stalk[1] /stɔ:k/ *n* tallo *m*

stalk[2] /stɔ:k/ *vi* andar majestuosamente. ● *vt* seguir; ‹*animal*› acechar

stall[1] /stɔ:l/ *n* (*stable*) cuadra *f*; (*in stable*) casilla *f*; (*in theatre*) butaca *f*; (*in market*) puesto *m*; (*kiosk*) quiosco *m*

stall[2] /stɔ:l/ *vt* parar ‹*engine*›. ● *vi* ‹*engine*› pararse; (*fig*) andar con rodeos

stallion /'stæljən/ *n* semental *m*

stalwart /'stɔ:lwət/ *n* partidario *m* leal

stamina /'stæmɪnə/ *n* resistencia *f*

stammer /'stæmə(r)/ *vi* tartamudear. ● *n* tartamudeo *m*

stamp /stæmp/ *vt* (*with feet*) patear; (*press*) estampar; poner un sello en ‹*envelope*›; (*with rubber stamp*) sellar; (*fig*) señalar. ● *vi* patear. ● *n* sello *m*; (*with foot*) patada *f*; (*mark*) marca *f*, señal *f*. ~ **out** (*fig*) acabar con

stampede /stæm'pi:d/ *n* desbandada *f*; (*fam*) pánico *m*. ● *vi* huir en desorden

stance /stɑ:ns/ *n* postura *f*

stand /stænd/ *vi* (*pt* **stood**) estar de pie; (*rise*) ponerse de pie; (*be*) encontrarse; (*stay firm*) permanecer; (*pol*) presentarse como candidato (**for** en). ~ **to reason** ser lógico. ● *vt* (*endure*) soportar; (*place*) poner; (*offer*) ofrecer. ~ **a chance** tener una posibilidad. ~ **one's ground** mantenerse firme. **I'll ~ you a drink** te invito a una copa.● *n* posición *f*, postura *f*; (*mil*) resistencia *f*; (*for lamp etc*) pie *m*, sostén *m*; (*at market*) puesto *m*; (*booth*) quiosco *m*; (*sport*) tribuna *f*. ~ **around** no hacer nada. ~ **back** retroceder. ~ **by** *vi* estar preparado. ● *vt* (*support*) apoyar. ~ **down** *vi* retirarse. ~ **for** *vt* representar. ~ **in for** suplir a. ~ **out** destacarse. ~ **up** *vi* ponerse de pie. ~ **up for** defender. ~ **up to** *vt* resistir a

standard /'stændəd/ *n* norma *f*; (*level*) nivel *m*; (*flag*) estandarte *m*. ● *a* normal, corriente. **~ize** *vt* uniformar. ~ **lamp** *n* lámpara *f* de pie. **~s** *npl* valores *mpl*

stand: **~-by** *n* (*person*) reserva *f*; (*at airport*) lista *f* de espera. **~-in** *n* suplente *m & f*. **~ing** /'stændɪŋ/ *a* de pie; (*upright*) derecho. ● *n* posición *f*; (*duration*) duración *f*. **~-offish** *a* (*fam*) frío. **~point** /'stændpɔɪnt/ *n* punto *m* de vista. **~still** /'stændstɪl/ *n*. **at a ~still** parado. **come to a ~still** pararse

stank /stæŋk/ *see* **stink**

staple[1] /'steɪpl/ *a* principal

staple[2] /'steɪpl/ *n* grapa *f*. ● *vt* sujetar con una grapa. **~r** /-ə(r)/ *n* grapadora *f*

star /stɑ:/ *n* (*incl cinema, theatre*) estrella *f*; (*asterisk*) asterisco *m*. ● *vi* (*pt* **starred**) ser el protagonista

starboard /'stɑ:bəd/ *n* estribor *m*

starch /stɑ:tʃ/ *n* almidón *m*; (*in food*) fécula *f*. ● *vt* almidonar. **~y** *a* almidonado; ‹*food*› feculento; (*fig*) formal

stardom /'stɑ:dəm/ *n* estrellato *m*

stare /steə(r)/ *n* mirada *f* fija. ● *vi*. ~ **at** mirar fijamente

starfish /'stɑ:fɪʃ/ *n* estrella *f* de mar

stark /stɑ:k/ *a* (**-er**, **-est**) rígido; (*utter*) completo. ● *adv* completamente

starlight /'stɑ:laɪt/ *n* luz *f* de las estrellas

starling /'stɑ:lɪŋ/ *n* estornino *m*

starry /'stɑ:rɪ/ *a* estrellado. **~-eyed** *a* (*fam*) ingenuo, idealista

start /stɑ:t/ *vt* empezar; poner en marcha ‹*machine*›; (*cause*) provocar. ● *vi* empezar; (*jump*) sobresaltarse; (*leave*) partir; ‹*car etc*› arrancar. ● *n* principio *m*; (*leaving*) salida *f*; (*sport*) ventaja *f*; (*jump*) susto *m*. **~er** *n* (*sport*) participante *m & f*; (*auto*) motor *m* de arranque; (*culin*) primer plato *m*. **~ing-point** *n* punto *m* de partida

startle /'stɑ:tl/ *vt* asustar

starv|ation /stɑ:'veɪʃn/ *n* hambre *f*. **~e** /stɑ:v/ *vt* hacer morir de hambre; (*deprive*) privar. ● *vi* morir de hambre

stash /stæʃ/ *vt* (*sl*) esconder

state /steɪt/ *n* estado *m*; (*grand style*) pompa *f*. **S~** *n* Estado *m*. **be in a ~** estar agitado. ● *vt* declarar; expresar ‹*views*›; (*fix*) fijar. ● *a* del Estado; (*schol*) público; (*with ceremony*) de gala. **~less** *a* sin patria

stately /'steɪtlɪ/ *a* (**-ier**, **-iest**) majestuoso

statement /'steɪtmənt/ *n* declaración *f*; (*account*) informe *m*. **bank ~** *n* estado *m* de cuenta

stateroom /'steɪtrʊm/ *n* (*on ship*) camarote *m*

statesman /'steɪtsmən/ *n* (*pl* **-men**) estadista *m*

static /'stætɪk/ *a* inmóvil. **~s** *n* estática *f*; (*rad, TV*) parásitos *mpl* atmosféricos, interferencias *fpl*
station /'steɪʃn/ *n* estación *f*; (*status*) posición *f* social. • *vt* colocar; (*mil*) estacionar
stationary /'steɪʃənərɪ/ *a* estacionario
stationer /'steɪʃənə(r)/ *n* papelero *m*. **~'s (shop)** *n* papelería *f*. **~y** *n* artículos *mpl* de escritorio
station-wagon /'steɪʃnwægən/ *n* furgoneta *f*
statistic /stə'tɪstɪk/ *n* estadística *f*. **~al** /stə'tɪstɪkl/ *a* estadístico. **~s** /stə'tɪstɪks/ *n* (*science*) estadística *f*
statue /'stætʃu:/ *n* estatua *f*. **~sque** /-ʊ'esk/ *a* escultural. **~tte** /-ʊ'et/ *n* figurilla *f*
stature /'stætʃə(r)/ *n* talla *f*, estatura *f*
status /'steɪtəs/ *n* posición *f* social; (*prestige*) categoría *f*; (*jurid*) estado *m*
statut|e /'stætʃu:t/ *n* estatuto *m*. **~ory** /-ʊtrɪ/ *a* estatutario
staunch /stɔ:nʃ/ *a* (**-er**, **-est**) leal. **~ly** *adv* lealmente
stave /'steɪv/ *n* (*mus*) pentagrama *m*. • *vt*. **~ off** evitar
stay /steɪ/ *n* soporte *m*, sostén *m*; (*of time*) estancia *f*; (*jurid*) suspensión *f*. • *vi* quedar; (*spend time*) detenerse; (*reside*) alojarse. • *vt* matar ‹*hunger*›. **~ the course** terminar. **~ in** quedar en casa. **~ put** mantenerse firme. **~ up** no acostarse. **~ing-power** *n* resistencia *f*
stays /steɪz/ *npl* (*old use*) corsé *m*
stead /sted/ *n*. **in s.o.'s ~** en lugar de uno. **stand s.o. in good ~** ser útil a uno
steadfast /'stedfɑ:st/ *a* firme
stead|ily /'stedɪlɪ/ *adv* firmemente; (*regularly*) regularmente. **~y** /'stedɪ/ *a* (**-ier**, **-iest**) firme; (*regular*) regular; (*dependable*) serio
steak /steɪk/ *n* filete *m*
steal /sti:l/ *vt* (*pt* **stole**, *pp* **stolen**) robar. **~ the show** llevarse los aplausos. **~ in** *vi* entrar a hurtadillas. **~ out** *vi* salir a hurtadillas
stealth /stelθ/ *n*. **by ~** sigilosamente. **~y** *a* sigiloso
steam /sti:m/ *n* vapor *m*; (*energy*) energía *f*. • *vt* (*cook*) cocer al vapor; empañar ‹*window*›. • *vi* echar vapor. **~ ahead** (*fam*) hacer progresos. **~ up** *vi* ‹*glass*› empañar. **~-engine** *n* máquina *f* de vapor. **~er** /'sti:mə(r)/ *n* (*ship*) barco *m* de vapor. **~-roller** /'sti:mrəʊlə(r)/ *n* apisonadora *f*. **~y** *a* húmedo
steel /sti:l/ *n* acero *m*. • *vt*. **~ o.s.** fortalecerse. **~ industry** *n* industria *f* siderúrgica. **~ wool** *n* estropajo *m* de acero. **~y** *a* acerado; (*fig*) duro, inflexible
steep /sti:p/ • *a* (**-er**, **-est**) escarpado; ‹*price*› (*fam*) exorbitante. • *vt* (*soak*) remojar. **~ed in** (*fig*) empapado de
steeple /'sti:pl/ *n* aguja *f*, campanario *m*. **~chase** /'sti:pltʃeɪs/ *n* carrera *f* de obstáculos
steep: **~ly** *adv* de modo empinado. **~ness** *n* lo escarpado
steer /stɪə(r)/ *vt* guiar; gobernar ‹*ship*›. • *vi* (*in ship*) gobernar. **~ clear of** evitar. **~ing** *n* (*auto*) dirección *f*. **~ing-wheel** *n* volante *m*
stem /stem/ *n* tallo *m*; (*of glass*) pie *m*; (*of word*) raíz *f*; (*of ship*) roda *f*. • *vt* (*pt* **stemmed**) detener. • *vi*. **~ from** provenir de
stench /stentʃ/ *n* hedor *m*
stencil /'stensl/ *n* plantilla *f*; (*for typing*) cliché *m*. • *vt* (*pt* **stencilled**) estarcir
stenographer /ste'nɒgrəfə(r)/ *n* (*Amer*) estenógrafo *m*
step /step/ *vi* (*pt* **stepped**) ir. **~ down** retirarse. **~ in** entrar; (*fig*) intervenir. **~ up** *vt* aumentar. • *n* paso *m*; (*surface*) escalón *m*; (*fig*) medida *f*. **in ~** (*fig*) de acuerdo con. **out of ~** (*fig*) en desacuerdo con. **~brother** /'stepbrʌðə(r)/ *n* hermanastro *m*. **~daughter** *n* hijastra *f*. **~-father** *n* padrastro *m*. **~-ladder** *n* escalera *f* de tijeras. **~mother** *n* madrastra *f*. **~ping-stone** /'stepɪŋstəʊn/ *n* pasadera *f*; (*fig*) escalón *m*. **~sister** *n* hermanastra *f*. **~son** *n* hijastro *m*
stereo /'sterɪəʊ/ *n* (*pl* **-os**) cadena *f* estereofónica. • *a* estereofónico. **~phonic** /sterɪəʊ'fɒnɪk/ *a* estereofónico. **~type** /'sterɪəʊtaɪp/ *n* estereotipo *m*. **~typed** *a* estereotipado
steril|e /'steraɪl/ *a* estéril. **~ity** /stə'rɪlətɪ/ *n* esterilidad *f*. **~ization** /-'zeɪʃn/ *n* esterilización *f*. **~ize** /'sterɪlaɪz/ *vt* esterilizar
sterling /'stɜ:lɪŋ/ *n* libras *fpl* esterlinas. • *a* ‹*pound*› esterlina; (*fig*) excelente. **~ silver** *n* plata *f* de ley

stern[1] /stɜːn/ *n* (*of boat*) popa *f*
stern[2] /stɜːn/ *a* (**-er, -est**) severo. **~ly** *adv* severamente
stethoscope /ˈsteθəskəʊp/ *n* estetoscopio *m*
stew /stjuː/ *vt/i* guisar. ● *n* guisado *m*. **in a ~** (*fam*) en un apuro
steward /stjʊəd/ *n* administrador *m*; (*on ship, aircraft*) camarero *m*. **~ess** /-ˈdes/ *n* camarera *f*; (*on aircraft*) azafata *f*
stick /stɪk/ *n* palo *m*; (*for walking*) bastón *m*; (*of celery etc*) tallo *m*. ● *vt* (*pt* **stuck**) (*glue*) pegar; (*put, fam*) poner; (*thrust*) clavar; (*endure, sl*) soportar. ● *vi* pegarse; (*remain, fam*) quedarse; (*jam*) bloquearse. **~ at** (*fam*) perseverar en. **~ out** sobresalir; (*catch the eye, fam*) resaltar. **~ to** aferrarse a; cumplir ‹*promise*›. **~ up for** (*fam*) defender. **~er** /ˈstɪkə(r)/ *n* pegatina *f*. **~ing-plaster** *n* esparadrapo *m*. **~-in-the-mud** *n* persona *f* chapada a la antigua
stickler /ˈstɪklə(r)/ *n*. **be a ~ for** insistir en
sticky /ˈstɪkɪ/ *a* (**-ier, -iest**) pegajoso; ‹*label*› engomado; (*sl*) difícil
stiff /stɪf/ *a* (**-er, -est**) rígido; (*difficult*) difícil; ‹*manner*› estirado; ‹*drink*› fuerte; ‹*price*› subido; ‹*joint*› tieso; ‹*muscle*› con agujetas. **~en** /ˈstɪfn/ *vt* poner tieso. **~ly** *adv* rígidamente. **~ neck** *n* tortícolis *f*. **~ness** *n* rigidez *f*
stifl|e /ˈstaɪfl/ *vt* sofocar. **~ing** *a* sofocante
stigma /ˈstɪgmə/ *n* (*pl* **-as**) estigma *m*. (*pl* **stigmata** /ˈstɪgmətə/) (*relig*) estigma *m*. **~tize** *vt* estigmatizar
stile /staɪl/ *n* portillo *m* con escalones
stiletto /stɪˈletəʊ/ *n* (*pl* **-os**) estilete *m*. **~ heels** *npl* tacones *mpl* aguja
still[1] /stɪl/ *a* inmóvil; (*peaceful*) tranquilo; ‹*drink*› sin gas. ● *n* silencio *m*. ● *adv* todavía; (*nevertheless*) sin embargo
still[2] /stɪl/ (*apparatus*) alambique *m*
still: **~born** *a* nacido muerto. **~ life** *n* (*pl* **-s**) bodegón *m*. **~ness** *n* tranquilidad *f*
stilted /ˈstɪltɪd/ *a* artificial
stilts /stɪlts/ *npl* zancos *mpl*
stimul|ant /ˈstɪmjʊlənt/ *n* estimulante *m*. **~ate** /ˈstɪmjʊleɪt/ *vt* estimular. **~ation** /-ˈleɪʃn/ *n* estímulo *m*. **~us** /ˈstɪmjʊləs/ *n* (*pl* **-li** /-laɪ/) estímulo *m*
sting /stɪŋ/ *n* picadura *f*; (*organ*) aguijón *m*. ● *vt/i* (*pt* **stung**) picar
sting|iness /ˈstɪndʒɪnɪs/ *n* tacañería *f*. **~y** /ˈstɪndʒɪ/ *a* (**-ier, -iest**) tacaño
stink /stɪŋk/ *n* hedor *m*. ● *vi* (*pt* **stank** *or* **stunk**, *pp* **stunk**) oler mal. ● *vt*. **~ out** apestar ‹*room*›; ahuyentar ‹*person*›. **~er** /-ə(r)/ *n* (*sl*) problema *m* difícil; (*person*) mal bicho *m*
stint /stɪnt/ *n* (*work*) trabajo *m*. ● *vi*. **~ on** escatimar
stipple /ˈstɪpl/ *vt* puntear
stipulat|e /ˈstɪpjʊleɪt/ *vt/i* estipular. **~ion** /-ˈleɪʃn/ *n* estipulación *f*
stir /stɜː(r)/ *vt* (*pt* **stirred**) remover, agitar; (*mix*) mezclar; (*stimulate*) estimular. ● *vi* moverse. ● *n* agitación *f*; (*commotion*) conmoción *f*
stirrup /ˈstɪrəp/ *n* estribo *m*
stitch /stɪtʃ/ *n* (*in sewing*) puntada *f*; (*in knitting*) punto *m*; (*pain*) dolor *m* de costado; (*med*) punto *m* de sutura. **be in ~es** (*fam*) desternillarse de risa. ● *vt* coser
stoat /stəʊt/ *n* armiño *m*
stock /stɒk/ *n* (*com, supplies*) existencias *fpl*; (*com, variety*) surtido *m*; (*livestock*) ganado *m*; (*lineage*) linaje *m*; (*finance*) acciones *fpl*; (*culin*) caldo *m*; (*plant*) alhelí *m*. **out of ~** agotado. **take ~** (*fig*) evaluar. ● *a* corriente; (*fig*) trillado. ● *vt* abastecer (**with** de). ● *vi*. **~ up** abastecerse (**with** de). **~broker** /ˈstɒkbrəʊkə(r)/ *n* corredor *m* de bolsa. **S~ Exchange** *n* bolsa *f*. **well-~ed** *a* bien provisto
stocking /ˈstɒkɪŋ/ *n* media *f*
stock: **~-in-trade** /ˈstɒkɪntreɪd/ *n* existencias *fpl*. **~ist** /ˈstɒkɪst/ *n* distribuidor *m*. **~pile** /ˈstɒkpaɪl/ *n* reservas *fpl*. ● *vt* acumular. **~-still** *a* inmóvil. **~-taking** *n* (*com*) inventario *m*
stocky /ˈstɒkɪ/ *a* (**-ier, -iest**) achaparrado
stodg|e /stɒdʒ/ *n* (*fam*) comida *f* pesada. **~y** *a* pesado
stoic /ˈstəʊɪk/ *n* estoico. **~al** *a* estoico. **~ally** *adv* estoicamente. **~ism** /-sɪzəm/ *n* estoicismo *m*
stoke /stəʊk/ *vt* alimentar. **~r** /ˈstəʊkə(r)/ *n* fogonero *m*
stole[1] /stəʊl/ *see* **steal**
stole[2] /stəʊl/ *n* estola *f*
stolen /ˈstəʊlən/ *see* **steal**
stolid /ˈstɒlɪd/ *a* impasible. **~ly** *adv* impasiblemente

stomach /ˈstʌmək/ *n* estómago *m*. ● *vt* soportar. **~-ache** *n* dolor *m* de estómago

ston|e /stəʊn/ *n* piedra *f*; (*med*) cálculo *m*; (*in fruit*) hueso *m*; (*weight, pl* **stone**) peso *m* de 14 libras (= *6,348 kg*). ● *a* de piedra. ● *vt* apedrear; deshuesar ‹*fruit*›. **~e-deaf** *a* sordo como una tapia. **~emason** /ˈstəʊnmeɪsn/ *n* albañil *m*. **~ework** /ˈstəʊnwɜ:k/ *n* cantería *f*. **~y** *a* pedregoso; (*like stone*) pétreo

stood /stʊd/ *see* **stand**

stooge /stu:dʒ/ *n* (*in theatre*) compañero *m*; (*underling*) lacayo *m*

stool /stu:l/ *n* taburete *m*

stoop /stu:p/ *vi* inclinarse; (*fig*) rebajarse. ● *n*. **have a ~** ser cargado de espaldas

stop /stɒp/ *vt* (*pt* **stopped**) parar; (*cease*) terminar; tapar ‹*a leak etc*›; (*prevent*) impedir; (*interrupt*) interrumpir. ● *vi* pararse; (*stay, fam*) quedarse. ● *n* (*bus etc*) parada *f*; (*gram*) punto *m*; (*mec*) tope *m*. **~ dead** *vi* pararse en seco. **~cock** /ˈstɒpkɒk/ *n* llave *f* de paso. **~gap** /ˈstɒpgæp/ *n* remedio *m* provisional. **~(-over)** *n* escala *f*. **~page** /ˈstɒpɪdʒ/ *n* parada *f*; (*of work*) paro *m*; (*interruption*) interrupción *f*. **~per** /ˈstɒpə(r)/ *n* tapón *m*. **~-press** *n* noticias *fpl* de última hora. **~ light** *n* luz *f* de freno. **~-watch** *n* cronómetro *m*

storage /ˈstɔ:rɪdʒ/ *n* almacenamiento *m*. **~ heater** *n* acumulador *m*. **in cold ~** almacenaje *m* frigorífico

store /stɔ:(r)/ *n* provisión *f*; (*shop, depot*) almacén *m*; (*fig*) reserva *f*. **in ~** en reserva. **set ~ by** dar importancia a. ● *vt* (*for future*) poner en reserva; (*in warehouse*) almacenar. **~ up** *vt* acumular

storeroom /ˈstɔ:ru:m/ *n* despensa *f*

storey /ˈstɔ:rɪ/ *n* (*pl* **-eys**) piso *m*

stork /stɔ:k/ *n* cigüeña *f*

storm /stɔ:m/ *n* tempestad *f*; (*mil*) asalto *m*. ● *vi* rabiar. ● *vt* (*mil*) asaltar. **~y** *a* tempestuoso

story /ˈstɔ:rɪ/ *n* historia *f*; (*in newspaper*) artículo *m*; (*fam*) mentira *f*, cuento *m*. **~-teller** *n* cuentista *m & f*

stout /staʊt/ *a* (**-er**, **-est**) (*fat*) gordo; (*brave*) valiente. ● *n* cerveza *f* negra. **~ness** *n* corpulencia *f*

stove /stəʊv/ *n* estufa *f*

stow /stəʊ/ *vt* guardar; (*hide*) esconder. ● *vi*. **~ away** viajar de polizón. **~away** /ˈstəʊəweɪ/ *n* polizón *m*

straddle /ˈstrædl/ *vt* estar a horcajadas

straggl|e /ˈstrægl/ *vi* rezagarse. **~y** *a* desordenado

straight /streɪt/ *a* (**-er**, **-est**) derecho, recto; (*tidy*) en orden; (*frank*) franco; ‹*drink*› solo, puro; ‹*hair*› lacio. ● *adv* derecho; (*direct*) directamente; (*without delay*) inmediatamente. **~ on** todo recto. **~ out** sin vacilar. **go ~** enmendarse. ● *n* recta *f*. **~ away** inmediatamente. **~en** /ˈstreɪtn/ *vt* enderezar. ● *vi* enderezarse. **~forward** /streɪtˈfɔ:wəd/ *a* franco; (*easy*) sencillo. **~forwardly** *adv* francamente. **~ness** *n* rectitud *f*

strain[1] /streɪn/ *n* (*tension*) tensión *f*; (*injury*) torcedura *f*. ● *vt* estirar; (*tire*) cansar; (*injure*) torcer; (*sieve*) colar

strain[2] /streɪn/ *n* (*lineage*) linaje *m*; (*streak*) tendencia *f*

strained /streɪnd/ *a* forzado; ‹*relations*› tirante

strainer /-ə(r)/ *n* colador *m*

strains /streɪnz/ *npl* (*mus*) acordes *mpl*

strait /streɪt/ *n* estrecho *m*. **~-jacket** *n* camisa *f* de fuerza. **~-laced** *a* remilgado, gazmoño. **~s** *npl* apuro *m*

strand /strænd/ *n* (*thread*) hebra *f*; (*sand*) playa *f*. ● *vi* ‹*ship*› varar. **be ~ed** quedarse sin recursos

strange /streɪndʒ/ *a* (**-er**, **-est**) extraño, raro; (*not known*) desconocido; (*unaccustomed*) nuevo. **~ly** *adv* extrañamente. **~ness** *n* extrañeza *f*. **~r** /ˈstreɪndʒə(r)/ *n* desconocido *m*

strang|le /ˈstræŋgl/ *vt* estrangular; (*fig*) ahogar. **~lehold** /ˈstræŋglhəʊld/ *n* (*fig*) dominio *m* completo. **~ler** /-ə(r)/ *n* estrangulador *m*. **~ulation** /stræŋgjʊˈleɪʃn/ *n* estrangulación *f*

strap /stræp/ *n* correa *f*; (*of garment*) tirante *m*. ● *vt* (*pt* **strapped**) atar con correa; (*flog*) azotar

strapping /ˈstræpɪŋ/ *a* robusto

strata /ˈstrɑ:tə/ *see* **stratum**

strat|agem /ˈstrætədʒəm/ *n* estratagema *f*. **~egic** /strəˈti:dʒɪk/ *a* estratégico. **~egically** *adv* estratégicamente. **~egist** *n* estratega *m & f.* **~egy** /'strætədʒɪ/ *n* estrategia *f*

stratum /'strɑ:təm/ *n* (*pl* **strata**) estrato *m*

straw /strɔ:/ *n* paja *f.* **the last ~** el colmo

strawberry /'strɔ:bərɪ/ *n* fresa *f*

stray /streɪ/ *vi* vagar; (*deviate*) desviarse (**from** de). ● *a* ‹*animal*› extraviado, callejero; (*isolated*) aislado. ● *n* animal *m* extraviado, animal *m* callejero

streak /stri:k/ *n* raya *f*; (*of madness*) vena *f.* ● *vt* rayar. ● *vi* moverse como un rayo. **~y** *a* (**-ier**, **-iest**) rayado; ‹*bacon*› entreverado

stream /stri:m/ *n* arroyo *m*; (*current*) corriente *f*; (*of people*) desfile *m*; (*schol*) grupo *m.* ● *vi* correr. **~ out** *vi* ‹*people*› salir en tropel

streamer /'stri:mə(r)/ *n* (*paper*) serpentina *f*; (*flag*) gallardete *m*

streamline /'stri:mlaɪn/ *vt* dar línea aerodinámica a; (*simplify*) simplificar. **~d** *a* aerodinámico

street /stri:t/ *n* calle *f.* **~car** /'stri:tkɑ:/ *n* (*Amer*) tranvía *m.* **~ lamp** *n* farol *m.* **~ map** *n*, **~ plan** *n* plano *m*

strength /streŋθ/ *n* fuerza *f*; (*of wall etc*) solidez *f.* **on the ~ of** a base de. **~en** /'streŋθn/ *vt* reforzar

strenuous /'strenjʊəs/ *a* enérgico; (*arduous*) arduo; (*tiring*) fatigoso. **~ly** *adv* enérgicamente

stress /stres/ *n* énfasis *f*; (*gram*) acento *m*; (*mec*, *med*, *tension*) tensión *f.* ● *vt* insistir en

stretch /stretʃ/ *vt* estirar; (*extend*) extender; (*exaggerate*) forzar. **~ a point** hacer una excepción. ● *vi* estirarse; (*extend*) extenderse. ● *n* estirón *m*; (*period*) período *m*; (*of road*) tramo *m.* **at a ~** seguido; (*in one go*) de un tirón. **~er** /'stretʃə(r)/ *n* camilla *f*

strew /stru:/ *vt* (*pt* **strewed**, *pp* **strewn** *or* **strewed**) esparcir; (*cover*) cubrir

stricken /'strɪkən/ *a.* **~ with** afectado de

strict /strɪkt/ *a* (**-er**, **-est**) severo; (*precise*) estricto, preciso. **~ly** *adv* estrictamente. **~ly speaking** en rigor

stricture /'strɪktʃə(r)/ *n* crítica *f*; (*constriction*) constricción *f*

stride /straɪd/ *vi* (*pt* **strode**, *pp* **stridden**) andar a zancadas. ● *n* zancada *f.* **take sth in one's ~** hacer algo con facilidad, tomarse las cosas con calma

strident /'straɪdnt/ *a* estridente

strife /straɪf/ *n* conflicto *m*

strike /straɪk/ *vt* (*pt* **struck**) golpear; encender ‹*match*›; encontrar ‹*gold etc*›; ‹*clock*› dar. ● *vi* golpear; (*go on strike*) declararse en huelga; (*be on strike*) estar en huelga; (*attack*) atacar; ‹*clock*› dar la hora. ● *n* (*of workers*) huelga *f*; (*attack*) ataque *m*; (*find*) descubrimiento *m.* **on ~** en huelga. **~ off**, **~ out** tachar. **~ up a friendship** trabar amistad. **~r** /'straɪkə(r)/ *n* huelguista *m & f*

striking /'straɪkɪŋ/ *a* impresionante

string /strɪŋ/ *n* cuerda *f*; (*of lies, pearls*) sarta *f.* **pull ~s** tocar todos los resortes. ● *vt* (*pt* **strung**) (*thread*) ensartar. **~ along** (*fam*) engañar. **~ out** extender(se). **~ed** *a* (*mus*) de cuerda

stringen|cy /'strɪndʒənsɪ/ *n* rigor *m.* **~t** /'strɪndʒənt/ *a* riguroso

stringy /'strɪŋɪ/ *a* fibroso

strip /strɪp/ *vt* (*pt* **stripped**) desnudar; (*tear away*, *deprive*) quitar; desmontar ‹*machine*›. ● *vi* desnudarse. ● *n* tira *f.* **~ cartoon** *n* historieta *f*

stripe /straɪp/ *n* raya *f*; (*mil*) galón *m.* **~d** *a* a rayas, rayado

strip: **~ light** *n* tubo *m* fluorescente. **~per** /-ə(r)/ *n* artista *m & f* de striptease. **~-tease** *n* número *m* del desnudo, striptease *m*

strive /straɪv/ *vi* (*pt* **strove**, *pp* **striven**). **~ to** esforzarse por

strode /strəʊd/ *see* **stride**

stroke /strəʊk/ *n* golpe *m*; (*in swimming*) brazada *f*; (*med*) apoplejía *f*; (*of pen etc*) rasgo *m*; (*of clock*) campanada *f*; (*caress*) caricia *f.* ● *vt* acariciar

stroll /strəʊl/ *vi* pasearse. ● *n* paseo *m*

strong /strɒŋ/ *a* (**-er**, **-est**) fuerte. **~-box** *n* caja *f* fuerte. **~hold** /'strɒŋhəʊld/ *n* fortaleza *f*; (*fig*) baluarte *m.* **~ language** *n* palabras *fpl* fuertes, palabras *fpl* subidas de tono. **~ly** *adv* (*greatly*) fuertemente; (*with energy*) enérgicamente; (*deeply*) profundamente. **~ measures** *npl* medidas *fpl* enérgicas. **~-minded** *a* resuelto. **~-room** *n* cámara *f* acorazada

stroppy /'strɒpɪ/ *a* (*sl*) irascible

strove /strəʊv/ *see* **strive**
struck /strʌk/ *see* **strike**. ~ **on** (*sl*) entusiasta de
structur|al /'strʌktʃərəl/ *a* estructural. ~**e** /'strʌktʃə(r)/ *n* estructura *f*
struggle /'strʌgl/ *vi* luchar. ~ **to one's feet** levantarse con dificultad. • *n* lucha *f*
strum /strʌm/ *vt/i* (*pt* **strummed**) rasguear
strung /strʌŋ/ *see* **string**. • *a*. ~ **up** (*tense*) nervioso
strut /strʌt/ *n* puntal *m*; (*walk*) pavoneo *m*. • *vi* (*pt* **strutted**) pavonearse
stub /stʌb/ *n* cabo *m*; (*counterfoil*) talón *m*; (*of cigarette*) colilla *f*; (*of tree*) tocón *m*. • *vt* (*pt* **stubbed**). ~ **out** apagar
stubble /'stʌbl/ *n* rastrojo *m*: (*beard*) barba *f* de varios días
stubborn /'stʌbən/ *a* terco. ~**ly** *adv* tercamente. ~**ness** *n* terquedad *f*
stubby /'stʌbɪ/ *a* (**-ier**, **-iest**) achaparrado
stucco /'stʌkəʊ/ *n* (*pl* **-oes**) estuco *m*
stuck /stʌk/ *see* **stick**. • *a* (*jammed*) bloqueado; (*in difficulties*) en un apuro. ~ **on** (*sl*) encantado con. ~**-up** *a* (*sl*) presumido
stud[1] /stʌd/ *n* tachón *m*; (*for collar*) botón *m*. • *vt* (*pt* **studded**) tachonar. ~**ded with** sembrado de
stud[2] /stʌd/ *n* (*of horses*) caballeriza *f*
student /'stju:dənt/ *n* estudiante *m* & *f*
studied /'stʌdɪd/ *a* deliberado
studio /'stju:dɪəʊ/ *n* (*pl* **-os**) estudio *m*. ~ **couch** *n* sofá *m* cama. ~ **flat** *n* estudio *m* de artista
studious /'stju:dɪəs/ *a* estudioso; (*studied*) deliberado. ~**ly** *adv* estudiosamente; (*carefully*) cuidadosamente
study /'stʌdɪ/ *n* estudio *m*; (*office*) despacho *m*. • *vt/i* estudiar
stuff /stʌf/ *n* materia *f*, sustancia *f*; (*sl*) cosas *fpl*. • *vt* rellenar; disecar ‹*animal*›; (*cram*) atiborrar; (*block up*) tapar; (*put*) meter de prisa. ~**ing** *n* relleno *m*
stuffy /'stʌfɪ/ *a* (**-ier**, **-iest**) mal ventilado; (*old-fashioned*) chapado a la antigua
stumbl|e /'stʌmbl/ *vi* tropezar. ~**e across**, ~**e on** tropezar con. • *n* tropezón *m*. ~**ing-block** *n* tropiezo *m*, impedimento *m*
stump /stʌmp/ *n* cabo *m*; (*of limb*) muñón *m*; (*of tree*) tocón *m*. ~**ed** /stʌmpt/ *a* (*fam*) perplejo. ~**y** /'stʌmpɪ/ *a* (**-ier**, **-iest**) achaparrado
stun /stʌn/ *vt* (*pt* **stunned**) aturdir; (*bewilder*) pasmar. ~**ning** *a* (*fabulous, fam*) estupendo
stung /stʌŋ/ *see* **sting**
stunk /stʌŋk/ *see* **stink**
stunt[1] /stʌnt/ *n* (*fam*) truco *m* publicitario
stunt[2] /stʌnt/ *vt* impedir el desarrollo de. ~**ed** *a* enano
stupefy /'stju:pɪfaɪ/ *vt* dejar estupefacto
stupendous /stju:'pendəs/ *a* estupendo. ~**ly** *adv* estupendamente
stupid /'stju:pɪd/ *a* estúpido. ~**ity** /-'pɪdətɪ/ *n* estupidez *f*. ~**ly** *adv* estúpidamente
stupor /'stju:pə(r)/ *n* estupor *m*
sturd|iness /'stɜ:dɪnɪs/ *n* robustez *f*. ~**y** /'stɜ:dɪ/ *a* (**-ier**, **-iest**) robusto
sturgeon /'stɜ:dʒən/ *n* (*pl* **sturgeon**) esturión *m*
stutter /'stʌtə(r)/ *vi* tartamudear. • *n* tartamudeo *m*
sty[1] /staɪ/ *n* (*pl* **sties**) pocilga *f*
sty[2] /staɪ/ *n* (*pl* **sties**) (*med*) orzuelo *m*
styl|e /staɪl/ *n* estilo *m*; (*fashion*) moda *f*. **in** ~ con todo lujo. • *vt* diseñar. ~**ish** /'staɪlɪʃ/ *a* elegante. ~**ishly** *adv* elegantemente. ~**ist** /'staɪlɪst/ *n* estilista *m* & *f*. **hair** ~**ist** *n* peluquero *m*. ~**ized** /'staɪlaɪzd/ *a* estilizado
stylus /'staɪləs/ *n* (*pl* **-uses**) aguja *f* (de tocadiscos)
suave /swɑ:v/ *a* (*pej*) zalamero
sub... /sʌb/ *pref* sub...
subaquatic /sʌbə'kwætɪk/ *a* subacuático
subconscious /sʌb'kɒnʃəs/ *a* & *n* subconsciente (*m*). ~**ly** *adv* de modo subconsciente
subcontinent /sʌb'kɒntɪnənt/ *n* subcontinente *m*
subcontract /sʌbkən'trækt/ *vt* subcontratar. ~**or** /-ə(r)/ *n* subcontratista *m* & *f*
subdivide /sʌbdɪ'vaɪd/ *vt* subdividir
subdue /səb'dju:/ *vt* dominar ‹*feelings*›; sojuzgar ‹*country*›. ~**d** *a* (*depressed*) abatido; ‹*light*› suave
subhuman /sʌb'hju:mən/ *a* infrahumano

subject /ˈsʌbdʒɪkt/ *a* sometido. **~ to** sujeto a. ● *n* súbdito *m*; (*theme*) asunto *m*; (*schol*) asignatura *f*; (*gram*) sujeto *m*; (*of painting, play, book etc*) tema *m*. /səbˈdʒekt/ *vt* sojuzgar; (*submit*) someter. **~ion** /-ʃn/ *n* sometimiento *m*

subjective /səbˈdʒektɪv/ *a* subjetivo. **~ly** *adv* subjetivamente

subjugate /ˈsʌbdʒʊgeɪt/ *vt* subyugar

subjunctive /səbˈdʒʌŋktɪv/ *a* & *n* subjuntivo (*m*)

sublet /sʌbˈlet/ *vt* (*pt* **sublet**, *pres p* **subletting**) subarrendar

sublimat|e /ˈsʌblɪmeɪt/ *vt* sublimar. **~ion** /-ˈmeɪʃn/ *n* sublimación *f*

sublime /səˈblaɪm/ *a* sublime. **~ly** *adv* sublimemente

submarine /sʌbməˈriːn/ *n* submarino *m*

submerge /səbˈmɜːdʒ/ *vt* sumergir. ● *vi* sumergirse

submi|ssion /səbˈmɪʃn/ *n* sumisión *f*. **~ssive** /-sɪv/ *a* sumiso. **~t** /səbˈmɪt/ *vt* (*pt* **submitted**) someter. ● *vi* someterse

subordinat|e /səˈbɔːdɪnət/ *a* & *n* subordinado (*m*). /səˈbɔːdɪneɪt/ *vt* subordinar. **~ion** /-ˈneɪʃn/ *n* subordinación *f*

subscri|be /səbˈskraɪb/ *vi* suscribir. **~be to** suscribir ‹*fund*›; (*agree*) estar de acuerdo con; abonarse a ‹*newspaper*›. **~ber** /-ə(r)/ *n* abonado *m*. **~ption** /-rɪpʃn/ *n* suscripción *f*

subsequent /ˈsʌbsɪkwənt/ *a* subsiguiente. **~ly** *adv* posteriormente

subservient /səbˈsɜːvjənt/ *a* servil

subside /səbˈsaɪd/ *vi* ‹*land*› hundirse; ‹*flood*› bajar; ‹*storm, wind*› amainar. **~nce** *n* hundimiento *m*

subsidiary /səbˈsɪdɪərɪ/ *a* subsidiario. ● *n* (*com*) sucursal *m*

subsid|ize /ˈsʌbsɪdaɪz/ *vt* subvencionar. **~y** /ˈsʌbsədɪ/ *n* subvención *f*

subsist /səbˈsɪst/ *vi* subsistir. **~ence** *n* subsistencia *f*

subsoil /ˈsʌbsɒɪl/ *n* subsuelo *m*

subsonic /sʌbˈsɒnɪk/ *a* subsónico

substance /ˈsʌbstəns/ *n* substancia *f*

substandard /sʌbˈstændəd/ *a* inferior

substantial /səbˈstænʃl/ *a* sólido; ‹*meal*› substancial; (*considerable*) considerable. **~ly** *adv* considerablemente

substantiate /səbˈstænʃɪeɪt/ *vt* justificar

substitut|e /ˈsʌbstɪtjuːt/ *n* substituto *m*. ● *vt/i* substituir. **~ion** /-ˈtjuːʃn/ *n* substitución *f*

subterfuge /ˈsʌbtəfjuːdʒ/ *n* subterfugio *m*

subterranean /sʌbtəˈreɪnjən/ *a* subterráneo

subtitle /ˈsʌbtaɪtl/ *n* subtítulo *m*

subtle /ˈsʌtl/ *a* (**-er**, **-est**) sutil. **~ty** *n* sutileza *f*

subtract /səbˈtrækt/ *vt* restar. **~ion** /-ʃn/ *n* resta *f*

suburb /ˈsʌbɜːb/ *n* barrio *m*. **the ~s** las afueras *fpl*. **~an** /səˈbɜːbən/ *a* suburbano. **~ia** /səˈbɜːbɪə/ *n* las afueras *fpl*

subvention /səbˈvenʃn/ *n* subvención *f*

subver|sion /səbˈvɜːʃn/ *n* subversión *f*. **~sive** /səbˈvɜːsɪv/ *a* subversivo. **~t** /səbˈvɜːt/ *vt* subvertir

subway /ˈsʌbweɪ/ *n* paso *m* subterráneo; (*Amer*) metro *m*

succeed /səkˈsiːd/ *vi* tener éxito. ● *vt* suceder a. **~ in doing** lograr hacer. **~ing** *a* sucesivo

success /səkˈses/ *n* éxito *m*. **~ful** *a* que tiene éxito; (*chosen*) elegido

succession /səkˈseʃn/ *n* sucesión *f*. **in ~** sucesivamente, seguidos

successive /səkˈsesɪv/ *a* sucesivo. **~ly** *adv* sucesivamente

successor /səkˈsesə(r)/ *n* sucesor *m*

succinct /səkˈsɪŋkt/ *a* sucinto

succour /ˈsʌkə(r)/ *vt* socorrer. ● *n* socorro *m*

succulent /ˈsʌkjʊlənt/ *a* suculento

succumb /səˈkʌm/ *vi* sucumbir

such /sʌtʃ/ *a* tal. ● *pron* los que, las que; (*so much*) tanto. **and ~** y tal. ● *adv* tan. **~ a big house** una casa tan grande. **~ and ~** tal o cual. **~ as it is** tal como es. **~like** *a* (*fam*) semejante, de ese tipo

suck /sʌk/ *vt* chupar; sorber ‹*liquid*›. **~ up** absorber. **~ up to** (*sl*) dar coba a. **~er** /ˈsʌkə(r)/ *n* (*plant*) chupón *m*; (*person, fam*) primo *m*

suckle /sʌkl/ *vt* amamantar

suction /ˈsʌkʃn/ *n* succión *f*

sudden /ˈsʌdn/ *a* repentino. **all of a ~** de repente. **~ly** *adv* de repente. **~ness** *n* lo repentino

suds /sʌds/ *npl* espuma *f* (de jabón)

sue /suː/ *vt* (*pres p* **suing**) demandar (**for** por)

suede /sweɪd/ *n* ante *m*

suet /'su:ɪt/ *n* sebo *m*

suffer /'sʌfə(r)/ *vt* sufrir; (*tolerate*) tolerar. ● *vi* sufrir. **~ance** /'sʌfərəns/ *n*. **on ~ance** por tolerancia. **~ing** *n* sufrimiento *m*

suffic|e /sə'faɪs/ *vi* bastar. **~iency** /sə'fɪʃənsɪ/ *n* suficiencia *f*. **~ient** /sə'fɪʃnt/ *a* suficiente; (*enough*) bastante. **~iently** *adv* suficientemente, bastante

suffix /'sʌfɪks/ *n* (*pl* **-ixes**) sufijo *m*

suffocat|e /'sʌfəkeɪt/ *vt* ahogar. ● *vi* ahogarse. **~ion** /-'keɪʃn/ *n* asfixia *f*

sugar /'ʃʊgə(r)/ *n* azúcar *m & f*. ● *vt* azucarar. **~-bowl** *n* azucarero *m*. **~ lump** *n* terrón *m* de azúcar. **~y** *a* azucarado.

suggest /sə'dʒest/ *vt* sugerir. **~ible** /sə'dʒestɪbl/ *a* sugestionable. **~ion** /-tʃən/ *n* sugerencia *f*; (*trace*) traza *f*. **~ive** /sə'dʒestɪv/ *a* sugestivo. **be ~ive of** evocar, recordar. **~ively** *adv* sugestivamente

suicid|al /su:ɪ'saɪdl/ *a* suicida. **~e** /'su:ɪsaɪd/ *n* suicidio *m*; (*person*) suicida *m & f*. **commit ~e** suicidarse

suit /su:t/ *n* traje *m*; (*woman's*) traje *m* de chaqueta; (*cards*) palo *m*; (*jurid*) pleito *m*. ● *vt* convenir; ‹*clothes*› sentar bien a; (*adapt*) adaptar. **be ~ed for** ser apto para. **~ability** *n* conveniencia *f*. **~able** *a* adecuado. **~ably** *adv* convenientemente. **~case** /'su:tkeɪs/ *n* maleta *f*, valija *f* (*LAm*)

suite /swi:t/ *n* (*of furniture*) juego *m*; (*of rooms*) apartamento *m*; (*retinue*) séquito *m*

suitor /'su:tə(r)/ *n* pretendiente *m*

sulk /sʌlk/ *vi* enfurruñarse. **~s** *npl* enfurruñamiento *m*. **~y** *a* enfurruñado

sullen /'sʌlən/ *a* resentido. **~ly** *adv* con resentimiento

sully /'sʌlɪ/ *vt* manchar

sulphur /'sʌlfə(r)/ *n* azufre *m*. **~ic** /-'fjʊərɪk/ *a* sulfúrico. **~ic acid** *n* ácido *m* sulfúrico

sultan /'sʌltən/ *n* sultán *m*

sultana /sʌl'tɑ:nə/ *n* pasa *f* gorrona

sultry /'sʌltrɪ/ *a* (**-ier**, **-iest**) ‹*weather*› bochornoso; (*fig*) sensual

sum /sʌm/ *n* suma *f*. ● *vt* (*pt* **summed**). **~ up** resumir ‹*situation*›; (*assess*) evaluar

summar|ily /'sʌmərɪlɪ/ *adv* sumariamente. **~ize** *vt* resumir. **~y** /'sʌmərɪ/ *a* sumario. ● *n* resumen *m*

summer /'sʌmə(r)/ *n* verano *m*. **~-house** *n* glorieta *f*, cenador *m*. **~time** *n* verano *m*. **~ time** *n* hora *f* de verano. **~y** *a* veraniego

summit /'sʌmɪt/ *n* cumbre *f*. **~ conference** *n* conferencia *f* cumbre

summon /'sʌmən/ *vt* llamar; convocar ‹*meeting, s.o. to meeting*›; (*jurid*) citar. **~ up** armarse de. **~s** /'sʌmənz/ *n* llamada *f*; (*jurid*) citación *f*. ● *vt* citar

sump /sʌmp/ *n* (*mec*) cárter *m*

sumptuous /'sʌmptjʊəs/ *a* suntuoso. **~ly** *adv* suntuosamente

sun /sʌn/ *n* sol *m*. ● *vt* (*pt* **sunned**). **~ o.s.** tomar el sol. **~bathe** /'sʌnbeɪð/ *vi* tomar el sol. **~beam** /'sʌnbi:m/ *n* rayo *m* de sol. **~burn** /'sʌnbɜ:n/ *n* quemadura *f* de sol. **~burnt** *a* quemado por el sol

sundae /'sʌndeɪ/ *n* helado *m* con frutas y nueces

Sunday /'sʌndeɪ/ *n* domingo *m*. **~ school** *n* catequesis *f*

sun: **~dial** /'sʌndaɪl/ *n* reloj *m* de sol. **~down** /'sʌndaʊn/ *n* puesta *f* del sol

sundry /'sʌndrɪ/ *a* diversos. **all and ~** todo el mundo. **sundries** *npl* artículos *mpl* diversos

sunflower /'sʌnflaʊə(r)/ *n* girasol *m*

sung /sʌŋ/ *see* **sing**

sun-glasses /'sʌnglɑ:sɪz/ *npl* gafas *fpl* de sol

sunk /sʌŋk/ *see* **sink**. **~en** /'sʌŋkən/ ● *a* hundido

sunlight /'sʌnlaɪt/ *n* luz *f* del sol

sunny /'sʌnɪ/ *a* (**-ier**, **-iest**) ‹*day*› de sol; ‹*place*› soleado. **it is ~** hace sol

sun: **~rise** /'sʌnraɪz/ *n* amanecer *m*, salida *f* del sol. **~-roof** *n* techo *m* corredizo. **~set** /'sʌnset/ *n* puesta *f* del sol. **~-shade** /'sʌnʃeɪd/ *n* quitasol *m*, sombrilla *f*; (*awning*) toldo *m*. **~shine** /'sʌnʃaɪn/ *n* sol *m*. **~spot** /'sʌnspɒt/ *n* mancha *f* solar. **~stroke** /'sʌnstrəʊk/ *n* insolación *f*. **~tan** *n* bronceado *m*. **~tanned** *a* bronceado. **~tan lotion** *n* bronceador *m*

sup /sʌp/ *vt* (*pt* **supped**) sorber

super /'su:pə(r)/ *a* (*fam*) estupendo

superannuation /su:pərænjʊ'eɪʃn/ *n* jubilación *f*

superb /su:'pɜ:b/ *a* espléndido. **~ly** *adv* espléndidamente

supercilious /su:pə'sɪlɪəs/ *a* desdeñoso

superficial /su:pə'fɪʃl/ *a* superficial. **~ity** /-ɪ'ælətɪ/ *n* superficialidad *f*. **~ly** *adv* superficialmente

superfluous /su:'pɜ:flʊəs/ *a* superfluo
superhuman /su:pə'hju:mən/ *a* sobrehumano
superimpose /su:pərɪm'pəʊz/ *vt* sobreponer
superintend /su:pərɪn'tend/ *vt* vigilar. **~ence** *n* dirección *f*. **~ent** *n* director *m*; (*of police*) comisario *m*
superior /su:'pɪərɪə(r)/ *a* & *n* superior (*m*). **~ity** /-'ɒrətɪ/ *n* superioridad *f*
superlative /su:'pɜ:lətɪv/ *a* & *n* superlativo (*m*)
superman /'su:pəmæn/ *n* (*pl* **-men**) superhombre *m*
supermarket /'su:pəmɑ:kɪt/ *n* supermercado *m*
supernatural /su:pə'nætʃrəl/ *a* sobrenatural
superpower /'su:pəpaʊə(r)/ *n* superpotencia *f*
supersede /su:pə'si:d/ *vt* reemplazar, suplantar
supersonic /su:pə'sɒnɪk/ *a* supersónico
superstitio|n /su:pə'stɪʃn/ *n* superstición *f*. **~us** *a* supersticioso
superstructure /'su:pəstrʌktʃə(r)/ *n* superestructura *f*
supertanker /'su:pətæŋkə(r)/ *n* petrolero *m* gigante
supervene /su:pə'vi:n/ *vi* sobrevenir
supervis|e /'su:pəvaɪz/ *vt* supervisar. **~ion** /-'vɪʒn/ *n* supervisión *f*. **~or** /-zə(r)/ *n* supervisor *m*. **~ory** *a* de supervisión
supper /'sʌpə(r)/ *n* cena *f*
supplant /sə'plɑ:nt/ *vt* suplantar
supple /sʌpl/ *a* flexible. **~ness** *n* flexibilidad *f*
supplement /'sʌplɪmənt/ *n* suplemento *m*. ● *vt* completar; (*increase*) aumentar. **~ary** /-'mentərɪ/ *a* suplementario
suppl|ier /sə'plaɪə(r)/ *n* suministrador *m*; (*com*) proveedor *m*. **~y** /sə'plaɪ/ *vt* proveer; (*feed*) alimentar; satisfacer ‹*a need*›. **~y with** abastecer de. ● *n* provisión *f*, suministro *m*. **~y and demand** oferta *f* y demanda
support /sə'pɔ:t/ *vt* sostener; (*endure*) soportar, aguantar; (*fig*) apoyar. ● *n* apoyo *m*; (*tec*) soporte *m*. **~er** /-ə(r)/ *n* soporte *m*; (*sport*) seguidor *m*, hincha *m* & *f*. **~ive** *a* alentador
suppos|e /sə'pəʊz/ *vt* suponer; (*think*) creer. **be ~ed to** deber. **not be ~ed to** (*fam*) no tener permiso para, no tener derecho a. **~edly** *adv* según cabe suponer; (*before adjective*) presuntamente. **~ition** /sʌpə'zɪʃn/ *n* suposición *f*
suppository /sə'pɒzɪtərɪ/ *n* supositorio *m*
suppress /sə'pres/ *vt* suprimir. **~ion** *n* supresión *f*. **~or** /-ə(r)/ *n* supresor *m*
suprem|acy /su:'preməsɪ/ *n* supremacía *f*. **~e** /su:'pri:m/ *a* supremo
surcharge /'sɜ:tʃɑ:dʒ/ *n* sobreprecio *m*; (*tax*) recargo *m*
sure /ʃʊə(r)/ *a* (**-er**, **-est**) seguro, cierto. **make ~** asegurarse. ● *adv* (*Amer*, *fam*) ¡claro! **~ enough** efectivamente. **~-footed** *a* de pie firme. **~ly** *adv* seguramente
surety /'ʃʊərətɪ/ *n* garantía *f*
surf /sɜ:f/ *n* oleaje *m*; (*foam*) espuma *f*
surface /'sɜ:fɪs/ *n* superficie *f*. ● *a* superficial, de la superficie. ● *vt* (*smoothe*) alisar; (*cover*) recubrir (**with** de). ● *vi* salir a la superficie; (*emerge*) emerger. **~ mail** *n* por vía marítima
surfboard /'sɜ:fbɔ:d/ *n* tabla *f* de surf
surfeit /'sɜ:fɪt/ *n* exceso *m*
surfing /'sɜ:fɪŋ/ *n*, **surf-riding** /'sɜ:fraɪdɪŋ/ *n* surf *m*
surge /sɜ:dʒ/ *vi* ‹*crowd*› moverse en tropel; ‹*waves*› encresparse. ● *n* oleada *f*; (*elec*) sobretensión *f*
surgeon /'sɜ:dʒən/ *n* cirujano *m*
surgery /'sɜ:dʒərɪ/ *n* cirugía *f*; (*consulting room*) consultorio *m*; (*consulting hours*) horas *fpl* de consulta
surgical /'sɜ:rdʒɪkl/ *a* quirúrgico
surl|iness /'sɜ:lɪnɪs/ *n* aspereza *f*. **~y** /'sɜ:lɪ/ *a* (**-ier**, **-iest**) áspero
surmise /sə'maɪz/ *vt* conjeturar
surmount /sə'maʊnt/ *vt* superar
surname /'sɜ:neɪm/ *n* apellido *m*
surpass /sə'pɑ:s/ *vt* sobrepasar, exceder
surplus /'sɜ:pləs/ *a* & *n* excedente (*m*)
surpris|e /sə'praɪz/ *n* sorpresa *f*. ● *vt* sorprender. **~ing** *a* sorprendente. **~ingly** *adv* asombrosamente
surrealis|m /sə'rɪəlɪzəm/ *n* surrealismo *m*. **~t** *n* surrealista *m* & *f*
surrender /sə'rendə(r)/ *vt* entregar. ● *vi* entregarse. ● *n* entrega *f*; (*mil*) rendición *f*

surreptitious /sʌrəp'tɪʃəs/ *a* clandestino
surrogate /'sʌrəgət/ *n* substituto *m*
surround /sə'raʊnd/ *vt* rodear; (*mil*) cercar. ● *n* borde *m*. **~ing** *a* circundante. **~ings** *npl* alrededores *mpl*
surveillance /sɜ:'veɪləns/ *n* vigilancia *f*
survey /'sɜ:veɪ/ *n* inspección *f*; (*report*) informe *m*; (*general view*) vista *f* de conjunto. /sə'veɪ/ *vt* examinar, inspeccionar; (*inquire into*) hacer una encuesta de. **~or** *n* topógrafo *m*, agrimensor
surviv|al /sə'vaɪvl/ *n* supervivencia *f*. **~e** /sə'vaɪv/ *vt/i* sobrevivir. **~or** /-ə(r)/ *n* superviviente *m & f*
susceptib|ility /səseptə'bɪlətɪ/ *n* susceptibilidad *f*. **~le** /sə'septəbl/ *a* susceptible. **~le to** propenso a
suspect /sə'spekt/ *vt* sospechar. /'sʌspekt/ *a & n* sospechoso (*m*)
suspend /sə'spend/ *vt* suspender. **~er** /səs'pendə(r)/ *n* liga *f*. **~er belt** *n* liguero *m*. **~ers** *npl* (*Amer*) tirantes *mpl*
suspense /sə'spens/ *n* incertidumbre *f*; (*in film etc*) suspense *m*
suspension /sə'spenʃn/ *n* suspensión *f*. **~ bridge** *n* puente *m* colgante
suspicion /sə'spɪʃn/ *n* sospecha *f*; (*trace*) pizca *f*
suspicious /sə'spɪʃəs/ *a* desconfiado; (*causing suspicion*) sospechoso
sustain /sə'steɪn/ *vt* sostener; (*suffer*) sufrir
sustenance /'sʌstɪnəns/ *n* sustento *m*
svelte /svelt/ *a* esbelto
SW *abbr* (*south-west*) sudoeste *m*
swab /swɒb/ *n* (*med*) tapón *m*
swagger /'swægə(r)/ *vi* pavonearse
swallow[1] /'swɒləʊ/ *vt/i* tragar. ● *n* trago *m*. **~ up** tragar; consumir ‹*savings etc*›
swallow[2] /'swɒləʊ/ *n* (*bird*) golondrina *f*
swam /swæm/ *see* **swim**
swamp /swɒmp/ *n* pantano *m*. ● *vt* inundar; (*with work*) agobiar. **~y** *a* pantanoso
swan /swɒn/ *n* cisne *m*
swank /swæŋk/ *n* (*fam*) ostentación *f*. ● *vi* (*fam*) fanfarronear
swap /swɒp/ *vt/i* (*pt* **swapped**) (*fam*) (inter)cambiar. ● *n* (*fam*) (inter) cambio *m*
swarm /swɔ:m/ *n* enjambre *m*. ● *vi* ‹*bees*› enjambrar; (*fig*) hormiguear
swarthy /'swɔ:ðɪ/ *a* (**-ier**, **-iest**) moreno
swastika /'swɒstɪkə/ *n* cruz *f* gamada
swat /swɒt/ *vt* (*pt* **swatted**) aplastar
sway /sweɪ/ *vi* balancearse. ● *vt* (*influence*) influir en. ● *n* balanceo *m*; (*rule*) imperio *m*
swear /sweə(r)/ *vt/i* (*pt* **swore**, *pp* **sworn**) jurar. **~ by** (*fam*) creer ciegamente en. **~-word** *n* palabrota *f*
sweat /swet/ *n* sudor *m*. ● *vi* sudar
sweat|er /'swetə(r)/ *n* jersey *m*. **~shirt** *n* sudadera *f*
swede /swi:d/ *n* naba *f*
Swede /swi:d/ *n* sueco *m*
Sweden /'swi:dn/ *n* Suecia *f*
Swedish /'swi:dɪʃ/ *a & n* sueco (*m*)
sweep /swi:p/ *vt* (*pt* **swept**) barrer; deshollinar ‹*chimney*›. **~ the board** ganar todo. ● *vi* barrer; ‹*road*› extenderse; (*go majestically*) moverse majestuosamente. ● *n* barrido *m*; (*curve*) curva *f*; (*movement*) movimiento *m*; (*person*) deshollinador *m*. **~ away** *vt* barrer. **~ing** *a* ‹*gesture*› amplio; ‹*changes etc*› radical; ‹*statement*› demasiado general. **~stake** /'swi:psteɪk/ *n* lotería *f*
sweet /swi:t/ *a* (**-er**, **-est**) dulce; (*fragrant*) fragante; (*pleasant*) agradable. **have a ~ tooth** ser dulcero. ● *n* caramelo *m*; (*dish*) postre *m*. **~bread** /'swi:tbred/ *n* lechecillas *fpl*. **~en** /'swi:tn/ *vt* endulzar. **~ener** /-ə(r)/ *n* dulcificante *m*. **~heart** /'swi:thɑ:t/ *n* amor *m*. **~ly** *adv* dulcemente. **~ness** *n* dulzura *f*. **~ pea** *n* guisante *m* de olor
swell /swel/ *vt* (*pt* **swelled**, *pp* **swollen** *or* **swelled**) hinchar; (*increase*) aumentar. ● *vi* hincharse; (*increase*) aumentarse; ‹*river*› crecer. ● *a* (*fam*) estupendo. ● *n* (*of sea*) oleaje *m*. **~ing** *n* hinchazón *m*
swelter /'sweltə(r)/ *vi* sofocarse de calor
swept /swept/ *see* **sweep**
swerve /swɜ:v/ *vi* desviarse
swift /swɪft/ *a* (**-er**, **-est**) rápido. ● *n* (*bird*) vencejo *m*. **~ly** *adv* rápidamente. **~ness** *n* rapidez *f*
swig /swɪg/ *vt* (*pt* **swigged**) (*fam*) beber a grandes tragos. ● *n* (*fam*) trago *m*

swill /swɪl/ *vt* enjuagar; (*drink*) beber a grandes tragos. ● *n* (*food for pigs*) bazofia *f*

swim /swɪm/ *vi* (*pt* **swam**, *pp* **swum**) nadar; ‹*room, head*› dar vueltas. ● *n* baño *m*. **~mer** *n* nadador *m*. **~ming-bath** *n* piscina *f*. **~mingly** /'swɪmɪŋlɪ/ *adv* a las mil maravillas. **~ming-pool** *n* piscina *f*. **~ming-trunks** *npl* bañador *m*. **~suit** *n* traje *m* de baño

swindle /'swɪndl/ *vt* estafar. ● *n* estafa *f*. **~r** /-ə(r)/ *n* estafador *m*

swine /swaɪn/ *npl* cerdos *mpl*. ● *n* (*pl* **swine**) (*person, fam*) canalla *m*

swing /swɪŋ/ *vt* (*pt* **swung**) balancear. ● *vi* oscilar; ‹*person*› balancearse; (*turn round*) girar. ● *n* balanceo *m*, vaivén *m*; (*seat*) columpio *m*; (*mus*) ritmo *m*. **in full ~** en plena actividad. **~ bridge** *n* puente *m* giratorio

swingeing /'swɪndʒɪŋ/ *a* enorme

swipe /swaɪp/ *vt* golpear; (*snatch, sl*) birlar. ● *n* (*fam*) golpe *m*

swirl /swɜːl/ *vi* arremolinarse. ● *n* remolino *m*

swish /swɪʃ/ *vt* silbar. ● *a* (*fam*) elegante

Swiss /swɪs/ *a & n* suizo (*m*). **~ roll** *n* bizcocho *m* enrollado

switch /swɪtʃ/ *n* (*elec*) interruptor *m*; (*change*) cambio *m*. ● *vt* cambiar; (*deviate*) desviar. **~ off** (*elec*) desconectar; apagar ‹*light*›. **~ on** (*elec*) encender; arrancar ‹*engine*›. **~back** /'swɪtʃbæk/ *n* montaña *f* rusa. **~board** /'swɪtʃbɔːd/ *n* centralita *f*

Switzerland /'swɪtsələnd/ *n* Suiza *f*

swivel /'swɪvl/ ● *vi* (*pt* **swivelled**) girar

swollen /'swəʊlən/ *see* **swell**. ● *a* hinchado

swoon /swuːn/ *vi* desmayarse

swoop /swuːp/ *vi* ‹*bird*› calarse; ‹*plane*› bajar en picado. ● *n* calada *f*; (*by police*) redada *f*

sword /sɔːd/ *n* espada *f*. **~fish** /'sɔːdfɪʃ/ *n* pez *m* espada

swore /swɔː(r)/ *see* **swear**

sworn /swɔːn/ *see* **swear**. ● *a* ‹*enemy*› jurado; ‹*friend*› leal

swot /swɒt/ *vt/i* (*pt* **swotted**) (*schol, sl*) empollar. ● *n* (*schol, sl*) empollón *m*

swum /swʌm/ *see* **swim**

swung /swʌŋ/ *see* **swing**

sycamore /'sɪkəmɔː(r)/ *n* plátano *m* falso

syllable /'sɪləbl/ *n* sílaba *f*

syllabus /'sɪləbəs/ *n* (*pl* **-buses**) programa *m* (de estudios)

symbol /'sɪmbl/ *n* símbolo *m*. **~ic(al)** /-'bɒlɪk(l)/ *a* simbólico. **~ism** *n* simbolismo *m*. **~ize** *vt* simbolizar

symmetr|ical /sɪ'metrɪkl/ *a* simétrico. **~y** /'sɪmətrɪ/ *n* simetría *f*

sympath|etic /sɪmpə'θetɪk/ *a* comprensivo; (*showing pity*) compasivo. **~ize** /-aɪz/ *vi* comprender; (*pity*) compadecerse (**with** de). **~izer** *n* (*pol*) simpatizante *m & f*. **~y** /'sɪmpəθɪ/ *n* comprensión *f*; (*pity*) compasión *f*; (*condolences*) pésame *m*. **be in ~y with** estar de acuerdo con

symphon|ic /sɪm'fɒnɪk/ *a* sinfónico. **~y** /'sɪmfənɪ/ *n* sinfonía *f*

symposium /sɪm'pəʊzɪəm/ *n* (*pl* **-ia**) simposio *m*

symptom /'sɪmptəm/ *n* síntoma *m*. **~atic** /-'mætɪk/ *a* sintomático

synagogue /'sɪnəgɒg/ *n* sinagoga *f*

synchroniz|ation /sɪnkrənaɪ'zeɪʃn/ *n* sincronización *f*. **~e** /'sɪŋkrənaɪz/ *vt* sincronizar

syncopat|e /'sɪnkəpeɪt/ *vt* sincopar. **~ion** /-'peɪʃn/ *n* síncopa *f*

syndicate /'sɪndɪkət/ *n* sindicato *m*

syndrome /'sɪndrəʊm/ *n* síndrome *m*

synod /'sɪnəd/ *n* sínodo *m*

synonym /'sɪnənɪm/ *n* sinónimo *m*. **~ous** /-'nɒnɪməs/ *a* sinónimo

synopsis /sɪ'nɒpsɪs/ *n* (*pl* **-opses** /-siːz/) sinopsis *f*, resumen *m*

syntax /'sɪntæks/ *n* sintaxis *f invar*

synthesi|s /'sɪnθəsɪs/ *n* (*pl* **-theses** /-siːz/) síntesis *f*. **~ze** *vt* sintetizar

synthetic /sɪn'θetɪk/ *a* sintético

syphilis /'sɪfɪlɪs/ *n* sífilis *f*

Syria /'sɪrɪə/ *n* Siria *f*. **~n** *a & n* sirio (*m*)

syringe /'sɪrɪndʒ/ *n* jeringa *f*. ● *vt* jeringar

syrup /'sɪrəp/ *n* jarabe *m*, almíbar *m*; (*treacle*) melaza *f*. **~y** *a* almibarado

system /'sɪstəm/ *n* sistema *m*; (*body*) organismo *m*; (*order*) método *m*. **~atic** /-ə'mætɪk/ *a* sistemático. **~atically** /-ə'mætɪklɪ/ *adv* sistemáticamente. **~s analyst** *n* analista *m & f* de sistemas

T

tab /tæb/ *n* (*flap*) lengüeta *f*; (*label*) etiqueta *f*. **keep ~s on** (*fam*) vigilar

tabby /'tæbɪ/ *n* gato *m* atigrado

tabernacle /'tæbənækl/ *n* tabernáculo *m*

table /'teɪbl/ *n* mesa *f*; (*list*) tabla *f*. **~ of contents** índice *m*. ● *vt* presentar; (*postpone*) aplazar. **~cloth** *n* mantel *m*. **~-mat** *n* salvamanteles *m invar*. **~spoon** /'teɪblspu:n/ *n* cucharón *m*, cuchara *f* sopera. **~spoonful** *n* (*pl* **-fuls**) cucharada *f*

tablet /'tæblɪt/ *n* (*of stone*) lápida *f*; (*pill*) tableta *f*; (*of soap etc*) pastilla *f*

table tennis /'teɪbltenɪs/ *n* tenis *m* de mesa, ping-pong *m*

tabloid /'tæblɔɪd/ *n* tabloide *m*

taboo /tə'bu:/ *a & n* tabú (*m*)

tabulator /'tæbjʊleɪtə(r)/ *n* tabulador *m*

tacit /'tæsɪt/ *a* tácito

taciturn /'tæsɪtɜ:n/ *a* taciturno

tack /tæk/ *n* tachuela *f*; (*stitch*) hilván *m*; (*naut*) virada *f*; (*fig*) línea *f* de conducta. ● *vt* sujetar con tachuelas; (*sew*) hilvanar. **~ on** añadir. ● *vi* virar

tackle /'tækl/ *n* (*equipment*) equipo *m*; (*football*) placaje *m*. ● *vt* abordar ‹*problem etc*›; (*in rugby*) hacer un placaje a

tacky /'tækɪ/ *a* pegajoso; (*in poor taste*) vulgar, de pacotilla

tact /tækt/ *n* tacto *m*. **~ful** *a* discreto. **~fully** *adv* discretamente

tactic|al /'tæktɪkl/ *a* táctico. **~s** /'tæktɪks/ *npl* táctica *f*

tactile /'tæktaɪl/ *a* táctil

tact: **~less** *a* indiscreto. **~lessly** *adv* indiscretamente

tadpole /'tædpəʊl/ *n* renacuajo *m*

tag /tæg/ *n* (*on shoe-lace*) herrete *m*; (*label*) etiqueta *f*. ● *vt* (*pt* **tagged**) poner etiqueta a; (*trail*) seguir. ● *vi*. **~ along** (*fam*) seguir

tail /teɪl/ *n* cola *f*. **~s** *npl* (*tailcoat*) frac *m*; (*of coin*) cruz *f*. ● *vt* (*sl*) seguir. ● *vi*. **~ off** disminuir. **~-end** *n* extremo *m* final, cola *f*

tailor /'teɪlə(r)/ *n* sastre *m*. ● *vt* confeccionar. **~-made** *n* hecho a la medida. **~-made for** (*fig*) hecho para

tailplane /'teɪlpleɪn/ *n* plano *m* de cola

taint /teɪnt/ *n* mancha *f*. ● *vt* contaminar

take /teɪk/ *vt* (*pt* **took**, *pp* **taken**) tomar, coger (*not LAm*), agarrar (*esp LAm*); (*contain*) contener; (*capture*) capturar; (*endure*) aguantar; (*require*) requerir; tomar ‹*bath*›; dar ‹*walk*›; (*carry*) llevar; (*accompany*) acompañar; presentarse para ‹*exam*›; sacar ‹*photo*›; ganar ‹*prize*›. **~ advantage of** aprovechar. **~ after** parecerse a. **~ away** quitar. **~ back** retirar ‹*statement etc*›. **~ in** achicar ‹*garment*›; (*understand*) comprender; (*deceive*) engañar. **~ off** quitarse ‹*clothes*›; (*mimic*) imitar; (*aviat*) despegar. **~ o.s. off** marcharse. **~ on** (*undertake*) emprender; contratar ‹*employee*›. **~ out** (*remove*) sacar. **~ over** tomar posesión de; (*assume control*) tomar el poder. **~ part** participar. **~ place** tener lugar. **~ sides** tomar partido. **~ to** dedicarse a; (*like*) tomar simpatía a ‹*person*›; (*like*) aficionarse a ‹*thing*›. **~ up** dedicarse a ‹*hobby*›; (*occupy*) ocupar; (*resume*) reanudar. **~ up with** trabar amistad con. **be ~n ill** ponerse enfermo. ● *n* presa *f*; (*photo, cinema, TV*) toma *f*

takings /'teɪkɪŋz/ *npl* ingresos *mpl*

take: **~-off** *n* despegue *m*. **~-over** *n* toma *f* de posesión.

talcum /'tælkəm/ *n*. **~ powder** *n* (polvos *mpl* de) talco (*m*)

tale /teɪl/ *n* cuento *m*

talent /'tælənt/ *n* talento *m*. **~ed** *a* talentoso

talisman /'tælɪzmən/ *n* talismán *m*

talk /tɔ:k/ *vt/i* hablar. **~ about** hablar de. **~ over** discutir. ● *n* conversación *f*; (*lecture*) conferencia *f*. **small ~** charla *f*. **~ative** *a* hablador. **~er** *n* hablador *m*; (*chatterbox*) parlanchín *m*. **~ing-to** *n* reprensión *f*

tall /tɔ:l/ *a* (**-er**, **-est**) alto. **~ story** *n* (*fam*) historia *f* inverosímil. **that's a ~ order** *n* (*fam*) eso es pedir mucho

tallboy /'tɔ:lbɔɪ/ *n* cómoda *f* alta

tally /'tælɪ/ *n* tarja *f*; (*total*) total *m*. ● *vi* corresponder (**with** a)

talon /'tælən/ *n* garra *f*

tambourine /tæmbə'ri:n/ *n* pandereta *f*

tame /teɪm/ *a* (**-er**, **-est**) ‹*animal*› doméstico; ‹*person*› dócil; (*dull*) insípido. ● *vt* domesticar; domar ‹*wild animal*›. **~ly** *adv* dócilmente. **~r** /-ə(r)/ *n* domador *m*

tamper /'tæmpə(r)/ *vi*. **~ with** manosear; (*alter*) alterar, falsificar

tampon /'tæmpən/ *n* tampón *m*

tan /tæn/ *vt* (*pt* **tanned**) curtir ‹*hide*›; ‹*sun*› broncear. ● *vi* ponerse moreno. ● *n* bronceado *m*. ● *a* (*colour*) de color canela

tandem /'tændəm/ *n* tándem *m*

tang /tæŋ/ *n* sabor *m* fuerte; (*smell*) olor *m* fuerte

tangent /'tændʒənt/ *n* tangente *f*

tangerine /tændʒə'ri:n/ *n* mandarina *f*

tangibl|e /'tændʒəbl/ *a* tangible. **~y** *adv* perceptiblemente

tangle /'tæŋgl/ *vt* enredar. ● *vi* enredarse. ● *n* enredo *m*

tango /'tæŋgəʊ/ *n* (*pl* **-os**) tango *m*

tank /tæŋk/ *n* depósito *m*; (*mil*) tanque *m*

tankard /'tæŋkəd/ *n* jarra *f*, bock *m*

tanker /'tæŋkə(r)/ *n* petrolero *m*; (*truck*) camión *m* cisterna

tantaliz|e /'tæntəlaɪz/ *vt* atormentar. **~ing** *a* atormentador; (*tempting*) tentador

tantamount /'tæntəmaʊnt/ *a*. **~ to** equivalente a

tantrum /'tæntrəm/ *n* rabieta *f*

tap[1] /tæp/ *n* grifo *m*. **on ~** disponible. ● *vt* explotar ‹*resources*›; interceptar ‹*phone*›

tap[2] /tæp/ *n* (*knock*) golpe *m* ligero. ● *vt* (*pt* **tapped**) golpear ligeramente. **~-dance** *n* zapateado *m*

tape /teɪp/ *n* cinta *f*. ● *vt* atar con cinta; (*record*) grabar. **have sth ~d** (*sl*) comprender perfectamente. **~-measure** *n* cinta *f* métrica

taper /'teɪpə(r)/ *n* bujía *f*. ● *vt* ahusar. ● *vi* ahusarse. **~ off** disminuir

tape: **~ recorder** *n* magnetofón *m*, magnetófono *m*. **~ recording** *n* grabación *f*

tapestry /'tæpɪstrɪ/ *n* tapicería *f*; (*product*) tapiz *m*

tapioca /tæpɪ'əʊkə/ *n* tapioca *f*

tar /tɑ:(r)/ *n* alquitrán *m*. ● *vt* (*pt* **tarred**) alquitranar

tard|ily /'tɑ:dɪlɪ/ *adv* lentamente; (*late*) tardíamente. **~y** /'tɑ:dɪ/ *a* (**-ier**, **-iest**) (*slow*) lento; (*late*) tardío

target /'tɑ:gɪt/ *n* blanco *m*; (*fig*) objetivo *m*

tariff /'tærɪf/ *n* tarifa *f*

tarmac /'tɑ:mæk/ *n* pista *f* de aterrizaje. **T~** *n* (*P*) macadán *m*

tarnish /'tɑ:nɪʃ/ *vt* deslustrar. ● *vi* deslustrarse

tarpaulin /tɑ:'pɔ:lɪn/ *n* alquitranado *m*

tarragon /'tærəgən/ *n* estragón *m*

tart[1] /tɑ:t/ *n* pastel *m*; (*individual*) pastelillo *m*

tart[2] /tɑ:t/ *n* (*sl, woman*) prostituta *f*, fulana *f* (*fam*). ● *vt*. **~ o.s. up** (*fam*) engalanarse

tart[3] /tɑ:t/ *a* (**-er**, **-est**) ácido; (*fig*) áspero

tartan /'tɑ:tn/ *n* tartán *m*, tela *f* escocesa

tartar /'tɑ:tə(r)/ *n* tártaro *m*. **~ sauce** *n* salsa *f* tártara

task /tɑ:sk/ *n* tarea *f*. **take to ~** reprender. **~ force** *n* destacamiento *m* especial

tassel /'tæsl/ *n* borla *f*

tast|e /teɪst/ *n* sabor *m*, gusto *m*; (*small quantity*) poquito *m*. ● *vt* probar. ● *vi*. **~e of** saber a. **~eful** *a* de buen gusto. **~eless** *a* soso; (*fig*) de mal gusto. **~y** *a* (**-ier**, **-iest**) sabroso

tat /tæt/ *see* **tit**[2]

tatter|ed /'tætəd/ *a* hecho jirones. **~s** /'tætəz/ *npl* andrajos *mpl*

tattle /'tætl/ *vi* charlar. ● *n* charla *f*

tattoo[1] /tə'tu:/ (*mil*) espectáculo *m* militar

tattoo[2] /tə'tu:/ *vt* tatuar. ● *n* tatuaje *m*

tatty /'tætɪ/ *a* (**-ier**, **-iest**) gastado, en mal estado

taught /tɔ:t/ *see* **teach**

taunt /tɔ:nt/ *vt* mofarse de. **~ s.o. with sth** echar algo en cara a uno. ● *n* mofa *f*

Taurus /'tɔ:rəs/ *n* (*astr*) Tauro *m*

taut /tɔ:t/ *a* tenso

tavern /'tævən/ *n* taberna *f*

tawdry /'tɔ:drɪ/ *a* (**-ier**, **-iest**) charro

tawny /'tɔ:nɪ/ *a* bronceado

tax /tæks/ *n* impuesto *m*. ● *vt* imponer contribuciones a ‹*person*›; gravar con un impuesto ‹*thing*›; (*fig*) poner a prueba. **~able** *a* imponible. **~ation** /-'seɪʃn/ *n* impuestos *mpl*. **~-collector** *n* recaudador *m* de contribuciones. **~-free** *a* libre de impuestos

taxi /'tæksɪ/ *n* (*pl* **-is**) taxi *m*. ● *vi* (*pt* **taxied**, *pres p* **taxiing**) ‹*aircraft*› rodar por la pista. **~ rank** *n* parada *f* de taxis

taxpayer /'tækspeɪə(r)/ *n* contribuyente *m & f*
te /ti:/ *n* (*mus, seventh note of any musical scale*) si *m*
tea /ti:/ *n* té *m*. **~-bag** *n* bolsita *f* de té. **~-break** *n* descanso *m* para el té
teach /ti:tʃ/ *vt/i* (*pt* **taught**) enseñar. **~er** *n* profesor *m*; (*primary*) maestro *m*. **~-in** *n* seminario *m*. **~ing** *n* enseñanza *f*. ● *a* docente. **~ing staff** *n* profesorado *m*
teacup /'ti:kʌp/ *n* taza *f* de té
teak /ti:k/ *n* teca *f*
tea-leaf /'ti:li:f/ *n* hoja *f* de té
team /ti:m/ *n* equipo *m*; (*of horses*) tiro *m*. ● *vi*. **~ up** unirse. **~-work** *n* trabajo *m* en equipo
teapot /'ti:pɒt/ *n* tetera *f*
tear[1] /teə(r)/ *vt* (*pt* **tore**, *pp* **torn**) rasgar. ● *vi* rasgarse; (*run*) precipitarse. ● *n* rasgón *m*. **~ apart** desgarrar. **~ o.s. away** separarse
tear[2] /tɪə(r)/ *n* lágrima *f*. **in ~s** llorando
tearaway /'teərəweɪ/ *n* gamberro *m*
tear /tɪə(r)/: **~ful** *a* lloroso. **~-gas** *n* gas *m* lacrimógeno
tease /ti:z/ *vt* tomar el pelo a; cardar ‹*cloth etc*›. ● *n* guasón *m*. **~r** /-ə(r)/ *n* (*fam*) problema *m* difícil
tea: **~-set** *n* juego *m* de té. **~spoon** /'ti:spu:n/ *n* cucharilla *f*. **~spoonful** *n* (*pl* **-fuls**) (*amount*) cucharadita *f*
teat /ti:t/ *n* (*of animal*) teta *f*; (*for bottle*) tetilla *f*
tea-towel /'ti:taʊəl/ *n* paño *m* de cocina
technical /'teknɪkl/ *a* técnico. **~ity** *n* /-'kælətɪ/ *n* detalle *m* técnico. **~ly** *adv* técnicamente
technician /tek'nɪʃn/ *n* técnico *m*
technique /tek'ni:k/ *n* técnica *f*
technolog|ist /tek'nɒlədʒɪst/ *n* tecnólogo *m*. **~y** /tek'nɒlədʒɪ/ *n* tecnología *f*
teddy bear /'tedɪbeə(r)/ *n* osito *m* de felpa, osito *m* de peluche
tedious /'ti:dɪəs/ *a* pesado. **~ly** *adv* pesadamente
tedium /'ti:dɪəm/ *n* aburrimiento *m*
tee /ti:/ *n* (*golf*) tee *m*
teem /ti:m/ *vi* abundar; (*rain*) llover a cántaros
teen|age /'ti:neɪdʒ/ *a* adolescente; (*for teenagers*) para jóvenes. **~ager** /-ə(r)/ *n* adolescente *m & f*, joven *m & f*. **~s** /ti:nz/ *npl*. **the ~s** la adolescencia *f*
teeny /'ti:nɪ/ *a* (**-ier**, **-iest**) (*fam*) chiquito
teeter /'ti:tə(r)/ *vi* balancearse
teeth /ti:θ/ *see* **tooth**. **~e** /ti:ð/ *vi* echar los dientes. **~ing troubles** *npl* (*fig*) dificultades *fpl* iniciales
teetotaller /ti:'təʊtələ(r)/ *n* abstemio *m*
telecommunications /telɪkəmju:nɪ'keɪʃnz/ *npl* telecomunicaciones *fpl*
telegram /'telɪgræm/ *n* telegrama *m*
telegraph /'telɪgrɑ:f/ *n* telégrafo *m*. ● *vt* telegrafiar. **~ic** /-'græfɪk/ *a* telegráfico
telepath|ic /telɪ'pæθɪk/ *a* telepático. **~y** /tɪ'lepəθɪ/ *n* telepatía *f*
telephon|e /'telɪfəʊn/ *n* teléfono *m*. ● *vt* llamar por teléfono. **~e booth** *n* cabina *f* telefónica. **~e directory** *n* guía *f* telefónica. **~e exchange** *n* central *f* telefónica. **~ic** /-'fɒnɪk/ *a* telefónico. **~ist** /tɪ'lefənɪst/ *n* telefonista *m & f*
telephoto /telɪ'fəʊtəʊ/ *a*. **~ lens** *n* teleobjetivo *m*
teleprinter /'telɪprɪntə(r)/ *n* teleimpresor *m*
telescop|e /'telɪskəʊp/ *n* telescopio *m*. **~ic** /-'kɒpɪk/ *a* telescópico
televis|e /'telɪvaɪz/ *vt* televisar. **~ion** /'telɪvɪʒn/ *n* televisión *f*. **~ion set** *n* televisor *m*
telex /'teleks/ *n* télex *m*. ● *vt* enviar por télex
tell /tel/ *vt* (*pt* **told**) decir; contar ‹*story*›; (*distinguish*) distinguir. ● *vi* (*produce an effect*) tener efecto; (*know*) saber. **~ off** *vt* reprender. **~er** /'telə(r)/ *n* (*in bank*) cajero *m*
telling /'telɪŋ/ *a* eficaz
tell-tale /'telteɪl/ *n* soplón *m*. ● *a* revelador
telly /'telɪ/ *n* (*fam*) televisión *f*, tele *f* (*fam*)
temerity /tɪ'merətɪ/ *n* temeridad *f*
temp /temp/ *n* (*fam*) empleado *m* temporal
temper /'tempə(r)/ *n* (*disposition*) disposición *f*; (*mood*) humor *m*; (*fit of anger*) cólera *f*; (*of metal*) temple *m*. **be in a ~** estar de mal humor. **keep one's ~** contenerse. **lose one's ~** enfadarse, perder la paciencia. ● *vt* templar ‹*metal*›
temperament /'temprəmənt/ *n* temperamento *m*. **~al** /-'mentl/ *a* caprichoso

temperance /'tempərəns/ *n* moderación *f*
temperate /'tempərət/ *a* moderado; ‹*climate*› templado
temperature /'temprɪtʃə(r)/ *n* temperatura *f*. **have a ~** tener fiebre
tempest /'tempɪst/ *n* tempestad *f*. **~uous** /-'pestjʊəs/ *a* tempestuoso
temple[1] /'templ/ *n* templo *m*
temple[2] /'templ/ (*anat*) sien *f*
tempo /'tempəʊ/ *n* (*pl* **-os** *or* **tempi**) ritmo *m*
temporar|ily /'tempərərəlɪ/ *adv* temporalmente. **~y** /'tempərərɪ/ *a* temporal, provisional
tempt /tempt/ *vt* tentar. **~ s.o. to** inducir a uno a. **~ation** /-'teɪʃn/ *n* tentación *f*. **~ing** *a* tentador
ten /ten/ *a* & *n* diez (*m*)
tenable /'tenəbl/ *a* sostenible
tenaci|ous /tɪ'neɪʃəs/ *a* tenaz. **~ty** /-æsətɪ/ *n* tenacidad *f*
tenan|cy /'tenənsɪ/ *n* alquiler *m*. **~t** /'tenənt/ *n* inquilino *m*
tend[1] /tend/ *vi*. **~ to** tener tendencia a
tend[2] /tend/ *vt* cuidar
tendency /'tendənsɪ/ *n* tendencia *f*
tender[1] /'tendə(r)/ *a* tierno; (*painful*) dolorido
tender[2] /'tendə(r)/ *n* (*com*) oferta *f*. **legal ~** *n* curso *m* legal. ● *vt* ofrecer, presentar
tender: **~ly** *adv* tiernamente. **~ness** *n* ternura *f*
tendon /'tendən/ *n* tendón *m*
tenement /'tenəmənt/ *n* vivienda *f*
tenet /'tenɪt/ *n* principio *m*
tenfold /'tenfəʊld/ *a* diez veces mayor, décuplo. ● *adv* diez veces
tenner /'tenə(r)/ *n* (*fam*) billete *m* de diez libras
tennis /'tenɪs/ *n* tenis *m*
tenor /'tenə(r)/ *n* tenor *m*
tens|e /tens/ *a* (**-er**, **-est**) tieso; (*fig*) tenso. ● *n* (*gram*) tiempo *m*. ● *vi*. **~ up** tensarse. **~eness** *n*, **~ion** /'tenʃn/ *n* tensión *f*
tent /tent/ *n* tienda *f*, carpa *f* (*LAm*)
tentacle /'tentəkl/ *n* tentáculo *m*
tentative /'tentətɪv/ *a* provisional; (*hesitant*) indeciso. **~ly** *adv* provisionalmente; (*timidly*) tímidamente
tenterhooks /'tentəhʊks/ *npl*. **on ~** en ascuas
tenth /tenθ/ *a* & *n* décimo (*m*)
tenuous /'tenjʊəs/ *a* tenue
tenure /'tenjʊə(r)/ *n* posesión *f*
tepid /'tepɪd/ *a* tibio
term /tɜ:m/ *n* (*of time*) período *m*; (*schol*) trimestre *m*; (*word etc*) término *m*. ● *vt* llamar. **~s** *npl* condiciones *fpl*; (*com*) precio *m*. **on bad ~s** en malas relaciones. **on good ~s** en buenas relaciones
terminal /'tɜ:mɪnl/ *a* terminal, final. ● *n* (*rail*) estación *f* terminal; (*elec*) borne *m*. **(air) ~** *n* término *m*, terminal *m*
terminat|e /'tɜ:mɪneɪt/ *vt* terminar. ● *vi* terminarse. **~tion** /-'neɪʃn/ *n* terminación *f*
terminology /tɜ:mɪ'nɒlədʒɪ/ *n* terminología *f*
terrace /'terəs/ *n* terraza *f*; (*houses*) hilera *f* de casas. **the ~s** *npl* (*sport*) las gradas *fpl*
terrain /tə'reɪn/ *n* terreno *m*
terrestrial /tɪ'restrɪəl/ *a* terrestre
terribl|e /'terəbl/ *a* terrible. **~y** *adv* terriblemente
terrier /'terɪə(r)/ *n* terrier *m*
terrific /tə'rɪfɪk/ *a* (*excellent*, *fam*) estupendo; (*huge*, *fam*) enorme. **~ally** *adv* (*fam*) terriblemente; (*very well*) muy bien
terrify /'terɪfaɪ/ *vt* aterrorizar. **~ing** *a* espantoso
territor|ial /terɪ'tɔ:rɪəl/ *a* territorial. **~y** /'terɪtrɪ/ *n* territorio *m*
terror /'terə(r)/ *n* terror *m*. **~ism** /-zəm/ *n* terrorismo *m*. **~ist** /'terərɪst/ *n* terrorista *m* & *f*. **~ize** /'terəraɪz/ *vt* aterrorizar
terse /tɜ:s/ *a* conciso; (*abrupt*) brusco
test /test/ *n* prueba *f*; (*exam*) examen *m*. ● *vt* probar; (*examine*) examinar
testament /'testəmənt/ *n* testamento *m*. **New T~** Nuevo Testamento. **Old T~** Antiguo Testamento
testicle /'testɪkl/ *n* testículo *m*
testify /'testɪfaɪ/ *vt* atestiguar. ● *vi* declarar
testimon|ial /testɪ'məʊnɪəl/ *n* certificado *m*; (*of character*) recomendación *f*. **~y** /'testɪmənɪ/ *n* testimonio *m*
test: **~ match** *n* partido *m* internacional. **~-tube** *n* tubo *m* de ensayo, probeta *f*
testy /'testɪ/ *a* irritable
tetanus /'tetənəs/ *n* tétanos *m invar*
tetchy /'tetʃɪ/ *a* irritable

tether /'teðə(r)/ *vt* atar. ● *n*. **be at the end of one's ~** no poder más
text /tekst/ *n* texto *m*. **~book** *n* libro *m* de texto
textile /'tekstaɪl/ *a & n* textil (*m*)
texture /'tekstʃə(r)/ *n* textura *f*
Thai /taɪ/ *a & n* tailandés (*m*). **~land** *n* Tailandia *f*
Thames /temz/ *n* Támesis *m*
than /ðæn, ðən/ *conj* que; (*with numbers*) de
thank /θæŋk/ *vt* dar las gracias a, agradecer. **~ you** gracias. **~ful** /'θæŋkfl/ *a* agradecido. **~fully** *adv* con gratitud; (*happily*) afortunadamente. **~less** /'θæŋklɪs/ *a* ingrato. **~s** *npl* gracias *fpl*. **~s!** (*fam*) ¡gracias! **~s to** gracias a
that /ðæt, ðət/ *a* (*pl* **those**) ese, aquel, esa, aquella. ● *pron* (*pl* **those**) ése, aquél, ésa, aquélla. **~ is** es decir. **~'s it!** ¡eso es! **~ is why** por eso. **is ~ you?** ¿eres tú? **like ~** así. ● *adv* tan. ● *rel pron* que; (*with prep*) el que, la que, el cual, la cual. ● *conj* que
thatch /θætʃ/ *n* techo *m* de paja. **~ed** *a* con techo de paja
thaw /θɔ:/ *vt* deshelar. ● *vi* deshelarse; ‹*snow*› derretirse. ● *n* deshielo *m*
the /ðə, ði:/ *def art* el, la, los, las. **at ~** al, a la, a los, a las. **from ~** del, de la, de los, de las. **to ~** al, a la, a los, a las. ● *adv*. **all ~ better** tanto mejor
theatr|e /'θɪətə(r)/ *n* teatro *m*. **~ical** /-'ætrɪkl/ *a* teatral
theft /θeft/ *n* hurto *m*
their /ðeə(r)/ *a* su, sus
theirs /ðeəz/ *poss pron* (el) suyo, (la) suya, (los) suyos, (las) suyas
them /ðem, ðəm/ *pron* (*accusative*) los, las; (*dative*) les; (*after prep*) ellos, ellas
theme /θi:m/ *n* tema *m*. **~ song** *n* motivo *m* principal
themselves /ðəm'selvz/ *pron* ellos mismos, ellas mismas; (*reflexive*) se; (*after prep*) sí mismos, sí mismas
then /ðen/ *adv* entonces; (*next*) luego, después. **by ~** para entonces. **now and ~** de vez en cuando. **since ~** desde entonces. ● *a* de entonces
theolog|ian /θɪə'ləʊdʒən/ *n* teólogo *m*. **~y** /θɪ'ɒlədʒɪ/ *n* teología *f*
theorem /'θɪərəm/ *n* teorema *m*
theor|etical /θɪə'retɪkl/ *a* teórico. **~y** /'θɪərɪ/ *n* teoría *f*
therap|eutic /θerə'pju:tɪk/ *a* terapéutico. **~ist** *n* terapeuta *m & f*. **~y** /'θerəpɪ/ *n* terapia *f*
there /ðeə(r)/ *adv* ahí, allí. **~ are** hay. **~ he is** ahí está. **~ is** hay. **~ it is** ahí está. **down ~** ahí abajo. **up ~** ahí arriba. ● *int* ¡vaya! **~, ~!** ¡ya, ya! **~abouts** *adv* por ahí. **~after** *adv* después. **~by** *adv* por eso. **~fore** /'ðeəfɔ:(r)/ *adv* por lo tanto.
thermal /'θɜ:ml/ *a* termal
thermometer /θə'mɒmɪtə(r)/ *n* termómetro *m*
thermonuclear /θɜ:məʊ'nju:klɪə(r)/ *a* termonuclear
Thermos /'θɜ:məs/ *n* (*P*) termo *m*
thermostat /'θɜ:məstæt/ *n* termostato *m*
thesaurus /θɪ'sɔ:rəs/ *n* (*pl* **-ri** /-raɪ/) diccionario *m* de sinónimos
these /ði:z/ *a* estos, estas. ● *pron* éstos, éstas
thesis /'θi:sɪs/ *n* (*pl* **theses** /-si:z/) tesis *f*
they /ðeɪ/ *pron* ellos, ellas. **~ say that** se dice que
thick /θɪk/ *a* (**-er, -est**) espeso; (*dense*) denso; (*stupid, fam*) torpe; (*close, fam*) íntimo. ● *adv* espesamente, densamente. ● *n*. **in the ~ of** en medio de. **~en** /'θɪkən/ *vt* espesar. ● *vi* espesarse
thicket /'θɪkɪt/ *n* matorral *m*
thick: **~ly** *adv* espesamente, densamente. **~ness** *n* espesor *m*
thickset /θɪk'set/ *a* fornido
thick-skinned /θɪk'skɪnd/ *a* insensible
thief /θi:f/ *n* (*pl* **thieves**) ladrón *m*
thiev|e /θi:v/ *vt/i* robar. **~ing** *a* ladrón
thigh /θaɪ/ *n* muslo *m*
thimble /'θɪmbl/ *n* dedal *m*
thin /θɪn/ *a* (**thinner, thinnest**) delgado; ‹*person*› flaco; (*weak*) débil; (*fine*) fino; (*sparse*) escaso. ● *adv* ligeramente. ● *vt* (*pt* **thinned**) adelgazar; (*dilute*) diluir. **~ out** hacer menos denso. ● *vi* adelgazarse; (*diminish*) disminuir
thing /θɪŋ/ *n* cosa *f*. **for one ~** en primer lugar. **just the ~** exactamente lo que se necesita. **poor ~!** ¡pobrecito! **~s** *npl* (*belongings*) efectos *mpl*; (*clothing*) ropa *f*
think /θɪŋk/ *vt* (*pt* **thought**) pensar, creer. ● *vi* pensar (**about, of** en); (*carefully*) reflexionar; (*imagine*) imaginarse. **~ better of it** cambiar de idea. **I ~ so** creo que sí. **~ over** *vt* pensar bien. **~ up** *vt* idear,

inventar. **~er** *n* pensador *m*. **~-tank** *n* grupo *m* de expertos

thin: **~ly** *adv* ligeramente. **~ness** *n* delgadez *f*; (*of person*) flaqueza *f*

third /θɜ:d/ *a* tercero. ● *n* tercio *m*, tercera parte *f*. **~-rate** *a* muy inferior. **T~ World** *n* Tercer Mundo *m*

thirst /θɜ:st/ *n* sed *f*. **~y** *a* sediento. **be ~y** tener sed

thirteen /θɜ:'ti:n/ *a* & *n* trece (*m*). **~th** *a* & *n* decimotercero (*m*)

thirt|ieth /'θɜ:tɪəθ/ *a* & *n* trigésimo (*m*). **~y** /'θɜ:tɪ/ *a* & *n* treinta (*m*)

this /ðɪs/ *a* (*pl* **these**) este, esta. **~ one** éste, ésta. ● *pron* (*pl* **these**) éste, ésta, esto. **like ~** así

thistle /'θɪsl/ *n* cardo *m*

thong /θɒŋ/ *n* correa *f*

thorn /θɔ:n/ *n* espina *f*. **~y** *a* espinoso

thorough /'θʌrə/ *a* completo; (*deep*) profundo; ‹*cleaning etc*› a fondo; ‹*person*› concienzudo

thoroughbred /'θʌrəbred/ *a* de pura sangre

thoroughfare /'θʌrəfeə(r)/ *n* calle *f*. **no ~** prohibido el paso

thoroughly /'θʌrəlɪ/ *adv* completamente

those /ðəʊz/ *a* esos, aquellos, esas, aquellas. ● *pron* ésos, aquéllos, ésas, aquéllas

though /ðəʊ/ *conj* aunque. ● *adv* sin embargo. **as ~** como si

thought /θɔ:t/ *see* **think**. ● *n* pensamiento *m*; (*idea*) idea *f*. **~ful** /'θɔ:tfl/ *a* pensativo; (*considerate*) atento. **~fully** *adv* pensativamente; (*considerately*) atentamente. **~less** /'θɔ:tlɪs/ *a* irreflexivo; (*inconsiderate*) desconsiderado

thousand /'θaʊznd/ *a* & *n* mil (*m*). **~th** *a* & *n* milésimo (*m*)

thrash /θræʃ/ *vt* azotar; (*defeat*) derrotar. **~ out** discutir a fondo

thread /θred/ *n* hilo *m*; (*of screw*) rosca *f*. ● *vt* ensartar. **~ one's way** abrirse paso. **~bare** /'θredbeə(r)/ *a* raído

threat /θret/ *n* amenaza *f*. **~en** /'θretn/ *vt/i* amenazar. **~ening** *a* amenazador. **~eningly** *adv* de modo amenazador

three /θri:/ *a* & *n* tres (*m*). **~fold** *a* triple. ● *adv* tres veces. **~some** /'θri:səm/ *n* conjunto *m* de tres personas

thresh /θreʃ/ *vt* trillar

threshold /'θreʃhəʊld/ *n* umbral *m*

threw /θru:/ *see* **throw**

thrift /θrɪft/ *n* economía *f*, ahorro *m*. **~y** *a* frugal

thrill /θrɪl/ *n* emoción *f*. ● *vt* emocionar. ● *vi* emocionarse; (*quiver*) estremecerse. **be ~ed with** estar encantado de. **~er** /'θrɪlə(r)/ *n* (*book*) libro *m* de suspense; (*film*) película *f* de suspense. **~ing** *a* emocionante

thriv|e /θraɪv/ *vi* prosperar. **~ing** *a* próspero

throat /θrəʊt/ *n* garganta *f*. **have a sore ~** dolerle la garganta

throb /θrɒb/ *vi* (*pt* **throbbed**) palpitar; (*with pain*) dar punzadas; (*fig*) vibrar. ● *n* palpitación *f*; (*pain*) punzada *f*; (*fig*) vibración *f*. **~bing** *a* ‹*pain*› punzante

throes /θrəʊz/ *npl*. **in the ~ of** en medio de

thrombosis /θrɒm'bəʊsɪs/ *n* trombosis *f*

throne /θrəʊn/ *n* trono *m*

throng /θrɒŋ/ *n* multitud *f*

throttle /'θrɒtl/ *n* (*auto*) acelerador *m*. ● *vt* ahogar

through /θru:/ *prep* por, a través de; (*during*) durante; (*by means of*) por medio de; (*thanks to*) gracias a. ● *adv* de parte a parte, de un lado a otro; (*entirely*) completamente; (*to the end*) hasta el final. **be ~** (*finished*) haber terminado. ● *a* ‹*train etc*› directo

throughout /θru:'aʊt/ *prep* por todo; (*time*) en todo. ● *adv* en todas partes; (*all the time*) todo el tiempo

throve /θrəʊv/ *see* **thrive**

throw /θrəʊ/ *vt* (*pt* **threw**, *pp* **thrown**) arrojar; (*baffle etc*) desconcertar. **~ a party** (*fam*) dar una fiesta. ● *n* tiro *m*; (*of dice*) lance *m*. **~ away** *vt* tirar. **~ over** *vt* abandonar. **~ up** *vi* (*vomit*) vomitar. **~-away** *a* desechable

thrush /θrʌʃ/ *n* tordo *m*

thrust /θrʌst/ *vt* (*pt* **thrust**) empujar; (*push in*) meter. ● *n* empuje *m*. **~ (up)on** imponer a

thud /θʌd/ *n* ruido *m* sordo

thug /θʌg/ *n* bruto *m*

thumb /θʌm/ *n* pulgar *m*. **under the ~ of** dominado por. ● *vt* hojear ‹*book*›. **~ a lift** hacer autostop. **~-index** *n* uñeros *mpl*

thump /θʌmp/ *vt* golpear. ● *vi* ‹*heart*› latir fuertemente. ● *n* porrazo *m*; (*noise*) ruido *m* sordo

thunder /'θʌndə(r)/ *n* trueno *m*. ● *vi* tronar. ~ **past** pasar con estruendo. ~**bolt** /'θʌndəbəʊlt/ *n* rayo *m*. ~**clap** /'θʌndəklæp/ *n* trueno *m*. ~**storm** /'θʌndəstɔ:m/ *n* tronada *f*. ~**y** *a* con truenos

Thursday /'θɜ:zdeɪ/ *n* jueves *m*

thus /ðʌs/ *adv* así

thwart /θwɔ:t/ *vt* frustrar

thyme /taɪm/ *n* tomillo *m*

thyroid /'θaɪrɔɪd/ *n* tiroides *m invar*

tiara /tɪ'ɑ:rə/ *n* diadema *f*

tic /tɪk/ *n* tic *m*

tick[1] /tɪk/ *n* tictac *m*; (*mark*) señal *f*, marca *f*; (*instant, fam*) momentito *m*. ● *vi* hacer tictac. ● *vt*. ~ **(off)** marcar. ~ **off** *vt* (*sl*) reprender. ~ **over** *vi* ‹*of engine*› marchar en vacío

tick[2] /tɪk/ *n* (*insect*) garrapata *f*

tick[3] /tɪk/ *n*. **on** ~ (*fam*) a crédito

ticket /'tɪkɪt/ *n* billete *m*, boleto *m* (*LAm*); (*label*) etiqueta *f*; (*fine*) multa *f*. ~**-collector** *n* revisor *m*. ~**-office** *n* taquilla *f*

tickl|e /'tɪkl/ *vt* hacer cosquillas a; (*amuse*) divertir. ● *n* cosquilleo *m*. ~**ish** /'tɪklɪʃ/ *a* cosquilloso; ‹*problem*› delicado. **be** ~**ish** tener cosquillas

tidal /'taɪdl/ *a* de marea. ~ **wave** *n* maremoto *m*

tiddly-winks /'tɪdlɪwɪŋks/ *n* juego *m* de pulgas

tide /taɪd/ *n* marea *f*; (*of events*) curso *m*. ● *vt*. ~ **over** ayudar a salir de un apuro

tidings /'taɪdɪŋz/ *npl* noticias *fpl*

tid|ily /'taɪdɪlɪ/ *adv* en orden; (*well*) bien. ~**iness** *n* orden *m*. ~**y** /'taɪdɪ/ *a* (**-ier**, **-iest**) ordenado; ‹*amount, fam*› considerable. ● *vt*/*i*. ~**y (up)** ordenar. ~**y o.s. up** arreglarse

tie /taɪ/ *vt* (*pres p* **tying**) atar; hacer ‹*a knot*›; (*link*) vincular. ● *vi* (*sport*) empatar. ● *n* atadura *f*; (*necktie*) corbata *f*; (*link*) lazo *m*; (*sport*) empate *m*. ~ **in with** relacionar con. ~ **up** atar; (*com*) inmovilizar. **be** ~**d up** (*busy*) estar ocupado

tier /tɪə(r)/ *n* fila *f*; (*in stadium etc*) grada *f*; (*of cake*) piso *m*

tie-up /'taɪʌp/ *n* enlace *m*

tiff /tɪf/ *n* riña *f*

tiger /'taɪgə(r)/ *n* tigre *m*

tight /taɪt/ *a* (**-er**, **-est**) ‹*clothes*› ceñido; (*taut*) tieso; ‹*control etc*› riguroso; ‹*knot, nut*› apretado; (*drunk, fam*) borracho. ● *adv* bien; (*shut*) herméticamente. ~ **corner** *n* (*fig*) apuro *m*. ~**en** /'taɪtn/ *vt* apretar. ● *vi* apretarse. ~**-fisted** *a* tacaño. ~**ly** *adv* bien; (*shut*) herméticamente. ~**ness** *n* estrechez *f*. ~**rope** /'taɪtrəʊp/ *n* cuerda *f* floja. ~**s** /taɪts/ *npl* leotardos *mpl*

tile /taɪl/ *n* (*decorative*) azulejo *m*; (*on roof*) teja *f*; (*on floor*) baldosa *f*. ● *vt* azulejar; tejar ‹*roof*›; embaldosar ‹*floor*›

till[1] /tɪl/ *prep* hasta. ● *conj* hasta que

till[2] /tɪl/ *n* caja *f*

till[3] /tɪl/ *vt* cultivar

tilt /tɪlt/ *vt* inclinar. ● *vi* inclinarse. ● *n* inclinación *f*. **at full** ~ a toda velocidad

timber /'tɪmbə(r)/ *n* madera *f* (de construcción); (*trees*) árboles *mpl*

time /taɪm/ *n* tiempo *m*; (*moment*) momento *m*; (*occasion*) ocasión *f*; (*by clock*) hora *f*; (*epoch*) época *f*; (*rhythm*) compás *m*. ~ **off** tiempo libre. **at** ~**s** a veces. **behind the** ~**s** anticuado. **behind** ~ atrasado. **for the** ~ **being** por ahora. **from** ~ **to** ~ de vez en cuando. **have a good** ~ divertirse, pasarlo bien. **in a year's** ~ dentro de un año. **in no** ~ en un abrir y cerrar de ojos. **in** ~ a tiempo; (*eventually*) con el tiempo. **on** ~ a la hora, puntual. ● *vt* elegir el momento; cronometrar ‹*race*›. ~ **bomb** *n* bomba *f* de tiempo. ~**-honoured** *a* consagrado. ~**-lag** *n* intervalo *m*

timeless /'taɪmlɪs/ *a* eterno

timely /'taɪmlɪ/ *a* oportuno

timer /'taɪmə(r)/ *n* cronómetro *m*; (*culin*) avisador *m*; (*with sand*) reloj *m* de arena; (*elec*) interruptor *m* de reloj

timetable /'taɪmteɪbl/ *n* horario *m*

time zone /'taɪmzəʊn/ *n* huso *m* horario

timid /'tɪmɪd/ *a* tímido; (*fearful*) miedoso. ~**ly** *adv* tímidamente

timing /'taɪmɪŋ/ *n* medida *f* del tiempo; (*moment*) momento *m*; (*sport*) cronometraje *m*

timorous /'tɪmərəs/ *a* tímido; (*fearful*) miedoso. ~**ly** *adv* tímidamente

tin /tɪn/ *n* estaño *m*; (*container*) lata *f*. ~ **foil** *n* papel *m* de estaño. ● *vt* (*pt* **tinned**) conservar en lata, enlatar

tinge /tɪndʒ/ *vt* teñir (**with** de); (*fig*) matizar (**with** de). ● *n* matiz *m*

tingle /'tɪŋgl/ *vi* sentir hormigueo; (*with excitement*) estremecerse

tinker /'tɪŋkə(r)/ *n* hojalatero *m*. ● *vi*. ~ **(with)** jugar con; (*repair*) arreglar

tinkle /'tɪŋkl/ *n* retintín *m*; (*phone call, fam*) llamada *f*

tin: ~**ned** *a* en lata. ~**ny** *a* metálico. ~**-opener** *n* abrelatas *m invar*. ~ **plate** *n* hojalata *f*

tinpot /'tɪnpɒt/ *a* (*pej*) inferior

tinsel /'tɪnsl/ *n* oropel *m*

tint /tɪnt/ *n* matiz *m*

tiny /'taɪnɪ/ *a* (**-ier**, **-iest**) diminuto

tip[1] /tɪp/ *n* punta *f*

tip[2] /tɪp/ *vt* (*pt* **tipped**) (*tilt*) inclinar; (*overturn*) volcar; (*pour*) verter● *vi* inclinarse; (*overturn*) volcarse. ● *n* (*for rubbish*) vertedero *m*. ~ **out** verter

tip[3] /tɪp/ *vt* (*reward*) dar una propina a. ~ **off** advertir. ● *n* (*reward*) propina *f*; (*advice*) consejo *m*

tip-off /'tɪpɒf/ *n* advertencia *f*

tipped /'tɪpt/ *a* ‹*cigarette*› con filtro

tipple /'tɪpl/ *vi* beborrotear. ● *n* bebida *f* alcohólica. **have a** ~ tomar una copa

tipsy /'tɪpsɪ/ *a* achispado

tiptoe /'tɪptəʊ/ *n*. **on** ~ de puntillas

tiptop /'tɪptɒp/ *a* (*fam*) de primera

tirade /taɪ'reɪd/ *n* diatriba *f*

tire /'taɪə(r)/ *vt* cansar. ● *vi* cansarse. ~**d** /'taɪəd/ *a* cansado. ~**d of** harto de. ~**d out** agotado. ~**less** *a* incansable

tiresome /'taɪəsəm/ *a* (*annoying*) fastidioso; (*boring*) pesado

tiring /'taɪərɪŋ/ *a* cansado

tissue /'tɪʃu:/ *n* tisú *m*; (*handkerchief*) pañuelo *m* de papel. ~**-paper** *n* papel *m* de seda

tit[1] /tɪt/ *n* (*bird*) paro *m*

tit[2] /tɪt/ *n*. ~ **for tat** golpe por golpe

titbit /'tɪtbɪt/ *n* golosina *f*

titillate /'tɪtɪleɪt/ *vt* excitar

title /'taɪtl/ *n* título *m*. ~**d** *a* con título nobiliario. ~**-deed** *n* título *m* de propiedad. ~**-role** *n* papel *m* principal

tittle-tattle /'tɪtltætl/ *n* cháchara *f*

titular /'tɪtjʊlə(r)/ *a* nominal

tizzy /'tɪzɪ/ *n* (*sl*). **get in a** ~ ponerse nervioso

to /tu:, tə/ *prep* a; (*towards*) hacia; (*in order to*) para; (*according to*) según; (*as far as*) hasta; (*with times*) menos; (*of*) de. **give it** ~ **me** dámelo. **I don't want to** no quiero. **twenty** ~ **seven** (*by clock*) las siete menos veinte. ● *adv*. **push** ~, **pull** ~ cerrar. ~ **and fro** *adv* de aquí para allá

toad /təʊd/ *n* sapo *m*

toadstool /'təʊdstu:l/ *n* seta *f* venenosa

toast /təʊst/ *n* pan *m* tostado, tostada *f*; (*drink*) brindis *m*. **drink a** ~ **to** brindar por. ● *vt* brindar por. ~**er** *n* tostador *m* de pan

tobacco /tə'bækəʊ/ *n* tabaco *m*. ~**nist** *n* estanquero *m*. ~**nist's shop** *n* estanco *m*

to-be /tə'bi:/ *a* futuro

toboggan /tə'bɒgən/ *n* tobogán *m*

today /tə'deɪ/ *n* & *adv* hoy (*m*). ~ **week** dentro de una semana

toddler /'tɒdlə(r)/ *n* niño *m* que empieza a andar

toddy /'tɒdɪ/ *n* ponche *m*

to-do /tə'du:/ *n* lío *m*

toe /təʊ/ *n* dedo *m* del pie; (*of shoe*) punta *f*. **big** ~ dedo *m* gordo (del pie). **on one's** ~**s** (*fig*) alerta. ● *vt*. ~ **the line** conformarse. ~**-hold** *n* punto *m* de apoyo

toff /tɒf/ *n* (*sl*) petimetre *m*

toffee /'tɒfɪ/ *n* caramelo *m*

together /tə'geðə(r)/ *adv* junto, juntos; (*at same time*) a la vez. ~ **with** junto con. ~**ness** *n* compañerismo *m*

toil /tɔɪl/ *vi* afanarse. ● *n* trabajo *m*

toilet /'tɔɪlɪt/ *n* servicio *m*, retrete *m*; (*grooming*) arreglo *m*, tocado *m*. ~**-paper** *n* papel *m* higiénico. ~**ries** /'tɔɪlɪtrɪz/ *npl* artículos *mpl* de tocador. ~ **water** *n* agua *f* de Colonia

token /'təʊkən/ *n* señal *f*; (*voucher*) vale *m*; (*coin*) ficha *f*. ● *a* simbólico

told /təʊld/ *see* **tell**. ● *a*. **all** ~ con todo

tolerabl|e /'tɒlərəbl/ *a* tolerable; (*not bad*) regular. ~**y** *adv* pasablemente

toleran|ce /'tɒlərəns/ *n* tolerancia *f*. ~**t** /'tɒlərənt/ *a* tolerante. ~**tly** *adv* con tolerancia

tolerate /'tɒləreɪt/ *vt* tolerar

toll[1] /təʊl/ *n* peaje *m*. **death** ~ número *m* de muertos. **take a heavy** ~ dejar muchas víctimas

toll[2] /təʊl/ *vi* doblar, tocar a muerto

tom /tɒm/ *n* gato *m* (macho)

tomato /tə'mɑ:təʊ/ *n* (*pl* ~**oes**) tomate *m*

tomb /tu:m/ *n* tumba *f*, sepulcro *m*

tomboy /'tɒmbɔɪ/ *n* marimacho *m*

tombstone /'tu:mstəʊn/ *n* lápida *f* sepulcral

tom-cat /'tɒmkæt/ *n* gato *m* (macho)
tome /təʊm/ *n* librote *m*
tomfoolery /tɒm'fu:lərɪ/ *n* payasadas *fpl*, tonterías *fpl*
tomorrow /tə'mɒrəʊ/ *n & adv* mañana (*f*). **see you ~!** ¡hasta mañana!
ton /tʌn/ *n* tonelada *f* (= *1,016 kg*). **~s of** (*fam*) montones de. **metric ~** tonelada *f* (métrica) (= *1,000 kg*)
tone /təʊn/ *n* tono *m*. ● *vt*. **~ down** atenuar. **~ up** tonificar ‹*muscles*›. ● *vi*. **~ in** armonizar. **~-deaf** *a* que no tiene buen oído
tongs /tɒŋz/ *npl* tenazas *fpl*; (*for hair, sugar*) tenacillas *fpl*
tongue /tʌŋ/ *n* lengua *f*. **~ in cheek** *adv* irónicamente. **~-tied** *a* mudo. **get ~-tied** trabársele la lengua. **~-twister** *n* trabalenguas *m invar*
tonic /'tɒnɪk/ *a* tónico. ● *n* (*tonic water*) tónica *f*; (*med, fig*) tónico *m*. **~ water** *n* tónica *f*
tonight /tə'naɪt/ *adv & n* esta noche (*f*); (*evening*) esta tarde (*f*)
tonne /tʌn/ *n* tonelada *f* (métrica)
tonsil /'tɒnsl/ *n* amígdala *f*. **~litis** /-'laɪtɪs/ *n* amigdalitis *f*
too /tu:/ *adv* demasiado; (*also*) también. **~ many** *a* demasiados. **~ much** *a & adv* demasiado
took /tʊk/ *see* **take**
tool /tu:l/ *n* herramienta *f*. **~-bag** *n* bolsa *f* de herramientas
toot /tu:t/ *n* bocinazo *m*. ● *vi* tocar la bocina
tooth /tu:θ/ *n* (*pl* **teeth**) diente *m*; (*molar*) muela *f*. **~ache** /'tu:θeɪk/ *n* dolor *m* de muelas. **~brush** /'tu:θbrʌʃ/ *n* cepillo *m* de dientes. **~comb** /'tu:θkəʊm/ *n* peine *m* de púa fina. **~less** *a* desdentado, sin dientes. **~paste** /'tu:θpeɪst/ *n* pasta *f* dentífrica. **~pick** /'tu:θpɪk/ *n* palillo *m* de dientes
top[1] /tɒp/ *n* cima *f*; (*upper part*) parte *f* de arriba; (*upper surface*) superficie *f*; (*lid, of bottle*) tapa *f*; (*of list*) cabeza *f*. **from ~ to bottom** de arriba abajo. **on ~ (of)** encima de; (*besides*) además. ● *a* más alto; (*in rank*) superior, principal; (*maximum*) máximo. **~ floor** *n* último piso *m*. ● *vt* (*pt* **topped**) cubrir; (*exceed*) exceder. **~ up** *vt* llenar
top[2] /tɒp/ *n* (*toy*) trompa *f*, peonza *f*
top: **~ hat** *n* chistera *f*. **~-heavy** *a* más pesado arriba que abajo
topic /'tɒpɪk/ *n* tema *m*. **~al** /'tɒpɪkl/ *a* de actualidad
top: **~less** /'tɒplɪs/ *a* ‹*bather*› con los senos desnudos. **~most** /'tɒpməʊst/ *a* (el) más alto. **~-notch** *a* (*fam*) excelente
topography /tə'pɒgrəfɪ/ *n* topografía *f*
topple /'tɒpl/ *vi* derribar; (*overturn*) volcar
top secret /tɒp'si:krɪt/ *a* sumamente secreto
topsy-turvy /tɒpsɪ'tɜ:vɪ/ *adv & a* patas arriba
torch /tɔ:tʃ/ *n* lámpara *f* de bolsillo; (*flaming*) antorcha *f*
tore /tɔ:(r)/ *see* **tear**[1]
toreador /'tɒrɪədɔ:(r)/ *n* torero *m*
torment /'tɔ:ment/ *n* tormento *m*. /tɔ:'ment/ *vt* atormentar
torn /tɔ:n/ *see* **tear**[1]
tornado /tɔ:'neɪdəʊ/ *n* (*pl* **-oes**) tornado *m*
torpedo /tɔ:'pi:dəʊ/ *n* (*pl* **-oes**) torpedo *m*. ● *vt* torpedear
torpor /'tɔ:pə(r)/ *n* apatía *f*
torrent /'tɒrənt/ *n* torrente *m*. **~ial** /tə'renʃl/ *a* torrencial
torrid /'tɒrɪd/ *a* tórrido
torso /'tɔ:səʊ/ *n* (*pl* **-os**) torso *m*
tortoise /'tɔ:təs/ *n* tortuga *f*. **~shell** *n* carey *m*
tortuous /'tɔ:tjʊəs/ *a* tortuoso
torture /'tɔ:tʃə(r)/ *n* tortura *f*, tormento *m*. ● *vt* atormentar. **~r** /-ə(r)/ *n* atormentador *m*, verdugo *m*
Tory /'tɔ:rɪ/ *a & n* (*fam*) conservador (*m*)
toss /tɒs/ *vt* echar; (*shake*) sacudir. ● *vi* agitarse. **~ and turn** (*in bed*) revolverse. **~ up** echar a cara o cruz
tot[1] /tɒt/ *n* nene *m*; (*of liquor, fam*) trago *m*
tot[2] /tɒt/ *vt* (*pt* **totted**). **~ up** (*fam*) sumar
total /'təʊtl/ *a & n* total (*m*). ● *vt* (*pt* **totalled**) sumar
totalitarian /təʊtælɪ'teərɪən/ *a* totalitario
total: **~ity** /təʊ'tælətɪ/ *n* totalidad *f*. **~ly** *adv* totalmente
totter /'tɒtə(r)/ *vi* tambalearse. **~y** *a* inseguro
touch /tʌtʃ/ *vt* tocar; (*reach*) alcanzar; (*move*) conmover. ● *vi* tocarse. ● *n* toque *m*; (*sense*) tacto *m*; (*contact*) contacto *m*; (*trace*) pizca *f*. **get in ~ with** ponerse en contacto con. **~ down** ‹*aircraft*› aterrizar. **~ off**

disparar ‹*gun*›; (*fig*) desencadenar. ~ **on** tratar levemente. ~ **up** retocar. ~**-and-go** *a* incierto, dudoso

touching /'tʌtʃɪŋ/ *a* conmovedor

touchstone /'tʌtʃstəʊn/ *n* (*fig*) piedra *f* de toque

touchy /'tʌtʃɪ/ *a* quisquilloso

tough /tʌf/ *a* (**-er**, **-est**) duro; (*strong*) fuerte, resistente. ~**en** /'tʌfn/ *vt* endurecer. ~**ness** *n* dureza *f*; (*strength*) resistencia *f*

toupee /'tu:peɪ/ *n* postizo *m*, tupé *m*

tour /tʊə(r)/ *n* viaje *m*; (*visit*) visita *f*; (*excursion*) excursión *f*; (*by team etc*) gira *f*. ● *vt* recorrer; (*visit*) visitar

touris|m /'tʊərɪzəm/ *n* turismo *m*. ~**t** /'tʊərɪst/ *n* turista *m & f*. ● *a* turístico. ~**t office** *n* oficina *f* de turismo

tournament /'tɔ:nəmənt/ *n* torneo *m*

tousle /'taʊzl/ *vt* despeinar

tout /taʊt/ *vi*. ~ **(for)** solicitar. ● *n* solicitador *m*

tow /təʊ/ *vt* remolcar. ● *n* remolque *m*. **on** ~ a remolque. **with his family in** ~ (*fam*) acompañado por su familia

toward(s) /tə'wɔ:d(z)/ *prep* hacia

towel /'taʊəl/ *n* toalla *f*. ~**ling** *n* (*fabric*) toalla *f*

tower /'taʊə(r)/ *n* torre *f*. ● *vi*. ~ **above** dominar. ~ **block** *n* edificio *m* alto. ~**ing** *a* altísimo; ‹*rage*› violento

town /taʊn/ *n* ciudad *f*, pueblo *m*. **go to** ~ (*fam*) no escatimar dinero. ~ **hall** *n* ayuntamiento *m*. ~ **planning** *n* urbanismo *m*

tow-path /'təʊpɑ:θ/ *n* camino *m* de sirga

toxi|c /'tɒksɪk/ *a* tóxico. ~**n** /'tɒksɪn/ *n* toxina *f*

toy /tɔɪ/ *n* juguete *m*. ● *vi*. ~ **with** jugar con ‹*object*›; acariciar ‹*idea*›. ~**shop** *n* juguetería *f*

trac|e /treɪs/ *n* huella *f*; (*small amount*) pizca *f*. ● *vt* seguir la pista de; (*draw*) dibujar; (*with tracing-paper*) calcar; (*track down*) encontrar. ~**ing** /'treɪsɪŋ/ *n* calco *m*. ~**ing-paper** *n* papel *m* de calcar

track /træk/ *n* huella *f*; (*path*) sendero *m*; (*sport*) pista *f*; (*of rocket etc*) trayectoria *f*; (*rail*) vía *f*. **keep** ~ **of** vigilar. **make** ~**s** (*sl*) marcharse. ● *vt* seguir la pista de. ~ **down** *vt* localizar. ~ **suit** *n* traje *m* de deporte, chandal *m*

tract[1] /trækt/ *n* (*land*) extensión *f*; (*anat*) aparato *m*

tract[2] /trækt/ *n* (*pamphlet*) opúsculo *m*

traction /'trækʃn/ *n* tracción *f*

tractor /'træktə(r)/ *n* tractor *m*

trade /treɪd/ *n* comercio *m*; (*occupation*) oficio *m*; (*exchange*) cambio *m*; (*industry*) industria *f*. ● *vt* cambiar. ● *vi* comerciar. ~ **in** (*give in part-exchange*) dar como parte del pago. ~ **on** aprovecharse de. ~ **mark** *n* marca *f* registrada. ~**r** /-ə(r)/ *n* comerciante *m & f*. ~**sman** /'treɪdzmən/ *n* (*pl* **-men**) (*shopkeeper*) tendero *m*. ~ **union** *n* sindicato *m*. ~ **unionist** *n* sindicalista *m & f*. ~ **wind** *n* viento *m* alisio

trading /'treɪdɪŋ/ *n* comercio *m*. ~ **estate** *n* zona *f* industrial

tradition /trə'dɪʃn/ *n* tradición *f*. ~**al** *a* tradicional. ~**alist** *n* tradicionalista *m & f*. ~**ally** *adv* tradicionalmente

traffic /'træfɪk/ *n* tráfico *m*. ● *vi* (*pt* **trafficked**) comerciar (**in** en). ~**-lights** *npl* semáforo *m*. ~ **warden** *n* guardia *m*, controlador *m* de tráfico

trag|edy /'trædʒɪdɪ/ *n* tragedia *f*. ~**ic** /'trædʒɪk/ *a* trágico. ~**ically** *adv* trágicamente

trail /treɪl/ *vi* arrastrarse; (*lag*) rezagarse. ● *vt* (*track*) seguir la pista de. ● *n* estela *f*; (*track*) pista *f*. (*path*) sendero *m*. ~**er** /'treɪlə(r)/ *n* remolque *m*; (*film*) avance *m*

train /treɪn/ *n* tren *m*; (*of dress*) cola *f*; (*series*) sucesión *f*; (*retinue*) séquito *m*. ● *vt* adiestrar; (*sport*) entrenar; educar ‹*child*›; guiar ‹*plant*›; domar ‹*animal*›. ● *vi* adiestrarse; (*sport*) entrenarse. ~**ed** *a* (*skilled*) cualificado; ‹*doctor*› diplomado. ~**ee** *n* aprendiz *m*. ~**er** *n* (*sport*) entrenador *m*; (*of animals*) domador *m*. ~**ers** *mpl* zapatillas *fpl* de deporte. ~**ing** *n* instrucción *f*; (*sport*) entrenamiento *m*

traipse /treɪps/ *vi* (*fam*) vagar

trait /treɪ(t)/ *n* característica *f*, rasgo *m*

traitor /'treɪtə(r)/ *n* traidor *m*

tram /træm/ *n* tranvía *m*

tramp /træmp/ *vt* recorrer a pie. ● *vi* andar con pasos pesados. ● *n* (*vagrant*) vagabundo *m*; (*sound*) ruido *m* de pasos; (*hike*) paseo *m* largo

trample /'træmpl/ *vt/i* pisotear. ~ **(on)** pisotear
trampoline /'træmpəli:n/ *n* trampolín *m*
trance /trɑ:ns/ *n* trance *m*
tranquil /'træŋkwɪl/ *a* tranquilo. ~**lity** /-'kwɪlətɪ/ *n* tranquilidad *f*
tranquillize /'træŋkwɪlaɪz/ *vt* tranquilizar. ~**r** /-ə(r)/ *n* tranquilizante *m*
transact /træn'zækt/ *vt* negociar. ~**ion** /-ʃn/ *n* transacción *f*
transatlantic /trænzət'læntɪk/ *a* transatlántico
transcend /træn'send/ *vt* exceder. ~**ent** *a* sobresaliente
transcendental /trænsen'dentl/ *a* trascendental
transcribe /træns'kraɪb/ *vt* transcribir; grabar ‹*recorded sound*›
transcript /'trænskrɪpt/ *n* copia *f*. ~**ion** /-ɪpʃn/ *n* transcripción *f*
transfer /træns'fɜ:(r)/ *vt* (*pt* **transferred**) trasladar; calcar ‹*drawing*›. ● *vi* trasladarse. ~ **the charges** (*on telephone*) llamar a cobro revertido. /'trænsfɜ:(r)/ *n* traslado *m*; (*paper*) calcomanía *f*. ~**able** *a* transferible
transfigur|ation /trænsfɪgjʊ'reɪʃn/ *n* transfiguración *f*. ~**e** /træns'fɪgə(r)/ *vt* transfigurar
transfix /træns'fɪks/ *vt* traspasar; (*fig*) paralizar
transform /træns'fɔ:m/ *vt* transformar. ~**ation** /-ə'meɪʃn/ *n* transformación *f*. ~**er** /-ə(r)/ *n* transformador *m*
transfusion /træns'fju:ʒn/ *n* transfusión *f*
transgress /træns'gres/ *vt* traspasar, infringir. ~**ion** /-ʃn/ *n* transgresión *f*; (*sin*) pecado *m*
transient /'trænzɪənt/ *a* pasajero
transistor /træn'zɪstə(r)/ *n* transistor *m*
transit /'trænsɪt/ *n* tránsito *m*
transition /træn'zɪʒn/ *n* transición *f*
transitive /'trænsɪtɪv/ *a* transitivo
transitory /'trænsɪtrɪ/ *a* transitorio
translat|e /trænz'leɪt/ *vt* traducir. ~**ion** /-ʃn/ *n* traducción *f*. ~**or** /-ə(r)/ *n* traductor *m*
translucen|ce /træns'lu:sns/ *n* traslucidez *f*. ~**t** /trænz'lu:snt/ *a* traslúcido
transmission /træns'mɪʃn/ *n* transmisión *f*
transmit /trænz'mɪt/ *vt* (*pt* **transmitted**) transmitir. ~**ter** /-ə(r)/ *n* transmisor *m*; (*TV, radio*) emisora *f*
transparen|cy /træns'pærənsɪ/ *n* transparencia *f*; (*photo*) diapositiva *f*. ~**t** /træns'pærənt/ *a* transparente
transpire /træn'spaɪə(r)/ *vi* transpirar; (*happen, fam*) suceder, revelarse
transplant /træns'plɑ:nt/ *vt* trasplantar. /'trænsplɑ:nt/ *n* trasplante *m*
transport /træn'spɔ:t/ *vt* transportar. /'trænspɔ:t/ *n* transporte *m*. ~**ation** /-'teɪʃn/ *n* transporte *m*
transpos|e /træn'spəʊz/ *vt* transponer; (*mus*) transportar. ~**ition** /-pə'zɪʃn/ *n* transposición *f*; (*mus*) transporte *m*
transverse /'trænzvɜ:s/ *a* transverso
transvestite /trænz'vestaɪt/ *n* travestido *m*
trap /træp/ *n* trampa *f*. ● *vt* (*pt* **trapped**) atrapar; (*jam*) atascar; (*cut off*) bloquear. ~**door** /'træpdɔ:(r)/ *n* trampa *f*; (*in theatre*) escotillón *m*
trapeze /trə'pi:z/ *n* trapecio *m*
trappings /'træpɪŋz/ *npl* (*fig*) atavíos *mpl*
trash /træʃ/ *n* pacotilla *f*; (*refuse*) basura *f*; (*nonsense*) tonterías *fpl*. ~ **can** *n* (*Amer*) cubo *m* de la basura. ~**y** *a* de baja calidad
trauma /'trɔ:mə/ *n* trauma *m*. ~**tic** /-'mætɪk/ *a* traumático
travel /'trævl/ *vi* (*pt* **travelled**) viajar. ● *vt* recorrer. ● *n* viajar *m*. ~**ler** /-ə(r)/ *n* viajero *m*. ~**ler's cheque** *n* cheque *m* de viaje. ~**ling** *n* viajar *m*
traverse /træ'vɜ:s/ *vt* atravesar, recorrer
travesty /'trævɪstɪ/ *n* parodia *f*
trawler /'trɔ:lə(r)/ *n* pesquero *m* de arrastre
tray /treɪ/ *n* bandeja *f*
treacher|ous *a* traidor; (*deceptive*) engañoso. ~**ously** *adv* traidoramente. ~**y** /'tretʃərɪ/ *n* traición *f*
treacle /'tri:kl/ *n* melaza *f*
tread /tred/ *vi* (*pt* **trod**, *pp* **trodden**) andar. ~ **on** pisar. ● *vt* pisar. ● *n* (*step*) paso *m*; (*of tyre*) banda *f* de rodadura. ~**le** /'tredl/ *n* pedal *m*. ~**mill** /'tredmɪl/ *n* rueda *f* de molino; (*fig*) rutina *f*
treason /'tri:zn/ *n* traición *f*
treasure /'treʒə(r)/ *n* tesoro *m*. ● *vt* apreciar mucho; (*store*) guardar

treasur|er /'treʒərə(r)/ *n* tesorero *m*. **~y** /'treʒərɪ/ *n* tesorería *f*. **the T~y** *n* el Ministerio *m* de Hacienda

treat /tri:t/ *vt* tratar; (*consider*) considerar. **~ s.o.** invitar a uno. ● *n* placer *m*; (*present*) regalo *m*

treatise /'tri:tɪz/ *n* tratado *m*

treatment /'tri:tmənt/ *n* tratamiento *m*

treaty /'tri:tɪ/ *n* tratado *m*

treble /'trebl/ *a* triple; ‹*clef*› de sol; ‹*voice*› de tiple. ● *vt* triplicar. ● *vi* triplicarse. ● *n* tiple *m & f*

tree /tri:/ *n* árbol *m*

trek /trek/ *n* viaje *m* arduo, caminata *f*. ● *vi* (*pt* **trekked**) hacer un viaje arduo

trellis /'trelɪs/ *n* enrejado *m*

tremble /'trembl/ *vi* temblar

tremendous /trɪ'mendəs/ *a* tremendo; (*huge, fam*) enorme. **~ly** *adv* tremendamente

tremor /'tremə(r)/ *n* temblor *m*

tremulous /'tremjʊləs/ *a* tembloroso

trench /trentʃ/ *n* foso *m*, zanja *f*; (*mil*) trinchera *f*. **~ coat** *n* trinchera *f*

trend /trend/ *n* tendencia *f*; (*fashion*) moda *f*. **~-setter** *n* persona *f* que lanza la moda. **~y** *a* (**-ier**, **-iest**) (*fam*) a la última

trepidation /trepɪ'deɪʃn/ *n* inquietud *f*

trespass /'trespəs/ *vi*. **~ on** entrar sin derecho; (*fig*) abusar de. **~er** /-ə(r)/ *n* intruso *m*

tress /tres/ *n* trenza *f*

trestle /'tresl/ *n* caballete *m*. **~-table** *n* mesa *f* de caballete

trews /tru:z/ *npl* pantalón *m*

trial /'traɪəl/ *n* prueba *f*; (*jurid*) proceso *m*; (*ordeal*) prueba *f* dura. **~ and error** tanteo *m*. **be on ~** estar a prueba; (*jurid*) ser procesado

triang|le /'traɪæŋgl/ *n* triángulo *m*. **~ular** /-'æŋgjʊlə(r)/ *a* triangular

trib|al /'traɪbl/ *a* tribal. **~e** /traɪb/ *n* tribu *f*

tribulation /trɪbjʊ'leɪʃn/ *n* tribulación *f*

tribunal /traɪ'bju:nl/ *n* tribunal *m*

tributary /'trɪbjʊtrɪ/ *n* (*stream*) afluente *m*

tribute /'trɪbju:t/ *n* tributo *m*. **pay ~ to** rendir homenaje a

trice /traɪs/ *n*. **in a ~** en un abrir y cerrar de ojos

trick /trɪk/ *n* trampa *f*; engaño *m*; (*joke*) broma *f*; (*at cards*) baza *f*; (*habit*) manía *f*. **do the ~** servir. **play a ~ on** gastar una broma a. ● *vt* engañar. **~ery** /'trɪkərɪ/ *n* engaño *m*

trickle /'trɪkl/ *vi* gotear. **~ in** (*fig*) entrar poco a poco. **~ out** (*fig*) salir poco a poco

trickster /'trɪkstə(r)/ *n* estafador *m*

tricky /'trɪkɪ/ *a* delicado, difícil

tricolour /'trɪkələ(r)/ *n* bandera *f* tricolor

tricycle /'traɪsɪkl/ *n* triciclo *m*

trident /'traɪdənt/ *n* tridente *m*

tried /traɪd/ *see* **try**

trifl|e /'traɪfl/ *n* bagatela *f*; (*culin*) bizcocho *m* con natillas, jalea, frutas y nata. ● *vi*. **~e with** jugar con. **~ing** *a* insignificante

trigger /'trɪgə(r)/ *n* (*of gun*) gatillo *m*. ● *vt*. **~ (off)** desencadenar

trigonometry /trɪgə'nɒmɪtrɪ/ *n* trigonometría *f*

trilby /'trɪlbɪ/ *n* sombrero *m* de fieltro

trilogy /'trɪlədʒɪ/ *n* trilogía *f*

trim /trɪm/ *a* (**trimmer**, **trimmest**) arreglado. ● *vt* (*pt* **trimmed**) cortar; recortar ‹*hair etc*›; (*adorn*) adornar. ● *n* (*cut*) recorte *m*; (*decoration*) adorno *m*; (*state*) estado *m*. **in ~** en buen estado; (*fit*) en forma. **~ming** *n* adorno *m*. **~mings** *npl* recortes *mpl*; (*decorations*) adornos *mpl*; (*culin*) guarnición *f*

trinity /'trɪnɪtɪ/ *n* trinidad *f*. **the T~** la Trinidad

trinket /'trɪŋkɪt/ *n* chuchería *f*

trio /'tri:əʊ/ *n* (*pl* **-os**) trío *m*

trip /trɪp/ *vt* (*pt* **tripped**) hacer tropezar. ● *vi* tropezar; (*go lightly*) andar con paso ligero. ● *n* (*journey*) viaje *m*; (*outing*) excursión *f*; (*stumble*) traspié *m*. **~ up** *vi* tropezar. ● *vt* hacer tropezar

tripe /traɪp/ *n* callos *mpl*; (*nonsense, sl*) tonterías *fpl*

triple /'trɪpl/ *a* triple. ● *vt* triplicar. ● *vi* triplicarse. **~ts** /'trɪplɪts/ *npl* trillizos *mpl*

triplicate /'trɪplɪkət/ *a* triplicado. **in ~** por triplicado

tripod /'traɪpɒd/ *n* trípode *m*

tripper /'trɪpə(r)/ *n* (*on day trip etc*) excursionista *m & f*

triptych /'trɪptɪk/ *n* tríptico *m*

trite /traɪt/ *a* trillado

triumph /'traɪʌmf/ *n* triunfo *m*. • *vi* trinufar (**over** sobre). **~al** /-'ʌmfl/ *a* triunfal. **~ant** /-'ʌmfnt/ *a* triunfante

trivial /'trɪvɪəl/ *a* insignificante. **~ity** /-'ælətɪ/ *n* insignificancia *f*

trod, trodden /trɒd, trɒdn/ *see* **tread**

trolley /'trɒlɪ/ *n* (*pl* **-eys**) carretón *m*. **tea ~** *n* mesita *f* de ruedas. **~bus** *n* trolebús *m*

trombone /trɒm'bəʊn/ *n* trombón *m*

troop /tru:p/ *n* grupo *m*. • *vi*. **~ in** entrar en tropel. **~ out** salir en tropel. • *vt*. **~ing the colour** saludo *m* a la bandera. **~er** *n* soldado *m* de caballería. **~s** *npl* (*mil*) tropas *fpl*

trophy /'trəʊfɪ/ *n* trofeo *m*

tropic /'trɒpɪk/ *n* trópico *m*. **~al** *a* tropical. **~s** *npl* trópicos *mpl*

trot /trɒt/ *n* trote *m*. **on the ~** (*fam*) seguidos. • *vi* (*pt* **trotted**) trotar. **~ out** (*produce, fam*) producir

trotter /'trɒtə(r)/ *n* (*culin*) pie *m* de cerdo

trouble /'trʌbl/ *n* problema *m*; (*awkward situation*) apuro *m*; (*inconvenience*) molestia *f*; (*conflict*) conflicto *m*; (*med*) enfermedad *f*; (*mec*) avería *f*. **be in ~** estar en un apuro. **make ~** armar un lío. **take ~** tomarse la molestia. • *vt* (*bother*) molestar; (*worry*) preocupar. • *vi* molestarse; (*worry*) preocuparse. **be ~d about** preocuparse por. **~-maker** *n* alborotador *m*. **~some** *a* molesto

trough /trɒf/ *n* (*for drinking*) abrevadero *m*; (*for feeding*) pesebre *m*; (*of wave*) seno *m*; (*atmospheric*) mínimo *m* de presión

trounce /traʊns/ *vt* (*defeat*) derrotar; (*thrash*) pegar

troupe /tru:p/ *n* compañía *f*

trousers /'traʊzəz/ *npl* pantalón *m*; pantalones *mpl*

trousseau /'tru:səʊ/ *n* (*pl* **-s** /-əʊz/) ajuar *m*

trout /traʊt/ *n* (*pl* **trout**) trucha *f*

trowel /'traʊəl/ *n* (*garden*) desplantador *m*; (*for mortar*) paleta *f*

truant /'tru:ənt/ *n*. **play ~** hacer novillos

truce /tru:s/ *n* tregua *f*

truck[1] /trʌk/ *n* carro *m*; (*rail*) vagón *m*; (*lorry*) camión *m*

truck[2] /trʌk/ *n* (*dealings*) trato *m*

truculent /'trʌkjʊlənt/ *a* agresivo

trudge /trʌdʒ/ *vi* andar penosamente. • *n* caminata *f* penosa

true /tru:/ *a* (**-er**, **-est**) verdadero; (*loyal*) leal; (*genuine*) auténtico; (*accurate*) exacto. **come ~** realizarse

truffle /'trʌfl/ *n* trufa *f*; (*chocolate*) trufa *f* de chocolate

truism /'tru:ɪzəm/ *n* perogrullada *f*

truly /'tru:lɪ/ *adv* verdaderamente; (*sincerely*) sinceramente; (*faithfully*) fielmente. **yours ~** (*in letters*) le saluda atentamente

trump /trʌmp/ *n* (*cards*) triunfo *m*. • *vt* fallar. **~ up** inventar

trumpet /'trʌmpɪt/ *n* trompeta *f*. **~er** /-ə(r)/ *n* trompetero *m*, trompeta *m & f*

truncated /trʌŋ'keɪtɪd/ *a* truncado

truncheon /'trʌntʃən/ *n* porra *f*

trundle /'trʌndl/ *vt* hacer rodar. • *vi* rodar

trunk /trʌŋk/ *n* tronco *m*; (*box*) baúl *m*; (*of elephant*) trompa *f*. **~-call** *n* conferencia *f*. **~-road** *n* carretera *f* (nacional). **~s** *npl* bañador *m*

truss /trʌs/ *n* (*med*) braguero *m*. **~ up** *vt* (*culin*) espetar

trust /trʌst/ *n* confianza *f*; (*association*) trust *m*. **on ~** a ojos cerrados; (*com*) al fiado. • *vi* confiar. **~ to** confiar en. • *vt* confiar en; (*hope*) esperar. **~ed** *a* leal

trustee /trʌ'sti:/ *n* administrador *m*

trust: **~ful** *a* confiado. **~fully** *adv* confiadamente. **~worthy** *a*, **~y** *a* digno de confianza

truth /tru:θ/ *n* (*pl* **-s** /tru:ðz/) verdad *f*. **~ful** *a* veraz; (*true*) verídico. **~fully** *adv* sinceramente

try /traɪ/ *vt* (*pt* **tried**) probar; (*be a strain on*) poner a prueba; (*jurid*) procesar. **~ on** *vt* probarse ‹*garment*›. **~ out** *vt* probar. • *vi* probar. **~ for** *vi* intentar conseguir. • *n* tentativa *f*, prueba *f*; (*rugby*) ensayo *m*. **~ing** *a* difícil; (*annoying*) molesto. **~-out** *n* prueba *f*

tryst /trɪst/ *n* cita *f*

T-shirt /'ti:ʃɜ:t/ *n* camiseta *f*

tub /tʌb/ *n* tina *f*; (*bath, fam*) baño *m*

tuba /'tju:bə/ *n* tuba *f*

tubby /'tʌbɪ/ *a* (**-ier**, **-iest**) rechoncho

tube /tju:b/ *n* tubo *m*; (*rail, fam*) metro *m*. **inner ~** *n* cámara *f* de aire

tuber /'tju:bə(r)/ *n* tubérculo *m*

tuberculosis /tju:bɜ:kjʊ'ləʊsɪs/ *n* tuberculosis *f*

tub|ing /'tju:bɪŋ/ *n* tubería *f*, tubos *mpl*. **~ular** *a* tubular

tuck /tʌk/ *n* pliegue *m*. ● *vt* plegar; (*put*) meter; (*put away*) remeter; (*hide*) esconder. **~ up** *vt* arropar ‹*child*›. ● *vi*. **~ in(to)** (*eat, sl*) comer con buen apetito. **~-shop** *n* confitería *f*

Tuesday /'tju:zdeɪ/ *n* martes *m*

tuft /tʌft/ *n* (*of hair*) mechón *m*; (*of feathers*) penacho *m*; (*of grass*) manojo *m*

tug /tʌg/ *vt* (*pt* **tugged**) tirar de; (*tow*) remolcar. ● *vi* tirar fuerte. ● *n* tirón *m*; (*naut*) remolcador *m*. **~-of-war** *n* lucha *f* de la cuerda; (*fig*) tira *m* y afloja

tuition /tju:'ɪʃn/ *n* enseñanza *f*

tulip /'tju:lɪp/ *n* tulipán *m*

tumble /'tʌmbl/ *vi* caerse. **~ to** (*fam*) comprender. ● *n* caída *f*

tumbledown /'tʌmbldaʊn/ *a* ruinoso

tumble-drier /tʌmbl'draɪə(r)/ *n* secadora *f* (eléctrica con aire de salida)

tumbler /'tʌmblə(r)/ *n* (*glass*) vaso *m*

tummy /'tʌmɪ/ *n* (*fam*) estómago *m*

tumour /'tju:mə(r)/ *n* tumor *m*

tumult /'tju:mʌlt/ *n* tumulto *m*. **~uous** /-'mʌltjʊəs/ *a* tumultuoso

tuna /'tju:nə/ *n* (*pl* **tuna**) atún *m*

tune /tju:n/ *n* aire *m*. **be in ~** estar afinado. **be out of ~** estar desafinado. ● *vt* afinar; sintonizar ‹*radio, TV*›; (*mec*) poner a punto. ● *vi*. **~ in (to)** ‹*radio, TV*› sintonizarse. **~ up** afinar. **~ful** *a* melodioso. **~r** /-ə(r)/ *n* afinador *m*; (*radio, TV*) sintonizador *m*

tunic /'tju:nɪk/ *n* túnica *f*

tuning-fork /'tju:nɪŋfɔ:k/ *n* diapasón *m*

Tunisia /tju:'nɪzɪə/ *n* Túnez *m*. **~n** *a* & *n* tunecino (*m*)

tunnel /'tʌnl/ *n* túnel *m*. ● *vi* (*pt* **tunnelled**) construir un túnel en

turban /'tɜ:bən/ *n* turbante *m*

turbid /'tɜ:bɪd/ *a* túrbido

turbine /'tɜ:baɪn/ *n* turbina *f*

turbo-jet /'tɜ:bəʊdʒet/ *n* turborreactor *m*

turbot /'tɜ:bət/ *n* rodaballo *m*

turbulen|ce /'tɜ:bjʊləns/ *n* turbulencia *f*. **~t** /'tɜ:bjʊlənt/ *a* turbulento

tureen /tjʊ'ri:n/ *n* sopera *f*

turf /tɜ:f/ *n* (*pl* **turfs** *or* **turves**) césped *m*; (*segment*) tepe *m*. **the ~** *n* las carreras *fpl* de caballos. ● *vt*. **~ out** (*sl*) echar

turgid /'tɜ:dʒɪd/ *a* ‹*language*› pomposo

Turk /tɜ:k/ *n* turco *m*

turkey /'tɜ:kɪ/ *n* (*pl* **-eys**) pavo *m*

Turk|ey /'tɜ:kɪ/ *f* Turquía *f*. **T~ish** *a* & *n* turco (*m*)

turmoil /'tɜ:mɔɪl/ *n* confusión *f*

turn /tɜ:n/ *vt* hacer girar, dar vueltas a; volver ‹*direction, page, etc*›; cumplir ‹*age*›; dar ‹*hour*›; doblar ‹*corner*›; (*change*) cambiar; (*deflect*) desviar. **~ the tables** volver las tornas. ● *vi* girar, dar vueltas; (*become*) hacerse; (*change*) cambiar. ● *n* vuelta *f*; (*in road*) curva *f*; (*change*) cambio *m*; (*sequence*) turno *m*; (*of mind*) disposición *f*; (*in theatre*) número *m*; (*fright*) susto *m*; (*of illness, fam*) ataque *m*. **bad ~** mala jugada *f*. **good ~** favor *m*. **in ~** a su vez. **out of ~** fuera de lugar. **to a ~** (*culin*) en su punto. **~ against** *vt* volverse en contra de. **~ down** *vt* (*fold*) doblar; (*reduce*) bajar; (*reject*) rechazar. **~ in** *vt* entregar. ● *vi* (*go to bed, fam*) acostarse. **~ off** *vt* cerrar ‹*tap*›; apagar ‹*light, TV, etc*›. ● *vi* desviarse. **~ on** *vt* abrir ‹*tap*›; encender ‹*light etc*›; (*attack*) atacar; (*attract, fam*) excitar. **~ out** *vt* expulsar; apagar ‹*light etc*›; (*produce*) producir; (*empty*) vaciar. ● *vi* (*result*) resultar. **~ round** *vi* dar la vuelta. **~ up** *vi* aparecer. ● *vt* (*find*) encontrar; levantar ‹*collar*›; poner más fuerte ‹*gas*›. **~ed-up** *a* ‹*nose*› respingona. **~ing** /'tɜ:nɪŋ/ *n* vuelta *f*; (*road*) bocacalle *f*. **~ing-point** *n* punto *m* decisivo.

turnip /'tɜ:nɪp/ *n* nabo *m*

turn: **~-out** *n* (*of people*) concurrencia *f*; (*of goods*) producción *f*. **~over** /'tɜ:nəʊvə(r)/ *n* (*culin*) empanada *f*; (*com*) volumen *m* de negocios; (*of staff*) rotación *f*. **~pike** /'tɜ:npaɪk/ *n* (*Amer*) autopista *f* de peaje. **~-stile** /'tɜ:nstaɪl/ *n* torniquete *m*. **~table** /'tɜ:nteɪbl/ *n* plataforma *f* giratoria; (*on record-player*) plato *m* giratorio. **~-up** *n* (*of trousers*) vuelta *f*

turpentine /'tɜ:pəntaɪn/ *n* trementina *f*

turquoise /'tɜ:kwɔɪz/ *a* & *n* turquesa (*f*)

turret /ˈtʌrɪt/ *n* torrecilla *f*; (*mil*) torreta *f*

turtle /ˈtɜːtl/ *n* tortuga *f* de mar. **~-neck** *n* cuello *m* alto

tusk /tʌsk/ *n* colmillo *m*

tussle /ˈtʌsl/ *vi* pelearse. ● *n* pelea *f*

tussock /ˈtʌsək/ *n* montecillo *m* de hierbas

tutor /ˈtjuːtə(r)/ *n* preceptor *m*; (*univ*) director *m* de estudios, profesor *m*. **~ial** /tjuːˈtɔːrɪəl/ *n* clase *f* particular

tuxedo /tʌkˈsiːdəʊ/ *n* (*pl* **-os**) (*Amer*) esmoquin *m*

TV /tiːˈviː/ *n* televisión *f*

twaddle /ˈtwɒdl/ *n* tonterías *fpl*

twang /twæŋ/ *n* tañido *m*; (*in voice*) gangueo *m*. ● *vt* hacer vibrar. ● *vi* vibrar

tweed /twiːd/ *n* tela *f* gruesa de lana

tweet /twiːt/ *n* piada *f*. ● *vi* piar

tweezers /ˈtwiːzəz/ *npl* pinzas *fpl*

twel|fth /twelfθ/ *a* & *n* duodécimo (*m*). **~ve** /twelv/ *a* & *n* doce (*m*)

twent|ieth /ˈtwentɪəθ/ *a* & *n* vigésimo (*m*). **~y** /ˈtwentɪ/ *a* & *n* veinte (*m*)

twerp /twɜːp/ *n* (*sl*) imbécil *m*

twice /twaɪs/ *adv* dos veces

twiddle /ˈtwɪdl/ *vt* hacer girar. **~ one's thumbs** (*fig*) no tener nada que hacer. **~ with** jugar con

twig[1] /twɪg/ *n* ramita *f*

twig[2] /twɪg/ *vt/i* (*pt* **twigged**) (*fam*) comprender

twilight /ˈtwaɪlaɪt/ *n* crepúsculo *m*

twin /twɪn/ *a* & *n* gemelo (*m*)

twine /twaɪn/ *n* bramante *m*. ● *vt* torcer. ● *vi* enroscarse

twinge /twɪndʒ/ *n* punzada *f*; (*fig*) remordimiento *m* (de conciencia)

twinkle /ˈtwɪŋkl/ *vi* centellear. ● *n* centelleo *m*

twirl /twɜːl/ *vt* dar vueltas a. ● *vi* dar vueltas. ● *n* vuelta *f*

twist /twɪst/ *vt* torcer; (*roll*) enrollar; (*distort*) deformar. ● *vi* torcerse; (*coil*) enroscarse; ‹*road*› serpentear. ● *n* torsión *f*; (*curve*) vuelta *f*; (*of character*) peculiaridad *f*

twit[1] /twɪt/ *n* (*sl*) imbécil *m*

twit[2] /twɪt/ *vt* (*pt* **twitted**) tomar el pelo a

twitch /twɪtʃ/ *vt* crispar. ● *vi* crisparse. ● *n* tic *m*; (*jerk*) tirón *m*

twitter /ˈtwɪtə(r)/ *vi* gorjear. ● *n* gorjeo *m*

two /tuː/ *a* & *n* dos (*m*). **in ~ minds** indeciso. **~-faced** *a* falso, insincero. **~-piece (suit)** *n* traje *m* (de dos piezas). **~some** /ˈtuːsəm/ *n* pareja *f*. **~-way** *a* ‹*traffic*› de doble sentido

tycoon /taɪˈkuːn/ *n* magnate *m*

tying /ˈtaɪɪŋ/ *see* **tie**

type /taɪp/ *n* tipo *m*. ● *vt/i* escribir a máquina. **~-cast** *a* ‹*actor*› encasillado. **~script** /ˈtaɪpskrɪpt/ *n* texto *m* escrito a máquina. **~writer** /ˈtaɪpraɪtə(r)/ *n* máquina *f* de escribir. **~written** /-ɪtn/ *a* escrito a máquina, mecanografiado

typhoid /ˈtaɪfɔɪd/ *n*. **~ (fever)** fiebre *f* tifoidea

typhoon /taɪˈfuːn/ *n* tifón *m*

typical /ˈtɪpɪkl/ *a* típico. **~ly** *adv* típicamente

typify /ˈtɪpɪfaɪ/ *vt* tipificar

typi|ng /ˈtaɪpɪŋ/ *n* mecanografía *f*. **~st** *n* mecanógrafo *m*

typography /taɪˈpɒgrəfɪ/ *n* tipografía *f*

tyran|nical /tɪˈrænɪkl/ *a* tiránico. **~nize** *vi* tiranizar. **~ny** /ˈtɪrənɪ/ *n* tiranía *f*. **~t** /ˈtaɪərənt/ *n* tirano *m*

tyre /ˈtaɪə(r)/ *n* neumático *m*, llanta *f* (*Amer*)

U

ubiquitous /juːˈbɪkwɪtəs/ *a* omnipresente, ubicuo

udder /ˈʌdə(r)/ *n* ubre *f*

UFO /ˈjuːfəʊ/ *abbr* (*unidentified flying object*) OVNI *m*, objeto *m* volante no identificado

ugl|iness /ʌglɪnɪs/ *n* fealdad *f*. **~y** /ˈʌglɪ/ *a* (**-ier**, **-iest**) feo

UK /juːˈkeɪ/ *abbr* (*United Kingdom*) Reino *m* Unido

ulcer /ˈʌlsə(r)/ *n* úlcera *f*. **~ous** *a* ulceroso

ulterior /ʌlˈtɪərɪə(r)/ *a* ulterior. **~ motive** *n* segunda intención *f*

ultimate /ˈʌltɪmət/ *a* último; (*definitive*) definitivo; (*fundamental*) fundamental. **~ly** *adv* al final; (*basically*) en el fondo

ultimatum /ʌltɪˈmeɪtəm/ *n* (*pl* **-ums**) ultimátum *m invar*

ultra... /ˈʌltrə/ *pref* ultra...

ultramarine /ʌltrəməˈriːn/ *n* azul *m* marino

ultrasonic /ʌltrəˈsɒnɪk/ *a* ultrasónico

ultraviolet /ʌltrə'vaɪələt/ *a* ultravioleta *a invar*
umbilical /ʌm'bɪlɪkl/ *a* umbilical. ~ **cord** *n* cordón *m* umbilical
umbrage /'ʌmbrɪdʒ/ *n* resentimiento *m*. **take** ~ ofenderse (**at** por)
umbrella /ʌm'brelə/ *n* paraguas *m invar*
umpire /'ʌmpaɪə(r)/ *n* árbitro *m*. ● *vt* arbitrar
umpteen /'ʌmpti:n/ *a* (*sl*) muchísimos. ~**th** *a* (*sl*) enésimo
UN /ju:'en/ *abbr* (*United Nations*) ONU *f*, Organización *f* de las Naciones Unidas
un... /ʌn/ *pref* in..., des..., no, poco, sin
unabated /ʌnə'beɪtɪd/ *a* no disminuido
unable /ʌn'eɪbl/ *a* incapaz (**to** de). **be** ~ **to** no poder
unabridged /ʌnə'brɪdʒd/ *a* íntegro
unacceptable /ʌnək'septəbl/ *a* inaceptable
unaccountabl|e /ʌnə'kaʊntəbl/ *a* inexplicable. ~**y** *adv* inexplicablemente
unaccustomed /ʌnə'kʌstəmd/ *a* insólito. **be** ~ **to** *a* no estar acostumbrado a
unadopted /ʌnə'dɒptɪd/ *a* ‹*of road*› privado
unadulterated /ʌnə'dʌltəreɪtɪd/ *a* puro
unaffected /ʌnə'fektɪd/ *a* sin afectación, natural
unaided /ʌn'eɪdɪd/ *a* sin ayuda
unalloyed /ʌnə'lɔɪd/ *a* puro
unanimous /ju:'nænɪməs/ *a* unánime. ~**ly** *adv* unánimemente
unannounced /ʌnə'naʊnst/ *a* sin previo aviso; (*unexpected*) inesperado
unarmed /ʌn'ɑ:md/ *a* desarmado
unassuming /ʌnə'sju:mɪŋ/ *a* modesto, sin pretensiones
unattached /ʌnə'tætʃt/ *a* suelto; (*unmarried*) soltero
unattended /ʌnə'tendɪd/ *a* sin vigilar
unattractive /ʌnə'træktɪv/ *a* poco atractivo
unavoidabl|e /ʌnə'vɔɪdəbl/ *a* inevitable. ~**y** *adv* inevitablemente
unaware /ʌnə'weə(r)/ *a* ignorante (**of** de). **be** ~ **of** ignorar. ~**s** /-eəz/ *adv* desprevenido
unbalanced /ʌn'bælənst/ *a* desequilibrado
unbearabl|e /ʌn'beərəbl/ *a* inaguantable. ~**y** *adv* inaguantablemente
unbeat|able /ʌn'bi:təbl/ *a* insuperable. ~**en** *a* no vencido
unbeknown /ʌnbɪ'nəʊn/ *a* desconocido. ~ **to me** (*fam*) sin saberlo yo
unbelievable /ʌnbɪ'li:vəbl/ *a* increíble
unbend /ʌn'bend/ *vt* (*pt* **unbent**) enderezar. ● *vi* (*relax*) relajarse. ~**ing** *a* inflexible
unbiased /ʌn'baɪəst/ *a* imparcial
unbidden /ʌn'bɪdn/ *a* espontáneo; (*without invitation*) sin ser invitado
unblock /ʌn'blɒk/ *vt* desatascar
unbolt /ʌn'bəʊlt/ *vt* desatrancar
unborn /ʌn'bɔ:n/ *a* no nacido todavía
unbounded /ʌn'baʊndɪd/ *a* ilimitado
unbreakable /ʌn'breɪkəbl/ *a* irrompible
unbridled /ʌn'braɪdld/ *a* desenfrenado
unbroken /ʌn'brəʊkən/ *a* (*intact*) intacto; (*continuous*) continuo
unburden /ʌn'bɜ:dn/ *vt*. ~ **o.s.** desahogarse
unbutton /ʌn'bʌtn/ *vt* desabotonar, desabrochar
uncalled-for /ʌn'kɔ:ldfɔ:(r)/ *a* fuera de lugar; (*unjustified*) injustificado
uncanny /ʌn'kænɪ/ *a* (**-ier**, **-iest**) misterioso
unceasing /ʌn'si:sɪŋ/ *a* incesante
unceremonious /ʌnserɪ'məʊnɪəs/ *a* informal; (*abrupt*) brusco
uncertain /ʌn'sɜ:tn/ *a* incierto; (*changeable*) variable. **be** ~ **whether** no saber exactamente si. ~**ty** *n* incertidumbre *f*
unchang|ed /ʌn'tʃeɪndʒd/ *a* igual. ~**ing** *a* inmutable
uncharitable /ʌn'tʃærɪtəbl/ *a* severo
uncivilized /ʌn'sɪvɪlaɪzd/ *a* incivilizado
uncle /'ʌŋkl/ *n* tío *m*
unclean /ʌn'kli:n/ *a* sucio
unclear /ʌn'klɪə(r)/ *a* poco claro
uncomfortable /ʌn'kʌmfətəbl/ *a* incómodo; (*unpleasant*) desagradable. **feel** ~ no estar a gusto
uncommon /ʌn'kɒmən/ *a* raro. ~**ly** *adv* extraordinariamente
uncompromising /ʌn'kɒmprəmaɪzɪŋ/ *a* intransigente
unconcerned /ʌnkən'sɜ:nd/ *a* indiferente

unconditional /ʌnkən'dɪʃənl/ *a* incondicional. **~ly** *adv* incondicionalmente
unconscious /ʌn'kɒnʃəs/ *a* inconsciente; (*med*) sin sentido. **~ly** *adv* inconscientemente
unconventional /ʌnkən'venʃənl/ *a* poco convencional
uncooperative /ʌnkəʊ'ɒpərətɪv/ *a* poco servicial
uncork /ʌn'kɔ:k/ *vt* descorchar, destapar
uncouth /ʌn'ku:θ/ *a* grosero
uncover /ʌn'kʌvə(r)/ *vt* descubrir
unctuous /'ʌŋktjʊəs/ *a* untuoso; (*fig*) empalagoso
undecided /ʌndɪ'saɪdɪd/ *a* indeciso
undeniabl|e /ʌndɪ'naɪəbl/ *a* innegable. **~y** *adv* indiscutible mente
under /'ʌndə(r)/ *prep* debajo de; (*less than*) menos de; (*in the course of*) bajo, en. ● *adv* debajo, abajo. **~ age** *a* menor de edad. **~ way** *adv* en curso; (*on the way*) en marcha
under... *pref* sub...
undercarriage /'ʌndəkærɪdʒ/ *n* (*aviat*) tren *m* de aterrizaje
underclothes /'ʌndəkləʊðz/ *npl* ropa *f* interior
undercoat /'ʌndəkəʊt/ *n* (*of paint*) primera mano *f*
undercover /ʌndə'kʌvə(r)/ *a* secreto
undercurrent /'ʌndəkʌrənt/ *n* corriente *f* submarina; (*fig*) tendencia *f* oculta
undercut /'ʌndəkʌt/ *vt* (*pt* **undercut**) (*com*) vender más barato que
underdeveloped /ʌndədɪ'veləpt/ *a* subdesarrollado
underdog /'ʌndədɒg/ *n* perdedor *m*. **the ~s** *npl* los de abajo
underdone /ʌndə'dʌn/ *a* ‹*meat*› poco hecho
underestimate /ʌndər'estɪmeɪt/ *vt* subestimar
underfed /ʌndə'fed/ *a* desnutrido
underfoot /ʌndə'fʊt/ *adv* bajo los pies
undergo /'ʌndəgəʊ/ *vt* (*pt* **-went**, *pp* **-gone**) sufrir
undergraduate /ʌndə'grædjʊət/ *n* estudiante *m & f* universitario (no licenciado)
underground /ʌndə'graʊnd/ *adv* bajo tierra; (*in secret*) clandestinamente. /'ʌndəgraʊnd/ *a* subterráneo; (*secret*) clandestino. ● *n* metro *m*
undergrowth /'ʌndəgrəʊθ/ *n* maleza *f*
underhand /'ʌndəhænd/ *a* (*secret*) clandestino; (*deceptive*) fraudulento
underlie /ʌndə'laɪ/ *vt* (*pt* **-lay**, *pp* **-lain**, *pres p* **-lying**) estar debajo de; (*fig*) estar a la base de
underline /ʌndə'laɪn/ *vt* subrayar
underling /'ʌndəlɪŋ/ *n* subalterno *m*
underlying /ʌndə'laɪɪŋ/ *a* fundamental
undermine /ʌndə'maɪn/ *vt* socavar
underneath /ʌndə'ni:θ/ *prep* debajo de. ● *adv* por debajo
underpaid /ʌndə'peɪd/ *a* mal pagado
underpants /'ʌndəpænts/ *npl* calzoncillos *mpl*
underpass /'ʌndəpa:s/ *n* paso *m* subterráneo
underprivileged /ʌndə'prɪvɪlɪdʒd/ *a* desvalido
underrate /ʌndə'reɪt/ *vt* subestimar
undersell /ʌndə'sel/ *vt* (*pt* **-sold**) vender más barato que
undersigned /'ʌndəsaɪnd/ *a* abajo firmante
undersized /ʌndə'saɪzd/ *a* pequeño
understand /ʌndə'stænd/ *vt/i* (*pt* **-stood**) entender, comprender. **~able** *a* comprensible. **~ing** /ʌndə'stændɪŋ/ *a* comprensivo. ● *n* comprensión *f*; (*agreement*) acuerdo *m*
understatement /ʌndə'steɪtmənt/ *n* subestimación *f*
understudy /'ʌndəstʌdɪ/ *n* sobresaliente *m & f* (en el teatro)
undertake /ʌndə'teɪk/ *vt* (*pt* **-took**, *pp* **-taken**) emprender; (*assume responsibility*) encargarse de
undertaker /'ʌndəteɪkə(r)/ *n* empresario *m* de pompas fúnebres
undertaking /ʌndə'teɪkɪŋ/ *n* empresa *f*; (*promise*) promesa *f*
undertone /'ʌndətəʊn/ *n*. **in an ~** en voz baja
undertow /'ʌndətəʊ/ *n* resaca *f*
undervalue /ʌndə'vælju:/ *vt* subvalorar
underwater /ʌndə'wɔ:tə(r)/ *a* submarino. ● *adv* bajo el agua
underwear /'ʌndəweə(r)/ *n* ropa *f* interior
underweight /'ʌndəweɪt/ *a* de peso insuficiente. **be ~** estar flaco
underwent /ʌndə'went/ *see* **undergo**

underworld /ˈʌndəwɜ:ld/ *n* (*criminals*) hampa *f*
underwrite /ʌndəˈraɪt/ *vt* (*pt* **-wrote**, *pp* **-written**) (*com*) asegurar. **~r** /-ə(r)/ *n* asegurador *m*
undeserved /ʌndɪˈzɜ:vd/ *a* inmerecido
undesirable /ʌndɪˈzaɪərəbl/ *a* indeseable
undeveloped /ʌndɪˈveləpt/ *a* sin desarrollar
undies /ˈʌndɪz/ *npl* (*fam*) ropa *f* interior
undignified /ʌnˈdɪgnɪfaɪd/ *a* indecoroso
undisputed /ʌndɪsˈpju:tɪd/ *a* incontestable
undistinguished /ʌndɪsˈtɪŋgwɪʃt/ *a* mediocre
undo /ʌnˈdu:/ *vt* (*pt* **-did**, *pp* **-done**) deshacer; (*ruin*) arruinar; reparar ‹*wrong*›. **leave ~ne** dejar sin hacer
undoubted /ʌnˈdaʊtɪd/ *a* indudable. **~ly** *adv* indudablemente
undress /ʌnˈdres/ *vt* desnudar. ● *vi* desnudarse
undue /ʌnˈdju:/ *a* excesivo
undulat|e /ˈʌndjʊleɪt/ *vi* ondular. **~ion** /-ˈleɪʃn/ *n* ondulación *f*
unduly /ʌnˈdju:lɪ/ *adv* excesivamente
undying /ʌnˈdaɪɪŋ/ *a* eterno
unearth /ʌnˈɜ:θ/ *vt* desenterrar
unearthly /ʌnˈɜ:θlɪ/ *a* sobrenatural; (*impossible, fam*) absurdo. **~ hour** *n* hora intempestiva
uneas|ily /ʌnˈi:zɪlɪ/ *adv* inquietamente. **~y** /ʌnˈi:zɪ/ *a* incómodo; (*worrying*) inquieto
uneconomic /ʌni:kəˈnɒmɪk/ *a* poco rentable
uneducated /ʌnˈedjʊkeɪtɪd/ *a* inculto
unemploy|ed /ʌnɪmˈplɔɪd/ *a* parado, desempleado; (*not in use*) inutilizado. **~ment** *n* paro *m*, desempleo *m*
unending /ʌnˈendɪŋ/ *a* interminable, sin fin
unequal /ʌnˈi:kwəl/ *a* desigual
unequivocal /ʌnɪˈkwɪvəkl/ *a* inequívoco
unerring /ʌnˈɜ:rɪŋ/ *a* infalible
unethical /ʌnˈeθɪkl/ *a* sin ética, inmoral
uneven /ʌnˈi:vn/ *a* desigual
unexceptional /ʌnɪkˈsepʃənl/ *a* corriente
unexpected /ʌnɪkˈspektɪd/ *a* inesperado
unfailing /ʌnˈfeɪlɪŋ/ *a* inagotable; (*constant*) constante; (*loyal*) leal
unfair /ʌnˈfeə(r)/ *a* injusto. **~ly** *adv* injustamente. **~ness** *n* injusticia *f*
unfaithful /ʌnˈfeɪθfl/ *a* infiel. **~ness** *n* infidelidad *f*
unfamiliar /ʌnfəˈmɪlɪə(r)/ *a* desconocido. **be ~ with** desconocer
unfasten /ʌnˈfɑ:sn/ *vt* desabrochar ‹*clothes*›; (*untie*) desatar
unfavourable /ʌnˈfeɪvərəbl/ *a* desfavorable
unfeeling /ʌnˈfi:lɪŋ/ *a* insensible
unfit /ʌnˈfɪt/ *a* inadecuado, no apto; (*unwell*) en mal estado físico; (*incapable*) incapaz
unflinching /ʌnˈflɪntʃɪŋ/ *a* resuelto
unfold /ʌnˈfəʊld/ *vt* desdoblar; (*fig*) revelar. ● *vi* ‹*view etc*› extenderse
unforeseen /ʌnfɔ:ˈsi:n/ *a* imprevisto
unforgettable /ʌnfəˈgetəbl/ *a* inolvidable
unforgivable /ʌnfəˈgɪvəbl/ *a* imperdonable
unfortunate /ʌnˈfɔ:tʃənət/ *a* desgraciado; (*regrettable*) lamentable. **~ly** *adv* desgraciadamente
unfounded /ʌnˈfaʊndɪd/ *a* infundado
unfriendly /ʌnˈfrendlɪ/ *a* poco amistoso, frío
unfurl /ʌnˈfɜ:l/ *vt* desplegar
ungainly /ʌnˈgeɪnlɪ/ *a* desgarbado
ungodly /ʌnˈgɒdlɪ/ *a* impío. **~ hour** *n* (*fam*) hora *f* intempestiva
ungrateful /ʌnˈgreɪtfl/ *a* desagradecido
unguarded /ʌnˈgɑ:dɪd/ *a* indefenso; (*incautious*) imprudente, incauto
unhapp|ily /ʌnˈhæpɪlɪ/ *adv* infelizmente; (*unfortunately*) desgraciadamente. **~iness** *n* tristeza *f*. **~y** /ʌnˈhæpɪ/ *a* (**-ier**, **-iest**) infeliz, triste; (*unsuitable*) inoportuno. **~y with** insatisfecho de ‹*plans etc*›
unharmed /ʌnˈhɑ:md/ *a* ileso, sano y salvo
unhealthy /ʌnˈhelθɪ/ *a* (**-ier**, **-iest**) enfermizo; (*insanitary*) malsano
unhinge /ʌnˈhɪndʒ/ *vt* desquiciar
unholy /ʌnˈhəʊlɪ/ *a* (**-ier**, **-iest**) impío; (*terrible, fam*) terrible
unhook /ʌnˈhʊk/ *vt* desenganchar
unhoped /ʌnˈhəʊpt/ *a*. **~ for** inesperado
unhurt /ʌnˈhɜ:t/ *a* ileso
unicorn /ˈju:nɪkɔ:n/ *n* unicornio *m*

unification /ju:nɪfɪ'keɪʃn/ *n* unificación *f*
uniform /'ju:nɪfɔ:m/ *a* & *n* uniforme (*m*). **~ity** /-'fɔ:mətɪ/ *n* uniformidad *f*. **~ly** *adv* uniformemente
unify /'ju:nɪfaɪ/ *vt* unificar
unilateral /ju:nɪ'lætərəl/ *a* unilateral
unimaginable /ʌnɪ'mædʒɪnəbl/ *a* inconcebible
unimpeachable /ʌnɪm'pi:tʃəbl/ *a* irreprensible
unimportant /ʌnɪm'pɔ:tnt/ *a* insignificante
uninhabited /ʌnɪn'hæbɪtɪd/ *a* inhabitado; (*abandoned*) despoblado
unintentional /ʌnɪn'tenʃənl/ *a* involuntario
union /'ju:njən/ *n* unión *f*; (*trade union*) sindicato *m*. **~ist** *n* sindicalista *m* & *f*. **U~ Jack** *n* bandera *f* del Reino Unido
unique /ju:'ni:k/ *a* único. **~ly** *adv* extraordinariamente
unisex /'ju:nɪseks/ *a* unisex(o)
unison /'ju:nɪsn/ *n*. **in ~** al unísono
unit /'ju:nɪt/ *n* unidad *f*; (*of furniture etc*) elemento *m*
unite /ju:'naɪt/ *vt* unir. ● *vi* unirse. **U~d Kingdom (UK)** *n* Reino *m* Unido. **U~d Nations (UN)** *n* Organización *f* de las Naciones Unidas (ONU). **U~d States (of America) (USA)** *n* Estados *mpl* Unidos (de América) (EE.UU.)
unity /'ju:nɪtɪ/ *n* unidad *f*; (*fig*) acuerdo *m*
univers|al /ju:nɪ'vɜ:sl/ *a* universal. **~e** /'ju:nɪvɜ:s/ *n* universo *m*
university /ju:nɪ'vɜ:sətɪ/ *n* universidad *f*. ● *a* universitario
unjust /ʌn'dʒʌst/ *a* injusto
unkempt /ʌn'kempt/ *a* desaseado
unkind /ʌn'kaɪnd/ *a* poco amable; (*cruel*) cruel. **~ly** *adv* poco amablemente. **~ness** *n* falta *f* de amabilidad; (*cruelty*) crueldad *f*
unknown /ʌn'nəʊn/ *a* desconocido
unlawful /ʌn'lɔ:fl/ *a* ilegal
unleash /ʌn'li:ʃ/ *vt* soltar; (*fig*) desencadenar
unless /ʌn'les, ən'les/ *conj* a menos que, a no ser que
unlike /ʌn'laɪk/ *a* diferente; (*not typical*) impropio de. ● *prep* a diferencia de. **~lihood** *n* improbabilidad *f*. **~ly** /ʌn'laɪklɪ/ *a* improbable
unlimited /ʌn'lɪmɪtɪd/ *a* ilimitado
unload /ʌn'ləʊd/ *vt* descargar
unlock /ʌn'lɒk/ *vt* abrir (con llave)
unluck|ily /ʌn'lʌkɪlɪ/ *adv* desgraciadamente. **~y** /ʌn'lʌkɪ/ *a* (**-ier, -iest**) desgraciado; ‹*number*› de mala suerte
unmanly /ʌn'mænlɪ/ *a* poco viril
unmanned /ʌn'mænd/ *a* no tripulado
unmarried /ʌn'mærɪd/ *a* soltero. **~ mother** *n* madre *f* soltera
unmask /ʌn'mɑ:sk/ *vt* desenmascarar. ● *vi* quitarse la máscara
unmentionable /ʌn'menʃənəbl/ *a* a que no se debe aludir
unmistakabl|e /ʌnmɪ'steɪkəbl/ *a* inconfundible. **~y** *adv* claramente
unmitigated /ʌn'mɪtɪgeɪtɪd/ *a* (*absolute*) absoluto
unmoved /ʌn'mu:vd/ *a* (*fig*) indiferente (**by** a), insensible (**by** a)
unnatural /ʌn'nætʃərəl/ *a* no natural; (*not normal*) anormal
unnecessar|ily /ʌn'nesəsərɪlɪ/ *adv* innecesariamente. **~y** /ʌn'nesəsərɪ/ *a* innecesario
unnerve /ʌn'nɜ:v/ *vt* desconcertar
unnoticed /ʌn'nəʊtɪst/ *a* inadvertido
unobtainable /ʌnəb'teɪnəbl/ *a* inasequible; (*fig*) inalcanzable
unobtrusive /ʌnəb'tru:sɪv/ *a* discreto
unofficial /ʌnə'fɪʃl/ *a* no oficial. **~ly** *adv* extraoficialmente
unpack /ʌn'pæk/ *vt* desempaquetar ‹*parcel*›; deshacer ‹*suitcase*›. ● *vi* deshacer la maleta
unpalatable /ʌn'pælətəbl/ *a* desagradable
unparalleled /ʌn'pærəleld/ *a* sin par
unpick /ʌn'pɪk/ *vt* descoser
unpleasant /ʌn'pleznt/ *a* desagradable. **~ness** *n* lo desagradable
unplug /ʌn'plʌg/ *vt* (*elec*) desenchufar
unpopular /ʌn'pɒpjʊlə(r)/ *a* impopular
unprecedented /ʌn'presɪdentɪd/ *a* sin precedente
unpredictable /ʌnprɪ'dɪktəbl/ *a* imprevisible
unpremeditated /ʌnprɪ'medɪteɪtɪd/ *a* impremeditado
unprepared /ʌnprɪ'peəd/ *a* no preparado; (*unready*) desprevenido
unprepossessing /ʌnpri:pə'zesɪŋ/ *a* poco atractivo
unpretentious /ʌnprɪ'tenʃəs/ *a* sin pretensiones, modesto

unprincipled /ʌn'prɪnsɪpld/ *a* sin principios

unprofessional /ʌnprə'feʃənəl/ *a* contrario a la ética profesional

unpublished /ʌn'pʌblɪʃt/ *a* inédito

unqualified /ʌn'kwɒlɪfaɪd/ *a* sin título; (*fig*) absoluto

unquestionabl|e /ʌn'kwestʃənəbl/ *a* indiscutible. **~y** *adv* indiscutiblemente

unquote /ʌn'kwəʊt/ *vi* cerrar comillas

unravel /ʌn'rævl/ *vt* (*pt* **unravelled**) desenredar; deshacer ‹*knitting etc*›. ● *vi* desenredarse

unreal /ʌn'rɪəl/ *a* irreal. **~istic** *a* poco realista

unreasonable /ʌn'ri:zənəbl/ *a* irrazonable

unrecognizable /ʌnrekəg'naɪzəbl/ *a* irreconocible

unrelated /ʌnrɪ'leɪtɪd/ *a* ‹*facts*› inconexo, sin relación; ‹*people*› no emparentado

unreliable /ʌnrɪ'laɪəbl/ *a* ‹*person*› poco formal; ‹*machine*› poco fiable

unrelieved /ʌnrɪ'li:vd/ *a* no aliviado

unremitting /ʌnrɪ'mɪtɪŋ/ *a* incesante

unrepentant /ʌnrɪ'pentənt/ *a* impenitente

unrequited /ʌnrɪ'kwaɪtɪd/ *a* no correspondido

unreservedly /ʌnrɪ'zɜ:vɪdlɪ/ *adv* sin reserva

unrest /ʌn'rest/ *n* inquietud *f*; (*pol*) agitación *f*

unrivalled /ʌn'raɪvld/ *a* sin par

unroll /ʌn'rəʊl/ *vt* desenrollar. ● *vi* desenrollarse

unruffled /ʌn'rʌfld/ ‹*person*› imperturbable

unruly /ʌn'ru:lɪ/ *a* indisciplinado

unsafe /ʌn'seɪf/ *a* peligroso; ‹*person*› en peligro

unsaid /ʌn'sed/ *a* sin decir

unsatisfactory /ʌnsætɪs'fæktərɪ/ *a* insatisfactorio

unsavoury /ʌn'seɪvərɪ/ *a* desagradable

unscathed /ʌn'skeɪðd/ *a* ileso

unscramble /ʌn'skræmbl/ *vt* descifrar

unscrew /ʌn'skru:/ *vt* destornillar

unscrupulous /ʌn'skru:pjʊləs/ *a* sin escrúpulos

unseat /ʌn'si:t/ *vt* (*pol*) quitar el escaño a

unseemly /ʌn'si:mlɪ/ *a* indecoroso

unseen /ʌn'si:n/ *a* inadvertido. ● *n* (*translation*) traducción *f* a primera vista

unselfish /ʌn'selfɪʃ/ *a* desinteresado

unsettle /ʌn'setl/ *vt* perturbar. **~d** *a* perturbado; ‹*weather*› variable; ‹*bill*› por pagar

unshakeable /ʌn'ʃeɪkəbl/ *a* firme

unshaven /ʌn'ʃeɪvn/ *a* sin afeitar

unsightly /ʌn'saɪtlɪ/ *a* feo

unskilled /ʌn'skɪld/ *a* inexperto. **~ worker** *n* obrero *m* no cualificado

unsociable /ʌn'səʊʃəbl/ *a* insociable

unsolicited /ʌnsə'lɪsɪtɪd/ *a* no solicitado

unsophisticated /ʌnsə'fɪstɪkeɪtɪd/ *a* sencillo

unsound /ʌn'saʊnd/ *a* defectuoso, erróneo. **of ~ mind** demente

unsparing /ʌn'speərɪŋ/ *a* pródigo; (*cruel*) cruel

unspeakable /ʌn'spi:kəbl/ *a* indecible

unspecified /ʌn'spesɪfaɪd/ *a* no especificado

unstable /ʌn'steɪbl/ *a* inestable

unsteady /ʌn'stedɪ/ *a* inestable; ‹*hand*› poco firme; ‹*step*› inseguro

unstinted /ʌn'stɪntɪd/ *a* abundante

unstuck /ʌn'stʌk/ *a* suelto. **come ~** despegarse; (*fail, fam*) fracasar

unstudied /ʌn'stʌdɪd/ *a* natural

unsuccessful /ʌnsək'sesfʊl/ *a* fracasado. **be ~** no tener éxito, fracasar

unsuitable /ʌn'su:təbl/ *a* inadecuado; (*inconvenient*) inconveniente

unsure /ʌn'ʃʊə(r)/ *a* inseguro

unsuspecting /ʌnsə'spektɪŋ/ *a* confiado

unthinkable /ʌn'θɪŋkəbl/ *a* inconcebible

untid|ily /ʌn'taɪdɪlɪ/ *adv* desordenadamente. **~iness** *n* desorden *m*. **~y** /ʌn'taɪdɪ/ *a* (**-ier**, **-iest**) desordenado; ‹*person*› desaseado

untie /ʌn'taɪ/ *vt* desatar

until /ən'tɪl, ʌn'tɪl/ *prep* hasta. ● *conj* hasta que

untimely /ʌn'taɪmlɪ/ *a* inoportuno; (*premature*) prematuro

untiring /ʌn'taɪərɪŋ/ *a* incansable

untold /ʌn'təʊld/ *a* incalculable

untoward /ʌntə'wɔ:d/ *a* (*inconvenient*) inconveniente

untried /ʌn'traɪd/ *a* no probado

untrue /ʌn'tru:/ *a* falso

unused /ʌn'ju:zd/ *a* nuevo. /ʌn'ju:st/ *a*. **~ to** no acostumbrado a

unusual /ʌn'ju:ʒʊəl/ *a* insólito; (*exceptional*) excepcional. **~ly** *adv* excepcionalmente

unutterable /ʌn'ʌtərəbl/ *a* indecible

unveil /ʌn'veɪl/ *vt* descubrir; (*disclose*) revelar

unwanted /ʌn'wɒntɪd/ *a* superfluo; ‹*child*› no deseado

unwarranted /ʌn'wɒrəntɪd/ *a* injustificado

unwelcome /ʌn'welkəm/ *a* desagradable; ‹*guest*› inoportuno

unwell /ʌn'wel/ *a* indispuesto

unwieldy /ʌn'wi:ldɪ/ *a* difícil de manejar

unwilling /ʌn'wɪlɪŋ/ *a* no dispuesto. **be ~** no querer. **~ly** *adv* de mala gana

unwind /ʌn'waɪnd/ *vt* (*pt* **unwound**) desenvolver. ● *vi* desenvolverse; (*relax, fam*) relajarse

unwise /ʌn'waɪz/ *a* imprudente

unwitting /ʌn'wɪtɪŋ/ *a* inconsciente; (*involuntary*) involuntario. **~ly** *adv* involuntariamente

unworthy /ʌn'wɜ:ðɪ/ *a* indigno

unwrap /ʌn'ræp/ *vt* (*pt* **unwrapped**) desenvolver, deshacer

unwritten /ʌn'rɪtn/ *a* no escrito; ‹*agreement*› tácito

up /ʌp/ *adv* arriba; (*upwards*) hacia arriba; (*higher*) más arriba; (*out of bed*) levantado; (*finished*) terminado. **~ here** aquí arriba. **~ in** (*fam*) versado en, fuerte en. **~ there** allí arriba. **~ to** hasta. **be one ~ on** llevar la ventaja a. **be ~ against** enfrentarse con. **be ~ to** tramar ‹*plot*›; (*one's turn*) tocar a; a la altura de ‹*task*›; (*reach*) llegar a. **come ~** subir. **feel ~ to it** sentirse capaz. **go ~** subir. **it's ~ to you** depende de tí. **what is ~?** ¿qué pasa? ● *prep* arriba; (*on top of*) en lo alto de. ● *vt* (*pt* **upped**) aumentar. ● *n*. **~s and downs** *npl* altibajos *mpl*

upbraid /ʌp'breɪd/ *vt* reprender

upbringing /'ʌpbrɪŋɪŋ/ *n* educación *f*

update /ʌp'deɪt/ *vt* poner al día

upgrade /ʌp'greɪd/ *vt* ascender ‹*person*›; mejorar ‹*equipment*›

upheaval /ʌp'hi:vl/ *n* trastorno *m*

uphill /'ʌphɪl/ *a* ascendente; (*fig*) arduo. ● *adv* /ʌp'hɪl/ cuesta arriba. **go ~** subir

uphold /ʌp'həʊld/ *vt* (*pt* **upheld**) sostener

upholster /ʌp'həʊlstə(r)/ *vt* tapizar. **~er** /-rə(r)/ *n* tapicero *m*. **~y** *n* tapicería *f*

upkeep /'ʌpki:p/ *n* mantenimiento *m*

up-market /ʌp'mɑ:kɪt/ *a* superior

upon /ə'pɒn/ *prep* en; (*on top of*) encima de. **once ~ a time** érase una vez

upper /'ʌpə(r)/ *a* superior. **~ class** *n* clases *fpl* altas. **~ hand** *n* dominio *m*, ventaja *f*. **~most** *a* (el) más alto. ● *n* (*of shoe*) pala *f*

uppish /'ʌpɪʃ/ *a* engreído

upright /'ʌpraɪt/ *a* derecho; ‹*piano*› vertical. ● *n* montante *m*

uprising /'ʌpraɪzɪŋ/ *n* sublevación *f*

uproar /'ʌprɔ:(r)/ *n* tumulto *m*. **~ious** /-'rɔ:rɪəs/ *a* tumultuoso

uproot /ʌp'ru:t/ *vt* desarraigar

upset /ʌp'set/ *vt* (*pt* **upset**, *presp* **upsetting**) trastornar; desbaratar ‹*plan etc*›; (*distress*) alterar. /'ʌpset/ *n* trastorno *m*

upshot /'ʌpʃɒt/ *n* resultado *m*

upside-down /ʌpsaɪd'daʊn/ *adv* al revés; (*in disorder*) patas arriba. **turn ~** volver

upstairs /ʌp'steəz/ *adv* arriba. /'ʌpsteəz/ *a* de arriba

upstart /'ʌpstɑ:t/ *n* arribista *m & f*

upstream /'ʌpstri:m/ *adv* río arriba; (*against the current*) contra la corriente

upsurge /'ʌpsɜ:dʒ/ *n* aumento *m*; (*of anger etc*) arrebato *m*

uptake /'ʌpteɪk/ *n*. **quick on the ~** muy listo

uptight /'ʌptaɪt/ *a* (*fam*) nervioso

up-to-date /ʌptə'deɪt/ *a* al día; ‹*news*› de última hora; (*modern*) moderno

upturn /'ʌptɜ:n/ *n* aumento *m*; (*improvement*) mejora *f*

upward /'ʌpwəd/ *a* ascendente. ● *adv* hacia arriba. **~s** *adv* hacia arriba

uranium /jʊ'reɪnɪəm/ *n* uranio *m*

urban /'ɜ:bən/ *a* urbano

urbane /ɜ:'beɪn/ *a* cortés

urbanize /'ɜ:bənaɪz/ *vt* urbanizar

urchin /'ɜ:tʃɪn/ *n* pilluelo *m*

urge /ɜ:dʒ/ *vt* incitar, animar. ● *n* impulso *m*. **~ on** animar

urgen|cy /'ɜ:dʒənsɪ/ *n* urgencia *f*. **~t** /'ɜ:dʒənt/ *a* urgente. **~tly** *adv* urgentemente

urin|ate /'jʊərɪneɪt/ *vi* orinar. **~e** /'jʊərɪn/ *n* orina *f*

urn /ɜ:n/ *n* urna *f*

Uruguay /jʊərəgwaɪ/ *n* el Uruguay *m*. **~an** *a & n* uruguayo (*m*)

us /ʌs, əs/ *pron* nos; (*after prep*) nosotros, nosotras

US(A) /ju:es'eɪ/ *abbr* (*United States* (*of America*)) EE.UU., Estados *mpl* Unidos

usage /'ju:zɪdʒ/ *n* uso *m*

use /ju:z/ *vt* emplear. /ju:s/ *n* uso *m*, empleo *m*. **be of ~** servir. **it is no ~** es inútil, no sirve para nada. **make ~ of** servirse de. **~ up** agotar, consumir. **~d** /ju:zd/ *a* ‹*clothes*› gastado. /ju:st/ *pt*. **he ~d to say** decía, solía decir. ● *a*. **~d to** acostumbrado a. **~ful** /'ju:sfl/ *a* útil. **~fully** *adv* útilmente. **~less** *a* inútil; ‹*person*› incompetente. **~r** /-zə(r)/ *n* usuario *m*

usher /'ʌʃə(r)/ *n* ujier *m*; (*in theatre etc*) acomodador *m*. ● *vt*. **~ in** hacer entrar. **~ette** *n* acomodadora *f*

USSR *abbr* (*history*) (*Union of Soviet Socialist Republics*) URSS

usual /'ju:ʒʊəl/ *a* usual, corriente; (*habitual*) acostumbrado, habitual. **as ~** como de costumbre, como siempre. **~ly** *adv* normalmente. **he ~ly wakes up early** suele despertarse temprano

usurer /'ju:ʒərə(r)/ *n* usurero *m*

usurp /jʊ'zɜ:p/ *vt* usurpar. **~er** /-ə(r)/ *n* usurpador *m*

usury /'ju:ʒərɪ/ *n* usura *f*

utensil /ju:'tensl/ *n* utensilio *m*

uterus /'ju:tərəs/ *n* útero *m*

utilitarian /ju:tɪlɪ'teərɪən/ *a* utilitario

utility /ju:'tɪlətɪ/ *n* utilidad *f*. **public ~** *n* servicio *m* público. ● *a* utilitario

utilize /'ju:tɪlaɪz/ *vt* utilizar

utmost /'ʌtməʊst/ *a* extremo. ● *n*. **one's ~** todo lo posible

utter[1] /'ʌtə(r)/ *a* completo

utter[2] /'ʌtə(r)/ *vt* (*speak*) pronunciar; dar ‹*sigh*›; emitir ‹*sound*›. **~ance** *n* expresión *f*

utterly /'ʌtəlɪ/ *adv* totalmente

U-turn /'ju:tɜ:n/ *n* vuelta *f*

V

vacan|cy /'veɪkənsɪ/ *n* (*job*) vacante *f*; (*room*) habitación *f* libre. **~t** *a* libre; (*empty*) vacío; ‹*look*› vago

vacate /və'keɪt/ *vt* dejar

vacation /və'keɪʃn/ *n* (*Amer*) vacaciones *fpl*

vaccin|ate /'væksɪneɪt/ *vt* vacunar. **~ation** /-'neɪʃn/ *n* vacunación *f*. **~e** /'væksi:n/ *n* vacuna *f*

vacuum /'vækjʊəm/ *n* (*pl* **-cuums** *or* **-cua**) vacío *m*. **~ cleaner** *n* aspiradora *f*. **~ flask** *n* termo *m*

vagabond /'vægəbɒnd/ *n* vagabundo *m*

vagary /'veɪgərɪ/ *n* capricho *m*

vagina /və'dʒaɪnə/ *n* vagina *f*

vagrant /'veɪgrənt/ *n* vagabundo *m*

vague /veɪg/ *a* (**-er**, **-est**) vago; ‹*outline*› indistinto. **be ~ about** no precisar. **~ly** *adv* vagamente

vain /veɪn/ *a* (**-er**, **-est**) vanidoso; (*useless*) vano, inútil. **in ~** en vano. **~ly** *adv* vanamente

valance /'væləns/ *n* cenefa *f*

vale /veɪl/ *n* valle *m*

valentine /'væləntaɪn/ *n* (*card*) tarjeta *f* del día de San Valentín

valet /'vælɪt, 'væleɪ/ *n* ayuda *m* de cámara

valiant /'vælɪənt/ *a* valeroso

valid /'vælɪd/ *a* válido; ‹*ticket*› valedero. **~ate** *vt* dar validez a; (*confirm*) convalidar. **~ity** /-'ɪdətɪ/ *n* validez *f*

valley /'vælɪ/ *n* (*pl* **-eys**) valle *m*

valour /'vælə(r)/ *n* valor *m*

valuable /'væljʊəbl/ *a* valioso. **~s** *npl* objetos *mpl* de valor

valuation /væljʊ'eɪʃn/ *n* valoración *f*

value /'vælju:/ *n* valor *m*; (*usefulness*) utilidad *f*. **face ~** *n* valor *m* nominal; (*fig*) significado *m* literal. ● *vt* valorar; (*cherish*) apreciar. **~ added tax (VAT)** *n* impuesto *m* sobre el valor añadido (IVA). **~d** *a* (*appreciated*) apreciado, estimado. **~r** /-ə(r)/ *n* tasador *m*

valve /vælv/ *n* válvula *f*

vampire /'væmpaɪə(r)/ *n* vampiro *m*

van /væn/ *n* furgoneta *f*; (*rail*) furgón *m*

vandal /'vændl/ *n* vándalo *m*. **~ism** /-əlɪzəm/ *n* vandalismo *m*. **~ize** *vt* destruir

vane /veɪn/ *n* (*weathercock*) veleta *f*; (*naut, aviat*) paleta *f*

vanguard /'vængɑ:d/ *n* vanguardia *f*

vanilla /və'nɪlə/ *n* vainilla *f*

vanish /'vænɪʃ/ *vi* desaparecer

vanity /'vænɪtɪ/ *n* vanidad *f*. **~ case** *n* neceser *m*

vantage /ˈvɑːntɪdʒ/ *n* ventaja *f*. **~-point** *n* posición *f* ventajosa
vapour /ˈveɪpə(r)/ *n* vapor *m*
variable /ˈveərɪəbl/ *a* variable
varian|ce /ˈveərɪəns/ *n*. **at ~ce** en desacuerdo. **~t** /ˈveərɪənt/ *a* diferente. ● *n* variante *m*
variation /veərɪˈeɪʃn/ *n* variación *f*
varicoloured /ˈveərɪkʌləd/ *a* multicolor
varied /ˈveərɪd/ *a* variado
varicose /ˈværɪkəʊs/ *a* varicoso. **~ veins** *npl* varices *fpl*
variety /vəˈraɪətɪ/ *n* variedad *f*. **~ show** *n* espectáculo *m* de variedades
various /ˈveərɪəs/ *a* diverso. **~ly** *adv* diversamente
varnish /ˈvɑːnɪʃ/ *n* barniz *m*; (*for nails*) esmalte *m*. ● *vt* barnizar
vary /ˈveərɪ/ *vt/i* variar. **~ing** *a* diverso
vase /vɑːz, *Amer* veɪs/ *n* jarrón *m*
vasectomy /vəˈsektəmɪ/ *n* vasectomía *f*
vast /vɑːst/ *a* vasto, enorme. **~ly** *adv* enormemente. **~ness** *n* inmensidad *f*
vat /væt/ *n* tina *f*
VAT /viːeɪˈtiː/ *abbr* (*value added tax*) IVA *m*, impuesto *m* sobre el valor añadido
vault /vɔːlt/ *n* (*roof*) bóveda *f*; (*in bank*) cámara *f* acorazada; (*tomb*) cripta *f*; (*cellar*) sótano *m*; (*jump*) salto *m*. ● *vt/i* saltar
vaunt /vɔːnt/ *vt* jactarse de
veal /viːl/ *n* ternera *f*
veer /vɪə(r)/ *vi* cambiar de dirección; (*naut*) virar
vegetable /ˈvedʒɪtəbl/ *a* vegetal. ● *n* legumbre *m*; (*greens*) verduras *fpl*
vegetarian /vedʒɪˈteərɪən/ *a & n* vegetariano (*m*)
vegetate /ˈvedʒɪteɪt/ *vi* vegetar
vegetation /vedʒɪˈteɪʃn/ *n* vegetación *f*
vehemen|ce /ˈviːəməns/ *n* vehemencia *f*. **~t** /ˈviːəmənt/ *a* vehemente. **~tly** *adv* con vehemencia
vehicle /ˈviːɪkl/ *n* vehículo *m*
veil /veɪl/ *n* velo *m*. **take the ~** hacerse monja. ● *vt* velar
vein /veɪn/ *n* vena *f*; (*mood*) humor *m*. **~ed** *a* veteado
velocity /vɪˈlɒsɪtɪ/ *n* velocidad *f*
velvet /ˈvelvɪt/ *n* terciopelo *m*. **~y** *a* aterciopelado
venal /ˈviːnl/ *a* venal. **~ity** /-ˈnælətɪ/ *n* venalidad *f*
vendetta /venˈdetə/ *n* enemistad *f* prolongada
vending-machine /ˈvendɪŋ məʃiːn/ *n* distribuidor *m* automático
vendor /ˈvendə(r)/ *n* vendedor *m*
veneer /vəˈnɪə(r)/ *n* chapa *f*; (*fig*) barniz *m*, apariencia *f*
venerable /ˈvenərəbl/ *a* venerable
venereal /vəˈnɪərɪəl/ *a* venéreo
Venetian /vəˈniːʃn/ *a & n* veneciano (*m*). **v~ blind** *n* persiana *f* veneciana
vengeance /ˈvendʒəns/ *n* venganza *f*. **with a ~** (*fig*) con creces
venison /ˈvenɪzn/ *n* carne *f* de venado
venom /ˈvenəm/ *n* veneno *m*. **~ous** *a* venenoso
vent /vent/ *n* abertura *f*; (*for air*) respiradero *m*. **give ~ to** dar salida a. ● *vt* hacer un agujero en; (*fig*) desahogar
ventilat|e /ˈventɪleɪt/ *vt* ventilar. **~ion** /-ˈleɪʃn/ *n* ventilación *f*. **~or** /-ə(r)/ *n* ventilador *m*
ventriloquist /venˈtrɪləkwɪst/ *n* ventrílocuo *m*
venture /ˈventʃə(r)/ *n* empresa *f* (arriesgada). **at a ~** a la ventura. ● *vt* arriesgar. ● *vi* atreverse
venue /ˈvenjuː/ *n* lugar *m* (de reunión)
veranda /vəˈrændə/ *n* terraza *f*
verb /vɜːb/ *n* verbo *m*
verbal /ˈvɜːbl/ *a* verbal. **~ly** *adv* verbalmente
verbatim /vɜːˈbeɪtɪm/ *adv* palabra por palabra, al pie de la letra
verbose /vɜːˈbəʊs/ *a* prolijo
verdant /ˈvɜːdənt/ *a* verde
verdict /ˈvɜːdɪkt/ *n* veredicto *m*; (*opinion*) opinión *f*
verge /vɜːdʒ/ *n* borde *m*. ● *vt*. **~ on** acercarse a
verger /ˈvɜːdʒə(r)/ *n* sacristán *m*
verif|ication /verɪfɪˈkeɪʃn/ *n* verificación *f*. **~y** /ˈverɪfaɪ/ *vt* verificar
veritable /ˈverɪtəbl/ *a* verdadero
vermicelli /vɜːmɪˈtʃelɪ/ *n* fideos *mpl*
vermin /ˈvɜːmɪn/ *n* sabandijas *fpl*
vermouth /ˈvɜːməθ/ *n* vermut *m*
vernacular /vəˈnækjʊlə(r)/ *n* lengua *f*; (*regional*) dialecto *m*
versatil|e /ˈvɜːsətaɪl/ *a* versátil. **~ity** /-ˈtɪlətɪ/ *n* versatilidad *f*
verse /vɜːs/ *n* estrofa *f*; (*poetry*) poesías *fpl*; (*of Bible*) versículo *m*

versed /vɜ:st/ *a*. ~ **in** versado en

version /'vɜ:ʃn/ *n* versión *f*

versus /'vɜ:səs/ *prep* contra

vertebra /'vɜ:tɪbrə/ *n* (*pl* **-brae** /-bri:/) vértebra *f*

vertical /'vɜ:tɪkl/ *a* & *n* vertical (*f*). ~**ly** *adv* verticalmente

vertigo /'vɜ:tɪgəʊ/ *n* vértigo *m*

verve /vɜ:v/ *n* entusiasmo *m*, vigor *m*

very /'verɪ/ *adv* muy. ~ **much** muchísimo. ~ **well** muy bien. **the** ~ **first** el primero de todos. ● *a* mismo. **the** ~ **thing** exactamente lo que hace falta

vespers /'vespəz/ *npl* vísperas *fpl*

vessel /'vesl/ *n* (*receptacle*) recipiente *m*; (*ship*) buque *m*; (*anat*) vaso *m*

vest /vest/ *n* camiseta *f*; (*Amer*) chaleco *m*. ● *vt* conferir. ~**ed interest** *n* interés *m* personal; (*jurid*) derecho *m* adquirido

vestige /'vestɪdʒ/ *n* vestigio *m*

vestment /'vestmənt/ *n* vestidura *f*

vestry /'vestrɪ/ *n* sacristía *f*

vet /vet/ *n* (*fam*) veterinario *m*. ● *vt* (*pt* **vetted**) examinar

veteran /'vetərən/ *n* veterano *m*

veterinary /'vetərɪnərɪ/ *a* veterinario. ~ **surgeon** *n* veterinario *m*

veto /'vi:təʊ/ *n* (*pl* **-oes**) veto *m*. ● *vt* poner el veto a

vex /veks/ *vt* fastidiar. ~**ation** /-'seɪʃn/ *n* fastidio *m*. ~**ed question** *n* cuestión *f* controvertida. ~**ing** *a* fastidioso

via /'vaɪə/ *prep* por, por vía de

viab|ility /vaɪə'bɪlətɪ/ *n* viabilidad *f*. ~**le** /'vaɪəbl/ *a* viable

viaduct /'vaɪədʌkt/ *n* viaducto *m*

vibrant /'vaɪbrənt/ *a* vibrante

vibrat|e /vaɪ'breɪt/ *vt/i* vibrar. ~**ion** /-ʃn/ *n* vibración *f*

vicar /'vɪkə(r)/ *n* párroco *m*. ~**age** /-rɪdʒ/ *n* casa *f* del párroco

vicarious /vɪ'keərɪəs/ *a* indirecto

vice[1] /vaɪs/ *n* vicio *m*

vice[2] /vaɪs/ *n* (*tec*) torno *m* de banco

vice... /'vaɪs/ *pref* vice...

vice versa /vaɪsɪ'vɜ:sə/ *adv* viceversa

vicinity /vɪ'sɪnɪtɪ/ *n* vecindad *f*. **in the** ~ **of** cerca de

vicious /'vɪʃəs/ *a* (*spiteful*) malicioso; (*violent*) atroz. ~ **circle** *n* círculo *m* vicioso. ~**ly** *adv* cruelmente

vicissitudes /vɪ'sɪsɪtju:dz/ *npl* vicisitudes *fpl*

victim /'vɪktɪm/ *n* víctima *f*. ~**ization** /-aɪ'zeɪʃn/ *n* persecución *f*. ~**ize** *vt* victimizar

victor /'vɪktə(r)/ *n* vencedor *m*

Victorian /vɪk'tɔ:rɪən/ *a* victoriano

victor|ious /vɪk'tɔ:rɪəs/ *a* victorioso. ~**y** /'vɪktərɪ/ *n* victoria *f*

video /'vɪdɪəʊ/ *a* video. ● *n* (*fam*) magnetoscopio *m*. ~ **recorder** *n* magnetoscopio *m*. ~**tape** *n* videocassette *f*

vie /vaɪ/ *vi* (*pres p* **vying**) rivalizar

view /vju:/ *n* vista *f*; (*mental survey*) visión *f* de conjunto; (*opinion*) opinión *f*. **in my** ~ a mi juicio. **in** ~ **of** en vista de. **on** ~ expuesto. **with a** ~ **to** con miras a. ● *vt* ver; (*visit*) visitar; (*consider*) considerar. ~**er** /-ə(r)/ *n* espectador *m*; (*TV*) televidente *m* & *f*. ~**finder** /'vju:faɪndə(r)/ *n* visor *m*. ~**point** /'vju:pɔɪnt/ *n* punto *m* de vista

vigil /'vɪdʒɪl/ *n* vigilia *f*. ~**ance** *n* vigilancia *f*. ~**ant** *a* vigilante. **keep** ~ velar

vigo|rous /'vɪgərəs/ *a* vigoroso. ~**ur** /'vɪgə(r)/ *n* vigor *m*

vile /vaɪl/ *a* (*base*) vil; (*bad*) horrible; ‹*weather, temper*› de perros

vilif|ication /vɪlɪfɪ'keɪʃn/ *n* difamación *f*. ~**y** /'vɪlɪfaɪ/ *vt* difamar

village /'vɪlɪdʒ/ *n* aldea *f*. ~**r** /-ə(r)/ *n* aldeano *m*

villain /'vɪlən/ *n* malvado *m*; (*in story etc*) malo *m*. ~**ous** *a* infame. ~**y** *n* infamia *f*

vim /vɪm/ *n* (*fam*) energía *f*

vinaigrette /vɪnɪ'gret/ *n*. ~ **sauce** *n* vinagreta *f*

vindicat|e /'vɪndɪkeɪt/ *vt* vindicar. ~**ion** /-'keɪʃn/ *n* vindicación *f*

vindictive /vɪn'dɪktɪv/ *a* vengativo. ~**ness** *n* carácter *m* vengativo

vine /vaɪn/ *n* vid *f*

vinegar /'vɪnɪgə(r)/ *n* vinagre *m*. ~**y** *a* ‹*person*› avinagrado

vineyard /'vɪnjəd/ *n* viña *f*

vintage /'vɪntɪdʒ/ *n* (*year*) cosecha *f*. ● *a* ‹*wine*› añejo; ‹*car*› de época

vinyl /'vaɪnɪl/ *n* vinilo *m*

viola /vɪ'əʊlə/ *n* viola *f*

violat|e /'vaɪəleɪt/ *vt* violar. ~**ion** /-'leɪʃn/ *n* violación *f*

violen|ce /'vaɪələns/ *n* violencia *f*. ~**t** /'vaɪələnt/ *a* violento. ~**tly** *adv* violentamente

violet /'vaɪələt/ *a* & *n* violeta (*f*)

violin /'vaɪəlɪn/ *n* violín *m*. ~**ist** *n* violinista *m* & *f*

VIP /vi:aɪ'pi:/ *abbr* (*very important person*) personaje *m*
viper /'vaɪpə(r)/ *n* víbora *f*
virgin /'vɜ:dʒɪn/ *a & n* virgen (*f*). **~al** *a* virginal. **~ity** /və'dʒɪnətɪ/ *n* virginidad *f*
Virgo /'vɜ:gəʊ/ *n* (*astr*) Virgo *f*
viril|e /'vɪraɪl/ *a* viril. **~ity** /-'rɪlətɪ/ *n* virilidad *f*
virtual /'vɜ:tʃʊəl/ *a* verdadero. **a ~ failure** prácticamente un fracaso. **~ly** *adv* prácticamente
virtue /'vɜ:tʃu:/ *n* virtud *f*. **by ~ of, in ~ of** en virtud de
virtuoso /vɜ:tjʊ'əʊzəʊ/ *n* (*pl* **-si** /-zi:/) virtuoso *m*
virtuous /'vɜ:tʃʊəs/ *a* virtuoso
virulent /'vɪrʊlənt/ *a* virulento
virus /'vaɪərəs/ *n* (*pl* **-uses**) virus *m*
visa /'vi:zə/ *n* visado *m*, visa *f* (*LAm*)
vis-a-vis /vi:zɑ:'vi:/ *adv* frente a frente. ● *prep* respecto a; (*opposite*) en frente de
viscount /'vaɪkaʊnt/ *n* vizconde *m*. **~ess** *n* vizcondesa *f*
viscous /'vɪskəs/ *a* viscoso
visib|ility /vɪzɪ'bɪlətɪ/ *n* visibilidad *f*. **~le** /'vɪzɪbl/ *a* visible. **~ly** *adv* visiblemente
vision /'vɪʒn/ *n* visión *f*; (*sight*) vista *f*. **~ary** /'vɪʒənərɪ/ *a & n* visionario (*m*)
visit /'vɪzɪt/ *vt* visitar; hacer una visita a ‹*person*›. ● *vi* hacer visitas. ● *n* visita *f*. **~or** *n* visitante *m & f*; (*guest*) visita *f*; (*in hotel*) cliente *m & f*
visor /'vaɪzə(r)/ *n* visera *f*
vista /'vɪstə/ *n* perspectiva *f*
visual /'vɪʒjʊəl/ *a* visual. **~ize** /'vɪʒjʊəlaɪz/ *vt* imaginar(se); (*foresee*) prever. **~ly** *adv* visualmente
vital /'vaɪtl/ *a* vital; (*essential*) esencial
vitality /vaɪ'tælətɪ/ *n* vitalidad *f*
vital: **~ly** /'vaɪtəlɪ/ *adv* extremadamente. **~s** *npl* órganos *mpl* vitales. **~ statistics** *npl* (*fam*) medidas *fpl*
vitamin /'vɪtəmɪn/ *n* vitamina *f*
vitiate /'vɪʃɪeɪt/ *vt* viciar
vitreous /'vɪtrɪəs/ *a* vítreo
vituperat|e /vɪ'tju:pəreɪt/ *vt* vituperar. **~ion** /-'reɪʃn/ *n* vituperación *f*
vivaci|ous /vɪ'veɪʃəs/ *a* animado, vivo. **~ously** *adv* animadamente. **~ty** /-'væsətɪ/ *n* viveza *f*
vivid /'vɪvɪd/ *a* vivo. **~ly** *adv* intensamente; (*describe*) gráficamente. **~ness** *n* viveza *f*
vivisection /vɪvɪ'sekʃn/ *n* vivisección *f*
vixen /'vɪksn/ *n* zorra *f*
vocabulary /və'kæbjʊlərɪ/ *n* vocabulario *m*
vocal /'vəʊkl/ *a* vocal; (*fig*) franco. **~ist** *n* cantante *m & f*
vocation /vəʊ'keɪʃn/ *n* vocación *f*. **~al** *a* profesional
vocifer|ate /və'sɪfəreɪt/ *vt/i* vociferar. **~ous** *a* vociferador
vogue /vəʊg/ *n* boga *f*. **in ~** de moda
voice /vɔɪs/ *n* voz *f*. ● *vt* expresar
void /vɔɪd/ *a* vacío; (*not valid*) nulo. **~ of** desprovisto de. ● *n* vacío *m*. ● *vt* anular
volatile /'vɒlətaɪl/ *a* volátil; ‹*person*› voluble
volcan|ic /vɒl'kænɪk/ *a* volcánico. **~o** /vɒl'keɪnəʊ/ *n* (*pl* **-oes**) volcán *m*
volition /və'lɪʃn/ *n*. **of one's own ~** de su propia voluntad
volley /'vɒlɪ/ *n* (*pl* **-eys**) (*of blows*) lluvia *f*; (*of gunfire*) descarga *f* cerrada
volt /vəʊlt/ *n* voltio *m*. **~age** *n* voltaje *m*
voluble /'vɒljʊbl/ *a* locuaz
volume /'vɒlju:m/ *n* volumen *m*; (*book*) tomo *m*
voluminous /və'lju:mɪnəs/ *a* voluminoso
voluntar|ily /'vɒləntərəlɪ/ *adv* voluntariamente. **~y** /'vɒləntərɪ/ *a* voluntario
volunteer /vɒlən'tɪə(r)/ *n* voluntario *m*. ● *vt* ofrecer. ● *vi* ofrecerse voluntariamente; (*mil*) alistarse como voluntario
voluptuous /və'lʌptjʊəs/ *a* voluptuoso
vomit /'vɒmɪt/ *vt/i* vomitar. ● *n* vómito *m*
voracious /və'reɪʃəs/ *a* voraz
vot|e /vəʊt/ *n* voto *m*; (*right*) derecho *m* de votar. ● *vi* votar. **~er** /-ə(r)/ *n* votante *m & f*. **~ing** *n* votación *f*
vouch /vaʊtʃ/ *vi*. **~ for** garantizar
voucher /'vaʊtʃə(r)/ *n* vale *m*
vow /vaʊ/ *n* voto *m*. ● *vi* jurar
vowel /'vaʊəl/ *n* vocal *f*
voyage /'vɔɪɪdʒ/ *n* viaje *m* (en barco)
vulgar /'vʌlgə(r)/ *a* vulgar. **~ity** /-'gærətɪ/ *n* vulgaridad *f*. **~ize** *vt* vulgarizar

vulnerab|ility /vʌlnərə'bɪlətɪ/ *n* vulnerabilidad *f*. **~le** /'vʌlnərəbl/ *a* vulnerable
vulture /'vʌltʃə(r)/ *n* buitre *m*
vying /'vaɪɪŋ/ *see* **vie**

W

wad /wɒd/ *n* (*pad*) tapón *m*; (*bundle*) lío *m*; (*of notes*) fajo *m*; (*of cotton wool etc*) bolita *f*
wadding /'wɒdɪŋ/ *n* relleno *m*
waddle /'wɒdl/ *vi* contonearse
wade /weɪd/ *vt* vadear. ● *vi*. ~ **through** abrirse paso entre; leer con dificultad ‹*book*›
wafer /'weɪfə(r)/ *n* barquillo *m*; (*relig*) hostia *f*
waffle[1] /'wɒfl/ *n* (*fam*) palabrería *f*. ● *vi* (*fam*) divagar
waffle[2] /'wɒfl/ *n* (*culin*) gofre *m*
waft /wɒft/ *vt* llevar por el aire. ● *vi* flotar
wag /wæg/ *vt* (*pt* **wagged**) menear. ● *vi* menearse
wage /weɪdʒ/ *n*. **~s** *npl* salario *m*. ● *vt*. ~ **war** hacer la guerra. **~r** /'weɪdʒə(r)/ *n* apuesta *f*. ● *vt* apostar
waggle /'wægl/ *vt* menear. ● *vi* menearse
wagon /'wægən/ *n* carro *m*; (*rail*) vagón *m*. **be on the ~** (*sl*) no beber
waif /weɪf/ *n* niño *m* abandonado
wail /weɪl/ *vi* lamentarse. ● *n* lamento *m*
wainscot /'weɪnskət/ *n* revestimiento *m*, zócalo *m*
waist /weɪst/ *n* cintura *f*. **~band** *n* cinturón *m*
waistcoat /'weɪstkəʊt/ *n* chaleco *m*
waistline /'weɪstlaɪn/ *n* cintura *f*
wait /weɪt/ *vt/i* esperar; (*at table*) servir. ~ **for** esperar. ~ **on** servir. ● *n* espera *f*. **lie in ~** acechar
waiter /'weɪtə(r)/ *n* camarero *m*
wait: **~ing-list** *n* lista *f* de espera. **~ing-room** *n* sala *f* de espera
waitress /'weɪtrɪs/ *n* camarera *f*
waive /weɪv/ *vt* renunciar a
wake[1] /weɪk/ *vt* (*pt* **woke**, *pp* **woken**) despertar. ● *vi* despertarse. ● *n* velatorio *m*. ~ **up** *vt* despertar. ● *vi* despertarse
wake[2] /weɪk/ *n* (*naut*) estela *f*. **in the ~ of** como resultado de, tras
waken /'weɪkən/ *vt* despertar. ● *vi* despertarse
wakeful /'weɪkfl/ *a* insomne
Wales /weɪlz/ *n* País *m* de Gales
walk /wɔ:k/ *vi* andar; (*not ride*) ir a pie; (*stroll*) pasearse. ~ **out** salir; ‹*workers*› declararse en huelga. ~ **out on** abandonar. ● *vt* andar por ‹*streets*›; llevar de paseo ‹*dog*›. ● *n* paseo *m*; (*gait*) modo *m* de andar; (*path*) sendero *m*. ~ **of life** clase *f* social. **~about** /'wɔ:kəbaʊt/ *n* (*of royalty*) encuentro *m* con el público. **~er** /-ə(r)/ *n* paseante *m* & *f*
walkie-talkie /wɔ:kɪ'tɔ:kɪ/ *n* transmisor-receptor *m* portátil
walking /'wɔ:kɪŋ/ *n* paseo *m*. **~-stick** *n* bastón *m*
Walkman /'wɔ:kmən/ *n* (*P*) estereo *m* personal, Walkman *m* (*P*), magnetófono *m* de bolsillo
walk: **~-out** *n* huelga *f*. **~-over** *n* victoria *f* fácil
wall /wɔ:l/ *n* (*interior*) pared *f*; (*exterior*) muro *m*; (*in garden*) tapia *f*; (*of city*) muralla *f*. **go to the ~** fracasar. **up the ~** (*fam*) loco. ● *vt* amurallar ‹*city*›
wallet /'wɒlɪt/ *n* cartera *f*, billetera *f* (*LAm*)
wallflower /'wɔ:lflaʊə(r)/ *n* alhelí *m*
wallop /'wɒləp/ *vt* (*pt* **walloped**) (*sl*) golpear con fuerza. ● *n* (*sl*) golpe *m* fuerte
wallow /'wɒləʊ/ *vi* revolcarse
wallpaper /'wɔ:lpeɪpə(r)/ *n* papel *m* pintado
walnut /'wɔ:lnʌt/ *n* nuez *f*; (*tree*) nogal *m*
walrus /'wɔ:lrəs/ *n* morsa *f*
waltz /wɔ:ls/ *n* vals *m*. ● *vi* valsar
wan /wɒn/ *a* pálido
wand /wɒnd/ *n* varita *f*
wander /'wɒndə(r)/ *vi* vagar; (*stroll*) pasearse; (*digress*) divagar; ‹*road, river*› serpentear. ● *n* paseo *m*. **~er** /-ə(r)/ *n* vagabundo *m*. **~lust** /'wɒndəlʌst/ *n* pasión *f* por los viajes
wane /weɪn/ *vi* menguar. ● *n*. **on the ~** disminuyendo
wangle /wæŋgl/ *vt* (*sl*) agenciarse
want /wɒnt/ *vt* querer; (*need*) necesitar; (*require*) exigir. ● *vi*. ~ **for** carecer de. ● *n* necesidad *f*; (*lack*) falta *f*; (*desire*) deseo *m*. **~ed** *a* ‹*criminal*› buscado. **~ing** *a* (*lacking*) falto de. **be ~ing** carecer de
wanton /'wɒntən/ *a* (*licentious*) lascivo; (*motiveless*) sin motivo
war /wɔ:(r)/ *n* guerra *f*. **at ~** en guerra

warble /'wɔ:bl/ *vt* cantar trinando. ● *vi* gorjear. ● *n* gorjeo *m*. **~r** /-ə(r)/ *n* curruca *f*

ward /wɔ:d/ *n* (*in hospital*) sala *f*; (*of town*) barrio *m*; (*child*) pupilo *m*. ● *vt*. **~ off** parar

warden /'wɔ:dn/ *n* guarda *m*

warder /'wɔ:də(r)/ *n* carcelero *m*

wardrobe /'wɔ:drəʊb/ *n* armario *m*; (*clothes*) vestuario *m*

warehouse /'weəhaʊs/ *n* almacén *m*

wares /weəz/ *npl* mercancías *fpl*

war: **~fare** /'wɔ:feə(r)/ *n* guerra *f*. **~head** /'wɔ:hed/ *n* cabeza *f* explosiva

warily /'weərɪlɪ/ *adv* cautelosamente

warlike /'wɔ:laɪk/ *a* belicoso

warm /wɔ:m/ *a* (**-er**, **-est**) caliente; (*hearty*) caluroso. **be ~** ‹*person*› tener calor. **it is ~** hace calor. ● *vt*. **~ (up)** calentar; recalentar ‹*food*›; (*fig*) animar. ● *vi*. **~ (up)** calentarse; (*fig*) animarse. **~ to** tomar simpatía a ‹*person*›; ir entusiasmándose por ‹*idea etc*›. **~-blooded** *a* de sangre caliente. **~-hearted** *a* simpático. **~ly** *adv* (*heartily*) calurosamente

warmonger /'wɔ:mʌŋgə(r)/ *n* belicista *m & f*

warmth /wɔ:mθ/ *n* calor *m*

warn /wɔ:n/ *vt* avisar, advertir. **~ing** *n* advertencia *f*; (*notice*) aviso *m*. **~ off** (*advise against*) aconsejar en contra de; (*forbid*) impedir

warp /wɔ:p/ *vt* deformar; (*fig*) pervertir. ● *vi* deformarse

warpath /'wɔ:pɑ:θ/ *n*. **be on the ~** buscar camorra

warrant /'wɒrənt/ *n* autorización *f*; (*for arrest*) orden *f*. ● *vt* justificar. **~-officer** *n* suboficial *m*

warranty /'wɒrəntɪ/ *n* garantía *f*

warring /'wɔ:rɪŋ/ *a* en guerra

warrior /'wɔ:rɪə(r)/ *n* guerrero *m*

warship /'wɔ:ʃɪp/ *n* buque *m* de guerra

wart /wɔ:t/ *n* verruga *f*

wartime /'wɔ:taɪm/ *n* tiempo *m* de guerra

wary /'weərɪ/ *a* (**-ier**, **-iest**) cauteloso

was /wəz, wɒz/ *see* **be**

wash /wɒʃ/ *vt* lavar; (*flow over*) bañar. ● *vi* lavarse. ● *n* lavado *m*; (*dirty clothes*) ropa *f* sucia; (*wet clothes*) colada *f*; (*of ship*) estela *f*. **have a ~** lavarse. **~ out** *vt* enjuagar; (*fig*) cancelar. **~ up** *vi* fregar los platos. **~able** *a* lavable. **~-basin** *n* lavabo *m*. **~ed-out** *a* (*pale*) pálido; (*tired*) rendido. **~er** /'wɒʃə(r)/ *n* arandela *f*; (*washing-machine*) lavadora *f*. **~ing** /'wɒʃɪŋ/ *n* lavado *m*; (*dirty clothes*) ropa *f* sucia; (*wet clothes*) colada *f*. **~ing-machine** *n* lavadora *f*. **~ing-powder** *n* jabón *m* en polvo. **~ing-up** *n* fregado *m*; (*dirty plates etc*) platos *mpl* para fregar. **~-out** *n* (*sl*) desastre *m*. **~-room** *n* (*Amer*) servicios *mpl*. **~-stand** *n* lavabo *m*. **~-tub** *n* tina *f* de lavar

wasp /wɒsp/ *n* avispa *f*

wastage /'weɪstɪdʒ/ *n* desperdicios *mpl*

waste /weɪst/ ● *a* de desecho; ‹*land*› yermo. ● *n* derroche *m*; (*rubbish*) desperdicio *m*; (*of time*) pérdida *f*. ● *vt* derrochar; (*not use*) desperdiciar; perder ‹*time*›. ● *vi*. **~ away** consumirse. **~-disposal unit** *n* trituradora *f* de basuras. **~ful** *a* dispendioso; ‹*person*› derrochador. **~-paper basket** *n* papelera *f*. **~s** *npl* tierras *fpl* baldías

watch /wɒtʃ/ *vt* mirar; (*keep an eye on*) vigilar; (*take heed*) tener cuidado con; ver ‹*TV*›. ● *vi* mirar; (*keep an eye on*) vigilar. ● *n* vigilancia *f*; (*period of duty*) guardia *f*; (*timepiece*) reloj *m*. **on the ~** alerta. **~ out** *vi* tener cuidado. **~-dog** *n* perro *m* guardián; (*fig*) guardián *m*. **~ful** *a* vigilante. **~maker** /'wɒtʃmeɪkə(r)/ *n* relojero *m*. **~man** /'wɒtʃmən/ *n* (*pl* **-men**) vigilante *m*. **~-tower** *n* atalaya *f*. **~word** /'wɒtʃwɜ:d/ *n* santo *m* y seña

water /'wɔ:tə(r)/ *n* agua *f*. **by ~** (*of travel*) por mar. **in hot ~** (*fam*) en un apuro. ● *vt* regar ‹*plants etc*›; (*dilute*) aguar, diluir. ● *vi* ‹*eyes*› llorar. **make s.o.'s mouth ~** hacérsele la boca agua. **~ down** *vt* diluir; (*fig*) suavizar. **~-closet** *n* wáter *m*. **~-colour** *n* acuarela *f*. **~course** /'wɔ:təkɔ:s/ *n* arroyo *m*; (*artificial*) canal *m*. **~cress** /'wɔ:təkres/ *n* berro *m*. **~fall** /'wɔ:təfɔ:l/ *n* cascada *f*. **~-ice** *n* sorbete *m*. **~ing-can** /'wɔ:tərɪŋkæn/ *n* regadera *f*. **~-lily** *n* nenúfar *m*. **~-line** *n* línea *f* de flotación. **~logged** /'wɔ:təlɒgd/ *a* saturado de agua, empapado. **~ main** *n* cañería *f* principal. **~ melon** *n* sandía *f*. **~-mill** *n* molino *m* de agua. **~ polo** *n* polo *m* acuático. **~-power** *n* energía *f* hidráulica. **~proof** /'wɔ:təpru:f/ *a* & *n* impermeable (*m*); ‹*watch*› sumergible. **~shed** /'wɔ:təʃed/ *n* punto *m* decisivo. **~-skiing** *n* esquí *m* acuático. **~-softener** *n* ablandador *m* de agua. **~tight** /'wɔ:tətaɪt/ *a* hermético, estanco; (*fig*) irrecusable. **~way** *n* canal *m* navegable. **~-wheel** *n* rueda *f* hidráulica. **~-wings** *npl* flotadores *mpl*. **~works** /'wɔ:təwɜ:ks/ *n* sistema *m* de abastecimiento de agua. **~y** /'wɔ:tərɪ/ *a* acuoso; ‹*colour*› pálido; ‹*eyes*› lloroso

watt /wɒt/ *n* vatio *m*

wave /weɪv/ *n* onda *f*; (*of hand*) señal *f*; (*fig*) oleada *f*. ● *vt* agitar; ondular ‹*hair*›. ● *vi* (*signal*) hacer señales con la mano; ‹*flag*› flotar. **~band** /'weɪvbænd/ *n* banda *f* de ondas. **~length** /'weɪvleŋθ/ *n* longitud *f* de onda

waver /'weɪvə(r)/ *vi* vacilar

wavy /'weɪvɪ/ *a* (**-ier**, **-iest**) ondulado

wax[1] /wæks/ *n* cera *f*. ● *vt* encerar

wax[2] /wæks/ *vi* ‹*moon*› crecer

wax: **~en** *a* céreo. **~work** /'wækswɜ:k/ *n* figura *f* de cera. **~y** *a* céreo

way /weɪ/ *n* camino *m*; (*distance*) distancia *f*; (*manner*) manera *f*, modo *m*; (*direction*) dirección *f*; (*means*) medio *m*; (*habit*) costumbre *f*. **be in the ~** estorbar. **by the ~** a propósito. **by ~ of** a título de, por. **either ~** de cualquier modo. **in a ~** en cierta manera. **in some ~s** en ciertos modos. **lead the ~** mostrar el camino. **make ~** dejar paso a. **on the ~** en camino. **out of the ~** remoto; (*extraordinary*) fuera de lo común. **that ~** por allí. **this ~** por aquí. **under ~** en curso. **~-bill** *n* hoja *f* de ruta. **~farer** /'weɪfeərə(r)/ *n* viajero *m*. **~ in** *n* entrada *f*

waylay /weɪ'leɪ/ *vt* (*pt* **-laid**) acechar; (*detain*) detener

way: **~ out** *n* salida *f*. **~-out** *a* ultramoderno, original. **~s** *npl* costumbres *fpl*. **~side** /'weɪsaɪd/ *n* borde *m* del camino

wayward /'weɪwəd/ *a* caprichoso

we /wi:/ *pron* nosotros, nosotras

weak /wi:k/ *a* (**-er**, **-est**) débil; ‹*liquid*› aguado, acuoso; (*fig*) flojo. **~en** *vt* debilitar. **~-kneed** *a* irresoluto. **~ling** /'wi:klɪŋ/ *n* persona *f* débil. **~ly** *adv* débilmente. ● *a* enfermizo. **~ness** *n* debilidad *f*

weal /wi:l/ *n* verdugón *m*

wealth /welθ/ *n* riqueza *f*. **~y** *a* (**-ier**, **-iest**) rico

wean /wi:n/ *vt* destetar

weapon /'wepən/ *n* arma *f*

wear /weə(r)/ *vt* (*pt* **wore**, *pp* **worn**) llevar; (*put on*) ponerse; tener ‹*expression etc*›; (*damage*) desgastar. ● *vi* desgastarse; (*last*) durar. ● *n* uso *m*; (*damage*) desgaste *m*; (*clothing*) ropa *f*. **~ down** *vt* desgastar; agotar ‹*opposition etc*›. **~ off** *vi* desaparecer. **~ on** *vi* ‹*time*› pasar. **~ out** *vt* desgastar; (*tire*) agotar. **~able** *a* que se puede llevar. **~ and tear** desgaste *m*

wear|ily /'wɪərɪlɪ/ *adv* cansadamente. **~iness** *n* cansancio *m*. **~isome** /'wɪərɪsəm/ *a* cansado. **~y** /'wɪərɪ/ *a* (**-ier**, **-iest**) cansado. ● *vt* cansar. ● *vi* cansarse. **~y of** cansarse de

weasel /'wi:zl/ *n* comadreja *f*

weather /'weðə(r)/ *n* tiempo *m*. **under the ~** (*fam*) indispuesto. ● *a* meteorológico. ● *vt* curar ‹*wood*›; (*survive*) superar. **~-beaten** *a* curtido. **~cock** /'weðəkɒk/ *n*, **~-vane** *n* veleta *f*

weave /wi:v/ *vt* (*pt* **wove**, *pp* **woven**) tejer; entretejer ‹*story etc*›; entrelazar ‹*flowers etc*›. **~ one's way** abrirse paso. ● *n* tejido *m*. **~r** /-ə(r)/ *n* tejedor *m*

web /web/ *n* tela *f*; (*of spider*) telaraña *f*; (*on foot*) membrana *f*. **~bing** *n* cincha *f*

wed /wed/ *vt* (*pt* **wedded**) casarse con; ‹*priest etc*› casar. ● *vi* casarse. **~ded to** (*fig*) unido a

wedding /'wedɪŋ/ *n* boda *f*. **~-cake** *n* pastel *m* de boda. **~-ring** *n* anillo *m* de boda

wedge /wedʒ/ *n* cuña *f*; (*space filler*) calce *m*. ● *vt* acuñar; (*push*) apretar

wedlock /'wedlɒk/ *n* matrimonio *m*

Wednesday /'wenzdeɪ/ *n* miércoles *m*

wee /wi:/ *a* (*fam*) pequeñito

weed /wi:d/ *n* mala hierba *f*. ● *vt* desherbar. **~-killer** *n* herbicida *m*. **~ out** eliminar. **~y** *a* ‹*person*› débil

week /wi:k/ *n* semana *f*. **~day** /'wi:kdeɪ/ *n* día *m* laborable. **~end** *n* fin *m* de semana. **~ly** /'wi:klɪ/ *a* semanal. ● *n* semanario *m*. ● *adv* semanalmente

weep /wi:p/ *vi* (*pt* **wept**) llorar. **~ing willow** *n* sauce *m* llorón

weevil /'wi:vɪl/ *n* gorgojo *m*
weigh /weɪ/ *vt/i* pesar. ~ **anchor** levar anclas. ~ **down** *vt* (*fig*) oprimir. ~ **up** *vt* pesar; (*fig*) considerar
weight /weɪt/ *n* peso *m*. ~**less** *a* ingrávido. ~**lessness** *n* ingravidez *f*. ~**-lifting** *n* halterofilia *f*, levantamiento *m* de pesos. ~**y** *a* (**-ier**, **-iest**) pesado; (*influential*) influyente
weir /wɪə(r)/ *n* presa *f*
weird /wɪəd/ *a* (**-er**, **-est**) misterioso; (*bizarre*) extraño
welcome /'welkəm/ *a* bienvenido. ~ **to do** libre de hacer. **you're** ~**e!** (*after thank you*) ¡de nada! ● *n* bienvenida *f*; (*reception*) acogida *f*. ● *vt* dar la bienvenida a; (*appreciate*) alegrarse de
welcoming /'welkəmɪŋ/ *a* acogedor
weld /weld/ *vt* soldar. ● *n* soldadura *f*. ~**er** *n* soldador *m*
welfare /'welfeə(r)/ *n* bienestar *m*; (*aid*) asistencia *f* social. **W**~ **State** *n* estado *m* benefactor. ~ **work** *n* asistencia *f* social
well[1] /wel/ *adv* (**better**, **best**) bien. ~ **done!** ¡bravo! **as** ~ también. **as** ~ **as** tanto... como. **be** ~ estar bien. **do** ~ (*succeed*) tener éxito. **very** ~ muy bien. ● *a* bien. ● *int* bueno; (*surprise*) ¡vaya! ~ **I never!** ¡no me digas!
well[2] /wel/ *n* pozo *m*; (*of staircase*) caja *f*
well: ~**-appointed** *a* bien equipado. ~**-behaved** *a* bien educado. ~**-being** *n* bienestar *m*. ~**-bred** *a* bien educado. ~**-disposed** *a* benévolo. ~**-groomed** *a* bien aseado. ~**-heeled** *a* (*fam*) rico
wellington /'welɪŋtən/ *n* bota *f* de agua
well: ~**-knit** *a* robusto. ~**-known** *a* conocido. ~**-meaning** *a*, ~ **meant** *a* bienintencionado. ~ **off** *a* acomodado. ~**-read** *a* culto. ~**-spoken** *a* bienhablado. ~**-to-do** *a* rico. ~**-wisher** *n* bienqueriente *m* & *f*
Welsh /welʃ/ *a* & *n* galés (*m*). ~ **rabbit** *n* pan *m* tostado con queso
welsh /welʃ/ *vi*. ~ **on** no cumplir con
wench /wentʃ/ *n* (*old use*) muchacha *f*
wend /wend/ *vt*. ~ **one's way** encaminarse
went /went/ *see* **go**
wept /wept/ *see* **weep**
were /wɜ:(r), wə(r)/ *see* **be**
west /west/ *n* oeste *m*. **the** ~ el Occidente *m*. ● *a* del oeste. ● *adv* hacia el oeste, al oeste. **go** ~ (*sl*) morir. **W**~ **Germany** *n* Alemania *f* Occidental. ~**erly** *a* del oeste. ~**ern** *a* occidental. ● *n* (*film*) película *f* del Oeste. ~**erner** /-ənə(r)/ *n* occidental *m* & *f*. **W**~ **Indian** *a* & *n* antillano (*m*). **W**~ **Indies** *npl* Antillas *fpl*. ~**ward** *a*, ~**ward(s)** *adv* hacia el oeste
wet /wet/ *a* (**wetter**, **wettest**) mojado; (*rainy*) lluvioso, de lluvia; (*person*, *sl*) soso. ~ **paint** recién pintado. **get** ~ mojarse. ● *vt* (*pt* **wetted**) mojar, humedecer. ~ **blanket** *n* aguafiestas *m* & *f invar*. ~ **suit** *n* traje *m* de buzo
whack /wæk/ *vt* (*fam*) golpear. ● *n* (*fam*) golpe *m*. ~**ed** /wækt/ *a* (*fam*) agotado. ~**ing** *a* (*huge*, *sl*) enorme. ● *n* paliza *f*
whale /weɪl/ *n* ballena *f*. **a** ~ **of a** (*fam*) maravilloso, enorme
wham /wæm/ *int* ¡zas!
wharf /wɔ:f/ *n* (*pl* **wharves** *or* **wharfs**) muelle *m*
what /wɒt/ *a* el que, la que, lo que, los que, las que; (*in questions & exclamations*) qué. ● *pron* lo que; (*interrogative*) qué. ~ **about going?** ¿si fuésemos? ~ **about me?** ¿y yo? ~ **for?** ¿para qué? ~ **if?** ¿y si? ~ **is it?** ¿qué es? ~ **you need** lo que te haga falta. ● *int* ¡cómo! ~ **a fool!** ¡qué tonto!
whatever /wɒt'evə(r)/ *a* cualquiera. ● *pron* (todo) lo que, cualquier cosa que
whatnot /'wɒtnɒt/ *n* chisme *m*
whatsoever /wɒtsəʊ'evə(r)/ *a* & *pron* = **whatever**
wheat /wi:t/ *n* trigo *m*. ~**en** *a* de trigo
wheedle /'wi:dl/ *vt* engatusar
wheel /wi:l/ *n* rueda *f*. **at the** ~ al volante. **steering-**~ *n* volante *m*. ● *vt* empujar ‹*bicycle etc*›. ● *vi* girar. ~ **round** girar. ~**barrow** /'wi:lbærəʊ/ *n* carretilla *f*. ~**chair** /'wi:ltʃeə(r)/ *n* silla *f* de ruedas
wheeze /wi:z/ *vi* resollar. ● *n* resuello *m*
when /wen/ *adv* cuándo. ● *conj* cuando
whence /wens/ *adv* de dónde
whenever /wen'evə(r)/ *adv* en cualquier momento; (*every time that*) cada vez que

where /weə(r)/ *adv & conj* donde; (*interrogative*) dónde. **~ are you going?** ¿adónde vas? **~ are you from?** ¿de dónde eres?

whereabouts /ˈweərəbaʊts/ *adv* dónde. ● *n* paradero *m*

whereas /weərˈæz/ *conj* por cuanto; (*in contrast*) mientras (que)

whereby /weəˈbaɪ/ *adv* por lo cual

whereupon /weərəˈpɒn/ *adv* después de lo cual

wherever /weərˈevə(r)/ *adv* (*in whatever place*) dónde (diablos). ● *conj* dondequiera que

whet /wet/ *vt* (*pt* **whetted**) afilar; (*fig*) aguzar

whether /ˈweðə(r)/ *conj* si. **~ you like it or not** que te guste o no te guste. **I don't know ~ she will like it** no sé si le gustará

which /wɪtʃ/ *a* (*in questions*) qué. **~ one** cuál. **~ one of you** cuál de vosotros. ● *pron* (*in questions*) cuál; (*relative*) que; (*object*) el cual, la cual, lo cual, los cuales, las cuales

whichever /wɪtʃˈevə(r)/ *a* cualquier. ● *pron* cualquiera que, el que, la que

whiff /wɪf/ *n* soplo *m*; (*of smoke*) bocanada *f*; (*smell*) olorcillo *m*

while /waɪl/ *n* rato *m*. ● *conj* mientras; (*although*) aunque. ● *vt*. **~ away** pasar ‹*time*›

whilst /waɪlst/ *conj* = **while**

whim /wɪm/ *n* capricho *m*

whimper /ˈwɪmpə(r)/ *vi* lloriquear. ● *n* lloriqueo *m*

whimsical /ˈwɪmzɪkl/ *a* caprichoso; (*odd*) extraño

whine /waɪn/ *vi* gimotear. ● *n* gimoteo *m*

whip /wɪp/ *n* látigo *m*; (*pol*) oficial *m* disciplinario. ● *vt* (*pt* **whipped**) azotar; (*culin*) batir; (*seize*) agarrar. **~-cord** *n* tralla *f*. **~ped cream** *n* nata *f* batida. **~ping-boy** /ˈwɪpɪŋbɔɪ/ *n* cabeza *f* de turco. **~-round** *n* colecta *f*. **~ up** (*incite*) estimular

whirl /wɜːl/ *vt* hacer girar rápidamente. ● *vi* girar rápidamente; (*swirl*) arremolinarse. ● *n* giro *m*; (*swirl*) remolino *m*. **~pool** /ˈwɜːlpuːl/ *n* remolino *m*. **~wind** /ˈwɜːlwɪnd/ *n* torbellino *m*

whirr /wɜː(r)/ *n* zumbido *m*. ● *vi* zumbar

whisk /wɪsk/ *vt* (*culin*) batir. ● *n* (*culin*) batidor *m*. **~ away** llevarse

whisker /ˈwɪskə(r)/ *n* pelo *m*. **~s** *npl* (*of man*) patillas *fpl*; (*of cat etc*) bigotes *mpl*

whisky /ˈwɪskɪ/ *n* güisqui *m*

whisper /ˈwɪspə(r)/ *vt* decir en voz baja. ● *vi* cuchichear; ‹*leaves etc*› susurrar. ● *n* cuchicheo *m*; (*of leaves*) susurro *m*; (*rumour*) rumor *m*

whistle /ˈwɪsl/ *n* silbido *m*; (*instrument*) silbato *m*. ● *vi* silbar. **~-stop** *n* (*pol*) breve parada *f* (en gira electoral)

white /waɪt/ *a* (**-er**, **-est**) blanco. **go ~** ponerse pálido. ● *n* blanco; (*of egg*) clara *f*. **~bait** /ˈwaɪtbeɪt/ *n* (*pl* **~bait**) chanquetes *mpl*. **~ coffee** *n* café *m* con leche. **~-collar worker** *n* empleado *m* de oficina. **~ elephant** *n* objeto *m* inútil y costoso

Whitehall /ˈwaɪthɔːl/ *n* el gobierno *m* británico

white: **~ horses** *n* cabrillas *fpl*. **~-hot** *a* ‹*metal*› candente. **~ lie** *n* mentirijilla *f*. **~n** *vt/i* blanquear. **~ness** *n* blancura *f*. **W~ Paper** *n* libro *m* blanco. **~wash** /ˈwaɪtwɒʃ/ *n* jalbegue *m*; (*fig*) encubrimiento *m*. ● *vt* enjalbegar; (*fig*) encubrir

whiting /ˈwaɪtɪŋ/ *n* (*pl* **whiting**) (*fish*) pescadilla *f*

whitlow /ˈwɪtləʊ/ *n* panadizo *m*

Whitsun /ˈwɪtsn/ *n* Pentecostés *m*

whittle /ˈwɪtl/ *vt*. **~ (down)** tallar; (*fig*) reducir

whiz /wɪz/ *vi* (*pt* **whizzed**) silbar; (*rush*) ir a gran velocidad. **~ past** pasar como un rayo. **~-kid** *n* (*fam*) joven *m* prometedor, promesa *f*

who /huː/ *pron* que, quien; (*interrogative*) quién; (*particular person*) el que, la que, los que, las que

whodunit /huːˈdʌnɪt/ *n* (*fam*) novela *f* policíaca

whoever /huːˈevə(r)/ *pron* quienquera que; (*interrogative*) quién (diablos)

whole /həʊl/ *a* entero; (*not broken*) intacto. ● *n* todo *m*, conjunto *m*; (*total*) total *m*. **as a ~** en conjunto. **on the ~** por regla general. **~-hearted** *a* sincero. **~meal** *a* integral

wholesale /ˈhəʊlseɪl/ *n* venta *f* al por mayor. ● *a & adv* al por mayor. **~r** /-ə(r)/ *n* comerciante *m & f* al por mayor

wholesome /ˈhəʊlsəm/ *a* saludable

wholly /ˈhəʊlɪ/ *adv* completamente

whom /hu:m/ *pron* que, a quien; (*interrogative*) a quién
whooping cough /'hu:pɪŋkɒf/ *n* tos *f* ferina
whore /hɔ:(r)/ *n* puta *f*
whose /hu:z/ *pron* de quién. ● *a* de quién; (*relative*) cuyo
why /waɪ/ *adv* por qué. ● *int* ¡toma!
wick /wɪk/ *n* mecha *f*
wicked /'wɪkɪd/ *a* malo; (*mischievous*) travieso; (*very bad, fam*) malísimo. **~ness** *n* maldad *f*
wicker /'wɪkə(r)/ *n* mimbre *m* & *f*. ● *a* de mimbre. **~work** *n* artículos *mpl* de mimbre
wicket /'wɪkɪt/ *n* (*cricket*) rastrillo *m*
wide /waɪd/ *a* (**-er**, **-est**) ancho; (*fully opened*) de par en par; (*far from target*) lejano; ‹*knowledge etc*› amplio. ● *adv* lejos. **far and ~** por todas partes. **~ awake** *a* completamente despierto; (*fig*) despabilado. **~ly** *adv* extensamente; (*believed*) generalmente; (*different*) muy. **~n** *vt* ensanchar
widespread /'waɪdspred/ *a* extendido; (*fig*) difundido
widow /'wɪdəʊ/ *n* viuda *f*. **~ed** *a* viudo. **~er** *n* viudo *m*. **~hood** *n* viudez *f*
width /wɪdθ/ *n* anchura *f*. **in ~** de ancho
wield /wi:ld/ *vt* manejar; ejercer ‹*power*›
wife /waɪf/ *n* (*pl* **wives**) mujer *f*, esposa *f*
wig /wɪg/ *n* peluca *f*
wiggle /'wɪgl/ *vt* menear. ● *vi* menearse
wild /waɪld/ *a* (**-er**, **-est**) salvaje; (*enraged*) furioso; ‹*idea*› extravagante; (*with joy*) loco; (*random*) al azar. ● *adv* en estado salvaje. **run ~** crecer en estado salvaje. **~s** *npl* regiones *fpl* salvajes
wildcat /'waɪldkæt/ *a*. **~ strike** *n* huelga *f* salvaje
wilderness /'wɪldənɪs/ *n* desierto *m*
wild: **~fire** /'waɪldfaɪl(r)/ *n*. **spread like ~fire** correr como un reguero de pólvera. **~-goose chase** *n* empresa *f* inútil. **~life** /'waɪldlaɪf/ *n* fauna *f*. **~ly** *adv* violentamente; (*fig*) locamente
wilful /'wɪlfʊl/ *a* intencionado; (*self-willed*) terco. **~ly** *adv* intencionadamente; (*obstinately*) obstinadamente

will¹ /wɪl/ *v aux*. **~ you have some wine?** ¿quieres vino? **he ~ be** será. **you ~ be back soon, won't you?** volverás pronto, ¿no?
will² /wɪl/ *n* voluntad *f*; (*document*) testamento *m*
willing /'wɪlɪŋ/ *a* complaciente. **~ to** dispuesto a. **~ly** *adv* de buena gana. **~ness** *n* buena voluntad *f*
willow /'wɪləʊ/ *n* sauce *m*
will-power /'wɪlpaʊə(r)/ *n* fuerza *f* de voluntad
willy-nilly /wɪlɪ'nɪlɪ/ *adv* quieras que no
wilt /wɪlt/ *vi* marchitarse
wily /'waɪlɪ/ *a* (**-ier**, **-iest**) astuto
win /wɪn/ *vt* (*pt* **won**, *pres p* **winning**) ganar; (*achieve, obtain*) conseguir. ● *vi* ganar. ● *n* victoria *f*. **~ back** *vi* reconquistar. **~ over** *vt* convencer
wince /wɪns/ *vi* hacer una mueca de dolor. **without wincing** sin pestañear. ● *n* mueca *f* de dolor
winch /wɪntʃ/ *n* cabrestante *m*. ● *vt* levantar con el cabrestante
wind¹ /wɪnd/ *n* viento *m*; (*in stomach*) flatulencia *f*. **get the ~ up** (*sl*) asustarse. **get ~ of** enterarse de. **in the ~** en el aire. ● *vt* dejar sin aliento.
wind² /waɪnd/ *vt* (*pt* **wound**) (*wrap around*) enrollar; dar cuerda a ‹*clock etc*›. ● *vi* ‹*road etc*› serpentear. **~ up** *vt* dar cuerda a ‹*watch, clock*›; (*provoke*) agitar, poner nervioso; (*fig*) terminar, concluir
wind /wɪnd/: **~bag** *n* charlatán *m*. **~-cheater** *n* cazadora *f*
winder /'waɪndə(r)/ *n* devanador *m*; (*of clock, watch*) llave *f*
windfall /'wɪndfɔ:l/ *n* fruta *f* caída; (*fig*) suerte *f* inesperada
winding /'waɪndɪŋ/ *a* tortuoso
wind instrument /'wɪndɪnstrəmənt/ *n* instrumento *m* de viento
windmill /'wɪndmɪl/ *n* molino *m* (de viento)
window /'wɪndəʊ/ *n* ventana *f*; (*in shop*) escaparate *m*; (*of vehicle, booking-office*) ventanilla *f*. **~-box** *n* jardinera *f*. **~-dresser** *n* escaparatista *m* & *f*. **~-shop** *vi* mirar los escaparates
windpipe /'wɪndpaɪp/ *n* tráquea *f*
windscreen /'wɪndskri:n/ *n*, **windshield** *n* (*Amer*) parabrisas *m invar*. **~ wiper** *n* limpiaparabrisas *m invar*

wind /wɪnd/: **~-swept** *a* barrido por el viento. **~y** *a* (**-ier**, **-iest**) ventoso, de mucho viento. **it is ~y** hace viento
wine /waɪn/ *n* vino *m*. **~-cellar** *n* bodega *f*. **~glass** *n* copa *f*. **~-grower** *n* vinicultor *m*. **~-growing** *n* vinicultura *f*. • *a* vinícola. **~ list** *n* lista *f* de vinos. **~-tasting** *n* cata *f* de vinos
wing /wɪŋ/ *n* ala *f*; (*auto*) aleta *f*. **under one's ~** bajo la protección de uno. **~ed** *a* alado. **~er** /-ə(r)/ *n* (*sport*) ala *m* & *f*. **~s** *npl* (*in theatre*) bastidores *mpl*
wink /wɪŋk/ *vi* guiñar el ojo; ‹*light etc*› centellear. • *n* guiño *m*. **not to sleep a ~** no pegar ojo
winkle /'wɪŋkl/ *n* bígaro *m*
win: **~ner** /-ə(r)/ *n* ganador *m*. **~ning-post** *n* poste *m* de llegada. **~ning smile** *n* sonrisa *f* encantadora. **~nings** *npl* ganancias *fpl*
winsome /'wɪnsəm/ *a* atractivo
wint|er /'wɪntə(r)/ *n* invierno *m*. • *vi* invernar. **~ry** *a* invernal
wipe /waɪp/ *vt* limpiar; (*dry*) secar. • *n* limpión *m*. **give sth a ~** limpiar algo. **~ out** (*cancel*) cancelar; (*destroy*) destruir; (*obliterate*) borrar. **~ up** limpiar; (*dry*) secar
wire /'waɪə(r)/ *n* alambre *m*; (*elec*) cable *m*; (*telegram*, *fam*) telegrama *m*
wireless /'waɪəlɪs/ *n* radio *f*
wire netting /waɪə'netɪŋ/ *n* alambrera *f*, tela *f* metálica
wiring *n* instalación *f* eléctrica
wiry /'waɪərɪ/ *a* (**-ier**, **-iest**) ‹*person*› delgado
wisdom /'wɪzdəm/ *n* sabiduría *f*. **~ tooth** *n* muela *f* del juicio
wise /waɪz/ *a* (**-er**, **-est**) sabio; (*sensible*) prudente. **~crack** /'waɪzkræk/ *n* (*fam*) salida *f*. **~ly** *adv* sabiamente; (*sensibly*) prudentemente
wish /wɪʃ/ *n* deseo *m*; (*greeting*) saludo *m*. **with best ~es** (*in letters*) un fuerte abrazo. • *vt* desear. **~ on** (*fam*) encajar a. **~ s.o. well** desear buena suerte a uno. **~bone** *n* espoleta *f* (de las aves). **~ful** *a* deseoso. **~ful thinking** *n* ilusiones *fpl*
wishy-washy /'wɪʃɪwɒʃɪ/ *a* soso; ‹*person*› sin convicciones, falto de entereza
wisp /wɪsp/ *n* manojito *m*; (*of smoke*) voluta *f*; (*of hair*) mechón *m*
wisteria /wɪs'tɪərɪə/ *n* glicina *f*
wistful /'wɪstfl/ *a* melancólico
wit /wɪt/ *n* gracia *f*; (*person*) persona *f* chistosa; (*intelligence*) ingenio *m*. **be at one's ~s' end** no saber qué hacer. **live by one's ~s** vivir de expedientes, vivir del cuento
witch /wɪtʃ/ *n* bruja *f*. **~craft** *n* brujería *f*. **~-doctor** *n* hechicero *m*
with /wɪð/ *prep* con; (*cause*, *having*) de. **be ~ it** (*fam*) estar al día, estar al tanto. **the man ~ the beard** el hombre de la barba
withdraw /wɪð'drɔ:/ *vt* (*pt* **withdrew**, *pp* **withdrawn**) retirar. • *vi* apartarse. **~al** *n* retirada *f*. **~n** *a* ‹*person*› introvertido
wither /'wɪðə(r)/ *vi* marchitarse. • *vt* (*fig*) fulminar
withhold /wɪð'həʊld/ *vt* (*pt* **withheld**) retener; (*conceal*) ocultar (**from** a)
within /wɪð'ɪn/ *prep* dentro de. • *adv* dentro. **~ sight** a la vista
without /wɪð'aʊt/ *prep* sin
withstand /wɪð'stænd/ *vt* (*pt* **~stood**) resistir a
witness /'wɪtnɪs/ *n* testigo *m*; (*proof*) testimonio *m*. • *vt* presenciar; firmar como testigo ‹*document*›. **~-box** *n* tribuna *f* de los testigos
witticism /'wɪtɪsɪzəm/ *n* ocurrencia *f*
wittingly /'wɪtɪŋlɪ/ *adv* a sabiendas
witty /'wɪtɪ/ *a* (**-ier**, **-iest**) gracioso
wives /waɪvz/ *see* **wife**
wizard /'wɪzəd/ *n* hechicero *m*. **~ry** *n* hechicería *f*
wizened /'wɪznd/ *a* arrugado
wobbl|e /'wɒbl/ *vi* tambalearse; ‹*voice*, *jelly*, *hand*› temblar; ‹*chair etc*› balancearse. **~y** *a* ‹*chair etc*› cojo
woe /wəʊ/ *n* aflicción *f*. **~ful** *a* triste. **~begone** /'wəʊbɪgɒn/ *a* desconsolado
woke, woken /wəʊk, 'wəʊkən/ *see* **wake**[1]
wolf /wʊlf/ *n* (*pl* **wolves**) lobo *m*. **cry ~** gritar al lobo. • *vt* zamparse. **~-whistle** *n* silbido *m* de admiración
woman /'wʊmən/ *n* (*pl* **women**) mujer *f*. **single ~** soltera *f*. **~ize** /'wʊmənaɪz/ *vi* ser mujeriego. **~ly** *a* femenino
womb /wu:m/ *n* matriz *f*
women /'wɪmɪn/ *npl see* **woman**. **~folk** /'wɪmɪnfəʊk/ *npl* mujeres *fpl*.

~'s lib *n* movimiento *m* de liberación de la mujer
won /wʌn/ *see* **win**
wonder /ˈwʌndə(r)/ *n* maravilla *f*; (*bewilderment*) asombro *m*. **no ~** no es de extrañarse (**that** que). ● *vi* admirarse; (*reflect*) preguntarse
wonderful /ˈwʌndəfl/ *a* maravilloso. **~ly** *adv* maravillosamente
won't /wəʊnt/ = **will not**
woo /wu:/ *vt* cortejar
wood /wʊd/ *n* madera *f*; (*for burning*) leña *f*; (*area*) bosque *m*; (*in bowls*) bola *f*. **out of the ~** (*fig*) fuera de peligro. **~cutter** /ˈwʊdkʌtə(r)/ *n* leñador *m*. **~ed** *a* poblado de árboles, boscoso. **~en** *a* de madera. **~land** *n* bosque *m*
woodlouse /ˈwʊdlaʊs/ *n* (*pl* **-lice**) cochinilla *f*
woodpecker /ˈwʊdpekə(r)/ *n* pájaro *m* carpintero
woodwind /ˈwʊdwɪnd/ *n* instrumentos *mpl* de viento de madera
woodwork /ˈwʊdwɜ:k/ *n* carpintería *f*; (*in room etc*) maderaje *m*
woodworm /ˈwʊdwɜ:m/ *n* carcoma *f*
woody /ˈwʊdɪ/ *a* leñoso
wool /wʊl/ *n* lana *f*. **pull the ~ over s.o.'s eyes** engañar a uno. **~len** *a* de lana. **~lens** *npl* ropa *f* de lana. **~ly** *a* (**-ier**, **-iest**) de lana; (*fig*) confuso. ● *n* jersey *m*
word /wɜ:d/ *n* palabra *f*; (*news*) noticia *f*. **by ~ of mouth** de palabra. **have ~s with** reñir con. **in one ~** en una palabra. **in other ~s** es decir. ● *vt* expresar. **~ing** *n* expresión *f*, términos *mpl*. **~-perfect** *a*. **be ~-perfect** saber de memoria. **~ processor** *n* procesador *m* de textos. **~y** *a* prolijo
wore /wɔ:(r)/ *see* **wear**
work /wɜ:k/ *n* trabajo *m*; (*arts*) obra *f*. ● *vt* hacer trabajar; manejar ‹*machine*›. ● *vi* trabajar; ‹*machine*› funcionar; ‹*student*› estudiar; ‹*drug etc*› tener efecto; (*be successful*) tener éxito. **~ in** introducir(se). **~ off** desahogar. **~ out** *vt* resolver; (*calculate*) calcular; elaborar ‹*plan*›. ● *vi* (*succeed*) salir bien; (*sport*) entrenarse. **~ up** *vt* desarrollar. ● *vi* excitarse. **~able** /ˈwɜ:kəbl/ *a* ‹*project*› factible. **~aholic** /wɜ:kəˈhɒlɪk/ *n* trabajador *m* obsesivo. **~ed up** *a* agitado. **~er** /ˈwɜ:kə(r)/ *n* trabajador *m*; (*manual*) obrero *m*
workhouse /ˈwɜ:khaʊs/ *n* asilo *m* de pobres
work: **~ing** /ˈwɜ:kɪŋ/ *a* ‹*day*› laborable; ‹*clothes etc*› de trabajo. ● *n* (*mec*) funcionamiento *m*. **in ~ing order** en estado de funcionamiento. **~ing class** *n* clase *f* obrera. **~ing-class** *a* de la clase obrera. **~man** /ˈwɜ:kmən/ *n* (*pl* **-men**) obrero *m*. **~manlike** /ˈwɜ:kmənlaɪk/ *a* concienzudo. **~manship** *n* destreza *f*. **~s** *npl* (*building*) fábrica *f*; (*mec*) mecanismo *m*. **~shop** /ˈwɜ:kʃɒp/ *n* taller *m*. **~-to-rule** *n* huelga *f* de celo
world /wɜ:ld/ *n* mundo *m*. **a ~ of** enorme. **out of this ~** maravilloso. ● *a* mundial. **~ly** *a* mundano. **~-wide** *a* universal
worm /wɜ:m/ *n* lombriz *f*; (*grub*) gusano *m*. ● *vi*. **~ one's way** insinuarse. **~eaten** *a* carcomido
worn /wɔ:n/ *see* **wear**. ● *a* gastado. **~-out** *a* gastado; ‹*person*› rendido
worr|ied /ˈwʌrɪd/ *a* preocupado. **~ier** /-ə(r)/ *n* aprensivo *m*. **~y** /ˈwʌrɪ/ *vt* preocupar; (*annoy*) molestar. ● *vi* preocuparse. ● *n* preocupación *f*. **~ying** *a* inquietante
worse /wɜ:s/ *a* peor. ● *adv* peor; (*more*) más. ● *n* lo peor. **~n** *vt/i* empeorar
worship /ˈwɜ:ʃɪp/ *n* culto *m*; (*title*) señor, su señoría. ● *vt* (*pt* **worshipped**) adorar
worst /wɜ:st/ *a* (el) peor. ● *adv* peor. ● *n* lo peor. **get the ~ of it** llevar la peor parte
worsted /ˈwʊstɪd/ *n* estambre *m*
worth /wɜ:θ/ *n* valor *m*. ● *a*. **be ~** valer. **it is ~ trying** vale la pena probarlo. **it was ~ my while** (me) valió la pena. **~less** *a* sin valor. **~while** /ˈwɜ:θwaɪl/ *a* que vale la pena
worthy /ˈwɜ:ðɪ/ *a* meritorio; (*respectable*) respetable; (*laudable*) loable
would /wʊd/ *v aux*. **~ you come here please?** ¿quieres venir aquí? **~ you go?** ¿irías tú? **he ~ come if he could** vendría si pudiese. **I ~ come every day** (*used to*) venía todos los días. **I ~ do it** lo haría yo. **~-be** *a* supuesto
wound[1] /wu:nd/ *n* herida *f*. ● *vt* herir
wound[2] /waʊnd/ *see* **wind**[2]

wove, woven /wəʊv, 'wəʊvn/ *see* **weave**
wow /waʊ/ *int* ¡caramba!
wrangle /'ræŋgl/ *vi* reñir. ● *n* riña *f*
wrap /ræp/ *vt* (*pt* **wrapped**) envolver. **be ~ped up in** (*fig*) estar absorto en. ● *n* bata *f*; (*shawl*) chal *m*. **~per** /-ə(r)/ *n*, **~ping** *n* envoltura *f*
wrath /rɒθ/ *n* ira *f*. **~ful** *a* iracundo
wreath /ri:θ/ *n* (*pl* **-ths** /-ðz/) guirnalda *f*; (*for funeral*) corona *f*
wreck /rek/ *n* ruina *f*; (*sinking*) naufragio *m*; (*remains of ship*) buque *m* naufragado. **be a nervous ~** tener los nervios destrozados. ● *vt* hacer naufragar; (*fig*) arruinar. **~age** *n* restos *mpl*; (*of building*) escombros *mpl*
wren /ren/ *n* troglodito *m*
wrench /rentʃ/ *vt* arrancar; (*twist*) torcer. ● *n* arranque *m*; (*tool*) llave *f* inglesa
wrest /rest/ *vt* arrancar (**from** a)
wrestl|e /'resl/ *vi* luchar. **~er** /-ə(r)/ *n* luchador *m*. **~ing** *n* lucha *f*
wretch /retʃ/ *n* desgraciado *m*; (*rascal*) tunante *m & f*. **~ed** *a* miserable; ‹*weather*› horrible, de perros; ‹*dog etc*› maldito
wriggle /'rɪgl/ *vi* culebrear. **~ out of** escaparse de. **~ through** deslizarse por. ● *n* serpenteo *m*
wring /rɪŋ/ *vt* (*pt* **wrung**) retorcer. **~ out of** (*obtain from*) arrancar. **~ing wet** empapado
wrinkle /'rɪŋkl/ *n* arruga *f*. ● *vt* arrugar. ● *vi* arrugarse
wrist /rɪst/ *n* muñeca *f*. **~-watch** *n* reloj *m* de pulsera
writ /rɪt/ *n* decreto *m* judicial
write /raɪt/ *vt/i* (*pt* **wrote**, *pp* **written**, *pres p* **writing**) escribir. **~ down** *vt* anotar. **~ off** *vt* cancelar; (*fig*) dar por perdido. **~ up** *vt* hacer un reportaje de; (*keep up to date*) poner al día. **~-off** *n* pérdida *f* total. **~r** /-ə(r)/ *n* escritor *m*; (*author*) autor *m*. **~-up** *n* reportaje *m*; (*review*) crítica *f*
writhe /raɪð/ *vi* retorcerse
writing /'raɪtɪŋ/ *n* escribir *m*; (*handwriting*) letra *f*. **in ~** por escrito. **~s** *npl* obras *fpl*. **~-paper** *n* papel *m* de escribir
written /'rɪtn/ *see* **write**
wrong /rɒŋ/ *a* incorrecto; (*not just*) injusto; (*mistaken*) equivocado. **be ~** no tener razón; (*be mistaken*) equivocarse. ● *adv* mal. **go ~** equivocarse; ‹*plan*› salir mal; ‹*car etc*› estropearse. ● *n* injusticia *f*; (*evil*) mal *m*. **in the ~** equivocado. ● *vt* ser injusto con. **~ful** *a* injusto. **~ly** *adv* mal; (*unfairly*) injustamente
wrote /rəʊt/ *see* **write**
wrought /rɔ:t/ *a*. **~ iron** *n* hierro *m* forjado
wrung /rʌŋ/ *see* **wring**
wry /raɪ/ *a* (**wryer, wryest**) torcido; ‹*smile*› forzado. **~ face** *n* mueca *f*

X

xenophobia /zenə'fəʊbɪə/ *n* xenofobia *f*
Xerox /'zɪərɒks/ *n* (*P*) fotocopiadora *f*. **xerox** *n* fotocopia *f*
Xmas /'krɪsməs/ *n abbr* (*Christmas*) Navidad *f*, Navidades *fpl*
X-ray /'eksreɪ/ *n* radiografía *f*. **~s** *npl* rayos *mpl* X. ● *vt* radiografiar
xylophone /'zaɪləfəʊn/ *n* xilófono *m*

Y

yacht /jɒt/ *n* yate *m*. **~ing** *n* navegación *f* a vela
yam /jæm/ *n* ñame *m*, batata *f*
yank /jæŋk/ *vt* (*fam*) arrancar violentamente
Yankee /'jæŋkɪ/ *n* (*fam*) yanqui *m & f*
yap /jæp/ *vi* (*pt* **yapped**) ‹*dog*› ladrar
yard[1] /jɑ:d/ *n* (*measurement*) yarda *f* (= *0.9144 metre*)
yard[2] /jɑ:d/ *n* patio *m*; (*Amer, garden*) jardín *m*
yardage /'jɑ:dɪdʒ/ *n* metraje *m*
yardstick /'jɑ:dstɪk/ *n* (*fig*) criterio *m*
yarn /jɑ:n/ *n* hilo *m*; (*tale, fam*) cuento *m*
yashmak /'jæʃmæk/ *n* velo *m*
yawn /jɔ:n/ *vi* bostezar. ● *n* bostezo *m*
year /jɪə(r)/ *n* año *m*. **be three ~s old** tener tres años. **~-book** *n* anuario *m*. **~ling** /'jɜ:lɪŋ/ *n* primal *m*. **~ly** *a* anual. ● *adv* anualmente
yearn /'jɜ:n/ *vi*. **~ for** anhelar. **~ing** *n* ansia *f*
yeast /ji:st/ *n* levadura *f*
yell /jel/ *vi* gritar. ● *n* grito *m*

yellow /'jeləʊ/ *a & n* amarillo (*m*). **~ish** *a* amarillento
yelp /jelp/ *n* gañido *m*. ● *vi* gañir
yen /jen/ *n* muchas ganas *fpl*
yeoman /'jəʊmən/ *n* (*pl* **-men**). **Y~ of the Guard** alabardero *m* de la Casa Real
yes /jes/ *adv & n* sí (*m*)
yesterday /'jestədeɪ/ *adv & n* ayer (*m*). **the day before ~** anteayer *m*
yet /jet/ *adv* todavía, aún; (*already*) ya. **as ~** hasta ahora. ● *conj* sin embargo
yew /ju:/ *n* tejo *m*
Yiddish /'jɪdɪʃ/ *n* judeoalemán *m*
yield /ji:ld/ *vt* producir. ● *vi* ceder. ● *n* producción *f*; (*com*) rendimiento *m*
yoga /'jəʊgə/ *n* yoga *m*
yoghurt /'jɒgət/ *n* yogur *m*
yoke /jəʊk/ *n* yugo *m*; (*of garment*) canesú *m*
yokel /'jəʊkl/ *n* patán *m*, palurdo *m*
yolk /jəʊk/ *n* yema *f* (de huevo)
yonder /'jɒndə(r)/ *adv* a lo lejos
you /ju:/ *pron* (*familiar form*) tú, vos (*Arg*), (*pl*) vosotros, vosotras, ustedes (*LAm*); (*polite form*) usted, (*pl*) ustedes; (*familiar, object*) te, (*pl*) os, les (*LAm*); (*polite, object*) le, la, (*pl*) les; (*familiar, after prep*) ti, (*pl*) vosotros, vosotras, ustedes (*LAm*); (*polite, after prep*) usted, (*pl*) ustedes. **with ~** (*familiar*) contigo, (*pl*) con vosotros, con vosotras, con ustedes (*LAm*); (*polite*) con usted, (*pl*) con ustedes; (*polite reflexive*) consigo. **I know ~** te conozco, le conozco a usted. **you can't smoke here** aquí no se puede fumar
young /jʌŋ/ *a* (**-er, -est**) joven. **~ lady** *n* señorita *f*. **~ man** *n* joven *m*. **her ~ man** (*boyfriend*) su novio *m*. **the ~** *npl* los jóvenes *mpl*; (*of animals*) la cría *f*. **~ster** /'jʌŋstə(r)/ *n* joven *m*
your /jɔ:(r)/ *a* (*familiar*) tu, (*pl*) vuestro; (*polite*) su
yours /jɔ:z/ *poss pron* (el) tuyo, (*pl*) (el) vuestro, el de ustedes (*LAm*); (*polite*) el suyo. **a book of ~s** un libro tuyo, un libro suyo. **Y~s faithfully, Y~s sincerely** le saluda atentamente
yourself /jɔ:'self/ *pron* (*pl* **yourselves**) (*familiar, subject*) tú mismo, tú misma, (*pl*) vosotros mismos, vosotras mismas, ustedes mismos (*LAm*), ustedes mismas (*LAm*); (*polite, subject*) usted mismo, usted misma, (*pl*) ustedes mismos, ustedes mismas; (*familiar, object*) te, (*pl*) os, se (*LAm*); (*polite, object*) se; (*familiar, after prep*) ti, (*pl*) vosotros, vosotras, ustedes (*LAm*); (*polite, after prep*) sí
youth /ju:θ/ *n* (*pl* **youths** /ju:ðz/) juventud *f*; (*boy*) joven *m*; (*young people*) jóvenes *mpl*. **~ful** *a* joven, juvenil. **~ hostel** *n* albergue *m* para jóvenes
yowl /jaʊl/ *vi* aullar. ● *n* aullido *m*
Yugoslav /'ju:gəslɑ:v/ *a & n* yugoslavo (*m*). **~ia** /-'slɑ:vɪə/ *n* Yugoslavia *f*
yule /ju:l/ *n*, **yule-tide** /'ju:ltaɪd/ *n* (*old use*) Navidades *fpl*

Z

zany /'zeɪnɪ/ *a* (**-ier, -iest**) estrafalario
zeal /zi:l/ *n* celo *m*
zealot /'zelət/ *n* fanático *m*
zealous /'zeləs/ *a* entusiasta. **~ly** /'zeləslɪ/ *adv* con entusiasmo
zebra /'zebrə/ *n* cebra *f*. **~ crossing** *n* paso *m* de cebra
zenith /'zenɪθ/ *n* cenit *m*
zero /'zɪərəʊ/ *n* (*pl* **-os**) cero *m*
zest /zest/ *n* gusto *m*; (*peel*) cáscara *f*
zigzag /'zɪgzæg/ *n* zigzag *m*. ● *vi* (*pt* **zigzagged**) zigzaguear
zinc /zɪŋk/ *n* cinc *m*
Zionis|m /'zaɪənɪzəm/ *n* sionismo *m*. **~t** *n* sionista *m & f*
zip /zɪp/ *n* cremallera *f*. ● *vt*. **~ (up)** cerrar (la cremallera)
Zip code /'zɪpkəʊd/ *n* (*Amer*) código *m* postal
zip fastener /zɪp'fɑ:snə(r)/ *n* cremallera *f*
zircon /'zɜ:kən/ *n* circón *m*
zither /'zɪðə(r)/ *n* cítara *f*
zodiac /'zəʊdɪæk/ *n* zodiaco *m*
zombie /'zɒmbɪ/ *n* (*fam*) autómata *m & f*
zone /zəʊn/ *n* zona *f*
zoo /zu:/ *n* (*fam*) zoo *m*, jardín *m* zoológico. **~logical** /zəʊə'lɒdʒɪkl/ *a* zoológico
zoolog|ist /zəʊ'ɒlədʒɪst/ *n* zoólogo *m*. **~y** /zəʊ'ɒlədʒɪ/ *n* zoología *f*
zoom /zu:m/ *vi* ir a gran velocidad. **~ in** (*photo*) acercarse rápidamente. **~ past** pasar zumbando. **~ lens** *n* zoom *m*
Zulu /'zu:lu:/ *n* zulú *m & f*

Numbers · Números

zero	0	cero
one (first)	1	uno (primero)
two (second)	2	dos (segundo)
three (third)	3	tres (tercero)
four (fourth)	4	cuatro (cuarto)
five (fifth)	5	cinco (quinto)
six (sixth)	6	seis (sexto)
seven (seventh)	7	siete (séptimo)
eight (eighth)	8	ocho (octavo)
nine (ninth)	9	nueve (noveno)
ten (tenth)	10	diez (décimo)
eleven (eleventh)	11	once (undécimo)
twelve (twelfth)	12	doce (duodécimo)
thirteen (thirteenth)	13	trece (decimotercero)
fourteen (fourteenth)	14	catorce (decimocuarto)
fifteen (fifteenth)	15	quince (decimoquinto)
sixteen (sixteenth)	16	dieciséis (decimosexto)
seventeen (seventeenth)	17	diecisiete (decimoséptimo)
eighteen (eighteenth)	18	dieciocho (decimoctavo)
nineteen (nineteenth)	19	diecinueve (decimonoveno)
twenty (twentieth)	20	veinte (vigésimo)
twenty-one (twenty-first)	21	veintiuno (vigésimo primero)
twenty-two (twenty-second)	22	veintidós (vigésimo segundo)
twenty-three (twenty-third)	23	veintitrés (vigésimo tercero)
twenty-four (twenty-fourth)	24	veinticuatro (vigésimo cuarto)
twenty-five (twenty-fifth)	25	veinticinco (vigésimo quinto)
twenty-six (twenty-sixth)	26	veintiséis (vigésimo sexto)
thirty (thirtieth)	30	treinta (trigésimo)
thirty-one (thirty-first)	31	treinta y uno (trigésimo primero)
forty (fortieth)	40	cuarenta (cuadragésimo)
fifty (fiftieth)	50	cincuenta (quincuagésimo)
sixty (sixtieth)	60	sesenta (sexagésimo)
seventy (seventieth)	70	setenta (septuagésimo)
eighty (eightieth)	80	ochenta

		(octogésimo)
ninety (ninetieth)	90	noventa (nonagésimo)
a/one hundred (hundredth)	100	cien (centésimo)
a/one hundred and one (hundred and first)	101	ciento uno (centésimo primero)
two hundred (two hundredth)	200	doscientos (ducentésimo)
three hundred (three hundredth)	300	trescientos (tricentésimo)
four hundred (four hundredth)	400	cuatrocientos (cuadringentésimo)
five hundred (five hundredth)	500	quinientos (quingentésimo)
six hundred (six hundredth)	600	seiscientos (sexcentésimo)
seven hundred (seven hundredth)	700	setecientos (septingentésimo)
eight hundred (eight hundredth)	800	ochocientos (octingentésimo)
nine hundred (nine hundredth)	900	novecientos (noningentésimo)
a/one thousand (thousandth)	1000	mil (milésimo)
two thousand (two thousandth)	2000	dos mil (dos milésimo)
a/one million (millionth)	1,000,000	un millón (millonésimo)

Spanish Verbs · Verbos españoles

Regular verbs:
in **-ar** (*e.g.* **comprar**)
Present; compr|o, **~as, ~a, ~amos, ~áis, ~an**
Future: comprar|é, **~ás, ~á, ~emos, ~éis, ~án**
Imperfect: compr|aba, **~abas, ~aba, ~ábamos, ~abais, ~aban**
Preterite: compr|é, **~aste, ~ó, ~amos, ~asteis, ~aron**
Present subjunctive: compr|e, **~es, ~e, ~emos, ~éis, ~en**
Imperfect subjunctive: compr|ara, **~aras ~ara, ~áramos, ~arais, ~aran**
compr|ase, **~ases, ~ase, ~ásemos, ~aseis, ~asen**
Conditional: comprar|ía, **~ías, ~ía, ~íamos, ~íais, ~ían**
Present participle: comprando
Past participle: comprado
Imperative: compra, comprad

in **-er** (*e.g.* **beber**)
Present: beb|o, **~es, ~e, ~emos, ~éis, ~en**
Future: beber|é, **~ás, ~á, ~emos, ~éis, ~án**
Imperfect: beb|ía, **~ías, ~ía, ~íamos, ~íais, ~ían**
Preterite: beb|í, **~iste, ~ió, ~imos, ~isteis, ~ieron**
Present subjunctive: beb|a, **~as, ~a, ~amos, ~áis, ~an**
Imperfect subjunctive: beb|iera, **~ieras, ~iera, ~iéramos, ~ierais, ~ieran**
beb|iese, **~ieses, ~iese, ~iésemos, ~ieseis, ~iesen**
Conditional: beber|ía, **~ías, ~ía, ~íamos, ~íais, ~ían**
Present participle: bebiendo
Past participle: bebido
Imperative: bebe, bebed

in **-ir** (*e.g.* **vivir**)
Present: viv|o, **~es, ~e, ~imos, ~ís, ~en**
Future: vivir|é, **~ás, ~á, ~emos, ~éis, ~án**
Imperfect: viv|ía, **~ías, ~ía, ~íamos, ~íais, ~ían**
Preterite: viv|í, **~iste, ~ió, ~imos, ~isteis, ~ieron**
Present subjunctive: viv|a, **~as, ~a, ~amos, ~áis, ~an**
Imperfect subjunctive: viv|iera, **~ieras, ~iera, ~iéramos, ~ierais, ~ieran**
viv|iese, **~ieses, ~iese, ~iésemos, ~ieseis, ~iesen**
Conditional: vivir|ía, **~ías, ~ía, ~íamos, ~íais, ~ían**
Present participle: viviendo
Past participle: vivido
Imperative: vive, vivid

Irregular verbs:
[1] **cerrar**
Present: cierro, cierras, cierra, cerramos, cerráis, cierran
Present subjunctive: cierre, cierres, cierre, cerremos, cerréis, cierren
Imperative: cierra, cerrad

[2] **contar, mover**
Present: cuento, cuentas, cuenta, contamos, contáis, cuentan
muevo, mueves, mueve, movemos, movéis, mueven
Present subjunctive: cuente, cuentes, cuente, contemos, contéis, cuenten
mueva, muevas mueva, movamos, mováis, muevan
Imperative: cuenta, contad mueve, moved

[3] **jugar**
Present: juego, juegas, juega, jugamos, jugáis, juegan
Preterite: jug|ué, jugaste, jugó, jugamos, jugasteis, jugaron
Present subjunctive: juegue, juegues, juegue, juguemos, juguéis, jueguen

[4] **sentir**
Present: siento, sientes, siente, sentimos, sentís, sienten
Preterite: sentí, sentiste, sintió, sentimos, sentisteis, sintieron
Present subjunctive: sienta, sientas, sienta, sintamos, sintáis, sientan
Imperfect subjunctive: sint|iera, **~ieras, ~iera, ~iéramos, ~ierais, ~ieran**

sint|iese, **~ieses, ~iese, ~iésemos, ~ieseis, ~iesen**
Present participle: sintiendo
Imperative: siente, sentid

[5] **pedir**
Present: pido, pides, pide, pedimos, pedís, piden
Preterite: pedí, pediste, pidió, pedimos, pedisteis, pidieron
Present subjunctive: pid|a, **~as, ~a, ~amos, ~áis, ~an**
Imperfect subjunctive: pid|iera, **~ieras, ~iera, ~iéramos, ~ierais, ~ieran**
pid|iese, **~ieses, ~iese, ~iésemos, ~ieseis, ~iesen**
Present participle: pidiendo
Imperative: pide, pedid

[6] **dormir**
Present: duermo, duermes, duerme, dormimos, dormís, duermen
Preterite: dormí, dormiste, durmió, dormimos, dormisteis, durmieron
Present subjunctive: duerma, duermas, duerma, durmamos, durmáis, duerman
Imperfect subjunctive: durm|iera, **~ieras, ~iera, ~iéramos, ~ierais, ~ieran**
durm|iese, **~ieses, ~iese, ~iésemos, ~ieseis, ~iesen**
Present participle: durmiendo
Imperative: duerme, dormid

[7] **dedicar**
Preterite: dediqué, dedicaste, dedicó, dedicamos, dedicasteis, dedicaron
Present subjunctive: dediqu|e, **~ues, ~e, ~emos, ~éis, ~en**

[8] **delinquir**
Present: delinco, delinques, delinque, delinquimos, delinquís, delinquen
Present subjunctive: delinc|a, **~as, ~a, ~amos, ~áis, ~an**

[9] **vencer**, **esparcir**
Present: venzo, vences, vence, vencemos, vencéis, vencen esparzo, esparces, esparce, esparcimos, esparcís, esparcen
Present subjunctive: venz|a, **~as, ~a, ~amos, ~áis, ~an** esparz|a, **~as, ~a, ~amos, ~áis, ~an**

[10] **rechazar**
Preterite: rechacé, rechazaste, rechazó, rechazamos, rechazasteis, rechazaron
Present subjunctive: rechac|e, **~es, ~e, ~emos, ~éis, ~en**

[11] **conocer**, **lucir**
Present: conozco, conoces, conoce, conocemos, conocéis, conocen luzco, luces, luce, lucimos, lucís, lucen
Present subjunctive: conozc|a, **~as, ~a, ~amos, ~áis, ~an** luzc|a, **~as, ~a, ~amos, ~áis, ~an**

[12] **pagar**
Preterite: pagué, pagaste, pagó, pagamos, pagasteis, pagaron
Present subjunctive: pagu|e, **~es, ~e, ~emos, ~éis, ~en**

[13] **distinguir**
Present: distingo, distingues, distingue, distinguimos, distinguís, distinguen
Present subjunctive: disting|a, **~as, ~a, ~amos, ~áis, ~an**

[14] **acoger**, **afligir**
Present: acojo, acoges, acoge, acogemos, acogéis, acogen aflijo, afliges, aflige, afligimos, afligís, afligen
Present subjunctive: acoj|a, **~as, ~a, ~amos, ~áis, ~an**
aflij|a, **~as, ~a, ~amos, ~áis, ~an**

[15] **averiguar**
Preterite: averigüé, averiguaste, averiguó, averiguamos, averiguasteis, averiguaron
Present subjunctive: averigü|e, **~es, ~e, ~emos, ~éis, ~en**

[16] **agorar**
Present: agüero, agüeras, agüera, agoramos, agoráis, agüeran
Present subjunctive: agüere, agüeres, agüere, agoremos, agoréis, agüeren
Imperative: agüera, agorad

[17] **huir**
Present: huyo, huyes, huye, huimos, huís, huyen

Preterite: huí, huiste, huyó, huimos, huisteis, huyeron
Present subjunctive: huy|a, **~as, ~a, ~amos, ~áis, ~an**
Imperfect subjunctive: huy|era, **~eras, ~era, ~éramos, ~erais, ~eran**
huy|ese, **~eses, ~ese, ~ésemos, ~eseis, ~esen**
Present participle: huyendo

[18] **creer**
Preterite: creí, creíste, creyó, creímos, creísteis, creyeron
Imperfect subjunctive: crey|era, **~eras, ~era, ~éramos, ~erais, ~eran**
crey|ese, **~eses, ~ese, ~ésemos, ~eseis, ~esen**
Present participle: creyendo
Past participle: creído

[19] **argüir**
Present: arguyo, arguyes, arguye, argüimos, argüís, arguyen
Preterite: argüí, argüiste, arguyó, argüimos, argüisteis, arguyeron
Present subjunctive: arguy|a, **~as, ~a, ~amos, ~áis, ~an**
Imperfect subjunctive: arguy|era, **~eras, ~era, ~éramos, ~erais, ~eran**
arguy|ese, **~eses, ~ese, ~ésemos, ~eseis, ~esen**
Present participle: arguyendo
Imperative: arguye, argüid

[20] **vaciar**
Present: vacío, vacías, vacía, vaciamos, vaciáis, vacían
Present subjunctive: vacíe, vacíes, vacíe, vaciemos, vaciéis, vacíen
Imperative: vacía, vaciad

[21] **acentuar**
Present: acentúo, acentúas, acentúa, acentuamos, acentuáis, acentúan
Present subjunctive: acentúe, acentúes, acentúe, acentuemos, acentuéis, acentúen
Imperative: acentúa, acentuad

[22] **ateñer**, **engullir**
Preterite: atañ|í, **~aste, ~ó, ~amos, ~asteis, ~eron** engull|í **~iste, ~ó, ~imos, ~isteis, ~eron**
Imperfect subjunctive: atañ|era, **~eras, ~era, ~éramos, ~erais, ~eran**
atañ|ese, **~eses, ~ese, ~ésemos, ~eseis, ~esen**
engull|era, **~eras, ~era, ~éramos, ~erais, ~eran**
engull|ese, **~eses, ~ese, ~ésemos, ~eseis, ~esen**
Present participle: atañendo
engullendo

[23] **aislar**, **aullar**
Present: aíslo, aíslas, aísla, aislamos, aisláis, aíslan
aúllo, aúllas, aúlla, aullamos aulláis, aúllan
Present subjunctive: aísle, aísles, aísle, aislemos, aisléis, aíslen
aúlle, aúlles, aúlle, aullemos, aulléis, aúllen
Imperative: aísla, aislad
aúlla, aullad

[24] **abolir**, **garantir**
Present: abolimos, abolís
garantimos, garantís
Present subjunctive: not used
Imperative: abolid
garantid

[25] **andar**
Preterite: anduv|e, **~iste, ~o, ~imos, ~isteis, ~ieron**
Imperfect subjunctive: anduv|iera, **~ieras, ~iera, ~iéramos, ~ierais, ~ieran**
anduv|iese, **~ieses, ~iese, ~iésemos, ~ieseis, ~iesen**

[26] **dar**
Present: doy, das, da, damos, dais, dan
Preterite: di, diste, dio, dimos, disteis, dieron
Present subjunctive: dé, des, dé, demos, deis, den
Imperfect subjunctive: diera, dieras, diera, diéramos, dierais, dieran
diese, dieses, diese, diésemos, dieseis, diesen

[27] **estar**
Present: estoy, estás, está, estamos, estáis, están
Preterite: estuv|e, **~iste, ~o, ~imos, ~isteis, ~ieron**
Present subjunctive: esté, estés, esté, estemos, estéis, estén

Imperfect subjunctive: estuv/iera, **~ieras, ~iera, ~iéramos, ~ierais, ~ieran**
estuv|iese, **~ieses, ~iese, ~iésemos, ~ieseis, ~iesen**
Imperative: está, estad

[28] **caber**
Present: quepo, cabes, cabe, cabemos, cabéis, caben
Future: cabr|é, **~ás, ~á, ~emos, ~éis, ~án**
Preterite: cup|e, **~iste, ~o, ~imos, ~isteis, ~ieron**
Present subjunctive: quep|a, **~as, ~a, ~amos, ~áis, ~an**
Imperfect subjunctive: cup|iera, **~ieras, ~iera, ~iéramos, ~ierais, ~ieran**
cup|iese, **~ieses, ~iese, ~iésemos, ~ieseis, ~iesen**
Conditional: cabr|ía, **~ías, ~ía, ~íamos, ~íais, ~ían**

[29] **caer**
Present: caigo, caes, cae, caemos, caéis, caen
Preterite: caí, caiste, cayó, caímos, caísteis, cayeron
Present subjunctive: caig|a, **~as, ~a, ~amos, ~áis, ~an**
Imperfect subjunctive: cay|era, **~eras, ~era, ~éramos, ~erais, ~eran**
cay|ese, **~eses, ~ese, ~ésemos, ~eseis, ~esen**
Present participle: cayendo
Past participle: caído

[30] **haber**
Present: he, has, ha, hemos, habéis, han
Future: habr|é **~ás, ~á, ~emos, ~éis, ~án**
Preterite: hub|e, **~iste, ~o, ~imos, ~isteis, ~ieron**
Present subjunctive: hay|a, **~as, ~a, ~amos, ~áis, ~an**
Imperfect subjunctive: hub|iera, **~ieras, ~iera, ~iéramos, ~ierais, ~ieran**
hub|iese, **~ieses, ~iese, ~iésemos, ~ieseis, ~iesen**
Conditional: habr|ía, **~ías, ~ía, ~íamos, ~íais, ~ían**
Imperative: habe, habed

[31] **hacer**
Present: hago, haces, hace, hacemos, hacéis, hacen
Future: har|é, **~ás, ~á, ~emos, ~éis, ~án**
Preterite: hice, hiciste, hizo, hicimos, hicisteis, hicieron
Present subjunctive: hag|a, **~as, ~a, ~amos, ~áis, ~an**
Imperfect subjunctive: hic|iera, **~ieras, ~iera, ~iéramos, ~ierais, ~ieran**
hic|iese, **~ieses, ~iese, ~iésemos, ~ieseis, ~iesen**
Conditional: har|ía, **~ías, ~ía, ~íamos, ~íais, ~ían**
Past participle: hecho
Imperative: haz, haced

[32] **placer**
Preterite: plació/plugo
Present subjunctive: plazca
Imperfect subjunctive: placiera/pluguiera
placiese/pluguiese

[33] **poder**
Present: puedo, puedes, puede, podemos, podéis, pueden
Future: podr|é, **~ás, ~á, ~emos, ~éis, ~án**
Preterite: pud|e, **~iste, ~o, ~imos, ~isteis, ~ieron**
Present subjunctive: pueda, puedas, pueda, podamos, podáis, puedan
Imperfect subjunctive: pud|iera, **~ieras, ~iera, ~iéramos, ~ierais, ~ieran**
pud|iese, **~ieses, ~iese, ~iésemos, ~ieseis, ~iesen**
Conditional: podr|ía, **~ías, ~ía, ~íamos, ~íais, ~ían**
Past participle: pudiendo

[34] **poner**
Present: pongo, pones, pone, ponemos, ponéis, ponen
Future: pondr|é, **~ás, ~á, ~emos, ~éis, ~án**
Preterite: pus|e, **~iste, ~o, ~imos, ~isteis, ~ieron**
Present subjunctive: pong|a, **~as, ~a, ~amos, ~áis, ~an**
Imperfect subjunctive: pus|iera, **~ieras, ~iera, ~iéramos, ~ierais, ~ieran**
pus|iese, **~ieses, ~iese, ~iésemos, ~ieseis, ~iesen**

Conditional: pondr|ía, **~ías, ~ía, ~íamos, ~íais, ~ían**
Past participle: puesto
Imperative: pon, poned

[35] **querer**
Present: quiero, quieres, quiere, queremos, queréis, quieren
Future: querr|é, **~ás, ~á, ~emos, ~éis, ~án**
Preterite: quis|e, **~iste, ~o, ~imos, ~isteis, ~ieron**
Present subjunctive: quiera, quieras, quiera, queramos, queráis, quieran
Imperfect subjunctive: quis|iera, **~ieras, ~iera, ~iéramos, ~ierais, ~ieran**
quis|iese, **~ieses, ~iese, ~iésemos, ~ieseis, ~iesen**
Conditional: querr|ía, **~ías, ~ía, ~íamos, ~íais, ~ían**
Imperative: quiere, quered

[36] **raer**
Present: raigo/rayo, raes, rae, raemos, raéis, raen
Preterite: raí, raíste, rayó, raímos, raísteis, rayeron
Present subjunctive: raig|a, **~as, ~a, ~amos, ~áis, ~an**
ray|a, **~as, ~a, ~amos, ~áis, ~an**
Imperfect subjunctive: ray|era, **~eras, ~era, ~éramos, ~erais, ~eran**
ray|ese, **~eses, ~ese, ~ésemos, ~eseis, ~esen**
Present participle: rayendo
Past participle: raído

[37] **roer**
Present: roo/roigo/royo, roes, roe, roemos, roéis, roen
Preterite: roí, roíste, royó, roímos, roísteis, royeron
Present subjunctive: roa/roiga/roya, roas, roa, roamos, roáis, roan
Imperfect subjunctive: roy|era, **~eras, ~era, ~éramos, ~erais, ~eran**
roy|ese, **~eses, ~ese, ~ésemos, ~eseis, ~esen**
Present participle: royendo
Past participle: roído

[38] **saber**
Present: sé, sabes, sabe, sabemos, sabéis, saben
Future: sabr|é, **~ás, ~á, ~emos, ~éis, ~án**
Preterite: sup|e, **~iste, ~o, ~imos, ~isteis, ~ieron**
Present subjunctive: sep|a, **~as, ~a, ~amos, ~áis, ~an**
Imperfect subjunctive: sup|iera, **~ieras, ~iera, ~iéramos, ~ierais, ~ieran**
sup|iese, **~ieses, ~iese, ~iésemos, ~ieseis, ~iesen**
Conditional: sabr|ía, **~ías, ~ía, ~íamos, ~íais, ~ían**

[39] **ser**
Present: soy, eres, es, somos, sois, son
Imperfect: era, eras, era, éramos, erais, eran
Preterite: fui, fuiste, fue, fuimos, fuisteis, fueron
Present subjunctive: se|a, **~as, ~a, ~amos, ~áis, ~an**
Imperfect subjunctive: fu|era, **~eras, ~era, ~éramos, ~erais, ~eran**
fu|ese, **~eses, ~ese, ~ésemos, ~eseis, ~esen**
Imperative: sé, sed

[40] **tener**
Present: tengo, tienes, tiene, tenemos, tenéis, tienen
Future: tendr|é, **~ás, ~á, ~emos, ~éis, ~án**
Preterite: tuv|e, **~iste, ~o, ~imos, ~isteis, ~ieron**
Present subjunctive: teng|a, **~as, ~a, ~amos, ~áis, ~an**
Imperfect subjunctive: tuv|iera, **~ieras, ~iera, ~iéramos, ~ierais, ~ieran**
tuv|iese, **~ieses, ~iese, ~iésemos, ~ieseis, ~iesen**
Conditional: tendr|ía, **~ías, ~ía, ~íamos, ~íais, ~ían**
Imperative: ten, tened

[41] **traer**
Present: traigo, traes, trae, traemos, traéis, traen
Preterite: traj|e, **~iste, ~o, ~imos, ~isteis, ~eron**
Present subjunctive: traig|a, **~as, ~a, ~amos, ~áis, ~an**
Imperfect subjunctive: traj|era, **~eras, ~era, ~éramos, ~erais, ~eran**

traj|ese, **~eses, ~ese, ~ésemos, ~eseis, ~esen**
Present participle: trayendo
Past participle: traído

[42] **valer**
Present: valgo, vales, vale, valemos, valéis, valen
Future: vald|ré, **~ás, ~á, ~emos, ~éis, ~án**
Present subjunctive: valg|a, **~as, ~a, ~amos ~áis, ~an**
Conditional: vald|ría, **~ías, ~ía, ~íamos, ~íais, ~ían**
Imperative: val/vale, valed

[43] **ver**
Present: veo, ves, ve, vemos, véis, ven
Imperfect: ve|ía, **~ías, ~ía, ~íamos, ~íais, ~ían**
Preterite: vi, viste, vio, vimos, visteis, vieron
Present subjunctive: ve|a, **~as, ~a, ~amos, ~áis, ~an**
Past participle: visto

[44] **yacer**
Present: yazco/yazgo/yago, yaces, yace, yacemos, yacéis, yacen
Present subjunctive: yazca/yazga/yaga, yazcas, yazca, yazcamos, yazcáis, yazcan
Imperative: yace/yaz, yaced

[45] **asir**
Present: asgo, ases, ase, asimos, asís, asen
Present subjunctive: asg|a, **~as, ~a, ~amos, ~áis, ~an**

[46] **decir**
Present: digo, dices, dice, decimos, decís, dicen
Future: dir|é, **~ás, ~á, ~emos, ~éis, ~án**
Preterite: dij|e, **~iste, ~o, ~imos, ~isteis, ~eron**
Present subjunctive: dig|a, **~as, ~a, ~amos, ~áis, ~an**
Imperfect subjunctive: dij|era, **~eras, ~era, ~éramos, ~erais, ~eran**
dij|ese, **~eses, ~ese, ~ésemos, ~eseis, ~esen**
Conditional: dir|ía, **~ías, ~ía, ~íamos, ~íais, ~ían**
Present participle: dicho
Imperative: di, decid

[47] **reducir**
Present: reduzco, reduces, reduce, reducimos, reducís, reducen
Preterite: reduj|e, **~iste, ~o, ~imos, ~isteis, ~eron**
Present subjunctive: reduzc|a, **~as, ~a, ~amos, ~áis, ~an**
Imperfect subjunctive: reduj|era, **~eras, ~era, ~éramos, ~erais, ~eran**
reduj|ese, **~eses, ~ese, ~ésemos, ~eseis, ~esen**

[48] **erguir**
Present: irgo, irgues, irgue, erguimos, erguís, irguen
yergo, yergues, yergue, erguimos, erguís, yerguen
Preterite: erguí, erguiste, irguió, erguimos, erguisteis, irguieron
Present subjunctive: irg|a, **~as, ~a, ~amos, ~áis, ~an**
yerg|a, **~as, ~a, ~amos, ~áis, ~an**
Imperfect subjunctive: irgu|iera, **~ieras, ~iera, ~iéramos, ~ierais, ~ieran**
irgu|iese, **~ieses, ~iese, ~iésemos, ~ieseis, ~iesen**
Present participle: irguiendo
Imperative: irgue/yergue, erguid

[49] **ir**
Present: voy, vas, va, vamos, vais, van
Imperfect: iba, ibas, iba, íbamos, ibais, iban
Preterite: fui, fuiste, fue, fuimos, fuisteis, fueron
Present subjunctive: vay|a, **~as, ~a, ~amos, ~áis, ~an**
Imperfect subjunctive: fu|era, **~eras, ~era, ~éramos, ~erais, ~eran**
fu|ese, **~eses, ~ese, ~ésemos, ~eseis, ~esen**
Present participle: yendo
Imperative: ve, id

[50] **oír**
Present: oigo, oyes, oye, oímos, oís, oyen
Preterite: oí, oíste, oyó, oímos, oísteis, oyeron
Present subjunctive: oig|a, **~as, ~a, ~amos, ~áis, ~an**

Imperfect subjunctive: oy|era, **~eras, ~era, ~éramos, ~erais, ~eran**
oy|ese, **~eses, ~ese, ~ésemos, ~eseis, ~esen**
Present participle: oyendo
Past participle: oído
Imperative: oye, oíd

[51] **reír**
Present: río, ríes, ríe, reímos, reís, ríen
Preterite: reí, reíste, rió, reímos, reísteis, rieron
Present subjunctive: ría, rías, ría, riamos, riáis, rían
Present participle: riendo
Past participle: reído
Imperative: ríe, reíd

[52] **salir**
Present: salgo, sales, sale, salimos, salís, salen
Future: saldr|é, **~ás, ~á, ~emos, ~éis, ~án**
Present subjunctive: salg|a, **~as, ~a, ~amos, ~áis, ~an**
Conditional: saldr|ía, **~ías, ~ía, ~íamos, ~íais, ~ían**
Imperative: sal, salid

[53] **venir**
Present: vengo, vienes, viene, venimos, venís, vienen
Future: vendr|é, **~ás, ~á, ~emos, ~éis, ~án**
Preterite: vin|e, **~iste, ~o, ~imos, ~isteis, ~ieron**
Present subjunctive: veng|a, **~as, ~a, ~amos, ~áis, ~an**
Imperfect subjunctive: vin|iera, **~ieras, ~iera, ~iéramos, ~ierais, ~ieran**
vin|iese, **~ieses, ~iese, ~iésemos, ~ieseis, ~iesen**
Conditional: vendr|ía, **~ías, ~ía, ~íamos, ~íais, ~ían**
Present participle: viniendo
Imperative: ven, venid

Verbos Irregulares Ingleses

Infinitivo	*Pretérito*	*Participio pasado*
arise	arose	arisen
awake	awoke	awoken
be	was	been
bear	bore	borne
beat	beat	beaten
become	became	become
befall	befell	befallen
beget	begot	begotten
begin	began	begun
behold	beheld	beheld
bend	bent	bent
beset	beset	beset
bet	bet, betted	bet, betted
bid	bade, bid	bidden, bid
bind	bound	bound
bite	bit	bitten
bleed	bled	bled
blow	blew	blown
break	broke	broken
breed	bred	bred
bring	brought	brought
broadcast	broadcast(ed)	broadcast
build	built	built
burn	burnt, burned	burnt, burned
burst	burst	burst
buy	bought	bought
cast	cast	cast
catch	caught	caught
choose	chose	chosen
cleave	clove, cleft, cleaved	cloven, cleft, cleaved
cling	clung	clung
clothe	clothed, clad	clothed, clad
come	came	come
cost	cost	cost
creep	crept	crept
crow	crowed, crew	crowed
cut	cut	cut
deal	dealt	dealt
dig	dug	dug
do	did	done
draw	drew	drawn
dream	dreamt, dreamed	dreamt, dreamed
drink	drank	drunk
drive	drove	driven
dwell	dwelt	dwelt
eat	ate	eaten
fall	fell	fallen
feed	fed	fed
feel	felt	felt
fight	fought	fought
find	found	found

Infinitivo	*Pretérito*	*Participio pasado*
flee	fled	fled
fling	flung	flung
fly	flew	flown
forbear	forbore	forborne
forbid	forbad(e)	forbidden
forecast	forecast(ed)	forecast(ed)
foresee	foresaw	foreseen
foretell	foretold	foretold
forget	forgot	forgotten
forgive	forgave	forgiven
forsake	forsook	forsaken
freeze	froze	frozen
gainsay	gainsaid	gainsaid
get	got	got
give	gave	given
go	went	gone
grind	ground	ground
grow	grew	grown
hang	hung, hanged	hung, hanged
have	had	had
hear	heard	heard
hew	hewed	hewn, hewed
hide	hid	hidden
hit	hit	hit
hold	held	held
hurt	hurt	hurt
inlay	inlaid	inlaid
keep	kept	kept
kneel	knelt	knelt
knit	knitted, knit	knitted, knit
know	knew	known
lay	laid	laid
lead	led	led
lean	leaned, leant	leaned, leant
leap	leaped, leapt	leaped, leapt
learn	learned, learnt	learned, learnt
leave	left	left
lend	lent	lent
let	let	let
lie	lay	lain
light	lit, lighted	lit, lighted
lose	lost	lost
make	made	made
mean	meant	meant
meet	met	met
mislay	mislaid	mislaid
mislead	misled	misled
misspell	misspelt	misspelt
mistake	mistook	mistaken
misunderstand	misunderstood	misunderstood
mow	mowed	mown
outbid	outbid	outbid
outdo	outdid	outdone
outgrow	outgrew	outgrown
overcome	overcame	overcome

Infinitivo	*Pretérito*	*Participio pasado*
overdo	overdid	overdone
overhang	overhung	overhung
overhear	overheard	overheard
override	overrode	overridden
overrun	overran	overrun
oversee	oversaw	overseen
overshoot	overshot	overshot
oversleep	overslept	overslept
overtake	overtook	overtaken
overthrow	overthrew	overthrown
partake	partook	partaken
pay	paid	paid
prove	proved	proved, proven
put	put	put
quit	quitted, quit	quitted, quit
read /ri:d/	read /red/	read /red/
rebuild	rebuilt	rebuilt
redo	redid	redone
rend	rent	rent
repay	repaid	repaid
rewrite	rewrote	rewritten
rid	rid	rid
ride	rode	ridden
ring	rang	rung
rise	rose	risen
run	ran	run
saw	sawed	sawn, sawed
say	said	said
see	saw	seen
seek	sought	sought
sell	sold	sold
send	sent	sent
set	set	set
sew	sewed	sewn, sewed
shake	shook	shaken
shear	sheared	shorn, sheared
shed	shed	shed
shine	shone	shone
shoe	shod	shod
shoot	shot	shot
show	showed	shown, showed
shrink	shrank	shrunk
shut	shut	shut
sing	sang	sung
sink	sank	sunk
sit	sat	sat
slay	slew	slain
sleep	slept	slept
slide	slid	slid
sling	slung	slung
slit	slit	slit
smell	smelt, smelled	smelt, smelled
smite	smote	smitten
sow	sowed	sown, sowed
speak	spoke	spoken

Infinitivo	*Pretérito*	*Participio pasado*
speed	speeded, sped	speeded, sped
spell	spelt, spelled	spelt, spelled
spend	spent	spent
spill	spilt, spilled	spilt, spilled
spin	spun	spun
spit	spat	spat
split	split	split
spoil	spoilt, spoiled	spoilt, spoiled
spread	spread	spread
spring	sprang	sprung
stand	stood	stood
steal	stole	stolen
stick	stuck	stuck
sting	stung	stung
stink	stank, stunk	stunk
strew	strewed	strewn, strewed
stride	strode	stridden
strike	struck	struck
string	strung	strung
strive	strove	striven
swear	swore	sworn
sweep	swept	swept
swell	swelled	swollen, swelled
swim	swam	swum
swing	swung	swung
take	took	taken
teach	taught	taught
tear	tore	torn
tell	told	told
think	thought	thought
thrive	thrived, throve	thrived, thriven
throw	threw	thrown
thrust	thrust	thrust
tread	trod	trodden, trod
unbend	unbent	unbent
undergo	underwent	undergone
understand	understood	understood
undertake	undertook	undertaken
undo	undid	undone
upset	upset	upset
wake	woke, waked	woken, waked
waylay	waylaid	waylaid
wear	wore	worn
weave	wove	woven
weep	wept	wept
win	won	won
wind	wound	wound
withdraw	withdrew	withdrawn
withhold	withheld	withheld
withstand	withstood	withstood
wring	wrung	wrung
write	wrote	written

OXFORD